BlackboxNLP Analyzing and Interpreting Neural Networks for NLP (BlackboxNLP 2022)

Abu Dhabi, United Arab Emirates
8 December 2022

ISBN: 978-1-7138-9104-8

Printed from e-media with permission by:

Curran Associates, Inc.
57 Morehouse Lane
Red Hook, NY 12571

CURRAN ASSOCIATES INC. proceedings.com

Some format issues inherent in the e-media version may also appear in this print version.

Printed with permission by Curran Associates, Inc. (2024)

Association for Computational Linguistics
209 N. Eighth Street
Stroudsburg, Pennsylvania 18360

Phone: 1-570-476-8006
Fax: 1-570-476-0860

acl@aclweb.org

Additional copies of this publication are available from:

Curran Associates, Inc.
57 Morehouse Lane
Red Hook, NY 12571 USA
Phone: 845-758-0400
Fax: 845-758-2633
Email: curran@proceedings.com
Web: www.proceedings.com

BlackboxNLP 2022

BlackboxNLP Analyzing and Interpreting Neural Networks for NLP

Proceedings of the Workshop

December 8, 2022

The BlackboxNLP organizers gratefully acknowledge the support from the following sponsors.

Main Sponsors

Google

Introduction

BlackboxNLP is the fifth workshop on analyzing and interpreting neural networks for NLP, hosted by the 2022 Conference on Empirical Methods in Natural Language Processing (EMNLP 2022) in Abu Dhabi, United Arab Emirates, and online (hybrid).

Many recent performance improvements in NLP have come at the cost of understanding of the systems. How do we assess what representations and computations models learn? How do we formalize desirable properties of interpretable models, and measure the extent to which existing models achieve them? How can we build models that better encode these properties? What can new or existing tools tell us about the inductive biases of systems?

The goal of this workshop is to bring together researchers focused on interpreting and explaining NLP models by taking inspiration from machine learning, psychology, linguistics, and neuroscience. We hope the workshop will serve as an interdisciplinary meetup that allows for cross-collaboration.

The topics of the workshop include, but are not limited to: Explanation methods such as saliency, attribution, free-text explanations, or explanations with structured properties; Probing methods for testing whether models have acquired or represent certain linguistic properties; Applying analysis techniques from other disciplines (e.g., neuroscience or computer vision); Examining model performance on simplified or formal languages; More interpretable model architectures; Open-source tools for analysis, visualization, or explanation; Evaluation of explanation methods; Opinion pieces about the state of explainable NLP.

We received an impressive number of 76 submissions (including both archival papers and extended abstracts), suggesting that the issue of interpretability of neural networks remains important within the NLP community. The final program contains three keynote talks, four oral presentations and 74 posters (33 archival papers, 13 extended abstracts, and 28 Findings papers). We hope this workshop provides a venue for bringing together ideas and stimulate new ways of building methods and resources for facilitating better analysis and understanding of the inner-dynamics of neural networks for NLP.

BlackboxNLP would not have been possible without the dedication of its program committee. We would like to thank them for their invaluable effort in providing high-quality reviews in a very short period of time. We are also grateful to our invited speakers, Lena Voita, Catherine Olsson and David Bau, for contributing to our program. Finally, we are very thankful to our sponsor, Google, that made it possible for some of our participants to attend the workshop.

Jasmijn Bastings, Yonatan Belinkov, Yanai Elazar, Dieuwke Hupkes, Naomi Saphra, Sarah Wiegreffe

Organizing Committee

Organizers

Jasmijn Bastings, Google Research
Yonatan Belinkov, Technion
Yanai Elazar, Allen Institute for AI
Dieuwke Hupkes, Meta AI
Naomi Saphra, NYU
Sarah Wiegreffe, Allen Institute for AI

Program Committee

Reviewers

Heike Adel, Sachin Agarwal, Leila Arras, Pepa Atanasova, Tania Avgustinova

Parsa Bagherzadeh, Vinayshekhar Bannihatti, Jonathan Brophy, Lisa Bylinina

Rahma Chaabouni, Stergios Chatzikyriakidis, Hanjie Chen

Arya D., Verna Dankers, Anubrata Das

Michael Eric

Ian F., Nils Feldhus, Ghazi Felhi, Richard Futrell

Mario Giulianelli, Seraphina Goldfarb-Tarrant

David Harwath, John Hewitt

Alon Jacovi, Carolyn Jane, Robin Jia, Jinhang Jiang, Zhiying Jiang, Richard Johansson, Jaap Jumelet

Sayantan Kumar, Jenny Kunz

Cassandra L, Minghan Li, Yuchen Lian, Sheng Liang, Jindřich Libovický, Tomasz Limisiewicz, Zhiyu Lin

Badr M, Valentin Malykh, Kate McCurdy, Francois Meyer, Janusz Milewski, Koji Mineshima, Marius Mosbach

Anmol Nayak, Joakim Nivre

Xiang Pan, Swetasudha Panda, Bhargavi Paranjape, Lis Pereira, Yuval Pinter, Jacob Portes, Aman Priyanshu

Shauli Ravfogel, Abhilasha Ravichander, Rudolf Rosa, Sara rajaee

Hassan Sajjad, Hendrik Schuff, Rico Sennrich, Mattia Setzu, Tatiana Shavrina, Victor Siemen, Sanchit Sinha, Pia Sommerauer, Shane Steinert-Threlkeld, Vinitra Swamy

Marc Tanti, Jörg Tiedemann

Jithendra Vepa

Eric Wallace, Alex Warstadt, Adina Williams

Lan Xiao, Zhouhang Xie

Dylan Z, Yichu Zhou

This page intentionally left blank.

Keynote Talk: The Two Viewpoints on the NMT Training Process

Lena Voita
Facebook AI Research

Abstract: In this talk, I illustrate how the same process (in this case, NMT training process) can be viewed from different perspectives: from the inside of the model and from the outside, i.e. in a black-box manner. In the first view, we look at the model's inner workings and try to understand how NMT balances two different types of context, the source and the prefix of the target sentence. In the second view, we look at model outputs (i.e. generated translations) at different steps during training and evaluate how the model acquires different competences. We find that NMT training consists of the stages where it focuses on the competences mirroring three core SMT components: target-side language modeling, lexical translation and reordering. Most importantly, the two views show the same process, and we will see how this process is reflected in these two types of analysis.

Bio: Elena (Lena) Voita is a Research Scientist joining Facebook AI Research. She is mostly interested in understanding what and how neural models learn. Her analysis works so far include looking at model components, adapting attribution methods to NLP models, black-box analysis of model outputs, as well as information-theoretic view on analysis (e.g., probing). Previously, she was a PhD student at the University of Edinburgh supervised by Ivan Titov and Rico Sennrich, was awarded Facebook PhD Fellowship, worked as a Research Scientist at Yandex Research side by side with the Yandex Translate team. She enjoys writing blog posts and teaching; a public version of (a part of) her NLP course is available at `lena-voita.github.io/nlp_course.html`.

Keynote Talk: In-Context Learning and Induction Heads

Catherine Olsson
Anthropic AI

Abstract: "Induction heads" are attention heads that implement a simple algorithm to complete token sequences like [A][B] ... [A] $\rightarrow$ [B]. In this work, we present preliminary and indirect evidence for a hypothesis that induction heads might constitute the mechanism for the majority of all "in-context learning" in large transformer models (i.e. decreasing loss at increasing token indices). We find that induction heads develop at precisely the same point as a sudden sharp increase in in-context learning ability, visible as a bump in the training loss. We present six complementary lines of evidence, arguing that induction heads may be the mechanistic source of general in-context learning in transformer models of any size. For small attention-only models, we present strong, causal evidence; for larger models with MLPs, we present correlational evidence.

Bio: Catherine Olsson is a research engineer at Anthropic, and the lead author on the recent mechanistic interpretability paper In-context Learning and Induction Heads. She has previously worked in technical research roles at Google Brain and OpenAI, and as a grantmaker at Open Philanthropy Project funding academic research in ML robustness.

Keynote Talk: Direct Model Editing

David Bau
Northeastern Khoury College

Abstract: Can we understand large deep networks well enough to reprogram them by changing their parameters directly? In this talk I will talk about Direct Model Editing: how to modify the weights of a large model directly by understanding its structure. We will consider examples in computer vision and NLP: how to probe and rewrite computations within an image synthesis model to alter compositional rules that govern rendering of realistic images, and how the ROME method can edit specific factual memories within a large language model, directly tracing and modifying parameters that store associations within GPT. I will talk about how causal mediation analysis can serve as a key to unlock the secrets of a huge model; the specificity-generalization trade-off when evaluating knowledge changes in a large model; and how recent results in our MEMIT work suggest that direct editing in huge models may scale orders-of-magnitudes better than traditional opaque fine-tuning.

Bio: David Bau is Assistant Professor at the Northeastern University Khoury College of Computer Science. He received his PhD from MIT and AB from Harvard. He is known for his network dissection studies of individual neurons in deep networks and has published research on the interpretable structure of large models in PNAS, CVPR, NeurIPS, and SIGGRAPH. Prof. Bau is also coauthor of the textbook, Numerical Linear Algebra.

Table of Contents

Program

Thursday, December 8, 2022

08:00 - 09:00 *Poster Session 0 - Virtual*

A Minimal Model for Compositional Generalization on gSCAN
Alice Hein and Klaus Diepold

Sparse Interventions in Language Models with Differentiable Masking
Nicola De Cao, Leon Schmid, Dieuwke Hupkes and Ivan Titov

Where's the Learning in Representation Learning for Compositional Semantics and the Case of Thematic Fit
Mughilan Muthupari, Samrat Halder, Asad B. Sayeed and Yuval Marton

Sentence Ambiguity, Grammaticality and Complexity Probes
Sunit Bhattacharya, Vilém Zouhar and Ondrej Bojar

Post-Hoc Interpretation of Transformer Hyperparameters with Explainable Boosting Machines
Kiron Deb, Xuan Zhang and Kevin Duh

Revisit Systematic Generalization via Meaningful Learning
Ning Shi, Boxin Wang, Wei Wang, Xiangyu Liu and Zhouhan Lin

Is It Smaller Than a Tennis Ball? Language Models Play the Game of Twenty Questions
Maxime De Bruyn, Ehsan Lotfi, Jeska Buhmann and Walter Daelemans

Post-hoc analysis of Arabic transformer models
Ahmed Abdelali, Nadir Durrani, Fahim Dalvi and Hassan Sajjad

Universal Evasion Attacks on Summarization Scoring
Wenchuan Mu and Kwan Hui Lim

How (Un)Faithful is Attention?
Hessam Amini and Leila Kosseim

Faithful, Interpretable Model Explanations via Causal Abstraction
Atticus Geiger, Zhengxuan Wu, Karel D'Oosterlinck, Elisa Kreiss, Noah Goodman, Thomas Icard and Christopher Potts

Behavioral Testing of Knowledge Graph Embedding Models for Link Prediction
Wiem Ben Rim, Carolin Lawrence, Kiril Gashteovski, Mathias Niepert and Naoaki Okazaki

Do LSTMs See Gender? Probing the Ability of LSTMs to Learn Abstract Syntactic Rules
Priyanka Sukumaran, Conor Houghton and Nina Kazanina

FRAME: Evaluating Rationale-Label Consistency Metrics for Free-Text Rationales
Aaron Chan, Shaoliang Nie, Liang Tan, Xiaochang Peng, Hamed Firooz, Maziar Sanjabi and Xiang Ren

Tracing and Manipulating Intermediate Results in Neural Math Problem Solvers
Yuta Matsumoto, Benjamin Heinzerling, Masashi Yoshikawa and Kentaro Inui

A Critical Look at Fine-tuning Generalization: Are Patterns All We Need?
Marius Mosbach, Shauli Ravfogel, Dietrich Klakow and Yanai Elazar

A Human-Centric Assessment Framework for AI
Sascha Saralajew, Ammar Shaker, Zhao Xu, Kiril Gashteovski, Bhushan Kotnis, Wiem Ben Rim, Jürgen Quittek and Carolin Lawrence

Do Language Models Understand Measurements?
Edward Choi, Seungwoo Ryu and Sungjin Park

Outlier Dimensions that Disrupt Transformers are Driven by Frequency
Felice Dell'Orletta, Aleksandr Drozd, Anna Rogers and Giovanni Puccetti

On the Impact of Temporal Concept Drift on Model Explanations
Nikolaos Aletras, Kalina Bontcheva, George Chrysostomou and Zhixue Zhao

Lexical Generalization Improves with Larger Models and Longer Training
Yanai Elazar, Yoav Goldberg and Elron Bandel

Thursday, December 8, 2022 (continued)

What Has Been Enhanced in my Knowledge-Enhanced Language Model?
Mrinmaya Sachan, Guoji Fu and Yifan Hou

SensePOLAR: Word sense aware interpretability for pre-trained contextual word embeddings
Markus Strohmaier, Marlene Lutz, Sandipan Sikdar and Jan Engler

Identifying Human Strategies for Generating Word-Level Adversarial Examples
Lewis Griffin, Bennett Kleinberg and Maximilian Mozes

Transformer Language Models without Positional Encodings Still Learn Positional Information
Omer Levy, Peter Izsak, Ofir Press, Ori Ram and Adi Haviv

Probing Relational Knowledge in Language Models via Word Analogies
Jose Camacho-Collados and Kiamehr Rezaee

Few-Shot Out-of-Domain Transfer Learning of Natural Language Explanations in a Label-Abundant Setup
Oana-Maria Camburu, Thomas Lukasiewicz, Vid Kocijan and Yordan Yordanov

The Curious Case of Absolute Position Embeddings
Adina Williams, Dieuwke Hupkes, Joelle Pineau, Siva Reddy, Amirhossein Kazemnejad and Koustuv Sinha

Evaluating the Faithfulness of Importance Measures in NLP by Recursively Masking Allegedly Important Tokens and Retraining
Siva Reddy, Vaibhav Adlakha, Nicholas Meade and Andreas Madsen

Are Large Pre-Trained Language Models Leaking Your Personal Information?
Kevin Chen-Chuan Chang, Hanyin Shao and Jie Huang

Exploring The Landscape of Distributional Robustness for Question Answering Models
Ludwig Schmidt, Hannaneh Hajishirzi, Ian Magnusson, Sewon Min, Gabriel Ilharco, Mitchell Wortsman and Anas Awadalla

Impact of Pretraining Term Frequencies on Few-Shot Numerical Reasoning
Sameer Singh, Matt Gardner, Robert L Logan IV and Yasaman Razeghi

Thursday, December 8, 2022 (continued)

	Influence Functions for Sequence Tagging Models Ani Nenkova, Byron Wallace, Varun Manjunatha and Sarthak Jain
	CORE: A Retrieve-then-Edit Framework for Counterfactual Data Generation Luke Zettlemoyer, Hannaneh Hajishirzi, Bhargavi Paranjape and Tanay Dixit
09:00 - 09:10	*Opening Remarks*
09:15 - 10:00	*Invited Talk 1 - Lena Voita*
10:00 - 10:30	*Oral Presentations 1 and 2*
	Human Ratings Do Not Reflect Downstream Utility: A Study of Free-Text Explanations for Model Predictions Jenny Kunz, Martin Jirenius, Oskar Holmström and Marco Kuhlmann
	Analyzing the Representational Geometry of Acoustic Word Embeddings Badr M. Abdullah and Dietrich Klakow
10:30 - 11:00	*Coffee Break*
11:00 - 12:30	*Poster Session 1 - Onsite*
	Where's the Learning in Representation Learning for Compositional Semantics and the Case of Thematic Fit Mughilan Muthupari, Samrat Halder, Asad B. Sayeed and Yuval Marton
	Sentence Ambiguity, Grammaticality and Complexity Probes Sunit Bhattacharya, Vilém Zouhar and Ondrej Bojar
	The Rediscovery Hypothesis: Language Models Need to Meet Linguistics Vassilina Nikoulina, Maxat Tezekbayev, Nuradil Kozhakhmet, Madina Babazhanova, Matthias Gallé and Zhenisbek Assylbekov
	The Solvability of Interpretability Evaluation Metrics Yilun Zhou and Julie Shah

Analyzing Transformers in Embedding Space
Guy Dar, Mor Geva, Ankit Gupta and Jonathan Berant

FIDAM-Eval: A Framework for Evaluating Feature Interaction Detection and Attribution Methods
Jaap Jumelet and Willem H. Zuidema

Understanding Domain Learning in Language Models Through Subpopulation Analysis
Zheng Zhao, Yftah Ziser and Shay B Cohen

Intermediate Entity-based Sparse Interpretable Representation Learning
Diego Garcia-Olano, Yasumasa Onoe, Joydeep Ghosh and Byron C Wallace

Investigating the Characteristics of a Transformer in a Few-Shot Setup: Does Freezing Layers in RoBERTa Help?
Digvijay Anil Ingle, Rishabh Kumar Tripathi, Ayush Kumar, Kevin Patel and Jithendra Vepa

It Is Not Easy To Detect Paraphrases: Analysing Semantic Similarity With Antonyms and Negation Using the New SemAntoNeg Benchmark
Teemu Vahtola, Mathias Creutz and Jörg Tiedemann

Controlling for Stereotypes in Multimodal Language Model Evaluation
Manuj Malik and Richard Johansson

Behavioral Testing of Knowledge Graph Embedding Models for Link Prediction
Wiem Ben Rim, Carolin Lawrence, Kiril Gashteovski, Mathias Niepert and Naoaki Okazaki

Do LSTMs See Gender? Probing the Ability of LSTMs to Learn Abstract Syntactic Rules
Priyanka Sukumaran, Conor Houghton and Nina Kazanina

Using Roark-Hollingshead Distance to Probe BERT's Syntactic Competence
Jingcheng Niu, Wenjie Lu, Eric Corlett and Gerald Penn

DALLE-2 is Seeing Double: Flaws in Word-to-Concept Mapping in Text2Image Models
Royi Rassin, Shauli Ravfogel and Yoav Goldberg

What Has Been Enhanced in my Knowledge-Enhanced Language Model?
Mrinmaya Sachan, Guoji Fu and Yifan Hou

Identifying Human Strategies for Generating Word-Level Adversarial Examples
Lewis Griffin, Bennett Kleinberg and Maximilian Mozes

Transformer Language Models without Positional Encodings Still Learn Positional Information
Omer Levy, Peter Izsak, Ofir Press, Ori Ram and Adi Haviv

Probing Relational Knowledge in Language Models via Word Analogies
Jose Camacho-Collados and Kiamehr Rezaee

The Curious Case of Absolute Position Embeddings
Adina Williams, Dieuwke Hupkes, Joelle Pineau, Siva Reddy, Amirhossein Kazemnejad and Koustuv Sinha

Evaluating the Faithfulness of Importance Measures in NLP by Recursively Masking Allegedly Important Tokens and Retraining
Siva Reddy, Vaibhav Adlakha, Nicholas Meade and Andreas Madsen

Exploring The Landscape of Distributional Robustness for Question Answering Models
Ludwig Schmidt, Hannaneh Hajishirzi, Ian Magnusson, Sewon Min, Gabriel Ilharco, Mitchell Wortsman and Anas Awadalla

Impact of Pretraining Term Frequencies on Few-Shot Numerical Reasoning
Sameer Singh, Matt Gardner, Robert L Logan IV and Yasaman Razeghi

How Much Does Attention Actually Attend? Questioning the Importance of Attention in Pretrained Transformers
Roy Schwartz, Noah A. Smith, Ivan Montero, Jungo Kasai, Daniel Rotem, Hao Peng and Michael Hassid

Probing for Constituency Structure in Neural Language Models
Hassan Sajjad, Laura Kallmeyer, Younes Samih and David Arps

Calibrating Trust of Multi-Hop Question Answering Systems with Decompositional Probes
Mark Riedl, Sarah Wiegreffe and Kaige Xie

Thursday, December 8, 2022 (continued)

CORE: A Retrieve-then-Edit Framework for Counterfactual Data Generation
Luke Zettlemoyer, Hannaneh Hajishirzi, Bhargavi Paranjape and Tanay Dixit

SensePOLAR: Word sense aware interpretability for pre-trained contextual word embeddings
Markus Strohmaier, Marlene Lutz, Sandipan Sikdar and Jan Engler

12:30 - 14:00 *Lunch Break*

14:00 - 14:45 *Invited Talk 2 - Catherine Olsson*

14:45 - 15:30 *Oral Presentations 3 and 4*

Investigating the Characteristics of a Transformer in a Few-Shot Setup: Does Freezing Layers in RoBERTa Help?
Digvijay Anil Ingle, Rishabh Kumar Tripathi, Ayush Kumar, Kevin Patel and Jithendra Vepa

Probing with Noise: Unpicking the Warp and Weft of Embeddings
Filip Klubicka and John D. Kelleher

15:30 - 16:00 *Coffee Break*

16:00 - 17:30 *Poster Session 2 - Virtual*

A Minimal Model for Compositional Generalization on gSCAN
Alice Hein and Klaus Diepold

Sparse Interventions in Language Models with Differentiable Masking
Nicola De Cao, Leon Schmid, Dieuwke Hupkes and Ivan Titov

Where's the Learning in Representation Learning for Compositional Semantics and the Case of Thematic Fit
Mughilan Muthupari, Samrat Halder, Asad B. Sayeed and Yuval Marton

Sentence Ambiguity, Grammaticality and Complexity Probes
Sunit Bhattacharya, Vilém Zouhar and Ondrej Bojar

A Critical Look at Fine-tuning Generalization: Are Patterns All We Need?
Marius Mosbach, Shauli Ravfogel, Dietrich Klakow and Yanai Elazar

A Human-Centric Assessment Framework for AI
Sascha Saralajew, Ammar Shaker, Zhao Xu, Kiril Gashteovski, Bhushan Kotnis, Wiem Ben Rim, Jürgen Quittek and Carolin Lawrence

Do Language Models Understand Measurements?
Edward Choi, Seungwoo Ryu and Sungjin Park

Outlier Dimensions that Disrupt Transformers are Driven by Frequency
Felice Dell'Orletta, Aleksandr Drozd, Anna Rogers and Giovanni Puccetti

On the Impact of Temporal Concept Drift on Model Explanations
Nikolaos Aletras, Kalina Bontcheva, George Chrysostomou and Zhixue Zhao

Lexical Generalization Improves with Larger Models and Longer Training
Yanai Elazar, Yoav Goldberg and Elron Bandel

What Has Been Enhanced in my Knowledge-Enhanced Language Model?
Mrinmaya Sachan, Guoji Fu and Yifan Hou

SensePOLAR: Word sense aware interpretability for pre-trained contextual word embeddings
Markus Strohmaier, Marlene Lutz, Sandipan Sikdar and Jan Engler

Identifying Human Strategies for Generating Word-Level Adversarial Examples
Lewis Griffin, Bennett Kleinberg and Maximilian Mozes

Transformer Language Models without Positional Encodings Still Learn Positional Information
Omer Levy, Peter Izsak, Ofir Press, Ori Ram and Adi Haviv

Probing Relational Knowledge in Language Models via Word Analogies
Jose Camacho-Collados and Kiamehr Rezaee

Few-Shot Out-of-Domain Transfer Learning of Natural Language Explanations in a Label-Abundant Setup
Oana-Maria Camburu, Thomas Lukasiewicz, Vid Kocijan and Yordan Yordanov

The Curious Case of Absolute Position Embeddings
Adina Williams, Dieuwke Hupkes, Joelle Pineau, Siva Reddy, Amirhossein Kazemnejad and Koustuv Sinha

Evaluating the Faithfulness of Importance Measures in NLP by Recursively Masking Allegedly Important Tokens and Retraining
Siva Reddy, Vaibhav Adlakha, Nicholas Meade and Andreas Madsen

Are Large Pre-Trained Language Models Leaking Your Personal Information?
Kevin Chen-Chuan Chang, Hanyin Shao and Jie Huang

Exploring The Landscape of Distributional Robustness for Question Answering Models
Ludwig Schmidt, Hannaneh Hajishirzi, Ian Magnusson, Sewon Min, Gabriel Ilharco, Mitchell Wortsman and Anas Awadalla

Impact of Pretraining Term Frequencies on Few-Shot Numerical Reasoning
Sameer Singh, Matt Gardner, Robert L Logan IV and Yasaman Razeghi

What do Large Language Models Learn beyond Language?
Shashank Srivastava and Avinash Madasu

How Much Does Attention Actually Attend? Questioning the Importance of Attention in Pretrained Transformers
Roy Schwartz, Noah A. Smith, Ivan Montero, Jungo Kasai, Daniel Rotem, Hao Peng and Michael Hassid

Probing for Constituency Structure in Neural Language Models
Hassan Sajjad, Laura Kallmeyer, Younes Samih and David Arps

Recursive Neural Networks with Bottlenecks Diagnose (Non-)Compositionality
Ivan Titov and Verna Dankers

CAT-probing: A Metric-based Approach to Interpret How Pre-trained Models for Programming Language Attend Code Structure
Ming Gao, Xuesong Lu, Xiang Li, Renyu Zhu, Qiushi Sun and Nuo Chen

Thursday, December 8, 2022 (continued)

ER-Test: Evaluating Explanation Regularization Methods for Language Models
Xiang Ren, Hamed Firooz, Maziar Sanjabi, Shaoliang Nie, Ziyi Liu, Aaron Chan and Brihi Joshi

Can Language Models Serve as Temporal Knowledge Bases?
Hai Jin, Sixiao Zhang, Guandong Xu, Feng Zhao and Ruilin Zhao

Baked-in State Probing
Kevin Gimpel, Karen Livescu, Sam Wiseman and Shubham Toshniwal

Towards Tracing Knowledge in Language Models Back to the Training Data
Kelvin Guu, Jacob Andreas, Ian Tenney, Binbin Xiong, Frederick Liu, Tolga Bolukbasi and Ekin Akyurek

Calibrating Trust of Multi-Hop Question Answering Systems with Decompositional Probes
Mark Riedl, Sarah Wiegreffe and Kaige Xie

CodeExp: Explanatory Code Document Generation
Nan Duan, Jianfeng Gao, Bo Wang, Todd Mytkowicz, Jeevana Priya Inala, Junjie Huang, Chenglong Wang and Haotian Cui

Influence Functions for Sequence Tagging Models
Ani Nenkova, Byron Wallace, Varun Manjunatha and Sarthak Jain

CORE: A Retrieve-then-Edit Framework for Counterfactual Data Generation
Luke Zettlemoyer, Hannaneh Hajishirzi, Bhargavi Paranjape and Tanay Dixit

17:30 - 17:45 *Mini Break*

17:45 - 18:45 *Invited Talk 3 - David Bau*

18:45 - 19:00 *Closing Remarks*

A Minimal Model for Compositional Generalization on gSCAN

Alice Hein **Klaus Diepold**
TUM School of Computation, Information and Technology
Department of Computer Engineering
Technical University of Munich, Munich, Germany
{alice.hein, kldi}@tum.de

Abstract

Whether neural networks are capable of compositional generalization has been a topic of much debate. Most previous studies on this subject investigate the generalization capabilities of state-of-the-art deep learning architectures. We here take a more bottom-up approach and design a minimal model that displays generalization on a compositional benchmark, namely, the gSCAN dataset. The model is a hybrid architecture that combines layers trained with gradient descent and a selective attention mechanism optimized with an evolutionary strategy. The architecture has around 60 times fewer trainable parameters than models previously tested on gSCAN, and achieves comparable accuracies on most test splits, even when trained only on a fraction of the dataset. On adverb to verb generalization accuracy, it outperforms previous approaches by 65 to 86%. Through ablation studies, neuron pruning, and error analyses, we show that weight decay and attention mechanisms facilitate compositional generalization by encouraging sparse representations divorced from irrelevant context. We find that the model's sample efficiency can mainly be attributed to its selective attention mechanism.

1 Introduction

Compositionality is a core aspect of human cognition. It is what allows us to produce and understand infinite combinations of known concepts, be it in the realm of language, vision, or motor skills. Regarding artificial intelligence (AI) systems, compositionality holds the promise of more human-like, robust generalization on out-of-distribution data, as well as increased sample efficiency. Compositionality in neural networks has thus been the subject of numerous empirical investigations – with mixed results. Several studies using a variety of deep neural network architectures have found that models either failed on compositional tasks or succeeded given enough data, but could do so without relying on systematic compositional rules (Baroni, 2020; Lake and Baroni, 2018; Loula et al., 2018; Subramanian et al., 2019; Keysers et al., 2019; Hupkes et al., 2020; Andreas et al., 2019; Chaabouni et al., 2020). Others found that such architectures could reach compositional solutions without being explicitly constrained to do so, but that this ability varied dramatically across random initializations of the same model (Liška et al., 2018; McCoy et al., 2020; Weber et al., 2018).

The main focus of these studies has been on testing whether state-of-the-art deep learning architectures are able to learn compositionally. We here take a different approach, namely that of specifically building a minimal model that is able to solve a set of compositional generalization tasks, then using this model as a tool for analyzing when and how generalization occurs. Our dataset of choice for this investigation is gSCAN, a challenge benchmark for systematic generalization in grounded language understanding.

The model we use is a hybrid architecture, containing some weights that are trained with gradient descent, some that are optimized with an evolutionary strategy, and some that are initialized randomly and left frozen. A detailed justification of these design choices is given in Section 4.2. The architecture has around 60 times fewer trainable parameters than models previously tested on gSCAN, which allows us to run extensive ablation studies and error analyses to investigate factors contributing to generalization performance. We find that our best-performing model breaks down the gSCAN tasks into simpler, reusable parts and combines them using only 13 neurons in its final decision layer. It achieves accuracies comparable with previously proposed models on most test splits and outperforms them on adverb to verb generalization by 65 to 86%, even when trained on as little as 2% of the full dataset.

Proceedings of the Fifth BlackboxNLP Workshop on Analyzing and Interpreting Neural Networks for NLP, pages 1 - 15
December 8, 2022 ©2022 Association for Computational Linguistics

2 Related Work

2.1 Compositional Generalization

A number of works have addressed the challenge of building AI systems that generalize compositionally. Neural Module Networks were designed for visual question answering and achieve systematicity by dynamically assembling question-specific models out of trainable reusable components (Andreas et al., 2016a,b). Other approaches explore ways of encouraging compositional representations in commonly used state-of-the-art models without major architectural changes. In this vein, Hupkes et al. (2018) and Baan et al. (2019) find that attentive guidance during training helps develop small functional groups of neurons that yield more compositional solutions by seq2seq models on lookup table tasks. Andreas (2020) and Akyürek et al. (2020) propose data augmentation schemes that promote compositional learning in instruction following and morphological analysis. Ontanon et al. (2022) focus on the effect that design decisions such as position encodings, weight sharing, or model hyper-parameters can have on the compositional generalization abilities of Transformer models. Finally Power et al. (2021) identify weight decay as being particularly effective at improving generalization on a binary operation table task.

2.2 Grounded instruction following

Several datasets have been proposed in recent years for training embodied agents to follow instructions in simulated 2D or 3D environments (Hermann et al., 2017; Yu et al., 2018a; Misra et al., 2018; Chaplot et al., 2018; Yu et al., 2018b; Deruyttere et al., 2019; Chevalier-Boisvert et al., 2019; Shridhar et al., 2020). One such task is gSCAN, which was specifically introduced as a benchmark for compositionality in grounded language understanding and contains 8 test splits for assessing different kinds of out-of-distribution generalization (Ruis et al., 2020). Previous approaches to solving gSCAN include language-conditioned message passing (Gao et al., 2020), compositional networks (Kuo et al., 2021), neuro-symbolic, dual-system models (Nye et al., 2021), and the introduction of auxiliary tasks (Jiang and Bansal, 2021; Heinze-Deml and Bouchacourt, 2020). The most successful model to date uses a general-purpose Transformer architecture with cross-modal attention and solves 5 out of 8 tasks (Qiu et al., 2021).

As outlined in the introduction, our goal is not necessarily to compete with these previous approaches. Instead we aim to devise a parameter-efficient model that can serve as a tool for a more in-depth investigation of the factors influencing performance on the different gSCAN test splits, and to contextualise the results with previous findings on out-of-distribution generalisation.

2.3 Neuroevolution

Evolutionary algorithms (EA) are stochastic, gradient-free methods that explore multiple areas of a search space in parallel. This work was particularly inspired by Tang et al. (2020), who combine neuroevolution techniques with self-attention to solve vision-based RL tasks. Their model extracts relevant patches from input images through a hard (non-differentiable) attention mechanism, optimized via an EA rather than more commonly used techniques like RL. The most attended-to patches are then passed on to an LSTM controller which determines the agent's action. The authors find that this approach significantly reduces the number of model parameters needed compared to previous methods, as well as offering increased interpretability and higher robustness to out-of-distribution modifications (Tang et al., 2020).

3 Background

Our architecture makes use of an Echo-State Network (ESN) and the covariance matrix adaptation evolution strategy (CMA-ES) to reduce the number of learnable parameters needed (see Section 4.2). As both are not commonly used in NLP, we here provide some background on these techniques.

3.1 Echo-State Networks

A basic ESN consists of an input layer W_i^r, a recurrent neural network (RNN) or so-called reservoir, and an output layer W_o. The reservoir's state is updated at each discrete time step as follows:

$$\begin{aligned}\mathbf{x}[n+1] =& (1-\alpha)\mathbf{x}[n] + \alpha f\big(W_i^r \mathbf{u}[n] \\ &+ W_r^r \mathbf{x}[n]\big),\end{aligned} \tag{1}$$

where α is a leak rate, $\mathbf{x}[n]$ is the current reservoir activation state, f is a the hyperbolic tangent function, $\mathbf{u}[n]$ is the external input, and W_r^r is the reservoir's internal weight matrix. The ESN's output is computed as

$$\mathbf{y}[n+1] = g(W_o \mathbf{x}[n+1]), \tag{2}$$

where g is an activation function. Crucially, W_i^r and W_r^r are randomly initialized and left untrained. Only W_o is optimized. This leads to considerably faster training times than for conventional RNNs where all weights are learned (Gauthier et al., 2021). ESNs' main areas of application therefore include resource-constrained contexts like robotics and edge computing (Nakajima, 2020).

3.2 CMA-ES

CMA-ES is a black-box optimization algorithm. It has been empirically shown to perform robustly on a range of tasks and requires very little parameter tuning (Hansen et al., 2010), making it the EA of choice for optimizing the model in Tang et al. (2020) which inspired our architecture. CMA-ES works by iteratively sampling λ candidate solutions from a multivariate normal distribution $\mathcal{N}(m, \sigma^2, C)$ with mean m, step size σ and covariance matrix C. At each generation, the candidate solutions' fitness is evaluated according to some function f, and m, σ, and C are adjusted to increase the probability of success. As the CMA-ES algorithm is not a main focus of this work, we relegate details on how the parameters are updated to Appendix A and refer the interested reader to Hansen and Ostermeier (2001) for a more in-depth description of the method.

4 Experiment setup

4.1 gSCAN Benchmark

The gSCAN environment is a grid with objects of various shapes, sizes, and colors. It is represented as a $16 \times 6 \times 6$ array, where 6 is the grid size and 16 is the dimension of the binary feature encoding for each grid cell. The agent receives synthetically generated English language instructions which it must carry out using 6 output actions, such as walking or turning. Some combinations are held out of the training set. Out-of-distribution generalization is then assessed on nine separate test splits, listed in Table 1, measured using exact match accuracy of predicted action sequences. The full dataset has $\approx 370,000$ training and $\approx 20,000$ test sequences. Hupkes et al. (2020) propose to distinguish between five interpretations of model compositionality, namely, the systematic recombination of known parts and rules (*systematicity*), the extension of predictions beyond lengths seen during training (*productivity*), robustness to synonym substitutions (*substitutivity*), dependence on local vs global structures (*localism*), and the preference for rules vs exceptions (*overgeneralization*). Following this taxonomy, split G tests the model's one-shot learning capabilities, or overgeneralization. Split I tests for productivity. We mainly consider splits B, C, D, E, F, and H, which focus on systematic generalization and substitutivity.

Table 1: Overview of gSCAN's compositional test splits

Test Split	Held-out Examples
A: Random	Random (in-distribution)
B: Yellow Squares	Yellow squares as targets if referred to as *yellow*
C: Red Squares	Red squares as targets
D: Novel Direction	Targets south-west of the agent
E: Relativity	Circles of size 2 referred to as *small* (references are relative to other grid objects, not tied to absolute sizes)
F: Class inference	Pushing squares of size 3 (*heavy* objects are pushed/pulled twice)
G: Adverb k = 1	All except *k* mentions of *cautiously* (looking both ways before each step)
H: Adverb to verb	Commands containing both *pull* and *while spinning* (turning 4 times)
I: Length	Action sequences of length ≥ 15

4.2 Model

To solve a gSCAN task, the agent requires knowledge of the command to carry out, the grid state, and its own past actions. The latter is needed to keep track of e.g. the number of turns completed when "spinning". In the following, we describe how these inputs are represented and processed.

Reservoir To create the representation of the language command we chose an ESN, due to its ability to capture information about all input words and their order in a single vector, without requiring any weight updates. This fit our goal of keeping the number of trainable parameters low. The instruction to the agent is tokenized, one-hot encoded, and input sequentially to a reservoir with 400 hidden neurons, which is updated after each token according to Equation 1. All reservoir neurons are randomly connected to an output layer W_o of size 64, yielding a 64-dimensional command embedding.

Selective attention The selective attention part of the model is responsible for extracting task-relevant information from the input grid. The command embedding $\mathbf{x}_{\text{lang}} \in \mathbb{R}^{1\times 64}$ is passed through a layer $W_{\text{lang}} \in \mathbb{R}^{64\times 16}$. The resulting vector is convolved with the input grid at each position to obtain a heatmap over grid $G \in \mathbb{R}^{16\times 6\times 6}$. The x-

and y-coordinates and the 16-dimensional feature vector for the most-attended grid cell $\mathbf{g}^*$ are then extracted:

$$\mathbf{g}^* = \arg\max\left((\mathbf{x}_{\text{lang}} \cdot W_{\text{lang}}) * G\right) \tag{3}$$

Because this $\arg\max$ operation is non-differentiable, we follow Tang et al. (2020)'s approach of using CMA-ES to optimize W_{lang}. However, in contrast to Tang et al., we apply the attention matrix to feature vectors rather than image patches, and we do not evolve all learnable parameters in our model. This is because our model has significantly more parameters than that of Tang et al. and the time and space complexity of CMA-ES is quadratic in the dimensionality of its objective function – restricting its application to problems with no more than a few hundred variables (Varelas et al., 2018). Therefore, only this selective attention part of the model is optimized using CMA-ES. The rest is trained using gradient descent. Inspired by joint attention mechanisms and parental guidance during child learning, the CMA-ES receives auxiliary feedback on whether the correct target object was most attended to. We also test and report the results for a version where the CMA-ES receives as feedback the cross-entropy loss produced by the agent's final prediction outputs (see Section 5.1).

Action attention The action attention part of the model serves as the agent's "memory" of past outputs. The command embedding undergoes self-attention, yielding a weighted embedding $\mathbf{a}_{\text{lang}} \in \mathbb{R}^{1\times 64}$. This is then passed through another attention layer $W_{\text{act}} \in \mathbb{R}^{64\times 200}$ and multiplied element-wise with a vector $\mathbf{x}_{\text{act}} \in \mathbb{R}^{200\times 1}$ containing the agent's one-hot encoded past 20 actions and orientations:

$$\mathbf{a}_{\text{act}} = (\mathbf{a}_{\text{lang}} \cdot W_{\text{act}}) \odot \mathbf{x}_{\text{act}} \tag{4}$$

As there is no $\arg\max$ operation involved, W_a is trained with conventional gradient descent.

Controller Finally, the outputs of the selective and action attention modules are concatenated with the agent's current x- and y-coordinates and orientation, as well as the unweighted command embedding and input to the agent's controller to predict the agent's next step. The controller consists of a layer normalization layer, a layer with 100 hidden ReLU units, and an output layer of size 6.

In total, the model has a little under $5 \cdot 10^4$ trainable parameters, compared to around $3 \cdot 10^6$ for models previously tested on gSCAN (Qiu et al., 2021). A schematic overview is shown in Figure 1.

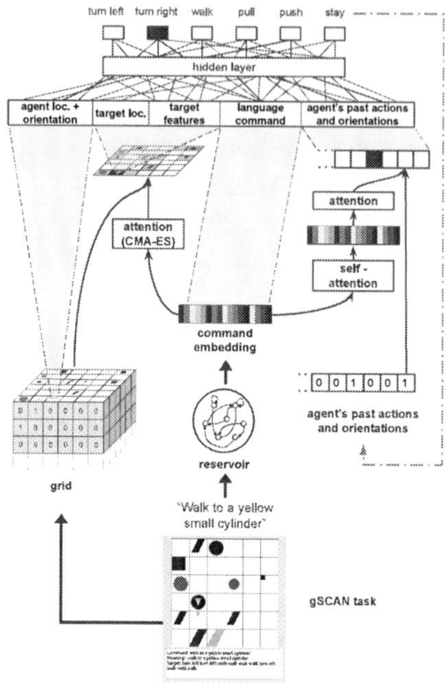

Figure 1: Schematic visualization of the proposed model

4.3 Training details

The weights of the ESN were initialized with a spectral radius of 0.99 and a density of $1e-2$. The leaking rate was set to $1e-1$. For the CMA-ES, we used a population size of 8 and an initial normal distribution with standard deviation $1e-1$. Optimization was implemented with the pycma library[1]. For the part of the model trained via gradient descent, we used the Adamax optimizer and a learning rate cycle with an upper boundary of $1e-2$. Weight decay was set to $1e-4$ and models were trained with batch size 4,096 for 100 epochs unless otherwise specified. All performance results are based on 10 runs. Each run used a different random seed for model weight initialization. However, the same 10 seeds were used for all tested modified or ablated architectures, so that all compared models started with the same 10 sets of weights. Experiments were implemented in Pytorch[2] and run on a server with 4 NVIDIA RTX 3090 GPUs and a 24 core Epyc CPU. The training time for one model was approximately 1.3 hours on the full

[1] `pypi.org/project/cma/`
[2] `pytorch.org`

dataset, 16 minutes on the 10% subset, and 9 minutes on the 2% subset. Code is publicly available at `https://github.com/lemonk6/minmodgscan`.

5 Results

5.1 Performance

As shown in Table 2, the model with auxiliary attention feedback reaches competitive accuracy on splits A, C, E, and F. On split H, it outperforms previous proposals by 65 to 86%. To see if generalization extended to other combinations, we also tested two custom splits. The first is a variation of task C, where not only red squares, but also yellow squares, green cylinders, and blue circles never appear as targets during training. The second is an extension of split H, where in addition to "pull while spinning", the agent is never told to "push while zigzagging" or to "walk hesitantly" during training. The model generalized to test sets containing only held-out shape-color and verb-adverb combinations, reaching 98.7% ± 1.5 and 98.9% ± 0.5 accuracy, respectively.

Table 3 compares the performance of models trained with and without an auxiliary feedback signal as well as models receiving perfect target location inputs, for reference. As can be seen, the model without an auxiliary signal does learn to focus on the target in some cases, but performance across the 10 runs exhibits a high variation. We also test a model which instead of absolute locations receives agent-centric row- and column-wise distances as input, which is sometimes used in RL goal navigation tasks. This stronger inductive bias seems to force the agent to more reliably employ the selective attention mechanism for target location, even when it only receives indirect feedback in the form of cross-entropy loss. Detailed evaluation results are given in B.

5.2 Sample Efficiency

One of the main advantages of our model is its sample efficiency. As shown in Figure 2, it achieves around 90% accuracy on splits A and C when trained on only 1% of the dataset, and 90 - 97% accuracy on splits A, C, E, and F with 2% of the data. This is well below the 40% data requirement threshold identified by Qiu et al. (2021) for their cross-modal transformer model. Interestingly, the exact match accuracy on splits B and C peaks at the 10% subset and declines slightly when given more data – something we take a closer look at in

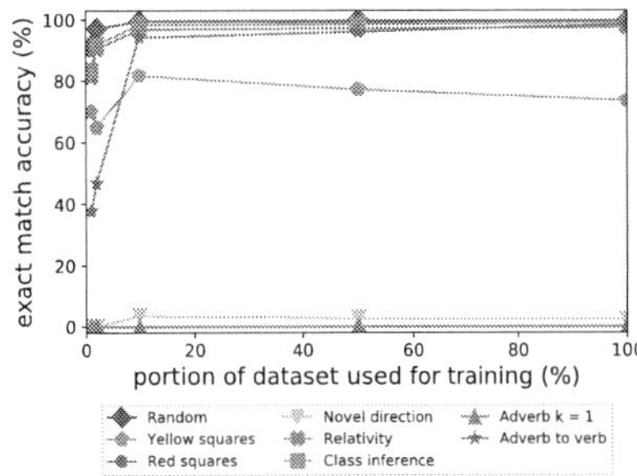

Figure 2: Sample efficiency on test splits for models with selective attention and auxiliary feedback

Section 5.3. Performance on task H increases more slowly than on other splits and requires at least 10% of the dataset to surpass 90% accuracy.

5.3 Error Analyses

Attention: We first analyze the mistakes made by the models trained without auxiliary feedback by treating the task of focusing on the correct target as a classification, and analyzing the feature-wise confusion matrices of the models. This reveals an accumulated false discovery rate of 66.5% for the "agent" dimension of the grid cell feature vectors, compared to 0% for the models trained with feedback. This means the models without attentive guidance tend to overly focus on the agent. The location of the agent does coincide with the target object's location around 18% of the time, which might lead to an overreliance on this dimension. We also find that the models trained without attention supervision struggle more with under-specified commands. For example, the models focus on an object of the correct color in ca. 96% of cases when the color is explicitly mentioned in the command. When the target object is only referred to by its shape or size, the accuracy drops to about 90%. Detailed confusion matrices can be found in D.1.

Yellow squares: In the case of split B, performance exhibits a large variation across instantiations of the same model. Out of 10 runs, approximately half always achieve accuracies in the range of 90 - 99% while the others only reach 35 - 55%. The best performance is achieved with a 10% subset of the training set, where all ten models reach at least 60% accuracy. A look at the confusion matrices shows that, on average, models correctly identify a square as their target object in 97% of test cases. However, their color accuracy is only around 75%. Taken together, this suggests that the

	Seq2Seq (2020)	GECA (2020)	Heinze (2020)	Gao (2020)	Kuo (2020)	Qiu (2021)	Jiang (2021)	Nye (2021)	Ours (100%)	Ours (10%)
A	97.69 ± 0.2	87.60 ± 1.2	94.19 ± 0.7	98.60 ± 1.0	96.73 ± 0.6	**99.95 ± 0.0**	-	74.7	99.7 ± 0.1	99.5 ± 0.1
B	54.96 ± 39.4	34.92 ± 39.3	86.45 ± 6.3	99.08 ± 0.7	94.91 ± 1.3	**99.90 ± 0.1**	-	81.3	73.5 ± 25.4	81.6 ± 14.3
C	23.51 ± 21.8	78.77 ± 6.6	81.07 ± 10.1	80.31 ± 24.5	67.72 ± 10.8	99.25 ± 0.9	-	78.1	99.4 ± 0.4	**99.5 ± 0.2**
D	0.00 ± 0.0	0.00 ± 0.0	-	0.16 ± 0.1	**11.52 ± 8.2**	0.00 ± 0.0	-	0.0	2.2 ± 1.5	3.5 ± 2.7
E	35.02 ± 2.4	33.19 ± 3.7	43.43 ± 7.0	87.32 ± 27.4	76.83 ± 2.3	**99.02 ± 1.2**	-	53.6	97.4 ± 2.0	96.8 ± 1.9
F	92.52 ± 6.8	85.99 ± 0.9	-	99.33 ± 0.5	98.67 ± 0.1	**99.98 ± 0.0**	-	76.2	99.1 ± 0.6	98.3 ± 1.7
G	0.00 ± 0.0	0.00 ± 0.0	-	-	1.14 ± 0.3	0.00 ± 0.0	**4.9**	0.00	0.00 ± 0.0	0.0 ± 0.1
H	22.70 ± 4.6	11.83 ± 0.3	-	33.6 ± 20.8	20.98 ± 1.4	22.2 ± 0.01	28.0	21.8	**98.4 ± 1.1**	94.2 ± 3.7

Table 2: Exact match accuracy on gSCAN compositional splits. For our proposed model, we report both the performance of models trained on the full dataset and of those trained on a 10% subset.

Table 3: Exact match accuracy and attention match accuracy on gSCAN compositional splits for models with selective attention, optimized with and without auxiliary feedback.

	perfect att.		**w/o aux. signal abs. loc.**				**w/o aux. signal rel. dist.**			
	seq. match		seq. match		att. match		seq. match		att. match	
A	100.0	± 0.0	59.3	± 29.1	74.2	± 21.4	83.0	± 3.4	92.8	± 2.2
B	100.0	± 0.0	50.8	± 21.1	61.6	± 17.0	59.5	± 15.7	70.0	± 16.7
C	100.0	± 0.0	70.0	± 29.5	73.8	± 24.8	89.7	± 9.3	91.1	± 8.4
D	1.9	± 1.7	0.1	± 0.2	66.6	± 28.9	0.8	± 0.9	91.3	± 2.6
E	100.0	± 0.0	50.3	± 20.4	62.1	± 17.9	74.1	± 6.2	84.1	± 7.6
F	100.0	± 0.0	52.6	± 25.0	70.4	± 20.7	67.5	± 9.3	84.4	± 8.0
G	0.0	± 0.0	0.0	± 0.0	63.0	± 15.7	0.0	± 0.0	73.0	± 5.8
H	99.3	± 1.0	37.5	± 20.2	74.4	± 14.9	56.4	± 6.2	89.9	± 3.9

models overfit to the absence of yellow squares. Depending on the random initialization of its selective attention matrix, a model may be more or less predisposed to generalization on this task. In the absence of any samples with yellow squares that could cause a course correction, this predisposition may be exacerbated with each update and thus deteriorate performance in the higher-data regimes.

Novel direction: Similar to previous architectures tested on gSCAN, our model has no trouble identifying the correct targets in split D (Ruis et al., 2020; Qiu et al., 2021). Its attention match accuracy is 100%. However, it cannot navigate to the identified target successfully. On average, it ends up in the correct row in 44% of cases, in the right column in 23% of cases, and never both.

5.4 Ablations

Weight Decay and Action Attention: As shown in Table 4, ablating weight decay or attention over past steps causes the most pronounced performance drops in splits E, F, and H. To compare structural differences between the ablated models, we perform a neuron pruning experiment (detailed results in C). For every neuron in the trained models' final hidden layer, we record the product of its activation and outgoing weights at each step when processing a 2% subset of the training set. We then disable neurons in ascending order of contribution to the models' outputs and assess the pruned model's exact match accuracy. All full models require only 13 hidden neurons to solve all tasks. Without attention over past actions, 16 neurons are needed to reach the final accuracy. Models without weight decay rely almost equally on all 100 neurons. Pruning any of them leads to decreased performance.

This difference in learned representations is also illustrated in Figure 3, which shows the weights between the agent's past actions and the hidden layer of three identically initialized models with different ablations applied. The model with weight decay and action attention learns the most sparse weights and focuses on recent steps. The hidden model without action attention has a similarly sparse hidden layer, but a longer "memory", i.e., it takes into account past actions from further back in the step sequence. The model without weight decay is very densely connected.

Selective Attention: To investigate the effect of selective attention, we train a soft attention version of the model. Instead of the isolated feature vector of the most attended grid cell, this model receives the attention-weighted whole grid as input, similar to the action attention mechanism. To account for the higher dimensionality of the input, we increase the number of neurons in the hidden units to 500. The relative amount of neurons needed to reach

	full model	**w/o weight decay**	**w/o action attention**	**w/o selective attention**
A	99.7 ± 0.1	92.5 ± 1.8	92.2 ± 2.5	89.6 ± 3.3
B	73.5 ± 25.4	74.2 ± 12.9	73.0 ± 21.1	69.5 ± 21.8
C	99.4 ± 0.4	95.9 ± 3.0	92.9 ± 7.6	78.6 ± 17.1
D	2.2 ± 1.5	0.1 ± 0.1	0.0 ± 0.0	0.3 ± 0.6
E	97.4 ± 2.0	73.9 ± 8.2	85.7 ± 6.6	72.1 ± 2.3
F	99.1 ± 0.6	73.7 ± 7.8	80.6 ± 9.3	81.6 ± 9.9
G	0.0 ± 0.0	0.4 ± 0.2	0.0 ± 0.0	0.0 ± 0.0
H	98.4 ± 1.1	39.5 ± 14.5	23.8 ± 3.7	65.5 ± 13.1

Table 4: Exact match accuracy on gSCAN compositional splits for ablated models

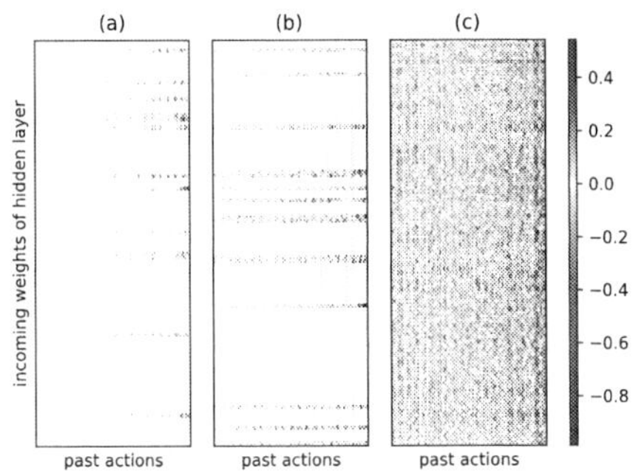

Figure 3: Weights between the agent's past actions and the model's hidden layer, as learned by (a) the full model, (b) the model with weight decay but no action attention, and (c) the model with action attention but no weight decay

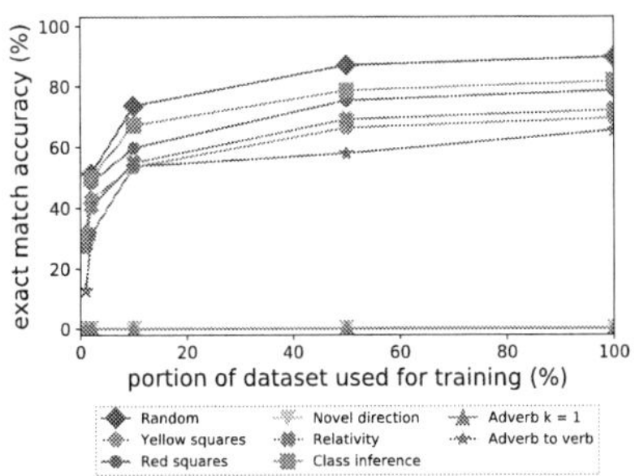

Figure 4: Sample efficiency on test splits for models without selective attention

full accuracy is similar to the model without action attention – around 18%. Performance-wise, the ablation causes a drop-off across the board but still achieves around 90% accuracy on in-distribution data when trained on the full dataset. However, the sample efficiency is greatly reduced (see Figure 4). I.e., models need to have seen a greater number of input combinations to start generalizing. This is also supported by a comparison of the confusion matrices for models with and without selective attention via a χ^2-test on split A (details in D.2). By far the most over-represented feature among misclassifications by the soft-attention model, as measured by standardized residuals, is the "square" dimension. Since squares are held out for splits B, C, and F, this shape is underrepresented in the training set. The model thus sees fewer examples during training, which seems to affect its ability to generalize to new combinations involving squares even for in-distribution data.

5.5 "Spontaneous" Generalization

During our ablation studies, we observed that generalization to the "adverb to verb" split did occur frequently in models without weight decay and action attention, but not in a linear fashion. As shown in Figure 5, performance on split H would spike on one training batch, then fall again. Higher systematic generalization ability is not necessarily evident from looking at the performance on in-distribution data – two models may have the same train loss or test accuracy, but very different out-of-distribution accuracies. Such spurious generalization behavior may also explain the variation in performance on split H observed by Gao et al. (2020) and Jiang and Bansal (2021).

One reason often cited for unstable generalization is sharp local minima (Keskar et al., 2017). However, a visualization of the loss landscape of the models at various points during training shows relatively flat planes. The landscapes for training and "adverb to verb" data are simply well aligned for some model-batch combinations, and less so for others (see Figure 6). We also investigated whether the batches used to update the models immediately before out-of-distribution performance spikes had any special properties that would facilitate generalization. We saved batches that preceded an increase on split H accuracy of at least 5%, injected them randomly into the training of other models, and recorded the difference in performance caused. However, we found no statistically significant improvement over random batches, and no statistically significant differences in feature or label distributions of such "spike" batches.

We did find that batch size had an impact on the likelihood of generalization spikes. We trained 10

[7] github.com/marcellodebernardi/loss-landscapes

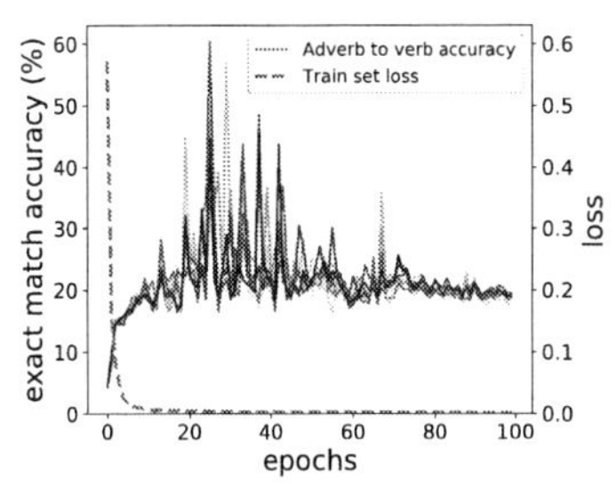

Figure 5: Accuracy on split H over the course of training for a model without action attention

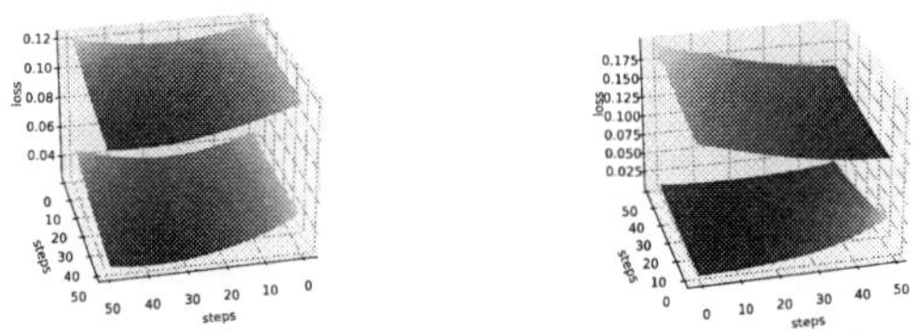

Figure 6: Examples of loss landscapes for models trained without weight decay, visualized with the loss-landscapes library [3]. Lower planes show the landscapes for a random training batch of size 256. Upper planes show the landscapes for the entire "adverb to verb" split. For some model-batch combinations, the two align well (left). For others, less so (right).

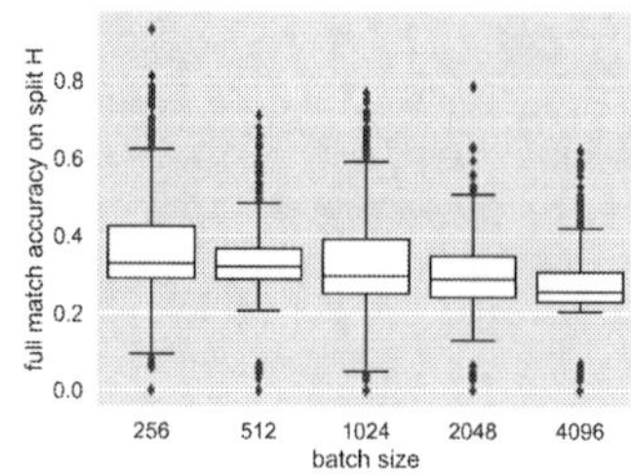

Figure 7: Distributions of split H accuracy sampled during training, for 5 different batch sizes

models without weight decay on 5 different batch sizes using a 2% subset of the training data. All models were trained for the same number of absolute updates. For all batch sizes, the random initialization of the ten models used the same random seeds. We then sampled the models' performance on split H at 50 points in regular intervals during training. As shown in Figure 7, generalization performance with smaller batches was higher but more volatile. Comparing the distribution of sampled "adverb to verb" accuracies across batch sizes yielded statistically significant Z-scores > 2 between batch sizes ≤ 512 and ≥ 2048. This is consistent with previous findings that smaller batch sizes facilitate better generalization (Smith and Le, 2018; Keskar et al., 2017; Smith et al., 2018; Hoffer et al., 2017; Masters and Luschi, 2018). Details on statistical tests are given in E.

6 Discussion

The core of systematic generalization, namely, the ability to flexibly compose known parts, is not something neural networks seem incapable of – as long as they receive atomic units as inputs that are separated from irrelevant context. Otherwise, they may overfit and learn solutions that only perform well on in-distribution data. Seen from this perspective, factors identified as helpful to generalization, both in the literature and in this study, are all mechanisms that can contribute to learning atomic input units. Weight decay facilitates this by serving as a kind of inductive simplicity bias (Power et al., 2021; Kirk et al., 2021). So do soft attention mechanisms, which filter out irrelevant inputs. So does the hard attention bottleneck employed in this paper, by decoupling content, which is only relevant for target identification, from location, which is only relevant for navigation (Heinze-Deml and Bouchacourt, 2020; Dubois et al., 2020).

7 Conclusion

In summary, we build on Tang et al.'s neuroevolution approach to selective attention and embed it in a hybrid model. We apply this model to the task of systematic generalization in grounded instruction following and explore the effect of various design decisions on out-of-distribution performance. We find that weight decay and attention mechanisms facilitate compositional generalization by encouraging sparse representations divorced from irrelevant context, and that selective attention dramatically improves the model's sample efficiency. We also find that, even without weight decay and attention, generalization performance may improve sporadically during training independent of in-distribution accuracy, especially with smaller batch sizes. Studies on out-of-distribution generalization should therefore employ a sufficiently high number of training runs to obtain a reliable estimate of a models' generalization robustness.

Although our architecture is specific to the dataset at hand, the factors contributing to its performance are consistent with related work on systematic generalization and likely to apply to other situations as well. However, compositional generalization encompasses a wide range of skills and even within systematic generalization, solving one task, e.g., recombining shapes and colors, may not translate to another, e.g. recombining directions. Several gSCAN tasks remain unsolved and likely require different inductive biases than the ones presented here. We hope that this closer look at the minimal requirements for generalization on the various gSCAN test splits can inform future work on this benchmark going forward.

References

Ekin Akyürek, Afra Feyza Akyürek, and Jacob Andreas. 2020. Learning to Recombine and Resample Data For Compositional Generalization. In *Proceedings of ICLR*.

Jacob Andreas. 2020. Good-Enough Compositional Data Augmentation. In *ACL*, pages 7556–7566.

Jacob Andreas, Marco Baroni, Alexis Conneau, Douwe Kiela, Holger Schwenk, Loïc Barrault, Antoine Bordes, Jacob Devlin, Alona Fyshe, Leila Wehbe, et al. 2019. Measuring Compositionality in Representation Learning. In *Proceedings of ICLR*, volume 375, pages 2227–2237.

Jacob Andreas, Marcus Rohrbach, Trevor Darrell, and Dan Klein. 2016a. Learning to Compose Neural Networks for Question Answering. In *Proceedings of NAACL-HTL*, pages 1545–1554.

Jacob Andreas, Marcus Rohrbach, Trevor Darrell, and Dan Klein. 2016b. Neural Module Networks. In *Proceedings of CVPR*, pages 39–48.

Joris Baan, Jana Leible, Mitja Nikolaus, David Rau, Dennis Ulmer, Tim Baumgärtner, Dieuwke Hupkes, and Elia Bruni. 2019. On the Realization of Compositionality in Neural Networks. In *BlackboxNLP@ ACL*, pages 127–137.

Marco Baroni. 2020. Linguistic generalization and compositionality in modern artificial neural networks. *Philosophical Transactions of the Royal Society B*, 375(1791):20190307.

Rahma Chaabouni, Eugene Kharitonov, Diane Bouchacourt, Emmanuel Dupoux, and Marco Baroni. 2020. Compositionality and Generalization in Emergent Languages. In *Proceedings of ACL*, pages 4427–4442.

Devendra Singh Chaplot, Kanthashree Mysore Sathyendra, Rama Kumar Pasumarthi, Dheeraj Rajagopal, and Ruslan Salakhutdinov. 2018. Gated-Attention Architectures for Task-Oriented Language Grounding. In *Proceedings of AAAI*, pages 2819–2826.

Maxime Chevalier-Boisvert, Dzmitry Bahdanau, Salem Lahlou, Lucas Willems, Chitwan Saharia, Thien Huu Nguyen, and Yoshua Bengio. 2019. BabyAI: A Platform to Study the Sample Efficiency of Grounded Language Learning. In *Proceedings of ICML*.

Thierry Deruyttere, Simon Vandenhende, Dusan Grujicic, Luc Van Gool, and Marie-Francine Moens. 2019. Talk2Car: Taking Control of Your Self-Driving Car. In *Proceedings of EMNLP/IJCNLP (1)*, pages 2088–2098.

Yann Dubois, Gautier Dagan, Dieuwke Hupkes, and Elia Bruni. 2020. Location Attention for Extrapolation to Longer Sequences. In *Proceedings of ACL*, pages 403–413.

Tong Gao, Qi Huang, and Raymond Mooney. 2020. Systematic Generalization on gSCAN with Language Conditioned Embedding. In *Proceedings of AACL-IJCNLP*, pages 491–503.

Daniel J. Gauthier, Erik Bollt, Aaron Griffith, and Wendson A. S. Barbosa. 2021. Next Generation Reservoir Computing. *Nature Communications*, 12(1):5564.

Nikolaus Hansen, Anne Auger, Raymond Ros, Steffen Finck, and Petr Posík. 2010. Comparing results of 31 algorithms from the black-box optimization benchmarking BBOB-2009. In *GECCO (Companion)*, pages 1689–1696. ACM.

Nikolaus Hansen, Sibylle D Müller, and Petros Koumoutsakos. 2003. Reducing the time complexity of the derandomized evolution strategy with covariance matrix adaptation (CMA-ES). *Evolutionary computation*, 11(1):1–18.

Nikolaus Hansen and Andreas Ostermeier. 2001. Completely Derandomized Self-Adaptation in Evolution Strategies. *Evol. Comput.*, 9(2):159–195.

Christina Heinze-Deml and Diane Bouchacourt. 2020. Think before you act: A simple baseline for compositional generalization. *arXiv preprint arXiv:2009.13962*.

Karl Moritz Hermann, Felix Hill, Simon Green, Fumin Wang, Ryan Faulkner, Hubert Soyer, David Szepesvari, Wojciech Marian Czarnecki, Max Jaderberg, Denis Teplyashin, Marcus Wainwright, Chris Apps, Demis Hassabis, and Phil Blunsom. 2017. Grounded Language Learning in a Simulated 3D World. *arXiv preprint arXiv:1706.06551*.

Elad Hoffer, Itay Hubara, and Daniel Soudry. 2017. Train longer, generalize better: closing the generalization gap in large batch training of neural networks. In *Proceedings of NeurIPS*, pages 1731–1741.

Dieuwke Hupkes, Verna Dankers, Mathijs Mul, and Elia Bruni. 2020. Compositionality Decomposed: How do Neural Networks Generalise? *Journal of Artificial Intelligence Research*, 67:757–795.

Dieuwke Hupkes, Anand Singh, Kris Korrel, German Kruszewski, and Elia Bruni. 2018. Learning compositionally through attentive guidance. *arXiv preprint arXiv:1805.09657*.

Yichen Jiang and Mohit Bansal. 2021. Inducing Transformer's Compositional Generalization Ability via Auxiliary Sequence Prediction Tasks. In *Proceedings of EMNLP*, pages 6253–6265.

Nitish Shirish Keskar, Dheevatsa Mudigere, Jorge Nocedal, Mikhail Smelyanskiy, and Ping Tak Peter Tang. 2017. On Large-Batch Training for Deep Learning: Generalization Gap and Sharp Minima. In *Proceedings of ICLR*.

Daniel Keysers, Nathanael Schärli, Nathan Scales, Hylke Buisman, Daniel Furrer, Sergii Kashubin, Nikola Momchev, Danila Sinopalnikov, Lukasz Stafiniak, Tibor Tihon, et al. 2019. Measuring Compositional Generalization: A Comprehensive Method on Realistic Data. In *Proceedings of ICLR*.

Robert Kirk, Amy Zhang, Edward Grefenstette, and Tim Rocktäschel. 2021. A Survey of Generalisation in Deep Reinforcement Learning. *arXiv preprint arXiv:2111.09794*.

Yen-Ling Kuo, Boris Katz, and Andrei Barbu. 2021. Compositional Networks Enable Systematic Generalization for Grounded Language Understanding. In *Findings of EMNLP*, pages 216–226.

Brenden M. Lake and Marco Baroni. 2018. Generalization without systematicity: On the compositional skills of sequence-to-sequence recurrent networks. In *Proceedings of ICLR*, pages 2873–2882. PMLR.

Adam Liška, Germán Kruszewski, and Marco Baroni. 2018. Memorize or generalize? Searching for a compositional RNN in a haystack. In *AEGAP Workshop@ ICML*.

João Loula, Marco Baroni, and Brenden M. Lake. 2018. Rearranging the Familiar: Testing Compositional Generalization in Recurrent Networks. In *BlackboxNLP@ EMNLP*.

Dominic Masters and Carlo Luschi. 2018. Revisiting Small Batch Training for Deep Neural Networks. *arXiv preprint arXiv:1804.07612*.

R. Thomas McCoy, Junghyun Min, and Tal Linzen. 2020. BERTs of a feather do not generalize together: Large variability in generalization across models with similar test set performance. In *BlackboxNLP@ EMNLP*, pages 217–227.

Dipendra Kumar Misra, Andrew Bennett, Valts Blukis, Eyvind Niklasson, Max Shatkhin, and Yoav Artzi. 2018. Mapping Instructions to Actions in 3D Environments with Visual Goal Prediction. In *Proceedings of EMNLP*, pages 2667–2678.

Kohei Nakajima. 2020. Physical reservoir computing—An introductory perspective. *Japanese Journal of Applied Physics*, 59(6):060501.

Maxwell Nye, Michael Tessler, Josh Tenenbaum, and Brenden M. Lake. 2021. Improving Coherence and Consistency in Neural Sequence Models with Dual-System, Neuro-Symbolic Reasoning. *Proceedings of NeurIPS*, 34.

Santiago Ontanon, Joshua Ainslie, Zachary Fisher, and Vaclav Cvicek. 2022. Making Transformers Solve Compositional Tasks. In *Proceedings of ACL*, pages 3591–3607.

Alethea Power, Yuri Burda, Harri Edwards, Igor Babuschkin, and Vedant Misra. 2021. Grokking: Generalization Beyond Overfitting on Small Algorithmic Datasets. In *MATH-AI@ ICLR*.

Linlu Qiu, Hexiang Hu, Bowen Zhang, Peter Shaw, and Fei Sha. 2021. Systematic Generalization on gSCAN: What is Nearly Solved and What is Next? In *Proceedings of EMNLP*, pages 2180–2188.

Laura Ruis, Jacob Andreas, Marco Baroni, Diane Bouchacourt, and Brenden M. Lake. 2020. A Benchmark for Systematic Generalization in Grounded Language Understanding. *Proceedings of NeurIPS*, 33:19861–19872.

Gresa Shala, André Biedenkapp, Noor Awad, Steven Adriaensen, Marius Lindauer, and Frank Hutter. 2020. Learning step-size adaptation in CMA-ES. In *International Conference on Parallel Problem Solving from Nature*, pages 691–706. Springer.

Mohit Shridhar, Jesse Thomason, Daniel Gordon, Yonatan Bisk, Winson Han, Roozbeh Mottaghi, Luke Zettlemoyer, and Dieter Fox. 2020. ALFRED: A Benchmark for Interpreting Grounded Instructions for Everyday Tasks. In *Proceedings of CVPR*, pages 10737–10746. Computer Vision Foundation / IEEE.

Samuel L. Smith, Pieter-Jan Kindermans, Chris Ying, and Quoc V. Le. 2018. Don't Decay the Learning Rate, Increase the Batch Size. In *Proceedings of ICLR*.

Samuel L. Smith and Quoc V. Le. 2018. A Bayesian Perspective on Generalization and Stochastic Gradient Descent. In *Proceedings of ICLR*.

Sanjay Subramanian, Sameer Singh, and Matt Gardner. 2019. Analyzing Compositionality in Visual Question Answering. *ViGIL@ NeurIPS*, 7.

Yujin Tang, Duong Nguyen, and David Ha. 2020. Neuroevolution of Self-Interpretable Agents. In *Proceedings of GECCO*, pages 414–424.

Konstantinos Varelas, Anne Auger, Dimo Brockhoff, Nikolaus Hansen, Ouassim Ait ElHara, Yann Semet, Rami Kassab, and Frédéric Barbaresco. 2018. A Comparative Study of Large-Scale Variants of CMA-ES. In *PPSN (1)*, volume 11101 of *Lecture Notes in Computer Science*, pages 3–15. Springer.

Noah Weber, Leena Shekhar, and Niranjan Balasubramanian. 2018. The Fine Line between Linguistic Generalization and Failure in Seq2Seq-Attention Models. In *Gen-Deep@ NAACL*, pages 24–27.

Haonan Yu, Xiaochen Lian, Haichao Zhang, and Wei Xu. 2018a. Guided Feature Transformation (GFT): A Neural Language Grounding Module for Embodied Agents. In *CoRL*, volume 87 of *PMLR*, pages 81–98.

Haonan Yu, Haichao Zhang, and Wei Xu. 2018b. Interactive Grounded Language Acquisition and Generalization in a 2D World. In *Proceedings of ICLR*.

A Background on CMA-ES

CMA-ES begins by sampling λ individual solutions $x_1^{(g+1)}, ..., x_\lambda^{(g+1)}$ from a multivariate Gaussian distribution $\mathcal{N}(m^{(g)}, \sigma^{(g)^2} C^{(g)})$ with mean $m^{(g)}$, step size $\sigma^{(g)}$ and covariance matrix $C^{(g)}$. The initial mean, step size and covariance matrix are then adapted iteratively to increase the likelihood of successful solutions as evaluated by some function f. Mean adaptation is done by shifting m by the weighted average of the μ best solutions of generation g (Shala et al., 2020):

$$m^{(g+1)} = m^{(g)} + c_m \sum_{i=1}^{\mu} w_i \big(x_{i:\sigma}^{(g+1)} - m^{(g)}\big), \quad (5)$$

where c_m is a learning rate. The new step size σ is determined as follows (Shala et al., 2020):

$$\sigma^{(g+1)} = \sigma^{(g)} exp\left(\frac{c_\sigma}{d_\sigma}\left(\frac{||\mathbf{p}_\sigma^{(g+1)}||}{E||\mathcal{N}(0,I)||} - 1\right)\right), \quad (6)$$

where c_σ is a separate learning rate, d_σ is a damping parameter, and $\mathbf{p}_\sigma^{(g+1)}$ is the next generation's conjugate evolution path computed as (Hansen et al., 2003):

$$\mathbf{p}_\sigma^{(g+1)} = (1 - c_\sigma) \cdot \mathbf{p}_\sigma^{(g)} + \sqrt{c_\sigma \cdot (2 - c_\sigma)} \cdot \frac{\sqrt{\mu}}{\sigma^{(g)}} \big(x_\mu^{(g+1)} - x_\mu^{(g)}\big). \quad (7)$$

Finally, the covariance matrix is updated (Hansen et al., 2003):

$$C^{(g+1)} = (1 - c_{cov}) \cdot C^{(g)} + c_{cov} \cdot \mathbf{p}_c^{(g+1)} \big(\mathbf{p}_c^{(g+1)}\big)^T, \quad (8)$$

where c_{cov} is another learning rate.

B Detailed Evaluation Results

Parameter	**Size**
Hidden layer	28,800
Layer normalization weights	100
Layer normalization biases	100
Output layer	600
Selective attention key matrix	1,024
Self-attention key matrix	4,096
Action attention key matrix	12,800
Total	**47,520**

Table 5: Overview of our model's trainable parameters

	0.01	0.02	0.1	0.5	1.0
A	0.996± 0.002	1.000± 0.000	1.000± 0.000	1.000± 0.000	1.000± 0.000
B	N/A	N/A	N/A	N/A	N/A
C	N/A	N/A	N/A	N/A	N/A
D	0.000± 0.000	0.000± 0.000	0.034± 0.032	0.021± 0.025	0.019 ± 0.017
E	0.997± 0.001	1.000± 0.000	1.000± 0.000	1.000± 0.000	1.000± 0.000
F	0.995± 0.002	1.000± 0.000	1.000± 0.000	1.000± 0.000	1.000± 0.000
G	0.000± 0.000	0.000± 0.000	0.000± 0.000	0.000± 0.000	0.000± 0.000
H	0.610± 0.182	0.790± 0.165	0.999± 0.001	0.988± 0.028	0.993± 0.01

Table 6: Sequence match accuracies on gSCAN compositional splits with perfect selective attention trained on 1%, 2%, 10%, 50%, and 100% of the dataset

	Att. Match	Exact Match	Exact Match if Att. Match
A	0.951± 0.015	0.925± 0.018	0.988± 0.006
B	0.786± 0.128	0.742± 0.129	0.988± 0.012
C	0.965± 0.028	0.959± 0.03	1.000± 0.000
D	0.934± 0.021	0.001± 0.001	0.001± 0.002
E	0.839± 0.109	0.739± 0.082	0.909± 0.066
F	0.878± 0.054	0.737± 0.078	0.886± 0.049
G	0.718± 0.07	0.004± 0.002	0.006± 0.003
H	0.918± 0.033	0.395± 0.145	0.441± 0.171

Table 7: Sequence and attention match accuracies on gSCAN compositional splits with selective attention but without weight decay (trained on the full dataset)

	Att. Match	Exact Match	Exact Match if Att. Match
A	0.947± 0.020	0.922± 0.025	0.996± 0.002
B	0.781± 0.188	0.730± 0.211	1.000± 0.000
C	0.947± 0.066	0.929± 0.076	1.000± 0.000
D	0.931± 0.027	0.000± 0.000	0.000± 0.000
E	0.901± 0.058	0.857± 0.066	0.996± 0.003
F	0.863± 0.073	0.806± 0.093	0.994± 0.005
G	0.772± 0.072	0.000± 0.000	0.000± 0.000
H	0.919 ± 0.032	0.238 ± 0.037	0.272 ± 0.034

Table 8: Sequence and attention match accuracies on gSCAN compositional splits with selective attention but without action attention (trained on the full dataset)

Table 9: Sequence and attention match accuracies with selective attention and auxiliary feedback, trained on 1%, 2%, 10%, 50%, and 100% of the dataset

	0.01			0.02			0.1			0.5			1.0		
	Att. Match	Exact Match	Exact Match if Att. Match	Att. Match	Exact Match	Exact Match if Att. Match	Att. Match	Exact Match	Exact Match if Att. Match	Att. Match	Exact Match	Exact Match if Att. Match	Att. Match	Exact Match	Exact Match if Att. Match
A	0.974 ± 0.005	0.916 ± 0.011	0.969 ± 0.004	0.990 ± 0.003	0.971 ± 0.006	0.995 ± 0.001	0.999 ± 0.000	0.995 ± 0.001	1.000 ± 0.000	0.999 ± 0.000	0.997 ± 0.001	1.000 ± 0.000	0.999 ± 0.000	0.997 ± 0.001	0.999 ± 0.000
B	0.772 ± 0.079	0.700 ± 0.086	0.978 ± 0.007	0.702 ± 0.175	0.649 ± 0.195	0.997 ± 0.004	0.846 ± 0.127	0.816 ± 0.143	1.000 ± 0.000	0.804 ± 0.212	0.771 ± 0.232	1.000 ± 0.000	0.781 ± 0.212	0.735 ± 0.254	0.999 ± 0.000
C	0.948 ± 0.030	0.900 ± 0.036	0.974 ± 0.011	0.985 ± 0.007	0.970 ± 0.009	0.997 ± 0.001	0.998 ± 0.001	0.995 ± 0.002	1.000 ± 0.000	0.996 ± 0.005	0.991 ± 0.008	1.000 ± 0.000	0.998 ± 0.003	0.994 ± 0.004	0.999 ± 0.000
D	0.977 ± 0.004	0.000 ± 0.000	0.000 ± 0.000	0.991 ± 0.003	0.000 ± 0.000	0.000 ± 0.000	1.000 ± 0.000	0.035 ± 0.027	0.035 ± 0.027	1.000 ± 0.000	0.026 ± 0.020	0.026 ± 0.020	1.000 ± 0.000	0.022 ± 0.015	0.022 ± 0.015
E	0.892 ± 0.062	0.811 ± 0.071	0.965 ± 0.006	0.941 ± 0.047	0.904 ± 0.054	0.997 ± 0.002	0.985 ± 0.014	0.968 ± 0.019	1.000 ± 0.001	0.985 ± 0.017	0.971 ± 0.031	1.000 ± 0.000	0.985 ± 0.016	0.974 ± 0.020	1.000 ± 0.000
F	0.930 ± 0.032	0.834 ± 0.042	0.946 ± 0.015	0.958 ± 0.026	0.918 ± 0.030	0.990 ± 0.007	0.992 ± 0.011	0.983 ± 0.017	1.000 ± 0.000	0.992 ± 0.013	0.984 ± 0.020	1.000 ± 0.000	0.997 ± 0.004	0.991 ± 0.006	1.000 ± 0.000
G	0.780 ± 0.050	0.000 ± 0.000	0.000 ± 0.000	0.805 ± 0.064	0.000 ± 0.000	0.000 ± 0.000	0.852 ± 0.050	0.000 ± 0.001	0.000 ± 0.001	0.804 ± 0.052	0.000 ± 0.000	0.000 ± 0.000	0.766 ± 0.101	0.000 ± 0.000	0.000 ± 0.000
H	0.957 ± 0.017	0.377 ± 0.082	0.406 ± 0.119	0.987 ± 0.005	0.468 ± 0.119	0.472 ± 0.130	0.994 ± 0.003	0.942 ± 0.037	0.956 ± 0.035	0.995 ± 0.005	0.960 ± 0.060	0.972 ± 0.062	0.998 ± 0.002	0.984 ± 0.011	0.992 ± 0.007

Table 10: Sequence and attention match accuracies with selective attention but without auxiliary feedback, trained on 1%, 2%, 10%, 50%, and 100% of the dataset, using relative target distances

	0.01			0.02			0.1			0.5			1.0		
	Att. Match	Exact Match	Exact Match if Att. Match	Att. Match	Exact Match	Exact Match if Att. Match	Att. Match	Exact Match	Exact Match if Att. Match	Att. Match	Exact Match	Exact Match if Att. Match	Att. Match	Exact Match	Exact Match if Att. Match
A	0.765 ± 0.154	0.604 ± 0.189	0.815 ± 0.17	0.946 ± 0.034	0.906 ± 0.044	0.984 ± 0.011	0.975 ± 0.008	0.976 ± 0.003	0.999 ± 0.001	0.978 ± 0.01	0.986 ± 0.003	1.000 ± 0.000	0.928 ± 0.022	0.83 ± 0.034	0.919 ± 0.017
B	0.502 ± 0.134	0.372 ± 0.154	0.791 ± 0.272	0.693 ± 0.195	0.618 ± 0.217	0.978 ± 0.013	0.73 ± 0.108	0.697 ± 0.118	0.999 ± 0.001	0.64 ± 0.198	0.603 ± 0.223	1.000 ± 0.000	0.7 ± 0.167	0.595 ± 0.157	0.928 ± 0.051
C	0.649 ± 0.205	0.507 ± 0.218	0.768 ± 0.264	0.939 ± 0.022	0.906 ± 0.033	0.985 ± 0.012	0.973 ± 0.012	0.967 ± 0.015	0.999 ± 0.003	0.975 ± 0.012	0.971 ± 0.018	0.999 ± 0.001	0.911 ± 0.084	0.897 ± 0.093	1.000 ± 0.000
D	0.749 ± 0.169	0.000 ± 0.000	0.000 ± 0.000	0.946 ± 0.039	0.000 ± 0.000	0.000 ± 0.000	0.983 ± 0.006	0.002 ± 0.002	0.002 ± 0.002	0.984 ± 0. 008	0.004 ± 0.006	0.005 ± 0.006	0.913 ± 0.026	0.008 ± 0.009	0.009 ± 0.010
E	0.615 ± 0.147	0.461 ± 0.144	0.736 ± 0.258	0.802 ± 0.074	0.731 ± 0.083	0.981 ± 0.01	0.938 ± 0.032	0.918 ± 0.028	0.994 ± 0.01	0.961 ± 0.024	0.954 ± 0.029	0.999 ± 0.003	0.841 ± 0.076	0.741 ± 0.062	0.91 ± 0.028
F	0.666 ± 0.175	0.502 ± 0.191	0.772 ± 0.267	0.911 ± 0.048	0.826 ± 0.058	0.942 ± 0.031	0.96 ± 0.022	0.944 ± 0.024	0.998 ± 0.003	0.971 ± 0.008	0.967 ± 0.016	0.999 ± 0.002	0.844 ± 0.08	0.675 ± 0.093	0.874 ± 0.038
G	0.624 ± 0.11	0.000 ± 0.000	0.000 ± 0.000	0.764 ± 0.083	0.000 ± 0.000	0.000 ± 0.000	0.800 ± 0.069	0.000 ± 0.000	0.000 ± 0.000	0.772 ± 0.045	0.000 ± 0.000	0.000 ± 0.000	0.73 ± 0.058	0.000 ± 0.000	0.000 ± 0.000
H	0.76 ± 0.15	0.311 ± 0.139	0.302 ± 0.17	0.922 ± 0.036	0.576 ± 0.056	0.615 ± 0.072	0.96 ± 0.023	0.744 ± 0.086	0.822 ± 0.058	0.962 ± 0.013	0.771 ± 0.097	0.822 ± 0.095	0.899 ± 0.039	0.564 ± 0.062	0.667 ± 0.055

Table 11: Sequence and attention match accuracies with selective attention but without auxiliary feedback, trained on 1%, 2%, 10%, 50%, and 100% of the dataset, using absolute target locations

	0.01			0.02			0.1			0.5			1.0		
	Att. Match	Exact Match	Exact Match if Att. Match	Att. Match	Exact Match	Exact Match if Att. Match	Att. Match	Exact Match	Exact Match if Att. Match	Att. Match	Exact Match	Exact Match if Att. Match	Att. Match	Exact Match	Exact Match if Att. Match
A	0.476 ± 0.005	0.228 ± 0.003	0.145 ± 0.226	0.541 ± 0.136	0.333 ± 0.182	0.203 ± 0.338	0.58 ± 0.201	0.41 ± 0.28	0.299 ± 0.457	0.68 ± 0.246	0.555 ± 0.347	0.399 ± 0.489	0.742 ± 0.214	0.593 ± 0.291	0.612 ± 0.415
B	0.435 ± 0.009	0.251 ± 0.006	0.025 ± 0.074	0.499 ± 0.145	0.353 ± 0.168	0.169 ± 0.342	0.493 ± 0.115	0.375 ± 0.155	0.245 ± 0.4	0.562 ± 0.193	0.469 ± 0.235	0.399 ± 0.489	0.616 ± 0.17	0.508 ± 0.211	0.591 ± 0.449
C	0.438 ± 0.018	0.266 ± 0.008	0.028 ± 0.085	0.481 ± 0.11	0.364 ± 0.128	0.161 ± 0.331	0.534 ± 0.203	0.454 ± 0.239	0.254 ± 0.406	0.647 ± 0.265	0.59 ± 0.31	0.400 ± 0.49	0.738 ± 0.248	0.700 ± 0.295	0.700 ± 0.458
D	0.313 ± 0.002	0.000 ± 0.000	0.000 ± 0.000	0.401 ± 0.192	0.000 ± 0.000	0.000 ± 0.000	0.446 ± 0.267	0.000 ± 0.000	0.000 ± 0.000	0.582 ± 0.330	0.013 ± 0.033	0.014 ± 0.036	0.666 ± 0.289	0.001 ± 0.002	0.001 ± 0.002
E	0.412 ± 0.003	0.249 ± 0.004	0.000 ± 0.000	0.464 ± 0.132	0.338 ± 0.155	0.163 ± 0.334	0.524 ± 0.22	0.407 ± 0.261	0.197 ± 0.395	0.623 ± 0.256	0.529 ± 0.317	0.399 ± 0.488	0.621 ± 0.179	0.503 ± 0.204	0.552 ± 0.451
F	0.462 ± 0.003	0.227 ± 0.006	0.032 ± 0.097	0.515 ± 0.117	0.332 ± 0.148	0.167 ± 0.339	0.554 ± 0.188	0.417 ± 0.245	0.199 ± 0.399	0.662 ± 0.247	0.544 ± 0.335	0.398 ± 0.488	0.704 ± 0.207	0.526 ± 0.25	0.53 ± 0.434
G	0.448 ± 0.01	0.000 ± 0.000	0.000 ± 0.000	0.493 ± 0.093	0.000 ± 0.000	0.000 ± 0.000	0.535 ± 0.167	0.000 ± 0.000	0.000 ± 0.000	0.596 ± 0.183	0.000 ± 0.000	0.000 ± 0.000	0.63 ± 0.157	0.000 ± 0.000	0.000 ± 0.000
H	0.557 ± 0.021	0.122 ± 0.012	0.000 ± 0.000	0.61 ± 0.109	0.248 ± 0.111	0.103 ± 0.206	0.648 ± 0.16	0.365 ± 0.224	0.173 ± 0.346	0.715 ± 0.183	0.37 ± 0.195	0.262 ± 0.334	0.744 ± 0.149	0.375 ± 0.202	0.394 ± 0.328

Table 12: Sequence and attention match accuracies without selective attention, trained on 1%, 2%, 10%, 50%, and 100% of the dataset

	0.01			0.02			0.1			0.5			1.0		
	Att. Match	Exact Match	Exact Match if Att. Match	Att. Match	Exact Match	Exact Match if Att. Match	Att. Match	Exact Match	Exact Match if Att. Match	Att. Match	Exact Match	Exact Match if Att. Match	Att. Match	Exact Match	Exact Match if Att. Match
A	0.498 ± 0.136	0.311 ± 0.12	0.282 ± 0.162	0.570 ± 0.222	0.512 ± 0.126	0.407 ± 0.271	0.578 ± 0.243	0.736 ± 0.028	0.617 ± 0.311	0.545 ± 0.216	0.869 ± 0.033	0.739 ± 0.372	0.548 ± 0.204	0.896 ± 0.033	0.652 ± 0.428
B	0.44 ± 0.1	0.273 ± 0.083	0.195 ± 0.167	0.566 ± 0.21	0.43 ± 0.127	0.352 ± 0.235	0.614 ± 0.229	0.535 ± 0.139	0.476 ± 0.24	0.579 ± 0.204	0.663 ± 0.199	0.572 ± 0.324	0.571 ± 0.195	0.695 ± 0.218	0.587 ± 0.343
C	0.492 ± 0.201	0.312 ± 0.105	0.256 ± 0.178	0.604 ± 0.274	0.484 ± 0.143	0.368 ± 0.249	0.631 ± 0.31	0.598 ± 0.175	0.457 ± 0.305	0.59 ± 0.278	0.753 ± 0.168	0.661 ± 0.335	0.557 ± 0.251	0.786 ± 0.171	0.696 ± 0.356
D	0.435 ± 0.174	0.001 ± 0.001	0.000 ± 0.000	0.548 ± 0.273	0.002 ± 0.004	0.002 ± 0.004	0.544 ± 0.284	0.002 ± 0.002	0.002± 0.004	0.504 ± 0.262	0.002 ± 0.005	0.002 ± 0.006	0.512 ± 0.245	0.003 ± 0.006	0.004 ± 0.012
E	0.334 ± 0.1	0.28 ± 0.077	0.199 ± 0.217	0.417 ± 0.133	0.405 ± 0.085	0.212 ± 0.26	0.422 ± 0.14	0.549 ± 0.019	0.255 ± 0.312	0.552 ± 0.255	0.691 ± 0.02	0.286 ± 0.351	0.561 ± 0.25	0.721 ± 0.023	0.296 ± 0.363
F	0.474 ± 0.101	0.311 ± 0.133	0.228 ± 0.234	0.522 ± 0.132	0.499 ± 0.126	0.447 ± 0.3	0.578 ± 0.203	0.672 ± 0.116	0.652 ± 0.334	0.575 ± 0.199	0.786 ± 0.099	0.534 ± 0.439	0.576 ± 0.195	0.816 ± 0.099	0.546 ± 0.448
G	0.487 ± 0.14	0.000 ± 0.000	0.000 ± 0.000	0.561 ± 0.21	0.000 ± 0.000	0.000 ± 0.000	0.571 ± 0.236	0.000 ± 0.000	0.000 ± 0.000	0.558 ± 0.214	0.000 ± 0.000	0.000 ± 0.000	0.562 ± 0.206	0.000 ± 0.000	0.000 ± 0.000
H	0.491 ± 0.117	0.127 ± 0.073	0.158 ± 0.167	0.535 ± 0.189	0.314 ± 0.139	0.337 ± 0.23	0.547 ± 0.209	0.537 ± 0.067	0.503 ± 0.331	0.528 ± 0.177	0.579 ± 0.163	0.636 ± 0.421	0.528 ± 0.164	0.655 ± 0.131	0.628 ± 0.427

	Att. Match	Exact Match	Exact Match if Att. Match
Pull while spinning, Push while zigzagging, Walk hesitantly	0.982± 0.008	0.989± 0.005	0.996± 0.002
H:Adverb to verb	0.996± 0.003	0.93± 0.059	0.943± 0.055

Table 13: Sequence and attention match accuracies on additional held-out verb-adverb combinations and split H with selective attention and auxiliary feedback (trained on the full dataset)

	Att. Match	Exact Match	Exact Match if Att. Match
Red squares, Yellow squares, Green cylinders, Blue circles	0.991± 0.013	0.987± 0.015	1.000± 0.000
B:Yellow squares	0.855± 0.144	0.829± 0.165	1.000± 0.000
C:Red squares	0.996± 0.006	0.992± 0.007	1.000± 0.000

Table 14: Sequence and attention match accuracies on additional held-out shape-color target combinations and splits B and C with selective attention and auxiliary feedback (trained on the full dataset)

C Neuron pruning

For each neuron in the final hidden layer of the model, we recorded its activation, multiplied by its outgoing weight (no biases were used in the model, except in the layer normalization layer). We then sorted neurons based on their accumulated contribution to the final model output and tested exact sequence accuracy on the gSCAN dev set with the top X% of neurons active. The rest were disabled by setting outgoing weights to 0. Detailed results are shown in Table 15.

% of top hidden neurons active	unablated model	w/o action attention	w/o selective attention	w/o weight decay
10%	0.538 ± 0.054	0.354 ± 0.096	0.576 ± 0.054	0.042 ± 0.023
11%	0.664 ± 0.111	0.442 ± 0.117	0.627 ± 0.057	0.044 ± 0.026
12%	0.855 ± 0.108	0.522 ± 0.158	0.671 ± 0.051	0.068 ± 0.027
13%	0.998 ± 0.001	0.649 ± 0.164	0.715 ± 0.045	0.073 ± 0.021
14%	-	0.824 ± 0.104	0.782 ± 0.034	0.079 ± 0.025
15%	-	0.876 ± 0.090	0.823 ± 0.033	0.083 ± 0.033
16%	-	0.904 ± 0.029	0.867 ± 0.034	0.093 ± 0.032
17%	-	-	0.902 ± 0.024	0.087 ± 0.031
18%	-	-	0.916 ± 0.025	0.097 ± 0.053
20%	-	-	-	0.126 ± 0.092
30%	-	-	-	0.119 ± 0.069
40%	-	-	-	0.263 ± 0.149
50%	-	-	-	0.486 ± 0.231
60%	-	-	-	0.741 ± 0.171
70%	-	-	-	0.810 ± 0.114
80%	-	-	-	0.874 ± 0.045
90%	-	-	-	0.880 ± 0.048
95%	-	-	-	0.885 ± 0.049
100%	-	-	-	0.906 ± 0.025

Table 15: Exact match accuracy on in-distribution data for ablated and unablated models with different percentages of disabled top contributing hidden neurons

D Error analyses

D.1 Confusion matrices

We collected the feature vectors for the grid cells that were most attended to by the models trained with selective attention, but without auxiliary feedback. We also collected the feature vectors of the actual target objects. We then created confusion matrices for the parts of the feature vector relating to the agent, to color, to size, and to shape (shown in Figures 8 - 13). For color and size, we distinguish between situations where the attribute is mentioned in the command and those where it is not.

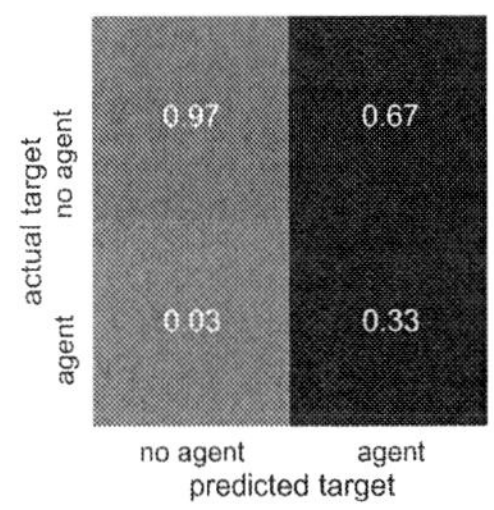

Figure 8: Confusion matrix for the agent dimension

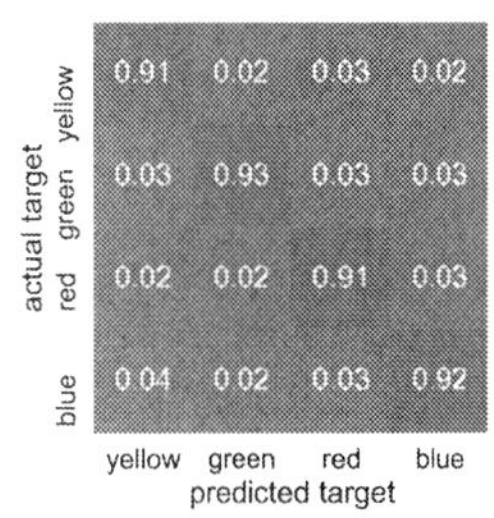

Figure 9: Confusion matrix for the color dimensions when color is specified in the command

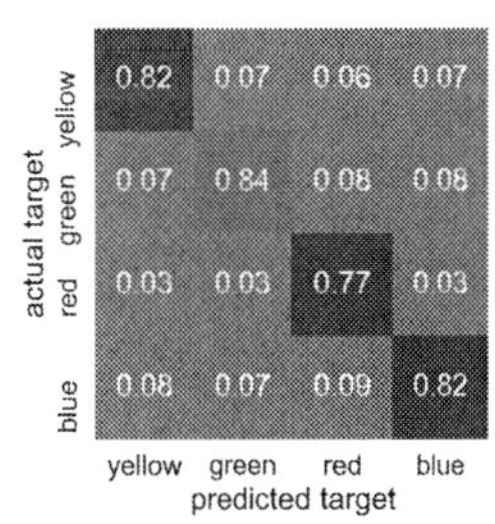

Figure 10: Confusion matrix for the color dimensions when color is not specified in the command

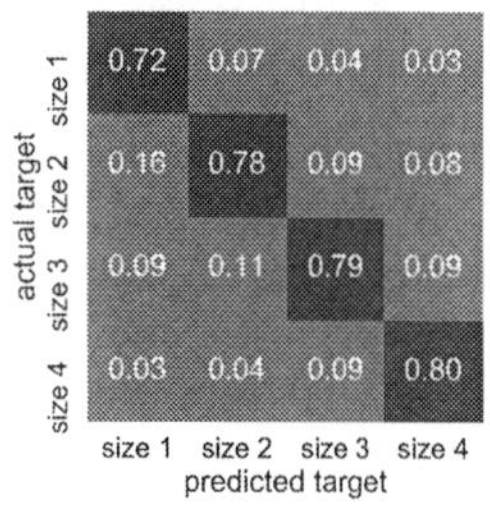

Figure 11: Confusion matrix for the color dimensions when size is specified in the command

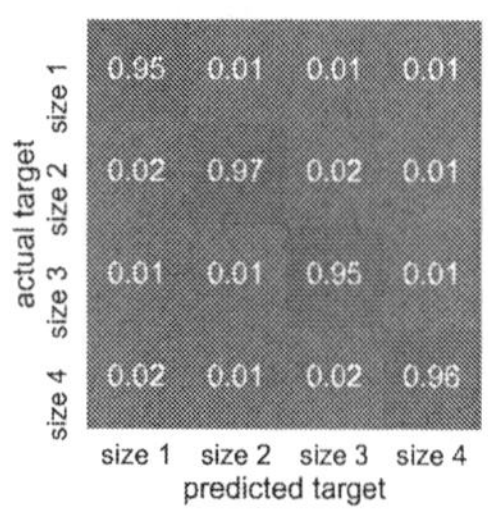

Figure 12: Confusion matrix for the color dimensions when size is not specified in the command

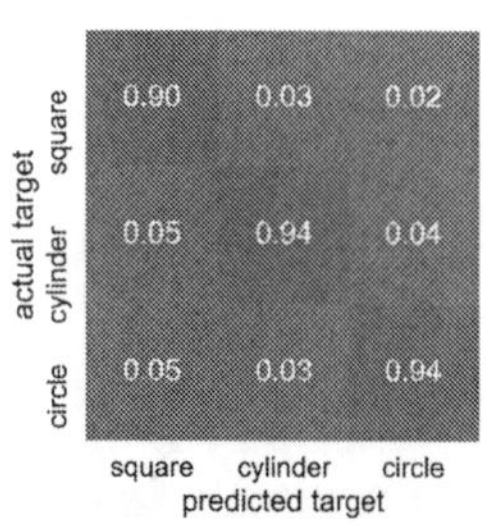

Figure 13: Confusion matrix for the shape dimensions (always specified in the command)

D.2 Ablated selective attention

We use a chi-squared test to compare the kind of target features that models tend to mis-identify when they are trained with vs. without selective attention. Figure 14 shows the test's standardized residuals for the model trained without selective attention, i.e., the strength of the difference between observed and expected values. Squares, the color yellow, and small object sizes are especially over-represented in the model's incorrect target predictions.

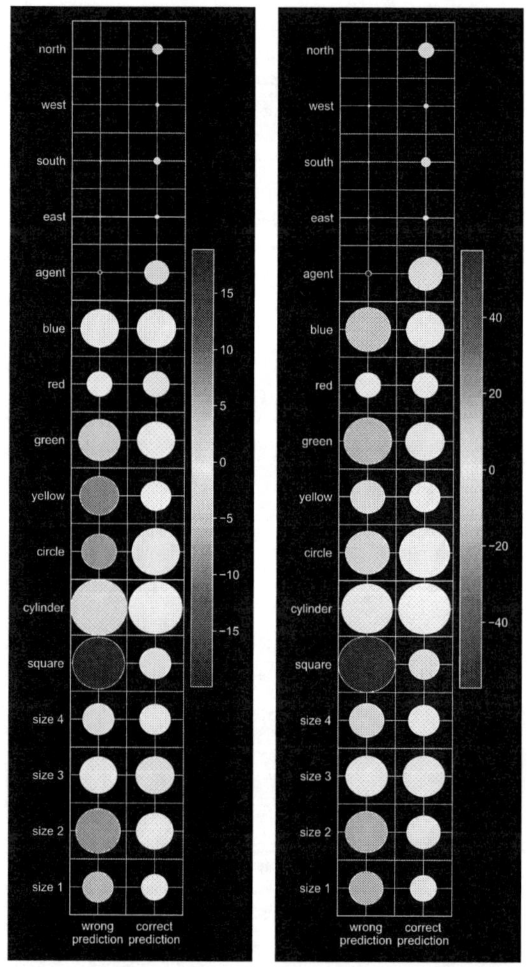

(a) dev set (b) test set

Figure 14: Plots of the standardized residuals of a Chi-square test comparing the wrong predictions of models trained with vs. without selective attention, on in-distribution data. We ran this test both on the dev set (14a) and the test set (14b) with similar results. Circle color represents absolute value of the residuals. Red indicates that a feature is over-represented, blue indicates a feature is under-represented. Circle size represents the number of occurrences in the tested set.

E "Spontaneous" generalization

E.1 "Spike" batches

To test if the batches used to update the model before a spike in performance on split H had any special properties, we trained a model with batch size 256 without action attention for 50 epochs and saved any batches that preceded at least a 5% increase in exact match accuracy on a 2% subset of split H. We then trained 10 additional models (with the same random seeds as used in the batch size experiments) and injected one of the "good" batches during training with a chance of 10%. We recorded the difference to the performance on the split H dev set before the batch update. A comparison of the distributions of split H performance differences after an update with "good" batch vs. a normal batch yields a Z-statistic of 0.665, which is not significant at the 0.05 level.

Injecting "good" batches also does not seem to increase the overall likelihood of higher performance on split H during training. We compared the distributions of split H accuracies sampled after each epoch for the models trained with and without "good" batch injections in the course of training. A two-sample Kolmogorov-Smirnov test yielded a p-value of 0.413, which is well above the threshold of 0.05 and indicates there is no difference between the distributions. Finally, we compare the distribution of labels in the "good" batches vs. the normal batches with a chi-squared test that yields a p-value of 0.445 – again, indicating little to no difference between the distributions.

E.2 Effect of batch size

We trained 10 models without weight decay on a 2% subset of the training data with batch sizes 256, 512, 1024, 2048, and 4096. The number of epochs was adjusted for each batch size so that all models were trained for the same number of absolute updates. For all batch sizes, the random initialization of the ten models used the same random seeds. We then sampled the models' performance on split H at 50 points in regular intervals during training and compared Z-scores for the resulting distributions. Results are given in Table 16

Batch size 1	Batch size 2	Z-score
256	512	1.35
256	1024	1.03
256	2048	**3**
256	4096	**4.09**
512	256	-1.35
512	1024	-0.09
512	2048	**2.33**
512	4096	**3.95**
1024	256	-1.03
1024	512	0.09
1024	1024	1.68
1024	4096	**2.74**
2048	256	**-3**
2048	512	**-2.33**
2048	1024	-1.68
2048	4096	1.77
4096	256	**-4.09**
4096	512	**-3.95**
4096	1024	**-2.74**
4096	2048	-1.77

Table 16: Pairwise comparison of distributions of split H performance sampled during training, for 5 different batch sizes. Statistically significant scores ($\geq |2|$) marked in bold.

Sparse Interventions in Language Models with Differentiable Masking

Nicola De Cao [*1,2], **Leon Schmid** [*3], **Dieuwke Hupkes** [4], **Ivan Titov** [1,2,5]
[1]University of Amsterdam, [2]University of Edinburgh
[3]University of Osnabrück, [4]Facebook AI Research, [5]Innopolis University
nicola.decao@gmail.com, lschmid@uos.de
dieuwkehupkes@fb.com, ititov@inf.ed.ac.uk

Abstract

There has been a lot of interest in understanding what information is captured by hidden representations of language models (LMs). Typically, interpretation methods i) do not guarantee that the model actually uses the information found to be encoded, and ii) do not discover small subsets of neurons responsible for a considered phenomenon. Inspired by causal mediation analysis, we propose a method that discovers a small subset of neurons within a neural LM responsible for a particular linguistic phenomenon, i.e., subsets causing a change in the corresponding token emission probabilities. We use a differentiable relaxation to approximately search through the combinatorial space. An L_0 regularization term ensures that the search converges to discrete and sparse solutions. We apply our method to analyze subject-verb number agreement and gender bias detection in LSTMs. We observe that it is fast and finds better solutions than alternatives such as REINFORCE and Integrated Gradients. Our experiments confirm that each of these phenomena is mediated through a small subset of neurons that do not play any other discernible role.

1 Introduction

The success of language models (LMs) in many natural language processing tasks is accompanied by an increasing interest in interpreting and analyzing such models. One goal in this direction is to identify how a model employs its hidden representations to arrive at a prediction (Belinkov and Glass, 2019; Jacovi and Goldberg, 2020). A popular line of research studies LMs with "diagnostic classifiers" or "probes" that are trained to predict linguistics properties from hidden units, with the purpose of analyzing what information is encoded by the network and where (Alain and Bengio, 2017; Adi et al., 2017; Hupkes et al., 2018; Voita and Titov, 2020). However, this method is sometimes criticized for generating unfaithful interpretations (Barrett et al., 2019) since the trained classifiers only measure the correlation between a model's representations and an external property and not whether such property is actually causing the model's predictions. Indeed, several studies pointed out limitations of probes (Belinkov and Glass, 2019; Vanmassenhove et al., 2017; Tamkin et al., 2020), including mismatches between the performance of the probe and the original model and the discrepancy between correlation and causation of hidden units and model outputs.

In response to these limitations, several recent studies have proposed to interpret neural models with *interventions* which aim to measure causal effects by intervening in representations of the model and observing a change in the model output (Giulianelli et al., 2018; Elazar et al., 2021; Feder et al., 2021). These techniques investigate directly if an LM represents a certain linguistic phenomenon but are limited when it comes to understanding where and how this information is represented. Therefore, an important question that they cannot answer is to what extent *modularity* – often believed to be a prerequisite for systematic generalization (Goyal and Bengio, 2020; Dittadi et al., 2021) – is a property that emerges naturally in such models. An adaptation of *causal mediation analysis* (Pearl, 2001) by Lakretz et al. (2019); Vig et al. (2020); Lakretz et al. (2021) makes an important step towards enabling such investigations. They consider neurons one by one by setting their activation to zero and measuring their effect on the output. However, these techniques suffer from two major shortcomings: i) they are restricted to detecting single neurons as systematically ablating combinations of multiple neurons is computationally infeasible, and ii) there is no guarantee that setting a unit activation to zero corresponds to switching the corresponding function on or off (Sturmfels et al., 2020).

Here, we use a differentiable relaxation of this

*Equal contributions.

Proceedings of the Fifth BlackboxNLP Workshop on Analyzing and Interpreting Neural Networks for NLP, pages 16 - 27
December 8, 2022 ©2022 Association for Computational Linguistics

search problem to overcome both these limitations. More specifically, our goal is to identify neurons responsible for shifting the probability from a word to its alternative in examples exemplifying the phenomena, without affecting other LM predictions. For example, when investigating subject-verb number agreement, we want to redistribute the probability mass from the singular form of an upcoming verb to the plural one (or vice versa), while discouraging changes in the distributions for other contexts. In this way, we ensure that the function is mediated through the detected neurons, and these neurons do not play any other discernible role.

Building on the framework of differentiable masking (De Cao et al., 2020; Schlichtkrull et al., 2021), we formalize this search for a *sparse intervention* as a constrained optimization problem. We aim to both detect the responsible neurons and learn the values to assign them when intervening. We use a continuous relaxation of the subset-selection problem, but ensure discreteness and encourage sparsity through L_0 regularization. The L_0 penalty determines how many neurons we want to discover. In our experiments, we use an LSTM-based LM, previously investigated by (Gulordava et al., 2018; Lakretz et al., 2019), and consider subject-verb number agreement and gender bias detection. We start with validating our method by showing that we can replicate findings reported in these previous studies and then dive into a deeper analysis. We show that our proposed method is effective as well as computationally efficient – it converges up to 7 times faster than REINFORCE (Williams, 1992) and surpasses Integrated Gradients (Sundararajan et al., 2017) in terms of accuracy/sparsity.

2 Related Work

The L_0 regularization was proposed by Louizos et al. (2018) in the context of pruning neural network weights and biases. It has been used in a variety of works in NLP as a tool for generating rationales and attribution (Bastings et al., 2019; De Cao et al., 2020; Schlichtkrull et al., 2021). Masking weights and groups of weights was also used by Csordás et al. (2021) to investigate the functional modularity of neural networks.

Studies suggested that some of the linguistic phenomena are encoded, at least to a large degree, in a disentangled and sparse fashion. For example, Radford et al. (2017) detected a neuron encoding sentiment polarity and Dai et al. (2021) showed that individual facts learned by an LM can be manipulated by modifying a small number of neurons. In a similar spirit, Voita et al. (2019) observed that many Transformer attention heads in a neural machine translation model are specialized; interestingly, they also used L_0 regularization but only to prune less important heads; the roles played by the heads were identified by studying their attention patterns. Our technique can facilitate such studies by effectively identifying sets of neural network's subcomponents playing a given function.

Bau et al. (2019) use different kinds of correlations between neurons from different models to measure their importance. The authors find that many individual neurons capture common linguistic phenomena, also showing how to control translations in predictable ways by modifying their activations. Similarly to Lakretz et al. (2021), the work of Finlayson et al. (2021) instead focuses on models' preferences for grammatical inflections, as well as whether neurons process subject-verb agreement. The authors include causal mediation analysis in their methodology.

Conversely, Antverg and Belinkov (2022) criticize recently proposed methodologies for analyzing individual neurons in LMs. In particular, they discuss methods that rely on an external probe to rank neurons according to their relevance to some linguistic attribute. They indicate two main pitfalls: 1) these methodologies confound probe quality and ranking quality, and 2) they focus on encoded information rather than information that the model uses. Their analysis does not apply to ours since we do not use probes explicit.

Finally, we refer the reader to Sajjad et al. (2021) for a recent survey of neuron-level interpretation of NLP models, which includes methods to discover neurons, evaluation methods, significant findings and future research directions.

3 Method

We investigate if we can find groups of neurons for which a modification of their value – which we call an *intervention* – systematically leads to a change of probability for the single token emission related to a specific phenomenon. Because there is no direct supervision for interventions, we need to learn them with a proxy objective. Let's assume we have an autoregressive model (e.g., an LSTM; Hochreiter and Schmidhuber 1997) that assigns a probability to sequences. For a set of input tokens

$x = \langle x_1, \ldots, x_n \rangle$, we obtain the model's probability of the token of interest $p(x_n|x_{<n})$ along with the hidden states $h = \langle h_1, \ldots, h_n \rangle$ where $h_i \in \mathbb{R}^k$ (one for each time step). We then intervene in the model's computation by modifying a group of neurons from one or multiple hidden states. The intervention at a certain time step $i < n$ consists of a binary mask $m \in \{0,1\}^k$ indicating which hidden units need intervention and which can be left unchanged. The intervention is then made substituting the ith hidden state with the altered state

$$\hat{h}_i = (1 - m) \odot h_i + m \odot b \,, \qquad (1)$$

where $\odot$ indicates the element-wise product and $b \in \mathbb{R}^k$ is a learned baseline vector that will lead the desired intervention. We denote $p(x_n|x_{<n}, \hat{h}_i)$ as the model's probability of the target token when its forward pass has been altered using $\hat{h}_i$.

In addition, as the main objective of this work, we are looking for sparse interventions, which we define as finding a defined small percentage (e.g., 1-5%) of neurons where to apply an intervention to while keeping all the rest untouched.

3.1 Learning to Intervene

Because there is no direct supervision to estimate the mask m and the baseline b, we minimize

$$\mathcal{L}_{\text{ratio}}(\hat{h}_i, x) = \frac{p(x_n = d|x_{<n}, \hat{h}_i)}{p(x_n = t|x_{<n}, \hat{h}_i)} \,, \qquad (2)$$

where we want to identify neurons responsible for a change in probability between a predicted word d and a target word t (e.g., a singular and plural verb form—where, independently from which form is correct, d is the form that the model assigns the highest probability to, and t to the other). In other words, we optimize to assign more probability mass to the token t rather than d. In addition, we desire interventions to be as sparse as possible, because we want to identify the least number of neurons responsible for the decision. Such *sparsity* corresponds to constraining most of the entries of m to be 0, which corresponds to not interfering. We cast this in the language of constrained optimization.

A practical way to express the sparsity constraint is through the L_0 'norm'. Our constraint is defined as the total number of neurons we intervene on:

$$\mathcal{C}_0(m) = \sum_{i=1}^{k} \mathbf{1}_{[\mathbb{R}_{\neq 0}]}(m_i) \,. \qquad (3)$$

The whole optimization problem is then:

$$\min_{m,b} \sum_{x \in \mathcal{D}} \mathcal{L}_{\text{ratio}}(\hat{h}_i, x) \;\; \text{s.t.} \;\; \mathcal{C}_0(m) \leq \alpha \,, \qquad (4)$$

where $\mathcal{D}$ is a dataset and the margin $\alpha \in (0, 1]$ is a hyperparameter that controls the desired sparsity (i.e., the lower α, the sparser the solution will be). Since non-linear constrained optimization is generally intractable, we employ Lagrangian relaxation (Boyd et al., 2004) optimizing

$$\max_{\lambda} \min_{m_i,b} \sum_{x \in \mathcal{D}} \mathcal{L}_{\text{ratio}}(\hat{h}_i) + \lambda(\mathcal{C}_0(m_i) - \alpha) \,, \qquad (5)$$

where $\lambda \in \mathbb{R}_{\geq 0}$ is the Lagrangian multiplier. Since we use binary masks, our loss is discontinuous and non-differentiable. A default option would be to use REINFORCE (Williams, 1992), but it is known to have a noisy gradient and thus slow convergence. To overcome both problems, we resort to a sparse relaxation to binary variables, namely using a Hard Concrete distribution (Louizos et al., 2018) (see Section 3.5 for more details).

3.2 Stochastic relaxation of the Mask

Our optimization problem poses two difficulties: i) $\mathcal{C}_0$ is discontinuous and has zero derivative almost everywhere, and ii) the altered state $\hat{h}_i$ is discontinuous w.r.t. the binary mask m. A simple way to overcome both issues is to treat the binary mask as stochastic and optimize the objective in expectation. In that case, one natural option is to resort to score function estimation (REINFORCE; Williams, 1992) while another is to use a sparse relaxation to binary variables (Louizos et al., 2018; Bastings et al., 2019; De Cao et al., 2020; Schlichtkrull et al., 2021). In Section 4 we discuss the two aforementioned options showing that the latter is much more effective (results in Table 6). Thus we opt to use the Hard Concrete distribution, a mixed discrete-continuous distribution on the closed interval $[0, 1]$. This distribution assigns a non-zero probability to exactly zero and one while it also admits continuous outcomes in the unit interval via the *reparameterization trick* (Kingma and Welling, 2014). We refer to Louizos et al. (2018) for details, but also provide a brief summary in Section 3.5. With a stochastic mask, the objective is computed in expectation, which addresses both sources of non-differentiability:

$$\mathcal{C}_0(m) = \sum_{i=1}^{k} \mathbb{E}_{p(m_i)}\left[m_i \neq 0\right] \,. \qquad (6)$$

Note that during training the mask is sampled and its values lies in the closed unit interval. After training, we set the mask entries to exact ones when their expected values are > 0.5 or to zero otherwise. To prevent issues due to the discrepancy between the values of the mask during training and during inference, we add another constraint

$$\mathcal{C}_{(0,1)} = \sum_{i=1}^{k} \mathbb{E}[m_i \in (0,1)] \ , \tag{7}$$

to be $\leq \beta$. $\mathcal{C}_{(0,1)}$ during training constrains the relaxed mask values not to lie in the open interval $(0,1)$ but rather to concentrate in $\{0,1\}$. $\beta \in (0,1]$ is a hyperparameter (the lower the less discrepancy is expected).

3.3 Single-step and Every-step intervention

We described how we apply an intervention at a certain time step $i < n$ as an intervention that directly modifies h_i. We refer to this type as a *single-step* intervention. The choice of the time step to intervene should be carefully set to investigate a particular phenomenon in the LM, and is task dependent; e.g., to explore subject-verb agreement, a reasonable choice is to do the intervention at the hidden state of the subject. As an extension, we also define an *every-step* intervention when instead of altering only h_i we modify all $h_1, \ldots, h_{n-1}$ with the same m and b (similar to Lakretz et al. 2019). The two types of intervention investigate different properties of an LM; we experiment with both variants.

3.4 Retaining other predictions

We train interventions to modify the model's prediction at a specific token position. However, there is little guarantee that all the other token positions will have the same output distribution as without the interventions. This is important as, when investigating modularity, we would like to ensure not only that a group of neurons plays a distinct interpretable role but also that they do not fulfil any other discernable role. For this reason, we employ a regularization term in addition to the constrained objective. This corresponds to minimizing a Kullback–Leibler divergence between the output distributions of the original model and the one from the model with interventions. The regularization term is a KL divergence between the output distributions of the original model p_O and the one from the model with interventions p_I averaged at every token position: $\mathcal{L}_{KL} =$

$$\frac{1}{T}\sum_{t=1}^{T} D_{KL}\left(p_O(x_t|x_{<t}) \parallel p_I(x_t|x_{<t})\right) \tag{8}$$

We sum $\mathcal{L}_{KL}$ to Equation 5 multiplied by a factor. This factor is a hyperparameter that controls the amount of regularization to apply, and we empirically found that 1.0 is a good value. In practice, as we will discuss in Section 5, the regularization term does not play an important role.

3.5 The Hard Concrete distribution

The Hard Concrete distribution, assigns density to continuous outcomes in the open interval $(0,1)$ and non-zero mass to exactly 0 and exactly 1. A particularly appealing property of this distribution is that sampling can be done via a differentiable reparameterization (Rezende et al., 2014; Kingma and Welling, 2014). In this way, the $\mathcal{C}_0$ constrain in Equation 3 becomes an expectation (Equation 6) whose gradient can be estimated via Monte Carlo sampling without the need for REINFORCE and without introducing biases. We did modify the original Hard Concrete, though only so slightly, in a way that it gives support to samples in the half-open interval $[0,1)$, that is, with non-zero mass only at 0. That is because we need only distinguish 0 from non-zero, and the value 1 is not particularly important.[1]

The distribution A stretched and rectified Binary Concrete (also known as Hard Concrete) distribution is obtained applying an affine transformation to the Binary Concrete distribution (Maddison et al., 2017; Jang et al., 2017) and rectifying its samples in the interval $[0,1]$. A Binary Concrete is defined over the open interval $(0,1)$ and it is parameterised by a location parameter $\gamma \in \mathbb{R}$ and temperature parameter $\tau \in \mathbb{R}_{>0}$. The location acts as a logit and it controls the probability mass skewing the distribution towards 0 in case of negative location and towards 1 in case of positive location. The temperature parameter controls the concentration of the distribution. The Binary Concrete is then stretched with an affine transformation extending its support to (l, r) with $l \leq 0$ and $r \geq 1$. Finally, we obtain a Hard Concrete distribution rectifying samples in the interval $[0,1]$. This corresponds to

[1]Only a true 0 is guaranteed to completely mask an input out, while any non-zero value, however small, may leak some amount of information.

collapsing the probability mass over the interval $(l, 0]$ to 0, and the mass over the interval $[1, r)$ to 1. This induces a distribution over the close interval $[0, 1]$ with non-zero mass at 0 and 1. Samples are obtained using

$$
\begin{aligned}
s &= \sigma\left((\log u - \log(1-u) + \gamma)/\tau\right) ,\\
z &= \min\left(1, \max\left(0, s \cdot (l - r) + r\right)\right) ,
\end{aligned}
\tag{9}
$$

where σ is the Sigmoid function $\sigma(x) = (1 + e^{-x})^{-1}$ and $u \sim \mathcal{U}(0, 1)$. We point to the Appendix B of Louizos et al. (2018) for more information about the density of the resulting distribution and its cumulative density function.

4 Experimental Setting

We study the pre-trained LSTM language model made available by Gulordava et al. (2018)[2], which has been studied extensively in previous works and therefore provides a good testing ground for our method. The studied model is a standard two-layered LSTM with a hidden dimension of 650. The embedding layer also has dimensionality 650, and it is not tied with the output layer. The vocabulary size is 50,000 and the model was trained on English Wikipedia data (with around 80M tokens training tokens and 10M for validation). We used this model to compare to previous findings of Lakretz et al. (2019). We also pre-train this LM several times with different weights initializations to make sure our results generalize.

We study the original model, as well as newly trained models with the same architecture, on two tasks described below: subject-verb number agreement and gender bias. The evaluation for tasks naturally follows the defined objective $\mathcal{L}_{\text{ratio}}(\hat{h}_i, x)$ (see § 3.1). Without intervention, the ratio is always > 1. Thus, we define a successful intervention when we find a mask and baseline values such that the ratio becomes < 1. Then, we define the *accuracy* of interventions as the average number of times that the ratio is < 1 across all datapoints in a given dataset/task. The accuracy thus reflects how often we can *flip* the model's decision.

Subject-verb number agreement Here, we seek the neurons responsible for predicting the number of verb forms: for a given sentence, we wish the intervention to change the number of the verb from singular to plural or vice versa. For this task, we employ data made available by Lakretz et al. (2019)[3]. The data are synthetic and generated with a modified version from Linzen et al. (2016) and Gulordava et al. (2018). Each synthetic number-agreement instance has a fixed syntax and varied lexical material. Sentences were randomly sampled by choosing words from pools of 20 subject/object nouns, 15 verbs, 10 adverbs, 5 prepositions, 10 proper nouns and 10 location nouns. We used a total of 11,000 training sentences and 1,000 evaluation sentences. We apply the single-step intervention to the subject of the (only) verb. We apply two intervention here (i.e., two sets of mask and baseline values): one where we train the model to turn the verb into the singular form and one into the plural one.

Gender bias detection In this task, we seek the neurons responsible for setting pronoun genders: for a given sentence, we wish the intervention to change the pronoun that refers to a person with a profession and an unspecified gender. For this task, we employ data made available by Vig et al. (2020)[4]. The data are synthetic and generated with a list of templates from Lu et al. (2020) and several other templates, instantiated with professions from Bolukbasi et al. (2016) (17 templates and 169 professions, resulting in 2,873 examples in total). We refer to Vig et al. (2020) for the full lists of templates and professions. The templates have the form "The [occupation] [verb] because [he/she]". Professions are definitionally gender-neutral. We used a total of 2,673 training sentences and 200 evaluation sentences. Also for his task, we apply the single-step intervention to the subject of the sentence, using different interventions for flipping the pronoun to "*he*" and to "*she*".

5 Results

For the single-step intervention (with regularization), our method achieves 91.5 and 93.9 accuracies for the number agreement and gender bias tasks, respectively. On average, our method finds 5.7 and 5.3 units for the two tasks, respectively. Considering that the LM has 1,300 hidden units, this intervention is relatively sparse as desired (we use $< 0.41\%$ of the total units). In Figure 1 and 2, we show examples of hidden state activations with

[2] https://github.com/facebookresearch/colorlessgreenRNNs

[3] https://github.com/FAIRNS/Number_and_syntax_units_in_LSTM_LMs

[4] https://github.com/sebastianGehrmann/CausalMediationAnalysis

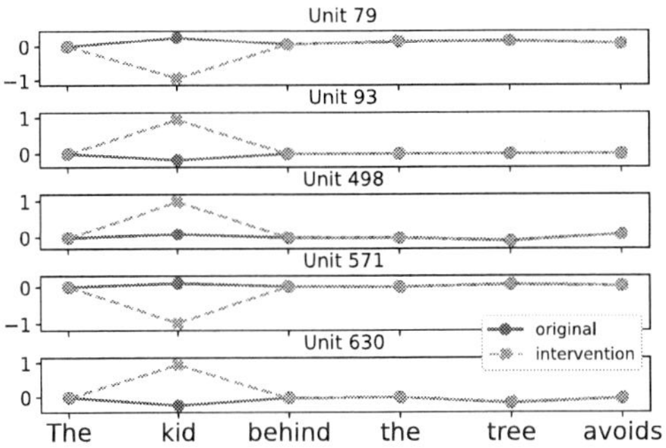

Figure 1: Activations of four units we intervene on (single step intervention at "kid") for changing number agreement (at "avoids").

Unit	Singular	Plural	Prevalence
79	-0.96 $\pm$0.02	0.99 $\pm$0.01	100%
93	0.95 $\pm$0.03	-0.84 $\pm$0.09	100%
243	0.91 $\pm$0.06	0.18 $\pm$0.15	20%
357	-0.99 $\pm$0.01	0.87 $\pm$0.03	40%
498	0.98 $\pm$0.01	-0.96 $\pm$0.03	100%
571	-0.99 $\pm$0.01	0.93 $\pm$0.06	80%
630	0.95 $\pm$0.03	0.11 $\pm$0.26	100%
776	-0.81 $\pm$0.05	0.96 $\pm$0.01	20%
988	1.00 $\pm$0.00	-0.99 $\pm$0.00	10%

Table 1: Subject-verb number agreement task with single-step interventions. Values are averages across 10 runs.

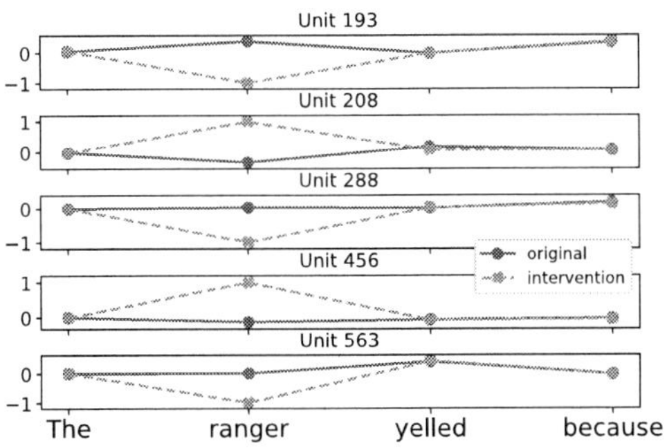

Figure 2: Activations of four units we intervene on (single step intervention at "ranger") for changing the pronoun (after "because").

Unit	He	She	Prevalence
193	-0.99 $\pm$0.00	0.91 $\pm$0.01	100%
208	0.99 $\pm$0.00	-0.96 $\pm$0.01	100%
288	-0.99 $\pm$0.00	-0.47 $\pm$0.14	100%
455	-0.99 $\pm$0.00	0.10 $\pm$0.01	20%
456	0.99 $\pm$0.00	-0.98 $\pm$0.00	100%
513	0.98 $\pm$0.00	-0.74 $\pm$0.00	10%
563	-0.99 $\pm$0.00	0.96 $\pm$0.01	100%

Table 2: Gender bias task with single-step interventions. Values are averages across 10 runs.

and without interventions for both tasks (see Appendix A for additional examples). From these figures, we can see that only one time-step is heavily affected (the one of the intervention) while the others are minimally corrupted after that time step. We hypothesize that the model stores the information of number or gender in other units (or in cell states), but the discovered units are the ones responsible for the *initialization* of such memory. In Table 1 and 2, we report the full list of discovered units and the learned baseline vectors for both tasks on the single-step intervention.

For the every-step intervention, our method achieved an almost perfect accuracy of 95.8 and 99.9 for the number agreement and gender bias tasks, respectively, while using 3 units or less on average for both tasks. This type of intervention is much more effective and more intrusive—the number of changes is larger as it happens at every step). In Table 3 we report the full list of discovered units and the learned baseline vectors, comparing to the one discovered by Lakretz et al. (2019) (every-step intervention). Noticeably, we *re-discover* unit 776 which validates our method and confirm their findings. Interestingly, we also discover an extra unit on average, highlighting that one of the limitations of Lakretz et al. (2019) was indeed an efficient way to search units. For a summary of all results see Table 4, and for the discovered units and baseline on the gender task see Table 5.

Efficiency To demonstrate the efficiency and efficacy of our estimation employing the Hard Concrete distribution, we compare to the standard Score Function Estimation (aka REINFORCE; Williams 1992) with a moving average baseline for variance reduction (Botev and Ridder, 2017) and trying different values of α to achieve a good trade-off between accuracy and number of units used. We also compare to Integrated Gradients (Sundararajan et al., 2017) where we intervene on the top-k influential neurons by setting them to zero. In Table 6, we summarize the results for the single-step intervention. REINFORCE takes at least 7 times more time to converge, and it always converges at using more units than our method with

Unit	Singular	Plural	Prevalence	**Found by** Lakretz et al. (2019)
79	-0.76 $\pm$0.023	0.99 $\pm$0.003	100%	✗
776	-0.99 $\pm$0.002	0.99 $\pm$0.002	100%	✓

Table 3: Subject-verb number agreement task with every-step interventions. Values are averages across 10 runs. "Found" indicates how many times our model decides to apply the intervention on a specific unit across runs.

	Accuracy	**Units**	**KL**
	Number agreement		
Single	90.9 $\pm$1.2	5.7 $\pm$0.5	0.034 $\pm$0.034
Single^R	91.5 $\pm$0.7	5.7 $\pm$0.9	0.035 $\pm$0.006
Every	96.8 $\pm$0.6	2.0 $\pm$0.0	0.131 $\pm$0.003
Every^R	95.8 $\pm$0.4	2.0 $\pm$0.0	0.084 $\pm$0.002
	Gender bias		
Single	93.1 $\pm$4.6	5.4 $\pm$1.1	0.009 $\pm$0.001
Single^R	93.9 $\pm$3.7	5.3 $\pm$0.5	0.009 $\pm$0.001
Every	98.3 $\pm$2.8	3.4 $\pm$0.5	0.176 $\pm$0.022
Every^R	99.9 $\pm$0.3	3.0 $\pm$0.0	0.117 $\pm$0.004

Table 4: Summary of results for both the number agreement and gender bias settings (average across 3 run for each setting). ^{R} indicates KL regularization. Single/ Every indicates single-step and every-step interventions respectively.

Unit	He	She	Prevalence
288	-0.98 $\pm$0.00	0.53 $\pm$0.05	100%
456	0.98 $\pm$0.00	-0.98 $\pm$0.01	100%
1184	-0.98 $\pm$0.00	0.99 $\pm$0.00	100%

Table 5: Gender bias task with every-step interventions. Values are averages across 10 runs.

lower accuracy. Note that doing an exact search for this problem has a time complexity of $O(2^k)$ where k is the number of neurons—this would amount to $> 10^{12}$ evaluations only for checking combinations up to 4 neurons.

Robustness To demonstrate that our method is robust, we tested it on 5 language models initialized with different seeds and trained with the original script by Gulordava et al. (2018). We run our method for the single-step intervention 3 times for each language model. The average accuracy at convergence is 88.7 ± 2.6, and we discover 4.7 ± 0.5 units on average. The variability in both accuracy and number of units is very low, indicating that our method is robust to different parameterizations of the model we applied it to.

	Acc. (↑)	Units (↓)	Speed (↓)
SFE ($\alpha = 0.05$)	**100.0**	20.0	5.2h
SFE ($\alpha = 0.02$)	87.6	6.0	3.6h
IG ($\alpha = 0.005$)	22.5	7.0	–
IG ($\alpha = 0.01$)	28.1	13.0	–
IG ($\alpha = 0.02$)	31.5	26.0	–
Ours ($\alpha = 0.02$)	91.5	**5.7**	**0.5h**

Table 6: Comparison between the solutions found by Score Function Estimation (SFE aka REINFORCE), Integrated Gradients (IG; Sundararajan et al., 2017), and our system (average across 10 runs on a single GPU device). Ours is much faster and finds a sparser solution with better accuracy.

Effect of Regularization We ablated the KL regularization to see whether it affects learning and the final convergence of our method. On the number agreement task, we found that the average KL divergence with respect to the original model predictions was $0.035/0.084$ with regularization and $0.034/0.131$ without regularization (for single-step and every-step intervention, respectively). We used different regularization coefficients (i.e., different weights), but we did not observe a substantial change in the convergence of our models. Moreover, the accuracy and the number of units found with regularization was almost the same as without regularization (see Table 4 for all results). This lack of effect of the regularization suggests the studied phenomenon is naturally captured by specialized neurons. In the gender bias task, regularization has a similar and negligible impact. The regularized method converges to finding fewer units on average and with worse accuracy (95.8 as opposed to 98.6) in the single-step intervention. In the every-step intervention, the accuracy stays invariant (for both settings is 100) while the model converges to using more units.

6 Conclusions

In this work, we present a new method that employs constraint optimization to efficiently find hidden units that are responsible for particular language phenomena of language models. We use an L_0 regularization to find a sparse solution—., our methodology discovers few units in the order of 2-6 that is $< 0.41\%$ of all units in the studied LM. We show such sparse solutions can be found for multiple phenomena (number and gender agreement) and is an useful tool for analysis of what a LM has learned and how units influence its token emissions. Although this work focuses on LSTM models, the proposed technique is not architecture-dependent and thus easily applicable to transformers, convolution-based models and many others.

Acknowledgements

Nicola De Cao and Ivan Titov are supported by SAP Innovation Center Network; Leon Schmid and Ivan Titov by the Dutch Organization for Scientific Research (NWO VIDI 639.022.518) and Ivan Titov by the Analytical Center for the Government of Russian Federation (agreement 70-2021-00143, dd. 01.11.2021, IGK 000000D730321P5Q0002).

References

Yossi Adi, Einat Kermany, Yonatan Belinkov, Ofer Lavi, and Yoav Goldberg. 2017. Fine-grained analysis of sentence embeddings using auxiliary prediction tasks. In *5th International Conference on Learning Representations, ICLR 2017, Toulon, France, April 24-26, 2017, Conference Track Proceedings*. OpenReview.net.

Guillaume Alain and Yoshua Bengio. 2017. Understanding intermediate layers using linear classifier probes. *International Conference on Learning Representations*.

Omer Antverg and Yonatan Belinkov. 2022. On the pitfalls of analyzing individual neurons in language models. In *The Tenth International Conference on Learning Representations, ICLR 2022, Virtual Event, April 25-29, 2022*. OpenReview.net.

Maria Barrett, Yova Kementchedjhieva, Yanai Elazar, Desmond Elliott, and Anders Søgaard. 2019. Adversarial removal of demographic attributes revisited. In *Proceedings of the 2019 Conference on Empirical Methods in Natural Language Processing and the 9th International Joint Conference on Natural Language Processing (EMNLP-IJCNLP)*, pages 6330–6335, Hong Kong, China. Association for Computational Linguistics.

Jasmijn Bastings, Wilker Aziz, and Ivan Titov. 2019. Interpretable neural predictions with differentiable binary variables. In *Proceedings of the 57th Annual Meeting of the Association for Computational Linguistics*, pages 2963–2977, Florence, Italy. Association for Computational Linguistics.

Anthony Bau, Yonatan Belinkov, Hassan Sajjad, Nadir Durrani, Fahim Dalvi, and James R. Glass. 2019. Identifying and controlling important neurons in neural machine translation. In *7th International Conference on Learning Representations, ICLR 2019, New Orleans, LA, USA, May 6-9, 2019*. OpenReview.net.

Yonatan Belinkov and James Glass. 2019. Analysis methods in neural language processing: A survey. *Transactions of the Association for Computational Linguistics*, 7:49–72.

Tolga Bolukbasi, Kai-Wei Chang, James Y. Zou, Venkatesh Saligrama, and Adam Tauman Kalai. 2016. Man is to computer programmer as woman is to homemaker? debiasing word embeddings. In *Advances in Neural Information Processing Systems 29: Annual Conference on Neural Information Processing Systems 2016, December 5-10, 2016, Barcelona, Spain*, pages 4349–4357.

Zdravko Botev and Ad Ridder. 2017. Variance reduction. *Wiley statsRef: Statistics reference online*, pages 1–6.

Stephen Boyd, Stephen P Boyd, and Lieven Vandenberghe. 2004. *Convex optimization*. Cambridge university press.

Róbert Csordás, Sjoerd van Steenkiste, and Jürgen Schmidhuber. 2021. Are neural nets modular? inspecting functional modularity through differentiable weight masks. In *9th International Conference on Learning Representations, ICLR 2021, Virtual Event, Austria, May 3-7, 2021*. OpenReview.net.

Damai Dai, Li Dong, Yaru Hao, Zhifang Sui, and Furu Wei. 2021. Knowledge neurons in pretrained transformers. *ArXiv preprint*, abs/2104.08696.

Nicola De Cao, Michael Sejr Schlichtkrull, Wilker Aziz, and Ivan Titov. 2020. How do decisions emerge across layers in neural models? interpretation with differentiable masking. In *Proceedings of the 2020 Conference on Empirical Methods in Natural Language Processing (EMNLP)*, pages 3243–3255, Online. Association for Computational Linguistics.

Andrea Dittadi, Frederik Träuble, Francesco Locatello, Manuel Wuthrich, Vaibhav Agrawal, Ole Winther, Stefan Bauer, and Bernhard Schölkopf. 2021. On the transfer of disentangled representations in realistic settings. In *9th International Conference on Learning Representations, ICLR 2021, Virtual Event, Austria, May 3-7, 2021*. OpenReview.net.

Yanai Elazar, Shauli Ravfogel, Alon Jacovi, and Yoav Goldberg. 2021. Amnesic Probing: Behavioral Explanation with Amnesic Counterfactuals. *Transactions of the Association for Computational Linguistics*, 9:160–175.

Amir Feder, Nadav Oved, Uri Shalit, and Roi Reichart. 2021. CausaLM: Causal Model Explanation Through Counterfactual Language Models. *Computational Linguistics*, 47(2):333–386.

Matthew Finlayson, Aaron Mueller, Sebastian Gehrmann, Stuart Shieber, Tal Linzen, and Yonatan Belinkov. 2021. Causal analysis of syntactic agreement mechanisms in neural language models. In *Proceedings of the 59th Annual Meeting of the Association for Computational Linguistics and the 11th International Joint Conference on Natural Language Processing (Volume 1: Long Papers)*, pages 1828–1843, Online. Association for Computational Linguistics.

Mario Giulianelli, Jack Harding, Florian Mohnert, Dieuwke Hupkes, and Willem Zuidema. 2018. Under the hood: Using diagnostic classifiers to investigate and improve how language models track agreement information. In *Proceedings of the 2018 EMNLP Workshop BlackboxNLP: Analyzing and Interpreting Neural Networks for NLP*, pages 240–248, Brussels, Belgium. Association for Computational Linguistics.

Anirudh Goyal and Yoshua Bengio. 2020. Inductive biases for deep learning of higher-level cognition. *ArXiv preprint*, abs/2011.15091.

Kristina Gulordava, Piotr Bojanowski, Edouard Grave, Tal Linzen, and Marco Baroni. 2018. Colorless green recurrent networks dream hierarchically. In *Proceedings of the 2018 Conference of the North American Chapter of the Association for Computational Linguistics: Human Language Technologies, Volume 1 (Long Papers)*, pages 1195–1205, New Orleans, Louisiana. Association for Computational Linguistics.

Sepp Hochreiter and Jürgen Schmidhuber. 1997. Long short-term memory. *Neural Computation*, 9(8):1735–1780.

Dieuwke Hupkes, Sara Veldhoen, and Willem Zuidema. 2018. Visualisation and 'diagnostic classifiers' reveal how recurrent and recursive neural networks process hierarchical structure. *Journal of Artificial Intelligence Research*, 61:907–926.

Alon Jacovi and Yoav Goldberg. 2020. Towards faithfully interpretable NLP systems: How should we define and evaluate faithfulness? In *Proceedings of the 58th Annual Meeting of the Association for Computational Linguistics*, pages 4198–4205, Online. Association for Computational Linguistics.

Eric Jang, Shixiang Gu, and Ben Poole. 2017. Categorical reparameterization with gumbel-softmax. In *5th International Conference on Learning Representations, ICLR 2017, Toulon, France, April 24-26, 2017, Conference Track Proceedings*. OpenReview.net.

Diederik P. Kingma and Max Welling. 2014. Autoencoding variational bayes. In *2nd International Conference on Learning Representations, ICLR 2014, Banff, AB, Canada, April 14-16, 2014, Conference Track Proceedings*.

Yair Lakretz, Dieuwke Hupkes, Alessandra Vergallito, Marco Marelli, Marco Baroni, and Stanislas Dehaene. 2021. Mechanisms for handling nested dependencies in neural-network language models and humans. *Cognition*, 213:104699. Special Issue in Honour of Jacques Mehler, Cognition's founding editor.

Yair Lakretz, German Kruszewski, Theo Desbordes, Dieuwke Hupkes, Stanislas Dehaene, and Marco Baroni. 2019. The emergence of number and syntax units in LSTM language models. In *Proceedings of the 2019 Conference of the North American Chapter of the Association for Computational Linguistics: Human Language Technologies, Volume 1 (Long and Short Papers)*, pages 11–20, Minneapolis, Minnesota. Association for Computational Linguistics.

Tal Linzen, Emmanuel Dupoux, and Yoav Goldberg. 2016. Assessing the ability of LSTMs to learn syntax-sensitive dependencies. *Transactions of the Association for Computational Linguistics*, 4:521–535.

Christos Louizos, Max Welling, and Diederik P. Kingma. 2018. Learning sparse neural networks through l_0 regularization. In *6th International Conference on Learning Representations, ICLR 2018, Vancouver, BC, Canada, April 30 - May 3, 2018, Conference Track Proceedings*. OpenReview.net.

Kaiji Lu, Piotr Mardziel, Fangjing Wu, Preetam Amancharla, and Anupam Datta. 2020. Gender Bias in Neural Natural Language Processing. *Logic, Language, and Security*, pages 189–202.

Chris J. Maddison, Andriy Mnih, and Yee Whye Teh. 2017. The concrete distribution: A continuous relaxation of discrete random variables. In *5th International Conference on Learning Representations, ICLR 2017, Toulon, France, April 24-26, 2017, Conference Track Proceedings*. OpenReview.net.

Judea Pearl. 2001. Direct and Indirect Effects. *Uncertainty in Artificial Intelligence*, page 411–420.

Alec Radford, Rafal Jozefowicz, and Ilya Sutskever. 2017. Learning to generate reviews and discovering sentiment. *ArXiv preprint*, abs/1704.01444.

Danilo Jimenez Rezende, Shakir Mohamed, and Daan Wierstra. 2014. Stochastic backpropagation and approximate inference in deep generative models. In *Proceedings of the 31th International Conference on Machine Learning, ICML 2014, Beijing,*

China, 21-26 June 2014, volume 32 of *JMLR Workshop and Conference Proceedings*, pages 1278–1286. JMLR.org.

Hassan Sajjad, Nadir Durrani, and Fahim Dalvi. 2021. Neuron-level interpretation of deep NLP models: A survey. *CoRR*, abs/2108.13138.

Michael Sejr Schlichtkrull, Nicola De Cao, and Ivan Titov. 2021. Interpreting graph neural networks for NLP with differentiable edge masking. In *9th International Conference on Learning Representations, ICLR 2021, Virtual Event, Austria, May 3-7, 2021*. OpenReview.net.

Pascal Sturmfels, Scott Lundberg, and Su-In Lee. 2020. Visualizing the Impact of Feature Attribution Baselines . *Distill*, 5(1):e22.

Mukund Sundararajan, Ankur Taly, and Qiqi Yan. 2017. Axiomatic attribution for deep networks. In *Proceedings of the 34th International Conference on Machine Learning*, volume 70 of *Proceedings of Machine Learning Research*, pages 3319–3328. PMLR.

Alex Tamkin, Trisha Singh, Davide Giovanardi, and Noah Goodman. 2020. Investigating transferability in pretrained language models. In *Findings of the Association for Computational Linguistics: EMNLP 2020*, pages 1393–1401, Online. Association for Computational Linguistics.

Eva Vanmassenhove, Jinhua Du, and Andy Way. 2017. Investigating 'Aspect'in NMT and SMT: Translating the English simple past and present perfect. *Computational Linguistics in the Netherlands Journal*, 7:109–128.

Jesse Vig, Sebastian Gehrmann, Yonatan Belinkov, Sharon Qian, Daniel Nevo, Yaron Singer, and Stuart M. Shieber. 2020. Investigating gender bias in language models using causal mediation analysis. In *Advances in Neural Information Processing Systems 33: Annual Conference on Neural Information Processing Systems 2020, NeurIPS 2020, December 6-12, 2020, virtual*.

Elena Voita, David Talbot, Fedor Moiseev, Rico Sennrich, and Ivan Titov. 2019. Analyzing multi-head self-attention: Specialized heads do the heavy lifting, the rest can be pruned. In *Proceedings of the 57th Annual Meeting of the Association for Computational Linguistics*, pages 5797–5808, Florence, Italy. Association for Computational Linguistics.

Elena Voita and Ivan Titov. 2020. Information-theoretic probing with minimum description length. In *Proceedings of the 2020 Conference on Empirical Methods in Natural Language Processing (EMNLP)*, pages 183–196, Online. Association for Computational Linguistics.

Ronald J. Williams. 1992. Simple statistical gradient-following algorithms for connectionist reinforcement learning. *Mach. Learn.*, 8(3–4):229–256.

A Additional results

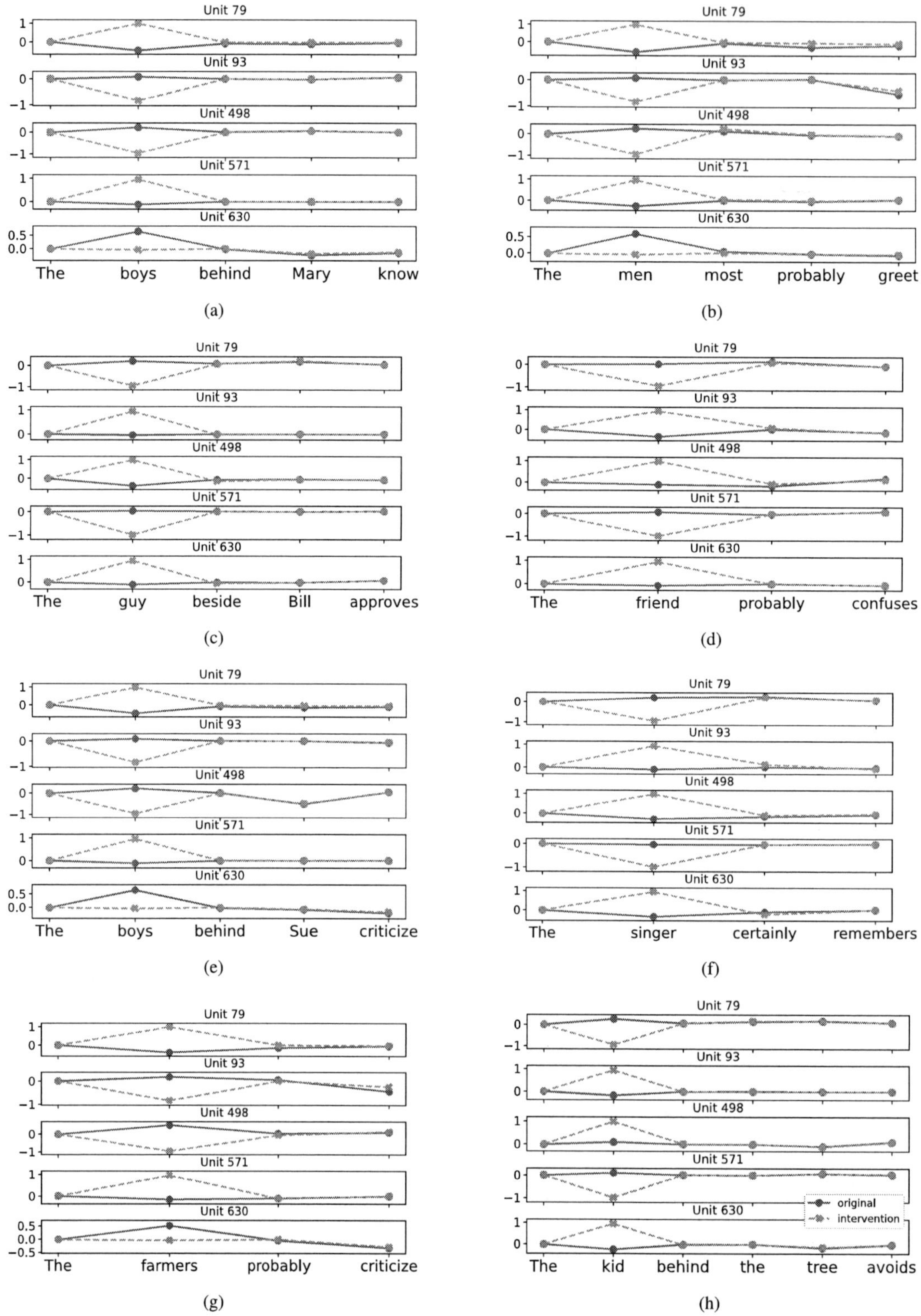

Figure 3: Subject-verb number agreement: activations of four units we intervene on (single step intervention at the second token from the left) for changing number agreement (at the last token).

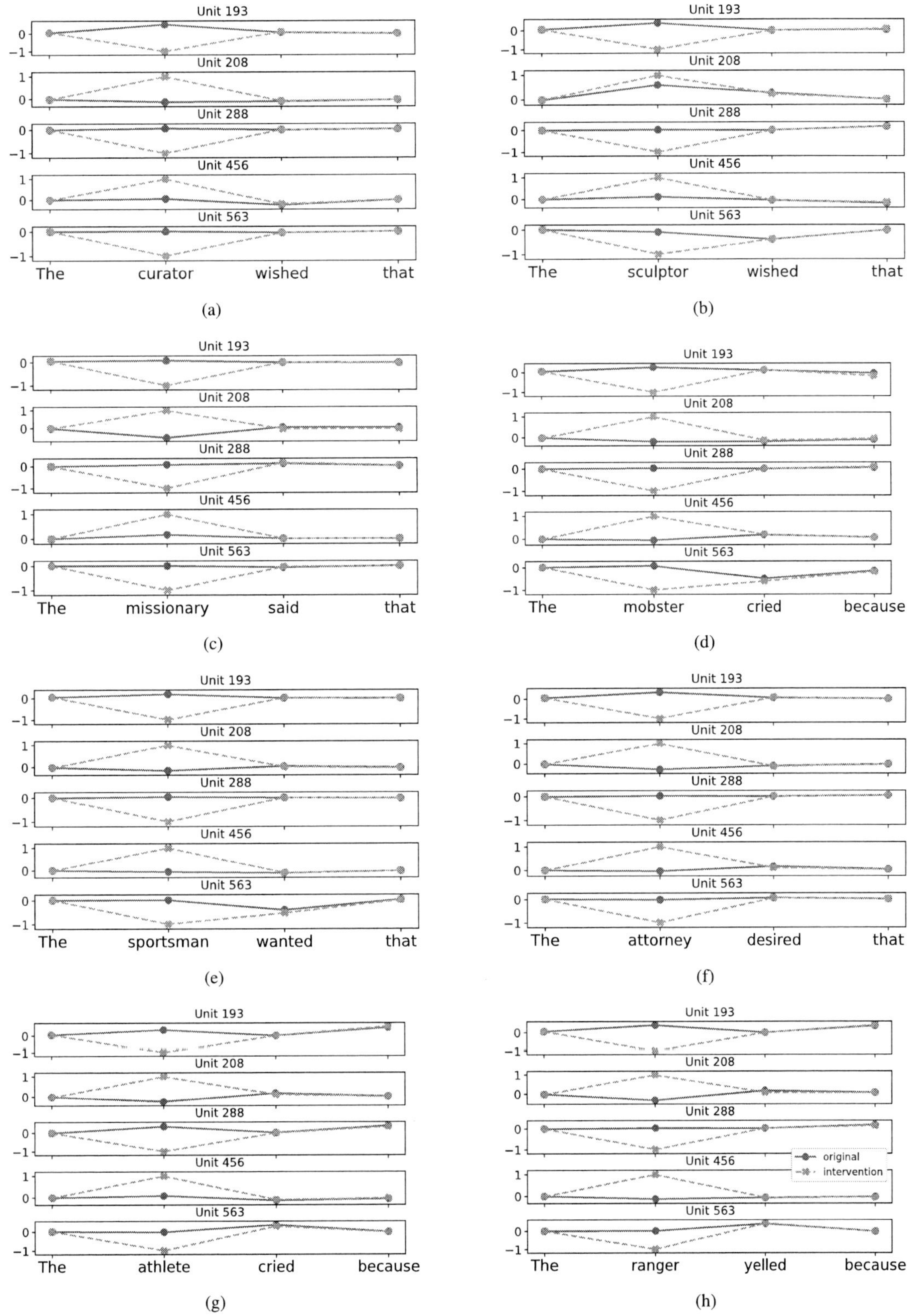

Figure 4: Gender bias: activations of four units we intervene on (single step intervention at the second token from the left) for changing the pronoun (after "because" or "that").

Where's the Learning in Representation Learning for Compositional Semantics and the Case of Thematic Fit

Mughilan Muthupari*
Columbia University
NY, USA
mm5569@columbia.edu

Samrat Halder*
Columbia University
NY, USA
sh3970@columbia.edu

Asad Sayeed
Dept. of Philosophy, Linguistics, and Theory of Science
University of Gothenburg, Sweden
asad.sayeed@gu.se

Yuval Marton
University of Washington
WA, USA
ymarton@uw.edu

Abstract

Observing that for certain NLP tasks, such as semantic role prediction or thematic fit estimation, random embeddings perform as well as pretrained embeddings, we explore what settings allow for this and examine where most of the learning is encoded: the word embeddings, the semantic role embeddings, or "the network". We find nuanced answers, depending on the task and its relation to the training objective. We examine these representation learning aspects in multi-task learning, where role prediction and role-filling are supervised tasks, while several thematic fit tasks are outside the models' direct supervision. We observe a non-monotonous relation between some tasks' quality score and the training data size. In order to better understand this observation, we analyze these results using easier, per-verb versions of these tasks.

1 Introduction

We examine to what extent models trained on a simplified semantic role labeling (SRL) task can estimate thematic fit (aka semantic fit), as the training set size grows – and where most of the learning is stored: in the word embeddings, the thematic role embeddings, or elsewhere in the neural net.

A major goal of natural language processing (NLP) is to understand the semantics of language. One traditional NLP task around this is SRL, which labels word spans in a sentence with thematic roles. Consider the sentence "I cut the cake with a knife". We can interpret 'cut' as the action, 'I' as the `Agent` (the performer of the action), 'cake' as the `Theme` of the action (the thing that underwent the action), and 'knife' as the `Instrument` of the action. These words, labeled with roles such as `Agent`, `Theme`, and `Instrument`, would be our representation of the event that the sentence conveys. Other sentences with similar meanings, e.g., "the cake was cut with the knife by me", should have the same (or very similar) event representations. In this work, we focus on model training with a simplified version of SRL: each event is represented only by the lemmatized syntactic head of each event argument (including the predicate), and the semantic roles are the simplified PropBank roles (`Arg0, Arg1`, etc.). The reason for this is the current limitations of available evaluation sets for thematic fit: they are all comprised of lemmatized syntactic argument heads as well.

Thematic fit is related to SRL. This task aims to identify how well a given word or concept fits into a role of an event. In our example sentence, consider these potential replacements for 'knife': scissors, fork, and brick. As humans, we understand that while 'knife' is the most typical object for this situation, both 'scissors' and 'fork' could also fit, even if not as naturally. This is because we have the general intuition that all three objects are plausible instruments for cutting. More so, we know that 'brick' is unlikely to fit given the context of cutting a cake. Since thematic fit datasets are scarce, one challenge in computational linguistics (and computational psycholinguistics) revolves around how machine learning models can learn thematic fit indirectly – perhaps from SRL training. To the best of our knowledge, the state-of-art in this line of work is the residual role-filler averaging model (ResRoFA-MT) proposed by Hong et al. (2018), with an adjusted embeddings representation and training data annotation in Marton and Sayeed (2022).

*These authors contributed equally to this work

Proceedings of the Fifth BlackboxNLP Workshop on Analyzing and Interpreting Neural Networks for NLP, pages 28 - 39
December 8, 2022

It has been repeatedly observed that in some settings, random word embeddings perform as well as pretrained ones, or very nearly, including in our baselines (Tilk et al., 2016; Hong et al., 2018; Marton and Sayeed, 2022). In this paper, we design experiments to answer the following questions: **Q1.** Why is this so in our compositional semantics and psycholinguistic tasks? **Q2.** For such semantic tasks and architecture, where is the learning encoded? Is it in the word embeddings, role embeddings, or elsewhere in the neural network? **Q3.** Training set size effect: is more data better for this indirect setting and tasks?

In this work, **1.** We compare updating the word embeddings during training to freezing them. **2.** We modify the ResRoFA-MT model architecture in various ways to understand what contributes the most to the learning: the pretrained (or random) word embeddings, the thematic role embeddings, or the rest of the network. **3.** In order to be able to train on larger data, we optimized the code of Hong et al. (2018) and Marton and Sayeed (2022). We release our optimized codebase[*], which trains 6 times faster and includes ablation architectures and a correction to the training data preparation step.

2 Related Work

In event representation models, the main goal is to predict the appropriate word in a sentence given both the role of that word and the surrounding context in the form of word-role pairs. One of the best early neural models was the non-incremental role-filler model (NNRF), by Tilk et al. (2016). This model was based on selectional preferences, or a probability distribution over the candidate words. However, one drawback of this model is that representations of two similarly-worded sentences differing hugely in meaning would closely resemble each other, e.g., "kid watches TV" and "TV watches kid". Another drawback is that the embeddings of the word-role pairs are summed together to represent the sentence, and so the resulting event representation vector does not weight the input vectors differently based on their importance and is not normalized for varying numbers of roles in a sample.

Hong et al. (2018) extend this model in three ways: First, in addition to the word prediction task of NNRF, the task of role prediction given the corresponding word is added, and the two tasks are trained simultaneously (multi-task learning). This model is known as the non-incremental role-filler multitask model (NNRF-MT). Second, they apply the parametric rectified linear unit (PReLU) non-linear function to each word-role embedding, which acts as weights on the composition of embeddings, and subsequently average the embeddings, which normalizes for variable length inputs. This model is called the role-filler averaging model (RoFA-MT). Third, in an effort to tackle the vanishing gradient problem, residual connections between the PReLU output and the averaging input were added together. This third iteration is known as the ResRoFA-MT model. They showed that it performs the best on our thematic fit tasks, and so we use it as our baseline.

Our work differs from Hong et al. (2018) and Marton and Sayeed (2022) in that while they focused more on state-of-the-art performance through new modeling and annotation methods, we aim to understand what controls the learning in such networks. Also, although Hong et al. confirm in private communication that they found pre-trained and random embeddings performance similar in preliminary studies, none of the surveyed previous work published experiments with pre-trained embeddings. We are the first to do so (using GloVe) and compare that to using random embeddings.

Previous work suggests a difference between "count" and "predict" models, where "count" models represent lexical semantics in terms of raw or adjusted unsupervised frequencies of correlations between words (such as Local Mutual Information; Baroni and Lenci, 2010) and syntactic or semantic phenomena; "predict" models involve supervised training to achieve their representations, e.g., neural models. Baroni et al. (2014) do a systematic exploration of tasks vs. state-of-the-art count and predict models and find that predict models are overall superior; for thematic fit, predict models are the same or better than count models on the best unsupervised setup for the task, although they are easily beaten by third-party baselines based on supervised learning over count models. More recently, Lenci et al. (2022) demonstrate that predict-models are not reliably superior to count-models, but depend on the task and the way the models are trained. They also show that even recent contextual models (e.g., BERT) are not necessarily better for out-of-context tasks than well-tuned static representations, predict or otherwise. See Appendix A for

[*]https://github.com/MughilM/RW-Eng-v3-src/tree/arxiv_release

details on why we do not use BERT in this work.

3 Datasets

We use the Rollenwechsel-English, Version 2 (RW-Eng v2) corpus (Marton and Sayeed, 2022) as the training set for all our experiments. This corpus is sentence-segmented, annotated with morphological analyses, syntactic parses, and syntax-independent PropBank-based semantic role labeling (SRL). The syntactic head word of each semantic argument is determined by using several heuristics to match the parses to the semantic argument spans. Note that a sentence may have multiple predicates (typically verbs) and therefore multiple semantic frames (sometimes called “events”), each with its own semantic arguments, whose span may overlap the argument span of other frames in the sentence.

The first version of this corpus contained NLTK lemmas, MaltParser parses, parts-of-speech (POS) tags, and SENNA SRL tags (Bird, 2006; Nivre et al., 2006; Collobert and Weston, 2007). The second version added layers from more modern taggers: Morfette lemmas, spaCy syntactic parses and POS tags, and LSGN SRL tags (Chrupala, 2011; Honnibal and Johnson, 2015; He et al., 2018). In our experiments here we use the lemmas of the semantic arguments' head words in v2.

The sentences themselves are taken from both the ukWaC (Ferraresi et al., 2008) and the British National Corpus (BNC). This corpus contains 78M sentences across 2.3M documents. This includes 210M verbal predicates with 700M associated role-fillers. We use the same training, validation, and test split as Hong et al. (2018). That is, we have 99.2% (201.5M samples) in the full training set, 0.4% in validation, and 0.4% in testing. We run our training experiments on different subsets of the training data, ranging from 0.1% up to the full dataset. We cap our vocabulary size at the 50,000 most common words in that specific subset.

We used the following psycholinguistic test sets:

Padó (Padó et al., 2006) 414 verb-argument pairs and the associated judgement scores. These were constructed from 18 verbs that are present in both FrameNet and PropBank. For each verb, the three most frequent subjects and objects from each of the underlying corpora were selected. This process yielded six arguments per verb per corpus, with some overlap between corpora. For each verb-argument pair, a judgement was collected online with an average of 21 ratings per item for the argument in subject and object role. The rating was collected on a Likert scale of 1-7 with the question "How common is it for [subject] to [verb]?" or "How common is it for [object] to be [verbed]?"

McRae (McRae et al., 1998) 1444 pairs of verb-argument pairs in a similar format to Padó. These were created using a similar rating question as the Padó dataset, but is a compilation of ratings collected over several studies with considerable overlap and heterogeneous selection criteria.

Ferretti-Instruments and Ferretti-Locations (Ferretti et al., 2001) 274 predicate-location pairs and 248 predicate-instrument pairs. Based on the McRae dataset (Psychological norms).

GDS (Greenberg et al., 2015) 720 predicate-object pairs and their ratings. Only objects (no subjects), matched for high and low polysemy and frequency, well fitting vs. poorly fitting. Greenberg and McRae overlap by about a third, but the human scores are obtained from new surveys.

Bicknell (Bicknell et al., 2010) 64 cases. Congruent vs incongruent `Patient` in an `Agent`-Verb-`Patient` paradigm. Hand crafted, not corpus-based, designed for event-related potentials-based neurolinguistic experiments.

4 Modeling and Methodology

In this setup, an input event is represented as role-word pairs, where the role is one of the following PropBank (Palmer et al., 2005) roles: `Arg0, Arg1, ArgM-Mnr, ArgM-Loc, ArgM-Tmp`, and the predicate. The word is the argument's syntactic head's lemma. Both the role and the head word are taken from RW-Eng v2.[*]

We train a feed-forward network in a multi-task learning setting to optimize word and role prediction accuracy. For target word prediction we give the prediction layer the target role and a context vector formed as a multiplication of the input word–role pairs. Similarly, for target role prediction we feed the same context vector along with the target word, following the ResRoFA-MT architecture (Hong et al., 2018) (Figure 1a). Since the network initialization is random, we perform 5 runs of each experiment and report the mean with a 95% confidence interval. Following Hong et al. (2018); Marton and Sayeed (2022), we test each model

[*]Note the input is *not* a full sentence, precluding the use of contextual models such as BERT. See Appendices for details.

on the psycholinguistic datasets (Section 3), for which the models were not directly optimized. The idea behind using the latter test battery is that the model, even though trained on (simplified) SRL and word prediction (aka role-filling) tasks, is expected to be able to make indirect generalizations about predicate–argument fit level from the training data and the related objectives. These psycholinguistic tasks are evaluated with Spearman's rank correlation between the sorted human scores and the sorted model scores, except for Bicknell, for which we take accuracy of predicting which argument in each `Patient` role-filler pair is (more) congruent (Lenci, 2011).

All prior work with the ResRoFA-MT model uses two random word embedding sets (one for input words and one for the target word) and similarly two role embedding sets. See Figure 1a.

Our implementation differs in these key aspects:

- **Modified model architecture** - Using a single word embeddings set, shared between the target and input words, and similarly a single role embeddings set (Section 5.1, Figure 1b). In our experiments, we find the non-shared, redundant embedding layers do not affect the performance while adding (vocab size 50,000 × word embedding size 300) 15,000,000 learnable parameters in the model.
- **Changes in Batching** - With previous implementations, one *epoch* only resulted in about a third of the data being traversed. The next epoch would start on the second third and so on. Now, we set the data preprocessing so that one *epoch* is one pass through all the training data. Additionally, the data is preprocessed during the training of each batch, so no time is lost during training in waiting for the next batch of data to be preprocessed.
- **Missing and unknown words handling** - Following Marton and Sayeed (2022) but unlike Hong et al. (2018), we represent out-of-vocabulary (OOV) words separately from missing words (empty slots in an event).
- **Architectural ablation experiments** - these are described in Section 5, for ease of readability.

5 Experiments and Discussion

5.1 Shared Embedding Layer

We modify the network to use a single embeddings set shared between the input words and target word, by using a single index-to-embedding mapping layer – and similarly a shared embedding-mapping layer for the input roles and target role (Figure 1b). This change results in 2x the training speed (Section 4) without degradation in performance: role accuracy remains at 96.6-96.7%, word accuracy at 13.6-13.7%, Padó at 52-54%, McRae at 32-33%, and so on (see first two rows in Tables 1 and 2). Therefore we use the faster shared architecture for the rest of the experiments. We train all models (until Section 5.5) on a uniformly sampled 1% subset, which is large enough to get indicative results while saving time and cost in experimentation. For comparison of our results to previous work, see Section 5.5.

5.2 Random vs. Pre-trained Embeddings

Hong et al. (2018) used random Glorot uniform to initialize the word embeddings. Private communication with the authors confirmed random embeddings do as well as pretrained ones for these tasks. We replicate this finding, comparing random word embeddings to pretrained GloVe embeddings (Pennington et al., 2014), both of size 300: role accuracy at 96.7%, word accuracy at 13.7%, Padó at 52.8-53.2%, McRae at 32.8-33.8%. Similar trend follows across all the thematic fit task results with overlapping 95% confidence intervals of the experiments with random and GloVe embeddings (rows 2 and 3 in the top part of Tables 1 and 2).

(**Q1**) Why is this so? We note that during training, embeddings get updated. To check if this update is responsible for bridging the gap between zero knowledge (random embeddings) and much knowledge (compressed in the pre-trained GloVe), we freeze the word embedding layer and rerun the experiments (see the middle part in the same two tables). Contrary to our previous experiment, we find fixed GloVe embeddings do much better than fixed random embeddings on all our tasks. We also see tuning helps the model converge much faster (from 25 epochs down to 11-15).

We conclude that indeed much of the learning is captured in the word embeddings. Tuning them even on only 1% of our training data bridges the knowledge gap from the pre-trained embeddings almost completely (with possible exceptions on Ferretti and Bicknell). But we note that although lower, the fixed embeddings results are not near-random. This leads us to (**Q2**) Where else is learning done, and to what extent?

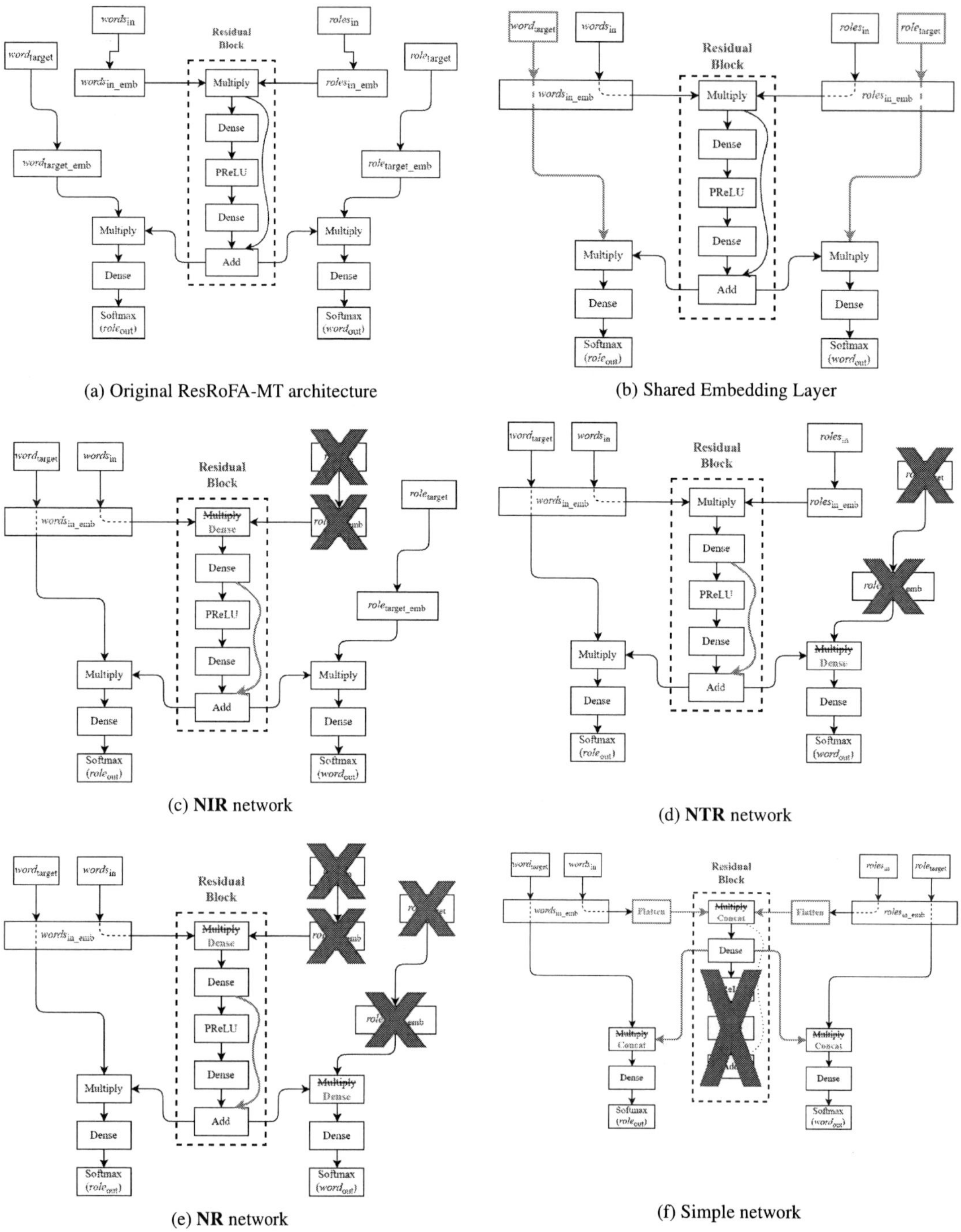

(a) Original ResRoFA-MT architecture

(b) Shared Embedding Layer

(c) **NIR** network

(d) **NTR** network

(e) **NR** network

(f) Simple network

Figure 1: The model architectures for our experiments

5.3 Role Contribution

We now turn to role ablation tests. First we take away the input roles from the context embeddings and call this the no-input-roles network **NIR** (see Figure 1c and the third part of Tables 1 and 2). We do not see large drops in word prediction (from 14.7% to 13.5%), or thematic fit tasks such as Padó (from 53.2% to 50.2%) and McRae (32.1% to 32.8%), except role prediction (from 96.7% to 90.4%), which we expect by construction. Note that when predicting the target word, the NIR network still receives the target role information,

Embedding	Shared?	Tuned?	Role?	Role Accuracy	Word Accuracy	Epochs*
Random	N	Y	Y	$.9655 \pm .0014$	$.1363 \pm .0020$	11(6)
Random	**Y**	Y	Y	$.9671 \pm .0003$	$.1372 \pm .0022$	11(6)
GloVe	Y	Y	Y	$.9669 \pm .0003$	$.1374 \pm .0005$	15(10)
Random	Y	**N**	Y	$.6609 \pm .0046$	$.1208 \pm .0012$	25(20)
GloVe	Y	N	Y	$.9510 \pm .0011$	$.1291 \pm .0006$	25(20)
GloVe	Y	Y	**NIR**†	$.9036 \pm .0013$	$.1348 \pm .0019$	11(6)
GloVe	Y	Y	**NTR**†	$.9677 \pm .0006$	$.1230 \pm .0017$	12(7)
GloVe	Y	Y	**NR**†	$.9007 \pm .0021$	$.1078 \pm .0010$	8(3)
RAND Network‡	Y	Y	Y	$.1530 \pm .0716$	$.0000 \pm .0000$	-
Simpler Network+	Y	N	Y	$.9987 \pm .0005$	$.1208 \pm .0020$	6(1)

Table 1: Word and Role accuracy on 1% training data.

† **NIR**=No input role (in context); **NTR**=No target role (in prediction); **NR**=No role
‡ Network with no training that uses previously fine tuned word/role embeddings as input
+ Simpler Feed forward Network with previously fine tuned word/role embeddings as input
* Epochs in parentheses: the epoch of the effective model (best model before early stopping after patience limit)

Embed.	Shrd	Tuned	Role	Padó	McRae	GDS	Ferretti-Loc	Ferretti-Instr	Bicknell
Random	N	Y	Y	$.5474 \pm .0345$	$.3231 \pm .0236$	$.4485 \pm .0314$	$.2611 \pm .0036$	$.2282 \pm .0623$	$.5260 \pm .1185$
Random	**Y**	Y	Y	$.5280 \pm .0274$	$.3384 \pm .0174$	$.4388 \pm .0206$	$.2532 \pm .1421$	$.2266 \pm .0391$	$.5000 \pm .0673$
GloVe	Y	Y	Y	$.5316 \pm .0320$	$.3280 \pm .0177$	$.4534 \pm .0209$	$.2851 \pm .0301$	$.2895 \pm .0258$	$.5438 \pm .0370$
Random	Y	**N**	Y	$.4396 \pm .0344$	$.2838 \pm .0109$	$.2841 \pm .0246$	$.1767 \pm .0273$	$.2086 \pm .0322$	$.4781 \pm .0450$
GloVe	Y	N	Y	$.4941 \pm .0247$	$.3090 \pm .0254$	$.4349 \pm .0229$	$.3011 \pm .0301$	$.3439 \pm .0421$	$.5563 \pm .0490$
GloVe	Y	Y	**NIR**	$.5079 \pm .0587$	$.3205 \pm .0580$	$.4217 \pm .0472$	$.3054 \pm .0791$	$.2543 \pm .0796$	$.6042 \pm .0896$
GloVe	Y	Y	**NTR**	$.2400 \pm .0294$	$.0937 \pm .0258$	$.3845 \pm .0083$	$.3071 \pm .0017$	$.2621 \pm .0531$	$.5469 \pm .0388$
GloVe	Y	Y	**NR**	$.2496 \pm .1088$	$.1139 \pm .0150$	$.3385 \pm .0363$	$.2955 \pm .1243$	$.2668 \pm .0375$	$.5885 \pm .0448$
RAND	Y	Y	Y	$-.0001 \pm .1090$	$.0109 \pm .1604$	$.0365 \pm .0784$	$.0165 \pm .1048$	$-.0346 \pm .0785$	$.4531 \pm .1027$
Simpler	Y	N	Y	$.3271 \pm .0555$	$.2175 \pm .0294$	$.3356 \pm .0345$	$.1055 \pm .0259$	$.0459 \pm .1239$	$.5365 \pm .0593$

Table 2: Thematic Fit tests on 1% training data (same models as in Table 1)

which, together with at least the predicate, is likely often sufficient information for prediction.

We find it surprising that input role ablation barely affects performance on the psycholinguistic tasks. Why is that? One possibility: the input role contribution is negligible. But another possibility is that in NIR, all (or almost all) the role information was *crammed* into the target role embeddings. To tease these apart, we next take away the target role from the penultimate layer of the network, but leave the input roles intact. We call this no-target-role network **NTR** (see Figure 1d and the row after NIR in the same tables). Now the role accuracy goes back to the base level of 96.7% (as expected by construction), but word accuracy drops (from 13.7% to 12.3%) and so does performance on the psycholinguistic tasks, e.g., Padó (from 53.2% to 24%), McRae (32.8% to 9.4%). We conclude that target role carries more crucial information than input roles for our psycholinguistic tasks, and that role information *cramming*, if it happens in NIR, does not happen in the other direction (NTR).

Finally, for completeness, we remove all role information from the network. We call this no-role network **NR** (see Figure 1e and same tables). This results in a drastic drop in word accuracy (from 13.7% to 10.8%) in addition to degradation of role accuracy from **NIR** experiment as well as the psycholinguistic tasks (Padó falls from 53.2% to 25%, McRae from 32.8% to 11.4%, and so on). This is an an interesting finding which supports previous knowledge about the importance of roles in multi-task learning setting while at the same time defies the importance of roles in the context vector (the output of the residual block in Figure 1). Next, we turn to learn more about the impact this vector and the block it is in.

5.4 "It's the Network!"... Or is it?

In order to see how much the particular ResRoFA-MT model architecture (aka "the network") contributes in our tasks, we first use the fine-tuned GloVe embedding from a previously trained base model (third row in Table 1) and assign the rest of the network random weights ("RAND Network" in Tables 1 and 2). To ensure the random weights are similar in size to the trained weights, we calculate the mean and standard deviation for each layer separately and assign that layer random weights using a Gaussian distribution with the same parameters. We see this new model does very poorly, near random prediction (word accuracy at 0%, role accuracy at 15.3%, Padó at 0%, McRae 1.1% and so on). This could be due to the learned representation in the network weights that were ablated here but also due to incompatibility of the non-trained random network weights with the very informative word embeddings.

Therefore next we replace the complex middle *residual block* with a plain dense layer but let this "Simpler Network" (Figure 1f, Tables 1 and 2) learn during training. In training here we use the fine-tuned word (and role) embeddings from our base model. Curiously, we see a notable jump in role accuracy (from 96.7% to 99.9%), but a drop in word accuracy (from 13.7% to 12.1%) as well as in the psycholinguistic tasks (Padó goes down from 53.2% to 32.7% , McRae from 32.8% to 21.8%, etc.) other than Bicknell's (53.7-54.4%). We speculate the latter task is an outlier here because it involves comparing the plausibility of two two-participant events with one participant changed. A simpler network may have an easier time representing binary distinctions within a pair of simple events, as opposed to predicting fine-grained scores of more complex inter-relationships, evaluated with Spearman's ρ in the other datasets. It may even be able to rely on general collocation statistics here, regardless of roles, but we leave this for future work. Note that here, we still do multi-task prediction as before, but in a much simpler network.

This, along with the role ablation experiments, suggest that while the potential incompatibility of the non-trained random network weights with the word embeddings may account for some of the drop in performance, the context vector formation through multiplication and likely also the improvements implemented in our base model have a large impact on the representation learning as tested on the thematic fit tasks (although not the same impact on word/role prediction).

We see again that there is no clear correlation between the increase in directly optimized for word/role prediction, and the performance on the psycholinguistic tasks for which the models were not directly optimized.

To recap, it seems the answer to **(Q2)** is nuanced: Padó and McRae are most sensitive to ablated roles; GDS, and perhaps Bicknell, to non-tuned random word embeddings; Ferretti to ablated (simplifiled) networks; and all are sensitive to RAND Networks, but Bicknell is surprisingly robust even there.

5.5 Training Data Size Effect

Often in machine learning and NLP, models learn better with more data. However, there are typically diminishing returns. To test the effect of training data size, we use our shared layer network with tuned GloVe embeddings (as in row 3 in Table 1) on uniformly sampled 1%, 10%, 20% 40% and 100% of the training dataset. See Table 3 and Table 4.

Sys	Role Accuracy	Word Accuracy	Epochs
B1†	.9470	-	-
B2‡	.9715 ± .0010	.1541 ± .0045	-
20%M+	.9707 ± .0002	.1450 ± .0004	-
0.1%	.9446 ± .0015	.0994 ± .0024	12(7)
1%	.9669 ± .0003	.1374 ± .0005	15(10)
10%	.9701 ± .0002	.1443 ± .0006	13(10)
20%	.9703 ± .0004	.1445 ± .0009	9(6)
40%	.9704 ± .0007	.1442 ± .0011	9(6)
100%*	.9708 ± .0006	.1444 ± .0019	7(4)

Table 3: Comparison of performance with GloVe (tuned) with varying training set sizes (Sys)

† Hong et al. (2018) 20%

‡ Marton and Sayeed (2022) 20%

+ The average of max value in each trial for fair comparison with benchmarks B1,B2

First, in order to compare fairly with previous work, we report the average of the *maximum* value in each training trial on 20% of the data. (Recall that our 20% of the data is a larger training set than our baselines' 20% due to improvements in our batcher). Our role accuracy (97.1%) is better than Hong et al. (2018) (94.7%) and similar to Marton and Sayeed (2022) (97.2%). Our word accuracy (14.5%) is a bit lower than the latter (15.4%). On the indirectly supervised thematic fit tasks, our results are better on Padó (58.6% compared to 53%), similar on McRae (42.5-43.4%), but lower for the rest. We suspect that in the previous work authors reported the *best* of all the epochs from all trials, which can explain why the previously reported scores are higher than our results; but we could not verify that.

In order to better understand the effect of training set size (**Q3**), we use next what we believe to be more realistic numbers: the average of the last saved model in each run (best model per our validation set) in each training subset size.

System	Padó	McRae	GDS	Ferretti-Loc	Ferretti-Instr	Bicknell
B1	.5300	.4250	.6080	.4630	.4770	.7450
B2	.5363 ± .0035	.4322 ± .0232	-	-	-	-
20%M	.5855 ± .0101	.4338 ± .0181	.5495 ± .0220	.3539 ± .0239	.4255 ± .0210	.6094 ± .0000
0.1%	.2992 ± .0441	.1856 ± .0157	.1699 ± .0180	.0891 ± .0306	.0367 ± .0203	.4906 ± .0402
1%	.5316 ± .0320	.3280 ± .0177	.4534 ± .0209	.2851 ± .0301	.2895 ± .0258	.5438 ± .0370
10%	.5572 ± .0247	.3993 ± .0137	.5409 ± .0150	.3410 ± .0358	.3765 ± .0320	.5906 ± .0320
20%	.5241 ± .0558	.3708 ± .1182†	.5245 ± .0148	.3191 ± .0312	.3853 ± .0454	.5813 ± .0210
40%	.3662 ± .1355	.3831 ± .0276	.5467 ± .0183	.3331 ± .0215	.3660 ± .0284	.5750 ± .0460
100%‡	.3375 ± .7293	.3733 ± .5203	.5338 ± .1328	.2736 ± .7846	.3416 ± .3297	.6094 ± .1985

Table 4: Thematic Fit with GloVe tuned (same models as in Table 3)

† 1 trial had an outlier score .2026

‡ All experiments had 5 runs per training subset, except for the 100% with only 2 runs, due to compute resource limitation.

We see incremental improvements from the 0.1% subset (role accuracy at 94.5%, word accuracy at 9.9%) to the 1% subset (role accuracy at 96.7%, word accuracy at 13.7%) to the 10% subset (role accuracy at 97.0%, word accuracy at 14.4%) across all our evaluation tasks; however, contrary to our null hypothesis, we see diminishing returns or no gains in role and word prediction when using 20% or more of the training set. In most of the psycholinguistic tasks (Table 4), results plateau at 10% or 20% (GDS at 52.5-54.1%, Ferretti-Loc at 32-34.1%, Ferretti-Instr at 36.6-38.5% and Bicknell at 57.5-59.1%) with the notable exception of Padó (best at 55.7% with 10% training data) and McRae (best at 40% at 10% training data) , where we see a negative trend at and beyond 20%. Why is it so, and only for these two tasks, with mainly Padó? The Padó dataset is constructed from high-frequency fillers. It behaves differently from the other datasets and gets a high maximum average score on the 20% subset probably because there is more training data available for high-frequency fillers, compared to the other datasets, including McRae. Considering the small samples in these test sets, they might quickly become victims of not only high variance, but also of overfitting, that is to say, the models may specialize on the corpus distribution, increasingly with training set size. This distribution is likely to be different from the WSJ distribution, from which Padó dataset is drawn (but see also Section 5.6).

How do word/role prediction and thematic fit tasks relate to each other? We leave this question for future research, but our hypothesis is that psycholinguistic meaning of natural language is grounded in interaction with other modalities (e.g., actions, vision, audio), which a model cannot learn just from more textual training data.

This leads potentially to a much bigger question: how much can a neural model learn natural language by just being trained on very large corpora or billions of parameters, and where is the saturation point? Furthermore, we see role information is important to our psycholinguistic tasks; how much does the role definition and granularity (e.g., PropBank or FrameNet), or the role set size, matter for these tasks? Possibly, with a richer roleset, we may see more alignment between word/role prediction and the psycholinguistic tasks. Perhaps PropBank roles are too coarse-grained to allow for an analysis of how a role-prediction task relates to a thematic fit task, which involves the fine-grained ranking (via Spearman's ρ) of event plausiblities derived from the underlying semantic characteristics of the nouns and verbs involved. If so, understanding how performance on a role-prediction task relates to thematic fit judgements may not be possible without a finer-grained inventory of semantic characteristics, such as Dowtyan proto-roles (Dowty, 1991).

5.6 Global and Local Correlation

We evaluate both Padó and McRae by computing Spearman's rank correlation between the sorted list of model's probability scores and the sorted list of averaged human scores, for each dataset. Why do Padó and McRae deteriorate with increasing training data size? To test if this is due to fluctuation of model scores for unrelated but near-in-score verb-noun pairs, we averaged correlations for *local* subsets, grouped by verb. This should be an easier task, since some of the globally close competition is not present in each by-verb subset. Indeed, we see high jumps of 5-8% for the *local* correlation scores in the larger subsets (40% and 100%). But in the smaller subsets we see changes of 2-3% up or down. Moreover, the trend of lower correlation with larger training sets remained. We leave it to future work to dig further into why Padó and McRae show such an anomaly.

6 Conclusions and Future Work

In this work, we explored why random word embeddings counter-intuitively perform as well as pretrained word embeddings on certain compositional semantic tasks (some being outside the models' explicit objective), where the learning is actually stored (teasing apart the word embeddings, role embeddings, and the rest of the network), and how training set size affects performance on these tasks. We found out that tuning (or further tuning) the word embeddings helps and can bridge the gap between random and pretrained embeddings. Moreover, our tuned embedding space is different from pretrained embeddings like GloVe. We saw that the target role is more important than the input roles on our tasks. Furthermore, our experiments suggested that much of the learning happens also in the rest of the network outside word and role embedding layers. No single factor (word and role embeddings or the network) is most important for all tasks.

Training set size had a surprising negative effect on Padó and McRae beyond 20% of the training data. We attempted explaining this with an alternative evaluation method, but this remains to be explained further.

We release our code, including our preferred network architecture – a modified version of ResRoFA-MT with shared embedding layers.

One avenue in which we want to invest is to better understand the complex relationship between word/role accuracy and our psycholinguistic tasks. While our initial hypothesis was that training the network to minimize loss on word/role prediction would also optimize performance on all our tasks, this did not always hold. We suspect that the groundedness is the missing link for (artificially and naturally) learning psycholinguistic tasks, and therefore adding grounding seems promising to us.

Another future avenue is to investigate the high variability in psycholinguistic task performance compared to the fairly stable results on the directly optimized-for word and role prediction tasks.

Limitations

There are certain limitations that were unavoidable in this work. One of them is the limited size of the available training and evaluation datasets for testing thematic fit tasks. It is likely that the high variance we observed is due to both our indirect supervision approach (in part due to lack of directly relevant data for training), and the small-size test sets. We are limited here by the state of the art in such datasets, not just by their size. It is a complex task to create and evaluate thematic fit with full phrases and sentences, i.e., not just with the arguments' syntactic heads. Since we do not know of any such datasets, our model was designed with only syntactic heads in mind.

Another limitation is the training dataset quality: due to its size, the training data was machine-annotated (for syntactic parsing, SRL and lemmas) and therefore unintended noise and bias may have been introduced in the models. In addition, even though our training datasets were collected with the goal of making them domain-general and balanced, it is hard to enforce and verify that in large sizes. We take issues such as toxicity and gender bias seriously, but we think that in our settings, where the model does not generate language and the test sets do not involve gendered examples, the related risks approach zero.

Semantic tasks such as thematic fit would most likely benefit from training on grounded language, e.g., combining text and vision, but working with such datasets is beyond the scope of this work.

Finally, a rather trivial limitation we have is the number of trials per experiment we could run due to time and computational constraints. We only ran 3-5 trials per experiment but a larger number of trials may yield more robust results. Despite all these limitations, we believe our work gives a very comprehensive analysis of the ResRoFaMT model and opens up some interesting avenues for future research work.

Ethical Considerations

Our work uses RW-Eng v2 (Marton and Sayeed, 2022), which in turn uses two corpora: ukWaC and the BNC. Therefore, we have similar ethical concerns as mentioned in that previous work, including the way the BNC data was collected. Those who so wish can easily exclude the BNC data (it comprises only a small part of the whole corpus) and retrain.

The RW-Eng corpus (v1 or v2) could introduce undesired bias in use outside the UK, since the data is sourced entirely from UK web pages and other UK sources from the 20th century. English used outside the UK, and more recent English anywhere, differ from this corpus in their word distributions, and therefore their input may yield sub-optimal or undesired results. Furthermore, models trained on it could encode a Western-centric view of the world.

The silver labels – the automatic parsing and tagging of the corpus – could introduce bias from the parsing / tagging algorithms. These parsers / taggers are also trained models, which could be affected by their data sources. If this is a concern for some users, we encourage them to perform validation of the data and its annotations.

Having said that, we believe that for most if not all conceivable applications, especially as long as one keep these limitations in mind, our work should not pose any practical risk.

Acknowledgements

This work started as a Masters Capstone project at the Columbia University Data Science Institute. We would like to thank Data Science Institute, and the Department of Computer Science at Columbia University for their support. Specifically, Smaranda Muresan for early discussions and Eleni Drinea for timely support with our computing resources in the initial stages of this project. We would like to thank Google Cloud Platform for an award of credits to Asad Sayeed, allowing us to use Google Cloud computing resources. We are grateful to the rest of the Capstone team members – Jake Stamell, Anjani Prasad Atluri and Priyadharshini Rajbabu – for their valuable contributions. This research was funded in part by a Swedish Research Council (VR) grant (2014-39) for the Centre for Linguistic Theory and Studies in Probability (CLASP).

References

Marco Baroni, Georgiana Dinu, and Germán Kruszewski. 2014. Don't count, predict! a systematic comparison of context-counting vs. context-predicting semantic vectors. In *ACL (1)*, pages 238–247.

Marco Baroni and Alessandro Lenci. 2010. Distributional memory: A general framework for corpus-based semantics. *Computational Linguistics*, 36(4):673–721.

Klinton Bicknell, Jeffrey L Elman, Mary Hare, Ken McRae, and Marta Kutas. 2010. Effects of event knowledge in processing verbal arguments. *Journal of Memory and Language*, 63(4):489–505.

Steven Bird. 2006. NLTK: the natural language toolkit. In *Proceedings of the COLING/ACL on Interactive presentation sessions*, pages 69–72. Association for Computational Linguistics.

Grzegorz Chrupala. 2011. Efficient induction of probabilistic word classes with LDA. In *Proceedings of 5th International Joint Conference on Natural Language Processing*, pages 363–372, Chiang Mai, Thailand. Asian Federation of Natural Language Processing.

Ronan Collobert and Jason Weston. 2007. Fast semantic extraction using a novel neural network architecture. In *Proceedings of the 45th Annual Meeting of the Association of Computational Linguistics*, pages 25–32.

David Dowty. 1991. Thematic proto-roles and argument selection. *Language*, 67(3):547–619.

Adriano Ferraresi, Eros Zanchetta, Marco Baroni, and Silvia Bernardini. 2008. Introducing and evaluating ukWaC, a very large web-derived corpus of english. *Proceedings of the 4th Web as Corpus Workshop (WAC-4) Can we beat Google*, pages 47–54.

Todd R Ferretti, Ken McRae, and Andrea Hatherell. 2001. Integrating verbs, situation schemas, and thematic role concepts. *Journal of Memory and Language*, 44(4):516–547.

Clayton Greenberg, Vera Demberg, and Asad Sayeed. 2015. Verb polysemy and frequency effects in thematic fit modeling. In *Proceedings of the 6th Workshop on Cognitive Modeling and Computational Linguistics*, pages 48–57, Denver, Colorado. Association for Computational Linguistics.

Luheng He, Kenton Lee, Omer Levy, and Luke Zettlemoyer. 2018. Jointly predicting predicates and arguments in neural semantic role labeling. *CoRR*, abs/1805.04787.

Alexander Henlein and Alexander Mehler. 2022. What do toothbrushes do in the kitchen? how transformers think our world is structured.

Xudong Hong, Asad Sayeed, and Vera Demberg. 2018. Learning distributed event representations with a multi-task approach. In *Proceedings of the Seventh Joint Conference on Lexical and Computational Semantics*, pages 11–21, New Orleans, Louisiana. Association for Computational Linguistics.

Matthew Honnibal and Mark Johnson. 2015. An improved non-monotonic transition system for dependency parsing. In *Proceedings of the 2015 Conference on Empirical Methods in Natural Language Processing*, pages 1373–1378, Lisbon, Portugal. Association for Computational Linguistics.

Alessandro Lenci. 2011. Composing and updating verb argument expectations: A distributional semantic model. In *Proceedings of the 2nd Workshop on Cognitive Modeling and Computational Linguistics*, CMCL 2011, pages 58–66, Stroudsburg, PA, USA. Association for Computational Linguistics.

Alessandro Lenci, Magnus Sahlgren, Patrick Jeuniaux, Amaru Cuba Gyllensten, and Martina Miliani. 2022. A comparative evaluation and analysis of three generations of distributional semantic models. *Language Resources and Evaluation*, pages 1–45.

Yuval Marton and Asad Sayeed. 2022. Thematic fit bits: Annotation quality and quantity interplay for event participant representation. In *Proceedings of the 13th Language Resources and Evaluation Conference*.

Ken McRae, Michael J Spivey-Knowlton, and Michael K Tanenhaus. 1998. Modeling the influence of thematic fit (and other constraints) in on-line sentence comprehension. *Journal of Memory and Language*, 38(3):283–312.

Joakim Nivre, Johan Hall, and Jens Nilsson. 2006. Malt-Parser: A data-driven parser-generator for dependency parsing. In *Proceedings of LREC*, volume 6, pages 2216–2219.

Ulrike Padó, Frank Keller, and Matthew W Crocker. 2006. Combining syntax and thematic fit in a probabilistic model of sentence processing. In *Proceedings of the 28th CogSci*, pages 657–662.

Martha Palmer, Daniel Gildea, and Paul Kingsbury. 2005. The proposition bank: An annotated corpus of semantic roles. *Computational Linguistics*, 31(1):71–106.

Jeffrey Pennington, Richard Socher, and Christopher Manning. 2014. Glove: Global vectors for word representation. In *Proceedings of the 2014 conference on empirical methods in natural language processing (EMNLP)*, pages 1532–1543.

Ottokar Tilk, Vera Demberg, Asad Sayeed, Dietrich Klakow, and Stefan Thater. 2016. Event participant modelling with neural networks. In *Proceedings of the 2016 Conference on Empirical Methods in Natural Language Processing*, pages 171–182, Austin, Texas. Association for Computational Linguistics.

Appendix A: Why Not Use BERT Here?

With the advent of contextual embeddings, static word embeddings are often regarded as inferior or outdated. While this is true in many cases, we wish to point out that **(a)** there are still cases where static word embeddings outperform BERT (Lenci et al. (2022); Henlein and Mehler (2022), *inter alia*) and more importantly, **(b)** not all NLP tasks and test sets are in the form of complete sentences, which may render contextual models useless there. More specifically for our tasks:

1. As we point out at the end of Section 2, "Lenci et al. (2022) demonstrate that ... even recent contextual models such as BERT are not necessarily better for out-of-context tasks than well-tuned static representations, predict or otherwise." Our tasks, as represented by several psycholinguistic test sets are such out-of-context tasks. This *is* the state-of-the-art in psycholinguistics datasets. The human judgments in these sets were given without a full sentence or other context beyond the verb-noun (or noun-verb-noun) items. There is no reason to assume that BERT, a contextual model trained on full sentences will do well on out-of-context tasks, and again, it has been shown BERT is not necessarily better than static word embeddings.

2. Even if we wanted to use BERT, we cannot use a lookup table the same way we can for static word embeddings. This means we will either have to decode each sentence on the fly every training (and evaluation) iteration, or decode once and save on disk. Simple calculation shows that the required storage demands, even for, say, 1% of the data, make this exercise computationally extremely expensive.

3. BERT may break words to several tokens. How to map these to the verb or noun in the training or test is not always straightforward, and this mapping makes embedding extraction speed 0.5x slower.

4. "Hallucinating" synthetic sentences from the verb-noun input in order for BERT to receive a sentence for input would invalidate the ratings given by the human raters without these (or other) sentences.

5. In order to validate our claims here, we experimented with BERT on-the-fly in preliminary studies, using a small training subset of a few thousand sentences with simple token mapping, and the results were dismal while the training already excruciatingly slow.

6. There is nothing wrong with systematically exploring models that use static word embeddings, even if contextual embeddings excite many people more. We don't think we should defend this choice.

Appendix B: Dataset Examples

For added clarity we give the readers a few examples of the training and evaluation data.

1. Each training example is a list of *word/role* pairs. Each of these examples are created with the head words from full sentences, i.e., our final training examples do not contain full context. We have 6 semantic roles such as *Arg0* and *Arg1* etc. + one placeholder *UNK* role for roles not included in our role set. A typical example could look like this: `{0: 6, 1: 97, 2: 43511, 3: 43511, 4: 239, 5: 143, 6: 64}`, where the numbers are pairs of role:word indices. The size of word vocabulary of the 0.1% training subset is 43,510 with tokenId 43,510 and 43,511 corresponding to *UNK* and *Missing* word (the corresponding role does not have a head word). Larger training subsets vocabulary is capped at 50,000.

   Each example is used in training 1 or more times, each time with a different target word/role pair (see Figures 1a, 1b, and Section 4), while the rest of the pairs are used for input. Note that a pair with a *Missing* word cannot serve as a target word/role.

2. Apart from the train / test split, we use multiple psycholinguistic evaluation sets that we do not optimize the model on, as mentioned in Section 3. While they all vary, a typical example is `{client, advise, Arg0, 3.7}`, which means that human raters gave an average of 3.7 to 'client' as Argument 0 (typically Agent) for 'advise' (as in "the client advised the banker that ..."). In contrast, `{client, advise, Arg1, 6.6}`, means that human raters gave an average of 6.6 to 'client' as Argument 1 (typically Theme/Patient) for 'advise' (as in "the banker advised the client that ..."). According to these human raters, 'client' fits semantically much better as Arg1 than Arg0 for 'advise'. During thematic fit evaluation, we sort these test examples by human rater average scores, and the model output by model score. Then, we compute Spearman's rank correlation between the two sorted lists, as explained in Section 5.6.

Sentence Ambiguity, Grammaticality and Complexity Probes

Sunit Bhattacharya[=] and **Vilém Zouhar**[=] and **Ondřej Bojar**
Charles University, Faculty Of Mathematics and Physics
Insititute of Formal and Applied Linguistics
{bhattacharya,zouhar,bojar}@ufal.mff.cuni.cz

Abstract

It is unclear whether, how and where large pre-trained language models capture subtle linguistic traits like ambiguity, grammaticality and sentence complexity. We present results of automatic classification of these traits and compare their viability and patterns across representation types. We demonstrate that template-based datasets with surface-level artifacts should not be used for probing, careful comparisons with baselines should be done and that t-SNE plots should not be used to determine the presence of a feature among dense vectors representations. We also show how features might be highly localized in the layers for these models and get lost in the upper layers.

1 Introduction

Pre-trained language models, such as BERT, M-BERT (Devlin et al., 2019) and GPT-2 (Radford et al., 2019), while being very efficient at solving NLP problems, are also notoriously difficult to interpret and their analysis and interpretation is an active area of research (Belinkov and Glass, 2019). One such technique of analysis is based on probing classifiers (Belinkov, 2021), which primarily consists of training and evaluating a shallow network multi-layer perceptron (MLP) as a classifier on top of the vector representations. Probing classifiers are now fairly established in NLP (Adi et al., 2016; Tenney et al., 2019; Ma et al., 2019).

In this work, we build sentence representations from layer-wise contextual embeddings obtained from three different pre-trained language models and probe them for three linguistic traits: sentence ambiguity, grammaticality, and complexity using some well-established datasets.

In the process, we show why having a reasonable baseline is a necessity for performance interpretation. We also demonstrate why simply visually checking the clustering of embeddings on datasets using t-SNE, a popular dimension-reduction technique in probing, can lead to incorrect conclusions.

Motivation. The study of these traits is important for example in machine translation where disambiguation is necessary and grammaticality correction and simplification sometimes happen implicitly without any control. For the tasks of text simplification and grammar correction, it is crucial to be aware of whether and how general-purpose models encode these traits or whether they abstract the meaning from them. Specifically, ambiguity detection has been investigated very little in contrast to other features. All of these three traits are orthogonal in their definitions, although their mutual relationships are unknown. For example, it may be that ambiguous sentences tend to be more complex and prone to lower grammaticality. We assimilate the definition of these traits from the respective datasets but nevertheless include examples in Table 1.

Contribution. We carry out text classification tasks of ambiguity, grammaticality and complexity and demonstrate empirically that:

- having a reasonable baseline is a necessity for performance interpretation;
- sentence ambiguity is represented much less than sentence complexity in the models;
- the template-based BLiMP dataset is not suitable for probing grammaticality because of surface-level artefacts;
- t-SNE is not always an adequate tool to see whether a feature is represented in vectors.

[=]Co-first authors.

Code for the experiments in this paper is open-source: github.com/ufal/ambiguity-grammaticality-complexity

Proceedings of the Fifth BlackboxNLP Workshop on Analyzing and Interpreting Neural Networks for NLP, pages 40 - 50
December 8, 2022 ©2022 Association for Computational Linguistics

Dataset	Class	Sentence
Ambiguous COCO	Ambiguous	A metal artwork displays a clock in the middle of a floor.
MS COCO	Unambiguous	A couple sitting under an umbrella on a park bench.
HCR English	Complex	For the year, net income tumbled 61% to $ 86 million, or $ 1.55 a share.
HCR English	Simple	In part, the trust cited the need to retain cash for possible acquisitions.
CoLA	Acceptable	The sailors rode the breeze clear of the rocks.
CoLA	Unacceptable	The problem perceives easily.
BLiMP-Morphology	Acceptable	The sketch of those trucks hasn't hurt Alan.
BLiMP-Morphology	Unacceptable	The sketch of those trucks haven't hurt Alan.
BLiMP-Syntax	Acceptable	Aaron breaks the glass.
BLiMP-Syntax	Unacceptable	Aaron appeared the glass.
BLiMP-Syn_Semantics	Acceptable	Mary can declare there to be some ladders falling.
BLiMP-Syn_Semantics	Unacceptable	Mary can entreat there to be some ladders falling.
BLiMP-Semantics	Acceptable	There was a rug disappearing.
BLiMP-Semantics	Unacceptable	There was every rug disappearing.

Table 1: Sentence examples from used datasets.

2 Related Work

Ambiguity. Word-sense disambiguation has been extensively studied and is a closely related task (Navigli, 2009). This has also been the focus of work done with recent NLP tools, which has mostly concentrated on the determination of ambiguity at the lexical level and not at the sentence level. Yaghoobzadeh et al. (2019); Şahin et al. (2020); Meyer and Lewis (2020) classify ambiguous words. Chen et al. (2020) explore the geometry of BERT and ELMo (Peters et al., 2018) using a structural probe to study the representational geometry of ambiguous sentences. Bordes et al. (2019) use a combination of visual and text data to ground the textual representations and make notes on disambiguation. Ambiguity modelling has also been a focus of the MT community because translation often requires disambiguation. This applies on many levels: lexical (Higinbotham, 1991; Zou and Zou, 2017; Do et al., 2020; Campolungo et al., 2022), syntactic (Pericliev, 1984) and semantic (Baker et al., 1994; Stahlberg and Kumar, 2022). Psycholinguists have also studied the effect of ambiguity resolution on cognitive load (Altmann, 1985; Trueswell, 1996; Papadopoulou, 2005), often motivated by issues in MT (Sammer et al., 2006; Scott, 2018). Bhattacharya et al. (2022) explore ambiguity by the task of translation by human annotators.

Grammaticality. This trait has been studied historically from the perspective of human sentence processing and acceptability (Nagata, 1992; Braze, 2002; Mirault and Grainger, 2020). Many real-world applications utilize tools for automatic grammaticality prediction (Heilman et al., 2014; Warstadt et al., 2019), such as automatic essay assessment (Foltz et al., 1999; Landauer, 2003; Dong et al., 2017) or machine translation (Riezler and Maxwell III, 2006). For MT, output acceptability, or fluency, is a standard evaluation direction for which many automated metrics exist (Hamon and Rajman, 2006; Lavie and Denkowski, 2009; Stymne and Ahrenberg, 2010). In contrast to our supervised classifier approach, perplexity-based approach has been used to measure acceptability (Meister et al., 2021).

Related more closely to our setup, Hewitt and Manning (2019) use a linear probe and identify syntax in contextual embeddings. Lu et al. (2020); Li et al. (2021) examine gramaticality in BERT layers. Hanna and Bojar (2021) assess BERTScore effectiveness in spotting grammatical errors.

Complexity. Similarly to other traits, complexity was first studied in the human processing of language (Richek, 1976; Just et al., 1996; Heinz and Idsardi, 2011). Brunato et al. (2018) perform a crowd-sourcing campaign for English along with an in-depth analysis of the annotator agreement and complexity perception. Automatic complexity estimation is vital, especially in the educational setting for predicting readability (McNamara et al., 2002; Weller et al., 2020). Ambati et al. (2016) estimate sentence complexity using a parser while Štajner et al. (2017) do so using n-grams. Sarti

(2020); Sarti et al. (2021) juxtapose the effect of complexity on language models and human assessment thereof. Martinc et al. (2021) survey multiple neural approaches to complexity estimation, including using pre-trained LM representation. In contrast to our work, they report only the final results and do not investigate the issue from the perspective of probing (e.g. what representation to extract and from which layer).

Probing. Earlier probing studies have shown that the early layers of BERT capture phrase-level information and the later layers tend to capture long-distance dependencies (Jawahar et al., 2019). The syntax is also captured more in the early layers of BERT and higher layers are better at representing semantic information (Tenney et al., 2019). It is not clear if and how pre-trained models achieve compositionality (Kalchbrenner and Blunsom, 2013; Nefdt, 2020; Kassner et al., 2020) and how linguistic knowledge is represented in sentence embeddings. Liu et al. (2019) use probing on a set of tasks including token labelling, segmentation and pairwise relation extraction to test the abilities of contextual embeddings. Mutual information can be used as a viable alternative to traditional probes that require optimization (Pimentel et al., 2020). A conceptual follow-up is $\mathcal{V}$-information (Hewitt et al., 2021) which is better suited for probing. In many cases, t-SNE is the prevalent method of visualization of class clusters in high-dimensional vector space (Jawahar et al., 2019; Jin et al., 2019; Wu and Xiong, 2020; Hoyt and Owen, 2021).

3 Data

For each trait, we use a different dataset. Their overall sizes are listed in Table 2 and example sentences in Table 1. We repurpose the datasets and derive binary labels (positive/negative) from each: ambiguous/unambiguous, complex/simple and grammatical/ungrammatical.

Ambiguity. We use sentences from the MS COCO (Lin et al., 2014) dataset, for our list of ambiguous and unambiguous sentences. The MS COCO dataset comprises of a set of captions describing an image. Captions containing ambiguous verbs corresponding to 461 images (Ambiguous COCO; Elliott et al., 2016) constitute the ambiguous sentences for our experiment. 461 captions that were randomly sampled from MS COCO constituted the unambiguous sentences for the experiment.

	Dataset	Sentences
Ambiguity	COCO	0.9k
Complexity	HCR English	1.2k
	PACCSS-IT	1.1k
Grammaticality	CoLA	5k
	BLiMP	67×2k

Table 2: Number of sentences for each dataset corresponding to each trait.

Complexity. Corpus of Sentences rated with Human Complexity Judgments[1] (Iavarone et al., 2021) and PACCSS-IT (Brunato et al., 2016) contain 20 human ratings on the scale from 1 (not complex) to 7 (very complex) about sentences. We binarize these ratings and consider sentences below the average to be simple sentences and others to be complex sentences. The resulting dataset is class-balanced (complex/simple) in terms of examples (592 sentences of each class for English and 551 sentences for Italian). The average sentence length for complex and simple examples is 24.84 and 13.95, respectively for English sentences. For Italian sentences, the average sentence length for complex and simple examples is 21.61 and 12.26, respectively. The complexity could therefore be encoded solely in the sentence length.

Grammaticality. For experiments under this category, we use the Benchmark of Linguistic Minimal Pairs (BLiMP; Warstadt et al., 2020) and the Corpus of Linguistic Acceptability (CoLA; Warstadt et al., 2019) datasets. BLiMP contains sentence pairs, one of which contains a mistake in syntax, morphology, or semantics while the other is correct. The dataset covers 67 different conditions, grouped into 12 phenomena. These phenomena are further categorized as 'syntax','morphology','syntax-semantics' and 'semantics'. The CoLA dataset is not contrastive but contains human annotations of acceptable grammaticality.

[1]English sentences were taken from the Wall Street Journal section of the Penn Treebank. Italian sentences were taken from the newspaper section of the Italian Universal Dependency Treebank.

4 Experiments

4.1 Task definition

In the following experiments, we are solving three classification tasks in parallel. The input is always the whole sentence and the output one of the two classes (ambiguous/unambiguous, complex/simple, acceptable/unacceptable), as shown in Table 1, applies to the whole sentence. The whole pipeline is also depicted in Figure 1. When using the TF-IDF feature extractor, it replaces the *pre-trained LM* block.

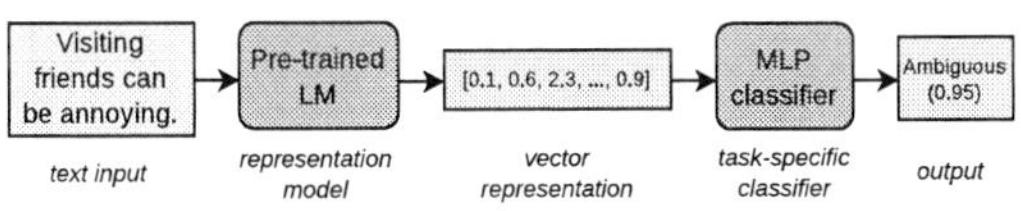

Figure 1: Example of the experiment pipeline for ambiguity classification. Ambiguous sentence from Stanley and Gendler Szabó (2000).

4.2 Setup

We use a simple MLP classifier to identify three linguistic traits from BERT (bert-base or multilingual bert-base) and GPT-2. The resulting vectors are 768-dimensional.[2] Both of these models are Transformer based models and contain 12 layers, which makes comparison convenient. We perform probing on each model separately.

- **CLS**: single vector at the `[CLS]` token.
- **Pooling:** single vector from the pooling layer.
- **Tokens:** vector representations of tokens aggregated with mean or (Hadamard) product to get a single 768-dimensional vector.

We obtain the layer-wise pre-trained model representations using Huggingface (Wolf et al., 2019) and use them to train a classifier that identifies if a sentence belongs to the positive class (e.g. ambiguous) or not. We perform a 10-fold cross-validation each with 10 runs of MLP.

Baseline. The most common class classifier (50% accuracy) is a poor baseline because it may be that the ambiguous and non-ambiguous sentences are distributed differently w.r.t. topic. In an attempt to alleviate this issue, we, therefore include as the baseline a TF-IDF-based vectorizer (with a varying number of maximum features). Probe performance of e.g. 65% would be considered at the first glance a positive result compared to 50%. However, in reality, it would be a false positive finding if a simple lexical feature extractor such as TF-IDF could yield 70%.

MLP Configuration. For probing we use `MLPClassifier` from scikit-learn 1.1.0 (Pedregosa et al., 2011) with most defaults preserved, as shown in Table 3.

Architecture	Single hidden layer (100)
Activation	ReLU
Optimizer	Adam
Learning rate	10^{-3}
Epochs	Early stopping, patience 1

Table 3: MLP classifier configuration.

4.3 Ambiguity & Complexity

Because the dataset is in Italian, we make use of multilingual BERT for both Complexity datasets. The probe performance for M-BERT is shown in Figure 2. At the first glance, it appears that the model does represent ambiguity internally since the ambiguity probe is systematically higher than 50%. However, because TF-IDF performs similarly and only uses surface-level features, the probe is very weak. This is supported by the fact that the most negative tokens from the classification (extracted from logistic regression coefficients) contained words such as *man* or *woman*, which disambiguate, based on gender, some unclear cases with an unclear referent.

In contrast, the complexity probe is systematically higher than the TF-IDF baseline. With minor exceptions, the accuracy remains high regardless of the layer. The performance for Italian (sentences taken from PACCSS-IT corpus) is identical to that for English using M-BERT (not shown). The CLS representation at layer 0 is 50% in both instances because it does not contain any information from the sentence (before the self-attention block).

4.4 Grammaticality

For the morphological task of determiner-noun agreement, Figure 3 shows a sudden drop in accuracy for the CLS representation at the 5th layer. In all the tasks concerning "Determiner-Noun Agreement", the sentence minimal pairs focus on the number agreement between the demonstrative determiners (like this/these) and an associated noun.

[2]The CLS and pooling representations apply only to BERT.

Acceptable Sentence	Unacceptable Sentence
Raymond is selling this sketch. Carmen hadn't shocked these customers.	Raymond is selling this sketches. Carmen hadn't shocked these customer.
Carl cures those horses. Sally thinks about that story.	Carl cures that horses. Sally thinks about those story.
Laurie hasn't lifted those cacti. The waitresses haven't cleaned this thesis.	Laurie hasn't lifted those cactus. The waitresses haven't cleaned this theses.
The teachers are running around this concealed oasis. Randolf buys those gray fungi.	The teachers are running around these concealed oasis. Randolf buys that gray fungi.
Cynthia scans these hard books. Jerry appreciates this lost report.	Cynthia scans this hard books. Jerry appreciates these lost report.

Table 4: Example minimal sentence pairs from the *determiner-noun* agreement task of BLiMP.

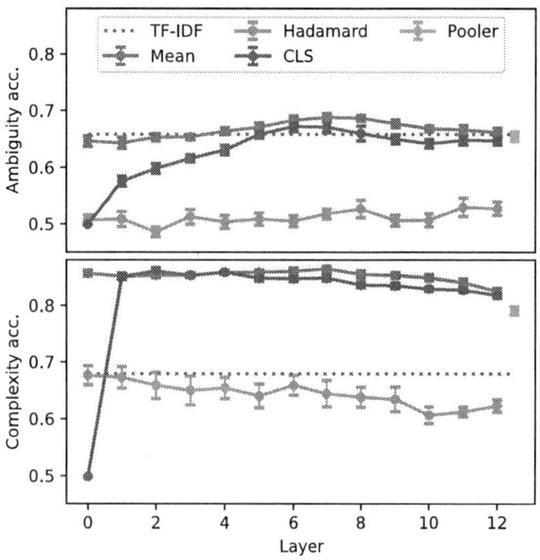

Figure 2: MLP dev accuracy for *ambiguity* and *complexity* BERT representation across layers.

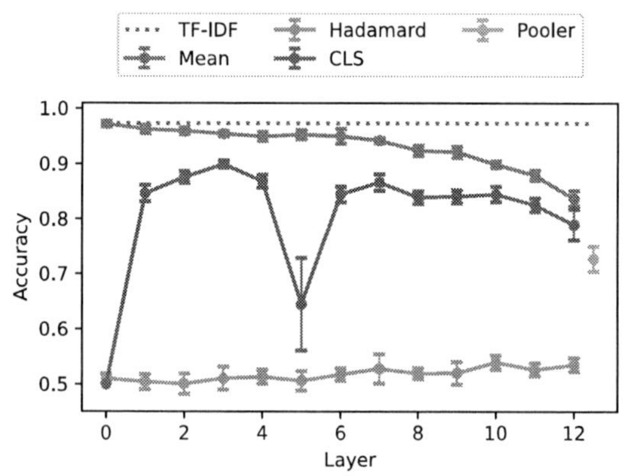

Figure 3: MLP dev accuracy for *determiner noun agreement irregular 1* task of BLiMP benchmark for BERT representation across layers. Each point is represented with a mean across 10 runs with a 95% confidence interval.

Examples of minimal pairs from the different tasks of this kind are shown in Table 4.

While the cause is unclear, it corresponds to the average norm of the representation being very low at that particular layer, making it harder for the classifier optimization.

As Figure 4 shows, many tasks can be "solved" with a simplistic TF-IDF featurizer, making them inadequate for determining the usefulness of large model representations. More adequate datasets need to be developed for probing stronger models. Systematically for all cases in morphology where the TF-IDF failed to work accurately, the performance of CLS representations was worse than the mean representations. Even in most semantics tasks, TF-IDF probes had near-perfect accuracy. For the 7 out of 26 syntactic tasks where the TF-IDF classifier was not accurate, the BERT models show a steep rise in accuracy from the 2nd/3rd layer for the mean and CLS representations, respectively. In comparison, GPT-2 does not exhibit this pattern.

5 Discussion

The experiments with ambiguity reveal that the representations of the pre-trained models do not encode the ambiguity trait well. The description detailing how the Ambiguous COCO was created (Elliott et al., 2017) states that the dataset was created with the intention of testing the capabilities of multimodal translation systems. We posit that ambiguity as a trait is not encoded in an accessi-

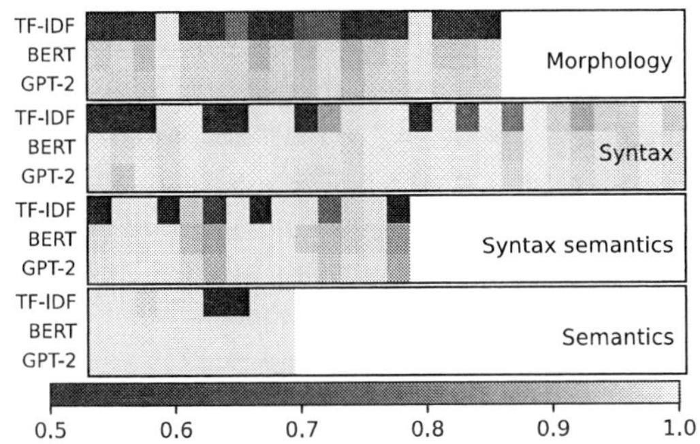

Figure 4: Accuracy on various BLiMP tasks with a max of BERT and GPT-2 representations and TF-IDF baseline. Each task+model is represented as one square. The lighter squares correspond to greater accuracy and are hence better.

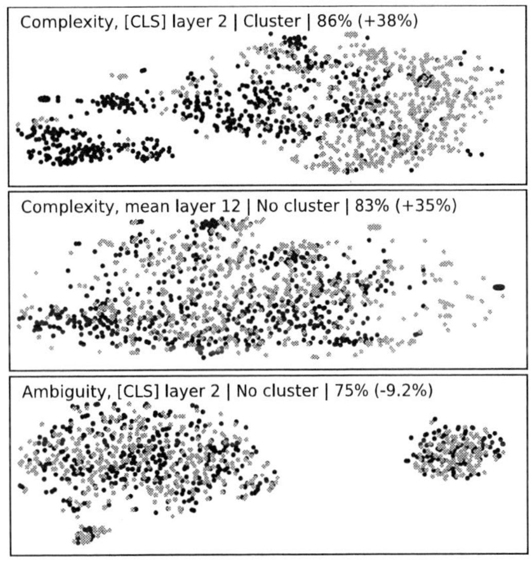

Figure 5: t-SNE projections from BERT-based embeddings. The first and the second row show high accuracy. The second and third rows show a lack of visual clusters. Red/black represent either complex/simple or ambiguous/unambiguous sentences. Percentages include classifier accuracy with the difference to the TF-IDF baseline in parentheses.

ble way in the layer representations of pre-trained models.

For BLiMP tasks related to morphology and syntax-semantics, the accuracy goes down in the upper layers, presumably because of increasing abstraction for both models (not shown in graphs). Although we perform experiments without fine-tuning, the findings are in line with the experimental results of Mosbach et al. (2020) where finetuning on 3 tasks from the GLUE benchmark (Wang et al., 2018) showed changes in probing performance mostly in the higher layers. Fine-tuning however led to modest gains. The present setup which probes sentence representations from pre-trained models shows that the middle layers fare far better in our probing tasks than the upper layers. This leads us to posit that the features of interest are highly localized and are lost in the upper layers (even with fine-tuning).

Although both BERT and GPT-2 employ the Transformer (Vaswani et al., 2017) architecture, they have very different ways and locations for storing knowledge in their internal representations (Rogers et al., 2020; Vulić et al., 2020; Lin et al., 2019; Kuznetsov and Gurevych, 2020; de Vries and Nissim, 2021; Liu et al., 2021). The CLS representations outperform the mean representations in only a few cases. This is expected since without fine-tuning the CLS token in BERT is trained to be used for the next sentence classification tasks.

6 t-SNE Inadequacy

Given appropriate optimization and classifier, if two or more classes in a vector space form clusters, they are linearly separable and therefore the classifier performs well. Furthermore, if a classifier probe performs well and is not affected by surface-level phenomena, it means that the features are represented in the vectors. Both these statements are one-way implications:

- clear clustering $\rightarrow$ high classifier accuracy
- high classifier acc. $\rightarrow$ feature present

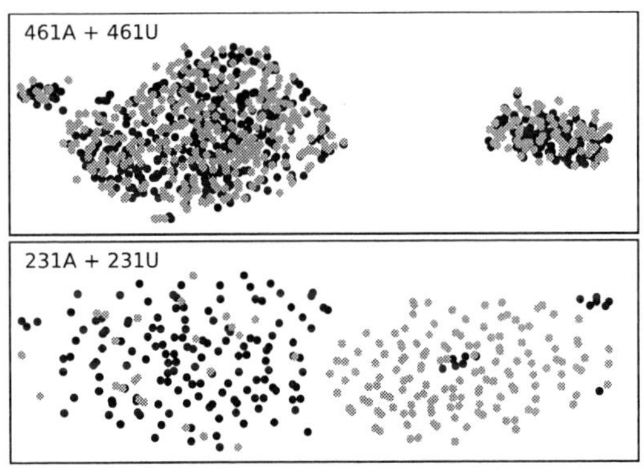

Figure 6: t-SNE projections from BERT-based embeddings (layer 1 of CLS) on ambiguous/unambiguous sentences (58% MLP and 66% TF-IDF accuracy). The first row is all the vectors and the second is half of them subsampled by Algorithm 1. Red/black represent ambiguous/unambiguous sentences.

Because t-SNE projects vectors from high dimensional space to lower dimensions in a manner that tries to preserve distances, it may be that visual clusters are created where there were none before and vice versa. The following scenarios are possible:

- clear clusters and high classifier accuracy
- no clusters and high classifier accuracy
- no clusters and low classifier accuracy

The last combination, "clear clusters and low classifier accuracy" is impossible with proper optimization. The three scenarios on probes from the previous experiments are shown in Figure 5. The conclusion is that probes should always precede visual clustering checks using t-SNE because it may be that the data does not form clear clusters in t-SNE but the classes are still linearly separable, meaning that the feature is encoded. The last image shows two clusters but not those that separate the two classes.

A plethora of work uses t-SNE to show clusters of vectors grouped by features (Chi et al., 2020; Nigam et al., 2020; Wu et al., 2020; Zhang et al., 2021; Subakti et al., 2022), though some follow-up with reporting classifier performance. Because t-SNE visual separation is not easily quantifiable, the negative results are often underreported (Fanelli, 2012; Mlinarić et al., 2017). This issue can be resolved by using other methods, such as probes.

Algorithm 1 Forcing t-SNE clusters

```
                    ▷ Vectors of sentences in the two classes
Load D_A, D_B
                              ▷ Cluster size, e.g. |D_A|/2
Input c', c ← c'/2
                       ▷ Two seeds from classes, most distant
s_A, s_B ← arg max_{v_A∈D_A, v_B∈D_B} ||v_A − v_B||

                              ▷ Closest points to own seeds
C'_A ← top-c_{v∈D_A}  −||s_A − v||
C'_B ← top-c_{v∈D_B}  −||s_B − v||
                        ▷ Furthest points to opposing seeds
C''_A ← top-c_{v∈D_A}  ||s_B − v||
C''_B ← top-c_{v∈D_B}  ||s_A − v||

C_A ← C'_A ∪ C''_A
C_B ← C'_B ∪ C''_B
t-SNE(C_A ∪ C_B)
```

6.1 Forcing t-SNE Clusters.

It is possible to start with sentence vectors that result in a t-SNE graph that does not show any visual clusters and select half of them such that running t-SNE will show clusters between the two classes. The algorithm is described in Algorithm 1. It is based on first finding two most distant "seeds" from the two classes and then selecting vectors of the same class which are closest to the seed or most distant to the other seed.

An example is shown in Figure 6. While the original does not show any clusters between the classes, the application of the algorithm selects such vectors that t-SNE shows visual clusters. Simplu randomly subsampling the vectors would not work but this shows that using t-SNE to visually determine the presence of a feature is not robust.

7 Conclusion

In this work, we showed how large pre-trained language models represent sentence ambiguity in a much less extractable way than sentence complexity and stress the importance of using reasonable baselines. We document that template-based datasets, such as BLiMP used for sentence acceptability, are not suitable for probing because of surface-level artefacts and more datasets should be developed for probing more performant models. Finally, we discuss why using t-SNE visually for determining whether some representations contain a specific feature is not always a suitable approach.

Future work

Because both t-SNE clustering and classification (inability to establish a rigid threshold for accuracy) can fail for determining whether a specific feature is represented in the model, more robust methods for this task should be devised. These probes should also be replicated in models used for machine translation, which is the primary motivation for studying these traits.

8 Acknowledgements

This work has been funded from the 19-26934X (NEUREM3) grant of the Czech Science Foundation. The work has also been supported by the Ministry of Education, Youth and Sports of the Czech Republic, Project No. LM2018101 LINDAT/CLARIAH-CZ.

References

Yossi Adi, Einat Kermany, Yonatan Belinkov, Ofer Lavi, and Yoav Goldberg. 2016. Fine-grained analysis of sentence embeddings using auxiliary prediction tasks.

Gerry Altmann. 1985. The resolution of local syntactic ambiguity by the human sentence processing mechanism. In *Second Conference of the European Chapter of the Association for Computational Linguistics*.

Bharat Ram Ambati, Siva Reddy, and Mark Steedman. 2016. Assessing relative sentence complexity using an incremental ccg parser. In *HLT-NAACL*, pages 1051–1057.

Kathryn Baker, Alexander Franz, Pamela Jordan, Teruko Mitamura, and Eric Nyberg. 1994. Coping with ambiguity in a large-scale machine translation system. In *COLING 1994 Volume 1: The 15th International Conference on Computational Linguistics*.

Yonatan Belinkov. 2021. Probing classifiers: Promises, shortcomings, and alternatives.

Yonatan Belinkov and James Glass. 2019. Analysis methods in neural language processing: A survey. *Transactions of the Association for Computational Linguistics*, 7:49–72.

Sunit Bhattacharya, Věra Kloudová, Vilém Zouhar, and Ondřej Bojar. 2022. EMMT: A simultaneous eye-tracking, 4-electrode eeg and audio corpus for multi-modal reading and translation scenarios. *arXiv preprint arXiv:2204.02905*.

Patrick Bordes, Eloi Zablocki, Laure Soulier, Benjamin Piwowarski, and Patrick Gallinari. 2019. Incorporating visual semantics into sentence representations within a grounded space. In *Proceedings of the 2019 Conference on Empirical Methods in Natural Language Processing and the 9th International Joint Conference on Natural Language Processing (EMNLP-IJCNLP)*, pages 696–707.

Forrest David Braze. 2002. *Grammaticality, acceptability and sentence processing: A psycholinguistic study*. University of Connecticut.

Dominique Brunato, Andrea Cimino, Felice Dell'Orletta, and Giulia Venturi. 2016. Paccss-it: A parallel corpus of complex-simple sentences for automatic text simplification. In *Proceedings of the 2016 Conference on Empirical Methods in Natural Language Processing*, pages 351–361.

Dominique Brunato, Lorenzo De Mattei, Felice Dell'Orletta, Benedetta Iavarone, and Giulia Venturi. 2018. Is this sentence difficult? do you agree? In *Proceedings of the 2018 Conference on Empirical Methods in Natural Language Processing*, pages 2690–2699.

Niccolò Campolungo, Federico Martelli, Francesco Saina, and Roberto Navigli. 2022. Dibimt: A novel benchmark for measuring word sense disambiguation biases in machine translation. In *Proceedings of the 60th Annual Meeting of the Association for Computational Linguistics (Volume 1: Long Papers)*, pages 4331–4352.

Boli Chen, Yao Fu, Guangwei Xu, Pengjun Xie, Chuanqi Tan, Mosha Chen, and Liping Jing. 2020. Probing bert in hyperbolic spaces. In *International Conference on Learning Representations*.

Ethan A Chi, John Hewitt, and Christopher D Manning. 2020. Finding universal grammatical relations in multilingual bert. In *Proceedings of the 58th Annual Meeting of the Association for Computational Linguistics*, pages 5564–5577.

Wietse de Vries and Malvina Nissim. 2021. As good as new. how to successfully recycle english GPT-2 to make models for other languages. In *Findings of the Association for Computational Linguistics: ACL-IJCNLP 2021*, pages 836–846.

Jacob Devlin, Ming-Wei Chang, Kenton Lee, and Kristina Toutanova. 2019. Bert: Pre-training of deep bidirectional transformers for language understanding. In *Proceedings of the 2019 Conference of the North American Chapter of the Association for Computational Linguistics: Human Language Technologies, Volume 1 (Long and Short Papers)*, pages 4171–4186.

Quang-Minh Do, Kungan Zeng, and Incheon Paik. 2020. Resolving lexical ambiguity in english-japanese neural machine translation. In *2020 3rd Artificial Intelligence and Cloud Computing Conference*, pages 46–51.

Fei Dong, Yue Zhang, and Jie Yang. 2017. Attention-based recurrent convolutional neural network for automatic essay scoring. In *Proceedings of the 21st conference on computational natural language learning (CoNLL 2017)*, pages 153–162.

D. Elliott, S. Frank, K. Sima'an, and L. Specia. 2016. Multi30k: Multilingual english-german image descriptions. In *Proceedings of the 5th Workshop on Vision and Language*, pages 70–74.

Desmond Elliott, Stella Frank, Loïc Barrault, Fethi Bougares, and Lucia Specia. 2017. Findings of the second shared task on multimodal machine translation and multilingual image description. In *Proceedings of the Second Conference on Machine Translation*, pages 215–233.

Daniele Fanelli. 2012. Negative results are disappearing from most disciplines and countries. *Scientometrics*, 90:891–904.

Peter W Foltz, Darrell Laham, and Thomas K Landauer. 1999. Automated essay scoring: Applications to educational technology. In *Edmedia+ innovate learning*, pages 939–944. Association for the Advancement of Computing in Education (AACE).

Olivier Hamon and Martin Rajman. 2006. X-score: Automatic evaluation of machine translation grammaticality. In *LREC*, pages 155–160.

Michael Hanna and Ondřej Bojar. 2021. A fine-grained analysis of bertscore. In *Proceedings of the Sixth Conference on Machine Translation*, pages 507–517.

Michael Heilman, Aoife Cahill, Nitin Madnani, Melissa Lopez, Matthew Mulholland, and Joel R Tetreault. 2014. Predicting grammaticality on an ordinal scale. In *ACL (2)*.

Jeffrey Heinz and William Idsardi. 2011. Sentence and word complexity. *Science*, 333(6040):295–297.

John Hewitt, Kawin Ethayarajh, Percy Liang, and Christopher D Manning. 2021. Conditional probing: measuring usable information beyond a baseline. In *Proceedings of the 2021 Conference on Empirical Methods in Natural Language Processing*, pages 1626–1639.

John Hewitt and Christopher D Manning. 2019. A structural probe for finding syntax in word representations. In *Proceedings of the 2019 Conference of the North American Chapter of the Association for Computational Linguistics: Human Language Technologies, Volume 1 (Long and Short Papers)*, pages 4129–4138.

Dan W Higinbotham. 1991. The resolution of lexical ambiguity in machine translation. In *Deseret Language and Linguistic Society Symposium*, volume 17, page 7.

Christopher R Hoyt and Art B Owen. 2021. Probing neural networks with t-sne, class-specific projections and a guided tour. *arXiv preprint arXiv:2107.12547*.

Benedetta Iavarone, Dominique Brunato, and Felice Dell'Orletta. 2021. Sentence complexity in context. In *Proceedings of the Workshop on Cognitive Modeling and Computational Linguistics*, pages 186–199.

Ganesh Jawahar, Benoît Sagot, and Djamé Seddah. 2019. What does BERT learn about the structure of language? In *ACL 2019-57th Annual Meeting of the Association for Computational Linguistics*.

Qiao Jin, Bhuwan Dhingra, William Cohen, and Xinghua Lu. 2019. Probing biomedical embeddings from language models. In *Proceedings of the 3rd Workshop on Evaluating Vector Space Representations for NLP*, pages 82–89.

Marcel Adam Just, Patricia A Carpenter, Timothy A Keller, William F Eddy, and Keith R Thulborn. 1996. Brain activation modulated by sentence comprehension. *Science*, 274(5284):114–116.

Nal Kalchbrenner and Phil Blunsom. 2013. Recurrent convolutional neural networks for discourse compositionality. In *Proceedings of the Workshop on Continuous Vector Space Models and their Compositionality*, pages 119–126.

Nora Kassner, Benno Krojer, and Hinrich Schütze. 2020. Are pretrained language models symbolic reasoners over knowledge? In *Proceedings of the 24th Conference on Computational Natural Language Learning*, pages 552–564.

Ilia Kuznetsov and Iryna Gurevych. 2020. A matter of framing: The impact of linguistic formalism on probing results. In *Proceedings of the 2020 Conference on Empirical Methods in Natural Language Processing (EMNLP)*, pages 171–182.

Thomas K Landauer. 2003. Automatic essay assessment. *Assessment in education: Principles, policy & practice*, 10(3):295–308.

Alon Lavie and Michael J Denkowski. 2009. The meteor metric for automatic evaluation of machine translation. *Machine translation*, 23(2):105–115.

Bai Li, Zining Zhu, Guillaume Thomas, Yang Xu, and Frank Rudzicz. 2021. How is BERT surprised? Layerwise detection of linguistic anomalies. In *Proceedings of the 59th Annual Meeting of the Association for Computational Linguistics and the 11th International Joint Conference on Natural Language Processing (Volume 1: Long Papers)*, pages 4215–4228.

Tsung-Yi Lin, Michael Maire, Serge Belongie, James Hays, Pietro Perona, Deva Ramanan, Piotr Dollár, and C Lawrence Zitnick. 2014. Microsoft coco: Common objects in context. In *European conference on computer vision*, pages 740–755. Springer.

Yongjie Lin, Yi Chern Tan, and Robert Frank. 2019. Open sesame: Getting inside bert's linguistic knowledge. In *Proceedings of the 2019 ACL Workshop BlackboxNLP: Analyzing and Interpreting Neural Networks for NLP*, pages 241–253.

Nelson F Liu, Matt Gardner, Yonatan Belinkov, Matthew E Peters, and Noah A Smith. 2019. Linguistic knowledge and transferability of contextual representations. In *Proceedings of the 2019 Conference of the North American Chapter of the Association for Computational Linguistics: Human Language Technologies, Volume 1 (Long and Short Papers)*, pages 1073–1094.

Xiao Liu, Yanan Zheng, Zhengxiao Du, Ming Ding, Yujie Qian, Zhilin Yang, and Jie Tang. 2021. GPT understands, too. *arXiv preprint arXiv:2103.10385*.

Zhibin Lu, Pan Du, and Jian-Yun Nie. 2020. Vgcn-bert: augmenting bert with graph embedding for text classification. In *European Conference on Information Retrieval*, pages 369–382. Springer.

Xiaofei Ma, Zhiguo Wang, Patrick Ng, Ramesh Nallapati, and Bing Xiang. 2019. Universal text representation from BERT: An empirical study. *arXiv preprint arXiv:1910.07973*.

Matej Martinc, Senja Pollak, and Marko Robnik-Šikonja. 2021. Supervised and unsupervised neural approaches to text readability. *Computational Linguistics*, 47(1):141–179.

Danielle S McNamara, Max M Louwerse, and Arthur C Graesser. 2002. Coh-metrix: Automated cohesion and coherence scores to predict text readability and facilitate comprehension. Technical report, Technical report, Institute for Intelligent Systems, University of Memphis ....

Clara Meister, Tiago Pimentel, Patrick Haller, Lena Jäger, Ryan Cotterell, and Roger Levy. 2021. Revisiting the uniform information density hypothesis. In *Proceedings of the 2021 Conference on Empirical Methods in Natural Language Processing*, pages 963–980.

Francois Meyer and Martha Lewis. 2020. Modelling lexical ambiguity with density matrices. In *Proceedings of the 24th Conference on Computational Natural Language Learning*, pages 276–290.

Jonathan Mirault and Jonathan Grainger. 2020. On the time it takes to judge grammaticality. *Quarterly Journal of Experimental Psychology*, 73(9):1460–1465.

Ana Mlinarić, Martina Horvat, and Vesna Šupak Smolčić. 2017. Dealing with the positive publication bias: Why you should really publish your negative results. *Biochemia medica*, 27(3):447–452.

Marius Mosbach, Anna Khokhlova, Michael A Hedderich, and Dietrich Klakow. 2020. On the interplay between fine-tuning and sentence-level probing for linguistic knowledge in pre-trained transformers. In *Proceedings of the Third BlackboxNLP Workshop on Analyzing and Interpreting Neural Networks for NLP*, pages 68–82.

Hiroshi Nagata. 1992. Anchoring effects in judging grammaticality of sentences. *Perceptual and Motor Skills*, 75(1):159–164.

Roberto Navigli. 2009. Word sense disambiguation: A survey. *ACM computing surveys (CSUR)*, 41(2):1–69.

Ryan M Nefdt. 2020. A puzzle concerning compositionality in machines. *Minds and Machines*, 30(1):47–75.

Amber Nigam, Shikha Tyagi, Kuldeep Tyagi, and Arpan Saxena. 2020. Skillbert:"skilling" the bert to classify skills!

Despina Papadopoulou. 2005. Reading-time studies of second language ambiguity resolution. *Second Language Research*, 21(2):98–120.

F. Pedregosa, G. Varoquaux, A. Gramfort, V. Michel, B. Thirion, O. Grisel, M. Blondel, P. Prettenhofer, R. Weiss, V. Dubourg, J. Vanderplas, A. Passos, D. Cournapeau, M. Brucher, M. Perrot, and E. Duchesnay. 2011. Scikit-learn: Machine learning in Python. *Journal of Machine Learning Research*, 12:2825–2830.

Vladimir Pericliev. 1984. Handling syntactical ambiguity in machine translation. In *10th International Conference on Computational Linguistics and 22nd Annual Meeting of the Association for Computational Linguistics*, pages 521–524.

Matthew E. Peters, Mark Neumann, Mohit Iyyer, Matt Gardner, Christopher Clark, Kenton Lee, and Luke Zettlemoyer. 2018. Deep contextualized word representations. In *Proceedings of the 2018 Conference of the North American Chapter of the Association for Computational Linguistics: Human Language Technologies, Volume 1 (Long Papers)*, pages 2227–2237, New Orleans, Louisiana. Association for Computational Linguistics.

Tiago Pimentel, Josef Valvoda, Rowan Hall Maudslay, Ran Zmigrod, Adina Williams, and Ryan Cotterell. 2020. Information-theoretic probing for linguistic structure. In *Proceedings of the 58th Annual Meeting of the Association for Computational Linguistics*, pages 4609–4622.

Alec Radford, Jeffrey Wu, Rewon Child, David Luan, Dario Amodei, Ilya Sutskever, et al. 2019. Language models are unsupervised multitask learners.

Margaret A Richek. 1976. Effect of sentence complexity on the reading comprehension of syntactic structures. *Journal of Educational Psychology*, 68(6):800.

Stefan Riezler and John T Maxwell III. 2006. Grammatical machine translation. In *Proceedings of the Human Language Technology Conference of the NAACL, Main Conference*, pages 248–255.

Anna Rogers, Olga Kovaleva, and Anna Rumshisky. 2020. A primer in bertology: What we know about how bert works. *Transactions of the Association for Computational Linguistics*, 8:842–866.

Gözde Gül Şahin, Clara Vania, Ilia Kuznetsov, and Iryna Gurevych. 2020. Linspector: Multilingual probing tasks for word representations. *Computational Linguistics*, 46(2):335–385.

Marcus Sammer, Kobi Reiter, Stephen Soderland, Katrin Kirchhoff, and Oren Etzioni. 2006. Ambiguity reduction for machine translation: Human-computer collaboration. In *Proceedings of the 7th Conference of the Association for Machine Translation in the Americas: Technical Papers*, pages 193–202.

Gabriele Sarti. 2020. Interpreting neural language models for linguistic complexity assessment. Master's thesis, University of Trieste, dec.

Gabriele Sarti, Dominique Brunato, and Felice Dell'Orletta. 2021. That looks hard: Characterizing linguistic complexity in humans and language models. In *Proceedings of the Workshop on Cognitive Modeling and Computational Linguistics*, pages 48–60.

Bernard Scott. 2018. *Translation, brains and the computer: A neurolinguistic solution to ambiguity and complexity in machine translation*, volume 2. Springer.

Felix Stahlberg and Shankar Kumar. 2022. Jam or cream first? modeling ambiguity in neural machine translation with SCONES. *arXiv preprint arXiv:2205.00704*.

Sanja Štajner, Simone Paolo Ponzetto, and Heiner Stuckenschmidt. 2017. Automatic assessment of absolute sentence complexity. In *Proceedings of the 26th International Joint Conference on Artificial Intelligence, IJCAI*, volume 17, pages 4096–4102.

Jason Stanley and Zoltan Gendler Szabó. 2000. On quantifier domain restriction. *Mind & Language*, 15(2-3):219–261.

Sara Stymne and Lars Ahrenberg. 2010. Using a grammar checker for evaluation and postprocessing of statistical machine translation. In *Proceedings of the Seventh International Conference on Language Resources and Evaluation (LREC'10)*.

Alvin Subakti, Hendri Murfi, and Nora Hariadi. 2022. The performance of bert as data representation of text clustering. *Journal of big Data*, 9(1):1–21.

Ian Tenney, Dipanjan Das, and Ellie Pavlick. 2019. Bert rediscovers the classical nlp pipeline. In *Proceedings of the 57th Annual Meeting of the Association for Computational Linguistics*, pages 4593–4601.

John C Trueswell. 1996. The role of lexical frequency in syntactic ambiguity resolution. *Journal of memory and language*, 35(4):566–585.

Ashish Vaswani, Noam Shazeer, Niki Parmar, Jakob Uszkoreit, Llion Jones, Aidan N Gomez, Łukasz Kaiser, and Illia Polosukhin. 2017. Attention is all you need. In *Advances in neural information processing systems*, pages 5998–6008.

Ivan Vulić, Edoardo Maria Ponti, Robert Litschko, Goran Glavaš, and Anna Korhonen. 2020. Probing pretrained language models for lexical semantics. In *Proceedings of the 2020 Conference on Empirical Methods in Natural Language Processing (EMNLP)*, pages 7222–7240.

Alex Wang, Amanpreet Singh, Julian Michael, Felix Hill, Omer Levy, and Samuel R Bowman. 2018. GLUE: A multi-task benchmark and analysis platform for natural language understanding. *EMNLP 2018*, page 353.

Alex Warstadt, Alicia Parrish, Haokun Liu, Anhad Mohananey, Wei Peng, Sheng-Fu Wang, and Samuel R Bowman. 2020. BLiMP: The benchmark of linguistic minimal pairs for english. *Transactions of the Association for Computational Linguistics*, 8:377–392.

Alex Warstadt, Amanpreet Singh, and Samuel R Bowman. 2019. Neural network acceptability judgments. *Transactions of the Association for Computational Linguistics*, 7:625–641.

Orion Weller, Jordan Hildebrandt, Ilya Reznik, Christopher Challis, E Shannon Tass, Quinn Snell, and Kevin Seppi. 2020. You don't have time to read this: An exploration of document reading time prediction. In *Proceedings of the 58th Annual Meeting of the Association for Computational Linguistics*, pages 1789–1794.

Thomas Wolf, Lysandre Debut, Victor Sanh, Julien Chaumond, Clement Delangue, Anthony Moi, Pierric Cistac, Tim Rault, Rémi Louf, Morgan Funtowicz, et al. 2019. Huggingface's transformers: State-of-the-art natural language processing. *arXiv preprint arXiv:1910.03771*.

Chien-Sheng Wu, Steven CH Hoi, Richard Socher, and Caiming Xiong. 2020. Tod-bert: Pre-trained natural language understanding for task-oriented dialogue. In *Proceedings of the 2020 Conference on Empirical Methods in Natural Language Processing (EMNLP)*, pages 917–929.

Chien-Sheng Wu and Caiming Xiong. 2020. Probing task-oriented dialogue representation from language models. In *Proceedings of the 2020 Conference on Empirical Methods in Natural Language Processing (EMNLP)*, pages 5036–5051.

Yadollah Yaghoobzadeh, Katharina Kann, Timothy J Hazen, Eneko Agirre, and Hinrich Schütze. 2019. Probing for semantic classes: Diagnosing the meaning content of word embeddings. In *Proceedings of the 57th Annual Meeting of the Association for Computational Linguistics*, pages 5740–5753.

Xiao-Chen Zhang, Cheng-Kun Wu, Zhi-Jiang Yang, Zhen-Xing Wu, Jia-Cai Yi, Chang-Yu Hsieh, Ting-Jun Hou, and Dong-Sheng Cao. 2021. Mg-bert: leveraging unsupervised atomic representation learning for molecular property prediction. *Briefings in bioinformatics*, 22(6):bbab152.

Shunpeng Zou and Xiaohui Zou. 2017. Understanding: how to resolve ambiguity. In *International Conference on Intelligence Science*, pages 333–343. Springer.

Post-Hoc Interpretation of Transformer Hyperparameters with Explainable Boosting Machines

Kiron Deb* **Xuan Zhang*** **Kevin Duh**
Johns Hopkins University
{kdeb1, xuanzhang}@jhu.edu, kevinduh@cs.jhu.edu

Abstract

Hyperparameter tuning is important for achieving high accuracy in deep learning models, yet little interpretability work has focused on hyperparameters. We propose to use the Explainable Boosting Machine (EBM), a glassbox method, as a post-hoc analysis tool for understanding how hyperparameters influence model accuracy. We present a case study on Transformer models in machine translation to illustrate the kinds of insights that may be gleaned, and perform extensive analysis to test the robustness of EBM under different data conditions.

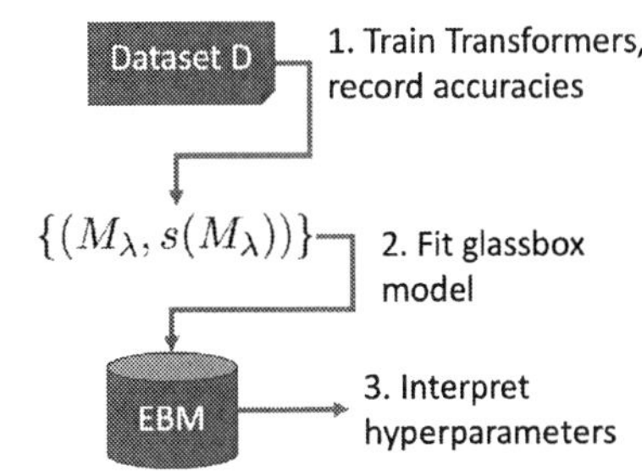

Figure 1: Proposed framework for post-hoc intepretation of hyperparameters with EBM.

1 Introduction

Deep neural networks have revolutionized the field of AI, bringing about impressive improvements in accuracy at various tasks. There is now a growing interest in interpreting what the model is doing that leads to these high accuracies (Bastings et al., 2021). A better understanding is useful in many ways: it can provide researchers a more in-depth view of the problem, assist developers to debug the model, or give users a way to act on the model result.

Our goal is to improve our understanding of neural network *hyperparameters*. While there are many research efforts on explaining a model's prediction or interpreting a model's parameters, there has been little work on hyperparameters. Hyperparameters like number of layers and learning rate are important factors that impact model performance. In practice, many engineering hours are spent on tuning hyperparameters. We believe methods and tools for interpreting hyperparameters are needed to help practitioners tune more effectively; there are also applications in the growing field of AutoML (Hutter et al., 2019), where our understanding of hyperparameters can help guide researchers design more effective search spaces.

In this paper, we advocate a *post-hoc interpretation framework* for hyperparameters. This framework requires that a set of neural network models with different hyperparameters are trained, and that their resulting accuracy metrics are recorded. Then, a glassbox model is fit on this data to reveal trends in hyperparameters. We use Explainable Boosting Machines (EBM, Lou et al. (2013)) as the glassbox model; it is a Generalized Additive Model similar to Boosted Trees, except that its additive feature function is visualizable in 1-D or 2-D plots, making it well-suited for understanding hyperparameters.

In the following, we first develop further the idea of post-hoc interpretation of hyperparameters and contrast it with other types of interpretability research (Section 3). Then we briefly describe the EBM, which is the glassbox model used in our interpretability framework (Section 2). Section 4 present a case study on Transformers in machine translation tasks, to illustrate how our framework can be used to understand which hyperparameters are important, how its influence changes according to different hyperparameter values, and whether pairwise interactions are present. Finally, Section 5 analyzes the robustness of EBM: it helps characterize under what conditions are the interpretability results valid.

The contribution of this paper is two-fold: First,

* These authors contributed equally to this work.

Proceedings of the Fifth BlackboxNLP Workshop on Analyzing and Interpreting Neural Networks for NLP, pages 51 - 61
December 8, 2022 ©2022 Association for Computational Linguistics

we advocate a framework for understanding hyperparameters with EBMs and present a case study on machine translation transformers to illustrate its usefulness. Second, we perform extensive experiments on EBMs to characterize the conditions where interpretability results are robust.

2 Explainable Boosting Machine

Let's define input x as a feature vector representing the hyperparameter setting model M_λ, and y as the scalar output response variable $s(M_\lambda)$. We use EBM as introduced in (Lou et al., 2012, 2013; Caruana et al., 2015) and implemented in Nori et al. (2019). EBM is a generalized additive model with the form:

$$g(y) = \beta_0 + \sum_j f_j(x_j) + \sum_{ij} f_{ij}(x_i, x_j), \quad (1)$$

where g is a link function that transforms the model to either a regression or classification setting (identity or logit, respectively). f_j is a feature function for feature x_j that is learnt through bagging and gradient boosting. Each f_j is trained separately at a time in round-robin fashion. Additionally, EBM also includes pairwise terms f_{ij} to increase accuracy and enable analysis of pairwise interactions between features. In our experiments, we focus on 6 Transformer hyperparameters, so x is a vector of dimension 6 and the EBM model $F(\cdot)$ is a sum of 6 single-hyperparameter functions f_j, up to $(6 \times 5)/2 = 15$ pairwise functions f_{ij}, and a bias term β_0.

An attractive aspect of EBM is that $f_j(x_j)$ is based on a single feature, and can be of arbitrary shape. See examples of f_j in Figure 3: on the left, we see that $f_{j=1}(x_1)$ decreases in score as the learning rate hyperparameter increases; on the right, we see a different $f_{j=2}(x_2)$ increase in score slightly as BPE hyperparameter from 10k to 30k, then drop sharply when BPE increases to 50k. Since the $f_j(\cdot)$ are summed *linearly* to predict the response variable (accuracy or BLEU score), we can obtain an intuitive understanding of how each hyperparameter impacts the final accuracy. In other words, since EBM is an additive model, it is straightforward to infer the contribution of each feature function; at the same time, the ability to learn arbitrary shapes for the feature function allows for enhanced interpretability. Refer to the aforementioned papers for details of how the EBM is trained.

3 Interpreting Hyperparameters

Proposed framework: Our goal is to gain insights about hyperparameters for a class of deep neural networks. We require the existence of a set of models with different hyperparameter settings trained on the same dataset. For example, assume a set of Transformer (Vaswani et al., 2017) models $\{M_\lambda\}, \lambda \in \Lambda$ where Λ represents the hyperparameter space, M_λ represents a model with a specific hyperparameter setting (e.g. 6-layer encoder, 2-layer decoder, 8 heads, 256 word embedding size); each model has an accuracy metric $s(M_\lambda)$, and a glassbox model is fit on pairs $P \triangleq \{(M_\lambda, s(M_\lambda))\}$. Assume there is a person building the models (model builder) and a person analyzing the models after the fact (model analyzer); they may or may not be the same person. Our framework consists of three steps:

1. On a dataset D, the model builder trains N models $\{M_\lambda\}$ and record their accuracy metric $s(M_\lambda)$. The metric can be any scalar in $\mathbb{R}$; for this paper, we focus on machine translation and use the development set BLEU score.

2. The model analyzer fits an EBM on $P \triangleq \{(M_\lambda, s(M_\lambda))\}$. The EBM is a function $F(\cdot)$ that maps from hyperparameter space to BLEU score, $F : \Lambda \rightarrow \mathbb{R}$. In practice, a small subset of P is held-out to measure EBM's generalization, and we would proceed only if we trust that the EBM has not over-fit or under-fit.

3. The model analyzer visualizes the internal features of EBM to glean insights about hyperparameters.

The overall framework is shown in Figure 1. Step 1 is critical because it provides the data for EBM fitting. How large must N be, and are there requirements for the samples from Λ to be independent, identically distributed (i.i.d.)? Neural models can be expensive to train, so we assume that Step 1 is the result of whatever hyperparameter search was performed by the model builder. Thus, the model analyzer may not have full control over the models available for analysis. Section 5 characterizes under what conditions is EBM robust over different sizes and distributions of P.

Step 2 is the core component of our framework. Different glassbox regression models are possible,

Type	Goal	Example Result
Prescriptive	Model building	Given past experience, we recommend setting embedding size to 256 and attention head to 8 on dataset D.
Descriptive (this work)	Post-hoc understanding	Given N models that are trained on dataset D, we find that embedding size influences BLEU more than attention heads.

Table 1: Two kinds of goals for Interpretability Research on hyperparameters.

but we choose EBM due to its excellent visualization ability. Note that while there is a considerable amount of work on interpreting a Transformer's parameters such as attention weights (Kobayashi et al., 2020; Abnar and Zuidema, 2020; Tay et al., 2021; Lim et al., 2018), these methods are not readily applicable due to the non-differentiability and heterogeneity of hyperparameters. Thus, an external model $F : \Lambda \rightarrow \mathbb{R}$ that treats hyperparameters as input features is more amenable. This external model is essentially finding hyperparameter "features" that are predictive of accuracy. As long as this model is glassbox in the sense that it's internals are viewable, then we are able to interpret the results in Step 3.

Broader context: We would like to provide context on what our framework does and does not do. In the Explainable AI literature, one way to characterize explainablity/interpretability research is to ask where the method sits on the local vs. global and self-explaining vs post-hoc continuum (Danilevsky et al., 2020). Local methods explain the model's behavior on a specific input, whereas global methods inspects the model generally. Our framework is global in the sense that it identifies hyperparameter trends based on accuracy on a batch of inputs. Self-explaining methods generate explanations as part of the model's prediction process, whereas post-hoc method builds an external model after the predictions have been made. Our framework sits squarely in the post-hoc camp because we work on top of trained Transformers, but it is interesting to note that the glassbox EBM employed can be called a self-explaining method.

In terms of research on hyperparameters, there is a branch of work (Bahar et al., 2017; Britz et al., 2017; Araabi and Monz, 2020) aiming at finding the optimal choices of hyperparameter values. In those work, hyperparameters are usually manually tuned based on experience and massive experiments are conducted to gather results. Those work would make recommendations on which hyperparameter combinations to use in general. We call this approach *prescriptive*; they are useful to inform the building of specific models.

In contrast, our framework is *descriptive*: models have already been trained, and we are interested in understanding the relationship between hyperparameters and accuracy. In other words, rather than predicting whether to set embedding size to 256 or 512, we are more interested in seeing how accuracy changes according to various embedding sizes and understanding whether other hyperparameters like number of layers would interact. This is an example of post-hoc analysis, which is also used in medicine (TDI, 2022; Srinivas et al., 2015) – after the effectiveness of a new treatment is tested, post-hoc analysis on both the failed and successful trials are conducted. It is not the intent of the original study, but it is the support for further trials. The distinctions between the two kinds of interpretation work are summarized in Table 1.

Post-hoc interpretation on hyperparameters is well-suit to the following two scenario: (a) Suppose a practitioner has already performed extensive hyperparameter tuning, and has deployed the best model. It would be a waste to throw away all the data pairs P. Running post-hoc interpretation allows us to extract more knowledge out of the data. Knowledge about which hyperparameters are important, for example, may inform future hyperparameter tuning experiments; it may also assist AutoML researchers to design more efficient search spaces for hyperparameter optimization and neural architecture search. (b) Suppose a researcher proposes a new neural network model. Providing a post-hoc analysis of hyperparameters is akin to showing feature ablation experiments. In sum, our work can be considered as an effort to unpack "blackbox" deep learning models at the level of hyperparameters.

4 Case Study: Post-hoc Interpretation

We now provide a case study on Transformer hyperparameters for machine translation to illustrate the kinds of insight we can learn from the proposed

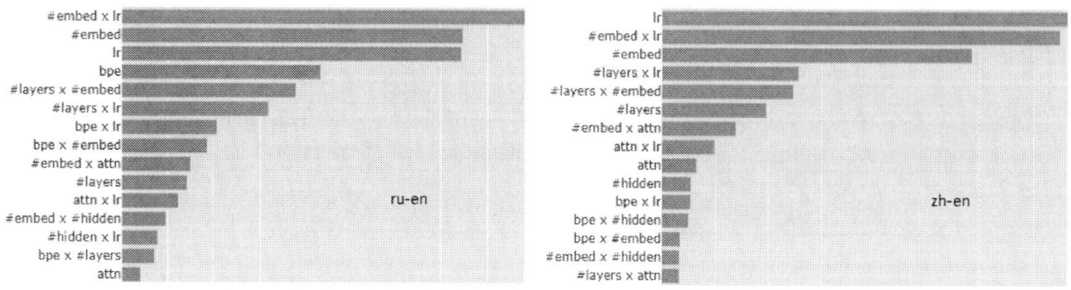

Figure 2: Hyperparameter contribution rank on ru-en (left) and zh-en (right). Hyperparameters are ordered by importance score – for ru-en, *#embed x lr* is the most important, while *attn* is the least important. Hyperparameters that are not included in the plots are in lower ranks than shown ones.

post-hoc interpretation framework.

4.1 Dataset and Setup

Machine Translation (MT) Datasets Our experiments are conducted on a tabular dataset published by Zhang and Duh (2020), which contains 1,983 pairs of hyperparameter configurations and BLEU scores in total. To obtain those pairs, they trained all the Transformers to convergence on 6 MT corpora. Those 6 MT datasets are distinct on sizes – ranging from 24K training samples to 4M; domains – either in a single domain like TED Talks or in mixed-domain; language pairs – including Chinese-English (zh-en), Russian-English (ru-en), Japanese-English (ja-en), English-Japanese (en-ja), Swahili-English (sw-en) and Somali-English (so-en). The large size of the tabular dataset enables efficient post-hoc investigation. Its diversity also allows further study on the generalization of the observations.

Following Zhang and Duh (2020), we will be focusing on the effect of 6 different hyperparameters.

- **Preprocessing configurations:** number of BPE symbols (bpe).
- **Training settings:** initial learning rate (lr) for the Adam optimizer.
- **Architecture designs:** number of layers (layers), embedding size (#embed), number of hidden units in each layer (#hidden), number of heads in self-attention (attn).

These hyperparameters appear frequently in MT literature as a part of the description of experiment setups. Practitioners aiming at a better model spend a large amount of time tuning them manually. We are interested in examining whether they are really equally important and deserve the efforts. We will answer these questions in the following section.

EBM Setup We adopt the implementation of EBM from Nori et al. (2019). To be specific, we train a EBM regressor on each of the language pair, which results in 6 models. Due to space limitation, we will only show results on selected language pairs, the rest can be found in Appendix.

4.2 Findings

In this section, we show how EBM can be used to interpret Transformer hyperparameters and report three types of findings.

4.2.1 Hyperparameter Importance

EBM learns an importance score for each feature, which indicates how much the model performance would change with varying feature values. It is computed as the absolute expected value of f_j over the dataset. Figure 2 plots the hyperparameter importance ranking on ru-en and zh-en. As shown in the figure, hyperparameters are not equally important and there is a large discrepancy between features. On ru-en, *#embed* and *lr* are the most critical hyperparameters in determining Transformer's performance followed by *bpe*; while adjusting *#layers*, *attn* and *#hidden* (not shown in the figure) would only slightly affect the results. On zh-en, *lr* and *#embed* are also at the top of the listing, but the overall ranking is different from ru-en. Some important hyperparameters for ru-en, e.g. *bpe*, rank low on zh-en. Some insignificant hyperparameters for ru-en, e.g. *#hidden*, are elevated to higher positions on zh-en.

https://github.com/interpretml/interpret

In summary, there are only a limited number of critical hyperparameters for Transformers, and it would be more efficient to focus more on tuning them when developing a model. Across 6 language pairs, *#attn* is always ranked low and can be probably dropped from future hyperparameter search.

4.2.2 Single Hyperparameter Analysis

Besides the macro view of contributions of all the hyperparameters, EBM also provides a micro view studying how the segments within each hyperparameter relate. Figure 3 depicts the single feature function extracted from the trained EBM model on en-ja. As *lr* increases from 0.0003 to 0.001, BLEU score decreases significantly. While it is not the case for *bpe*, where the BLEU score does not change monotonically – it rises a little when *bpe* increases from 10k to 30k, then drops notably when *bpe* becomes 50k. This finding tell us both 10k and 30k are positively correlated with BLEU and the difference is not so distinct, but 50k is definitely not desirable.

4.2.3 Pairwise Interactions

EBM can automatically detect and include pairwise interaction terms in its modeling. Figure 4 shows an example of how two hyperparameters interact to determine Transformer's performance. On en-ja, *#embed* with size of 1024 and *lr* with the size of 0.0003 produce the highest BLEU score among all the combinations. On the contrary, *#embed* 1024 and *lr* 0.001 output the worst Transformer. This is consistent with Figure 3 Left – larger *lr* worsens the performance.

However, this does not hold true for *#embed* 256 and 512: given these values, there is not so strong of a (negative) correlation between *lr* and BLEU score. This seems to imply that while lr is sensitive for a large *#embed* 1024, it is less sensitive when *#embed* is small. We do have to interpret this result carefully because there may be confounding factors from the individual feature functions f_j that are added, but this is illustrative of the potential insights we may gain from this case study.

Theoretically, the EBM formulation can allow for higher-order interactions (e.g. three-way). This may be a promising direction for future work.

5 Analysis of EBM Robustness

To ensure the validity of our post-hoc interpretation framework, we need to analyze the robustness of EBM to different kinds of data sizes and distributions. Specifically, one important requirement for our framework is the availability of $P \triangleq \{(M_\lambda, s(M_\lambda))\}$; one might not be able to fully control how this data is acquired. It may be a by-product of an extensive grid search, a manual and focused hyperparameter tuning guided by an engineer's intuition, or an AutoML experiment. This implies the that hyperparameters may not be sampled uniformly from the space Λ, and the number of samples for EBM fitting may not be very large.

In order to gain better understanding of EBM's robustness under different conditions, we conduct four experiments. We first study how EBM's fitting ability would be affected if the size or the distribution of training data changes. We then make connections to Hyperparameter Optimization (HPO), and examine EBM's performance on data generated by sampling from two different HPO methods. Finally, we investigate the generalization ability of EBM. To be more specific, we test whether a EBM model trained on one dataset can perform well on another dataset.

The experiments following are all conducted on sw-en except for the one in Section 5.4. We split the sw-en dataset, the largest dataset among the six datasets provided by Zhang and Duh (2020) which contains 767 (configuration, BLEU score) pairs, into a train set with 614 samples and a test set with 153 samples. An EBM regressor is trained on a subset of the train set and its performance on the test set is reported. We repeat the process 5 times with different random seeds to generate 5 different train-test splits. Thus, results reported below are all averaged over 5 runs.

5.1 Varying Data Sizes

In practice, it is often infeasible to get a tabular dataset as large as the one in Zhang and Duh (2020), where around 2,000 Transformers are trained. This raises the question how EBM would perform with insufficient training data. In other words, it is in doubt if its interpretations on hyperparameters (e.g. observations shown in Section 4.2) are trustworthy when it is trained with less data.

In order to answer the questions above, we create datasets with different sizes by randomly sampling from the train set of sw-en. We experimented with subsets ranging from containing only 5% of the training samples, that is 31 samples, to the whole

Data here refers to the (hyperparameter configuration, BLEU score) pairs, instead of the sentence pairs that are used to train a MT Transformer.

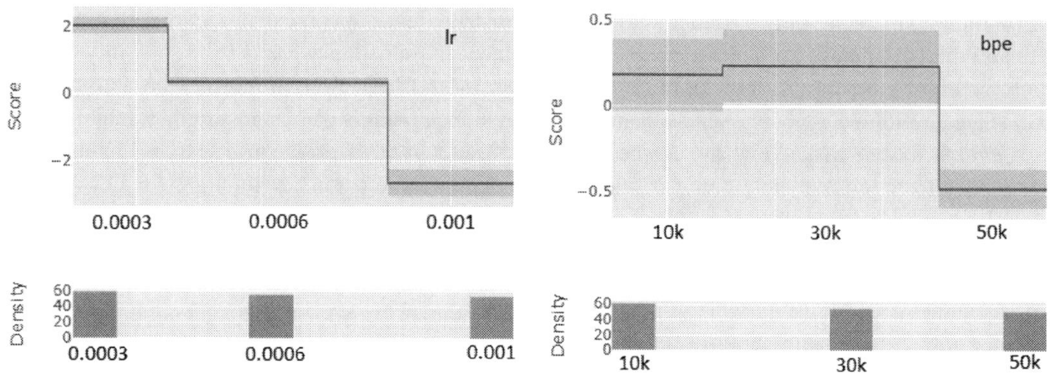

Figure 3: Single hyperparameter feature function on en-ja. Left: initial learning rate. Right: bpe symbols. Higher *score* indicates a higher chance to get a high BLEU score. *Density* refers to the number of samples in the dataset.

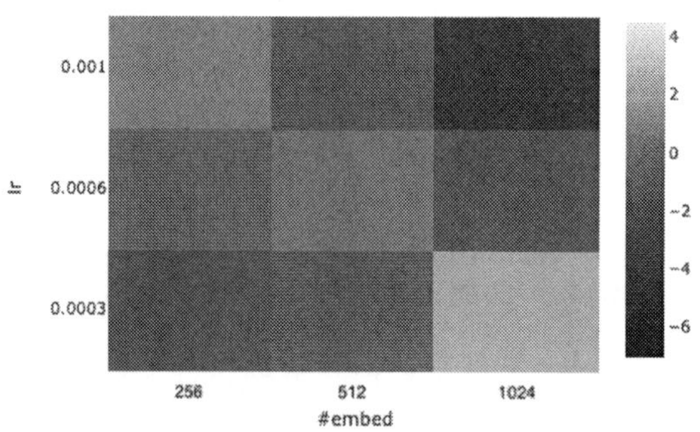

Figure 4: Pairwise interaction between embedding size and initial learning rate on en-ja. Higher *score* (yellow) indicates higher odds to get higher BLEU scores.

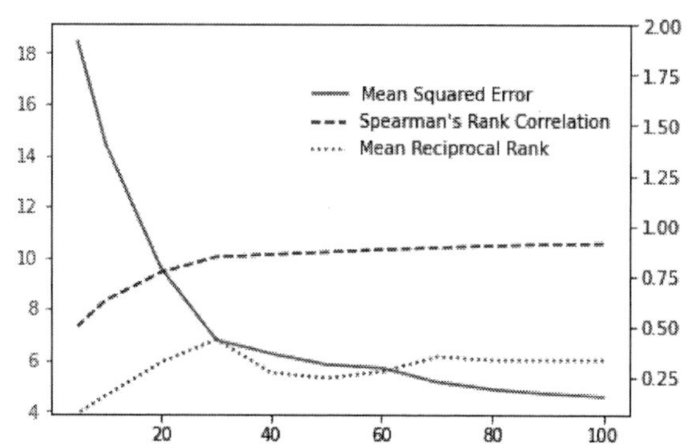

Figure 5: EBM's fitting ability with varying data sizes of sw-en. Subsets are generated by randomly sampling from the train set. Results are averaged over 5 runs with different random seeds.

train set, i.e. 614 samples.

We use the following metrics to measure EBM's performance:

- **Mean Squared Error (MSE)** We calculate the average of the squared difference between the actual BLEU scores and EBM regressor's predictions given hyperparameter configurations. As a widely used measure of an estimator's quality, MSE is useful when compared between estimators. To be more specific, when there are multiple MSE scores, a lower one indicates a stronger estimator. While when there is only a single MSE score, it is hard to judge whether it is low enough to testify a good EBM model. Thus, we propose the following metrics as complements to MSE.

- **Spearman's Rank Correlation Coefficient (SRC)** We measure SRC between the ranking of real BLEU scores and EBM's predictions. For the purpose of interpreting hyperparameters, it is not necessary that EBM would predict the exact BLEU scores. Instead, it is more important that it recovers the ranking. For SRC, higher is better.

- **Mean Reciprocal Rank (MRR)** In some cases, for example, in hyperparameter search, one might be more interested in getting the best configuration and would be less concerned with the ranking of all the configurations. Reciprocal rank is defined as $\frac{1}{rank}$, where $rank$ is the position of the best configuration predicted by EBM in the real ranking. MRR, in our case, is the average over 5 runs. It is better if MRR is closer to 1.

Size(%)	5	10	20	30	40	50	60	70	80	90	100
Mean	18.43	14.40	9.58	6.79	6.26	5.84	5.72	5.17	4.88	4.73	4.59
Std	3.51	1.56	0.84	0.54	0.41	0.57	0.32	0.16	0.31	0.13	0.10

Table 2: The mean and standard deviation of MSE on sw-en test set. EBM is trained on subsets of train set with various sizes and data compositions. Each subset is sampled 5 times with different random seeds.

We plot EBM's performance with varying data sizes in Figure 5. It can be observed that although MSE rises drastically when the data size shrinks from 30% to 5%, it remains roughly at the same level when the size is larger than 30%. This means that a relatively accurate EBM model can be obtained with only 185 samples, and data sizes smaller than that would worsen the model significantly.

Same trend is also shown in other metrics and 30% is the turning point for all the lines. SRC ends up getting close to 1 when the data size increases, suggesting EBM's great ability to recover the ranking. MRR stops at $\frac{1}{3}$, that means EBM mistakes the third best configuration as the best one. However, the difference between the BLEU score of the top three and top one is small, which is only 0.41.

5.2 Varying Data Distributions

Section 5.1 shows that a comparably good EBM model can be obtained by training on as few as 185 samples. Would this stay true if those 185 samples are replaced with other 185 samples? In other words, would EBM be robust to varying data distributions?

We evaluate EBM models trained with different data compositions and data sizes. Results are summarized in Table 2. As the amount of training data increases, the standard deviation of MSE decreases gradually, i.e. the EBM model becomes more robust. When given limited data, EBM is more prone to underfitting and generalize poorly to the test set. It can be inferred that hyperparameter interpretations produced by EBM models trained with more samples are more trustworthy and accurate than those trained with limited data.

5.3 Connections to HPO

The goal of HPO is to find an optimal hyperparameter configuration with as few evaluations of the model as possible. Most of the HPO methods

100% refers to using all the samples in the train set, which takes up 80% of the original sw-en dataset. MSE here is not determined because we also randomly sampled train set from the whole dataset multiple times.

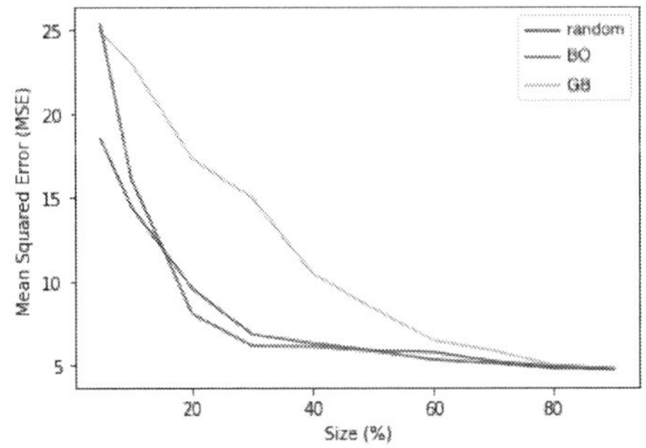

Figure 6: The performance of EBM trained on sw-en data sampled by BO, GB and randomly sampling. EBM is evaluated on a held-out test set, which takes up 20% of the sw-en data.

can be classified as sequential model-based optimization (SMBO). SMBO employs 1) a **surrogate model** to approximate the underlying function between hyperparameters and model performance, 2) an **acquisition function** to propose hyperparameter configurations to explore. SMBO works iteratively. Considering applying HPO to MT Transformer, at each iteration, the acquisition function selects configuration candidates to query the Transformer; after training and evaluation, a BLEU score is returned; the surrogate model then fits on the resulting pairs of configurations and BLEU scores and make predictions on unevaluated configurations, which are further used by the acquisition function as bases for making candidate suggestions. Thus, the fitting ability of the surrogate model is crucial to the success of the HPO method.

In this section, we focus on investigating how EBM would fit the sampling by HPO methods, where sampling refers to the candidates proposed by acquisition function along one complete run of HPO – this is related to Section 5.2, since HPO sampling generates another unique data distribution for EBM to train on.

We experiment with two HPO methods, Bayesian Optimization (BO) and a Graph-Based HPO method (GB, Zhang and Duh (2020)). For BO, we use Gaussian Processes as surrogate model and expected improvement as acquisition function.

For GB, we use Matérn52 kernel and expected influence. We run BO and GB separately on sw-en and record the sampling order of hyperparameter configurations. We then compare the performance of EBM models trained on the first $n\%$ data points in the sampling with those trained on randomly sampled data. Results are plotted in Figure 6.

BO and *random* show similar trends with MSE falling sharply when the training data increases from 5% to 30%. While GB drops at a slower pace with MSE always staying the highest among the three. The discrepancy between the curves testifies the discrepancy between the sampling of BO and GB. Compared to *random* and BO, the distribution of GB sampling is more skewed. At size 15%, BO surpasses *random* and maintains the lowest MSE till size 100%. This suggests that BO sampling makes EBM a better model than random sampling.

EBM can be used in combination with HPO in two ways: 1) During the run of HPO, EBM can be adopted as an analysis tool. By fitting the HPO sampling, it can provide insights on hyperparameter importance (Section 4.2.1) and make suggestions on hyperparameter values (Section 4.2.2). The HPO algorithm can then adjust its search space accordingly for later runs. But one should be cautious when the HPO algorithm in employment generates poor sampling distribution like GB does. 2) EBM can also be adopted as an alternative surrogate model considering its good fitting ability.

5.4 Transferability

So far, we have examined EBM's behaviours on specific language pairs. We have trained isolated EBM models on 6 MT tasks. Next, we explore whether EBM can leverage knowledge learned from one task and transfer it to another. Specifically, we evaluate each trained model on the test set of each of the language pair respectively. Figure 7 summarizes the results.

EBM faces difficulty on some of the transfers, for example, from sw-en (y-axis) to so-en (x-axis) and from so-en to sw-en. Meanwhile, there are also some successful transfers, for example, from en-ja to ru-en and from ru-en to en-ja. Surprisingly, EBM trained on en-ja generalizes so well on ja-en and ru-en that MSE obtained on those two test sets is even lower than that obtained on en-ja's test set. However, overall, there does not exist a single dataset that can produce a good EBM that can generalize well on all the other datasets.

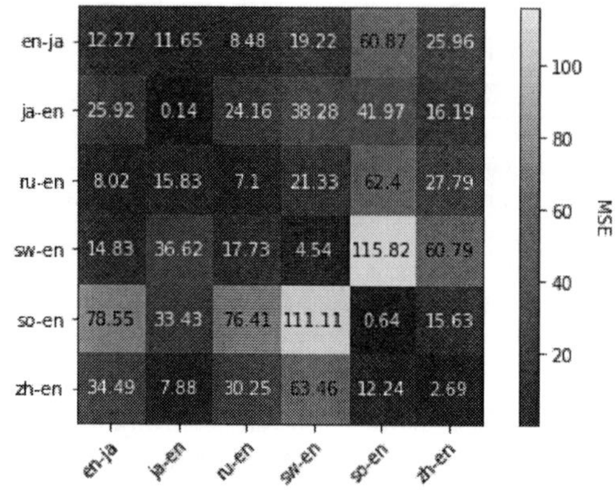

Figure 7: MSE of EBMs trained on one dataset (x-axis) and tested on another (y-axis).

An interesting future work is to implement interpretability tools to analyze when transfer works and when it does not.

6 Related Work

Previous work that explores the effect of choices of hyperparameters can be mainly divided into two categories: the prescriptive approach aims to offer advice on the configurations by large-scale experimental runs and those developing tools to improve the understanding of the hyperparameters, as cited in Section 3. Our work follows the descriptive approach, which seeks to interpret trends from a set of already-trained models. Related are some studies that measure hyperparameter importance: Hutter et al. (2014) and Sharma et al. (2019) applied a functional ANOVA framework to assess the importance, while Probst et al. (2019) adopted a variant term, hyperparameter tunability, conditioned on the difference on the performance of default and optimal settings of hyperparameters.

Exploration of the hyperparameter space also appears in research on HPO interpretability (Pfisterer et al., 2019; Freitas, 2019; Xanthopoulos et al., 2020). Moosbauer et al. (2021) attempted to interpret the HPO process with a variant of the partial dependence plot and showed what the surrogate model learned about the search space and how the final model is found.

7 Conclusions

In this work, we propose a framework for interpreting the hyperparameters of a set of Transformer models. Our framework work uses EBM as a post-hoc analysis tool, and we show that as a glassbox model, EBM is effectively at interpreting hyperparameters. While the computational needs of generating training data for EBM may seem large at first glance, we emphasize that we advocate for *post-hoc* analysis. In other words, the analysis is performed on the results of whatever hyperparameter search the model builder needs to perform to deploy a model.

Our MT case study demonstrates the kinds of insights one can glean regarding the relationship between hyperparameter configurations and Transformer performance; for example, we discover that that not all hyperparameters are equally important, and some hyperparameters exhibit non-monotic corelation with BLEU scores. Further, we conducted a series of analyses to test the robustness of EBM's fitting ability under varying data sizes and distributions. We show that EBM fits well under limited data, yet struggles with transfer across different MT datasets. It should also be noted that the conclusions drawn from MT tasks might not be applicable to other Transformer-based tasks.

Hyperparameter tuning is often viewed as a critical yet un-intuitive part of the model building process. We hope that our proposal provides a first step in unveiling the mysterious masks of hard-to-interpret hyperparameters in deep learning models.

References

Samira Abnar and Willem Zuidema. 2020. Quantifying attention flow in transformers. In *Proceedings of the 58th Annual Meeting of the Association for Computational Linguistics*, pages 4190–4197, Online. Association for Computational Linguistics.

Ali Araabi and Christof Monz. 2020. Optimizing transformer for low-resource neural machine translation. *arXiv preprint arXiv:2011.02266*.

Parnia Bahar, Tamer Alkhouli, Jan-Thorsten Peter, Christopher Jan-Steffen Brix, and Hermann Ney. 2017. Empirical investigation of optimization algorithms in neural machine translation. *The Prague Bulletin of Mathematical Linguistics*, 108(1):13–25.

Jasmijn Bastings, Yonatan Belinkov, Emmanuel Dupoux, Mario Giulianelli, Dieuwke Hupkes, Yuval Pinter, and Hassan Sajjad, editors. 2021. *Proceedings of the Fourth BlackboxNLP Workshop on Analyzing and Interpreting Neural Networks for NLP*. Association for Computational Linguistics, Punta Cana, Dominican Republic.

Denny Britz, Anna Goldie, Minh-Thang Luong, and Quoc Le. 2017. Massive exploration of neural machine translation architectures. *arXiv preprint arXiv:1703.03906*.

Rich Caruana, Paul Koch, Yin Lou, Marc Sturm , Johannes Gehrke, and Noemie Elhadad. 2015. Intelligible models for healthcare: Predicting pneumonia risk and hospital 30-day readmission. In *KDD'15, August 10-13, 2015, Sydney, NSW, Australia*. ACM.

Marina Danilevsky, Kun Qian, Ranit Aharonov, Yannis Katsis, Ban Kawas, and Prithviraj Sen. 2020. A survey of the state of explainable AI for natural language processing. In *Proceedings of the 1st Conference of the Asia-Pacific Chapter of the Association for Computational Linguistics and the 10th International Joint Conference on Natural Language Processing*, pages 447–459, Suzhou, China. Association for Computational Linguistics.

Alex A Freitas. 2019. Automated machine learning for studying the trade-off between predictive accuracy and interpretability. In *International Cross-Domain Conference for Machine Learning and Knowledge Extraction*, pages 48–66. Springer.

Frank Hutter, Holger Hoos, and Kevin Leyton-Brown. 2014. An efficient approach for assessing hyperparameter importance. In *International conference on machine learning*, pages 754–762. PMLR.

Frank Hutter, Lars Kotthoff, and Joaquin Vanschoren, editors. 2019. *Automated Machine Learning - Methods, Systems, Challenges*. Springer.

Goro Kobayashi, Tatsuki Kuribayashi, Sho Yokoi, and Kentaro Inui. 2020. Attention is not only a weight: Analyzing transformers with vector norms. In *Proceedings of the 2020 Conference on Empirical Methods in Natural Language Processing (EMNLP)*, Online. Association for Computational Linguistics.

Robert Lim, Kenneth Heafield, Hieu Hoang, Mark Briers, and Allen Malony. 2018. Exploring hyper-parameter optimization for neural machine translation on gpu architectures. *arXiv preprint arXiv:1805.02094*.

Yin Lou, Rich Caruana, and Johannes Gehrke. 2012. Intelligible models for classification and regression. In *Proceedings of the 18th ACM SIGKDD International Conference on Knowledge Discovery and Data Mining*, KDD '12, page 150–158, New York, NY, USA. Association for Computing Machinery.

Yin Lou, Rich Caruana, Johannes Gehrke, and Giles Hooker. 2013. Accurate intelligible models with pairwise interactions. In *Proceedings of the 19th ACM SIGKDD International Conference on Knowledge Discovery and Data Mining*, KDD '13, page 623–631, New York, NY, USA. Association for Computing Machinery.

Julia Moosbauer, Julia Herbinger, Giuseppe Casalicchio, Marius Lindauer, and Bernd Bischl. 2021. Explaining hyperparameter optimization via partial dependence plots. *Advances in Neural Information Processing Systems*, 34.

Harsha Nori, Samuel Jenkins, Paul Koch, and Rich Caruana. 2019. Interpretml: A unified framework for machine learning interpretability. *arXiv preprint arXiv:1909.09223*.

Florian Pfisterer, Janek Thomas, and Bernd Bischl. 2019. Towards human centered automl. *arXiv preprint arXiv:1911.02391*.

Philipp Probst, Anne-Laure Boulesteix, and Bernd Bischl. 2019. Tunability: importance of hyperparameters of machine learning algorithms. *The Journal of Machine Learning Research*, 20(1):1934–1965.

Abhinav Sharma, Jan N van Rijn, Frank Hutter, and Andreas Müller. 2019. Hyperparameter importance for image classification by residual neural networks. In *International Conference on Discovery Science*, pages 112–126. Springer.

Titte R Srinivas, Bing Ho, Joseph Kang, and Bruce Kaplan. 2015. Post hoc analyses: After the facts. *Transplantation*, 99.

Yi Tay, Dara Bahri, Donald Metzler, Da-Cheng Juan, Zhe Zhao, and Che Zheng. 2021. Synthesizer: Rethinking self-attention for transformer models. In *International conference on machine learning*, pages 10183–10192. PMLR.

ALS TDI. 2022. What is post-hoc analysis in a clinical trial.

Ashish Vaswani, Noam Shazeer, Niki Parmar, Jakob Uszkoreit, Llion Jones, Aidan N Gomez, Łukasz Kaiser, and Illia Polosukhin. 2017. Attention is all you need. *Advances in neural information processing systems*, 30.

Iordanis Xanthopoulos, Ioannis Tsamardinos, Vassilis Christophides, Eric Simon, and Alejandro Salinger. 2020. Putting the human back in the automl loop. In *EDBT/ICDT Workshops*.

Xuan Zhang and Kevin Duh. 2020. Reproducible and efficient benchmarks for hyperparameter optimization of neural machine translation systems. *Transactions of the Association for Computational Linguistics*, 8:393–408.

A Hyperparameter Importance

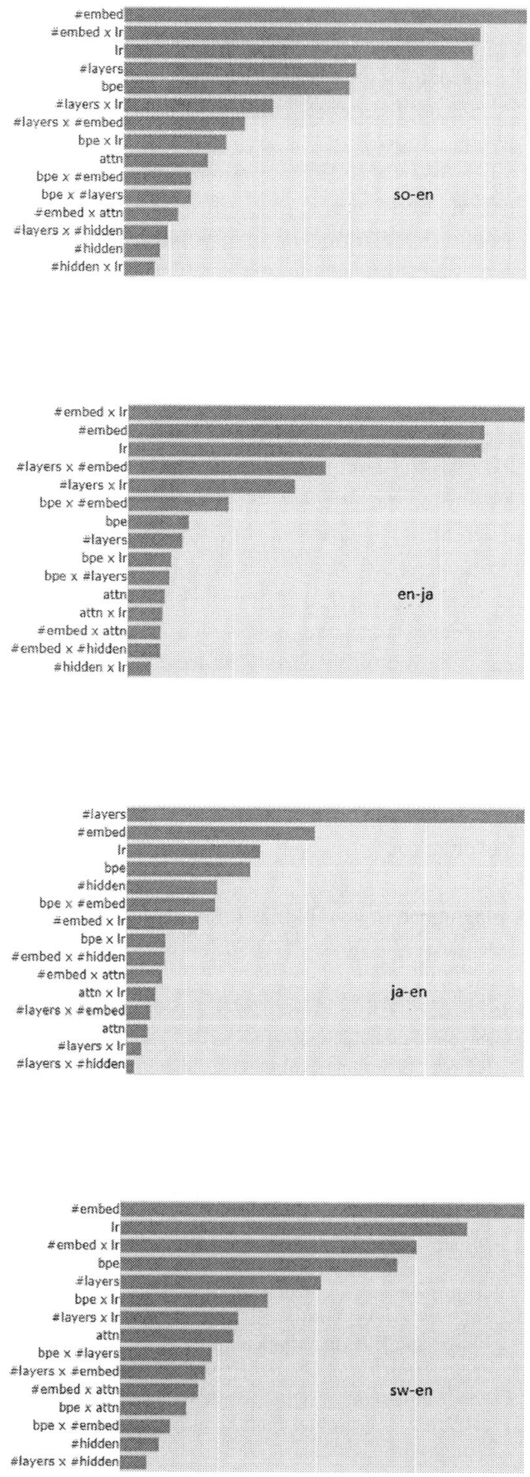

Figure 8: Hyperparameter contribution rank on so-en, en-ja, ja-en and sw-en.

B Single Hyperparameter Analysis

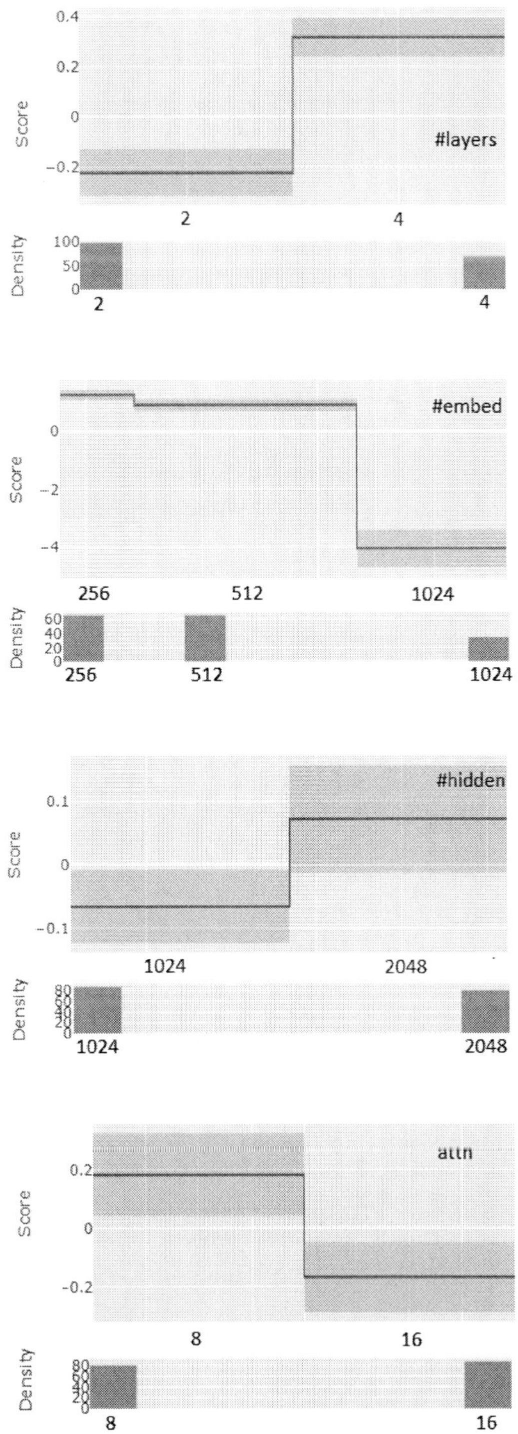

Figure 9: Single hyperparameter feature functions for en-ja. Higher *score* indicates a higher chance to get a high BLEU score. *Density* refers to the number of samples in the dataset.

C Pairwise Interactions

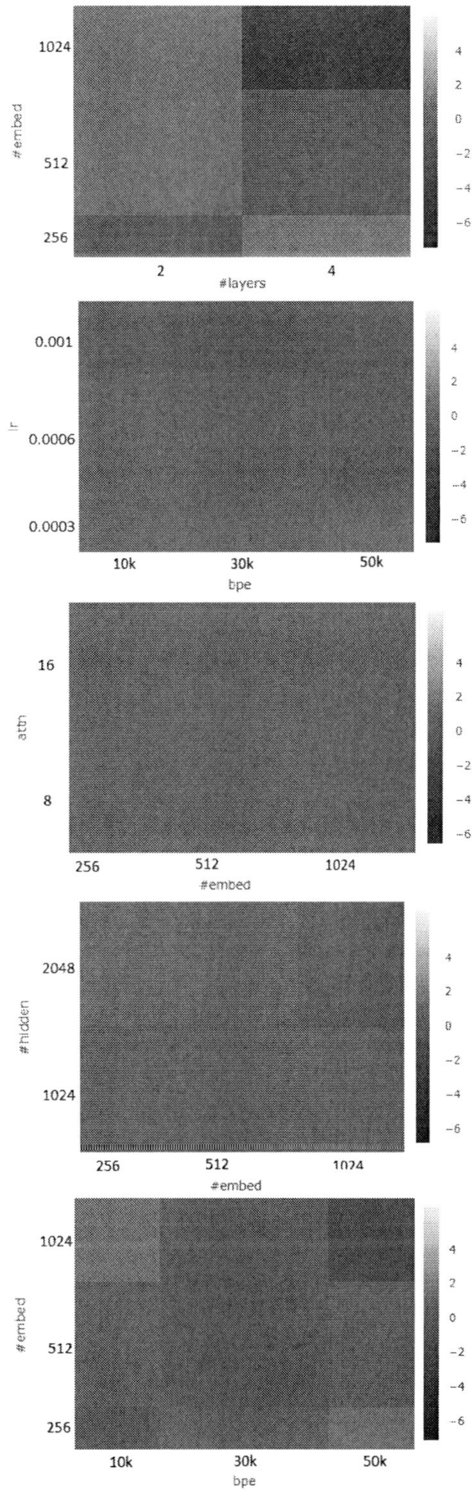

Figure 10: Pairwise interaction between features on en-ja. Higher *score* (yellow) indicates higher odds to get higher BLEU scores.

Revisit Systematic Generalization via Meaningful Learning

*Ning Shi♠♡ *Boxin Wang♣ Wei Wang♡ Xiangyu Liu♡ †Zhouhan Lin★
♠Alberta Machine Intelligence Institute, Dept. of Computing Science, University of Alberta
♣University of Illinois at Urbana-Champaign
♡Alibaba Group ★Shanghai Jiao Tong University
ning.shi@ualberta.ca, boxinw2@illinois.edu
{luyang.ww,eason.lxy}@alibaba-inc.com, lin.zhouhan@gmail.com

Abstract

Humans can systematically generalize to novel compositions of existing concepts. Recent studies argue that neural networks appear inherently ineffective in such cognitive capacity, leading to a pessimistic view and a lack of attention to optimistic results. We revisit this controversial topic from the perspective of meaningful learning, an exceptional capability of humans to learn novel concepts by connecting them with known ones. We reassess the compositional skills of sequence-to-sequence models conditioned on the semantic links between new and old concepts. Our observations suggest that models can successfully one-shot generalize to novel concepts and compositions through semantic linking, either inductively or deductively. We demonstrate that prior knowledge plays a key role as well. In addition to synthetic tests, we further conduct proof-of-concept experiments in machine translation and semantic parsing, showing the benefits of meaningful learning in applications. We hope our positive findings will encourage excavating modern neural networks' potential in systematic generalization through more advanced learning schemes.

1 Introduction

As a crucial characteristic of human cognition, systematic generalization reflects people's talents to learn infinite combinations of finite concepts (Chomsky, 1956; Montague et al., 1970). Whether connectionist networks can express language and thoughts systematically has been controversial for many years (Fodor and Pylyshyn, 1988; Hadley, 1994; Marcus, 1998; Fodor and Lepore, 2002; Brakel and Frank, 2009; Frank et al., 2009; Marcus, 2018). To date, the systematic compositionality in neural networks remains an appealing research topic. Evidence on multiple explicitly proposed language-based generalization challenges suggests

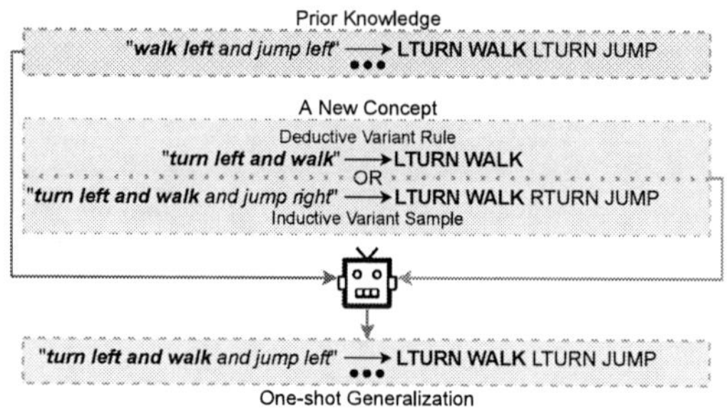

Figure 1: An example of the one-shot compositional generalization from the old concept "***walk left***" to the new one "***turn left and walk***" in SCAN. The model is able to generalize from the command "***walk left*** *and jump left*" to "***turn left and walk*** *and jump left*" through the semantic relationship between the old and new concepts because they refer to the same action "**LTURN WALK**". Such semantic linking can be established by either an inductive sample or a deductive rule.

that models lack such cognitive capacity (Bastings et al., 2018; Loula et al., 2018; Sinha et al., 2019; Keysers et al., 2020; Hupkes et al., 2020; Kim and Linzen, 2020; Li et al., 2021). Tremendous efforts are made to tackle these challenges through architectural modifications (Li et al., 2019; Gordon et al., 2020; Oren et al., 2020; Akyurek and Andreas, 2021; Chaabouni et al., 2021), meta-learning (Lake, 2019; Conklin et al., 2021), grammar (Kim, 2021; Shaw et al., 2021), neuro-symbolic models (Chen et al., 2020; Liu et al., 2020; Nye et al., 2020), data augmentation (Andreas, 2020; Akyürek et al., 2021; Auersperger and Pecina, 2021; Jiang and Bansal, 2021; Patel et al., 2022), and loss design (Yin et al., 2021). Despite their astounding accomplishments, standard sequence-to-sequence (seq2seq) models (Sutskever et al., 2014) appear to have relatively weak inductive biases, failing to capture underlying hierarchical structure.

In contrast, the successful one-shot generalization in the turn-left experiment on the **S**implified **C**omm**AI** **N**avigation (SCAN) task reveals the potential of seq2seq recurrent networks in controlled

* Work was done at Alibaba Group.
† Zhouhan Lin is the corresponding author.

Proceedings of the Fifth BlackboxNLP Workshop on Analyzing and Interpreting Neural Networks for NLP, pages 62 - 79
December 8, 2022 ©2022 Association for Computational Linguistics

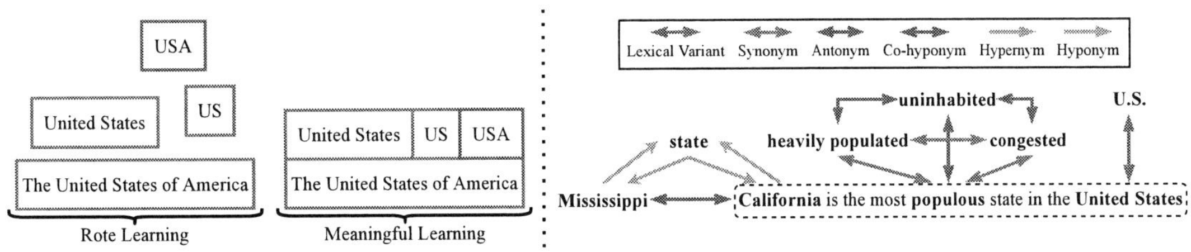

Figure 2: Adapted examples from Geography. In the left one, intuitively, knowing how the new concept (e.g., "*USA*") relates to the other existing ones (e.g., "*US*") can boost the learning and memory of this knowledge as a whole. In the right one, bidirectional arrows denote symmetric relations. "*Mississippi*" and "*California*" are two specific states, and thus both are hyponyms of "*state*". In turn, "*state*" is a hypernym of them. Due to a common hypernym, "*Mississippi*" and "*California*" become a co-hyponym for each other. {"*heavily populated*", "*congested*", "*populus*"} is a group of synonyms as sharing similar semantics. Finally, "*U.S.*", as a kind of abbreviation, is a lexical variant of "*United States*".

environments (Lake and Baroni, 2018). Although models are only exposed to the primitive command before, they are able to understand most composed commands of "*turn left*". One assumption is that models study new commands with a primitive from other action sequences containing the basic action it denotes. However, there is still a missing formal exploration to answer the question raised by Lake and Baroni (2018) on page 8 that "*what are, precisely, the generalization mechanisms that subtend the networks' success in these experiments*".

In this work, as a response to the call, we question whether neural networks are indeed deficient or just conventional learning protocols unable to exploit their full potential (Csordás et al., 2021; Dankers et al., 2022b). We revisit the systematic generalization of seq2seq models from a *meaningful learning* perspective (Ausubel, 1963; Okebukola and Jegede, 1988; Mayer, 2002). Given the idea that humans are used to memorizing concepts in a relational manner, we hypothesize that the success of the turn-left experiment results from the semantic relationships between old concepts and new ones. For example, in Figure 1, a model can understand the meaning of "***turn left and walk** and jump left*" from "***walk left** and jump left*" via the semantic link between two concepts (in bold) since both denote to the same action "LTURN WALK".

To validate our hypothesis, we reproduce the one-shot compositional generalization by *semantic linking* that exposes semantic relationships through either *inductive learning* or *deductive learning* (Hammerly, 1975; Shaffer, 1989; Thornbury, 1999). On the one hand, by introducing new concepts sharing the same context, we hope the model can capture the underlying semantic connections inductively. On the other hand, by involving a rule-like concept dictionary without specific context information, we hope the model can utilize the general cross-lingual supervised signals as anchor points so as to launch the semantic linking deductively.

In experiments, we treat concepts in the initial data set as primitives and generate variant samples and rules accordingly. Next, we mix them up and construct a seq2seq task after a random split. We repeatedly train and evaluate models but slowly decrease the number of times they see each variant until one-shot learning. We observe there is hardly a performance drop in SCAN for three representative model structures. This evidences that, with semantic linking, even canonical neural networks can generalize systematically to new concepts and compositions. Such observation holds consistently across two more semantic parsing (SP) datasets. The followed sensitivity analysis shows that prior knowledge also takes essential parts. Lastly, as a proof-of-concept, we demonstrate how meaningful learning already benefits models in standard machine translation (MT) and SP. Overall, our contributions[1] are as follows:

- We revisit systematic generalization from a meaningful learning perspective by either inductive or deductive semantic linking.
- We find that modern seq2seq models can generalize to new concepts and compositions after semantic linking, which empirically answers the question by Lake and Baroni (2018).
- We show in the sensitivity analysis that both semantic linking and prior knowledge play a key role, in line with meaningful learning theory.
- We extend to standard MT and SP and demonstrate how meaningful learning already benefits models in solving realistic problems.

[1]Code and data are publicly available at GitHub.

2 Meaningful Learning

In educational psychology, meaningful learning refers to learning new concepts by relating them to old ones (Ausubel, 1963; Mayer, 2002). In Figure 2, intuitively, the utilization of meaningful learning can encourage learners to understand information continuously built on concepts the learners already understand (Okebukola and Jegede, 1988). Following this, we intend to examine models' systematic compositionality by exploring semantic linking that establishes semantic relations between primitives (old concepts) and their variants (new concepts). We propose to spoon-feed semantic knowledge to models for semantic linking in two ways, that is, inductive learning and deductive learning (Hammerly, 1975; Shaffer, 1989; Thornbury, 1999). In this section, we discuss the process of semantic linking and take "*jump*" from SCAN as an example primitive to illustrate the learning scheme.

2.1 Semantic links

We focus on three semantic relationships, namely, *lexical variant*, *co-hyponym*, and *synonym*. Lexical Variant refers to an alternative expression form for the same concept. Co-hyponym is a linguistic term to designate a semantic relation between two group members belonging to the same broader class, where each member is a hyponym and the class is a hypernym (Lyons and John, 1995). Synonym stands for a word, morpheme, or phrase that shares exactly or nearly the same semantics with another one. We provide an example in Figure 2 and a detailed description in Appendix A.

2.2 Inductive learning

Inductive learning is a bottom-up approach from the more specific to the more general. In grammar teaching, inductive learning is a rule-discovery approach starting with the presentation of specific examples from which a general rule can be inferred (Thornbury, 1999). In semantic linking, we propose to introduce variant samples sharing the same context with their primitives during training. The assumption is that models can observe the interchange of primitives and their variants surrounded by the same context in the hope of coming up with a general hypothesis that there is a semantic linking between primitives and their variants (Harris, 1954). To test the generalization, we design a prompt "*[concept] twice*" from a primitive sample "*jump twice*". After that, we fill in the concept slot with "*jump_0*" and generate the variant sample "*jump_0 twice*". There is no change from the target side. Finally, by training models on the generated variant sample in combination with prior knowledge (all the other primitive samples), we aim to establish the semantic relationship between "*jump*" and "*jump_0*" inductively.

2.3 Deductive learning

Deductive Learning, the opposite of inductive learning, is a top-down approach from the more general to the more specific. As a rule-driven approach, teaching in a deductive manner often begins with presenting a general rule followed by specific examples in practice where the rule is applied (Thornbury, 1999). To align with this definition, we intend to do semantic linking deductively by combining a bilingual dictionary that maps primitives and their variants to the same in the target domain. This additional dictionary, hence, mixes the original training task with word translation (Mikolov et al., 2013b). Without any specific context, we hope the model can utilize the general cross-lingual supervised signals as anchor points so as to launch the semantic linking. We want to point out that deductive learning is partially different from *deductive reasoning*. Although there is an overlap, it is not necessary for the former to extract rules from observations like the inference conducted by the latter. In this work, we care more about the learning outcomes, rather than the reasoning process, through empirical evaluations. In practice, given the same example above, we directly make use of primitive "*jump*" and its variant "*jump_0*" as the source sequences, as well as the action "JUMP" as their identical target sequences. Words and phrases can be treated as text sequences of relatively short length. By exposing both the primitive rule "*jump*" $\rightarrow$ "JUMP" and the variants rule "*jump_0*"$\rightarrow$ "JUMP" during training, we aim to build the semantic connections between "*jump*" and "*jump_0*" deductively.

3 Systematic Generalization

The following section specifies the setup and outcome of the experiments. We first employ SCAN as the initial testbed to reproduce the one-shot generalization conditioned on the semantic linking. Then, we examine neural networks' potential to achieve this on SCAN and two real-world tasks of SP, followed by a sensitivity analysis.

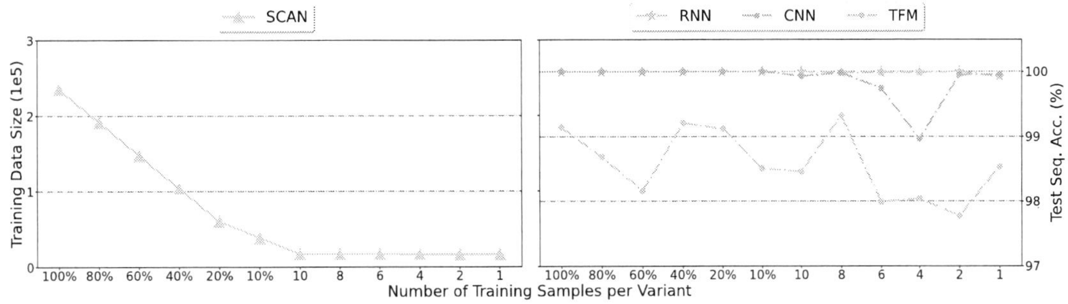

Figure 3: Experiments on SCAN expressing the total training size (left) and the test sequence accuracy (right) when the number of training samples per variant decreases from the complete set (100%) to a single sample (1).

3.1 Datasets

Some suggest SCAN is not enough to fully verify compositionality (Bastings et al., 2018; Keysers et al., 2020; Dankers et al., 2022a). Thus, we introduce GEO and ADV generated respectively from real SP datasets: Geography and Advising.[2] Example inputs and outputs can be found in Table 6.

SCAN (Lake and Baroni, 2018) is a diagnostic dataset proposed to investigate neural networks' compositionality.[3] It includes 20,910 pairs of commands to their instructed actions such as the example in Figure 1. We select {"*jump*", "*look*", "*run*", "*walk*" } as 4 primitives to be in line with previous works. We focus on lexical variants and create them by adding a suffix that consists of an underline and a unique number. We control the size of the variants set by setting the upper limit of this number. An example variant of "*jump*" is "*jump_0*" and both mean the same action "JUMP".

Geography is a common SP dataset (Zelle and Mooney, 1996; Srinivasan et al., 2017), containing 880 examples of queries paired with corresponding expressions. It is later formatted to SQL language with variables in the target sequences (Finegan-Dollak et al., 2018). **GEO** is generated from Geography. We regard 4 of 9 annotated variables as hypernyms and keep them as they are in SQL sequences. The other variables are restored by entities from the source sequence accordingly. As a result, the overall data size is 618 after processing. We can make use of the "is-a" hypernymy relation for semantic linking. Specifically, we select {"*new york city*", "*mississippi rivier*", "*dc*", "*dover*" } as 4 primitives[4] with their variants consisting of entities as co-hyponyms sharing the same variable group with primitives. An example variant of "*new york city*" is "*houston city*" and both are in the same variable group "CITY_NAME".

Advising includes 4,570 questions on course information paired with SQL queries (Finegan-Dollak et al., 2018). **ADV** is generated from Advising. We treat 4 of 26 annotated variables as hypernyms. Precisely, we select { "*a history of american film*", "*aaron magid*", "*aaptis*", "*100*" } as 4 primitives with their variants as co-hyponyms sharing the same variables. For instance, "*advanced at ai techniques*" is a co-hyponym of "*a history of american film*" sharing the same variable "TOPIC".

3.2 Models and experimental setup

Models. After testing many adapted versions, we employ three dominant model candidates, that is, RNN, CNN, and TFM. In terms of RNN, we reproduce bi-directional recurrent networks (Schuster and Paliwal, 1997) with long short-term memory units (Hochreiter and Schmidhuber, 1997) and an attention mechanism (Bahdanau et al., 2015). We follow the convolutional seq2seq architecture presented by Gehring et al. (2017) with regard to CNN and the attention-based structure proposed by Vaswani et al. (2017) in the case of TFM. More details are in Appendix B.

Training. We apply the mini-batch strategy to sample 128 sequence pairs for each training step. We use Adam optimizer (Kingma and Ba, 2015) with an ℓ_2 gradient clipping of 5.0 (Pascanu et al., 2013) and a learning rate of $1e^{-4}$. We freeze the maximum training epoch at 320 for CNN and 640 for RNN and TFM. To prevent uncontrolled interference, we train all models from scratch instead of fine-tuning (Devlin et al., 2019). For the same reason, we break words by whitespace tokenization rather than subword modeling. So, we can guarantee that words are treated separately as distinct

[2] github.com/jkkummerfeld/text2sql-data

[3] github.com/brendenlake/SCAN

[4] We randomly select 4 primitives from GEO and ADV to align with SCAN.

Data	SCAN					GEO					ADV				
	Exp. IL			Exp. DL		Exp. IL			Exp. DL		Exp. IL			Exp. DL	
	Sta.	Dif.	Cha.	Sta.	Dif.	Sta.	Dif.	Cha.	Sta.	Dif.	Sta.	Dif.	Cha.	Sta.	Dif.
Train Size	20946	20942	20928	20950	20946	724	720	711	728	724	6038	6034	5969	6040	6036
Test Size	308240	308240	308240	308240	308240	21350	21350	21350	21350	21350	107614	107614	107614	107614	107614

Table 1: Dataset statistics for inductive learning (IL) and deductive learning (DL) across Standard (Sta.), Difficult (Dif.), and Challenging (Cha.) in Section 3.4.

tokens with completely different embeddings.

Evaluation. Token and sequence accuracy serve as two primary metrics. The former allows partial errors in a sequence, while the latter strictly does not. Every reported number, along with the standard deviation, is the mean of five runs.

3.3 Experiment: meaningful learning

Thanks to their incredible algebraic compositionality (Chomsky, 1956), humans can effectively capture the underlying semantic connections between new and old concepts and generalize the prior knowledge to novel combinations by meaningful learning (Ausubel, 1963). To investigate the extent to which models can do the same, we probe the models' compositionality by introducing semantic linking. It is reasonable to illustrate the function of semantic linking through an ablation study, while its missing will lead to an out-of-vocabulary (OOV) issue since there will be no sample to expose variants during training. Replacing variants with other tokens (e.g., "*[unk]*") goes against our intent to investigate the generalization from primitives to their variants. It also leads to an unfair comparison, where all the variants, for example, go to the same unknown token and cause poor test accuracy. Instead, we gradually remove training samples for each variant until the one-shot learning scenario. We hope to observe the presence of models' meaningful learning by measuring the corresponding performance loss.

Experimental setup. Following section 2.2, we make use of 40 variants for 4 primitives and produce a total of 329,190 samples, including both primitive and variant samples. We randomly split them into a training set (80%) and a test set (20%). The training set is further processed to remove samples having multiple variants to ensure that each variant occurs only once in each sample. Eventually, the training set contains 235,002 samples. Models directly trained on this full dataset serve as baselines. Then, to format a gradual transition from baselines to the meaningful learning, we train the same models on various datasets with a decreasing number of augmented samples for each variant until the one-shot learning setting. Besides, we use the variant rule "*jump_0*" $\rightarrow$ "JUMP" as the only training sample for "*jump_0*" in the end as a case of our deductive learning introduced in Section 2.3 and consider the rest as our inductive learning.

Results. As elaborated in Figure 3, the solid line (SCAN) in green denotes the total training data size against the decreasing number of training samples per variant. The dashed line in other colors denotes the test sequence accuracy against the same horizontal axis. RNN has no significant performance drop when the training size is reduced from 100% to 1. It still achieves 99.92% test sequence accuracy when there is only one training sample for each variant. The same happens for CNN and TFM. Despite a slight fluctuation, they keep the results almost consistent regardless of whether the number of training variant samples is all or 1. It is not necessary to augment the training set nearly 14 times from 16,736 to 235,002 to cover all the possible variant compositions. The participation of a single sample is able to launch semantic linking via either inductive learning (a variant sample) or deductive learning (a variant rule), thus enabling models to achieve one-shot generalization. We put two plots in one figure to emphasize such a surprising observation through the strong contrast.

3.4 Experiment: semantic linking injection

The following two experiments evaluate models' systematic generalization, particularly for prior knowledge and semantic linking. A sliding scale of difficulty is carefully designed by weakening these two factors according to the assumption that the greater the difficulty, the more compositional skills are required. We further validate our findings on GEO and ADV. We use the same evaluation protocol across different datasets in this section.

Taking the base dataset as prior knowledge, we replace the primitives in source sequences with their variants to generate novel compositions, as introduced in Section 2.2. So far, the produced variant samples are not in the training set but in the

Data	Model	Token Acc.%			Seq. Acc.%		
		Standard	Difficult	Challenging	Standard	Difficult	Challenging
SCAN	RNN	99.99 ± 0.03	99.89 ± 0.19	99.96 ± 0.02	99.95 ± 0.08	99.85 ± 0.08	99.80 ± 0.31
	CNN	99.96 ± 0.08	99.76 ± 0.54	98.89 ± 2.44	99.85 ± 0.34	99.52 ± 1.07	97.57 ± 5.24
	TFM	98.91 ± 0.78	98.90 ± 1.10	98.76 ± 0.85	97.35 ± 1.62	96.86 ± 2.64	96.38 ± 2.81
GEO	RNN	75.71 ± 8.42	75.69 ± 6.12	73.46 ± 3.05	44.95 ± 14.69	43.27 ± 13.47	36.77 ± 5.60
	CNN	87.99 ± 2.67	79.51 ± 6.03	77.40 ± 2.48	69.46 ± 5.78	51.20 ± 8.64	48.58 ± 3.40
	TFM	75.37 ± 7.84	75.11 ± 4.88	68.41 ± 4.76	45.93 ± 12.42	44.59 ± 9.76	36.93 ± 7.47
ADV	RNN	58.61 ± 6.18	59.74 ± 5.67	58.11 ± 5.82	36.18 ± 5.75	35.69 ± 6.05	35.45 ± 6.69
	CNN	57.83 ± 7.55	54.05 ± 5.74	53.66 ± 2.57	45.08 ± 9.32	42.14 ± 6.90	41.37 ± 4.04
	TFM	53.43 ± 2.80	51.51 ± 4.50	49.17 ± 2.58	42.59 ± 3.65	41.28 ± 4.35	38.88 ± 2.68

Table 2: Evaluation results over RNN, CNN, and TFM on SCAN, GEO, and ADV across Standard, Difficult, and Challenging in Section 3.4.1.

test set. Hence, variants exist as OOV now. Then, we either incorporate one variant sample to introduce variants in training inductively or one variant rule to do so deductively. In the one-shot learning scenario, we ensure each variant only has a single sample and appears only once during training. For convenience, we keep the same settings for each primitive to have 10 variants in SCAN and a full variant set in GEO (e.g., 39 variants for "*new york city*"). It is noted in ADV that we randomly sample 5 variants for each primitive so that we cover all the variants with an appropriate test size.

3.4.1 Inductive learning

Experimental setup. We increase the difficulty by excluding primitive samples from the training set. It is worth noting that models have to generalize to not only new concepts but also their new compositions with a higher level of difficulty.

- **Standard**: Models are trained on prior knowledge and one variant sample per variant.
- **Difficult**: We remove from the prior knowledge primitive samples sharing the same context with their variant samples. For example, we remove "*jump twice*" due to "*jump_0 twice*", and thus models have to generalize to "*jump_0 twice*" without seeing "*jump twice*".
- **Challenging:** We also exclude from the prior knowledge primitive samples of the same length as their variant samples. For instance, models have to reproduce the same generalization to "*jump_0 twice*" without seeing primitive samples of length 2, including "*jump twice*", "*jump right*", "*jump left*", to name a few.[5]

SCAN. What stands out in Table 2 is an excellent one-shot generalization for all three networks.

[5]We remove samples that will not lead to unknown tokens.

Data	Model	Token Acc.%		Seq. Acc.%	
		Standard	Difficult	Standard	Difficult
SCAN	RNN	99.48 ± 0.71	98.70 ± 0.92	98.27 ± 2.38	95.39 ± 2.72
	CNN	99.99 ± 0.01	98.59 ± 3.10	99.96 ± 0.03	96.66 ± 7.27
	TFM	96.90 ± 1.78	96.68 ± 2.21	91.94 ± 4.04	91.26 ± 5.80
GEO	RNN	54.44 ± 7.15	39.71 ± 18.38	13.61 ± 7.08	7.76 ± 5.34
	CNN	41.86 ± 3.38	41.07 ± 7.48	4.85 ± 4.66	4.04 ± 2.18
	TFM	67.02 ± 6.91	65.97 ± 5.17	36.38 ± 10.08	31.57 ± 7.42
ADV	RNN	36.50 ± 7.66	36.42 ± 7.39	12.84 ± 4.31	12.66 ± 5.19
	CNN	43.51 ± 11.31	35.34 ± 14.68	32.33 ± 12.93	23.58 ± 16.04
	TFM	56.82 ± 3.79	53.33 ± 3.85	47.43 ± 3.71	43.24 ± 5.14

Table 3: Evaluation results over RNN, CNN, and TFM on SCAN, GEO, and ADV across Standard and Difficult in Section 3.4.2.

The participation of variant samples induces a near-perfect generalization. Even the worst results obtained by TFM in Challenging are around 98.76% and 96.38% in terms of token and sequence accuracy. The outcomes confirm that networks can inductively learn semantic relations from the context after semantic linking. The disappearance of training samples in Difficult and Challenging causes a performance drop. This is well in line with the widely accepted belief in meaningful learning theory that prior knowledge matters to generalization.

GEO & ADV. The more apparent changes in metrics again verify that prior knowledge is essential. Either excluding primitive samples containing the same context or those of the same sequence length can produce a steep fall in the generalization. On GEO, CNN can lose an absolute sequence accuracy of 18.26% from Standard to Difficult, and that for TFM drops 7.66%. This upholds our argument that generalization via meaningful learning is inseparable from sufficient prior knowledge. The overall decline in performance can be attributed to the switch from toy sets to actual datasets since both GEO and ADV own a much more complex encoding and decoding space than SCAN. Therefore, we conclude that both prior knowledge and semantic linking exert powerful effects upon the potential of models to generalize systematically.

3.4.2 Deductive learning

Experimental setup. We increase the difficulty of compositional learning by excluding primitive rules from the training set as follows:

- **Standard**: Models are trained on the prior knowledge, primitive rules, and variant rules.
- **Difficult**: We remove primitive rules from the training set. Consequently, semantic links are weakened and depend on variant rules only.

SCAN. By incorporating deductive semantic linking, all three networks attain satisfying compositional generalization as shown in Table 3. CNN achieves the highest 99.96% in Standard, while TFM takes the lowest 91.26% in Difficult with regard to sequence accuracy. We can see a consistent decline in accuracy when we undermine the semantic linking by removing primitive rules from the training set. The most significant sequence accuracy drop of 3.3% comes from CNN when the difficulty upgrades. However, in Difficult, even the lowest one is impressive as there is only one variant rule to introduce each variant during training.

GEO & ADV. There is a persistent performance loss because of the absence of primitive rules from the training set across models. Concretely in GEO, the grade of CNN declines from 32.33% in Standard to 23.58% in Difficult in terms of sequence accuracy. The causal role of semantic linking is also demonstrated by varying the difficulty. The difference between Standard and Difficult indicated that either concept rules and just variant rules can connect primitives with their variants semantically, though the former is better than the latter. Moreover, models appear to realize systematic generalization better in an inductive way. By comparing Table 2 with Table 3, we find that current black-box neural nets are more capable of exploring patterns from specific samples with context information rather than understanding knowledge from general rules in our experiments. This sheds light on why current machine learning is still highly data-driven and can hardly break through the bottleneck to conduct advanced logic reasoning as human beings.

3.5 Sensitivity analysis

Regarding deductive learning, we conduct sensitivity analysis with a varying number of primitives (#primitives) from {1,2,3,4} and that of variants

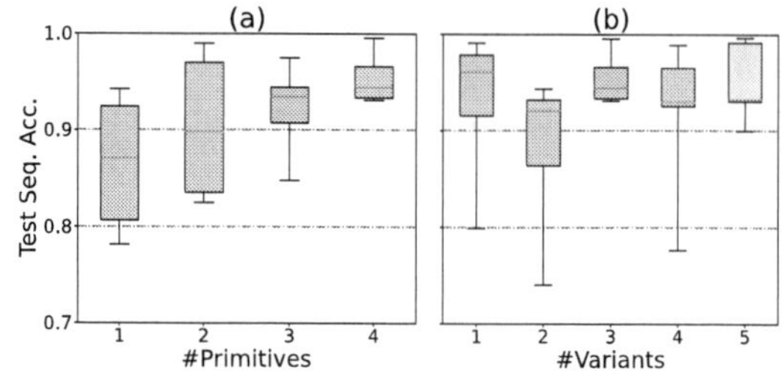

Figure 4: Experiments over RNN on SCAN with varying #primitives (a) and #variants (b).

per primitive (#variants) from {1,5,10,15,20} over RNN on SCAN. The experimental setup is borrowed from Standard in Section 3.4.2.

Impact of #primitives. In Figure 4 (a), the generalization performance improves w.r.t. accuracy boosting and variance reduction when #primitives grows simultaneously. This is counter-intuitive as we thought primitive rules should work independently. A potential reason is semantic linking built by various *independent* primitive rules can profit each other to trigger a more robust and stable generalization. For example, "*jump*" $\rightarrow$ "JUMP" and "*look*" $\rightarrow$ "LOOK" may separate them from the context such as "***jump** right*" and "***look** right*". So, "*[concept] right*" functions as a compositional rule shared among primitive samples and finally encourages models to generalize more effectively.

Impact of #variants. As presented in Figure 4 (b), RNN generalizes consistently well when #variants goes up. Therefore, we report that the generalization among variants of the same primitive has a certain degree of independence within a reasonable range (e.g., #variants $\leq$ 20).

4 From SCAN to Real Data

Thus far, we have argued the feasibility of systematic generalization activated by semantic linking. We move on to discuss how it already benefits machines in solving real problems. Many recent papers propose to improve systematic generalization by techniques such as data augmentation (Andreas, 2020; Akyürek et al., 2021) and meta-learning (Lake, 2019; Conklin et al., 2021). The success is reasonable given our findings. Replacing fragments in real training samples with others that share similar contexts is supported by our inductive learning. We have demonstrated that similar context information can help establish the semantic links between new concepts and old ones, thus enabling models to generalize compositionally. By

Model	IWSLT'14				IWSLT'15			
	En-De		De-En		En-Fr		Fr-En	
	BLEU	SacreBLEU	BLEU	SacreBLEU	BLEU	SacreBLEU	BLEU	SacreBLEU
Baselines								
LSTM (Luong et al., 2015)	24.98	24.88	30.18	32.62	38.06	42.93	37.34	39.36
Transformer (Vaswani et al., 2017)	28.95	28.85	35.24	37.60	41.82	46.41	40.45	42.61
Dynamic Conv. (Wu et al., 2019)	27.39	27.28	33.33	35.54	40.41	45.32	39.61	41.42
+Vocabulary Augmentation								
LSTM (Luong et al., 2015)	$25.35\uparrow_{0.37}$	$25.38\uparrow_{0.50}$	$30.99\uparrow_{0.81}$	$33.63\uparrow_{1.01}$	$38.32\uparrow_{0.26}$	$43.30\uparrow_{0.37}$	$37.77\uparrow_{0.43}$	$39.83\uparrow_{0.47}$
Transformer (Vaswani et al., 2017)	$29.40\uparrow_{0.45}$	$29.29\uparrow_{0.44}$	$35.72\uparrow_{0.48}$	$38.07\uparrow_{0.47}$	$42.19\uparrow_{0.37}$	$46.68\uparrow_{0.27}$	$41.04\uparrow_{0.59}$	$43.15\uparrow_{0.54}$
Dynamic Conv. (Wu et al., 2019)	$27.60\uparrow_{0.21}$	$27.50\uparrow_{0.22}$	$33.62\uparrow_{0.29}$	$36.00\uparrow_{0.46}$	$40.87\uparrow_{0.46}$	$45.95\uparrow_{0.63}$	$39.95\uparrow_{0.34}$	$41.86\uparrow_{0.44}$

Table 4: Evaluation results over LSTM, Transformer, and Dynamic Conv. on IWSLT'14 En-De (English-German) and De-En, IWSLT'15 En-Fr (English-French) and Fr-En translations.

considering concepts as pointers in the memory, meta-learning equips models with memory loading to make connections between new and old concepts as semantic linking. The utility of similar unsupervised techniques (Xie et al., 2020) in both compositional generalization and real tasks can be attributed to inductive learning as well. Besides, our sensitivity analysis in Section 3.5 shows that adding seemingly independent primitive samples or rules can also improve the generalization, which has been further validated recently (Auersperger and Pecina, 2021; Patel et al., 2022).

In addition to inductive-based methods, some works (Mikolov et al., 2013b; Arthur et al., 2016; Nag et al., 2020), incorporating bilingual dictionaries in low-resource MT, can fall in the field of deductive-based ones. As a proof-of-concept, we reproduce the word-to-word augmentation, or called deductive learning in this work, by training models on not only the base training set but also concept rules. Intuitively, we wonder to which extent deductive semantic linking can promote models' performance in MT (IWSLT'14 and IWSLT'15) and SP (Geography and Advising). We report the evaluation results in Table 4 and Table 5. Details of models and data can be found in Appendix B and Appendix C.

4.1 Machine translation

Setup. We evaluate our approach on IWSLT'14 (Cettolo et al., 2014) English-German (En-De) and German-English (De-En), IWSLT'15 (Cettolo et al., 2015) English-French (En-Fr) and French-English (Fr-En) translation tasks. We follow the standard evaluation protocol (Ott et al., 2019) that keeps the original training set and validation set but combines multiple previous test sets for final evaluation. The test set of IWSLT'14 consists of IWSLT14.TED.dev{2010, 2012} and IWSLT14.TED.tst{2010, 2011, 2012}. That of IWSLT'15 includes IWSLT15.TED.tst{2014, 2015} (Ott et al., 2019). We apply BPE with 10K tokens for all tasks and report both BLEU (Papineni et al., 2002) and SacreBLEU (Post, 2018) scores for three baselines: LSTM (Luong et al., 2015), Transformer (Vaswani et al., 2017), and Dynamic Conv. (Wu et al., 2019) in comparsion with same structures augmented by our method.

Vocabulary augmentation. We introduce concept rules as *vocabulary augmentation* in MT. The semantic links between primitives and their variants can be built upon the synonymous relations between tokens such as "*heavily populated*" and "*populous*". From this, the source words paired with translated ones can be regarded as concept rules. It is noted that such relationships are reversible as shown in Figure 2, so a primitive can be a variant of the other primitive as well. In practice, we collect a dictionary of tokens in the source language and feed them to the Google Translation[6] so as to obtain a token map from the source language to the target one. The same operation can be repeated from the target language to the source one. Two dictionaries are combined into one with duplicates removed. Consequently, we get 144,874 token-level samples as a training supplementary for IWSLT'14 En-De and De-En, and 110,099 for IWSLT'15 En-Fr and Fr-En, which leads to a total of 305,113 training samples for IWSLT'14 En-De and De-En and 315,671 for IWSLT'15 En-Fr and Fr-En after such vocabulary augmentation.

Results. From Table 4, we observe a consistent improvement in both BLEU and SacreBLEU over all baselines after vocabulary augmentation, particularly up to 1 in SacreBlEU. The additional synonym pairs not only construct the semantic linking between tokens in two languages explicitly, but also create a complicated semantic linking network im-

[6] `cloud.google.com/translate`

Model	Geography				Advising			
	Train		Test		Train		Test	
	Token Acc.%	Seq. Acc.%	Token Acc.%	Seq. Acc.%	Token Acc.%	Seq. Acc.%	Token Acc.%	Seq. Acc.%
Baselines								
RNN	89.05	17.39	69.81	9.68	92.22	3.64	60.41	6.11
CNN	98.45	70.74	78.44	55.91	99.74	81.62	81.74	51.13
TFM	99.45	84.95	80.24	49.82	99.68	76.90	78.51	29.67
+Entity Augmentation								
RNN	87.47	29.96	$72.39\uparrow_{2.58}$	$15.05\uparrow_{5.37}$	88.82	30.97	$71.17\uparrow_{10.76}$	$16.06\uparrow_{9.95}$
CNN	97.54	76.03	$80.32\uparrow_{1.88}$	$60.93\uparrow_{5.02}$	99.65	87.01	$84.50\uparrow_{2.76}$	$56.02\uparrow_{4.89}$
TFM	99.30	85.73	$81.09\uparrow_{0.85}$	$54.84\uparrow_{5.02}$	99.57	86.94	$84.26\uparrow_{5.75}$	$35.08\uparrow_{5.41}$

Table 5: Evaluation results over RNN, CNN, and TFM on Geography and Advising.

plicitly because of synonyms within the single language and the transitivity nature of synonym relation. Our experiments prove that semantic linking, which allows models to generalize systematically, can be beneficial for improving MT performance.

4.2 Semantic parsing

Setup. We evaluate our method on two SP benchmarks, Geography, and Advising. We train the same models (i.e., RNN, CNN, and TFM) as we analyzed before without further hyperparameter tuning. There are some changes for CNN, where the learning rate is $5e^{-4}$ in Geography, and the maximum sequence length for the decoder position embedding is 312 in Advising. We split 10% training samples as the validation set to find the converged epoch and then add it back to the training set for the final report.

Entity augmentation. We introduce concept rules as *entity augmentation* in SP. The semantic links are established among co-hyponyms. We consider a variable as a hypernym for its values. By that, entities belonging to the same variable are co-hyponyms. Thus, we can regard entity values as primitives and the translations from primitives (e.g., "*new york city*") to their variables (e.g., "CITY_NAME") as primitive rules. To be specific, We construct entity dictionaries by collecting entities such as "*new york city*". They are translated to themselves since they do not change from the source natural language to the target SQL. For a fair comparison, a token from this extra dataset will be marked as a unique unknown mark, "*[unk]*", if it does not exist in the original base training set. After that, we have a map of 103 entity translations for Geography and 1846 for Advising, resulting in a training size change from 701 to 804 for Geography and from 3814 to 5660 for Advising.

Results. As elaborated in Table 5, all three networks can achieve better performance in terms of both accuracy and variance. A 10.76% token accuracy and 9.95% sequence accuracy boosting are observed from RNN on Advising after such entity augmentation. The results suggest that models can learn semantic linking or be more familiar with similar contexts from those primitive rules in a deductive way to enhance model systematic generalization and finally lead to better outcomes.

5 Conclusion

We revisit systematic generalization from a meaningful learning perspective. According to the theory, we conduct semantic linking to expose semantic relations between new and old concepts via either inductive learning or deductive learning. Experimental results on SCAN, GEO, and ADV support that seq2seq neural networks, as a class of modern machine learning methods, can behave systematically after semantic linking. Testing with various difficulties indicates that both semantic linking and prior knowledge are two essential factors in such generalization, in agreement with what humans do in meaningful learning. Finally, we group recent methods in either the inductive-based or deductive-based category, followed by a proof-of-concept, to highlight the already-existing advantages of meaningful learning in applications such as machine translation and semantic parsing.

We want to underline that, to the best of our knowledge, this work is the first one exploring the optimistic results observed by Lake and Baroni (2018). Our positive findings oppose the recent prevailing view that neural networks appear inherently ineffective in such cognitive capacity, thus confirming the mixed picture. By rationalizing recent findings from a meaningful learning perspective, we hope to encourage followers to interpret the exceptional generalization ability through the connection between neural nets and human cognition.

Limitations

We establish semantic relationships between primitives and their variants by either inductive or deductive learning. The incorporation of both learning skills is worth exploring further. We primarily utilize data augmentation techniques to expose the semantic information to models. Apart from that, there should be many other methods to achieve the same goal. Which method is most appropriate to realize semantic linking remains an open topic. Meanwhile, the application of meaningful learning to promote systematic generalization in practice (e.g., MT and SP) could have been expanded.

Acknowledgements

We gratefully appreciate Yewen Pu, Guan (Royal) Wang, Yichen Gong, Rong Zhang, and Hui Xue for sharing their pearls of wisdom. We also would like to express our special thanks of graitude to Yingying Huo for the support, as well as BlackboxNLP anonymous reviewers for their constructive feedback. This work was supported by Shining Lab, Learnable, Inc., and Alibaba Group.

References

Ekin Akyürek, Afra Feyza Akyürek, and Jacob Andreas. 2021. Learning to recombine and resample data for compositional generalization. In *International Conference on Learning Representations*.

Ekin Akyurek and Jacob Andreas. 2021. Lexicon learning for few shot sequence modeling. In *Proceedings of the 59th Annual Meeting of the Association for Computational Linguistics and the 11th International Joint Conference on Natural Language Processing (Volume 1: Long Papers)*, pages 4934–4946, Online. Association for Computational Linguistics.

Jacob Andreas. 2020. Good-enough compositional data augmentation. In *Proceedings of the 58th Annual Meeting of the Association for Computational Linguistics*, pages 7556–7566, Online. Association for Computational Linguistics.

Philip Arthur, Graham Neubig, and Satoshi Nakamura. 2016. Incorporating discrete translation lexicons into neural machine translation. In *Proceedings of the 2016 Conference on Empirical Methods in Natural Language Processing*, pages 1557–1567, Austin, Texas. Association for Computational Linguistics.

Michal Auersperger and Pavel Pecina. 2021. Solving SCAN tasks with data augmentation and input embeddings. In *Proceedings of the International Conference on Recent Advances in Natural Language Processing (RANLP 2021)*, pages 86–91, Held Online. INCOMA Ltd.

D.P. Ausubel. 1963. *The Psychology of Meaningful Verbal Learning*. Grune & Stratton.

Dzmitry Bahdanau, Kyunghyun Cho, and Yoshua Bengio. 2015. Neural machine translation by jointly learning to align and translate. In *3rd International Conference on Learning Representations, ICLR 2015, San Diego, CA, USA, May 7-9, 2015, Conference Track Proceedings*.

Timothy Baldwin, Marie Catherine de Marneffe, Bo Han, Young-Bum Kim, Alan Ritter, and Wei Xu. 2015. Shared tasks of the 2015 workshop on noisy user-generated text: Twitter lexical normalization and named entity recognition. In *Proceedings of the Workshop on Noisy User-generated Text*, pages 126–135, Beijing, China. Association for Computational Linguistics.

Fabian Barteld. 2017. Detecting spelling variants in non-standard texts. In *Proceedings of the Student Research Workshop at the 15th Conference of the European Chapter of the Association for Computational Linguistics*, pages 11–22, Valencia, Spain. Association for Computational Linguistics.

Joost Bastings, Marco Baroni, Jason Weston, Kyunghyun Cho, and Douwe Kiela. 2018. Jump to better conclusions: SCAN both left and right. In *Proceedings of the 2018 EMNLP Workshop BlackboxNLP: Analyzing and Interpreting Neural Networks for NLP*, pages 47–55, Brussels, Belgium. Association for Computational Linguistics.

Philémon Brakel and Stefan Frank. 2009. Strong systematicity in sentence processing by simple recurrent networks. In *31th Annual Conference of the Cognitive Science Society (COGSCI-2009)*, pages 1599–1604. Cognitive Science Society.

M. Cettolo, J. Niehues, S. Stüker, L. Bentivogli, R. Cattoni, and Marcello Federico. 2015. The iwslt 2015 evaluation campaign. In *IWSLT*.

Mauro Cettolo, Jan Niehues, Sebastian Stüker, Luisa Bentivogli, and Marcello Federico. 2014. Report on the 11th iwslt evaluation campaign, iwslt 2014. In *Proceedings of the International Workshop on Spoken Language Translation, Hanoi, Vietnam*, volume 57.

Rahma Chaabouni, Roberto Dessì, and Eugene Kharitonov. 2021. Can transformers jump around right in natural language? assessing performance transfer from SCAN. In *Proceedings of the Fourth BlackboxNLP Workshop on Analyzing and Interpreting Neural Networks for NLP*, pages 136–148, Punta Cana, Dominican Republic. Association for Computational Linguistics.

Xinyun Chen, Chen Liang, Adams Wei Yu, Dawn Song, and Denny Zhou. 2020. Compositional generalization via neural-symbolic stack machines. In *Advances in Neural Information Processing Systems 33: Annual Conference on Neural Information Processing Systems 2020, NeurIPS 2020, December 6-12, 2020, virtual*.

Noam Chomsky. 1956. Syntactic structures.

Henry Conklin, Bailin Wang, Kenny Smith, and Ivan Titov. 2021. Meta-learning to compositionally generalize. In *Proceedings of the 59th Annual Meeting of the Association for Computational Linguistics and the 11th International Joint Conference on Natural Language Processing (Volume 1: Long Papers)*, pages 3322–3335, Online. Association for Computational Linguistics.

Róbert Csordás, Kazuki Irie, and Jürgen Schmidhuber. 2021. The devil is in the detail: Simple tricks improve systematic generalization of transformers. In *Proc. Conf. on Empirical Methods in Natural Language Processing (EMNLP)*, Punta Cana, Dominican Republic.

Verna Dankers, Elia Bruni, and Dieuwke Hupkes. 2022a. The paradox of the compositionality of natural language: A neural machine translation case study. In *Proceedings of the 60th Annual Meeting of the Association for Computational Linguistics (Volume 1: Long Papers)*, pages 4154–4175, Dublin, Ireland. Association for Computational Linguistics.

Verna Dankers, Christopher Lucas, and Ivan Titov. 2022b. Can transformer be too compositional? analysing idiom processing in neural machine translation. In *Proceedings of the 60th Annual Meeting of the Association for Computational Linguistics (Volume 1: Long Papers)*, pages 3608–3626, Dublin, Ireland. Association for Computational Linguistics.

Sarthak Dash, Md Faisal Mahbub Chowdhury, Alfio Gliozzo, Nandana Mihindukulasooriya, and Nicolas Rodolfo Fauceglia. 2020. Hypernym detection using strict partial order networks. *Proceedings of the AAAI Conference on Artificial Intelligence*, 34(05):7626–7633.

Jacob Devlin, Ming-Wei Chang, Kenton Lee, and Kristina Toutanova. 2019. BERT: Pre-training of deep bidirectional transformers for language understanding. In *Proceedings of the 2019 Conference of the North American Chapter of the Association for Computational Linguistics: Human Language Technologies, Volume 1 (Long and Short Papers)*, pages 4171–4186, Minneapolis, Minnesota. Association for Computational Linguistics.

Catherine Finegan-Dollak, Jonathan K. Kummerfeld, Li Zhang, Karthik Ramanathan, Sesh Sadasivam, Rui Zhang, and Dragomir Radev. 2018. Improving text-to-SQL evaluation methodology. In *Proceedings of the 56th Annual Meeting of the Association for Computational Linguistics (Volume 1: Long Papers)*, pages 351–360, Melbourne, Australia. Association for Computational Linguistics.

Jerry A Fodor and Ernest Lepore. 2002. *The compositionality papers*. Oxford University Press.

Jerry A Fodor and Zenon W Pylyshyn. 1988. Connectionism and cognitive architecture: A critical analysis. *Cognition*, 28(1-2):3–71.

Stefan L Frank, Willem FG Haselager, and Iris van Rooij. 2009. Connectionist semantic systematicity. *Cognition*, 110(3):358–379.

Jonas Gehring, Michael Auli, David Grangier, Denis Yarats, and Yann N Dauphin. 2017. Convolutional sequence to sequence learning. In *International Conference on Machine Learning*, pages 1243–1252. PMLR.

Jonathan Gordon, David Lopez-Paz, Marco Baroni, and Diane Bouchacourt. 2020. Permutation equivariant models for compositional generalization in language. In *International Conference on Learning Representations*.

Robert F Hadley. 1994. Systematicity in connectionist language learning. *Mind & Language*, 9(3):247–272.

Hector Hammerly. 1975. The deduction/induction controversy. *The Modern Language Journal*, 59(1/2):15–18.

Zellig S Harris. 1954. Distributional structure. *Word*, 10(2-3):146–162.

Sepp Hochreiter and Jürgen Schmidhuber. 1997. Long short-term memory. *Neural computation*, 9(8):1735–1780.

Dieuwke Hupkes, Verna Dankers, Mathijs Mul, and Elia Bruni. 2020. Compositionality decomposed: how do neural networks generalise? *Journal of Artificial Intelligence Research*, 67:757–795.

Shaoxiong Ji, Shirui Pan, Erik Cambria, Pekka Marttinen, and Philip S. Yu. 2021. A survey on knowledge graphs: Representation, acquisition, and applications. *IEEE Transactions on Neural Networks and Learning Systems*, pages 1–21.

Yichen Jiang and Mohit Bansal. 2021. Inducing transformer's compositional generalization ability via auxiliary sequence prediction tasks. In *Proceedings of the 2021 Conference on Empirical Methods in Natural Language Processing*, pages 6253–6265, Online and Punta Cana, Dominican Republic. Association for Computational Linguistics.

Daniel Keysers, Nathanael Schärli, Nathan Scales, Hylke Buisman, Daniel Furrer, Sergii Kashubin, Nikola Momchev, Danila Sinopalnikov, Lukasz Stafiniak, Tibor Tihon, Dmitry Tsarkov, Xiao Wang, Marc van Zee, and Olivier Bousquet. 2020. Measuring compositional generalization: A comprehensive method on realistic data. In *International Conference on Learning Representations*.

Najoung Kim and Tal Linzen. 2020. COGS: A compositional generalization challenge based on semantic interpretation. In *Proceedings of the 2020 Conference on Empirical Methods in Natural Language Processing (EMNLP)*, pages 9087–9105, Online. Association for Computational Linguistics.

Yoon Kim. 2021. Sequence-to-sequence learning with latent neural grammars. *Advances in Neural Information Processing Systems*, 34.

Diederik P. Kingma and Jimmy Ba. 2015. Adam: A method for stochastic optimization. In *3rd International Conference on Learning Representations, ICLR 2015, San Diego, CA, USA, May 7-9, 2015, Conference Track Proceedings*.

William Labov. 1963. The social motivation of a sound change. *Word*, 19(3):273–309.

Brenden M Lake. 2019. Compositional generalization through meta sequence-to-sequence learning. In *Advances in Neural Information Processing Systems*, volume 32. Curran Associates, Inc.

Brenden M. Lake and Marco Baroni. 2018. Generalization without systematicity: On the compositional skills of sequence-to-sequence recurrent networks. In *Proceedings of the 35th International Conference on Machine Learning, ICML 2018, Stockholmsmässan, Stockholm, Sweden, July 10-15, 2018*, volume 80 of *Proceedings of Machine Learning Research*, pages 2879–2888. PMLR.

Yafu Li, Yongjing Yin, Yulong Chen, and Yue Zhang. 2021. On compositional generalization of neural machine translation. In *Proceedings of the 59th Annual Meeting of the Association for Computational Linguistics and the 11th International Joint Conference on Natural Language Processing (Volume 1: Long Papers)*, pages 4767–4780, Online. Association for Computational Linguistics.

Yuanpeng Li, Liang Zhao, Jianyu Wang, and Joel Hestness. 2019. Compositional generalization for primitive substitutions. In *Proceedings of the 2019 Conference on Empirical Methods in Natural Language Processing and the 9th International Joint Conference on Natural Language Processing (EMNLP-IJCNLP)*, pages 4293–4302, Hong Kong, China. Association for Computational Linguistics.

Qian Liu, Shengnan An, Jian-Guang Lou, Bei Chen, Zeqi Lin, Yan Gao, Bin Zhou, Nanning Zheng, and Dongmei Zhang. 2020. Compositional generalization by learning analytical expressions. In *Advances in Neural Information Processing Systems*, volume 33, pages 11416–11427. Curran Associates, Inc.

Joao Loula, Marco Baroni, and Brenden Lake. 2018. Rearranging the familiar: Testing compositional generalization in recurrent networks. In *Proceedings of the 2018 EMNLP Workshop BlackboxNLP: Analyzing and Interpreting Neural Networks for NLP*, pages 108–114, Brussels, Belgium. Association for Computational Linguistics.

Thang Luong, Hieu Pham, and Christopher D. Manning. 2015. Effective approaches to attention-based neural machine translation. In *Proceedings of the 2015 Conference on Empirical Methods in Natural Language Processing*, pages 1412–1421, Lisbon, Portugal. Association for Computational Linguistics.

John Lyons and Lyons John. 1995. *Linguistic semantics: An introduction*. Cambridge University Press.

Gary F Marcus. 1998. Rethinking eliminative connectionism. *Cognitive psychology*, 37(3):243–282.

Gary F Marcus. 2018. *The algebraic mind: Integrating connectionism and cognitive science*. MIT press.

Richard E Mayer. 2002. Rote versus meaningful learning. *Theory into practice*, 41(4):226–232.

Tomás Mikolov, Kai Chen, Greg Corrado, and Jeffrey Dean. 2013a. Efficient estimation of word representations in vector space. In *1st International Conference on Learning Representations, ICLR 2013, Scottsdale, Arizona, USA, May 2-4, 2013, Workshop Track Proceedings*.

Tomas Mikolov, Quoc V Le, and Ilya Sutskever. 2013b. Exploiting similarities among languages for machine translation. *arXiv preprint arXiv:1309.4168*.

Richard Montague et al. 1970. Universal grammar. *1974*, pages 222–46.

Sreyashi Nag, Mihir Kale, Varun Lakshminarasimhan, and Swapnil Singhavi. 2020. Incorporating bilingual dictionaries for low resource semi-supervised neural machine translation. In *International Conference on Learning Representations, Learning with Limited Labeled Data*.

Dong Nguyen and Jack Grieve. 2020. Do word embeddings capture spelling variation? In *Proceedings of the 28th International Conference on Computational Linguistics*, pages 870–881, Barcelona, Spain (Online). International Committee on Computational Linguistics.

Maxwell Nye, Armando Solar-Lezama, Josh Tenenbaum, and Brenden M Lake. 2020. Learning compositional rules via neural program synthesis. In *Advances in Neural Information Processing Systems*, volume 33, pages 10832–10842. Curran Associates, Inc.

Peter Akinsola Okebukola and Olugbemiro J Jegede. 1988. Cognitive preference and learning mode as determinants of meaningful learning through concept mapping. *Science Education*, 72(4):489–500.

Inbar Oren, Jonathan Herzig, Nitish Gupta, Matt Gardner, and Jonathan Berant. 2020. Improving compositional generalization in semantic parsing. In *Findings of the Association for Computational Linguistics: EMNLP 2020*, pages 2482–2495, Online. Association for Computational Linguistics.

Myle Ott, Sergey Edunov, Alexei Baevski, Angela Fan, Sam Gross, Nathan Ng, David Grangier, and Michael Auli. 2019. fairseq: A fast, extensible toolkit for sequence modeling. In *Proceedings of NAACL-HLT 2019: Demonstrations*.

Kishore Papineni, Salim Roukos, Todd Ward, and Wei-Jing Zhu. 2002. Bleu: a method for automatic evaluation of machine translation. In *Proceedings of the 40th annual meeting of the Association for Computational Linguistics*, pages 311–318.

Razvan Pascanu, Tomas Mikolov, and Yoshua Bengio. 2013. On the difficulty of training recurrent neural networks. In *Proceedings of the 30th International Conference on International Conference on Machine Learning - Volume 28*, ICML'13, page III–1310–III–1318. JMLR.org.

Arkil Patel, Satwik Bhattamishra, Phil Blunsom, and Navin Goyal. 2022. Revisiting the compositional generalization abilities of neural sequence models. In *Proceedings of the 60th Annual Meeting of the Association for Computational Linguistics (Volume 2: Short Papers)*, pages 424–434, Dublin, Ireland. Association for Computational Linguistics.

Matt Post. 2018. A call for clarity in reporting BLEU scores. In *Proceedings of the Third Conference on Machine Translation: Research Papers*, pages 186–191, Brussels, Belgium. Association for Computational Linguistics.

Lutz Prechelt. 1998. Early stopping-but when? In *Neural Networks: Tricks of the trade*, pages 55–69. Springer.

Herbert Rubenstein and John B. Goodenough. 1965. Contextual correlates of synonymy. *Commun. ACM*, 8(10):627–633.

Mike Schuster and Kuldip K Paliwal. 1997. Bidirectional recurrent neural networks. *IEEE transactions on Signal Processing*, 45(11):2673–2681.

Constance Shaffer. 1989. A comparison of inductive and deductive approaches to teaching foreign languages. *The Modern Language Journal*, 73(4):395–403.

Peter Shaw, Ming-Wei Chang, Panupong Pasupat, and Kristina Toutanova. 2021. Compositional generalization and natural language variation: Can a semantic parsing approach handle both? In *Proceedings of the 59th Annual Meeting of the Association for Computational Linguistics and the 11th International Joint Conference on Natural Language Processing (Volume 1: Long Papers)*, pages 922–938, Online. Association for Computational Linguistics.

Koustuv Sinha, Shagun Sodhani, Jin Dong, Joelle Pineau, and William L. Hamilton. 2019. CLUTRR: A diagnostic benchmark for inductive reasoning from text. In *Proceedings of the 2019 Conference on Empirical Methods in Natural Language Processing and the 9th International Joint Conference on Natural Language Processing (EMNLP-IJCNLP)*, pages 4506–4515, Hong Kong, China. Association for Computational Linguistics.

Iyer Srinivasan, Konstas Ioannis, Cheung Alvin, Krishnamurthy Jayant, and Zettlemoyer Luke. 2017. Learning a neural semantic parser from user feedback. In *Proceedings of the 55th Annual Meeting of the Association for Computational Linguistics (Volume 1: Long Papers)*, pages 963–973.

Nitish Srivastava, Geoffrey Hinton, Alex Krizhevsky, Ilya Sutskever, and Ruslan Salakhutdinov. 2014. Dropout: a simple way to prevent neural networks from overfitting. *The journal of machine learning research*, 15(1):1929–1958.

Maja Stanojević et al. 2009. Cognitive synonymy: A general overview. *FACTA UNIVERSITATIS-Linguistics and Literature*, 7(2):193–200.

Ilya Sutskever, Oriol Vinyals, and Quoc V Le. 2014. Sequence to sequence learning with neural networks. In Z. Ghahramani, M. Welling, C. Cortes, N. D. Lawrence, and K. Q. Weinberger, editors, *Advances in Neural Information Processing Systems 27*, pages 3104–3112. Curran Associates, Inc.

Scott Thornbury. 1999. *How to teach grammar*, volume 3. Longman Harlow.

Ashish Vaswani, Noam Shazeer, Niki Parmar, Jakob Uszkoreit, Llion Jones, Aidan N Gomez, Ł ukasz Kaiser, and Illia Polosukhin. 2017. Attention is all you need. In I. Guyon, U. V. Luxburg, S. Bengio, H. Wallach, R. Fergus, S. Vishwanathan, and R. Garnett, editors, *Advances in Neural Information Processing Systems 30*, pages 5998–6008. Curran Associates, Inc.

Chengyu Wang and Xiaofeng He. 2020. Birre: learning bidirectional residual relation embeddings for supervised hypernymy detection. In *Proceedings of the 58th Annual Meeting of the Association for Computational Linguistics*, pages 3630–3640.

Ronald J Williams and David Zipser. 1989. A learning algorithm for continually running fully recurrent neural networks. *Neural computation*, 1(2):270–280.

Felix Wu, Angela Fan, Alexei Baevski, Yann Dauphin, and Michael Auli. 2019. Pay less attention with lightweight and dynamic convolutions. In *International Conference on Learning Representations*.

Qizhe Xie, Zihang Dai, Eduard H. Hovy, Thang Luong, and Quoc Le. 2020. Unsupervised data augmentation for consistency training. In *Advances in Neural Information Processing Systems*.

Pengcheng Yin, Hao Fang, Graham Neubig, Adam Pauls, Emmanouil Antonios Platanios, Yu Su, Sam Thomson, and Jacob Andreas. 2021. Compositional generalization for neural semantic parsing via span-level supervised attention. In *Proceedings of the 2021 Conference of the North American Chapter of the Association for Computational Linguistics: Human Language Technologies*, pages 2810–2823, Online. Association for Computational Linguistics.

Jiale Yu, Yongliang Shen, Xinyin Ma, Chenghao Jia, Chen Chen, and Weiming Lu. 2020a. Synet: Synonym expansion using transitivity. In *Proceedings of the 2020 Conference on Empirical Methods in Natural Language Processing: Findings*, pages 1961–1970.

Yue Yu, Yinghao Li, Jiaming Shen, Hao Feng, Jimeng Sun, and Chao Zhang. 2020b. Steam: Self-supervised taxonomy expansion with mini-paths. In *Proceedings of the 26th ACM SIGKDD International Conference on Knowledge Discovery & Data Mining*, pages 1026–1035.

John M. Zelle and Raymond J. Mooney. 1996. Learning to parse database queries using inductive logic programming. In *Proceedings of the Thirteenth National Conference on Artificial Intelligence - Volume 2*, pages 1050–1055.

A Semantic Links

Lexical Variant refers to an alternative expression form for the same concept, where the various forms may derive from foreign languages, abbreviations, and even mistakes. A basic assumption is that all languages change over time due to non-linguistic factors. Since the rise of sociolinguistics in the 1960s, studies on linguistic variability, a characteristic of language, are central to the language use and motivations for speakers to vary the pronunciation, word choice, or morphology of existing concepts (Labov, 1963). Taking "*United States of America*" as an example, people have generally accepted the semantic connections among its lexical variants in history, including "*America*" and "*United States*", as well as the initialisms "*U.S.*" and "*U.S.A*". Many efforts have been devoted on lexical variants representation (Nguyen and Grieve, 2020), detection (Barteld, 2017), normalization (Baldwin et al., 2015) to keep machines up with the trend of the times.

Co-hyponym is a linguistic term to designate a semantic relation between two group members belonging to the same broader class, where each member is a hyponym, also called subtype or subordinate, and the class is a hypernym (Lyons and John, 1995). The "is-a" hypernymy relation between a generic hypernym and its specific hyponyms builds semantic connections among co-hyponyms. An example of such a hierarchical structure can be "*Mississippi*" and "*California*" in the domain of "*state*". Specifically, "*Mississippi*" and "*California*" are two hyponyms, and "*state*" is a hypernym. Thus, "*Mississippi*" and "*California*" are semantically connected to be co-hyponyms for each other. Harvesting hypernymy relations (Wang and He, 2020) plays an essential role for downstream knowledge graph construction (Ji et al., 2021), out-vocabulary generalization (Dash et al., 2020), and taxonomy expansion (Yu et al., 2020b).

Synonym stands for a word, morpheme, or phrase that shares exactly or nearly the same semantics with another one. Many tend to assume synonyms are utterances that occur in most contexts in common, so they are semantically closely related enough to be synonyms for each other (Rubenstein and Goodenough, 1965; Harris, 1954). The existence of the association to contexts is a basic assumption supporting the advance of recent masked language modeling (Devlin et al., 2019). Given that, one of the definitions of a synonymous relation is a semantic link between two expressions if substitution of one for the other never hurts the true value of the context (Stanojević et al., 2009). For instance, the substitution of "*heavily populated*" for "*populous*" will seldom alter the truth of the sentence in Figure 2. Such semantic similarity can be observed in continuous vector space from a trained representation as well (Mikolov et al., 2013a). Synonym discovery (Yu et al., 2020a) has been a fundamental job to construct knowledge base and thus benefits substantial researches.

B Models

All models are built within the encoder-decoder framework (Sutskever et al., 2014). We reproduce RNN, CNN, and TFM by ourselves to have fewer parameters than the original versions for the experimental purposes. The dropout rate is 0.5 for RNN, CNN, and TFM (Srivastava et al., 2014). We implement LSTM, Transformer, and Dynamic Conv. within the library *fairseq*.[7] (Ott et al., 2019) and inherit its default model structures.[8] In contrast to early stopping (Prechelt, 1998), we prefer a fixed training regime sufficient enough for models to fully converge in practice with a focus on the systematic generalization observation instead of superior structure exploration. Training is on a single Nvidia Tesla V100. Without specific notes, hyperparameters are shared throughout the work.

RNN denotes bi-directional recurrent network (Schuster and Paliwal, 1997; Hochreiter and Schmidhuber, 1997) with long short-term memory

[7] `https://github.com/pytorch/fairseq`

[8] LSTM is adapted from *lstm_luong_wmt_en_de*; Transformer is adapted from *transformer_iwslt_de_en*; Dynamic Conv. is adapted from *lightconv_iwslt_de_en*.

Data	Sequence	
SCAN	Source	*jump twice*
	Target	JUMP JUMP
GEO	Source	*how many people in new york city*
	Target	SELECT CITY alias0 . POPULATION FROM CITY AS CITY alias0 WHERE CITY alias0 . CITY_NAME = CITY_NAME ;
ADV	Source	*Which department includes a history of american film ?*
	Target	SELECT DISTINCT COURSE alias0 . DEPARTMENT FROM COURSE AS COURSE alias0 WHERE COURSE alias0 . NAME LIKE TOPIC ;
Geography	Source	*how many people live in new york*
	Target	SELECT STATE alias0 . POPULATION FROM STATE AS STATE alias0 WHERE STATE alias0 . STATE_NAME = " new york " ;
Advising	Source	*I would like to see A History of American Film courses of 2 credits .*
	Target	SELECT DISTINCT COURSE alias0 . DEPARTMENT , COURSE alias0 . NAME , COURSE alias0 . NUMBER FROM COURSE AS COURSE alias0 WHERE (COURSE alias0 . DESCRIPTION LIKE "% A History of American Film %" OR COURSE alias0 . NAME LIKE "% A History of American Film %") AND COURSE alias0 . CREDITS = 2 ;

Table 6: Example source and target sequences from SCAN, GEO, ADV, Geography, and Advising.

Data	Primitive	Semantic Links	Variant	Concept Rule	
				Primitive Rule	Variant Rule
SCAN	*jump*	Lexical Variant	*jump_0*	*jump* → JUMP	*jump_0* → JUMP
	look		*look_0*	*look* → LOOK	*look_0* → LOOK
	run		*run_0*	*run* → RUN	*run_0* → RUN
	walk		*walk_0*	*walk* → WALK	*walk_0* → WALK
GEO	*new york city*	Co-hyponym	*houston city*	*new york city* → CITY_NAME	*houston city* → CITY_NAME
	mississippi rivier		*red rivier*	*mississippi rivier* → RIVER_NAME	*red rivier* → RIVER_NAME
	dc		*kansas*	*dc* → STATE_NAME	*kansas* → STATE_NAME
	dover		*salem*	*dover* → CAPITAL_NAME	*salem* → CAPITAL_NAME
ADV	*a history of american film*	Co-hyponym	*advanced ai techniques*	*a history of american film* → TOPIC	*advanced ai techniques* → TOPIC
	aaron magid		*cargo*	*aaron magid* → INSTRUCTOR	*cargo* → INSTRUCTOR
	aaptis		*survmeth*	*aaptis* → DEPARTMENT	*survmeth* → DEPARTMENT
	100		*171*	*100* → NUMBER	*171* → NUMBER

Table 7: Concept rules with primitives and their example variants.

units and an attention mechanism (Bahdanau et al., 2015). Its encoder consists of two layers with a hidden size of 256 in each direction, and its decoder has one layer with a hidden size of 512. The embedding size is 512 for both encoder and decoder. There are a total of $5.29M$ trainable parameters. Teacher forcing with a rate of 0.5 serves to spur up the training process (Williams and Zipser, 1989).
CNN denotes the fully convolutional seq2seq network (Gehring et al., 2017). The size of the position embedding layer is 128 for encoding and 256 for decoding, while that of the token embedding layer is 512 for both encoding and decoding. There are 10 convolutional layers with 512 as the hidden size and 3 as the kernel size in both encoder and decoder, resulting in a total of $33.55M$ trainable parameters.
TFM denotes transformers, an attention-based network (Vaswani et al., 2017). As a tiny version, TFM has 2 layers for each encoder and decoder with 8 attention heads and a dimension of 512. The size of the feedforward layer is 2048. We utilize the cyclic nature of sin and cos functions to represent token positions. There are a total of $15.02M$ trainable parameters.
LSTM is adapted from the recurrent network used by Luong et al. (2015) for statistical MT. The size of the embedding layer is 1000. There are 4 layers in both encoder and decoder with a hidden size of 512 and a dropout rate of 0.2.
Transformer, the same as TFM, is adapted from the base version of transformers in the work of Vaswani et al. (2017), while TFM is a tiny version to test systematic generalization. The dimension is 512 for the embedding layer, 1024 for the feedforward layer, and 512 for the attention layer. There are 6 attention blocks in both encoder and decoder with 4 attention heads and 0.3 dropout probability.
Dynamic Conv. is adapted from the seq2seq convolutional network proposed by Wu et al. (2019), where the hidden size of the embedding layer, encoder layer, and decoder layer is 512. The number of attention heads is 4, and the dimension of the feedforward layer is 1024 for both encoder and encoder. There are 6 layers in the encoder and 7 layers in the decoder. The dropout rate is 0.1 for both attention and weight units.

C Data

IWSLT involves IWSLT'14 (Cettolo et al., 2014) English-German (En-De) and German-English (De-En), IWSLT'15 (Cettolo et al., 2015) English-French (En-Fr) and French-English (Fr-En) translation tasks. The goal is to translate a sen-

Data	Primitive	Variant	#Variants	Prompt
SCAN	*jump*	*jump_0*	10	*[concept] twice*
GEO	*new york city*	*houston city*	39	*how many people in [concept]*
	mississippi rivier	*red rivier*	9	*how long is [concept]*
	dc	*kansas*	49	*where is [concept]*
	dover	*salem*	8	*what states capital is [concept]*
ADV	*a history of american film*	*advanced ai techniques*	5/424	*who teaches [concept] ?*
	aaron magid	*cargo*	5/492	*does [concept] give upper-level courses ?*
	aaptis	*survmeth*	5/1720	*name core courses for [concept] .*
	100	*171*	5/1895	*can undergrads take [concept] ?*

Table 8: Prompts with example primitives and sampled variants. In SCAN, primitives share the same prompt and the number of variants can be changed. In GEO, we make use of the full variants set. In ADV, we randomly sample 5 variants for each source sequence so that we cover all the variants with a test set of an appropriate size. We generate variant samples by filling the prompt with variants accordingly.

Data	SCAN					GEO					ADV					Geography		Advising	
	Exp. 1			Exp. 2		Exp. 1			Exp. 2		Exp. 1			Exp. 2		Bas.	Aug.	Bas.	Aug.
	Sta.	Dif.	Cha.	Sta.	Dif.	Sta.	Dif.	Cha.	Sta.	Dif.	Sta.	Dif.	Cha.	Sta.	Dif.				
Train Size	20946	20942	20928	20950	20946	724	720	711	728	724	6038	6034	5969	6040	6036	598	701	3814	5660
Test Size	308240	308240	308240	308240	308240	21350	21350	21350	21350	21350	107614	107614	107614	107614	107614	279	279	573	573
Time RNN			21					5					19			4	5	27	35
Time CNN			17					1.2					11			1	1.2	12	19
Time TFM			7					0.5					5			0.4	0.5	6	8

Table 9: Data statistics and training time per epoch in seconds. The batch size of each epoch for GEO and Geography is 32, and that for the others is 128.

tence from one language to the other. The IWSLT'14 En-De and De-EN have 160,239 sequence pairs for training and 7,283 for validation. We make use of IWSLT14.TED.dev{2010, 2012} and IWSLT14.TED.tst{2010, 2011, 2012} to measure translation performance, resulting in a total of 6,750 test samples. In terms of IWSLT'15 En-Fr and Fr-En, there are 205,572 sequence pairs for training. We employ IWSLT15.TED.dev2010 and IWSLT15.TED.tst{2010, 2011, 2012, 2013} as the validation set and IWSLT15.tst{2014, 2015} as the test set. As a consequence, there are 5,519 samples for validation and 2,385 for evaluation. For all four translation tasks, we apply BPE with 10K tokens to share.

D Experiments

D.1 Inductive learning

Semantic linking can be operated via inductive learning, where we replace the concept in the prompt with primitives and their variants. The learning rate to train CNN in GEO is changed to $5e^{-4}$. Prompts used in SCAN, GEO, and ADV are expressed in Table 8. Detailed experimental results with respect to three levels can be found in Table 10, Table 11, and Table 12.

D.2 Deductive learning

Semantic linking can be established via deductive learning, where we put concept rules without context information in the training set instead of specific sequence samples. Example concept rules for SCAN, GEO, and ADV are presented in Table 7. Detailed experimental results with respect to two levels can be found in Table 13 and Table 14.

D.3 Sensitivity analysis

In sensitivity analysis, we adjust the number of primitives (#primitives) and the number of variants per primitive (#variants) over RNN on SCAN. The complete versions of Figure 4 in Section 3.5 are presented as Figure 5 and Figure 6 for #primitives and #variants respectively.

Data	Model	Train			Test		
		Loss	Token Acc.%	Seq. Acc.%	Loss	Token Acc.%	Seq. Acc.%
SCAN	RNN	0.00 ± 0.00	100.00 ± 0.00	99.99 ± 0.02	0.00 ± 0.00	99.99 ± 0.03	99.95 ± 0.08
	CNN	0.00 ± 0.00	99.81 ± 0.09	98.78 ± 0.55	0.00 ± 0.00	99.96 ± 0.08	99.85 ± 0.34
	TFM	0.00 ± 0.00	99.82 ± 0.02	98.83 ± 0.12	0.06 ± 0.03	98.91 ± 0.78	97.35 ± 1.62
GEO	RNN	0.15 ± 0.02	97.73 ± 0.42	80.25 ± 2.81	1.36 ± 0.48	75.71 ± 8.42	44.95 ± 14.69
	CNN	0.07 ± 0.01	98.23 ± 0.39	76.80 ± 2.25	9.01 ± 4.26	87.99 ± 2.67	69.46 ± 5.78
	TFM	0.02 ± 0.00	99.63 ± 0.07	91.60 ± 1.41	4.55 ± 1.39	75.37 ± 7.84	45.93 ± 12.42
ADV	RNN	0.03 ± 0.01	99.40 ± 0.13	82.74 ± 2.78	6.04 ± 0.95	58.61 ± 6.18	36.18 ± 5.75
	CNN	0.01 ± 0.01	99.59 ± 0.07	85.13 ± 1.95	23.56 ± 4.95	57.83 ± 7.55	45.08 ± 9.32
	TFM	0.00 ± 0.00	99.92 ± 0.01	96.14 ± 0.28	15.12 ± 1.00	53.43 ± 2.80	42.59 ± 3.65

Table 10: Results of Standard inductive learning.

Data	Model	Train			Test		
		Loss	Token Acc.%	Seq. Acc.%	Loss	Token Acc.%	Seq. Acc.%
SCAN	RNN	0.00 ± 0.00	100.00 ± 0.00	99.99 ± 0.01	0.00 ± 0.00	99.96 ± 0.02	99.85 ± 0.08
	CNN	0.00 ± 0.00	99.77 ± 0.19	98.62 ± 1.13	0.03 ± 0.06	99.76 ± 0.54	99.52 ± 1.07
	TFM	0.00 ± 0.00	99.79 ± 0.03	98.59 ± 0.12	0.06 ± 0.03	98.90 ± 1.10	96.86 ± 2.64
GEO	RNN	0.16 ± 0.03	97.39 ± 0.67	78.33 ± 4.31	1.29 ± 0.27	75.69 ± 6.12	43.27 ± 13.47
	CNN	0.07 ± 0.01	98.25 ± 0.13	76.53 ± 1.68	13.87 ± 3.19	79.51 ± 6.03	51.20 ± 8.64
	TFM	0.00 ± 0.11	99.60 ± 0.11	91.33 ± 1.46	4.50 ± 0.80	75.11 ± 4.88	44.59 ± 9.76
ADV	RNN	0.03 ± 0.01	99.26 ± 0.21	79.57 ± 4.12	5.80 ± 0.92	59.74 ± 5.67	35.69 ± 6.05
	CNN	0.02 ± 0.00	99.56 ± 0.05	84.06 ± 1.57	24.58 ± 3.40	54.05 ± 5.74	42.14 ± 6.90
	TFM	0.00 ± 0.00	99.91 ± 0.01	95.88 ± 0.23	15.84 ± 1.51	51.51 ± 4.50	41.28 ± 4.35

Table 11: Results of Difficult inductive learning.

Data	Model	Train			Test		
		Loss	Token Acc.%	Seq. Acc.%	Loss	Token Acc.%	Seq. Acc.%
SCAN	RNN	0.00 ± 0.00	100.00 ± 0.00	99.99 ± 0.02	0.20 ± 0.45	99.95 ± 0.08	99.80 ± 0.31
	CNN	0.00 ± 0.00	99.85 ± 0.05	99.00 ± 0.30	0.14 ± 0.31	98.89 ± 2.44	97.57 ± 5.24
	TFM	0.00 ± 0.00	99.82 ± 0.05	98.85 ± 0.27	0.07 ± 0.05	98.76 ± 0.85	96.38 ± 2.81
GEO	RNN	0.15 ± 0.04	97.76 ± 0.74	79.77 ± 4.19	1.52 ± 0.29	73.46 ± 3.05	36.77 ± 5.60
	CNN	0.07 ± 0.01	98.23 ± 0.17	75.98 ± 1.46	15.83 ± 4.56	77.40 ± 2.48	48.53 ± 3.40
	TFM	0.02 ± 0.00	99.60 ± 0.06	91.00 ± 1.20	6.01 ± 1.03	68.41 ± 4.76	36.93 ± 7.47
ADV	RNN	0.03 ± 0.01	99.23 ± 0.13	79.90 ± 1.85	5.95 ± 0.90	58.11 ± 5.82	35.45 ± 6.69
	CNN	0.01 ± 0.01	99.68 ± 0.15	87.90 ± 5.05	23.08 ± 6.34	53.66 ± 2.57	41.37 ± 4.04
	TFM	0.00 ± 0.00	99.93 ± 0.01	96.41 ± 0.24	16.59 ± 0.98	49.17 ± 2.58	38.88 ± 2.68

Table 12: Results of Challenging inductive learning.

Data	Model	Train			Test		
		Loss	Token Acc.%	Seq. Acc.%	Loss	Token Acc.%	Seq. Acc.%
SCAN	RNN	0.00 ± 0.00	99.99 ± 0.03	99.90 ± 0.23	0.05 ± 0.06	99.48 ± 0.71	98.27 ± 2.38
	CNN	0.00 ± 0.00	99.79 ± 0.14	98.78 ± 0.79	0.00 ± 0.00	99.99 ± 0.01	99.96 ± 0.03
	TFM	0.00 ± 0.00	99.82 ± 0.03	98.78 ± 0.17	0.27 ± 0.22	96.90 ± 1.78	91.94 ± 4.04
GEO	RNN	0.17 ± 0.03	97.50 ± 0.30	78.54 ± 2.16	2.83 ± 0.69	54.44 ± 7.15	13.61 ± 7.08
	CNN	0.08 ± 0.01	97.97 ± 0.24	77.03 ± 1.42	51.08 ± 25.97	41.86 ± 3.38	4.85 ± 4.66
	TFM	0.02 ± 0.00	99.54 ± 0.31	91.82 ± 2.27	6.03 ± 1.56	67.02 ± 6.91	36.38 ± 10.08
ADV	RNN	0.08 ± 0.02	98.64 ± 0.31	68.84 ± 4.57	7.95 ± 1.13	36.50 ± 7.66	12.84 ± 4.31
	CNN	0.02 ± 0.00	99.53 ± 0.07	84.64 ± 1.20	31.12 ± 4.76	43.51 ± 11.31	32.33 ± 12.93
	TFM	0.00 ± 0.00	99.91 ± 0.02	96.33 ± 0.37	13.72 ± 1.41	56.82 ± 3.79	47.43 ± 3.71

Table 13: Results of Standard deductive learning.

Data	Model	Train			Test		
		Loss	Token Acc.%	Seq. Acc.%	Loss	Token Acc.%	Seq. Acc.%
SCAN	RNN	0.00 ± 0.00	99.99 ± 0.01	99.95 ± 0.07	0.08 ± 0.08	98.70 ± 0.92	95.39 ± 2.72
	CNN	0.00 ± 0.00	99.62 ± 0.34	98.82 ± 1.09	0.13 ± 0.29	98.59 ± 3.10	96.66 ± 7.27
	TFM	0.00 ± 0.00	99.82 ± 0.03	98.78 ± 0.12	0.21 ± 0.20	96.68 ± 2.21	91.26 ± 5.80
GEO	RNN	0.20 ± 0.03	96.93 ± 0.71	75.35 ± 3.57	4.40 ± 2.50	39.71 ± 18.38	7.67 ± 5.34
	CNN	0.08 ± 0.01	97.77 ± 0.76	76.41 ± 2.80	32.94 ± 4.26	41.07 ± 7.48	4.04 ± 2.18
	TFM	0.02 ± 0.00	99.56 ± 0.11	91.08 ± 1.56	5.97 ± 1.05	65.97 ± 5.17	31.57 ± 7.42
ADV	RNN	0.08 ± 0.02	98.54 ± 0.28	67.10 ± 3.45	7.87 ± 1.01	36.42 ± 7.39	12.66 ± 5.19
	CNN	0.04 ± 0.05	98.78 ± 1.91	77.14 ± 23.28	32.44 ± 6.07	35.34 ± 14.68	23.58 ± 16.04
	TFM	0.00 ± 0.00	99.92 ± 0.02	96.41 ± 0.26	14.92 ± 1.31	53.33 ± 3.85	43.24 ± 5.14

Table 14: Results of Difficult deductive learning.

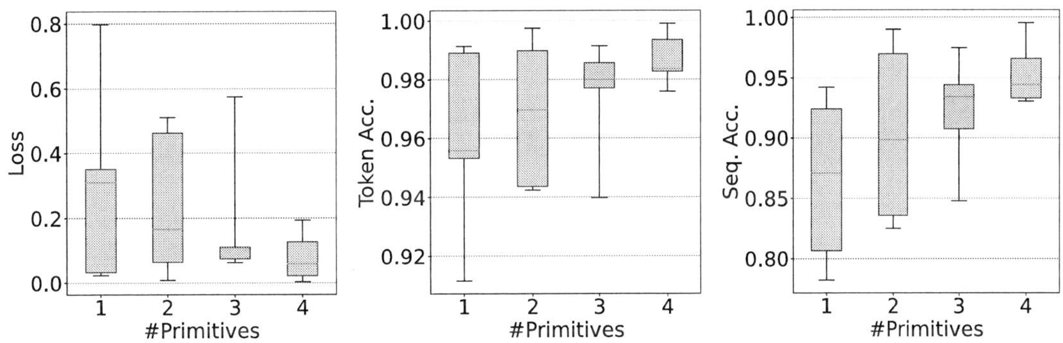

Figure 5: The complete version of Figure 4 in Section 3.5 regarding #primitives.

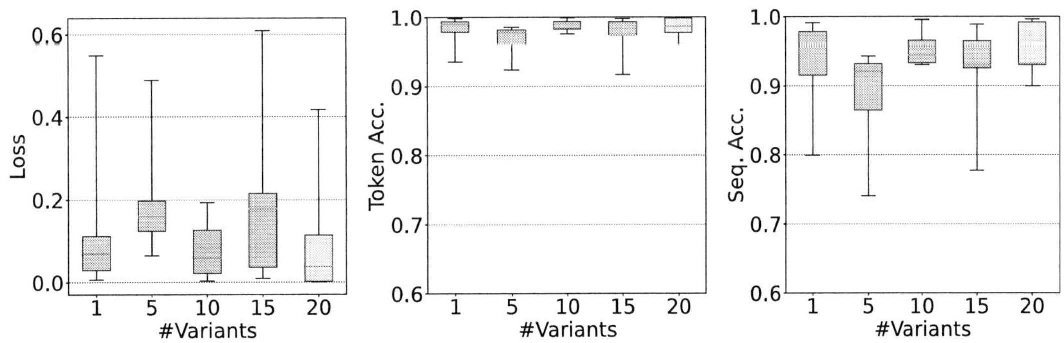

Figure 6: The complete version of Figure 4 in Section 3.5 regarding #variants.

Is It Smaller Than a Tennis Ball?
Language Models Play the Game of Twenty Questions

Maxime De Bruyn, Ehsan Lotfi, Jeska Buhmann, Walter Daelemans
CLiPS Research Center
University of Antwerp, Belgium
maxime.debruyn@uantwerpen.be

Abstract

Researchers often use games to analyze the abilities of Artificial Intelligence models. In this work, we use the game of Twenty Questions to study the world knowledge of language models. Despite its simplicity for humans, this game requires a broad knowledge of the world to answer yes/no questions. We evaluate several language models on this task and find that only the largest model has enough world knowledge to play it well, although it still has difficulties with the shape and size of objects. We also present a new method to improve the knowledge of smaller models by leveraging external information from the web. Finally, we release our dataset and Twentle, a website to interactively test the knowledge of language models by playing Twenty Questions.

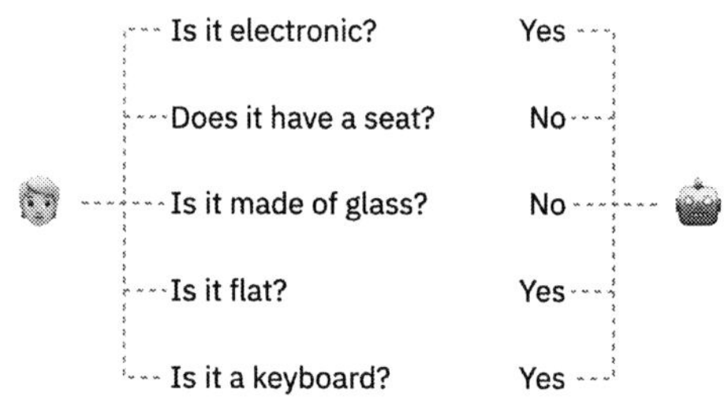

Figure 1: Example Twenty Questions game: a human must discover the hidden entity (a keyboard) by asking yes/no questions to the language model. In this case, the model needs to know about the shape, composition, and purpose of a keyboard to correctly answer all questions. While trivial for humans, our results show that this is not the case for most language models, except for GPT-3, which displays fantastic world knowledge on all questions except size-related questions.

1 Introduction

Generative language models achieve strong performance on multiple NLP tasks by using an unsupervised training objective: predicting the next token in a string of text (Brown et al., 2020; Chowdhery et al., 2022; Zhang et al., 2022).

Despite the simple training objective, these models capture a significant amount of world knowledge (Roberts et al., 2020; Jiang et al., 2020; Talmor et al., 2020). However, we can quickly uncover some limitations by asking simple questions. For example, GPT-3 (Brown et al., 2020) is more likely to complete the following sentence *question: is a kettle smaller than a tennis ball? answer:* ___ with *yes* than *no*. While trivial for a human, GPT-3 has trouble comparing the size of a kettle and a tennis ball.

We can use the *let's think step by step* method to look into the chain of reasoning of GPT-3 (Kojima et al., 2022): *question: is a kettle smaller than a tennis ball? answer: let's think step by step. [...] a tennis ball is about 6 inches in diameter [...] a typical kettle is about 8-10 inches tall and has a diameter of about 4-5 inches. So, a kettle is smaller than a tennis ball.* According to this example, GPT-3 predicts that a tennis ball is twice its actual size, leading to the wrong conclusion that a kettle is smaller than a tennis ball.

In this work, we try to analyze the world knowledge of language models through the game of Twenty Questions. We collected a dataset of 2000+ questions and tried to understand the strength and weaknesses of language models by classifying questions into nine categories of knowledge (usage, size & shape, appearance).

Our results show that GPT-3, a 175 billion parameters language model, can play Twenty Questions thanks to a consistent world knowledge on all categories identified, except for size & shape questions (e.g., *is it bigger than a foot*). Unfortunately, we also show that smaller models do not display the same consistency. However, leveraging the web improved the knowledgeability of T0 by 10% and brought it to a level competitive with GPT-3, despite having 16 times fewer parameters.

Proceedings of the Fifth BlackboxNLP Workshop on Analyzing and Interpreting Neural Networks for NLP, pages 80 - 90
December 8, 2022

Our contributions are the following:

- We release the first dataset consisting of Twenty Questions games.
- We show that very large language models have a consistent world knowledge, while smaller models do not.
- We provide a method to improve the knowledgeability of smaller models using background information from the web.

We publicly release our dataset on HuggingFace (Wolf et al., 2020).[1] We also present *Twentle*, a website to interactively test the world knowledge of language model by playing the game of Twenty Questions.

2 Related Work

Although analyzing the capabilities of language models through the game of Twenty Questions is new, researching the amount of general knowledge and common sense of language models is not.

Unfortunately, the knowledge stored by language models is not symbolic. Therefore, we cannot look into the model and inspect its knowledge. Instead, previous work relied on multiple proxy tasks.

One option is to use regular reading comprehension datasets in a closed-book format. Roberts et al. (2020) follow this approach. They evaluate how much knowledge can be stored inside the weights of a text-to-text T5 model (Raffel et al., 2020). The authors repurposed three reading comprehension datasets to closed-book question answering: Web Questions (Berant et al., 2013), Trivia QA (Joshi et al., 2017) and Natural Questions (Kwiatkowski et al., 2019). They concluded that T5 performs on par with specialized machine comprehension models. GPT-3 (Brown et al., 2020) was also evaluated on the same closed-book question-answering datasets. The largest model (175B parameters) achieved state-of-the-art results on TriviaQA despite not being trained for the task.

Unfortunately, it has been demonstrated later by Lewis et al. (2021) that the datasets used by Roberts et al. (2020) and Brown et al. (2020) suffer from a considerable overlap between the training and test set, invalidating the authors' conclusion based on these datasets. Furthermore, when the overlap between the training and test set is removed, the performance of BART (Lewis et al., 2020a) diminishes from 26.7% to 0.8% on TriviaQA (Joshi et al., 2017), suggesting that the model is unable to generalize to previously unseen questions.

To overcome the previously mentioned overlap problem, Wang et al. (2021) repurposed SQuAD (Rajpurkar et al., 2016), a popular reading comprehension dataset, as a closed-book question answering dataset. They evaluated the performance of BART on this new dataset and concluded that it was still challenging for generative models to perform closed-book question answering.

Another approach is to look at how a language model fills in blanks (i.e., masking). One can estimate what the language model knows by carefully analyzing the model's suggestion. This is the approach followed by Petroni et al. (2019). The authors introduce a new dataset LAMA to test the factual and commonsense knowledge in language models. It provides a set of cloze tasks, e.g., *ravens can* _____ with the associated answer *fly*.

The *oLMpic Games* (Talmor et al., 2020) tests the symbolic reasoning of language models through eight synthetic tasks. While very similar to our work, the dataset uses masking to probe the language model. Mask tokens are only applicable to encoder language models, while we are interested in generative language models.

Previous studies have shown that providing generative language models with background information improves their performance. (Borgeaud et al., 2021; Lewis et al., 2020b; Komeili et al., 2022; De Bruyn et al., 2020; Lazaridou et al., 2022) Similar to Lazaridou et al. (2022), we find that including external knowledge improves the language model's performance, however, we obtain better results by restricting the source of knowledge to Wikipedia instead of the entire Internet.

To summarize, we are the first to analyze the world knowledge of generative language models through the game of Twenty Questions. We depart from the work of Roberts et al. (2020) and Wang et al. (2021) in several ways. First, we only have yes/no answers, which simplifies the evaluation and removes the surface-form problem (Holtzman et al., 2021). Second, using generic questions allows disentangling the understanding of the object and the question.

[1] https://huggingface.co/datasets/maximedb/twentle

	Twenty Questions
Questions	2,832
Generic questions	915
Entities	126
Words (per question)	6.8
Yes	35%
No	65%

Table 1: Summary of the Twenty Questions dataset. We collected 2,832 questions from 126 different entities. We make the distinction between generic and regular questions. Generic questions refer to the entity as "it" (e.g. does it [a rake] have a seat). Generic questions are asked multiple times over different entities (on average 3). We use this unique feature to disentangle the understanding of the question and the entity.

3 Data

This section presents our dataset based on the Twenty Questions game — the first boolean closed-book question answering dataset regarding world and commonsense knowledge. We start this section by introducing the Twenty Questions game. We then explain our data collection process. Finally, we analyze the type of knowledge required to perform well on this dataset.

3.1 Twenty Questions Game

Wikipedia describes Twenty Questions as a spoken parlor game that encourages deductive reasoning and creativity. In the traditional game, one player (the answerer) chooses a subject and does not reveal it. The other players are questioners and must find the hidden entity by asking yes/no questions.

Previous research focused on playing the questioner (Hu et al., 2018; Chen et al., 2018), however, we are interested in the role of the answerer — the player responsible for answering the yes/no questions using his knowledge of the world. According to our research, this is the first attempt at playing the role of the answerer.

3.2 Akinator

Instead of organizing games using Amazon Mechanical Turk, we used Akinator[2] to collect many questions. Akinator is an online game where users can play games of Twenty Questions against a probabilistic model.

Users first pick an entity (without revealing it), and Akinator will then ask yes/no questions to find the hidden entity. It can guess animals, objects, or characters. The player can answer with 5 possible options: *yes*, *no*, *probably yes*, *probably not*, and *don't know*. Although the original Twenty Questions game used a maximum of 20 questions, Akinator will ask questions until it finds the correct entity. We provide examples of questions and entities in Table 2. We were pleasantly surprised by the quality of the Akinator model. It was able to find our hidden entities in most instances. We removed questions from the few instances where it was not capable of finding the correct entity.

3.2.1 Generic Questions

Akinator does not know the entity when asking the question and refers to the entity using *"it"*. Because of its probabilistic nature, Akinator will likely ask the same generic question for multiple entities. We list the most common generic questions in Table 3. For example *is a rake bigger than a foot* and *is a tennis ball bigger than a foot* are two different questions but share the same generic question *is it bigger than a foot*. The average generic question (e.g., *is it bigger than a foot*) is asked for three different entities. However, the distribution is highly skewed, with many specific questions asked only once.

3.2.2 Choice of Entities

We restricted our choice of entities to objects, as we think characters and animals are too culture-dependent to be deemed general knowledge. As much as possible, we tried to choose objects which are not specific to a particular place or culture.

3.2.3 Post-processing

As we are interested in yes/no questions, we remove all questions with *probably yes*, *probably not*, or *don't know* as answer. We use simple regex rules to inject entities into generic questions. We removed all questions about sex or the user's personal experience (e.g., *do you have one at home?*) as these require personal knowledge.

3.3 Knowledge Category

In order to understand the reasoning abilities of the language model, we need to understand the type of knowledge required to answer each question correctly.

After carefully reviewing the questions in our dataset, we classified each question into one of the following nine categories: usage, size & shape,

[2]https://akinator.com/

Generic Question	Entity	Answer
Is it bigger than a foot?	Padlock	No
Does it work with electricity?	Magnifying glass	No
Does it have a seat?	Forklift	Yes
Does it work with the feet?	Lawn mowner	No
Can it be made of wood?	Rake	Yes
Is it mostly for girls?	Belt	No
Does it have a relationship with school?	Wallet	No
Can it be read?	Worldmap	Yes
Is it made of rubber?	Balloon	Yes
Is it bigger than a foot?	Saw	Yes

Table 2: Example questions in our dataset. Akinator does not know the entity when asking the question, and refers to the entity using "it". To avoid any bias toward a specific culture we only used well-known objects as hidden entities. We did not use animals or characters.

Question	Entities
Is it bigger than a foot?	68
Does it go into the mouth?	67
Is it something we wear?	56
Can we buy it?	55
Is it a toy?	50
Is it made of metal?	48
Is it soft?	45
Can it be opened or closed?	42
Is it electronic?	34
Can it be found in a kitchen?	31

Table 3: Most common generic questions in the dataset.

location, composition, description, relatedness, appearance, functioning, and purpose. Finally, we provide an overview with examples in Table 4.

Shape and Size To answer this kind of question, the model should understand an object's shape and be able to compare it with others. For example, *is it bigger than a foot?*

Usage The model should know how an object is used in everyday life to answer these questions. For example, the model should know that a question like *is it something we wear?* applies to a pair of sunglasses, but not a forklift.

Location The model must know in which place or circumstances an object is used. For example, *can we find it in a bathroom* or, *is it outside*.

Composition These questions require knowing the composition of an object. For example, *is it liquid*, or *is it made of glass*.

Description The model should know how humans describe this object with adjectives. For example, *is it heavy*, or *is it sticky*.

Relatedness To answer these questions, the model must be able to relate two categories of objects or concepts together. For example, *does it have a relation with water*, or *is it a toy*.

Functioning These questions require knowing how an object works. This category is broad and includes questions such as *can it be opened or closed*, or *does it work with electricity*.

Appearance This category is related to the description category but focuses on how an object looks. For example, it includes questions such as *does it have a seat*, or *does it have eyes*.

Purpose This kind of question focuses on the purpose of objects. It is related to the usage category but focuses on why we use objects instead of how. It includes questions like *is it useful to sleep*, or *do we use it for travel*.

3.4 Human Agreement

Answering yes/no question is not always straightforward. A single question can be approached in multiple ways. For example, some people answer the question, " *is a DVD smaller than a tennis ball* with yes because the height of a DVD is smaller than that of a tennis ball, while others look at the diameter and answer *no*. We asked four annotators to answer 100 randomly sampled questions. On average, they share the same answer as the one in the dataset 94% of the time. The inter-annotator agreement is good, with a Cohen's Kappa score of 0.76 (Cohen, 1968).

Object Knowledge	Example Question	Percentage
Shape and Size	Is it bigger than a foot? Is it flat?	12.7
Usage	Is it something we wear? Do we use it for a sport?	15.5
Location	Can it be found in houses? Is it outside?	10.9
Composition	Is it liquid? Is it made of glass?	7.8
Description	Is it heavy? Is it sticky?	7.1
Relatedness	Does it have a relation with water? Is it a toy?	14.5
Functioning	Does it work with electricity? Can it be opened or closed?	14.8
Appearance	Does it have eyes? Does it have a seat?	6.9
Purpose	Is it useful to sleep? Do we use it for travel?	7.4

Table 4: We classified each question of the dataset into nine categories depending on the type of knowledge required to answer the question.

4 Language Models

In this section, we review the subjects of this work: generative language models. Language models come in all forms and shapes. However, we focus on two types: encoder-decoder and decoder-only models.

4.1 Encoder-Decoder Models

Encoder-decoder models treat every NLP task as a text-to-text problem using an encoder-decoder Transformer. When this framework is applied to question answering, the model is trained to generate the literal text of the answer in a free-form fashion (Roberts et al., 2020).

T5 is a text-to-text model pre-trained on multiple tasks simultaneously: translation, summarization, classification, reading comprehension, and an unsupervised span corruption task (Raffel et al., 2020). We experiment with the 11 billion parameters version.

T0 further trains T5 on 1700 English datasets (Sanh et al., 2022). The resulting model outperforms GPT-3 (Brown et al., 2020) on several tasks despite being 16x smaller. We use the T0pp version with 11 billion parameters. Conveniently, T0 has already been pre-trained on BoolQ (Clark et al., 2019), a reading comprehension dataset with boolean answers.

4.2 Decoder Models

Decoder models use the decoder part of the original Transformer (Vaswani et al., 2017) model. These models were not trained for a specific task but with an unsupervised objective: predict the next token in a piece of text. Due to their extensive training corpora, these models have already seen many examples of Trivia style questions.

GPT-3 is an auto-regressive language model (Brown et al., 2020). The largest version has 175 billion parameters. The model weights are not publicly available, although the model's predictions are available through a paid API.[3]

GPT-J is a 6 billion parameters autoregressive language model (Wang and Komatsuzaki, 2021) trained on the Pile (Gao et al., 2021).

GPT-Neo-X is a 20 billion parameters autoregressive language model (Black et al., 2022) trained on the Pile (Gao et al., 2021).

OPT is a similar model to GPT-3, but the models' weights were publicly released (Zhang et al., 2022), except for the largest version (175 billion parameters), which is available upon request. Similar to GPT-J, it was trained on the Pile along with data from Reddit. We experiment with the 30 billion parameters version.

5 Experiments

In this section, we report on our experiments using our dataset of Twenty Questions. We experimented with three setups: zero-shot, few-shot, and zero-shot with knowledge augmentation. We use these results in the section to understand the scale of the world knowledge stored by language models.

5.1 Experimental Settings

Our experiments do not require any training, we use language models as-is without fine-tuning. We use the entirety of our dataset for evaluation. We

[3] https://openai.com/api/

Model	Size	F1	Accuracy
Majority	-	0	65.0
GPT-J	6B	48.6	49.0
T5	11B	24.6	68.4
T0	11B	**68.5**	**81.9**
GPT-Neo-X	20B	51.8	34.9
OPT	30B	52.8	38.2
GPT-3	13 B	59.4	60.2
GPT-3	175B	66.4	81.3

Table 5: Result of the zero-shot evaluation. Best performance is achieved by GPT-3 and T0. The other models struggle to reach the majority vote baseline.

measure the probability of the *yes* answer by summing the probability of the *yes*, *Yes*, *true*, and *True* tokens. The same is done for the *no* answer with *no*, *No*, *false* and *False*. Our dataset contains 65% of *no* answers, we use F1 (binary) as primary evaluation metric and also report accuracy.

5.2 Zero-shot

In the zero-shot setting, models answer the question with only a textual description of the task. We expect T5 and T0 to perform well in this setup as they were pre-trained using the same setup, while this is not the case for decoder-only models.

Prompt We use the same prompt for both encoder-decoders and decoder-only models.

```
You are playing a game of 20 questions.
Answer the following question with yes or no.
Question: {{ question }}
Answer:
```

Results We report the results of our zero-shot experiment in Table 5. As expected, T0 achieves the best results with an F1 of 68.5% and an accuracy of 81.9%. GPT-3 also performs nicely in this setup, with 16x more parameters than T0. However, all the other models show an accuracy lower than the majority vote baseline.

5.3 Few-shot

In the few-shot setup, models receive identical instructions as in the zero-shot setup, in addition to a few examples. This setup benefits decoder-only models as they can now learn the task on the fly using in-context learning (Beltagy et al., 2022).

Prompt We augment the zero-shot prompt with four examples. There are two examples with *yes* and two with *no*. We randomly select examples from different entities and generic questions.[4]

Model	Size	F1	Accuracy
Majority	-	0,0	65.0
GPT-J	6B	57.7	57.7
T5	11B	0.0	65.8
T0	11B	6.7	65.8
GPT-Neo-X	20B	58.4	58.3
OPT	30B	60.4	71.6
GPT-3	13B	58.2	60.2
GPT-3	175B	**83.0**	**87.9**

Table 6: Result of the few-shot evaluation. GPT-3's F1 improves by 9% to reach 83%. The performance of OPT barely improves compared to the zero-shot reasoning, while as expected the performance of encoder-decoder models plummets.

```
You are playing a game of 20 questions.
Answer the following question with yes or no.
Question: {{ question_example_1 }}
Answer: {{ answer_example_1 }}
...
Question: {{ question_example_n }}
Answer: {{ answer_example_n }}
Question: {{ question }}
Answer:
```

Results We provide an overview of the few-shots results in Table 6. As expected, the performance of decoder-only models increases, while the performance of encoder-decoder decreases[5]. For example, GPT-3's F1 increased from 66.4% to a record 83.0%. Unfortunately, these results also show that (relatively) smaller decoder-only models do not reach T0's performance in a zero-shot setup.

5.4 Zero-shot with Knowledge Augmentation

The performance of GPT-3 is exceptional. However, it comes at a steep computational and environmental cost. Moreover, as T0 has fewer parameters than GPT-3, it has less "space" to store world knowledge. In this section, we try to augment T0 with external knowledge to help it bridge the performance gap with GPT-3. We use two sources of background knowledge: the entire Internet using Bing search and the Wikipedia page of the entity.

Prompt We follow the same prompt as in the zero-shot analysis. In addition, we augment it with a space for background knowledge.

[4]This setup is similar to the start of a Twenty Questions game where the model does not have previous examples for the same entity.

[5]These models were zero-shot inference, not few-shot.

Model	Size	F1	Accuracy
T0 (ZS)	11B	68.5	81.9
T0 (Bing)	11B	69.7	75.7
T0 (Wiki)	11B	**79.3**	**86.0**
GPT-3 (FS)	175B	**83.0**	**87.9**

Table 7: Augmenting T0 with background information improves its F1 score by 10% and brings it to a competitive level with GPT-3.

```
Text: {{ background_knowledge }}
You are playing a game of 20 questions.
Answer the following question with yes or no.
Question: {{ question }}
Answer:
```

Bing We run a bing search for every question and only keep the text snippet returned by Bing. We compare each text snippet to the question using a cross-encoder from Sentence Transformers (Reimers and Gurevych, 2019). We then keep the snippet with the highest score. We do not restrict Bing, so it can also choose to return pages from Wikipedia.

Wikipedia We chunk the Wikipedia page of each entity into passages of around 256 tokens. Then, we re-rank the passages using the same cross-encoder.

Results We provide an overview of the few-shots results in Table 7. The Bing search results are disappointing. The F1 score barely improves by 1%. On the other hand, the Wikipedia search results are outstanding: F1 improves by over 10% and accuracy by 4%.

This section concludes that GPT-3 (few-shot) is the best model for playing the answerer in a game of Twenty Questions. However, GPT-3 is computationally and environmentally costly. We showed that incorporating background knowledge from Wikipedia can improve T0's performance to a competitive level with GPT-3 despite having 16 times fewer parameters.

6 World Knowledge Analysis

We now use the results of the previous section to analyze the world knowledge of the three best models: GPT-3, T0, and T0 Knowledge Grounded (KG).

6.1 Knowledge Category

We list the accuracy by category of knowledge in Table 8. The most striking result is the low performance of the three models in the Shape &

Knowledge Type	GPT-3	T0	T0-KG	OPT
Shape & Size	66	56	69	60
Usage	86	82	86	75
Location	88	74	89	60
Composition	90	78	78	69
Description	81	69	73	65
Relatedness	95	94	88	79
Functioning	87	79	74	71
Appearance	91	83	83	89
Purpose	91	88	82	75

Table 8: Accuracy (%) by category of knowledge. GPT-3 outperforms T0 on every knowledge type. Shape & Size questions stand out as a weak spot for GPT-3 and T0.

Size category. For example, GPT-3 has a difference of 20% between the worst category (Shape & Size) and the second-worst category (Usage).

On the other hand, GPT-3 and T0 can answer questions relating to two objects or concepts exceptionally well (e.g., *is it related to water* or *is it a toy*). Intriguingly, incorporating knowledge into the prompt diminishes the score on relatedness for T0-KG.

We now dig deeper into *size & shape* questions and try to understand if there are specific kinds of questions mishandled by the language models. We list the average accuracy by questions in the Shape & Size category in Table 9. We notice that questions 1, 3 & 4 are not specific enough. On which dimension should we compare the size of the tennis ball? [6] The inter-annotator score on Shape & Size question is 0.75, almost equivalent to the global inter-annotator score of 0.76. We believe humans have enough common sense to decide on which dimension to evaluate the size of objects.

6.2 Entities

Inspired by previous research (Razeghi et al., 2022), we look for a correlation between the average accuracy of an entity and its frequency in the pretraining data.[7] We do not find any significant correlation, except a small 0.05 correlation for T0. We believe the conclusion would be different with lesser-known objects.

We notice that ambiguous entities such as *a rule*[8]

[6] Is a DVD smaller than a tennis ball because of its thickness?

[7] We use the first 10 billion tokens of the C4 dataset (Raffel et al., 2020) to estimate the frequency of entities in the pretraining data.

[8] As in a 30 cm rule/ruler

Question	GPT-3	T0	T0-KG
Is it smaller than a tennis ball?	50	55	60
Is it globe-shaped?	55	77	77
Is it bigger than a foot?	60	47	67
Can we transport it in a pocket?	62	50	50
Is it flat?	66	55	61
Is it round?	68	43	69
Is it long?	71	28	57
Is it rectangular?	72	81	72
Is it taller than a man?	78	78	71
Does it have a square shape?	80	80	100
Is it pointed?	85	71	71
Is it bigger than a bus?	100	100	100

Table 9: Accuracy (%) of GPT-3, T0, and T0-KG on Shape & Size questions. GPT-3 struggles with comparing the size of entities with the size of a tennis ball.

and *a racket*[9] are not well managed by all models for understandable reasons.

6.3 Knowledge Augmentation

In this section, we try to understand why Wikipedia is a much better source of background knowledge than Bing's search over the Internet.

Knowledge Source We manually reviewed and compared the background knowledge provided by Bing and Wikipedia. We found that the knowledge returned by Bing can be specific, whereas the game of Twenty Questions requires general knowledge. For example, when asked *does a printer have a seat*, the obvious answer is no. However, Bing returns a text saying *[...] each used printer takes one license seat. [...]* confusing the model into thinking printers do have seats. Another example is the question *is a litter box a weapon*. The correct answer is no. Bing, however, returns a text saying *[...] cat litter box used as a weapon in fight over prescription drugs [...]* confusing the model into thinking a litter box is a weapon. In both instances, the knowledge returned by Wikipedia is the introductory paragraph describing the entity.

Knowledge Category According to Table 8, incorporating background knowledge helps in Location (+15%) and Usage (+13%) questions. On the other hand, it hurts performance on Relatedness questions (-6%).

This section concludes that GPT-3 performs consistently on all categories of questions, except Shape and Size. Although competitive, T0 does not show the same consistency as GPT-3, even when augmented with background information.

[9]As in a tennis racket

7 Twentle

We present an interactive website to let anyone test the world knowledge of T0-KG by playing the game of Twenty Questions. Inspired by Wordle, we named our website Twentle, available at twentle.com.

8 Future Work

Reducing the world to yes/no questions is not an easy task. Our human agreement section demonstrates that humans do not agree on all answers. Future work is needed to compare the agreement of humans and language models by category of question. In this study, we limited ourselves to the study of the answerer. However, GPT-3 could potentially also play the role of the questioner. Future work is needed to study the knowledgeability of language models on lesser-known objects. In this case, we anticipate that large models will also need to leverage the web for information.

9 Conclusion

In this work, we analyzed the world knowledge of language models through the game of Twenty Questions. Our analysis reveals that most language models do not have the world knowledge required to play this game. GPT-3 is a notable exception. It displays impressive world knowledge on all categories of questions identified, except for shape & size questions — *is it smaller than a tennis ball*. Furthermore, we showed how grounding smaller models on information from the web improves their knowledgeability. Through this work, we demonstrated the need for more clarity on which model architecture and pre-training method best captures world knowledge.

10 Limitations

We intentionally limited our analysis to well-known objects. We anticipate a lower performance on lesser-known objects. Furthermore, our work uses well-defined questions with little noise, whereas real-world questions by humans could be more challenging for language models to understand. The dataset we collected could contain biases already present in our society. Unfortunately, the same is true for the answers given by the language model.

Acknowledgement

We thank the reviewers for their helpful feedback. This research received funding from the Flemish Government under the *Onderzoeksprogramma Artificiële Intelligentie (AI) Vlaanderen* programme.

References

Iz Beltagy, Arman Cohan, Robert Logan IV, Sewon Min, and Sameer Singh. 2022. Zero- and few-shot NLP with pretrained language models. In *Proceedings of the 60th Annual Meeting of the Association for Computational Linguistics: Tutorial Abstracts*, pages 32–37, Dublin, Ireland. Association for Computational Linguistics.

Jonathan Berant, Andrew Chou, Roy Frostig, and Percy Liang. 2013. Semantic parsing on Freebase from question-answer pairs. In *Proceedings of the 2013 Conference on Empirical Methods in Natural Language Processing*, pages 1533–1544, Seattle, Washington, USA. Association for Computational Linguistics.

Sidney Black, Stella Biderman, Eric Hallahan, Quentin Anthony, Leo Gao, Laurence Golding, Horace He, Connor Leahy, Kyle McDonell, Jason Phang, Michael Pieler, Usvsn Sai Prashanth, Shivanshu Purohit, Laria Reynolds, Jonathan Tow, Ben Wang, and Samuel Weinbach. 2022. GPT-NeoX-20B: An open-source autoregressive language model. In *Proceedings of BigScience Episode #5 – Workshop on Challenges & Perspectives in Creating Large Language Models*, pages 95–136, virtual+Dublin. Association for Computational Linguistics.

Sebastian Borgeaud, Arthur Mensch, Jordan Hoffmann, Trevor Cai, Eliza Rutherford, Katie Millican, George van den Driessche, Jean-Baptiste Lespiau, Bogdan Damoc, Aidan Clark, Diego de Las Casas, Aurelia Guy, Jacob Menick, Roman Ring, Tom Hennigan, Saffron Huang, Loren Maggiore, Chris Jones, Albin Cassirer, Andy Brock, Michela Paganini, Geoffrey Irving, Oriol Vinyals, Simon Osindero, Karen Simonyan, Jack W. Rae, Erich Elsen, and Laurent Sifre. 2021. Improving language models by retrieving from trillions of tokens. *CoRR*, abs/2112.04426.

Tom Brown, Benjamin Mann, Nick Ryder, Melanie Subbiah, Jared D Kaplan, Prafulla Dhariwal, Arvind Neelakantan, Pranav Shyam, Girish Sastry, Amanda Askell, Sandhini Agarwal, Ariel Herbert-Voss, Gretchen Krueger, Tom Henighan, Rewon Child, Aditya Ramesh, Daniel Ziegler, Jeffrey Wu, Clemens Winter, Chris Hesse, Mark Chen, Eric Sigler, Mateusz Litwin, Scott Gray, Benjamin Chess, Jack Clark, Christopher Berner, Sam McCandlish, Alec Radford, Ilya Sutskever, and Dario Amodei. 2020. Language models are few-shot learners. In *Advances in Neural Information Processing Systems*, volume 33, pages 1877–1901. Curran Associates, Inc.

Yihong Chen, Bei Chen, Xuguang Duan, Jian-Guang Lou, Yue Wang, Wenwu Zhu, and Yong Cao. 2018. Learning-to-ask: Knowledge acquisition via 20 questions. In *Proceedings of the 24th ACM SIGKDD International Conference on Knowledge Discovery, Data Mining*, KDD '18, page 1216–1225, New York, NY, USA. Association for Computing Machinery.

Aakanksha Chowdhery, Sharan Narang, Jacob Devlin, Maarten Bosma, Gaurav Mishra, Adam Roberts, Paul Barham, Hyung Won Chung, Charles Sutton, Sebastian Gehrmann, Parker Schuh, Kensen Shi, Sasha Tsvyashchenko, Joshua Maynez, Abhishek Rao, Parker Barnes, Yi Tay, Noam Shazeer, Vinodkumar Prabhakaran, Emily Reif, Nan Du, Ben Hutchinson, Reiner Pope, James Bradbury, Jacob Austin, Michael Isard, Guy Gur-Ari, Pengcheng Yin, Toju Duke, Anselm Levskaya, Sanjay Ghemawat, Sunipa Dev, Henryk Michalewski, Xavier Garcia, Vedant Misra, Kevin Robinson, Liam Fedus, Denny Zhou, Daphne Ippolito, David Luan, Hyeontaek Lim, Barret Zoph, Alexander Spiridonov, Ryan Sepassi, David Dohan, Shivani Agrawal, Mark Omernick, Andrew M. Dai, Thanumalayan Sankaranarayana Pillai, Marie Pellat, Aitor Lewkowycz, Erica Moreira, Rewon Child, Oleksandr Polozov, Katherine Lee, Zongwei Zhou, Xuezhi Wang, Brennan Saeta, Mark Diaz, Orhan Firat, Michele Catasta, Jason Wei, Kathy Meier-Hellstern, Douglas Eck, Jeff Dean, Slav Petrov, and Noah Fiedel. 2022. Palm: Scaling language modeling with pathways.

Christopher Clark, Kenton Lee, Ming-Wei Chang, Tom Kwiatkowski, Michael Collins, and Kristina Toutanova. 2019. BoolQ: Exploring the surprising difficulty of natural yes/no questions. In *Proceedings of the 2019 Conference of the North American Chapter of the Association for Computational Linguistics: Human Language Technologies, Volume 1 (Long and Short Papers)*, pages 2924–2936, Minneapolis, Minnesota. Association for Computational Linguistics.

J. Cohen. 1968. Weighted kappa: nominal scale agreement with provision for scaled disagreement or partial credit. *Psychological bulletin*, 70 4:213–20.

Maxime De Bruyn, Ehsan Lotfi, Jeska Buhmann, and Walter Daelemans. 2020. Bart for knowledge grounded conversations. In *Converse@ KDD*.

Leo Gao, Stella Biderman, Sid Black, Laurence Golding, Travis Hoppe, Charles Foster, Jason Phang, Horace He, Anish Thite, Noa Nabeshima, Shawn Presser, and Connor Leahy. 2021. The pile: An 800gb dataset of diverse text for language modeling.

Ari Holtzman, Peter West, Vered Shwartz, Yejin Choi, and Luke Zettlemoyer. 2021. Surface form competition: Why the highest probability answer isn't always right. In *Proceedings of the 2021 Conference on Empirical Methods in Natural Language Processing*, pages 7038–7051, Online and Punta Cana, Dominican Republic. Association for Computational Linguistics.

Huang Hu, Xianchao Wu, Bingfeng Luo, Chongyang Tao, Can Xu, Wei Wu, and Zhan Chen. 2018. Playing 20 question game with policy-based reinforcement learning. In *Proceedings of the 2018 Conference on Empirical Methods in Natural Language Processing*, pages 3233–3242, Brussels, Belgium. Association for Computational Linguistics.

Zhengbao Jiang, Frank F. Xu, Jun Araki, and Graham Neubig. 2020. How can we know what language models know? *Transactions of the Association for Computational Linguistics*, 8:423–438.

Mandar Joshi, Eunsol Choi, Daniel Weld, and Luke Zettlemoyer. 2017. TriviaQA: A large scale distantly supervised challenge dataset for reading comprehension. In *Proceedings of the 55th Annual Meeting of the Association for Computational Linguistics (Volume 1: Long Papers)*, pages 1601–1611, Vancouver, Canada. Association for Computational Linguistics.

Takeshi Kojima, Shixiang Shane Gu, Machel Reid, Yutaka Matsuo, and Yusuke Iwasawa. 2022. Large language models are zero-shot reasoners.

Mojtaba Komeili, Kurt Shuster, and Jason Weston. 2022. Internet-augmented dialogue generation. In *Proceedings of the 60th Annual Meeting of the Association for Computational Linguistics (Volume 1: Long Papers)*, pages 8460–8478, Dublin, Ireland. Association for Computational Linguistics.

Tom Kwiatkowski, Jennimaria Palomaki, Olivia Redfield, Michael Collins, Ankur Parikh, Chris Alberti, Danielle Epstein, Illia Polosukhin, Jacob Devlin, Kenton Lee, Kristina Toutanova, Llion Jones, Matthew Kelcey, Ming-Wei Chang, Andrew M. Dai, Jakob Uszkoreit, Quoc Le, and Slav Petrov. 2019. Natural questions: A benchmark for question answering research. *Transactions of the Association for Computational Linguistics*, 7:452–466.

Angeliki Lazaridou, Elena Gribovskaya, Wojciech Stokowiec, and Nikolai Grigorev. 2022. Internet-augmented language models through few-shot prompting for open-domain question answering.

Mike Lewis, Yinhan Liu, Naman Goyal, Marjan Ghazvininejad, Abdelrahman Mohamed, Omer Levy, Veselin Stoyanov, and Luke Zettlemoyer. 2020a. BART: Denoising sequence-to-sequence pre-training for natural language generation, translation, and comprehension. In *Proceedings of the 58th Annual Meeting of the Association for Computational Linguistics*, pages 7871–7880, Online. Association for Computational Linguistics.

Patrick Lewis, Ethan Perez, Aleksandra Piktus, Fabio Petroni, Vladimir Karpukhin, Naman Goyal, Heinrich Küttler, Mike Lewis, Wen-tau Yih, Tim Rocktäschel, Sebastian Riedel, and Douwe Kiela. 2020b. Retrieval-augmented generation for knowledge-intensive nlp tasks. In *Proceedings of the 34th International Conference on Neural Information Processing Systems*, NIPS'20, Red Hook, NY, USA. Curran Associates Inc.

Patrick Lewis, Pontus Stenetorp, and Sebastian Riedel. 2021. Question and answer test-train overlap in open-domain question answering datasets. In *Proceedings of the 16th Conference of the European Chapter of the Association for Computational Linguistics: Main Volume*, pages 1000–1008, Online. Association for Computational Linguistics.

Fabio Petroni, Tim Rocktäschel, Sebastian Riedel, Patrick Lewis, Anton Bakhtin, Yuxiang Wu, and Alexander Miller. 2019. Language models as knowledge bases? In *Proceedings of the 2019 Conference on Empirical Methods in Natural Language Processing and the 9th International Joint Conference on Natural Language Processing (EMNLP-IJCNLP)*, pages 2463–2473, Hong Kong, China. Association for Computational Linguistics.

Colin Raffel, Noam Shazeer, Adam Roberts, Katherine Lee, Sharan Narang, Michael Matena, Yanqi Zhou, Wei Li, and Peter J. Liu. 2020. Exploring the limits of transfer learning with a unified text-to-text transformer. *Journal of Machine Learning Research*, 21(140):1–67.

Pranav Rajpurkar, Jian Zhang, Konstantin Lopyrev, and Percy Liang. 2016. SQuAD: 100,000+ questions for machine comprehension of text. In *Proceedings of the 2016 Conference on Empirical Methods in Natural Language Processing*, pages 2383–2392, Austin, Texas. Association for Computational Linguistics.

Yasaman Razeghi, Robert L. Logan, Matt Gardner, and Sameer Singh. 2022. Impact of pretraining term frequencies on few-shot reasoning.

Nils Reimers and Iryna Gurevych. 2019. Sentence-BERT: Sentence embeddings using Siamese BERT-networks. In *Proceedings of the 2019 Conference on Empirical Methods in Natural Language Processing and the 9th International Joint Conference on Natural Language Processing (EMNLP-IJCNLP)*, pages 3982–3992, Hong Kong, China. Association for Computational Linguistics.

Adam Roberts, Colin Raffel, and Noam Shazeer. 2020. How much knowledge can you pack into the parameters of a language model? In *Proceedings of the 2020 Conference on Empirical Methods in Natural Language Processing (EMNLP)*, pages 5418–5426, Online. Association for Computational Linguistics.

Victor Sanh, Albert Webson, Colin Raffel, Stephen Bach, Lintang Sutawika, Zaid Alyafeai, Antoine Chaffin, Arnaud Stiegler, Teven Le Scao, Arun Raja, et al. 2022. Multitask prompted training enables zero-shot task generalization. In *The Tenth International Conference on Learning Representations*.

Alon Talmor, Yanai Elazar, Yoav Goldberg, and Jonathan Berant. 2020. oLMpics-on what language model pre-training captures. *Transactions of the Association for Computational Linguistics*, 8:743–758.

Ashish Vaswani, Noam Shazeer, Niki Parmar, Jakob Uszkoreit, Llion Jones, Aidan N Gomez, Ł ukasz Kaiser, and Illia Polosukhin. 2017. Attention is all you need. In *Advances in Neural Information Processing Systems*, volume 30. Curran Associates, Inc.

Ben Wang and Aran Komatsuzaki. 2021. GPT-J-6B: A 6 Billion Parameter Autoregressive Language Model. https://github.com/kingoflolz/mesh-transformer-jax.

Cunxiang Wang, Pai Liu, and Yue Zhang. 2021. Can generative pre-trained language models serve as knowledge bases for closed-book QA? In *Proceedings of the 59th Annual Meeting of the Association for Computational Linguistics and the 11th International Joint Conference on Natural Language Processing (Volume 1: Long Papers)*, pages 3241–3251, Online. Association for Computational Linguistics.

Thomas Wolf, Lysandre Debut, Victor Sanh, Julien Chaumond, Clement Delangue, Anthony Moi, Pierric Cistac, Tim Rault, Remi Louf, Morgan Funtowicz, Joe Davison, Sam Shleifer, Patrick von Platen, Clara Ma, Yacine Jernite, Julien Plu, Canwen Xu, Teven Le Scao, Sylvain Gugger, Mariama Drame, Quentin Lhoest, and Alexander Rush. 2020. Transformers: State-of-the-art natural language processing. In *Proceedings of the 2020 Conference on Empirical Methods in Natural Language Processing: System Demonstrations*, pages 38–45, Online. Association for Computational Linguistics.

Susan Zhang, Stephen Roller, Naman Goyal, Mikel Artetxe, Moya Chen, Shuohui Chen, Christopher Dewan, Mona Diab, Xian Li, Xi Victoria Lin, Todor Mihaylov, Myle Ott, Sam Shleifer, Kurt Shuster, Daniel Simig, Punit Singh Koura, Anjali Sridhar, Tianlu Wang, and Luke Zettlemoyer. 2022. Opt: Open pre-trained transformer language models.

A Computing Infrastructure

We ran all our experiments on a server running 8 NVIDIA GPU (12GB) with 128GB of RAM and 24 CPU. All models ran in parallel using the device_map argument of the from_pretained method.

B Hyperparameter Search

We did not engage in a hyperparameter search. Future research could look for the optimal prompt, balance of yes and no examples.

C Correlation With Token Frequency

We display the correlation between the average accuracy of an entity and its relative frequency in the pre-training data in Table 10.

Model	**Correlation**	**P-value**
GPT-3	-0.02	0.35
T0	0.05	0.01
T0-KG	-0.01	0.45

Table 10: Spearman correlation of the average accuracy of an entity with its frequency in the pre-training data.

Post-hoc analysis of Arabic transformer models

Ahmed Abdelali[◇] **Nadir Durrani**[◇] **Fahim Dalvi**[◇] **Hassan Sajjad**[♣*]
[◇]Qatar Computing Research Institute, Hamad Bin Khalifa University, Qatar
[♣]Faculty of Computer Science, Dalhousie University, Canada
{aabdelali, ndurrani,faimaduddin}@hbku.edu.qa, hsajjad@dal.ca

Abstract

Arabic is a Semitic language which is widely spoken with many dialects. Given the success of pre-trained language models, many transformer models trained on Arabic and its dialects have surfaced. While there have been an extrinsic evaluation of these models with respect to downstream NLP tasks, no work has been carried out to analyze and compare their internal representations. We probe how linguistic information is encoded in the transformer models, trained on different Arabic dialects. We perform a layer and neuron analysis on the models using morphological tagging tasks for different dialects of Arabic and a dialectal identification task. Our analysis enlightens interesting findings such as: i) word morphology is learned at the lower and middle layers, ii) while syntactic dependencies are predominantly captured at the higher layers, iii) despite a large overlap in their vocabulary, the MSA-based models fail to capture the nuances of Arabic dialects, iv) we found that neurons in embedding layers are polysemous in nature, while the neurons in middle layers are exclusive to specific properties.

1 Introduction

Arabic is a linguistically rich language, with its structures realized using both concatenative and templatic morphology. The agglutinating aspect of the language adds to the complexity where a given word could be formed using multiple morphemes. For example, the word فأسقيناكموه (fOsqynAkmwh[1] – and we gave it to you to drink) combines a conjunction, a verb, and three pronouns. At another longitude, Arabic has three variants: Classical Arabic (CA), Modern Standard Arabic (MSA) and Dialectal Arabic (DA). While the MSA is traditionally considered as the de facto standard in the written medium and DA being the predominantly spoken counterpart, this has changed recently (Mubarak and Darwish, 2014; Zaidan and Callison-Burch, 2014; Durrani et al., 2014). Due to the recent influx of Social Media platforms, dialectal Arabic also enjoys a significant presence in the written medium.

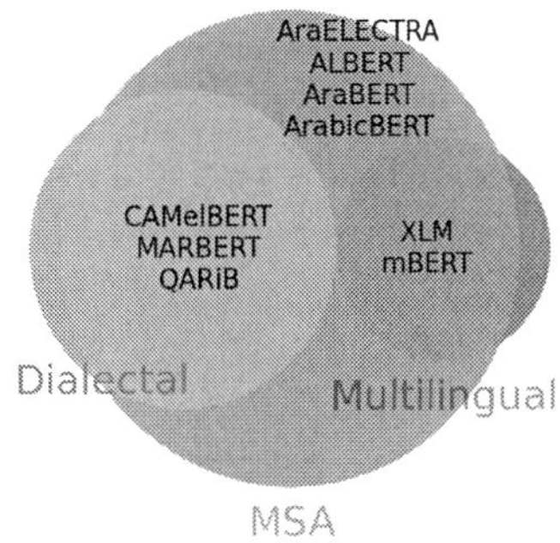

Figure 1: Data regimes of various pre-trained Transformer models of Arabic

Transfer learning using contextualized representations in pre-trained language models have revolutionized the arena of downstream NLP tasks. A plethora of transformer-based language models, trained in dozens of languages are uploaded every day now. Arabic is no different. Several researchers have released and benchmarked pre-trained Arabic transformer models such as AraBERT (Antoun et al., 2020), ArabicBERT (Safaya et al., 2020), CAMeLBERT (Inoue et al., 2021), MARBERT (Abdul-Mageed et al., 2020) and QARIB (Abdelali et al., 2021) etc. These models have demonstrated state-of-the-art performance on many tasks as well as their ability to learn salient features for Arabic. One of the main differences among these models is the genre and amount of Arabic data they are trained on. For example, AraBERT was trained only on the MSA (Modern Standard Arabic),

*The work was done while the author was at QCRI
[1]Using Safe Buckwalter Arabic (SBA) encoding.

Proceedings of the Fifth BlackboxNLP Workshop on Analyzing and Interpreting Neural Networks for NLP, pages 91 - 103
December 8, 2022 ©2022 Association for Computational Linguistics

ArabicBERT additionally used DA during training, and CAMelBERT-mix used a combination of all types of Arabic text for training. Multilingual models such as mBERT and XLM are mostly trained on Wikipedia and CommonCrawl data which is predominantly MSA (Suwaileh et al., 2016). Figure 1 summarizes the training data regimes of these models.

This large variety of Arabic pre-trained models motivates us to question **how their representations encode various linguistic concepts?** To this end, **we present the first work on interpreting deep Arabic models.** We experiment with nine transformer models including: five Arabic BERT models, Arabic ALBERT, Arabic Electra, and two multilingual models (mBERT and XLM). We analyze their representations using MSA and dialectal parts-of-speech tagging and dialect identification tasks. This allows us to compare the representations of Arabic transformer models using tasks involving different varieties of Arabic dialects.

We analyze representations of the network at layer-level and at neuron-level using diagnostic classifier framework (Belinkov et al., 2017; Hupkes et al., 2018). The overall idea is to extract feature vectors from the learned representations and train probing classifiers towards understudied auxiliary tasks (of predicting morphology or identifying dialect). We additionally use the *Linguistic Correlation Analysis* method (Dalvi et al., 2019a; Durrani et al., 2020) to identify salient neurons with respect to a downstream task. Our results show that:

Network and Layer Analysis

- Lower and middle layers capture word morphology
- The long-range contextual knowledge required to solve the dialectal identification is preserved in the higher layers

Neuron Analysis

- The salient neurons with respect to a property are well distributed across the network
- First (embedding) and last layers of the models contribute a substantial amount of salient neurons for any downstream task
- The neurons of embedding layer layer are polysemous in nature while the neurons of middle layers specializes in specific properties

MSA vs. Dialect

- Although dialects of Arabic are closely related to MSA, the pre-trained models trained using MSA only do not implicitly learn nuances of dialectal Arabic

2 Methodology

Our methodology is based on the class of interpretation methods called as the *Probing Classifiers*. The central idea is to extract the activation vectors from a pre-trained language model as static features. These activation vectors are then trained towards the task of predicting a property of interest, a linguistic task that we would like to probe the representation against. The underlying assumption is that if the classifier can predict the property, the representations implicitly encode this information. We train layer (Belinkov et al., 2020) and neuron probes (Durrani et al., 2022) using logistic-regression classifiers.

Formally, consider a pre-trained neural language model $\mathbb{M}$ with L layers: $\{l_1, l_2, \ldots, l_L\}$. Given a dataset $\mathbb{D} = \{w_1, w_2, ..., w_N\}$ with a corresponding set of linguistic annotations $\mathbb{T} = \{t_{w_1}, t_{w_2}, ..., t_{w_N}\}$, we map each word w_i in the data $\mathbb{D}$ to a sequence of latent representations: $\mathbb{D} \xmapsto{\mathbb{M}} \mathbf{z} = \{\mathbf{z}_1, \ldots, \mathbf{z}_N\}$. The layer-wise probing classifier is trained by minimizing the following loss function:

$$\mathcal{L}(\theta) = -\sum_i \log P_\theta(t_{w_i}|w_i)$$

where $P_\theta(t_{w_i}|w_i) = \frac{\exp(\theta_l \cdot \mathbf{z}_i)}{\sum_{l'} \exp(\theta_{l'} \cdot \mathbf{z}_i)}$ is the probability that word i is assigned property t_{w_i}.

For neuron analysis, we use *Linguistic Correlation Analysis* (LCA) as described in (Dalvi et al., 2019a). LCA is also based on the probing classifier paradigm. However, they used elastic-net regularization (Zou and Hastie, 2005) that enables the selection of both focused and distributed neurons. The loss function is as follows:

$$\mathcal{L}(\theta) = -\sum_i \log P_\theta(t_{w_i}|w_i) + \lambda_1\|\theta\|_1 + \lambda_2\|\theta\|_2^2$$

The regularization parameters λ_1 and λ_2 are tuned using a grid-search algorithm. The classifier assigns weight to each feature (neuron) which serves as their importance with respect to a class like Noun. We ranked the neurons based on the absolute weights for every class. We select salient neurons for the task such as POS by iteratively selecting top neurons of every class.

A minimum set of neurons is identified by iteratively selecting top neurons that achieves classification performance comparable (within a certain threshold) to the *Oracle* – accuracy of the classifier trained using all the features in the network.

Data	Size	Tokens	Vocab	Type
AraBERT	23GB	2.7B	64K	MSA
ArabicBERT	95GB	8.2B	32K	MSA
CAMeLBERT	167B	17.3B	30K	MSA/CA/DA
MARBERT	128GB	15.6B	100K	MSA/DA
mBERT	-	1.5B	110K	MSA
QARiB	127GB	14.0B	64K	MSA/DA
AraELECTRA	77GB	8.6B	64K	MSA
ALBERT	-	4.4B	30K	MSA
XLM	2.5TB	-	250K	MSA

Table 1: Pretrained Models data and statistics.

3 Experimental Setup

In this section, we describe our experimental setup including the Arabic transformer models, probing tasks that we have used to carry the analysis and the classifier settings.

3.1 Pre-trained Models

We select a number of Arabic transformer models, trained using various varieties of Arabic and based on different architectures. Table 1 provides a summary of these models. In the following, we describe each model and the dataset used for their training.

AraBERT was trained using a combination of 70 million sentences from Arabic Wikipedia Dumps, 1.5B words Arabic Corpus (El-khair, 2016) and the Open Source International Arabic News Corpus (OSIAN) from (Zeroual et al., 2019). The final corpus contained mostly MSA news from different Arab regions.

ArabicBERT Safaya et al. (2020) pretrained a BERT model using a concatenation of Arabic version of OSCAR (Ortiz Suárez et al., 2019), a filtered subset from Common Crawl and a dump of Arabic Wikipedia totalling to 8.2B words.

CAMeLBERT Inoue et al. (2021) combined a mixed collection of MSA, Dialectal and Classical Arabic texts with a total of 17.3B tokens. They used the data to pre-train CAMeLBERT-Mix model.

MARBERT Abdul-Mageed et al. (2020) combined a dataset of 1B tweets that covering mostly Arabic dialects and Arabic Gigaword 5th Edition,[2] OSCAR (Ortiz Suárez et al., 2019), OSIAN (Zeroual et al., 2019) and Wikipedia dump totally up to 15.6B tokens.

QARIB Abdelali et al. (2021) combined Arabic Gigaword Fourth Edition,[3] 1.5B words Arabic Corpus (El-khair, 2016), the Arabic part of Open Subtitles (Lison and Tiedemann, 2016) and 440M tweets collected between 2012 and 2020. The data was processed using Farasa (Abdelali et al., 2016).

ALBERT used a subset of OSCAR (Ortiz Suárez et al., 2019) and a dump of Wikipedia, selecting around 4.4 Billion words (Safaya, 2020). The model differs from BERT using factorized embedding and repeating layers which results in a small memory footprint (Lan et al., 2020).

AraELECTRA ELECTRA, model Clark et al. (2020) is trained to distinguish "real" vs "fake" input tokens generated by another neural network. The Arabic ELECTRA was trained on 77GB of data combining OSCAR dataset, Arabic Wikipedia dump, the 1.5B words Arabic Corpus, the OSIAN Corpus and Assafir news articles (Antoun et al., 2021). Different than other models, AraELECTRA uses a hidden layer size of 256 while all other models have 768 neurons per layer.

Multilingual BERT Google research released BERT multilingual base model pretrained on the concatenation of monolingual Wikipedia corpora from 104 languages with a shared word piece vocabulary of 110K.

XLM Conneau et al. (2020) is a multilingual version of RoBERTa, trained on 2.5TB CommonCrawl data. The model is trained on 100 different languages.

3.2 Probing Tasks

We consider morphological tagging on a variety of Arabic dialects and dialectal identification tasks to analyze and compare the models. Below we describe the task details.

POS Tagging on Arabic Treebank (ATB): The Arabic Treebank Part1 v2.0 and Part3 v1.0 with a total of 515k tokens labeled at the segment level with POS tags. The data is a combination of

[2]LDC Catalogue LDC2011T11

[3]LDC Catalogue LDC2009T30

ATB	Text	واعرب بيرسول عن دهشته ازاء تطور مستواه المتواصل ،
	Labels	VBD NNP IN NN NN NN NN DT+JJ PUNC
	SBA	wAErb byrswl En dhcth AzAC tTwr mstwAh AlmtwASl ,
	Gloss.	And Peirsol expressed his surprise at the continuous development of his level ,
CRS	Text	! نط أخوي الصغير وجبلي مي
	Labels	VERB NOUN+PRON DET+ADJC PREP+VERB+PREP+PRON NOUN PUNC
	SBA	nT Oxwy AlSgyr wjbly my !
	Gloss.	My little brother jumped and brought me water !
DIA	Text	في ناس مناح ما في متلن ، و في ناس منيح اللي ما في متلن
	Labels	ADV NOUN ADJ PART ADV NOUN PUNC CONJ ADV NOUN ADJ PART PART ADV NOUN
	SBA	fy nAs mnAH mA fy mtln , w fy nAs mnyH Ally mA fy mtln
	Gloss.	There are good people who are unparalleled, and there are people that it is good they are unparalleled.
DID	Text	! له مجددا أقول مفقوسة أوي
	Labels	lang1 lang1 ambiguous lang2 lang2 other
	SBA	lh mjddA Oqwl mfqwsp Owy
	Gloss.	For him again I say (I am) very upset !
GMR	Text	سيف : انا ما غلطت قلت صدق
	Labels	NOUN_PROP:MS PUNC:- PRON:1S PART:- VERB:P1S VERB:P1S NOUN:MS
	SBA	syf : AnA mA glTt qlt Sdq
	Gloss.	Saif: I wasn't wrong, I said the truth.

Table 2: Examples of Arabic annotated text and their corresponding labels for each task.

newswire text from An-Nahar and Agence France Presse corpus (Maamouri et al., 2004). The data is labeled with 42 distinct tags.

Gumar POS Tagging on Gulf Arabic (GMR): Khalifa et al.(2020) compiled a collection of 15,225 sentences from eight different novels written in the Emirati Arabic dialect from the Gumar Corpus (Khalifa et al., 2018). The data was manually annotated for tokenization, part-of-speech, lemmatization, spelling adjustment, English glosses and sentence level dialect identification, using 169 tags.

Curras POS Tagging on Palestinian Arabic dialect (CRS): Jarrar et al.(2017) collected around 5K sentences written in Palestinian Arabic dialect from web blogs, Twitter and Facebook comments and transcripts from a TV Shows Watan Aa Watar. The sentences were manually annotated for part-of-speech (POS), stem, prefix, suffix, lemma, and gloss using 260 tags.

POS Multidialects (DIA): A total of 1.4k tweets from four Arabic dialects, namely Egyptian (EGY), Levantine (LEV), Gulf (GLF), and Maghrebi (MGR). The tweets were morphologically tagged (Samih et al., 2017) using a reduced subset of 22 tags.

Dialect IDentification (DID): This task is related to code switching and language identification (LID) between MSA and Egyptian dialect on social media content. The data comprises intrasentential code switched sentences (mixing languages between utterances) used for the Second Shared Task on Language Identification in Code-Switched Data. The data contains over 11k sentences, where each token in the sentences is labeled with one of the eight labels:lang1, lang2, fw, mixed, unk, ambiguous, other and named entities (ne) (Molina et al., 2016).

Figure2 shows examples for each of the probing tasks with their respective labels.

3.3 Post-hoc Classifier

We used the NeuroX toolkit (Dalvi et al., 2019b) to perform our analysis. Our probe is a linear classifier with categorical cross-entropy loss, optimized by Adam (Kingma and Ba, 2014). For neuron-analysis, the classifier additionally used the elastic-net regularization (Zou and Hastie, 2005). The regularization weights are trained using grid-search algorithm. Training is run with shuffled mini-batches of size 512 and stopped after 10 epochs. Linear classifiers are a popular choice in analyzing deep NLP models due to their better interpretability (Qian et al., 2016). Hewitt and Liang (2019) have also shown linear probes to have higher *Selectivity*, a property deemed desirable for more interpretable probes. We perform control task experiments to ensure that our probes are reflective of the linguistic knowledge that representations capture. For sub-word based models, we use the average activation value (Durrani et al., 2019) to be the representative of the word. We additionally

Task	ATB		CRS		DIA		DID		GMR		Avg. Acc.
Model	Acc.	Sel.	Acc.	Sel.	Acc.	Sel.	Acc.	Sel.	Acc.	Sel.	
AraBERT	93.9	48.1	77.3	22.1	79.0	58.1	84.7	37.4	90.4	06.4	85.06
ArabicBERT	95.2	48.2	80.5	24.7	83.6	50.4	91.2	34.7	91.6	05.1	88.43
CAMelBERT	**95.8**	39.2	82.9	23.6	**86.0**	37.2	92.0	21.3	93.0	05.6	89.94
MARBERT	95.6	51.4	**84.2**	27.5	84.8	48.8	93.1	33.9	**93.4**	07.3	90.22
QARiB	**95.8**	50.6	84.0	28.9	85.4	45.0	**93.3**	28.8	93.3	06.7	**90.38**
mBERT	94.4	48.8	73.7	22.7	77.6	58.4	81.7	36.3	88.0	04.4	83.08
AraELECTRA	94.4	46.9	72.7	28.4	79.0	56.2	87.9	34.3	89.1	08.1	84.64
ALBERT	95.2	40.9	77.0	28.3	82.1	39.8	88.3	27.1	90.2	09.4	86.56
XLM	95.7	43.7	75.0	20.6	78.9	42.1	86.7	29.3	88.2	06.0	84.90

Table 3: Classifier performance on Test sets using **top layers**

Task	ATB		CRS		DIA		DID		GMR	
Threshold δ	5%		10%		10%		7%		5%	
Model	Acc.	Sel.	Acc.	Sel.	Acc.	Sel.	Acc.	Sel.	Acc.	Sel.
AraBERT	93.4	48.8	82.1	33.5	79.3	39.9	86.0	21.5	89.9	18.1
ArabicBERT	94.0	50.8	83.6	31.6	83.3	44.9	90.1	26.3	91.0	12.5
CAMelBERT	94.9	51.1	86.1	37.0	85.1	47.5	91.0	27.2	92.6	22.6
MARBERT	94.5	51.6	86.2	30.0	84.2	48.5	91.6	29.2	92.3	15.0
QARiB	95.0	52.7	86.1	31.0	83.6	46.7	91.7	30.0	92.4	11.6
mBERT	94.1	48.5	78.4	33.1	77.5	37.7	83.2	17.0	87.6	13.4
AraELECTRA	91.2	53.3	79.0	33.9	79.4	45.0	88.2	25.6	87.6	13.1
ALBERT	94.7	56.8	80.7	33.7	81.8	47.4	88.5	25.9	89.8	12.0
XLM	95.3	51.8	78.5	27.9	79.0	44.5	86.5	21.7	88.0	12.4

Table 4: Classifier performance on Test sets using **top neurons** as features

normalize the embeddings using znorm as it has shown to provide better ranking of neurons with respect to a property (Sajjad et al., 2021a).

4 Analysis and Discussion

Our goal is to carry out a comparative investigation of the knowledge encoded in different Arabic transformer models. First we compare the representations in terms of how much linguistic information is preserved in the network using the overall accuracy on the understudied auxiliary tasks. Then we analyze how such information is preserved across individual layers of the model. Lastly, we analyze the distribution of neurons across the model with respect to these tasks.

4.1 Network Analysis

We use the feature vectors[4] generated from different dialects of Arabic to train post-hoc classifiers towards the task of predicting morphology in these dialects or predicting the dialect themselves. Table 3 gives accuracy of the classifiers on different dialectal tasks. Firstly, the high accuracy numbers show that the representations learn non-trivial linguistic knowledge. We found all the models to do well on the task of predicting MSA morphology unsurprisingly, since all these models have been trained on a large amount of MSA data. Contrastingly, the performance varied a lot on the dialectal tasks with different models giving optimal performance on different dialects. Note that the models that were trained only using MSA performed much worse despite the fact that MSA and dialect have a significant vocabulary overlap. This shows that **to capture specific dialectal nuances these transformer models need to train on dialectal data.** Comparing the models, we found dialectal models (QARiB, MARBERT and CAMeLBERT) to perform considerably well across all the tasks. Lastly the high selectivity numbers in Table 3 validate the fact that our classifiers are not memorizing the tasks and are a true reflection of the knowledge captured within the underlying representations.

4.2 Layer-wise Analysis

We now analyze how the understudied linguistic knowledge is distributed across the layers. We train a classifier for each probing task using representations of individual layers as features. The

[4]We concatenated the features from all layers of the network to train the classifier.

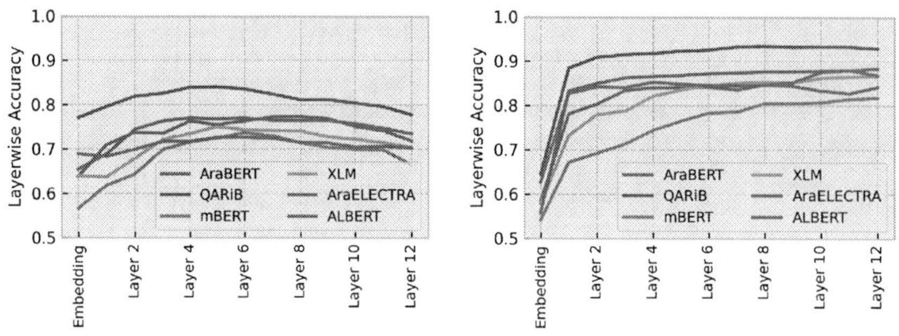

(a) CRS

(b) DID

Figure 2: Layer-wise accuracy for different selected tasks.

performance of the classifier serves as a proxy to the amount of task knowledge learned in each layer representation. Figure 2 provides per-layer accuracy for the CRS (morphological tagging for Palestinian dialect) and DID (Dialect Identification) tasks.[5] We found that **the word morphology is captured predominantly in the lower layers of the model**, retained in the middle layers before declining in the final layers. **The higher layers are reserved for complex phenomenon such as capturing non-local dependencies.** This is confirmed from our DID results. Identifying dialect requires learning non-local dependencies and sentence level phenomenon to accurately predict the dialect. For example, a lexical form can belong to two different dialects depending on the context to disambiguate the dialect of the word. For example, حاجة "HAjp" (thing or need) is MSA in the context: لست في حاجة لأن "lst fy HAjp lOn" (I am not in **need** to) or Egyptian: مفيش حاجة أصعب من "mfyc HAjp OSEb mn" (there is no **thing** difficult than). The contextual knowledge is essential to disambiguate in such cases.

4.3 Neurons Analysis

We now study how the information is spread across neurons instead of layer by carrying a fine-grained analysis. We discover neurons that learn a particular linguistic property using LCA (Dalvi et al., 2019a) and analyze: i) how many neurons can sufficiently capture a concept, ii) how these neurons are distributed across the layers. LCA provides a ranked list of neurons with respect to the understudied property. We select a minimumal set of top neurons from the ranked list that yield close to the oracle performance.[6]

Minimal Neurons: We found 5% neurons to be optimal for ATB, and GMR; while 10% for both CRS and DIA tasks, due to their more granular tag-set. For the DID task, we found 7% neurons to be optimal (Table 4 shows results – please also see Appendix for a more detailed result using different neuron thresholds). Our results show that **a small subset of features can achieve close to oracle performance.** This entails that re-trainable features are available in the network as also shown by Dalvi et al. (2020). Such a finding entails interesting frontier in efficient feature-based transfer learning, which is considered as a viable alternative to the traditional fine-tuning based transfer learning (Peters et al., 2019; Durrani et al., 2021; Alrowili and Shanker, 2021).

Neuron Distribution: Let us now turn our attention towards how these neurons are distributed in the network. In Figure 3 we plot salient neurons across the layers (See Appendix for all the tasks). A dominant pattern that we observed was that the **embedding and final layers of the model consistently contribute the most number of salient neurons**. This entails that while the neurons in middle layers capture intricate details of the task, the input and output layers of the model that are closer to the actual words possess most lexical information required to for accurate predictions. The model uses the embedding layer to focus on more localized information and final layers to capture contextual dependencies. An exception to this overall pattern was the ALBERT

[5]We limit the presentation to fewer models for clarity purposes. Our observations consistently hold for all dialectal tasks. See Appendix for complete results.

[6]Accuracy when using the entire network or best layer, whichever is higher.

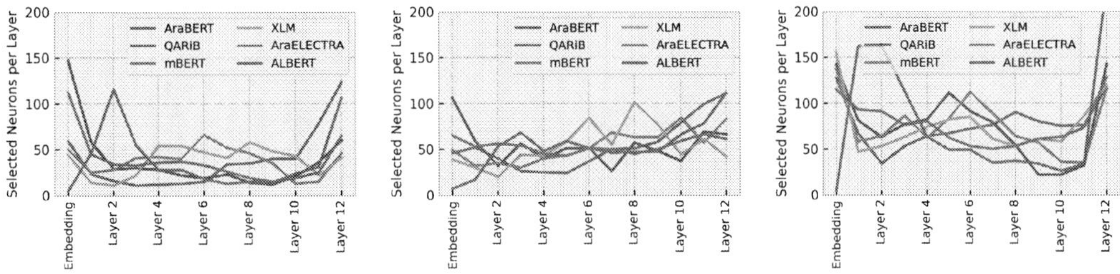

(a) ATB (b) DIA (c) DID

Figure 3: Distribution of selected neurons across the layers

model, where the embedding layer has close to zero contribution in the salient neurons and relatively higher number of neurons from the initial contextualized layers. Recall that ALBERT has a different architecture where parameters are shared across the encoder layers. Moreover the model factorizes the embedding layer. These architectural choices perhaps explain the difference of neuron distribution pattern. A detailed analysis of word embedding layers using lexical tasks such as word similarity and word relatedness is required to fully understand this.

Property Distribution: We have seen how salient neurons distribute across the network. Now we analyze how these neurons distribute across sub-properties within a task. A morphological tagging task for example is composed of different properties such as Noun, Verb, Adjective etc. In Figure 4 we plot the number of salient neurons required to capture different properties on the task of predicting classes in the ATB task. We observed that **closed class categories such as personal pronoun (PRP) are localized to fewer neurons, where as the open-class words such as past-tense verbs (VBD) that exhibit a variety of roles in different contexts require a large number of neurons.** We found this observation to be true for all the models across different dialectal tasks (Please see Appendix for more results).

Layer-wise Property Distribution: We also analyzed **how individual properties are encoded across the layers in the network**, Do they have similar neuron distribution pattern or are the specific properties learned more on higher layers than lower layers and vice versa? Figure 5 shows the distribution of selected neurons of ALBERT, AraBERT and QARiB for a few properties. We observed a very consistent pattern to the overall neuron distribution that we saw in Figure 3. For most of the properties salient neurons were contributed from the embedding and final layers, and middle layers contributed less than 20 neurons. Another interesting pattern to be noted is that noun neurons were more prevalent in the embedding layer (layer 1-2 for ALBERT) but verb neurons were dominantly found in the final layers. Verbs are considered to be structural center in linguistic theories as they connect to all other syntactic units in a sentence (Hudson, 2010). This further reinforces our result that **the higher layers of the model capture long distance dependencies**.

Polysemous Neurons: Neurons are multi-variate in nature and may capture multiple concepts. For example Bau et al. (2019) discovered switch neurons that activate positively for present-tense verbs and negatively for the past-tense verbs in LSTM encoders. We also analyzed the overlaps between salient neurons that learn different linguistic properties in an attempt to discover polysemous neurons. Figure 6 shows the overlap of neurons across properties in different layers in the QARiB model. The zeros means that none of the top neurons between the properties overlap. Note that there is a high concentration of overlapping neurons between determiners (DT), adjectives (JJ) and nouns (NN) or between determiners and verbs. The intersection was around 54% in the case of Determiner "DT" and Noun "NN". We believe this is an artifact of concatenative morphology that Arabic exhibits, where it is common for affixes such as preposition or determiner to join with nouns or adjectives to form composite constructions. We also observed that the number of polysemous neurons exist more dominantly in the embedding layer. Higher layers (Exp. Figure 6e and 6f) show less shared and overlapping neurons.

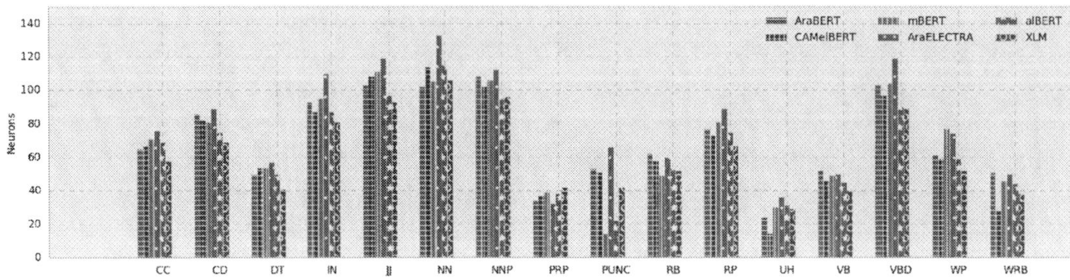

Figure 4: Distribution of neurons per property (ATB)

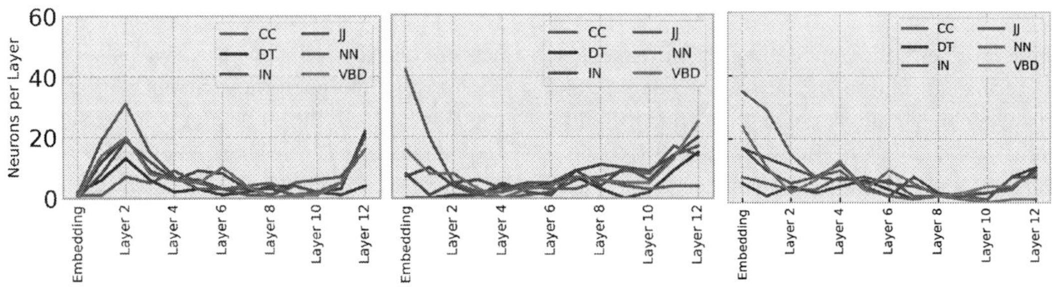

(a) ALBERT

(b) AraBERT

(c) QARiB

Figure 5: Property-wise distribution of neurons across the layers in ATB

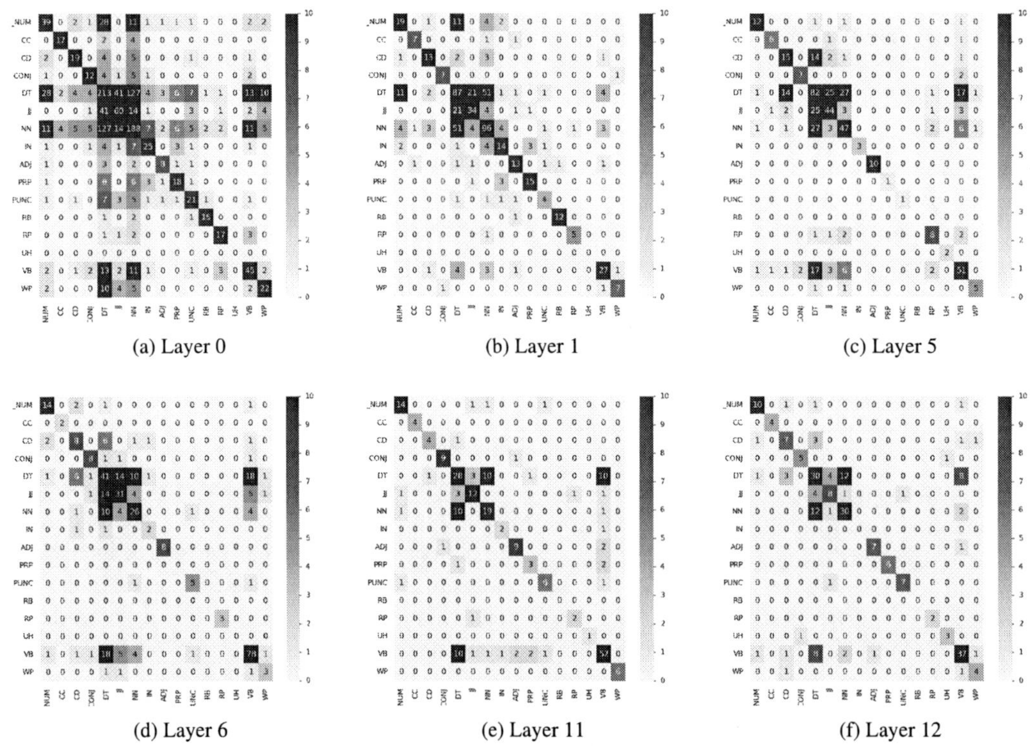

(a) Layer 0

(b) Layer 1

(c) Layer 5

(d) Layer 6

(e) Layer 11

(f) Layer 12

Figure 6: QARiB: Neurons overlap across the ATB properties

5 Related Work

Work done on interpreting deep NLP models can be broadly classified into *Concept Analysis* and *Attribution Analysis*. The former thrives on post-hoc decomposability, where we analyze representations to uncover linguistic (and non-linguistic) phenomenon that are captured as the network is trained towards any NLP task (Conneau et al., 2018; Liu et al., 2019; Tenney et al., 2019; Sajjad et al., 2022; Dalvi et al., 2022) and the latter characterize the role of model components and input features towards a specific prediction (Linzen et al., 2016; Gulordava et al., 2018; Marvin and Linzen, 2018). Our work falls into the former category. We carry out a layer and neuron-wise analysis on the Arabic transformer models. We used Diagnostic classifiers (Belinkov et al., 2017) to train layer and neuron-wise probes towards predicting linguistic properties of interest. **To the best of our knowledge this is the first work on analyzing Arabic transformer models.** Suau et al. (2020) used *max-pooling* to identify relevant neurons (aka *Expert units*) in pre-trained models, with respect to a specific concept (for example word-sense). Mu and Andreas (2020) proposed a *Masked-based Corpus Selection* method to determine important neurons with respect to a concept. See Sajjad et al. (2021b) for a comprehensive survey of these techniques. We used the *Linguistic Correlation Analysis* of Dalvi et al. (2019a) to perform neuron analysis.

6 Conclusion and Future Work

In this paper we carry out a post-hoc analysis on a number of Arabic transformer models using five linguistic tasks. Our results enlighten interesting insights: i) neural networks learn non-trivial amount of linguistic knowledge with lower and middle layers capturing word morphology and higher layers learning more universal phenomenon, ii) we found that salient neurons are distributed across the network, but some layers contribute more salient neurons towards a task, iii) we found some neurons to be polysemous in nature while other capturing very specialized properties, iv) lastly we showed that MSA-based models do not capture dialectal nuances despite having a large overlap with dialects. For future work, we aim to expand this analysis to include more tasks and explore related languages such as the families of Semitic, Germanic or Latin languages.

References

Ahmed Abdelali, Kareem Darwish, Nadir Durrani, and Hamdy Mubarak. 2016. Farasa: A fast and furious segmenter for Arabic. In *Proceedings of the 2016 Conference of the North American Chapter of the Association for Computational Linguistics: Demonstrations*, pages 11–16, San Diego, California. Association for Computational Linguistics.

Ahmed Abdelali, Sabit Hassan, Hamdy Mubarak, Kareem Darwish, and Younes Samih. 2021. Pre-training bert on arabic tweets: Practical considerations.

Muhammad Abdul-Mageed, AbdelRahim Elmadany, and El Moatez Billah Nagoudi. 2020. Arbert & marbert: Deep bidirectional transformers for arabic.

Sultan Alrowili and Vijay Shanker. 2021. ArabicTransformer: Efficient large Arabic language model with funnel transformer and ELECTRA objective. In *Findings of the Association for Computational Linguistics: EMNLP 2021*, pages 1255–1261, Punta Cana, Dominican Republic. Association for Computational Linguistics.

Wissam Antoun, Fady Baly, and Hazem Hajj. 2020. Arabert: Transformer-based model for arabic language understanding. In *LREC 2020 Workshop Language Resources and Evaluation Conference 11–16 May 2020*, page 9.

Wissam Antoun, Fady Baly, and Hazem Hajj. 2021. Araelectra: Pre-training text discriminators for arabic language understanding.

D. Anthony Bau, Yonatan Belinkov, Hassan Sajjad, Nadir Durrani, Fahim Dalvi, and James Glass. 2019. Identifying and Controlling Important Neurons in Neural Machine Translation. *arXiv preprint arXiv:1811.01157*.

Yonatan Belinkov, Nadir Durrani, Fahim Dalvi, Hassan Sajjad, and James Glass. 2017. What do Neural Machine Translation Models Learn about Morphology? In *Proceedings of ACL*, Vancouver. Association for Computational Linguistics.

Yonatan Belinkov, Nadir Durrani, Fahim Dalvi, Hassan Sajjad, and James Glass. 2020. On the linguistic representational power of neural machine translation models. *Computational Linguistics*, 46(1):1–52.

Kevin Clark, Minh-Thang Luong, Quoc V. Le, and Christopher D. Manning. 2020. Electra: Pre-training text encoders as discriminators rather than generators.

Alexis Conneau, Kartikay Khandelwal, Naman Goyal, Vishrav Chaudhary, Guillaume Wenzek, Francisco Guzmán, Edouard Grave, Myle Ott, Luke Zettlemoyer, and Veselin Stoyanov. 2020. Unsupervised cross-lingual representation learning at scale.

Alexis Conneau, German Kruszewski, Guillaume Lample, Loïc Barrault, and Marco Baroni. 2018. What you can cram into a single vector: Probing sentence embeddings for linguistic properties. In *Proceedings of ACL*.

Fahim Dalvi, Nadir Durrani, Hassan Sajjad, Yonatan Belinkov, D. Anthony Bau, and James Glass. 2019a. What is one grain of sand in the desert? analyzing individual neurons in deep nlp models. In *Proceedings of the Thirty-Third AAAI Conference on Artificial Intelligence (AAAI, Oral presentation)*.

Fahim Dalvi, Abdul Rafae Khan, Firoj Alam, Nadir Durrani, Jia Xu, and Hassan Sajjad. 2022. Discovering latent concepts learned in BERT. In *International Conference on Learning Representations*.

Fahim Dalvi, Avery Nortonsmith, D. Anthony Bau, Yonatan Belinkov, Hassan Sajjad, Nadir Durrani, and James Glass. 2019b. NeuroX: A toolkit for analyzing individual neurons in neural networks. In *Proceedings of the AAAI Conference on Artificial Intelligence (AAAI)*, Honolulu, US.

Fahim Dalvi, Hassan Sajjad, Nadir Durrani, and Yonatan Belinkov. 2020. Analyzing redundancy in pretrained transformer models. In *Proceedings of the 2020 EMNLP (EMNLP)*, pages 4908–4926, Online. Association for Computational Linguistics.

Nadir Durrani, Yaser Al-Onaizan, and Abraham Ittycheriah. 2014. Improving egyptian-to-english SMT by mapping egyptian into MSA. In *Computational Linguistics and Intelligent Text Processing - 15th International Conference, CICLing 2014, Kathmandu, Nepal, April 6-12, 2014, Proceedings, Part II*, volume 8404 of *Lecture Notes in Computer Science*, pages 271–282. Springer.

Nadir Durrani, Fahim Dalvi, and Hassan Sajjad. 2022. Linguistic correlation analysis: Discovering salient neurons in deepnlp models.

Nadir Durrani, Fahim Dalvi, Hassan Sajjad, Yonatan Belinkov, and Preslav Nakov. 2019. One size does not fit all: Comparing NMT representations of different granularities. In *Proceedings of the 2019 Conference of the NAACL-HLT, Volume 1 (Long and Short Papers)*, pages 1504–1516, Minneapolis, Minnesota. Association for Computational Linguistics.

Nadir Durrani, Hassan Sajjad, and Fahim Dalvi. 2021. How transfer learning impacts linguistic knowledge in deep NLP models? In *Findings of the Association for Computational Linguistics: ACL-IJCNLP 2021*, pages 4947–4957, Online. Association for Computational Linguistics.

Nadir Durrani, Hassan Sajjad, Fahim Dalvi, and Yonatan Belinkov. 2020. Analyzing individual neurons in pre-trained language models. In *Proceedings of the 2020 EMNLP (EMNLP)*, pages 4865–4880, Online. Association for Computational Linguistics.

Ibrahim Abu El-khair. 2016. 1.5 billion words arabic corpus.

Kristina Gulordava, Piotr Bojanowski, Edouard Grave, Tal Linzen, and Marco Baroni. 2018. Colorless green recurrent networks dream hierarchically. In *Proceedings of the 2018 Conference of NAACL-HLT, Volume 1 (Long Papers)*, pages 1195–1205, New Orleans, Louisiana. Association for Computational Linguistics.

Shilan Hameed. 2018. Filter-wrapper combination and embedded feature selection for gene expression data. *International Journal of Advances in Soft Computing and its Applications*, 10:90–105.

John Hewitt and Percy Liang. 2019. Designing and interpreting probes with control tasks. In *Proceedings of the 2019 EMNLP-IJCNLP*, pages 2733–2743, Hong Kong, China. Association for Computational Linguistics.

Richard Hudson. 2010. *An Introduction to Word Grammar*. Cambridge Textbooks in Linguistics. Cambridge University Press.

Dieuwke Hupkes, Sara Veldhoen, and Willem Zuidema. 2018. Visualisation and 'diagnostic classifiers' reveal how recurrent and recursive neural networks process hierarchical structure.

Go Inoue, Bashar Alhafni, Nurpeiis Baimukan, Houda Bouamor, and Nizar Habash. 2021. The interplay of variant, size, and task type in Arabic pre-trained language models. In *Proceedings of the Sixth Arabic Natural Language Processing Workshop*, Kyiv, Ukraine (Online). Association for Computational Linguistics.

Mustafa Jarrar, Nizar Habash, Faeq Alrimawi, Diyam Akra, and Nasser Zalmout. 2017. Curras: an annotated corpus for the palestinian arabic dialect. *Lang. Resour. Evaluation*, 51(3):745–775.

Salam Khalifa, Nizar Habash, Fadhl Eryani, Ossama Obeid, Dana Abdulrahim, and Meera Al Kaabi. 2018. A morphologically annotated corpus of Emirati Arabic. In *Proceedings of LREC 2018*, Miyazaki, Japan. European Language Resources Association (ELRA).

Salam Khalifa, Nasser Zalmout, and Nizar Habash. 2020. Morphological analysis and disambiguation for Gulf Arabic: The interplay between resources and methods. In *Proceedings of LREC 2020*, pages 3895–3904, Marseille, France. European Language Resources Association.

Diederik Kingma and Jimmy Ba. 2014. Adam: A Method for Stochastic Optimization. *arXiv preprint arXiv:1412.6980*.

Zhenzhong Lan, Mingda Chen, Sebastian Goodman, Kevin Gimpel, Piyush Sharma, and Radu Soricut. 2020. Albert: A lite bert for self-supervised learning of language representations.

Tal Linzen, Emmanuel Dupoux, and Yoav Goldberg. 2016. Assessing the ability of LSTMs to learn syntax-sensitive dependencies. *Transactions of the Association for Computational Linguistics*, 4:521–535.

Pierre Lison and Jörg Tiedemann. 2016. OpenSubtitles2016: Extracting large parallel corpora from movie and TV subtitles. In *Proceedings of LREC'16*, pages 923–929, Portorož, Slovenia. European Language Resources Association (ELRA).

Nelson F. Liu, Matt Gardner, Yonatan Belinkov, Matthew E. Peters, and Noah A. Smith. 2019. Linguistic knowledge and transferability of contextual representations. In *Proceedings of the 2019 Conference of the NAACL-HLT, Volume 1 (Long and Short Papers)*, Minneapolis, Minnesota. Association for Computational Linguistics.

M. Maamouri, Ann Bies, Tim Buckwalter, and Wigdan Mekki. 2004. The penn arabic treebank : Building a large-scale annotated arabic corpus. *NEMLAR Conference on Arabic Language Resources and Tools*.

Rebecca Marvin and Tal Linzen. 2018. Targeted syntactic evaluation of language models. In *Proceedings of the 2018 EMNLP*, pages 1192–1202, Brussels, Belgium. Association for Computational Linguistics.

Giovanni Molina, Fahad AlGhamdi, Mahmoud Ghoneim, Abdelati Hawwari, Nicolas Rey-Villamizar, Mona Diab, and Thamar Solorio. 2016. Overview for the second shared task on language identification in code-switched data. In *Proceedings of the Second Workshop on Computational Approaches to Code Switching*, pages 40–49, Austin, Texas. Association for Computational Linguistics.

Jesse Mu and Jacob Andreas. 2020. Compositional explanations of neurons. *CoRR*, abs/2006.14032.

Hamdy Mubarak and Kareem Darwish. 2014. Using Twitter to collect a multi-dialectal corpus of Arabic. In *Proceedings of the EMNLP 2014 Workshop on Arabic Natural Language Processing (ANLP)*, pages 1–7, Doha, Qatar. Association for Computational Linguistics.

Pedro Javier Ortiz Suárez, Benoît Sagot, and Laurent Romary. 2019. Asynchronous Pipeline for Processing Huge Corpora on Medium to Low Resource Infrastructures. In *7th Workshop on the Challenges in the Management of Large Corpora (CMLC-7)*, Cardiff, United Kingdom. Leibniz-Institut für Deutsche Sprache.

Matthew E. Peters, Sebastian Ruder, and Noah A. Smith. 2019. To tune or not to tune? adapting pretrained representations to diverse tasks. In *Proceedings of the 4th Workshop on Representation Learning for NLP (RepL4NLP-2019)*, Florence, Italy. Association for Computational Linguistics.

Peng Qian, Xipeng Qiu, and Xuanjing Huang. 2016. Analyzing Linguistic Knowledge in Sequential Model of Sentence. In *Proceedings of the 2016 EMNLP*, pages 826–835, Austin, Texas. Association for Computational Linguistics.

Ali Safaya. 2020. Arabic-albert, zenodo, 10.5281/zenodo.4718724.

Ali Safaya, Moutasem Abdullatif, and Deniz Yuret. 2020. KUISAIL at SemEval-2020 task 12: BERT-CNN for offensive speech identification in social media. In *Proceedings of the Fourteenth Workshop on Semantic Evaluation*, pages 2054–2059, Barcelona (online). International Committee for Computational Linguistics.

Hassan Sajjad, Firoj Alam, Fahim Dalvi, and Nadir Durrani. 2021a. Effect of post-processing on contextualized word representations. *CoRR*, abs/2104.07456.

Hassan Sajjad, Nadir Durrani, and Fahim Dalvi. 2021b. Neuron-level interpretation of deep NLP models: A survey. *CoRR*, abs/2108.13138.

Hassan Sajjad, Nadir Durrani, Fahim Dalvi, Firoj Alam, Abdul Khan, and Jia Xu. 2022. In *Proceedings of the 2022 Conference of NAACL-HLT*, pages 3082–3101, Seattle, United States. Association for Computational Linguistics. [link].

Younes Samih, Mohamed Eldesouki, Mohammed Attia, Kareem Darwish, Ahmed Abdelali, Hamdy Mubarak, and Laura Kallmeyer. 2017. Learning from relatives: Unified dialectal Arabic segmentation. In *Proceedings of the 21st Conference on Computational Natural Language Learning (CoNLL 2017)*, pages 432–441, Vancouver, Canada. Association for Computational Linguistics.

Xavier Suau, Luca Zappella, and Nicholas Apostoloff. 2020. Finding experts in transformer models. *CoRR*, abs/2005.07647.

Reem Suwaileh, Mucahid Kutlu, Nihal Fathima, Tamer Elsayed, and Matthew Lease. 2016. Arabicweb16: A new crawl for today's arabic web. In *Proceedings of the 39th International ACM SIGIR Conference on Research and Development in Information Retrieval*, SIGIR '16, page 673–676, New York, NY, USA. Association for Computing Machinery.

Ian Tenney, Dipanjan Das, and Ellie Pavlick. 2019. BERT rediscovers the classical NLP pipeline. In *Proceedings of ACL*, pages 4593–4601, Florence, Italy. Association for Computational Linguistics.

Omar F. Zaidan and Chris Callison-Burch. 2014. Arabic dialect identification. *Computational Linguistics*, 40(1):171–202.

Imad Zeroual, Dirk Goldhahn, Thomas Eckart, and Abdelhak Lakhouaja. 2019. OSIAN: Open source international Arabic news corpus - preparation and integration into the CLARIN-infrastructure. In *Proceedings of the Fourth Arabic Natural Language Processing Workshop*, pages 175–182, Florence, Italy. Association for Computational Linguistics.

Hui Zou and Trevor Hastie. 2005. Regularization and variable selection via the elastic net. *Journal of the Royal Statistical Society, Series B*, 67:301–320.

A Appendix

Table 5 shows the performance loss for different thresholds. Highlighted thresholds were selected based on the 1% average performance loss. For the case of DIA, some overfitting is noticeable. Such case is reported in literature where the classifiers with large contextualized vectors tend to overfit when supervised data is insufficient (Hameed, 2018).

Task	Threshold	AraBERT	ArabicBERT	CAMelBERT	MARBERT	QARiB	mBERT	AraELECTRA	ALBERT	XLM
ATB	3.00%	0.914	0.915	0.929	0.916	0.924	0.924	0.868	0.935	0.938
	5.00%	0.934	0.940	0.949	0.945	0.950	0.941	0.912	0.947	0.953
	7.00%	0.939	0.949	0.957	0.952	0.957	0.945	0.934	0.953	0.957
	10.00%	0.943	0.953	0.960	0.957	0.961	0.947	0.945	0.954	0.960
	20.00%	0.945	0.956	0.960	0.958	0.962	0.948	0.954	0.953	0.961
	50.00%	0.940	0.953	0.955	0.954	0.958	0.941	0.957	0.948	0.955
	100.00%	0.937	0.954	0.957	0.955	0.955	0.938	0.954	0.947	0.953
CRS	3.00%	0.769	0.767	0.803	0.784	0.787	0.725	0.658	0.763	0.714
	5.00%	0.798	0.809	0.834	0.831	0.828	0.757	0.723	0.791	0.755
	7.00%	0.791	0.811	0.842	0.840	0.845	0.755	0.789	0.782	0.761
	10.00%	0.821	0.836	0.861	0.862	0.861	0.784	0.790	0.807	0.785
	20.00%	0.822	0.844	0.868	0.864	0.866	0.796	0.824	0.809	0.797
	50.00%	0.804	0.827	0.858	0.857	0.861	0.776	0.825	0.792	0.792
	100.00%	0.788	0.824	0.839	0.845	0.847	0.763	0.816	0.779	0.780
DIA	3.00%	0.753	0.780	0.798	0.766	0.783	0.732	0.683	0.779	0.753
	5.00%	0.774	0.812	0.835	0.809	0.820	0.748	0.747	0.808	0.767
	7.00%	0.788	0.831	0.847	0.830	0.834	0.757	0.776	0.815	0.783
	10.00%	0.793	0.833	0.851	0.842	0.836	0.775	0.794	0.818	0.790
	20.00%	0.794	0.840	0.857	0.850	0.851	0.768	0.809	0.814	0.806
	50.00%	0.784	0.832	0.840	0.844	0.847	0.752	0.814	0.798	0.799
	100.00%	0.770	0.818	0.831	0.826	0.829	0.734	0.803	0.790	0.776
DID	3.00%	0.829	0.876	0.879	0.879	0.885	0.809	0.840	0.864	0.833
	5.00%	0.854	0.892	0.897	0.907	0.908	0.821	0.868	0.881	0.860
	7.00%	0.860	0.901	0.910	0.916	0.917	0.832	0.882	0.885	0.865
	10.00%	0.872	0.905	0.914	0.918	0.920	0.837	0.887	0.892	0.878
	20.00%	0.880	0.908	0.917	0.922	0.923	0.846	0.900	0.893	0.878
	50.00%	0.876	0.902	0.909	0.915	0.915	0.840	0.906	0.888	0.871
	100.00%	0.864	0.892	0.896	0.903	0.903	0.823	0.906	0.877	0.858
GMR	3.00%	0.881	0.891	0.913	0.907	0.912	0.856	0.833	0.885	0.856
	5.00%	0.899	0.910	0.926	0.923	0.924	0.876	0.876	0.898	0.880
	7.00%	0.913	0.925	0.929	0.936	0.934	0.892	0.892	0.909	0.891
	10.00%	0.908	0.920	0.931	0.930	0.929	0.890	0.901	0.905	0.897
	20.00%	0.907	0.920	0.926	0.929	0.925	0.891	0.914	0.904	0.898
	50.00%	0.899	0.909	0.918	0.919	0.915	0.876	0.911	0.889	0.884
	100.00%	0.890	0.900	0.910	0.909	0.908	0.865	0.901	0.880	0.878

Table 5: Performance per models using different threshold δ

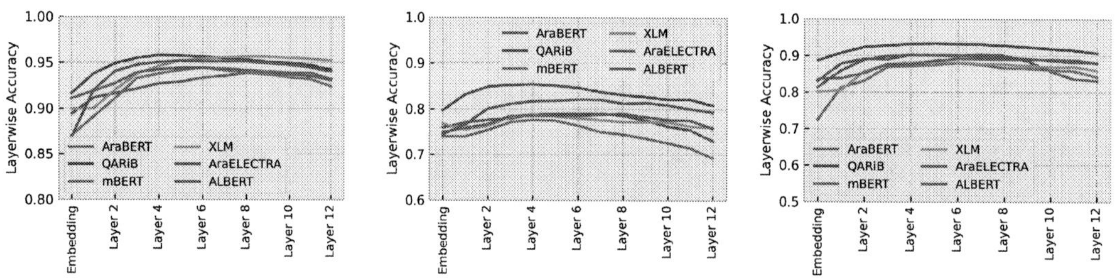

(a) ATB (b) DIA (c) GMR

Figure 7: Layer-wise accuracy for ATB, DIA, GMR tasks.

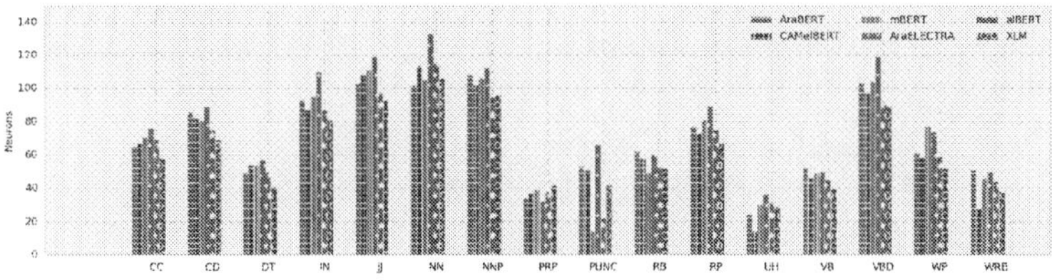

(a) ATB

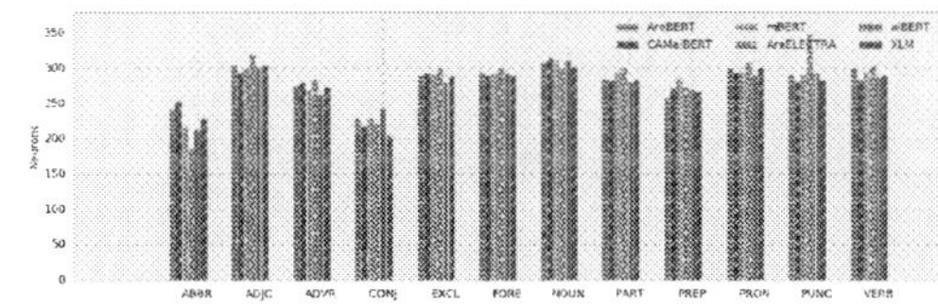

(b) CRS

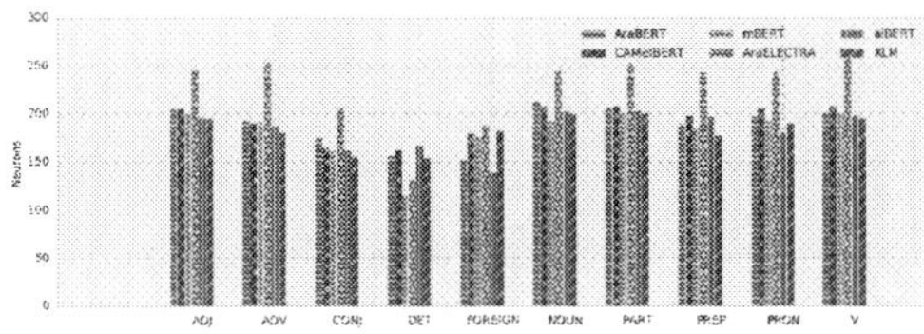

(c) DIA

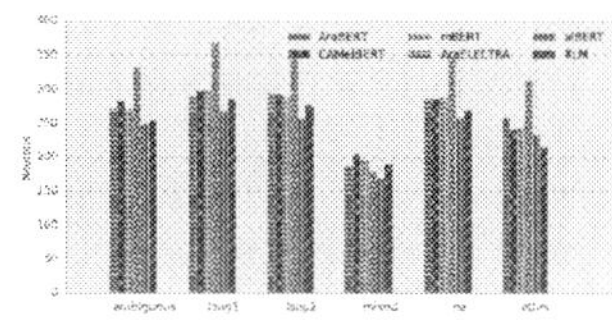

(d) DID

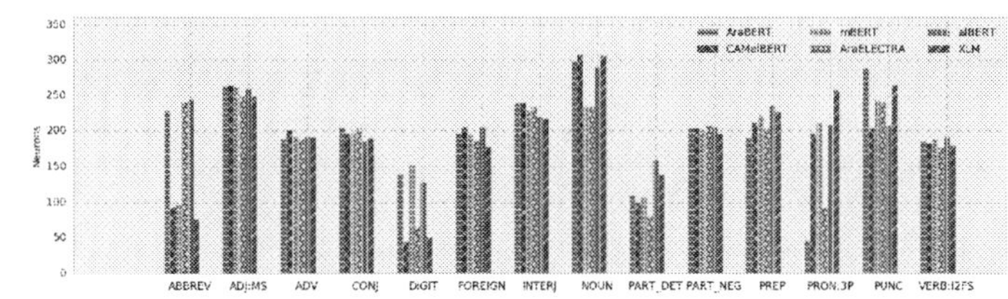

(e) GMR

Figure 8: Distribution of neurons per property

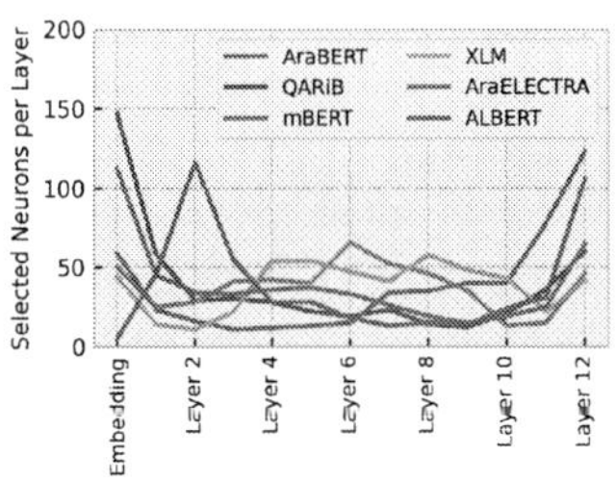

(a) ATB

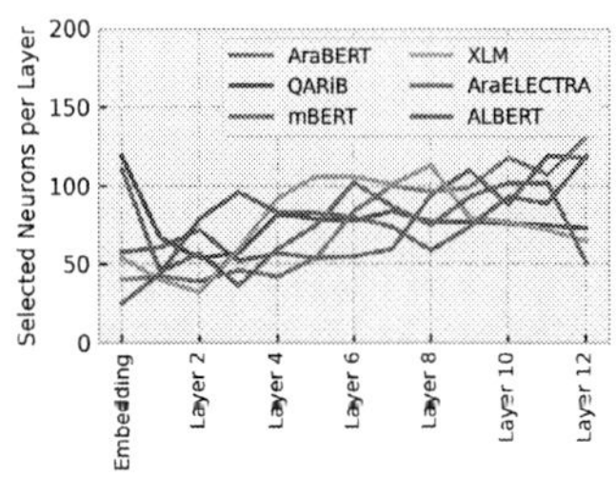

(b) CRS

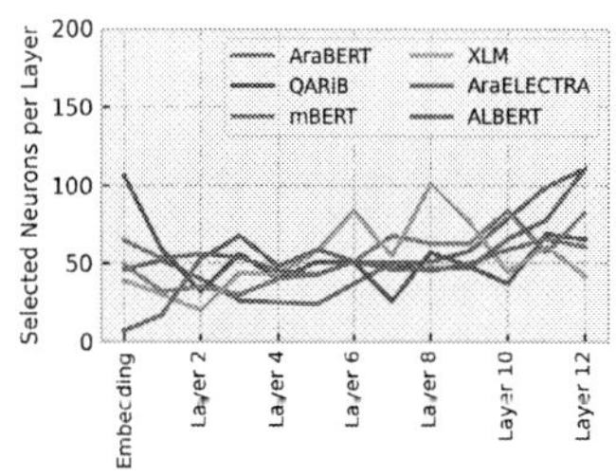

(c) DIA

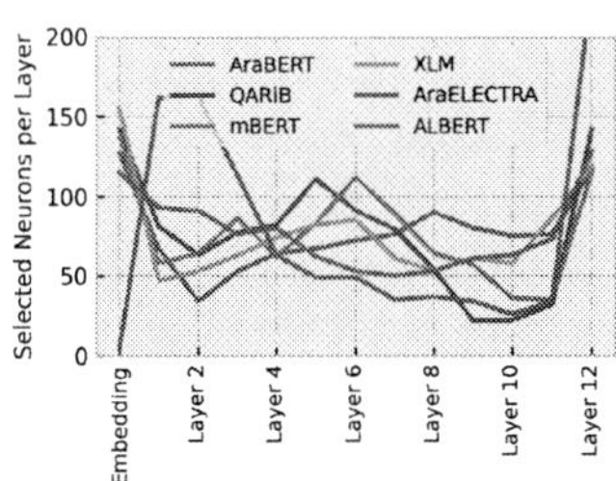

(d) DID

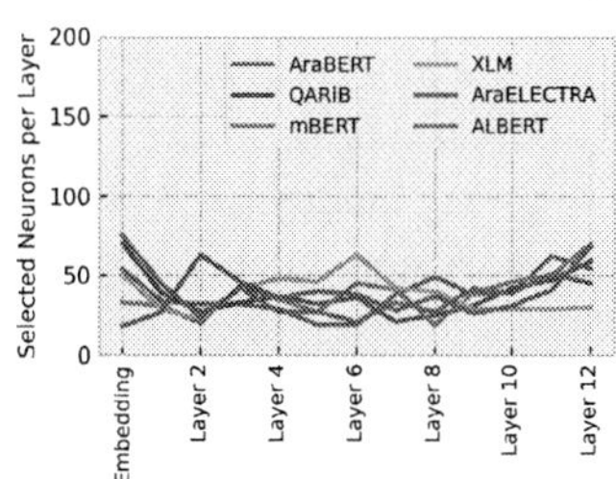

(e) GMR

Figure 9: Distribution of selected neurons across the layers

Universal Evasion Attacks on Summarization Scoring

Wenchuan Mu Kwan Hui Lim
Singapore University of Technology and Design
{wenchuan_mu,kwanhui_lim}@sutd.edu.sg

Abstract

The automatic scoring of summaries is important as it guides the development of summarizers. Scoring is also complex, as it involves multiple aspects such as fluency, grammar, and even textual entailment with the source text. However, summary scoring has not been considered a machine learning task to study its accuracy and robustness. In this study, we place automatic scoring in the context of regression machine learning tasks and perform evasion attacks to explore its robustness. Attack systems predict a non-summary string from each input, and these non-summary strings achieve competitive scores with good summarizers on the most popular metrics: ROUGE, METEOR, and BERTScore. Attack systems also "outperform" state-of-the-art summarization methods on ROUGE-1 and ROUGE-L, and score the second-highest on METEOR. Furthermore, a BERTScore backdoor is observed: a simple trigger can score higher than any automatic summarization method. The evasion attacks in this work indicate the low robustness of current scoring systems at the system level. We hope that our highlighting of these proposed attacks will facilitate the development of summary scores.

1 Introduction

A long-standing paradox has plagued the task of automatic summarization. On the one hand, for about 20 years, there has not been any automatic scoring available as a sufficient or necessary condition to demonstrate summary quality, such as adequacy, grammaticality, cohesion, fidelity, etc. On the other hand, contemporaneous research more often uses one or several automatic scores to endorse a summarizer as state-of-the-art. More than 90% of works on language generation neural models choose automatic scoring as the main basis, and about half of them rely on automatic scoring only (van der Lee et al., 2021). However, these scoring methods have been found to be insufficient (Novikova et al., 2017), oversimplified (van der Lee et al., 2021), difficult to interpret (Sai et al., 2022), inconsistent with the way humans assess summaries (Rankel et al., 2013; Böhm et al., 2019), or even contradict each other (Gehrmann et al., 2021; Bhandari et al., 2020).

Figure 1: Automatic summarization (left) and automatic scoring (right) should be considered as two systems of the same rank, representing conditional language generation and natural language understanding, respectively. As a stand-alone system, the accuracy and robustness of automatic scoring are also important. In this study, we create systems that use bad summaries to fool existing scoring systems. This work shows that optimizing towards a flawed scoring does more harm than good, and flawed scoring methods are *not* able to indicate the true performance of summarizers, even at a system level.

Why do we have to deal with this paradox? The current work may not have suggested that summarizers assessed by automatic scoring are de facto ineffective. However, optimizing for flawed evaluations (Gehrmann et al., 2021; Peyrard et al., 2017), directly or indirectly, ultimately harms the development of automatic summarization (Narayan et al., 2018; Kryscinski et al., 2019; Paulus et al., 2018). One of the most likely drawbacks is shortcut learning (surface learning, Geirhos et al., 2020), where summarizing models may fail to generate text with more widely accepted qualities such as adequacy and authenticity, but instead pleasing scores. Here,

Proceedings of the Fifth BlackboxNLP Workshop on Analyzing and Interpreting Neural Networks for NLP, pages 104 - 118
December 8, 2022 ©2022 Association for Computational Linguistics

we quote and adapt[1] this hypothetical story by Geirhos et al..

"Alice loves literature. Always has, probably always will. At this very moment, however, she is cursing the subject: After spending weeks immersing herself in the world of Shakespeare's The Tempest, she is now faced with a number of exam questions that are (in her opinion) to equal parts dull and difficult. 'How many times is Duke of Milan addressed'... Alice notices that Bob, sitting in front of her, seems to be doing very well. Bob of all people, who had just boasted how he had learned the whole book chapter by rote last night ..."

According to Geirhos et al., Bob might get better grades and consequently be considered a better student than Alice, which is an example of surface learning. The same could be the case with automatic summarization, where we might end up with significant differences between expected and actual learning outcomes (Paulus et al., 2018). To avoid going astray, it is important to ensure that the objective is correct.

In addition to understanding the importance of correct justification, we also need to know what caused the fallacy of the justification process for these potentially useful summarizers. There are three mainstream speculations that are not mutually exclusive. (1) The transition from extractive summarization to abstractive summarization (Kryscinski et al., 2019) could have been underestimated. For example, the popular score ROUGE (Lin, 2004) was originally used to judge the ranking of sentences selected from documents. Due to constraints on sentence integrity, the generated summaries can always be fluent and undistorted, except sometimes when anaphora is involved. However, when it comes to free-form language generation, sentence integrity is no longer guaranteed, but the metric continues to be used. (2) Many metrics, while flawed in judging individual summaries, often make sense at the system level (Reiter, 2018; Gehrmann et al., 2021; Böhm et al., 2019). In other words, it might have been believed that few summarization systems can *consistently* output poor-quality but high-scoring strings. (3) Researchers have not figured out how humans interpret or understand texts (van der Lee et al., 2021; Gehrmann et al., 2021; Schluter, 2017), thus the decision about how good a summary really is varies from person to person, let alone automated scoring. In fact, automatic scoring is more of a natural language understanding (NLU) task, a task that is far from solved. From this viewpoint, automatic scoring itself is fairly challenging.

Nevertheless, the current work is not to advocate (and certainly does not disparage) human evaluation. Instead, we argue that automatic scoring itself is not just a sub-module of automatic summarization, and that automatic scoring is a stand-alone system that needs to be studied for its *own* accuracy and robustness. The primary reason is that NLU is clearly required to characterize summary quality, *e.g.*, semantic similarity to determine adequacy (Morris, 2020), or textual entailment (Dagan et al., 2006) to determine fidelity. Besides, summary scoring is similar to automated essay scoring (AES), which is a 50-year-old task measuring grammaticality, cohesion, relevance etc. of written texts (Ke and Ng, 2019). Moreover, recent advances in automatic scoring also support this argument well. Automatic scoring is gradually transitioning from well-established metrics measuring N-gram overlap (BLEU (Papineni et al., 2002), ROUGE (Lin, 2004), METEOR (Banerjee and Lavie, 2005), etc.) to emerging metrics aimed at computing semantic similarity through pre-trained neural models (BERTScore (Zhang et al., 2019b), MoverScore (Zhao et al., 2019), BLEURT (Sellam et al., 2020), etc.) These emerging scores exhibit two characteristics that stand-alone machine learning systems typically have: one is that some *can be fine-tuned* for human cognition; the other is that they *still have room to improve* and still have to learn how to match human ratings.

Machine learning systems can be attacked. Attacks can help improve their generality, robustness, and interpretability. In particular, evasion attacks are an intuitive way to further expose the weaknesses of current automatic scoring systems. Evasion attack is the parent task of adversarial attack, which aims to make the system fail to correctly identify the input, and thus requires defence against certain exposed vulnerabilities.

In this work, we try to answer the question: do current representative automatic scoring systems really work well at the system level? How hard is it to say they do not work well at the system level? In summary, we make the following major contributions in this study:

- We are the first to treat automatic summariza-

[1] We underline adaptations.

System	Summary	Document
Gold	Kevin Pietersen was sacked by England 14 months ago after Ashes defeat. Batsman scored 170 on his county cricket return for Surrey last week. Pietersen wants to make a sensational return to the England side this year. But Andrew Flintoff thinks time is running out for him to resurrect career. (ROUGE-1, ROUGE-2, ROUGE-L, METEOR, BERTScore)	Andrew Flintoff fears Kevin Pietersen is 'running out of time' to resurrect his England career. The dual Ashes-winning all-rounder is less convinced, however, about Pietersen's prospects of forcing his way back into Test contention. Kevin Pietersen scored 170 for Surrey in The Parks as he bids to earn a recall to the England squad... ... Flintoff senses he no longer has age on his side. Pietersen has not featured for England since he was unceremoniously sacked 14 months ago. ... ... Flintoff said ... 'If he'd started the season last year with Surrey, and scored run after run and put himself in the position... whereas now I think he's looking at the Ashes ... ... you get the sense everyone within the England set-up wants him as captain,' he said.' ... The former England star is hoping to win back his Test place with a return to red ball cricket. ... ... 'this stands up as a competition.'
Good (Liu and Liu, 2021)	Kevin pietersen scored 170 for surrey against mccu oxford. Former england star andrew flintoff fears pietersen is 'running out of time' to resurrect his england career. Pietersen has been surplus to requirements since being sacked 14 months ago. Flintoff sees a bright future for 'probably the premier tournament' in this country. (55.45, 18.18, 41.58, 40.03, 85.56)	
Broken	Andrew Flintoff fears Kevin Pietersen is running out of time to resurrect his England career Flintoff. Pietersen scored 170 for Surrey in The. Former England star Andrew. batsman has been . since being sacked 14 months ago after. three in the. the Ashes and he s. (**56.84**, **21.51**, **44.21**, **47.26**, 85.95)	
A dot	. (0, 0, 0, 0, **88.47**)	
Scrambled code	\x03\x18$\x18...\x03$\x03|...\x0f\x01<<$$\x04...\x0e \x04# $...\x0f\x0f\x0f...\x0e...\x0f...\x0f\x0f$\x0f \x04\x0f\x0f (many tokens omitted) (0, 0, 0, 0, 87.00)	
Scrambled code + broken	\x03\x18$\x18...\x03$\x03|...\x0f\x01<<$$\x04...\x0e \x04# $...\x0f\x0f\x0f...\x0e...\x0f...\x0f\x0f$\x0f \x04\x0f\x0f... Andrew Flintoff fears Kevin Pietersen is running out of time to resurrect his England career Flintoff. Pietersen scored 170 for Surrey in The. Former England star Andrew. batsman has been . since being sacked 14 months ago after. three in the. the Ashes and he s. (many tokens omitted) (**56.84**, **21.51**, **44.21**, **47.26**, 87.00)	

Table 1: We created non-summarizing systems, each of which produces bad text when processing any document. Broken sentences get higher lexical scores; non-alphanumeric characters outperform good summaries on BERTScore. Concatenating two strings produces equally bad text, but scores high on both. The example is from CNN/DailyMail (for visualization, document is abridged to keep content most consistent with the corresponding gold summary).

tion scoring as an NLU regression task and perform evasion attacks.

- We are the first to perform a *universal, targeted* attack on NLP *regression* models.
- Our evasion attacks support that it is not difficult to deceive the three most popular automatic scoring systems simultaneously.
- The proposed attacks can be directly applied to test emerging scoring systems.

2 Related Work

2.1 Evasion Attacks in NLP

In an evasion attack, the attacker modifies the input data so that the NLP model incorrectly identifies the input. The most widely studied evasion attack is the adversarial attack, in which insignificant changes are made to the input to make "adversarial examples" that greatly affect the model's output (Szegedy et al., 2014). There are other types of evasion attacks, and evasion attacks can be classified from at least three perspectives. (1) Targeted evasion attacks and untargeted evasion attacks (Cao and Gong, 2017). The former is intended for the model to predict a specific wrong output for that example. The latter is designed to mislead the model to predict any incorrect output. (2) Universal attacks and input-dependent attacks (Wallace et al., 2019; Song et al., 2021). The former, also known as an "input-agnostic" attack, is a "unique model analysis tool". They are more threatening and expose more general input-output patterns learned by the model. The opposite is often referred to as an input-dependent attack, and is sometimes referred to as a local or typical attack. (3) Black-box attacks and white-box attacks. The difference is whether the attacker has access to the detailed computation of the victim model. The former does not, and the latter does. Often, targeted, universal, black-box attacks are more challenging. Evasion attacks have been used to expose vulnerabilities in sentiment analysis, natural language inference (NLI), automatic short answer grading (ASAG), and natural language generation (NLG) (Alzantot et al., 2018; Wallace et al., 2019; Song et al., 2021; Filighera et al., 2020, 2022; Zang et al., 2020; Behjati et al., 2019).

2.2 Universal Triggers in Attacks on Classification

A prefix can be a universal trigger. When a prefix is added to any input, it can cause the classifier to misclassify sentiment, textual entailment (Wallace et al., 2019), or if a short answer is correct (Filighera et al., 2020). These are usually untargeted attacks in a white-box setting[2], where the gradients of neural models are computed during the trigger search phase.

[2]When the number of categories is small, the line between targeted and non-targeted attacks is blurred, especially when there are only two categories.

Wallace et al. also used prefixes to trigger a reading comprehension model to specifically choose an odd answer or an NLG model to generate something similar to an egregious set of targets. These two are universal, targeted attacks, but are mainly for classification tasks. Given that automatic scoring is a regression task, more research is needed.

2.3 Adversarial Examples Search for Regression Models

Compared with classification tasks in NLP, regression tasks (such as determining text similarity) are fewer and less frequently attacked. For example, the Universal Sentence Encoder (USE, Cer et al., 2018) and BERTScore (Zhang et al., 2019b) are often taken as two constraints when searching adversarial examples for other tasks (Alzantot et al., 2018). However, these regression models may also be flawed, vulnerable or not robust, which may invalidate the constraints (Morris, 2020).

Morris (2020) shows that adversarial attacks could also threaten these regression models. For example, Maheshwary et al. (2021) adopt a black-box setting to maximize the semantic similarity between the altered input text sequence and the original text. Similar attacks are mostly input-dependent, probably because these regression models are mostly used as constraints. In contrast, universal attacks may better reveal the vulnerabilities of these regression models.

2.4 Victim Scoring Systems

Every (existing) automatic summary scoring is a monotonic regression model. Most scoring requires at least one gold-standard text to be compared to the output from summarizers. One can opt to combine multiple available systems in one super system (Lamontagne and Abi-Zeid, 2006). We will focus on the three most frequently used systems, including rule-based systems and neural systems. ROUGE (Recall-Oriented Understudy for Gisting Evaluation Lin, 2004) measures the number of overlapping N-grams or the longest common subsequence (LCS) between the generated summary and a set of gold reference summaries. Particularly, ROUGE-1 corresponds to unigrams, ROUGE-2 to bigrams, and ROUGE-L to LCS. F-measures of ROUGE are often used (See et al., 2017). METEOR (Banerjee and Lavie, 2005) measures overlapping unigrams, equating a unigram with its stemmed form, synonyms, and paraphrases. BERTScore (Zhang et al., 2019b) measures soft overlap between two token-aligned texts, by selecting alignments, BERTScore returns the maximum cosine similarity between contextual BERT (Devlin et al., 2019) embeddings.

2.5 Targeted Threshold for Attacks

We use a threshold to determine whether a targeted attack on the regression model was successful. Intuitively, the threshold is given by the scores of the top summarizers, and we consider our attack to be successful if an attacker obtains a score higher than the threshold using clearly inferior summaries. We use representative systems that once achieved the state-of-the-art in the past five years: Pointer Generator (See et al., 2017), Bottom-Up (Gehrmann et al., 2018), PNBERT (Zhong et al., 2019), T5 (Raffel et al., 2019), BART (Lewis et al., 2020), and SimCLS (Liu and Liu, 2021).

3 Universal Evasion Attacks

We develop universal evasion attacks for individual scoring system, and make sure that the combined attacker can fool ROUGE, METEOR, and BERTScore at the same time. It incorporates two parts, a white-box attacker on ROUGE, and a black-box universal trigger search algorithm for BERTScore, based on genetic algorithms. METEOR can be attacked directly by the one designed for ROUGE. Concatenating output strings from black-box and white-box attackers leads to a sole universal evasion attacking string.

3.1 Problem Formulation

Summarization is conditional generation. A system σ that performs this conditional generation takes an input text ($\mathbf{a}$) and outputs a text ($\hat{\mathbf{s}}$), *i.e.*, $\hat{\mathbf{s}} = \sigma(\mathbf{a})$. In single-reference scenario, there is a gold reference sequence $\mathbf{s}_{\text{ref}}$. A summary scoring system γ calculates the "closeness" between sequence $\hat{\mathbf{s}}$ and $\mathbf{s}_{\text{ref}}$. In order for a scoring system to be sufficient to justify a good summarizer, the following condition should always be avoided:

$$\gamma(\sigma_{\text{far worse}}(\mathbf{a}), \mathbf{s}_{\text{ref}}) > \gamma(\sigma_{\text{better}}(\mathbf{a}), \mathbf{s}_{\text{ref}}). \quad (1)$$

Indeed, to satisfy the condition above is our attacking task. In this section, we detail how we find a suitable $\sigma_{\text{far worse}}$.

3.2 White-box Input-agnostic Attack on ROUGE and METEOR

In general, attacking ROUGE or METEOR can only be done with a white-box setup, since even the most novice attacker (developer) will understand how these two formulae calculate the overlap between two strings. We choose to game ROUGE with the most obvious bad system output (broken sentences) such that no additional human evaluation is required. In contrast, for other gaming methods, such as reinforcement learning (Paulus et al., 2018), even if a high score is achieved, human evaluation is still needed to measure how bad the quality of the text is.

We utilize a hybrid approach (we refer to it as σ_{ROUGE}) of token classification neural models and simple rule-based ordering, since we know that ROUGE compares each pair of sequences $(\mathrm{s}_1, \mathrm{s}_2)$ via hard N-gram overlapping. In bag algebra, extended from set algebra (Bertossi et al., 2018), two trendy variants of ROUGE: ROUGE-N ($R_{\text{N}}(n, \mathrm{s}_1, \mathrm{s}_2), n \in \mathbb{Z}^+$) and ROUGE-L($R_{\text{L}}(\mathrm{s}_1, \mathrm{s}_2)$) calculate as follows:

$$R_{\text{N}}(n, \mathrm{s}_1, \mathrm{s}_2) = \frac{2 \cdot |b(n, \mathrm{s}_1) \cap b(n, \mathrm{s}_2)|}{|b(n, \mathrm{s}_1)| + |b(n, \mathrm{s}_2)|}, \quad (2)$$

$$R_{\text{L}}(\mathrm{s}_1, \mathrm{s}_2) = \frac{2 \cdot |b(1, \text{LCS}(\mathrm{s}_1, \mathrm{s}_1))|}{|b(1, \mathrm{s}_1)| + |b(1, \mathrm{s}_2)|}, \quad (3)$$

where $|\cdot|$ denotes the size of a bag, $\cap$ denotes *bag* intersection, and bag of N-grams is calculated as follows:

$$b(n, \mathrm{s}) = \{\, x \mid x \text{ is an } n\text{-gram in s} \,\}_{\text{bag}}. \quad (4)$$

In our hybrid approach, the first step is that the neural model tries to predict the target's bag of words $b(1, \mathrm{s}_{\text{ref}})$, given any input $\mathbf{a}$ and corresponding target s_{ref}. Then, words in the predicted bag are ordered according to their occurrence in the input $\mathbf{a}$. Formally, training of the neural model (ϕ) is:

$$\min_{\phi} \frac{1}{|\mathcal{A}|} \sum_{\mathbf{a} \in \mathcal{A}} \sum_{w \in \mathbf{a}} H(P_{\text{ref}}(\cdot \mid w), P(\cdot \mid w, \phi)), \quad (5)$$

where H is the cross-entropy between the probability distribution of the reference word count and the predicted word count. An approximation is that the model tries to predict $b(1, \mathrm{s}_{\text{ref}}) \cap b(1, \mathbf{a})$. Empirically, three-quarters of words in reference summaries can be found in their corresponding input texts.

Referencing the input text ($\mathbf{a}$) and predicted bag of words ($\hat{W}$) to construct a sequence is straightforward, as seen in Algorithm 1.

Algorithm 1 From bag of words to sequence

Require: $\mathbf{a}, \hat{W}$ **return** $\hat{\mathrm{s}}$
  $\hat{\mathrm{s}} \leftarrow ()$
  while $|\hat{W}| > 0$ **do**
    Salient Sequence $\mathrm{l} \leftarrow (x \mid \text{for } x \in \mathbf{a} \text{ if } [x \in \hat{W}])$
    $\mathbf{c} \leftarrow$ Longest Consecutive Salient Subsequence of l
    if $|\mathbf{c}| < C$ **then** ▷ Constant about 3
      break
    end if
    $\hat{\mathrm{s}} \leftarrow \hat{\mathrm{s}} + \mathbf{c}$ ▷ Concatenate $\mathbf{c}$ to $\hat{\mathrm{s}}$
    $\hat{W} \leftarrow \hat{W} - \mathbf{c}$ ▷ Remove used words
  end while

Algorithm 1 uses salient words to highlight the longest consecutive salient subsequences in $\mathbf{a}$, until the words in $\hat{W}$ are exhausted, or when each consecutive salient sequence is less than three words ($C = 3$).

3.3 Black-box Universal Trigger Search on BERTScore

Finding a $\sigma_{\text{far worse}}$ for BERTScore alone to satisfy condition1 is easy. A single dot (".") is an imitator of *all* strings, as if it is a "backdoor" left by developers. We notice that, on default setting of BERTScore[3], using a single dot can achieve around 0.892 on average when compared with any natural sentences. This figure "outperforms" all existing summarizers, making *outputing a dot* a good enough $\sigma_{\text{far worse}}$ instance.

This example is very intriguing because it highlights the extent to which many vulnerabilities go unnoticed, although it cannot be combined directly with the attacker for ROUGE. Intuitively, there could be various clever methods to attack BERTScore as well, such as adding a prefix to each string (Wallace et al., 2019; Song et al., 2021). However, we here opt to develop a system that could output (one of) the most obviously bad strings (scrambled codes) to score high.

BERTScore is generally classified as a neural, untrained score (Sai et al., 2022). In other words, part of its forward computation (*e.g.*, greedy matching) is rule-based, while the rest (*e.g.*, getting every token embedded in the sequence) is not. Therefore, it is difficult to "design" an attack rationally. Gradient methods (white-box) or discrete optimization (black-box) are preferable. Likewise, while letting BERTScore generate soft predictions (Jauregi Unanue et al., 2021) may allow attacks in a

[3] `https://huggingface.co/metrics/bertscore`

white-box setting, we found that black-box optimization is sufficient.

Inspired by the single-dot backdoor in BERTScore, we hypothesize that we can form longer catch-all emulators by using only non-alphanumeric tokens. Such an emulator has two benefits: first, it requires a small fitting set, which is important in targeted attacks on regression models. We will see that once an emulator is optimized to fit one natural sentence, it can also emulate almost any other natural sentence. The total number of natural sentences that need to be fitted before it can imitate decently is usually less than ten. Another benefit is that using non-alphanumeric tokens does not affect ROUGE.

Genetic Algorithm (GA, Holland, 2012) was used to discretely optimize the proposed non-alphanumeric strings. Genetic algorithm is a search-based optimization technique inspired by the natural selection process. GA starts by initializing a population of candidate solutions and iteratively making them progress towards better solutions. In each iteration, GA uses a fitness function to evaluate the quality of each candidate. High-quality candidates are likely to be selected and crossover-ed to produce the next set of candidates. New candidates are mutated to ensure search space diversity and better exploration. Applying GA to attacks has shown effectiveness and efficiency in maximizing the probability of a certain classification label (Alzantot et al., 2018) or the semantic similarity between two text sequences (Maheshwary et al., 2021). Our single fitness function is as follows,

$$\hat{\mathrm{s}}_{\text{emu}} = \arg\min_{\hat{\mathrm{s}}} -B(\hat{\mathrm{s}}, \mathrm{s}_{\text{ref}}), \quad (6)$$

where B stands for BERTScore. As for termination, we either use a threshold of -0.88, or maximum of 2000 iterations.

To fit $\hat{\mathrm{s}}_{\text{emu}}$ to a set of natural sentences, we calculate BERTScore for each sentence in the set after each termination. We then select a proper s_{ref} to fit for the next round. We always select the natural sentence (in a finite set) that has the lowest BERTScore with the optimized $\hat{\mathrm{s}}_{\text{emu}}$ at the current stage. We then repeat this process till the average BERTScore achieved by this string is higher than many reputable summarizers.

Finally, to simultaneously game ROUGE and BERTScore, we concatenate $\hat{\mathrm{s}}_{\text{emu}}$ and the input-agnostic $\sigma_{\text{ROUGE}}(\mathbf{a})$. If we set the number of tokens in $\hat{\mathrm{s}}_{\text{emu}}$ greater than 512 (the max sequence length for BERT), $\sigma_{\text{ROUGE}}(\mathbf{a})$ would then not affect the effectiveness of $\hat{\mathrm{s}}_{\text{emu}}$, and we technically game them both. Additionally, this concatenated string games METEOR, too.

4 Experiments

We instantiate our evasion attack by conducting experiments on non-anonymized CNN/DailyMail (CNNDM, Nallapati et al., 2016; See et al., 2017), a dataset that contains news articles and associated highlights as summaries. CNNDM includes 287,226 training pairs, 13,368 validation pairs and 11,490 test pairs.

For σ_{ROUGE} we use RoBERTa (base model, Liu et al., 2019) to instantiate ϕ, which is an optimized pretrained encoding with a randomly initialized linear layer on top of the hidden states. Number of classes is set to three because we assume that each word appears at most twice in a summary. All 124,058,116 parameters are trained as a whole on CNNDM train split for one epoch. When the batch size is eight, the training time on an NVIDIA Tesla K80 graphics processing unit (GPU) is less than 14 hours. It then takes about 20 minutes to predict (including word ordering) all 11,490 samples in the CNNDM test split. Scripts and results are available at `https://github.com/cestwc/universal-evasion.git`.

For the universal trigger to BERTScore, we use the library from Blank and Deb (2020) for discrete optimizing, set population size at 10, and terminate at 2000 generations. $\hat{\mathrm{s}}_{\text{emu}}$ is a sequence of independent randomly initialized non-alphanumeric characters. For a reference s_{ref} from CNNDM, we start from randomly pick a summary text from train split and optimize for $\hat{\mathrm{s}}_{\text{emu},i=0}$. We then pick the s_{ref} that is farthest away from $\hat{\mathrm{s}}_{\text{emu},i=0}$ to optimize for $\hat{\mathrm{s}}_{\text{emu},i=1}$, with $\hat{\mathrm{s}}_{\text{emu},i=1}$ as initial population. Practically, we found that we can stop iterating when $i = 5$. Each iteration takes less than two hours on a 2vCPU (Intel Xeon @ 2.30GHz).

5 Results

We compare ROUGE-1/2/L, METEOR, and BERTScore of our threat model with that achieved by the top summarizers in Table 2. We present two versions of threat models with a minor difference. As the results indicate, each version alone can exceed state-of-the-art summarizing algorithms on both ROUGE-1 and ROUGE-L. For METEOR,

System	ROUGE-1	ROUGE-2	ROUGE-L	ROUGE-A.M.	ROUGE-G.M.	METEOR	BERTScore
Pointer-generator(coverage) (See et al., 2017)	39.53	17.28	36.38	31.06	29.18	33.1	86.44
Bottom-Up (Gehrmann et al., 2018)	41.22	18.68	38.34	32.75	30.91	34.2	87.71
PNBERT (Zhong et al., 2019)	42.69	19.60	38.85	33.71	31.91	**41.2**	87.73
T5 (Raffel et al., 2019)	43.52	21.55	40.69	35.25	33.67	38.6	88.66
BART (Lewis et al., 2020)	44.16	21.28	40.90	35.45	33.75	40.5	88.62
SimCLS (Liu and Liu, 2021)	46.67	**22.15**	43.54	37.45	**35.57**	40.5	**88.85**
Scrambled code + broken	46.71	20.39	43.56	36.89	34.62	39.6	87.80
Scrambled code + broken (alter)	**48.18**	19.84	**45.35**	**37.79**	35.13	40.6	87.80

Table 2: Results on CNNDM. Besides ROUGE-1/2/L, METEOR, and BERTScore, we also compute the arithmetic mean (A.M.) and geometric mean (G.M.) of ROUGE-1/2/L, which is commonly adopted (Zhang et al., 2019a; Bae et al., 2019; Chowdhery et al., 2022). The best score in each column is in bold, the runner-up underlined. Our attack system is compared with well-known summarizers from the past five years. The alternative version (last row) of our system changes C in Algorithm 1 from 3 to 2.

the threat model ranks second. As for ROUGE-2 and BERTScore, the threat model can score higher than other BERT-based summarizing algorithms[4]. Overall, we rank the systems by averaging their three relative ranking on ROUGE[5], METEOR, and BERTScore; our threat model gets runner-up (2.7), right behind SimCLS (1.7) and ahead of BART (3.3). This suggests that at the system level, even a combination of mainstream metrics is questionable in justifying the excellence of the summarizer.

These results reveal low robustness of popular metrics and how certain models can obtain high scores with inferior summaries. For example, our threat model is able to grasp the essence of ROUGE-1/2/L using a general but lightweight model, which requires less running time than summarizing algorithms. The training strategies for the model and word order are trivial. Not surprisingly, its output texts do not resemble human understandable "summaries" (Table 1).

6 Discussion

6.1 How does Shortcut Learning Come about?

As suggested in the hypothetical story by Geirhos et al., scoring draws students' attention (Filighera et al., 2022) and Bob is thus considered a better student. Similarly, in automatic summarization, there are already works that are explicitly optimized for various scoring systems (Jauregi Unanue et al., 2021; Pasunuru and Bansal, 2018). Even in some cases, people subscribe more to automatic scoring than "aspects of good summarization". For example, Pasunuru and Bansal (2018) employ reinforcement learning where entailment is one of the rewards, but in the end, ROUGE, not textual entailment, is the only justification for this summarizer.

We use a threat model to show that optimizing toward a flawed indicator does more harm than good. This is consistent with the findings by Paulus et al. but more often, not everyone scrutinizes the output like Paulus et al. do, and these damages can be overshadowed by a staggering increase in metrics, or made less visible by optimizing with other objectives. This is also because human evaluations are usually only used as a supplement, and it is only one per cent of the scale of automatic scoring, and how human evaluations are done also varies from group to group (van der Lee et al., 2021).

6.2 Simple defence

For score robustness, we believe that simply taking more scores as benchmark (Gehrmann et al., 2021) may not be enough. Instead, fixing the existing scoring system might be a better option. A well-defined attack leads to a well-defined defence. Our attacks can be detected, or neutralised through a few defences such as adversarial example detection (Xu et al., 2018; Metzen et al., 2017; Carlini and Wagner, 2017). During the model inference phase, detectors, determining if the sample is fluent/grammatical, can be applied before the input samples are scored. An even easier defence is to check whether there is a series of non-alphanumeric characters. Practically, grammar-based measures, like grammatical error correction (GEC[6]), could be promising (Napoles et al., 2016; Novikova et al., 2017), although they are also under development. To account for grammar in text, one can also try to parse predictions and references, and calculate

[4]except MatchSum (Zhong et al., 2020) and DiscoBERT (Xu et al., 2020), where our method is about 0.5 lower in ROUGE-2. We present the same results in tables with additional target thresholds in Appendix B

[5]Conservatively, We take geometric mean (Chowdhery et al., 2022). Combining metrics in other ways shows similar trends.

[6]`https://github.com/PrithivirajDamodaran/Gramformer`

System	Parse	GEC
Pointer-generator(coverage) (See et al., 2017)	0.131	<u>1.73</u>
Bottom-Up (Gehrmann et al., 2018)	0.145	1.88
PNBERT (Zhong et al., 2020)	0.179	2.15
T5 (Raffel et al., 2019)	<u>0.198</u>	**1.59**
BART (Lewis et al., 2020)	0.170	2.07
SimCLS (Liu and Liu, 2021)	**0.202**	2.17
Scrambled code + broken	0.168	2.64

Table 3: Input sanitization checks, Parse and GEC, on the 100-sample CNNDM test split given by Graham (2015). They penalize non-summary texts, but may introduce more disagreement with human evaluation, *e.g.*, high-scoring Pointer-generator on GEC. Thus, their actual summary-evaluating capabilities on linguistic features (grammar, dependencies, or co-reference) require further investigation.

F1-score of dependency triple overlap (Riezler et al., 2003; Clarke and Lapata, 2006). Dependency triples compare grammatical relations of two texts. We found both useful to ensure input sanitization (Table 3).

6.3 Potential Objections on the Proposed Attacks

The Flaw was Known. That many summarization scoring can be gamed is well known. For example, ROUGE grows when prediction length increases (Sun et al., 2019). ROUGE-L is not reliable when output space is relatively large (Krishna et al., 2021). That ROUGE correlates badly with human judgments at a system level has been revealed by findings of Paulus et al.. And, BERTScore does not improve upon the correlation of ROUGE (Fabbri et al., 2021; Gehrmann et al., 2021).

The current work goes beyond most conventional arguments and analyses against the metrics, and actually constructs a system that sets out to game ROUGE, METEOR, and BERTScore together. We believe that clearly showing the vulnerability is beneficial for scoring remediation efforts. From a behavioural viewpoint, each step of defence against an attack makes the scoring more robust. Compared with findings by Paulus et al., we cover more metrics, and provide a more thorough overthrow of the monotonicity of the scoring systems, *i.e.*, outputs from our threat model are significantly worse.

Shoddy Attack? The proposed attack is easy to detect, so its effectiveness may be questioned. In fact, since we are the first to see automatic scoring as a decent NLU task and attack the most widely used systems, evasion attacks are relatively easy. This just goes to show that even the crudest attack can work on these scoring systems. Certainly, as the scoring system becomes more robust, the attack has to be more crafted. For example, if the minimum accepted input to the scoring system is a "grammatically correct" sentence, an attacker may have to search for fluent but factually incorrect sentences. With a contest like this, we may end up with a robust scoring system.

As for attack scope, we believe it is more urgent to explore popular metrics, as they currently have the greatest impact on summarization. Nonetheless, we will expand to a wider range of scoring and catch up with emerging ratings such as BLEURT (Sellam et al., 2020).

6.4 Potential Difficulties

Performing evasion attacks with bad texts is easy, when texts are as bad as broken sentences or scrambled codes in Table 1. In this case, the output of the threat system does not need to be scrutinized by human evaluators. However, human evaluation of attack examples may be required to identify more complex flaws, such as untrue statements or those that the document does not entail. Therefore, more effort may be required when performing evasion attacks on more robust scoring systems.

7 Conclusion

We hereby answer the question: it is easy to create a threat system that simultaneously scores high on ROUGE, METEOR, and BERTScore using worse text. In this work, we treat automatic scoring as a regression machine learning task and conduct evasion attacks to probe its robustness or reliability. Our attacker, whose score competes with top-level summarizers, actually outputs non-summary strings. This further suggests that current mainstream scoring systems are not a sufficient condition to support the plausibility of summarizers, as they ignore the linguistic information required to compute sentence proximity. Intentionally or not, optimizing for flawed scores can prevent algorithms from summarizing well. The practical effectiveness of existing summarizing algorithms is not affected by this, since most of them optimize maximum likelihood estimation. Based on the exposed vulnerabilities, careful fixes to scoring systems that measure summary quality and sentence similarity are necessary.

Ethical considerations

The techniques developed in this study can be recognized by programs or humans, and we also provide defences. Our intention is not to harm, but to publish such attacks publicly so that better scores can be developed in the future and to better guide the development of summaries. This is similar to how hackers publicly expose bugs/vulnerabilities in software. This shows that our work has long-term benefits for the community. Our attacks are not against real-world machine learning systems.

Limitations

We have only attacked the three most widely adopted scoring schemes that have already in summarization literature. However, there are emerging scoring schemes like BLEURT (Sellam et al., 2020), which will be studied in our future work.

References

Moustafa Alzantot, Yash Sharma, Ahmed Elgohary, Bo-Jhang Ho, Mani Srivastava, and Kai-Wei Chang. 2018. Generating natural language adversarial examples. In *Proceedings of the 2018 Conference on Empirical Methods in Natural Language Processing*, pages 2890–2896, Brussels, Belgium. Association for Computational Linguistics.

Sanghwan Bae, Taeuk Kim, Jihoon Kim, and Sang-goo Lee. 2019. Summary level training of sentence rewriting for abstractive summarization. In *Proceedings of the 2nd Workshop on New Frontiers in Summarization*, pages 10–20, Hong Kong, China. Association for Computational Linguistics.

Satanjeev Banerjee and Alon Lavie. 2005. METEOR: An automatic metric for MT evaluation with improved correlation with human judgments. In *Proceedings of the ACL Workshop on Intrinsic and Extrinsic Evaluation Measures for Machine Translation and/or Summarization*, pages 65–72, Ann Arbor, Michigan. Association for Computational Linguistics.

Melika Behjati, Seyed-Mohsen Moosavi-Dezfooli, Mahdieh Soleymani Baghshah, and Pascal Frossard. 2019. Universal adversarial attacks on text classifiers. In *ICASSP 2019 - 2019 IEEE International Conference on Acoustics, Speech and Signal Processing (ICASSP)*, pages 7345–7349.

Leopoldo E. Bertossi, Georg Gottlob, and Reinhard Pichler. 2018. Datalog: Bag semantics via set semantics. *CoRR*, abs/1803.06445.

Manik Bhandari, Pranav Narayan Gour, Atabak Ashfaq, and Pengfei Liu. 2020. Metrics also disagree in the low scoring range: Revisiting summarization evaluation metrics. In *Proceedings of the 28th International Conference on Computational Linguistics*, pages 5702–5711, Barcelona, Spain (Online). International Committee on Computational Linguistics.

J. Blank and K. Deb. 2020. pymoo: Multi-objective optimization in python. *IEEE Access*, 8:89497–89509.

Florian Böhm, Yang Gao, Christian M. Meyer, Ori Shapira, Ido Dagan, and Iryna Gurevych. 2019. Better rewards yield better summaries: Learning to summarise without references. In *Proceedings of the 2019 Conference on Empirical Methods in Natural Language Processing and the 9th International Joint Conference on Natural Language Processing (EMNLP-IJCNLP)*, pages 3110–3120, Hong Kong, China. Association for Computational Linguistics.

Xiaoyu Cao and Neil Zhenqiang Gong. 2017. Mitigating evasion attacks to deep neural networks via region-based classification. In *Proceedings of the 33rd Annual Computer Security Applications Conference, Orlando, FL, USA, December 4-8, 2017*, pages 278–287. ACM.

Nicholas Carlini and David Wagner. 2017. *Adversarial Examples Are Not Easily Detected: Bypassing Ten Detection Methods*, page 3–14. Association for Computing Machinery, New York, NY, USA.

Asli Celikyilmaz, Antoine Bosselut, Xiaodong He, and Yejin Choi. 2018. Deep communicating agents for abstractive summarization. In *Proceedings of the 2018 Conference of the North American Chapter of the Association for Computational Linguistics: Human Language Technologies, Volume 1 (Long Papers)*, pages 1662–1675, New Orleans, Louisiana. Association for Computational Linguistics.

Daniel Cer, Yinfei Yang, Sheng-yi Kong, Nan Hua, Nicole Limtiaco, Rhomni St. John, Noah Constant, Mario Guajardo-Cespedes, Steve Yuan, Chris Tar, Brian Strope, and Ray Kurzweil. 2018. Universal sentence encoder for English. In *Proceedings of the 2018 Conference on Empirical Methods in Natural Language Processing: System Demonstrations*, pages 169–174, Brussels, Belgium. Association for Computational Linguistics.

Yen-Chun Chen and Mohit Bansal. 2018. Fast abstractive summarization with reinforce-selected sentence rewriting. In *Proceedings of the 56th Annual Meeting of the Association for Computational Linguistics (Volume 1: Long Papers)*, pages 675–686, Melbourne, Australia. Association for Computational Linguistics.

Aakanksha Chowdhery, Sharan Narang, Jacob Devlin, Maarten Bosma, Gaurav Mishra, Adam Roberts, Paul Barham, Hyung Won Chung, Charles Sutton, Sebastian Gehrmann, Parker Schuh, Kensen Shi, Sasha Tsvyashchenko, Joshua Maynez, Abhishek Rao, Parker Barnes, Yi Tay, Noam Shazeer, Vinodkumar Prabhakaran, Emily Reif, Nan Du, Ben Hutchinson, Reiner Pope, James Bradbury, Jacob Austin, Michael Isard, Guy Gur-Ari, Pengcheng Yin,

Toju Duke, Anselm Levskaya, Sanjay Ghemawat, Sunipa Dev, Henryk Michalewski, Xavier Garcia, Vedant Misra, Kevin Robinson, Liam Fedus, Denny Zhou, Daphne Ippolito, David Luan, Hyeontaek Lim, Barret Zoph, Alexander Spiridonov, Ryan Sepassi, David Dohan, Shivani Agrawal, Mark Omernick, Andrew M. Dai, Thanumalayan Sankaranarayana Pillai, Marie Pellat, Aitor Lewkowycz, Erica Moreira, Rewon Child, Oleksandr Polozov, Katherine Lee, Zongwei Zhou, Xuezhi Wang, Brennan Saeta, Mark Diaz, Orhan Firat, Michele Catasta, Jason Wei, Kathy Meier-Hellstern, Douglas Eck, Jeff Dean, Slav Petrov, and Noah Fiedel. 2022. Palm: Scaling language modeling with pathways. *CoRR*, abs/2204.02311.

James Clarke and Mirella Lapata. 2006. Models for sentence compression: A comparison across domains, training requirements and evaluation measures. In *Proceedings of the 21st International Conference on Computational Linguistics and 44th Annual Meeting of the Association for Computational Linguistics*, pages 377–384, Sydney, Australia. Association for Computational Linguistics.

Ido Dagan, Oren Glickman, and Bernardo Magnini. 2006. The pascal recognising textual entailment challenge. In *Machine Learning Challenges. Evaluating Predictive Uncertainty, Visual Object Classification, and Recognising Tectual Entailment*, pages 177–190, Berlin, Heidelberg. Springer Berlin Heidelberg.

Jacob Devlin, Ming-Wei Chang, Kenton Lee, and Kristina Toutanova. 2019. BERT: Pre-training of deep bidirectional transformers for language understanding. In *Proceedings of the 2019 Conference of the North American Chapter of the Association for Computational Linguistics: Human Language Technologies, Volume 1 (Long and Short Papers)*, pages 4171–4186, Minneapolis, Minnesota. Association for Computational Linguistics.

Li Dong, Nan Yang, Wenhui Wang, Furu Wei, Xiaodong Liu, Yu Wang, Jianfeng Gao, Ming Zhou, and Hsiao-Wuen Hon. 2019. Unified language model pre-training for natural language understanding and generation. In *Advances in Neural Information Processing Systems 32: Annual Conference on Neural Information Processing Systems 2019, NeurIPS 2019, December 8-14, 2019, Vancouver, BC, Canada*, pages 13042–13054.

Yue Dong, Yikang Shen, Eric Crawford, Herke van Hoof, and Jackie Chi Kit Cheung. 2018. BanditSum: Extractive summarization as a contextual bandit. In *Proceedings of the 2018 Conference on Empirical Methods in Natural Language Processing*, pages 3739–3748, Brussels, Belgium. Association for Computational Linguistics.

Zi-Yi Dou, Pengfei Liu, Hiroaki Hayashi, Zhengbao Jiang, and Graham Neubig. 2021. GSum: A general framework for guided neural abstractive summarization. In *Proceedings of the 2021 Conference of the North American Chapter of the Association for Computational Linguistics: Human Language Technologies*, pages 4830–4842, Online. Association for Computational Linguistics.

Alexander R. Fabbri, Wojciech Kryściński, Bryan McCann, Caiming Xiong, Richard Socher, and Dragomir Radev. 2021. SummEval: Re-evaluating summarization evaluation. *Transactions of the Association for Computational Linguistics*, 9:391–409.

Anna Filighera, Sebastian Ochs, Tim Steuer, and Thomas Tregel. 2022. Cheating automatic short answer grading: On the adversarial usage of adjectives and adverbs. *CoRR*, abs/2201.08318.

Anna Filighera, Tim Steuer, and Christoph Rensing. 2020. Fooling automatic short answer grading systems. In *Artificial Intelligence in Education*, pages 177–190, Cham. Springer International Publishing.

Sebastian Gehrmann, Tosin Adewumi, Karmanya Aggarwal, Pawan Sasanka Ammanamanchi, Anuoluwapo Aremu, Antoine Bosselut, Khyathi Raghavi Chandu, Miruna-Adriana Clinciu, Dipanjan Das, Kaustubh Dhole, Wanyu Du, Esin Durmus, Ondřej Dušek, Chris Chinenye Emezue, Varun Gangal, Cristina Garbacea, Tatsunori Hashimoto, Yufang Hou, Yacine Jernite, Harsh Jhamtani, Yangfeng Ji, Shailza Jolly, Mihir Kale, Dhruv Kumar, Faisal Ladhak, Aman Madaan, Mounica Maddela, Khyati Mahajan, Saad Mahamood, Bodhisattwa Prasad Majumder, Pedro Henrique Martins, Angelina McMillan-Major, Simon Mille, Emiel van Miltenburg, Moin Nadeem, Shashi Narayan, Vitaly Nikolaev, Andre Niyongabo Rubungo, Salomey Osei, Ankur Parikh, Laura Perez-Beltrachini, Niranjan Ramesh Rao, Vikas Raunak, Juan Diego Rodriguez, Sashank Santhanam, João Sedoc, Thibault Sellam, Samira Shaikh, Anastasia Shimorina, Marco Antonio Sobrevilla Cabezudo, Hendrik Strobelt, Nishant Subramani, Wei Xu, Diyi Yang, Akhila Yerukola, and Jiawei Zhou. 2021. The GEM benchmark: Natural language generation, its evaluation and metrics. In *Proceedings of the 1st Workshop on Natural Language Generation, Evaluation, and Metrics (GEM 2021)*, pages 96–120, Online. Association for Computational Linguistics.

Sebastian Gehrmann, Yuntian Deng, and Alexander Rush. 2018. Bottom-up abstractive summarization. In *Proceedings of the 2018 Conference on Empirical Methods in Natural Language Processing*, pages 4098–4109, Brussels, Belgium. Association for Computational Linguistics.

Robert Geirhos, Jörn-Henrik Jacobsen, Claudio Michaelis, Richard S. Zemel, Wieland Brendel, Matthias Bethge, and Felix A. Wichmann. 2020. Shortcut learning in deep neural networks. *Nat. Mach. Intell.*, 2(11):665–673.

Yvette Graham. 2015. Re-evaluating automatic summarization with BLEU and 192 shades of ROUGE. In *Proceedings of the 2015 Conference on Empirical*

Methods in Natural Language Processing, pages 128–137, Lisbon, Portugal. Association for Computational Linguistics.

Han Guo, Ramakanth Pasunuru, and Mohit Bansal. 2018. Soft layer-specific multi-task summarization with entailment and question generation. In *Proceedings of the 56th Annual Meeting of the Association for Computational Linguistics (Volume 1: Long Papers)*, pages 687–697, Melbourne, Australia. Association for Computational Linguistics.

John H. Holland. 2012. Genetic algorithms. *Scholarpedia*, 7(12):1482.

Wan-Ting Hsu, Chieh-Kai Lin, Ming-Ying Lee, Kerui Min, Jing Tang, and Min Sun. 2018. A unified model for extractive and abstractive summarization using inconsistency loss. In *Proceedings of the 56th Annual Meeting of the Association for Computational Linguistics (Volume 1: Long Papers)*, pages 132–141, Melbourne, Australia. Association for Computational Linguistics.

Inigo Jauregi Unanue, Jacob Parnell, and Massimo Piccardi. 2021. BERTTune: Fine-tuning neural machine translation with BERTScore. In *Proceedings of the 59th Annual Meeting of the Association for Computational Linguistics and the 11th International Joint Conference on Natural Language Processing (Volume 2: Short Papers)*, pages 915–924, Online. Association for Computational Linguistics.

Yichen Jiang and Mohit Bansal. 2018. Closed-book training to improve summarization encoder memory. In *Proceedings of the 2018 Conference on Empirical Methods in Natural Language Processing*, pages 4067–4077, Brussels, Belgium. Association for Computational Linguistics.

Zixuan Ke and Vincent Ng. 2019. Automated essay scoring: A survey of the state of the art. In *Proceedings of the Twenty-Eighth International Joint Conference on Artificial Intelligence, IJCAI-19*, pages 6300–6308. International Joint Conferences on Artificial Intelligence Organization.

Kalpesh Krishna, Aurko Roy, and Mohit Iyyer. 2021. Hurdles to progress in long-form question answering. In *Proceedings of the 2021 Conference of the North American Chapter of the Association for Computational Linguistics: Human Language Technologies*, pages 4940–4957, Online. Association for Computational Linguistics.

Wojciech Kryscinski, Nitish Shirish Keskar, Bryan McCann, Caiming Xiong, and Richard Socher. 2019. Neural text summarization: A critical evaluation. In *Proceedings of the 2019 Conference on Empirical Methods in Natural Language Processing and the 9th International Joint Conference on Natural Language Processing (EMNLP-IJCNLP)*, pages 540–551, Hong Kong, China. Association for Computational Linguistics.

Wojciech Kryściński, Romain Paulus, Caiming Xiong, and Richard Socher. 2018. Improving abstraction in text summarization. In *Proceedings of the 2018 Conference on Empirical Methods in Natural Language Processing*, pages 1808–1817, Brussels, Belgium. Association for Computational Linguistics.

Luc Lamontagne and Irène Abi-Zeid. 2006. Combining multiple similarity metrics using a multicriteria approach. In *Advances in Case-Based Reasoning*, pages 415–428, Berlin, Heidelberg. Springer Berlin Heidelberg.

Alon Lavie and Abhaya Agarwal. 2007. METEOR: An automatic metric for MT evaluation with high levels of correlation with human judgments. In *Proceedings of the Second Workshop on Statistical Machine Translation*, pages 228–231, Prague, Czech Republic. Association for Computational Linguistics.

Mike Lewis, Yinhan Liu, Naman Goyal, Marjan Ghazvininejad, Abdelrahman Mohamed, Omer Levy, Veselin Stoyanov, and Luke Zettlemoyer. 2020. BART: Denoising sequence-to-sequence pre-training for natural language generation, translation, and comprehension. In *Proceedings of the 58th Annual Meeting of the Association for Computational Linguistics*, pages 7871–7880, Online. Association for Computational Linguistics.

Wei Li, Xinyan Xiao, Yajuan Lyu, and Yuanzhuo Wang. 2018a. Improving neural abstractive document summarization with explicit information selection modeling. In *Proceedings of the 2018 Conference on Empirical Methods in Natural Language Processing*, pages 1787–1796, Brussels, Belgium. Association for Computational Linguistics.

Wei Li, Xinyan Xiao, Yajuan Lyu, and Yuanzhuo Wang. 2018b. Improving neural abstractive document summarization with structural regularization. In *Proceedings of the 2018 Conference on Empirical Methods in Natural Language Processing*, pages 4078–4087, Brussels, Belgium. Association for Computational Linguistics.

Chin-Yew Lin. 2004. ROUGE: A package for automatic evaluation of summaries. In *Text Summarization Branches Out*, pages 74–81, Barcelona, Spain. Association for Computational Linguistics.

Chin-Yew Lin and Eduard Hovy. 2003. Automatic evaluation of summaries using n-gram co-occurrence statistics. In *Proceedings of the 2003 Human Language Technology Conference of the North American Chapter of the Association for Computational Linguistics*, pages 150–157.

Yang Liu and Mirella Lapata. 2019. Text summarization with pretrained encoders. In *Proceedings of the 2019 Conference on Empirical Methods in Natural Language Processing and the 9th International Joint Conference on Natural Language Processing (EMNLP-IJCNLP)*, pages 3730–3740, Hong Kong, China. Association for Computational Linguistics.

Yinhan Liu, Myle Ott, Naman Goyal, Jingfei Du, Mandar Joshi, Danqi Chen, Omer Levy, Mike Lewis, Luke Zettlemoyer, and Veselin Stoyanov. 2019. Roberta: A robustly optimized BERT pretraining approach. *CoRR*, abs/1907.11692.

Yixin Liu and Pengfei Liu. 2021. SimCLS: A simple framework for contrastive learning of abstractive summarization. In *Proceedings of the 59th Annual Meeting of the Association for Computational Linguistics and the 11th International Joint Conference on Natural Language Processing (Volume 2: Short Papers)*, pages 1065–1072, Online. Association for Computational Linguistics.

Rishabh Maheshwary, Saket Maheshwary, and Vikram Pudi. 2021. Generating natural language attacks in a hard label black box setting. In *Thirty-Fifth AAAI Conference on Artificial Intelligence, AAAI 2021, Thirty-Third Conference on Innovative Applications of Artificial Intelligence, IAAI 2021, The Eleventh Symposium on Educational Advances in Artificial Intelligence, EAAI 2021, Virtual Event, February 2-9, 2021*, pages 13525–13533. AAAI Press.

Jan Hendrik Metzen, Tim Genewein, Volker Fischer, and Bastian Bischoff. 2017. On detecting adversarial perturbations. In *5th International Conference on Learning Representations, ICLR 2017, Toulon, France, April 24-26, 2017, Conference Track Proceedings*. OpenReview.net.

Edward Moroshko, Guy Feigenblat, Haggai Roitman, and David Konopnicki. 2019. An editorial network for enhanced document summarization. In *Proceedings of the 2nd Workshop on New Frontiers in Summarization*, pages 57–63, Hong Kong, China. Association for Computational Linguistics.

John Morris. 2020. Second-order NLP adversarial examples. In *Proceedings of the Third BlackboxNLP Workshop on Analyzing and Interpreting Neural Networks for NLP*, pages 228–237, Online. Association for Computational Linguistics.

Ramesh Nallapati, Feifei Zhai, and Bowen Zhou. 2017. Summarunner: A recurrent neural network based sequence model for extractive summarization of documents. In *Proceedings of the Thirty-First AAAI Conference on Artificial Intelligence, February 4-9, 2017, San Francisco, California, USA*, pages 3075–3081. AAAI Press.

Ramesh Nallapati, Bowen Zhou, Caglar Gulcehre, Bing Xiang, et al. 2016. Abstractive text summarization using sequence-to-sequence rnns and beyond. *arXiv preprint arXiv:1602.06023*.

Courtney Napoles, Keisuke Sakaguchi, and Joel Tetreault. 2016. There's no comparison: Referenceless evaluation metrics in grammatical error correction. In *Proceedings of the 2016 Conference on Empirical Methods in Natural Language Processing*, pages 2109–2115, Austin, Texas. Association for Computational Linguistics.

Shashi Narayan, Shay B. Cohen, and Mirella Lapata. 2018. Ranking sentences for extractive summarization with reinforcement learning. In *Proceedings of the 2018 Conference of the North American Chapter of the Association for Computational Linguistics: Human Language Technologies, Volume 1 (Long Papers)*, pages 1747–1759, New Orleans, Louisiana. Association for Computational Linguistics.

Jekaterina Novikova, Ondřej Dušek, Amanda Cercas Curry, and Verena Rieser. 2017. Why we need new evaluation metrics for NLG. In *Proceedings of the 2017 Conference on Empirical Methods in Natural Language Processing*, pages 2241–2252, Copenhagen, Denmark. Association for Computational Linguistics.

Kishore Papineni, Salim Roukos, Todd Ward, and Wei-Jing Zhu. 2002. Bleu: a method for automatic evaluation of machine translation. In *Proceedings of the 40th Annual Meeting of the Association for Computational Linguistics*, pages 311–318, Philadelphia, Pennsylvania, USA. Association for Computational Linguistics.

Ramakanth Pasunuru and Mohit Bansal. 2018. Multi-reward reinforced summarization with saliency and entailment. In *Proceedings of the 2018 Conference of the North American Chapter of the Association for Computational Linguistics: Human Language Technologies, Volume 2 (Short Papers)*, pages 646–653, New Orleans, Louisiana. Association for Computational Linguistics.

Romain Paulus, Caiming Xiong, and Richard Socher. 2018. A deep reinforced model for abstractive summarization. In *International Conference on Learning Representations*.

Maxime Peyrard, Teresa Botschen, and Iryna Gurevych. 2017. Learning to score system summaries for better content selection evaluation. In *Proceedings of the Workshop on New Frontiers in Summarization*, pages 74–84, Copenhagen, Denmark. Association for Computational Linguistics.

Weizhen Qi, Yu Yan, Yeyun Gong, Dayiheng Liu, Nan Duan, Jiusheng Chen, Ruofei Zhang, and Ming Zhou. 2020. ProphetNet: Predicting future n-gram for sequence-to-SequencePre-training. In *Findings of the Association for Computational Linguistics: EMNLP 2020*, pages 2401–2410, Online. Association for Computational Linguistics.

Colin Raffel, Noam Shazeer, Adam Roberts, Katherine Lee, Sharan Narang, Michael Matena, Yanqi Zhou, Wei Li, and Peter J. Liu. 2019. Exploring the limits of transfer learning with a unified text-to-text transformer. *CoRR*, abs/1910.10683.

Peter A. Rankel, John M. Conroy, Hoa Trang Dang, and Ani Nenkova. 2013. A decade of automatic content evaluation of news summaries: Reassessing the state of the art. In *Proceedings of the 51st Annual Meeting of the Association for Computational Linguistics*

(Volume 2: Short Papers), pages 131–136, Sofia, Bulgaria. Association for Computational Linguistics.

Ehud Reiter. 2018. A structured review of the validity of BLEU. *Computational Linguistics*, 44(3):393–401.

Stefan Riezler, Tracy H. King, Richard Crouch, and Annie Zaenen. 2003. Statistical sentence condensation using ambiguity packing and stochastic disambiguation methods for Lexical-Functional Grammar. In *Proceedings of the 2003 Human Language Technology Conference of the North American Chapter of the Association for Computational Linguistics*, pages 197–204.

Ananya B. Sai, Akash Kumar Mohankumar, and Mitesh M. Khapra. 2022. A survey of evaluation metrics used for nlg systems. *ACM Comput. Surv.*, 55(2).

Natalie Schluter. 2017. The limits of automatic summarisation according to ROUGE. In *Proceedings of the 15th Conference of the European Chapter of the Association for Computational Linguistics: Volume 2, Short Papers*, pages 41–45, Valencia, Spain. Association for Computational Linguistics.

Abigail See, Peter J. Liu, and Christopher D. Manning. 2017. Get to the point: Summarization with pointer-generator networks. In *Proceedings of the 55th Annual Meeting of the Association for Computational Linguistics (Volume 1: Long Papers)*, pages 1073–1083, Vancouver, Canada. Association for Computational Linguistics.

Thibault Sellam, Dipanjan Das, and Ankur Parikh. 2020. BLEURT: Learning robust metrics for text generation. In *Proceedings of the 58th Annual Meeting of the Association for Computational Linguistics*, pages 7881–7892, Online. Association for Computational Linguistics.

Liwei Song, Xinwei Yu, Hsuan-Tung Peng, and Karthik Narasimhan. 2021. Universal adversarial attacks with natural triggers for text classification. In *Proceedings of the 2021 Conference of the North American Chapter of the Association for Computational Linguistics: Human Language Technologies*, pages 3724–3733, Online. Association for Computational Linguistics.

Simeng Sun, Ori Shapira, Ido Dagan, and Ani Nenkova. 2019. How to compare summarizers without target length? pitfalls, solutions and re-examination of the neural summarization literature. In *Proceedings of the Workshop on Methods for Optimizing and Evaluating Neural Language Generation*, pages 21–29, Minneapolis, Minnesota. Association for Computational Linguistics.

Christian Szegedy, Wojciech Zaremba, Ilya Sutskever, Joan Bruna, Dumitru Erhan, Ian J. Goodfellow, and Rob Fergus. 2014. Intriguing properties of neural networks. In *2nd International Conference on Learning Representations, ICLR 2014, Banff, AB, Canada, April 14-16, 2014, Conference Track Proceedings*.

Chris van der Lee, Albert Gatt, Emiel van Miltenburg, and Emiel Krahmer. 2021. Human evaluation of automatically generated text: Current trends and best practice guidelines. *Computer Speech & Language*, 67:101151.

Eric Wallace, Shi Feng, Nikhil Kandpal, Matt Gardner, and Sameer Singh. 2019. Universal adversarial triggers for attacking and analyzing NLP. In *Proceedings of the 2019 Conference on Empirical Methods in Natural Language Processing and the 9th International Joint Conference on Natural Language Processing (EMNLP-IJCNLP)*, pages 2153–2162, Hong Kong, China. Association for Computational Linguistics.

Danqing Wang, Pengfei Liu, Yining Zheng, Xipeng Qiu, and Xuanjing Huang. 2020. Heterogeneous graph neural networks for extractive document summarization. In *Proceedings of the 58th Annual Meeting of the Association for Computational Linguistics*, pages 6209–6219, Online. Association for Computational Linguistics.

Jiacheng Xu, Zhe Gan, Yu Cheng, and Jingjing Liu. 2020. Discourse-aware neural extractive text summarization. In *Proceedings of the 58th Annual Meeting of the Association for Computational Linguistics*, pages 5021–5031, Online. Association for Computational Linguistics.

Weilin Xu, David Evans, and Yanjun Qi. 2018. Feature squeezing: Detecting adversarial examples in deep neural networks. In *25th Annual Network and Distributed System Security Symposium, NDSS 2018, San Diego, California, USA, February 18-21, 2018*. The Internet Society.

Yuan Zang, Fanchao Qi, Chenghao Yang, Zhiyuan Liu, Meng Zhang, Qun Liu, and Maosong Sun. 2020. Word-level textual adversarial attacking as combinatorial optimization. In *Proceedings of the 58th Annual Meeting of the Association for Computational Linguistics*, pages 6066–6080, Online. Association for Computational Linguistics.

Haoyu Zhang, Jingjing Cai, Jianjun Xu, and Ji Wang. 2019a. Pretraining-based natural language generation for text summarization. In *Proceedings of the 23rd Conference on Computational Natural Language Learning (CoNLL)*, pages 789–797, Hong Kong, China. Association for Computational Linguistics.

Jingqing Zhang, Yao Zhao, Mohammad Saleh, and Peter J. Liu. 2020. PEGASUS: pre-training with extracted gap-sentences for abstractive summarization. In *Proceedings of the 37th International Conference on Machine Learning, ICML 2020, 13-18 July 2020, Virtual Event*, volume 119 of *Proceedings of Machine Learning Research*, pages 11328–11339. PMLR.

Tianyi Zhang, Varsha Kishore, Felix Wu, Kilian Q. Weinberger, and Yoav Artzi. 2019b. Bertscore: Evaluating text generation with BERT. *CoRR*, abs/1904.09675.

Xingxing Zhang, Mirella Lapata, Furu Wei, and Ming Zhou. 2018. Neural latent extractive document summarization. In *Proceedings of the 2018 Conference on Empirical Methods in Natural Language Processing*, pages 779–784, Brussels, Belgium. Association for Computational Linguistics.

Xingxing Zhang, Furu Wei, and Ming Zhou. 2019c. HIBERT: Document level pre-training of hierarchical bidirectional transformers for document summarization. In *Proceedings of the 57th Annual Meeting of the Association for Computational Linguistics*, pages 5059–5069, Florence, Italy. Association for Computational Linguistics.

Wei Zhao, Maxime Peyrard, Fei Liu, Yang Gao, Christian M. Meyer, and Steffen Eger. 2019. MoverScore: Text generation evaluating with contextualized embeddings and earth mover distance. In *Proceedings of the 2019 Conference on Empirical Methods in Natural Language Processing and the 9th International Joint Conference on Natural Language Processing (EMNLP-IJCNLP)*, pages 563–578, Hong Kong, China. Association for Computational Linguistics.

Ming Zhong, Pengfei Liu, Yiran Chen, Danqing Wang, Xipeng Qiu, and Xuanjing Huang. 2020. Extractive summarization as text matching. In *Proceedings of the 58th Annual Meeting of the Association for Computational Linguistics*, pages 6197–6208, Online. Association for Computational Linguistics.

Ming Zhong, Pengfei Liu, Danqing Wang, Xipeng Qiu, and Xuanjing Huang. 2019. Searching for effective neural extractive summarization: What works and what's next. In *Proceedings of the 57th Annual Meeting of the Association for Computational Linguistics*, pages 1049–1058, Florence, Italy. Association for Computational Linguistics.

Qingyu Zhou, Nan Yang, Furu Wei, Shaohan Huang, Ming Zhou, and Tiejun Zhao. 2018. Neural document summarization by jointly learning to score and select sentences. In *Proceedings of the 56th Annual Meeting of the Association for Computational Linguistics (Volume 1: Long Papers)*, pages 654–663, Melbourne, Australia. Association for Computational Linguistics.

A Packages

For evaluation metrics, we used the following packages:

- For ROUGE metrics (Lin and Hovy, 2003), we used the public *rouge-score* package from Google Research: `https://github.com/google-research/google-research/tree/master/rouge`
- For METEOR (Lavie and Agarwal, 2007), we used the public Natural Language Toolkit: `https://www.nltk.org/_modules/nltk/translate/meteor_score.html`
- For BERTScore (Zhang et al., 2019b), we used the public *datasets* package from Huggingface: `https://huggingface.co/metrics/bertscore`

B Additional Comparison with More Summarization Systems

We present the same results in Table 2 with additional systems in Table 4. Table 4 also shows that about half of the listed works employ human evaluation to support the effectiveness of summarization systems.

System	ROUGE-1	ROUGE-2	ROUGE-L	Average R-Rank	ROUGE-A.M.	ROUGE-G.M.	METEOR	BERTScore	Average Rank	Human Eval
Pointer-generator + coverage See et al., 2017	39.53 (34)	17.28 (33)	36.38 (33)	33.33	31.06	29.18	33.1 (16)	86.44 (15)	26.20	
SummaRuNNer Nallapati et al., 2017	39.6 (33)	16.2 (34)	35.3 (34)	33.67	30.37	28.29			33.67	
Pointer + EntailmentGen Guo et al., 2018	39.81 (32)	17.64 (31)	36.54 (31)	31.33	31.33	29.50			31.33	yes
REFRESH Narayan et al., 2018	40.00 (31)	18.20 (25)	36.60 (30)	28.67	31.60	29.87	**43.2** (1)	87.15 (14)	20.20	yes
ML+RL ROUGE Kryściński et al., 2018	40.19 (30)	17.38 (32)	37.52 (25)	29.00	31.70	29.70			29.00	yes
Li et al., 2018b	40.30 (29)	18.02 (27)	37.36 (26)	27.33	31.89	30.05			27.33	yes
ROUGESal+Ent RL Pasunuru and Bansal, 2018	40.43 (28)	18.00 (28)	37.10 (28)	28.00	31.84	30.00			28.00	
RL + pg + cbdec Jiang and Bansal, 2018	40.66 (27)	17.87 (30)	37.06 (29)	28.67	31.86	29.97			28.67	yes
end2end w/ inconsistency loss Hsu et al., 2018	40.68 (26)	17.97 (29)	37.13 (27)	27.33	31.93	30.05			27.33	yes
Latent Zhang et al., 2018	41.05 (25)	18.77 (21)	37.54 (24)	23.33	32.45	30.70			23.33	
Bottom-Up Summarization Gehrmann et al., 2018	41.22 (24)	18.68 (24)	38.34 (19)	22.33	32.75	30.91	34.2 (15)	87.71 (11)	18.60	
EditNet Moroshko et al., 2019	41.42 (23)	19.03 (19)	38.36 (18)	20.00	32.94	31.15			20.00	
rnn-ext + RL Chen and Bansal, 2018	41.47 (22)	18.72 (22)	37.76 (22)	22.00	32.65	30.83	36.7 (13)	87.37 (13)	18.40	yes
BanditSum Dong et al., 2018	41.50 (21)	18.70 (23)	37.60 (23)	22.33	32.60	30.79	39.2 (9)	87.41 (12)	17.60	yes
Li et al., 2018a	41.54 (20)	18.18 (26)	36.47 (32)	26.00	32.06	30.20			26.00	yes
NeuSUM Zhou et al., 2018	41.59 (19)	19.01 (20)	37.98 (20)	19.67	32.86	31.08	39.9 (7)	88.18 (5)	14.20	yes
DCA Celikyilmaz et al., 2018	41.69 (18)	19.47 (18)	37.92 (21)	19.00	33.03	31.34			19.00	yes
Two-Stage + RL Zhang et al., 2019a	41.71 (17)	19.49 (17)	38.79 (17)	17.00	33.33	31.59	35.3 (14)	87.97 (6)	14.20	
HIBERT Zhang et al., 2019c	42.37 (16)	19.95 (12)	38.83 (16)	14.67	33.72	32.02			14.67	yes
PNBERT Zhong et al., 2019	42.69 (15)	19.60 (16)	38.85 (15)	15.33	33.71	31.91	40.3 (6)	87.73 (9)	12.20	
BERT-ext + RL Bae et al., 2019	42.76 (14)	19.87 (13)	39.11 (14)	13.67	33.91	32.15			13.67	yes
UniLM Dong et al., 2019	43.33 (12)	20.21 (11)	40.51 (11)	11.33	34.68	32.86	38.6 (10)	88.51 (4)	9.60	
T5 Raffel et al., 2019	43.52 (11)	21.55 (3)	40.69 (8)	7.33	35.25	33.67	38.6 (10)	88.66 (2)	6.80	
DiscoBERT Xu et al., 2020	43.77 (10)	20.85 (8)	40.67 (9)	9.00	35.10	33.36			9.00	yes
BertSum Liu and Lapata, 2019	43.85 (9)	20.34 (10)	39.90 (12)	10.33	34.70	32.89			10.33	
BART Lewis et al., 2020	44.16 (8)	21.28 (5)	40.90 (7)	6.67	35.45	33.75	40.5 (4)	88.62 (3)	5.40	yes
PEGASUS Zhang et al., 2020	44.17 (7)	21.47 (4)	41.11 (6)	5.67	35.58	33.91			5.67	
HeterGraph Wang et al., 2020	42.95 (13)	19.76 (15)	39.23 (13)	13.67	33.98	32.17	39.7 (8)		12.25	
ProphetNet Qi et al., 2020	44.20 (6)	21.17 (6)	41.30 (5)	5.67	35.56	33.81			5.67	
MatchSum Zhong et al., 2020	44.41 (5)	20.86 (7)	40.55 (10)	7.33	35.27	33.49	41.4 (2)	87.72 (10)	6.80	
Gsum Dou et al., 2021	45.94 (4)	**22.32** (1)	42.48 (4)	3.00	36.91	35.18			3.00	yes
SimCLS Liu and Liu, 2021	46.67 (3)	22.15 (2)	43.54 (3)	**2.67**	37.45	**35.57**	40.5 (4)	**88.85** (1)	**2.60**	
Scrambled code + broken	46.71 (2)	20.39 (9)	43.56 (2)	4.33	36.89	34.62	37.5 (12)	87.8 (7)	6.40	
Scrambled code + broken (alter)	**48.18** (1)	19.84 (14)	**45.35** (1)	5.33	**37.79**	35.13	40.6 (3)	87.8 (7)	5.20	

Table 4: ROUGE, METEOR, and BERTScore of various summarizers on the CNNDM test set. Ranking of each number in each column is indicated in parentheses. We calculate the average of the ranking, and the smaller the number, the better the ranking. The arithmetic mean (A.M.) and geometric mean (G.M.) of ROUGE-1/2/L obtained by each system (each row) are computed. The **best score** in each column is in bold, the runner-up is underlined, and the second runner-up is underlined with two lines. Our attack system is compared with well-known summarizers from the past five years. The alternative version (last row) of our system changes C in Algorithm 1 from 3 to 2.

How (Un)Faithful is Attention?

Hessam Amini and **Leila Kosseim**
Computational Linguistics at Concordia (CLaC) Laboratory
Department of Computer Science and Software Engineering
Concordia University, Montreal, Canada
hessam.amini@mail.concordia.ca; leila.kosseim@concordia.ca

Abstract

Although attention weights have been commonly used as a means to provide explanations for deep learning models, the approach has been widely criticized due to its lack of *faithfulness*. In this work, we present a simple approach to compute the newly proposed metric *AtteFa*, which can quantitatively represent the degree of faithfulness of the attention weights. Using this metric, we further validate the effect of the frequency of informative input elements and the use of contextual vs. non-contextual encoders on the faithfulness of the attention mechanism. Finally, we apply the approach on several real-life binary classification datasets to measure the faithfulness of attention weights in real-life settings.

1 Introduction

Attention mechanism (Bahdanau et al., 2015) has become an indispensable part of many state-of-the-art NLP models, and its application is becoming more and more prevalent in non-NLP use cases. In simple words and from a functionality perspective, attention can be described as a module which generates outputs from the representations of input elements by performing the following two steps:

1. Automatically compute weights corresponding to each input element
2. Use the computed weights to run a weighted average over the input representations

Due to attention's explicit mechanism to assign weights to input elements, attention weights have been frequently used as explanations for model predictions. A common approach has been to provide attention heat maps to which input elements the attention component has attended to (e.g. Wang et al., 2016; Lee et al., 2017; Lin et al., 2017; Ghaeini et al., 2018).

However, the use of attention weights as explanations has been widely challenged, with regards to the observation that they are not *faithful*, meaning that different attention weights can result in similar model predictions (Jain and Wallace, 2019; Serrano and Smith, 2019; Wiegreffe and Pinter, 2019). Therefore, the explanations provided by the attention weights are neither unique nor closely related.

In this work, we extend the work of Wiegreffe and Pinter (2019) to a one-shot adversarial setup that can be used to compute a quantitative metric for the faithfulness of attention weights. We call the metric *AtteFa* which simply stands for *Attention Faithfulness*. We consider the adversarial training setup one-shot in the sense that it can provide us with the AtteFa metric by running the adversarial training only once.

To perform a sanity check on AtteFa, we run experiments in a controlled setting using synthetic datasets and two types of encoders (a non-contextual MLP and a contextual LSTM) that could help us validate if the values of this metric reflect what we expect it to. We later compute this metric on some real-life binary text classification datasets to validate how faithful the attention weights are in those settings.

2 Related Work

Since the rise of deep learning models, researchers have focused on devising techniques that could provide an explanation for the functioning of these so-called "black-box" models. Among different classes of explainability techniques, the following can be mentioned:

Gradient-based methods attribute model decisions to input features using gradient signals (Sundararajan et al., 2017; Selvaraju et al., 2017; Aubakirova and Bansal, 2016; Karlekar et al., 2018). Perturbation-based methods try to provide an explanation for the model behavior by evaluating its reactions to perturbations in input features (Ribeiro et al., 2016; Zintgraf et al., 2017).

Proceedings of the Fifth BlackboxNLP Workshop on Analyzing and Interpreting Neural Networks for NLP, pages 119 - 130
December 8, 2022

Attention-based methods act as an intuitive way of interpreting the model's decision. They use the probability distribution or weights provided by an attention mechanism as a feature importance measure to find the features that the model is attending to (Luong et al., 2015; Xie et al., 2017; Mullenbach et al., 2018).

Despite the popularity of the attention-based explainability approaches, the reliability of these methods has been called into question, with the special focus on the faithfulness of the explanations provided by the attention mechanism. Jain and Wallace (2019) perform different experiments to evaluate the meaningfulness of explanations provided by attention weights. Their results show that attention weights are not correlated with gradient-based feature importance scores. Furthermore, they show that it is often possible to have different attention probability distributions that result in a similar output, arguing that a specific distribution cannot be treated as the definitive cause behind a model decision.

Serrano and Smith (2019) investigate the ability of attention weights to act as importance measures through a different lens. They state that it is not sufficient for the weights to make sense to humans. The weights should also provide a faithful explanation for the model output in order to be considered reliable. Through performing multi-weight tests, they show that although there is a certain level of correlation between attention weights and the importance of features in the final prediction of the model, these weights in many cases cannot successfully identify the features that heavily impact a model's decision.

Wiegreffe and Pinter (2019) propose additional tests for evaluating the ability of the attention mechanism to provide explainability. They challenged the findings reported by Jain and Wallace (2019) as they treated the attention as a stand-alone component within a network that is independent from the rest of the components. Through an end-to-end adversarial setup to train models to similar outputs while coming up with different attention distributions in binary classification tasks, they show that the explanations provided by attention are not as unfaithful as Jain and Wallace (2019) found them to be.

In this paper, we extend the adversarial setup by Wiegreffe and Pinter (2019) so that it can be used in a one-shot pass, i.e. training the adversarial models only once. This approach results in a metric, which we call *AtteFa*, that can provide us with a quantitative insight on how faithful the explanations by the attention component are, given a specific model and a specific dataset. To the best of our knowledge, this is the first work that provides such a quantitative measure to evaluate the faithfulness of attention.

3 Method

3.1 Base Model Training

First, we train a base model on the data. The base model is comprised of an embedding layer, followed by an encoder (LSTM or MLP), which is in turn followed by an attention component, and finally a classification head. To train the base model, cross-entropy loss is used, and training is done for 8 epochs. The final base model is the trained model at the end of the epoch where the ROC-AUC score on the test dataset is minimum.

3.2 Adversarial Model Training

With the base model at hand, we train an adversarial model with the same architecture as the base model, but with the following two characteristics:

1. Having predictions as similar as possible to the base model, and
2. Having attention weight distributions as different as possible from the base model

In order to measure the difference between the two models' predictions, namely $\hat{y}_a$ and $\hat{y}_b$, we use Total Variation Distance (TVD), which is computed using Equation 1:

$$\mathrm{TVD}(\hat{y}_a^j, \hat{y}_b^j) = \frac{1}{2} \sum_{j=1}^{|\mathcal{Y}|} |\hat{y}_a^j - \hat{y}_b^j| \quad (1)$$

where $|\mathcal{Y}|$ represents the number of output heads (which is equal to 1 in our binary classification setting).

To compute the difference between attention distributions α_a and α_b, Jensen-Shannon Divergence (JSD) is used, which is computed using Equation 2:

$$\mathrm{JSD}(\alpha_a, \alpha_b) = \frac{1}{2}\mathrm{KL}(\alpha_a||\bar{\alpha}) + \frac{1}{2}\mathrm{KL}(\alpha_b||\bar{\alpha}) \quad (2)$$

where $\bar{\alpha} = \frac{\alpha_a + \alpha_b}{2}$ and the Kullback–Leibler (KL) divergence is computed using Equation 3:

$$\mathrm{KL}(\alpha_a||\alpha_b) = \sum_{k=1}^{|\alpha|} \alpha_a^k \times \left(\log(\alpha_a^k + \epsilon) - \log(\alpha_b^k + \epsilon)\right) \quad (3)$$

where $|\alpha|$ corresponds to the size of the attention weight vector. The inclusion of ϵ in the KL equation is to prevent the logs from becoming infinite in cases where the values of α become equal to zero due to mathematical underflow. In our experiments, we set the value of ϵ equal to 1e-10.

Having the TVD of the predictions and the JSD of the attention weight distributions, we design the loss function so that it tries to minimize TVD and maximize JSD. The final loss formula is given in Equation 4:

$$\mathcal{L}(\mathcal{M}_a, \mathcal{M}_b)^{(i)} = \text{sTVD}(\hat{y}_a^{(i)}, \hat{y}_b^{(i)}) - \text{sJSD}(\alpha_a^{(i)}, \alpha_b^{(i)}) \quad (4)$$

In Equation 4, we use sTVD and sJSD to denote the scaled values of TVD and JSD, respectively. We apply the scaling in order to make sure that the value ranges for the TVD and JSD components of the loss are equal, and therefore the final value of the loss is affected equally by the two components. Knowing that the value of TVD is always between 0 and 0.5, sTVD is computed using Equation 5:

$$\text{sTVD}(\hat{y}_a, \hat{y}_b) = \text{TVD}(\hat{y}_a, \hat{y}_b)/0.5 \quad (5)$$

To compute sJSD Equation 6 is used:

$$\text{sJSD}(\alpha_a, \alpha_b) = \text{JSD}(\alpha_a, \alpha_b)/JSD_{max} \quad (6)$$

where JSD_{max} is the calculated upper-bound for JSD when Equations 2 and 3 are used. JSD_{max} is approximately equal to 0.6931, and is reached when α_1 and α_2 in Equation 2 are two one-hot vectors with the element 1 located in different indices.

The value of the loss is computed per sample. In order to compute the backpropagated loss value for each batch, we compute the average over the per-sample losses in the batch.

The training process is continued until the loss value on the test data does not improve for 10 consecutive epochs, or a maximum number of 80 epochs is reached. To calculate the total loss on the test data, instead of computing the per-sample losses and averaging them over the dataset, for simplicity and to leverage the metric implementations by Wiegreffe and Pinter (2019), we first average over the per-sample TVD and JSD in this dataset, and then compute the total loss using these averages. As the final adversarial model, we pick the one from the training epoch with the lowest value of loss on test data.

The key difference between our adversarial training setup with the one from Wiegreffe and Pinter (2019) is in the way the adversarial loss is computed. In Wiegreffe and Pinter (2019), KL divergence is used instead of JSD to compute the distribution divergence between the base model's attentions and the adversarial one. Since the value of KL is un-bounded, it is mandatory to use an additional hyperparameter λ to avoid the final value of the loss getting dragged fully towards the attention divergence. Knowing that JSD has a specific lower and upper bound, including that in the adversarial loss formula allows us to do away with the additional hyperparameter λ, and to be able to do the adversarial training in one shot, which in turn provides us with an easy and systematic way to compute a metric value for the attention faithfulness.

3.3 Computing *AtteFa*

Having the TVD of the predictions and the JSD of the attention distributions on the test data between the base model $\mathcal{M}_b$ and adversarial version of the model $\mathcal{M}_a$, we compute the faithfulness score *AtteFa* of the attention module $\mathcal{A}_\mathcal{M}$ using Equation 7:

$$\text{AtteFa}(\mathcal{A}_\mathcal{M}) = \min\left(\frac{\text{sTVD}(\hat{y}_a, \hat{y}_b)}{\text{sJSD}(\alpha_a, \alpha_b)}, 1\right) \quad (7)$$

The formula is motivated by the assumption that, the degree of attention faithfulness has a direct relation with the value of the TVD of predictions, and an inverse relation with the value of the JSD of the attention weights. In other words, if the attention is faithful, meaning that the attention can find a limited set of informative sources, the adversarial setup will either converge to a point where both the TVD of predictions and the JSD of attention weights are low, or both of them are high. We believe that the second scenario is more probable, as the adversarial model has a much higher degree of freedom in order to converge to a different attention distribution from the base model than to achieve a similar output prediction. This will later be shown in Section 6 that, with the current adversarial setup, the adversarial model usually achieves a JSD close to its maximum value.

With this assumption, we believe that in most cases, the final value for $\text{sTVD}(\hat{y}_a, \hat{y}_b)$ should be lower than $\text{sJSD}(\alpha_a, \alpha_b)$, but we still do not rule out the opposite scenario, which is why we force the value of AtteFa to be bounded between 0 and 1 through the use of the min function in Equation 7.

4 Datasets

4.1 Synthetic Datasets

In principle, we hypothesize that the faithfulness of the attention has a direct relation with the rareness of the informative elements in the input. In the task of text classification, considering the input elements being textual tokens and with an attention that assigns weight to each token, if there are very few informative tokens that could help with the task, our assumption is that the attention should probably focus on those and not the other tokens, and finding alternative attention weight distributions that would lead to a similar outcome would be difficult. Whereas in cases when many input tokens are informative and helpful to the task, the attention can simply shift its focus from one set of tokens to another, therefore the faithfulness will be low.

In order to verify this scenario, we designed a set of synthetic sentiment analysis datasets that include different proportions of informative texts. To that end, we synthetically created samples in a way that a specific portion of their tokens are words with sentiment weights that align with the sentiment label of the sample[1], while filling the rest of the token slots with the uninformative token "something". This results in a simple-to-classify sentiment dataset that allows us to investigate the effect of the frequency of informative input elements on the faithfulness of attention, without the need to take into account the effectiveness of attention for the task at hand.

Our *Mock* datasets are comprised of 8000 training and 1000 testing samples. The distribution of the positive/negative labels is 50/50 in the datasets, and each sample has a random length between 50 and 100 tokens. These synthetic datasets are comprised of **Mock-1**, **Mock-2**, **Mock-5**, and **Mock-10** datasets with 1, 2, 5, and 10 informative tokens in each sample, respectively, and **Mock-1q**, **Mock-2q**, **Mock-3q**, and **Mock-4q**, in which 25%, 50%, 75%, and 100% of the tokens in each sample are informative.

4.2 Real-life Datasets

The datasets used are the ones utilized in the work of Jain and Wallace (2019) and Wiegreffe and Pinter (2019). The description of the datasets are provided in section 3 of Jain and Wallace (2019).

4.3 Dataset Statistics

Table 1 shows the average number of tokens across samples, along with the distribution of the positive/negative samples for each dataset. Since all the synthetic datasets include the same number of samples, class distributions, and average number of tokens across samples, we have included the statistics for them under *Mock-**.

Dataset	Train		Test	
	Size (neg/pos)	Avg Len (Tokens)	Size (neg/pos)	Avg Len (Tokens)
Mock-*	4000/4000	75	500/500	75
Diabetes	6650/1416	1985	1389/340	2385
Anemia	1742/2912	2368	512/857	2396
IMDB	8673/8539	180	2189/2174	176
SST	3310/3610	17	912/909	17
AgNews	25508/25492	36	1900/1900	36
20News	612/624	159	192/195	206

Table 1: Summary statistics of the datasets.

5 Experimental Setup

The *LSTM* models are comprised of the following components:

1. A 300d word embedding layer
2. A bidirectional LSTM layer (Hochreiter and Schmidhuber, 1997) with 128 units
3. The attention module
4. A fully-connected layer

The *MLP* models include embedding, attention, and fully-connected modules similar to the *LSTM* models, but utilize a feed-forward projection layer with 128 nodes followed by a *tanh* activation, instead of the bi-LSTM layer.

The attention has a two layer fully-connected network that first projects the input to half its size in its first layer, applies a *tanh* activation, and then maps it to a single logit in the second layer. A softmax function is then used to convert the logit to a probability distribution, which is used to compute a weighted average over the inputs and form the output of the attention.

Similar to Jain and Wallace (2019) and Wiegreffe and Pinter (2019), for the Diabetes and Anemia datasets, 300d Word2Vec embeddings (Mikolov et al., 2013) are pre-trained on the combined text from the two datasets. The training is done using CBOW with a window size of 10. For the rest of the datasets, 300d publicly-pretrained FastText embeddings (Bojanowski et al., 2017) are used.

Adam (Kingma and Ba, 2015) is used as the optimizer during training, and the learning rate and

[1]We picked words with positive and negative sentiment from the following gazetteers, respectively: `https://ptrckprry.com/course/ssd/data/positive-words.txt`, `https://ptrckprry.com/course/ssd/data/negative-words.txt`

weight decay rates are set to 1e-3 and 1e-5, respectively. Weight decay is applied to every component in the network except the attention module.

6 Results and Discussion

First, we have included the F1 scores achieved by the base models in Table 2. In order to verify the correctness of our experiments, we have also included in the table the F1 scores reported by Wiegreffe and Pinter (2019).

Dataset	LSTM		MLP	
	Reported	Reproduced	Reported	Reproduced
Mock-1	-	0.974	-	0.975
Mock-2	-	0.988	-	0.989
Mock-5	-	0.999	-	1.000
Mock-10	-	1.000	-	0.999
Mock-1q	-	1.000	-	1.000
Mock-2q	-	1.000	-	1.000
Mock-3q	-	1.000	-	1.000
Mock-4q	-	1.000	-	1.000
Diabetes	0.775	0.733	0.699	0.665
Anemia	0.938	0.935	0.920	0.915
IMDB	0.902	0.908	0.888	0.882
SST	0.831	0.830	0.817	0.816
AgNews	0.964	0.959	-	0.956
20News	0.942	0.935	-	0.878

Table 2: F1 scores by the base model achieved on the test datasets. The F1 scores reported by Wiegreffe and Pinter (2019) have been included under the *Reported* columns. The MLP setup is equivalent to the *Trained MLP* setup from Wiegreffe and Pinter (2019).

Table 3 contains the results achieved by the adversarial setup. It includes the F1 scores of the adversarial models, the TVD of their predictions from the base models, the JSD of their attention distributions from the base models, the number of epochs that resulted in the best loss on test, and their attention faithfulness score *AtteFa*. The numbers are reported in terms of average and standard deviation runs with 9 different random seeds. Individual results for each seed is available in Tables 4 and 5 in Appendix A.

6.1 Effect of Contextualization

Comparing the *AtteFa* columns for the *LSTM* and *MLP* models in Table 3, we can observe that the attentions incorporated in models with LSTM as their encoder are significantly less faithful than their counterparts in the models with MLP as their encoder. This observation was not surprising, as a lower degree of contextualization in token representations should inherently result in higher faithfulness in the attention that is applied on top of those representations.

To better understand this, imagine the task of detecting whether a text is about sports or fruits. Now imagine that you want to classify the following sample: `football is life`. We can simply agree that the only informative word in the sample is `football`, as it clearly indicates a sport. In an ideal scenario, a faithful attention should have a distribution highly centered on this word. Using an MLP encoder, the input tokens will retain their information, therefore the representation of token `football` retains its informativeness. This is, however, not necessarily the case if a contextual encoder such as LSTM is used to compute the token representations, as it can simply manipulate the tokens in a way that another word, such as `is`, has the informative representation.

Going back to our adversarial setting, when LSTM is used, the encoder has the capacity to manipulate the token representations so that a different set of tokens bear the useful information to achieve the task. In this setting, the attention can simply focus on the new set and obtain similar information. On the other hand, a non-contextual MLP encoder does not have the capacity that LSTM holds, and will retain the informativeness of the representation for each token. Therefore, it becomes more challenging for the attention to find a new set of tokens to attend to. That is why the prediction TVD in the MLP models is significantly lower than the LSTM ones, resulting in the MLP models having a noticeably higher AtteFa.

Simply put, our results show that attention components applied on top of contextual encoders are generally less faithful than the ones on top of non-contextual encoders.

6.2 Effect of the Frequency of Informative Sources

Looking at the rows corresponding to the results on the *Mock-** datasets and the MLP model in Table 3, we can observe the general trend towards the reduction of AtteFa as the number of informative tokens increase. For the case of the MLP model, a relatively high AtteFa of 0.82 is achieved on the Mock-1 dataset, which only includes one informative token in each sample text, and the value drops to close to 0 for the case of Mock-3q and Mock-4q datasets. This shows that the faithfulness of the attention mechanism has an inverse correlation with the number of informative sources in the input.

The trend is still observable in the case of the

dataset	LSTM					MLP				
	epoch	F1	TVD	JSD	AtteFa	epoch	F1	TVD	JSD	AtteFa
Mock-1	12±5	0.947±0.020	0.015±0.009	0.693±0.000	0.0304±0.0176	20±24	0.221±0.312	0.231±0.012	0.393±0.000	0.8153±0.0425
Mock-2	9±7	0.977±0.010	0.016±0.005	0.693±0.000	0.0329±0.0096	1±0	0.221±0.312	0.246±0.003	0.670±0.000	0.5086±0.0064
Mock-5	7±5	1.000±0.001	0.002±0.000	0.693±0.000	0.0037±0.0008	9±11	0.147±0.275	0.247±0.001	0.686±0.000	0.4987±0.0027
Mock-10	14±8	1.000±0.000	0.001±0.000	0.693±0.000	0.0012±0.0000	23±31	0.147±0.275	0.249±0.001	0.686±0.000	0.5028±0.0027
Mock-1q	23±12	1.000±0.000	0.000±0.000	0.693±0.000	0.0006±0.0000	37±31	0.465±0.480	0.135±0.120	0.689±0.001	0.2721±0.2407
Mock-2q	35±32	1.000±0.001	0.000±0.000	0.678±0.004	0.0008±0.0010	42±35	0.751±0.324	0.099±0.109	0.691±0.000	0.1983±0.2188
Mock-3q	21±21	1.000±0.000	0.000±0.000	0.681±0.008	0.0003±0.0001	13±13	0.999±0.001	0.001±0.001	0.691±0.000	0.0013±0.0011
Mock-4q	8±4	1.000±0.000	0.000±0.000	0.680±0.004	0.0002±0.0003	3±0	1.000±0.000	0.000±0.000	0.690±0.000	0.0002±0.0000
Diabetes	22±5	0.729±0.003	0.018±0.001	0.693±0.000	0.0367±0.0020	42±27	0.134±0.076	0.147±0.004	0.691±0.000	0.2945±0.0072
Anemia	20±6	0.901±0.018	0.058±0.011	0.693±0.000	0.1164±0.0211	23±10	0.832±0.007	0.093±0.004	0.692±0.000	0.1861±0.0083
SST	21±6	0.823±0.002	0.034±0.002	0.626±0.006	0.0760±0.0034	23±15	0.605±0.028	0.173±0.001	0.656±0.002	0.3645±0.0024
IMDB	49±12	0.889±0.006	0.038±0.004	0.691±0.001	0.0769±0.0090	21±14	0.158±0.056	0.190±0.001	0.689±0.000	0.3826±0.0019
AgNews	49±18	0.958±0.001	0.007±0.001	0.683±0.002	0.0136±0.0015	24±12	0.610±0.032	0.172±0.005	0.671±0.001	0.3558±0.0097
20News	18±5	0.865±0.013	0.046±0.007	0.689±0.001	0.0931±0.0149	24±18	0.340±0.149	0.208±0.004	0.650±0.008	0.4444±0.0133

Table 3: Average and standard deviation of the results from our adversarial setup. The results for every row are reported from 9 different runs with different random seed initializations. The column *epoch* includes the the number of training epoch for each selected model.

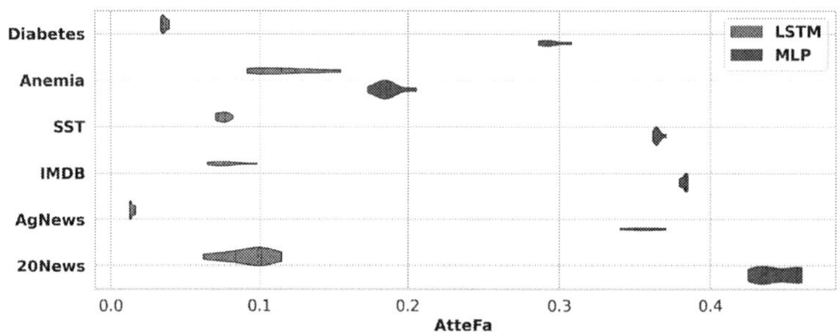

Figure 1: Distribution of AtteFa across different models and real-life datasets.

LSTM models, but with a magnitude that is considerably lower than what we have for the MLP models, as the AtteFa on the Mock-1 dataset is only 0.03. As discussed in Section 6.1, the contextualized LSTM encoder has the flexibility to re-distribute the task-relative information across different input tokens. Regardless of that, we can still observe the general trend towards the drop of AtteFa as we move from Mock-1 to Mock-4, which shows that, even with the case of contextualization, the frequency of informative elements in the source input can still affect the faithfulness of the attention mechanism.

We can observe anomalies in the trend mentioned before. For example, we can observe bumps in the AtteFa in Mock-1 to Mock-2 and Mock-1q to Mock-2q for the case of the LSTM model, and from Mock-5 to Mock-10 in the case of the MLP model. This can be partially justified by the behavior of the base model in terms of how successful it is in detecting informative tokens. An example of this can be found in Table 2, where the MLP model has achieved a lower F1 score on Mock-5 in comparison to Mock-10, meaning that the attention used in the MLP model was more successful in identifying informative tokens in the Mock-5 dataset than in Mock-10.

We can also observe a 19% gap between the AtteFa of the MLP model trained on the Mock-1 dataset and the maximum value of AtteFa (i.e. 1). We argue that this is also related (at least partially) to how the base model performs. We can see in Table 2 that the base model trained on the Mock-1 dataset does not have an F1 score of 1 on the test dataset. This could partially be due to the failure of attention to detect the informative tokens and highly focus on them.

Overall, we conclude that there is generally an inverse relation between the frequency of informative sources in the input data and the faithfulness of the attention module trained on it. But there is still some noise in the AtteFa metric which is attributed to how well the base model performs. Although we do not think that this rules out AtteFa as a suitable metric to compute the faithfulness of attention, we believe there is room for exploring alternative metrics that, for example, also incorporate the performance of the base models in their computation.

6.3 AtteFa on Real-life Datasets

Looking at Table 3, we can see that, for the case of the MLP models, the values of AtteFa on all the real-life datasets are significantly lower than the ones on Mock-1 to Mock-10. As discussed in Section 6.2, this could show that there is quite a large number of informative tokens in the samples belonging to these datasets, which allows the attention to shift its focus among them. This shows that, the attention mechanism in MLP models trained on all these datasets is not very faithful.

For the case of the LSTM model, however, we can observe that the AtteFa on these real-life datasets is comparable and sometimes higher than their counterparts on the Mock-* datasets. However, focusing only on the real-life datasets, the AtteFa of the LSTM models are still lower than the MLP ones. This can also be visually observed in Figure 1, which includes the violin plots of the distribution of AtteFa across the different datasets and models. We hypothesize that, in real-life datasets, we have a significantly lower number of completely uninformative tokens as we had in the Mock-* datasets. Although the LSTM encoder still retains its flexibility to redistribute information across different tokens, the lower number of completely uninformative tokens reduces the degree of the information redistribution capacity. This is something that we have not explored in our experiments with the synthetic datasets, and therefore, leaves room for more studies on this aspect.

One may argue that the number of input tokens on its own can affect the distribution of attention weights and can in turn affect the value of the attention JSD of the adversarial models, hence the final value of AtteFa. While we do not rule this out, we believe that it is not merely the input lengths that would affect the attention JSD, but rather the frequency of informative input tokens that could increase as the input lengths become higher. We also believe that the way information is distributed among their representations used by the attention component also plays a big role here.

In Figure 1, we can see that for the case of the MLP models, the values of AtteFa on datasets with lengthier samples, namely Diabetes and Anemia, are generally lower than the ones on the other datasets. This is, however, not the case for the LSTM models, as we can observe a relatively high AtteFa on the Anemia dataset with respect to the rest of the datasets. Even for the case of the MLP model, we can see that the AtteFa on the 20News dataset is higher than SST and AgNews that have lower average input lengths (see Table 1).

We therefore conclude that the distribution of task-related information across the input token representations used by the attention component plays a key role in the faithfulness of the attention.

6.4 Comparison of Our Adversial Setup with Wiegreffe and Pinter's

In Figure 2, we have plotted the prediction TVD and attention JSD of our adversarial LSTM models against the results reported in Wiegreffe and Pinter (2019). The dotted lines in the plots resemble the ones in figure 5 from Wiegreffe and Pinter (2019).

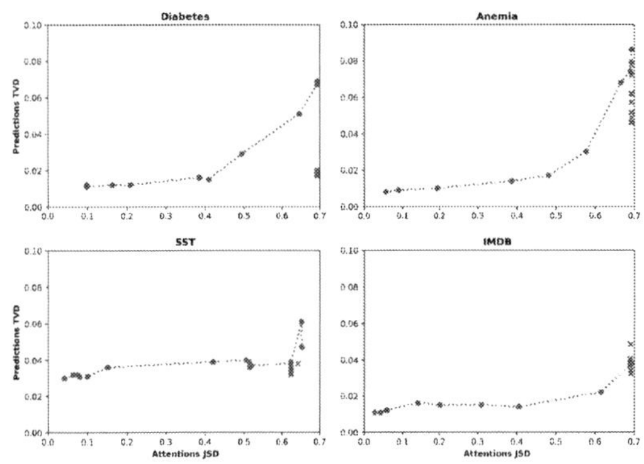

Figure 2: Visual comparison of averaged per-instance test set JSD and TVD from base model for each model variant between our adversarial setup and the one from Wiegreffe and Pinter (2019). The • show results from Wiegreffe and Pinter (2019), and the × show results from our setup.

We can see that, with our adversarial setup, we have achieved comparable prediction TVDs to Wiegreffe and Pinter's on the Anemia, SST and IMDB datasets. However, on the Diabetes dataset, our prediction TVDs are significantly lower than Wiegreffe and Pinter's. Given that our adversarial setups are pretty similar, we believe that this is mainly due to our inability to properly reproduce their base LSTM model on the Diabetes dataset. We can observe this from the 0.042 drop in the F1 score of our model from what was reported in Wiegreffe and Pinter (2019).

Looking at Figure 2, we can see that the adversarial results that we have achieved are towards the higher-end of the attention JSDs reported by Wiegreffe and Pinter (2019). This is very close to the calculated upper-bound for JSD, which is

0.6931. Wiegreffe and Pinter used the hyperparameter λ in order to reduce the effect of the attention JSD in the value of their loss. With the removal of this hyperparameter in our setup (which is the equivalent of setting it to 1), the adversarial training leads the model to primarily maximize the attention JSD, as it is an easier objective than to minimize the prediction TVD. Therefore, we usually end up with an almost maxed-out attention JSD, and it is mainly the prediction TVD that determines the value of AtteFa. However, we argue that the JSD is not always fully maxed-out (see the plot for the SST dataset in Figure 2), and therefore, we cannot simply disregard it in the computation of AtteFa.

7 Limitations

There are certain limitations with the current work, in terms of both the methodology used to compute AtteFa, and the different factors affecting the attention faithfulness. In this section, we explore the ones that we believe are the most important:

The current methodology to compute AtteFa is scoped solely on binary text classification. In order to have AtteFa as a widely accepted metric in the NLP community, the methodology needs to be extended to other NLP tasks, such as multi-class classification, text retrieval, question answering, machine translation, etc.

In the current work, we have studied the effect of the frequency of informative tokens on the faithfulness of attention through running experiments on the Mock-* datasets, which are synthetic datasets for sentiment classification. The current selection of sentiment words and their positioning within the input texts were done in a random fashion. A more thorough experiment would explore the effect of the distribution of informative tokens across the input texts (centered towards the start/end/middle vs. scattered evenly), along with a more careful selection of the words to be used as the informative tokens (e.g. differentiating between words with strong vs. weak sentiments).

In terms of investigating the effect of encoder contextualization on the faithfulness of attention, we have explored using token-level MLP as a non-contextual encoder and LSTM as a contextual one. This can be extended to exploring other encoder architectures, such as CNNs (LeCun et al., 1999), GRUs (Cho et al., 2014), and transformers (Vaswani et al., 2017).

Another aspect in the current study which has room for exploration is the evaluation of the effect of softmax temperature on the faithfulness of attention. We believe that higher faithfulness may be achieved by using lower temperatures in the case of datasets with infrequent informative tokens, and higher temperature in the case of datasets with frequent informative tokens within their input.

Last, but not least, the experiments in this work are only focused on a specific type of single-head attention. We believe that the current approach does not transfer properly to multi-headed attentions, as we may still consider a multi-headed attention faithful if the only way for the adversarial model to come up with the same predictions as the base model is to change the order of the attention heads and not the attention weights computed by them. Due to the frequent use of multi-headed attentions in state-of-the-art NLP models, the extension of AtteFa to multi-headed attentions would play a big role in its widespread adoption by the NLP community.

8 Conclusion

In this paper, we presented an adversarial training approach for binary text classification tasks, which can provide us with the metric *AtteFa* that quantitatively measures the degree of faithfulness in the attention weights. We, then, measured the effect of contextualization, as well as the effect of the frequency of informative tokens on the attention faithfulness. Finally, we computed and evaluated AtteFa for models trained on several real-life binary text classification datasets.

We hope that the presented approach can act as a motivation for researchers to further explore automatic approaches to quantitatively measure the degree of model explainability or its different aspects (e.g. faithfulness, plausibility, sufficiency, etc.).

As future directions, we plan to address the limitations specified in Section 7 to come up with a more reliable and more widely applicable metric to measure the faithfulness of attention. We also plan to measure attention faithfulness in other settings, e.g. the use of different types of attention such as multi-headed and scaled dot-product (Vaswani et al., 2017), the use of attention components in different layers of a model, etc.

Acknowledgments

We would like to express our gratitude to Sarah Wiegreffe, Yuval Pinter, Sarthak Jain, and Byron Wallace for the availability of their high quality code, which greatly helped us with the current work. We also thank the anonymous reviewers for their comments on an earlier version of this paper.

This work was financially supported by the Natural Sciences and Engineering Research Council of Canada (NSERC).

References

Malika Aubakirova and Mohit Bansal. 2016. Interpreting neural networks to improve politeness comprehension. In *Proceedings of the 2016 Conference on Empirical Methods in Natural Language Processing*, pages 2035–2041, Austin, Texas, USA.

Dzmitry Bahdanau, Kyunghyun Cho, and Yoshua Bengio. 2015. Neural machine translation by jointly learning to align and translate. In *Proceedings of the 3rd International Conference on Learning Representations, (ICLR 2015)*, San Diego, California, USA.

Piotr Bojanowski, Edouard Grave, Armand Joulin, and Tomas Mikolov. 2017. Enriching word vectors with subword information. *Transactions of the Association for Computational Linguistics*, 5:135–146.

Kyunghyun Cho, Bart van Merrienboer, Caglar Gulcehre, Dzmitry Bahdanau, Fethi Bougares, Holger Schwenk, and Yoshua Bengio. 2014. Learning phrase representations using RNN encoder–decoder for statistical machine translation. In *Proceedings of the 2014 Conference on Empirical Methods in Natural Language Processing (EMNLP 2014)*, pages 1724–1734, Doha, Qatar.

Reza Ghaeini, Xiaoli Fern, and Prasad Tadepalli. 2018. Interpreting recurrent and attention-based neural models: a case study on natural language inference. In *Proceedings of the 2018 Conference on Empirical Methods in Natural Language Processing (EMNLP 2018)*, pages 4952–4957, Brussels, Belgium.

Sepp Hochreiter and Jürgen Schmidhuber. 1997. Long short-term memory. *Neural Computation*, 9(8):1735–1780.

Sarthak Jain and Byron C. Wallace. 2019. Attention is not explanation. In *Proceedings of the 2019 Conference of the North American Chapter of the Association for Computational Linguistics: Human Language Technologies (NAACL-HLT 2019)*, pages 3543–3556, Minneapolis, Minnesota, USA.

Sweta Karlekar, Tong Niu, and Mohit Bansal. 2018. Detecting linguistic characteristics of Alzheimer's dementia by interpreting neural models. In *Proceedings of the 2018 Conference of the North American Chapter of the Association for Computational Linguistics: Human Language Technologies, Volume 2 (Short Papers)*, pages 701–707, New Orleans, Louisiana.

Diederik P. Kingma and Jimmy Ba. 2015. Adam: A method for stochastic optimization. In *Proceedings of the 3rd International Conference for Learning Representations (ICLR 2015)*, San Diego, California, USA.

Yann LeCun, Patrick Haffner, Léon Bottou, and Yoshua Bengio. 1999. Object recognition with gradient-based learning. In *Shape, Contour and Grouping in Computer Vision*, pages 319–345.

Jaesong Lee, Joong-Hwi Shin, and Jun-Seok Kim. 2017. Interactive visualization and manipulation of attention-based neural machine translation. In *Proceedings of the 2017 Conference on Empirical Methods in Natural Language Processing (EMNLP 2017): System Demonstrations*, pages 121–126, Copenhagen, Denmark.

Zhouhan Lin, Minwei Feng, Cícero Nogueira dos Santos, Mo Yu, Bing Xiang, Bowen Zhou, and Yoshua Bengio. 2017. A structured self-attentive sentence embedding. In *Proceedings of the 5th International Conference on Learning Representations (ICLR 2017)*, Toulon, France.

Thang Luong, Hieu Pham, and Christopher D. Manning. 2015. Effective approaches to attention-based neural machine translation. In *Proceedings of the 2015 Conference on Empirical Methods in Natural Language Processing*, pages 1412–1421, Lisbon, Portugal.

Tomas Mikolov, Kai Chen, Greg Corrado, and Jeffrey Dean. 2013. Efficient estimation of word representations in vector space. In *Workshop Proceedings of the International Conference on Learning Representations (ICLR 2013)*, Scottsdale, Arizona, USA.

James Mullenbach, Sarah Wiegreffe, Jon Duke, Jimeng Sun, and Jacob Eisenstein. 2018. Explainable prediction of medical codes from clinical text. In *Proceedings of the 2018 Conference of the North American Chapter of the Association for Computational Linguistics: Human Language Technologies (NAACL-HLT 2018)*, pages 1101–1111, New Orleans, Louisiana.

Marco Ribeiro, Sameer Singh, and Carlos Guestrin. 2016. "why should I trust you?": Explaining the predictions of any classifier. In *Proceedings of the 2016 Conference of the North American Chapter of the Association for Computational Linguistics (NAACL 2016): Demonstrations*, pages 97–101, San Diego, California, USA.

Ramprasaath R Selvaraju, Michael Cogswell, Abhishek Das, Ramakrishna Vedantam, Devi Parikh, and Dhruv Batra. 2017. Grad-cam: Visual explanations from deep networks via gradient-based localization.

In *Proceedings of the 2017 IEEE international conference on computer vision (ICCV 2017)*, pages 618–626, Venice, Italy.

Sofia Serrano and Noah A. Smith. 2019. Is attention interpretable? In *Proceedings of the 57th Annual Meeting of the Association for Computational Linguistics (ACL 2019)*, pages 2931–2951, Florence, Italy.

Mukund Sundararajan, Ankur Taly, and Qiqi Yan. 2017. Axiomatic attribution for deep networks. In *Proceedings of the 2017 International Conference on Machine Learning (ICML 2017)*, pages 3319–3328, Sydney, Australia.

Ashish Vaswani, Noam Shazeer, Niki Parmar, Jakob Uszkoreit, Llion Jones, Aidan N Gomez, Łukasz Kaiser, and Illia Polosukhin. 2017. Attention is all you need. In I. Guyon, U. V. Luxburg, S. Bengio, H. Wallach, R. Fergus, S. Vishwanathan, and R. Garnett, editors, *Proceedings of the 2017 Conference on Advances in Neural Information Processing Systems (NIPS 2017)*, pages 5998–6008. Long Beach, California, USA.

Yequan Wang, Minlie Huang, Xiaoyan Zhu, and Li Zhao. 2016. Attention-based LSTM for aspect-level sentiment classification. In *Proceedings of the 2016 Conference on Empirical Methods in Natural Language Processing (EMNLP 2016)*, pages 606–615, Austin, Texas, USA.

Sarah Wiegreffe and Yuval Pinter. 2019. Attention is not not explanation. In *Proceedings of the 2019 Conference on Empirical Methods in Natural Language Processing and the 9th International Joint Conference on Natural Language Processing (EMNLP-IJCNLP 2019)*, pages 11–20, Hong Kong, China.

Qizhe Xie, Xuezhe Ma, Zihang Dai, and Eduard Hovy. 2017. An interpretable knowledge transfer model for knowledge base completion. In *Proceedings of the 55th Annual Meeting of the Association for Computational Linguistics (ACL 2017)*, pages 950–962, Vancouver, Canada.

Luisa M Zintgraf, Taco S. Cohen, Tameem Adel, and Max Welling. 2017. Visualizing deep neural network decisions: Prediction difference analysis. In *Proceedings of the 2017 International Conference on Learning Representations (ICLR 2017)*.

A All Results on the Adversarial Setup

Tables 4 and 5 are the extended versions of Table 3, which include the results from the adversarial setup for each individual random seed that was used in the training of the adversarial models.

dataset	seed	LSTM					MLP				
		epoch	F1	TVD	JSD	AtteFa	epoch	F1	TVD	JSD	AtteFa
Mock-1	10	7	0.923	0.025	0.693	0.050	47	0.662	0.222	0.393	0.784
	50	16	0.971	0.004	0.693	0.008	1	0.000	0.244	0.393	0.860
	257	15	0.943	0.017	0.693	0.033	1	0.000	0.219	0.393	0.774
	500231	20	0.960	0.011	0.693	0.021	76	0.662	0.223	0.393	0.787
	100078	13	0.968	0.006	0.693	0.011	9	0.000	0.247	0.393	0.872
	12504	7	0.916	0.029	0.693	0.057	11	0.000	0.249	0.393	0.879
	90754789	16	0.963	0.008	0.693	0.015	7	0.000	0.218	0.393	0.767
	8988812	3	0.926	0.026	0.693	0.052	30	0.662	0.223	0.393	0.785
	2	9	0.952	0.012	0.693	0.025	2	0.000	0.235	0.393	0.828
Mock-2	10	2	0.982	0.015	0.692	0.030	1	0.662	0.243	0.670	0.504
	50	4	0.977	0.016	0.693	0.032	1	0.000	0.248	0.670	0.513
	257	12	0.978	0.016	0.693	0.032	1	0.000	0.244	0.670	0.506
	500231	5	0.964	0.024	0.693	0.047	2	0.662	0.242	0.670	0.502
	100078	15	0.975	0.016	0.693	0.033	1	0.000	0.247	0.670	0.510
	12504	19	0.960	0.024	0.693	0.048	1	0.000	0.250	0.670	0.519
	90754789	3	0.978	0.017	0.693	0.034	1	0.000	0.242	0.670	0.502
	8988812	4	0.984	0.012	0.693	0.024	1	0.662	0.243	0.670	0.504
	2	19	0.997	0.007	0.693	0.015	1	0.000	0.250	0.670	0.519
Mock-5	10	12	1.000	0.002	0.693	0.003	1	0.662	0.249	0.686	0.504
	50	3	1.000	0.002	0.693	0.003	17	0.000	0.246	0.686	0.497
	257	2	0.998	0.003	0.693	0.006	4	0.000	0.246	0.686	0.497
	500231	20	1.000	0.002	0.693	0.003	2	0.000	0.247	0.686	0.499
	100078	5	0.999	0.002	0.693	0.004	16	0.000	0.246	0.686	0.497
	12504	7	1.000	0.002	0.693	0.003	2	0.000	0.246	0.686	0.497
	90754789	3	1.000	0.002	0.693	0.003	34	0.000	0.246	0.686	0.497
	8988812	5	1.000	0.002	0.693	0.003	1	0.662	0.249	0.686	0.504
	2	7	1.000	0.002	0.693	0.003	2	0.000	0.246	0.686	0.497
Mock-10	10	21	1.000	0.001	0.693	0.001	1	0.662	0.251	0.686	0.508
	50	25	1.000	0.001	0.693	0.001	80	0.000	0.248	0.686	0.501
	257	6	1.000	0.001	0.693	0.001	13	0.000	0.248	0.686	0.501
	500231	8	1.000	0.001	0.693	0.001	2	0.000	0.249	0.686	0.503
	100078	16	1.000	0.001	0.693	0.001	80	0.000	0.248	0.686	0.501
	12504	4	1.000	0.001	0.693	0.001	6	0.000	0.248	0.686	0.501
	90754789	9	1.000	0.001	0.693	0.001	24	0.000	0.248	0.686	0.501
	8988812	28	1.000	0.001	0.693	0.001	1	0.662	0.251	0.686	0.508
	2	12	1.000	0.001	0.693	0.001	4	0.000	0.248	0.686	0.501
Mock-1q	10	20	1.000	0.000	0.693	0.001	70	0.000	0.247	0.690	0.497
	50	40	1.000	0.000	0.693	0.001	10	1.000	0.001	0.688	0.002
	257	39	1.000	0.000	0.693	0.001	79	0.093	0.235	0.690	0.473
	500231	13	1.000	0.000	0.693	0.001	80	0.093	0.235	0.690	0.473
	100078	17	1.000	0.000	0.693	0.001	6	1.000	0.002	0.688	0.003
	12504	14	1.000	0.000	0.693	0.001	6	1.000	0.002	0.689	0.003
	90754789	12	1.000	0.000	0.693	0.001	44	0.000	0.247	0.690	0.497
	8988812	15	1.000	0.000	0.693	0.001	28	0.000	0.247	0.690	0.497
	2	39	1.000	0.000	0.693	0.001	6	1.000	0.002	0.689	0.004
Mock-2q	10	25	1.000	0.000	0.678	0.001	80	0.305	0.203	0.690	0.408
	50	80	1.000	0.000	0.681	0.000	79	0.700	0.212	0.690	0.426
	257	79	1.000	0.000	0.681	0.000	4	0.997	0.002	0.691	0.003
	500231	5	0.998	0.002	0.678	0.003	40	0.995	0.003	0.691	0.005
	100078	23	0.999	0.001	0.681	0.001	80	0.089	0.236	0.690	0.474
	12504	8	1.000	0.000	0.682	0.000	79	0.683	0.230	0.690	0.461
	90754789	12	1.000	0.000	0.681	0.000	4	0.998	0.001	0.691	0.002
	8988812	3	1.000	0.000	0.670	0.000	10	0.997	0.002	0.691	0.004
	2	79	1.000	0.000	0.670	0.000	6	0.999	0.001	0.690	0.001
Mock-3q	10	5	1.000	0.000	0.674	0.000	5	0.998	0.001	0.691	0.002
	50	16	1.000	0.000	0.675	0.000	4	0.997	0.002	0.691	0.003
	257	9	1.000	0.000	0.674	0.001	2	1.000	0.000	0.690	0.000
	500231	12	1.000	0.000	0.691	0.000	44	1.000	0.000	0.691	0.000
	100078	10	1.000	0.000	0.691	0.000	13	1.000	0.000	0.691	0.000
	12504	4	1.000	0.000	0.689	0.000	5	0.999	0.001	0.691	0.001
	90754789	46	1.000	0.000	0.675	0.000	11	1.000	0.000	0.691	0.000
	8988812	71	1.000	0.000	0.686	0.000	25	0.999	0.001	0.691	0.001
	2	12	1.000	0.000	0.674	0.000	5	0.998	0.001	0.691	0.002
Mock-4q	10	6	1.000	0.000	0.683	0.000	3	1.000	0.000	0.690	0.000
	50	7	1.000	0.000	0.683	0.000	3	1.000	0.000	0.690	0.000
	257	5	1.000	0.000	0.683	0.000	3	1.000	0.000	0.690	0.000
	500231	12	1.000	0.000	0.683	0.000	2	1.000	0.000	0.690	0.000
	100078	9	1.000	0.000	0.683	0.000	3	1.000	0.000	0.690	0.000
	12504	16	1.000	0.000	0.682	0.000	3	1.000	0.000	0.691	0.000
	90754789	7	0.999	0.001	0.670	0.001	3	1.000	0.000	0.690	0.000
	8988812	8	1.000	0.000	0.674	0.000	3	1.000	0.000	0.690	0.000
	2	4	1.000	0.000	0.683	0.000	4	1.000	0.000	0.690	0.000

Table 4: All results from our adversarial setup on the synthetic datasets.

dataset	seed	LSTM					MLP				
		epoch	F1	TVD	JSD	AtteFa	epoch	F1	TVD	JSD	AtteFa
	10	21	0.732	0.017	0.693	0.035	58	0.180	0.145	0.691	0.291
	50	25	0.730	0.018	0.693	0.037	76	0.203	0.142	0.691	0.286
	257	23	0.730	0.018	0.693	0.037	66	0.167	0.146	0.690	0.293
	500231	22	0.730	0.018	0.693	0.035	21	0.112	0.147	0.690	0.295
Diabetes	100078	25	0.726	0.020	0.693	0.040	34	0.227	0.143	0.691	0.287
	12504	20	0.735	0.019	0.693	0.038	80	0.159	0.146	0.691	0.292
	90754789	31	0.728	0.018	0.693	0.035	24	0.151	0.145	0.691	0.291
	8988812	10	0.723	0.020	0.693	0.040	15	0.006	0.153	0.690	0.307
	2	18	0.729	0.017	0.692	0.034	5	0.000	0.153	0.691	0.308
	10	32	0.900	0.057	0.693	0.115	30	0.833	0.094	0.692	0.189
	50	14	0.877	0.072	0.693	0.144	13	0.842	0.086	0.692	0.173
	257	15	0.923	0.047	0.692	0.093	45	0.841	0.095	0.693	0.190
	500231	19	0.914	0.049	0.693	0.098	11	0.829	0.091	0.693	0.182
Anemia	100078	26	0.894	0.061	0.693	0.123	23	0.828	0.093	0.692	0.185
	12504	14	0.877	0.077	0.693	0.155	29	0.817	0.103	0.693	0.206
	90754789	26	0.912	0.052	0.693	0.104	19	0.835	0.093	0.692	0.186
	8988812	19	0.888	0.062	0.693	0.124	23	0.831	0.091	0.692	0.183
	2	17	0.927	0.046	0.692	0.092	14	0.834	0.091	0.693	0.182
	10	23	0.825	0.038	0.643	0.082	23	0.657	0.172	0.658	0.362
	50	16	0.822	0.033	0.624	0.072	10	0.598	0.172	0.656	0.363
	257	29	0.821	0.032	0.624	0.071	28	0.577	0.172	0.655	0.364
	500231	11	0.823	0.033	0.624	0.073	22	0.580	0.173	0.657	0.365
SST	100078	30	0.822	0.035	0.624	0.078	15	0.576	0.174	0.653	0.370
	12504	20	0.828	0.033	0.624	0.074	61	0.590	0.173	0.660	0.365
	90754789	18	0.818	0.035	0.624	0.078	21	0.630	0.173	0.657	0.364
	8988812	24	0.823	0.035	0.624	0.077	9	0.636	0.173	0.654	0.366
	2	18	0.823	0.035	0.624	0.078	14	0.599	0.172	0.656	0.363
	10	62	0.896	0.034	0.691	0.069	13	0.210	0.191	0.689	0.385
	50	42	0.889	0.040	0.689	0.081	18	0.230	0.188	0.689	0.379
	257	50	0.891	0.037	0.691	0.074	10	0.101	0.191	0.689	0.384
	500231	26	0.893	0.038	0.691	0.077	45	0.073	0.190	0.689	0.382
IMDB	100078	44	0.889	0.033	0.691	0.066	11	0.180	0.191	0.689	0.384
	12504	41	0.892	0.035	0.691	0.070	12	0.195	0.190	0.689	0.382
	90754789	60	0.890	0.040	0.691	0.081	29	0.100	0.191	0.690	0.384
	8988812	65	0.875	0.049	0.691	0.098	45	0.215	0.189	0.689	0.380
	2	54	0.890	0.038	0.691	0.077	10	0.120	0.191	0.689	0.385
	10	27	0.959	0.006	0.680	0.013	11	0.630	0.164	0.670	0.340
	50	28	0.958	0.006	0.681	0.013	17	0.567	0.174	0.671	0.359
	257	33	0.957	0.008	0.685	0.016	10	0.653	0.169	0.671	0.349
	500231	60	0.958	0.006	0.680	0.012	49	0.639	0.172	0.670	0.356
AgNews	100078	37	0.958	0.006	0.680	0.013	17	0.610	0.167	0.671	0.345
	12504	78	0.957	0.008	0.685	0.016	19	0.597	0.176	0.672	0.362
	90754789	68	0.959	0.007	0.685	0.015	27	0.633	0.171	0.671	0.352
	8988812	66	0.958	0.007	0.686	0.014	23	0.549	0.179	0.673	0.369
	2	47	0.958	0.006	0.680	0.012	39	0.611	0.179	0.671	0.370
	10	23	0.849	0.057	0.689	0.115	34	0.246	0.207	0.661	0.433
	50	26	0.863	0.038	0.690	0.077	34	0.176	0.200	0.653	0.425
	257	21	0.850	0.050	0.688	0.100	23	0.315	0.207	0.656	0.437
	500231	17	0.858	0.050	0.687	0.101	57	0.397	0.206	0.659	0.434
20News	100078	16	0.894	0.031	0.689	0.063	3	0.460	0.211	0.639	0.457
	12504	13	0.859	0.052	0.689	0.105	4	0.440	0.211	0.641	0.456
	90754789	16	0.874	0.049	0.688	0.099	44	0.043	0.205	0.654	0.435
	8988812	7	0.863	0.047	0.688	0.094	11	0.495	0.214	0.644	0.461
	2	19	0.875	0.042	0.689	0.084	10	0.492	0.213	0.642	0.461

Table 5: All results from our adversarial setup on the real-life datasets.

Are Multilingual Sentiment Models Equally Right for the Right Reasons?

Rasmus Kær Jørgensen[1,2], **Fiammetta Caccavale**[3], **Christian Igel**[1] and **Anders Søgaard**[1]
[1]University of Copenhagen, Denmark
[2]PricewaterhouseCoopers (PwC), Denmark
[3]Technical University of Denmark
rasmuskj,igel,soegaard@di.ku.dk
fiacac@kt.dtu.dk

Abstract

Multilingual NLP models provide potential solutions to *the digital language divide*, i.e., cross-language performance disparities. Early analyses of such models have indicated good performance across training languages and good generalization to unseen, related languages. This work examines whether, between related languages, multilingual models are equally *right for the right reasons*, i.e., if interpretability methods reveal that the models put emphasis on the same words as humans. To this end, we provide a new trilingual, parallel corpus of rationale annotations for English, Danish, and Italian sentiment analysis models and use it to benchmark models and interpretability methods. We propose rank-biased overlap as a better metric for comparing input token attributions to human rationale annotations. Our results show: (i) models generally perform well on the languages they are trained on, and align best with human rationales in these languages; (ii) performance is higher on English, even when not a source language, but this performance is not accompanied by higher alignment with human rationales, which suggests that language models favor English, but do not facilitate successful transfer of rationales.

EN	**A**	**deep**	**and**	**meaningful**	**film**
	2.34	1.69	2.70	1.92	0.09
DA	**En**	**dyb**	**og**	**meningsfuld**	**film**
	0.20	0.79	0.67	2.32	0.11
IT	**Un**	**film**	**profondo**	**e**	**significativo**
	0.44	0.28	1.72	1.79	1.43

Table 1: Tokens with machine generated importance scores for direct translations of the same sentence into English, Danish, and Italian. We see machine rationales are nevertheless quite different; e.g., consider the importance scores for the connectives *and*, *og* and *e*.

1 Introduction

NLP models are sometimes right for the wrong reasons, e.g., when sentiment analysis models correctly predict a movie review to be positive because it contains the word *Shrek* (Sindhwani and Melville, 2008). Human rationale annotations can be used to evaluate the extent to which models are right for the right reasons, i.e., whether model rationales align with human rationales. Datasets with rationale annotations exist for sentiment analysis (Zaidan and Eisner, 2008), fact-checking (Thorne et al., 2018), natural language inference (Camburu et al., 2018a), and hate speech detection (Mathew et al., 2020),[1] but so far only for the English language. While multilingual language models often fail to generalize across distant languages (Singh et al., 2019a; Pires et al., 2019; Rust et al., 2020), they do bridge between related languages and have become a standard solution to data sparsity (Zheng et al., 2021), as well as a way to reduce the overall energy consumption of training language-specific language models (Sahlgren et al., 2021). Benchmark performance does not tell us whether multilingual models are more prone to spurious correlations in some languages rather than others, i.e., whether models are *equally right for the right reasons* or to different degrees, see Table 1.

This paper presents a trilingual parallel corpus of human rationale annotations in Danish, Italian, and English, for the task of sentiment analysis. To this end, we translate an existing sentiment analysis dataset into different languages following a similar procedure as Hu et al. (2020), with human post-correction. We then collect rationales from native speakers of these languages. We evaluate the quality of our human rationale annotations in two ways: using inter-annotator agreement metrics and using human forward prediction experiments (Nguyen, 2018). We then use the corpus to evaluate the extent to which multilingual language models are equally right for the right reasons across languages, and whether agreement with human rationales aligns

[1]Several of these datasets can also be found in the ERASER Benchmark (DeYoung et al., 2020).

Proceedings of the Fifth BlackboxNLP Workshop on Analyzing and Interpreting Neural Networks for NLP, pages 131 - 141
December 8, 2022 ©2022 Association for Computational Linguistics

with downstream performance.

Contributions Our contributions are as follows: (a) We present a trilingual corpus of human rationales, based on post-corrected translations of the Stanford Sentiment Treebank (Socher et al., 2013) and annotated by native speakers. The corpus is made publicly available at `https://github.com/RasmusKaer/BlackBox2022`. (b) We propose better metrics for comparing ranked rationales than has previously been used, as well as a sequence-wise normalization of LIME's token scores to make scores comparable across sequences. (c) We evaluate MBERT (Devlin et al., 2019) and XLM-R (Conneau et al., 2019), in conjunction with two interpretability methods, LIME (Ribeiro et al., 2016) and SHAP (Lundberg and Lee, 2017), across three languages, quantifying the extent to which these models are *equally right for the right reasons*.

2 Multilingual Rationale Annotation

Our multilingual corpus of human rationales is based on post-corrected translations of the Stanford Sentiment Treebank. We obtain Danish and Italian translations of a sample of validation data, correct the translations manually, and have native speakers annotate the original English sentences, as well as their post-corrected translations. We then validate the annotations by quantifying human inter-annotator agreement and by performing human forward prediction experiments (Doshi-Velez and Kim, 2017; Nguyen, 2018; Hase and Bansal, 2020; Gonzalez and Søgaard, 2020; González et al., 2021). We describe each step in detail in this section.

Stanford Sentiment Treebank (SST) Our dataset builds on a sample of the Stanford Sentiment Treebank, which originally consists of 11,855 sentences from movie reviews, annotated with sentiment labels, and split in training, validation and evaluation sections of 8,544, 1,101, and 2,210 sentences. The sample selected for annotation of the rationales consists of 250 sentences from the validation section.

Translation We translate the English dataset into the target languages using Google Cloud API[2]. We carefully correct the translations of the rationales set manually and assess the quality of corpus through a language analysis. The post-correction process is presented in 6. We are aware that it would have been beneficial to have a set of languages that was more representative of linguistic diversity, but for this work we only had access to professional annotators in the three languages.

Annotation We ask native speakers of English, Danish and Italian to annotate the sample with rationales. Our aim is to identify two types of information for each sentence: the rationales span, snippets of text that support the outcome; and the rank, the most meaningful words to justify the sentiment of the sentence. Inspired by previous explainability work in NLP using human rationale annotations (Mathew et al., 2020; DeYoung et al., 2019; Zhang et al., 2016), we follow the annotation guidelines in Zaidan et al. (2007). For the rank, we are interested in single words that carry a semantic meaning for the output (positive or negative sentiment). Annotators are asked to rank up to five words from most (1) to least (5) meaningful. See Table 2 for an example. The four annotators used in this study had linguistic training and participated on a voluntary basis.

S	John and Adam are such likeable actors.
R	John and Adam are such [2] likeable [1] actors.
S	A warm , funny , engaging film.
R	A warm [3], funny [1], engaging [2] film.

Table 2: Text annotation showing span (S) annotation and rank (R) annotation.

Annotator agreement The inter-annotator agreement is measured as Cohen's κ (Cohen, 1960) and accuracy; see Table 3. The κ coefficients suggest that the two annotators for each language have substantial agreement across all languages.

Lang.	κ	Acc.	Span	Rank	Tokens
DA	0.705	0.882	1,114	722	4157
EN	0.731	0.890	1,250	770	4232
IT	0.642	0.857	1,067	736	4411

Table 3: Annotator agreement and rationales by token. The minimum sentence length is 3 tokens for all three languages. The average length for both EN and DA is 17 and the maximum is 42 tokens per sentence, while in IT it is, respectively, 18 and 44 tokens per sentence.

Forward prediction Besides calculating the inter-annotator agreement, we also validate the

[2]Advanced version (v3), September 2021

quality of our annotations through human forward prediction (Doshi-Velez and Kim, 2017; Nguyen, 2018; Hase and Bansal, 2020; Gonzalez and Søgaard, 2020; González et al., 2021). We recruited 9 annotators from our professional network, and everyone had degrees in computer science or linguistics. In a small-scale side experiment, we show participants 28 examples in which rationales identified by the annotators are highlighted. Participants are then asked to guess the ground truth (positive or negative sentiment) from these highlighted spans. We compare this to a baseline setting in which our participants have to guess the ground truth from raw text. We explicitly mentioned in the task that the results will be used for scientific research. If the rationales help participants predict the ground truth, they have been shown to be good rationales. Humans predicted the ground-truth for 82% of the examples with rationales, compared to 70% of the examples *without* rationales. For example, without rationales provided, 22.2% of annotators struggled in identifying the correct sentiment of a review such as *"Turns a potentially forgettable formula into something strangely diverting"*, while having less difficulties with equally challenging reviews when the rationales are provided. The high inter-annotator agreement and the usefulness of our rationales together indicate that our annotations are of high quality.

3 Comparing Ranked Rationale Lists

To evaluate the agreement between human rationales and rationales identified by interpretability methods applied to automatic sentiment analyses, we need a similarity measure for comparing ranked rationale lists. Common correlation tests are not sufficient, because the measure must be applicable to non-conjoint, uneven lists and should put a higher weight on higher-ranked words.

The human annotator selects the most relevant words in a sentence until exhausted. The ranking is ordered, but may only contain a few words. On the other hand, the interpretability methods provide by design a rank for each word in a sentence. Thus, the annotator's ranking is typically *incomplete* (not all items are ranked), while the automatically computed ranking is *complete*. That is, the two rankings are mutually *non-conjoint*. Furthermore, we need to deal with *indefiniteness* (Webber et al., 2010) in the sense that the annotator may truncate the complete list at an arbitrary depth. The measure we propose for evaluating rationale rankings is the extrapolated version of the *rank-biased overlap* (Webber et al., 2010), RBO_{EXT}, which is a generalization of average based overlap for indefinite rankings. It ranges from 0 (disjoint) to 1 (identical). The RBO_{EXT} measure satisfy the criteria needed for evaluating the agreement of list rationale rankings of both sentences and documents by being able to handle tied ranks, rankings of different lengths and top-weighted rankings.

The degree of top-weightedness is determined by a parameter $p \in [0, 1]$. Consider a person comparing two rankings by sequentially going through the lists starting with the highest rank. In each step, one additional rank is considered. That is, in the beginning only the highest ranked elements are compared, then additionally the top two elements are compared, and so on. At each step, the person stops the comparison with a probability $1 - p$. Roughly speaking, RBO_{EXT} measures the expected similarity computed by this randomized comparison. The parameter p induces a weighting of the ranks that decreases with decreasing rank (i.e., decreasing importance). Following Webber et al. (2010), we choose p such that 86% of the weight is concentrated on the first d ranks. They show that the concentration of weights on the first d ranks given p can be computed as

$$1 - p^{d-1} + \frac{1-p}{p} d \left(\ln \frac{1}{1-p} - \sum_{i=1}^{d-1} \frac{p^i}{i} \right) .$$

Table 3 shows that annotators on average rank 3 words per sentence. Hence, we set $p = 0.68$, because this leads to a concentration of roughly 86% for $d = 3$. The annotators were asked to rank up to 5 words. Therefore, we also considered only the top-5 elements in the rankings produced by the interpretability methods (still, we apply RBO_{EXT} as derived for indefinite rankings).

4 Experiments

Our experiments below rely on two pretrained multilingual language models, which we briefly introduce, three different experimental protocols, and two different interpretability methods.

Pretrained language models The experimental protocol is based on two pretrained multilingual transformer language models (Vaswani et al., 2017), namely MBERT (Devlin et al., 2019)[3] and

[3]https://huggingface.co/bert-base-multilingual-cased

XLM-R (Conneau et al., 2019)[4]. We used the base, cased version from the Hugging Face transformers library[5]. Following (Devlin et al., 2019), we added a classification layer on top of the [CLS] token. We fine-tuned these models for 3 epochs on a single Tesla K80 GPU, with a training batch size of 16 and a learning rate of $3 \cdot 10^{-5}$. The parameters were found using manual hyperparameter tuning based on the authors' recommendations of batch-sizes $\{16, 32\}$, epochs $\{2, 3, 4\}$. The learning rate was fine-tuned over $\{2 \cdot 10^{-5}, 3 \cdot 10^{-5}, 5 \cdot 10^{-5}\}$ with 3 trials each.

Experimental protocols In our experiments, we fine-tune MBERT and XLM-R on the SST training data and/or translations thereof (into Danish or Italian). We rely on three standard protocols, which we call the BASE-SETTING, the CROSS-SETTING, and the MULTI-SETTING. In the BASE-SETTING, we fine-tune MBERT and XLM-R on a single language, e.g., English, and evaluate them on the evaluation data in the *same* language. This corresponds to the situation in which you use a multilingual language model to learn a monolingual model in the presence of training data. This scenario is common for *medium-resourced* languages. In the CROSS-SETTING, we evaluate such models, e.g., trained on English, on another language. This scenario is common for *low-resourced* languages. Finally, in the MULTI-SETTING, we train and evaluate on all three languages, inducing a *multilingual* sentiment analysis model for three languages. In all three settings, we evaluate the extent to which the fine-tuned MBERT and XLM-R models align with human rationales, relying on interpretability methods.

Interpretability methods A variety of methods for deriving explanations are currently being used by the NLP community. Examples of such methods are LIME (Ribeiro et al., 2016) and SHAP (Lundberg and Lee, 2017), LRP (Bach et al., 2015), and DTD (Montavon et al., 2017). For this study, we consider SHAP and LIME, since they are two of the most widely used post-hoc model interpretability methods, also used in similar studies such as ERASER (DeYoung et al., 2020) and HateXplain (Mathew et al., 2020). LIME is a model-agnostic approach that returns an explanation for a prediction on an input example (a text) by virtue of a local linear approximation of the model's behavior around that example. The linear approximation is a sparse linear model induced from hundreds of perturbations of the example. In the case of text examples, perturbations are obtained by randomly removing tokens or words. SHAP is also model-agnostic and based on Shapley values (Shapley, 1953), a concept from cooperative game theory, which refers to the average of the marginal contributions to all possible coalitions. When applied to text, the method, like LIME, produces explanations in terms of tokens or words. We kept the hyperparameters of the two methods to their default-setting, except for the size of neighbourhood used to learn linear models for LIME, which we set to 500 for computational reasons.

[4]https://huggingface.co/xlm-roberta-base

[5]https://huggingface.co/docs/transformers, V4.15.0

5 Results

Table 4 presents the results of the experimental protocol on our trilingual corpus. We compare the effectiveness of LIME and SHAP on human rationales. The agreements is evaluated using ROC AUC for rationale span and RBO_{EXT} for rank similarity based on all 250 samples. The protocol sets two properties for fine-tuning: a single language, denoted by DA, EN and IT, or multiple languages, denoted MULTI. The fine-tuned models are tested across DA, EN and IT with 3 runs per setting.

Performance of MBERT and XLM-R The accuracy of the multilingual models across languages and settings is presented in Table 4. The results confirm the findings of the original works (Conneau et al., 2019), that XLM-R is consistently better than MBERT.

While MBERT-based models consistently obtain their highest accuracy in the BASE-SETTING, XLM-R-based models always perform best on English as the target language, independently from the source language. MBERT-based models exhibit a high variation in the CROSS-SETTING (5.11 p.p. difference between the average accuracy of the BASE compared to the CROSS settings), e.g., EN-MBERT achieves 81.48% accuracy when tested on the English test set, but has only 70.42% accuracy on Danish. In contrast, XLM-R shows less variation between BASE and CROSS settings (0.52 p.p. difference).

But does a higher performance correspond to higher agreement with human rationales? Table 4 presents the results for agreement, evaluated using ROC AUC for rationale span and RBO_{EXT} for rank similarity of the two list rankings. The results sug-

Protocol settings				SHAP		LIME	
Source	Model	Target	Acc.	ROC AUC	RBO_{EXT}	ROC AUC	RBO_{EXT}
English	EN-MBERT	EN	81.48 ± 0.3	68.69 ± 0.7	51.63 ± 0.0	67.08 ± 0.0	53.76 ± 0.0
		IT	74.28 ± 0.6	70.11 ± 1.0	49.92 ± 0.0	66.18 ± 0.0	47.77 ± 0.0
		DA	70.42 ± 0.9	67.41 ± 1.0	44.38 ± 0.0	62.05 ± 0.0	42.35 ± 0.0
	EN-XLM-R	EN	85.37 ± 0.2	69.95 ± 1.4	52.78 ± 0.0	66.83 ± 0.0	56.87 ± 0.0
		IT	82.16 ± 0.2	69.80 ± 0.4	48.52 ± 0.0	68.05 ± 0.0	54.48 ± 0.0
		DA	82.50 ± 0.3	68.85 ± 0.7	50.68 ± 0.0	66.19 ± 0.0	53.33 ± 0.0
Italian	IT-MBERT	IT	80.66 ± 1.2	69.24 ± 1.1	53.24 ± 0.0	68.23 ± 0.0	55.37 ± 0.0
		EN	76.08 ± 1.7	68.79 ± 1.0	50.46 ± 0.0	66.04 ± 0.0	48.62 ± 0.0
		DA	68.94 ± 0.5	65.13 ± 0.6	43.11 ± 0.0	62.66 ± 0.0	43.95 ± 0.0
	IT-XLM-R	IT	82.56 ± 0.0	71.79 ± 1.2	52.79 ± 0.0	69.94 ± 0.0	56.72 ± 0.0
		EN	84.15 ± 0.7	70.62 ± 0.8	55.48 ± 0.0	66.79 ± 0.0	55.22 ± 0.0
		DA	81.24 ± 1.0	69.59 ± 0.4	53.03 ± 0.0	66.16 ± 0.0	52.98 ± 0.0
Danish	DA-MBERT	DA	79.17 ± 0.5	67.40 ± 2.0	49.07 ± 0.0	66.37 ± 0.0	51.33 ± 0.0
		IT	72.10 ± 0.3	68.36 ± 0.8	45.84 ± 0.0	64.74 ± 0.0	45.39 ± 0.0
		EN	75.60 ± 0.7	69.95 ± 0.5	49.50 ± 0.0	66.17 ± 0.0	48.37 ± 0.0
	DA-XLM-R	DA	83.41 ± 0.5	69.74 ± 1.6	55.88 ± 0.0	65.99 ± 0.0	53.27 ± 0.0
		IT	82.07 ± 0.6	69.16 ± 0.6	49.75 ± 0.0	67.57 ± 0.0	52.12 ± 0.0
		EN	84.80 ± 0.2	70.39 ± 1.1	53.63 ± 0.0	66.34 ± 0.0	52.59 ± 0.0
Multi	MULTI-MBERT	EN	81.51 ± 0.1	65.02 ± 2.1	43.49 ± 0.0	65.97 ± 0.0	51.68 ± 0.0
		IT	80.62 ± 0.2	66.16 ± 1.6	45.57 ± 0.0	66.21 ± 0.0	49.60 ± 0.0
		DA	78.34 ± 0.9	63.99 ± 0.4	42.65 ± 0.0	63.89 ± 0.0	49.71 ± 0.0
	MULTI-XLM-R	EN	85.83 ± 0.4	67.79 ± 0.8	50.45 ± 0.0	64.48 ± 0.0	48.66 ± 0.0
		IT	83.67 ± 0.3	69.10 ± 0.7	46.41 ± 0.0	66.52 ± 0.0	51.88 ± 0.0
		DA	82.88 ± 0.7	66.99 ± 1.3	48.89 ± 0.0	64.61 ± 0.0	49.59 ± 0.0

Table 4: Evaluation results on the multilingual corpus of rationales. All results are averaged over three trials. We report the results in percentages. We observe that generally models perform well on the languages they are trained on (source languages), and align best with human rationales in these languages. Generally, MBERT aligns better with human rationales, but XLM-R performs better. We also observe, however, that performance is high on English, even when not a source language, but that this performance is not accompanied by higher alignment with human rationales. This suggests that language models favor English, but do not facilitate successful transfer of rationales.

gest that the accuracy of the models does not generally seem to influence ROC AUC and RBO_{EXT} scores, since a much higher accuracy does not imply better span prediction.

Interpretability methods Our evaluation of the span agreement shows an average across all models and languages of 68.50% for SHAP and 66.04% for LIME, indicating that SHAP has a higher (2.46 p.p.) agreement with human span rationales than LIME. The average rank agreement across all models and languages measured using RBO_{EXT} is 49.46% for SHAP and 51.07% for LIME, the latter being 1.61 p.p. higher in agreement than SHAP. These experiments show that we do not have a single best method across rank and span. Our results suggest a trend of SHAP being a more successful method for capturing good weights for span agreement and LIME being slightly more in accordance with human ranking.

Languages The best rank agreement is achieved when English is used as target language, with the overall highest for both LIME (51.97%) and SHAP (50.93%), as presented in Table 5.

Metric	Method	Target-EN	Target-IT	Target-DA
RBO_{EXT}	SHAP	50.93	49.01	48.46
	LIME	51.97	51.67	49.56
ROC AUC	SHAP	68.90	69.22	67.39
	LIME	66.21	67.18	64.74
Overall		59.50	59.27	57.54

Table 5: To investigate whether explanations are in equal agreement across languages, we group target languages together across the BASE, CROSS and MULTI settings.

The second best rank agreement is obtained in Italian, while the worst is in Danish for both LIME and SHAP. The highest average span score is achieved on Italian, while English follows close and Danish again remain the lowest in agreement. While English is slightly higher in rank agreement, Italian obtains a better span agreement. The lowest span and rank agreement is generally seen with Danish as target language. As we are interested in how languages compare across models, settings and metrics, we can derive the total from the target languages column in Table 5. Altogether, these results indicate that we have better explanations for English (59.50%) than we have for Italian (59.27%)

and Danish (57.54%). The explanations for English are 1.96 p.p. higher in agreement with human rationales than the explanations derived from Danish, while Italian is 1.73 p.p. higher than Danish.

Evaluation metrics An interpretation of the evaluation metrics across settings and languages shows a span agreement that ranges from 62.05% to 71.79%, with an average of 67.27%. What we can interpret from the score is a satisfactory span agreement, suggesting that there is a $\frac{2}{3}$ chance that the model is able to distinguish a token inside a span and a token outside a span. That is, the machine rationale agrees with a human rationale. Regarding the rank agreement across all settings and languages, we see it ranges from 42.35% to 56.87% with an overall average of 50.27%. The score can be interpreted as neither disjoint nor identical, thus implying a fair agreement.

6 Analysis

In this section, we present our analysis of our results and findings. First, we address whether models are *equally right for the right reasons* and how performance compares to agreement. Next, we analyze the translations and the post-corrections. Lastly, we examine whether token scores predict human rationales.

Are models equally right for the right reasons across languages? The idea of being right for the right reasons refers to learning from reliable signals in your data, which are causally related to the ground truth classification. While some models can be used to illuminate complex causal dynamics, others adapt Clever Hans strategies of relying on pervasive, yet spurious correlations in the training data. In this paper, we ask if multilingual language models such as MBERT and XLM-R are equally prone to spurious correlations across languages? Or could it be that these models adopt Clever Hans strategies for some languages, but not for others?

Our results show, very consistently, that MBERT and XLM-R are *less* right for the right reasons for Danish: When the training language is English or Italian, or when multilingual training language is used, Danish never aligns best with human rationales. For English and Italian, it comes in worst in 18/20 cases, and in the multilingual setting, Danish is least right for the right reasons in 6/10 cases. For English and Italian, things are more or less *on par*. While English is slightly higher in rank agreement, then Italian obtains a better span agreement, but the lowest span and rank agreement is generally seen with Danish as the target language. We conclude that multilingual language models are *not* equally right for the right reasons across languages.

How indicative is accuracy for agreement? It seems intuitive that a good model with high performance will also align better with human rationales, but theoretically, models may adopt radically different strategies, if multiple strategies are possible. Even if we expect a positive correlation between performance and alignment, how strong is this correlation in practice? To answer this question, we compute the correlation between the accuracy of the language models and the agreement of span and rank. We use Spearman's rank-order correlation test and Pearson's correlation test, across both explanation methods and all datasets. Both tests show that performance is only weakly (positively) correlated with alignment with human rationales; see Table 6 for details. That is, we see better alignment if models are better, but performance explains only a little of the variance, suggesting multiple possible strategies for prediction exist. This aligns well with our results, also, where a larger difference in accuracy between models does not transfer into a significant difference in agreement.

Lang.	Spearman's ρ	Pearson's ρ
Acc/AUC	0.059**	0.092**
Acc/RBO	0.076**	0.153**

Table 6: Correlation scores for performance (Acc) and alignment with human rationales (AUC/RBO).

Humans may base their rationales on different parts than machine-based rationales. While humans consider *and* necessary for the snippet of *deep and meaningful* (see example in Table 1), a model may not find it a useful predictor of sentiment. Humans and models may agree on the sentiment, but for slightly different reasons.

Language analysis The translated corpus is post-corrected to obtain a high overall quality, ensuring that the corpus can be used to evaluate the interpretability methods in our experiments. To quantify the translations quality, we report the number or sentences that needed corrections and the average number of corrected words in Table 7. The percentage of sentences that needed to have corrections in Italian and Danish are, respectively, 17.20% and

Lang.	% corrected sentences	Avg. corrected words
DA	15.60	1.46
IT	17.20	1.74

Table 7: Percentage of corrected sentences and average number of corrected words per sentence in Italian and Danish.

15.60%. Among these corrected sentences, 1.74 words were corrected on average in Italian, 1.46 in Danish. The results indicate that overall the quality of the translations is high. This is also supported by the performance of the fine-tuned models in Table 4. A selection of original translation and the post-corrected equivalent is presented in Table 8. We can highlight some limitations found during post-correction. The original sentences sometimes present an informal register, sprinkled with colloquial and slang words, which may result in suboptimal and literal translations. Some of the original sentences present idiomatic expressions that might result in a literal translation, as in A-DA, not corresponding to actual terms in the target language. Moreover, some translations may contain

A-IT ORG.	..., sbalorditivo, assurdamente *cattivo.*
A-IT COR.	..., sbalorditivo, assurdamente **brutto**
B-IT ORG.	Questo film *fa impazzire*.
B-IT COR.	Questo film **è esasperante**.
A-DA ORG.	Der er *parcelhuller*, der er store nok til, ...
A-DA COR.	Der er **plothuller**, der er store nok til, ...
B-DA ORG.	Det er en *greb taske* med genrer, ...
B-DA COR.	Det er en **rodekasse** med genrer, ...

Table 8: Examples of corrected translations (COR.) and the original translations (ORG.).

subpar syntactic structure or lexicon, e.g., in A-IT *brutto* is more suiting to refer to *films*, although it presents the same polarity and magnitude of the original adjective. In B-IT the sentiment of the expression could be misinterpreted, since *fa impazzire* is sometimes used in a positive connotation. Lastly, sometimes the original English sentences contain typos and other errors, which the model is understandably not able to correct or process, therefore transferred into the translations.

Do token scores predict human rationales Meaningful token scores produced by an interpretability method should be predictive of human rationales (Doshi-Velez and Kim, 2017; Nguyen, 2018; DeYoung et al., 2019). To verify this, we map the token score $s(w)$ of a word w to an estimate of the probability that the word is in the rationales span. We assume a logistic model

$$P(w \text{ in rationales span} \mid s(w)) = \sigma_{a,b}(|s(w)|) \ ,$$

where $\sigma_{a,b}(x) = (1 + \exp(ax + b))^{-1}$ with scalar parameters a and b. These parameters are determined by maximum likelihood estimation on a training set pairing token scores and corresponding human annotations. We consider the absolute value of the score because we are interested in the importance of a word regardless of whether it contributes to a positive or negative sentiment. This approach corresponds to calibrating the (absolute) scores to posterior probabilities as suggested by Platt (Platt, 1999; Niculescu-Mizil and Caruana, 2005). It can also be viewed as logistic regression from the absolute score to the dependent variable indicating whether a word is in the rationale span or not.

The logistic model gives us the probability of a word being a rationale, which allows for an interpretation of token scores and a comparison of scores across different interpretability methods. In particular, the model suggests a criterion for deciding whether a word should be considered part of the rationales span or not by applying the natural 50% threshold on the probabilities (we pay for this additional information by using training data to fit the models). To fit the model and to compare the different interpretability methods, we split our data into a training and a validation set. We used 25 positive and 25 negative samples for validation and trained on the remaining 200 data points.

Let $\boldsymbol{s} = (s(w_1), s(w_2), \dots)^{\mathrm{T}}$ denote the vector of scores for a word sequence $w_1, w_2, \dots$ and $\min(\boldsymbol{s})$ and $\max(\boldsymbol{s})$ the minimum and maximum element of $\boldsymbol{s}$, respectively. To compare token scores across sequences, their scaling should not differ across the sequences. That is, because we can assume that each sequence contains at least one word within and one outside the span, for two sequence $\boldsymbol{s}$ and $\boldsymbol{s}'$ we should have $\min(\boldsymbol{s}) = \min(\boldsymbol{s}')$ and $\max(\boldsymbol{s}) = \max(\boldsymbol{s}')$. We found this property to be violated, in particular for LIME. Thus, we normalized the scores at the sequence level using

$$s(w) \leftarrow \frac{s(w) - \min(\boldsymbol{s})}{\max(\boldsymbol{s}) - \min(\boldsymbol{s})}$$

for each score $s(w)$ in a sequence with scores $\boldsymbol{s}$.

Table 9 shows the accuracies on the held-out sets in BASE-SETTING. Both methods performed better

		LIME MBERT	LIME XLM-R	SHAP MBERT	SHAP XLM-R	BASE LINE
(A)	EN	70.03	71.51	71.68	72.76	67.74
	DA	69.50	70.23	70.83	72.75	67.49
	IT	70.94	72.73	72.73	73.78	67.80
(B)	EN	73.75	73.03	70.97	71.68	67.74
	DA	72.34	72.75	71.47	72.70	67.49
	IT	73.47	75.44	73.30	73.13	67.80

Table 9: The accuracies on the hold-out sets in BASESETTING. The BASELINE is a majority classifier that naively predicts all tokens as not a rationale. (A) refers to the original token scores and (B) to the normalized token scores.

than simply predicting the majority class. Without normalization, SHAP outperformed LIME on our (rather small) validation data set. LIME was only slightly better than the baseline, but after normalization LIME surpassed SHAP, which did not profit from the normalization. When evaluating explanations on how well the token scores generalize to human rationales, we see a similar pattern of Italian and English sharing the highest agreement where Danish consistently shows the lowest agreement.

Human annotated rationales include connectives, determiners, and similar, which are irrelevant for our binary task and are therefore not used by the logistic models. This suggests that methods for adding the relevance of these could be a promising direction for improving our approach and the evaluation between human and machine rationales.

7 Related work

Transformer-based multilingual models have been analyzed in many ways: Researchers have, for example, looked at performance differences across languages (Singh et al., 2019b), looked at their organization of language types (Rama et al., 2020), used similarity analysis to probe their representations (Kudugunta et al., 2019), and investigated how learned self-attention in the Transformer blocks affects different languages (Ravishankar et al., 2021). Human rationales have been used to supervise attention for various text classification tasks, such as sentiment analysis (Zhong et al., 2019) and machine translation (Yin et al., 2021). Feature attribution methods such as LIME and SHAP have also been applied to multilingual models: LIME has been applied to MBERT for analysis of hate speech models (Aluru et al., 2020), and SHAP has been applied to MBERT in biomedical NLP (Zaragoza, 2021). LIME has also been applied to XLM-R in the context of hate speech (Socha, 2020), as well as in a biomedical context (Koloski et al., 2021). Shapley values have also been used to estimate the influence of source languages on the final predictions of models based on MBERT (Parvez and Chang, 2021). None of these applications have been evaluated, however. Feature attributions have been applied to monolingual models, especially for English, more often than multilingual models. For English, we have a set of datasets with human rationales that we can use to evaluate feature attribution methods. These include BeerAdvocate (Bastings et al., 2019) and e-SNLI (Camburu et al., 2018b), as well as other datasets, several of which were collected in the ERASER benchmark (DeYoung et al., 2020). The reason feature attribution methods have not been properly evaluated in a multilingual context, is simple: There was, until now, no gold standard with which to evaluate the rationales produced by multilingual models.

8 Conclusions

We introduced a new trilingual, parallel corpus of human rank and span rationales in three related languages, English, Danish and Italian. We proposed rank-biased overlap as a better metric for rank evaluation when common correlation tests are not sufficient. We found that a sequence-wise normalization of LIME's token scores is required to make scores comparable across sequences. Evaluations on the corpus showed that generally, models perform well on the languages they are trained on, and align best with human rationales in these languages. Models can be right for different reasons. The main results suggest that multilingual models are *not* equally right for the right reasons in the sense that interpretability methods indicate that the models not necessarily put emphasis on the same words as humans. We also observed that performance is high on English, even when it is not a source language, but that this superior performance is not accompanied by higher alignment with human rationales. In other words, this zero-shot advantage of English as a target language seems to come at the cost of being more prone to spurious correlations. With this work, we hope to inspire further progress on multilingual interpretation and collection of rationales in different languages.

9 Limitations

All the languages chosen for the presented work belong to the Indo-European language family, since we only had access to professional annotators in the three languages. A clear limitation of this study is the lack of linguistic diversity in the set of languages used. It would be beneficial in the future to build larger rationale datasets for less related languages, including languages from different language families. Another limitation to be highlighted is the limited size of the multilingual parallel corpus of rationales, consisting on 250 annotations per language. Finally, although the parallel corpus was post-corrected, the language models are fine-tuned on the translations.

References

Sai Saketh Aluru, Binny Mathew, Punyajoy Saha, and Animesh Mukherjee. 2020. Deep learning models for multilingual hate speech detection.

Sebastian Bach, Alexander Binder, Grégoire Montavon, Frederick Klauschen, Klaus-Robert Müller, and Wojciech Samek. 2015. On pixel-wise explanations for non-linear classifier decisions by layer-wise relevance propagation. *PLOS ONE*, 10(7):1–46.

Jasmijn Bastings, Wilker Aziz, and Ivan Titov. 2019. Interpretable neural predictions with differentiable binary variables. In *Proceedings of the 57th Annual Meeting of the Association for Computational Linguistics*, pages 2963–2977, Florence, Italy. Association for Computational Linguistics.

Oana-Maria Camburu, Tim Rocktäschel, Thomas Lukasiewicz, and Phil Blunsom. 2018a. e-SNLI: Natural language inference with natural language explanations. In *Advances in Neural Information Processing Systems*, volume 31.

Oana-Maria Camburu, Tim Rocktäschel, Thomas Lukasiewicz, and Phil Blunsom. 2018b. e-snli: Natural language inference with natural language explanations. In *Advances in Neural Information Processing Systems*, volume 31. Curran Associates, Inc.

Jacob Cohen. 1960. A coefficient of agreement for nominal scales. *Educational and Psychological Measurement*, 20(1):37–46.

Alexis Conneau, Kartikay Khandelwal, Naman Goyal, Vishrav Chaudhary, Guillaume Wenzek, Francisco Guzmán, Edouard Grave, Myle Ott, Luke Zettlemoyer, and Veselin Stoyanov. 2019. Unsupervised cross-lingual representation learning at scale. *arXiv preprint arXiv:1911.02116*.

Jacob Devlin, Ming-Wei Chang, Kenton Lee, and Kristina Toutanova. 2019. BERT: Pre-training of deep bidirectional transformers for language understanding. In *Proceedings of the 2019 Conference of the North American Chapter of the Association for Computational Linguistics: Human Language Technologies, Volume 1 (Long and Short Papers)*, pages 4171–4186, Minneapolis, Minnesota. Association for Computational Linguistics.

Jay DeYoung, Sarthak Jain, Nazneen Fatema Rajani, Eric Lehman, Caiming Xiong, Richard Socher, and Byron C Wallace. 2019. Eraser: A benchmark to evaluate rationalized nlp models. *arXiv preprint arXiv:1911.03429*.

Jay DeYoung, Sarthak Jain, Nazneen Fatema Rajani, Eric Lehman, Caiming Xiong, Richard Socher, and Byron C. Wallace. 2020. ERASER: A benchmark to evaluate rationalized NLP models. In *Proceedings of the 58th Annual Meeting of the Association for Computational Linguistics*, pages 4443–4458, Online. Association for Computational Linguistics.

Finale Doshi-Velez and Been Kim. 2017. Towards a rigorous science of interpretable machine learning. *arXiv preprint arXiv:1702.08608*.

Ana Valeria González, Anna Rogers, and Anders Søgaard. 2021. On the interaction of belief bias and explanations. In *Findings of the Association for Computational Linguistics: ACL-IJCNLP 2021*, pages 2930–2942, Online. Association for Computational Linguistics.

Ana Valeria Gonzalez and Anders Søgaard. 2020. The reverse turing test for evaluating interpretability methods on unknown tasks. In *NeurIPS 2020 Workshop on Human And Model in the Loop Evaluation and Training Strategies*.

Peter Hase and Mohit Bansal. 2020. Evaluating explainable AI: Which algorithmic explanations help users predict model behavior? In *Proceedings of the 58th Annual Meeting of the Association for Computational Linguistics*, pages 5540–5552, Online. Association for Computational Linguistics.

Junjie Hu, Sebastian Ruder, Aditya Siddhant, Graham Neubig, Orhan Firat, and Melvin Johnson. 2020. XTREME: A massively multilingual multitask benchmark for evaluating cross-lingual generalisation. In *Proceedings of the 37th International Conference on Machine Learning*, volume 119 of *Proceedings of Machine Learning Research*, pages 4411–4421. PMLR.

Boshko Koloski, Timen Stepišnik-Perdih, Senja Pollak, and Blaž Škrlj. 2021. Identification of covid-19 related fake news via neural stacking. In *Combating Online Hostile Posts in Regional Languages during Emergency Situation*, pages 177–188, Cham. Springer International Publishing.

Sneha Kudugunta, Ankur Bapna, Isaac Caswell, and Orhan Firat. 2019. Investigating multilingual NMT representations at scale. In *Proceedings of the*

2019 Conference on Empirical Methods in Natural Language Processing and the 9th International Joint Conference on Natural Language Processing (EMNLP-IJCNLP), pages 1565–1575, Hong Kong, China. Association for Computational Linguistics.

Scott M. Lundberg and Su-In Lee. 2017. A unified approach to interpreting model predictions. In *Advances in Neural Information Processing Systems*, pages 4768–4777.

Binny Mathew, Punyajoy Saha, Seid Muhie Yimam, Chris Biemann, Pawan Goyal, and Animesh Mukherjee. 2020. Hatexplain: A benchmark dataset for explainable hate speech detection.

Grégoire Montavon, Sebastian Lapuschkin, Alexander Binder, Wojciech Samek, and Klaus-Robert Müller. 2017. Explaining nonlinear classification decisions with deep taylor decomposition. *Pattern Recognition*, 65:211–222.

Dong Nguyen. 2018. Comparing automatic and human evaluation of local explanations for text classification. In *Proceedings of the 2018 Conference of the North American Chapter of the Association for Computational Linguistics: Human Language Technologies, Volume 1 (Long Papers)*, pages 1069–1078, New Orleans, Louisiana. Association for Computational Linguistics.

Alexandru Niculescu-Mizil and Rich Caruana. 2005. Predicting good probabilities with supervised learning. In *Proceedings of the 22nd International Conference on Machine Learning*, pages 625–632.

Md Rizwan Parvez and Kai-Wei Chang. 2021. Evaluating the values of sources in transfer learning. In *Proceedings of the 2021 Conference of the North American Chapter of the Association for Computational Linguistics: Human Language Technologies*, pages 5084–5116, Online. Association for Computational Linguistics.

Telmo Pires, Eva Schlinger, and Dan Garrette. 2019. How multilingual is multilingual BERT? In *Proceedings of the 57th Annual Meeting of the Association for Computational Linguistics*, pages 4996–5001, Florence, Italy. Association for Computational Linguistics.

John C. Platt. 1999. Probabilistic outputs for support vector machines and comparisons to regularized likelihood methods. In Alex J. Smola, Peter Bartlett, Bernhard Schölkopf, and Dale Schuurmans, editors, *Advances in Large Margin Classifiers*, pages 61–74. MIT Press.

Taraka Rama, Lisa Beinborn, and Steffen Eger. 2020. Probing multilingual BERT for genetic and typological signals. In *Proceedings of the 28th International Conference on Computational Linguistics*, pages 1214–1228, Barcelona, Spain (Online). International Committee on Computational Linguistics.

Vinit Ravishankar, Artur Kulmizev, Mostafa Abdou, Anders Søgaard, and Joakim Nivre. 2021. Attention can reflect syntactic structure (if you let it). In *Proceedings of the 16th Conference of the European Chapter of the Association for Computational Linguistics: Main Volume*, pages 3031–3045, Online. Association for Computational Linguistics.

Marco Tulio Ribeiro, Sameer Singh, and Carlos Guestrin. 2016. "Why should I trust you?" Explaining the predictions of any classifier. In *Proceedings of the 22nd ACM SIGKDD International Conference on Knowledge Discovery and Data Mining*, pages 1135–1144.

Phillip Rust, Jonas Pfeiffer, Ivan Vulić, Sebastian Ruder, and Iryna Gurevych. 2020. How good is your tokenizer? On the monolingual performance of multilingual language models. *arXiv preprint arXiv:2012.15613*.

Magnus Sahlgren, Fredrik Carlsson, Fredrik Olsson, and Love Börjeson. 2021. It's basically the same language anyway: the case for a nordic language model. In *Proceedings of the 23rd Nordic Conference on Computational Linguistics (NoDaLiDa)*, pages 367–372, Reykjavik, Iceland (Online). Linköping University Electronic Press, Sweden.

Lloyd S. Shapley. 1953. *A Value for n-Person Games*, pages 307–318. Princeton University Press.

Vikas Sindhwani and Prem Melville. 2008. Document-word co-regularization for semi-supervised sentiment analysis. In *2008 Eighth IEEE International Conference on Data Mining*, pages 1025–1030.

Jasdeep Singh, Bryan McCann, Richard Socher, and Caiming Xiong. 2019a. Bert is not an interlingua and the bias of tokenization. In *Proceedings of the 2nd Workshop on Deep Learning Approaches for Low-Resource NLP (DeepLo 2019)*, pages 47–55.

Jasdeep Singh, Bryan McCann, Richard Socher, and Caiming Xiong. 2019b. BERT is not an interlingua and the bias of tokenization. In *Proceedings of the 2nd Workshop on Deep Learning Approaches for Low-Resource NLP (DeepLo 2019)*, pages 47–55, Hong Kong, China. Association for Computational Linguistics.

Kasper Socha. 2020. KS@LTH at SemEval-2020 task 12: Fine-tuning multi- and monolingual transformer models for offensive language detection. In *Proceedings of the Fourteenth Workshop on Semantic Evaluation*, pages 2045–2053, Barcelona (online). International Committee for Computational Linguistics.

Richard Socher, Alex Perelygin, Jean Wu, Jason Chuang, Christopher D. Manning, Andrew Ng, and Christopher Potts. 2013. Recursive deep models for semantic compositionality over a sentiment treebank. In *Proceedings of the 2013 Conference on Empirical Methods in Natural Language Processing*, pages

1631–1642, Seattle, Washington, USA. Association for Computational Linguistics.

James Thorne, Andreas Vlachos, Christos Christodoulopoulos, and Arpit Mittal. 2018. FEVER: a large-scale dataset for fact extraction and VERification. In *Proceedings of the 2018 Conference of the North American Chapter of the Association for Computational Linguistics: Human Language Technologies, Volume 1 (Long Papers)*, pages 809–819, New Orleans, Louisiana. Association for Computational Linguistics.

Ashish Vaswani, Noam Shazeer, Niki Parmar, Jakob Uszkoreit, Llion Jones, Aidan N Gomez, Łukasz Kaiser, and Illia Polosukhin. 2017. Attention is all you need. In *Advances in Neural Information Processing Systems*, pages 5998–6008.

William Webber, Alistair Moffat, and Justin Zobel. 2010. A similarity measure for indefinite rankings. *ACM Transactions on Information Systems (TOIS)*, 28(4):1–38.

Kayo Yin, Patrick Fernandes, Danish Pruthi, Aditi Chaudhary, André F. T. Martins, and Graham Neubig. 2021. Do context-aware translation models pay the right attention? In *Proceedings of the 59th Annual Meeting of the Association for Computational Linguistics and the 11th International Joint Conference on Natural Language Processing (Volume 1: Long Papers)*, pages 788–801, Online. Association for Computational Linguistics.

Omar Zaidan and Jason Eisner. 2008. Modeling annotators: A generative approach to learning from annotator rationales. In *Proceedings of the 2008 Conference on Empirical Methods in Natural Language Processing*, pages 31–40, Honolulu, Hawaii. Association for Computational Linguistics.

Omar Zaidan, Jason Eisner, and Christine Piatko. 2007. Using "annotator rationales" to improve machine learning for text categorization. In *Human Language Technologies 2007: The Conference of the North American Chapter of the Association for Computational Linguistics; Proceedings of the Main Conference*, pages 260–267, Rochester, New York. Association for Computational Linguistics.

Omar Emilio Contreras Zaragoza. 2021. Explainable antibiotics prescriptions in nlp with transformer models. Master's thesis, Stockholm University.

Ye Zhang, Iain Marshall, and Byron C. Wallace. 2016. Rationale-augmented convolutional neural networks for text classification. In *Proceedings of the 2016 Conference on Empirical Methods in Natural Language Processing*, pages 795–804, Austin, Texas. Association for Computational Linguistics.

Francis Zheng, Machel Reid, Edison Marrese-Taylor, and Yutaka Matsuo. 2021. Low-resource machine translation using cross-lingual language model pretraining. In *Proceedings of the First Workshop on Natural Language Processing for Indigenous Languages of the Americas*, pages 234–240, Online. Association for Computational Linguistics.

Ruiqi Zhong, Steven Shao, and Kathleen McKeown. 2019. Fine-grained sentiment analysis with faithful attention. *arXiv preprint arXiv:1908.06870*.

Probing for Understanding of English Verb Classes and Alternations in Large Pre-trained Language Models

David K. Yi, James V. Bruno, Jiayu Han, Peter Zukerman, Shane Steinert-Threlkeld
Department of Linguistics, University of Washington
{davidyi6, jbruno, jyhan126, pzuk, shanest}@uw.edu

Abstract

We investigate the extent to which verb alternation classes, as described by Levin (1993), are encoded in the embeddings of Large Pre-trained Language Models (PLMs) such as BERT, RoBERTa, ELECTRA, and DeBERTa using selectively constructed diagnostic classifiers for word and sentence-level prediction tasks. We follow and expand upon the experiments of Kann et al. (2019), which aim to probe whether static embeddings encode frame-selectional properties of verbs. At both the word and sentence level, we find that contextual embeddings from PLMs not only outperform non-contextual embeddings, but achieve astonishingly high accuracies on tasks across most alternation classes. Additionally, we find evidence that the middle-to-upper layers of PLMs achieve better performance on average than the lower layers across all probing tasks.

1 Introduction

We investigate the extent to which verb alternation classes are represented in word and sentence embeddings produced by Pre-trained Language Model (PLM) embeddings (Qiu et al., 2020). As first comprehensively cataloged by Levin (1993), verbs pattern together into classes according to the syntactic alternations in which they can and cannot participate. For example, (1) illustrates the *causative-inchoative* alternation. *Break* can be a transitive verb in which the subject of the sentence is the agent and the direct object is the theme, as in example (1a). It can also alternate with the form in (1b), in which the subject of the sentence is the theme and the agent is unexpressed. However, (2) demonstrates that *cut* cannot participate in the same alternation, despite its semantic similarity.

(1) a. Janet broke the cup.
    b. The cup broke.

(2) a. Margaret cut the bread.
    b. * The bread cut.

(3) demonstrates an alternation of a different class – namely, the *spray-load* class, in which the theme and locative arguments can be syntactically realized as either direct objects or objects of the preposition. *Spray* can participate in the alternation, but as shown in (4), *pour* cannot.

(3) a. Jack sprayed paint on the wall.
    b. Jack sprayed the wall with paint.

(4) a. Tamara poured water into the bowl.
    b. * Tamara poured the bowl with water.

The alternations in which a verb may participate is taken to be a lexical property of the verb (e.g. Pinker, 1989; Levin, 1993; Levin et al., 1995; Schafer, 2009). Moreover, we hypothesize that the alternations should be observable within large text corpora, and are therefore available during the pre-training procedure for PLMs such as BERT (Devlin et al., 2018). In contrast, ungrammatical examples such as (2b) and (4b) should be virtually absent from the training data. This leads us to hypothesize that PLM embeddings should encode whether particular verbs are allowed to participate in syntactic frames of various alternation classes. Our research questions are as follows:

1. Do PLM word-level contextual representations encode information about which syntactic frames an individual verb can participate in?

2. At the sentence level, do PLM embeddings encode the frame-selectional properties of their main verb?

Through our series of experiments, we find that PLM embeddings indeed encode information about verb alternation classes at both the word and sentence level. While performance is relatively consistent on the word-level task for the four PLMs

Proceedings of the Fifth BlackboxNLP Workshop on Analyzing and Interpreting Neural Networks for NLP, pages 142 - 152
December 8, 2022 ©2022 Association for Computational Linguistics

we analyze, we find that ELECTRA (Clark et al., 2020) significantly outperforms the other models for the sentence-level task. Furthermore, we find evidence suggesting that middle-to-upper layers encode more information about verb alternation classes since they consistently improve upon the lower layers across all tasks.

The rest of the paper is organized as follows: after a brief review of related literature in Section 2, we present datasets and models that are relevant to our experiment in Sections 3 and 4. We then present two experiments to answer our research questions in Sections 5 and 7. Section 6 presents an additional *control task* (Hewitt and Liang, 2019) to test whether our linear probes are selective for the given tasks. Finally, we offer a discussion in Section 8 and overall conclusions in Section 9.

2 Related work

Our work follows Kann et al. (2019), who attempt to predict verb class membership and sentence grammaticality judgments on the basis of GloVe embeddings (Pennington et al., 2014) and embeddings derived from the 100M-token British National Corpus with a single-directional LSTM (Warstadt et al., 2019). For the sentence-level task, they further process the input embeddings using a sentence encoder trained on a "real/fake" sentence classification task. Varying multi-layer perceptron (MLP) architectures are used for the classification step. Because their primary research focus has to do with how neural language models inform learnability (in the sense of human language acquisition), they intentionally use smaller language models derived from "an amount of data similar to what humans are exposed to during language acquisition" and avoid models trained on "several orders of magnitude more data than humans see in a lifetime" (p. 291).

As described in Section 5, we depart and build upon Kann et al. 2019 by examining the embedding representations of PLMs instead of static embeddings. We then use an intentionally simple and selective linear diagnostic classifier to probe the representations, as our research questions focuses on the PLM embeddings themselves. We note that Kann et al. (2019) achieves only modest performance in prediction accuracy and MCC, and only for a limited number of verb classes. While this is a valuable result for their research goals, our hypothesis is that PLMs will achieve better performance due to a combination of their contextual representations, complex architectures, and larger training corpora.

To our knowledge, attempting to predict verb alternation class membership along the lines of Levin 1993 from PLM representations is novel. However, two very closely related lines of work include the experiments of Warstadt and Bowman (2019), which respectively evaluate the performance of various PLMs on the CoLA (Warstadt et al., 2019) and BLiMP (Warstadt et al., 2020) benchmarks, which include acceptability judgment examples from a wide variety of linguistic phenomena (including verb argument structures). We distinguish our experiments from these papers in two major ways. First, we attempt to directly probe the linguistic knowledge of individual PLM embedding layers with a classification probe instead of specifically finetuning the models to a specific task. Second, we limit our focus to verb alternation classes and present detailed analysis about patterns and trends across different alternations and their corresponding syntactic frames.

3 Data

In our experiments, we use two dataset created by Kann et al. (2019). One is the **L**exic**a**l **V**erb-frame **A**lternations dataset (LaVA), which is based on the verbs and alternation classes defined in Levin (1993). It contains a mapping of 516 verbs to 5 alternation classes, which are further subdivided into two syntactic frames for each alternation. The broad categories of the alternation classes are: *Spray-Load*, *Causative-Inchoative*, *Dative*, *There-insertion*, and *Understood-object*. Table 1[1] provides the class distributions for each syntactic frame. **F**rames and **A**lternations of **V**erbs (FAVA), the other dataset, is a corpus of 9413 semi-automatically generated sentences formed from the verbs in LaVA along with human grammaticality judgments. The sentences in FAVA are categorized according to the relevant alternation class, and are separated into train, development, and test sets by the authors for each category.

[1]A similar table appears in Kann et al. (2019), but we present it again here because of discrepancies that we found in the distribution counts. Notably, it appears that the authors flipped the positive and negative counts for the *there-Insertion* and *Understood-Object* alternation classes which carries over to their results.

LEVIN-CLASS	CAUS-INCH		DATIVE		SPRAY-LOAD		there-INSERTION		UNDERSTOOD-OBJECT	
	Inch.	Caus.	Prep.	2-Obj	with	loc.	no-there	there	Refl	No-Refl
Positive	73	124	65	74	101	86	149	50	84	11
Negative	144	0	377	442	242	257	0	192	419	503
Total	217	124	442	516	343	343	149	242	503	514

Table 1: An updated overview of the LaVA dataset based on verb membership class distributions for each syntactic frame. "Postitive" refers to the number of verbs that can participate in the specified syntactic frame, while "Negative" refers to the number of verbs that cannot participate.

4 Models

In addition to BERT, we perform experiments on several recent Transformer-based PLMs including RoBERTa (Liu et al., 2019), DeBERTa (He et al., 2021), and ELECTRA (Clark et al., 2020) which vary from BERT in a few ways including modifications to BERT's tokenization and pre-training procedure and the size of their training corpus. To make comparisons between each model fair, we use the base architectures for each model which have 12 layers, 12 attention heads, and a hidden layer size of 768.[2]

4.1 Model differences

For pre-training, BERT uses standard Masked Language Modeling (MLM) wherein tokens from a given input sequence are masked at random and the model attempts to recover the masked tokens from the unmasked tokens and Next Sentence Prediction (NSP), in which the model tries to predict whether one sentence follows another in a given text sequence. The other PLMs drop NSP from their pre-training procedure but make other significant changes to the architecture and the MLM approach. RoBERTa introduces "dynamic" masking, in which different tokens are masked across different training epochs (as opposed to the same training mask being used across epochs). DeBERTa uses a "disentangled attention mechanism" which computes attention weights using distinctly encoded position and context vectors, and also moves absolute position encodings from the input layer to the second-to-last layer. Lastly, instead of randomly masking input tokens, ELECTRA strategically replaces tokens with plausible alternatives using a trained generator network, and separately trains a discriminative model which aims to predict whether each token in an input sequence was replaced by a generator sample.

[2]All further references to these models refer to their *base* architectures.

4.2 Training Data

In addition to variations in the pre-training methods, the models are also trained on different datasets. BERT and ELECTRA are both trained on the English Wikipedia Dump and BookCorpus (Zhu et al., 2015). DeBERTa is additionally trained on CC-Stories (Trinh and Le, 2018) and OpenWebText (Gokaslan and Cohen, 2019). Finally, RoBERTa is pretrained on all of the aforementioned datasets as well as the CC-News corpus (Mackenzie et al., 2020).

5 Experiment 1: Frame Membership from Word Embeddings

5.1 Method

In order to answer the first question: "Do PLM token-level representations encode information about which syntactic frames an individual verb can participate in?", we build a diagnostic classifier for each syntactic frame which takes a verb's layer embedding representation as input. For example, to probe the *Spray-Load* alternation, we build two binary classifiers: one that predicts whether a verb can participate in the "locative" frame and one that predicts whether a verb can participate in the "with" frame.

Furthermore, we build a separate classifier for each model layer based on the embedding representations from that particular layer. For the token-embedding layer, the verb embedding is formed by averaging the pretrained token embeddings that correspond to a particular verb. For layers 1–12, the verb embedding is formed by incorporating contextual information from the sentences in FAVA. Specifically, for each verb, we pass the grammatical sentences from FAVA that contain the verb as input to the PLM and average over the token embeddings corresponding to the verb. We choose to only include grammatical examples in the construction of the word-level contextual embeddings since we hypothesize that they represent sentences

	MCC					Accuracy				
	Ref.	BERT	DeBERTa	ELECTRA	RoBERTa	Ref.	BERT	DeBERTa	ELECTRA	RoBERTa
CAUSATIVE-INCHOATIVE										
Inchoative	0.555	0.948 [11]	0.969 [11]	0.959 [5]	0.969 [7]	0.855	0.977	0.986	0.982	0.986
Causative *	0.000	0.000	0.000	0.000	0.000	1.000	1.000	1.000	1.000	1.000
DATIVE										
Preposition	0.320	**0.954 [8]**	0.937 [12]	0.945 [11]	0.928 [9]	0.850	**0.989**	0.984	0.986	0.982
Double-Object	0.482	0.976 [10]	0.968 [10]	0.976 [12]	0.936 [9]	0.853	0.994	0.992	0.994	0.984
SPRAY-LOAD										
With	0.645	0.972 [10]	0.972 [12]	**0.979 [8]**	0.930 [10]	0.839	0.988	0.988	**0.991**	0.971
Locative	0.253	**0.969 [10]**	0.961 [12]	0.961 [9]	0.953 [11]	0.734	**0.989**	0.985	0.985	0.983
THERE										
No-There *	0.000	0.000	0.000	0.000	0.000	1.000	1.000	1.000	1.000	1.000
There	0.459	1.000 [9]	0.987 [7]	1.000 [10]	0.962 [10]	0.858	1.000	1.00	1.000	0.988
UNDERSTOOD OBJECT										
Refl	0.000	0.868 [6]	0.869[12]	0.860 [5]	**0.884 [11]**	0.732	0.964	0.964	0.962	**0.968**
Non-Refl	0.219	0.850 [7]	0.850 [10]	**0.855 [11]**	0.794 [8]	0.976	0.994	0.994	0.994	0.992

Table 2: Results from Word-Level experiments with static embeddings. Reference MCC is from Kann et al. (2019)'s CoLA word-level experiments. The * symbol indicates syntactic frames which only have positive examples, which trivially achieve 100% accuracy and 0 MCC (see Footnote 1). The best performing model for a given frame is denoted in **bold** (ties are not bolded), and the best performing layer for each model is denoted in brackets '[]'.

in the actual training corpora of the PLMs more accurately than the ungrammatical examples.[3] We then average over the verb representations for all input sentences in each layer to form the "layer-embedding" for the verb.

We choose a Logistic Regression classifier without regularization as our diagnostic probe as implemented in `scikit-learn` (Buitinck et al., 2013) and show that it is sufficiently *selective* in Section 6. Following Kann et al. (2019), we use stratified k-fold cross-validation to split the verbs into 4 equally-sized folds: 3 of which are chosen to be the training set and the remaining fold chosen to be the test set.

Also following Kann et al. (2019), we report Matthews correlation coefficient (MCC) (Matthews, 1975) in addition to accuracy for model evaluation. MCC is better suited to data such as ours, in which there is an extreme majority class bias for all syntactic frames.[4]

5.2 Results

In Figure 1, we present the layer-by-layer performance of each PLM and in Table 2, we report a comparison between the best-performing layer for each PLM alongside the performance of the "CoLA-style" reference embeddings from Kann et al. (2019). Overall, we find that the contextual PLM embeddings dramatically outperform the reference embeddings in terms of both MCC and accuracy.

Surprisingly, the PLMs perform well even for the more challenging frames; for the "locative" frame, BERT achieves 0.969 MCC compared to 0.253 when using the reference embeddings, and for the "non-reflexive" frame, ELECTRA achieves 0.855 MCC compared to 0.219 when using the reference embeddings. Furthermore, we observe consistent patterns in performance across different layers of each PLM. As shown in Figure 2, the lower layers achieve low-to-moderate correlation on average while the middle-to-upper layers consistently achieve strong correlation.

6 Control Task

A control task as described by (Hewitt and Liang, 2019) aims to combat the *Probe Confounder Problem*, which highlights the issue of supervised probe classifiers "learning" a linguistic task by combining signals in the data that are irrelevant to the linguistic property of interest. In the context of our first experiment, a confounding probe would

[3] A potential issue with constructing the embeddings in this manner is that the classifier may simply "memorize" whether there is a corresponding grammatical example for each verb in FAVA to trivially determine frame membership. However, we included ungrammatical examples as well in preliminary experiments and found negligible differences from our final results.

[4] All code and data needed to replicate our analysis can be found at `https://github.com/kvah/analyzing_verb_alternations_plms`

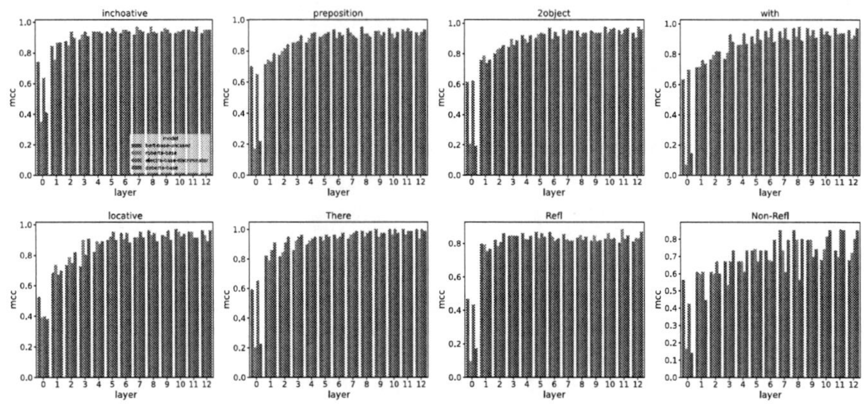

Figure 1: MCC for each model layer across all syntactic frames on LAVA.

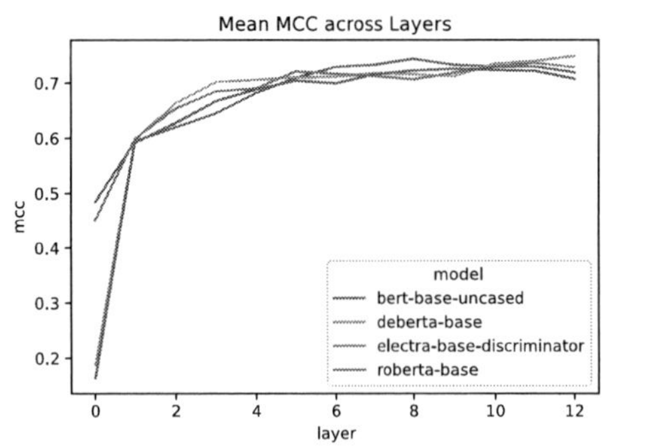

Figure 2: Mean MCC for each model layer across all syntactic frames on LAVA.

be problematic since it suggests that good model performance may be attributed to arbitrary signals picked up by the probe, as opposed to the PLM embeddings actually containing linguistic information about the syntactic frames. To mitigate the Probe Confounder Problem, we implement an example control task for the *Spray-Load* "with" syntactic frame for BERT.

For each verb v_i in LaVA with a binary label y_i denoting whether v_i can participate in the syntax frame SL-WITH, we independently sample a control behavior $C(v)$ by randomly assigning a binary "membership" value to v_i based on the empirical membership distribution of verbs that participate in the SL-WITH syntax frame. The control task is the function that maps each verb, v_i, to the label specified by the control behavior $C(V_i)$:

$$f_{control}(v_i) = C(v_i)$$

Following the experiment design of Hewitt and Liang (2019), we compare the *selectivity* of a linear probe, an Multi-layer Perceptron with 1-hidden layer (MLP-1), and an MLP with 2-hidden layers (MLP-2) where the *selectivity* of a model is defined by the difference between its accuracy on the real task (i.e. predicting verb membership for the SL-WITH frame) and the control task. In addition, we explore several "complexity control" methods including limitation of feature dimensionality, reducing the number of training examples, and increasing regularization.

6.1 Complexity Hyperparameters

In this section, we describe the complexity control methods in more detail and enumerate the hyperparameters that we tried for each method. The control parameters were chosen based on the three most effective methods from the experiments of Hewitt and Liang (2019). To isolate the effect of each control method, we only change one of the complexity parameters in each experiment.

6.1.1 Limiting Dimensionality

For the Logistic Regression model, we reduce the dimensionality of the feature embeddings by performing a Truncated Singular Value Decomposition and limiting the output matrix to rank k. For the MLP models, we simply limit the size of the hidden layer(s) to k.

Considering the input BERT embeddings which have 768 dimensions, we limit k to the following values: $\{20, 100, 300, 500\}$.

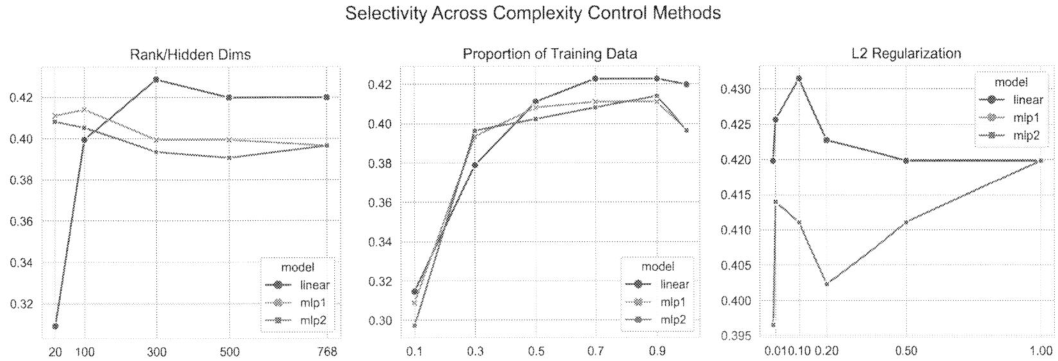

Figure 3: Linguistic Task selectivities for the three complexity control methods.

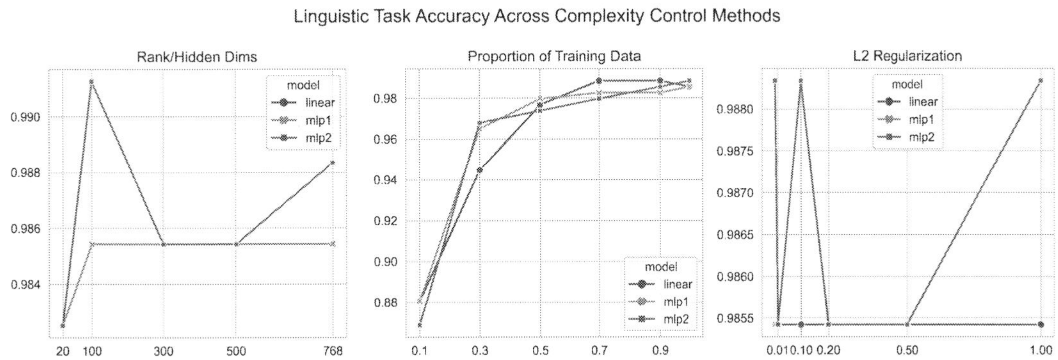

Figure 4: Linguistic Task accuracies for the three complexity control methods.

6.1.2 Reducing Proportion of Training Data

Because LaVA is not split into train and test sets, we use 4-fold cross validation as done in Kann et al. (2019) with 3 training folds and one test fold for evaluation on the control task. As an additional constraint, we reduce the number of training samples in each training fold by randomly sampling a proportion p of the samples and discarding the rest.

Although Zhang and Bowman (2018) recommend training on 1%, 10% and, 100% of the training data, our training data is relatively small and imbalanced (71% of the train set verbs do not participate in the SL-WITH frame). Hence, we experiment with larger values of p: $\{0.1, 0.3, 0.5, 0.7, 0.9\}$

6.1.3 L_2 Regularization

For both the linear and MLP models, we add L_2 regularization with the following strength values: $\{0.01, 0.1, 0.2, 0.5, 1\}$

6.2 Results

Figure 3 shows the high-level trends across experiment configurations for model selectivity. We observe that the linear model with default parameters ($k = 768, p = 1, L_2 = 0$) outperforms both the MLP-1 and MLP-2 model in selectivity (0.420 v.s. 0.397) with no significant decrease in linguistic task accuracy (0.985 for the linear and MLP-1 models v.s. 0.988 for the MLP-2 model).

Looking at the effect of complexity control methods on model accuracy in Figure 4, we find that limiting dimensionality and L_2 regularization has little impact across all configurations, with the worst model (linear: $k = 20$) achieving an accuracy of 0.983 and the best model (MLP-2: $k = 100$) achieving only a slightly higher accuracy of 0.991. On the other hand, reducing the proportion of data in each training fold appears to have significant impact on model performance. For the linear model, there is a huge discrepancy in accuracy between training on 10% of the data (0.869) and the full training set (0.988). A nearly identical pattern can be observed for both of the MLP models as well.

Comparing selectivity, the linear models outperform both MLPs across all complexity control methods. For dimensionality control, we see a lower selectivity in the linear model for lower values of k ($k = 20, 100$) but the best linear model ($k = 300$) achieved a higher selectivity (0.429) than the best MLP model (0.414). Similarly, the best performing configuration for reduced training samples and L_2 regularization are linear models with $p = 0.9$ (0.423) and $L_2 = 0.1$ (0.431) respectively.

We arrive at two major conclusions from the control task experiments. The first is that a linear probe is a good choice for our linguistic task since it achieves higher selectivity than the MLP models without substantial loss in model accuracy across a wide range of complexity control methods. The second is that limiting dimensionality, reducing training samples, and L_2 regularization are all effective methods for increasing model selectivity for both the linear and MLP models. However, the best configurations are not significantly better (> 0.01 improvement in selectivity) than the default linear model so we did not make any modifications to our classification probe. As we only performed these experiments for BERT and the SL-WITH syntactic frame specifically, a great avenue for future work is to test whether our results extend to other PLMs and syntactic frames.

7 Experiment 2: Grammar Judgments from Sentence-embeddings

7.1 Method

In the second experiment, we investigate the extent to which PLMs encode frame-selectional properties of their main verb. For each PLM and embedding layer, we fit a binary Logistic Regression classifier on the FAVA training set for a given alternation class which predicts whether a given sentence is grammatical. We ignore the held out development set because the probe hyperparameters do not need to be tuned and directly evaluate each model on the test set. The whole process can be described by the following equation:

$$c_{s_i} = f(\mathbf{W}\mathbf{s}_i + \mathbf{b})$$

where $\mathbf{s}_i$ refers to the embedding of the whole sentence for layer i (by averaging all i layer's hidden states of words in the sentence s), f refers to the logistic regression classifier, $\mathbf{W}$ and $\mathbf{b}$ are the parameters of f, and c_{s_i} is a binary value corresponding to whether the sentence is grammatical. We then extract the best performing layer for each model and compare the results with the reference acceptability judgment model proposed by Kann et al. (2019).

7.2 Results

The MCC and accuracy scores for each model and layer are shown in Figure 5. From the figure, we can see that there is significant variation in layer performance aside from the *Understood-object* alternation. Generally, we observe a trend in which performance increases substantially from the lower (1-4) layers to the middle layers (5-9), with some models, most notably ELECTRA, continuing to improve through the upper layers (10-12). This can be seen more clearly in Figure 6, which shows the mean layer performance across each category. Furthermore, ELECTRA achieves the best MCC on 5 of the 6 categories: *Combined* (0.818), *Inchoative* (0.864), *Spray_Load* (0.830), *There* (0.828), and *Understood-Object* (0.869). The outlier frame is RoBERTa, which achieves the best MCC (0.802) on the *Dative* frame.

Table 3 provides a comparison between the best performing layer from each PLM and the reference embeddings from Kann et al. (2019) for each alternation class. As defined by Kann et al. (2019) an MCC value between 0.5 and 0.7 demonstrates a moderate correlation between predicted and true labels while an MCC greater than 0.7 implies strong correlation. From the table, we see all models are able to obtain strong correlation for the *Understood-Object* alternation, the *There* frame, and the *Causative-Inchoative* frame. In contrast, BERT and RoBERTa are only able to achieve moderate correlation on the *Spray-Load* frame, while all models except RoBERTa only achieve moderate correlation on the *Dative* alternation. Consistent with the CoLA-style embeddings, we find that the PLMs achieve the best performance on average for sentences from the *Understood-Object* alternation class. This is surprising since frames from the *Understood-Object* alternation were the hardest to predict for the word-level task for both the CoLA-style embeddings and the PLMs. Nevertheless, all PLM outperform the reference model across all alternation categories for the sentence acceptability judgment task.

8 Discussion

On the word level prediction task, all PLMs achieve strong correlation (> 0.7 MCC) across all syntactic frames with the strongest performance in the "there" frame (1.00, achieved by BERT and ELECTRA) and the weakest performance on the "non-reflexive" frame (0.794, achieved by RoBERTa). When look-

	COMBINED	CAUSATIVE-INCHOATIVE	DATIVE	SPRAY-LOAD	THERE	UNDERSTOOD
MCC						
REF.	0.290	0.603	0.413	0.323	0.528	0.753
BERT	0.642 (10)	0.760 (8)	0.678 (6)	0.625 (10)	0.716 (10)	0.842 (9)
DEBERTA	0.653 (9)	0.776 (5)	0.633 (8)	0.704 (12)	0.744 (6)	0.826 (1)
ELECTRA	**0.818 (11)**	**0.864 (11)**	0.670 (8)	**0.830 (12)**	**0.828 (12)**	**0.869 (11)**
ROBERTA	0.496 (8)	0.725 (8)	**0.802 (2)**	0.470 (5)	0.725 (11)	0.793 (1)
ACCURACY						
REF.	0.646	0.854	0.760	0.662	0.729	0.874
BERT	0.840 (10)	0.920 (8)	0.880 (6)	0.820 (10)	0.890 (10)	0.921 (9)
DEBERTA	0.847 (9)	0.924 (5)	0.902 (8)	0.858 (12)	0.912 (6)	0.909 (1)
ELECTRA	**0.920 (11)**	**0.954 (11)**	0.897 (8)	**0.918 (12)**	**0.937 (12)**	**0.934 (11)**
ROBERTA	0.787 (8)	0.909 (8)	**0.944 (2)**	0.747 (5)	0.899 (11)	0.893 (1)

Table 3: Results from Sentence-Level experiments. REF refers to the reference probing model in (Kann et al., 2019). Bolded values show the best result for each alternation class. '()' indicates the best performing layer for each model.

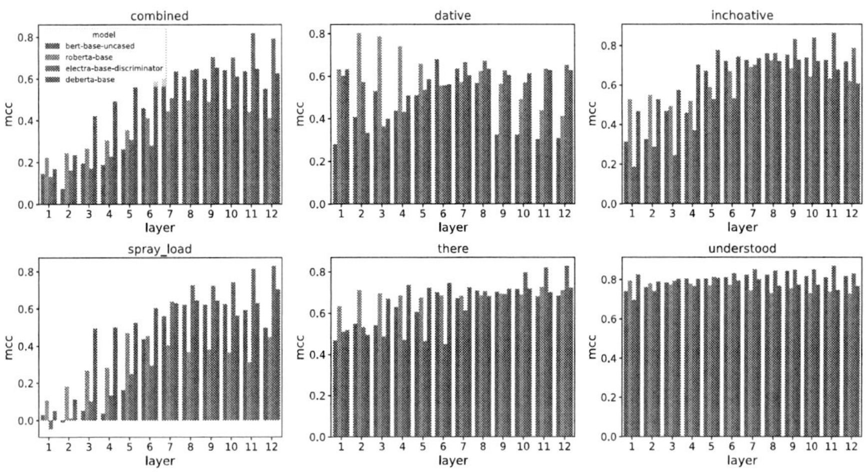

Figure 5: Layer-by-layer MCC score for each alternation class on FAVA.

ing at accuracies, each model is able to predict whether a verb belongs to a particular syntactic frame with excellent accuracy (> 0.95 across all alternation frames). Morever, looking at Table 2, we see that the middle (5-9) and upper (10-12) layers consistently achieve the highest MCC, which is reinforced by the trend shown in Figure 2.

For the sentence-level experiments, we see a similar outcome wherein the upper-middle PLM layers achieve the best performance on average. However, we observe that there is much more variation in performance between each PLM. ELECTRA and BERT are relatively consistent, since their best performing layer for all alternation classes either come from the middle or upper layers. In contrast, the lower layers of RoBERTa achieve the best performance on the *Dative* alternation, and both RoBERTa and DeBERTa achieve the best performance on the *Understood-Object* alternation from the first layer. These anomalies can potentially be explained by the claim that different alternation classes require different types of linguistic knowledge (i.e. syntactic v.s. semantic) which are encoded in different PLM layers. However, the consistently strong performance of the upper layers for BERT and ELECTRA across all alternation classes provides counter evidence against the claim.

ELECTRA is the best performing model overall on the sentence-level acceptability task, achieving the best MCC and accuracy on four of the five alternation classes (all except *Dative*). Unsurprisingly, ELECTRA also excels on the combined dataset compared to the other models (0.165 MCC over the second-best performing model, DeBERTa). While it is difficult to attribute the model's success to a specific property, one hypothesis is that its generator/discriminator architecture closely resembles the FAVA task of identifying acceptable sentences from linguistic minimal pairs. This idea is reinforced by the authors as well, who note that the model's relatively strong performance on CoLA potentially stems from the fact that the acceptability judgment task of CoLA "closely matches ELECTRA's pre-training task of identifying fake tokens" (Clark et al., 2020, p.15).

While we are optimistic about our results, there are several limitations to our experiments. First, we only analyze five different alternation classes which is a small subset of the 83 classes presented in Levin (1993). In addition – although our control task ensures that our classifier probe is relatively *selective* for the first experiment and BERT, it may not necessarily generalize well to the second experiment, other syntactic frames, and other models. In the future, we hope to expand our selectivity experiments to a wider array of syntactic frames and models.

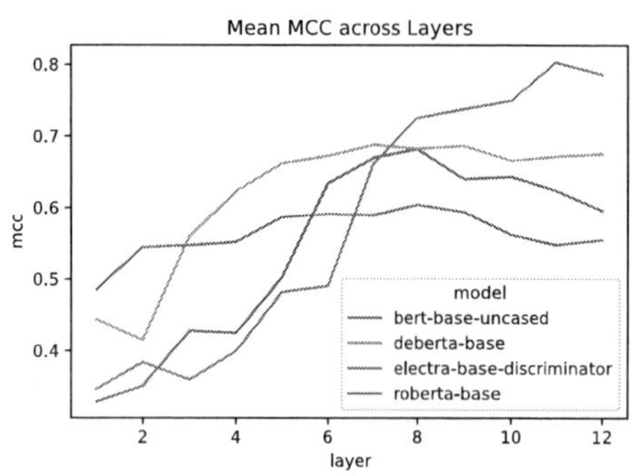

Figure 6: Mean layer MCC score across all alternation classes on FAVA.

9 Conclusion and Future Work

Overall, our results support the hypothesis that PLM contextual embeddings encode linguistic information about verb alternation classes at both the word and sentence level. For the frame-selectional verb classification task, all PLMs achieve significant improvement upon the reference CoLA-style embeddings from Kann et al. (2019), especially for frames in which the CoLA-style embeddings obtain weak correlation (i.e. "locative", "reflexive", and "non-reflexive"). Also, it is clear that model performance tends to improve from lower to upper layers, which can be seen the most easily from the mean performance across layer figures. For the sentence acceptability task, we arrive at similar conclusions, albeit with greater distinction in results between different models and layers. While there are numerous factors that may be responsible for the improved performance from PLMs, we hypothesize that the improvement can largely be attributed to the attention-based encodings of transformer models since we only saw modest improvements in performance from the reference embeddings when using the bottom "static" layers for each PLM.

In terms of future work, there are several interesting avenues that we hope to explore. From the data perspective, it would certainly be worthwhile to test whether our insights and conclusions extends to the dozens of alternations described in Levin (1993) that are not present in the LAVA and FaVA datasets. There are also several interesting adaptations that can be made to our experiment methodology. For example, instead of just analyzing the base architecture for each PLM, we could also analyze *small* and *large* variants to directly evaluate the effect of scaling training data and model size within the same model. Moreover, while we attempt to control the *Probe Confounder Problem* by building a selective probe, there is no guarantee that the classifier probes do not pick up on arbitrary signals in the training data that lead to non-meaningful improvements in performance. Two promising alternative approaches that mitigate this risk include unsupervised evaluation of minimal pairs as shown in Warstadt et al. (2020) and "amnesic probing", which tests whether a property that can be extracted from a probe is actually relevant to task importance (Elazar et al., 2021).

References

Lars Buitinck, Gilles Louppe, Mathieu Blondel, Fabian Pedregosa, Andreas Mueller, Olivier Grisel, Vlad Niculae, Peter Prettenhofer, Alexandre Gramfort, Jaques Grobler, Robert Layton, Jake VanderPlas, Arnaud Joly, Brian Holt, and Gaël Varoquaux. 2013. API design for machine learning software: experiences from the scikit-learn project. In *ECML PKDD Workshop: Languages for Data Mining and Machine Learning*, pages 108–122.

Kevin Clark, Minh-Thang Luong, Quoc V. Le, and Christopher D. Manning. 2020. ELECTRA: Pre-training text encoders as discriminators rather than generators. In *ICLR*.

Jacob Devlin, Ming-Wei Chang, Kenton Lee, and Kristina Toutanova. 2018. BERT: pre-training of deep bidirectional transformers for language understanding. *CoRR*, abs/1810.04805.

Yanai Elazar, Shauli Ravfogel, Alon Jacovi, and Yoav Goldberg. 2021. Amnesic probing: Behavioral explanation with amnesic counterfactuals. *Transactions of the Association for Computational Linguistics*, 9:160–175.

Aaron Gokaslan and Vanya Cohen. 2019. Openwebtext corpus.

Pengcheng He, Xiaodong Liu, Jianfeng Gao, and Weizhu Chen. 2021. Deberta: Decoding-enhanced bert with disentangled attention. In *International Conference on Learning Representations*.

John Hewitt and Percy Liang. 2019. Designing and interpreting probes with control tasks. In *Proceedings of the 2019 Conference on Empirical Methods in Natural Language Processing and the 9th International Joint Conference on Natural Language Processing (EMNLP-IJCNLP)*, pages 2733–2743.

Katharina Kann, Alex Warstadt, Adina Williams, and Samuel R. Bowman. 2019. Verb argument structure alternations in word and sentence embeddings. In *Proceedings of the Society for Computation in Linguistics (SCiL) 2019*, pages 287–297.

Beth Levin. 1993. *English verb classes and alternations: A preliminary investigation*. University of Chicago press.

Beth Levin, Malka Rappaport Hovav, and Samuel Jay Keyser. 1995. *Unaccusativity: At the syntax-lexical semantics interface*, volume 26. MIT press.

Yinhan Liu, Myle Ott, Naman Goyal, Jingfei Du, Mandar Joshi, Danqi Chen, Omer Levy, Mike Lewis, Luke Zettlemoyer, and Veselin Stoyanov. 2019. Roberta: A robustly optimized bert pretraining approach. *arXiv preprint arXiv:1907.11692*.

Joel Mackenzie, Rodger Benham, Matthias Petri, Johanne R. Trippas, J. Shane Culpepper, and Alistair Moffat. 2020. Cc-news-en: A large english news corpus. *Proceedings of the 29th ACM International Conference on Information & Knowledge Management*.

Brian W Matthews. 1975. Comparison of the predicted and observed secondary structure of t4 phage lysozyme. *Biochimica et Biophysica Acta (BBA)-Protein Structure*, 405(2):442–451.

Jeffrey Pennington, Richard Socher, and Christopher D Manning. 2014. Glove: Global vectors for word representation. In *Proceedings of the 2014 conference on empirical methods in natural language processing (EMNLP)*, pages 1532–1543.

Steven Pinker. 1989. *Learnability and cognition: The acquisition of argument structure*. Cambridge, MA: MIT Press.

XiPeng Qiu, TianXiang Sun, YiGe Xu, YunFan Shao, Ning Dai, and XuanJing Huang. 2020. Pre-trained models for natural language processing: A survey. *Science China Technological Sciences*, 63(10):1872–1897.

Florian Schafer. 2009. The causative alternation. *Language and linguistics compass*, 3(2):641–681.

Trieu H. Trinh and Quoc V. Le. 2018. A simple method for commonsense reasoning.

Alex Warstadt and Samuel R. Bowman. 2019. Linguistic analysis of pretrained sentence encoders with acceptability judgments.

Alex Warstadt, Alicia Parrish, Haokun Liu, Anhad Mohananey, Wei Peng, Sheng-Fu Wang, and Samuel R. Bowman. 2020. BLiMP: A benchmark of linguistic minimal pairs for English. In *Proceedings of the Society for Computation in Linguistics 2020*, pages 409–410, New York, New York. Association for Computational Linguistics.

Alex Warstadt, Amanpreet Singh, and Samuel R Bowman. 2019. Neural network acceptability judgments. *Transactions of the Association for Computational Linguistics*, 7:625–641.

Kelly Zhang and Samuel Bowman. 2018. Language modeling teaches you more than translation does: Lessons learned through auxiliary syntactic task analysis. In *Proceedings of the 2018 EMNLP Workshop BlackboxNLP: Analyzing and Interpreting Neural Networks for NLP*, pages 359–361, Brussels, Belgium. Association for Computational Linguistics.

Yukun Zhu, Ryan Kiros, Rich Zemel, Ruslan Salakhutdinov, Raquel Urtasun, Antonio Torralba, and Sanja Fidler. 2015. Aligning books and movies: Towards story-like visual explanations by watching movies and reading books. In *The IEEE International Conference on Computer Vision (ICCV)*.

A Complexity Control Results

	Dimensions (k)	Training Prop. (p)	L_2 Reg.	Accuracy	Selectivity
DEFAULT PARAMS					
Linear	768	1.0	0.0	0.985	**0.420**
MLP-1	768	1.0	0.0	0.985	0.397
MLP-2	768	1.0	0.0	0.988	0.397
LIMITING DIMENSIONS					
Linear	300	1.0	0.0	0.985	**0.429**
MLP-1	100	1.0	0.0	0.985	0.414
MLP-2	20	1.0	0.0	0.983	0.408
REDUCING TRAINING SAMPLES					
Linear	768	0.9	0.0	0.988	**0.423**
MLP-1	768	0.9	0.0	0.983	0.411
MLP-2	768	0.9	0.0	0.985	0.414
L_2 REGULARIZATION					
Linear	768	1.0	0.1	0.985	**0.431**
MLP-1	768	1.0	1.0	0.988	0.420
MLP-2	768	1.0	1.0	0.988	0.420

Table A1: Results from the Complexity Control Experiments. For each experiment, only the best performing configuration for each model is reported.

Analyzing Gender Translation Errors to Identify Information Flows between the Encoder and Decoder of an NMT System

Guillaume Wisniewski and **Lichao Zhu**
LLF, Université Paris Cité & CNRS F-75013 Paris, France
{guillaume.wisniewski,lichao.zhu}@u-paris.fr

Nicolas Ballier
CLILLAC-ARP, Université Paris Cité
F-75013 Paris, France
nicolas.ballier@u-paris.fr

François Yvon
Université Paris-Saclay & CNRS, LISN
91403 Orsay, France
francois.yvon@cnrs.fr

Abstract

Multiple studies have shown that existing NMT systems demonstrate some kind of gender bias. As a result, MT output appears to err more often for feminine forms and to amplify social gender misrepresentations, which is potentially harmful to users and practioners of these technologies.

This paper continues this line of investigations and reports results obtained with a new test set in strictly controlled conditions. This setting allows us to better understand the multiple inner mechanisms that are causing these biases, which include the linguistic expressions of gender, the unbalanced distribution of masculine and feminine forms in the language, the modelling of morphological variation and the training process dynamics. To counterbalance these effects, we formulate several proposals and notably show that modifying the training loss can effectively mitigate such biases.

1 Introduction

State-of-the-art machine translation models (TMs) have been shown to suffer from gender-bias (Prates et al., 2020) and works trying to mitigate this problem constitute a very active line of research (e.g. Costa-jussà and de Jorge (2020); Saunders and Byrne (2020); Savoldi et al. (2021)). We here adopt a different point of view and try to understand why the TM, often incorrectly, chooses a masculine rather than a feminine form. For this, we identify the mechanisms which the neural network uses to extract gender information from the source side and transfer it to the target side. This study of the causes of gender bias illustrates in a more general way the inner working of neural translation systems and notably reveals information flows between the encoder and the decoder involved in a TM.

To study gender transfer, we introduce a new French-English test set specifically designed to highlight the difficulties of translating gender information between these two languages. Using a controlled test set allows us to precisely pinpoint where and how gender is expressed in source and target sentences and to quantify the information flow in an encoder-decoder architecture. Our experiments rely on both well-known methods such as probing or new methods tailored to identify gender bias such as comparing the predictions of a language model and those of a TM to better analyze the possible causes of gender bias. Considering a controlled experimental setting also allows us to assess the impact of training conditions such as subword segmentation or training data distributions.

The rest of the paper is organized as follows. In §2, we describe our test set and use it to highlight gender bias in state-of-the-art systems. In §3 we describe several experiments aiming to study how information flows between the encoder and the decoder can explain these biases. To counterbalance these effects, we formulate several proposals in §4, and notably show that a simple modification of the training loss can effectively mitigate gender bias.

2 Observing Gender biases in MT

2.1 A Controlled Set to Study Gender Bias

We first describe the controlled test set used in our experiments and explain why (and how) we use it to identify the flow of information in an encoder-decoder architecture.

This test set, built on an idea introduced in Wis-

Proceedings of the Fifth BlackboxNLP Workshop on Analyzing and Interpreting Neural Networks for NLP, pages 153 - 163
December 8, 2022 ©2022 Association for Computational Linguistics

niewski et al. (2021), is made of 3,394 parallel sentences perfectly balanced between genders. All sentences use the following template:

- `[DET] [N]` a terminé son travail.
- The `[N]` has finished `[PRO]` work.

where `[N]` is an occupational noun chosen from the list of Dister and Moreau (2014) that matches feminine and masculine professions and occupations in French. This list was automatically translated in English with `DeepL` and manually corrected by two professional translators.[1] `[DET]` is the French determiner in agreement with the `[N]` (the feminine form la_F, the masculine form le_M or the epicene form *l'* that is used for both grammatical genders when the job noun starts with a vowel); `[PRO]` is the English possessive pronoun `her` $_F$ or `his` $_M$. For English, in the case of indefinite reference or generic NPs like "the writer", since the 1980's different strategies have been used to avoid the use of resumption by "his" and style guides for authors have recommended the use of "his or her", then "her" for generic references as well and the same period has seen the rise of the use of singular "their" (see, among others, (Bodine, 1975; Pauwels, 2000)). For the sake of simplicity and to keep our test set gender-balanced, we have only considered two forms of the possessive pronoun and our test set contains a feminine sentence (with `her`) and a masculine sentence (with `his`) for each occupational noun, even if its gender is ambiguous in the source sentence (see below).

In English, gender is unambiguously expressed in the possessive pronoun; it may also be expressed by the occupational noun, when it has different feminine and masculine forms (e.g. *actress-actor*). In most sentences, however, the occupational noun is epicene and its gender can not be inferred from the surface form. In French, gender can be expressed by the determiner, the occupational noun, or both; in rarer cases, both the determiner and the occupational noun are epicene, and the feminine and masculine versions are identical. In the latter case, as explained above, the English translation should use the possessive pronoun `their` to mark that gender is not specified. The choice we made to associate the same sentence once with the masculine pronoun and once with the feminine pronoun is a way to identify the biases of the translation system: an unbiased system would be expected to err one out of two times in the choice of pronoun, a higher error rate indicates that the system prefers one pronoun to the other. Table 1 illustrates the various ways that gender can be expressed in English and French as well as their proportion in our test set.

When translating sentences from our controlled set from French into English, the prediction of the English possessive pronoun can rely on two kinds of evidence: *i)* using cross-attention, the model can encode information about the French subject gender into the representation of the possessive pronoun;[2] *ii)* because of the decoder self-attention, the possessive pronoun representation can also encode information about the target context. This is notably the case of the English subject that encodes gender information either directly, or because its representation depends on the French subject (through cross-attention).

2.2 Direct Evidence of a Gender Bias

Before investigating the roots of gender bias in MT systems, we would first like to describe the experimental setting that will be used throughout this work and highlight the difficulties of predicting gender information. Most observations reported in this section have already been described for other models, language pairs and datasets (see e.g. (Stanovsky et al., 2019; Saunders et al., 2020) or (Stanczak and Augenstein, 2021) for an overview).

NMT System We use `JoeyNMT` (Kreutzer et al., 2019), an implementation of a translation system based on the `Transformer` model of Vaswani et al. (2017). Encoder and decoder are composed of 6 layers, each with 8 attention heads; hidden representations have dimension $d = 512$, while *feed-forward* layers has dimension 2,048. Our model comprises a grand total of about 76M parameters.

We consider the English-French parallel corpus from the WMT'15 'News' task (Bojar et al., 2015) that contains 4.8M sentences and nearly 141M French running words. All raw corpora

[1] As our sentences have a fixed structure, most translation issues were related to occupational nouns, and were resolved by mining reference dictionaries and corpora such as the COCA corpus (Davies, 2009). The resulting resource is more than three times larger than the list used in (Niu et al., 2021).

[2] The French subject can have either a direct impact through cross-attention or an indirect impact as the representation of all source tokens depends on it (via encoder self-attention). We will not try to distinguish these two effects.

Gender-marked Determiner	Gender-marked Noun	Proportion	Example
French			
yes	yes	53.0%	• (**la**$_F$ **boulangère**$_F$|**le**$_M$ **boulanger**$_M$) a fini son travail • the baker has finished (his$_M$|her$_F$) job.
yes	no	24.2%	• (**la**$_F$ **cinéaste**|**le**$_M$ **cinéaste**) a fini son travail • the film-maker has finished (his$_M$|her$_F$) job.
no	yes	14.9%	• (**l'adjointe**$_F$|**l'adjoint**$_M$) a fini son travail • the assistant has finished (his$_M$|her$_F$) job.
no	no	7.9%	• **l'artiste** a fini son travail • the artist has finished (his$_M$|her$_F$) job.
English			
no	yes	5.5%	• (**the actress**$_F$|**the actor**$_M$) has finished her$_F$|his$_M$ work • (**l'actrice**$_F$|**l'acteur**$_M$) a terminé son travail.
no	no	94.5%	• **the user** has finished her$_F$|his$_M$ work • (**l'usagère**$_F$x|**l'usager**$_M$) a terminé son travail.

Table 1: Examples of the various ways by which gender is expressed in our test corpus.

are segmented into sub-lexical units using the unigram model of `SentencePiece` (Kudo, 2018); the vocabularies contain 32,000 units in each language. Our model is trained by optimizing the cross-entropy with ADAM and achieves a BLEU score of 34.0 on the WMT'14 test set.

Results We report in Table 2 the accuracy with which our NMT systems are able to predict the English possessive pronoun gender and therefore to correctly capture and transfer gender information between French and English. These numbers are broken down by context, where we distinguish between the various cases of Table 1. Note that when both the determiner and the noun are epicene, both `his` and `her` (as well as `their`) are equally correct: we nonetheless report the number of mispredictions for this category - as our test set is perfectly balanced, an unbiased system predicting only `his` and `her` should have an accuracy of 50%. We also report the performance achieved by `mBART`,[3] the multilingual model of Tang et al. (2020). Note that `mBART` is a strong baseline with 610M parameters trained on, at least, a hundred times more English sentences than our system.

It appears that our system, `JoeyNMT`, has many difficulties in predicting the correct form of the possessive pronoun, with a striking difference between the accuracy of the prediction of `his` and `her`. For `mBART`, which is doing much better overall, the difference in accuracy between the two genders is about 20 points. For both systems, the accuracy is slightly better when both the determiner and noun are unambiguous. Also note

Gender in source: Determiner	Gender in source: Epicene Noun	Accuracy: `JoeyNMT`	Accuracy: `mBART`
Masc.	no	76.5	72.8
	yes	84.7	84.1
Fem.	no	33.1	60.6
	yes	31.9	65.4
Epicene	no	40.4	66.1
	yes	40.4	45.9

Table 2: Accuracy (in %) of possessive pronoun prediction by `JoeyNMT` and a strong baseline (`mBART`).

that mispredictions are not only due to error on gender: the system sometimes generates sentences that do not contain any possessive pronoun or in which the possessive pronoun was either `their` or `its`. This may be because in French, occupational nouns may also refer to technical devices or machines that are used to perform the occupation, especially for the feminine form: one such example is *cafetière* that can either mean *coffeemaker*, the machine that makes coffee or (female) barkeeper, the person that makes coffee (in a bar).

3 Uncovering the Flows of Gender Information

In this Section, we report experiments aimed to explain the results reported in Table 2 using either well-known probing methods (§3.1) or, as suggested by Fernandes et al. (2021), by comparing the prediction of a translation and a language models (§3.2). In Section 3.3 we describe the impact of our findings on training.

[3]We used the model through the HuggingFace API (Wolf et al., 2020).

	layer	encoder					
		a	terminé	son	travail	.	eos
Gender weakening							
chaque surveillant a terminé son travail.	1	73.1	73.6	65.7	63.5	53.9	56.7
	6	71.0	71.4	70.4	68.2	71.2	69.7
Gender strengthening							
le surveillant *français* a terminé son travail.	1	99.9	98.5	95.0	80.6	62.0	80.4
	6	100.0	99.7	99.7	98.9	98.8	96.9
Gender change for the direct object							
le surveillant a terminé son *travail*.	1	79.4	74.6	79.0	75.0	58.8	72.0
	6	90.3	88.8	89.2	85.3	86.2	83.3
le surveillant a terminé son *activité*.	1	80.5	75.5	78.6	62.6	57.6	67.2
	6	89.7	88.3	89.6	84.3	86.1	84.1
Syntactical distancing							
le surveillant *qui a chanté formidablement hier* a terminé son travail.	1	71.1	66.3	68.8	81.1	56.8	65.4
	6	91.5	91.0	90.5	86.8	81.2	82.1
Distractor							
.without gender weakening							
le surveillant *que cette femme critiquait* a terminé son travail.	1	65.7	66.6	69.3	79.50	62.8	68.5
	6	90.6	89.6	89.1	85.91	81.9	80.2
le surveillant *que cet homme critiquait* a terminé son travail.	1	65.4	67.0	68.7	80.0	63.4	68.2
	6	90.3	89.3	89.7	86.6	81.0	79.9
.with gender weakening							
chaque surveillant *que cet homme critiquait* a terminé son travail.	1	63.1	63.5	64.3	62.4	56.2	55.8
	6	72.1	71.4	69.7	69.9	71.8	69.2
chaque surveillant *que cette femme critiquait* a terminé son travail.	1	63.3	64.6	65.9	63.4	55.4	55.2
	6	71.8	71.8	70.0	69.2	70.2	69.5

Table 3: Accuracy (in %) of probes when manipulating the test sentences corpus

3.1 Probing

We use *probing* (Belinkov, 2022) to analyze which words in the source sentences convey gender information: a *probe* (Alain and Bengio, 2017) is trained to predict linguistic properties from the representations of language (e.g. token embeddings); achieving high accuracy at this task implies these properties are encoded in the representations.

Experimental Setup We collected the 512 dimensional representations at the output of the first and last layer of the encoder and the decoder for all tokens except the French subject and associate each of them to a label indicating the occupational noun gender in the French sentence.

For each of these examples, we randomly split all sentences between a train (75%) and a test (25%) set. We use `scikit-learn` (Pedregosa et al., 2011) to learn a logistic regression to predict the occupational noun gender from a single token representation. This experiment is repeated on 10 random train/test splits and 95% confidence intervals are computed. As advocated by Hewitt and Liang (2019), we use a linear classifier to be sure that gender information is actually encoded in token representations and not learned by the probe and report, as a control score, the performance achieved after a random permutation of labels.

layer	decoder	
	the	other tokens
1	89.5 $\pm$0.2	71.6 $\pm$0.6
2	92.0 $\pm$0.1	76.3 $\pm$0.7
3	91.8 $\pm$0.1	78.1 $\pm$0.6
4	90.9 $\pm$0.2	79.1 $\pm$0.6
5	89.3 $\pm$0.2	82.4 $\pm$0.5
6	87.7 $\pm$0.2	84.7 $\pm$0.3

Table 4: Accuracy (in %) of probing the gender of the French occupational noun in decoder representations.

Results The probe achieves an average accuracy of 74.1% (resp. 87.9%) for the first (resp. last) layer of the encoder and of 80.5% and 86.2% for the decoder (detailed results are in Table 4 for the decoder and Table 5 for the encoder), showing that gender information is encoded in the representations of all source and target tokens. Note that, for the decoder, the diversity of the automatically generated structures makes it impossible to carry out a position-by-position analysis.

In the spirit of the analyses of Marvin and Linzen (2018) for monolingual representations, we have also manipulated source sentences to evaluate the robustness of our observations. We consider transformations that consist in:

1. weakening the gender expression in the subject by replacing `[DET]` (which can vary in gender) by *chaque* (each), which is epicene;

layer	encoder						random labels
	a	terminé	son	travail	.	eos	son
1	80.4 ±1.1	75.1 ±0.3	80.6 ±0.3	76.4 ±0.6	59.5 ±1.0	73.3 ±1.0	45,3 ±0.9
2	85.8 ±1.0	80.8 ±0.2	81.6 ±0.3	78.3 ±0.7	87.6 ±0.6	88.3 ±0.7	50,7 ±0.8
3	89.5 ±0.6	88.2 ±0.2	89.2 ±0.2	82.0 ±1.1	86.5 ±1.0	87.6 ±0.6	48,8 ±0.9
4	90.8 ±0.4	89.3 ±0.2	90.6 ±0.2	85.9 ±0.9	85.7 ±1.0	85.6 ±0.7	48,6 ±0.8
5	90.4 ±1.0	89.3 ±0.2	90.4 ±0.2	85.5 ±0.8	86.4 ±0.8	85.2 ±1.2	49,6 ±0.8
6	91.0 ±0.6	89.3 ±0.2	90.0 ±0.2	86.0 ±1.0	86.4 ±1.1	85.1 ±0.8	49,2 ±0.8

Table 5: Accuracy (in %) of a probe predicting the gender of the French subject given the encoder representations

2. strengthening the gender expression in the subject group by introducing an adjective that is always marked in gender (*français*$_M$/*française*$_F$, French);
3. replacing the direct object *travail*$_M$ (work) by *activité*$_F$ (activity) to evaluate the impact of the object noun phrase on the gender information encoded in the sentence;
4. increasing the distance between the subject group in which the gender is expressed and the possessive pronoun by inserting a relative clause containing no word marked in gender;
5. inserting a distractor (e.g. a word whose gender is different from the subject gender) between the subject, likely to introduce noise in the propagation of gender information.

Results in Table 3 show that the encoder is able to capture gender information even in convoluted contexts (e.g. presence of a distractor, insertion of an extraneous relative clause, etc.). In all these cases, accuracy remains much higher than chance for each input token, especially for the last layer of the encoder. Note, however, the strong effect obtained with weakening, where we observe a drop in accuracy of about 20 points. This corroborates the analysis of Table 2, where we see a drop in accuracy with an epicene determiner. A cumulative effect seems to be at play, whereby the encoding of gender is stronger with a double marking (on `[DET]` and `[N]`), and even more so when an additional unambiguous adjective also comes into play (the strengthening condition).

3.2 Translation Model as Conditional Language Model

Our probing experiments have confirmed that information about the gender of the nominal subject in the source was actually encoded in the source representations, and also available in the hidden states of target tokens. We now investigate whether this information is actually used: a well-known weakness of probes is that they can detect the presence of linguistic information in representations, but cannot measure how much it is used in the model predictions (Ravichander et al., 2021).

For this, we compare the predictions of a target language model (LM), that only knows about previous target tokens $t_{<i} = t_0, ..., t_{i-1}$; with the predictions of a translation model (TM), which additionally conditioned the output probabilities on the entire source sequence s. The TM can be viewed as a *conditional language model* which computes $p(t_i|t_{<i}, \mathrm{s})$ where the LM computes $p(t_i|t_{<i})$. By comparing the predictions of these two models, we can evaluate the impact of information from the source. Other attempts at disentangling the influence of the source *vs.* the target context in NMT, using other methods and tools, are in (Ma et al., 2018; Fernandes et al., 2021; Voita et al., 2021).

Experimental Setting We compare the predictions of our NMT system (described in §2.2) with our in-house implementation of a TRANSFORMER language model with the same dimensions as the MT decoder using the PYTORCH library (Paszke et al., 2019).[4] To mimic the decoder, we use an autoregressive (causal) LM in which the representation of the i-th token is computed based on the $(i-1)$ previous tokens.[5] The model is trained by optimizing the cross-entropy with ADAM on the same corpus as for our TM (considering only the English side of the parallel corpus) and achieves a perplexity of 43.0 on the WMT'14 test set.

Method We investigate the ability of a TM or an LM to predict the correct form of the possessive pronoun in English sentences by comparing $p(\texttt{her}|c)$ and $p(\texttt{his}|c)$, where the context c is either the target prefix *The [occupational noun] has finished* for a LM or the target prefix and the

[4]Code and models are available at `https://github.com/neuroviz/neuroviz/tree/main/blackbox2022`

[5]An alternative to this experiment, more economical in terms of computational cost, would have been to consider only the predictions of a translation system in which all the words of the source sentence would be masked.

source sentence, for a TM. These probabilities can be easily computed with a forced decoding, e.g. by compelling the model to generate the reference English sentence up to the possessive pronoun. Comparing the probabilities rather than the predicted token allows us to conduct a more precise analysis, as we can include all sentences (rather than only the ones in which the sentence contains `his` or `her`) and also evaluate the confidence with which the model prefers one form to the other. This "contrastive" methodology has also been used in (Sennrich, 2017; Müller et al., 2018) to evaluate the quality of pronoun translation in MT.

Results Table 6 reports the average values for these probabilities.The LM that has only access to the prefix (and not to the source sentence) always generates `his` with a much higher probability than `her`. This is because the prefix context rarely contains information about the gender (Table 1). In this situation the model can only rely on associations between the target words and their frequency, and prefers to generate `his`, which is twice as frequent in the train set as `her`.

The TM probabilities of generating `his` or `her` are much higher than those estimated by the LM, showing that the TM actually uses source information, notably the presence of `son` in the French input, to increase these two probabilities. In almost all cases, nevertheless, the probability of generating `his` is reinforced more strongly than that of generating `her`, except when the determiner is la_F. Even in the latter case, where the context unambiguously marks feminine (cf. Table 6, the TM fails to give a clear preference for `her`). This result shows that the initial preference for a masculine pronoun is hard to be overturned, even in the presence of strong evidence that the feminine should be preferred.

Impact of tokenization Several factors may influence these observations and explain why the TM is able (or not) to predict the correct gender. The first factor is the tokenization of the occupational noun into lexical subword units. Recall that the number of subword units that a word is tokenized into is directly related to its frequency in the train set.

To assess the impact of tokenization, we report in Table 7 the probability that a TM generates `her` or `his` as a function of the number of subword units the occupational noun is broken into. Here we only consider the source sentences in which gender is expressed (either by the determiner, the occupational noun or both of them). These results show that the TM is more likely to increase the probability of generating `her` for a feminine source context when the occupational noun is sufficiently frequent to be kept as one single token. In all other cases, the increase in probability is not large enough to surpass that of the masculine form. This effect of subword splitting on gender prediction confirms the hypothesis of Savoldi et al. (2021) regarding the effect of morphological variation on gender bias.

Going one step further, we observe (Table 8) the 15 most frequent suffixes in feminine occupational nouns (e.g. the last token in their segmentation) in our test set. These suffixes appear to often correspond to feminine endings (*-ienne*, *-ière*, *-atrice*), with several of them only appearing in feminine nouns. Yet, except for two cases, `his` remains more likely than `her` showing that TM is not able to take advantage of the suffixes uncovered by the subword segmentation. We see here that using statistical subword segmentation yields morphologically inconsistent segmentations,[6] which has the effect of weakening gender information that could be learned from good predictors of the feminine form.

Replacing `SentencePiece` with a morphological segmentation would likely result in more consistent analyses and may have positive effects on gender transfer, at least for rare words. However, for the frequent words, which are not split into subwords, the effect could be somehow reversed. It is safe to say, still, that architectural decisions related to word segmentations have an impact on the transfer of gender across languages, at least for languages where gender is morphologically expressed like French. The impact of using a morphological *vs.* non-morphological segmentation in NMT is also documented in e.g. (Huck et al., 2017; Ataman et al., 2017; Banerjee and Bhattacharyya, 2018; Weller-Di Marco and Fraser, 2020).

3.3 Impact on training

The results reported in the previous Sections show that, for a TM, the target side priors for predicting `his` are much larger than for predicting `her`,

[6]Note, for instance, the competition between the two "suffixes" *-use* and *-euse*, the former corresponding to a "wrong" morphological segmentation of the latter.

Gender source sentence		TM		LM	
Determiner	Epicene noun	$p(\texttt{his}\|c)$	$p(\texttt{her}\|c)$	$p(\texttt{his}\|c)$	$p(\texttt{her}\|c)$
Feminine	no	0.278	0.216	0.158	0.022
	yes	0.213	0.248	0.098	0.022
Masculine	no	0.589	0.037	0.158	0.022
	yes	0.548	0.036	0.104	0.016
Epicene	no	0.588	0.055	0.182	0.021
	yes	0.485	0.074	0.109	0.016

Table 6: Average probabilities of his and her when conditioning on the source sentence (TM) or not (LM).

gender	# tokens	# occ.	$p(\texttt{his}\|c)$	$p(\texttt{her}\|c)$
Feminine	1	155	0.232	0.315
	2	601	0.251	0.238
	3	526	0.295	0.185
	≥ 4	279	0.289	0.176
Masculine	1	386	0.569	0.040
	2	529	0.547	0.035
	3	460	0.546	0.038
	≥ 4	200	0.544	0.039

Table 7: Probability of his or her estimated by a TM broken down by the number of tokens of the French occupational noun. Only French sentences in which the gender is marked are considered.

and that they get an additional boost when taking the source context into account. In comparison, the LM probabilities of her are always very small, and on average very similar to his for a feminine source context.

This unbalance is likely to have a negative impact during training. To see this, recall that the gradient of the training loss, the cross-entropy, is small when the system makes correct predictions with a high confidence. This is the case for the predictions of his, which also happens to be much more frequent in the data than her. As a result, the cumulated gradient flow that propagates to the encoder layers through the cross-attention module is not sufficiently strong for a system to correctly learn the dependency between the gendered words in the source and the target pronoun prediction.

To measure the strength of this effect, we perform the following experiment: after training the MT system, we consider all sentences with a feminine source subject in our test set and perform a single learning step (forward pass, cross-entropy computation and backward pass) and compute for each layer of the encoder and of the decoder the gradients accumulated during the backward pass. We carry out the same computation with sentences with a masculine subject. Note that we have ignored the 136 sentences having an epicene subject. Overall, there are as many words in sentences with a feminine subject as with a masculine subject.

We report in Table 9 the ratio between the norms of gradients computed on feminine and masculine examples. As predicted, gradients computed on feminine examples are on average larger than those computed on masculine examples, showing that the system errs more for the former cases. More interestingly, the difference is more significant for the encoder's parameters than for the decoder's: to correct the mispredictions for feminine examples, the training process attempts, as it were, to update the encoder parameters so as to better extract gender information from the source. When processing masculine sentences, the errors are less common and the parameter updates on the encoder side are comparatively smaller.

One conclusion of this experiment is that feminine and masculine examples do not have the same impact on the parameter estimation and the learning procedure fails to faithfully capture the dependency between source and target: only parameter updates for feminine occurrences that are often mispredicted, go a long way towards correcting the prior preference for the masculine pronoun.

4 Towards Mitigating Gender Bias

4.1 Increasing the cost of gender errors

In support of our analyses, we propose to slightly modify the loss function and to replace the cross-entropy, which penalizes mispredicted words according to the system confidence, by the softmax-margin loss (Gimpel and Smith, 2010):

$$- \text{logit}[y_{\text{gold}}] + \log\left(\sum_{y \in \mathcal{V}} \exp\left(\text{logit}[y] + \text{cost}\left(y, y_{\text{gold}}\right)\right)\right) \quad (1)$$

where $\text{logit}[y]$ is the score computed by the translation model (the logit) for token y, $\mathcal{V}$ is the system vocabulary and y_{gold} is the gold token that

	-iste	**-use**	**-euse**	-ologue	**-ière**	-e	**-atrice**	-graphe	**-ienne**	-ologiste	**-trice**	-liste	-niste	**-rice**
# occurrences in occupational noun														
masculine	168	0	0	76	0	18	0	32	0	27	0	18	17	0
feminine	167	208	199	76	129	110	76	30	54	25	46	18	17	30
$p(\texttt{his}\|c)$	**0.51**	**0.25**	**0.27**	**0.61**	**0.26**	**0.34**	0.28	**0.40**	**0.31**	**0.55**	0.26	**0.47**	**0.56**	0.30
$p(\texttt{her}\|c)$	0.12	0.19	0.21	0.08	0.15	0.18	**0.34**	0.08	0.18	0.11	**0.30**	0.07	0.07	0.27

Table 8: Most frequent sub-lexical suffixes in feminine occupational nouns and the probability, estimated by the TM, that the translation hypothesis contains `her` or `his`. Suffixes in bold only appear in feminine nouns.

	layer	$\frac{\nabla \text{param}_{\text{masc}}}{\nabla \text{param}_{\text{fem}}}$
decoder	0	0.719
	1	0.756
	2	0.758
	3	0.720
	4	0.780
	5	0.950
encoder	0	0.652
	1	0.649
	2	0.713
	3	0.661
	4	0.729
	5	0.770

Table 9: Ratio of the gradients norm for masculine and feminine sentences, in each of the encoder and decoder layer. Feminine sentences yield larger gradients, especially on the encoder side.

Gender in source		Accuracy	
Determiner	Epicene Noun		
Masculine	no	76.6	+0.1
	yes	84.5	-0.2
Feminine	no	35.3	+2.2
	yes	35.1	+3.2
Epicene	no	39.2	-1.2
	yes	41.1	+0.7

Table 10: Accuracy (in %) of possessive pronoun prediction when the TM is trained with the softmax-margin loss and difference with the accuracy achieved by system trained with cross-entropy loss.

should have been predicted. In comparison to the standard cross-entropy (in black), the loss function of Equation (1) includes an additional term (in cyan) that can been implemented using a $\mathcal{V} \times \mathcal{V}$ cost matrix cost $\left(y^{(i)}, y\right)$ where we specify how much the system should be penalized (in addition to the usual penalty) when predicting y instead of $y^{(i)}$. This loss function allows us to associate an extra penalty for each pair of (predicted word, gold word). In practice, in our experiments, we use a cost matrix where all elements except four are zero: the system receives an additional penalty when it predicts `its` instead of `her`, `its` instead of `his`, `his` instead of `her` and `her` instead of `his`. This means that for all other tokens, the system is trained as usual, meaning that the overall impact on translation quality remains circumscribed to these words.This penalty is fixed at 10% of the average value of the logits on the last layer of the decoder. Preliminary experiments with other values of the penalty or other pairs of tokens that are penalized did not improve these results.

By increasing the penalty incurred by mistakes in predicting the possessive pronoun, we are actually instructing the TM to be more careful when choosing them. This is mathematically expressed through reinforced gradients for these examples, which should ultimately result in parameters that are better at extracting and transferring gender information between the source and the target.

Experimental Results Table 10 reports the accuracy of pronoun prediction achieved by system trained with a softmax-margin loss. This system appears to be, on average, better at predicting the correct form of the possessive pronouns, especially for feminine source subjects. This observation confirms our conclusions: reinforcing gradients does result in better possessive pronoun predictions, illustrating again the fact that the cross-entropy loss fails to fully transfer gender information from the source, mainly because, as explained above, masculine pronoun can be correctly predicted without taking any source side information into account.

5 Conclusions

We have presented a new series of experimental evidence highlighting the causes of gender biases in NMT. Our analyses are based on observing pronoun translation errors in a controlled setting, using a new French-English test set of more than 3,000 occupational nouns. They mostly confirm the findings of previous studies that have amply documented the fact that errors were more likely to occur for feminine than for masculine pronouns, the latter being used as the default option in most context. Additional analyses based (a) on systematic probes, (b) on the comparison of LM *vs.* TM probabilities, (c) on subword splitting, (d) on the gradient flow in the encoder and decoder layers show that the cause of these biases are multifactorial. We have finally proposed a new way to mitigate these errors via a margin augmented training loss, specifically aimed at improving the information flow between source and target.

In our future work, we intend to continue exploring the potential of margin augmented losses, with the aim to also train the cost matrix, and to perform more systematic experiments with other systems and language pairs. Another line of investigation will be considering other linguistic phenomena posing difficult challenges for MT systems, such as the prediction of tense (Vanmassenhove et al., 2017) or mood information (Burchardt et al., 2017).

6 Ethics Statement

This supplemental description tries to follow (Larson, 2017) recommendations for gender as a variable in NLP. We cannot avoid gender as it is necessary to achieve our objectives, that is the study of gender biases. To make our theory of gender explicit, we follow Corbett's analysis of gender as a grammatical category (Corbett, 1991), defined for English as a pronominal gender system. For human referents in our corpus and in our experiments, we operationalize grammatical gender as a binary feature in French and English, which, on the one hand, can be felt as excluding, and, on the other hand, does not take into consideration more recent uses in these languages. As explained in lines 116–125, we resort to this simplistic representation of gender to highlight the gender bias in current NMT systems. For a more complete approach to the variety of gender-inclusive linguistic strategies currently in use in English, see for instance (Cao and Daumé III, 2020).

Acknowledgements

This work was partially funded by the NeuroViz project (Explorations and visualizations of a neural translation system), supported by the Région Ile-de-France within the DIM RFSI 2020 funding framework. This publication has emanated from research supported in part by the 2020 émergence research project SPECTRANS, under the ANR grant (ANR-18-IDEX-0001, Financement IdEx Université Paris Cité). We gratefully acknowledge support from the CNRS/TGIR HUMA-NUM and IN2P3 Computing Center (Lyon - France) for providing computing and data-processing resources needed for this work.

References

Guillaume Alain and Yoshua Bengio. 2017. Understanding intermediate layers using linear classifier probes. In *5th International Conference on Learning Representations, ICLR 2017, Toulon, France, April 24-26, 2017, Workshop Track Proceedings*. OpenReview.net.

Duygu Ataman, Matteo Negri, Marco Turchi, and Marcello Federico. 2017. Linguistically motivated vocabulary reduction for neural machine translation from turkish to english. *The Prague Bulletin of Mathematical Linguistics*, 108(1):331 – 342.

Tamali Banerjee and Pushpak Bhattacharyya. 2018. Meaningless yet meaningful: Morphology grounded subword-level NMT. In *Proceedings of the Second Workshop on Subword/Character LEvel Models*, pages 55–60, New Orleans. Association for Computational Linguistics.

Yonatan Belinkov. 2022. Probing classifiers: Promises, shortcomings, and advances. *Computational Linguistics*, 48(1):207–219.

Ann Bodine. 1975. Androcentrism in prescriptive grammar: singular they, sex-indefinite he, and he or she. *Language in society*, 4(2):129–146.

Ondřej Bojar, Rajen Chatterjee, Christian Federmann, Barry Haddow, Matthias Huck, Chris Hokamp, Philipp Koehn, Varvara Logacheva, Christof Monz, Matteo Negri, Matt Post, Carolina Scarton, Lucia Specia, and Marco Turchi. 2015. Findings of the 2015 workshop on statistical machine translation. In *Proceedings of the Tenth Workshop on Statistical Machine Translation*, pages 1–46, Lisbon, Portugal. Association for Computational Linguistics.

Aljoscha Burchardt, Vivien Macketanz, Jon Dehdari, Georg Heigold, Peter Jan-Thorsten, and Philip Williams. 2017. A linguistic evaluation of rule-based, phrase-based, and neural MT engines. *The Prague Bulletin of Mathematical Linguistics*, 108(1):159–170.

Yang Trista Cao and Hal Daumé III. 2020. Toward gender-inclusive coreference resolution. In *Proceedings of the 58th Annual Meeting of the Association for Computational Linguistics*, pages 4568–4595, Online. Association for Computational Linguistics.

Greville Corbett. 1991. *Gender*. Cambridge University Press.

Marta R. Costa-jussà and Adrià de Jorge. 2020. Fine-tuning neural machine translation on gender-balanced datasets. In *Proceedings of the Second*

Workshop on Gender Bias in Natural Language Processing, pages 26–34, Barcelona, Spain (Online). Association for Computational Linguistics.

Mark Davies. 2009. The 385+ million word corpus of contemporary american english (1990–2008+): Design, architecture, and linguistic insights. *International journal of corpus linguistics*, 14(2):159–190.

Anne Dister and Marie-Louise Moreau. 2014. *Mettre au féminin : guide de féminisation des noms de métier, fonction, grade ou titre*, 3e édition edition. Fédération Wallonie-Bruxelles.

Patrick Fernandes, Kayo Yin, Graham Neubig, and André F. T. Martins. 2021. Measuring and increasing context usage in context-aware machine translation. In *Proceedings of the 59th Annual Meeting of the Association for Computational Linguistics and the 11th International Joint Conference on Natural Language Processing (Volume 1: Long Papers)*, pages 6467–6478, Online. Association for Computational Linguistics.

Kevin Gimpel and Noah A. Smith. 2010. Softmax-margin CRFs: Training log-linear models with cost functions. In *Human Language Technologies: The 2010 Annual Conference of the North American Chapter of the Association for Computational Linguistics*, pages 733–736, Los Angeles, California. Association for Computational Linguistics.

John Hewitt and Percy Liang. 2019. Designing and interpreting probes with control tasks. In *Proceedings of the 2019 Conference on Empirical Methods in Natural Language Processing and the 9th International Joint Conference on Natural Language Processing (EMNLP-IJCNLP)*, pages 2733–2743, Hong Kong, China. Association for Computational Linguistics.

Matthias Huck, Simon Riess, and Alexander Fraser. 2017. Target-side word segmentation strategies for neural machine translation. In *Proceedings of the Second Conference on Machine Translation*, pages 56–67, Copenhagen, Denmark. Association for Computational Linguistics.

Julia Kreutzer, Jasmijn Bastings, and Stefan Riezler. 2019. Joey NMT: A minimalist NMT toolkit for novices. In *Proceedings of the 2019 Conference on Empirical Methods in Natural Language Processing and the 9th International Joint Conference on Natural Language Processing (EMNLP-IJCNLP): System Demonstrations*, pages 109–114, Hong Kong, China. Association for Computational Linguistics.

Taku Kudo. 2018. Subword regularization: Improving neural network translation models with multiple subword candidates. In *Proceedings of the 56th Annual Meeting of the Association for Computational Linguistics (Volume 1: Long Papers)*, pages 66–75, Melbourne, Australia. Association for Computational Linguistics.

Brian Larson. 2017. Gender as a variable in natural-language processing: Ethical considerations. In *Proceedings of the First ACL Workshop on Ethics in Natural Language Processing*, pages 1–11, Valencia, Spain. Association for Computational Linguistics.

Xutai Ma, Ke Li, and Philipp Koehn. 2018. An analysis of source context dependency in neural machine translation. In *21st Annual Conference of the European Association for Machine Translation*, pages 189–197.

Rebecca Marvin and Tal Linzen. 2018. Targeted syntactic evaluation of language models. In *Proceedings of the 2018 Conference on Empirical Methods in Natural Language Processing*, pages 1192–1202, Brussels, Belgium. Association for Computational Linguistics.

Mathias Müller, Annette Rios, Elena Voita, and Rico Sennrich. 2018. A large-scale test set for the evaluation of context-aware pronoun translation in neural machine translation. In *Proceedings of the Third Conference on Machine Translation: Research Papers*, pages 61–72, Brussels, Belgium. Association for Computational Linguistics.

Xing Niu, Georgiana Dinu, Prashant Mathur, and Anna Currey. 2021. Faithful target attribute prediction in neural machine translation. *CoRR*, abs/2109.12105.

Adam Paszke, Sam Gross, Francisco Massa, Adam Lerer, James Bradbury, Gregory Chanan, Trevor Killeen, Zeming Lin, Natalia Gimelshein, Luca Antiga, Alban Desmaison, Andreas Kopf, Edward Yang, Zachary DeVito, Martin Raison, Alykhan Tejani, Sasank Chilamkurthy, Benoit Steiner, Lu Fang, Junjie Bai, and Soumith Chintala. 2019. Pytorch: An imperative style, high-performance deep learning library. In H. Wallach, H. Larochelle, A. Beygelzimer, F. d'Alché-Buc, E. Fox, and R. Garnett, editors, *Advances in Neural Information Processing Systems 32*, pages 8024–8035. Curran Associates, Inc.

Anne Pauwels. 2000. Inclusive language is good business: gender, language and equality in the workplace. In Janet Holmes, editor, *Gendered Speech in Social Context: Perspectives from Gown and Town*, pages 134–151. Victoria University Press.

F. Pedregosa, G. Varoquaux, A. Gramfort, V. Michel, B. Thirion, O. Grisel, M. Blondel, P. Prettenhofer, R. Weiss, V. Dubourg, J. Vanderplas, A. Passos, D. Cournapeau, M. Brucher, M. Perrot, and E. Duchesnay. 2011. Scikit-learn: Machine learning in Python. *JMLR*, 12:2825–2830.

Marcelo O. R. Prates, Pedro H. Avelar, and Luís C. Lamb. 2020. Assessing gender bias in machine translation: a case study with Google Translate. *Neural Computing and Applications*, 32(10):6363–6381.

Abhilasha Ravichander, Yonatan Belinkov, and Eduard Hovy. 2021. Probing the probing paradigm: Does probing accuracy entail task relevance? In *Proceedings of the 16th Conference of the European Chapter of the Association for Computational Linguistics: Main Volume*, pages 3363–3377, Online. Association for Computational Linguistics.

Danielle Saunders and Bill Byrne. 2020. Reducing gender bias in neural machine translation as a domain adaptation problem. In *Proceedings of the 58th Annual Meeting of the Association for Computational Linguistics*, pages 7724–7736, Online. Association for Computational Linguistics.

Danielle Saunders, Rosie Sallis, and Bill Byrne. 2020. Neural machine translation doesn't translate gender coreference right unless you make it. In *Proceedings of the Second Workshop on Gender Bias in Natural Language Processing*, pages 35–43, Barcelona, Spain (Online). Association for Computational Linguistics.

Beatrice Savoldi, Marco Gaido, Luisa Bentivogli, Matteo Negri, and Marco Turchi. 2021. Gender bias in machine translation. *Transactions of the Association for Computational Linguistics*, 9:845–874.

Rico Sennrich. 2017. How grammatical is character-level neural machine translation? assessing MT quality with contrastive translation pairs. In *Proceedings of the 15th Conference of the European Chapter of the Association for Computational Linguistics: Volume 2, Short Papers*, pages 376–382, Valencia, Spain. Association for Computational Linguistics.

Karolina Stanczak and Isabelle Augenstein. 2021. A survey on gender bias in natural language processing. *CoRR*, abs/2112.14168.

Gabriel Stanovsky, Noah A. Smith, and Luke Zettlemoyer. 2019. Evaluating gender bias in machine translation. In *Proceedings of the 57th Annual Meeting of the Association for Computational Linguistics*, pages 1679–1684, Florence, Italy. Association for Computational Linguistics.

Yuqing Tang, Chau Tran, Xian Li, Peng-Jen Chen, Naman Goyal, Vishrav Chaudhary, Jiatao Gu, and Angela Fan. 2020. Multilingual translation with extensible multilingual pretraining and finetuning. *CoRR*, abs/2008.00401.

Eva Vanmassenhove, Jinhua Du, and Andy Way. 2017. Investigating 'aspect' in NMT and SMT: translating the English simple past and present perfect. *Computational Linguistics in the Netherlands Journal (CLIN)*, 7:109–128.

Ashish Vaswani, Noam Shazeer, Niki Parmar, Jakob Uszkoreit, Llion Jones, Aidan N Gomez, Ł ukasz Kaiser, and Illia Polosukhin. 2017. Attention is all you need. In *NeurIPS*, pages 5998–6008.

Elena Voita, Rico Sennrich, and Ivan Titov. 2021. Analyzing the source and target contributions to predictions in neural machine translation. In *Proceedings of the 59th Annual Meeting of the Association for Computational Linguistics and the 11th International Joint Conference on Natural Language Processing (Volume 1: Long Papers)*, pages 1126–1140, Online. Association for Computational Linguistics.

Marion Weller-Di Marco and Alexander Fraser. 2020. Modeling word formation in English–German neural machine translation. In *Proceedings of the 58th Annual Meeting of the Association for Computational Linguistics*, pages 4227–4232. Association for Computational Linguistics.

Guillaume Wisniewski, Lichao Zhu, Nicolas Bailler, and François Yvon. 2021. Screening gender transfer in neural machine translation. In *Proceedings of the Fourth BlackboxNLP Workshop on Analyzing and Interpreting Neural Networks for NLP*, pages 311–321, Punta Cana, Dominican Republic. Association for Computational Linguistics.

Thomas Wolf, Lysandre Debut, Victor Sanh, Julien Chaumond, Clement Delangue, Anthony Moi, Pierric Cistac, Tim Rault, Remi Louf, Morgan Funtowicz, Joe Davison, Sam Shleifer, Patrick von Platen, Clara Ma, Yacine Jernite, Julien Plu, Canwen Xu, Teven Le Scao, Sylvain Gugger, Mariama Drame, Quentin Lhoest, and Alexander Rush. 2020. Transformers: State-of-the-art natural language processing. In *Proceedings of the 2020 Conference on Empirical Methods in Natural Language Processing: System Demonstrations*, pages 38–45, Online. Association for Computational Linguistics.

Human Ratings Do Not Reflect Downstream Utility: A Study of Free-Text Explanations for Model Predictions

Jenny Kunz[1], **Martin Jirénius**[2], **Oskar Holmström**[1], **Marco Kuhlmann**[1]
Dept. of Computer and Information Science
Linköping University
[1]firstname.lastname@liu.se, [2]martin.jirenius@gmail.com

Abstract

Models able to generate free-text rationales that explain their output have been proposed as an important step towards interpretable NLP for "reasoning" tasks such as natural language inference and commonsense question answering. However, the relative merits of different architectures and types of rationales are not well understood and hard to measure. In this paper, we contribute two insights to this line of research: First, we find that models trained on gold explanations learn to rely on these but, in the case of the more challenging question answering data set we use, fail when given generated explanations at test time. However, additional fine-tuning on generated explanations teaches the model to distinguish between reliable and unreliable information in explanations. Second, we compare explanations by a generation-only model to those generated by a self-rationalizing model and find that, while the former score higher in terms of validity, factual correctness, and similarity to gold explanations, they are not more useful for downstream classification. We observe that the self-rationalizing model is prone to hallucination, which is punished by most metrics but may add useful context for the classification step.

1 Introduction

Adding free-text explanations to NLP models is appealing as such explanations are easy to understand to human users and can include richer reasoning than methods that assign relevance scores to the input, such as LIME (Ribeiro et al., 2016) or saliency maps (Simonyan et al., 2014). Therefore, several commonsense reasoning data sets have been enriched with natural language explanations (Camburu et al., 2018; Rajani et al., 2019; Aggarwal et al., 2021). However, there is also significant scepticism, as the association between the model's predictions and its generated explanations is unclear. Bommasani et al. (2021) note that explanations may seem plausible but do not provide true insight into the model's reasoning, which fits the observation that open-ended generation models are prone to hallucinating unfaithful content (Maynez et al., 2020). Also, human explanations are not designed to be valid (or even complete) mechanisms leading to a correct prediction (Tan, 2022).

In this work, we study the effects of different design choices and properties of automatically generated explanations on the predictive performance of rationale-augmented models. To this end, we make targeted modifications to the model architecture and compare with gold-standard explanations. A common architecture for rationale-augmented models is a *pipeline* that maps the input to a rationale and the rationale to the output (I $\rightarrow$ R; R $\rightarrow$ O). Pipeline models are faithful by construction, but inferior in their performance. *Self-rationalizing models* that generate the rationale along with the output (I $\rightarrow$ OR) show good performance, but it is hard to assess the faithfulness of their explanations (Wiegreffe et al., 2021). We focus on a less-studied usage of free-text explanations, a rationale-enriched pipeline mapping the input to the rationale and the input along with the rationale to the output (I $\rightarrow$ R; IR $\rightarrow$ O). This architecture was originally proposed by Rajani et al. (2019) in their CAGE (Commonsense Auto-Generated Explanations) model. In the taxonomy of Hase et al. (2020), we are dealing with *serial-task reasoning models*. While not inherently faithful, as a causal path from input to predicted label remains open, these models allow us to study interactions between inputs and explanations more directly than self-rationalizing models because they allow for interventions at the explanation level, prior to the classification step. At the same time, Wiegreffe et al. (2021) show that the performance is superior to R $\rightarrow$ O, particularly when annotators are not instructed to provide self-contained explanations.

We use the framework of rationale-enriched pipelines to generate insights along two lines:

Proceedings of the Fifth BlackboxNLP Workshop on Analyzing and Interpreting Neural Networks for NLP, pages 164 - 177
December 8, 2022 ©2022 Association for Computational Linguistics

1. We compare classification models solely trained on ground-truth explanations with models additionally fine-tuned on generated explanations. We find that the latter always perform notably better, while the former fail completely on the more challenging of our data sets.

2. We ask how explanations generated by a serial-task model (I $\rightarrow$ R) compare to those generated by a multi-task model (I $\rightarrow$ OR). We find that, while the serial-task explanations are more similar to gold explanations and their validity and factual correctness are ranked higher by human annotators, there is no clear difference in terms of utility for the classification step (IR $\rightarrow$ O).

2 Background

Annotating free-form explanations for NLP data sets has gained attention in recent years as language generation models became stronger. The popular natural language inference dataset SNLI (Bowman et al., 2015) has been enriched with crowd-sourced text explanations, resulting in e-SNLI Camburu et al. (2018). Two extensions were created for CommonsenseQA (Talmor et al., 2019), called CoS-E (Rajani et al., 2019) and ECQA (Aggarwal et al., 2021). In SemEval-2020 Task 4, a subtask was to generate a reason why a natural language statement does not makes sense to humans (Wang et al., 2020). Ling et al. (2017) solve algebraic word problems and generate a series of small steps necessary to derive the answer. Textual explanations have also been proposed for self-driving vehicles (Kim et al., 2018). The need for manual annotations of natural language explanations creates challenges, such as annotation costs (Belinkov and Glass, 2019). Also, human explanations can take various forms and have different goals (Miller, 2019) and do not necessarily verbalize valid reasoning paths (Tan, 2022).

2.1 Automatic Evaluation and Diagnostics

Two main characteristics are commonly included into the evaluation of explanations: Similarity with human-generated explanations and faithfulness towards the model's true decision-making process. Evaluating *extractive* explanations is straightforward at the first glance: If overlap with human importance assignments is desired, classical metrics such as F_n-scores can be used. Distinguishing between faithful and unfaithful explanations is harder, as there is no ground truth to compare to (Jacovi and Goldberg, 2020). Faithfulness is often evaluated by testing the model's performance after perturbing the input in relevant parts; see e.g. DeYoung et al. (2020) and Atanasova et al. (2020). The results obtained from such metrics are however not always consistent (Chan et al., 2022).

The evaluation of free-text explanations, which typically include input-external facts and reasoning, is a topic of ongoing discussion. Surface-level text generation metrics that measure the textual similarity of the generated explanation with the gold explanation have been employed, like BLEU (Papineni et al., 2002) and ROUGE (Lin, 2004), which measure n-gram overlap, or BERTScore (Zhang et al., 2020), which sums cosine similarities between the BERT (Devlin et al., 2019) embeddings of the tokens in two sentences. BERTScore has been reported to correlate better with human judgement than other metrics in generation tasks (Zhang et al., 2020). The inconsistency of free-form explanations presents an obvious problem however, as there can be a large number of valid explanations that differ not only in surface form but also in reasoning paths. Also, humans and models may prefer different reasoning paths, resulting in a disconnect of generated explanations and model decisions.

To evaluate the faithfulness of explanations, Hase et al. (2020) suggest the Leakage-Adjusted Simulatability (LAS) metric, where the performance of a classifier with access to explanations is compared to its input-only version. In addition, they control for label leakage in the explanations by grouping data for which the label can be predicted solely with the explanation. Wiegreffe et al. (2021) show that a self-rationalizing T5 model (Raffel et al., 2020) fulfills two necessary conditions for faithful explanations: the robustness of output and explanations to input noise is correlated, and labels and rationales have a high feature importance agreement. While such approaches to evaluate the connection between explanations and predictions are insightful first steps, we are still scratching the surface. Evaluating faithfulness remains an unsolved problem.

2.2 Human Evaluation

While human evaluation is costly, it can provide important insights about properties such as factual correctness, which are not caught by automated metrics. A manual evaluation of explanation plausibility conducted by Marasovic et al. (2021) shows that the qualitative difference of human and generated explanations remains substantial even with the largest available models. Wiegreffe et al. (2022) show that humans often prefer explanations generated by GPT-3 (Brown et al., 2020) over crowdsourced explanations. While the automatically generated explanations were rated low on qualitative criteria such as support of the label and novelty of information by default, a supervised acceptability filtering model based on human ratings of explanations improved explanation quality.

Other Domains Abstractive summarization is an insightful use case to evaluate generation faithfulness, as it is straightforward to judge if facts were in the original text. Maynez et al. (2020) show that the majority of summaries contain erroneous hallucinated content. Monsen and Rennes (2022) conduct a user study on abstractive versus extractive summaries. Their results show that abstractive summaries are much worse aligned with the meaning of the original text, resulting in factual incorrectness. Kryscinski et al. (2019) also report factual inconsistencies in a large number of abstractive summaries with a manual evaluation, and weak correlation between human ratings and ROUGE scores.

3 Experimental Setup

We generate and evaluate explanations in reasoning pipeline models using the following setups:

3.1 Data Sets

We use two English-language commonsense reasoning data sets that include human-annotated free-text explanations: ECQA and e-SNLI.

ECQA The Explanations for CommonsenseQA (ECQA) dataset (Aggarwal et al., 2021) extends the multiple-choice commonsense question answering data set CommonsenseQA (Talmor et al., 2019). For each question, five answer choices are provided. While Rajani et al. (2019) proposed the first extension of CommonsenseQA, their CoS-E data set has been reported to be of low quality: answers are ungrammatical (Narang et al., 2020) and rated exceptionally bad by humans (Wiegreffe et al., 2022). Explanations in ECQA are more detailed than in CoS-E. ECQA also includes refuting explanations for incorrect answer choices.

In our models, we provide one answer option with the respective explanation at a time, and use the target label *justify* if the answer is the correct one and *refute* if it is a wrong one. We create one training example for each annotated positive property and sample the data to get a ratio of 50/50 for positives/negatives during training.

e-SNLI The second data set we use is the natural language inference data set e-SNLI (Camburu et al., 2018). It is based on the popular SNLI (Bowman et al., 2015) that classifies the logical relation between a premise and a hypothesis sentence. It has three labels: *entailment*, *neutral* and *contradiction*. SNLI has been shown to contain annotation artifacts (label-specific lexical choices and the length of the hypothesis) that allow for correct classifications without solving the task (Gururangan et al., 2018), making explanation annotations to guide the model even more interesting. In fact, Camburu et al. (2018) show that correct explanations are much less likely to emerge from artifacts than correct labels. Explanations in e-SNLI are largely self-contained: Camburu et al. (2018) report that the classification accuracy conditioned only on the explanation is 96.83%.

3.2 Models

As previously mentioned, our reasoning models consist of a generator and a classifier. We implement all models on top of the PyTorch (Paszke et al., 2019) and Hugging Face Transformers (Wolf et al., 2020) libraries and follow standard fine-tuning strategies.[1]

3.2.1 Generation Models

We use two models to collect explanations.

- Our single-task model (called **GPT-ST** in the following sections) is a GPT-2 (Radford et al., 2019) model that we fine-tune on the task-specific data using a language modelling head.
- The multi-task model (**GPT-MT**) is a GPT-2 model with *two* heads, one for language modeling and one for label classification. We use a weighted additive loss to combine the LM and the classification loss.

The prompt for the GPT-2 components is: "Statement: + *Question or Premise* + Statement: + *Answer Option or Hypothesis* + Explanation: + *Explanation*". We only account for tokens in the

[1]All code with dependencies and parameters is available at `https://github.com/martinjirenius/reasoning-pipeline-models`

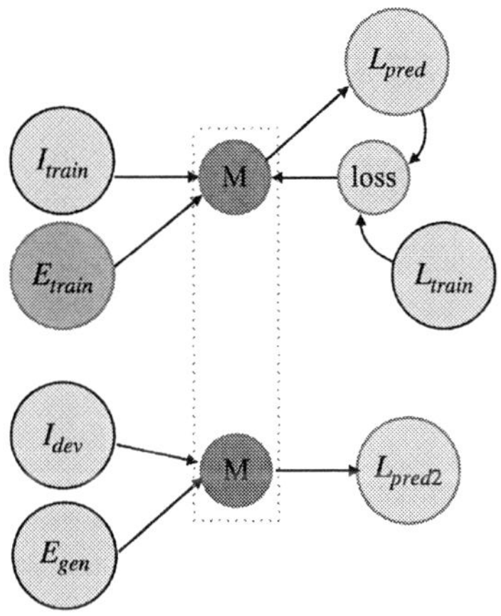

Figure 1: Experimental setup for training (upper half) and testing (lower half) on gold versus generated explanations as a causal graph (Pearl, 1995). I_{train}, I_{dev}, E_{train}, L_{train} and L_{dev} are the inputs, explanations and labels from the train and dev set, respectively. E_{gen} are generated explanations from the GPT-models, M is the BERT classification model, L_{pred} are the labels predicted by M. All variables affected by the intervention on E_{train} are marked with a red border line.

generated explanation when calculating the cross-entropy loss.

3.2.2 Classification Models

For classification, we use fine-tuned BERT base models (Devlin et al., 2019) and present the input in the format "`[CLS]` + *Question or Premise* + `[SEP]` + *Answer Option or Hypothesis* + `[SEP]` + *Explanation* + `[SEP]`". We evaluate six different setups for each data set as specified in Table 1.

BERT$_{\text{none}}$ is a lower-bound baseline that does not use any explanations. BERT$_{\text{gold}}$ is an upper-bound baseline that uses gold explanations both for training and at test time. BERT$_{\text{ST}}$ uses gold explanations for training and the explanations generated by GPT-ST at test time. BERT$_{\text{ST-ft}}$ uses explanations of GPT-ST at test time, but different from BERT$_{\text{ST}}$ it is also fine-tuned on GPT-ST explanations. BERT$_{\text{MT}}$ uses gold explanations for training and the explanations from GPT-MT at test time. BERT$_{\text{MT-ft}}$ is fine-tuned and tested on GPT-MT explanations.

	Trained with:	Tested with:
BERT$_{\text{none}}$	–	–
BERT$_{\text{gold}}$	Gold	Gold
BERT$_{\text{ST}}$	Gold	GPT-ST
BERT$_{\text{ST-ft}}$	GPT-ST	GPT-ST
BERT$_{\text{MT}}$	Gold	GPT-MT
BERT$_{\text{MT-ft}}$	GPT-MT	GPT-MT

Table 1: Overview of our classification setups. The table indicates the source of the explanations that the model is trained and tested with.

Figure 1 illustrates the latter four models with regard to the intervention of fine-tuning the model on generated explanations, i.e. going from BERT$_{\text{ST}}$ to BERT$_{\text{ST-ft}}$ and from BERT$_{\text{MT}}$ to BERT$_{\text{MT-ft}}$.

3.3 Evaluation

Quantitative Metrics Our primary evaluation criteria are the similarity between the generated explanations and the gold explanations, as well as the predictive performance of the complete pipeline. To quantify the similarity, we use BERTScore (F1). To evaluate the classifiers, we compute their macro-averaged F1 score and accuracy on the test data.

Note that the native labels for our ECQA models are *justify* and *refute* for each possible answer. To make our evaluation comparable to other work, we calculate accuracy based on the answer with the highest score for *justify*.

Human Evaluation To assess qualitative properties of the generated explanations, we conduct a human evaluation over 200 random samples for each of the data sets. Inspired by the human evaluation studies by Monsen and Rennes (2022) and Wiegreffe et al. (2022), we ask annotators the following questions for each e out of the gold, GPT-ST and GPT-MT explanations of each sample:

- Is e a well-formed sentence?
- Does e support the label?
- Is the content of e factually correct?
- Does e provide a valid reasoning path for the label?
- Does e add new information, rather than recombining information from the input?

The possible answers for each question are *yes* or *no*. Each sample is rated by three persons familiar with the tasks (the first three authors). We report the average score across reviewers as well as Krippendorf's α ($n = 3$, interval from -1 to 1) for inter-rater agreement (Krippendorff, 2011). The full instructions for the annotators can be found in Appendix A. The data is available at `https://github.com/jekunz/bbnlp22_human`.

	GPT-ST	GPT-MT
ECQA	**0.3108**	0.2502
e-SNLI	0.3989	0.4009

Table 2: BERTScores (F1) for the single-task (GPT-ST) and multi-task (GPT-MT) models.

4 Results

We present our main results together with some additional follow-up experiments.

4.1 BERTScores and Surface Features

First, we test if GPT-ST or GPT-MT generates better explanations as evaluated by BERTScores. We see in Table 2 that GPT-ST explanations are more similar to the human reference explanations than GPT-MT solutions, at 0.3108 vs. 0.2502. For e-SNLI, the BERTScores for both models are very close, and much higher than those for ECQA, at 0.3989 resp. 0.4009.

We also compare the generated explanations in terms of simple surface features: explanation length, vocabulary size and vocabulary overlap with gold explanations (Table 3), and find that for e-SNLI, GPT-ST and GPT-MT explanations have almost identical characteristics. For ECQA, the difference is more substantial: While GPT-ST explanations are shorter than both GPT-MT and gold explanations, the former's vocabulary is larger than that of GPT-MT. The overlap with gold explanations is slightly higher for GPT-MT.

4.2 Classification

Results for the classification models are reported in Tables 4 and 5 (macro-averaged F1, accuracy).

	GPT-ST	GPT-MT	Gold
ECQA: Words	9.14	10.28	10.54
ECQA: Chars	48.08	49.74	57.48
ECQA: Vocab	7,946	4,436	11,033
ECQA: Overl.	0.772	0.735	–
e-SNLI: Words	11.79	11.77	13.32
e-SNLI: Chars	60.11	60.01	68.75
e-SNLI: Vocab	9,398	9,346	14,935
e-SNLI: Overl.	0.860	0.860	–

Table 3: Surface features: average word and character length, vocabulary size and vocabulary overlap with gold explanations for each set of explanations (dev. set).

Baselines As expected, the baseline $\text{BERT}_{\text{gold}}$ performs best across all metrics, models and data sets. For e-SNLI, $\text{BERT}_{\text{none}}$ performs better than all models that utilize generated explanations. For ECQA, BERT_{ST} and BERT_{MT} get a classification accuracy below the $\text{BERT}_{\text{none}}$ accuracy, with 0.253 and 0.231 compared to a random baseline of 0.2. However, looking at the F1 scores, we see that the $\text{BERT}_{\text{none}}$ baseline is outperformed by all ECQA explanation models.

Fine-tuning on generated explanations improves results When fine-tuning on generated explanations in the $\text{BERT}_{\text{ST-ft}}$ and $\text{BERT}_{\text{MT-ft}}$ models, the explanation models outperform the $\text{BERT}_{\text{none}}$ baseline for ECQA consistently, showing that the additional supervision with generated explanations is helpful. While for e-SNLI $\text{BERT}_{\text{none}}$ is not outperformed, the *ft* models still perform consistently better than the models trained on gold explanations, although the gap is smaller than for ECQA.

As an ablation, we also train two ECQA BERT models ($\text{BERT}_{\text{ST-abl}}$ and $\text{BERT}_{\text{MT-abl}}$) on generated explanations only, and evaluate them on gold explanations. $\text{BERT}_{\text{ST-abl}}$ achieves an accuracy of 0.522 on gold explanations and $\text{BERT}_{\text{MT-abl}}$ achieves 0.479, improving over comparable models that utilize generated explanations by at least 0.062 ($\text{BERT}_{\text{ST-ft}}$: 0.460) and 0.011 ($\text{BERT}_{\text{MT-ft}}$: 0.468). The accuracies of the ablation models on generated explanations are 0.406 ($\text{BERT}_{\text{ST-abl}}$) and 0.469 ($\text{BERT}_{\text{MT-abl}}$). Still, the gap to the gold-trained and gold-evaluated model remains substantial.

Single-task versus multi-task explanations While the BERTScore differences between GPT-ST and GPT-MT explanations are large for ECQA, using these explanations downstream in the classification model gives very similar results. For ECQA, the MT model even appears to have a slight advantage at least for the *ft* models, while for e-SNLI, it is the other way round.

4.3 Human Evaluation

The results of the human evaluation are reported in Table 6. In the case of ECQA, we see that the annotators have a preference for the GPT-ST explanations, giving them considerably higher scores for *support*, *correctness* and *validity*. The GPT-MT model adds more novel information. A closer look at the novel information shows that in the examples that were flagged to contain novel information, the majority (0.637) are factually incorrect. The

	$BERT_{none}$	$BERT_{gold}$	$BERT_{ST}$	$BERT_{ST\text{-}ft}$	$BERT_{MT}$	$BERT_{MT\text{-}ft}$
ECQA	0.378	**0.906**	0.514	0.631	0.489	**0.634**
e-SNLI	0.898	**0.980**	0.836	**0.861**	0.836	0.861

Table 4: Results for the classification models, macro-averaged F1 scores.

	$BERT_{none}$	$BERT_{gold}$	$BERT_{ST}$	$BERT_{ST\text{-}ft}$	$BERT_{MT}$	$BERT_{MT\text{-}ft}$
ECQA	0.338	**0.945**	0.253	0.460	0.231	**0.468**
e-SNLI	0.898	**0.993**	0.844	**0.866**	0.843	0.863

Table 5: Results for the classification models, accuracy.

annotators anecdotally report a large amount of nonsensical hallucinations in the GPT-MT model; we include examples in Appendix B.1. The overall scores are low, with shares of *yes* answers to the validity criterion being only 0.285 (GPT-ST) and 0.107 (GPT-MT). However, the gold answers do not get good scores either, with a *yes* share of 0.49. The highest-scoring criterion is *well-formedness*, where GPT-MT gets scores comparable to the gold explanations. With 0.607 vs. 0.603, the share of well-formed answers is however still low, with the generation models probably mirroring sloppy explanations in the training set.

For e-SNLI, the scores for all criteria except *novelty* are considerably higher. There is a slight preference for GPT-MT in the criteria *support*, *correctness* and *validity*, and a slight preference for GPT-ST in *well-formedness*, where GPT-ST even surpasses the gold explanations (0.868 vs. 0.833). Annotators noted that the ease of creating well-formed explanation may be due to the explanation often following clear templates; examples are given in Appendix B.2. e-SNLI explanations almost never add new information; the highest share is in the gold set with only 0.052.

For both data sets we note that the inter-annotator agreement on gold explanations is much lower than on both sets of generated explanations.

5 Discussion

We now discuss or results and method.

5.1 Results

The downstream utility of explanations is not reflected by BERTScores or human ratings The rationale-enriched pipeline helps us to better understand interactions between predictions and explanations by comparing the usefulness of different sets of explanations. Perhaps not surprisingly, we see that BERTScores do not reflect the usefulness of the explanations generated by different models. Large drops in BERTScores go along with at most very slight drops in the model's performance on the respective predictions. This is in line with results by Hase et al. (2020), who report that BLEU scores are not correlated with LAS.

Perhaps surprisingly however, the same effect is observed for the interplay of the human ratings and the downstream usefulness: Large differences in the human ratings of the validity and factual correctness of the explanations are not at all reflected in the downstream utility of the explanations. We hypothesize that a key property that leads to this behavior is the tendency of GPT-MT to hallucinate in ECQA (§ 4.3): While novel but factually incorrect information is punished in human ratings and BERTScore, the new information can still help the downstream model by adding possible context. GPT-ST on the other hand tends to "play safe" by creating more template-like explanations, with often sensible results but without novel information, and thereby without additional features for the classifier. Consider this example:

> **Q:** The archaeologist was seeing artifacts that he knew were fake, how did he feel?
> **A:** painful memories
> **Label:** refute
> **GPT-ST:** Painful memories is not a feeling.
> **GPT-MT:** A person who is in fear of being embarrassed is called a bad person.

The GPT-ST explanation is reasonable but merely re-combines words from the question and answer. GPT-MT on the other hand creates an off-topic explanation that could, however, help the reasoning of the classifier by giving hints on alternative answers (like *embarrassed* or *fear*). We leave an investigation of this to future work.

	Well-formed	Support	Correctness	Validity	Novelty
ECQA gold	0.603 (+0.22)	0.682 (+0.13)	0.593 (−0.03)	0.490 (+0.18)	0.173 (+0.20)
ECQA GPT-ST	0.573 (+0.25)	0.513 (+0.45)	0.443 (+0.19)	0.285 (+0.48)	0.126 (+0.28)
ECQA GPT-MT	0.607 (+0.32)	0.320 (+0.43)	0.333 (+0.15)	0.107 (+0.43)	0.211 (+0.23)
e-SNLI gold	0.833 (+0.04)	0.873 (+0.06)	0.860 (+0.08)	0.772 (−0.06)	0.052 (−0.02)
e-SNLI GPT-ST	0.868 (+0.10)	0.807 (+0.57)	0.755 (+0.73)	0.670 (+0.65)	0.018 (+0.26)
e-SNLI GPT-MT	0.830 (+0.24)	0.813 (+0.56)	0.813 (+0.56)	0.688 (+0.54)	0.012 (−0.01)

Table 6: Human evaluation: average share of *yes* answers across all samples that were not flagged as invalid. The numbers in parentheses show Krippendorf's α ($n = 3$, interval from -1 to $+1$) for inter-rater agreement.

Fine-tuning on generated explanations is crucial Another important finding is the failure of BERT_{ST} and BERT_{MT} when encountering generated explanations in ECQA, which shows that our generator models do not catch the relevant semantic aspects sufficiently well for the classifier to rely on them. However, after fine-tuning with generated explanations, the BERT classifier can improve over the baseline without access to explanations. This shows that the model can still profit from the imperfect explanations if it learns to handle their limitations better. Our ablation with a model trained on generated and evaluated gold explanations suggests that it is not surface differences that make the transfer hard: The ablation model can in fact handle the gold explanations quite well, performing even better than on generated explanations. The fact that it still performs much worse than $\text{BERT}_{\text{gold}}$ on gold explanations shows that the model is far from perfect in identifying reliable information in the explanations; however, it is able to differentiate *to some extent.*

In previous work, Rajani et al. (2019) use a similar model consisting of GPT-2 and BERT, and succeed with gold-explanation training and generated-explanation testing for CoS-E. One reason for the contradictory results could be a more sophisticated optimization of their model, but we find it worth discussing that the success does not necessarily come by default. Another hypothesis is that the cause is the (reportedly) low-quality annotations in CoS-E (Narang et al., 2020) having a similar noise-adding effect as the generated explanations, and therefore allow the model to transfer.

e-SNLI is easy, ECQA problematic to explain On e-SNLI, all models get higher scores in all metrics than on ECQA. The only exception is novelty in the human evaluation: Novel information is not necessary to explain e-SNLI instances; it is sufficient to re-combine parts of premise and hypothesis. This is commonly done in a template-like manner:

- *[Part of premise] is [part of hypothesis]* for the *entailment* label,
- *Not all [part of premise] are [part of hypothesis]* for *neutral*, and
- *[Subject] cannot [part of premise] and [part of hypothesis] at the same time* for *contradiction*.

For full examples containing these patterns, we refer to Appendix B.2. The template-like explanations in e-SNLI have also been noted by Camburu et al. (2018) and Brahman et al. (2021). Such observations could raise the question if templates could be a more appropriate form of explanation for this data set, as they would improve clarity and reliability. Wiegreffe and Marasovic (2021) review explanation data sets and question the popular perception that template-like explanations are generally dismissed as uninformative. The authors suggest to instead embrace naturally occurring structures.

ECQA explanations rarely follow simple patterns and more often include external information. The low *validity* scores even for the gold explanations show that the data set is rather hard to explain. Our annotators noted that "incorrect" answer options in ECQA are not generally implausible but often just less likely than the "correct" option. This makes it hard to write explanations that do not explicitly consider the correct answer option in a contrastive manner (arguing why it is more likely than the current candidate). Examples are given in Appendix B.3. ECQA contains a notable number of uninformative explanations for the *refute* label both in the gold and the generated explanations, e.g. *[Answer] is not a correct option* (see Appendix B.4 for examples). This is possibly a result of annotators not being able to formulate satisfying reasons why the answer option is incorrect. ECQA also has a large amount of ungrammatical and low-quality annotations, which affects the generation models negatively.

5.2 Limitations

We conclude this section with a discussion of the limitations of our study.

Model An obvious limitation of our work is that our results on SNLI and CommonsenseQA are below the current state of the art, due to the moderate size of our models. While combining GPT-2 and BERT is a common setup for free-form explanation generating models (Wang et al., 2020), Hase et al. (2020) report much higher results using T5 models, and Marasovic et al. (2021) clearly document the effect of scale in a few-shot setup, with e-SNLI climbing from 79.2% to 87.4% and ECQA from 41.4% to 65.9% in classification accuracy when going from T5-base to T5-3B. While repeating the experiments with larger models could lead to different conclusions, we believe that investigating the smaller, more accessible and widely used models remains valuable.

Evaluation Another limitation in our analysis is the possibility that the multi-task explanations are affected by error propagation when the system makes wrong predictions.[2] This issue may affect both BERTScores and human evaluations. We suggest that a promising fix to this potential problem is to over-generate explanations and randomly choose one that accompanies a correct prediction.

Data sets That explanations do not increase the overall performance of SNLI models is known in the literature. Camburu et al. (2018) report a decline in accuracy with explanations: 84.01% for SNLI, but 83.96% for the best explanation model. Note that their models were BiLSTM models trained from scratch, as their work preceded current pre-trained models. Another work reports an improvement in accuracy, but with 0.3% it is extremely slight (Zhao and Vydiswaran, 2021). As pre-trained models get a superhuman performance on SNLI, and because of the known presence of annotation artifacts (Gururangan et al., 2018), recent improvements may however not be meaningful for solving the actual task. In addition, the high performance of models is not aligned with human agreement on natural language understanding tasks. In a human evaluation of SNLI by (Bowman et al., 2015), all annotators agree only on 58% of the labels.

[2]This limitation was rightfully noted by one of the reviewers of this paper, which we gratefully acknowledge.

Both data sets we use consist of crowd-sourced explanations of mixed quality. Doing a manual inspection of either of them, it is easy to find incorrect and logically inconsistent explanations, or explanations that contribute no additional information (§§ B.3, B.4). Our low inter-annotator agreement on gold explanations is an indicator of these problems. Related observations have also been raised in previous evaluations (Wiegreffe et al., 2022). Besides data quality, the tasks of natural language inference and multiple-choice question are arguably artificial. It is unclear how the results would transfer to explanation generation in general.

The status of free-text explanations We believe it is appropriate to remain sceptical about the utility of generated free-text explanations. Large models produce better explanations by all metrics, but there is still a huge qualitative difference of human and generated explanations (Marasovic et al., 2021). The acceptability filtering system proposed by Wiegreffe et al. (2022) improves human ratings of model-generated explanations substantially, but may, as these authors state themselves, be more relevant for goals such as creating trust in the system than for creating explanations faithful to the model's prediction process. In fact, generating explanations without guarantees of a causal connection between explanation and label is not faithful, and evidence that there is such a connection is sparse. Still, while we would strongly advise against using generated explanations as evidence about how a prediction was made, we argue that they can generate valuable insights into the "reasoning" capabilities of models, and thereby help improving models, task formulations and data sets. Unfortunately, the current lack of high-quality annotated data sets with explanations for diverse tasks makes it hard to fully assess their potential.

6 Conclusion

In this paper we compared free-text explanations in variants of a rationale-enriched pipeline: using a single-task versus a self-rationalizing generation model, and training the classifier on gold explanation only versus doing further fine-tuning with generated explanations. An extensive evaluation with similarity-based metrics, utility in downstream classification, and human ratings based on five different criteria shows limitations but also chances of free-text explanations. We see indications that hallucinations occur more frequently in explanations by a self-rationalizing generation model. However, they do not appear to be generally harmful, and may even be useful for downstream predictions in rationale-enriched pipelines if the classification model has the chance to learn to differentiate between reliable and unreliable information. Further investigation of hallucinations in rationale-enriched pipelines, e.g. with extractive explanation methods, is an interesting avenue for future research.

That human ratings do not reflect classification utility indicates that it is crucial to design annotations and models targeted towards a use case: Explanations that convince human raters are not ideal for the goal of performance improvements by providing useful guidance to the model. However, the latter goal is not explicitly accounted for in popular data sets, but the former is not sufficiently met either, as particularly for ECQA, human annotators rate gold explanations low. Specialized explanations that maximize one goal at a time would help us understand the differences between human and model "reasoning", and thereby allow us to move towards more faithful free-text explanations.

Acknowledgements

This work was partially supported by the Wallenberg AI, Autonomous Systems and Software Program (WASP) funded by the Knut and Alice Wallenberg Foundation. We thank the anonymous reviewers for their valuable and constructive feedback that contributed to improving this work.

References

Shourya Aggarwal, Divyanshu Mandowara, Vishwajeet Agrawal, Dinesh Khandelwal, Parag Singla, and Dinesh Garg. 2021. Explanations for CommonsenseQA: New Dataset and Models. In *Proceedings of the 59th Annual Meeting of the Association for Computational Linguistics and the 11th International Joint Conference on Natural Language Processing (Volume 1: Long Papers)*, pages 3050–3065, Online. Association for Computational Linguistics.

Pepa Atanasova, Jakob Grue Simonsen, Christina Lioma, and Isabelle Augenstein. 2020. A diagnostic study of explainability techniques for text classification. In *Proceedings of the 2020 Conference on Empirical Methods in Natural Language Processing (EMNLP)*, pages 3256–3274, Online. Association for Computational Linguistics.

Yonatan Belinkov and James Glass. 2019. Analysis methods in neural language processing: A survey. *Transactions of the Association for Computational Linguistics*, 7:49–72.

Rishi Bommasani, Drew A. Hudson, Ehsan Adeli, Russ Altman, Simran Arora, Sydney von Arx, Michael S. Bernstein, Jeannette Bohg, Antoine Bosselut, Emma Brunskill, Erik Brynjolfsson, Shyamal Buch, Dallas Card, Rodrigo Castellon, Niladri S. Chatterji, Annie S. Chen, Kathleen Creel, Jared Quincy Davis, Dorottya Demszky, Chris Donahue, Moussa Doumbouya, Esin Durmus, Stefano Ermon, John Etchemendy, Kawin Ethayarajh, Li Fei-Fei, Chelsea Finn, Trevor Gale, Lauren Gillespie, Karan Goel, Noah D. Goodman, Shelby Grossman, Neel Guha, Tatsunori Hashimoto, Peter Henderson, John Hewitt, Daniel E. Ho, Jenny Hong, Kyle Hsu, Jing Huang, Thomas Icard, Saahil Jain, Dan Jurafsky, Pratyusha Kalluri, Siddharth Karamcheti, Geoff Keeling, Fereshte Khani, Omar Khattab, Pang Wei Koh, Mark S. Krass, Ranjay Krishna, Rohith Kuditipudi, and et al. 2021. On the opportunities and risks of foundation models. *CoRR*, abs/2108.07258.

Samuel R. Bowman, Gabor Angeli, Christopher Potts, and Christopher D. Manning. 2015. A large annotated corpus for learning natural language inference. In *Proceedings of the 2015 Conference on Empirical Methods in Natural Language Processing*, pages 632–642, Lisbon, Portugal. Association for Computational Linguistics.

Faeze Brahman, Vered Shwartz, Rachel Rudinger, and Yejin Choi. 2021. Learning to rationalize for nonmonotonic reasoning with distant supervision. *Proceedings of the AAAI Conference on Artificial Intelligence*, 35(14):12592–12601.

Tom Brown, Benjamin Mann, Nick Ryder, Melanie Subbiah, Jared D Kaplan, Prafulla Dhariwal, Arvind Neelakantan, Pranav Shyam, Girish Sastry, Amanda Askell, Sandhini Agarwal, Ariel Herbert-Voss, Gretchen Krueger, Tom Henighan, Rewon Child, Aditya Ramesh, Daniel Ziegler, Jeffrey Wu, Clemens Winter, Chris Hesse, Mark Chen, Eric Sigler, Mateusz Litwin, Scott Gray, Benjamin Chess, Jack Clark, Christopher Berner, Sam McCandlish, Alec Radford, Ilya Sutskever, and Dario Amodei. 2020. Language models are few-shot learners. In *Advances in Neural Information Processing Systems*, volume 33, pages 1877–1901. Curran Associates, Inc.

Oana-Maria Camburu, Tim Rocktäschel, Thomas Lukasiewicz, and Phil Blunsom. 2018. e-snli: Natural language inference with natural language explanations. In *Advances in Neural Information Processing Systems*, volume 31. Curran Associates, Inc.

Chun Sik Chan, Huanqi Kong, and Liang Guanqing. 2022. A comparative study of faithfulness metrics for model interpretability methods. In *Proceedings of the 60th Annual Meeting of the Association for Computational Linguistics (Volume 1: Long Papers)*, pages 5029–5038, Dublin, Ireland. Association for Computational Linguistics.

Jacob Devlin, Ming-Wei Chang, Kenton Lee, and Kristina Toutanova. 2019. BERT: Pre-training of deep bidirectional transformers for language understanding. In *Proceedings of the 2019 Conference of the North American Chapter of the Association for Computational Linguistics: Human Language Technologies, Volume 1 (Long and Short Papers)*, pages 4171–4186, Minneapolis, Minnesota. Association for Computational Linguistics.

Jay DeYoung, Sarthak Jain, Nazneen Fatema Rajani, Eric Lehman, Caiming Xiong, Richard Socher, and Byron C. Wallace. 2020. ERASER: A benchmark to evaluate rationalized NLP models. In *Proceedings of the 58th Annual Meeting of the Association for Computational Linguistics*, pages 4443–4458, Online. Association for Computational Linguistics.

Suchin Gururangan, Swabha Swayamdipta, Omer Levy, Roy Schwartz, Samuel Bowman, and Noah A. Smith. 2018. Annotation artifacts in natural language inference data. In *Proceedings of the 2018 Conference of the North American Chapter of the Association for Computational Linguistics: Human Language Technologies, Volume 2 (Short Papers)*, pages 107–112, New Orleans, Louisiana. Association for Computational Linguistics.

Peter Hase, Shiyue Zhang, Harry Xie, and Mohit Bansal. 2020. Leakage-adjusted simulatability: Can models generate non-trivial explanations of their behavior in natural language? In *Findings of the Association for Computational Linguistics: EMNLP 2020*, pages 4351–4367, Online. Association for Computational Linguistics.

Alon Jacovi and Yoav Goldberg. 2020. Towards faithfully interpretable NLP systems: How should we define and evaluate faithfulness? In *Proceedings of the 58th Annual Meeting of the Association for Computational Linguistics*, pages 4198–4205, Online. Association for Computational Linguistics.

Jinkyu Kim, Anna Rohrbach, Trevor Darrell, John Canny, and Zeynep Akata. 2018. Textual explanations for self-driving vehicles. In *Proceedings of the European conference on computer vision (ECCV)*, pages 563–578.

Klaus Krippendorff. 2011. Computing Krippendorff's Alpha-Reliability.

Wojciech Kryscinski, Nitish Shirish Keskar, Bryan McCann, Caiming Xiong, and Richard Socher. 2019. Neural text summarization: A critical evaluation. In *Proceedings of the 2019 Conference on Empirical Methods in Natural Language Processing and the 9th International Joint Conference on Natural Language Processing (EMNLP-IJCNLP)*, pages 540–551, Hong Kong, China. Association for Computational Linguistics.

Chin-Yew Lin. 2004. ROUGE: A package for automatic evaluation of summaries. In *Text Summarization Branches Out*, pages 74–81, Barcelona, Spain. Association for Computational Linguistics.

Wang Ling, Dani Yogatama, Chris Dyer, and Phil Blunsom. 2017. Program induction by rationale generation: Learning to solve and explain algebraic word problems. In *Proceedings of the 55th Annual Meeting of the Association for Computational Linguistics (Volume 1: Long Papers)*, pages 158–167, Vancouver, Canada. Association for Computational Linguistics.

Ana Marasovic, Iz Beltagy, Doug Downey, and Matthew E. Peters. 2021. Few-shot self-rationalization with natural language prompts. *CoRR*, abs/2111.08284.

Joshua Maynez, Shashi Narayan, Bernd Bohnet, and Ryan McDonald. 2020. On faithfulness and factuality in abstractive summarization. In *Proceedings of the 58th Annual Meeting of the Association for Computational Linguistics*, pages 1906–1919, Online. Association for Computational Linguistics.

Tim Miller. 2019. Explanation in artificial intelligence: Insights from the social sciences. *Artificial intelligence*, 267:1–38.

Julius Monsen and Evelina Rennes. 2022. Perceived text quality and readability in extractive and abstractive summaries. In *Proceedings of the 13th international conference on Language Resources and Evaluation (LREC), Marseille, France.*

Sharan Narang, Colin Raffel, Katherine Lee, Adam Roberts, Noah Fiedel, and Karishma Malkan. 2020. Wt5?! training text-to-text models to explain their predictions. *CoRR*, abs/2004.14546.

Kishore Papineni, Salim Roukos, Todd Ward, and Wei-Jing Zhu. 2002. Bleu: a method for automatic evaluation of machine translation. In *Proceedings of the 40th Annual Meeting of the Association for Computational Linguistics*, pages 311–318, Philadelphia, Pennsylvania, USA. Association for Computational Linguistics.

Adam Paszke, Sam Gross, Francisco Massa, Adam Lerer, James Bradbury, Gregory Chanan, Trevor Killeen, Zeming Lin, Natalia Gimelshein, Luca Antiga, Alban Desmaison, Andreas Kopf, Edward Yang, Zachary DeVito, Martin Raison, Alykhan Tejani, Sasank Chilamkurthy, Benoit Steiner, Lu Fang, Junjie Bai, and Soumith Chintala. 2019. Pytorch: An imperative style, high-performance deep learning library. In H. Wallach, H. Larochelle, A. Beygelzimer, F. d'Alché-Buc, E. Fox, and R. Garnett, editors, *Advances in Neural Information Processing Systems 32*, pages 8024–8035. Curran Associates, Inc.

Judea Pearl. 1995. Causal diagrams for empirical research. *Biometrika*, 82(4):669–688.

Alec Radford, Jeffrey Wu, Rewon Child, David Luan, Dario Amodei, Ilya Sutskever, et al. 2019. Language models are unsupervised multitask learners. *OpenAI blog*, 1(8):9.

Colin Raffel, Noam Shazeer, Adam Roberts, Katherine Lee, Sharan Narang, Michael Matena, Yanqi Zhou, Wei Li, and Peter J. Liu. 2020. Exploring the limits of transfer learning with a unified text-to-text transformer. *Journal of Machine Learning Research*, 21(140):1–67.

Nazneen Fatema Rajani, Bryan McCann, Caiming Xiong, and Richard Socher. 2019. Explain yourself! leveraging language models for commonsense reasoning. In *Proceedings of the 57th Annual Meeting of the Association for Computational Linguistics*, pages 4932–4942, Florence, Italy. Association for Computational Linguistics.

Marco Ribeiro, Sameer Singh, and Carlos Guestrin. 2016. "why should I trust you?": Explaining the predictions of any classifier. In *Proceedings of the 2016 Conference of the North American Chapter of the Association for Computational Linguistics: Demonstrations*, pages 97–101, San Diego, California. Association for Computational Linguistics.

Karen Simonyan, Andrea Vedaldi, and Andrew Zisserman. 2014. Deep inside convolutional networks: Visualising image classification models and saliency maps. In *2nd International Conference on Learning Representations, ICLR 2014, Banff, AB, Canada, April 14-16, 2014, Workshop Track Proceedings*.

Alon Talmor, Jonathan Herzig, Nicholas Lourie, and Jonathan Berant. 2019. CommonsenseQA: A question answering challenge targeting commonsense knowledge. In *Proceedings of the 2019 Conference of the North American Chapter of the Association for Computational Linguistics: Human Language Technologies, Volume 1 (Long and Short Papers)*, pages 4149–4158, Minneapolis, Minnesota. Association for Computational Linguistics.

Chenhao Tan. 2022. On the diversity and limits of human explanations. In *Proceedings of the 2022 Conference of the North American Chapter of the Association for Computational Linguistics: Human Language Technologies*, pages 2173–2188, Seattle, United States. Association for Computational Linguistics.

Cunxiang Wang, Shuailong Liang, Yili Jin, Yilong Wang, Xiaodan Zhu, and Yue Zhang. 2020. SemEval-2020 task 4: Commonsense validation and explanation. In *Proceedings of the Fourteenth Workshop on Semantic Evaluation*, pages 307–321, Barcelona (online). International Committee for Computational Linguistics.

Sarah Wiegreffe, Jack Hessel, Swabha Swayamdipta, Mark Riedl, and Yejin Choi. 2022. Reframing human-AI collaboration for generating free-text explanations. In *Proceedings of the 2022 Conference of the North American Chapter of the Association for Computational Linguistics: Human Language Technologies*, pages 632–658, Seattle, United States. Association for Computational Linguistics.

Sarah Wiegreffe and Ana Marasovic. 2021. Teach me to explain: A review of datasets for explainable natural language processing. In *Proceedings of the Neural Information Processing Systems Track on Datasets and Benchmarks*, volume 1.

Sarah Wiegreffe, Ana Marasović, and Noah A. Smith. 2021. Measuring association between labels and free-text rationales. In *Proceedings of the 2021 Conference on Empirical Methods in Natural Language Processing*, pages 10266–10284, Online and Punta Cana, Dominican Republic. Association for Computational Linguistics.

Thomas Wolf, Lysandre Debut, Victor Sanh, Julien Chaumond, Clement Delangue, Anthony Moi, Pierric Cistac, Tim Rault, Remi Louf, Morgan Funtowicz, Joe Davison, Sam Shleifer, Patrick von Platen, Clara Ma, Yacine Jernite, Julien Plu, Canwen Xu, Teven Le Scao, Sylvain Gugger, Mariama Drame, Quentin Lhoest, and Alexander Rush. 2020. Transformers: State-of-the-art natural language processing. In *Proceedings of the 2020 Conference on Empirical Methods in Natural Language Processing: System Demonstrations*, pages 38–45, Online. Association for Computational Linguistics.

Tianyi Zhang, Varsha Kishore, Felix Wu, Kilian Q. Weinberger, and Yoav Artzi. 2020. Bertscore: Evaluating text generation with BERT. In *8th International Conference on Learning Representations, ICLR 2020, Addis Ababa, Ethiopia, April 26-30, 2020*. OpenReview.net.

Xinyan Zhao and VG Vinod Vydiswaran. 2021. Lirex: Augmenting language inference with relevant explanations. In *Proceedings of the AAAI Conference on Artificial Intelligence*, volume 35, pages 14532–14539.

A Full Instructions to Human Annotators

In the following box we provide the full instructions given to the human annotators for the manual evaluation. As all of our annotators are Master students or doctoral students who work with NLP, they were familiar with the e-SNLI and the ECQA data sets, so that we only needed to clarify the criteria and provide specific instructions.

If you disagree with the label or find the example to be non-sense: Flag the example with *N/A*.

Step 1: Look only at e internally:

- Is e a well-formed sentence? (e is grammatical and structurally sensible.)
- Is the content of e factually correct? (e itself is a true statement about the real world. e is factually and logically correct.)

Step 2: Look at e and the label:

- Does e support the label? (Looking at e alone, it is reasonable that the label is correct.)

Step 3: Use all available context:

- Does e provide a valid reasoning path for the label? (e convincingly explains how to get from the context to the label.)
- Does e add new information? (Rather than re-combining information from the context, e comes up with new information.)

B Anecdotical Examples for Observed Characteristics

In this appendix section we provide further examples for four phenomena mentioned in this paper that raters noticed during the human evaluation. These phenomena were not systematically reviewed at evaluation time but are anecdotal observations.

B.1 Hallucinations in GPT-MT

The following five examples from GPT-MT include novel, "hallucinated" information that has no connection to the question or answer option.

Q: When old conservative people observe a changing society, what do the experience?
A: acceptance
Label: refute
GPT-MT: The experience of dying is a feeling

Q: Where can I put a coin to stop my car from being towed?
A: piggy bank
Label: refute
GPT-MT: A person can put a coin in a cowgy bank to stop his car from being washed from the water.

Q: After I urinate and flush the toilet and wash my hands, what should I do next?
A: zip pants
Label: refute
GPT-MT: A person should not put bag under shirt.

Q: The stud bull was brought in to breed with the prize winning what?
A: female
Label: refute
GPT-MT: Cats are not called horses

Q: Who might wear dark glasses indoors?
A: ray charles
Label: refute
GPT-MT: A person might wear dark glasses in a ring in the house.

B.2 Template-like explanations in e-SNLI

In the following we provide six examples from e-SNLI, two for each label, where the explanations follow a clear template that is consistently followed by all explanation models.

Premise: A dog biting a man's rear
Hypothesis: An animal is biting a man.
Label: entailment
GPT-ST: A dog is an animal.
GPT-MT: A dog is an animal.
Gold: A dog is an animal.

Premise: A group of men playing music, the man holding a guitar is talking to a man with drums.
Hypothesis: A band is playing music.
Label: entailment
GPT-ST: A group of men playing music is a band.
GPT-MT: A group of men playing music is a band.
Gold: A group playing music together is know as a band.

Premise: Man holding torch of fire.
Hypothesis: The fire is large.
Label: neutral
GPT-ST: Not all fires are large.
GPT-MT: The fire is not necessarily large.
Gold: Not all the fires are large.

Premise: A woman in a bright pink and green skirt carries a large wicker basket on her back up a stone-cobbled street.
Hypothesis: The woman is carrying a basket down the street in Nepal.
Label: neutral
GPT-ST: Not all stone-cobbled streets are in Nepal.
GPT-MT: Not all stone-cobbled streets are in Nepal.
Gold: Just because a woman is carrying a basket does not mean that she is in Nepal.

Premise: A woman in a teal apron prepares a meal at a restaurant.
Hypothesis: A woman is walking in park
Label: contradiction
GPT-ST: The woman cannot be walking and preparing a meal at the same time.
GPT-MT: The woman cannot prepare a meal at a restaurant and walk in a park at the same time.
Gold: A restaurant is not a park.

Premise: A man in a blue shirt, blue jeans, and a red apron standing at a grill.
Hypothesis: A man bakes a cake.
Label: contradiction
GPT-ST: A man cannot bake a cake and stand at a grill at the same time.
GPT-MT: The man cannot be standing at a grill and baking a cake at the same time.
Gold: Standing at a grill cannot be done simultaneously with baking a cake.

B.3 Plausible but "incorrect" answer options

The answer options in the following five examples are plausible, but not the most likely option. Reasons include too general or rather far-fetched but still possible options.

Q: Sean was a native English speaker, a fact that he found helpful. Ludwig didn't speak the language well because he was what?
A: alien
Label: refute
GPT-ST: Alien is not a person.
GPT-MT: A person cannot speak the language well if he is an island.
Gold: A human being is not an alien.

Q: Billy found that his toilet was overflowing. Water was splashing onto the floor and making a huge mess. He got a mop and tried to clean it up. Where might the toilet be located?
A: apartment
Label: refute
GPT-ST: Apartment is a community having 10 to 20 homes or a block of apartments. Apartment is not where toilet overflowed.
GPT-MT: Apartment is a room or set of rooms or a building where people live permanently, especially as a member of a family or household.
Gold: His toilet was not in the apartment.

Q: They really needed the information prisoner, so they did the least human thing and began to what the prisoner?
A: hurt
Label: refute
GPT-ST: Prisoners do not hurt when they are being hurt
GPT-MT: When a person is hurt, he gets hurt.
Gold: Hurt is not the least human thing they can do.

Q: When old conservative people observe a changing society, what do the experience?
A: acceptance
Label: refute
GPT-ST: Acceptance is not related to changing society
GPT-MT: The experience of dying is a feeling
Gold: Acceptance is not an emotion

Q: How can one's views change after learning about science?
A: appreciation of nature
Label: refute
GPT-ST: One can't change his views after learning about science.
GPT-MT: A person can change his ideas by learning about science.
Gold: Appreciation of nature is the act of recognising or understanding that nature is valuable, important or as described. Appreciation of nature is the act of recognising that nature is valuable while learning about science is all about greater knowledge and not appreciation.

B.4 Uninformative "refute" answers

These five examples show explanations that do not contain incorrect facts, but are completely uninformative and therefore unfit as explanations.

Q: What can happen as a result of a business spending money and having to make a declaration?
A: poverty
Label: refute
Gold: Poverty is not an appropriate option.

Q: What animal has quills all over it?
A: calligraphy
Label: refute
Gold: Calligraphy dont suits in this sentence.

Q: What is unlikely to get bugs on its windshield due to bugs' inability to reach it when it is moving?
A: car
Label: refute
GPT-MT: Car is not a correct option.

Q: There was a cloud or two out but overall it was very what?
A: bringing rain
Label: refute
GPT-MT: Rain is not a correct option.

Q: Sam tried to go to sleep, but he couldn't. He suffered from what?
A: bed
Label: refute
GPT-ST: Bed is not a correct option.

Q: The coach decided to make a lineup change, the team's effort was suffering from what?
A: paper money
Label: refute
GPT-ST: Paper money is not a correct option.

Analyzing the Representational Geometry of Acoustic Word Embeddings

Badr M. Abdullah and **Dietrich Klakow**
Language Science and Technology (LST), Saarland University, Germany
Saarland Informatics Campus
{ babdullah | dietrich }@lsv.uni-saarland.de

Abstract

Acoustic word embeddings (AWEs) are vector representations such that different acoustic exemplars of the same word are projected nearby in the embedding space. In addition to their use in speech technology applications such as spoken term discovery and keyword spotting, AWE models have been adopted as models of spoken-word processing in several cognitively motivated studies and have been shown to exhibit human-like performance in some auditory processing tasks. Nevertheless, the representational geometry of AWEs remains an underexplored topic that has not been studied in the literature. In this paper, we take a closer analytical look at AWEs learned from English speech and study how the choice of the learning objective and the architecture shapes their representational profile. To this end, we employ a set of analytic techniques from machine learning and neuroscience in three different analyses: embedding space uniformity, word discriminability, and representational consistency. Our main findings highlight the prominent role of the learning objective on shaping the representation profile compared to the model architecture.

1 Introduction

Due to their ubiquity, word embeddings are nowadays a central component in natural language processing (NLP). Inducing word embeddings from text yields representations such that words occurring in similar contexts are nearby in the vector space (Mikolov et al., 2013; Pennington et al., 2014). Therefore, the representational geometry of text-based word embeddings captures lexical similarity and semantic relatedness at multiple levels of granularity. Word embeddings, and their underlying distributional semantic models, have also been adopted as models of human semantic memory in cognitive science research (Pereira et al., 2016; Nematzadeh et al., 2017; Grand et al., 2022).

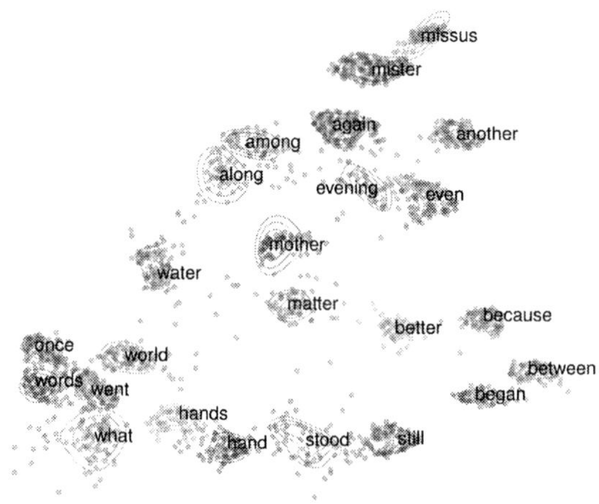

Figure 1: UMAP projection (McInnes et al., 2018) of a sample of acoustic word embeddings (AWEs) produced by a correspondence autoencoder (CAE) model trained on English read speech. AWE models project different exemplars of the same word type closer in the embedding space while abstracting away from speaker and context variability.

In the speech processing domain, researchers have independently developed representations of acoustic segments that correspond to linguistic units (Levin et al., 2013; Bengio and Heigold, 2014; Kamper et al., 2016b; Settle and Livescu, 2016a, *inter alia*). A notable example of such representations are acoustic word embeddings (AWEs)—vector representations that encode the sound structure of words, not their semantic and syntactic structure—see Fig. 1. AWEs support voice-based speech technology applications such as query-by-example spoken term discovery (Zhang and Glass, 2009; Jansen and Durme, 2012; Metze et al., 2013) and keyword spotting (Myers et al., 1980; Rohlicek, 1995). In addition, AWEs can be leveraged to facilitate access to speech recordings of endangered spoken languages that might lack standardized writing systems (Bird, 2021; San et al., 2021)

However, there are fundamental differences be-

Proceedings of the Fifth BlackboxNLP Workshop on Analyzing and Interpreting Neural Networks for NLP, pages 178 - 191
December 8, 2022 ©2022 Association for Computational Linguistics

tween text-based and speech-based word embeddings that have to do with the degree of variability between the two modalities. Contrary to written words which have context-invariant orthographic realizations,[1] spoken words are notoriously variable. The underlying sources of variability in speech include speaker-related factors such as vocal tract shape, gender, age, and dialect. In addition, two acoustic instances, or exemplars, of the same word will vary in different phonological and semantic contexts even if they are produced by the same speaker (Jurafsky, 2003). Therefore, acoustic word embeddings are not static, but have to be computed "on the fly" given a speech segment as input. Models of AWEs need to abstract away from speaker and context variability to project different acoustic exemplars of the same word onto (ideally) the same point of the embedding space.

Nevertheless, AWEs have not yet been extensively studied in the literature from a neural network interpretability point of view. We are only aware of a few prior efforts in this direction that have either analyzed the representational geometry of AWEs from a cognitively motivated angle (Matusevych et al., 2020a; Abdullah et al., 2021a) or from a cross-linguistic perspective (Abdullah et al., 2021b). In this paper, we make a contribution in this direction and use analytic techniques from machine learning and neuroscience in three different analytic studies: embedding space uniformity (§4), word discriminability (§5), and representational consistency (§6).

2 Acoustic Word Embedding Models

Given an acoustic signal that corresponds to a spoken word represented as a temporal sequence of T acoustic feature vectors, i.e., $\boldsymbol{a} = (\boldsymbol{a}^1, \boldsymbol{a}^2, ..., \boldsymbol{a}^T)$, the goal of an AWE model is to transform $\boldsymbol{a}$ into a fixed-dimensionality vector representation e. Due to the variability in speech production (i.e., speech rate, emotional state, etc), the length of the acoustic segment T varies between different exemplars, or instances, of the same word type. Therefore, this task is modeled as a mapping $\mathcal{F} : \mathcal{A} \rightarrow \mathbb{R}^D$, where $\mathcal{A}$ is the (continuous) space of acoustic sequences and D is the dimensionality of the embedding. Formally, transforming a variable-length acoustic input into a D-dimensional AWE is described as

$$\mathrm{e} = \mathcal{F}(\boldsymbol{a}; \boldsymbol{\theta}_\mathcal{F}) \in \mathbb{R}^D \tag{1}$$

[1]although some orthographic variation exists in informal, user-generated text such as tweets.

where $\boldsymbol{\theta}_\mathcal{F}$ are the parameters of the encoder function $\mathcal{F}$. In a supervised setting of training AWE models, one assumes a dataset $\mathcal{D} = \{(\boldsymbol{a}_1, w_1), (\boldsymbol{a}_2, w_2), \ldots, (\boldsymbol{a}_N, w_N)\}$ of N spoken word instances where w_i is the word type, or lexical category, of the ith acoustic sample. In this paper, we experiment with two architectural choices—recurrent and convolutional—and employ four different learning objectives for training AWE models from the literature. Next, we formally describe each of the objectives.

2.1 Correspondence Autoencoder

In the correspondence autoencoder (CAE) (Kamper, 2019), each training acoustic word sample $\boldsymbol{a}$ is paired with another sample that corresponds to the same word type $\boldsymbol{a}_+ = (\boldsymbol{a}_+^1, \boldsymbol{a}_+^2, ..., \boldsymbol{a}_+^S)$. The acoustic encoder $\mathcal{F}$ takes $\boldsymbol{a}$ as input and produces an embedding e, which is then fed to an acoustic decoder $\mathcal{H}$ that aims to sequentially reconstruct the corresponding acoustic sequence $\boldsymbol{a}_+$—see Fig. 6(a). The objective is to minimize the L_2 distance at each timestep in the decoder, which is equivalent to

$$J = \sum_{i=1}^{S} \|\boldsymbol{a}_+^i - \mathcal{H}^i(\mathrm{e})\|_2 \tag{2}$$

where $\boldsymbol{a}_i^+$ is the ground-truth acoustic feature vector at timestep i and $\mathcal{H}_i(\mathrm{e})$ is the reconstructed acoustic vector at timestep i as a function of the embedding e. Learning the correspondence between different acoustic realizations of the same word type seems to encourage the encoder to build up speaker-invariant word representations while preserving linguistically-relevant phonetic information (Matusevych et al., 2020b). When the target acoustic sequence to generate is the same as the input signal $\boldsymbol{a}$, this corresponds to a conventional autoencoder (AE) which we consider as one of our learning objectives in this paper.

2.2 Phonologically Guided Encoder

The phonologically guided encoder (PGE) is trained as component in a sequence-to-sequence model to map acoustics into phonology (Abdullah et al., 2021a). Given the output of the encoder as an embedding e, a phonological decoder $\mathcal{G}(.; \boldsymbol{\theta}_\mathcal{G})$ is trained to decode the corresponding phonological sequence $\boldsymbol{\varphi} = (\varphi^1, \ldots, \varphi^\tau)$ of the word-form —see Fig. 6(b). The objective is to minimize a categorical cross-entropy loss at each decoder timestep, which is equivalent to minimizing the term

$$J = -\sum_{(a_i,w_i)\in\mathcal{D}} \log \mathbf{P}(\varphi|\mathbf{e}_i;\boldsymbol{\theta}_{\mathcal{G}}) = -\sum_{(a_i,w_i)\in\mathcal{D}} \sum_{t=1}^{\mathcal{T}} \log \mathbf{P}(\varphi^t|t,\mathbf{e}_i;\boldsymbol{\theta}_{\mathcal{G}}) \tag{3}$$

where $\mathbf{P}(\varphi^t|t,\mathbf{e}_i;\boldsymbol{\theta}_{\mathcal{G}})$ is the probability of the phoneme φ^t at the tth timestep, conditioned on the previous phoneme sequence $\varphi^{<t}$ and the AWE $\mathbf{e}$, and $\boldsymbol{\theta}_{\mathcal{G}}$ are the parameters of the decoder. The intuition of this learning objective is the following: although their acoustic realizations vary due to speaker and context variability, different exemplars of the same word category would have identical phonological sequences. We thus expect the encoder to project exemplars of the same lexical category nearby in the embedding space while embedding similarity in the vector space should correlate with phonological similarity.

2.3 Contrastive Siamese Encoder

The contrastive siamese encoder (CSE) has been explored in the context of AWEs with both recurrent and convolutional architectures in several studies (Settle and Livescu, 2016b; Kamper et al., 2016a; Jacobs et al., 2021). Contrary to the previously described objectives, the CSE explicitly minimizes the distance between exemplar embeddings of the same word type—see Fig. 6(c). First, each acoustic word instance is paired with another instance of the same word type $(\boldsymbol{a}, \boldsymbol{a}_+)$. Given their embeddings $(\mathbf{e}_a, \mathbf{e}_+)$, the objective is then to minimize a triplet margin loss

$$J = \max\left[0, m + d(\mathbf{e}_a, \mathbf{e}_+) - d(\mathbf{e}_a, \mathbf{e}_-)\right] \tag{4}$$

Here, $d(.,.)$ is the cosine distance and $\mathbf{e}_-$ is an AWE that corresponds to a different word type sampled from the mini-batch such that the term $d(\mathbf{e}_a, \mathbf{e}_-)$ is minimized. This objective clusters acoustic instances of the same word type closer in the embedding space while pushing away instances of other word types by a distance defined by the margin hyperparameter m.

3 Data, Setup, and Intrinsic Evaluation

3.1 Experimental Data

The data in our study is drawn from the the LibriSpeech dataset which contains read speech recordings of American-English (Panayotov et al., 2015), which is a public dataset under the CC BY 4.0 license. We sample 384 speakers from for training and 128 for evaluation—disjoint sets—and obtain word-aligned speech samples using the Montreal Forced Aligner (McAuliffe et al., 2017). To make our models comparable with prior work, which has focused on AWEs for low-resource languages, we sample $\sim$ 39.4k samples for training and $\sim$ 9.7k for evaluation. The phonetic transcription for each word is produced using the online *WebMaus* G2P tool (Strunk et al., 2014). Then, each acoustic segment is parametrized as a sequence of 39-dimensional Mel-frequency spectral coefficients of 25ms frames with 15ms overlap—the conventional feature representation of speech in automatic speech recognition (ASR). It is worth pointing out that in this paper we consider each morphological variant of a lexeme as a separate lexical category. For example, different inflections of the lexeme MAKE such as {MADE, MAKING, MAKER, etc.} represent different lexical categories, each with its own exemplars.

3.2 Architectures, Hyperparameters, and Training Details

CNN Acoustic Encoder. We employ a 3-layer temporal convolutional network (1D-CNN) with 256, 384, and 512 filters and widths of 4, 8, and 16 for each layer and keep stride step at 1. Following each convolutional operation, we apply batch normalization, ReLU non-linearity, and dropout. We apply average pooling to downsample the representation at the end of the convolution block, then apply one non-linear layer with Tanh on the CNN output, which yields a 512-dimensional AWE.

RNN Acoustic Encoder. We employ a 3-layer directional Gated Recurrent Unit (GRU) with a hidden state dimension of 512, then apply one non-linear layer with Tanh on the GRU output, which yields a 512-dimensional AWE. We apply layer-wise dropout with a probability of 0.1.

Phonological Decoder $\mathcal{G}(.;\boldsymbol{\theta}_{\mathcal{G}})$. We employ a 1-layer GRU of 512 units hidden state that takes the 512-dimensional AWE as the initial hidden state and decodes the corresponding phonological sequence without teacher forcing.

Acoustic Decoder $\mathcal{H}(.;\boldsymbol{\theta}_{\mathcal{H}})$. We employ a 1-layer GRU of 512 units hidden state that takes the 512-dimensional AWE as the initial hidden state and decodes the corresponding acoustic sequence with a teacher forcing ratio of 0.2.

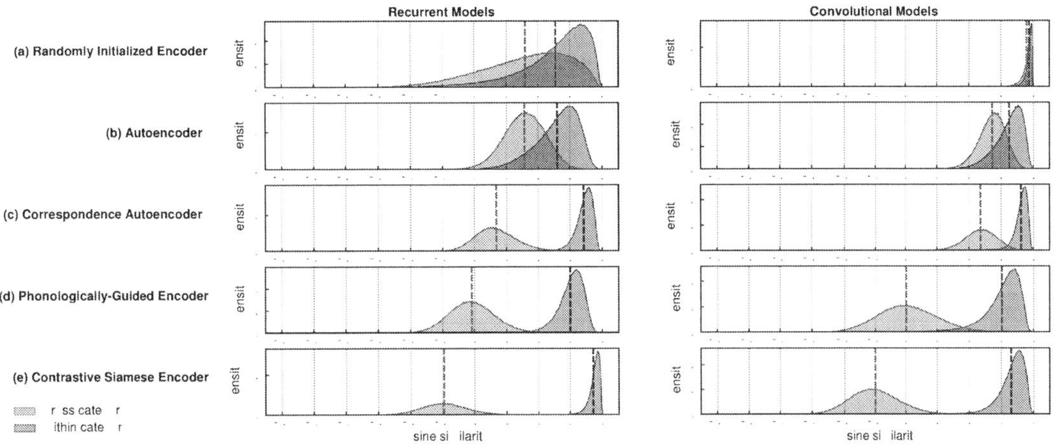

Figure 2: Distribution of cosine similarity scores of the different models for within category samples (i.e., exemplar pairs of the same word type) and cross-category samples (i.e., sample pairs that correspond to different word types). Each row in the figure corresponds to one learning objective and each column corresponds to one architecture.

Contrastive Loss. For the CSE, we experiment with different values of the margin hyperparameter $m = \{0.2, 0.3, 0.4, 0.5\}$, out of which 0.4 yields the best performance on the validation set.

Training Details. All models in this study are randomly initialized with each parameter drawn uniformly from $[-0.05, 0.05]$. Then, each model is trained for 100 epochs with a batch size of 256 using the ADAM optimizer (Kingma and Ba, 2015) and an initial learning rate of 0.001. The learning rate is reduced by a factor of 0.5 if the mAP on the validation set does not improve for 10 epochs.

Implementation. We build our models using PyTorch (Paszke et al., 2019) and use FAISS (Johnson et al., 2017) for efficient similarity search. Our code is based on our prior work in building and analyzing AWEs (Abdullah et al., 2021a,b).

3.3 Quantitative Evaluation

We conduct an intrinsic evaluation for the AWEs to assess the performance of our models using the same-different acoustic word discrimination task with the mean average precision (mAP) metric (Carlin et al., 2011; Kamper et al., 2015; Settle et al., 2019; Algayres et al., 2020). This task evaluates the ability of the model to determine whether two given speech segments correspond to the same word type—that is, whether or not two acoustic segments are exemplars of the same category. The results of the evaluation is shown in Fig. 7 in the appendix. We observe that each recurrent encoder outperforms its convolutional counterpart within each objective. Moreover, the performance largely depends on the strength of the supervision signal where the contrastive encoders outperform other objectives that lack explicit loss to group exemplars of the same category closer in the embedding space.

4 Analysis 1: Embedding Space Uniformity

In our first analysis, we take a closer look at how uniform are representational spaces of AWE models by analyzing the distribution of cosine similarity for each model type and the degree to which the embeddings are isotropic.

4.1 Distribution of Cosine Similarity

One way of analyzing the geometry of representation spaces in the acoustic domain is by inspecting the similarity distributions of exemplars of the same lexical category (or word type) versus randomly sampled, cross-category exemplars. We perform this analysis on the training samples and depict the result in Fig. 2. We observe that the difference between the means of the within-category and those of cross-category distributions is largely dependent on the strength of the supervision signal with the randomly initialized encoders (RIE) having the smallest mean differences for both architectures. The contrastive encoders have the largest mean difference–with mean cross-category scores centered at the zero—which is intuitive given the explicit supervision signal they receive in grouping exemplars of the same category closer in the embedding space. One surprising observation is the

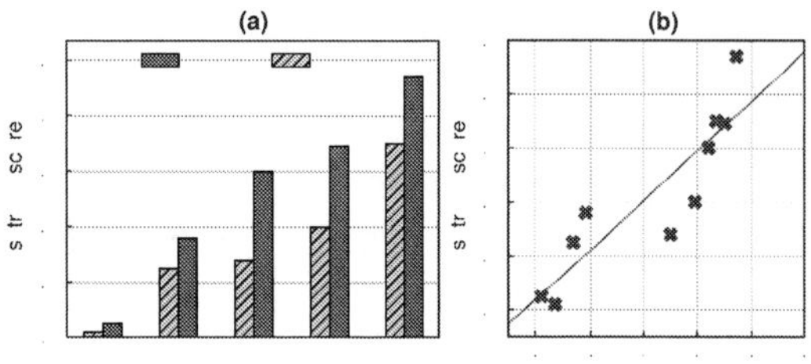

Figure 3: (a). The degree of isotropy of AWE for each model. (b) Correlation between the word discrimination performance measured by mAP and isotropy score (Pearson $r = 0.89, p < 0.001$).

behavior of the untrained convolutional encoder which gives cosine similarity scores very close to 1 for each input pair. In appendix C, we demonstrate that this behavior is mainly caused by the unbounded activation function (i.e., ReLU) in the convolutional layers.

4.2 Degree of Isotropy

Although inspecting the cosine similarity distributions is an insightful analysis, it does not enable us to make well-informed judgments about the uniformity of the representation spaces. Here, we ask two questions: (1) do AWE models utilize all dimensions of the vector space to represent the speech samples and separate the categories? and (2) how do architecture and learning objective affect the distributivity of information in the embedding space? To answer these questions, we inspect the degree of isotropy in the representation spaces. An embedding space is said to be maximally isotropic if the variance is uniformly distributed across all dimensions. Prior work in NLP has found that semantic word embeddings tend to be anisotropic since they only utilize a few dimensions of the vector space—an effect that has been observed for word embeddings that are static (Mimno and Thompson, 2017; Mu and Viswanath, 2018) as well as contextualized (Ethayarajh, 2019; Cai et al., 2020; Rudman et al., 2022). The degree of isotropy in acoustic embeddings, however, remains so far unknown. To inspect the degree of isotropy of the AWE vector spaces, we use the IsoScore metric recently proposed by Rudman et al. (2022), which is—to the best of our knowledge—the only metric in the literature that is grounded on the mathematical definition of isotropy. The IsoScore metric operates on the covariance matrix of the embedding dimensions and returns values between 0 (minimally isotropic) and 1 (maximally isotropic). We quantify the degree of isotropy using IsoScore for each model type and show the result in Fig. 3(a). We observe that IsoScore returns values that are within the range $[0.002, 0.095]$, which indicates that embedding spaces for all models tend towards being minimally isotropic. However, the embeddings of untrained, randomly initialized encoders (RIE) tend to be extremely anisotropic (i.e., IsoScore values close to 0). This observation suggests that the anisotropic space does not "emerge" during the model training but rather that it is an inherent property of the encoder architecture. We are not aware of prior work in NLP that has studied the degree of isotropy in untrained NLP models to investigate whether anisotropic spaces are an emergent or inherent feature. In our case, training with a learning objective that encourages the model to separate word categories moves the representation space more towards utilizing more dimensions, therefore resulting in a higher degree of isotropy. Moreover, recurrent encoders tend to be more isotropic than their convolutional counterparts within the same learning objective.

Despite the tendency of all models to be anisotropic, we find a strong positive correlation between the degree of isotropy and the performance on word discrimination—see Fig. 3(b). That is, the more dimensions the model utilizes in the representation space, the better it performs on the intrinsic evaluation task.

5 Analysis 2: Word Discriminability

Ideally, AWE models should project exemplars of the same word category onto the same point in the embedding space. However, there are no strong constraints during training to encourage maximal separability between different word categories. In this analysis, we seek to answer two questions: (1) how well-separated are the word categories of the training samples? and (2) to what degree do lexical properties predict the discriminability of word categories?

5.1 Category Discriminability Index

In order to investigate the geometric density of each word category in the representation space, we need to measure within-category compactness and cross-category separability. Inspired by the exemplar discriminability index proposed in the neuroscience literature (Nili et al., 2020), we define

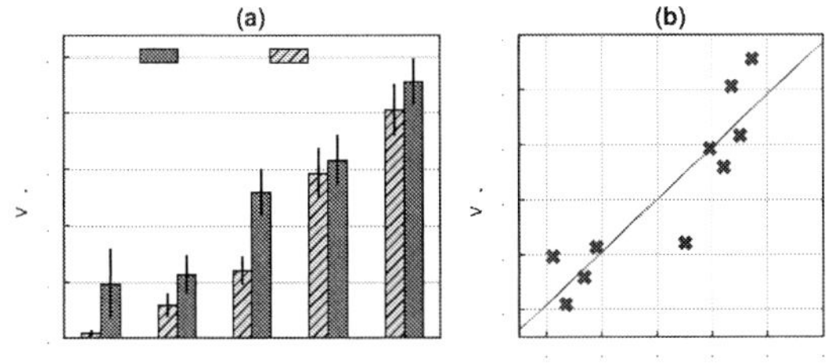

Figure 4: Averaged Category Discriminability Index (CDI) for each AWE model with error bars showing standard deviation over word categories. (b) Correlation between the word discrimination performance measured by mAP and averaged CDI (Pearson $r = 0.90, p < 0.001$).

category discriminability index (CDI) as a metric that operates on within-category and cross-category distances. If we consider each lexical category in the training set as a set of its exemplar embeddings $\mathcal{C} = \{\mathbf{e}_1, \dots, \mathbf{e}_{|\mathcal{C}|}\}$, CDI is defined for a single category $\mathcal{C}$ as

$$\text{CDI}(\mathcal{C}) = \frac{1}{|\mathcal{C}|} \sum_{\forall \mathbf{e}_i \in \mathcal{C}} \Big(\sum_{\forall \mathbf{e}_j \sim \mathcal{C} | j \neq i} d(\mathbf{e}_i, \tilde{\mathbf{e}}_j) - d(\mathbf{e}_i, \mathbf{e}_j) \Big) \quad (5)$$

where $d(.,.)$ is the cosine distance and $\mathbf{e}_j$ is a within-category sample while $\tilde{\mathbf{e}}_j$ is an embedding sampled from a different category. If we normalize the embeddings, CDI $\in [-1, 1]$ with values closer to 1 indicating higher word discriminability. We compute CDI for each word category in the training set and take the average over categories to estimate how well the categories are separated in the embedding space of each model type. The result of this analysis is shown in Fig. 4(a). For each learning objective, we observe that word discriminability is higher in the recurrent encoders compared to their convolutional counterparts. Besides that, the contrastive objective yields encoders with a higher word discriminability index regardless of the architecture type—recurrent vs. convolutional. Furthermore, we report a strong positive correlation between average CDI and the performance on the evaluation task—see Fig. 4(b), indicating that word discrimination performance on future, held-out samples can be predicted based on the CDI computed on the training samples.

5.2 Effect of Frequency and Distinctiveness

The CDI quantifies the separability and compactness for each lexical category in the representation space. Next, we aim to identify the factors that could make a lexical category compact and well-separable.

In this analysis, we study the effect of two lexical properties that could be quantified in a data-driven approach: word frequency and acoustic distinctiveness. Our initial hypothesis is that a word category with many training exemplars becomes more discriminable in the embedding space as the repeated exposure to samples of various degrees of variability should enable the model to learn compact and precise representation for categories with high frequency. Also, words that are acoustically distinct have fewer competitors in the perceptual space, thus they should be more separable than words with many phonological neighbours that sound similar. Therefore, we expect word acoustic distinctiveness (WAD) to positively correlate with CDI. In this analysis, we operationalize WAD using two metrics: word length (i.e., the number of phonemes) and phonological distinctiveness. Word length contributes to WAD since word formation in natural languages is a combinatorial process. That is, increasing the number of phonemes in a word-form decreases the likelihood of encountering a similarly sounding word-form which makes it less confusable. However, the word formation process is governed by language-specific phonotactic rules which makes some sound combinations more probable than others. To capture the probabilistic nature of sound sequences, we employ phonological information content (PIC), an information-theoretic metric that estimates WAD based on its phoneme-to-phoneme transition probabilities (Meylan and Griffiths, 2017). Given a word-form as a sequence of phonemes $\varphi = (\varphi_1, \dots, \varphi_T)$, PIC is defined as

$$\text{PIC}(\varphi) = -\sum_{i=1}^{T} \log p_{\theta}(\varphi_i | \varphi_{<i}) \quad (6)$$

where p_{θ} is a probabilistic phoneme-level language model (PLM). We estimate p_{θ} using a trigram PLM with the counts of the phonemes in the training word categories. Higher values of PIC indicate less probable phoneme sequences thus more distinct word-forms. Note that PIC is not length normalized and therefore shorter words tend to have lower PIC.

Next, we conduct a correlation analysis between word CDI and the three lexical predictors: fre-

Objective	Arch.	Frequency	Length	PIC
AE	CNN	-0.081†	0.315†	0.263†
	RNN	-0.087†	0.357†	0.306†
CAE	CNN	0.021	0.376†	0.274†
	RNN	0.077†	0.447†	0.359†
PGE	CNN	0.035	0.039*	-0.011
	RNN	-0.043*	0.325†	0.263†
CSE	CNN	0.131†	0.075†	0.031
	RNN	0.109†	0.100†	0.030

Table 1: Pearson correlation (r) between word category discriminability index (CDI) and three lexical properties: frequency, length, and phonological information content (PIC). Statistical significance is marked with * and † for $p < 0.05$ and $p < 0.001$, respectively.

quency, length, and PIC. The result of this analysis is shown in Table 1. Surprisingly, our correlation analysis shows that lexical frequency is a poor predictor of CDI. Although in five out of eight models the frequency positively correlates with CDI, the correlation is rather weak. However, measures of acoustic distinctiveness have a stronger correlation with CDI compared to frequency, and the strength of the correlation is more noticeable in all decoding-based models—except the convolutional PGE—compared to contrastive models. We also find it surprising that PIC is not a better predictor of CDI than word length. However, it has been shown in a related work that autoencoder-based AWEs encode duration as an acoustic feature (Matusevych et al., 2021). Taken together with our findings, this suggests that the models exploit and rely on acoustic word length as a feature to discriminate between the lexical categories. Arguably, word length is a more accessible feature to learn from the acoustic signal compared to structural phonological regularities in the training data.

6 Analysis 3: Network Representational Consistency

Suppose we train two instances of the same architecture and learning objective on the same training samples, but each with different random initializations. Do these two neural network instances exhibit differences in their representational geometries? In this section, we shed light on the representational discrepancies caused by different initializations. In other words, we are interested in quantifying the degree to which variability in the initial conditions affects the way two models separate the same set of speech samples.

6.1 Performance Stability

First, we quantify the effect of the initial weights on the evaluation task performance. To this end, we train six model instances—in identical setup but with different initializations—for each architecture and each learning objective, which yields 48 model instances in total (6×4 RNN runs and 6×4 CNN runs). We evaluate each model instance on the acoustic word discrimination task while observing the result variation per model type. The result of the performance stability analysis is shown in Table 2 in Appendix D. We observe that all instances have converged and the performance is fairly stable across different runs.

6.2 Representational Discrepancies

Our previous performance stability analysis has demonstrated that different DNN instances exhibit only trivial quantitative differences. However, a stable performance on the evaluation task does not entail an identical representational geometry across different instances. That is, two network instances could have have an identical performance on the evaluation task while each having a distinct representational geometry. To closely investigate representational discrepancies between network instances, we employ the representational consistency (RC) analysis (Mehrer et al., 2020), which is a neuroscience-inspired technique based on the representational similarity analysis (RSA) framework (Kriegeskorte et al., 2008). For our analysis, we operationalize the RC using linear Centered Kernal Alignment (CKA) as a representational similarity measure of two views of the same input samples (Kornblith et al., 2019). CKA abstracts away from the embeddings themselves and operates on pairwise distances between the sample representations. Concretely, given K spoken-word samples $\boldsymbol{a}_1^K = \{\boldsymbol{a}_1, \ldots, \boldsymbol{a}_K\}$, we embed the samples using two encoder instances to obtain two different views of the samples $\mathbf{X} \in \mathbb{R}^{K \times D}$ and $\mathbf{Y} \in \mathbb{R}^{K \times D}$. Then, each view matrix is multiplied by a centering matrix $\mathbf{H} = \mathbf{I}_K - \mathbf{1}_K / K$ to make each column's mean equal to zero and obtain centered second moment matrices as

$$\begin{aligned} \mathbf{G_X} &= \mathbf{H}\mathbf{X}\mathbf{X}^\top\mathbf{H}^\top / D, \\ \mathbf{G_Y} &= \mathbf{H}\mathbf{Y}\mathbf{Y}^\top\mathbf{H}^\top / D \end{aligned} \tag{7}$$

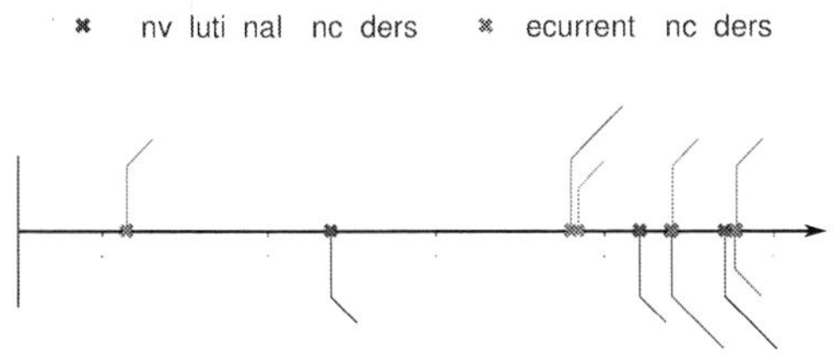

Figure 5: Network representational consistency (RC): (top) recurrent encoders and (bottom) convolutional encoders. Values closer to 1 indicates higher RC.

Then, the representational similarity of the two views is computed using CKA as

$$\text{CKA}(\mathbf{X}, \mathbf{Y}) = \frac{\langle \text{vec}(\mathbf{G_X}), \text{vec}(\mathbf{G_Y}) \rangle}{||\mathbf{G_X}||_F ||\mathbf{G_Y}||_F} \quad (8)$$

where vec(.) is the vector-reshaped matrix, $\langle ., . \rangle$ is the inner product, and $||.||_F$ is the Frobenius norm to ensure that CKA $\in [0, 1]$ where values close to 1 indicate that the two instances are highly consistent, while values close to 0 indicate low consistency.

Using CKA, we conduct pairwise similarity analysis across all six instances which yields 15 comparisons for each model type. We report the mean of the resulting CKA values for each model type in Fig. 5. First, we observe that randomly initialized encoders (RIE) are highly consistent for both architectures (mean $\text{CKA}_{RIE/RNN} \approx$ mean $\text{CKA}_{RIE/CNN} = 0.98$). However, after training the encoder instances, convolutional networks are more consistent than their recurrent counterparts. Note that this behaviour cannot be attributed to a difference in the number of trainable parameters between the two architectures since they are comparable. Moreover, all decoding-based learning objectives return mean CKA values above 0.87, which indicates that their representational profiles are similar despite some noticeable differences especially among the recurrent encoders. The only exception to this trend are model instances trained with contrastive loss since they are significantly less consistent compared to the other learning objectives (mean $\text{CKA}_{CSE/RNN} = 0.61$ and mean $\text{CKA}_{CSE/CNN} = 0.74$). We emphasize that CKA is a second-order isomorphismic approach that operates on the similarity of the pairwise sample similarity matrices across different views. Therefore, the anisotropic nature of AWEs reported in §4 cannot explain their similarity-based representational profiles, and by implication, their representational consistency.

7 Discussion

Acoustic word embeddings (AWEs) are vector representations that encode the sound structure and acoustic-phonetic features of spoken words. AWEs are induced from actual acoustic realizations of speech, and therefore AWE models have to abstract away from non-linguistic dimensions of variability in speech signals (e.g., speaker characteristics, speech rate, recording conditions, etc). While analyzing the representational geometry of semantic word embeddings is a topic that has received a substantial attention in the NLP research community, the interpretability of AWEs remains an under-explored topic and we are aware of a few prior studies in this direction (Matusevych et al., 2020b; Abdullah et al., 2021a,b). In this article, we made a number contributions in analyzing the representational geometry of AWEs and obtained research findings which we discuss and summarize in this section.

Learning objective affects the geometry more than architecture. Our three analyses in this paper have shown that the learning objective shapes the representational geometry of the AWE encoders more than their underlying architectures. This finding suggests that recurrent and convolutional encoders exhibit similar inductive biases while the learning process is mainly guided by the loss function.

AWE models tend to be anisotropic. Our analysis in §4 has shown that AWEs tend towards being minimally isotropic. However, this behavior is not an emergent property of the training process, but rather an inherent behavior of the neural network. Moreover, the degree of isotropy after training the model positively correlates with the acoustic word discrimination evaluation task. Since different models have different degree of isotropy and the representation space is not always uniform, we conclude that any comparison between different models based on absolute distance metrics such cosine distance will definitely lead to inaccurate observations.

Word distinctiveness, but not frequency, predicts category discriminability. While word acoustic distinctiveness has been found in §5 to be a good predictor of the degree to which a word category is compact and well-separated in the embedding space, word frequency does not correlate with category discriminability. In retrospective, this finding should not be surprising as frequent words tend to have shorter lengths. Shorter words have more phonological neighbours that are perceptually similar in form and thus they are more confusable with other words. Future work could employ more sophisticated linear mixed effects models to analyse the interaction between different lexical properties such as frequency, phonological neighbourhood density, and word length and their effect on word category discriminability.

AWE models exhibit individual differences. Although AWE model instances trained with different random initializations are stable with respect to the performance of the evaluation task, they exhibit individual differences in their representational profiles as shown in §6. However, the degree of the network representational consistency across different initializations depends on both the architecture and the learning objective. Contrastive objectives are less consistent than decoding-based objectives, while recurrent encoder are less consistent than their convolutional counterparts.

Contrastive models have distinct representational profiles. In the analyses we presented in this paper, we observed that the contrastive encoders behave differently than other encoders trained with non-contrastive losses. For example, word distinctiveness has been found to be a weak predictor of category discriminability in the embedding spaces of the contrastive encoders. Recall that our contrastive encoders have a stronger constraint in grouping exemplars of the same category closer in the embedding space guided by the margin hyperparameter, while decoding-based model lack this constraint. We hypothesize that this constraint forces the models to emphasize the separability of the lexical categories in the embedding space. Therefore, a stronger constraint seems to make contrastive encoders different compared to other learning objectives and different instances of the same contrastive encoder are less consistent in their representational geometry.

8 Conclusion

In this paper, we have taken a closer, analytical look at the representational geometry of acoustic word embeddings (AWEs) from three different, but complementary perspectives: (1) embedding space uniformity, (2) word discriminability, and (3) network representational consistency. We have shown that the representational spaces of AWEs tend towards being minimally isotropic, or in other words, they utilize only a few dimensions of the embedding space. Another finding was that most AWE models rely on word length as a feature to discriminate between lexical categories since the word discriminability index positively correlates with the number of phonemes in a word. Furthermore, our representational consistency analysis have shown that AWE models exhibit individual differences in their representational profiles, with the contrastive encoders being the most inconsistent across different random initializations.

Even though we focused on acoustic word embeddings in this paper, our analytic methodology can also be employed for the interpretability of self-supervised speech representation models such as contrastive predictive coding (Oord et al., 2018) and wav2vec (Schneider et al., 2019). Also, the emergent representations of sublexical units such phonemes and syllables in speech neural networks can be analyzed using the our proposed methodology in this paper.

9 Acknowledgements

The authors would like to thank the anonymous reviewers for their encouraging feedback and insightful comments on the paper. We express our heartfelt thanks to Miriam Schulz for proofreading the paper. This research is funded by the Deutsche Forschungsgemeinschaft (DFG, German Research Foundation), Project-ID 232722074 – SFB 1102.

References

Badr M. Abdullah, Marius Mosbach, Iuliia Zaitova, Bernd Mobius, and Dietrich Klakow. 2021a. Do acoustic word embeddings capture phonological similarity? An empirical study. In *Interspeech*.

Badr M. Abdullah, Iuliia Zaitova, Tania Avgustinova, Bernd Möbius, and Dietrich Klakow. 2021b. How familiar does that sound? cross-lingual representational similarity analysis of acoustic word embeddings. In *Proceedings of the Fourth BlackboxNLP Workshop on Analyzing and Interpreting Neural Networks for NLP*, pages 407–419, Punta Cana, Dominican Republic. Association for Computational Linguistics.

Robin Algayres, Mohamed Salah Zaiem, Benoît Sagot, and Emmanuel Dupoux. 2020. Evaluating the Reliability of Acoustic Speech Embeddings. In *Proc. Interspeech*.

Samy Bengio and Georg Heigold. 2014. Word embeddings for speech recognition. In *Proc. Interspeech*.

Steven Bird. 2021. Sparse transcription. *Computational Linguistics*, 46(4):713–744.

Xingyu Cai, Jiaji Huang, Yuchen Bian, and Kenneth Church. 2020. Isotropy in the contextual embedding space: Clusters and manifolds. In *International Conference on Learning Representations*.

Michael A Carlin, Samuel Thomas, Aren Jansen, and Hynek Hermansky. 2011. Rapid evaluation of speech representations for spoken term discovery. In *Proc. Interspeech*.

Kawin Ethayarajh. 2019. How contextual are contextualized word representations? Comparing the geometry of BERT, ELMo, and GPT-2 embeddings. In *Proceedings of the 2019 Conference on Empirical Methods in Natural Language Processing and the 9th International Joint Conference on Natural Language Processing (EMNLP-IJCNLP)*, pages 55–65, Hong Kong, China. Association for Computational Linguistics.

Gabriel Grand, Idan Asher Blank, Francisco Pereira, and Evelina Fedorenko. 2022. Semantic projection recovers rich human knowledge of multiple object features from word embeddings. *Nature Human Behaviour*, pages 1–13.

Christiaan Jacobs, Yevgen Matusevych, and Herman Kamper. 2021. Acoustic word embeddings for zero-resource languages using self-supervised contrastive learning and multilingual adaptation. In *2021 IEEE Spoken Language Technology Workshop (SLT)*, pages 919–926. IEEE.

Aren Jansen and Benjamin Van Durme. 2012. Indexing raw acoustic features for scalable zero resource search. In *Proc. Interspeech*.

Jeff Johnson, Matthijs Douze, and Hervé Jégou. 2017. Billion-scale similarity search with GPUs. *IEEE Transactions on Big Data*.

Dan Jurafsky. 2003. Probabilistic modeling in psycholinguistics: Linguistic comprehension and production. *Probabilistic linguistics*, 21.

H. Kamper, W. Wang, and Karen Livescu. 2016a. Deep convolutional acoustic word embeddings using word-pair side information. In *Proc. ICASSP*.

Herman Kamper. 2019. Truly unsupervised acoustic word embeddings using weak top-down constraints in encoder-decoder models. In *Proc. ICASSP*.

Herman Kamper, Micha Elsner, Aren Jansen, and Sharon Goldwater. 2015. Unsupervised neural network based feature extraction using weak top-down constraints. In *Proc. ICASSP*.

Herman Kamper, Weiran Wang, and Karen Livescu. 2016b. Deep convolutional acoustic word embeddings using word-pair side information. In *Proc. ICASSP*.

Diederik P. Kingma and Jimmy Ba. 2015. Adam: A method for stochastic optimization. In *Proc. ICLR*.

Simon Kornblith, Mohammad Norouzi, Honglak Lee, and Geoffrey Hinton. 2019. Similarity of neural network representations revisited. In *International Conference on Machine Learning*, pages 3519–3529. PMLR.

Nikolaus Kriegeskorte, Marieke Mur, and Peter A Bandettini. 2008. Representational similarity analysis-connecting the branches of systems neuroscience. *Frontiers in systems neuroscience*, 2:4.

Keith Levin, Katharine Henry, Aren Jansen, and Karen Livescu. 2013. Fixed-dimensional acoustic embeddings of variable-length segments in low-resource settings. In *IEEE Workshop on Automatic Speech Recognition and Understanding (ASRU)*.

Yevgen Matusevych, Herman Kamper, and Sharon Goldwater. 2020a. Analyzing autoencoder-based acoustic word embeddings. In *BAICS Workshop ICLR*.

Yevgen Matusevych, Herman Kamper, and Sharon Goldwater. 2020b. Analyzing autoencoder-based acoustic word embeddings. In *Bridging AI and Cognitive Science Workshop, ICLR 2020*.

Yevgen Matusevych, Herman Kamper, Thomas Schatz, Naomi Feldman, and Sharon Goldwater. 2021. A phonetic model of non-native spoken word processing. In *Proceedings of the 16th Conference of the European Chapter of the Association for Computational Linguistics: Main Volume*, pages 1480–1490, Online. Association for Computational Linguistics.

Michael McAuliffe, Michaela Socolof, Sarah Mihuc, Michael Wagner, and Morgan Sonderegger. 2017. Montreal Forced Aligner: Trainable text-speech alignment using Kaldi. In *Interspeech*.

Leland McInnes, John Healy, Nathaniel Saul, and Lukas Großberger. 2018. Umap: Uniform manifold approximation and projection. *Journal of Open Source Software*, 3(29):861.

Johannes Mehrer, Courtney J Spoerer, Nikolaus Kriegeskorte, and Tim C Kietzmann. 2020. Individual differences among deep neural network models. *Nature communications*, 11(1):1–12.

Florian Metze, Xavier Anguera, Etienne Barnard, Marelie Davel, and Guillaume Gravier. 2013. The spoken web search task at MediaEval 2012. In *Proc. ICASSP*.

Stephan C. Meylan and Thomas L. Griffiths. 2017. Word forms - not just their lengths- are optimized for efficient communication. *ArXiv*, abs/1703.01694.

Tomas Mikolov, Ilya Sutskever, Kai Chen, Greg S Corrado, and Jeff Dean. 2013. Distributed representations of words and phrases and their compositionality. *Advances in neural information processing systems*, 26.

David Mimno and Laure Thompson. 2017. The strange geometry of skip-gram with negative sampling. In *Proceedings of the 2017 Conference on Empirical Methods in Natural Language Processing*, pages 2873–2878, Copenhagen, Denmark. Association for Computational Linguistics.

Jiaqi Mu and Pramod Viswanath. 2018. All-but-the-top: Simple and effective postprocessing for word representations. In *International Conference on Learning Representations*.

Cory Myers, Lawrence Rabiner, and Andrew Rosenberg. 1980. An investigation of the use of dynamic time warping for word spotting and connected speech recognition. In *ICASSP'80. IEEE International Conference on Acoustics, Speech, and Signal Processing*, volume 5, pages 173–177. IEEE.

Aida Nematzadeh, Stephan C. Meylan, and Thomas L. Griffiths. 2017. Evaluating vector-space models of word representation, or, the unreasonable effectiveness of counting words near other words. *Cognitive Science*.

Hamed Nili, Alexander Walther, Arjen Alink, and Nikolaus Kriegeskorte. 2020. Inferring exemplar discriminability in brain representations. *Plos one*, 15(6):e0232551.

Aaron van den Oord, Yazhe Li, and Oriol Vinyals. 2018. Representation learning with contrastive predictive coding. *arXiv preprint arXiv:1807.03748*.

Vassil Panayotov, Guoguo Chen, Daniel Povey, and Sanjeev Khudanpur. 2015. Librispeech: an asr corpus based on public domain audio books. In *2015 IEEE international conference on acoustics, speech and signal processing (ICASSP)*, pages 5206–5210. IEEE.

Adam Paszke, Sam Gross, Francisco Massa, Adam Lerer, James Bradbury, Gregory Chanan, Trevor Killeen, Zeming Lin, Natalia Gimelshein, Luca Antiga, et al. 2019. Pytorch: An imperative style, high-performance deep learning library. In *Proc. NeuRIPS*.

Jeffrey Pennington, Richard Socher, and Christopher D Manning. 2014. Glove: Global vectors for word representation. In *Proceedings of the 2014 conference on empirical methods in natural language processing (EMNLP)*, pages 1532–1543.

Francisco Pereira, Samuel Gershman, Samuel Ritter, and Matthew Botvinick. 2016. A comparative evaluation of off-the-shelf distributed semantic representations for modelling behavioural data. *Cognitive neuropsychology*, 33(3-4):175–190.

Jan Robin Rohlicek. 1995. Word spotting. In *Modern Methods of Speech Processing*, pages 123–157. Springer.

William Rudman, Nate Gillman, Taylor Rayne, and Carsten Eickhoff. 2022. IsoScore: Measuring the uniformity of embedding space utilization. In *Findings of the Association for Computational Linguistics: ACL 2022*, pages 3325–3339, Dublin, Ireland. Association for Computational Linguistics.

Nay San, Martijn Bartelds, Mitchell Browne, Lily Clifford, Fiona Gibson, John Mansfield, David Nash, Jane Simpson, Myfany Turpin, Maria Vollmer, et al. 2021. Leveraging pre-trained representations to improve access to untranscribed speech from endangered languages. In *2021 IEEE Automatic Speech Recognition and Understanding Workshop (ASRU)*, pages 1094–1101. IEEE.

Steffen Schneider, Alexei Baevski, Ronan Collobert, and Michael Auli. 2019. wav2vec: Unsupervised pre-training for speech recognition. *arXiv preprint arXiv:1904.05862*.

Shane Settle, Kartik Audhkhasi, Karen Livescu, and Michael Picheny. 2019. Acoustically grounded word embeddings for improved acoustics-to-word speech recognition. In *Proc. ICASSP*.

Shane Settle and Karen Livescu. 2016a. Discriminative acoustic word embeddings: Recurrent neural network-based approaches. In *IEEE Spoken Language Technology Workshop (SLT)*.

Shane Settle and Karen Livescu. 2016b. Discriminative acoustic word embeddings: Recurrent neural network-based approaches. In *Proc. IEEE Spoken Language Technology Workshop (SLT)*.

Jan Strunk, Florian Schiel, and Frank Seifart. 2014. Untrained forced alignment of transcriptions and audio for language documentation corpora using webmaus. In *Proceedings of the Ninth International Conference on Language Resources and Evaluation (LREC'14)*, pages 3940–3947.

Yaodong Zhang and James R Glass. 2009. Unsupervised spoken keyword spotting via segmental DTW on Gaussian posteriorgrams. In *IEEE Workshop on Automatic Speech Recognition & Understanding (ASRU)*.

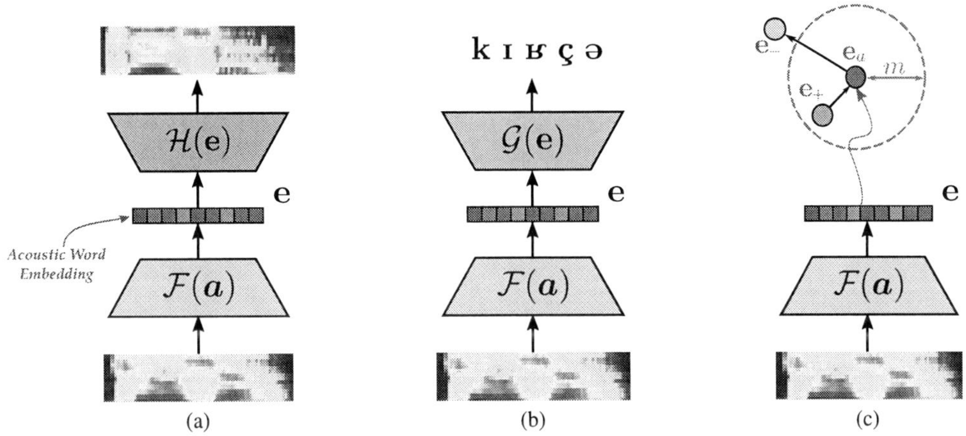

Figure 6: A visual illustration of the different learning objectives for training AWE encoders: (a) correspondence auto-encoder (CAE): a sequence-to-sequence network with an acoustic decoder, (b) phonologically guided encoder (PGE): a sequence-to-sequence network with a phonological decoder, and (c) contrastive siamese encoder (CSE): a contrastive network trained via triplet margin loss. After training the model, only the encoder component of the model $\mathcal{F}$ is used to produce AWEs.

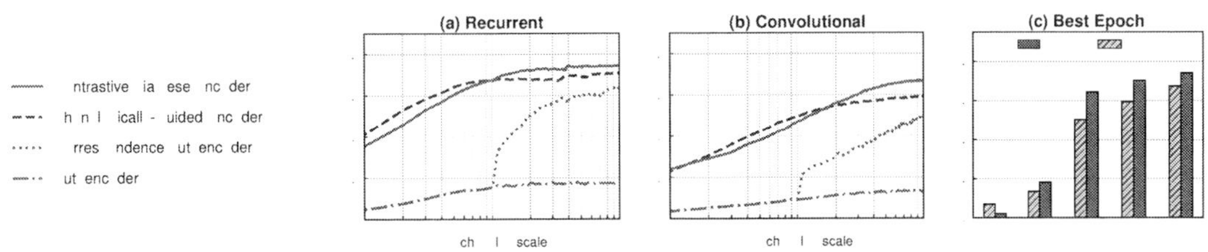

Figure 7: Evaluation on the same-different acoustic word discrimination task quantified by the word discrimination task and the mAP metric: Learning curves of 100 training epochs for (a) the recurrent encoder and (b) convolutional encoders. (c) mAP of the best epoch.

Appendices

A AWE Models

See Fig. 6 for a visual illustration of the different learning objectives in our paper.

B Intrinsic Evaluation

The results of the intrinsic evaluation—same-different word discrimination task quantified by the mAP metric—is shown in Fig. 7. Note that the CAE model is pre-trained as autoencoder for 10 epochs, following prior work (Kamper, 2019).

C Randomly Initialized CNN Encoder

To further investigate the minimally isotropic behavior and the near 1 values of cosine similarities of the untrained, randomly initialized convolutional encoder reported in §4, we examine the potential contribution of two factors to this observation; batch normalization (BN) and the activation function of the convolutional layers. The result of this analysis is depicted in Fig. 8. We observe that removing the BN layer has no effect on the distributions of cosine similarities as they remain almost identical to the encoder that has a BN layer—see Fig. 8(b). However, changing the activation function from the unbounded ReLU to the bounded Tanh in the convolutional layers makes the distributions of cosine similarities move towards zero mean, even though they remain closer to 1 than 0. Therefore, this behavior seems to be related to the inner dynamics of the convolutional operation and gets amplified where the activation function in the convolutional layers are unbounded. Nevertheless, identifying the source of this behavior requires further investigation with different activation functions and a controlled ablation study.

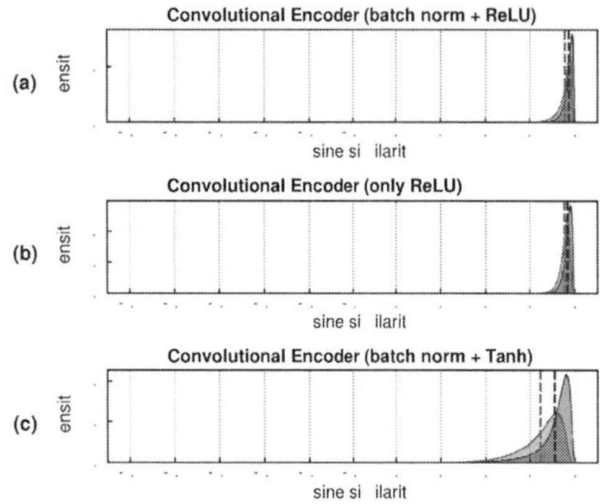

Figure 8: Cosine similarity distributions across three different variants of convolutional encoders: (a) convolutional layers with batch normalization and ReLU non-linearity, (b) convolutional layers with ReLU non-linearity but without batch normalization, and (3) convolutional layers with batch normalization and Tanh non-linearity.

D Performance Stability across Different Runs

For the analysis in §6, we have trained six neural network instances for each encoder type using the same training samples to investigate the performance stability and representational consistency of training runs that differ in their random seeds. A summary statistics for the performance on the evaluation task measured by the mAP metric is shown in Table 2. One can observe only trivial differences on the evaluation tasks. Therefore, we conclude that the performance of different training runs is stable and our findings on the network representational consistency reported in §6 cannot be explained by quantitative differences, but rather by representational discrepancies due to disagreement in the geometric arrangement of the speech samples in the embedding space.

E Qualitative Analysis

To further inspect the representation space and its neighborhood structure, we conduct a qualitative analysis by querying the representation space with a few word samples. In this analysis, we compute word category centroids by averaging the word embeddings of the training samples, then we use a word centroid as a query and obtain the top-10 ranked nearest neighbors. The result of this analysis is shown in Fig. 3. For the majority of the examples in Fig. 3, we observe that there is a strong word onset bias where the most similar words are those that begin with a similar sounding prefix as the query word.

Objective	Arch.	mean	max	min	std
AE	CNN	0.137	0.141	0.133	0.0026
	RNN	0.183	0.186	0.179	0.0024
CAE	CNN	0.505	0.510	0.500	0.0040
	RNN	0.646	0.650	0.643	0.0029
PGE	CNN	0.595	0.599	0.592	0.0033
	RNN	0.704	0.710	0.687	0.1000
CSE	CNN	0.676	0.680	0.674	0.0023
	RNN	0.742	0.745	0.739	0.0027

Table 2: mAP statistics across six different runs for each model type.

Query (↓)	Convolutional Encoders (CNN)				Recurrent Encoders (RNN)			
	AE	CAE	PGE	CSE	AE	CAE	PGE	CSE
mentioned	mention	mention	mention	mention	mention	mention	mention	mention
	wretched	mansion	mansion	mansion	wretched	mansion	mansion	mansion
	nation	motion	legends	merchant	nation	merchant	merchant	merchant
	midst	merchant	management	mission	merchant	motion	legends	mission
	merchants	making	merchants	mental	motion	nation	mountain	pinching
	motion	wilson	magic	vincent	merchants	making	merchants	massive
	merchant	nation	matrons	pinching	midst	vincent	mission	mental
	message	midst	mission	medicine	milking	nineteen	magician	transient
	regiment	missing	merchant	crouching	winter	nature	motion	motion
	winter	nature	magician	midst	vessel	rachel	wretched	hudson
intellectual	individual	introduction	intellect	intellect	individual	individual	individual	introduction
	interesting	individual	individual	adjoining	interesting	introduction	intelligence	individual
	indifferent	interrupted	introduction	recollection	neglected	uncomfortable	introduction	immature
	newton	indifference	intelligent	delightful	petition	intelligent	intellect	objection
	institution	attraction	encouragement	individual	magician	intelligence	uncomfortable	implacable
	departure	intellect	interrupted	employing	hokosa	interesting	intelligent	delightful
	imitation	immature	intelligence	impetuous	compassion	invisible	interpretation	theatrical
	hokosa	indifferent	indifferently	employed	departure	interrupted	industrial	thoughtful
	encountered	encouragingly	unconditional	natural	convention	imperfectly	incapable	industrial
	neglected	implacable	impetuous	accumulated	consulted	incredible	insensible	election
maker	labor	naked	naked	baker	labor	nature	baker	liquor
	liquor	natured	liquor	naked	nature	local	nature	negro
	labored	nature	natured	negro	walker	naked	liquor	eaten
	labour	local	nature	liquor	local	labour	labour	baker
	wicker	labour	baker	local	naked	labor	labor	nature
	leaping	major	major	native	labour	major	major	labor
	lifted	labor	negro	nature	rachel	natured	negro	naked
	walker	native	native	major	liquor	baker	neighbors	newspaper
	local	making	wicker	matrons	labored	liquor	vapor	mink
	nature	navy	labor	vigor	leaping	negro	labors	vigour
profession	position	procession	procession	professor	position	procession	procession	professor
	proceed	professor	professor	sufficient	professors	possession	proportion	procession
	positions	position	position	procession	possessions	position	perfection	perfection
	physician	possession	petition	professors	proceeded	professor	possession	sufficient
	proceeded	professors	pushing	efficiency	physician	possessions	protection	proposition
	possessed	pushing	professors	efficient	condition	permission	proportions	proportion
	prison	perfection	possession	petition	procession	discussion	position	production
	possessions	positions	physician	prevent	presumption	positions	possessions	petition
	perfect	discussion	positions	position	protested	commission	professor	compassion
	discussion	preferred	precious	physician	proceed	physician	petition	pushing
seized	ceased	ceased	ceased	thieves	ceased	ceased	ceased	thieves
	freedom	season	seizing	ceased	faded	feasts	thieves	ceased
	seated	thieves	season	season	cities	scenes	saves	fuse
	faded	saves	thieves	feast	singing	thieves	seats	jesus
	singing	seems	saves	seizing	scenes	saves	seems	spheres
	scenes	scenes	ceasing	feared	feeding	seems	scenes	feels
	season	ceasing	seems	ceasing	season	feast	seemed	cities
	cities	saints	feast	saves	sweetest	saints	feast	season
	field	feast	seats	species	seated	faced	saved	seats
	seeming	sins	seemed	speed	saying	seemed	seizing	scenes
experiments	experiment	experiment	experiment	experiment	experiment	experiment	experiment	experiment
	experience	experienced	experience	experienced	experienced	experienced	experienced	attendants
	experienced	experience	experienced	garments	experience	experience	experience	extremities
	experiences	experiences	experiences	extermination	extinguished	experiences	experiences	islands
	extinguished	extremities	expense	expense	experiences	exposed	expressions	experienced
	exchange	established	embarrassment	experience	expected	extremities	extermination	prominence
	extremities	extraordinary	expanse	aramis	exchange	expense	extremities	edmunds
	expressions	extinguished	extraordinary	disturbance	expressions	expanse	extremity	instruments
	extremely	extremity	extremities	examined	extremities	extinguished	expression	attendance
	extremity	expanse	expressions	vanished	extent	exclusion	expensive	commons

Table 3: Top-10 nearest word embedding centroids for a word sample.

Understanding Domain Learning in Language Models Through Subpopulation Analysis

Zheng Zhao Yftah Ziser Shay B. Cohen
Institute for Language, Cognition and Computation
School of Informatics, University of Edinburgh
10 Crichton Street, Edinburgh, EH8 9AB
{zheng.zhao,yftah.ziser}@ed.ac.uk, scohen@inf.ed.ac.uk

Abstract

We investigate how different domains are encoded in modern neural network architectures. We analyze the relationship between natural language domains, model size, and the amount of training data used. The primary analysis tool we develop is based on subpopulation analysis with Singular Vector Canonical Correlation Analysis (SVCCA), which we apply to Transformer-based language models (LMs). We compare the latent representations of such a language model at its different layers from a pair of models: a model trained on multiple domains (an experimental model) and a model trained on a single domain (a control model). Through our method, we find that increasing the model capacity impacts how domain information is stored in upper and lower layers differently. In addition, we show that larger experimental models simultaneously embed domain-specific information as if they were conjoined control models. These findings are confirmed qualitatively, demonstrating the validity of our method.

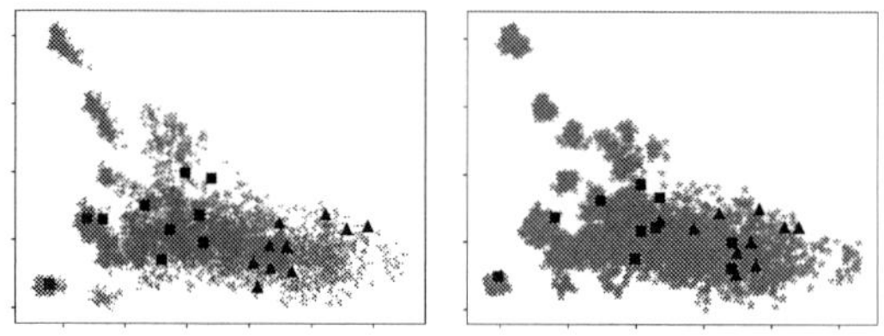

(a) Experimental model (b) Control model

Figure 1: An example of a visualization used with our subpopulation analysis tool. The experimental model, which includes all domain data, separates in its latent representations words related to the `Books` domain (▲) from general words (■). The control model, on the other hand, mixes them together.

1 Introduction

Pre-trained language models (PLMs) have become an essential modeling component for state-of-the-art natural language processing (NLP) models. They process text into latent representations in such a way that allows an NLP practitioner to seamlessly use these representations for prediction problems of various degrees of difficulty (Wang et al., 2018, 2019). The opaqueness in obtaining these representations has been an important research topic in the NLP community. PLMs, and more generally, neural models, are currently studied to understand their process and behavior in obtaining their latent representations. These PLMs are often trained on large datasets, with inputs originating from different sources. In this paper, we further develop our understanding of how neural networks obtain their latent representation and study the effect of learning from various domains on the characteristics of the corresponding latent representations.

Texts come from various domains that differ in their writing styles, authors and topics (Plank, 2016). In this work, we follow a simple definition of a domain as *a corpus of documents sharing a common topic*. We rely on a simple tool of subpopulation analysis to compare and contrast latent representations obtained with and without a specific domain. Our analysis relies on constructing two types of models: *experimental* models, from multi-domain data, and *control* models, from single-domain data. Figure 1 describes an example in which this analysis is applied to study the way embeddings for domain-specific words cluster together in the experimental and control model representations.

We believe training in an implicit multi-domain setup is widespread and often overlooked. For example, SQuAD (Rajpurkar et al., 2016), a widely used question-answering dataset composed of Wikipedia articles from multiple domains, is often referred to as a single-domain dataset in domain adaptation works for simplicity (Hazen et al., 2019; Shakeri et al., 2020; Yue et al., 2021). This scenario is also common in text summarization, where

Proceedings of the Fifth BlackboxNLP Workshop on Analyzing and Interpreting Neural Networks for NLP, pages 192 - 209
December 8, 2022 ©2022 Association for Computational Linguistics

many datasets consist of a bundle of domains for news articles (Grusky et al., 2018), academic papers (Cohan et al., 2018; Fonseca et al., 2022), and do-it-yourself (DIY) guides (Cohen et al., 2021). While models that learn from multiple domains are frequently used, their nature and behavior have hardly been explored.

Our work sheds light on the way state-of-the-art multi-domain models encode domain-specific information. We focus on two main aspects highly relevant for many training procedures: model capacity and data size. We discover that model capacity, indicated by the number of its parameters, strongly impacts the amount of domain-specific information multi-domain models store. This property might explain the performance gains of larger models (Devlin et al., 2019; Raffel et al., 2020; Clark et al., 2020; Srivastava et al., 2022). While this paper focuses on studying the effect of domains on latent representations, the subpopulation analysis tool could be used for studying other NLP setups, such as multitask and multimodal learning.[1]

2 Methodology

For an integer n, we denote by $[n]$ the set $\{1, \ldots, n\}$. Our analysis tool assumes a distribution $p(\mathbf{X})$ from which a set of examples $\mathcal{X} = \{\mathbf{x}^{(i)} \mid i \in [n]\}$ is drawn. It also assumes a family of binary indicators $\pi_1, \ldots, \pi_d$ such that $\pi_i(\mathbf{x})$ indicates whether the example $\mathbf{x}$ satisfies a certain *subpopulation* attribute i. For example, in this paper we focus on domain analysis, so π_5 could indicate if an example belongs to a `Books` domain.

We denote by $\mathcal{X}\big|_{\pi_i}$ the set $\{\mathbf{x}^{(j)} \mid \pi_i(\mathbf{x}^{(j)}) = 1\}$, the subset of $\mathcal{X}$ that satisfies attribute i. Unlike standard diagnostic classifier methods (Belinkov et al., 2017a,b; Giulianelli et al., 2018), rather than building a model to *predict* the attribute, we perform subpopulation analysis by training a set of models: $\mathbf{E}$, trained from $\mathcal{X}$ (the *experimental* model), and $\mathbf{C}_i$, trained from $\mathcal{X}\big|_{\pi_i}$ (the *control* model). We borrow the terminology of "experimental" and "control" from experimental design such as in clinical trials (Hinkelmann and Kempthorne, 2007). The experimental model corresponds to the experimental (or "treatment" in the case of medical trials) group in such trials and the control model corresponds to the control group. Unlike a standard experimental design, rather than comparing a function (such as squared difference) between the outcomes of the two groups to calculate a statistic with an underlying distribution, we instead calculate the similarity values between the representations of the two models. Our analysis is also related to Representational Similarity Analysis (Dimsdale-Zucker and Ranganath, 2018), aimed at studying similarities (across different experimental settings) between activation levels in brain neurons.

Through their latent representations, the set of models $\mathbf{C}_i$ represent the information that is captured about $p(\mathbf{X})$ from the relevant subpopulation of data. By comparing the different models to each other, we can learn what information is captured in the latent representations when a subset of the data is used and whether this information is different from the one captured when the whole set of data is used. With a proper control for model size and subpopulation sizes, we can determine the relationship between the different attributes π_i and the corresponding representations in different model components. The remaining question now is *how do we compare these representations?* Here, we follow previous work (Saphra and Lopez, 2019; Bau et al., 2019; Kudugunta et al., 2019), and apply Singular Vector Canonical Correlation Analysis (SVCCA; Raghu et al. 2017) to the latent representations of the experimental and control models.

We assume that each example $\mathbf{x}^{(i)}$ is associated with a latent representation $\mathbf{h}_j^{(i)}$ given by $\mathbf{C}_j$. For example, this could be the representation in the embedding layer for the input example, or the representation in the final pre-output layer. We define $\mathcal{H}_j$ to be a set of latent representations $\mathcal{H}_j = \{\mathbf{h}_j^{(k)} \mid k \in [n]\}$ for model $\mathbf{C}_j$. We define $\mathcal{H}_j\big|_{\pi_i} = \{\mathbf{h}_j^{(k)} \mid \pi_i(\mathbf{x}^{(k)}) = 1\}$ – the latent representations of $\mathbf{C}_j$ for which attribute i fires. Similarly, we define $\mathcal{H}_0$ for the model $\mathbf{E}$. We calculate the SVCCA value between subsets of $\mathcal{H}_0$ and subsets of $\mathcal{H}_j$ for $j \geq 1$. The procedure of SVCCA in this case follows:

- Performing Singular Value Decomposition (SVD) on the matrix forms of $\mathcal{H}_0$ and $\mathcal{H}_j$ (matching the representations in each through the index of the example $\mathbf{x}^{(i)}$ from which they originate). We use the lowest number of principal directions that preserve 99% of the variance in the data to project the latent representations.
- Performing Canonical Correlation Analysis (CCA; Hardoon et al. 2004) between the pro-

[1]Our code is available at: `https://github.com/zsquaredz/subpopulation_analysis`

jections of the latent representations from the SVD step, and calculating the average correlation value, denoted by ρ_{0j}.

The SVD step, which may seem redundant, is actually crucial, as it had been shown that low variance directions in neural network representations are primarily noise (Raghu et al., 2017; Frankle and Carbin, 2019). The intensity of ρ_{0j} indicates the level of overlap between the latent representations of each model (Saphra and Lopez, 2019).

In the rest of this paper, we use the tool of subpopulation analysis with **E**/$\mathbf{C}_i$ as above for the case of domain learning in neural networks. We note that each time we use this tool, the following decisions need to be made: (a) what training set we use for each **E** and $\mathbf{C}_i$; (b) the subset of $\mathcal{H}_j$ for $j \geq 0$ for which we perform the similarity analysis; (c) the component in the model from which we take the latent representations. For (c), the component can be, for example, a layer. Indeed, for most of our experiments, we use the first and last layer to create the latent representation sets, as they stand in stark contrast to each other in their behavior (see § 4). We provide an illustration of our proposed pipeline in Figure 2. We are particularly interested in studying the effect of two aspects of learning: dataset size and model capacity.

The case of domains In this paper, we define a domain as a corpus of documents with a common topic. Since a single massive web-crawled corpus used to pre-train language models usually contains many domains, we examine to what extent domain-specific information is encoded in the pre-trained model learned on this corpus. Such domain membership is indicated by our attribute functions π_i. For example, we may use $\pi_5(\mathbf{x})$ to indicate whether $\mathbf{x}$ is an input example from the domain `Books`. Given this notion of a domain, we can readily use subpopulation analysis through experimental and control models to analyze the effect on neural representations of learning from multiple domains or a single domain.

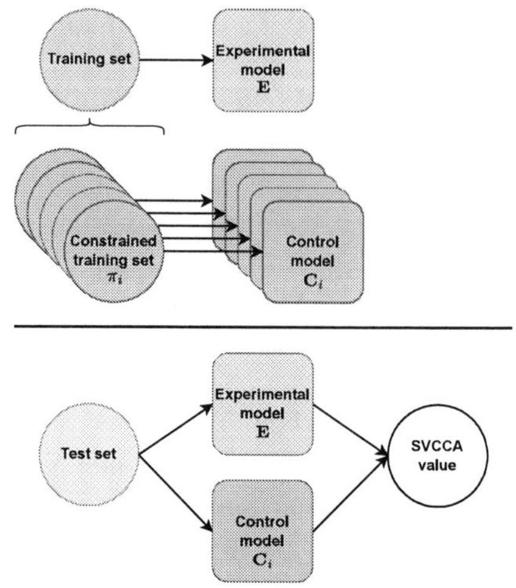

Figure 2: A diagram explaining the analysis we perform. At the top, during training, we create two sets of models from constrained datasets (based on different π_i) and a dataset that is not constrained. The result of this training is two set of models, the experimental model (**E**) and control models ($\mathbf{C}_i$). To perform the similarity analysis, we compute latent representation from a common test set for both models, and then run SVCCA (bottom).

3 Experimental Setup

Data We use the Amazon Reviews dataset (Ni et al., 2019), a dataset that facilitates research in tasks like sentiment analysis (Zhang et al., 2020), aspect-based sentiment analysis, and recommendation systems (Wang et al., 2020). The reviews in this dataset are explicitly divided into different product categories that serve as domains, which makes it a natural testbed for many multi-domain studies. A noteworthy example of a research field that heavily relies on this dataset is domain adaptation (Blitzer et al., 2007; Ziser and Reichart, 2018; Du et al., 2020; Lekhtman et al., 2021; Long et al., 2022), which is the task of learning robust models across different domains, closely related to our research.[2] We sort the domains by their review counts and pick the top five, which results in: `Books`, `Clothing Shoes and Jewelry`, `Electronics`, `Home and Kitchen`, and `Movies and TV` domains. To further validate our data quality, we use the 5-core subset of the data, ensuring that all reviewed items have at least five reviews authored by reviewers who wrote at least five reviews.

A representative dataset sample is presented in Table 1. We consider the different domains within the Amazon review dataset as *lexical domains*, i.e., domains that share a similar textual structure and functionality but differ with respect to their vocabulary. For example, we see the review snippet from the `Books` domain contains an aspect ("ending") for which a negative sentiment is conveyed ("didn't have a proper"). Similarly, we find an aspect ("han-

[2]We use the latest version of the dataset, consisting reviews from 1996 up to 2019.

Books: ... the book didn't have a proper ending but rather a rushed attempt to conclude the story and put everyone away neatly ...
Clothing: ... clearly of awful quality, the design and paint was totally wrong, the mask was short and stumpy as well as slightly deformed and bent to the left ...
Home: ... there are no handles, and the plastic gets too hot to hold, so you have to awkwardly pour by the top ...

Table 1: A representative sample of review snippets.

dle") with a corresponding conveyed sentiment ("too hot") for the `Home` domain. We can see this shared pattern across all domains, with different aspects and sentiment terms. We would not expect this to be the case for other datasets, which might have different differentiators for domains. For example, Amazon reviews and Wikipedia pages on `Books` domain may have a similar vocabulary, however, a review is more likely to convey sentiment toward a particular book, and a Wikipedia article is more likely to focus on describing the book. Thus, the Amazon Reviews dataset is an ideal testbed for our analysis.

In addition to the Amazon Reviews dataset, we experimented on the WikiSum dataset (Cohen et al., 2021) to further validate our findings. The WikiSum dataset is a coherent paragraph summarization dataset based on the WikiHow website.[3] WikiHow consists of do-it-yourself (DIY) guides for the general public, thus is written using simple English and ranges over many domains. Similar to Amazon Reviews, we also pick the top five domains for our experiments: `Education`, `Food`, `Health`, `Home`, and `Pets`. Since the dataset is designed for summarization, we concatenate the document and summary together for our MLM task. We present the results for this dataset at the end of § 4.

Task We study the language modeling task to understand the nature of multi-domain learning better. More precisely, we experiment with the masked language modeling (MLM) task, which randomly masks some of the tokens from the input, then predicts the masked word based on the context as the training objective. We focus on the MLM task as it is a prevalent pre-training task for many standard models such as BERT (Devlin et al., 2019) and RoBERTa (Liu et al., 2019) that serve as building blocks for many downstream tasks. Using examples from a set of pre-defined domains, we train a BERT model from scratch to fully control our experiment and isolate the effect of different domains. This is crucial since a pre-trained BERT model is already trained on multiple domains, hence hard to drive correct conclusions through our analysis from such a model. Moreover, recent studies (Magar and Schwartz, 2022; Brown et al., 2020) showed the risk of exposure of large language models to test data in the pre-training phase, also known as *data contamination*.

Model We use the $\text{BERT}_{\text{BASE}}$ (Devlin et al., 2019) architecture for all of our experiments. We train two types of models: the experimental model $\mathbf{E}$, trained on all five domains with the MLM objective, and the control model $\mathbf{C}_i$ for $i \in [5]$ trained on the ith domain. We are particularly interested in the effect of two aspects on the model representation: model capacity and data size. We use the capacity of 100% for $\text{BERT}_{\text{BASE}}$ size. $\text{BERT}_{\text{BASE}}$ has 768-dimensional vectors for each layer, adding up to a total of 110M parameters. We also experiment with a reduced model capacity of 75%, 50%, 25%, and 10% by reducing the dimension of the hidden layers. We follow Devlin et al. (2019) design choices, e.g., 12 layers with 12 attention heads per layer. We set the base training data size (100%) for $\mathbf{E}$ to be 50K, composed of 10K reviews per domain. Each $\mathbf{C}_i$ is trained on single domain data containing 10K reviews. $\mathbf{E}$ and $\mathbf{C}_i$ *share all the examples of domain* i. To study the effect of data size on model representation, we take subsets from the data split and create smaller datasets: a 10% split and a 50% split. We also create a 200% split to simulate the case with abundant data. We provide additional details about our training procedure in Appendix A.

4 Experiments and Results

Our research questions (RQs) examine how domain-specific information is encoded in $\mathbf{E}$ by calculating its SVCCA score with $\mathbf{C}_i$ for a specific i. For a given domain, we use a held-out test set for getting the experimental and control model representations as an input for the SVCCA method. Intuitively, a high SVCCA score between $\mathbf{E}$ and $\mathbf{C}_i$ indicates $\mathbf{E}$ stores domain-specific information for domain i, as $\mathbf{C}_i$ was train solely on data from domain i. A low SVCCA score between $\mathbf{E}$ and $\mathbf{C}_i$ could mean one of two things: a) $\mathbf{E}$ can generalize to data from d_i without explicitly storing domain-specific information about it, or b) $\mathbf{E}$ can not store information about $\mathbf{C}_i$, as a result of, for

[3] `https://www.wikihow.com`

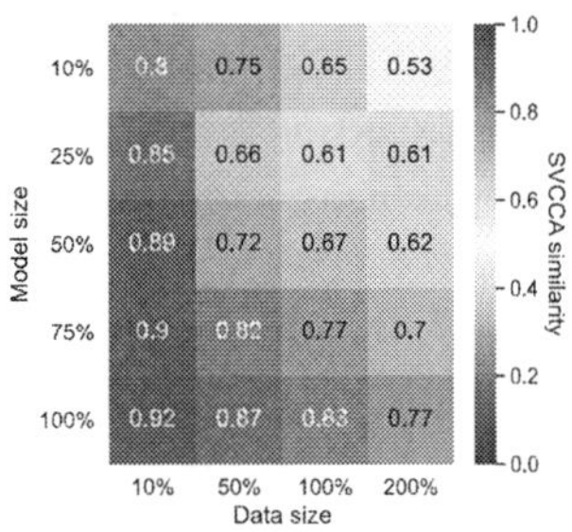

(a) $\mathbf{C}_{Books}$: ℓ_0

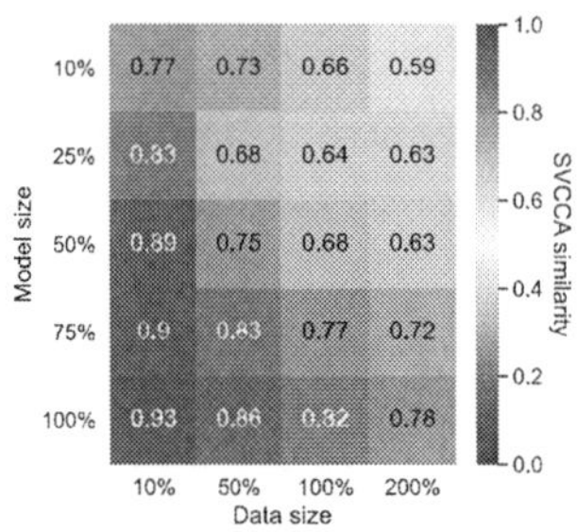

(b) $\mathbf{C}_{Clothing}$: ℓ_0

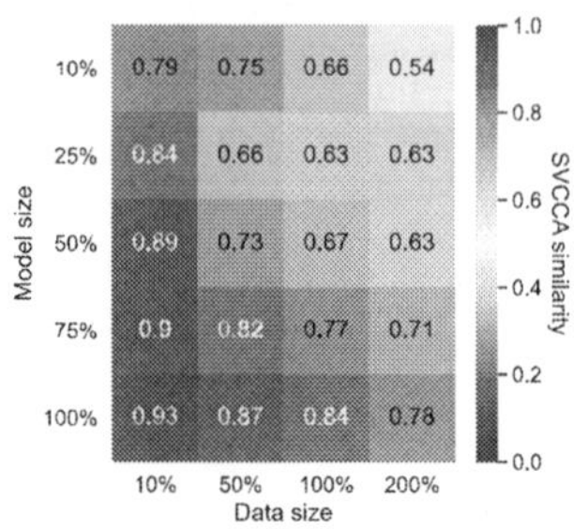

(c) $\mathbf{C}_{Electronics}$: ℓ_0

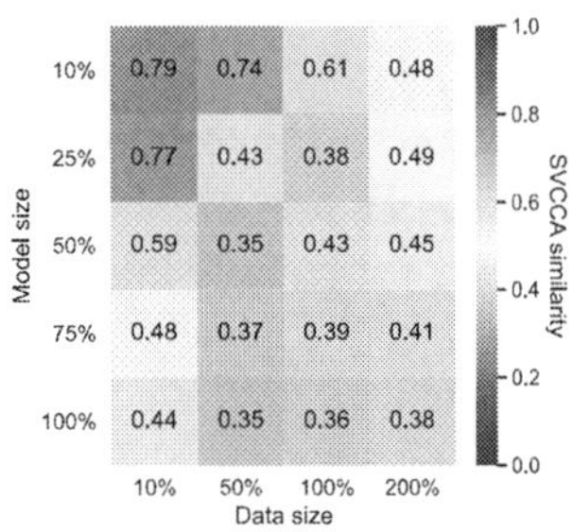

(d) $\mathbf{C}_{Books}$: ℓ_{12}

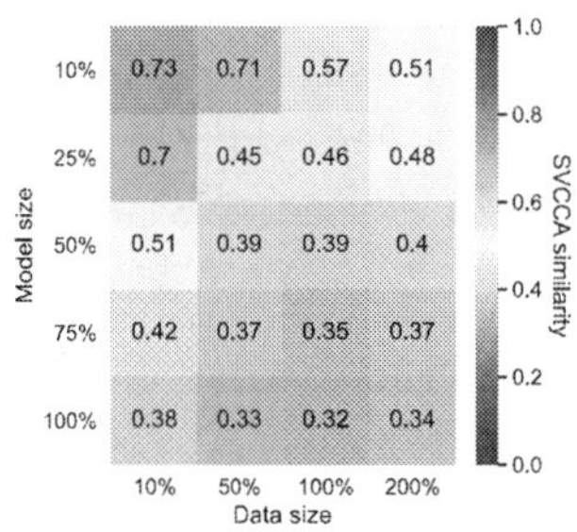

(e) $\mathbf{C}_{Clothing}$: ℓ_{12}

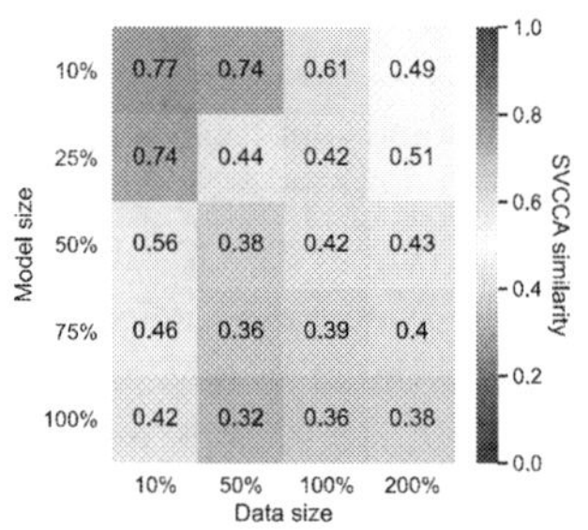

(f) $\mathbf{C}_{Electronics}$: ℓ_{12}

Figure 3: The SVCCA scores between $\mathbf{E}$ and different $\mathbf{C}_i$s for different data sizes and model capacities. We only display for three domains here, and we provide the rest in Appendix B.2. The top row presents the results for the embedding layer ℓ_0, and the bottom row presents them for the last layer ℓ_{12}.

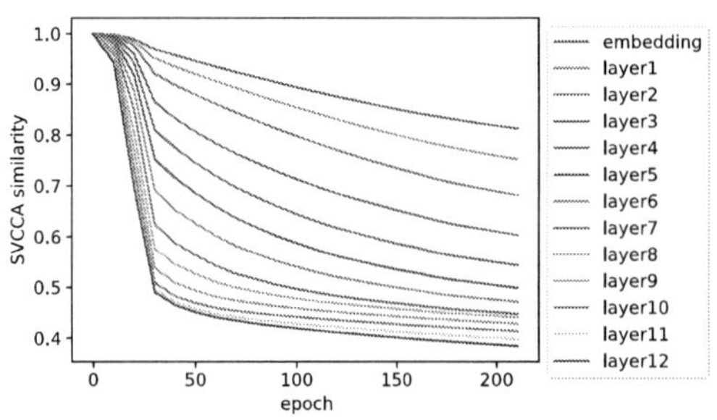

Figure 4: Training dynamics for all layers between $\mathbf{E}$ and $\mathbf{C}_{Books}$. Here both model and data size are 100%.

example, lack of model capacity. The way to distinguish between the two is subjective and depends on whether one finds $\mathbf{E}$ performance when applied to data from d_i to be satisfactory. This paper analyzes how information is stored at the model layers. As we inspect highly complex models consisting of multiple layers, it is challenging to determine to what extent a certain layer contributes to a model's overall performance. For those reasons, when comparing equivalent layers of different models, we focus on the amount of domain-specific information encoded in $\mathbf{E}$ for a given layer. With these preliminaries in mind, we are now ready to ask the following research questions:

RQ1: How does the similarity between the corresponding layers in E and C evolve over training? We perform an iterative comparison between the $\mathbf{E}$ and $\mathbf{C}_i$ for each $i \in [5]$. After each epoch, we calculate the SVCCA score between corresponding layers of the models, i.e., layer j of $\mathbf{E}$ is compared to layer j of $\mathbf{C}_i$. As $\mathbf{E}$ is trained on more data points than $\mathbf{C}_i$, and both use the same batch size, for any given epoch, $\mathbf{E}$ had more weights' updates than $\mathbf{C}_i$. More precisely, after the kth epoch, $\mathbf{C}_i$ and $\mathbf{E}$ had completed k passes on data points from d_i, but $\mathbf{E}$ used additional data points from the rest of the domains. We choose this alignment to examine the effect of the additional training data drawn from other domains.

Figure 4 presents the training dynamics analysis for the `Books` domain (we denote the `Books` control model as $\mathbf{C}_{Books}$). We include training dynamics analyses of other control models and domains in Appendix B.1, as they demonstrate similar trends. Since both $\mathbf{C}_{Books}$ and $\mathbf{E}$ are initialized with the same weights, the initial SVCCA score is 1 for all layers before training. We observe that as training progresses, the SVCCA values of higher layers (closer to the output) consistently become lower compared to the first layer. The order of SVCCA values is almost perfectly preserved with respect to the order of the layers in the network. The separation is higher for lower layers, with higher layers receiving similar SVCCA values. This is evidence that ***E** stores more domain-specific information in lower layers than in deeper layers throughout the training procedure.* Singh et al. (2019), who researched the nature of multilingual models, observed a similar pattern of dissimilarity in deeper layers for multilingual model representations of parallel sentences in different languages.

The alignment between the similarity of the layer pairs (**E** and **C**) and their depth also exists for models with random weights. It can be partially attributed to the mathematical artifact of decreasing correlation values for layers that are deeper because of the use of nonlinear activation units. To see to what extent this artifact plays a role in this alignment, we created ten models with random weights (no training, so there is no longer an experimental/control distinction) and calculated SVCCA between all 45 pairs for the first and last layers. We discovered that the mean difference between SVCCA scores of the first layer comparison and the last layer comparison is 0.139 (with a standard deviation of 0.001 over 45 pairs). In Figure 4, the difference is much larger when comparing the control model to the experimental model (0.428), indicating that the difference in layer SVCCA score cannot be only attributed to the mathematical artifact of increasing depth with more nonlinear activation. We still note that one should exercise caution when using linear methods, such as SVCCA, to analyze nonlinear processes.

The observed training dynamics motivates us to focus on the embedding layer (ℓ_0) and final layer (ℓ_{12}) for the rest of our analysis, as they serve as a lower bound (ℓ_0) and an upper bound (ℓ_{12}) with respect to the SVCCA scores of $\mathbf{C}_i$ and **E** throughout the training process. In addition, those layers have interesting attributes that we would like to explore. ℓ_0, a non-contextualized word embeddings layer, is known for encoding mainly lexical information (de Vries et al., 2020; Vulić et al., 2020). The highly contextualized ℓ_{12} is fed directly to the masked word classifier, thus playing a significant role in the MLM task. Our interest in the fully-trained models leads us to the following question:

RQ2: How do data size and model capacity affect domain encoding in ℓ_0 and ℓ_{12}? To answer this question, we measure the SVCCA score between variants of **E** and their corresponding $\mathbf{C}_i$ for different domains. The variants differ with respect to two parameters, data size and model capacity.

Figure 3 presents our results. We observe training the model on larger datasets decreases the SVCCA scores across all model capacities and domains for both ℓ_0 and ℓ_{12}. For each data point we add to the control model, we add d data points to the general model, where $d-1$ out of them belong to other domains. This means while we keep a constant ratio between the number of datapoints for the domains, the absolute gap between a given domain and the rest of the domains is growing for larger data sizes. This might explain why adding more data points increase **E** and **C** divergence.

A possible explanation for these trends might be how we define domains. The Amazon reviews dataset is divided by product categories which can be seen as lexical domains (see § 3). More precisely, all the domains share a similar structure and writing style of Amazon product reviews. The differences lie in the vocabulary of each domain. We hypothesize that the ***E** uses the increased capacity to keep more domain-specific information in ℓ_0, where the lexical information is kept and diverges from **C** in ℓ_{12}, where the highly contextualized representations are stored.* As we hypothesize that our domains differ mostly with respect to their vocabularies, we refine the mentioned above experiment by raising the following research question:

RQ3: To what extent does E encode domain-specific information for domain-specific words? To shed light on the domains' lexical nature, we inspect the patterns of domain-specific and general words. Domain-specific words need to appear with at least 20 reviews in the domain in hand and no more than 10 reviews in total for the rest of the other domains. General words must appear in at least 20 reviews in each domain. Those definitions are often used in domain adaptation works to describe domain discrepancy and find adaptable features (Blitzer et al., 2007; Ziser and Reichart, 2017). We provide some examples of domain-specific and general words in Appendix B.3. It is noteworthy that the union of the domain-specific and general words is not the complete vocabulary. To calculate the SVCCA scores for a subset of words, we first apply SVD to all inputs. Then we use the corre-

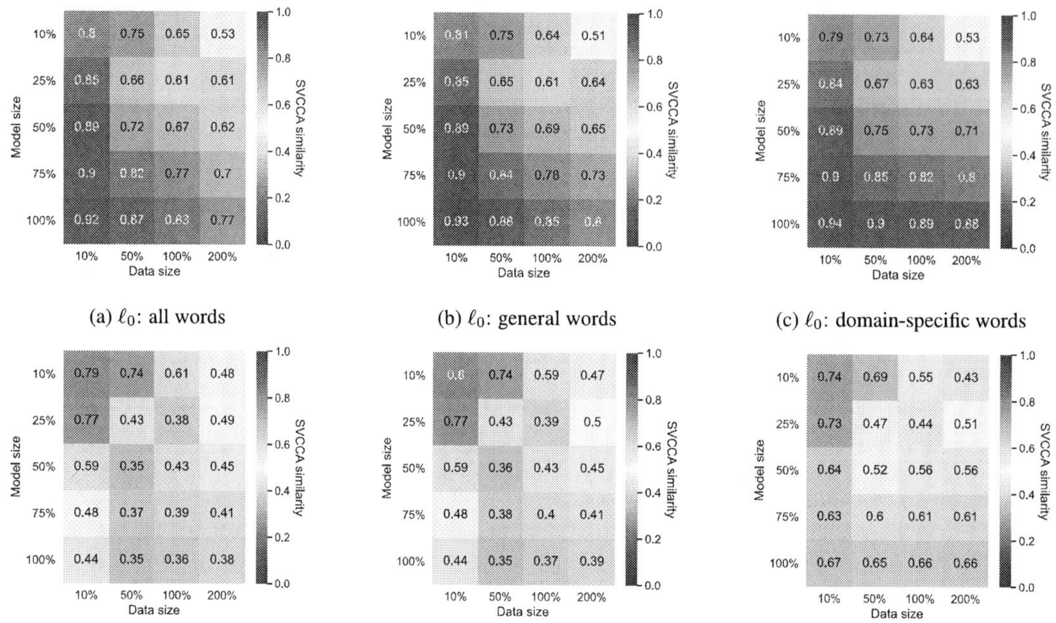

(a) ℓ_0: all words
(b) ℓ_0: general words
(c) ℓ_0: domain-specific words
(d) ℓ_{12}: all words
(e) ℓ_{12}: general words
(f) ℓ_{12}: domain-specific words

Figure 5: The SVCCA score between **E** and $\mathbf{C}_{Books}$ for different subsets of tokens. The top row presents the results for the embedding layer ℓ_0, and the bottom row presents them for the last layer ℓ_{12}.

sponding representations of the subset tokens to calculate the CCA similarity.

Figure 5 presents our results for the `Books` domain.[4] We present the `Books` domain analysis for all the words taken from RQ2 for reference (on the left-hand side of the figure). We observe high SVCCA scores for domain-specific words for ℓ_{12}. For large data sizes (100% and 200%), the trends of domain-specific words are opposite to the ones of RQ2, i.e., **E** uses the additional capacity to encode more domain-specific information. This indicates that as model capacity increases, **E** can capture similar information to $\mathbf{C}_{Books}$ for domain-specific words. This justifies the construction of large language models, mixing multiple subpopulations, as it demonstrates that *if the **E** model has large enough capacity, it separately creates representations for the different subpopulations that are similar to $\mathbf{C}_i$ model, which is a specialized model for a given domain.* Domain-specific words and their representations are crucial for the success of many NLP tasks, for example, Named Entity Recognition (Rocktäschel et al., 2013; Shang et al., 2018; Gu et al., 2021). We can see that the SVCCA scores for all the words and general words are almost identical. These findings make us suspect that word frequency and domain specificity are strongly connected. Indeed, we find out that the average frequency for `Books` domain-specific words is 75 with a median of 43. For general words, the average is 7696, and the median is 1440, making general words the main factor in the SVCCA scores for all words.

Finally, we would like to ensure the patterns we observe throughout this paper affect the behavior of the model:

RQ4: Do the observed trends manifest in the models' behavior? We conducted two qualitative analyses to understand better if the models' behavior expresses our findings. For the first analysis, we compare MLM predictions of **E** and **C** to check whether higher SVCCA values are associated with similar word predictions. For ℓ_0, we calculate the k-nearest neighbors of the word embeddings for a given word as a proxy to make predictions. For ℓ_{12}, we follow the standard procedure by feeding the last layer representation to the final MLM classifier in BERT. Table 2 presents our analyses. We can see that for ℓ_0, as we increase the model capacity, we get more similar predictions for both domain-specific and general words. This finding agrees

[4] The rest of the domains exhibit similar patterns. We provide all results in Appendix B.4

m=50%		m=100%	
E	$\mathbf{C}_i$	**E**	$\mathbf{C}_i$
blackberry	proxy	linux	mac
linux	linux	mac	linux
biologist	peer	blackberry	computers
viking	windows	vista	windows
samsung	servers	xp	xp

(a) 5-nearest neighbors for the domain-specific word **Macintosh** with i=`Electronics`.

m=50%		m=100%	
E	$\mathbf{C}_i$	**E**	$\mathbf{C}_i$
functioning	riding	functioning	functioning
work	running	work	repair
worked	work	worked	work
playing	walking	looking	riding
responding	cleaning	works	looking

(b) 5-nearest neighbors for the general word **working** with i=`Home and Kitchen`.

m=50%		m=100%	
E	$\mathbf{C}_i$	**E**	$\mathbf{C}_i$
networks	connections	routers	router
phones	networks	products	networks
devices	ports	systems	connections
problems	computers	mice	computers
models	cables	connections	products

(c) *Other wired and wireless [MASK] I had never had this problem.* The masked word is a domain-specific word **routers** with i=`Electronics`.

m=50%		m=100%	
E	$\mathbf{C}_i$	**E**	$\mathbf{C}_i$
away	apart	apart	aside
apart	off	flat	apart
aside	away	short	down
downhill	downhill	out	back
asleep	asleep	off	along

(d) *Sadly, those hopes began to fall [MASK] shortly after I finished the Prologue.* The masked word is a general word **apart** with i=`Books`.

Table 2: (a) and (b) are the 5-nearest neighbors using the embedding layer weights. (c) and (d) are model predictions using last layer representations. m denotes model capacity. All models here use a data size of 100%.

with the trend in Figure 3 that higher model capacity is associated with higher SVCCA similarity for ℓ_0. For ℓ_{12}, we can see that as model capacity increases, predictions for the general word becomes inconsistent, whereas, for domain-specific words, it is the opposite. This finding also agrees with our findings in RQ2 and RQ3, in which we observe the ℓ_{12} SVCCA values are decreasing for general words as we increase the model capacity and decrease for domain-specific words. We provide additional examples in Appendix B.5.

For the second analysis, we employ principal component analysis (PCA) to reduce the dimension of general and domain-specific representations for ℓ_0 and ℓ_{12} for both **E** and $\mathbf{C}_{Books}$. We provide visualizations in Figure 6. We can see that as model capacity increases, ℓ_0 representations of both general and domain-specific words from **E** and $\mathbf{C}_{Books}$ are aligned to a similar subspace. Additionally, ℓ_{12} representations of general words and domain-specific words for both models exhibit opposite behavior: domain-specific words are more aligned with increasing model capacity while general words start to detach. All of these agree with our findings in corresponding SVCCA scores trends in Figure 5. Even though we did not explicitly examine the relations between general and specific words in our work, we can observe that general and domain-specific word representations form different clusters in both models. Those clusters are more separated in ℓ_0 than in ℓ_{12}, suggesting that models use their increased capacity to keep more domain-specific information in ℓ_0.

WikiSum results Due to the lack of computational resources required, we only validate our main findings, namely, RQ2 and RQ3, using WikiSum. We present the results in Appendix B.6. We choose `Health` domain as it is the largest domain of this dataset. We observe that the trend in SVCCA scores across different scenarios on WikiSum is generally the same as those on Amazon Reviews, demonstrating that our findings are consistent.

5 Related Work

Analyzing neural representations Raghu et al. (2017) proposed SVCCA for comparing representations for the same data points from different layers and networks invariant to an affine transform. They also discovered that lower layers in a multi layer neural network converge more quickly to their final representations in contrast to higher layers. Building off of SVCCA, Morcos et al. (2018) developed projection weighted CCA (PWCCA) using an aggregation technique. Using the SVCCA tool, Saphra and Lopez (2019) studied the learning dynamics of neural language models by probing the evolution of syntactic, semantic, and topic representations across time and models. Kudugunta et al. (2019) used SVCCA to understand massively multilingual neural machine translation representations over 100 languages. Their major findings are that encoder representations of different languages form clusters based on their linguistic similarities.

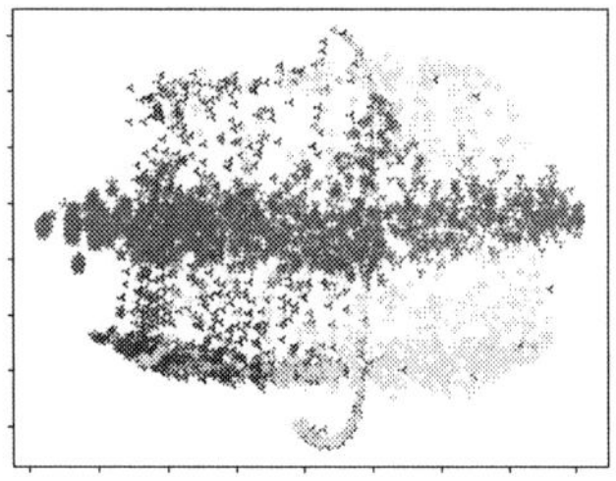

(a) ℓ_0: m=10%

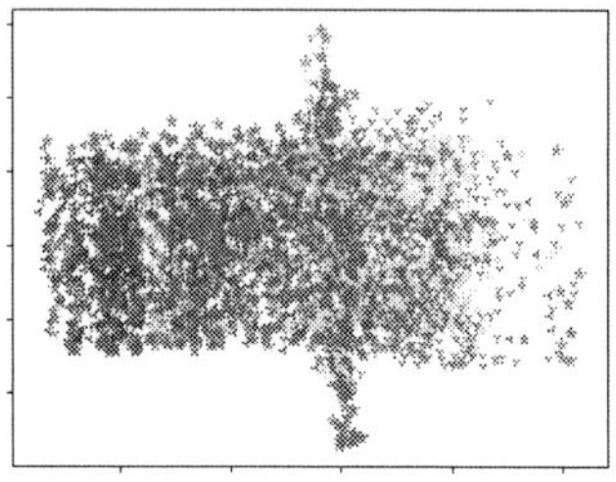

(b) ℓ_0: m=50%

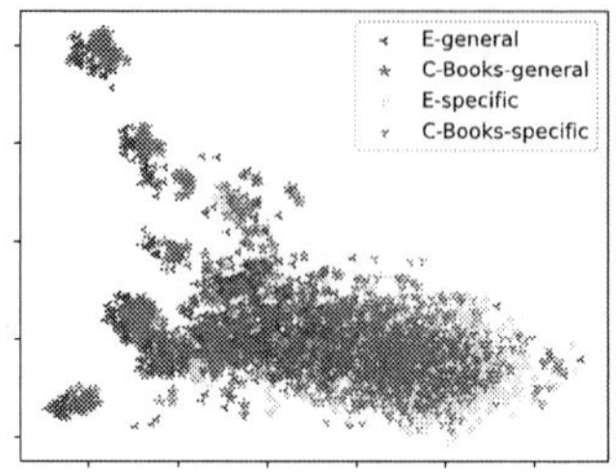

(c) ℓ_0: m=100%

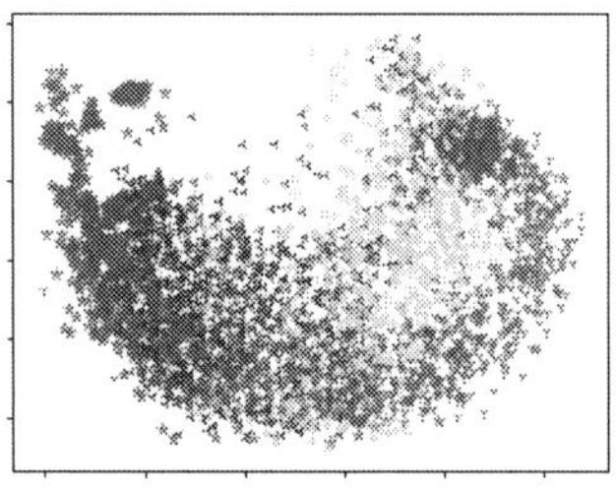

(d) ℓ_{12}: m=10%

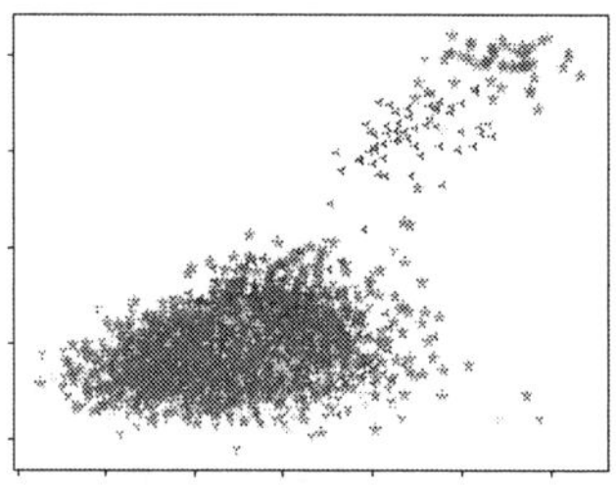

(e) ℓ_{12}: m=50%

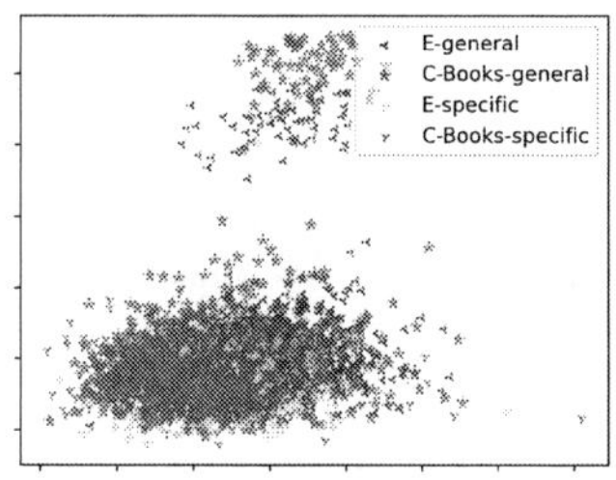

(f) ℓ_{12}: m=100%

Figure 6: Visualization for ℓ_0 and ℓ_{12} representations for **E** and $\mathbf{C}_{Books}$. We use colors (blue/cyan for **E** and red/magenta for $\mathbf{C}_{Books}$) to separate representations for generals and domain-specific words. m denotes model capacity. All models here use a data size of 100%.

Diagnostic Classifiers Another prominent tool for analyzing learned representations is diagnostic classifiers (DCs; Belinkov et al., 2017a,b; Giulianelli et al., 2018). DCs measure the amount of information encoded in representations about a particular task by using them as input to a classifier, which is trained on the task in a supervised manner. DC users assume that the higher their performance for this task, the more task-specific information is encoded in the representations. While widely adopted, DCs have several pitfalls. For example, Zhang and Bowman (2018) showed that learning a classifier on top of random embeddings is often competitive and, in some cases, even better than doing so with representations taken from a pre-trained model when trained on enough data. Saphra and Lopez (2019) demonstrated that, unlike SVCCA, DCs showed a stable correlation between language models and target labels throughout training epochs, in contrast to the language models' immense improvement over time.

6 Conclusions and Future Work

We present a novel methodology based on subpopulation analysis which helps understand how subdomains are represented in a multi-domain model. Our findings show that neural models encode domain information differently in lower and upper layers and that larger models (in our case, **E**) tend to "preserve a copy" of small, more specialized models (**C**). Generally, we observe rapid model improvements in NLP tasks when model capacity and dataset size, the two dimensions we study, increase. We encourage the research community to study the cause for these improvements from a multi-domain angle (i.e., the ability to encode specific information about many domains at once using the increased capacity). In future work, we would like to apply our methodology to examine the behavior of multilingual, multitask, and multimodal models.

Acknowledgments

This work was supported by the UKRI Centre for Doctoral Training (CDT) in Natural Language Processing through UKRI grant EP/S022481/1 and CDT funding from Huawei. We would like to thank Bonnie Webber, Ivan Titov and the anonymous reviewers for their helpful feedback. We appreciate the use of computing resources through the CSD3 cluster at the University of Cambridge.

Limitations

Throughout this work, we use the $\text{BERT}_{\text{BASE}}$ model. While it is widely adopted in the NLP community, there are other more advanced models (such as $\text{BERT}_{\text{LARGE}}$, RoBERTa and GPT3) that we do not experiment with due to a lack of resources. Given that the differences between models of the BERT family are mostly irrelevant to the way we conduct our experiments, we believe our results would generalize, at the very least, to this family of models.

In addition, we do not experiment with a large amount of training data for two reasons: a) We want to control for the domains from which we draw examples, and those have a size limitation, and b) Training many models on a large dataset is computationally expensive. Our multi-domain setup is comprised of five domains. We believe a higher number of domains should be considered for real-world scenarios.

To control our experiments, we train all models from scratch. For real-world scenarios, it would be harder to divide the training data into homogeneous and natural domains. While our proposed methodology can be easily adapted to different similarity measurement methods, we focus on SVCCA, which restricts us to linear correlations. In future work, we plan to investigate the nature of domains using non-linear techniques.

We identify domains through a common topic, and as a result, the shared lexical choices within the domain. This is the most common case for classifying domains, but we acknowledge that there are additional valuable ways to define domains. For example, domains could be separated based on writing style while still having a significant shared vocabulary (Amazon book reviews and Wikipedia articles about books).

References

Anthony Bau, Yonatan Belinkov, Hassan Sajjad, Nadir Durrani, Fahim Dalvi, and James R. Glass. 2019. Identifying and controlling important neurons in neural machine translation. In *7th International Conference on Learning Representations, ICLR 2019, New Orleans, LA, USA, May 6-9, 2019*. OpenReview.net.

Yonatan Belinkov, Nadir Durrani, Fahim Dalvi, Hassan Sajjad, and James Glass. 2017a. What do neural machine translation models learn about morphology? In *Proceedings of the 55th Annual Meeting of the Association for Computational Linguistics (Volume 1: Long Papers)*, pages 861–872, Vancouver, Canada. Association for Computational Linguistics.

Yonatan Belinkov, Lluís Màrquez, Hassan Sajjad, Nadir Durrani, Fahim Dalvi, and James Glass. 2017b. Evaluating layers of representation in neural machine translation on part-of-speech and semantic tagging tasks. In *Proceedings of the Eighth International Joint Conference on Natural Language Processing (Volume 1: Long Papers)*, pages 1–10, Taipei, Taiwan. Asian Federation of Natural Language Processing.

John Blitzer, Mark Dredze, and Fernando Pereira. 2007. Biographies, Bollywood, boom-boxes and blenders: Domain adaptation for sentiment classification. In *Proceedings of the 45th Annual Meeting of the Association of Computational Linguistics*, pages 440–447, Prague, Czech Republic. Association for Computational Linguistics.

Tom B. Brown, Benjamin Mann, Nick Ryder, Melanie Subbiah, Jared Kaplan, Prafulla Dhariwal, Arvind Neelakantan, Pranav Shyam, Girish Sastry, Amanda Askell, Sandhini Agarwal, Ariel Herbert-Voss, Gretchen Krueger, Tom Henighan, Rewon Child, Aditya Ramesh, Daniel M. Ziegler, Jeffrey Wu, Clemens Winter, Christopher Hesse, Mark Chen, Eric Sigler, Mateusz Litwin, Scott Gray, Benjamin Chess, Jack Clark, Christopher Berner, Sam McCandlish, Alec Radford, Ilya Sutskever, and Dario Amodei. 2020. Language models are few-shot learners. In *Proceedings of the 34th International Conference on Neural Information Processing Systems*, NIPS'20, Red Hook, NY, USA. Curran Associates Inc.

Kevin Clark, Minh-Thang Luong, Quoc V. Le, and Christopher D. Manning. 2020. ELECTRA: Pre-training text encoders as discriminators rather than generators. In *ICLR*.

Arman Cohan, Franck Dernoncourt, Doo Soon Kim, Trung Bui, Seokhwan Kim, Walter Chang, and Nazli Goharian. 2018. A discourse-aware attention model for abstractive summarization of long documents. In *Proceedings of the 2018 Conference of the North American Chapter of the Association for Computational Linguistics: Human Language Technologies, Volume 2 (Short Papers)*, pages 615–621, New Orleans, Louisiana. Association for Computational Linguistics.

Nachshon Cohen, Oren Kalinsky, Yftah Ziser, and Alessandro Moschitti. 2021. WikiSum: Coherent summarization dataset for efficient human-evaluation. In *Proceedings of the 59th Annual Meeting of the Association for Computational Linguistics and the 11th International Joint Conference on Natural Language Processing (Volume 2: Short Papers)*, pages 212–219, Online. Association for Computational Linguistics.

Wietse de Vries, Andreas van Cranenburgh, and Malvina Nissim. 2020. What's so special about BERT's layers? a closer look at the NLP pipeline in monolingual and multilingual models. In *Findings of the Association for Computational Linguistics: EMNLP 2020*, pages 4339–4350, Online. Association for Computational Linguistics.

Jacob Devlin, Ming-Wei Chang, Kenton Lee, and Kristina Toutanova. 2019. BERT: Pre-training of deep bidirectional transformers for language understanding. In *Proceedings of the 2019 Conference of the North American Chapter of the Association for*

Computational Linguistics: Human Language Technologies, Volume 1 (Long and Short Papers), pages 4171–4186, Minneapolis, Minnesota. Association for Computational Linguistics.

Halle R Dimsdale-Zucker and Charan Ranganath. 2018. Representational similarity analyses: a practical guide for functional mri applications. In *Handbook of behavioral neuroscience*, volume 28, pages 509–525. Elsevier.

Chunning Du, Haifeng Sun, Jingyu Wang, Qi Qi, and Jianxin Liao. 2020. Adversarial and domain-aware BERT for cross-domain sentiment analysis. In *Proceedings of the 58th Annual Meeting of the Association for Computational Linguistics*, pages 4019–4028, Online. Association for Computational Linguistics.

Marcio Fonseca, Yftah Ziser, and Shay B. Cohen. 2022. Factorizing content and budget decisions in abstractive summarization of long documents by sampling summary views. In *Proceedings of the Conference on Empirical Methods in Natural Language Processing (EMNLP)*.

Jonathan Frankle and Michael Carbin. 2019. The lottery ticket hypothesis: Finding sparse, trainable neural networks. In *7th International Conference on Learning Representations, ICLR 2019, New Orleans, LA, USA, May 6-9, 2019*. OpenReview.net.

Mario Giulianelli, Jack Harding, Florian Mohnert, Dieuwke Hupkes, and Willem Zuidema. 2018. Under the hood: Using diagnostic classifiers to investigate and improve how language models track agreement information. In *Proceedings of the 2018 EMNLP Workshop BlackboxNLP: Analyzing and Interpreting Neural Networks for NLP*, pages 240–248, Brussels, Belgium. Association for Computational Linguistics.

Max Grusky, Mor Naaman, and Yoav Artzi. 2018. Newsroom: A dataset of 1.3 million summaries with diverse extractive strategies. In *Proceedings of the 2018 Conference of the North American Chapter of the Association for Computational Linguistics: Human Language Technologies, Volume 1 (Long Papers)*, pages 708–719, New Orleans, Louisiana. Association for Computational Linguistics.

Yu Gu, Robert Tinn, Hao Cheng, Michael Lucas, Naoto Usuyama, Xiaodong Liu, Tristan Naumann, Jianfeng Gao, and Hoifung Poon. 2021. Domain-specific language model pretraining for biomedical natural language processing. *ACM Trans. Comput. Healthcare*, 3(1).

David R. Hardoon, Sándor Szedmák, and John Shawe-Taylor. 2004. Canonical correlation analysis: An overview with application to learning methods. *Neural Comput.*, 16(12):2639–2664.

Timothy J Hazen, Shehzaad Dhuliawala, and Daniel Boies. 2019. Towards domain adaptation from limited data for question answering using deep neural networks. *arXiv preprint arXiv:1911.02655*.

Klaus Hinkelmann and Oscar Kempthorne. 2007. *Design and analysis of experiments, volume 1: Introduction to experimental design*, volume 1. John Wiley & Sons.

Sneha Kudugunta, Ankur Bapna, Isaac Caswell, and Orhan Firat. 2019. Investigating multilingual NMT representations at scale. In *Proceedings of the 2019 Conference on Empirical Methods in Natural Language Processing and the 9th International Joint Conference on Natural Language Processing (EMNLP-IJCNLP)*, pages 1565–1575, Hong Kong, China. Association for Computational Linguistics.

Entony Lekhtman, Yftah Ziser, and Roi Reichart. 2021. DILBERT: Customized pre-training for domain adaptation with category shift, with an application to aspect extraction. In *Proceedings of the 2021 Conference on Empirical Methods in Natural Language Processing*, pages 219–230, Online and Punta Cana, Dominican Republic. Association for Computational Linguistics.

Yinhan Liu, Myle Ott, Naman Goyal, Jingfei Du, Mandar Joshi, Danqi Chen, Omer Levy, Mike Lewis, Luke Zettlemoyer, and Veselin Stoyanov. 2019. Roberta: A robustly optimized bert pretraining approach. *arXiv preprint arXiv:1907.11692*.

Quanyu Long, Tianze Luo, Wenya Wang, and Sinno Pan. 2022. Domain confused contrastive learning for unsupervised domain adaptation. In *Proceedings of the 2022 Conference of the North American Chapter of the Association for Computational Linguistics: Human Language Technologies*, pages 2982–2995, Seattle, United States. Association for Computational Linguistics.

Inbal Magar and Roy Schwartz. 2022. Data contamination: From memorization to exploitation. In *Proceedings of the 60th Annual Meeting of the Association for Computational Linguistics (Volume 2: Short Papers)*, pages 157–165, Dublin, Ireland. Association for Computational Linguistics.

Ari S. Morcos, Maithra Raghu, and Samy Bengio. 2018. Insights on representational similarity in neural networks with canonical correlation. In *Advances in Neural Information Processing Systems 31: Annual Conference on Neural Information Processing Systems 2018, NeurIPS 2018, December 3-8, 2018, Montréal, Canada*, pages 5732–5741.

Jianmo Ni, Jiacheng Li, and Julian McAuley. 2019. Justifying recommendations using distantly-labeled reviews and fine-grained aspects. In *Proceedings of the 2019 Conference on Empirical Methods in Natural Language Processing and the 9th International Joint Conference on Natural Language Processing (EMNLP-IJCNLP)*, pages 188–197, Hong Kong, China. Association for Computational Linguistics.

Adam Paszke, Sam Gross, Francisco Massa, Adam Lerer, James Bradbury, Gregory Chanan, Trevor

Killeen, Zeming Lin, Natalia Gimelshein, Luca Antiga, Alban Desmaison, Andreas Kopf, Edward Yang, Zachary DeVito, Martin Raison, Alykhan Tejani, Sasank Chilamkurthy, Benoit Steiner, Lu Fang, Junjie Bai, and Soumith Chintala. 2019. Pytorch: An imperative style, high-performance deep learning library. In *NeurIPS*.

Barbara Plank. 2016. What to do about non-standard (or non-canonical) language in NLP. In *Proceedings of the 13th Conference on Natural Language Processing, KONVENS 2016, Bochum, Germany, September 19-21, 2016*, volume 16 of *Bochumer Linguistische Arbeitsberichte*.

Colin Raffel, Noam Shazeer, Adam Roberts, Katherine Lee, Sharan Narang, Michael Matena, Yanqi Zhou, Wei Li, and Peter J. Liu. 2020. Exploring the limits of transfer learning with a unified text-to-text transformer. *JMLR*.

Maithra Raghu, Justin Gilmer, Jason Yosinski, and Jascha Sohl-Dickstein. 2017. SVCCA: singular vector canonical correlation analysis for deep learning dynamics and interpretability. In *Advances in Neural Information Processing Systems 30: Annual Conference on Neural Information Processing Systems 2017, December 4-9, 2017, Long Beach, CA, USA*, pages 6076–6085.

Pranav Rajpurkar, Jian Zhang, Konstantin Lopyrev, and Percy Liang. 2016. SQuAD: 100,000+ questions for machine comprehension of text. In *Proceedings of the 2016 Conference on Empirical Methods in Natural Language Processing*, pages 2383–2392, Austin, Texas. Association for Computational Linguistics.

Tim Rocktäschel, Torsten Huber, Michael Weidlich, and Ulf Leser. 2013. WBI-NER: The impact of domain-specific features on the performance of identifying and classifying mentions of drugs. In *Second Joint Conference on Lexical and Computational Semantics (*SEM), Volume 2: Proceedings of the Seventh International Workshop on Semantic Evaluation (SemEval 2013)*, pages 356–363, Atlanta, Georgia, USA. Association for Computational Linguistics.

Naomi Saphra and Adam Lopez. 2019. Understanding learning dynamics of language models with SVCCA. In *Proceedings of the 2019 Conference of the North American Chapter of the Association for Computational Linguistics: Human Language Technologies, Volume 1 (Long and Short Papers)*, pages 3257–3267, Minneapolis, Minnesota. Association for Computational Linguistics.

Siamak Shakeri, Cicero Nogueira dos Santos, Henghui Zhu, Patrick Ng, Feng Nan, Zhiguo Wang, Ramesh Nallapati, and Bing Xiang. 2020. End-to-end synthetic data generation for domain adaptation of question answering systems. In *Proceedings of the 2020 Conference on Empirical Methods in Natural Language Processing (EMNLP)*, pages 5445–5460, Online. Association for Computational Linguistics.

Jingbo Shang, Liyuan Liu, Xiaotao Gu, Xiang Ren, Teng Ren, and Jiawei Han. 2018. Learning named entity tagger using domain-specific dictionary. In *Proceedings of the 2018 Conference on Empirical Methods in Natural Language Processing*, pages 2054–2064, Brussels, Belgium. Association for Computational Linguistics.

Jasdeep Singh, Bryan McCann, Richard Socher, and Caiming Xiong. 2019. BERT is not an interlingua and the bias of tokenization. In *Proceedings of the 2nd Workshop on Deep Learning Approaches for Low-Resource NLP (DeepLo 2019)*, pages 47–55, Hong Kong, China. Association for Computational Linguistics.

Aarohi Srivastava, Abhinav Rastogi, Abhishek Rao, Abu Awal Md Shoeb, Abubakar Abid, Adam Fisch, Adam R Brown, Adam Santoro, Aditya Gupta, Adrià Garriga-Alonso, et al. 2022. Beyond the imitation game: Quantifying and extrapolating the capabilities of language models. *arXiv preprint arXiv:2206.04615*.

Ivan Vulić, Edoardo Maria Ponti, Robert Litschko, Goran Glavaš, and Anna Korhonen. 2020. Probing pretrained language models for lexical semantics. In *Proceedings of the 2020 Conference on Empirical Methods in Natural Language Processing (EMNLP)*, pages 7222–7240, Online. Association for Computational Linguistics.

Alex Wang, Yada Pruksachatkun, Nikita Nangia, Amanpreet Singh, Julian Michael, Felix Hill, Omer Levy, and Samuel R. Bowman. 2019. Superglue: A stickier benchmark for general-purpose language understanding systems. In *Advances in Neural Information Processing Systems 32: Annual Conference on Neural Information Processing Systems 2019, NeurIPS 2019, December 8-14, 2019, Vancouver, BC, Canada*, pages 3261–3275.

Alex Wang, Amanpreet Singh, Julian Michael, Felix Hill, Omer Levy, and Samuel Bowman. 2018. GLUE: A multi-task benchmark and analysis platform for natural language understanding. In *Proceedings of the 2018 EMNLP Workshop BlackboxNLP: Analyzing and Interpreting Neural Networks for NLP*, pages 353–355, Brussels, Belgium. Association for Computational Linguistics.

Jianling Wang, Kaize Ding, Liangjie Hong, Huan Liu, and James Caverlee. 2020. Next-item recommendation with sequential hypergraphs. In *Proceedings of the 43rd international ACM SIGIR conference on research and development in information retrieval*, pages 1101–1110.

Thomas Wolf, Lysandre Debut, Victor Sanh, Julien Chaumond, Clement Delangue, Anthony Moi, Pierric Cistac, Tim Rault, Remi Louf, Morgan Funtowicz, Joe Davison, Sam Shleifer, Patrick von Platen, Clara Ma, Yacine Jernite, Julien Plu, Canwen Xu, Teven Le Scao, Sylvain Gugger, Mariama Drame, Quentin Lhoest, and Alexander Rush. 2020. Transformers:

State-of-the-art natural language processing. In *Proc. of EMNLP*.

Zhenrui Yue, Bernhard Kratzwald, and Stefan Feuerriegel. 2021. Contrastive domain adaptation for question answering using limited text corpora. In *Proceedings of the 2021 Conference on Empirical Methods in Natural Language Processing*, pages 9575–9593, Online and Punta Cana, Dominican Republic. Association for Computational Linguistics.

Kelly Zhang and Samuel Bowman. 2018. Language modeling teaches you more than translation does: Lessons learned through auxiliary syntactic task analysis. In *Proceedings of the 2018 EMNLP Workshop BlackboxNLP: Analyzing and Interpreting Neural Networks for NLP*, pages 359–361, Brussels, Belgium. Association for Computational Linguistics.

Shaozhong Zhang, Dingkai Zhang, Haidong Zhong, and Guorong Wang. 2020. A multiclassification model of sentiment for e-commerce reviews. *IEEE Access*, 8:189513–189526.

Yftah Ziser and Roi Reichart. 2017. Neural structural correspondence learning for domain adaptation. In *Proceedings of the 21st Conference on Computational Natural Language Learning (CoNLL 2017)*, pages 400–410, Vancouver, Canada. Association for Computational Linguistics.

Yftah Ziser and Roi Reichart. 2018. Pivot based language modeling for improved neural domain adaptation. In *Proceedings of the 2018 Conference of the North American Chapter of the Association for Computational Linguistics: Human Language Technologies, Volume 1 (Long Papers)*, pages 1241–1251, New Orleans, Louisiana. Association for Computational Linguistics.

A Additional Details for Experiments

Here we provide some additional details for our experiments.

Training We set the validation data size for $\mathbf{E}$ to be 10K, which is composed of 2K reviews from each domain. For validation set of each $\mathbf{C}_i$, we use the same 2K reviews used for $\mathbf{E}$ from each domain. For consistency, we use the same validation set for all data sizes. We use a test set with 2.5K reviews for each domain. The same test set is fed to both $\mathbf{E}$ and $\mathbf{C}_i$ across all model capacities and data sizes to obtain representations for subpopulation analysis. When it is clear from the context which $\mathbf{C}_i$ for $i \in [5]$ we are referring to (and under which training regime), we will use the simplification $\mathbf{C}$.

All models use the validation set cross-entropy loss to perform early stopping, and we train a model for a maximum of 500 epochs. We provide the validation loss (cross-entropy) for the $\mathbf{E}$ model in Table 3. From the results, we can see that for fixed data size, model performance saturates when reaching model capacity of 100%. Thus, unlike data size, we do not perform further experiments with model capacity larger than 100%.

	10%d	50%d	100%d	200%d
10%m	6.052	5.541	4.788	3.886
25%m	5.764	3.257	2.745	2.354
50%m	4.366	2.758	2.451	2.144
75%m	4.017	2.781	2.435	2.149
100%m	4.012	2.786	2.436	2.16

Table 3: Validation cross-entropy loss on the experimental model for different model capacities and data sizes where m refers to model capacity and d refers to data size used to train the model.

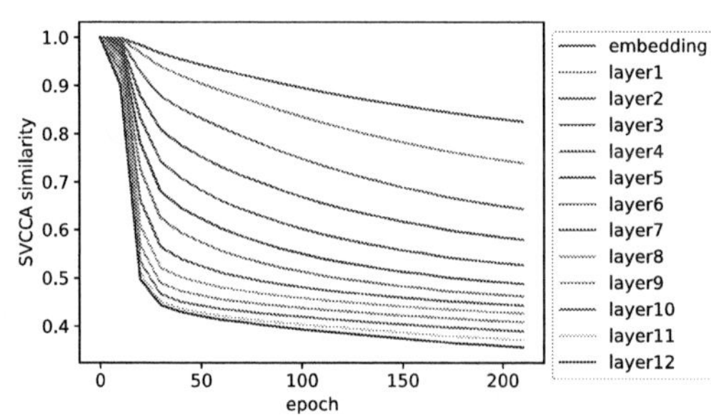

Figure 7: Training dynamics for all layers between $\mathbf{E}$ and $\mathbf{C}_{Clothing}$. Here both model and data size are 100%.

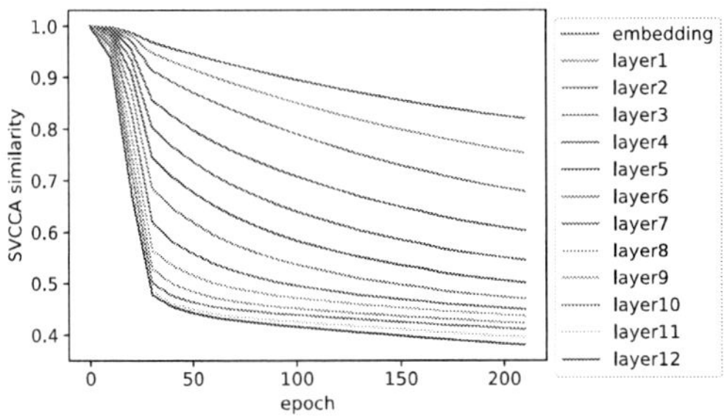

Figure 8: Training dynamics for all layers between $\mathbf{E}$ and $\mathbf{C}_{Electronics}$. Here both model and data size are 100%.

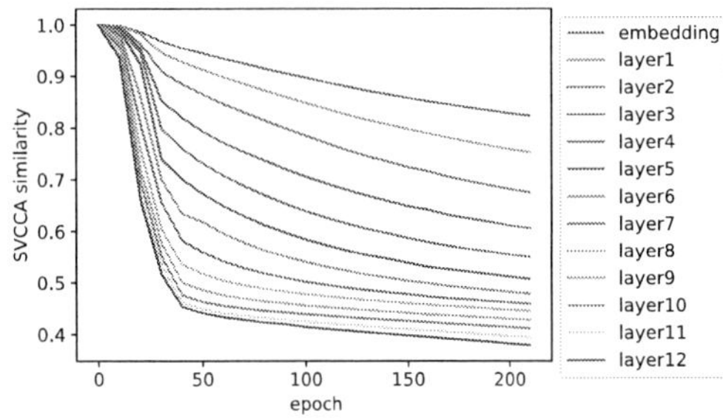

Figure 10: Training dynamics for all layers between $\mathbf{E}$ and $\mathbf{C}_{Movies}$. Here both model and data size are 100%.

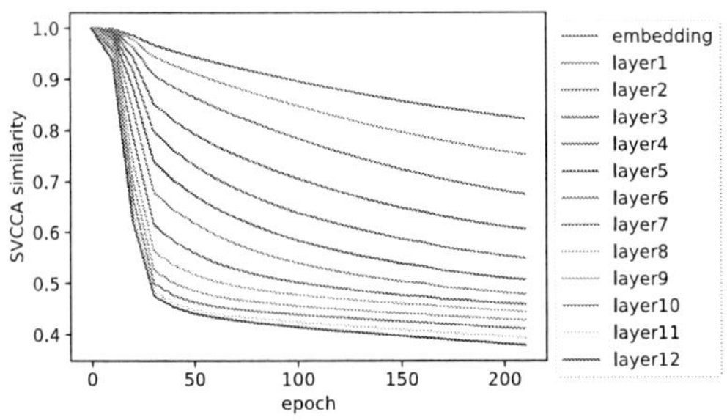

Figure 9: Training dynamics for all layers between $\mathbf{E}$ and $\mathbf{C}_{Home}$. Here both model and data size are 100%.

All models are trained on 4 NVIDIA A100 GPUs with a batch size of 32 per GPU. We use PyTorch (Paszke et al., 2019) and the HuggingFace library (Wolf et al., 2020) for all model implementation.

B Additional Details for Results

B.1 Additional Results for RQ1

We provide additional experimental results for training dynamics on `Clothing Shoes and Jewelry` (Figure 7), `Electronics` (Figure 8), `Home and Kitchen` (Figure 9), and `Movies and TV` (Figure 10).

B.2 Additional Results for RQ2

In § 4, we provided SVCCA results between $\mathbf{E}$ and different $\mathbf{C}_i$s for three domains. Here we present the results for the rest of the two domains in Figure 13a, 13d, 14a, and 14d.

B.3 Example of General and Domain-specific Words

We provide a sample of general words and domain specific words for each domain in Table 4. Note that list of general words are domain independent, i.e., the general word list is the same for all domains.

B.4 Additional Results for RQ3

Here we present additional results for SVCCA score between $\mathbf{E}$ and $\mathbf{C}_i$ for different subsets of tokens. Figure 11 illustrates for $\mathbf{C}_{Clothing}$, Figure 12 illustrates for $\mathbf{C}_{Electronics}$, Figure 13 illustrates for $\mathbf{C}_{Home}$, and Figure 14 illustrates for $\mathbf{C}_{Movies}$.

B.5 Additional Results for RQ4

Here we provide more example MLM predictions of $\mathbf{E}$ and $\mathbf{C}_i$. Table 5 presents predictions using k-nearest neighbors of the word embeddings. Table 6 presents predictions using the final layer representation.

B.6 Additional Results on WikiSum

Here we provide additional results on WikiSum `Health` domain in Figure 15, including SVCCA results between $\mathbf{E}$ and $\mathbf{C}_{Health}$, as well as results for different subsets of tokens.

General words: totally, preference, cost, mistake, hello, noticeable, play, factor, common, friend, previously, upon, explain, future, everyone
Books: gutenberg, appendix, autobiographical, grammatically, bookshelves, democrat, asides, arabic, stagnant, curriculum, minutiae, gripped, publishers, referencing, socialism **Clothing**: marten, docker, florsheim, rockports, skechers, buckles, 38d, fleece, nylons, insoles, tees, pantyhose, puckered, slippers, footwear **Electronics**: printable, wifi, 105mm, aux, energizer, recordable, directories, reinstall, gigabit, reboots, portability, vga, hitachi, configurations, wirelessly **Home**: cupcakes, kitchenaid, undercooked, ikea, chopper, mugs, steamers, juices, fiesta, kettles, aroma, toasted, rinsed ovens, airtight **Movie**: scenic, 16x9, nightclub, cheesiest, filmakers, supernova, serials, weepy, purists, incarnations, lionsgate, reportedly, suggestive, 1931, choreography

Table 4: A representative sample of general words (top row) and domain specific words (bottom rows) taken from different categories (domains) of the dataset.

m=50%		m=100%	
E	$\mathbf{C}_i$	**E**	$\mathbf{C}_i$
editors	volumns	editors	editors
publisher	buyer	publisher	publisher
heirs	listing	editor	editor
libraries	edit	writers	authors
universities	hardcover	authors	reviewers

(a) 5-nearest neighbors for the domain-specific word **publishers** with i=`Books`.

m=50%		m=100%	
E	$\mathbf{C}_i$	**E**	$\mathbf{C}_i$
towards	towards	towards	towards
beside	settled	against	at
surrounding	at	onto	onto
beneath	concerning	at	against
against	behind	beside	near

(b) 5-nearest neighbors for the general word **toward** with i=`Books`.

m=50%		m=100%	
E	$\mathbf{C}_i$	**E**	$\mathbf{C}_i$
comics	jokes	comics	comics
jokes	joke	comedian	joke
comedian	accolades	laughs	comedian
directors	critics	comedies	critics
commentators	reviewers	jokes	laughs

(c) 5-nearest neighbors for the domain-specific word **comedians** with i=`Movies and TV`.

m=50%		m=100%	
E	$\mathbf{C}_i$	**E**	$\mathbf{C}_i$
print	vinyl	plastic	plastic
plastic	bonded	print	vinyl
cloth	plastic	materials	cardboard
cardboard	junk	paperback	print
printed	cardboard	cardboard	tissue

(d) 5-nearest neighbors for the general word **paper** with i=`Clothing Shoes and Jewelry`.

Table 5: Example predictions of **E** and $\mathbf{C}_i$ using 5-nearest neighbors from embedding layer weights. m denotes model capacity. All models here use data size of 100%.

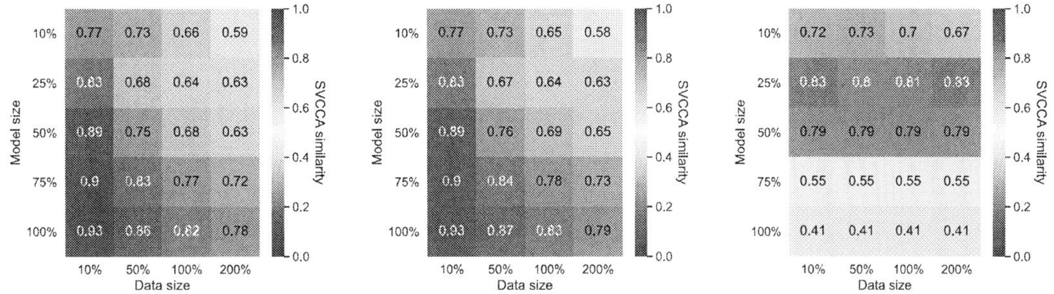

(a) ℓ_0: all words (b) ℓ_0: general words (c) ℓ_0: domain-specific words

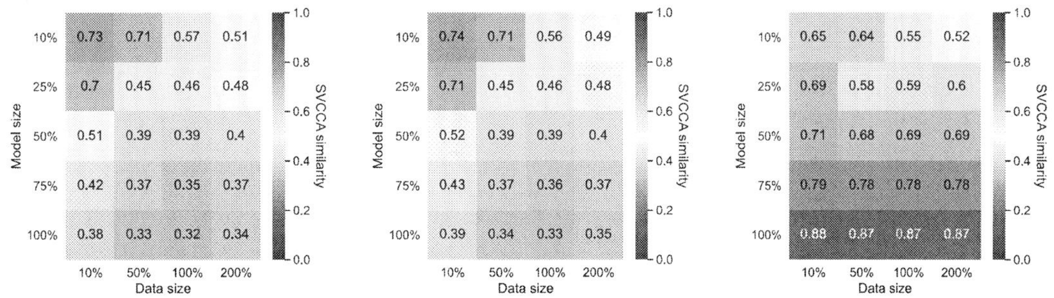

(d) ℓ_{12}: all words (e) ℓ_{12}: general words (f) ℓ_{12}: domain-specific words

Figure 11: The SVCCA score between $\mathbf{E}$ and $\mathbf{C}_{Clothing}$ for different subsets of tokens. The top row presents the results for the embedding layer ℓ_0, and the bottom row presents them for the last layer ℓ_{12}.

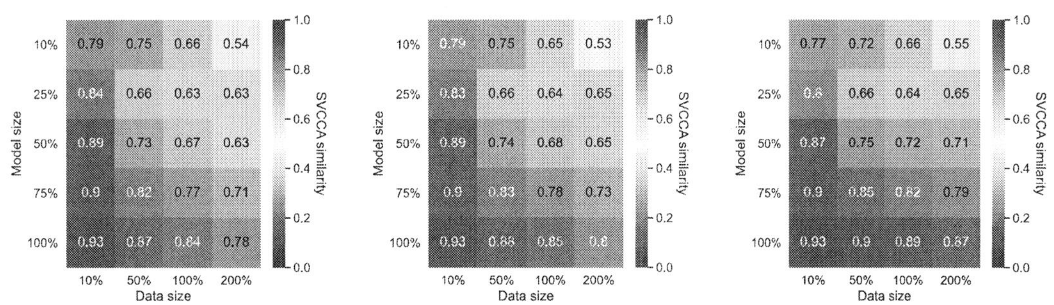

(a) ℓ_0: all words (b) ℓ_0: general words (c) ℓ_0: domain-specific words

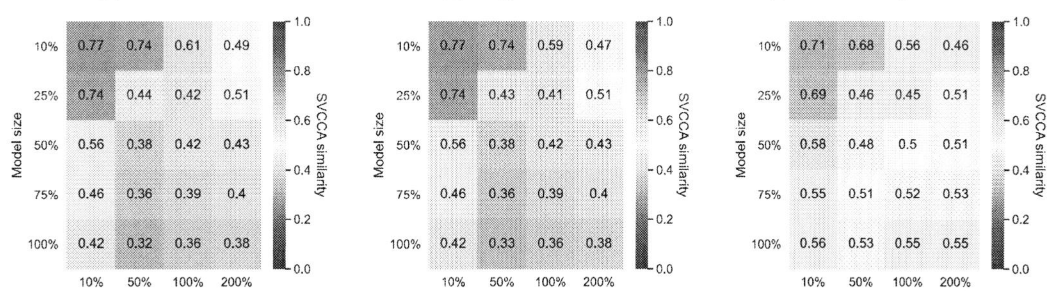

(d) ℓ_{12}: all words (e) ℓ_{12}: general words (f) ℓ_{12}: domain-specific words

Figure 12: The SVCCA score between $\mathbf{E}$ and $\mathbf{C}_{Electronics}$ for different subsets of tokens. The top row presents the results for the embedding layer ℓ_0, and the bottom row presents them for the last layer ℓ_{12}.

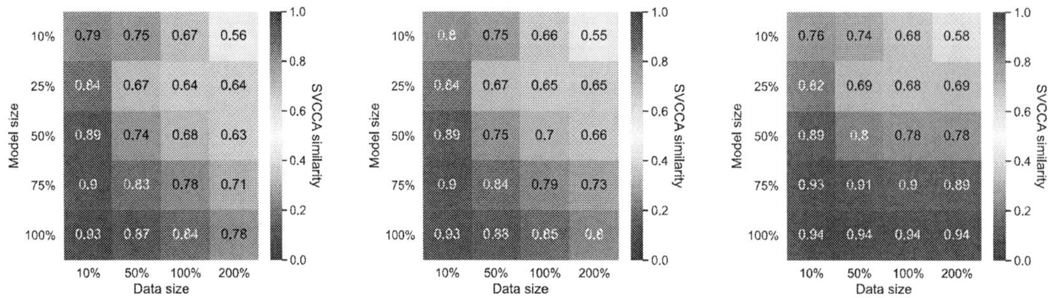

(a) ℓ_0: all words (b) ℓ_0: general words (c) ℓ_0: domain-specific words

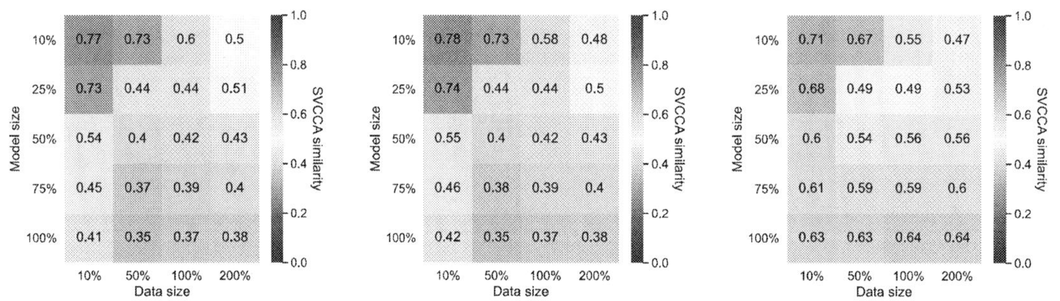

(d) ℓ_{12}: all words (e) ℓ_{12}: general words (f) ℓ_{12}: domain-specific words

Figure 13: The SVCCA score between $\mathbf{E}$ and $\mathbf{C}_{Home}$ for different subsets of tokens. The top row presents the results for the embedding layer ℓ_0, and the bottom row presents them for the last layer ℓ_{12}.

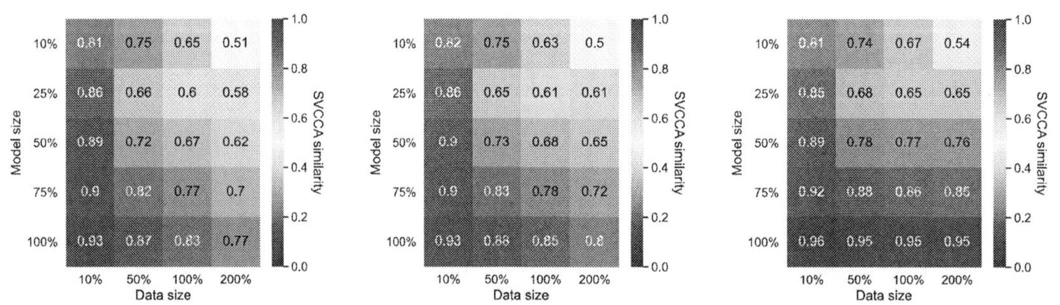

(a) ℓ_0: all words (b) ℓ_0: general words (c) ℓ_0: domain-specific words

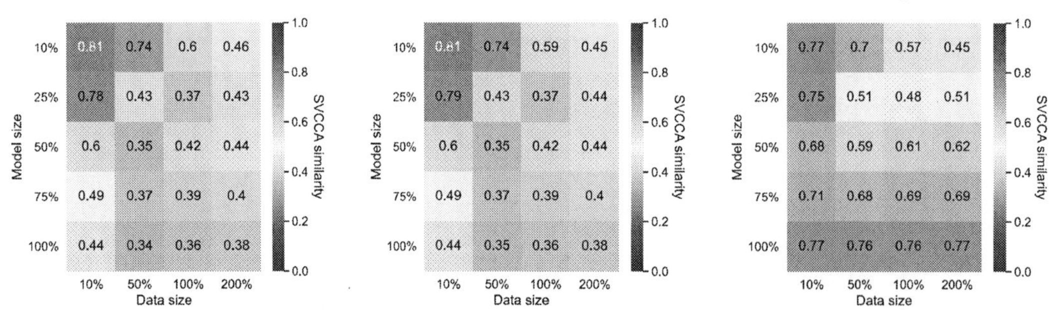

(d) ℓ_{12}: all words (e) ℓ_{12}: general words (f) ℓ_{12}: domain-specific words

Figure 14: The SVCCA score between $\mathbf{E}$ and $\mathbf{C}_{Movies}$ for different subsets of tokens. The top row presents the results for the embedding layer ℓ_0, and the bottom row presents them for the last layer ℓ_{12}.

m=50%		m=100%	
E	$\mathbf{C}_i$	**E**	$\mathbf{C}_i$
food	counter	bottle	counter
counter	hands	refrigerator	bottle
wine	oil	wine	hands
oil	food	food	sink
salad	salad	fridge	stove

(a) *I realize the point of my purchase was to reduce the amount of olive oil I sprayed on my [MASK] but I do end up having to pump it up and mist twice.* The masked word is a domain-specific word **salad** with i=`Home and Kitchen`.

m=50%		m=100%	
E	$\mathbf{C}_i$	**E**	$\mathbf{C}_i$
guy	guy	girl	guy
musician	woman	guy	woman
dude	man	killer	hero
kid	kid	gal	cop
vampire	person	dude	man

(b) *There had to be the four friends-a hypochondriac, a smoothing-talking [MASK] who gets everyone in trouble, the joker's friend who's a bit of a ham but has slightly more brains, and a girl.* The masked word is a domain-specific word **joker** with i=`Movies and TV`.

m=50%		m=100%	
E	$\mathbf{C}_i$	**E**	$\mathbf{C}_i$
say	have	worry	worry
think	say	complain	say
complain	know	wonder	know
know	care	know	think
worry	understand	say	complain

(c) *Amazon replaced it with no hassle, but I always have to [MASK] about these drives.* The masked word is a general word **worry** with i=`Electronics`.

m=50%		m=100%	
E	$\mathbf{C}_i$	**E**	$\mathbf{C}_i$
instructed	expected	suggested	suggested
suggested	instructed	stated	instructed
well	stated	instructed	expected
usual	advertised	advertised	well
indicated	normal	well	stated

(d) *I ordered a half size down as [MASK] and the size 11 eclipses my foot.* The masked word is a general word **suggested** with i=`Clothing Shoes and Jewelry`.

Table 6: Example MLM predictions of **E** and $\mathbf{C}_i$ using last layer representation. m denotes model capacity. All models here use a data size of 100%.

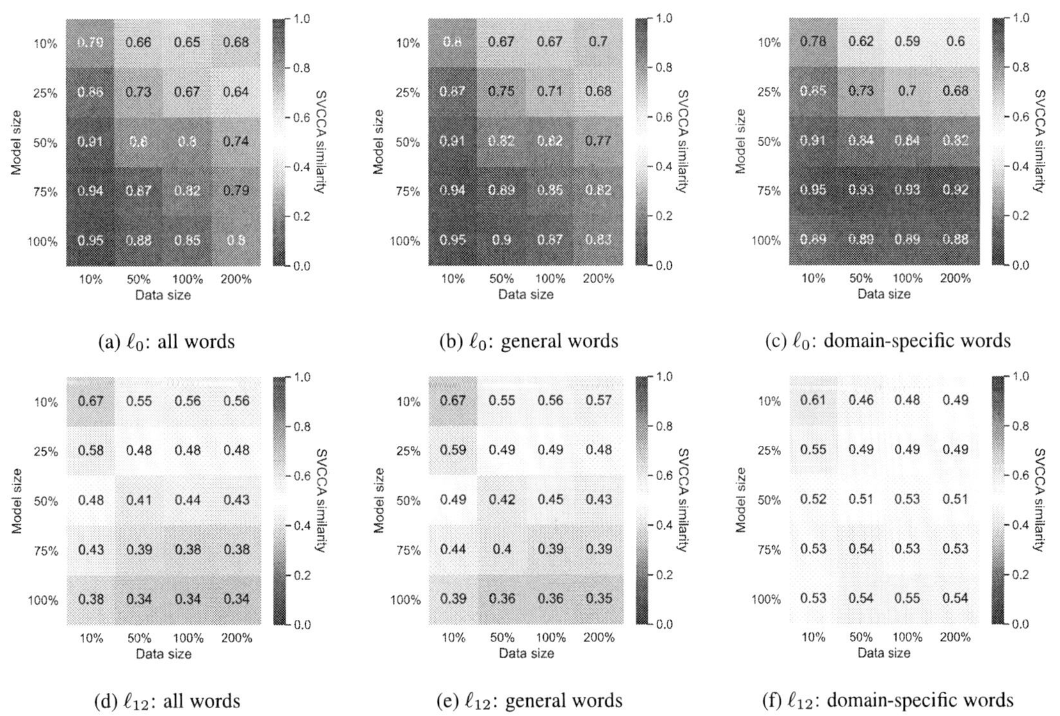

(a) ℓ_0: all words (b) ℓ_0: general words (c) ℓ_0: domain-specific words

(d) ℓ_{12}: all words (e) ℓ_{12}: general words (f) ℓ_{12}: domain-specific words

Figure 15: The SVCCA score between **E** and $\mathbf{C}_{Health}$ for different subsets of tokens. The top row presents the results for the embedding layer ℓ_0, and the bottom row presents them for the last layer ℓ_{12}.

Intermediate Entity-based Sparse Interpretable Representation Learning

Diego Garcia-Olano[1,3*] **Yasumasa Onoe**[1]
Joydeep Ghosh[1] **Byron C. Wallace**[2]
[1]University of Texas at Austin, [2]Northeastern University, [3]Meta AI
diegoolano@meta.com, {yasumasa,ghosh}@utexas.edu, b.wallace@northeastern.edu,

Abstract

Interpretable entity representations (IERs) are sparse embeddings that are "human-readable" in that dimensions correspond to fine-grained entity types and values are predicted probabilities that a given entity is of the corresponding type. These methods perform well in zero-shot and low supervision settings. Compared to standard dense neural embeddings, such interpretable representations may permit analysis and debugging. However, while fine-tuning sparse, interpretable representations improves accuracy on downstream tasks, it destroys the semantics of the dimensions which were enforced in pre-training. Can we maintain the interpretable semantics afforded by IERs while improving predictive performance on downstream tasks? Toward this end, we propose Intermediate enTity-based Sparse Interpretable Representation Learning (ItsIRL). ItsIRL realizes improved performance over prior IERs on biomedical tasks, while maintaining "interpretability" generally and their ability to support model debugging specifically. The latter is enabled in part by the ability to perform "counterfactual" fine-grained entity type manipulation, which we explore in this work. Finally, we propose a method to construct entity type based class prototypes for revealing global semantic properties of classes learned by our model.[1]

1 Introduction

Deep pre-trained models yield SOTA performance on a range of NLP tasks, but do so by learning and exploiting dense continuous representations of inputs which complicate model interpretation. That is, the dimensions in learned representations have no *a priori* semantics, and consequently are not directly human readable. Indeed, this has inspired an entire line of work on "probing" dense representations to recover the implicit knowledge stored within them (Petroni et al., 2019; Poerner et al., 2019).

An alternative is to design architectures that explicitly imbue embeddings with semantics. To this end, recent work has proposed learning high-dimensional sparse interpretable entity representations (IERs) for general and biomedical domains (Onoe and Durrett, 2020; Garcia-Olano et al., 2021). IERs are composed of a Transformer-based (Vaswani et al., 2017) entity typing model with a corresponding fine-grained static type system that accepts an entity mention and its context, and outputs individual probabilities that the mention is an instance of the respective types. These embeddings may then be used as features for downstream tasks.

IERs afford a variety of model transparency (dimensions have semantics) which may facilitate model debugging and/or instill confidence in model outputs. For example, if one defines a linear layer on top of entity-type representations, learned coefficients are interpretable as weights assigned to specific entity types. One could learn rules or manually debug models by reviewing incorrect predictions and inspecting the corresponding induced representations to identify potentially systematic erroneous type assignments. In addition to providing this type of interpretability, IERs have been shown to perform comparatively well in zero- and few-shot settings (Onoe and Durrett, 2020; Garcia-Olano et al., 2021).

A limitation of IERs is that they do not naturally permit fine-tuning, because doing so destroys the semantically meaningful entity typing representations learned during pre-training. This requirement is a limitation because fine-tuned models will in general achieve stronger predictive performance when supervision is available.

In this work we aim to improve the predictive performance of IERs without sacrificing their interpretability. Specifically, we propose Intermediate

* Work completed during PhD at UT Austin

[1]Code for pre-training and experiments available at `https://github.com/diegoolano/itsirl`

Proceedings of the Fifth BlackboxNLP Workshop on Analyzing and Interpreting Neural Networks for NLP, pages 210 - 224
December 8, 2022 ©2022 Association for Computational Linguistics

enTity-based Sparse Interpretable Representation Learning (ItsIRL). We show that this model outperforms prior IERs by a substantial margin on experiments over biomedical datasets — a domain where interpretability is often paramount — while providing natural mechanisms for model debugging by virtue of the representational semantics inherent to the architecture.

We then propose a counterfactual analysis of our intermediate interpretable layer to measure the effect of *entity type manipulation* on downstream predictions. This intervention is made possible by virtue of the model design. Using manually constructed, class-specific entity type sets we show that this intervention can be used to fix errors made by the proposed ItsIRL model automatically, ultimately allowing the model to outperform dense (uninterpretable) models in terms of test accuracy. We then propose a method in which we combine entity types over classes on training data to create positive and negative class prototypes that can be used to better understand the "global" semantics learned by ItsIRL for downstream tasks.

Our specific contributions are as follows:

- We introduce an intermediate interpretable layer into IERs; this layer output (representation) is then "decoded" into a dense layer which can be used for downstream predictions. The decoding step can be fine-tuned for specific tasks.

- We show that this approach empirically outperforms prior IER methods on two diverse biomedical benchmark tasks, often by a substantial margin.

- We propose a counterfactual entity type manipulation analysis made possible by our architecture which facilitates model debugging in an automated fashion with minimal, noisy supervision. This analysis allows our model to outperform dense (uninterpretable) models in terms of test accuracy and shows that the entity typing layer affects output classifications in an interpretable and intuitive way.

- We show how combining entity types over classes on the training set to create positive and negative class prototypes can be used to reveal task specific global semantics learned by our model.

2 Background: Interpretable Entity Representations Model

We first review the IER model architecture. Much of the material and notation here comes directly from (Onoe and Durrett, 2020; Garcia-Olano et al., 2021). Let $s = (w_1, ..., w_N)$ denote a sequence of input context words, $m = (w_i, ..., w_j)$ denote an entity mention span in s (over positions i through j), and $\mathbf{t} \in [0,1]^{|\mathcal{T}|}$ denote a vector whose values are predicted probabilities corresponding to fine-grained entity types $\mathcal{T}$ from a predefined type system.

Given a labeled dataset $\mathcal{D} = \{(m, s, \mathbf{t}^*)^{(1)}, ..., (m, s, \mathbf{t}^*)^{(k)}\}$ the IERs' objective is to estimate parameters θ of a function f_θ that maps the mention m and its context s to a vector $\mathbf{t}$ that captures salient features (fine-grain types) of the entity mention within its context. The entity embedding $\mathbf{t}$ whose individual dimensions have explicit semantics can then be used directly as input for downstream tasks using standard similarity measures (e.g., dot products). Note that fine-tuning these representations would destroy their interpretability because dimensions would no longer be readable as the probability of the input representing specific entity types.

The model f_θ that produces these embeddings is depicted as the "encoder" in Figure 1. First, a BERT-based encoder (Devlin et al., 2019) maps inputs m and s to an intermediate dense vector representation. The encoder input is a token sequence $\mathbf{x} = \texttt{[CLS]}\ m\ \texttt{[SEP]}\ s\ \texttt{[SEP]}$, where the mention m and context s are segmented into WordPiece tokens (Wu et al., 2016). The vector output `[CLS]` token serves as a d-dimensional dense mention and context representation: $\mathbf{h}_{\texttt{[CLS]}} = \text{BERTENCODER}(\mathbf{x}) \in \mathcal{R}^d$.

The key ingredient of IERs is a *type embedding layer*, which projects this intermediate representation to a vector whose dimensions correspond to the entity types in $\mathcal{T}$ using a single linear layer with parameters $\mathbf{E} \in \mathcal{R}^{|\mathcal{T}| \times d}$. Finally, each dimension (individually) is passed through the sigmoid function, yielding the predicted probabilities that form the interpretable entity representation $\mathbf{t}$ (the "intermediate layer" in Figure 1). More concisely: $\mathbf{t} = \sigma(\mathbf{E} \cdot \mathbf{h}_{\texttt{[CLS]}})$. To estimate parameters we optimize the sum of binary cross-entropy losses entity types $\mathcal{T}$ over training examples $\mathcal{D}$.

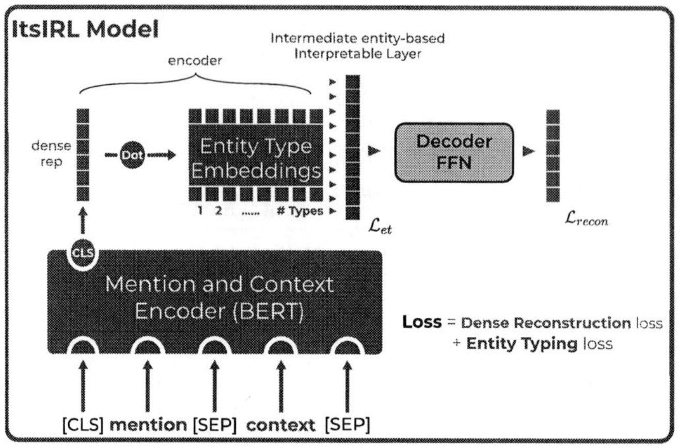

Figure 1: ItsIRL uses a LM and type supervision during pre-training to encode entity mention and context inputs for learning a matrix of entity type embeddings, an intermediate interpretable layer of type scores and a decoder to reconstruct the initial LM representation. The decoder can be fine-tuned on downstream tasks for better performance than IERs while keeping the semantics of the type layer.

3 Intermediate Entity-based Sparse Interpretable Representation Learning

We modify the IER model just described as follows:

- We project down the sparse entity typing layer and add pass its output through a three layer feed forward "decoder" network.
- We add an additional reconstruction component to our loss which is simply the mean squared error between the model's output and the initial `[CLS]` representation given by the Transformer based model.

This proposed model architecture — which we have called ItsIRL — is depicted in Figure 1. During pre-training, we adopt a loss $\mathcal{L}$ that combines entity typing loss over the sparse intermediate interpretable layer $\mathcal{L}_{\text{et}}$ and the reconstruction loss of the output representation $\mathcal{L}_{\text{recon}}$

$$\mathcal{L} = \mathcal{L}_{\text{recon}} + \lambda \mathcal{L}_{\text{et}}$$

where λ is a hyperparameter to be tuned.

The motivation behind the additional reconstruction loss is to pre-train a sort of auto-encoder with a sparse, high dimensional, interpretable latent space and rich dense output representations. Here the encoder induces a sparse embedding of entity types as in prior work on IERs, but now for downstream tasks we can freeze the encoder (which yields interpretable entity representations) and *fine-tune the decoder*. That hope is that this allows for both interpretable entity types and improved task performance.

In contrast to prior IER work in which sparse entity type representations were used directly for downstream tasks, here we pass the intermediate interpretable representation into a feed forward decoder network that produces a new representation which is used for prediction. This choice leads to differences in interpretability between IERs and our proposed architecture. We explore this in Section 5, along with how these intermediate predicted entity types affect task performance and how user or automated mechanisms to manipulate (i.e., up or down weight) these intermediate types affects performance.

This approach in some ways resembles *concept bottleneck* models (Koh et al. 2020; Chen et al. 2020; reviewed further in Section 6). However, these methods generally use low dimensional, *human-labeled concept supervision* to guide learning *for a single task*. By contrast, in our approach we exploit large-scale, possibly noisy entity type supervision to learn to induce interpretable representations which might be useful across tasks, i.e., for general pre-training.

We could pre-train such models in a few ways: (i) Train them end-to-end, or, (ii) Use existing IER models as points of initialization. In the latter case, we freeze the IER model originally trained using only $\mathcal{L}_{\text{et}}$ and train/update the rest of the model weights using only $\mathcal{L}_{\text{recon}}$ as the loss on our pre-training data.

For our experiments we use the publicly available biomedical IER model checkpoint, entity type system, and pre-training data from (Garcia-Olano et al., 2021). The model checkpoint is based on an underlying PubMedBERT model (Gu et al., 2020). The type system contains 68,304 entity types and the training data consists of 37,357,141 triples of the form (`mention, context, [list of entity types]`) derived from PubMed linked Wikipedia pages where entity types are Wikipedia categories.

4 Experimental Setup

We evaluate the proposed ItsIRL architecture on two biomedical benchmark tasks: Entity label classification for Cancer Genetics (Pyysalo et al., 2013) and sentence similarity regression for the BIOSSES dataset found in the BLURB benchmark (Gu et al., 2020).

4.1 Cancer Genetics Entity Label Classification

The Cancer Genetics dataset (Pyysalo et al., 2013) consists of 10,935 training, 3,634 dev, and 6,955 test examples from 300, 100, and 200 unique PubMed articles, respectively. Given an article title/abstract and an entity mention, the objective is to categorize the entity into one of 16 classes which cover different subdomains in cancer biology.

For the downstream task we simply add a linear layer that accepts as its input the output of our pre-trained ItsIRL model and we then fine-tune the ItsIRL decoder and linear layer to minimize cross entropy loss. We stop training when the model accuracy ceases to improve on the dev set. We also provide numbers for how ItsIRL performs if we fine-tune on training data in an end-to-end fashion (ItsIRL E2E; i.e., unfreezing and updating the encoder weights and intermediate type layer); this destroys the interpretability of the intermediate layer enforced in pre-training. Results for using the prior Biomedical Interpretable Entity Representations (BIERs) dot product based model and PubMedBERT dense model are from (Garcia-Olano et al., 2021). We provide ablations to explore the effect of decoder network layer size and pre-training.

Results We report task results in Table 1. Compared to the prior IERs work (87.5%), the ItsIRL model gives improved performance (91.9%) while keeping the semantic interpretable entity type layer intact. ItsIRL E2E realizes performance comparable to fine-tuning PubMedBERT alone (95.7% and 96.1%, respectively), but in both cases we no longer have interpretable models which can be diagnosed and fixed at run time.

As a point of reference, we also report results achieved by dense models. However, we emphasize that these do not provide the transparency afforded by ItsIRL; we are interested in achieving both accuracy *and* interpretability — models which strictly optimize the former may be viewed as a reasonable "upper-bound" with respect to accuracy alone, and in general we expect that realizing interpretability (and specifically in our case, "debuggability") will entail some trade-off in accuracy.[2]

We observe this expected trade-off here (ItsIRL performs better than BIER, but worse than end-to-end models which lack semantic representations). We also confirm that the proposed model can be fine-tuned end-to-end to achieve the same accuracy as the dense PubMedBERT model, at the expense of interpretability. Perhaps more interestingly, in section 5 we show that leveraging entity type manipulation at inference time allows the ItsIRL model to outperform both uninterpretable models.

We perform a few ablations to assess which parts of ItsIRL affect performance. We perform fine-tuning on the task data using a decoder whose weights are randomly initialized to test the effect of pre-training on 37 million triples. The bottom of Table 1 shows that this degrades performance (88.9% vs. 91.9%) and suggests that pre-training the decoder network is important for task performance.

We additionally explored varying layer depths for our decoder (3, 5, 8) and observed similar performance across them; we therefore opted to use the smaller decoder network of 3 layers. We note that prior work (Garcia-Olano et al., 2021) explored adding a single linear layer on top of the entity type representation (which is identical to ours) and fine-tuning it for the task. This single layer "decoder" yields 68.1% test accuracy, indicating that the additional network capacity and pre-training are both important.

4.2 BIOSSES sentence similarity regression

The Sentence Similarity Estimation System for the Biomedical Domain (Soğancıoğlu et al., 2017)

[2]Related works (e.g., Koh et al. 2020; Alvarez Melis and Jaakkola 2018 have tended to report results for *only* other "interpretable" models as baselines; we include standard dense models here for completeness.

Model	Q	Test Acc
BIER-PMB*	✓	87.5
ItsIRL	✓	91.9
ItsIRL E2E*	-	95.7
PubMedBERT	-	96.1

Ablations	Test Acc
ItsIRL - random init	88.9
ItsIRL - 1 layer decoder	68.1

Table 1: Cancer Genetics results
Q = interpretable types

			Type Sparsity		
Model	Q	MSE	@.01	@.1	@.25
BIER-PMB*	✓	5.05	33.6	8.1	4.4
ItsIRL	✓	1.59	33.6	8.1	4.4
ItsIRL E2E*	-	1.15	5723	780	330
PubMedBERT	-	1.14	-	-	-

Table 2: BIOSSES sentence similarity results.

PMB* = PubMedBERT
E2E* = End-To-End fine-tuned

(BIOSSES) contains 100 pairs of PubMed sentences, each annotated by five expert annotators with an estimated similarity score in the range from 0 (no relation) to 4 (equivalent meanings). Predicting these scores (averaged over annotators) is a regression task used in the BLURB benchmark (Gu et al., 2020).

We use the train/dev/test splits from the BLUE benchmark (Peng et al., 2019). We feed each sentence pair with a `SEP` between them as input and use mean squared error as our loss and for evaluation purposes amongst our model variants. In contrast to the Cancer Genetics task which has >10k training samples, this dataset is small, comprising 64, 16, and 20 train, dev, and test instances, respectively. We also evaluate the sparsity of the entity type layer induced by ItsIRL using different thresholds to numerically quantify the interpretability of these entity types, where having fewer types is more easily human interpretable.[3] Entity types whose weights are larger than a threshold are semantically meaningful at that threshold.

Results We show results for the sentence similarity regression task in Table 2. The pattern in our results is similar to above: ItsIRL outperforms BIERs due to its being fine-tuned on task specific data. ItsIRL is competitive with, but slightly underperforms, the end-to-end fine-tuned ItsIRL E2E variant and the dense PubMedBERT model (neither of these offer an interpretable entity layer after fine-tuning).

In Table 2 we also observe that the number of entity types shown to be semantically meaningful is much less and hence more interpretable when comparing ItsIRL with ItsIRL E2E which removes the semantic meaning of the entity types space. Figure 4 in the Appendix shows this sparsity value as a percentage over many different thresholds, showing the fine-tuned ItsIRL is more sparse and interpretable than both the ItsIRL E2E model and the dense non-interpretable PubMedBERT model.

5 Entity Type Counterfactual Manipulation and Global Explainability

We have claimed that (sparse) entity type representations permit "interpretability", but this is an ill-defined term in general. Here we demonstrate that ItsIRL provides a specific type of "interpretability" in that it can help facilitate model understanding and error analysis via "counterfactual" entity type manipulation, made possible by the intermediate entity type layer. Specifically, we consider the Cancer Genetics classification task (Pyysalo et al., 2013), and focus on revealing learned global structure of classes. We then show how manipulating predicted types on erroneous test cases affects the ItsIRL model's performance.

5.1 Entity Type Global Explainability

To better understand the representations learned by ItsIRL for each class, we apply the task, decoder fine-tuned model over the training data. We gather all correctly predicted instances for each class, sum their interpretable entity type representations and normalize them.[4] We refer to each of these as a *positive class prototype*.

Results In Table 3 we show the "top" entity types — those with the highest weights — for 7 of 16 class prototypes (for space); on inspection, these intuitively seem semantically meaningful with respect

[3]As the prior BIER-PubMedBERT and ItsIRL share the same model checkpoint and hence interpretable entity typing layer, BIER-PMB will have the same type sparsity as ItsIRL.

[4]Positive class prototype $= \frac{v-\min(v)}{\max(v)-\min(v)}$ where v is the sum of entity type representations for correctly predicted training instances of a given class.

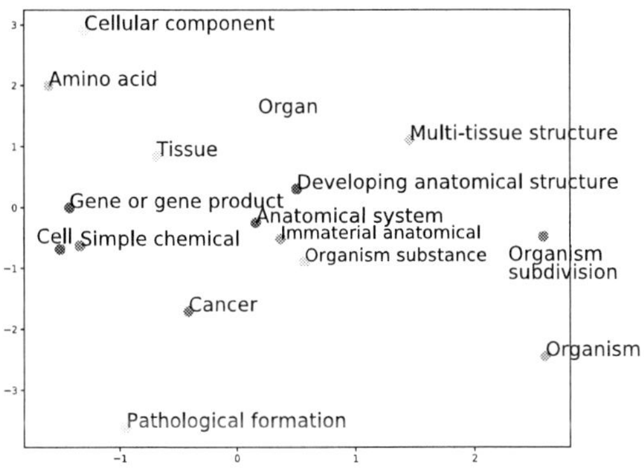

Figure 2: Positive Class Prototypes in 2D via PaCMAP

to the classes. In Appendix Table 7 we also show the weights and index of each entity type in the 68k type system, with lower indices denoting types that appeared more often in pre-training data. We also provide the F1 scores and support of these classes on the test set. Looking at the indices of top entity terms per class prototypes, we note that they tend to be in the tens or hundreds range, implying that more frequent entity types in the training data dominate the positive prototypes. However, consider two classes for which we observe lower than average F1 scores: *Multi-tissue structure* and *Tissue*. These prototypes include rare "top" entity types (e.g., "soft tissue", "nephron" and "barcode") with indices in the 1000s (3067, 1951 & 2351) that were seen less during pre-training which shows the model may have learned weaker representations for entity types that appeared less frequently.

Similarly, we can gather all training predictions that were incorrect, group them by the true labels, and then sum and normalize their entity type layers to generate negative prototypes. In Appendix Table 9 we show the most common error patterns and their negative prototypes' most important entity types. We note the negative prototypes predicted align with the positive prototypes true classes.

Finally, in Figure 2 we use PaCMAP (Wang et al., 2021) to visualize our positive prototypes in two dimensions.[5] The distance between classes aligns well with the most common error patterns (i.e., Cell, Cancer, Chemical, and Gene cluster near each other) while "anatomical" and "organism" related classes also cluster near each other.

[5] PacMAP is a dimensionality reduction method shown to preserve the global and local structure of the data in its original space better than techniques such as TSNE and UMAP.

5.2 Counterfactual Entity Type Manipulation

To explore how intermediate entity types affect downstream performance, and more specifically how predictions *would have changed* had relevant types been manipulated, we first construct sets of entity types for each class as approximations of what a non-expert might come up with by simple string matching per class against the 68K entity types in the type system provided in (Garcia-Olano et al., 2021). These terms for inclusion and exclusion from the sets along with the resulting type set sizes are provided in Appendix Table 6. We emphasize that these were easy to assemble and are coarse, noisy sets that roughly approximate entity types we would expect to be associated with each class.

Some classes such as Organism, Organism substance, Organism subdivision and Organ have sets containing the same entity types to show even quite noisy sets can be useful. Our intent here is not to obtain the maximum possible accuracy we can get via entity type manipulation for error cases, but rather to show the utility of this model even when paired with noisy term sets.

After constructing coarse sets of entity types, we identify three strategies of interest for manipulating entity types during inference time:

- "Fixing" bad entity types (i.e., minimize the weights of entity types from the incorrectly predicted class's coarse type set).
- "Promoting" good types (i.e., maximize the weights of entity types associated with the true label's type set).
- Using both the fix and promote strategies together.

For our experiment, we take test error cases and for each, run them through our model and either lower ("fix") types associated with the incorrect class set, increase ("promote") types associated with the true class set or do "both" to the corresponding entity type weights in the intermediate entity types layer. We then observe how the final class probabilities for the task are affected by the manipulation. Appendix Figure 3 shows how a single test example's class prediction distribution, derived from its original inferred types and logits, are changed by these techniques.

	Gene or gene product	Cell	Cancer	Simple chemical	Organism	Multi-tissue structure	Tissue
1	protein	cell	disease	ingredient	taxonomy	blood	tissue
2	ingredient	elementary particle	neoplasm	acid	mammals in 1758	angiology	cell
3	human	human cells	oncology	rtt	humans	soft tissue	human body
4	gene	battery	tissue	who essential medicines	tool-using mammals	nephron	connective tissue
5	coagulation	gene	abnormality	chemical compound	anatomically modern humans	blood vessel	endocrine system
6	cell	protein	cancer	measurement	postmodernism	human body	epithelium
7	cell growth	pancreas	syndrome	calcium	patient	lymphatic sys	angiology
8	endothelium	system	malignancy	hydroxyl	medical term.	lymphoid org.	blood vessel
9	homology	carboxylic acid	cell growth	glucose	prothrombin time	mononuclear phagocyte sys	histology
10	oncogene	ester	paraneoplastic syndromes	methyl group	bbc	gland	barcode

Table 3: Top 10 Entity Types by weight for 7 most frequent positive Prototype class embeddings

Model	Test Accuracy
ItsIRL	91.48
+ Fix types	93.91
+ Promote types	95.74
+ Both fix & promote	95.68
+ Best of 3 "oracle"	**96.78**
PubMedBERT*	96.10

Table 4: Entity type manipulation results using class-specific coarse type sets

Results In Table 4 we report the results for our three entity manipulation techniques using coarse term sets including the best accuracy that could have been achieved amongst them for each error pattern. The model predicting `Gene` when the true class label was `Chemical` is the most common test error pattern and in Table 5 we show the most frequent error patterns observed on the test set. Promoting entity types of the true class improves our model results from 91.48 to 95.74, while both promoting and fixing leads to a similar 95.68. These strategies give results on par with using a dense non-interpretable PubMedBert model while using the best among them outperforms PubMedBert. For future work, determining the best method for each error case could be done by observing performance of the techniques on a holdout set. Fixing incorrect entity types alone under performs the other techniques possibly since down weighing incorrect types alone does not necessarily push the embedding towards the correct class. We note these automated methods require knowledge of if and in what way initial predictions may be erroneous, and our intent is to show that manipulating entity types in ItsIRL affects classification in an intuitive way which amongst other things allows them to be used with the rule based diagnostics from prior IERs.

In Table 5 we show how the entity type manipulation techniques perform on each error pattern. Using the best technique for each error pattern allows us to correct 361 out of 592 test errors (~61%). "Promoting" types is best or tied 11 out of 15 times, "Both" gives 10 out of 15 while "Fixing" gives 6 out of 15. Given the coarse type sets, all methods work poorly on the following error patterns (True Class-Predicted): Pathological Formation-Cancer, Organism-Cell, Organism-Gene, Organ-Multi-Tissue, and Multi-Tissue-Cancer. This suggests these sets should be edited in order to better discriminate between these classes. Resolving errors is dependent on the distance between two classes and for Cell-Cancer, Cell-Gene, Cancer-Cell and Cancer-Organism subdivision, fixing incorrect types does poorly (0 errors resolved out of 101) while at the same time, promoting types from the true class does very well resolving 99 out of 101 error cases. We note that this process was entirely automated and having experts edit or choose better terms to form type sets associated with each class would easily improve its performance in particular with regard to error patterns where all strategies performed poorly.

6 Related Work

In this work we introduced an architecture with an encoder that uses supervision from a pre-defined

True	Predicted	Errs	T1+2	T1	T2	Best%
Chemical	Gene	65	64	48	59	98.4
Cell	Cancer	41	31	41	0	100
Cell	Gene	34	34	34	0	100
Multi-Tis	Tissue*	22	0	0	7	31.8
Gene	Chemical	17	3	3	10	58.8
Organ	Tissue	16	12	10	12	75
Cancer	Cell	16	0	14	0	87
Gene	Organism	15	6	0	15	100
Cell	Chemical	14	14	14	4	100
Amino	Gene	14	14	14	14	100
Pathol	Cancer	14	0	0	0	0
Organism	Cell	14	0	0	0	0
Organism	Gene	12	0	2	0	16.7
Organ	Multi-Tissue	10	0	1	0	10
Multi-Tis	Cancer	10	0	0	0	0
Chemical	Amino	10	10	10	10	100
Cancer	Org. Sub.	10	10	10	0	100
Cell	Tissue	10	10	10	5	100
Cell	Celu Comp*	10	10	10	0	100
	Raw Total	592	292	296	169	361
	Percent	100	49.3	50	46.8	61

Table 5: Most frequent error patterns and manipulation results on test data for "Promote" (T1), "Fix" (T2) and "Both" (T1+2) techniques. * means the term sets are equal and as "Fix" is first applied followed by "Promote", the "Both" results for these cases are identical to the "Promote" ones.

static entity type system to learn an intermediate, interpretable high dimension, sparse entity type layer which is then used by a decoder network for downstream tasks. The most similar area of work to ours is that of Concept Bottlenecks (CBs) (Chen et al., 2020; Koh et al., 2020) which use an encoder and supervision to learn a low dimensional, dense representation for a single task. Supervision for CBs are hand collected by experts, dense (mostly nonzero) and exist in a low dimensional space (tens to hundreds of dimensions). For the two experiments in (Koh et al., 2020) 112 binary (CUB) and 10 ordinal (OAI) concepts were gathered from experts. On the other hand, IERs and our work use static, noisy entity systems gathered via weak supervision that exist in a high dimensional space (68,340 entity types) and are pre-trained for use in downstream tasks. Due to its size compared to layers in the rest of the network, our intermediate entity type layer is not a "bottleneck" in the usual sense of latent spaces of autoencoders, such as those from the CB literature.

Our use of the intermediate interpretable entity layer to represent classes for global explainability is reminiscent of work for learning prototypes for images (Li et al., 2018), timeseries (Garcia-Olano et al., 2019) or text (Das et al., 2022), however in our case constructing the prototypes of each class is done post-hoc and as such the prototypes are used for analysis rather than classification or learning. Additionally, our method is interpretable at the vector component level whereas the latent representations used for constructing prototypes are not. Also, our pre-trained representations are not tied to a classification task like prototypes and as such can be used for various different tasks.

Our model could be viewed as including an internal Probing task which tests a models' ability to induce type information by measuring the accuracy of a probe (Peters et al., 2018; Hewitt and Manning, 2019; Hewitt and Liang, 2019). However, probing is usually a post-hoc means of revealing the information implicitly stored within internal dense output representations, whereas our model was defined and pre-trained in such a way as to explicitly provide intermediate interpretable entity type representations.

7 Conclusions

In this work we proposed Intermediate Entity-based Sparse Interpretable Representation Learning (ItsIRL), an extension to the IERs architecture which provides an intermediate interpretable layer whose decoded dense representation output can be fine-tuned and leveraged for performance on downstream tasks. Empirically we show the model substantially outperforms prior IERs work on two diverse benchmark biomedical tasks.

To demonstrate the utility of the kind of interpretability afforded by ItsIRL, we proposed a counterfactual entity type manipulation analysis which allows for modeling debugging. This is a fine-grained, human interaction inquiry made possible by the proposed model architecture and pre-training scheme. Using coarse class type sets, we show this technique can allow ItsIRL to surpass performance against dense non-interpretable models. This analysis establishes that entity type manipulation works intuitively as expected in ItsIRL, which is important for future work on methods for flagging when a predicted answer should be inspected and possibly manipulated at the entity type level.

We finally show how combining entity types over classes on the training set to create positive and negative class prototypes can be used to explain task specific global structure and semantics learned by our model.

Ethical Considerations

NLP models are increasingly used in biomedicine, where some applications can be quite high-stakes. Establishing trust in such models is therefore paramount; unfortunately, deep neural networks tend to be opaque in their operations, potentially precluding their use in certain areas of biomedicine where they might otherwise be beneficial. This work is a step towards more transparent NLP models.

References

David Alvarez Melis and Tommi Jaakkola. 2018. Towards robust interpretability with self-explaining neural networks. In *Advances in Neural Information Processing Systems*.

Zhi Chen, Yijie Bei, and Cynthia Rudin. 2020. Concept whitening for interpretable image recognition. In *Nature Machine Intelligence*.

Anubrata Das, Chitrank Gupta, Venelin Kovatchev, Matthew Lease, and Junyi Jessy Li. 2022. PROTOTEX: Explaining Model Decisions with Prototype Tensors. In *Proceedings of the 60th Annual Meeting of the Association for Computational Linguistics (ACL)*. 12 pages.

Jacob Devlin, Ming-Wei Chang, Kenton Lee, and Kristina Toutanova. 2019. BERT: Pre-training of Deep Bidirectional Transformers for Language Understanding. In *Proceedings of the Conference of the North American Chapter of the Association for Computational Linguistics: Human Language Technologies (NAACL-HLT)*.

Diego Garcia-Olano, Alan H. Gee, Joydeep Ghosh, and David Paydarfar. 2019. Explaining deep classification of time-series data with learned prototypes. In *Proceedings of the International Conference on Machine Learning (ICML) Time-series workshop*.

Diego Garcia-Olano, Yasumasa Onoe, Ioana Baldini, Joydeep Ghosh, Byron Wallace, and Kush Varshney. 2021. Biomedical interpretable entity representations. In *Findings of the 59th Annual Meeting of the Association for Computational Linguistics*. Association for Computational Linguistics.

Yu Gu, Robert Tinn, Hao Cheng, Michael Lucas, Naoto Usuyama, Xiaodong Liu, Tristan Naumann, Jianfeng Gao, and Hoifung Poon. 2020. Domain-Specific Language Model Pretraining for Biomedical Natural Language Processing.

John Hewitt and Percy Liang. 2019. Designing and Interpreting Probes with Control Tasks. In *Proceedings of the Conference on Empirical Methods in Natural Language Processing (EMNLP)*.

John Hewitt and Christopher D. Manning. 2019. A Structural Probe for Finding Syntax in Word Representations. In *Proceedings of the Conference of the North American Chapter of the Association for Computational Linguistics: Human Language Technologies (NAACL-HLT)*.

Pang Wei Koh, Thao Nguyen, Yew Siang Tang, Stephen Mussmann, Emma Pierson, Been Kim, and Percy Liang. 2020. Concept bottleneck models. In *Proceedings of the 37th International Conference on Machine Learning*, volume 119 of *Proceedings of Machine Learning Research*, pages 5338–5348. PMLR.

Oscar Li, Hao Liu, Chaofan Chen, and Cynthia Rudin. 2018. Deep learning for case-based reasoning through prototypes: A neural network that explains its predictions. AAAI'18/IAAI'18/EAAI'18. AAAI Press.

Yasumasa Onoe and Greg Durrett. 2020. Interpretable Entity Representations through Large-Scale Typing. In *Findings of the Association for Computational Linguistics: EMNLP*.

Yifan Peng, Shankai Yan, and Zhiyong Lu. 2019. Transfer learning in biomedical natural language processing: An evaluation of BERT and ELMo on ten benchmarking datasets. In *Proceedings of the 18th BioNLP Workshop and Shared Task*, pages 58–65, Florence, Italy. Association for Computational Linguistics.

Matthew Peters, Mark Neumann, Mohit Iyyer, Matt Gardner, Christopher Clark, Kenton Lee, and Luke Zettlemoyer. 2018. Deep Contextualized Word Representations. In *Proceedings of the Conference of the North American Chapter of the Association for Computational Linguistics: Human Language Technologies (NAACL-HLT)*.

Fabio Petroni, Tim Rocktäschel, Sebastian Riedel, Patrick Lewis, Anton Bakhtin, Yuxiang Wu, and Alexander Miller. 2019. Language Models as Knowledge Bases? In *Proceedings of the Conference on Empirical Methods in Natural Language Processing (EMNLP)*.

Nina Poerner, Ulli Waltinger, and Hinrich Schütze. 2019. BERT is Not a Knowledge Base (Yet): Factual Knowledge vs. Name-Based Reasoning in Unsupervised QA. *ArXiv*, abs/1911.03681.

Sampo Pyysalo, Tomoko Ohta, and Sophia Ananiadou. 2013. Overview of the Cancer Genetics (CG) task of BioNLP Shared Task 2013. In *Proceedings of the BioNLP Shared Task 2013 Workshop*.

Gizem Soğancıoğlu, Hakime Öztürk, and Arzucan Özgür. 2017. BIOSSES: a semantic sentence similarity estimation system for the biomedical domain. *Bioinformatics*, 33(14):i49–i58.

Ashish Vaswani, Noam Shazeer, Niki Parmar, Jakob Uszkoreit, Llion Jones, Aidan N. Gomez, Lukasz Kaiser, and Illia Polosukhin. 2017. Attention is All you Need. In *Proceedings of Advances in Neural Information Processing Systems (NeurIPS)*.

Yingfan Wang, Haiyang Huang, Cynthia Rudin, and Yaron Shaposhnik. 2021. Understanding how dimension reduction tools work: An empirical approach to deciphering t-sne, umap, trimap, and pacmap for data visualization. *Journal of Machine Learning Research*, 22(201):1–73.

Yonghui Wu, Mike Schuster, Zhifeng Chen, Quoc V. Le, Mohammad Norouzi, Wolfgang Macherey, Maxim Krikun, Yuan Cao, Qin Gao, Klaus Macherey, Jeff Klingner, Apurva Shah, Melvin Johnson, Xiaobing Liu, Lukasz Kaiser, Stephan Gouws, Yoshikiyo Kato, Taku Kudo, Hideto Kazawa, Keith Stevens, George Kurian, Nishant Patil, Wei Wang, Cliff Young, Jason Smith, Jason Riesa, Alex Rudnick, Oriol Vinyals, Gregory S. Corrado, Macduff Hughes, and Jeffrey Dean. 2016. Google's Neural Machine Translation System: Bridging the Gap between Human and Machine Translation. *ArXiv*, abs/1609.08144.

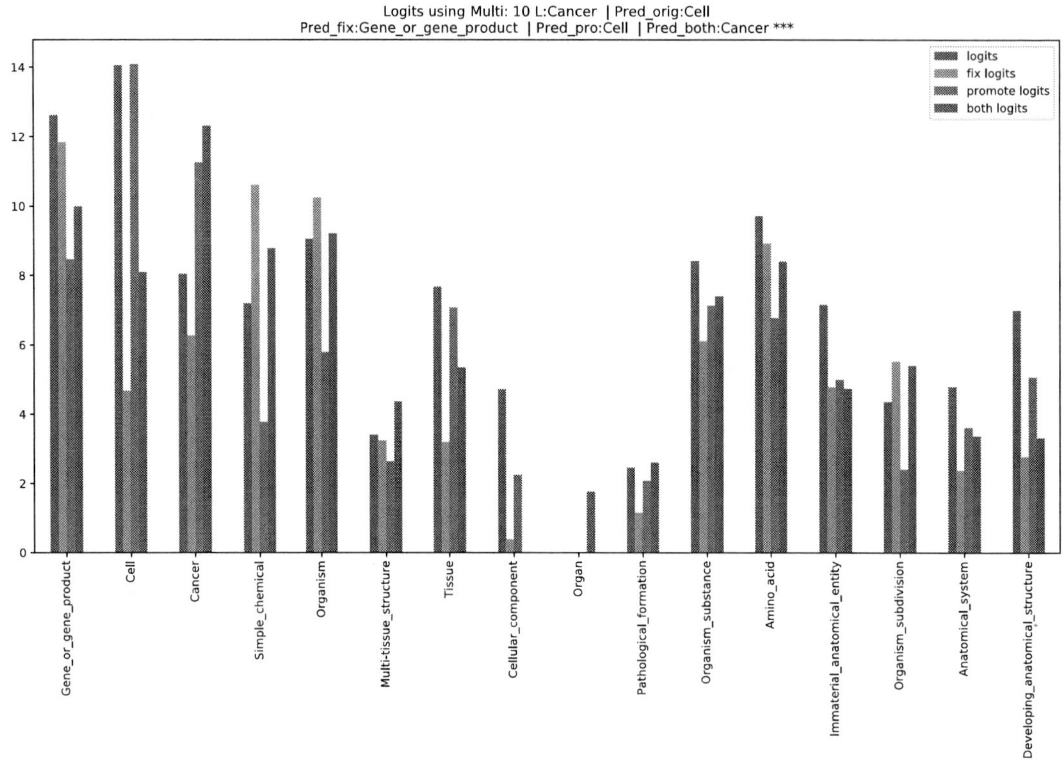

Figure 3: Class shifts using type manipulation techniques for single example

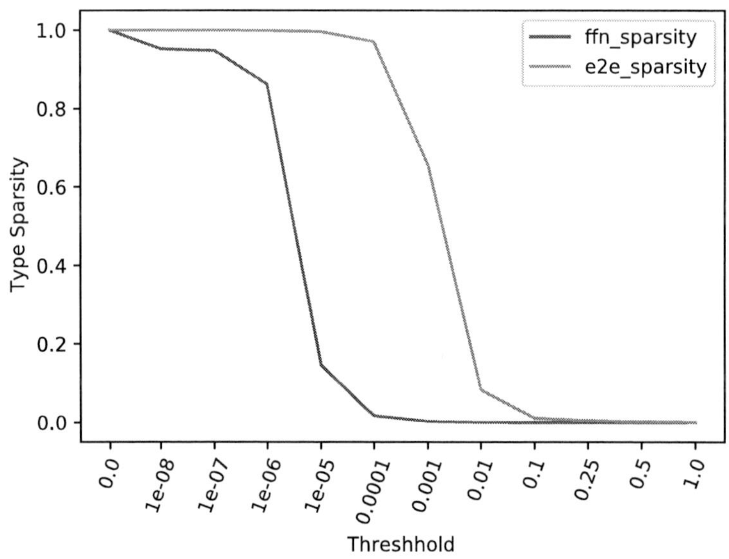

Figure 4: Entity Type Sparsity at various thresholds on BIOSSES test set

Class	Term Rules Inclusion/Exclusion	Terms in Set
Cell	[cell]	357
Cellular component	[cell]	357
Cancer	[cancer, neoplasm]	155
Gene or gene product	[‘ gene’, ‘gene ’, ‘ genes’, ‘genes ’] , not in [‘generation’, ‘general’] ,	434
Simple chemical	[chemical, chemical]	80
Organism	[‘ organ’, ‘organ ’, ‘organism’] not in [‘organization’]	172
Organism substance	[‘ organ’, ‘organ ’, ‘organism’] not in [‘organization’]	172
Organism subdivision	[‘ organ’, ‘organ ’, ‘organism’] not in [‘organization’]	172
Organ	[‘ organ’, ‘organ ’, ‘organism’] not in [‘organization’]	172
Tissue	[tissue, tissue]	15
Multi-tissue structure	[tissue, tissue]	15
Amino acid	[amino, amino , amino acid]	22
Pathological formation	[pathological]	3
Immaterial anatomical entity	[anatomical , anatomical, anatomical]	11
Developing anatomical structure	[anatomical , anatomical, anatomical]	11
Anatomical system	[anatomical , anatomical, anatomical]	11

Table 6: Terms used to create coarse Class specific Entity Type sets

Gene or gene product	Cell	Cancer	Simple chemical	Organism	Multi-tissue structure	Tissue
protein (1.0, 5)	cell (biology) (1.0, 3)	disease (1.0, 2)	ingredient (1.0, 1)	taxonomy (biology) (1.0, 45)	blood (1.0, 47)	tissue (biology) (1.0, 34)
ingredient (0.742, 1)	elementary particle (0.346, 314)	neoplasm (0.897, 8)	acid (0.304, 18)	mammals described in 1758 (0.943,169)	angiology (0.843, 857)	cell (biology) (0.878, 3)
human (0.729, 7)	human cells (0.201, 145)	oncology (0.684, 28)	rtt (0.301, 4)	humans (0.943, 187)	soft tissue (0.792, 3067)	human body (0.814, 30)
gene (0.679, 6)	battery (electricity) (0.192, 485)	tissue (biology) (0.646, 34)	world health organization essential medicines (0.269, 25)	tool-using mammals (0.943, 186)	nephron (0.761, 1951)	connective tissue (0.385, 937)
coagulation (0.361, 37)	gene (0.184, 6)	abnormality (behavior) (0.604, 56)	chemical compound (0.206, 14)	anatomically modern humans (0.943,188)	blood vessel (0.682, 327)	endocrine system (0.345, 482)
cell (biology) (0.353, 3)	protein (0.177, 5)	cancer (0.582, 9)	measurement (0.19, 12)	post-modernism (0.943, 177)	human body (0.538, 30)	epithelium (0.325, 144)
cell growth (0.314, 46)	pancreas (0.167, 498)	syndrome (0.492, 48)	calcium in biology (0.175, 40)	patient (0.863, 13)	lymphatic system (0.52, 789)	angiology (0.322, 857)
endothelium (0.265, 192)	system (0.166, 166)	malignancy (0.467, 20)	hydroxyl (0.16, 76)	medical terminology (0.84, 11)	lymphoid organ (0.498, 1640)	blood vessel (0.319, 327)
homology (biology) (0.241, 111)	carboxylic acid (0.164, 577)	cell growth (0.466, 46)	glucose (0.142, 278)	prothrombin time (0.836, 22)	mononuclear phagocyte system (0.493, 979)	histology (0.317, 391)
oncogene (0.24, 285)	ester (0.164, 208)	paraneoplastic syndromes (0.458,380)	methyl group (0.131, 72)	bbc (0.739, 180)	gland (0.471, 174)	barcode (0.311, 2351)
F1score - 96.29	90.71	92.73	90.24	94.10	81.65	74.94
Support - 2520	1054	925	727	543	303	190

Table 7: Top 10 Entity Types for 7 most frequent positive Prototype classes with weights and index of type. F1 score and support for each class over test data is given in final two rows.

Cellular component	Organ	Pathological formation	Organism substance	Amino acid	Immaterial anatomical entity	Organism subdivision	Anatomical system	Developing anatomical structure
dna (1.0, 127)	tongue (1.0, 158)	disease (1.0, 2)	blood (1.0, 47)	ingredient (1.0, 1)	cell anatomy (1.0, 464)	anatomical terms of location (1.0, 373)	organ (1.0, 138)	embryology (1.0, 3496)
ingredient (0.97, 1)	ecosystem (0.88, 268)	wound (0.85, 2492)	tetrahydrogestrinone (0.51, 828)	amino acid (0.97, 98)	cell biology (0.99, 84)	human body (0.93, 30)	system (0.91, 166)	childbirth (0.07, 101)
molecule (0.89, 82)	organs (0.75, 321)	medical emergencies (0.77, 532)	nitrous oxide (0.48, 16)	glucogenic amino acids (0.96, 757)	cell (0.77, 3)	leg (0.91, 2382)	nervous system (0.72, 566)	midwifery (0.07, 1835)
acid (0.89, 18)	human body (0.69, 30)	injury (0.75, 463)	psychosis (0.48, 26)	proteinogenic amino acids (0.96, 657)	intracellular (0.74, 328)	limb (0.85, 3675)	central nervous system (0.59, 721)	health issues in pregnancy (0.07, 2873)
biotechnology (0.89, 140)	organ (0.64, 138)	morphology (0.75, 137)	hematology (0.39, 236)	acid (0.93, 18)	molecular biology (0.73, 55)	tongue (0.71, 158)	central african republic (0.58, 4155)	health care (0.07, 272)
polymer (0.89, 1204)	articles containing video clips (0.54, 19)	injuries (0.75, 3237)	ingredient (0.32, 1)	calcium in biology (0.90, 40)	middle east (0.28, 1229)	lower limb anatomy (0.67, 8420)	chemical structure (0.57, 1315)	fetus (0.07, 1172)
helices (0.87, 2487)	human anatomy by organ (0.44, 1430)	acute pain (0.75, 923)	articles containing video clips (0.29,19)	measurement (0.83, 12)	route of administration (0.24, 209)	anatomy (0.63, 287)	cerebrospinal fluid (0.56, 2756)	obstetrical procedures (0.0, 146)
nucleic acids (0.89, 1426)	gland (0.43, 174)	first aid (0.74, 5588)	cell anatomy (0.27, 464)	amine (0.67, 61)	abdomen (0.24, 503)	animal locomotion (0.62, 672)	musical quintets (0.5, 1926)	blood cells (0.0, 2195)
cell (0.83, 3)	digestion (0.39, 607)	physical therapy (0.73, 1765)	tissues (0.27, 791)	isomer (0.48, 800)	drug (0.19, 24)	foot (0.59, 5959)	radiophar macology (0.49, 3611)	developmental biology (0.0, 352)
cell membrane (0.58, 288)	tissue (0.38, 34)	tongue (0.37, 158)	body fluids (0.19, 617)	ketogenic amino acids (0.42, 1974)	pharmaceutical drug (0.18, 17)	animal (0.59, 273)	earache records (0.48, 5219)	transformation (genetics) (0.0, 752)

Table 8: Top 10 Entity Types for remaining 9 positive Prototype classes with weights and index of type. F1 score and support for each class over test data is given in final two rows.

Truth Pred	Cell Cancer	Chemical Gene	Cell Gene	Organism Gene	Tissue Multi-tissue	Gene Chemical	Cancer Cell
1	cancer (1.0, 9)	ingredient (1.0, 1)	gene (1.0, 6)	gene (1.0, 6)	histology (1.0, 391)	ingredient (1.0, 1)	cell (biology) (1.0, 3)
2	disease (0.87, 2)	protein (0.61, 5)	protein (0.65, 5)	protein (0.93, 5)	blood (0.96, 47)	acid (0.58, 18)	neoplasm (0.41, 8)
3	neoplasm (0.73, 8)	receptor (biochemistry) (0.53, 52)	human (0.50, 7)	human (0.65, 7)	blood vessel (0.96, 327)	chemical compound (0.53, 14)	disease (0.38, 2)
4	malignancy (0.66, 20)	gene (0.49, 6)	allele (0.34, 71)	allele (0.43, 71)	angiology (0.92, 857)	derivative (chemistry) (0.42, 58)	t cell (0.36, 429)
5	rtt (0.55, 4)	human (0.41, 7)	ingredient (0.28, 1)	apoptosis (0.37, 87)	nephron (0.74, 1951)	protein (0.34, 5)	lymphocyte (0.35, 112)
6	oncology (0.46, 28)	enzyme (0.34, 29)	receptor (biochemistry) (0.25, 52)	wild type (0.35, 159)	circulatory system (0.64, 664)	purine (0.32, 781)	cancer (0.25, 9)
7	squamous-cell carcinoma (0.37, 163)	blood (0.29, 47)	transcription factors (0.25, 219)	ingredient (0.34, 1)	tongue (0.58, 158)	deciduous teeth (0.28, 3292)	lymphoblast (0.25, 1200)
8	tissue (biology) (0.35, 34)	receptor antagonist (0.28, 922)	coagulation (0.23, 37)	fas receptor (0.33, 5278)	heart (0.54, 353)	cell (biology) (0.27, 3)	thymus (0.23, 506)
9	cell (biology) (0.31, 3)	enzyme inhibitor (0.28, 41)	cell growth (0.23, 46)	tumor necrosis factor alpha (0.30, 604)	kidney (0.52, 430)	tooth (0.27, 2205)	human (0.22, 7)
10	infectious causes of cancer (0.30, 73)	antigen (0.27, 64)	dna (0.21, 127)	antigen (0.23, 64)	soft tissue (0.51, 3067)	receptor (biochemistry) (0.27, 52)	precursor cell (0.17, 2220)

Table 9: Top 10 Entity Types for 7 most frequent negative Prototypes

Towards Procedural Fairness: Uncovering Biases in How a Toxic Language Classifier Uses Sentiment Information

Isar Nejadgholi, Esma Balkır, Kathleen C. Fraser, and Svetlana Kiritchenko
National Research Council Canada
Ottawa, Canada
{Isar.Nejadgholi,Esma.Balkir,Kathleen.Fraser,Svetlana.Kiritchenko}@nrc-cnrc.gc.ca

Abstract

Previous works on the fairness of toxic language classifiers compare the output of models with different identity terms as input features but do not consider the impact of other important concepts present in the context. Here, besides identity terms, we take into account high-level latent features learned by the classifier and investigate the interaction between these features and identity terms. For a multi-class toxic language classifier, we leverage a concept-based explanation framework to calculate the sensitivity of the model to the concept of *sentiment*, which has been used before as a salient feature for toxic language detection. Our results show that although for some classes the classifier has learned the sentiment information as expected, this information is outweighed by the influence of identity terms as input features. This work is a step towards evaluating procedural fairness, where unfair processes lead to unfair outcomes. The produced knowledge can guide debiasing techniques to ensure that important concepts besides identity terms are well-represented in training datasets.

1 Introduction

Previous NLP works have studied the fairness of toxicity detection classifiers by comparing the distributions of prediction scores across different demographic groups as input features (Dixon et al., 2018; Borkan et al., 2019). However, other toxicity-related concepts are often present in the text and affect the differences in score distribution between identity groups. Here, we introduce a framework that uses *concept-based global explanations* to uncover unintended biases for different identity groups, while controlling for a certain toxicity-related concept. To demonstrate the effectiveness of concept-based explanations in uncovering biases, we specifically focus on *sentiment*, although the general methodology can be applied to any other relevant human-defined concept. Negative sentiment is a salient toxicity feature, which has been used in designing feature-based and neural toxicity detection systems (Fortuna and Nunes, 2018; Zhou et al., 2021; Chiril et al., 2022), and highly correlates with toxic language when targeted at demographic groups.

Assessing the differences in score distributions for various demographics is an example of outcome fairness. In fact, most fairness criteria used in machine learning measure outcome fairness, such as accuracy parity (equal accuracy for protected and unprotected groups), equality of opportunity (equal true positive rates), or equalized odds (equal true positive and false positive rates) (Morse et al., 2021). While valuable, outcome fairness metrics are costly to compute as they require large labelled datasets and do not provide any information about the model's decision making processes.

More recently, work has begun to focus on the complementary notion of *process fairness* (also known as *procedural fairness*), or the idea that the decision-making process itself must be fair. Grgic-Hlaca et al. (2016) conducted one of the first studies on process fairness in machine learning, measuring the extent to which people believed it was permissible to use various features as input to a criminal recidivism prediction algorithm. For example, they found that people generally felt that *criminal history* was fair to use as an input feature, but that it was unfair to use *family criminality* as input. Another aspect of process fairness is that the importance given to an attribute in the decision-making process shouldn't be very different for different demographic groups. An example of this is the recent *SFFA vs. Harvard* court case where it was argued that academic and extracurricular achievements of Asian-American applicants are given less weight in the admissions process compared to their White-American counterparts (Arcidiacono et al., 2022). We take a similar view of process fairness and consider a classifier as unfair if it either ignores or over-utilizes a feature for some demographic

Proceedings of the Fifth BlackboxNLP Workshop on Analyzing and Interpreting Neural Networks for NLP, pages 225 - 237
December 8, 2022

groups compared to others.

In the current NLP landscape, one major barrier to assessing process fairness is that predictive models rarely use human-understandable concepts as input features, and so it is increasingly difficult to understand what high-level features[1] are actually being learned and used by the classifier. In this work, we use an interpretability framework of concept-based explanations (Yeh et al., 2022), which enables us to explain a machine learning model's decision-making via conceptual units understandable to humans.

Concept-based explanations have been studied mostly in the context of computer vision, where it is fairly straightforward to define concepts of interest with a set of representative examples. However for textual data, it is much less clear how to define a concept in an effective and intuitive manner, and global explainability methods that operate on high-level abstractions remain under-explored (Danilevsky et al., 2020; Balkır et al., 2022a). Ghorbani et al. (2019) define a concept to be a meaningful, human-defined abstraction, which is expected to be important for the task at hand and which can be specified by a coherent set of examples. Following this definition, we identify *sentiment* as a concept for toxicity classification.[2] To the best of our knowledge, this is one of the first works to apply concept-based explanations to the domain of NLP, and the first one to explore its effectiveness in identifying high-level fairness issues in models that work with textual data.

In this work, we show how to use concept-based explanations to determine whether a trained toxicity classifier uses the information of *sentiment* as an important feature in its predictions. For that we use a multi-class model, described in Section 2, and compare the importance of the concept of sentiment in predicting different subtypes of toxicity. Although intuitively, negative sentiment should be an important signal for toxicity detection, its presence is neither necessary nor sufficient for an utterance to be tagged as toxic. For example, "*Muslims are grieving*" carries a negative sentiment but is not abusive, whereas "*You are so smart for a woman*" is perceived as an insult despite including a positive sentiment word. Also, sentiment might not be a distinguishing feature for some variations or subtypes of toxic language, such as threats or cyberbullying. For all the classes of our multi-class model, we ask, "Has the classifier learned the concept of sentiment as a coherent and important high-level feature associated with this label?", and answer this question with concept-based explanations (Section 5). We then assess how the presence of identity terms impacts the use of sentiment information by the classifier. For that, we control the context for sentiment and ask if the learned sentiment information is used similarly and fairly across identity groups (Section 6). Our code and data is available at `https://github.com/IsarNejad/Procedural-Fairness-Sentiment`.

Our main contributions are:

- We propose a concept-based explanation framework to determine whether a trained text classifier uses a human-defined concept fairly in its decision making process. To the best of our knowledge, this is the first work that uses concept-based explanations to uncover biases in text classifiers, and the first to formalize concepts with short textual templates.
- To demonstrate the utility of the proposed method, we apply it to a multi-class toxicity classifier and show that when the subject of the sentiment is not specified (e.g., "*They are <SENTIMENT-WORD>*"), the classifier is sensitive to the concept of negative sentiment, for some of the classes.
- Further, we show that when the subject of the sentiment is a specific identity term (e.g., "*<IDENTITY-TERM> are <SENTIMENT-WORD>*"), for some classes, the classifier becomes sensitive to neutral and in some cases even positive sentiment. This demonstrates that the process by which the classifier makes its decision is not the same for all identity groups, and for some groups may even be unfairly associating positive sentiment with toxicity.

2 Multi-Class Toxicity Model

For our experiments, we use an open-source, RoBERTa-based model[3] (Hanu, 2020) trained on the English dataset released as part of a Kaggle competition on identifying and reducing bias in

[1] Here, by "feature" we mean the latent representations of a semantic concept learned by a classifier, as opposed to the low-level input features.

[2] We distinguish between the *concept* of sentiment, as defined by a human through a set of examples, and the *feature* of sentiment, which is implicitly learned by the classifier, although our assumption is that they are closely aligned.

[3] `https://huggingface.co/unitary/unbiased-toxic-roberta`

toxicity classification of online comments.[4]. The dataset includes public comments from the Civil Comments platform manually annotated for *Toxicity* as well as six toxicity subtypes: *Severe Toxicity*, *Obscene*, *Identity Attack*, *Insult*, *Threat*, and *Sexual Explicit*. The values for each label represent the fraction of the annotators that assigned the label to the comment. There are over 1.8M examples in the training set and around 195K examples in the test set. We exclude the class *Severe Toxicity* from our experiments, since there are only eight training examples with values higher than 0.5 for this class. Further, a subset of the data is annotated for various identity groups mentioned in the text. The most frequently mentioned identity groups include *male, female, homosexual (gay or lesbian), Christian, Jewish, Muslim, Black, white, people with psychiatric or mental illness*. The classification model optimizes the competition's official evaluation metric that combines the overall AUC with Bias AUCs for the identity groups (Hanu, 2020). For this, the model's loss function combines the weighted loss functions for two tasks, toxicity prediction and identity prediction. This simple and straight-forward model has been shown to effectively reduce bias on non-toxic sentences that mention identity terms, and results in a competitive score of 93.74 on the test set.

We chose this model for two reasons. First, the model is publicly available and is trained on one of the largest available toxicity dataset, annotated for multiple types of toxicity. An alternative choice for our experiments would be using multiple toxicity classifiers. However, the definitions of subtypes of toxicity are usually ambiguous and similar labels might be used for different subtypes of toxicity across datasets. In the case of our multi-class model, the disparities in using sentiment information can be reliably attributed to differences in subtype definitions. Second, the model is debiased to some extent with regards to outcome fairness metrics. Uncovering biases in such a model highlights the issue that optimizing for outcome fairness does not guarantee the procedural fairness in decision making.

3 Sentiment Lexicon

To formalize sentiment concepts, we employ the NRC Valence, Arousal, and Dominance (NRC-VAD) lexicon (Mohammad, 2018), which provides manually annotated real-valued scores of valence, arousal, and dominance for 20,000 English words. We use the valence scores and convert them into the range from -1 (the most negative) to 1 (the most positive). We automatically select single words from the lexicon that are predominantly used as adjectives in the British National Corpus (BNC)[5] and sort them in decreasing order by their frequency in the BNC. The N most frequent adjectives that can be used to describe humans or groups of humans are manually selected as the sentiment words to define the sentiment concepts. The sentiment range [-1, 1] is divided into five intervals: *very negative* [-1, -0.75], *negative* (-0.75, -0.25), *neutral* [-0.25, 0.25], *positive* (0.25, 0.75), and *very positive* [0.75, 1]. For each interval, $N = 100$ adjectives are selected.[6] These sets of adjectives are then used to populate the sentence templates to define the sentiment concepts as described in Section 5.

4 Concept-Based Explanations

Concept-based explanation is an emerging area in black-box model explainability, aiming to explain neural network models at the abstraction level defined by a human user (Yeh et al., 2022). Most explainability methods provide importance weights for low-level input features such as pixels in images or tokens for text (Sundararajan et al., 2017; Smilkov et al., 2017; Selvaraju et al., 2017; Shrikumar et al., 2017). However, a user might want to evaluate the model's functionality at the level of a concept that is expected to be important for the model's prediction, which can be achieved with concept-based explanations (Koh et al., 2020). Ghorbani et al. (2019) states that a concept needs to satisfy the properties of *meaningfulness*, *coherency* and *importance* for the task at hand. Some examples of concepts in computer vision tasks are the concept of *stripes* for the class of *zebra* (Kim et al., 2018), the concept of *white coat* for the class of *doctor* (Pandey, 2021), and the concept of *nuclei texture* in the detection of tumor tissue in breast lymph node samples (Graziani et al., 2018). In the case of text, Nejadgholi et al. (2022) used concept-based explanations to measure the sensitivity of a

[4] `https://www.kaggle.com/c/jigsaw-unintended-bias-in-toxicity-classification/`

[5] The British National Corpus, version 3 (BNC XML Edition), `http://www.natcorp.ox.ac.uk/`

[6] The full list of the selected adjectives is available in the Supplemental Material. We also conducted similar experiments with the full NRC-VAD lexicon and obtained similar results.

abusive language classifier to the emerging concept of COVID-related anti-Asian hate speech, and Yeh et al. (2020) explained a text classifier with respect to the concepts identified through topic modeling.

Here, our goal is to explain the prediction of a toxicity classifier at the level of sentiment information learned by the trained model. Since sentiment is not one of the direct input features of the model, feature importance metrics such as LIME (Ribeiro et al., 2016) and SHAP (Lundberg and Lee, 2017) cannot be used to provide its importance. Instead, we consider each level of sentiment as a concept and calculate the importance of these concepts for the model's predictions with Testing Concept Activation Vectors (TCAV) algorithm. In the following section, we explain the TCAV algorithm in detail.

4.1 Testing Concept Activation Vectors

Testing Concept Activation Vectors (TCAV) is an algorithm from the family of concept-based explainability methods, which measures the importance of a human-defined concept for model's predictions (Kim et al., 2018). In TCAV, each concept is defined with a set of examples and represented as Concept Activation Vectors (CAVs), in the activation layer of the trained model. TCAV formalizes the importance of a concept as the fraction of input examples for which the prediction scores of the model increase if the input representation is infinitesimally moved towards the concept representation. The prediction increase is measured by calculating the directional derivatives of the prediction layer to CAVs. To calculate the statistical significance of a concept, multiple subsets of concept examples are used to form multiple CAVs, and a TCAV score is calculated for each CAV. A concept is considered to be important for a class if the distribution of its TCAV scores is significantly different from the TCAV scores of a random concept defined by random examples.

Here, we explain how the TCAV procedure measures the importance of a concept for a class of a RoBERTa-base classifier, in more detail. Similar to Nejadgholi et al. (2022), we define each concept C with N_C concept examples, and map them to RoBERTa representations of the [CLS] token $r_C^j, j = 1, ..., N_C$. Then, P number of Concept Activation Vectors (CAVs), v_C^p, are generated by averaging the RoBERTa representations of N_v randomly chosen concept examples, to represent C in the activation space:

$$v_C^p = \frac{1}{N_v} \sum_{j=1}^{N_v} r_C^j \quad p = 1, .., P \qquad (1)$$

where $N_v < N_C$. With f_{emb}, which maps an input text x to its RoBERTa representation r_x, the *conceptual sensitivity* of a class to the v_C^p, at input x can be computed as the directional derivative $S_{C,p}(x)$:

$$S_{C,p}(x) = \lim_{\epsilon \to 0} \frac{h(f_{emb}(x) + \epsilon v_C^p) - h(f_{emb}(x))}{\epsilon}$$
$$= \nabla h(f_{emb}(x)).v_C^p \qquad (2)$$

where h is the function that maps the RoBERTa representation to the logit value of the class of interest. For a set of input examples, X, we calculate the TCAV score as the fraction of inputs for which small changes in the direction of C increase the logit:

$$TCAV_{C,p} = \frac{|x \in X : S_{C,p}(x) > 0|}{|X|} \qquad (3)$$

When calculated for all CAVs, Equation 3 results in a distribution of scores for the concept C. The mean and standard deviation of this distribution determines the overall sensitivity of the classifier to the concept C for the class of interest.

Intuitively, the derivatives in Equation 2 indicate whether a label's likelihood increases when a small vector in the direction of the concept's representation is added to a random context. For example, the predicted probability of the class *Toxic* for sentence *"I saw these people."* is 0.01. The comment *"I saw these people. They are terrible."* is labeled as toxic with the probability of 0.56, but the statement *"I saw these people. They are wonderful."* receives the toxicity probability of 0.01. If this observation holds systematically across many negative and positive sentiment words, the classifier has learned negative sentiment as an important feature of the toxicity class, but the positive sentiment does not contribute to the toxicity estimation.

In contrast to the previous concept-based explanation works in NLP, which either require annotated data (Nejadgholi et al., 2022), or are limited to the topics extracted by the topic modeling procedure (Yeh et al., 2020), we define the sentiment concepts with a set of minimal templates, that are easy to generate and minimize extra contextual information. Using concept examples, described in Sections 5 and 6, TCAV first encodes the information of sentiment in the RoBERTa embedding

Class label	Sentiment level concepts					Control concepts	
	Very negative	Negative	Neutral	Positive	Very positive	Explicit	Non-coherent
Toxicity	**0.87 (0.04)**	**0.47 (0.26)**	0 (0)	0 (0)	0 (0)	**0.88 (0.02)**	0 (0)
Obscene	0 (0)	0 (0)	0 (0)	0 (0)	0 (0)	**0.75 (0.1)**	0 (0)
Identity Attack	0 (0)	0 (0)	0 (0)	0 (0)	0 (0)	0.01 (0.03)	0 (0)
Insult	**0.92 (0.02)**	**0.77 (0.14)**	0 (0)	0 (0)	0 (0)	**0.89 (0.02)**	0 (0)
Threat	0.01 (0.03)	0 (0)	0 (0)	0 (0)	0 (0)	0 (0)	0 (0)
Sexual Explicit	0 (0)	0 (0)	0 (0)	0 (0)	0 (0)	**0.70 (0.18)**	0 (0)

Table 1: Means and standard deviations of TCAV score distributions for the six types of toxicity with respect to five sentiment categories and two control concepts. Scores statistically significantly different from random are in bold.

space. Then, it populates the directional derivatives of the prediction layer with respect to these vectors. If the derivatives are positive for a significant number of the sentiment concept representations, a high average TCAV score is obtained, i.e, sentiment is learned as a coherent and important feature for the label of interest.

In our implementation, for each concept, 100 CAVs are generated, each of which is the average representation of 50 randomly selected concept examples. For 1000 random input texts (random tweets collected with stop words), the TCAV scores of each CAV are calculated. Average and standard deviation of TCAV scores are reported to quantify the importance of the concept for this class.

5 Classifier Sensitivity to Sentiment

In this section, we analyze the sensitivity of the classifier described in Section 2 and identify the classes for which the classifier is sensitive to sentiment as a coherent and important feature. For the concepts of sentiment level, we create concept examples and use the TCAV technique to test the importance of the concepts for each class.

To create concept examples for each level of sentiment described in Section 3, we use the template *"They are <SENTIMENT-WORD>."*. This simple template ensures minimal extra semantic information other than sentiment level and avoids the problem of encoding unwanted biases in the concept itself, as described by Tong and Kagal (2020). It is important to note that such minimal templates cannot be labeled for toxicity without more context. Consider a sentence such as *"They are terrible."*. This sentence expresses a negative sentiment but lacks any other significant information. Only with more context can we say whether this sentence is toxic or not. The statement *"These people are immigrants. They are terrible."* is toxic, while the comment *"I don't like these computers. They are terrible."* is non-toxic, and *"I don't like these singers. They are terrible."* can be toxic depending on the specific definition of toxicity in a use case. Therefore, the fairness analysis methods that rely on labels cannot be used to study the impact of these templates on the model's predictions.

In addition to five levels of sentiment, we use two control concepts with predictable sensitivities: 1) A non-coherent concept, defined by a set of random tweets collected with stop words, for which we expect low average TCAV scores for all labels; 2) The concept of *explicit offence* defined by inserting a profane word[7] in the template *"They are <PROFANE-WORD>"*, for which we expect high sensitivity from at least some of the labels. As the creators of the toxicity model mention, this classifier shows high sensitivity to profanity because of the over-representation of these words in its training data.[8] Table 1 shows the average and standard deviation of TCAV scores calculated for the seven concepts described above.

We observe that the TCAV scores for the control concepts are as expected—zero sensitivity for a non-coherent, random concept and high sensitivity to the concept of explicit offence for the labels *Toxicity*, *Obscene*, *Insult* and *Sexual Explicit*. For the sentiment concepts, we observe that the classifier is sensitive to *Very Negative* and *Negative* sentiment for the labels *Toxicity* and *Insult*. [9] We also observe that the classifier is not sensitive to the *Neutral*, *Positive* and *Very Positive* sentiment concepts for any of the labels, which rules out the sensitivity of the classifier to the specific sentence structure of the templates.

Literature suggests that a high TCAV score indicates: 1) the concept is learned by the classifier as

[7]We use the words from `https://github.com/chucknorris-io/swear-words/blob/master/en`

[8]`https://github.com/unitaryai/detoxify`

[9]Intuitively, the classes *Obscene*, *Identity Attack*, *Threat* and *Sexual Explicit* rely on features other than negative sentiment, i.e., profanity, identity terms, violence or intention of harming, and lewdness, respectively.

Class label	Sentiment level concepts					Control concepts	
	Very negative	Negative	Neutral	Positive	Very positive	Explicit	Non-coherent
Toxicity	**0.22**	**0.12**	0.01	0	-0.01	**0.27**	0.03
Obscene	0.01	0	0	0	0	**0.10**	0
Identity Attack	0.01	0	0	0	0	0.03	0
Insult	**0.17**	**0.10**	0.02	0	0	**0.16**	0
Threat	0	0	0	0	0	0	0
Sexual Explicit	0	0	0	0	0	**0.09**	0

Table 2: Average increase in probabilities when concept templates are added to random texts. Cells in equivalent positions to Table 1 are in bold.

Class label	Increase in Probability		TCAV scores	
	non-coherent	coherent	non-coherent	coherent
Toxicity	0.11	0.12	0.01 (0.07)	**0.47 (0.26)**
Insult	0.09	0.10	0.09 (0.19)	**0.77 (0.14)**

Table 3: Average increase in probability and mean and standard deviation of TCAV scores for the non-coherent concept (Very negative or Very positive sentiment) and the coherent concept (Negative sentiment).

a coherent feature, and 2) that feature is important for the classifiers' predictions (Kim et al., 2018). We evaluate the TCAV scores shown in Table 1, in terms of the *importance* and *coherency* of a concept. We first confirm that the *importance* of a concept can be interpreted as the *increase in the predicted probability due to the addition of a concept to input sentences*. Then, we show that *increase in probability* is not an equivalent metric to *TCAV score*, since increase in probability can be due to the addition of a non-coherent concept to input sentences.

High average TCAV scores indicate a significant increase of prediction probabilities when the concept is added to random contexts. We append the concept examples to random tweets and measure the prediction probabilities before and after the addition of the concept examples. The average increase of probabilities for all concepts and labels is shown in Table 2. We observe that in all cases where the average TCAV scores are high (i.e., significantly different from the control random concept) in Table 1, the probability increase is notable in Table 2. For example, for the *Toxic* label, the addition of sentences with *Very Negative* and *Negative* sentiment on average increases the prediction probability by 0.22 and 0.12, whereas the addition of *Neutral*, *Positive* and *Very Positive* sentiments increases the prediction probability by 0.01 or less. This is in line with our observation from Table 1 that the classifier is sensitive to *Negative* and *Very Negative* sentiments for the label *Toxic*.

TCAV scores differentiate between coherent and non-coherent concepts whereas the probability increase does not. To test this hypothesis, we create a non-coherent concept by combining the *Very Negative* and the *Very Positive* sentiment examples, and compare the average increase in probability and the TCAV score for this concept with those for the *Negative* sentiment concept. The comparison is demonstrated in Table 3. Although the increase in probability is similar for the coherent and non-coherent concepts, the TCAV score indicates that the classifier has only learned the coherent concept as an important feature.

6 Sensitivity to Sentiment Towards an Identity Group

In the previous section, we demonstrated how the TCAV framework can be used to assess whether a human-defined concept is learned by a classifier as an important feature. With that we showed that for some labels our model is sensitive to the presence of *Very Negative* and *Negative* sentiments in broader contexts. Here, we turn to the concept of *"associating a sentiment with an identity group"*[10] and ask if similar levels of sensitivity to sentiment are observed in the presence of certain demographic terms as input features. For creating the concept examples, we use the template "<SUBJECTS> are <SENTIMENT-WORD>", where <SUBJECTS> are the protected identity terms used in HateCheck (Röttger et al., 2021): *Women*, *Gay people*, *Trans people*, *Muslims*, *Immigrants*, *Black people*, and *Disabled people*. We also add

[10]Note that this concept is composed of more basic concepts, similar to the concept of *white coat* used in (Pandey, 2021). Still, it satisfies the three criteria of meaningfulness, coherency and importance as stated by (Ghorbani et al., 2019) and can be considered as a relevant concept for toxicity.

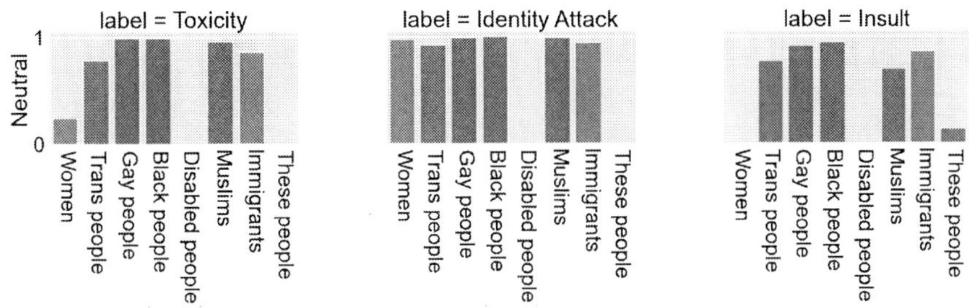

Figure 1: Sensitivity to identity terms in neutral contexts, for which a low sensitivity is expected.

the terms *These people* and *These things*, to assess the sensitivity of the model to the concepts of *"associating a sentiment with people in general"* and *"associating a sentiment with objects"* as two baselines. As expected, we observe that the classifier is not sensitive to any level of sentiment when associated with objects. We discuss some of the most salient results below. (The full results are presented in Appendix in Table A.1.)

We first assess the influence of identity terms by analysing the classifiers' sensitivities to the neutral sentiment towards the identity groups. Figure 1 visualizes the column of Table A.1 related to the *Neutral* sentiment. From the findings in Table 1, as well as human intuition, the association of identity terms with neutral sentiment should not increase the probability of the classifier predicting a toxic label. However, we observe high sensitivities for the labels *Toxicity* and *Insult* and all identity groups, except for *Women* and *Disabled people*. The classifier is also sensitive to the *Neutral* sentiment associated with *Women* for the label *Identity Attack*. We conclude that in neutral contexts the classifier is more sensitive to some identity terms than others.

Figure 2 visualizes the results of Table A.1 from a different perspective. In this figure, we assess the sensitivity of the classifier to different levels of sentiment across the identity groups. For the relevant classes, we expect to see that the classifier is sensitive to negative sentiment but not sensitive to positive sentiment; i.e., the average TCAV score should be high for negative sentiment and low for positive sentiment. Consistent with results in Table 1, we observe this expected pattern for the subject *These people* and the two classes *Insult* and *Toxicity*. Taking this as our baseline, we expect to see similar patterns across all the identity groups for an unbiased classifier. However, we observe that the pattern only holds for certain classes, and certain identity groups. Notably, the classifier loses its sensitivity to the *Negative* sentiment for the classes *Insult* and *Toxicity* when the mentioned identity group is *Disabled people*. In addition to classes *Insult* and *Toxicity*, in the presence of an identity term, the classifier becomes sensitive to *Negative* and *Very Negative* sentiment for the class *Identity Attack*. This is expected given the class definition, but again the pattern does not hold for the identity term *Disabled people*.

Another anomalous result with respect to the *Negative* sentiment is that the classifier is sensitive to *Negative* and *Very Negative* sentiment for the class *Sexual Explicit*, but only in the context of the identity group *Gay people*. Additionally, for the label of *Threat* the classifier shows some sensitivity to the *Very Negative* and *Negative* sentiment, but only when used with the identity term *Muslims*.

We then turn to assessing the sensitivities to positive sentiment. In general, the expected pattern of sensitivities is only observed for the labels *Toxicity* and *Insult* and the identity term *Women*. For other cases, as the level of sentiment changes from *Very Negative* and *Negative* to *Positive* and *Very Positive*, the sensitivity of the classifier does not decrease as expected and remains high, specifically for identity groups *Gay people*, *Black people* and *Muslims*. This observation indicates that a sentence such as "*Black people are wonderful*" in a conversation will increase the probability of that text being labeled as *Toxic*, *Identity Attack* and *Insult*. Also, for *Sexual Explicit* the classifier is sensitive to the mention of *Gay people* for all levels of sentiment. We conclude that the classifier is oversensitive to the presence of these identity terms regardless of the level of sentiment, and even highly positive sentiment cannot cancel out the impact of the identity terms. One exception is the term *Disabled people*, for which the model is under-sensitive, i.e, not sensitive to even *Negative* and *Very Negative* sentiments associated with this group.

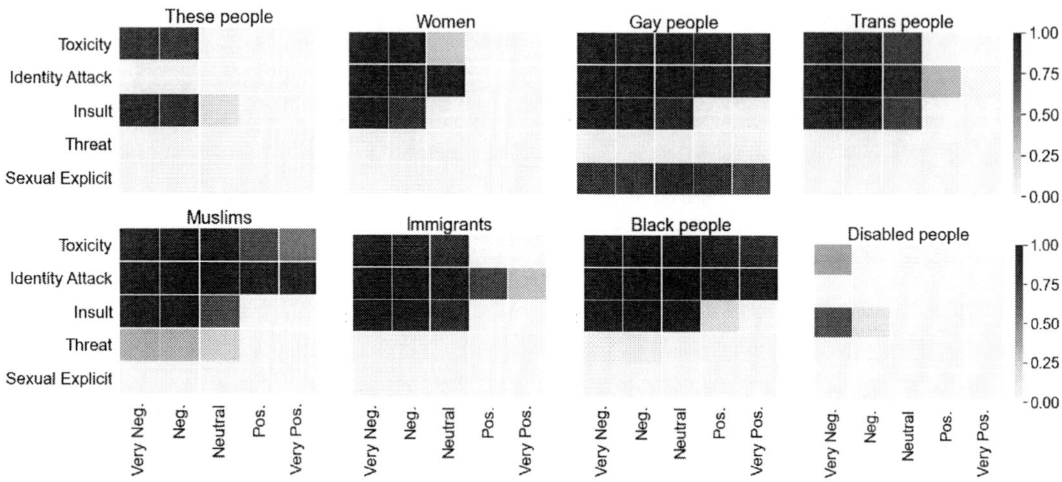

Figure 2: Sensitivity to various levels of sentiment for all demographic groups.

7 Discussion

Our results demonstrate that while a multi-class toxicity classifier generally shows high sensitivities to negative sentiment for certain classes, and zero sensitivities to neutral or positive sentiment, the picture changes when the sentiment is applied to certain marginalized identity groups. Then, counter-intuitively, even positive sentiment can increase the probability of a toxicity label. This suggests an over-reliance on the identity group term.

Previous work in computer vision has underscored the difficulty in finding unbiased examples with which to define concepts, e.g., when searching for images of men or women to examine gender bias, the examples invariably also contain information about age, race, and so on. Here, in the context of NLP, we propose a generalizable solution to that problem, by generating examples rather than collecting them, and carefully controlling the variable of interest (here, sentiment, although the method could extend to other features). For this we use existing lexicons, without the need to label the examples for the various toxicity classes, as would be required for an analysis of outcome fairness.

This knowledge of how the model uses the sentiment information can guide debiasing techniques. For example, a data augmentation approach can ensure important features are present in the training dataset. In the case of our model, a data balancing procedure should collect and label positive and very positive sentiments associated with gay people, Black people and Muslims, as well as very negative sentiments associated with disabled people and add them to the training dataset.

It is important to note that evaluating models for the sensitivity to human-defined concepts is a tool to reveal flaws of a trained model, where prior knowledge about expected sensitivities is available. Similar to previous test suits such as HateCheck (Röttger et al., 2021), our method should not be considered as a standalone evaluation of models. Moreover, observing the expected sensitivities does not guarantee the fairness of the model. Only where unexpected sensitivity patterns are observed, the biases can be detected and mitigated accordingly.

Our method has limitations. We carry our analysis for one grammatical construction that expresses the concept of *associating sentiment to identity groups*. Future work is needed to assess the generalizability of our results to other expressions of sentiment. Moreover, TCAV requires access to at least some model layers and cannot be applied when the model itself is unavailable.

8 Related work

Identifying and mitigating unintended biases in NLP systems to ensure fair treatment of various demographic groups has been focus of intensive research in the past decade (Blodgett et al., 2020; Shah et al., 2020). Various metrics to quantify biases in system outputs have been proposed, including group fairness metrics and individual fairness metrics (Castelnovo et al., 2022; Czarnowska et al., 2021). However, to apply such metrics, the datasets need to be annotated with demographic attributes, which is costly and sometimes infeasible to do (e.g., the demographics of the authors of social media posts are often unknown). Alternatively, the bias metrics are applied on synthetic data automatically generated using simple templates (Kiritchenko and Mohammad, 2018; Borkan et al., 2019). In both cases, the test data are limited, and the evaluation is restricted to a set of pre-defined contexts.

Explainability techniques (XAI) can potentially help in discovering and quantifying biases. Much work on XAI has been motivated by the need to assist in bias detection and mitigation (Doshi-Velez and Kim, 2017; Das and Rad, 2020). However, only a handful of NLP studies have actually employed explainability methods for bias detection and to a limited extent (Prabhakaran et al., 2019; Kennedy et al., 2020; Aksenov et al., 2021; Balkır et al., 2022b). Balkır et al. (2022a) surveyed the works at the intersection of fairness and XAI in NLP and discussed conceptual and practical challenges in applying current explainability approaches for debiasing NLP models. Multiple outlined issues stem from the fact that most current XAI methods employed in NLP provide explanations on a local level through post-hoc processing, and it is still an open question how to generalize these local explanations to reveal systematic model biases. The TCAV framework used in this paper produces global explanations and can therefore uncover unfair processes in the model's decision making.

Probing classifiers are well-known interpretability tools used to examine the encoded information in the representation layers of NLP models (Conneau et al., 2018). Probes are trained independently from the original model to predict an externally defined property (e.g., linguistic properties such as part of speech) from the model's representations. Despite being widely used, several studies revealed that probes are not well-controlled, and caution should be taken when drawing behavioural conclusions about the original model from the performance of probing classifiers (Belinkov, 2022). Also, probes can only assess whether the information about the property of interest is encoded in the representations (e.g., (Tenney et al., 2019; Rogers et al., 2020)) but do not provide evidence about how the model uses this information. To that end, extensions of probing classifiers were proposed, which assess the effect of removing the property's information with counterfactual interventions to provide causal explanations and mitigate biases in NLP classifiers (Ravfogel et al., 2020; Elazar et al., 2021). However, several concerns are raised about the effectiveness and the unintended consequences of removing attributes (Kumar et al., 2022). While causality-driven probing methods assess the necessity of the property for the classifier's decision, TCAV determines whether the model uses the encoded information as an important signal for a particular class. Also, TCAV allows us to quantify the relative importance of different properties encoded in the representation, which is not feasible with probing classifiers.

The TCAV framework has been developed and mostly applied in image classification. In the original paper, Kim et al. (2018) showed how gender and racial biases can be discovered with TCAV in image classifiers. Wei et al. (2021) extended the method to regression problems, and applied it to detect gender and first language biases in automatic spoken language assessment. Tong and Kagal (2020) studied the effectiveness of TCAV in discovering gender biases in image classification and discussed the difficulties in obtaining quality examples to represent a concept while not introducing new sources of bias (e.g., introducing a racial bias when selecting gendered examples). Adhikari (2021) used TCAV to measure gender bias when classifying faces as young or old, and discussed the difficulty of defining 'disentangled' concepts that only encode the concept of interest. To the best of our knowledge, our work is the first in applying TCAV to discover biases in text classifiers.

9 Conclusion

Building on previous studies that measured group fairness in toxic language detection, this work is a step toward a more systematic and fine-grained analysis of procedural fairness in neural model's predictions. We use a global explainability metric to uncover the disparities in how the classifier learns to associate identity terms with domain-relevant concepts, e.g. sentiment. Future work will focus on extending the analysis to other concepts known to be important to toxic language detection (profanity, threats of violence, dehumanizing or othering language, and so on) as well as additional classifiers, domains, and types of bias.

Ethical Statement

The presented framework aims to identify fairness issues in text classifiers when identity terms are mentioned in the text. As stated above, such evaluation cannot attest for the absence of any biases, but can indicate potential areas of concern. This framework is a complementary approach to other methods of bias detection that are based on the notion of outcome fairness (e.g., using fairness metrics on held-out test sets annotated for mentions of demographics or on specifically designed test suits, such as HateCheck). The proposed method cannot be applied to assessing fairness on texts *written by* different demographic groups.

The method requires the identity groups of interest to be specified in advance. In the current study, we have included several protected groups, but the list is by no means exhaustive. More protected groups should be included in the future. Additionally, it is known that the label used to refer to a social group can itself communicate bias (consider, for example, the difference between *immigrants* versus *migrants* versus *expats*) (Beukeboom and Burgers, 2019). We have not analyzed the effect of this form of bias on the explanations here. Furthermore, other, legally non-protected groups (e.g., based on physical appearances, education, etc.), should also be considered as we strive towards inclusive and safe online spaces.

As most AI technology, this approach can be used adversely to exploit the system's vulnerabilities and produce toxic texts that would be undetectable by the studied classifier. Specifically, for methods that require access to the model's inner layers, care should be taken so that only trusted parties could gain such access. The obtained knowledge should only be used for model transparency purposes, and the security concerns should be adequately addressed.

Regarding environmental concerns, contemporary NLP systems based on pre-trained large language models, such as RoBERTa, require significant computational resources to train and even fine-tune. Larger training datasets, such as the one used in this study with almost 2M training examples, used for fine-tuning, usually result in a better classification performance, but also an even higher computational cost. To lower the cost of this study and its negative impact on the environment, we chose to use an existing, publicly available classification model.

References

Rittika Adhikari. 2021. Fair-doctor: Detecting and mitigating unfairness in neural networks. Master's thesis, University of Illinois Urbana-Champaign.

Dmitrii Aksenov, Peter Bourgonje, Karolina Zaczynska, Malte Ostendorff, Julian Moreno Schneider, and Georg Rehm. 2021. Fine-grained classification of political bias in German news: A data set and initial experiments. In *Proceedings of the 5th Workshop on Online Abuse and Harms (WOAH 2021)*, pages 121–131.

Peter Arcidiacono, Josh Kinsler, and Tyler Ransom. 2022. Asian american discrimination in harvard admissions. *European Economic Review*, 144:104079.

Esma Balkır, Svetlana Kiritchenko, Isar Nejadgholi, and Kathleen C. Fraser. 2022a. Challenges in applying explainability methods to improve the fairness of NLP models. In *Proceedings of the Second Workshop on Trustworthy Natural Language Processing (TrustNLP @ NAACL)*, Seattle, WA, USA.

Esma Balkır, Isar Nejadgholi, Kathleen Fraser, and Svetlana Kiritchenko. 2022b. Necessity and sufficiency for explaining text classifiers: A case study in hate speech detection. In *Proceedings of the 2022 Conference of the North American Chapter of the Association for Computational Linguistics: Human Language Technologies*, pages 2672–2686, Seattle, United States. Association for Computational Linguistics.

Yonatan Belinkov. 2022. Probing classifiers: Promises, shortcomings, and advances. *Computational Linguistics*, 48(1):207–219.

Camiel J Beukeboom and Christian Burgers. 2019. How stereotypes are shared through language: A review and introduction of the social categories and stereotypes communication (SCSC) framework. *Review of Communication Research*, 7:1–37.

Su Lin Blodgett, Solon Barocas, Hal Daumé III, and Hanna Wallach. 2020. Language (technology) is power: A critical survey of "bias" in NLP. In *Proceedings of the 58th Annual Meeting of the Association for Computational Linguistics*, pages 5454–5476.

Daniel Borkan, Lucas Dixon, Jeffrey Sorensen, Nithum Thain, and Lucy Vasserman. 2019. Nuanced metrics for measuring unintended bias with real data for text classification. In *Companion Proceedings of the 2019 World Wide Web Conference*, pages 491–500.

Alessandro Castelnovo, Riccardo Crupi, Greta Greco, Daniele Regoli, Ilaria Giuseppina Penco, and Andrea Claudio Cosentini. 2022. A clarification of the nuances in the fairness metrics landscape. *Scientific Reports*, 12.

Patricia Chiril, Endang Wahyu Pamungkas, Farah Benamara, Véronique Moriceau, and Viviana Patti. 2022. Emotionally informed hate speech detection: a multi-target perspective. *Cognitive Computation*, 14(1):322–352.

Alexis Conneau, German Kruszewski, Guillaume Lample, Loïc Barrault, and Marco Baroni. 2018. What you can cram into a single vector: Probing sentence embeddings for linguistic properties. *arXiv preprint arXiv:1805.01070*.

Paula Czarnowska, Yogarshi Vyas, and Kashif Shah. 2021. Quantifying social biases in NLP: A generalization and empirical comparison of extrinsic fairness metrics. *Transactions of the Association for Computational Linguistics*, 9:1249–1267.

Marina Danilevsky, Kun Qian, Ranit Aharonov, Yannis Katsis, Ban Kawas, and Prithviraj Sen. 2020. A survey of the state of explainable ai for natural language processing. In *Proceedings of the 1st Conference of the Asia-Pacific Chapter of the Association for Computational Linguistics and the 10th International Joint Conference on Natural Language Processing*, pages 447–459.

Arun Das and Paul Rad. 2020. Opportunities and challenges in explainable artificial intelligence (xai): A survey. *arXiv preprint arXiv:2006.11371*.

Lucas Dixon, John Li, Jeffrey Sorensen, Nithum Thain, and Lucy Vasserman. 2018. Measuring and mitigating unintended bias in text classification. In *Proceedings of the 2018 AAAI/ACM Conference on AI, Ethics, and Society*, pages 67–73.

Finale Doshi-Velez and Been Kim. 2017. Towards a rigorous science of interpretable machine learning. *arXiv preprint arXiv:1702.08608*.

Yanai Elazar, Shauli Ravfogel, Alon Jacovi, and Yoav Goldberg. 2021. Amnesic probing: Behavioral explanation with amnesic counterfactuals. *Transactions of the Association for Computational Linguistics*, 9:160–175.

Paula Fortuna and Sérgio Nunes. 2018. A survey on automatic detection of hate speech in text. *ACM Computing Surveys (CSUR)*, 51(4):1–30.

Amirata Ghorbani, James Wexler, James Y Zou, and Been Kim. 2019. Towards automatic concept-based explanations. *Advances in Neural Information Processing Systems*, 32.

Mara Graziani, Vincent Andrearczyk, and Henning Müller. 2018. Regression concept vectors for bidirectional explanations in histopathology. In *Understanding and Interpreting Machine Learning in Medical Image Computing Applications*, pages 124–132. Springer.

Nina Grgic-Hlaca, Muhammad Bilal Zafar, Krishna P Gummadi, and Adrian Weller. 2016. The case for process fairness in learning: Feature selection for fair decision making. In *Proceedings of the NIPS Symposium on Machine Learning and the Law*, volume 1, page 2. Barcelona, Spain.

Laura Hanu. 2020. How well can we detoxify comments online? Unitary, accessed on 15 June, 2022.

Brendan Kennedy, Xisen Jin, Aida Mostafazadeh Davani, Morteza Dehghani, and Xiang Ren. 2020. Contextualizing hate speech classifiers with post-hoc explanation. In *Proceedings of the 58th Annual Meeting of the Association for Computational Linguistics*, pages 5435–5442.

Been Kim, Martin Wattenberg, Justin Gilmer, Carrie Cai, James Wexler, Fernanda Viegas, et al. 2018. Interpretability beyond feature attribution: Quantitative testing with concept activation vectors (tcav). In *Proceedings of the International Conference on Machine Learning*, pages 2668–2677. PMLR.

Svetlana Kiritchenko and Saif Mohammad. 2018. Examining gender and race bias in two hundred sentiment analysis systems. In *Proceedings of the Seventh Joint Conference on Lexical and Computational Semantics*, pages 43–53.

Pang Wei Koh, Thao Nguyen, Yew Siang Tang, Stephen Mussmann, Emma Pierson, Been Kim, and Percy Liang. 2020. Concept bottleneck models. In *Proceedings of the International Conference on Machine Learning*, pages 5338–5348. PMLR.

Abhinav Kumar, Chenhao Tan, and Amit Sharma. 2022. Probing classifiers are unreliable for concept removal and detection. *arXiv preprint arXiv:2207.04153*.

Scott M Lundberg and Su-In Lee. 2017. A unified approach to interpreting model predictions. *Advances in Neural Information Processing Systems*, 30.

Saif M. Mohammad. 2018. Obtaining reliable human ratings of valence, arousal, and dominance for 20,000 English words. In *Proceedings of The Annual Conference of the Association for Computational Linguistics (ACL)*, Melbourne, Australia.

Lily Morse, Mike Horia M Teodorescu, Yazeed Awwad, and Gerald C Kane. 2021. Do the ends justify the means? variation in the distributive and procedural fairness of machine learning algorithms. *Journal of Business Ethics*, pages 1–13.

Isar Nejadgholi, Kathleen Fraser, and Svetlana Kiritchenko. 2022. Improving generalizability in implicitly abusive language detection with concept activation vectors. In *Proceedings of the 60th Annual Meeting of the Association for Computational Linguistics (Volume 1: Long Papers)*, pages 5517–5529, Dublin, Ireland. Association for Computational Linguistics.

Parul Pandey. 2021. Tcav: Interpretability beyond feature attribution. Breaking the Jargons, accessed on 13 June, 2022.

Vinodkumar Prabhakaran, Ben Hutchinson, and Margaret Mitchell. 2019. Perturbation sensitivity analysis to detect unintended model biases. In *Proceedings of the 2019 Conference on Empirical Methods in Natural Language Processing and the 9th International Joint Conference on Natural Language Processing (EMNLP-IJCNLP)*, pages 5740–5745.

Shauli Ravfogel, Yanai Elazar, Hila Gonen, Michael Twiton, and Yoav Goldberg. 2020. Null it out: Guarding protected attributes by iterative nullspace projection. In *Proceedings of the 58th Annual Meeting of the Association for Computational Linguistics*, pages 7237–7256.

Marco Tulio Ribeiro, Sameer Singh, and Carlos Guestrin. 2016. "Why should i trust you?" Explaining the predictions of any classifier. In *Proceedings of the 22nd ACM SIGKDD International Conference on Knowledge Discovery and Data Mining*, pages 1135–1144.

Anna Rogers, Olga Kovaleva, and Anna Rumshisky. 2020. A primer in bertology: What we know about how bert works. *Transactions of the Association for Computational Linguistics*, 8:842–866.

Paul Röttger, Bertie Vidgen, Dong Nguyen, Zeerak Waseem, Helen Margetts, and Janet Pierrehumbert. 2021. HateCheck: Functional tests for hate speech detection models. In *Proceedings of the 59th Annual Meeting of the Association for Computational Linguistics and the 11th International Joint Conference on Natural Language Processing (Volume 1: Long Papers)*, pages 41–58, Online. Association for Computational Linguistics.

Ramprasaath R Selvaraju, Michael Cogswell, Abhishek Das, Ramakrishna Vedantam, Devi Parikh, and Dhruv Batra. 2017. Grad-cam: Visual explanations from deep networks via gradient-based localization. In *Proceedings of the IEEE International Conference on Computer Vision*, pages 618–626.

Deven Santosh Shah, H Andrew Schwartz, and Dirk Hovy. 2020. Predictive biases in natural language processing models: A conceptual framework and overview. In *Proceedings of the 58th Annual Meeting of the Association for Computational Linguistics*, pages 5248–5264.

Avanti Shrikumar, Peyton Greenside, and Anshul Kundaje. 2017. Learning important features through propagating activation differences. In *Proceedings of the International Conference on Machine Learning*, pages 3145–3153.

Daniel Smilkov, Nikhil Thorat, Been Kim, Fernanda Viégas, and Martin Wattenberg. 2017. Smoothgrad: removing noise by adding noise. *arXiv preprint arXiv:1706.03825*.

Mukund Sundararajan, Ankur Taly, and Qiqi Yan. 2017. Axiomatic attribution for deep networks. In *Proceedings of the International Conference on Machine Learning*, pages 3319–3328.

Ian Tenney, Patrick Xia, Berlin Chen, Alex Wang, Adam Poliak, R Thomas McCoy, Najoung Kim, Benjamin Van Durme, Samuel R Bowman, Dipanjan Das, et al. 2019. What do you learn from context? probing for sentence structure in contextualized word representations. *arXiv preprint arXiv:1905.06316*.

Schrasing Tong and Lalana Kagal. 2020. Investigating bias in image classification using model explanations. In *Proceedings of the ICML Workshop on Human Interpretability in Machine Learning (WHI 2020)*.

Xizi Wei, Mark JF Gales, and Kate M Knill. 2021. Analysing bias in spoken language assessment using concept activation vectors. In *Proceedings of the IEEE International Conference on Acoustics, Speech and Signal Processing (ICASSP)*, pages 7753–7757. IEEE.

Chih-Kuan Yeh, Been Kim, Sercan Arik, Chun-Liang Li, Tomas Pfister, and Pradeep Ravikumar. 2020. On completeness-aware concept-based explanations in deep neural networks. *Advances in Neural Information Processing Systems*, 33:20554–20565.

Chih-Kuan Yeh, Been Kim, and Pradeep Ravikumar. 2022. Human-centered concept explanations for neural networks. In P. Hitzler and M. K. Sarker, editors, *Neuro-Symbolic Artificial Intelligence: The State of the Art*, volume 342, page 2. IOS Press.

Xianbing Zhou, Yang Yong, Xiaochao Fan, Ge Ren, Yunfeng Song, Yufeng Diao, Liang Yang, and Hongfei Lin. 2021. Hate speech detection based on sentiment knowledge sharing. In *Proceedings of the 59th Annual Meeting of the Association for Computational Linguistics and the 11th International Joint Conference on Natural Language Processing (Volume 1: Long Papers)*, pages 7158–7166, Online. Association for Computational Linguistics.

A Sensitivities to Sentiment in Presence of Identity Terms

The full results of the experiments described in Section 6 are presented in Table A.1.

Target	Class label	Very negative	Negative	Neutral	Positive	Very positive
Women	*Toxicity*	**0.99(0.00)**	**0.99(0.00)**	0.24(0.22)	0(0)	0(0)
	Obscene	0(0)	0(0)	0(0)	0(0)	0(0)
	Identity Attack	**1.00(0)**	**0.99(0.00)**	**0.98(0.02)**	0(0.01)	0(0)
	Insult	**0.98(0.01)**	**0.87(0.11)**	0(0)	0(0)	0(0)
	Threat	0(0)	0(0)	0(0)	0(0)	0(0)
	Sexual Explicit	0(0)	0(0)	0(0)	0(0)	0(0)
Trans people	*Toxicity*	**0.97(0.01)**	**0.93(0.01)**	**0.78(0.04)**	0(0)	0(0)
	Obscene	0(0)	0(0)	0(0)	0(0)	0(0)
	Identity Attack	**1.00(0)**	**1.00(0)**	**0.92(0.01)**	**0.32(0.20)**	0.02(0.05)
	Insult	**0.97(0.007)**	**0.94(0.01)**	**0.77(0.07)**	0(0)	0(0)
	Threat	0(0)	0(0)	0(0)	0(0)	0(0)
	Sexual Explicit	0(0)	0(0)	0(0)	0(0)	0(0)
Gay people	*Toxicity*	**1.00(0)**	**0.99(0.00)**	**0.99(0.00)**	**0.97(0.00)**	**0.93(0.01)**
	Obscene	0.25(0.12)	0.01(0.02)	0(0)	0(0)	0(0)
	Identity Attack	**1.00(0)**	**1.00(0)**	**0.99(0.00)**	**0.99(0.00)**	**0.99(0.00)**
	Insult	**0.99(0.001)**	**0.99(0.003)**	**0.91(0.04)**	0(0)	0(0)
	Threat	0(0)	0(0)	0(0)	0(0)	0(0)
	Sexual Explicit	**0.82(0.02)**	**0.84(0.01)**	**0.88(0.01)**	**0.82(0.02)**	**0.73(0.02)**
Black people	*Toxicity*	**1.00(0)**	**1.00(0)**	**0.99(0.00)**	**0.95(0.00)**	**0.92(0.01)**
	Obscene	0.05(0.06)	0.00(0.00)	0(0)	0(0)	0(0)
	Identity Attack	**1.00(0)**	**1.00(0)**	**1.00(0)**	**0.99(0.00)**	**0.99(0.00)**
	Insult	**0.99(0.001)**	**0.99(0.002)**	**0.95(0.01)**	0.14(0.12)	0(0)
	Threat	0.03(0.02)	0.04(0.02)	0(0)	0(0)	0(0)
	Sexual Explicit	0(0)	0(0)	0(0)	0(0)	0(0)
Disabled people	*Toxicity*	**0.41(0.2)**	0.01(0.06)	0(0)	0(0)	0(0)
	Obscene	0(0)	0(0)	0(0)	0(0)	0(0)
	Identity Attack	0(0)	0(0)	0(0)	0(0)	0(0)
	Insult	**0.70(0.2)**	0.13(0.21)	0(0)	0(0)	0(0)
	Threat	0(0)	0(0)	0(0)	0(0)	0(0)
	Sexual Explicit	0(0)	0(0)	0(0)	0(0)	0(0)
Muslims	*Toxicity*	**1.00(0)**	**0.99(0.00)**	**0.96(0.01)**	**0.75(0.04)**	**0.57(0.07)**
	Obscene	0(0.02)	0(0)	0(0)	0(0)	0(0)
	Identity Attack	**1.00(0)**	**1.00(0)**	**0.99(0.00)**	**0.98(0.00)**	**0.97(0.00)**
	Insult	**0.99(0.00)**	**0.98(0.007)**	**0.69(0.15)**	0(0)	0(0)
	Threat	**0.33(0.07)**	**0.32(0.07)**	**0.20(0.06)**	0(0)	0(0)
	Sexual Explicit	0(0)	0(0)	0(0)	0(0)	0(0)
Immigrants	*Toxicity*	**0.98(0)**	**0.95(0.01)**	**0.86(0.03)**	0(0)	0(0)
	Obscene	0(0)	0(0)	0(0)	0(0)	0(0)
	Identity Attack	**1.00(0)**	**0.99(0)**	**0.95(0.01)**	**0.74(0.11)**	**0.30(0.23)**
	Insult	**0.98(0.005)**	**0.96(0.01)**	**0.86(0.03)**	0(0)	0(0)
	Threat	0(0)	0(0)	0(0)	0(0)	0(0)
	Sexual Explicit	0(0)	0(0)	0(0)	0(0)	0(0)
These people	*Toxicity*	**0.93(0.02)**	**0.83(0.07)**	**0(0.03)**	0(0)	0(0)
	Obscene	0(0)	0(0)	0(0)	0(0)	0(0)
	Identity Attack	0(0)	0(0)	0(0)	0(0)	0(0)
	Insult	**0.97(0.01)**	**0.92(0.02)**	0.13(0.21)	0(0)	0(0)
	Threat	0(0)	0(0)	0(0)	0(0)	0(0)
	Sexual Explicit	0(0)	0(0)	0(0)	0(0)	0(0)
These things	*Toxicity*	0(0)	0(0)	0(0)	0(0)	0(0)
	Obscene	0(0)	0(0)	0(0)	0(0)	0(0)
	Identity Attack	0(0)	0(0)	0(0)	0(0)	0(0)
	Insult	0(0.03)	0(0)	0(0)	0(0)	0(0)
	Threat	0(0)	0(0)	0(0)	0(0)	0(0)
	Sexual Explicit	0(0)	0(0)	0(0)	0(0)	0(0)

Table A.1: Average and standard deviation of TCAV scores for all the labels and different levels of sentiment ranging from Very Negative to Very Positive for the template **"<SUBJECTS> are <SENTIMENT-WORD>"**. All the sensitivities that are significantly different from random are in bold.

Investigating the Characteristics of a Transformer in a Few-Shot Setup: Does Freezing Layers in RoBERTa Help?

Digvijay Ingle **Rishabh Tripathi** **Ayush Kumar** **Kevin Patel** **Jithendra Vepa**
Observe.AI, India
{digvijay.ingle, rishabh.tripathi, ayush}@observe.ai
{kevin.patel, jithendra}@observe.ai

Abstract

Transformer based language models have been widely adopted by industrial and research organisations in developing machine learning applications in the presence of limited annotated data. While these models show remarkable results, their functioning in few-shot settings is still poorly understood. Hence, we perform an investigative study to understand the characteristics of such models fine-tuned in few-shot setups. Specifically, we compare the intermediate layer representations obtained from a few-shot model and a pre-trained language model. We observe that pre-trained and few-shot models show similar representations over initial layers, whereas the later layers show a stark deviation. Based on these observations, we propose to freeze the initial Transformer layers to fine-tune the model in a constrained text classification setup with K annotated data points per class, where K ranges from 8 to 64. In our experiments across six benchmark sentence classification tasks, we discover that freezing initial 50% Transformer layers not only reduces training time but also surprisingly improves Macro F1 (upto 8%) when compared to fully trainable layers in few-shot setup. We also observe that this idea of layer freezing can very well be generalized to state-of-the-art few-shot text classification techniques, like DNNC and LM-BFF, leading to significant reduction in training time while maintaining comparable performance.

1 Introduction

The immense success of pre-trained language models (PLMs), such as BERT (Devlin et al., 2019) has significantly fueled their adoption to several real world NLP applications. However, the massive parameterization of these models inherently assumes access to large training data to fine-tune them for specific tasks. Collection of such large high quality annotated data is not only time-consuming but also a costly exercise. This gives rise to a research stream specifically focused towards developing techniques that help adoption of these models in a highly constrained setting, where only a small annotated dataset is available, a setup commonly referred to as *low resource setting*. Recent years have witnessed significant advancements in popular low-resource settings like - *Weak Supervised Learning* (Zhang et al., 2022; Wang et al., 2019), *Zero-Shot Learning* (Zhong et al., 2021; Ye et al., 2022) and *Few-Shot Learning* (Brown et al., 2020; Gao et al., 2021). Despite the success of these techniques, their functioning still remains a mystery. There has been a significant amount of work done on interpretability of representations learnt by these language models in presence of large task-specific data (Phang et al., 2021; Fayyaz et al., 2021; Kumar et al., 2021). However, understanding the representations learnt in presence of few-shot examples is relatively less studied. Hence, in this paper, we attempt to compare and contrast the characteristics of representations learnt by a BERT-style language model in presence of large as well as few-shot training examples with the intention to learn better few-shot models.

Our work is primarily motivated from the findings of Phang et al. (2021), where the authors perform a study to investigate the similarities and differences between the representations learned by PLMs and task-tuned models. We replicate a similar analysis on RoBERTa-base model, where we compare the representations obtained from the PLM and those obtained by fine-tuning it on SST-2 task in an oracle setup. We refer to an oracle setup, as an ideal setting where the entire PLM is fine-tuned on a specific task in presence of a large training dataset. We use centered kernel alignment (CKA; (Kornblith et al., 2019)) to measure similarity of representations as this is also the metric used by the authors for comparison. We observe that the representations obtained from initial layers of a fine-tuned model show high degree of similarity with those obtained from a pre-trained RoBERTa-

Proceedings of the Fifth BlackboxNLP Workshop on Analyzing and Interpreting Neural Networks for NLP, pages 238 - 248
December 8, 2022 ©2022 Association for Computational Linguistics

base model (Figure 1a). On the other hand, the representations from later layers highly deviate from the pre-trained model. This is also coherent with the observations reported by Phang et al. (2021) on ALBERT (Lan et al., 2020) model. Additionally, we compare the similarity of representations obtained from PLM to those obtained by fine-tuning it with K-shot examples, where we randomly sample $K = 8$ training examples per class for fine-tuning. We find that a similar nature of observations exists in case of K-shot model (Figure 1b), implying that most of the task-specific information is learnt in later half of the Transformer layers irrespective of the size of training data used for fine-tuning.

Thus, based on the results from Figure 1, we observe that the representations from models fine-tuned in both oracle and few-shot setups capture linguistic properties similar to that of PLMs at the initial layers. Hence, we conjecture that the initial layers can be frozen while training models in few-shot setup. We hypothesize that the reduced parameter space post such layer freezing would help learn better few-shot models.

In this work, we perform a comprehensive study of the impact of freezing specific layers while fine-tuning language models on six popular sequence classification tasks in a constrained setup where we have access to limited dataset of K annotated examples per class, where $K \in \{8, 16, 32, 64\}$. Specifically, our research contributions include:

- We show that initial 50% of the Transformer layers can be safely frozen while maintaining performance equivalent to or better than model fine-tuned with fully trainable layers in a few-shot setup. Our results indicate that this observation not only holds true for vanilla fine-tuning but also can be generalized to state-of-the-art (SOTA) few-shot techniques.

- We observe significant reductions in training time across K values for SOTA few-shot models and specifically lower K values for vanilla fine-tuning. This further helps justify our hypothesis that the reduction in parameter space due to freezing Transformer layers helps in faster convergence of the model in a few-shot setup. Moreover, the reduced training time further leads to broader environmental impact due to reduced carbon footprint (Patterson et al., 2021).

- While simply fine-tuning the classification head (100% of the Transformer layers frozen) might seem to be an intuitive choice for training few-shot models, given the significantly low size of training data, our experiments demonstrate that this strategy never helps and some proportion of Transformer layers are always required to be trainable.

- Most notably, while there has been a significant work on studying the representations of PLMs and the impact of freezing specific layers on a variety of NLU tasks, to the best of our knowledge, this is the first work that studies these aspects in a few-shot setup.

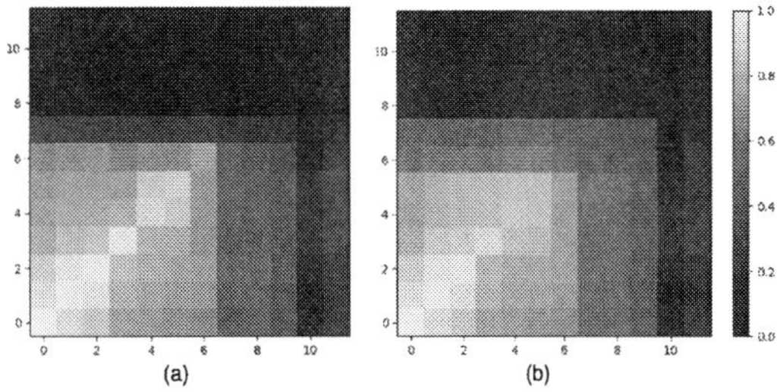

Figure 1: CKA similarity matrix based on <s> representations for: a) Pre-Trained (X-axis) vs Fine-Tuned on full training set (Y-axis), b) Pre-Trained (X-axis) vs Fine-Tuned with 8-shot examples (Y-axis)

2 Problem Setup

2.1 Task Formulation

For the purpose of this study, we assume access to a pre-trained language model, $\mathcal{L}$. The end goal is to utilize $\mathcal{L}$ to learn a text classifier $\mathcal{M}$ for task $\mathcal{D}$ with a label space $\mathcal{C} = \{c_1, c_2, ..., c_n\}$. We further assume a training set $\mathcal{D}_{train}$ for the task $\mathcal{D}$, with only K training examples per class such that the total number of training examples, $K_{total} = K \times |\mathcal{C}|$ and $\mathcal{D}_{train} = \{x_i, y_i\}_{i=1}^{K_{total}}$. For model selection and hyper-parameter tuning, we assume a validation set $\mathcal{D}_{val}$ which is of the same size as that of the training set $\mathcal{D}_{train}$, i.e, $|\mathcal{D}_{val}| = |\mathcal{D}_{train}|$. This constraint is significantly important as it conforms to the goal of learning in a low resource setting. Finally, we assume an access to an unseen test set, $\mathcal{D}_{test} = \{x_i^{test}, y_i^{test}\}$ for evaluation of $\mathcal{M}$ on task $\mathcal{D}$. For all our experiments, unless stated otherwise, we use $\mathcal{L}$ = RoBERTa-base and $K \in \{8, 16, 32, 64\}$.

2.2 Datasets

We conduct a systematic study across three binary classification tasks - CoLA (Warstadt et al., 2019), SST-2 (Socher et al., 2013) and Subj (Pang and Lee, 2004) and three multi-class classification tasks - AG News (Zhang et al., 2015), SST-5 (Socher et al., 2013) and SNIPS (Coucke et al., 2018). For AG News and Subj tasks, we do not have readily available validation sets, $\mathcal{U}_{val}$. Hence, we randomly sample 20% of the examples from the training set to create a validation set for these tasks. For CoLA, SST-2 and SST-5 tasks, we use their official validation sets. Similarly, for CoLA, SST-2 and SST-5 we do not have annotated test sets, $\mathcal{U}_{test}$. Hence, we randomly sample 10% of the examples from the training set to create unseen test sets, whereas we use the official test sets for AG News and Subj tasks. The remainder of the training set is referred to as $\mathcal{U}_{train}$. For model development, we finally obtain subsamples $\mathcal{D}_{train}$ and $\mathcal{D}_{val}$ from $\mathcal{U}_{train}$ and $\mathcal{U}_{val}$ respectively for each $K \in \{8, 16, 32, 64\}$ as described in section 2.1 such that $\mathcal{D}_{train} \subset \mathcal{U}_{train}$ and $\mathcal{D}_{val} \subset \mathcal{U}_{val}$. Note that for each of the tasks, we use a common test set for reporting model performance, i.e. $\mathcal{D}_{test} = \mathcal{U}_{test}$ for each $K \in \{8, 16, 32, 64\}$.

3 Experimental Setup

Based on the findings of Phang et al. (2021) and our experimental results in Figure 1, we investigate the impact of freezing Transformer layers on training a model in a K-shot setup, where $K \in \{8, 16, 32, 64\}$. We hypothesize that freezing particular layers would significantly reduce the parameter space which would in-turn benefit the process of fine-tuning a PLM specifically when we are operating in a constrained setup where we have access to only a limited number of annotated training examples. In order to test this hypothesis, we freeze the first $N\%$ of Transformer layers while fine-tuning $\mathcal{L}$ on task $\mathcal{D}$. Specifically, we start with $N = 0$ which resembles fully trainable Transformer layers and sequentially vary N in steps of 25. We continue this until $N = 100$ where we freeze the entire RoBERTa architecture allowing only the classification head to train. We study this setup on both vanilla fine-tuning and state-of-the-art (SOTA) few-shot techniques for fine-tuning RoBERTa-base model on each of the benchmark datasets described in Section 2.2.

3.1 Vanilla Fine-Tuning

Given a pre-trained language model $\mathcal{L}$ and text sequence x, we first obtain a tokenized sequence $\bar{x}$. Each sequence $\bar{x}$ is prefixed with a start of sentence token `<s>` and suffixed with end of sentence token `</s>`. The language model $\mathcal{L}$ is then used to map $\bar{x}$ to a sequence of hidden states h_p, such that $h_p \in \mathbb{R}^d$, where d = dimensionality of the hidden vector space. For fine-tuning the model on task $\mathcal{D}$, we add a task specific classification head, $softmax(\mathbf{W}h_{<s>})$, which returns a probability distribution over the label space C. Here, $\mathbf{W} \in \mathbb{R}^{|C| \times d}$ represents the randomly initialized weights at the start of the training, whereas $h_{<s>}$ is the hidden vector representation of `<s>` token. We further freeze $N\%$ of layers as per the approach described in Section 3. Finally, we train the entire network for a maximum of 10 epochs on a T4 GPU to minimize the cross-entropy loss. However, during training, we use early stopping criteria, where we utilize validation loss as the metric to choose the best checkpoint. Specifically, we stop the training, if validation loss does not improve for five consecutive evaluation steps. We perform a hyper-parameter sweep over the range - learning rate $\in \{1e-5, 5e-5, 1e-4\}$, batch size $\in \{4, 8, 16, 32\}$ and choose the best setting as evaluated on $\mathcal{D}_{val}$. Additionally, it is well-known that fine-tuning based on small data suffers from instability and the results may significantly vary based on choice of data split (Zhang et al., 2021). Hence, we report average performance and training times across 5 different $\mathcal{D}_{train}$ and $\mathcal{D}_{val}$ splits.

We specifically use vanilla fine-tuning approach for our experiments because it coheres with the standard fine-tuning of language models and is usually quoted as a baseline in SOTA few-shot techniques. Hence, benchmarking our methodology on vanilla fine-tuning allows us an opportunity to test the limits to which the performance of such a simple yet effective system can be pushed to.

3.2 SOTA Few-Shot Classification

In order to investigate the generalizability of our observations, we validate our experimental settings with layer freezing on following SOTA few-shot techniques. We utilize the original code-base open-sourced by the authors for the following techniques and report the results in terms of Macro F1 and training times as obtained from their training pipelines.

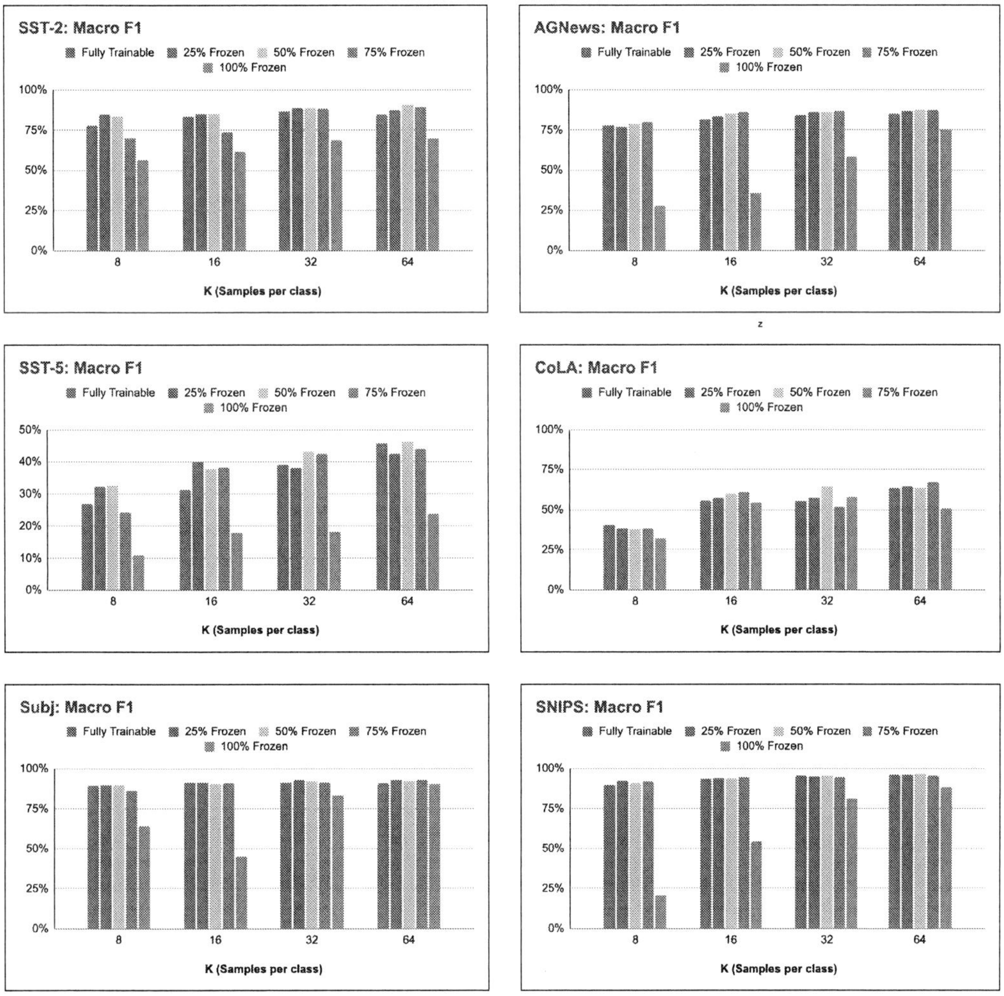

Figure 2: Comparison of Macro F1 (Y-axis) using vanilla fine-tuning post freezing of Transformer layers. In about 77% of the settings with upto 50% layers frozen, we observe an improvement in Macro F1 over fully trainable setup.

3.2.1 DNNC

DNNC (Zhang et al., 2020) is a state-of-the-art model that leverages nearest neighbor classification schema to perform few-shot text classification. Specifically, it uses the training data to create positive and negative examples that include ordered pairs of training data points belonging to the same class and different classes, respectively. It further uses BERT-style model pre-trained on natural language inference (NLI) task to fine-tune a binary classifier to estimate the best matching training example for a user input. The matched training example is then used to infer output class label. We specifically choose this model for benchmarking our setup since it is one of the commonly adopted few-shot techniques that demonstrated comparable performances in few-shot and oracle setups.

3.2.2 LM-BFF

We utilize LM-BFF (Gao et al., 2021), that uses a prompt-based approach to fine-tune a PLM in few-shot setup. A prompt refers to a human or machine generated natural language instruction that is indicative of the underlying task that a PLM is supposed to be fine-tuned on. Specifically, LM-BFF augments the input with a prompt consisting of a `<mask>` token. This re-formulates the text classification task into a masked language modelling (MLM) task, wherein $\mathcal{L}$ can be fine-tuned using MLM objective to maximize the probability

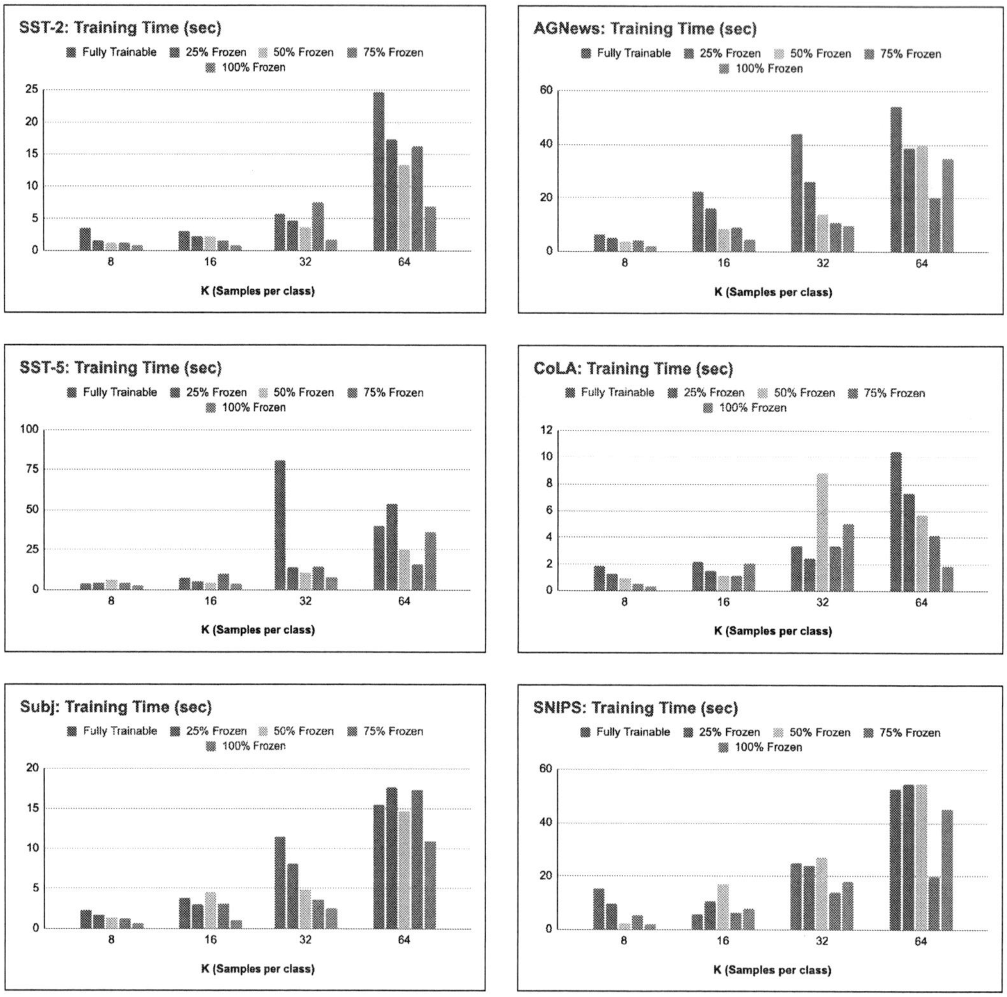

Figure 3: Comparison of training time (Y-axis) using vanilla fine-tuning post freezing of Transformer layers. In 79% of the settings with $K = 8$ and $K = 16$, we observe an improvement in training time over fully trainable setup.

of predicting the word that best resembles the task label corresponding to the input. We choose this approach for our benchmarking since it resulted in state-of-the-art performance over standard few-shot fine-tuning techniques. Moreover, prompt-based setups are becoming increasingly popular in the field of few-shot learning and benchmarking on LM-BFF allows us to validate the generalizability of our proposed method on recent approaches.

4 Results and Discussions

The results obtained from experiments with vanilla fine-tuning and few-shot classification methods have been summarized in Figures 2, 3, 4 and 5.

4.1 Effect of Freezing Layers on Vanilla Fine-Tuning

4.1.1 On Model Performance

For SST-2 task, we observe that freezing 25% and 50% of Transformer layers outperforms fully trainable setup by an absolute margin of 6% and 5% in Macro F1, respectively for $K = 8$ (refer Figure 2). A similar trend is also observed for higher values of K (=16, 32 and 64) where freezing upto 50% of Transformer layers consistently improves Macro F1 over fully trainable setup by a margin of upto 6%. This implies that the reduction in parameter space indeed benefits fine-tuning when we are operating in a few-shot setup. This further co-

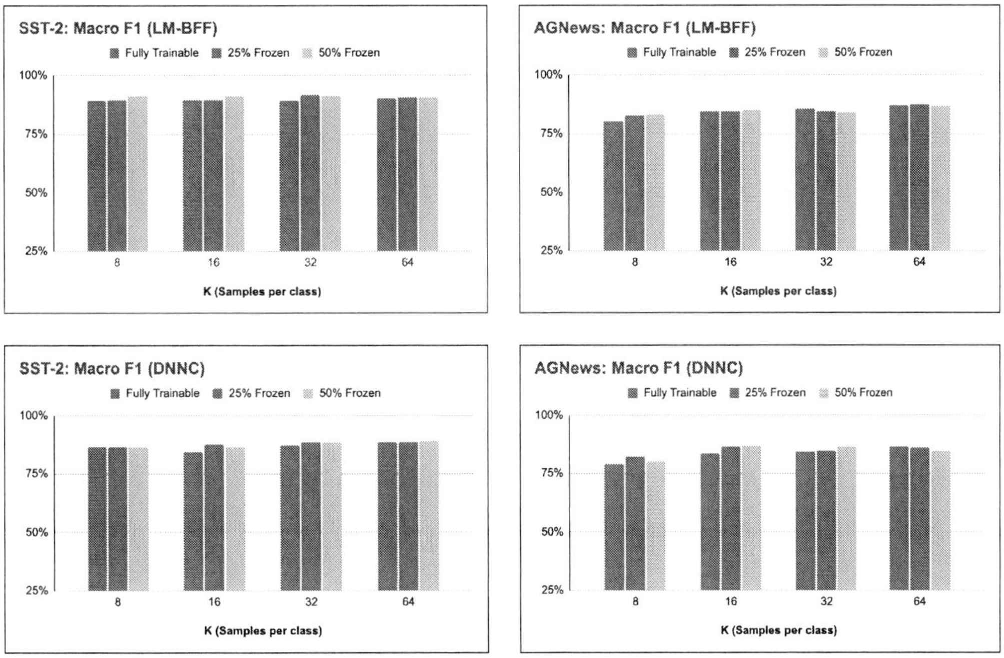

Figure 4: Comparison of Macro F1 (Y-axis) using few-shot methods post freezing of Transformer layers. In 81% of the settings experimented above, we observe an improvement in Macro F1 over fully trainable setup.

heres with our observations in Figure 1, where the representations obtained from initial layers of task-tuned model show a high degree of similarity with those obtained from the pre-trained model. Thus, making these layers trainable does not help learn any additional properties specific to the SST-2 task, instead it hurts the performance when trained in a few-shot setup. Furthermore, we observe a similar trend for other tasks (AG News, SST-5, CoLA, Subj and SNIPS) where freezing upto 50% of the transformer layers generally results in comparable or better performance. This further strengthens our claim that the first 50% of the Transformer layers can be safely frozen while fine-tuning the model in a few-shot setup.

Interestingly, further freezing of layers (>50%) starts showing a downward trend in Macro F1 over SST-2 task for $K \in \{8, 16, 32, 64\}$ implying that freezing these layers prevents the model from learning information useful for the task, which it was able to learn when only 50% of the layers were frozen. These observations are consistent with our findings in Figure 1, where the representations from later half of the Transformer layers show stark dissimilarity with those from the PLM implying that these layers are primarily responsible for learning task-specific information. Specifically, when we freeze 100% of the Transformer layers, we observe that the results show strong alignment with the above findings where it consistently leads to lower performance compared to other setups. It is a common practice to freeze the entire encoder while allowing only the classification head to be trainable while working with low resource setups. Surprisingly, our results suggest that this approach leads to sub-optimal results on all our datasets and one can achieve significantly better results with partial or no layer freezing.

On the other hand, when we freeze 75% of the layers, we see some uncertainty in the trend across tasks and K-values. We hypothesize that this could either be due to proximity to the inflection point where the behavior between similarities of representations between task-tuned and pre-trained model changes or due to certain characteristics in the similarity pattern that are peculiar to specific tasks. However, we leave this idea for further exploration as a part of future work.

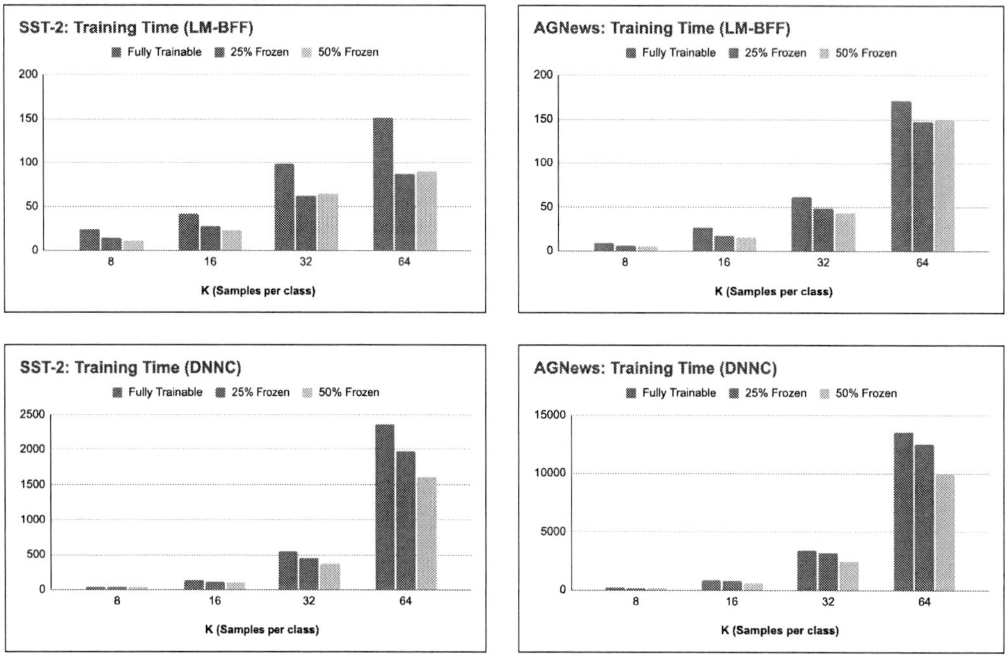

Figure 5: Comparison of training time (Y-axis) using few-shot methods post freezing of Transformer layers. In 100% of the settings experimented above, we observe an improvement in training time over fully trainable setup.

4.1.2 On Model Convergence

For SST-2 task, we observe that increasing the number of frozen layers from $0 - 100\%$ leads to a decreasing trend in training times for lower values of $K(= 8, 16)$. Since we are using early stopping criteria, this ensures that we are specifically looking for convergence of the evaluation loss. Thus, the reduction in training time is not only due to reduced computations due to layer freezing but also an effect of faster convergence due to the reduced parameter space. Moreover, we observe a similar trend for other datasets which further strengthens our claim that layer freezing results in reduced training time for vanilla fine-tuning. We do observe certain exceptions, for example higher training time on CoLA for $K = 16$ with 100% frozen layers which could be due to the general instability of few-shot setups (Zhang et al., 2021; Dodge et al., 2020).

Furthermore, for higher values of K, we observe a mixed trend in training time with increasing number of frozen layers. This is primarily because higher K leads to more gradient updates leading to higher possibility of deviations from local optima thus affecting the model convergence. We consistently observe this uncertainty in training times for higher values of K across tasks.

4.2 Effects of Freezing Layers on SOTA Few-Shot Classification Techniques

We further investigate the generalizability of proposed layer freezing approach on SOTA few-shot techniques. Based on our experimental results on vanilla fine-tuning, we observe that freezing beyond 50% of the layers generally degrades performance across our experiments (Figure 2). Hence, we only experiment with freezing upto 50% of the Transformer layers in case of SOTA few-shot models. We observe a similar trend in Macro F1 where freezing upto 50% of the layers generally leads to comparable performance. Moreover, freezing layers leads to significant drop in training time across tasks and K values implying that reduced parameter space consistently helps in faster convergence even in case of SOTA few-shot techniques. Refer to figures 4 and 5 for detailed results [1].

4.3 Meta Analysis and Key Takeaways

Table 1 consolidates a summary of absolute gains in Macro F1 and training time with layer freezing for

[1] We also extend the study to CoLA and Subj tasks and observe directionally similar results

	25% Layers Frozen						50% Layers Frozen					
	SST-2											
K	Vanilla Fine-Tuning		DNNC		LM-BFF		Vanilla Fine-Tuning		DNNC		LM-BFF	
	Δ_{F1}	Δ_{Time}	Δ_{F1}	Δ_{Time}	Δ_{F1}	Δ_{Time}	Δ_{F1}	Δ_{Time}	Δ_{F1}	Δ_{Time}	Δ_{F1}	Δ_{Time}
8	8.25	56	0.01	12	0.34	39	6.89	66	0.03	21	2.33	49
16	1.60	27	3.69	16	0.11	34	1.92	26	2.18	30	1.82	45
32	2.37	19	1.47	17	2.77	36	2.62	37	1.64	32	2.40	35
64	3.57	30	-0.11	16	0.06	42	7.49	46	0.44	32	0.35	40
	AG News											
8	-1.15	18	4.00	10	3.26	29	1.93	42	1.34	27	3.57	42
16	2.56	28	3.38	8	0.07	33	4.12	62	3.75	28	0.37	42
32	2.22	41	0.17	7	-0.94	22	2.28	68	2.33	27	-1.63	30
64	1.91	28	-0.64	8	0.49	14	2.32	27	-2.04	27	-0.38	13

Table 1: Comparison of layer freezing strategy across modelling setups averaged across 5 different data splits. **How to read the table?:** Let M_N be a K-shot model fine-tuned over PLM, $\mathcal{L}$, with $N\%$ of the Transformer layers frozen. (Note that, M_0 implies a model with all Transformer layers trainable.) Say, M_0 achieves a Macro F1 of $S_0\%$ with a training time of T_0 seconds and M_N achieves a Macro F1 of $S_N\%$ with a training time of T_N seconds, where $N \in \{25, 50\}$. We quote the improvement in Macro F1 with $N\%$ layer freezing over fully trainable setup as $\Delta_{F1} = 100 \times \frac{S_N - S_0}{S_0}\%$. Additionally, we quote the improvement in training time as $\Delta_{Time} = 100 \times \frac{T_0 - T_N}{T_0}\%$. Also, a negative value of Δ_{F1} implies layer freezing degrades the performance as compared to fully trainable setup.

SST-2 and AG News tasks across our experimental setups. Following are some of the macro-level insights and takeaways from the analysis:

- In 85% (41 out of 48) of the settings we experimented with, we observe that freezing upto 50% of the layers results in performance better than fully trainable setup. Specifically, we observe that 81% (26 out of 32) of the setups with DNNC and LM-BFF outperform fully trainable setup. This further reinforces that proposed layer freezing can very well be generalized to SOTA few-shot models.

- We obtain upto 56% and 68% reduction in training time with vanilla fine-tuning and SOTA few-shot methods respectively, which reinforces that freezing transformer layers leads to faster convergence. Resulting improvement in training efficiency leads to a significant reduction in carbon footprint (Patterson et al., 2021).

- Finally, we note that the reduced parameter space due to freezing of Transformer layers prevents the representations from losing out on the universal linguistic properties learnt by the pre-trained language model due to overfitting on few-shot examples, while allowing more freedom for later layers to learn task-specific features from few-shot examples. While, we observe degradation in performance with layer freezing in 6 settings using DNNC and LM-BFF, we note that 4 of these settings deviate marginally (less than 1%). We hypothesize that this could be due to use of default hyperparameters in the training pipelines released by the authors. We believe, an exhaustive hyperparameter sweep can help eliminate these inconsistencies.

5 Prior Work

Recent years have seen significant development in the field of language modelling using Transformer (Vaswani et al., 2017) based models like GPT (Radford and Narasimhan, 2018), BERT (Devlin et al., 2019), RoBERTa (Liu et al., 2019), etc. A number of studies have been conducted to identify better techniques to fine-tune these models on NLU tasks in both oracle and few-shot settings. Dodge et al. (2020), Lee et al. (2020), Zhang et al. (2021) focus on regularization techniques that help stabilize the fine-tuning of BERT-style models. Specifically, Zhang et al. (2021) demonstrate that standard process of fine-tuning for fixed epochs is sub-optimal for BERT-like models especially in few-shot setting and hence training for large epochs is required. Further, Dodge et al. (2020) show that fine-tuning on small datasets often leads to divergence during training and a simple yet effective approach like early stopping can lead to a better model selection.

Due to the tedious and time-consuming nature of data collection process, few-shot learning has recently started gaining popularity. Zhang et al. (2020) propose DNNC, a nearest neighbor classification approach that uses NLI-style training to predict if two inputs belong to the same class. Additionally, Gao et al. (2021) use a prompting based approach to fine-tune a pre-trained language model in few-shot setup leading to state-of-the-art performance without introducing any new parameters.

Parallelly, there has been a surge in works on interpretability of language models and understanding the patterns in representations learnt by them. Li et al. (2020) probe attention heads to understand certain linguistic patterns learnt by BERT. Kumar et al. (2021) design probing tasks to investigate the ability of BERT-based language models in understanding properties in spoken language. Fayyaz et al. (2021) discover different localizations of linguistic properties learnt by ELECTRA (Clark et al., 2020) and XLNET (Yang et al., 2019). On the other hand, Phang et al. (2021) perform a layer wise comparison of representations learnt by pre-trained and task-tuned models. While they perform an extensive analysis to compare the models in a setup where a large training data is available, the validation of these findings in the few-shot setup is largely unexplored.

6 Conclusions

In this work, we compare the representations obtained from intermediate Transformer layers of RoBERTa-base model and task-tuned models in few-shot setup and discover that the linguistic properties learnt by pre-trained and task-tuned models at the initial layers are very similar and hence can potentially be frozen for training models in few-shot settings. We further study the impact of such freezing of Transformer layers in a few-shot setting. Our experimental results indicate that freezing upto initial 50% of the Transformer layers surprisingly leads to performance either comparable to or better than fully trainable layers in both vanilla fine-tuning as well as SOTA few-shot models. We also observe that the reduced parameter space due to layer freezing leads to faster convergence which in turn leads to reduction in training time for 8-shot and 16-shot setups on both vanilla fine-tuning and SOTA few-shot models across tasks. Specifically, for few-shot models, this observation can even be extended to 32-shot and 64-shot setups. Moreover, layer freezing can be viewed as a medium to foster sustainable NLP research by reducing carbon footprint due to improvement in training efficiency. Finally, our results also establish that a commonly followed practice of completely frozen encoder (100% Transformer layers frozen) never helps in a few-shot setup and a proportion of Transformer layers are always required to be trainable.

7 Future Work

As discussed in Section 4.1.1, we observe an uncertainty in performance trends with 75% of the Transformer layers frozen. In future, we would like to dive deeper into understanding the potential reasons for such an uncertainty. Additionally, in this paper, we primarily focused on studying a K-shot setups with $K \in \{8, 16, 32, 64\}$, however, we believe that the idea of partially freezing Transformer layers can very well be extended to other classes of low-resource settings, like weak supervision and hence we would like to further our experiments in this direction.

References

Tom B. Brown, Benjamin Mann, Nick Ryder, Melanie Subbiah, Jared Kaplan, Prafulla Dhariwal, Arvind Neelakantan, Pranav Shyam, Girish Sastry, Amanda Askell, Sandhini Agarwal, Ariel Herbert-Voss, Gretchen Krueger, Tom Henighan, Rewon Child, Aditya Ramesh, Daniel M. Ziegler, Jeffrey Wu, Clemens Winter, Christopher Hesse, Mark Chen, Eric Sigler, Mateusz Litwin, Scott Gray, Benjamin Chess, Jack Clark, Christopher Berner, Sam McCandlish, Alec Radford, Ilya Sutskever, and Dario Amodei. 2020. Language models are few-shot learners. In *Advances in Neural Information Processing Systems 33: Annual Conference on Neural Information Processing Systems 2020, NeurIPS 2020, December 6-12, 2020, virtual.*

Kevin Clark, Minh-Thang Luong, Quoc V. Le, and Christopher D. Manning. 2020. ELECTRA: pre-training text encoders as discriminators rather than generators. In *8th International Conference on Learning Representations, ICLR 2020, Addis Ababa, Ethiopia, April 26-30, 2020*. OpenReview.net.

Alice Coucke, Alaa Saade, Adrien Ball, Théodore Bluche, Alexandre Caulier, David Leroy, Clément Doumouro, Thibault Gisselbrecht, Francesco Caltagirone, Thibaut Lavril, Maël Primet, and Joseph Dureau. 2018. Snips voice platform: an embedded spoken language understanding system for private-by-design voice interfaces. *CoRR*, abs/1805.10190.

Jacob Devlin, Ming-Wei Chang, Kenton Lee, and Kristina Toutanova. 2019. BERT: pre-training of deep bidirectional transformers for language understanding. In *Proceedings of the 2019 Conference of the North American Chapter of the Association for Computational Linguistics: Human Language Technologies, NAACL-HLT 2019, Minneapolis, MN, USA, June 2-7, 2019, Volume 1 (Long and Short Papers)*, pages 4171–4186. Association for Computational Linguistics.

Jesse Dodge, Gabriel Ilharco, Roy Schwartz, Ali Farhadi, Hannaneh Hajishirzi, and Noah A. Smith. 2020. Fine-tuning pretrained language models: Weight initializations, data orders, and early stopping. *CoRR*, abs/2002.06305.

Mohsen Fayyaz, Ehsan Aghazadeh, Ali Modarressi, Hosein Mohebbi, and Mohammad Taher Pilehvar. 2021. Not all models localize linguistic knowledge in the same place: A layer-wise probing on bertoids' representations. In *Proceedings of the Fourth BlackboxNLP Workshop on Analyzing and Interpreting Neural Networks for NLP, BlackboxNLP@EMNLP 2021, Punta Cana, Dominican Republic, November 11, 2021*, pages 375–388. Association for Computational Linguistics.

Tianyu Gao, Adam Fisch, and Danqi Chen. 2021. Making pre-trained language models better few-shot learners. In *Proceedings of the 59th Annual Meeting of the Association for Computational Linguistics and the 11th International Joint Conference on Natural Language Processing, ACL/IJCNLP 2021, (Volume 1: Long Papers), Virtual Event, August 1-6, 2021*, pages 3816–3830. Association for Computational Linguistics.

Simon Kornblith, Mohammad Norouzi, Honglak Lee, and Geoffrey E. Hinton. 2019. Similarity of neural network representations revisited. In *Proceedings of the 36th International Conference on Machine Learning, ICML 2019, 9-15 June 2019, Long Beach, California, USA*, volume 97 of *Proceedings of Machine Learning Research*, pages 3519–3529. PMLR.

Ayush Kumar, Mukuntha Narayanan Sundararaman, and Jithendra Vepa. 2021. What BERT based language models learn in spoken transcripts: An empirical study. *CoRR*, abs/2109.09105.

Zhenzhong Lan, Mingda Chen, Sebastian Goodman, Kevin Gimpel, Piyush Sharma, and Radu Soricut. 2020. ALBERT: A lite BERT for self-supervised learning of language representations. In *8th International Conference on Learning Representations, ICLR 2020, Addis Ababa, Ethiopia, April 26-30, 2020*. OpenReview.net.

Cheolhyoung Lee, Kyunghyun Cho, and Wanmo Kang. 2020. Mixout: Effective regularization to finetune large-scale pretrained language models. In *8th International Conference on Learning Representations, ICLR 2020, Addis Ababa, Ethiopia, April 26-30, 2020*. OpenReview.net.

Liunian Harold Li, Mark Yatskar, Da Yin, Cho-Jui Hsieh, and Kai-Wei Chang. 2020. What does BERT with vision look at? In *Proceedings of the 58th Annual Meeting of the Association for Computational Linguistics, ACL 2020, Online, July 5-10, 2020*, pages 5265–5275. Association for Computational Linguistics.

Yinhan Liu, Myle Ott, Naman Goyal, Jingfei Du, Mandar Joshi, Danqi Chen, Omer Levy, Mike Lewis, Luke Zettlemoyer, and Veselin Stoyanov. 2019. Roberta: A robustly optimized BERT pretraining approach. *CoRR*, abs/1907.11692.

Bo Pang and Lillian Lee. 2004. A sentimental education: Sentiment analysis using subjectivity summarization based on minimum cuts. In *Proceedings of the 42nd Annual Meeting of the Association for Computational Linguistics, 21-26 July, 2004, Barcelona, Spain*, pages 271–278. ACL.

David Patterson, Joseph Gonzalez, Quoc Le, Chen Liang, Lluis-Miquel Munguia, Daniel Rothchild, David So, Maud Texier, and Jeff Dean. 2021. Carbon emissions and large neural network training. *arXiv preprint arXiv:2104.10350*.

Jason Phang, Haokun Liu, and Samuel R. Bowman. 2021. Fine-tuned transformers show clusters of similar representations across layers. In *Proceedings of the Fourth BlackboxNLP Workshop on Analyzing and Interpreting Neural Networks for NLP, BlackboxNLP@EMNLP 2021, Punta Cana, Dominican Republic, November 11, 2021*, pages 529–538. Association for Computational Linguistics.

Alec Radford and Karthik Narasimhan. 2018. Improving language understanding by generative pretraining.

Richard Socher, Alex Perelygin, Jean Wu, Jason Chuang, Christopher D. Manning, Andrew Y. Ng, and Christopher Potts. 2013. Recursive deep models for semantic compositionality over a sentiment treebank. In *Proceedings of the 2013 Conference on Empirical Methods in Natural Language Processing, EMNLP 2013, 18-21 October 2013, Grand Hyatt Seattle, Seattle, Washington, USA, A meeting of SIGDAT, a Special Interest Group of the ACL*, pages 1631–1642. ACL.

Ashish Vaswani, Noam Shazeer, Niki Parmar, Jakob Uszkoreit, Llion Jones, Aidan N. Gomez, Lukasz Kaiser, and Illia Polosukhin. 2017. Attention is all you need. In *Advances in Neural Information Processing Systems 30: Annual Conference on Neural Information Processing Systems 2017, December 4-9, 2017, Long Beach, CA, USA*, pages 5998–6008.

Hao Wang, Bing Liu, Chaozhuo Li, Yan Yang, and Tianrui Li. 2019. Learning with noisy labels for sentence-level sentiment classification. In *Proceedings of the 2019 Conference on Empirical Methods in Natural Language Processing and the 9th International Joint Conference on Natural Language Processing, EMNLP-IJCNLP 2019, Hong Kong, China, November 3-7, 2019*, pages 6285–6291. Association for Computational Linguistics.

Alex Warstadt, Amanpreet Singh, and Samuel R. Bowman. 2019. Neural network acceptability judgments. *Trans. Assoc. Comput. Linguistics*, 7:625–641.

Zhilin Yang, Zihang Dai, Yiming Yang, Jaime G. Carbonell, Ruslan Salakhutdinov, and Quoc V. Le. 2019. Xlnet: Generalized autoregressive pretraining for language understanding. In *Advances in Neural Information Processing Systems 32: Annual Conference on Neural Information Processing Systems 2019, NeurIPS 2019, December 8-14, 2019, Vancouver, BC, Canada*, pages 5754–5764.

Jiacheng Ye, Jiahui Gao, Qintong Li, Hang Xu, Jiangtao Feng, Zhiyong Wu, Tao Yu, and Lingpeng Kong. 2022. Zerogen: Efficient zero-shot learning via dataset generation. *CoRR*, abs/2202.07922.

Jian-Guo Zhang, Kazuma Hashimoto, Wenhao Liu, Chien-Sheng Wu, Yao Wan, Philip S. Yu, Richard Socher, and Caiming Xiong. 2020. Discriminative nearest neighbor few-shot intent detection by transferring natural language inference. In *Proceedings of the 2020 Conference on Empirical Methods in Natural Language Processing, EMNLP 2020, Online, November 16-20, 2020*, pages 5064–5082. Association for Computational Linguistics.

Jieyu Zhang, Cheng-Yu Hsieh, Yue Yu, Chao Zhang, and Alexander Ratner. 2022. A survey on programmatic weak supervision. *CoRR*, abs/2202.05433.

Tianyi Zhang, Felix Wu, Arzoo Katiyar, Kilian Q. Weinberger, and Yoav Artzi. 2021. Revisiting few-sample BERT fine-tuning. In *9th International Conference on Learning Representations, ICLR 2021, Virtual Event, Austria, May 3-7, 2021*. OpenReview.net.

Xiang Zhang, Junbo Jake Zhao, and Yann LeCun. 2015. Character-level convolutional networks for text classification. In *Advances in Neural Information Processing Systems 28: Annual Conference on Neural Information Processing Systems 2015, December 7-12, 2015, Montreal, Quebec, Canada*, pages 649–657.

Ruiqi Zhong, Kristy Lee, Zheng Zhang, and Dan Klein. 2021. Adapting language models for zero-shot learning by meta-tuning on dataset and prompt collections. In *Findings of the Association for Computational Linguistics: EMNLP 2021, Virtual Event / Punta Cana, Dominican Republic, 16-20 November, 2021*, pages 2856–2878. Association for Computational Linguistics.

It Is Not Easy To Detect Paraphrases: Analysing Semantic Similarity With Antonyms and Negation Using the New *SemAntoNeg* Benchmark

Teemu Vahtola and **Mathias Creutz** and **Jörg Tiedemann**
Department of Digital Humanities
Faculty of Arts
University of Helsinki
Finland
{teemu.vahtola, mathias.creutz, jorg.tiedemann}helsinki.fi

Abstract

We investigate to what extent a hundred publicly available, popular neural language models capture meaning systematically. Sentence embeddings obtained from pretrained or fine-tuned language models can be used to perform particular tasks, such as paraphrase detection, semantic textual similarity assessment or natural language inference. Common to all of these tasks is that paraphrastic sentences, that is, sentences that carry (nearly) the same meaning, should have (nearly) the same embeddings regardless of surface form.

We demonstrate that performance varies greatly across different language models when a specific type of meaning-preserving transformation is applied: two sentences should be identified as paraphrastic if one of them contains a negated antonym in relation to the other one, such as *I am not guilty* versus *I am innocent.*

We introduce and release *SemAntoNeg*, a new test suite containing 3152 entries for probing paraphrasticity in sentences incorporating negation and antonyms. Among other things, we show that language models fine-tuned for natural language inference outperform other types of models, especially the ones fine-tuned to produce general-purpose sentence embeddings, on the test suite. Furthermore, we show that most models designed explicitly for paraphrasing are rather mediocre in our task.

1 Introduction

Large pretrained language language models have pushed NLP forward in many sub-fields, and their ability to embed essential linguistic properties makes them applicable across a wide range of tasks. However, it is still an open question how well they cope with systematic compositionality and to what level of abstraction they reflect the actual meaning behind a given sentence.

This work is in line with other experiments based on dedicated test suites that study specific linguistic phenomena in connection with neural representation models. In particular, we publish a novel benchmark called *SemAntoNeg*[1], that tests the ability of language models to properly represent expressions that contain antonymy and negation, embedded into a paraphrase task.

Our test suite consists of contrastive examples where the task is to select the correct paraphrase for a given input sentence among three candidate expressions that include combinations of negated sentences and antonym substitutions. To provide a simple example, a semantic opposite to an input sentence *I am guilty* would be *I am not guilty*, where the opposite meaning is invoked by an insertion of a negation marker. Similarly, instead of inserting the negation marker, substituting the adjective to its antonym inverses the meaning of the sentence: *I am innocent.* To maintain paraphrasticity with respect to the original sentence, performing both of the operations is necessary, resulting in: *I am not innocent.* Thus, for a model to succeed in the *SemAntoNeg* test suite, the models need to understand that insertion or deletion of a negation accompanied with antonym substitution produces a sentence that is semantically equivalent to the original sentence, and the sentence embeddings should represent this relationship.

Using this benchmark, we study the following questions:

- How well do sentence embeddings from general-purpose language models fare in this task?
- Does fine-tuning on paraphrase tasks help to improve the performance on our test suite?
- What is the best fine-tuning task that supports our benchmark?

[1]The challenge set is available at: https://github.com/teemuvh/antonym-substitution

Proceedings of the Fifth BlackboxNLP Workshop on Analyzing and Interpreting Neural Networks for NLP, pages 249 - 262
December 8, 2022 ©2022 Association for Computational Linguistics

In order to answer those questions, we systematically evaluate a large number of publicly available pretrained language models on the novel test suite. We notice a large amount of variation between different models, mostly depending on the fine-tuning objective and data, but, in some cases, also between models fine-tuned for the same task. Selecting an appropriate model becomes a challenge considering the sea of releases available on public model hubs. Simply selecting among the most popular ones might be a poor strategy, as we can see in Table 1.

Model	Accuracy
all-MiniLM-L6-v2	1.9
paraphrase-MiniLM-L6-v2	43.3
bert-base-nli-mean-tokens	83.3
all-mpnet-base-v2	31.9
distiluse-base-multilingual-cased-v2	1.5
all-MiniLM-L12-v2	8.2
multi-qa-mpnet-base-dot-v1	17.5
paraphrase-multilingual-MiniLM-L12-v2	61.8
paraphrase-mpnet-base-v2	76.1
distilbert-multilingual-nli-stsb-quora-ranking	47.1

Table 1: Testing our new benchmark on the ten most downloaded models from the Hugging Face sentence-transformers library in a descending order based on download counts.

Our analysis below provides new insights into the semantic abstraction abilities with respect to antonyms and negation and gives additional guidance for the selection of an appropriate model for tasks that require proper inference with such constructions.

2 Description of the Task

The objective of our test suite is to test to what extent sentence representation models succeed in distinguishing sentences similar in meaning when the change in semantics is realised only by a substitution of a distributionally similar (Grefenstette, 1992) word token (antonym in this case) or by an insertion or deletion of a negation marker. Performing either of the operations results in a sentence that conveys the semantic opposite of the original sentence while maintaining a high lexical overlap between both sentences.

We cast the benchmark in terms of a paraphrase detection task: a model is confronted with three alternatives of potential reformulations of an input sentence and only one of them is a proper equivalent on a semantic level. The candidates are designed to include negations and antonyms of adjectives to create the specific challenge of the test suite. More details about the data sets and its creation are given in Section 3 below.

The idea is not to fine-tune any model for this particular task (because any model would quickly overfit to such regular constructions) but rather to test independently trained sentence embedding models that can be used to measure semantic distance to make the decision. As such, it is in line with other natural language understanding benchmarks such as SentEval (Conneau and Kiela, 2018) and GLUE (Wang et al., 2018) but it represents a dedicated linguistic probing task rather than a general-purpose evaluation framework.

The work is motivated by previous research that identified deficiencies in the popular sentence representation benchmarks. For instance, existing paraphrase detection data sets (e.g., QQP[2]) lack examples that are characterised by a high lexical overlap without paraphrastic meaning (Zhang et al., 2019). Classification models can simply learn to measure lexical overlap to make proper decisions and, therefore, Zhang et al. (2019) generate a more difficult test suite of paraphrases and non-paraphrases with a high bag-of-words overlap by word scrambling. The same problem has been observed in natural language inference, where contradicting sentences typically exhibit low lexical overlap. Word permutations have been proposed (Dasgupta et al., 2018) to generate difficult cases that require better knowledge of compositionality.

In our test suite, we go beyond the creation of more challenging distractors (e.g., better negative examples with high vocabulary overlaps) by introducing more challenging positive candidates that are explicitly different from the source by adding antonyms from a lexical resource. In connection with negation, the model is now forced to disregard surface features (such as matching tokens) and to properly understand negated messages to make the correct decision. Thus, we test not only for semantic similarity but also evaluate the ability to understand the relationship between antonyms as well as the effect of negation on meaning representations.

Before discussing the experimental setup (Section 4) and the results of our practical experiments (Section 5), we will present details of the data set and how it was created in the section below.

[2] https://www.kaggle.com/c/quora-question-pairs

Label	Input	Options
2	No, that's true.	{No, that's false., No, that's not true., No, that's not false.}
2	I'm guilty.	{I'm innocent., I'm not guilty., I'm not innocent.}
2	I'm not sure.	{I'm not uncertain., I'm sure., I'm uncertain.}
2	That is good.	{That is bad., That is not good., That is not bad.}
2	I know you're not asleep.	{I know you're not awake., I know you're asleep., I know you're awake.}

Table 2: Examples from the test suite. Based on the input sentence, the model is supposed to select the equivalent sentence from the alternative hypotheses in the Options column. Values on the Label column indicate the index of the true paraphrase in the options column.

3 Data Creation

We created the test suite in a semi-automatic way. First, we downloaded 1.5 million sentence pairs from the English training set of the Opusparcus paraphrase corpus (Creutz, 2018). Next, we removed sentence pairs where the length of either of the sentences was less than four tokens. Furthermore, we retained only sentence pairs, where either one, but not both, of the sentences contains a negation (e.g., *I'm innocent. – I'm not guilty.*) After this filtering process, our data consisted of approximately 7500 sentence pairs. At this point we realised that, even though many of the sentence pairs were meaningful for our experiments, our filtered set also contained pairs that were paraphrastic but did not include antonymous relations, such as *Aren't you cold? – Are you cold?* Therefore, we proceeded with a second round of filtering, where we POS-tagged the sentences using NLTK (Bird et al., 2009) and retained sentences containing explicit negation (*not*) as an adverb (RB) as well as adjectives (JJ). Finally, we removed duplicate sentences. This process resulted in 1317 sentences, all of which included an explicit negation marker and an adjective.

For each of the 1317 sentences, we generated three hypotheses from which the model is supposed to choose the one that conveys the same meaning as the input sentence. First, we queried an antonym for the adjective in the input sentence from the WordNet Electrical Lexical Database (Fellbaum, 1998) to get a an opposing sentence. To obtain the second contradicting sentence, we deleted the negator from the input sentence. Finally, we substituted the adjective from the second contradicting sentence to its antonym to obtain the paraphrase of the input sentence. Examples of entries in the test suite are provided in Table 2.

We reviewed the resulting test suite manually to ensure its good quality. The antonym substitution procedure introduced some grammatical errors to the data, such as wrong agreement of articles (*a evil idea*) or a question tag not agreeing with the main clause (*You're not serious, aren't you?*). We corrected such phrases manually. The sentences also included some examples where the automatically retrieved antonyms were not considered to carry opposite meanings, such as *Are you hungry? – Are you not thirsty?* We removed such examples from the final test suite.

Eventually, we obtained 788 examples, from which we permuted all possible input sentences to result in 3152 test examples, containing 209 unique adjectives, which constitute the *SemAntoNeg* test suite.

4 Experimental Setup

To compare sentence representations derived from different Transformer-based pretrained language models, we ran 114 of the 120 pretrained Sentence-BERT (Reimers and Gurevych, 2019) models that are publicly available in the Hugging Face transformers library (Wolf et al., 2020).[3] We provide the full list of the models we tested accompanied with the accuracy they acquired on the *SemAntoNeg* test suite in Appendix A.

We embed the sentences in our test suite using the different language models. To create the embeddings we apply the same pooling strategy used in training the original sentence-transformers. We then evaluate each model by its ability to produce embeddings such that the input sentence and its true paraphrase are closest to each other in the vector space. To compare embeddings we use cosine similarity.

Basically, we have run a systematic loop over all

[3]We did not include four image-to-text models, nor did we include two T5-xxl models that we could not fit into the GPU.

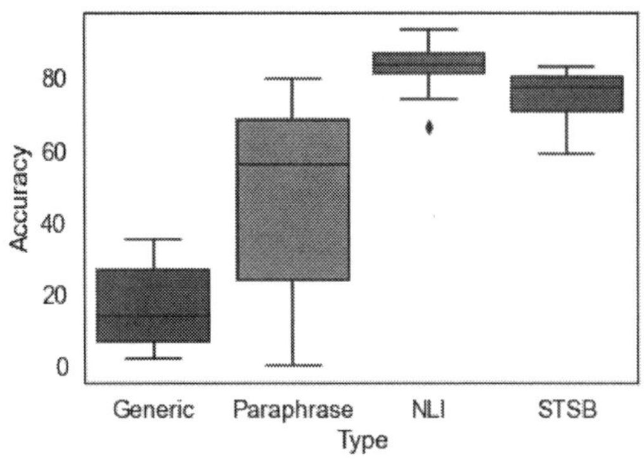

Figure 1: Results of the different model types. The accuracy [%] of the models is labeled on the y-axis and the different model types are labeled on the x-axis. "Generic" refers to the general-purpose models fine-tuned for a large range of transfer tasks. "Paraphrase", "NLI", and "STSB" refer to models fine-tuned for paraphrase detection, natural language inference, and semantic textual similarity, respectively.

available models but we are especially interested in specific groups of models, which we will discuss next. First of all, we want to see the performance of general-purpose models before looking at dedicated paraphrase models. Finally, we discuss other task-specific models before we present a detailed error analysis and conclude with prospects for future work.

5 Results

We analyse the results of our experiments by grouping the language models into four different categories, determined by the fine-tuning objective of the models: general-purpose embeddings, as well as embeddings specialised for paraphrasing, natural language inference and semantic textual similarity. Figure 1 shows average accuracies and variances for these four types of models. Individual results of all models are provided in Appendix A.

Since there are three possible choices in our task, a random selection yields a baseline level of 33.3% accuracy. We observe models that diverge clearly from the baseline level, either positively or negatively. This means that many tested models make good or bad choices systematically. We return to these findings in the error analysis in Section 6. The following sections summarise the analyses of the separate model groups.

Model	Accuracy
sentence-t5-xl	81.2
sentence-t5-large	78.4
sentence-t5-base	67.2
all-roberta-large-v1	35.4
all-mpnet-base-v2	31.9
all-mpnet-base-v1	25.1
all-distilroberta-v1	18.5
all-MiniLM-L12-v1	9.7
all-MiniLM-L12-v2	8.2
all-MiniLM-L6-v1	3.1
all-MiniLM-L6-v2	1.9

Table 3: Results of the general-purpose models. The dashed line represents results from random choice (33.3%)

5.1 General-Purpose Sentence Representations

Table 3 provides results on the general-purpose sentence representation models. These models are trained to generate representations that have the capacity to be highly useful for a large range of natural language understanding tasks. When extensively evaluated on different benchmarks related to sentence embeddings and semantic search, the aggregated results reported on the sentence-transformers website indicate good performance.[4] The performance on the *SemAntoNeg* test suite probing for understanding of negation and antonymy, however, suggests that especially the fine-tuned general-purpose models lack in this crucial aspect of natural language understanding.

The T5 models (Raffel et al., 2020) are not fine-tuned for any specific objective. The all-* models, instead, are fine-tuned for a wide range of natural language understanding tasks and are thus expected to produce general-purpose sentence embeddings that have the capacity to capture a diverse range of linguistic properties in order to be successful in different transfer tasks. Analysis of the predicted sentences from the only fine-tuned general-purpose model that outperforms the random baseline (all-roberta-large-v1) suggests that the model is prone to predicting the sentence with the highest lexical overlap while ignoring the negation. Thus, the model often predicts the semantic opposite of the input sentence by simply connecting lexical similarity with semantic similarity, which explains the

[4]https://www.sbert.net/docs/pretrained_models.html

Model	Accuracy
paraphrase-multilingual-mpnet-base-v2	79.9
paraphrase-mpnet-base-v2	76.1
paraphrase-TinyBERT-L6-v2	72.1
paraphrase-distilroberta-base-v2	68.4
quora-distilbert-base	67.2
paraphrase-multilingual-MiniLM-L12-v2	61.8
paraphrase-albert-small-v2	60.8
paraphrase-albert-base-v2	58.7
paraphrase-MiniLM-L12-v2	55.9
quora-distilbert-multilingual	47.1
paraphrase-MiniLM-L6-v2	43.3
paraphrase-xlm-r-multilingual-v1	23.9
xlm-r-distilroberta-base-paraphrase-v1	23.9
paraphrase-distilroberta-base-v1	19.4
paraphrase-MiniLM-L3-v2	0.03

Table 4: Results [%] of the models fine-tuned for paraphrase detection. The dashed line represents results from random choice (33.3%)

poor performance.

5.2 Paraphrase Models

We report the results of the paraphrase models on the test suite in Table 4. One would expect the paraphrase models, whose objective is to recognise sentences that carry the same meaning but use a different wording (Bhagat and Hovy, 2013) to be successful on our test suite. This is, however, not the case for all of the models, and none of the models actually outperform the best performing general-purpose model.

The paraphrase models seem to vary greatly in their ability to generate representations that capture meaning regardless of surface form. Some of the differences between the results can be traced back to the data used for fine-tuning the models. For instance, the two distilled implementations of RoBERTa (Liu et al., 2019) perform very differently on the test suite (19.4% vs. 68.4%). However, "version 2" (paraphrase-distilroberta-base-v2), which obtains the higher accuracy, was fine-tuned with much more training examples[5].

Some of the variation can be traced back to the methodology, such as with the MiniLM models (Wang et al., 2020). The difference in performance between the MiniLM models may be explained by the layer from which the representations are extracted. Previous research has demonstrated how Transformer-based models accumulate different types of knowledge on different layers, semantics being predominantly encoded in the last layers of the network (Jawahar et al., 2019). The results obtained for the MiniLM models are in line with the previous findings: embeddings from layer 12 outperform embeddings from layer 6, which in turn outperform embeddings from layer 3. To a smaller extent, the same effect is seen on the general-purpose models (Table 3) where the representations derived from the MiniLM models perform differently based on the layer they are extracted from.

[5] https://www.sbert.net/examples/training/paraphrases/README.html

Model	Accuracy
roberta-large-nli-mean-tokens	93.6
roberta-base-nli-mean-tokens	89.5
bert-large-nli-mean-tokens	87.4
nli-bert-large-cls-pooling	86.8
nli-bert-large-max-pooling	86.4
xlm-r-large-en-ko-nli-ststb	85.4
xlm-r-bert-base-nli-mean-tokens	83.9
bert-base-nli-cls-token	83.7
bert-base-nli-mean-tokens	83.3
nli-distilbert-base-max-pooling	83.2
distilbert-base-nli-mean-tokens	81.2
bert-base-nli-max-tokens	80.8
nli-roberta-base-v2	79.6
nli-mpnet-base-v2	74.1
nli-distilroberta-base-v2	66.6

Table 5: Results [%] of the models that are fine-tuned for natural language inference.

5.3 Other Fine-Tuning Objectives

In addition to paraphrasing, we hypothesise that models which have been fine-tuned on other similar objectives could perform well on the *SemAntoNeg* test suite.

Table 5 provides results for all models fine-tuned for natural language inference (NLI) that are available in the sentence-transformers library. Natural language inference probes the model for recognising whether an input sentence (the premise) entails, contradicts or is neutral with respect to another sentence (the hypothesis).

Compared to the general-purpose models (Table 3) and the paraphrase models (Table 4), the NLI models are, for the most part, considerably more successful on the test suite. The success of the NLI models might arise due to a more prominent use of negation in the training data, giving a model more knowledge about the proper treatment of such constructions. Furthermore, models trained for NLI have been shown to understand the effect of ex-

Model	Accuracy
stsb-bert-large	83.3
stsb-roberta-large	82.4
stsb-roberta-base	80.3
stsb-xlm-r-multilingual	79.8
stsb-bert-base	77.3
stsb-distilbert-base	76.5
stsb-roberta-base-v2	70.8
stsb-mpnet-base-v2	70.2
stsb-distilroberta-base-v2	58.7

Table 6: Results [%] of the models fine-tuned for the Semantic textual similarity benchmark.

plicit negation (i.e., *not*) to the sentence semantics rather well (Kim et al., 2019). Additionally, entailment examples may get very close to instances in our test suite and, in this way, provide better support for the expressions we test. Paraphrase data sets, on the other hand, tend to emphasise the use of synonyms and therefore fail to learn a better treatment of negation and antonyms. Even though NLI models seem to be successful on our test suite, they do not necessarily perform well on other paraphrase tasks. BERT-large fine-tuned for NLI obtains 87.4% accuracy on the *SemAntoNeg* test suite, while only reaching 75.9% on the Microsoft Research Paraphrase Corpus (Reimers and Gurevych, 2019), where the best-performing models fine-tuned explicitly for paraphrasing obtain results exceeding 90% accuracy (e.g., fine-tuned RoBERTa achieves 92.3% on that task (Liu et al., 2019)). In future work, we will investigate the qualitative difference in training data in more depth in order to provide a better picture about the influence of fine-tuning objectives on *SemAntoNeg* performance.

In addition to NLI, we believe that fine-tuning sentence representation models on the Semantic Textual Similarity Benchmark (STSB) data (Cer et al., 2017) can produce embeddings that can distinguish between semantically similar sentences regardless of their surface forms and be successful on the test suite. The results of the models fine-tuned for STSB are presented in Table 6. The STSB data is designed to comprise sentences that share some level of semantic similarity, and the task probes the representations for "gradations of meaning overlap" (Agirre et al., 2016; Cer et al., 2017). Fine-tuning on the STSB data potentially encourages models to learn more fine-grained (dis-)similarities from the sentence pairs, which is valuable for succeeding in the *SemAntoNeg* test suite.

Model	Accuracy
roberta-large-nli-mean-tokens	93.6
roberta-base-nli-mean-tokens	89.5
bert-large-nli-mean-tokens	87.4
nli-bert-large-cls-pooling	86.8
nli-bert-large-max-pooling	86.4
xlm-r-large-en-ko-nli-ststb	85.4
xlm-r-bert-base-nli-mean-tokens	83.9
bert-base-nli-cls-token	83.7
bert-base-nli-mean-tokens	83.3
stsb-bert-large	83.3
bert-large-nli-stsb-mean-tokens	83.3
distilbert-base-nli-max-tokens	83.2

Table 7: Results [%] of the best performing models.

The sentence-transformers library also includes models that are not suited to the *SemAntoNeg* task by design. Such models include for instance models trained for machine reading comprehension and question answering on the MS MARCO data set (Bajaj et al., 2016). The results of these models are included in Appendix A, and affirm the hypothesis that the models are not suitable for this task.

6 Error Analysis

We have analysed misclassified examples from a set of different models. Naturally, the errors the best-performing models make differ from the ones made by the worst-performing models.

We have studied an intersection of the examples that were misclassified by all of the best models (listed in Table 7). Antonym pairs that are rare and highly contextual seem to be difficult for the models. For instance, the antonym pair *possible – actual* (e.g., in the sentence pair *No, that's actual. – No, that's not possible.*) is very often misclassified. The antonym pair *possible – actual* comprises the majority of the common misclassified examples of the best performing models: 70 out of 105 examples. The antonym pair is retrieved from WordNet, but in the test suite they rarely occur in a natural context (in which they would refer to a possibility, as opposed to an actual event). The example would probably demand some contextual priming for the models to be able to connect the relationship between the antonyms.

Another frequently shared incorrectly predicted antonym pair includes the words *same* and *other*

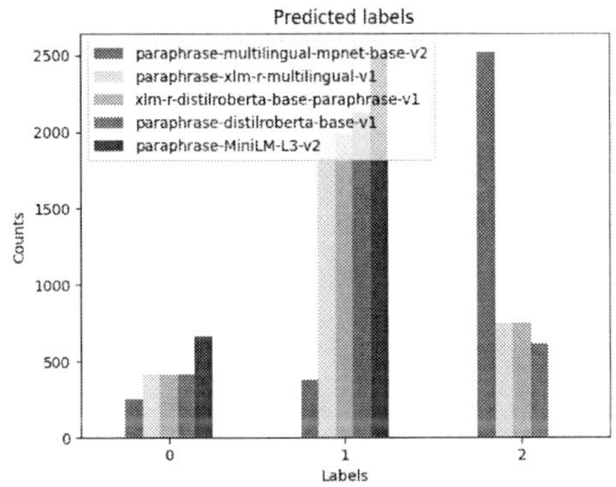

Figure 2: The best and the four worst performing paraphrase models. Labels in the test suite are presented on the x-axis. The number of times the labels are predicted by the models is presented on the y-axis. Labels 0 and 1 denote errors, 0 meaning sentences where only antonym substitution is performed, and 1 meaning only polarity swap (insertion or deletion of negation). Label 2 indicates that both operations are performed, which is the correct choice.

in the definite form, for instance: *It is not the same. – It is the other.* Here, the definite form *the other* could be the cause of incorrect predictions, whereas a more suitable opposing relation could be expressed using for example *some* as an indefinite article as in *some other*. The antonym pair *the same – the other* comprises 17 of the remaining 35 incorrectly predicted examples shared by the best performing models.

A bar chart of the best paraphrase model and the four paraphrase models that obtain accuracy below random choice is presented in Figure 2. The results indicate that the poor performance of the worst paraphrase models is explained by them systematically preferring the sentence with the highest lexical overlap disregarding the negation completely, which is reflected by a high proportion of label 1 in the figure. The trend seems similar for the other models whose accuracies are below random choice. Compared to the models that perform well, the poorly performing models seem more prone to associating lexical similarity with semantic similarity, leading them to predict the sentence with the opposite meaning with respect to the input sentence.

7 Limitations

The test suite comes with some limitations that we find important to discuss. We acknowledge that the proposed task is not difficult to solve using a simple rule-based model and that it is rather easy to overfit a neural network-based model to the data. Therefore, the kind of data the test suite instantiates is supposed to be used for evaluating models by probing sentence representations for the certain kinds of linguistic phenomena exclusively.

The test suite includes overrepresentation of certain frequent adjectives. The adjective *good* occurs more than 270 times in the input sentence, whereas some rarer adjectives, such as *opaque* only occur twice. Adding more unique adjectives to make the data even more representative and balancing the data is left for future work.

Another caveat of the test suite is that for now it only probes the sentence representations for a set of negated antonyms that belong to the adjective class. As some of the other word classes also include words that have a related opposing concept (e.g., *accept – reject* in the verb class), and it would be equally important to assess how language models understand the relation of the words in other word classes. Additionally, the test suite consists only of one certain negation pattern: not + adjective. Adding examples with more variable negation patterns would require an adapted filtering method to extract the sentences from a paraphrase corpus or more manual work to ensure high-quality paraphrases of the sort (e.g., *I walked – I didn't stand still.*) Augmenting the test suite with test examples of more varied negation patterns, as well as antonymous tokens from different word classes is left for future work.

8 Related Work

Previous work has focused on understanding negation, on the one hand, and antonymy, on the other.

Kassner and Schütze (2020) show that pretrained language models (Transformer-XL (Dai et al., 2019), ELMO (Peters et al., 2018) and BERT (Devlin et al., 2019) in this case) are poor at recognising the difference between a sentence in affirmative or negative form when they are queried with a negative cloze test, and are prone to predict the same token regardless of the polarity of the sentence. Ettinger (2020) study how BERT understands negation with similar minimal pairs to our test suite. However, they probe BERT for predicting one word token in a sentence pair where one sentence is a negated version of the other (e.g., *Most smokers find that quitting is very __. – Most smokers find that quitting isn't very __.*) BERT does not seem to be highly robust for the transformation, and it does not seem that negation alone suffices to prime the model for systematically predicting the opposite of the prediction in the affirmative sentence (Ettinger, 2020).

Hossain et al. (2020) show that NLI models are not robust to negation by analysing models on a new benchmark designed to assess how models understand negation. In a similar spirit, assessing a multilingual language model fine-tuned for NLI on a test suite of minimal pairs of label-changing and label-preserving negations, Hartmann et al. (2021) find that multilingual language models are not fully aware of the effects that a negation marker can have on sentence semantics. Furthermore, NLI models' difficulty to represent negations reliably has been traced to training data, suggesting that models trained on SNLI (Bowman et al., 2015) or MNLI (Williams et al., 2018) do not properly learn to reason with expressions that include negation (Geiger et al., 2020; Richardson et al., 2020).

Kim et al. (2019) analyse different pretraining objectives for predicting textual entailment on various function word probing tasks, one of which assesses models' understanding of negation in a similar manner to our test suite. They find that the natural language inference models outperform other pretraining objectives in representing negation, mostly owing to NLI models' capability to represent explicit negation. However, analysis of examples that were difficult for a state-of-the-art NLI model has suggested that antonymy and negation are challenging phenomena to represent reliably, as models do not recognise antonymous relations as semantically opposing and may associate explicit negation to contradiction in neutral or entailed examples (Naik et al., 2018).

In addition to analysing language models' understanding of natural language in textual entailment, representation of antonyms has been studied for instance by comparing the mapping of negated adjectives in vector space (Rimell et al., 2017). BERT has also been adapted to perform a cloze problem for predicting antonyms in context (Niwa et al., 2021).

Additionally, previous research has focused on learning vector-based representations of word semantics that can model the relationship between distributionally similar but semantically opposing words better (e.g., Pham et al., 2015; Ono et al., 2015). Jumelet and Hupkes (2018) study how language models understand semantic compositionality with respect to contrasting meanings but focus on transformations of (negative) polarity items.

9 Conclusions

We have presented a novel test suite, *SemAntoNeg*, designed to probe pretrained language models for the understanding of the relationship between negation and antonymy. Contradicting examples in the test suite are close to the input by design and lead to a challenging benchmark. In order to succeed on our test suite, a model needs to recognise the semantic opposites invoked either by antonym substitution or by an insertion or a deletion of a negation marker. Equally, the model needs understanding of semantic compositionality to understand how the operations affect semantics of the sentence when performed together.

We have evaluated publicly available pretrained sentence representation models and reported results that display a large amount of variation when assessed on the new test suite. Surprisingly, dedicated paraphrase models are not among the best performing models and deliver rather poor results in many cases, whereas fine-tuning to natural language inference seems very beneficial for the task. General-purpose models are overall not very good at recognising our examples either, except for recent very large multi-task models such as T5-xl.

Our findings highlight that models that fare well in established natural language understanding benchmarks may still have crucial deficiencies in representing certain, rather typical, linguistic constructions and may produce critical mistakes. As a result, more structured test suites are necessary for assessing how the pretrained models understand language. This paper provides another contribution in that direction.

There are various avenues in future work we would like to explore. First of all, we need to further test the scaling effects when moving to very large language models such as GPT-3 (Brown et al., 2020). The T5 results already indicate that size matters but it is too early to draw general conclusions. Furthermore, we plan to investigate prompting as an alternative to vector similarity. However, prompt engineering is a challenging task in itself and we will need to explore the influence of prompts on results we can expect. Finally, we would also like to move to other languages and potentially cross-lingual setups.

Acknowledgements

The research reported in this paper was supported by the Behind the Words project, funded by the Academy of Finland. We would like to acknowledge *CSC – The Finnish IT Center for Science* for the computational resources they have generously provided. We would also like to thank the anonymous reviewers for their insightful comments.

References

Eneko Agirre, Carmen Banea, Daniel Cer, Mona Diab, Aitor Gonzalez-Agirre, Rada Mihalcea, German Rigau, and Janyce Wiebe. 2016. SemEval-2016 task 1: Semantic textual similarity, monolingual and cross-lingual evaluation. In *Proceedings of the 10th International Workshop on Semantic Evaluation (SemEval-2016)*, pages 497–511, San Diego, California. Association for Computational Linguistics.

Payal Bajaj, Daniel Campos, Nick Craswell, Li Deng, Jianfeng Gao, Xiaodong Liu, Rangan Majumder, Andrew McNamara, Bhaskar Mitra, Tri Nguyen, et al. 2016. Ms marco: A human generated machine reading comprehension dataset. *arXiv preprint arXiv:1611.09268*.

Rahul Bhagat and Eduard Hovy. 2013. What Is a Paraphrase? *Computational Linguistics*, 39(3):463–472.

Steven Bird, Ewan Klein, and Edward Loper. 2009. *Natural language processing with Python: analyzing text with the natural language toolkit.* " O'Reilly Media, Inc.".

Samuel R. Bowman, Gabor Angeli, Christopher Potts, and Christopher D. Manning. 2015. A large annotated corpus for learning natural language inference. In *Proceedings of the 2015 Conference on Empirical Methods in Natural Language Processing*, pages 632–642, Lisbon, Portugal. Association for Computational Linguistics.

Tom Brown, Benjamin Mann, Nick Ryder, Melanie Subbiah, Jared D Kaplan, Prafulla Dhariwal, Arvind Neelakantan, Pranav Shyam, Girish Sastry, Amanda Askell, Sandhini Agarwal, Ariel Herbert-Voss, Gretchen Krueger, Tom Henighan, Rewon Child, Aditya Ramesh, Daniel Ziegler, Jeffrey Wu, Clemens Winter, Chris Hesse, Mark Chen, Eric Sigler, Mateusz Litwin, Scott Gray, Benjamin Chess, Jack Clark, Christopher Berner, Sam McCandlish, Alec Radford, Ilya Sutskever, and Dario Amodei. 2020. Language models are few-shot learners. In *Advances in Neural Information Processing Systems*, volume 33, pages 1877–1901. Curran Associates, Inc.

Daniel Cer, Mona Diab, Eneko Agirre, Iñigo Lopez-Gazpio, and Lucia Specia. 2017. SemEval-2017 task 1: Semantic textual similarity multilingual and crosslingual focused evaluation. In *Proceedings of the 11th International Workshop on Semantic Evaluation (SemEval-2017)*, pages 1–14, Vancouver, Canada. Association for Computational Linguistics.

Alexis Conneau and Douwe Kiela. 2018. SentEval: An evaluation toolkit for universal sentence representations. In *Proceedings of the Eleventh International Conference on Language Resources and Evaluation (LREC 2018)*, Miyazaki, Japan. European Language Resources Association (ELRA).

Mathias Creutz. 2018. Open subtitles paraphrase corpus for six languages. In *Proceedings of the Eleventh International Conference on Language Resources and Evaluation (LREC 2018)*, Miyazaki, Japan. European Language Resources Association (ELRA).

Zihang Dai, Zhilin Yang, Yiming Yang, Jaime Carbonell, Quoc Le, and Ruslan Salakhutdinov. 2019. Transformer-XL: Attentive language models beyond a fixed-length context. In *Proceedings of the 57th Annual Meeting of the Association for Computational Linguistics*, pages 2978–2988, Florence, Italy. Association for Computational Linguistics.

Ishita Dasgupta, Demi Guo, Andreas Stuhlmüller, Samuel J. Gershman, and Noah D. Goodman. 2018. Evaluating compositionality in sentence embeddings. *CoRR*, abs/1802.04302.

Jacob Devlin, Ming-Wei Chang, Kenton Lee, and Kristina Toutanova. 2019. BERT: Pre-training of deep bidirectional transformers for language understanding. In *Proceedings of the 2019 Conference of the North American Chapter of the Association for Computational Linguistics: Human Language Technologies, Volume 1 (Long and Short Papers)*, pages 4171–4186, Minneapolis, Minnesota. Association for Computational Linguistics.

Allyson Ettinger. 2020. What BERT Is Not: Lessons from a New Suite of Psycholinguistic Diagnostics for Language Models. *Transactions of the Association for Computational Linguistics*, 8:34–48.

Christiane Fellbaum. 1998. *WordNet: An Electronic Lexical Database*. The MIT Press.

Atticus Geiger, Kyle Richardson, and Christopher Potts. 2020. Neural natural language inference models partially embed theories of lexical entailment and negation. In *Proceedings of the Third BlackboxNLP Workshop on Analyzing and Interpreting Neural Networks for NLP*, pages 163–173, Online. Association for Computational Linguistics.

Gregory Grefenstette. 1992. Finding semantic similarity in raw text: The deese antonyms. In *Fall Symposium Series, Working Notes, Probabilistic Approaches to Natural Language*, pages 61–65.

Mareike Hartmann, Miryam de Lhoneux, Daniel Hershcovich, Yova Kementchedjhieva, Lukas Nielsen, Chen Qiu, and Anders Søgaard. 2021. A multilingual benchmark for probing negation-awareness with minimal pairs. In *Proceedings of the 25th Conference on*

Computational Natural Language Learning, pages 244–257, Online. Association for Computational Linguistics.

Md Mosharaf Hossain, Venelin Kovatchev, Pranoy Dutta, Tiffany Kao, Elizabeth Wei, and Eduardo Blanco. 2020. An analysis of natural language inference benchmarks through the lens of negation. In *Proceedings of the 2020 Conference on Empirical Methods in Natural Language Processing (EMNLP)*, pages 9106–9118, Online. Association for Computational Linguistics.

Ganesh Jawahar, Benoît Sagot, and Djamé Seddah. 2019. What does BERT learn about the structure of language? In *Proceedings of the 57th Annual Meeting of the Association for Computational Linguistics*, pages 3651–3657, Florence, Italy. Association for Computational Linguistics.

Jaap Jumelet and Dieuwke Hupkes. 2018. Do language models understand anything? on the ability of LSTMs to understand negative polarity items. In *Proceedings of the 2018 EMNLP Workshop BlackboxNLP: Analyzing and Interpreting Neural Networks for NLP*, pages 222–231, Brussels, Belgium. Association for Computational Linguistics.

Nora Kassner and Hinrich Schütze. 2020. Negated and misprimed probes for pretrained language models: Birds can talk, but cannot fly. In *Proceedings of the 58th Annual Meeting of the Association for Computational Linguistics*, pages 7811–7818, Online. Association for Computational Linguistics.

Najoung Kim, Roma Patel, Adam Poliak, Patrick Xia, Alex Wang, Tom McCoy, Ian Tenney, Alexis Ross, Tal Linzen, Benjamin Van Durme, Samuel R. Bowman, and Ellie Pavlick. 2019. Probing what different NLP tasks teach machines about function word comprehension. In *Proceedings of the Eighth Joint Conference on Lexical and Computational Semantics (*SEM 2019)*, pages 235–249, Minneapolis, Minnesota. Association for Computational Linguistics.

Yinhan Liu, Myle Ott, Naman Goyal, Jingfei Du, Mandar Joshi, Danqi Chen, Omer Levy, Mike Lewis, Luke Zettlemoyer, and Veselin Stoyanov. 2019. Roberta: A robustly optimized bert pretraining approach. *arXiv preprint arXiv:1907.11692*.

Aakanksha Naik, Abhilasha Ravichander, Norman Sadeh, Carolyn Rose, and Graham Neubig. 2018. Stress test evaluation for natural language inference. In *Proceedings of the 27th International Conference on Computational Linguistics*, pages 2340–2353, Santa Fe, New Mexico, USA. Association for Computational Linguistics.

Ayana Niwa, Keisuke Nishiguchi, and Naoaki Okazaki. 2021. Predicting antonyms in context using BERT. In *Proceedings of the 14th International Conference on Natural Language Generation*, pages 48–54, Aberdeen, Scotland, UK. Association for Computational Linguistics.

Masataka Ono, Makoto Miwa, and Yutaka Sasaki. 2015. Word embedding-based antonym detection using thesauri and distributional information. In *Proceedings of the 2015 Conference of the North American Chapter of the Association for Computational Linguistics: Human Language Technologies*, pages 984–989, Denver, Colorado. Association for Computational Linguistics.

Matthew E. Peters, Mark Neumann, Mohit Iyyer, Matt Gardner, Christopher Clark, Kenton Lee, and Luke Zettlemoyer. 2018. Deep contextualized word representations. In *Proceedings of the 2018 Conference of the North American Chapter of the Association for Computational Linguistics: Human Language Technologies, Volume 1 (Long Papers)*, pages 2227–2237, New Orleans, Louisiana. Association for Computational Linguistics.

Nghia The Pham, Angeliki Lazaridou, and Marco Baroni. 2015. A multitask objective to inject lexical contrast into distributional semantics. In *Proceedings of the 53rd Annual Meeting of the Association for Computational Linguistics and the 7th International Joint Conference on Natural Language Processing (Volume 2: Short Papers)*, pages 21–26, Beijing, China. Association for Computational Linguistics.

Colin Raffel, Noam Shazeer, Adam Roberts, Katherine Lee, Sharan Narang, Michael Matena, Yanqi Zhou, Wei Li, and Peter J. Liu. 2020. Exploring the limits of transfer learning with a unified text-to-text transformer. *Journal of Machine Learning Research*, 21(140):1–67.

Nils Reimers and Iryna Gurevych. 2019. Sentence-BERT: Sentence embeddings using Siamese BERT-networks. In *Proceedings of the 2019 Conference on Empirical Methods in Natural Language Processing and the 9th International Joint Conference on Natural Language Processing (EMNLP-IJCNLP)*, pages 3982–3992, Hong Kong, China. Association for Computational Linguistics.

Kyle Richardson, Hai Hu, Lawrence Moss, and Ashish Sabharwal. 2020. Probing natural language inference models through semantic fragments. *Proceedings of the AAAI Conference on Artificial Intelligence*, 34(05):8713–8721.

Laura Rimell, Amandla Mabona, Luana Bulat, and Douwe Kiela. 2017. Learning to negate adjectives with bilinear models. In *Proceedings of the 15th Conference of the European Chapter of the Association for Computational Linguistics: Volume 2, Short Papers*, pages 71–78, Valencia, Spain. Association for Computational Linguistics.

Alex Wang, Amanpreet Singh, Julian Michael, Felix Hill, Omer Levy, and Samuel Bowman. 2018. GLUE: A multi-task benchmark and analysis platform for natural language understanding. In *Proceedings of the 2018 EMNLP Workshop BlackboxNLP: Analyzing and Interpreting Neural Networks for NLP*, pages 353–355, Brussels, Belgium. Association for Computational Linguistics.

Wenhui Wang, Furu Wei, Li Dong, Hangbo Bao, Nan Yang, and Ming Zhou. 2020. Minilm: Deep self-attention distillation for task-agnostic compression of pre-trained transformers. In *Advances in Neural Information Processing Systems*, volume 33, pages 5776–5788. Curran Associates, Inc.

Adina Williams, Nikita Nangia, and Samuel Bowman. 2018. A broad-coverage challenge corpus for sentence understanding through inference. In *Proceedings of the 2018 Conference of the North American Chapter of the Association for Computational Linguistics: Human Language Technologies, Volume 1 (Long Papers)*, pages 1112–1122. Association for Computational Linguistics.

Thomas Wolf, Lysandre Debut, Victor Sanh, Julien Chaumond, Clement Delangue, Anthony Moi, Pierric Cistac, Tim Rault, Remi Louf, Morgan Funtowicz, Joe Davison, Sam Shleifer, Patrick von Platen, Clara Ma, Yacine Jernite, Julien Plu, Canwen Xu, Teven Le Scao, Sylvain Gugger, Mariama Drame, Quentin Lhoest, and Alexander Rush. 2020. Transformers: State-of-the-art natural language processing. In *Proceedings of the 2020 Conference on Empirical Methods in Natural Language Processing: System Demonstrations*, pages 38–45, Online. Association for Computational Linguistics.

Yuan Zhang, Jason Baldridge, and Luheng He. 2019. PAWS: Paraphrase adversaries from word scrambling. In *Proceedings of the 2019 Conference of the North American Chapter of the Association for Computational Linguistics: Human Language Technologies, Volume 1 (Long and Short Papers)*, pages 1298–1308, Minneapolis, Minnesota. Association for Computational Linguistics.

A Results of All Models

Results of the 114 Transformer-based models from the Hugging Face Transformers library on the test suite.

Model	Accuracy
msmarco-distilbert-base-tas-b	0.0
multi-qa-MiniLM-L6-cos-v1	0.3
all-MiniLM-L6-v2	1.9
multi-qa-distilbert-cos-v1	1.4
all-MiniLM-L12-v2	8.2
all-distilroberta-v1	18.5
multi-qa-mpnet-base-dot-v1	17.5
all-mpnet-base-v2	31.9
paraphrase-MiniLM-L3-v2	0.0
paraphrase-albert-small-v2	60.8
sentence-t5-base	67.2
distiluse-base-multilingual-cased	1.5
distilroberta-base-msmarco-v1	1.7
nli-bert-large-cls-pooling	86.8
xlm-r-base-en-ko-nli-ststb	79.5
bert-large-nli-cls-token	86.8
nli-distilbert-base-max-pooling	83.2
nli-bert-large-max-pooling	86.4
xlm-r-bert-base-nli-mean-tokens	83.9
msmarco-roberta-base-v2	4.3
distilbert-base-nli-max-tokens	83.2
xlm-r-100langs-bert-base-nli-mean-tokens	83.9
msmarco-MiniLM-L-12-v3	0.0
msmarco-MiniLM-L12-cos-v5	0.0
nli-distilbert-base	81.2
xlm-r-large-en-ko-nli-ststb	85.4
quora-distilbert-base	67.2
facebook-dpr-question_encoder-single-nq-base	6.8
facebook-dpr-question_encoder-multiset-base	5.9
nli-bert-base	83.3
bert-large-nli-max-tokens	86.4
msmarco-roberta-base-ance-firstp	3.1
bert-base-nli-cls-token	83.7
stsb-bert-large	83.3
facebook-dpr-ctx_encoder-multiset-base	9.4
bert-large-nli-stsb-mean-tokens	83.3
multi-qa-MiniLM-L6-dot-v1	0.5
msmarco-distilbert-multilingual-en-de-v2-tmp-trained-scratch	0.0
nli-roberta-base-v2	79.6
nli-roberta-base	89.5
stsb-distilroberta-base-v2	58.7
bert-base-wikipedia-sections-mean-tokens	7.1
stsb-bert-base	77.3
paraphrase-albert-base-v2	58.7
msmarco-distilbert-base-dot-prod-v3	0.4
msmarco-distilbert-multilingual-en-de-v2-tmp-lng-aligned	0.9

bert-large-nli-mean-tokens	87.4
xlm-r-distilroberta-base-paraphrase-v1	23.9
msmarco-roberta-base-v3	3.1
bert-base-nli-max-tokens	80.8
distilbert-base-nli-stsb-quora-ranking	67.2
msmarco-MiniLM-L6-cos-v5	0.0
msmarco-distilroberta-base-v2	0.4
nli-distilroberta-base-v2	66.6
roberta-base-nli-mean-tokens	89.5
distilroberta-base-paraphrase-v1	19.4
msmarco-MiniLM-L-6-v3	0.0
distilroberta-base-msmarco-v2	0.4
nq-distilbert-base-v1	2.3
msmarco-distilbert-cos-v5	0.0
msmarco-distilbert-base-v2	0.7
msmarco-distilbert-base-v3	0.0
stsb-xlm-r-multilingual	79.8
allenai-specter	0.1
roberta-large-nli-stsb-mean-tokens	82.4
roberta-base-nli-stsb-mean-tokens	80.3
use-cmlm-multilingual	3.6
xlm-r-100langs-bert-base-nli-stsb-mean-tokens	79.8
stsb-roberta-base	80.3
msmarco-bert-base-dot-v5	0.0
quora-distilbert-multilingual	47.1
stsb-roberta-large	82.4
xlm-r-bert-base-nli-stsb-mean-tokens	79.8
paraphrase-MiniLM-L12-v2	55.9
clip-ViT-B-32-multilingual-v1	Image-text model
msmarco-distilbert-dot-v5	0.0
nli-mpnet-base-v2	74.1
paraphrase-TinyBERT-L6-v2	72.1
distiluse-base-multilingual-cased-v1	1.4
distilbert-base-nli-stsb-mean-tokens	76.5
stsb-roberta-base-v2	70.8
paraphrase-distilroberta-base-v1	19.4
bert-base-nli-stsb-mean-tokens	77.3
LaBSE	11.7
stsb-distilbert-base	76.5
paraphrase-distilroberta-base-v2	68.4
paraphrase-multilingual-mpnet-base-v2	79.9
distilbert-base-nli-mean-tokens	81.2
distilbert-multilingual-nli-stsb-quora-ranking	47.1
msmarco-distilbert-base-v4	0.0
paraphrase-xlm-r-multilingual-v1	23.9
distiluse-base-multilingual-cased-v2	1.5
paraphrase-mpnet-base-v2	76.1
paraphrase-multilingual-MiniLM-L12-v2	61.8
paraphrase-MiniLM-L6-v2	43.3
bert-base-nli-mean-tokens	83.3
clip-ViT-B-16	Image-text model

clip-ViT-L-14	Image-text model
clip-ViT-B-32	Image-text model
sentence-t5-xxl	–
sentence-t5-xl	81.2
sentence-t5-large	78.4
gtr-t5-large	17.4
gtr-t5-xl	17.4
gtr-t5-base	9.5
gtr-t5-xxl	–
msmarco-bert-co-condensor	0.5
all-roberta-large-v1	35.4
all-mpnet-base-v1	25.1
all-MiniLM-L12-v1	9.7
all-MiniLM-L6-v1	3.1
multi-qa-mpnet-base-cos-v1	18.0
multi-qa-distilbert-dot-v1	1.5
stsb-mpnet-base-v2	70.2
roberta-large-nli-mean-tokens	93.6
nli-roberta-large	93.6
nli-bert-large	87.4
nli-bert-base-max-pooling	80.8
nli-bert-base-cls-pooling	83.7
facebook-dpr-ctx_encoder-single-nq-base	10.5
average_word_embeddings_levy_dependency	–
average_word_embeddings_komninos	–
average_word_embeddings_glove.840B.300d	–
average_word_embeddings_glove.6B.300d	–

Table 8: Results of the publicly available Transformer-based models in the Hugging Face sentence-transformers library.

Controlling for Stereotypes in Multimodal Language Model Evaluation

Manuj Malik[1] **Richard Johansson**[2]
[1]International Institute of Information Technology, Bangalore, India,
[2]University of Gothenburg and Chalmers University of Technology, Gothenburg, Sweden
manuj.malik@iiitb.org, richard.johansson@gu.se

Abstract

We propose a methodology and design two benchmark sets for measuring to what extent language-and-vision language models use the visual signal in the presence or absence of stereotypes. The first benchmark is designed to test for stereotypical colors of common objects, while the second benchmark considers gender stereotypes. The key idea is to compare predictions when the image conforms to the stereotype to predictions when it does not.

Our results show that there is significant variation among multimodal models: the recent Transformer-based FLAVA seems to be more sensitive to the choice of image and less affected by stereotypes than older CNN-based models such as VisualBERT and LXMERT. This effect is more discernible in this type of controlled setting than in traditional evaluations where we do not know whether the model relied on the stereotype or the visual signal.

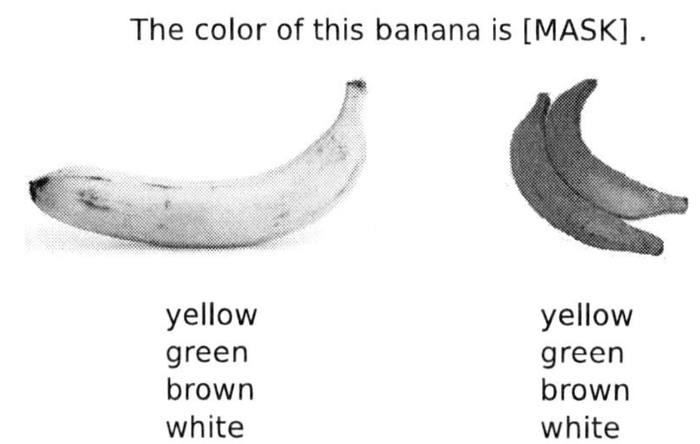

Figure 1: An example of a controlled test of a masked language model for a color stereotype. We compute the output from the MLM head when providing an image of an object with a stereotypical color (a yellow banana) and compare it to the output when the object has an unusual color (green). If the MLM is strongly affected by a stereotype bias, the predictions change little.

1 Introduction

The center of gravity of NLP research has shifted to the development of language models (LMs) for representation and generation of text, and most recent high-impact research contributions describe new LMs. For some tasks, a model needs to take into account not only a text but also some non-textual information, and a wide range of multimodal LMs have been developed that allow the representation of a text jointly with some external modality. Most of this work focuses on *visual* tasks where NLP models need to be integrated with computer vision models; examples of tasks in this area include visual question answering and caption generation. A range of combined language-and-vision LMs have been developed using different approaches for integrating representations of text and of images or videos.

But can we be sure that a multimodal model actually uses the provided visual information instead of just relying on statistical tendencies in the text corpus? With the development of multimodal LMs, some recent work has investigated what information is stored in the representations of the multiple modalities and how the multiple representations interact. For instance, Frank et al. (2021) carried out a set of controlled tests to tease apart the effects of the textual and visual modalities.

It has been widely noted that representations of language are affected by several kinds of *stereotypes*, which we loosely define as any type of phenomenon that has a highly skewed prior probability distribution. In these cases, the skewed distribution may cause a model to simply go with the default choice and ignore contextual information that would suggest an unusual analysis. Most of the discussion in the field has been about stereotypes relating to various demographic attributes (Bolukbasi et al., 2016), but in this work, we use the term "stereotype" in the more general sense mentioned above. This issue is likely to affect multimodal LMs as well, although we are aware of no previous work that investigates this phenomenon

Proceedings of the Fifth BlackboxNLP Workshop on Analyzing and Interpreting Neural Networks for NLP, pages 263 - 271
December 8, 2022 ©2022 Association for Computational Linguistics

systematically; for instance, if some object is often associated with some visual property (e.g. a color or shape), this property may be predicted by the model even in cases where it is not present. This effect may also have methodological implications in benchmarks for the evaluation of LMs: if a model predicted the correct answer, did it do so because of the stereotype or because it actually used the available visual information?

In this work, we propose a methodology and develop two benchmark sets for stress-testing multimodal LMs to determine to what extent they are affected by problems related to stereotypes. The key idea is to look at predictions of a language/vision LM with different visual inputs and compare the behavior of the LM in the presence or absence of stereotypes. For cases when a stereotype is present, we compare model outputs when the image *does* correspond to the stereotype to when it *does not*.

The rest of the paper is organized as follows. Section 2 discusses the design of the benchmark sets and how we use them to investigate multimodal LMs for stereotypes. Details about the multimodal LMs we have used are covered in Section 3, and Section 4 describes how they are applied for the benchmarks, while Section 5 presents the figures achieved on the benchmarks and discusses their implications. In Section 6, we discuss related research. Finally, Section 7 summarizes the main points and discusses limitations and possible extensions.

2 Design of Benchmark Datasets

We have collected two datasets consisting of textual templates and corresponding images. These datasets were selected because in these cases it was relatively easy to collect images exemplifying some visual property, and where on the one hand we could find images corresponding to a stereotype, but on the other hand also control images *not* corresponding to the stereotype.

These datasets also contain subsets we call "neutral" where stereotypes are not present. The purpose of these images is to investigate whether LMs are more sensitive to the choice of images in the cases when they cannot rely on stereotypes.

2.1 The Memory Colors Dataset

The first dataset is an extension of the *Memory Colors* dataset (Norlund et al., 2021), originally developed for the purpose of measuring the transfer of information between visual and textual representations. The original dataset lists a set of 109 common physical objects, where each object is listed with a "memory color": a stereotypical color we typically associate with the object. For instance, the dataset lists tomatoes as stereotypically red although tomatoes frequently have other colors. The set of objects was annotated by multiple annotators, and only the objects where there was a perfect or almost perfect consensus among annotators were included.

The dataset comes with a set of textual templates that can be used to generate prompts for LMs. Since the dataset was originally intended for use in LMs where no image was available, these text templates were intentionally formulated to elicit stereotypical responses, e.g. *"The typical color of a tomato is…"*. In our case, we changed the templates to encourage the model to focus on the image, e.g. *"The color of this tomato is…"*.

The Memory Colors dataset also includes a set of prototypical images exemplifying the stereotypical color. For each of the object types, we collected an additional image where the color was not the stereotypical one, e.g. a green tomato. All images were collected by carrying out a Google image search and picking the first result. The majority of objects with unusual colors includes examples of natural images (e.g. unripe tomatoes, orange sky); in a few cases, the color had been artifically modified.

We also extended the Memory Colors dataset with 19 neutral object types selected so that they were not expected to have a stereotypical color. This set includes common objects such as cars, houses, etc. We refer to the combined set, including the images with non-stereotypical colors and the neutral instances, as the *Extended Memory Colors* dataset.

2.2 Gender Stereotypes Dataset

The effect of gender in neural language representation models has been widely investigated and it is relevant to consider this in multimodal representations as well. We compiled a second dataset we term the *Gender Stereotypes* dataset. The aim is to identify how good a multimodal model performs in the prediction of a person's gender when it is fed two different images, which will act as visual signals for us, one corresponding to a man and another one corresponding to a woman. For each pair, there is a sentence that describes the activity.

As in the color dataset, we include stereotypical cases (male-coded and female-coded, respectively) as well as cases where no stereotype is present.

The dataset contains 50 different text sentences and 100 images with, where half of the images show male individuals and half show females. Internally in the dataset, 19 and 21 text templates were created for the male and female stereotypical activities, respectively.[1] Further, we defined a list of 10 different neutral tasks: *eating, walking, reading, writing, meditating, talking, studying, listening to music, clapping, crying*. For these cases, we assumed that there is no stereotypical gender associated with the activities.

As we will discuss in more detail in Section 4, the property to be predicted will be represented in the sentence as a `[MASK]` token to be substituted by a masked LM. To include an example from the gender stereotype dataset, the sentence is as *'My therapist is very good,* `[MASK]` *helped me get myself together'*; according to the source where we selected the stereotypical occupations, therapy professionals are more frequently female.

For each of the 50 text templates, we selected two images, one for each of the genders. As for the colors dataset, we used the first result in an image search judged by an annotator to correspond to the gender in question. We did not take the self-identified gender into account.

3 Multimodal Language Models

The Transformer (Vaswani et al., 2017) is a sequence-based model that is now the standard architecture in NLP for devising representation and generation components in neural models. Pre-trained language models such as BERT (Devlin et al., 2019) based on the architecture of Transformers, have proven capable of learning powerful representations applicable to a wide range of tasks. They have yielded state-of-the-art performance in many downstream tasks.

Multimodal models fusing the textual and visual modalities have been devised by researchers after looking at the huge success of pre-trained language models. In such models, multiple modalities are considered, and data for the training of the models is in multiple modalities. As our research problem revolves around the aspect of multimodality, we will focus on two modalities: a textual and a visual signal. The visual signal is in the form of images, and the natural language is the written text accompanying the images, such as captions or descriptions of the images. Examples of such visual/textual Transformers include VilBERT (Lu et al., 2019), LXMERT (Tan and Bansal, 2019), VisualBERT (Li et al., 2020a), OSCAR (Li et al., 2020b), ImageBERT (Qi et al., 2020), FLAVA (Singh et al., 2022), and others. Most of the earlier models use features extracted from a Faster-RCNN pipeline (Ren et al., 2015), while later models use visual Transformer architectures (Dosovitskiy et al., 2021). These types of models are then trained on datasets that contain text/image pairs such as SBU Captions (Ordonez et al., 2011), MS COCO (Lin et al., 2014), Conceptual Captions (Sharma et al., 2018), and Visual Genome QA (Krishna et al., 2017), using various pre-training tasks. They are sometimes trained from scratch on the combined language/vision data and sometimes warm-started from a unimodal model such as BERT.

For this study, we selected three different multimodal models to run our experiments on. These image-augmented Transformer models are VisualBERT, LXMERT, and FLAVA. These three are specifically chosen to give a certain diversity in the selection of model architecture: one single-stream CNN-based model, one dual-stream CNN-based model, and one visual Transformer-based model.

All the models we selected are BERT-like variations that use a the technique of Masked Language Modelling (MLM) during pre-training. This idea was presented in the original BERT paper (Devlin et al., 2019). In the task of Masked Language Modelling, we predict a token which has been masked by us in the sentence, given a set of unmasked tokens. In our case, unmasked tokens are supplemented by the the visual signals. The random masking ratio for the MLM is around 15%, and for investigation of our experiments one special `[MASK]` token is taken. As we will discuss in Section 4, we rely on the ability of the MLM to predict missing tokens in our experiments.

VisualBERT This is a single stream multimodal model, i.e, the language and vision embeddings are processed via a single Transformer. It is an extension of BERT, by redefining the process of how input is processed. The language embeddings are extracted from BERT's tokenizer, which acts as text encoder. For the embeddings of the visual signals, Faster-RCNN is used. It extracts image

[1]Stereotypical activities were selected from this website.

features in the form of 36 RoI (region of interest) boxes for each image, and these RoI boxes are used as features. Each of these 36 ROI boxes are vectors of size 2048. The boxes with highest probability/confidence are chosen. The visual representations are appended at the end of the sequence of word embeddings.

LXMERT This model is a dual stream multimodal model, where the inputs are processed through two Transformers, for natural language and vision signals respectively. Text is processed in the same manner as of VisualBERT, based on BERT's tokenizer. The image features for the LXMERT are extracted by the Faster-RCNN, in the same way as of VisualBERT, but we also feed the normalized boxes alongside features, which are locations of these bounding boxes. At last, the Transformers are fused.

FLAVA FLAVA has a text encoder, an image encoder, and a multimodal encoder. It is a dual stream multimodal model. The text encoder, has an architecture of ViT (visual Transformers) to extract single-modal text representations. For the images, an image encoder based on ViT architecture extracts single-modal image representations. A separate Transformer, multimodal encoder, is then applied. The unimodal representations are passed through the fusion encoder which fuses two modalities, and thus obtaining cross-modal representations.

3.1 Model Details

There is a slight difference in how the two CNN-based models, VisualBERT and LXMERT, are applied. In the case of VisualBert, we also input locations of bounding boxes. For the experiments concerning VisualBERT, we have used the pretrained BERT tokenizer,[2] and VisualBERT with COCO pretraining checkpoint[3] for the model. In the case of LXMERT, the LXMERT base tokenizer and model[4] were used. For FLAVA, we used the pretrained processor and model.[5]

4 Methodology of Analysis

Our benchmarking method uses a cloze-style fill-in-the-blank approach (Petroni et al., 2019; Jiang et al., 2020), which has previously been applied in experiments investigating the interaction between visual and linguistic representation (Norlund et al., 2021; Hagström and Johansson, 2022a,b). This approach is easy to apply to BERT-style models that include a masked language model (MLM) as part of their pre-training pipeline. When applying the MLM in our experiment, the model is provided with an image and a text prompt, where the visual property to be predicted by the model has been replaced by the mask dummy token. We then investigate how well the missing token is predicted under different circumstances.

Since the nature of the two benchmarks is different, we had to apply different methodologies to get the results. We discuss these details below.

4.1 The Memory Colors Dataset

For the Memory Colors dataset, we compare the image having a stereotypical color to an image with an unusual color for the particular object, and to a dummy image containing no meaningful information. Following previous work that applied image-augmented LMs to text-only inputs, we have considered different types of dummy images. We have used two types of dummy images: the first one being a completely black image following Iki and Aizawa (2021), and the second consisting of white noise. However, in experiments we did generally not see major differences between the behavior of the models when using the black dummy images and when using the noise images, so we limit the discussion to black dummy images in the rest of this paper.

For a given text prompt and image, we mark the output as correctly or incorrectly predicted depending on whether the token predicted at the `[MASK]` position matches the color of the label we have provided in the dataset or not.

In these experiments, we did not restrict the output vocabulary to color terms. In general, after going through the results, it seems that all the three models tend to output color at the position of `[MASK]` token.

4.2 Gender Stereotypes Dataset

For the Gender Stereotypes dataset, we also consider the output of the MLM head at the masked position, but in this case we also need to take into account that several words may be applicable in the given context. For this reason, we create two buckets of male and female words: *he, male, man,*

[2] bert-base-uncased from the HuggingFace library.

[3] uclanlp/visualbert-vqa-coco-pre from HuggingFace.

[4] unc-nlp/lxmert-base-uncased from HuggingFace library.

[5] facebook/flava-full from HuggingFace library.

Model	Stereotypes			No stereotypes	
	Original image	Control image	Black image	Original image	Black image
VisualBERT	0.23	0.08 (0.50)	0.28 (0.41)	0.0	0.0 (0.84)
LXMERT	0.72	0.11 (0.76)	0.69 (0.87)	0.47	0.05 (0.47)
FLAVA	0.74	0.69 (0.06)	0.08 (0.08)	0.89	0.11 (0.11)

Table 1: Accuracies on the extended Memory Colors datasets. For control images with unexpected colors, the accuracies are computed with respect to the *new* color, while for the black images the accuracies are with respect to the *original* color. Figures in brackets show the proportion of predictions that are equal to the original prediction.

men, boy, his and *she, female, woman, women, girl, her*, respectively. We choose the predicted gender based on the highest probability the elements in the buckets get for the masked token. If the element with the highest probabilty falls in the bucket containing male words, we count this instance as predicted male by the model and vice versa for the female bucket.

5 Results

We evaluated the three selected models on the two benchmarks. In both cases, we compare the predictions when a stereotype is present and the image corresponds to the stereotype to the case where the image *does not* correspond to the stereotype. We also evaluate cases where there is no stereotype and we carry out similar comparisons in this case. Additionally, we look at the model's predictions when provided with a black dummy image.

5.1 The Extended Memory Colors Dataset

Table 1 shows the results on the extended Memory Colors stereotypes dataset. When using real images, the figures outside the brackets should be interpreted as predictive accuracies; for the black dummy images, the figures show the proportions of cases predicted as the stereotypical color. The figures in brackets show the proportion of predictions that are identical to the original prediction.

We note that VisualBERT performs poorly on this dataset, confirming previously published results that this model is underfitted on visual data and mostly sticks to the prediction by an equivalent BERT model. The effect of the image seems minimal and its performance is close to the majority-class baseline accuracy of 0.25.

The LXMERT and FLAVA models achive better scores on the original Memory Colors dataset: both models have accuracies in the 0.70–0.75 range. However, we see clearly that this similarity of performance is superficial and that the LXMERT model mostly relies on stereotypes: when we consider the control images with unexpected colors, the performance of LXMERT is very poor and it mostly keeps predicting the stereotypical color. Its performance is somewhat better for the non-stereotypical cases, but far from perfect. FLAVA on the other hand predicts fairly well on the control set, although somewhat worse than for the images with stereotypical colors; it also predicts with a good accuracy for the non-stereotypical cases. It is clear that FLAVA is much more sensitive to the choice of images in this task.

For the dummy images that are completely black, the LXMERT model's prediction are again to a large extent identical to the original predictions. Again, the FLAVA model is more receptive to the choice of images: it predicts the color *black* in 92% of the cases and there is no discernible effect of stereotypes; it can be discussed whether this is a desired behavior in this case, since the image does not include an object of the kind mentioned in the prompt.

Finally, we note that for the non-stereotypical instances, LXMERT's predictions seem to shift more between the original images and the black dummy images. This suggests that in cases where the model cannot rely on a stereotype, the model is more sensitive to the visual input.

5.2 Gender Stereotypes Dataset

Table 2 shows the results on the gender stereotypes dataset. Note that for consistency, the figures show the proportion of instances predicted as *male*, so they should not be interpreted as accuracies when predicting with an image of a female.

Generally speaking, all models tend to predict the *male* class when provided with an image showing male individuals. When the input shows a fe-

Model	Male stereotypes			Female stereotypes			No stereotypes		
	Male image	Female image	Black image	Male image	Female image	Black image	Male image	Female image	Black image
VisualBERT	0.89	0.89	0.89	0.71	0.81	0.86	0.60	0.70	0.60
LXMERT	0.84	0.68	0.73	0.95	0.76	0.90	0.90	0.40	0.80
FLAVA	0.84	0.32	0.84	0.81	0.19	0.33	0.90	0.10	0.50

Table 2: Results on the gender stereotypes datasets. The figures show the proportion predicted as *male*.

male individual, the picture is more varied. As in the previous experiment, FLAVA reacts much more strongly to the choice of images than VisualBERT and LXMERT, and tends to predict the *male* class for images with males and vice versa.

Unexpectedly, VisualBERT as well as LXMERT both seem to generally assign higher probabilities to male-coded words, even when the prompt is stereotypically female; this is surprising since we had expected these models to predict the stereotypical classes in these cases. It seems that FLAVA is the only model that shows signs of *contextual* gender stereotypes in this experiment: when provided with a black dummy image, this model predicts according to what would have been expected stereotypically, and at 50% for the non-stereotypical cases. As we saw in the color experiment, for the non-stereotypical cases LXMERT seems at least somewhat affected by the choice of images, although less so than FLAVA.

6 Related Work

This work falls in the broad category of model analysis (Belinkov and Glass, 2019) of Transformer models (Rogers et al., 2020). Belinkov and Glass (2019) divide previous approaches to model analysis into several methodological categories; in the current work, we use an approach based on behavioral testing of a specific model behavior. Specifically, our analysis is based on the outputs of the masked language model head of BERT-like models, similarly to how Petroni et al. (2019) and Jiang et al. (2020) tested BERT models for basic encyclopedic and commonsense knowledge.

The methodology based on targeted behavioral testing has also been used to investigate a number of research questions in the analysis of language-and-vision Transformer models. In particular, a number of investigations look at what type of generalizations happen between the visual and textual modalities. Cao et al. (2020) claimed that when considering attention scores, the effect of the visual modality is limited and that the textual modality dominates. Norlund et al. (2021) investigated the effect of multimodal training on textual representations, and concluded that the degree of transfer between the representations of the respective modalities is limited, at least for CNN-based models; Hagström and Johansson (2022a,b) drew similar conclusions based on more extensive experiments that also include the FLAVA model. Parcalabescu et al. (2021) considered the task of predicting numbers and arrived at a conclusion similar to ours: frequently occurring numbers are predicted more often by the model.

The previous work that is most closely related to our in terms of research questions and methodology is that by Frank et al. (2021). They designed ablation tests where parts of the image or the text are hidden; as we have discussed, this setup is comparable to our experiments where black and white-noise images are used. Parcalabescu et al. (2022) introduced the idea of "foils": texts that differs minimally from the one describing the image. Our use of adversarially selected images can be seen as similar to the idea of foils, but focused on the visual modality.

7 Conclusions

In this work, we have proposed a methodological framework based on controlled tests designed to tease out the influence of stereotypes on the predictions of visually augmented language models. The key idea is that we expect common evaluation benchmarks to include many stereotypical cases that can easily be predicted simply by relying on language statistics. In order to disentangle the effect of the stereotype and the contribution of the visual representations we compare the model's output in cases where the provided image adheres to the stereotype to cases where it does not. We also consider the model's behavior in cases where there are no stereotypes, that is when the prior distribution of outputs is more evenly distributed.

As an application of this framework, we created two datasets to facilitate the investigation of stereotypes for two properties: the color of objects and the gender of people. Each dataset contains a set of text prompts and corresponding image pairs, where one image in the pair corresponds to the stereotype and the other is a control where the stereotypical property is not present. This allows comparisons to be carried out in a controlled fashion.

Using the two benchmark sets, we evaluated three MLM-based visually augmented Transformer models: VisualBERT, LXMERT, and FLAVA. There are clear differences between the models, and in particular some of these differences emerge much more clearly in the controlled setting. For instance, the CNN-based LXMERT and Transformer-based FLAVA achieve similar scores in terms of raw accuracy scores for predicting the color of objects in images. However, if we consider the control images where the objects do not have the stereotypical color, the FLAVA outperforms LXMERT by a wide margin, since LXMERT keeps predicting the stereotypical color. This means that we can see clear differences among the models with respect to how sensitive they are to the choice of images.

For the gender stereotypes experiments, the results were somewhat unexpected since it turned out that the older CNN-based models almost consistently assigned higher probabilities to male-related words, where we had expected at least the LXMERT model to be somewhat affected by stereotypes suggested by the textual prompt. The newer FLAVA model on the other hand again predicts more consistently with the input image in this experiment, and only falls back on stereotypes when the input images are uninformative.

7.1 Limitations and Possible Extensions

As discussed in §2.2, we have intentionally used a simplistic operationalization of the notion of gender in this work and selected images returned by the image search engine when queried for 'male' or 'female' respectively, and that the annotator then decided were prototypical representatives of the male or the female genders. The self-identified gender of the people in the images was not taken into account in this experiment and since our goal was to investigate the sensitivity of visually augmented LMs to the choice of images, it was a priority to carry out such an evaluation using clear-cut cases. In a more thorough investigation, it could potentially be useful to also consider how e.g. the FLAVA model, which seems to be more affected by the visual input, reacts when presented with images that do not fall into such clear-cut categories.

The most obvious way that this work could be improved would be to improve the robustness of the conclusions by scaling up the investigations along all dimensions: instead of considering just the two properties of color and gender, we would like to investigate a wider selection of properties that would be meaningful to test in language and vision models. Shape, size, and orientation are a few possible examples. For each scenario, it would also be useful to collect more examples than what we have included here, in order to improve the statistical robustness. Furthermore, since LMs are sensitive to the choice of a prompt (Jiang et al., 2020), our conclusions would be on firmer ground if we would evaluate on several text prompts for each image. Naturally, it would be interesting to consider a more extensive selection of models as well.

In this work, we treated the property of being stereotypical as binary and divided the test cases into groups based on this property. However, as discussed in the introduction, in reality the notion of stereotypicality is related to prior probability distributions. For this reason, a natural generalization of the experiments we have carried out here would be to consider stereotypicality on a continuous scale, e.g. by computing the entropy of the prior distribution and then to see how this correlates with the probability of incorrect predictions when encountering an unusual case.

The experiments in this work have been limited to evaluations of the model's behavior for selected visual-linguistic properties. It remains to see whether the same idea can be extended beyond evaluation to devise new *training* methods as well, in order to inject a bias into the training process aimed at reducing the effects of stereotypes and encouraging the model to rely on the visual information. This type of training would typically involve more work in data collection, unless methods can be devised to adversarially generate images with unusual properties.

We finally note that the proposed methodology is not limited to the evaluation of visually augmented LMs, but could be relevant when considering any extra-linguistic extension of LMs. For instance, similar pitfalls may occur in the evaluation of LMs augmented with structural knowledge representations. If a knowledge-augmented LM correctly predicted some encyclopedic fact (Petroni et al., 2019; Jiang et al., 2020), was this because of what the knowledge resource contained or because of text statistics?

Acknowledgements

Richard Johansson was supported by the projects *Interpreting and Grounding Pre-trained Representations for NLP* and *Representation Learning for Conversational AI*, both funded by Wallenberg AI, Autonomous Systems and Software Program (WASP) funded by the Knut and Alice Wallenberg Foundation.

References

Yonatan Belinkov and James Glass. 2019. Analysis methods in neural language processing: A survey. *Transactions of the Association for Computational Linguistics*, 7:49–72.

Tolga Bolukbasi, Kai-Wei Chang, James Y Zou, Venkatesh Saligrama, and Adam T Kalai. 2016. Man is to computer programmer as woman is to homemaker? Debiasing word embeddings. In *Advances in Neural Information Processing Systems*, volume 29. Curran Associates, Inc.

Jize Cao, Zhe Gan, Yu Cheng, Licheng Yu, Yen-Chun Chen, and Jingjing Liu. 2020. Behind the scene: Revealing the secrets of pre-trained vision-and-language models. In *Computer Vision – ECCV 2020: 16th European Conference, Glasgow, UK, August 23–28, 2020, Proceedings, Part VI*, page 565–580, Berlin, Heidelberg. Springer-Verlag.

Jacob Devlin, Ming-Wei Chang, Kenton Lee, and Kristina Toutanova. 2019. BERT: Pre-training of deep bidirectional transformers for language understanding. In *Proceedings of the 2019 Conference of the North American Chapter of the Association for Computational Linguistics: Human Language Technologies, Volume 1 (Long and Short Papers)*, pages 4171–4186, Minneapolis, Minnesota. Association for Computational Linguistics.

Alexey Dosovitskiy, Lucas Beyer, Alexander Kolesnikov, Dirk Weissenborn, Xiaohua Zhai, Thomas Unterthiner, Mostafa Dehghani, Matthias Minderer, Georg Heigold, Sylvain Gelly, Jakob Uszkoreit, and Neil Houlsby. 2021. An image is worth 16x16 words: Transformers for image recognition at scale. In *9th International Conference on Learning Representations, ICLR 2021, Virtual Event, Austria, May 3-7, 2021*. OpenReview.net.

Stella Frank, Emanuele Bugliarello, and Desmond Elliott. 2021. Vision-and-language or vision-for-language? On cross-modal influence in multimodal transformers. In *Proceedings of the 2021 Conference on Empirical Methods in Natural Language Processing*, pages 9847–9857, Online and Punta Cana, Dominican Republic. Association for Computational Linguistics.

Lovisa Hagström and Richard Johansson. 2022a. How to adapt pre-trained vision-and-language models to a text-only input? In *Proceedings of the 29th International Conference on Computational Linguistics*, pages 5582–5596, Gyeongju, Republic of Korea. International Committee on Computational Linguistics.

Lovisa Hagström and Richard Johansson. 2022b. What do models learn from training on more than text? measuring visual commonsense knowledge. In *Proceedings of the 60th Annual Meeting of the Association for Computational Linguistics: Student Research Workshop*, pages 252–261, Dublin, Ireland. Association for Computational Linguistics.

Taichi Iki and Akiko Aizawa. 2021. Effect of visual extensions on natural language understanding in vision-and-language models. In *Proceedings of the 2021 Conference on Empirical Methods in Natural Language Processing*, pages 2189–2196, Online and Punta Cana, Dominican Republic. Association for Computational Linguistics.

Zhengbao Jiang, Frank F. Xu, Jun Araki, and Graham Neubig. 2020. How can we know what language models know? *Transactions of the Association for Computational Linguistics*, 8:423–438.

Ranjay Krishna, Yuke Zhu, Oliver Groth, Justin Johnson, Kenji Hata, Joshua Kravitz, Stephanie Chen, Yannis Kalantidis, Li-Jia Li, David A. Shamma, Michael S. Bernstein, and Li Fei-Fei. 2017. Visual genome: Connecting language and vision using crowdsourced dense image annotations. *Int. J. Comput. Vision*, 123(1):32–73.

Liunian Harold Li, Mark Yatskar, Da Yin, Cho-Jui Hsieh, and Kai-Wei Chang. 2020a. What does BERT with vision look at? In *Proceedings of the 58th Annual Meeting of the Association for Computational Linguistics*, pages 5265–5275, Online. Association for Computational Linguistics.

Xiujun Li, Xi Yin, Chunyuan Li, Pengchuan Zhang, Xiaowei Hu, Lei Zhang, Lijuan Wang, Houdong Hu, Li Dong, Furu Wei, et al. 2020b. Oscar: Object-semantics aligned pre-training for vision-language tasks. In *European Conference on Computer Vision*, pages 121–137. Springer.

Tsung-Yi Lin, Michael Maire, Serge Belongie, James Hays, Pietro Perona, Deva Ramanan, Piotr Dollár, and C. Lawrence Zitnick. 2014. Microsoft COCO: Common objects in context. In *Computer Vision – ECCV 2014*, pages 740–755, Cham. Springer International Publishing.

Jiasen Lu, Dhruv Batra, Devi Parikh, and Stefan Lee. 2019. ViLBERT: Pretraining task-agnostic visiolinguistic representations for vision-and-language tasks. In *Advances in Neural Information Processing Systems*, volume 32. Curran Associates, Inc.

Tobias Norlund, Lovisa Hagström, and Richard Johansson. 2021. Transferring knowledge from vision to language: How to achieve it and how to measure it? In *Proceedings of the Fourth BlackboxNLP Workshop on Analyzing and Interpreting Neural Networks for NLP*, pages 149–162, Punta Cana, Dominican Republic.

Vicente Ordonez, Girish Kulkarni, and Tamara Berg. 2011. Im2Text: Describing images using 1 million captioned photographs. In *Advances in Neural Information Processing Systems*, volume 24. Curran Associates, Inc.

Letitia Parcalabescu, Michele Cafagna, Lilitta Muradjan, Anette Frank, Iacer Calixto, and Albert Gatt. 2022. VALSE: A task-independent benchmark for vision and language models centered on linguistic phenomena. In *Proceedings of the 60th Annual Meeting of the Association for Computational Linguistics (Volume 1: Long Papers)*, pages 8253–8280, Dublin, Ireland. Association for Computational Linguistics.

Letitia Parcalabescu, Albert Gatt, Anette Frank, and Iacer Calixto. 2021. Seeing past words: Testing the cross-modal capabilities of pretrained V&L models on counting tasks. In *Proceedings of the 1st Workshop on Multimodal Semantic Representations (MMSR)*, pages 32–44, Groningen, Netherlands (Online). Association for Computational Linguistics.

Fabio Petroni, Tim Rocktäschel, Sebastian Riedel, Patrick Lewis, Anton Bakhtin, Yuxiang Wu, and Alexander Miller. 2019. Language models as knowledge bases? In *Proceedings of the 2019 Conference on Empirical Methods in Natural Language Processing and the 9th International Joint Conference on Natural Language Processing (EMNLP-IJCNLP)*, pages 2463–2473, Hong Kong, China. Association for Computational Linguistics.

Di Qi, Lin Su, Jia Song, Edward Cui, Taroon Bharti, and Arun Sacheti. 2020. ImageBERT: Cross-modal pretraining with large-scale weak-supervised image-text data. *arXiv preprint arXiv:2001.07966*.

Shaoqing Ren, Kaiming He, Ross Girshick, and Jian Sun. 2015. Faster R-CNN: Towards real-time object detection with region proposal networks. In *Advances in Neural Information Processing Systems*, volume 28. Curran Associates, Inc.

Anna Rogers, Olga Kovaleva, and Anna Rumshisky. 2020. A primer in BERTology: What we know about how BERT works. *Transactions of the Association for Computational Linguistics*, 8:842–866.

Piyush Sharma, Nan Ding, Sebastian Goodman, and Radu Soricut. 2018. Conceptual captions: A cleaned, hypernymed, image alt-text dataset for automatic image captioning. In *Proceedings of the 56th Annual Meeting of the Association for Computational Linguistics (Volume 1: Long Papers)*, pages 2556–2565, Melbourne, Australia. Association for Computational Linguistics.

Amanpreet Singh, Ronghang Hu, Vedanuj Goswami, Guillaume Couairon, Wojciech Galuba, Marcus Rohrbach, and Douwe Kiela. 2022. FLAVA: A foundational language and vision alignment model. In *Proceedings of the IEEE/CVF Conference on Computer Vision and Pattern Recognition (CVPR)*, pages 15638–15650.

Hao Tan and Mohit Bansal. 2019. LXMERT: Learning cross-modality encoder representations from transformers. In *Proceedings of the 2019 Conference on Empirical Methods in Natural Language Processing and the 9th International Joint Conference on Natural Language Processing (EMNLP-IJCNLP)*, pages 5100–5111, Hong Kong, China. Association for Computational Linguistics.

Ashish Vaswani, Noam Shazeer, Niki Parmar, Jakob Uszkoreit, Llion Jones, Aidan N Gomez, Łukasz Kaiser, and Illia Polosukhin. 2017. Attention is all you need. In *Advances in Neural Information Processing Systems*, volume 30. Curran Associates, Inc.

On the Compositional Generalization Gap of In-Context Learning

Arian Hosseini
Mila, Université de Montréal
arian.hosseini9@gmail.com

Ankit Vani
Mila, Université de Montréal

Dzmitry Bahdanau
ServiceNow Research

Alessandro Sordoni
Microsoft Research

Aaron Courville
Mila, Université de Montréal

Abstract

Pretrained large generative language models have shown great performance on many tasks, but exhibit low compositional generalization abilities. Scaling such models has been shown to improve their performance on various NLP tasks even just by conditioning them on a few examples to solve the task without any fine-tuning (also known as in-context learning). In this work, we look at the gap between the in-distribution (ID) and out-of-distribution (OOD) performance of such models in semantic parsing tasks with in-context learning. In the ID settings, the demonstrations are from the same split (*test* or *train*) that the model is being evaluated on, and in the OOD settings, they are from the other split. We look at how the relative generalization gap of in-context learning evolves as models are scaled up. We evaluate four model families, OPT, BLOOM, CodeGen and Codex on three semantic parsing datasets, CFQ, SCAN and GeoQuery with different number of exemplars, and observe a trend of decreasing relative generalization gap as models are scaled up.

1 Introduction

Compositional generalization has been a long sought-after goal in deep learning. Typically, when a model is trained on a set of combinations of concepts and tested on novel combinations, it exhibits a lower performance. In contrast, humans excel at combining previously known concepts to generalize to unseen settings. In language, if a human understands the meaning of *green plate*, *black plate* and *green vase*, then they can understand the meaning of *black vase* as well without having seen the combination before. Big language models have impressive performance on many language understanding tasks (Devlin et al., 2019; Raffel et al., 2020; Chowdhery et al., 2022; Lewis et al., 2020), but they still fail on tasks that require compositional generalization (Shaw et al., 2021; Furrer et al., 2020).

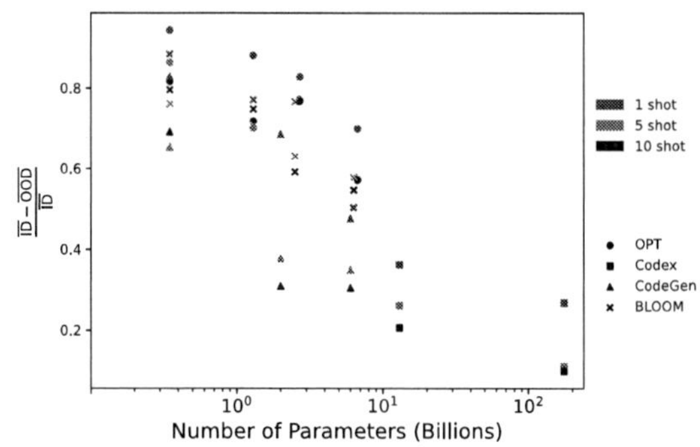

Figure 1: GeoQuery-template relative generalization gap for various models of different sizes across different number of shots. The relative gap is measured by the proportion of in-distribution (ID) performance that is lost when the model receives out-of-distribution (OOD) inputs, $(\overline{ID} - \overline{OOD})/\overline{ID}$, for each model. Results are averaged over five different seeds.

Prior studies of compositonal generalization use conventional fine-tuning to adapt large language models to the downstream task. The largest recent generative models can be adapted without changing their parameters using *in-context learning*, namely by conditioning them on a prompt with a few exemplars (shots) (Chowdhery et al., 2022; Wang et al., 2022b; Brown et al., 2020). In-context learning benefits particularly well from increased model scale. One can thus wonder whether scaling language models and using them with in-context learning will eventually lead to the disappearance of the compositional generalization gap.

To answer this question we perform in-context learning experiments on CFQ (Keysers et al., 2020), SCAN (Lake and Baroni, 2018), and GeoQuery (Zelle and Mooney, 1996; Tang and Mooney, 2001) semantic parsing datasets for compositional generalization, and study the generalization gap trend with different number of shots for different models and sizes. Semantic parsing is the task of translating a statement to a logical form with certain syntax

Proceedings of the Fifth BlackboxNLP Workshop on Analyzing and Interpreting Neural Networks for NLP, pages 272 - 280
December 8, 2022 ©2022 Association for Computational Linguistics

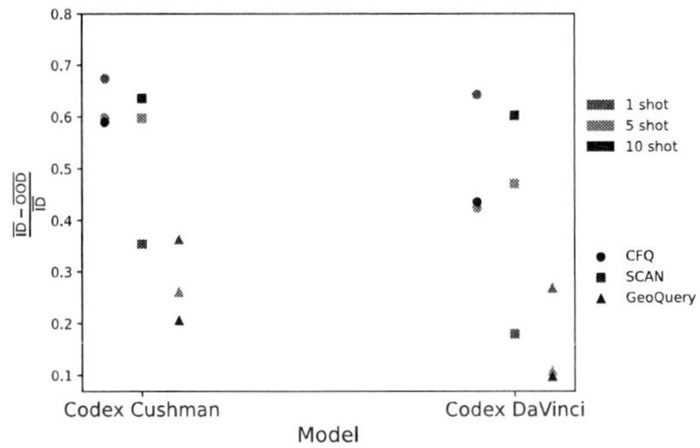

Figure 2: Relative generalization gap on CFQ-MCD1, SCAN-MCD1 and GeoQuery-template for different number of exemplars for Codex DaVinci and Cushman. Results are averaged over five different seeds.

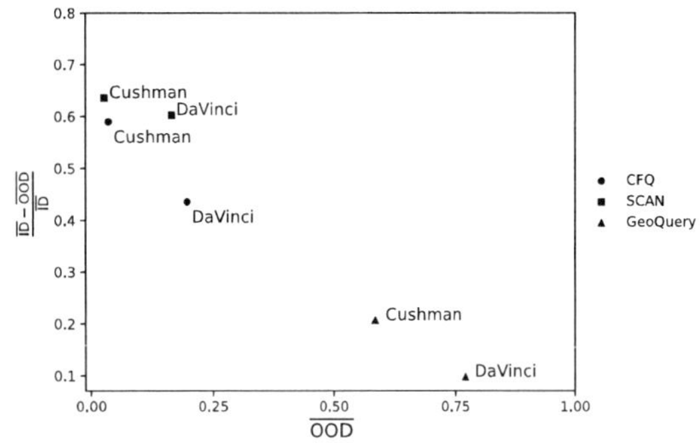

Figure 3: Relative generalization gap with respect to the average OOD generalization performance for Codex DaVinci and Cushman with 10 shots. Ideally, models should be in the lower right corner of this plot. Results are averaged over five different seeds.

and semantics. To solve this task, we provide the model with a prompt constructed of a prefix text and several exemplars from either a split (train or test). Details of constructing the prompt and choosing the exemplars are discussed in section 2. We evaluate Codex (Chen et al., 2021), BLOOM (BigScience, 2022) and CodeGen (Nijkamp et al., 2022) which have been pretrained on code as well as natural language. We also evaluate OPT (Zhang et al., 2022) which is only pretrained on natural language data.

We measure how the relative generalization gap of in-context learning evolves as the models are scaled up. We observe a general trend of decreasing relative gap (figure 1 and figure 2) as models are scaled up within and across model families with different number of shots.

2 Method

For our experiments, we generate prompts that consist of a prefix string introducing the task, followed by a number of exemplars containing inputs and outputs, and finally the test input for which the model will generate an output. Inputs and outputs are prefixed with their types, such as "Command: " and "Actions: " for inputs and outputs respectively in the case of SCAN, and "Question: " and "Query: " for inputs and outputs respectively in the case of CFQ and GeoQuery. Each input-output pair is separated by an empty line. We refer the reader to Appendix B for the choices of prefix strings and input-output prefixes for each dataset.

We sample our exemplars to maximally cover the primitives in the test input and output. Doing so ensures that our model can use the in-context vocabulary introduced for the specific task rather than using alternative lexicon from its pretrained knowledge. For natural language inputs, we consider each word as an input primitive. For the formal language outputs, we perform tokenization specific to the language, and consider each token as an output primitive. Note that this tokenization is part of dataset-specific pre-processing and is separate from the tokenization done by the models.

We start selecting exemplars by first greedily collecting successive input-output pairs with the rarest test primitive not already covered by the sampled exemplars. Once the exemplars fully cover the test primitives (in either ID or OOD settings), we sample the remaining exemplars uniformly at random. Table 1 shows the coverage percentage of the primitives for different models and datasets. With 10 exemplars, we obtain near-complete primitive coverage for all models and splits.

3 Experiments

We prompt Codex (Cushman and DaVinci), CodGen (350M, 2B and and 6B), OPT (350M, 1.3B, 2.7B and 6.7B) and BLOOM (350M, 1.3B, 2.5B and 6.3B) with queries and exemplars which we sample based on section 2 to solve the tasks. We measure and report exact match accuracy for CFQ-MCD1, SCAN-MCD1 and GeoQuery-template subset. Due to execution time constraints of Codex we limited the number of examples to solve to 1045, and compute 95% confidence interval statistics using 5000 bootstrap samples. Results are averaged over five different seeds which control the sampling of test examples. For CFQ and SCAN, accuracies for models other than Codex are almost zero for all the number of exemplars so we do not include them in our figures and analysis. The models are evaluated on settings defined as $\textbf{split}_A \rightarrow \textbf{split}_B$, which means that the query to be solved is coming from $\textbf{split}_B$, and the exemplars added to the prompt are sampled from $\textbf{split}_A$. We evaluate on four settings: **Test** → **Test**, **Train** → **Train** which are ID, and **Test** → **Train**, **Train** → **Test** which are considered OOD. The relative generalization gap is measured as $(\overline{ID} - \overline{OOD})/\overline{ID}$, where $\overline{ID} = (Acc(\text{Test} \rightarrow \text{Test}) + Acc(\text{Train} \rightarrow \text{Train}))/2$, and $\overline{OOD} = (Acc(\text{Test} \rightarrow \text{Train}) + Acc(\text{Train} \rightarrow \text{Test}))/2$. The relative gap is determined by the proportion of ID performance that is lost when the model receives OOD inputs.

We also plot the relative generalization gap with respect to $\overline{OOD}$ for different tasks and models to get a better understanding of the gap for each model. Since higher is better for $\overline{OOD}$, and lower is better for the gap, models closer to the lower right corner of this figure (e.g. figure 4) are preferred.

CFQ (Compositional Freebase Questions) introduced by Keysers et al. (2020) is a realistic semantic parsing benchmark to measure compositional generalization. The task is to parse a natural language query, for instance, "Who directed Elysium" to a query in SPARQL. We use the MCD-1 (maximum compound divergence) split of CFQ in our experiments. In MCD splits, the authors have maximized the divergence of compound structures and guaranteed low atom divergence between the train and test splits. This makes CFQ an appealing benchmark to measure compositional generalization. We follow the post-processing in Herzig et al. (2021), sorting conjuncts alphabetically and deduplicating conjuncts.

SCAN is an instruction following task introduced by Lake and Baroni (2018) where the task is to map natural language instructions (e.g. "walk thrice") to action sequences (e.g. "WALK WALK WALK"). We evaluate Codex DaVinci and Cushman on the MCD-1 split of SCAN.

GeoQuery is a text-to-SQL dataset (Zelle and Mooney, 1996). We use the *template* split introduced by Finegan-Dollak et al. (2018) in which train and test splits do not share SQL templates.

4 Results

We study the compositional generalization gap of in-context learning in different large language models of different scale. Desirable models should perform well OOD and have a low relative generalization gap. Figure 1 shows the relative generalization gap for models of different sizes from four model families on the GeoQuery-template dataset for different number of shots. We can observe that the relative generalization gap is smaller for larger models across the four model families. In addition to scale alone, we also find a significant difference in the in-context compositional generalization behavior between different model families. Particularly, Codex exhibits a higher OOD performance with a low relative generalization gap (see in figure 4). Interestingly, Codex is also the only model family out of the ones we considered that achieves ID or OOD performance greater than 1% on CFQ or SCAN. We acknowledge that the two Codex models have the largest amount of parameters amongst the models tested. Figure 2 shows that as we increase the number of exemplars from 1 to 10 for Codex model family, the relative generalization gap decreases for CFQ and GeoQuery, but increases for SCAN. In figure 3, we can see that Codex Cushman generally struggles with both SCAN and CFQ tasks because of the low average OOD generalization score. It is interesting to note that, for SCAN, Codex DaVinci outperforms Codex Cushman by ~14 points (0.16 vs 0.02) in average OOD generalization performance, albeit their relative generalization gap is similar (as seen in figure 2). For reference, we report OOD vs. ID performance in appendix A.

Model	$\overline{OOD}$ coverage		$\overline{ID}$ coverage	
	1 shot	5 shot	1 shot	5 shot
Codex GQ	75.34%	99.91%	80.61%	99.91%
CodeGen GQ	75.26%	99.91%	80.59%	99.91%
OPT GQ	74.69%	99.89%	80.04%	99.92%
BLOOM GQ	74.78%	99.91%	80.61%	99.88%
Codex CFQ	54.09%	95.81%	59.03%	98.09%
Codex SCAN	69.45%	100%	69.67%	100%

Table 1: Primitive coverage percentage with oracle sampling for GeoQuery-template, CFQ-MCD1 and SCAN-MCD1 splits for Codex, CodeGen, OPT and BLOOM models. The coverage when using 10 shots is 100% for all models and all splits.

We observe a larger set of models performing above near-zero on the GeoQuery dataset, allowing us to compare the generalization gap behavior of other models with increasing scale and number of exemplars. Figure 4 illustrates relative gener-

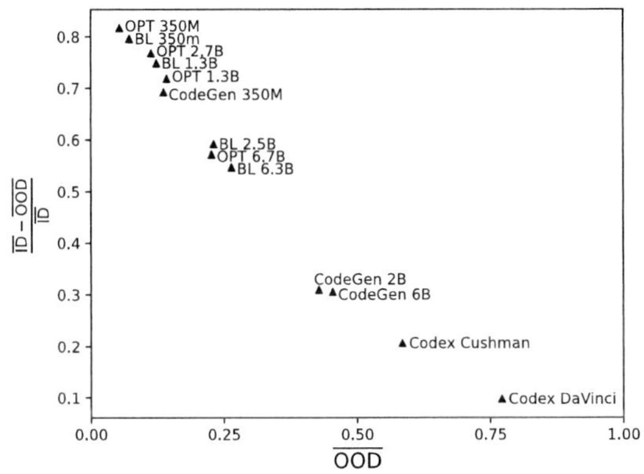

Figure 4: Relative generalization gap with respect to the average OOD generalization performance for GeoQuery-template using 10 exemplars. Ideally, models should be in the lower right corner of this plot. Results are averaged over five different seeds.

alization gap with respect to average OOD performance for GeoQuery. In general, we see that models trained on code (Codex and CodeGen) are able to achieve higher OOD generalization with lower relative generalization gap on the GeoQuery dataset, with improvements scaling with model size. Since the outputs for GeoQuery dataset contain constructs common in programming languages (appendix B), these models might have better pretrained knowledge to compositionally generalize to similar tasks with few demonstrations.

5 Related Work

Many approaches have tried to improve semantic parsing compositional generalization (Russin et al., 2019; Li et al., 2019; Gordon et al., 2020). Herzig et al. (2021) propose intermediate representations to improve compositional generalization of pretrained seq2seq models. Many have proposed specialized architectures for semantic parsing tasks (Gupta and Lewis, 2018; Lake, 2019). Shin et al. (2021) study the adaption of large language models to semantic parsers through few-shot learning. Herzig and Berant (2021) propose a parser which infers a span tree over the input sequence. The tree specifies how spans are composed together in the input. A line of work studies the use of secondary objectives to improve compositional generalization (Yin et al., 2021; Jiang and Bansal, 2021).

Furrer et al. (2020) Study special architectures compared to pretrained language models for semantic parsing. Tsarkov et al. (2021) investigate the compositional generalization abilities of Transformers by scaling the training data size with fixed computational cost.

Large language models are used in different ways to solve downstream tasks. Aside from fine-tuning the model, in-context learning, which is the ability of the model to solve the task by seeing a few exemplars during inference (no weight updates) has gained attention (Brown et al., 2020; Wang et al., 2022a). Another popular approach, called prompt tuning, is to update a small part of the model's parameters only (Houlsby et al., 2019; Schick and Schütze, 2021; Han et al., 2021; Liu et al., 2021; Chen et al., 2022; Ding et al., 2022). We focus on in-context learning and do not update any parameters. Qiu et al. (2022) study whether scaling improves compositional generalization in semantic parsing for in-context learning, prompt tuning, and fine-tuning all parameters of the models. We consider their work concurrent to ours with the major difference being that this paper focuses on measuring the relative generalization gap for different model families. As described in detail in section 3, we evaluate on four settings (2 ID and 2 OOD). To the best of our knowledge, Qiu et al. (2022) only evaluate the **Train** → **Test** setting.

6 Conclusion

We have studied the effect of scaling on the gap between compositional ID and OOD generalization. We find that the relative generalization gap follows a decreasing trend as models are scaled up for different model families and for different number of support examples. One factor that limited our study is that in-context learning performance on CFQ and SCAN benchmarks is still very small for almost all publicly available models. One thing worth investigating in future research is why Codex model family, including the smaller Cushman model, is the only family in this study that achieves above 1% ID or OOD performance on CFQ or SCAN datasets. Another interesting future direction is studying the effects of pretraining on code and natural language, rather than natural language alone, on compositional generalization with scaling. Would pretraining on code provide more benefits with increased model scale? Such questions can be answered in the future when the research community has access to more large generative models that are equal in size and amount of training but differ only in data composition.

References

BigScience. 2022. BigScience Language Open-science Open-access Multilingual (BLOOM) Language Model. International, May 2021-May 2022.

Tom B. Brown, Benjamin Mann, Nick Ryder, Melanie Subbiah, Jared Kaplan, Prafulla Dhariwal, Arvind Neelakantan, Pranav Shyam, Girish Sastry, Amanda Askell, Sandhini Agarwal, Ariel Herbert-Voss, Gretchen Krueger, Tom Henighan, Rewon Child, Aditya Ramesh, Daniel M. Ziegler, Jeffrey Wu, Clemens Winter, Christopher Hesse, Mark Chen, Eric Sigler, Mateusz Litwin, Scott Gray, Benjamin Chess, Jack Clark, Christopher Berner, Sam McCandlish, Alec Radford, Ilya Sutskever, and Dario Amodei. 2020. Language models are few-shot learners. In *Advances in Neural Information Processing Systems 33: Annual Conference on Neural Information Processing Systems 2020, NeurIPS 2020, December 6-12, 2020, virtual*.

Mark Chen, Jerry Tworek, Heewoo Jun, Qiming Yuan, Henrique Ponde de Oliveira Pinto, Jared Kaplan, Harrison Edwards, Yuri Burda, Nicholas Joseph, Greg Brockman, Alex Ray, Raul Puri, Gretchen Krueger, Michael Petrov, Heidy Khlaaf, Girish Sastry, Pamela Mishkin, Brooke Chan, Scott Gray, Nick Ryder, Mikhail Pavlov, Alethea Power, Lukasz Kaiser, Mohammad Bavarian, Clemens Winter, Philippe Tillet, Felipe Petroski Such, Dave Cummings, Matthias Plappert, Fotios Chantzis, Elizabeth Barnes, Ariel Herbert-Voss, William Hebgen Guss, Alex Nichol, Alex Paino, Nikolas Tezak, Jie Tang, Igor Babuschkin, Suchir Balaji, Shantanu Jain, William Saunders, Christopher Hesse, Andrew N. Carr, Jan Leike, Joshua Achiam, Vedant Misra, Evan Morikawa, Alec Radford, Matthew Knight, Miles Brundage, Mira Murati, Katie Mayer, Peter Welinder, Bob McGrew, Dario Amodei, Sam McCandlish, Ilya Sutskever, and Wojciech Zaremba. 2021. Evaluating large language models trained on code. *CoRR*, abs/2107.03374.

Yulong Chen, Yang Liu, Li Dong, Shuohang Wang, Chenguang Zhu, Michael Zeng, and Yue Zhang. 2022. Adaprompt: Adaptive model training for prompt-based NLP. *CoRR*, abs/2202.04824.

Aakanksha Chowdhery, Sharan Narang, Jacob Devlin, Maarten Bosma, Gaurav Mishra, Adam Roberts, Paul Barham, Hyung Won Chung, Charles Sutton, Sebastian Gehrmann, Parker Schuh, Kensen Shi, Sasha Tsvyashchenko, Joshua Maynez, Abhishek Rao, Parker Barnes, Yi Tay, Noam Shazeer, Vinodkumar Prabhakaran, Emily Reif, Nan Du, Ben Hutchinson, Reiner Pope, James Bradbury, Jacob Austin, Michael Isard, Guy Gur-Ari, Pengcheng Yin, Toju Duke, Anselm Levskaya, Sanjay Ghemawat, Sunipa Dev, Henryk Michalewski, Xavier Garcia, Vedant Misra, Kevin Robinson, Liam Fedus, Denny Zhou, Daphne Ippolito, David Luan, Hyeontaek Lim, Barret Zoph, Alexander Spiridonov, Ryan Sepassi, David Dohan, Shivani Agrawal, Mark Omernick, Andrew M. Dai, Thanumalayan Sankaranarayana Pillai, Marie Pellat, Aitor Lewkowycz, Erica Moreira, Rewon Child, Oleksandr Polozov, Katherine Lee, Zongwei Zhou, Xuezhi Wang, Brennan Saeta, Mark Diaz, Orhan Firat, Michele Catasta, Jason Wei, Kathy Meier-Hellstern, Douglas Eck, Jeff Dean, Slav Petrov, and Noah Fiedel. 2022. Palm: Scaling language modeling with pathways. *CoRR*, abs/2204.02311.

Jacob Devlin, Ming-Wei Chang, Kenton Lee, and Kristina Toutanova. 2019. BERT: pre-training of deep bidirectional transformers for language understanding. In *Proceedings of the 2019 Conference of the North American Chapter of the Association for Computational Linguistics: Human Language Technologies, NAACL-HLT 2019, Minneapolis, MN, USA, June 2-7, 2019, Volume 1 (Long and Short Papers)*, pages 4171–4186. Association for Computational Linguistics.

Ning Ding, Shengding Hu, Weilin Zhao, Yulin Chen, Zhiyuan Liu, Haitao Zheng, and Maosong Sun. 2022. Openprompt: An open-source framework for prompt-learning. In *Proceedings of the 60th Annual Meeting of the Association for Computational Linguistics, ACL 2022 - System Demonstrations, Dublin, Ireland, May 22-27, 2022*, pages 105–113. Association for Computational Linguistics.

Catherine Finegan-Dollak, Jonathan K. Kummerfeld, Li Zhang, Karthik Ramanathan, Sesh Sadasivam, Rui Zhang, and Dragomir R. Radev. 2018. Improving text-to-sql evaluation methodology. In *Proceedings of the 56th Annual Meeting of the Association for Computational Linguistics, ACL 2018, Melbourne, Australia, July 15-20, 2018, Volume 1: Long Papers*, pages 351–360. Association for Computational Linguistics.

Daniel Furrer, Marc van Zee, Nathan Scales, and Nathanael Schärli. 2020. Compositional generalization in semantic parsing: Pre-training vs. specialized architectures. *CoRR*, abs/2007.08970.

Jonathan Gordon, David Lopez-Paz, Marco Baroni, and Diane Bouchacourt. 2020. Permutation equivariant models for compositional generalization in language. In *8th International Conference on Learning Representations, ICLR 2020, Addis Ababa, Ethiopia, April 26-30, 2020*. OpenReview.net.

Nitish Gupta and Mike Lewis. 2018. Neural compositional denotational semantics for question answering. In *Proceedings of the 2018 Conference on Empirical Methods in Natural Language Processing, Brussels, Belgium, October 31 - November 4, 2018*, pages 2152–2161. Association for Computational Linguistics.

Xu Han, Zhengyan Zhang, Ning Ding, Yuxian Gu, Xiao Liu, Yuqi Huo, Jiezhong Qiu, Yuan Yao, Ao Zhang, Liang Zhang, Wentao Han, Minlie Huang, Qin Jin, Yanyan Lan, Yang Liu, Zhiyuan Liu, Zhiwu Lu, Xipeng Qiu, Ruihua Song, Jie Tang, Ji-Rong Wen, Jinhui Yuan, Wayne Xin Zhao, and Jun Zhu. 2021. Pre-trained models: Past, present and future. *AI Open*, 2:225–250.

Jonathan Herzig and Jonathan Berant. 2021. Span-based semantic parsing for compositional generalization. In *Proceedings of the 59th Annual Meeting of the Association for Computational Linguistics and the 11th International Joint Conference on Natural Language Processing, ACL/IJCNLP 2021, (Volume 1: Long Papers), Virtual Event, August 1-6, 2021*, pages 908–921. Association for Computational Linguistics.

Jonathan Herzig, Peter Shaw, Ming-Wei Chang, Kelvin Guu, Panupong Pasupat, and Yuan Zhang. 2021. Unlocking compositional generalization in pre-trained models using intermediate representations. *CoRR*, abs/2104.07478.

Neil Houlsby, Andrei Giurgiu, Stanislaw Jastrzebski, Bruna Morrone, Quentin de Laroussilhe, Andrea Gesmundo, Mona Attariyan, and Sylvain Gelly. 2019. Parameter-efficient transfer learning for NLP. In *Proceedings of the 36th International Conference on Machine Learning, ICML 2019, 9-15 June 2019, Long Beach, California, USA*, volume 97 of *Proceedings of Machine Learning Research*, pages 2790–2799. PMLR.

Yichen Jiang and Mohit Bansal. 2021. Inducing transformer's compositional generalization ability via auxiliary sequence prediction tasks. In *Proceedings of the 2021 Conference on Empirical Methods in Natural Language Processing, EMNLP 2021, Virtual Event / Punta Cana, Dominican Republic, 7-11 November, 2021*, pages 6253–6265. Association for Computational Linguistics.

Daniel Keysers, Nathanael Schärli, Nathan Scales, Hylke Buisman, Daniel Furrer, Sergii Kashubin, Nikola Momchev, Danila Sinopalnikov, Lukasz Stafiniak, Tibor Tihon, Dmitry Tsarkov, Xiao Wang, Marc van Zee, and Olivier Bousquet. 2020. Measuring compositional generalization: A comprehensive method on realistic data. In *8th International Conference on Learning Representations, ICLR 2020, Addis Ababa, Ethiopia, April 26-30, 2020*. OpenReview.net.

Brenden M. Lake. 2019. Compositional generalization through meta sequence-to-sequence learning. In *Advances in Neural Information Processing Systems 32: Annual Conference on Neural Information Processing Systems 2019, NeurIPS 2019, December 8-14, 2019, Vancouver, BC, Canada*, pages 9788–9798.

Brenden M. Lake and Marco Baroni. 2018. Generalization without systematicity: On the compositional skills of sequence-to-sequence recurrent networks. In *Proceedings of the 35th International Conference on Machine Learning, ICML 2018, Stockholmsmässan, Stockholm, Sweden, July 10-15, 2018*, volume 80 of *Proceedings of Machine Learning Research*, pages 2879–2888. PMLR.

Mike Lewis, Yinhan Liu, Naman Goyal, Marjan Ghazvininejad, Abdelrahman Mohamed, Omer Levy, Veselin Stoyanov, and Luke Zettlemoyer. 2020. BART: Denoising sequence-to-sequence pre-training for natural language generation, translation, and comprehension. In *Proceedings of the 58th Annual Meeting of the Association for Computational Linguistics*, pages 7871–7880, Online. Association for Computational Linguistics.

Yuanpeng Li, Liang Zhao, Jianyu Wang, and Joel Hestness. 2019. Compositional generalization for primitive substitutions. In *Proceedings of the 2019 Conference on Empirical Methods in Natural Language Processing and the 9th International Joint Conference on Natural Language Processing, EMNLP-IJCNLP 2019, Hong Kong, China, November 3-7, 2019*, pages 4292–4301. Association for Computational Linguistics.

Pengfei Liu, Weizhe Yuan, Jinlan Fu, Zhengbao Jiang, Hiroaki Hayashi, and Graham Neubig. 2021. Pre-train, prompt, and predict: A systematic survey of prompting methods in natural language processing. *CoRR*, abs/2107.13586.

Erik Nijkamp, Bo Pang, Hiroaki Hayashi, Lifu Tu, Huan Wang, Yingbo Zhou, Silvio Savarese, and Caiming Xiong. 2022. A conversational paradigm for program synthesis. *arXiv preprint*.

Linlu Qiu, Peter Shaw, Panupong Pasupat, Tianze Shi, Jonathan Herzig, Emily Pitler, Fei Sha, and Kristina Toutanova. 2022. Evaluating the impact of model scale for compositional generalization in semantic parsing. *CoRR*, abs/2205.12253.

Colin Raffel, Noam Shazeer, Adam Roberts, Katherine Lee, Sharan Narang, Michael Matena, Yanqi Zhou, Wei Li, and Peter J. Liu. 2020. Exploring the limits of transfer learning with a unified text-to-text transformer. *J. Mach. Learn. Res.*, 21:140:1–140:67.

Jake Russin, Jason Jo, Randall C. O'Reilly, and Yoshua Bengio. 2019. Compositional generalization in a deep seq2seq model by separating syntax and semantics. *CoRR*, abs/1904.09708.

Timo Schick and Hinrich Schütze. 2021. It's not just size that matters: Small language models are also few-shot learners. In *Proceedings of the 2021 Conference of the North American Chapter of the Association for Computational Linguistics: Human Language Technologies, NAACL-HLT 2021, Online, June 6-11, 2021*, pages 2339–2352. Association for Computational Linguistics.

Peter Shaw, Ming-Wei Chang, Panupong Pasupat, and Kristina Toutanova. 2021. Compositional generalization and natural language variation: Can a semantic parsing approach handle both? In *Proceedings of the 59th Annual Meeting of the Association for Computational Linguistics and the 11th International Joint Conference on Natural Language Processing, ACL/IJCNLP 2021, (Volume 1: Long Papers), Virtual Event, August 1-6, 2021*, pages 922–938. Association for Computational Linguistics.

Richard Shin, Christopher H. Lin, Sam Thomson, Charles Chen, Subhro Roy, Emmanouil Antonios Platanios, Adam Pauls, Dan Klein, Jason Eisner, and Benjamin Van Durme. 2021. Constrained language models yield few-shot semantic parsers. In *Proceedings of the 2021 Conference on Empirical Methods in Natural Language Processing, EMNLP 2021, Virtual Event / Punta Cana, Dominican Republic, 7-11 November, 2021*, pages 7699–7715. Association for Computational Linguistics.

Lappoon R. Tang and Raymond J. Mooney. 2001. Using multiple clause constructors in inductive logic programming for semantic parsing. In *Machine Learning: EMCL 2001, 12th European Conference on Machine Learning, Freiburg, Germany, September 5-7, 2001, Proceedings*, volume 2167 of *Lecture Notes in Computer Science*, pages 466–477. Springer.

Dmitry Tsarkov, Tibor Tihon, Nathan Scales, Nikola Momchev, Danila Sinopalnikov, and Nathanael Schärli. 2021. *-cfq: Analyzing the scalability of machine learning on a compositional task. In *Thirty-Fifth AAAI Conference on Artificial Intelligence, AAAI 2021, Thirty-Third Conference on Innovative Applications of Artificial Intelligence, IAAI 2021, The Eleventh Symposium on Educational Advances in Artificial Intelligence, EAAI 2021, Virtual Event, February 2-9, 2021*, pages 9949–9957. AAAI Press.

Thomas Wang, Adam Roberts, Daniel Hesslow, Teven Le Scao, Hyung Won Chung, Iz Beltagy, Julien Launay, and Colin Raffel. 2022a. What language model architecture and pretraining objective works best for zero-shot generalization? In *International Conference on Machine Learning, ICML 2022, 17-23 July 2022, Baltimore, Maryland, USA*, volume 162 of *Proceedings of Machine Learning Research*, pages 22964–22984. PMLR.

Zhenhailong Wang, Manling Li, Ruochen Xu, Luowei Zhou, Jie Lei, Xudong Lin, Shuohang Wang, Ziyi Yang, Chenguang Zhu, Derek Hoiem, Shih-Fu Chang, Mohit Bansal, and Heng Ji. 2022b. Language models with image descriptors are strong few-shot video-language learners. *CoRR*, abs/2205.10747.

Pengcheng Yin, Hao Fang, Graham Neubig, Adam Pauls, Emmanouil Antonios Platanios, Yu Su, Sam Thomson, and Jacob Andreas. 2021. Compositional generalization for neural semantic parsing via span-level supervised attention. In *Proceedings of the 2021 Conference of the North American Chapter of the Association for Computational Linguistics: Human Language Technologies, NAACL-HLT 2021, Online, June 6-11, 2021*, pages 2810–2823. Association for Computational Linguistics.

John M. Zelle and Raymond J. Mooney. 1996. Learning to parse database queries using inductive logic programming. In *Proceedings of the Thirteenth National Conference on Artificial Intelligence and Eighth Innovative Applications of Artificial Intelligence Conference, AAAI 96, IAAI 96, Portland, Oregon, USA, August 4-8, 1996, Volume 2*, pages 1050–1055. AAAI Press / The MIT Press.

Susan Zhang, Stephen Roller, Naman Goyal, Mikel Artetxe, Moya Chen, Shuohui Chen, Christopher Dewan, Mona Diab, Xian Li, Xi Victoria Lin, Todor Mihaylov, Myle Ott, Sam Shleifer, Kurt Shuster, Daniel Simig, Punit Singh Koura, Anjali Sridhar, Tianlu Wang, and Luke Zettlemoyer. 2022. OPT: open pre-trained transformer language models. *CoRR*, abs/2205.01068.

A Average OOD generalization with respect to average ID generalization performance

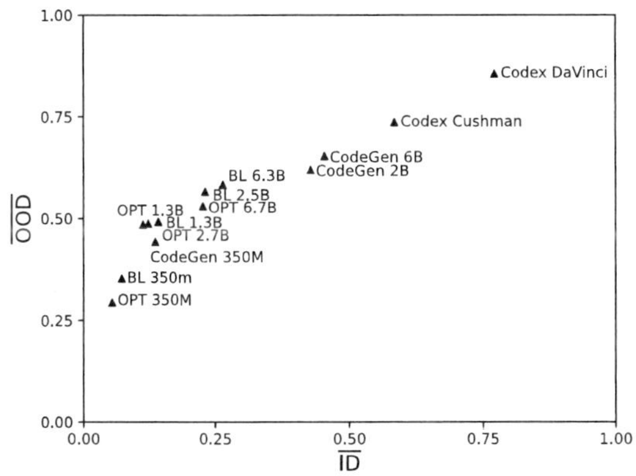

Figure 5: Average OOD generalization vs. average ID generalization performance on GeoQuery-template using 10 exemplars. Results are averaged over five different seeds.

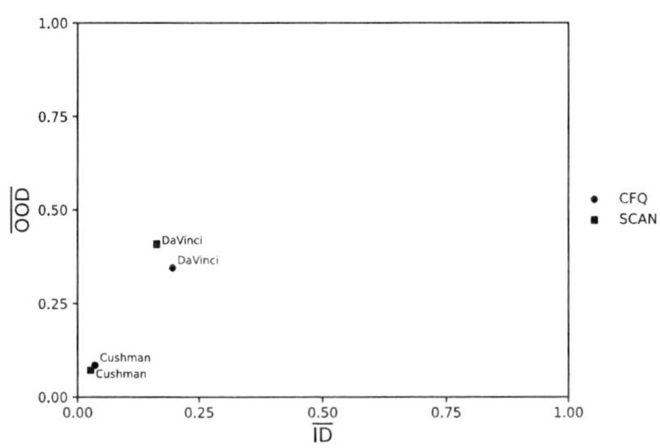

Figure 6: Average OOD generalization vs. average ID generalization performance on CFQ-MCD1 and SCAN-MCD1 using 10 exemplars for Codex DaVinci and Cushman. Results are averaged over five different seeds

B Prompt design

Our prompts include a prefix string that introduces the task, followed by a number of input-output examples where inputs and outputs have dataset-specific prefixes. The templates used for producing the prompts are illustrated in Table 2.

Dataset	Prompt template
CFQ	As a programmer, I can correctly translate any complicated question to a SPARQL query. Question: Was a employer of M1 a film distributor? Query: SELECT count(*) WHERE { ?x0 a film.film_distributor . ?x0 employment_tenure.person M1 } Question: <example 2 input> Query: <example 2 output> ... Question: <evaluation input> Query:
SCAN	Here are some examples of converting complicated commands to correct navigation actions. Command: run opposite right thrice and jump around right thrice. Actions: TURN_RIGHT TURN_RIGHT RUN TURN_RIGHT TURN_RIGHT RUN TURN_RIGHT TURN_RIGHT RUN TURN_RIGHT JUMP TURN_RIGHT JUMP TURN_RIGHT JUMP TURN_RIGHT JUMP TURN_RIGHT JUMP TURN_RIGHT JUMP TURN_RIGHT JUMP TURN_RIGHT JUMP TURN_RIGHT JUMP TURN_RIGHT JUMP TURN_RIGHT JUMP TURN_RIGHT JUMP. Command: <example 2 input> Actions: <example 2 output> ... Command: <evaluation input> Actions:
GeoQuery	As a programmer, I can correctly translate any complicated question to a meaning representation query. Question: how high is the highest point in m0. Query: answer (elevation_1 (highest (intersection (place , loc_2 (m0))))). Question: <example 2 input> Query: <example 2 output> ... Question: <evaluation input> Query:

Table 2: Templates used for generating the prompts for CFQ, SCAN, and GeoQuery.

Explaining Translationese: why are Neural Classifiers Better and what do they Learn?

Kwabena Amponsah-Kaakyire[*1,2], **Daria Pylypenko**[*1], **Josef van Genabith**[1,2], and **Cristina España-Bonet**[2]
[1]Saarland University, [2]German Research Center for Artificial Intelligence (DFKI)
Saarland Informatics Campus, Saarbrücken, Germany
amponsahkaakyirek@gmail.com
daria.pylypenko@uni-saarland.de
{cristinae, Josef.Van_Genabith}@dfki.de

Abstract

Recent work has shown that neural feature- and representation-learning, e.g. BERT, achieves superior performance over traditional manual feature engineering based approaches, with e.g. SVMs, in translationese classification tasks. Previous research did not show (i) whether the difference is because of the features, the classifiers or both, and (ii) what the neural classifiers actually learn. To address (i), we carefully design experiments that swap features between BERT- and SVM-based classifiers. We show that an SVM fed with BERT representations performs at the level of the best BERT classifiers, while BERT learning and using handcrafted features performs at the level of an SVM using handcrafted features. This shows that the performance differences are due to the features. To address (ii) we use integrated gradients and find that (a) there is indication that information captured by hand-crafted features is only a subset of what BERT learns, and (b) part of BERT's top performance results are due to BERT learning topic differences and spurious correlations with translationese.

1 Introduction

Translationese is a descriptive (non-negative) cover term for the systematic differences between translated and originally authored text in same language (Gellerstam, 1986). Some aspects of translationese such as source interference (Toury, 1980; Teich, 2003) are language dependent, others are presumed universal, e.g. simplification, explicitation, overadherence to target language linguistic norms (Volansky et al., 2015) in the products of translations. While translationese effects can be subtle, especially for professional human translation, corpus-based studies (Baker et al., 1993) and, in particular, machine-learning and classifier based studies (Rabinovich and Wintner, 2015; Volansky et al., 2015; Rubino et al., 2016; Pylypenko et al., 2021) clearly reveal the differences.

While research on translationese is important from a theoretical point of view (translation universals, specific interference), it has a direct impact on machine translation research: (Kurokawa et al., 2009; Stymne, 2017; Toral et al., 2018; Zhang and Toral, 2019; Freitag et al., 2019; Graham et al., 2020; Riley et al., 2020), amongst others, show that translation direction in training and test data impacts on results, that already translated test data are easier to translate than original data, that machine translation and post-editing result in translationese, and that mitigating translationese in MT output can improve results. Translationese impacts cross-lingual applications, e.g. question answering and natural language inference (Singh et al., 2019; Clark et al., 2020; Artetxe et al., 2020).

In this paper we focus on machine-learning-classifier-based research on translationese. Here, typically a classifier is trained to distinguish between original and translated texts (in the same language). Until recently, most of this research (Baroni and Bernardini, 2005; Volansky et al., 2015; Rubino et al., 2016) used manually defined, often linguistically inspired, feature-engineering based sets of features, mostly using support vector machines (SVM). Once a classifier is trained, feature importance and ranking methods are used to reason back to what aspects of the input is responsible for (i.e. explains) the classification (and whether this accords with linguistic theorisation). More recently, a small number of papers explored feature- and representation-learning neural network based approaches to translationese classification (Sominsky and Wintner, 2019). In a systematic study Pylypenko et al. (2021) show that feature- and representation-learning deep neural network-based approaches (in particular BERT-based, but also other neural approaches) to translationese

[*]Equal contribution.

Proceedings of the Fifth BlackboxNLP Workshop on Analyzing and Interpreting Neural Networks for NLP, pages 281 - 296
December 8, 2022 ©2022 Association for Computational Linguistics

classification substantially outperform handcrafted feature-engineering based approaches using SVMs. However, to date, two important questions remain: (i) it is not clear whether the substantial performance differences are due to learned vs. handcrafted features, the classifiers (SVM, the BERT classification head, or full BERT), or the combination of both, and (ii) what the neural feature and representation learning approaches actually learn and how that explains the superior classification. The contributions of our paper are as follows:

1. we address (i) by carefully crossing features and classifiers, feeding BERT-based learned features to feature-engineering models (SVMs), feeding the BERT classification head with hand-crafted features, and by making BERT architectures learn handcrafted features, as well as feeding embeddings of handcrafted features into BERT. Our experiments show that SVMs using BERT-learned features perform on a par with our best BERT-translationese classifiers, while BERT using handcrafted features only performs at the level of feature-engineering-based classifiers. This shows that it is the features and not the classifiers, that lead to the substantial (up to 20% points accuracy absolute) difference in performance.

2. we present the first steps to address (ii) using integrated gradients, an attribution-based approach, on the BERT models trained in various settings. Based on striking similarities in attributions between BERT trained from scratch and BERT pretrained on handcrafted features and fine-tuned on text data, as well as comparable classification accuracies, we find evidence that the hand-crafted features do not bring any additional information over the set learnt by BERT. it is therefore likely that the hand-crafted features are a (possibly partial) subset of the features learnt by BERT. Inspecting the most attributed tokens, we present evidence of 'Clever Hans' behaviour: at least part of the high classification accuracy of BERT is due to names of places and countries, suggesting that part of the classification is topic- and not translationese-based. Moreover, some top features suggest that there may be some punctuation-based spurious correlation in the data.

2 Related Work

Combining learned and hand-crafted features. (Kaas et al., 2020; Prakash and Tayyar Madabushi, 2020; Lim and Tayyar Madabushi, 2020) combine BERT-based and manual features in order to improve accuracy. (Kazameini et al., 2020; Ray and Garain, 2020; Zhang and Yamana, 2020) concatenate BERT pooled output embeddings with handcrafted feature vectors for classification, often using an SVM, where the handcrafted feature vector might be further encoded by a neural network or used as it is. Our work differs in that we do not combine features from both models but swap them in order to decide whether it is the features, the classifiers or the combination that explains the performance difference between neural and feature engineering based models. Additionally, our approach allows us to examine whether or not representation learning learns features similar to hand-crafted features.

Explainability for the feature-engineering approach to translationese classification. To date, explainability in translationese research has mainly focused on quantifying handcrafted feature importance. Techniques include inspecting SVM feature weights (Avner et al., 2016; Pylypenko et al., 2021), correlation (Rubino et al., 2016), information gain (Ilisei et al., 2010), chi-square (Ilisei et al., 2010), decision trees or random forests (Rubino et al., 2016; Ilisei et al., 2010), ablating features and observing the change in accuracy (Baroni and Bernardini, 2005; Ilisei et al., 2010), training separate classifiers on each individual feature (or feature set) and comparing accuracies (Volansky et al., 2015; Avner et al., 2016). For n-grams, the difference in frequencies between the original and translationese classes (Koppel and Ordan, 2011; van Halteren, 2008), and the contribution to the symmetrized Kullback-Leibler Divergence between the classes (Kurokawa et al., 2009) have been used.

Explainability for the neural approach to translationese classification. To date, explainability methods for neural networks have not been widely explored. Pylypenko et al. (2021) quantify to which extent handcrafted features can explain the variance in the predictions of neural models, such as BERT, LSTMs, and a simplified Transformer, by training per-feature linear regression models to output the predicted probabilities of the neural models and computing the R^2 measure. They find that most of the top features are either POS-perplexity-based, or bag-of-POS features. However, their method treats the neural network as a black-box, whereas we use a method that accesses the internals of the model.

Integrated Gradients (IG). In our work we use the Integrated Gradients method (Sundararajan et al., 2017) for explainability. This method provides attribution scores for the input with respect to a certain class. IG calculates the integral of gradients of the model F with respect to the input x (token embedding), along the path from a baseline x' (in our case, PAD token embedding) to the input x:

$$\texttt{IntegratedGrads}_i(x) ::= (x_i - x'_i) \times \int_{\alpha=0}^{1} \frac{\partial F(x' + \alpha \times (x - x'))}{\partial x_i} d\alpha \quad (1)$$

The strength of the Integrated Gradients method is that it satisfies two fundamental axioms (Sensitivity and Implementation Invariance), while many other popular attribution methods, like Gradients (Simonyan et al., 2014), DeepLift (Shrikumar et al., 2017) and LRP (Bach et al., 2015) violate one or both of them. IG also satisfies the completeness axiom, that is, IG is comprehensive in accounting for attributions and does not just to pick the top label (Sundararajan et al., 2017).

3 Experimental Settings

3.1 Data

For our experiments, we use the monolingual German dataset in the Multilingual Parallel Direct Europarl (MPDE) (Amponsah-Kaakyire et al., 2021) corpus. The set contains 42k paragraphs with half of the texts German originals and the other half translations into German from Spanish (see statistics in Appendix A.1). We perform paragraph-level classification with an average length of 80 tokens per training sample.

We additionally use an in-domain Europarl-based heldout corpus of around 30k paragraphs for training language models and n-gram quartile distributions on it. This corpus consists of original German texts only.

3.2 Base Setup

We compare the traditional SVM-based feature engineering approach, which has demonstrated high performance in previous translationese research, to the BERT model known to be very successful for various NLP tasks, including classification. As base setup, we reproduce the models from Pylypenko et al. (2021) for the two architectures and a new baseline:

1. a linear **SVM** on 108-dimensional **handcrafted feature** vectors (with surface, lexical, unigram bag-of-PoS, language modelling and n-gram frequency distribution features[1]). **[handcr.-features+SVM]**
2. a **linear classifier** (BERT classification head, simple linear FFN, except for difference in input dimension) trained on the 108-dimensional **handcrafted feature** vectors. **[handcr.-features+LinearClassifier]**
3. off-the-shelf Google's **pretrained BERT**-base model (12 layers, 768 hidden dimensions, 12 attention heads) which we **fine-tune** on the MPDE corpus for translationese classification. **[pretrained-BERT-ft]**
4. a BERT-base model with the same settings trained **from scratch** on MPDE for translationese classification. **[fromScratch-BERT]**

For 1, we estimate n-gram language models with SRILM (Stolcke, 2002) and do POS-tagging with SpaCy.[2] For 3, we use multilingual BERT (Devlin et al., 2019) (BERT-base-multilingual-uncased), and fine-tune with the *simpletransformers*[3] library. We use a batch size of 32, learning rate of $4 \cdot 10^{-5}$, and the Adam optimiser with epsilon $1 \cdot 10^{-8}$.

To ensure fair and comprehensive treatment, we carefully explore many experiments and variations below: we exchange input features between BERT and SVM architectures by (i) feeding BERT-learned features into SVMs (Section 3.3), handcrafted features into the BERT classification head, and $(ii\text{-}a)$ letting the full BERT architecture learn handcrafted feature vectors used by SVMs and $(ii\text{-}b)$ feeding handcrafted feature vectors as embeddings into the BERT model (Section 3.4).

3.3 SVM Classifier with BERT Features

We train an SVM with linear kernel on the features learnt by the pretrained BERT model fine-tuned on

[1]See (Pylypenko et al., 2021) for the detailed list of features.

[2]`https://spacy.io/`

[3]`github.com/ThilinaRajapakse/simpletransformers`

the translationese classification task. We use the output of the BERT pooler, which selects the last layer $[CLS]$ token vector, with linear projection and $tanh$ activation as our feature vector. We use:

1. BERT's 768-dim pooled vector output, **[pretrained-BERT-ft+SVM]**
2. a 108-dim PCA projection of this vector. **[pretrained-BERT-ft+PCA$_{108}$+SVM]**

The PCA projection allows us to match the handcrafted feature vector dimensionality.

3.4 BERT with Handcrafted Features

Apart from feeding hand-crafted feature vectors into a suitably adjusted BERT classification head **[handcr.-features+LinearClassifier]**, we carefully design two strategies to force the full BERT architecture use the handcrafted features.

Pretraining on handcrafted feature prediction. First, we train a BERT-base model from scratch on the MPDE dataset to predict the handcrafted features. This regression model **[BERT-reg-full]** takes unmasked text as input and predicts continuous values (the 108 dimension vectors representing handcrafted features originally used in training the SVM). The complete feature vector is predicted at once, and the pretraining is done by minimizing MSE loss between the predicted and the ground truth vector. The weights of this model encode the information of the handcrafted features. With this pretrained model,

1. we freeze the weights, replace the regression head (linear layer predicting 108 features) with a linear classifier (a BERT classification head predicting the original or translationese label) and train the classifier on the MPDE data for translationese classification, **[BERT-r2c-full-frozen]**[4]
2. we do not freeze but fine-tune on MPDE for the translationese classification task. **[BERT-r2c-full-ft]**

The comparison between frozen and unfrozen weights is designed to provide us insights on the importance of representation learning in BERT.

We reproduce the same approach as above with a smaller BERT model with only 6 layers instead of 12 **[BERT-reg-half]**. Interestingly, according to the losses when training for predicting the handcrafted features, the smaller BERT-reg-half performs comparably to BERT-reg-full (0.0041136 vs 0.0041148 MSE). We then load the weights of the small 6 layer model into the embedding layer and the first 6 layers of a 12 layer non-pretrained BERT-base model and, similarly as before:

3. we freeze the loaded weights in the first 6 layers and train the remaining 6 layers and classifier on the translationese classification task, **[BERT-r2c-half-frozen]**
4. we do not freeze but fine-tune on the translationese classification task with randomly-initialised weights for the other 6 layers. **[BERT-r2c-half-ft]**

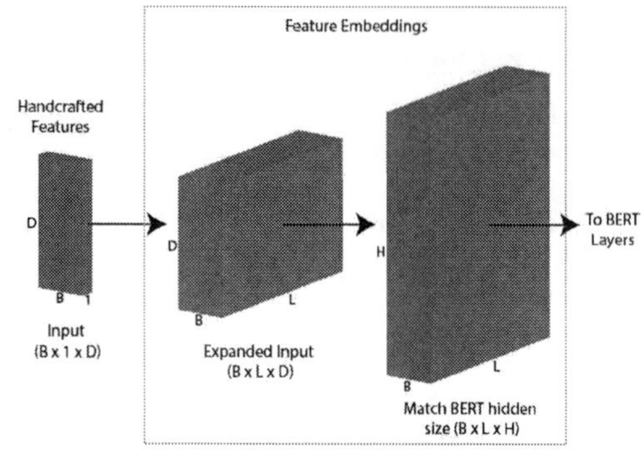

Figure 1: Mapping handcrafted features to embeddings.

Mapping handcrafted features to embeddings. Even though the very low MSE results indicate that both versions of BERT-reg are able to learn handcrafted features well, using them in terms of frozen layers in translationese classification leads to low classification performance (Section 4). This could be attributed to the fact that, not being an end-to-end approach, information losses accumulate: first, even though MSE is low in BERT-reg, we do not have exactly the same features; and second, the features are not used directly for classification, but are encoded again by the network. This motivates us to explore an alternative way of encoding handcrafted features in an end-to-end manner.

We convert the single vector of handcrafted features of dimension D (108 in our experiments) into a sequence of embeddings in BERT's layer format, that is, length of feature embedding sequence L times the dimension of the hidden states H (768), while preserving the information of the single vector (Figure 1). To do this, we consider a batch of

[4] **r2c** – regression-to-classification

Model	Accuracy (%)
handcr.-features+SVM	73.2±0.1
handcr.-features+LinearClassifier	72.0±0.4
pretrained-BERT-ft	92.2±0.2
fromScratch-BERT	89.3±0.3
pretrained-BERT-ft+SVM	92.0±0.0
pretrained-BERT-ft+PCA$_{108}$+SVM	92.0±0.0
BERT-r2c-full-frozen+SVM	74.9±0.7
BERT-r2c-full-frozen+PCA$_{108}$+SVM	70.3±0.1
BERT-r2c-full-frozen	59.6±0.1
BERT-r2c-full-ft	89.3±0.4
BERT-r2c-half-frozen	67.5±0.4
BERT-r2c-half-ft	89.0±0.3
BERT-f2c $L = 1$	57±10
BERT-f2c $L = 80$	72.8±0.2
BERT-f2c $L = 256$	72.7±0.2
pretrained-BERT-f2c $L = 80$	68.0±2.1

Table 1: Translationese classification accuracy for all settings (average and standard deviation over 5 runs). All of the models were trained/fine-tuned for the translationese classification task.

tokens with size B and take in the handcrafted features as a $(B \times D)$-dimensional input to the BERT model and generate feature embeddings by passing the features through 2 linear layers as follows. We first pass the $(B \times 1 \times D)$ input to the first linear layer. The resulting $(B \times L \times D)$-dimensional output is fed as input to the second linear layer which outputs a $(B \times L \times H)$-dimensional output as the feature embeddings.

This reshaped handcrafted feature embedding layer replaces BERT's embedding layer. Weights are randomly initialised and the modified BERT model is trained on the translationese classification task. We experiment with three different values for sequence length L: 1, 80 (average length of our training samples) and 256 (half of maximum input for BERT). All three variants are trained from scratch [**BERT-f2c**[5] **L=1**, **BERT-f2c L=80**, **BERT-f2c L=256**]. For further comparison, we also take BERT-f2c L=80, load the weights of pretrained BERT-base layers into the 12 layers of the modified model and fine-tune on the task **[pretrained BERT-f2c L=80]**.

Training and hyperparameter settings for these models are given in Appendix A.2.

4 Translationese Classification

Table 1 summarises results of the different translationese classification settings. For the base models, BERT outperforms the SVM by 16% when trained from scratch and 19% when finetuned.

Feeding pooled output of BERT into the SVM model [**pretrained-BERT-ft+SVM**], accuracy increases by 19% percentage points absolute over using handcrafted features [**handcr.-features+SVM**], even when PCA is used to reduce the BERT vector dimensionality to match the size of the handcrafted feature vector. Feeding handcrafted features directly to the linear BERT classification head [**handcr.-features+LinearClassifier**] reduces accuracy by about 20% points compared to pretrained and fine-tuned BERT [**pretrained-BERT-ft**]. This shows that features learnt by BERT are superior to our set of manual features, as used in previous high performing classical feature engineering-based approaches to translationese classification. When BERT is trained from scratch on the MPDE data [**fromScratch-BERT**], translationese classification accuracy reduces by $\sim$ 3 percentage points, compared to pretrained-BERT-ft. This suggests that pretraining on large data helps to encode additional information that turns out to be helpful in the translationese classification task.

One can assume that BERT pretrained to predict the handcrafted features and subsequently frozen [**BERT-r2c-full-frozen**] has learnt to encode the handcrafted features during pretraining (Section 3.4). Nevertheless, its accuracy, albeit higher than a random guess, is lower by $\sim$ 13 percentage points than the SVM classifier. We perform an additional experiment, in order to check whether the difference in accuracy is due to BERT failing to sufficiently encode the handcrafted features during pretraining, or due to the SVM classifier being superior to the linear classification head of the BERT model. Namely, we train the SVM classifier on the pooled output of BERT-r2c-full-frozen model [**BERT-r2c-full-frozen+SVM**] and on the PCA-reduced dimensionality [**BERT-r2c-full-frozen+PCA$_{108}$+SVM**]. The accuracy is around 75% for both settings which is as high as using SVM on handcrafted feature vectors. We conclude that BERT encodes the handcrafted features sufficiently well, but the linear classifier performs worse than an SVM in these conditions.

Further fine-tuning BERT fully pretrained for handcrafted feature prediction [**BERT-r2c-full-ft**] for translationese classification results in accuracy comparable to BERT that was not pretrained on this task [**fromScratch-BERT**]. This could suggest that our handcrafted feature set is either a sub-

[5]**f2c** – feature-embeddings to classification

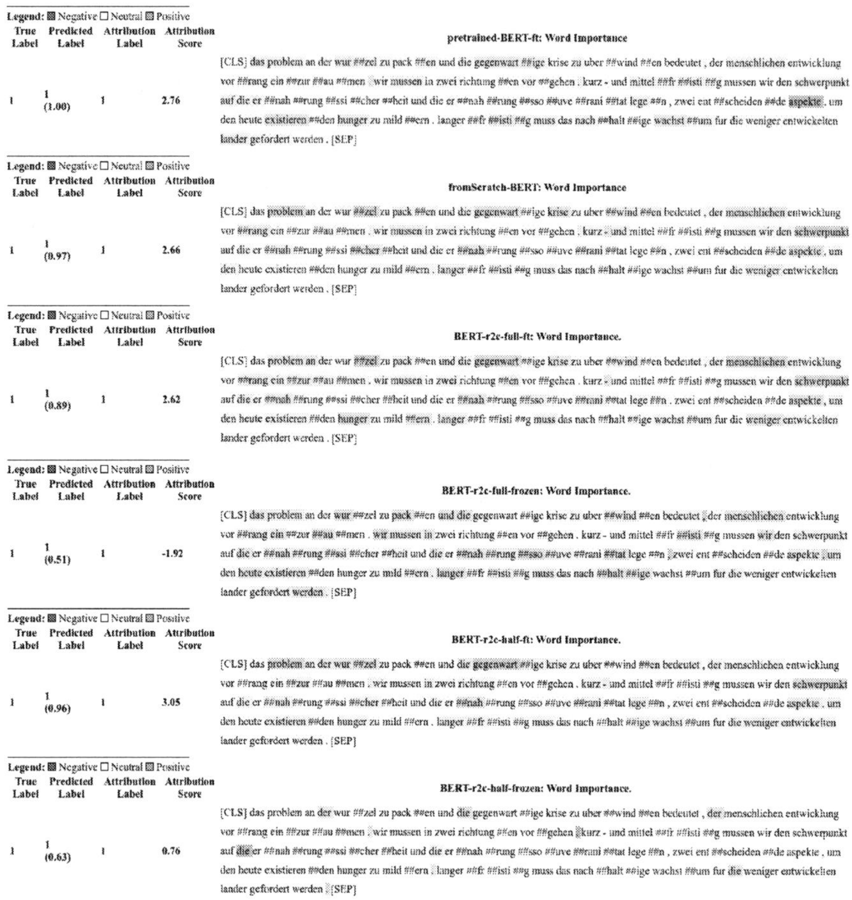

Figure 2: Layer Integrated Gradient saliency maps of input tokens contributing to the ground truth translationese label (here: translation). Comparison of different models.

set of features learned by fromScratch-BERT, or that the handcrafted features are discarded during fine-tuning. The model where only the first 6 layers were pretrained [**BERT-r2c-half-ft**], achieves similar accuracy, likely due to the same reasons. By contrast, freezing the 6 handcrafted feature prediction pretrained layers [**BERT-r2c-half-frozen**] largely reduces the accuracy with respect to BERT-r2c-half-ft, because the model only has access to the 6th layer embeddings that supposedly encode the information about the handcrafted features, and does not have ability to extract its own features. The remaining (higher) 6 layers are responsible for the increment in accuracy with respect to BERT-r2c-full-frozen.

The results of BERT-f2c models show that BERT, when fed the handcrafted features in the form of embeddings, can reach at most the same accuracy as the hancdr.-features+SVM approach, which suggests that the BERT architecture has no advantage over the SVM classifier in utilizing the handcrafted features for classification. This is again evidence that the features, and not the classifier, cause the better performance of the feature and representation learning method.[6]

5 Layer Integrated Gradients Saliency

We compare input attributions of the ground truth classification label amongst **pretrained-BERT-ft**, **fromScratch-BERT** and four different settings of the translationese classification models pretrained on the handcrafted feature prediction task: **BERT-r2c-full-ft**, **BERT-r2c-full-frozen**, **BERT-r2c-half-ft** and **BERT-r2c-half-frozen**. We use Layer Integrated Gradients from the Captum library (Kokhlikyan et al., 2020), which computes the attribution for all the individual neurons in the

[6]As a sanity check, we ran an experiment using a gradient boosting classifier instead of an SVM, with the exact same 108 hand-crafted features and obtain accuracy of 72.3%.

	Translationese				Original			
	BERT-r2c-full-ft		pretrained-BERT-ft		BERT-r2c-full-ft		pretrained-BERT-ft	
Rank	Token	AAS	Token	AAS	Token	AAS	Token	AAS
1	sagte	0.60	entstand	0.70	##wegen	0.61	situations	0.37
2	gebiet	0.46	virus	0.63	•	0.55	•	0.36
3	##dies	0.44	inti	0.60	eu	0.49	ria	0.34
4	ansicht	0.43	sagte	0.58	daraufhin	0.49	##lk	0.33
5	bezug	0.42	entdeckte	0.57	finde	0.45	##iet	0.32
6	neige	0.40	gras	0.57	##vo	0.45	golden	0.32
7	amt	0.40	nuts	0.56	gerne	0.43	sak	0.30
8	pre	0.40	nicaragua	0.55	##abb	0.42	turm	0.30
9	spanien	0.39	rekord	0.53	##lute	0.42	##emen	0.27
10	sprechen	0.38	bilbao	0.53	ausbau	0.42	orange	0.27
11	nuts	0.36	verfugte	0.53	!	0.42	hang	0.26
12	barcelona	0.34	bol	0.51	bekommen	0.42	##wald	0.25
13	;	0.33	colombia	0.51	trips	0.41	1732	0.25
14	##bien	0.32	nis	0.51	ez	0.41	dobe	0.24
15	spanischen	0.32	och	0.49	##gemeinde	0.40	##pas	0.23
16	wiederholt	0.31	vorkommen	0.49	vot	0.36	profits	0.22
17	einige	0.30	oecd	0.49	won	0.36	stuttgart	0.22
18	##sprache	0.29	;	0.46	geplant	0.35	soja	0.21
19	weder	0.29	erklarte	0.45	demnach	0.35	r	0.21
20	territorium	0.28	clinton	0.45	ja	0.35	ruth	0.21

Table 2: Top-20 tokens with highest average attribution score (AAS) towards original and translationese classes in the test set. BERT-r2c-full-ft and pretrained-BERT-ft.

embedding layer, and calculate the salience score for each token by averaging the attributions over the embedding dimension.

Comparing Models. Figure 2 displays Integrated Gradients attributions for a translated paragraph across different BERT models. The trends for the original paragraph are similar to those that we observe for the translated paragraph, therefore attributions for the original paragraph are given in Appendix A.3.

Comparing the attributions of classification labels to sample inputs amongst the various settings of BERT, we observe that attributions are similar for **fromScratch-BERT** and the fine-tuned models: **BERT-r2c-full-ft** and **BERT-r2c-half-ft**. This suggests that fine-tuning "dissolves" the pre-learned information about the hand-crafted features in the **r2c** models, no matter how much of the model was pre-trained. By contrast, freezing the weights in **BERT-r2c-full-frozen** and **BERT-r2c-half-frozen** resulted in very different attributions compared to the **fromScratch-BERT**. Since these frozen models only utilize the information they have learnt about the handcrafted features, this shows that this information is not identical to the information that **fromScratch-BERT** learns for the translationese classification task. For **BERT-r2c-half-frozen** the attributions are more peaked than for other models, with only a few tokens receiving large scores, and most tokens having scores close to zero. Notably, **pretrained-BERT-ft** displays a pattern that is overall similar to BERT trained from scratch, but some attributions are reversed, and the peaks are on different tokens. This supports the observation that off-the-shelf BERT pretrained on a large amount of data encodes some useful additional information.

For **BERT-r2c-full-frozen**, a substantial number of tokens with negative attributions have positive attributions in the model trained from scratch and also the fine-tuned models. However some attributions overlap, which suggests that **fromScratch-BERT** may be using something like the hand-crafted features. We investigate this further by examining the fine-tuning checkpoints.

Comparing Checkpoints. We aim to study how **fromScratch-BERT** learns information about translationese classification over the epochs, and how this compares to the fine-tuning of **BERT-r2c-full-ft**, when the information about the hand-crafted features is gradually modified over the epochs turn into the final feature set used for translationese classification. In Appendix A.3 we provide additional results on examining training checkpoints for **fromScratch-BERT** and **BERT-r2c-full-ft** for an original and a translated paragraph.

Results indicate that for **fromScratch-BERT**

some attributions change into their opposite during training, whereas for **BERT-r2c-full-ft** the pattern appears to be already settled from the early checkpoints onwards, and does not change much over the course of fine-tuning. This supports the hypothesis that the handcrafted features are a subset of features learnt by **fromScratch-BERT**, and thus provide a useful initialization of weights for fine-tuning for translationese classification.

Highest Average Attribution. In order to make the interpretation less local, and to generalize the observations, we compute the top tokens with highest attribution on average across the test set. The results for each class for best-performing models (**pretrained-BERT-ft** and **BERT-r2c-full-ft**) are given in Table 2.

For German translationese data translated from Spanish, some top tokens correspond to the geographical areas, where Spanish is spoken, e.g. "spanien", "barcelona", "spanischen" for BERT-r2c-full-ft; "nicaragua", "colombia", "bilbao" for pretrained-BERT-ft. (Moreover, in this example it appears that off-the-shelf pretrained-BERT-ft, pretrained on the Wikipedia data, better utilizes the non-European toponyms, unlike the BERT-r2c-full-ft that was only trained on the European-focused Europarl data.) Likewise for original German data, some of the top tokens are German geographical names, e.g. "stuttgart" for pretrained-BERT-ft. The subword "##wald" also appears to be a common German toponymic suffix. This suggests that topic is one of the spurious clues that is used by BERT to determine the correct translationese class. This is also supported by the fact that some nouns that likely correspond to certain recurring discussion topics for only one class within our data sample, receive high attribution, e.g. "virus", "soja", "clinton", "orange" etc. The "ez" token, salient for the original class, appears to be a starting subword unit of the *EZB* abbreviation (Europäische Zentralbank).

The "•" token (bullet point) having a high attribution for the class *originals* for both models might suggest a spurious correlation within the dataset, that is apparently utilized by BERT. The ";" token is deemed important for the translationese class by both models, which might also be a spurious correlation. Conversely, this could be an indication that clauses in Spanish are more often joint with the semi-colon, than in German, which was preserved in the translation. This corroborates findings from other works that deep networks exploit spurious statistical cues for better performance (Mudrakarta et al., 2018; Niven and Kao, 2019).

For both models the Präteritum forms "sagte", "erklärte" etc. are also among the top tokens important for recognizing translationese. One possible explanation could be that the Perfekt form ("hat gesagt") is more common in German spoken language, and Präteritum is more common in writing. Therefore the translators, while translating Spanish speeches into German, may have preferred to use the Präteritum form more common for writing.

6 Summary and Conclusions

We address two open questions in classification-based translationese research: (1) are the substantial performance differences between feature- and representation-learning and classical handcrafted feature based approaches is due to (i) the difference in the features, (ii) the classifiers, or (iii) both, and (2) what do feature- and representation-learning based approaches actually learn?

We address (1) by exchanging features from both models, examining a broad variety of settings, to ensure that this is done in a fair an unbiased way. We show that SVMs perform as good as BERT when fed with features learnt by BERT. Likewise, the BERT classification head and the full BERT architecture perform at the level of traditional SVM-based classification with handcrafted features, when fed with handcrafted features only. This shows that it is the feature and representation learning and not the classifiers that are responsible for the translationese classification performance difference.

To address question (2), we examine BERT's input attributions using Integrated Gradients Saliency for various settings and observe that attributions are indeed similar for the model trained from scratch (fromScratch-BERT) on just the text data and the fine-tuned models that were pretrained on handcrafted feature prediction (BERT-r2c-full-ft and BERT-r2c-half-ft). This suggests that pretraining on the handcrafted features does not make a visible difference in attributions, and, together with the accuracy result that also does not change, suggests that no extra information is learnt during pretraining on handcrafted features. Based on these findings, and the fact that some attributions appear to overlap for BERT pretrained on handcrafted features and where the pretrained layers were subsequently frozen (BERT-r2c-full-frozen), and BERT trained from scratch (fromScratch-BERT), it is consistent to assume that handcrafted features are a (possibly partial) subset of the features automatically learnt by BERT.

Finally, analysis of top activated tokens suggests that at least part of BERT's strong translationese classification accuracy is based on topic differences between the classes as well as on some spurious correlations, rather than "proper" translationese phenomena. We are currently working on quantifying the 'Clever Hans' behaviour using named entity masking and cleaning/normalizing the data.

Acknowledgements

We would like to thank the reviewers for their insightful comments and feedback. This research is funded by the German Research Foundation (Deutsche Forschungsgemeinschaft) under grant SFB 1102: Information Density and Linguistic Encoding.

References

Kwabena Amponsah-Kaakyire, Daria Pylypenko, Cristina España-Bonet, and Josef van Genabith. 2021. Do not rely on relay translations: Multilingual parallel direct Europarl. In *Proceedings for the First Workshop on Modelling Translation: Translatology in the Digital Age*, pages 1–7, online. Association for Computational Linguistics.

Mikel Artetxe, Gorka Labaka, and Eneko Agirre. 2020. Translation artifacts in cross-lingual transfer learning. In *Proceedings of the 2020 Conference on Empirical Methods in Natural Language Processing (EMNLP)*, pages 7674–7684, Online. Association for Computational Linguistics.

Ehud Alexander Avner, Noam Ordan, and Shuly Wintner. 2016. Identifying translationese at the word and sub-word level. *Digit. Scholarsh. Humanit.*, 31:30–54.

Sebastian Bach, Alexander Binder, Grégoire Montavon, Frederick Klauschen, Klaus-Robert Müller, and Wojciech Samek. 2015. On pixel-wise explanations for non-linear classifier decisions by layer-wise relevance propagation. *PLoS ONE*, 10:e0130140.

Mona Baker, Gill Francis, and Elena Tognini-Bonelli. 1993. Corpus linguistics and translation studies: Implications and applications. In *Text and Technology: In Honour of John Sinclair*, page 233–, Netherlands. John Benjamins Publishing Company.

Marco Baroni and Silvia Bernardini. 2005. A New Approach to the Study of Translationese: Machine-learning the Difference between Original and Translated Text. *Literary and Linguistic Computing*, 21(3):259–274.

Jonathan H. Clark, Eunsol Choi, Michael Collins, Dan Garrette, Tom Kwiatkowski, Vitaly Nikolaev, and Jennimaria Palomaki. 2020. TyDi QA: A benchmark for information-seeking question answering in typologically diverse languages. *Transactions of the Association for Computational Linguistics*, 8:454–470.

Jacob Devlin, Ming-Wei Chang, Kenton Lee, and Kristina Toutanova. 2019. BERT: Pre training of deep bidirectional transformers for language understanding. In *Proceedings of the 2019 Conference of the North American Chapter of the Association for Computational Linguistics: Human Language Technologies, Volume 1 (Long and Short Papers)*, pages 4171–4186, Minneapolis, Minnesota. Association for Computational Linguistics.

Markus Freitag, Isaac Caswell, and Scott Roy. 2019. APE at scale and its implications on MT evaluation biases. In *Proceedings of the Fourth Conference on Machine Translation (Volume 1: Research Papers)*, pages 34–44, Florence, Italy. Association for Computational Linguistics.

Martin Gellerstam. 1986. Translationese in Swedish novels translated from English. *Translation studies in Scandinavia*, 1:88–95.

Yvette Graham, Barry Haddow, and Philipp Koehn. 2020. Statistical power and translationese in machine translation evaluation. In *Proceedings of the 2020 Conference on Empirical Methods in Natural Language Processing (EMNLP)*, pages 72–81, Online. Association for Computational Linguistics.

Iustina Ilisei, Diana Inkpen, Gloria Corpas Pastor, and Ruslan Mitkov. 2010. Identification of translationese: A machine learning approach. In *Computational Linguistics and Intelligent Text Processing*, pages 503–511, Berlin, Heidelberg. Springer Berlin Heidelberg.

Anders Kaas, Viktor Torp Thomsen, and Barbara Plank. 2020. Team DiSaster at SemEval-2020 task 11: Combining BERT and hand-crafted features for identifying propaganda techniques in news. In *Proceedings of the Fourteenth Workshop on Semantic Evaluation*, pages 1817–1822, Barcelona (online). International Committee for Computational Linguistics.

Amirmohammad Kazameini, Samin Fatehi, Yash Mehta, Sauleh Eetemadi, and Erik Cambria. 2020. Personality trait detection using bagged SVM over BERT word embedding ensembles. *CoRR*, abs/2010.01309.

Narine Kokhlikyan, Vivek Miglani, Miguel Martin, Edward Wang, Bilal Alsallakh, Jonathan Reynolds, Alexander Melnikov, Natalia Kliushkina, Carlos Araya, Siqi Yan, and Orion Reblitz-Richardson. 2020. Captum: A unified and generic model interpretability library for pytorch.

Moshe Koppel and Noam Ordan. 2011. Translationese and its dialects. In *Proceedings of the 49th Annual Meeting of the Association for Computational Linguistics: Human Language Technologies*, pages 1318–1326, Portland, Oregon, USA. Association for Computational Linguistics.

David Kurokawa, Cyril Goutte, and Pierre Isabelle. 2009. Automatic detection of translated text and its impact on machine translation. In *Proceedings of Machine Translation Summit XII: Papers*, Ottawa, Canada.

Wah Meng Lim and Harish Tayyar Madabushi. 2020. UoB at SemEval-2020 task 12: Boosting BERT with corpus level information. In *Proceedings of the Fourteenth Workshop on Semantic Evaluation*, pages 2216–2221, Barcelona (online). International Committee for Computational Linguistics.

Pramod Kaushik Mudrakarta, Ankur Taly, Mukund Sundararajan, and Kedar Dhamdhere. 2018. Did the model understand the question? In *Proceedings of the 56th Annual Meeting of the Association for Computational Linguistics (Volume 1: Long Papers)*, pages 1896–1906, Melbourne, Australia. Association for Computational Linguistics.

Timothy Niven and Hung-Yu Kao. 2019. Probing neural network comprehension of natural language arguments. In *Proceedings of the 57th Annual Meeting of the Association for Computational Linguistics*, pages 4658–4664, Florence, Italy. Association for Computational Linguistics.

Anushka Prakash and Harish Tayyar Madabushi. 2020. Incorporating count-based features into pre-trained models for improved stance detection. In *Proceedings of the 3rd NLP4IF Workshop on NLP for Internet Freedom: Censorship, Disinformation, and Propaganda*, pages 22–32, Barcelona, Spain (Online). International Committee on Computational Linguistics (ICCL).

Daria Pylypenko, Kwabena Amponsah-Kaakyire, Koel Dutta Chowdhury, Josef van Genabith, and Cristina España-Bonet. 2021. Comparing feature-engineering and feature-learning approaches for multilingual translationese classification. In *Proceedings of the 2021 Conference on Empirical Methods in Natural Language Processing*, pages 8596–8611, Online and Punta Cana, Dominican Republic. Association for Computational Linguistics.

Ella Rabinovich and Shuly Wintner. 2015. Unsupervised identification of translationese. *Transactions of the Association for Computational Linguistics*, 3:419–432.

Biswarup Ray and Avishek Garain. 2020. Factuality classification using bert embeddings and support vector machines. In *IberLEF@SEPLN*.

Parker Riley, Isaac Caswell, Markus Freitag, and David Grangier. 2020. Translationese as a language in "multilingual" NMT. In *Proceedings of the 58th Annual Meeting of the Association for Computational Linguistics*, pages 7737–7746, Online. Association for Computational Linguistics.

Raphael Rubino, Ekaterina Lapshinova-Koltunski, and Josef van Genabith. 2016. Information density and quality estimation features as translationese indicators for human translation classification. In *Proceedings of the 2016 Conference of the North American Chapter of the Association for Computational Linguistics: Human Language Technologies*, pages 960–970, San Diego, California. Association for Computational Linguistics.

Avanti Shrikumar, Peyton Greenside, and Anshul Kundaje. 2017. Learning important features through propagating activation differences. In *Proceedings of the 34th International Conference on Machine Learning - Volume 70*, ICML'17, page 3145–3153. JMLR.org.

Karen Simonyan, Andrea Vedaldi, and Andrew Zisserman. 2014. Deep inside convolutional networks: Visualising image classification models and saliency maps. In *Workshop at International Conference on Learning Representations*.

Jasdeep Singh, Bryan McCann, Nitish Shirish Keskar, Caiming Xiong, and Richard Socher. 2019. XLDA: Cross-Lingual Data Augmentation for Natural Language Inference and Question Answering. *ArXiv*, abs/1905.11471.

Ilia Sominsky and Shuly Wintner. 2019. Automatic detection of translation direction. In *Proceedings of the International Conference on Recent Advances in Natural Language Processing (RANLP 2019)*, pages 1131–1140, Varna, Bulgaria. INCOMA Ltd.

Andreas Stolcke. 2002. SRILM – An extensible language modeling toolkit. In *Proceedings of the 7th International Conference on Spoken Language Processing (ICSLP 2002)*, pages 901–904.

Sara Stymne. 2017. The effect of translationese on tuning for statistical machine translation. In *The 21st Nordic Conference on Computational Linguistics*, pages 241–246.

Mukund Sundararajan, Ankur Taly, and Qiqi Yan. 2017. Axiomatic attribution for deep networks. In *Proceedings of the 34th International Conference on Machine Learning - Volume 70*, ICML'17, page 3319–3328. JMLR.org.

Elke Teich. 2003. *Cross-Linguistic Variation in System und Text. A Methodology for the Investigation of Translations and Comparable Texts*. Mouton de Gruyter, Berlin.

Antonio Toral, Sheila Castilho, Ke Hu, and Andy Way. 2018. Attaining the Unattainable? Reassessing Claims of Human Parity in Neural Machine Translation. In *Proceedings of the Third Conference on Machine Translation: Research Papers*, pages 113–123, Brussels, Belgium. Association for Computational Linguistics.

Gideon Toury. 1980. *In Search of a Theory of Translation*. The Porter Institute for Poetics and Semiotics, Tel Aviv University, Tel Aviv.

Hans van Halteren. 2008. Source language markers in EUROPARL translations. In *Proceedings of the 22nd International Conference on Computational Linguistics (Coling 2008)*, pages 937–944, Manchester, UK. Coling 2008 Organizing Committee.

Vered Volansky, Noam Ordan, and Shuly Wintner. 2015. On the features of translationese. *Digital Scholarship in the Humanities*, 30(1):98–118.

Cheng Zhang and Hayato Yamana. 2020. WUY at SemEval-2020 task 7: Combining BERT and naive Bayes-SVM for humor assessment in edited news headlines. In *Proceedings of the Fourteenth Workshop on Semantic Evaluation*, pages 1071–1076, Barcelona (online). International Committee for Computational Linguistics.

Mike Zhang and Antonio Toral. 2019. The effect of translationese in machine translation test sets. In *Proceedings of the Fourth Conference on Machine Translation (Volume 1: Research Papers)*, pages 73–81, Florence, Italy. Association for Computational Linguistics.

A Appendix

A.1 Extra Information on the MPDE Dataset

We use version 2.0.0 of the MPDE dataset licensed under CC-BY 4.0. Specifically we use the *mono_de_es* train/dev/test splits of the German-Spanish language pair. Table 3 contains summary statistics of the data.

Split	Number of Examples
Train set	29580
Validation set	6366
Test	6344

Table 3: Dataset statistics.

A.2 Extra Information on BERT Models

With the exception of pretrained-BERT-ft, we use the *transformers* library.[7] Training is done across 4 NVIDIA GeForce GTX TITAN X GPUs with a batch size of 8 per GPU. We use a learning rate of $3 \cdot 10^{-5}$ and train or fine-tune for 5 epochs. Table 4 shows the number of parameters of the different BERT variants. Parameter counts include the embedding and respective prediction (classifier or regression) layers.

Model	Num. Params (M)
fromScratch-BERT	177.85
BERT-reg-full	177.94
BERT-reg-half	135.41
BERT-r2c-*	177.85
BERT-f2c $L = 1$	177.46
BERT-f2c $L = 80$	177.52
BERT-f2c $L = 256$	177.66
pretrained-BERT-f2c $L = 80$	177.52

Table 4: Number of parameters of the various BERT models.

[7]https://huggingface.co/transformers/model_doc/bert.html

A.3 Additional Layer Integrated Gradients saliency maps

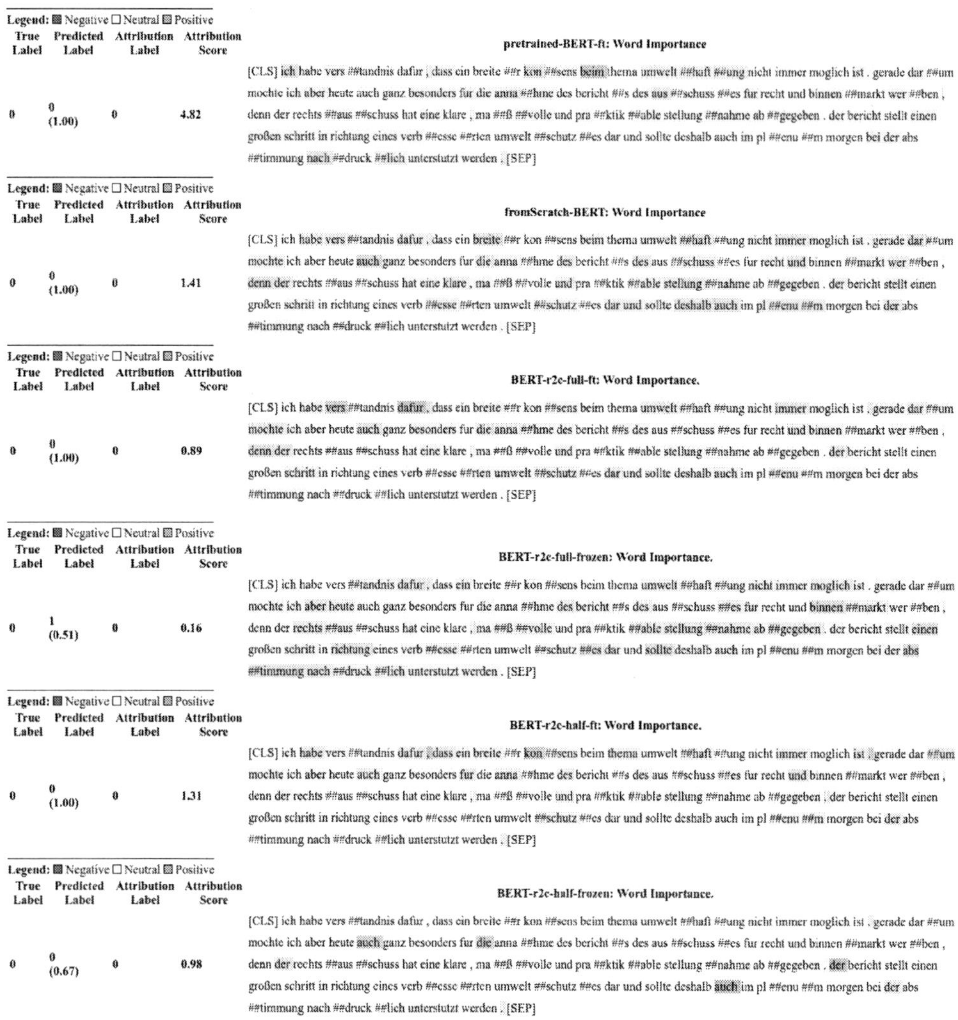

Figure 3: Layer Integrated Gradient saliency maps of input tokens contributing to the ground truth translationese label (here: original). Comparison of different models.

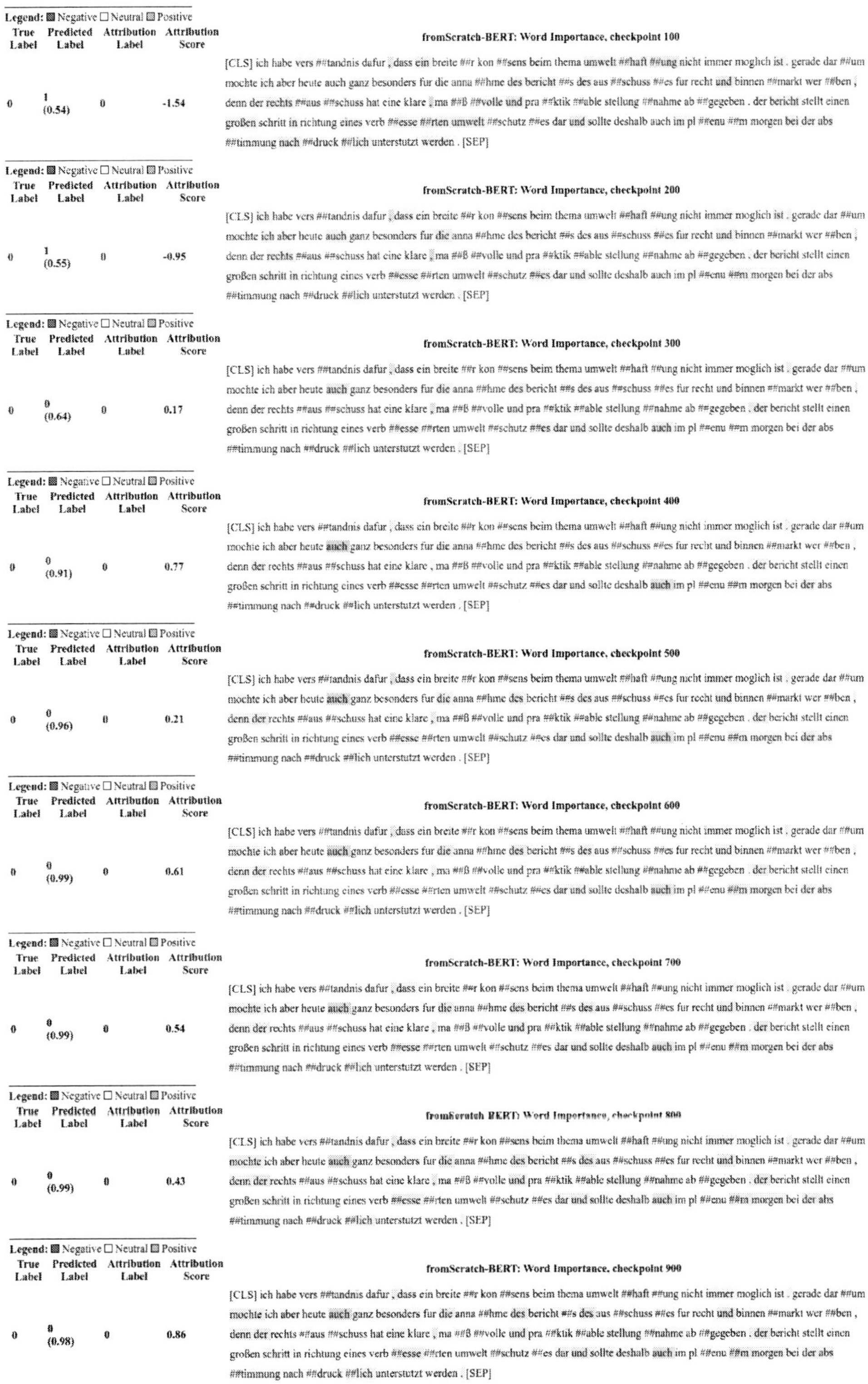

Figure 4: Layer Integrated Gradient saliency maps of input tokens contributing to the ground truth translationese label (here: original). BERT trained from scratch for translationese classification. Changes in attribution over the training checkpoints.

Figure 5: Layer Integrated Gradient saliency maps of input tokens contributing to the ground truth translationese label (here: original). BERT pretrained for handcrafted feature prediction, and fine-tuned for translationese classification. Changes in attribution over the training checkpoints.

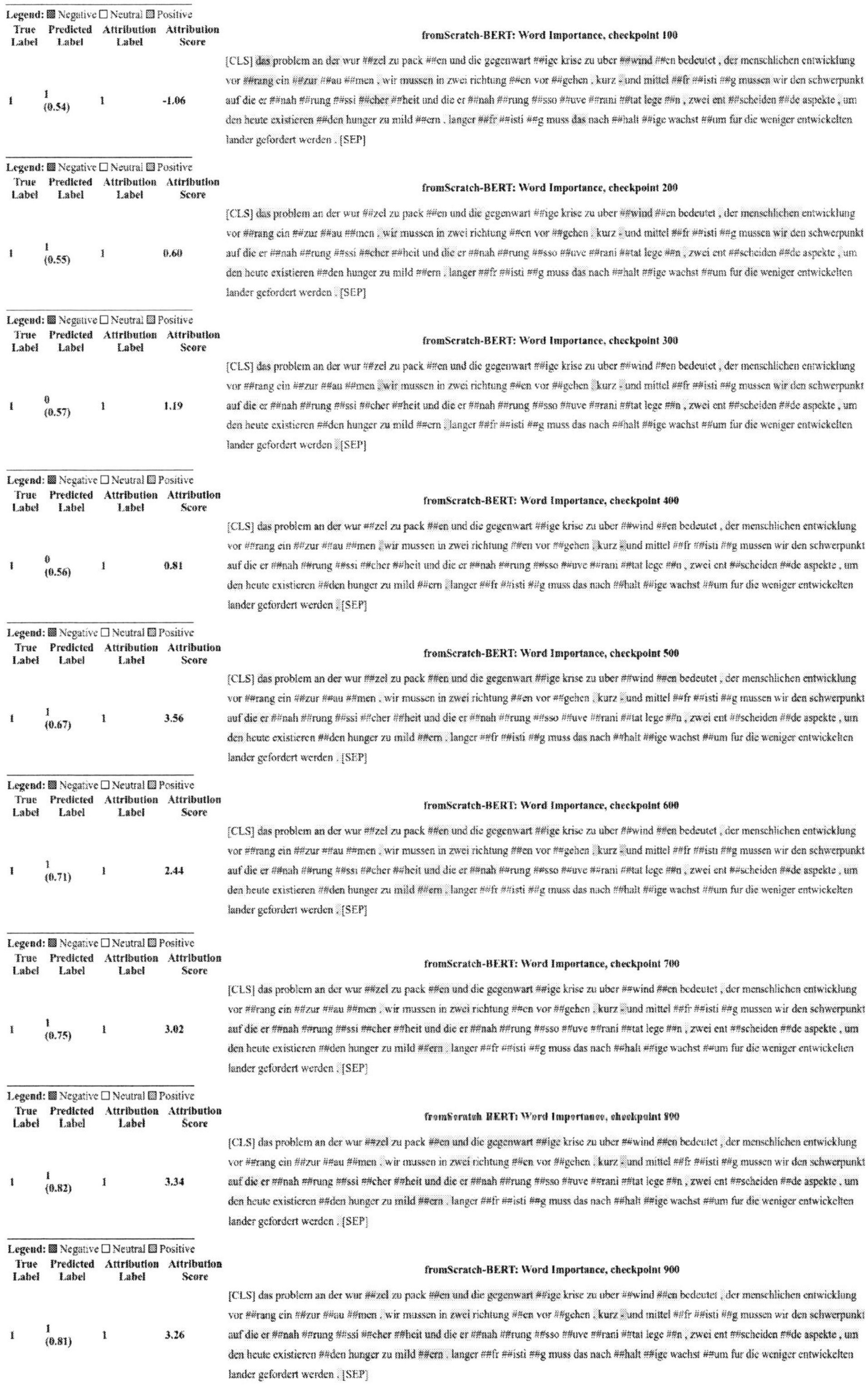

Figure 6: Layer Integrated Gradient saliency maps of input tokens contributing to the ground truth translationese label (here: translation). BERT trained from scratch for translationese classification. Changes in attribution over the training checkpoints.

Legend: ■ Negative □ Neutral ■ Positive

True Label	Predicted Label	Attribution Label	Attribution Score
1	1 (0.76)	1	1.11

BERT-r2c-full-ft: Word Importance, checkpoint 100

[CLS] das problem an der wur ##zel zu pack ##en und die gegenwart ##ige krise zu uber ##wind ##en bedeutet , der menschlichen entwicklung vor ##rang ein ##zur ##au ##men . wir mussen in zwei richtung ##en vor ##gehen . kurz - und mittel ##fr ##isti ##g mussen wir den schwerpunkt auf die er ##nah ##rung ##ssi ##cher ##heit und die er ##nah ##rung ##sso ##uve ##rani ##tat lege ##n , zwei ent ##scheiden ##de aspekte . um den heute existieren ##den hunger zu mild ##ern . langer ##fr ##isti ##g muss das nach ##halt ##ige wachst ##um fur die weniger entwickelten lander gefordert werden . [SEP]

Legend: ■ Negative □ Neutral ■ Positive

True Label	Predicted Label	Attribution Label	Attribution Score
1	0 (0.82)	1	0.98

BERT-r2c-full-ft: Word Importance, checkpoint 200

[CLS] das problem an der wur ##zel zu pack ##en und die gegenwart ##ige krise zu uber ##wind ##en bedeutet , der menschlichen entwicklung vor ##rang ein ##zur ##au ##men . wir mussen in zwei richtung ##en vor ##gehen . kurz - und mittel ##fr ##isti ##g mussen wir den schwerpunkt auf die er ##nah ##rung ##ssi ##cher ##heit und die er ##nah ##rung ##sso ##uve ##rani ##tat lege ##n , zwei ent ##scheiden ##de aspekte , um den heute existieren ##den hunger zu mild ##ern . langer ##fr ##isti ##g muss das nach ##halt ##ige wachst ##um fur die weniger entwickelten lander gefordert werden . [SEP]

Legend: ■ Negative □ Neutral ■ Positive

True Label	Predicted Label	Attribution Label	Attribution Score
1	1 (0.93)	1	2.64

BERT-r2c-full-ft: Word Importance, checkpoint 300

[CLS] das problem an der wur ##zel zu pack ##en und die gegenwart ##ige krise zu uber ##wind ##en bedeutet , der menschlichen entwicklung vor ##rang ein ##zur ##au ##men . wir mussen in zwei richtung ##en vor ##gehen . kurz - und mittel ##fr ##isti ##g mussen wir den schwerpunkt auf die er ##nah ##rung ##ssi ##cher ##heit und die er ##nah ##rung ##sso ##uve ##rani ##tat lege ##n , zwei ent ##scheiden ##de aspekte . um den heute existieren ##den hunger zu mild ##ern . langer ##fr ##isti ##g muss das nach ##halt ##ige wachst ##um fur die weniger entwickelten lander gefordert werden . [SEP]

Legend: ■ Negative □ Neutral ■ Positive

True Label	Predicted Label	Attribution Label	Attribution Score
1	1 (0.91)	1	2.69

BERT-r2c-full-ft: Word Importance, checkpoint 400

[CLS] das problem an der wur ##zel zu pack ##en und die gegenwart ##ige krise zu uber ##wind ##en bedeutet , der menschlichen entwicklung vor ##rang ein ##zur ##au ##men . wir mussen in zwei richtung ##en vor ##gehen . kurz - und mittel ##fr ##isti ##g mussen wir den schwerpunkt auf die er ##nah ##rung ##ssi ##cher ##heit und die er ##nah ##rung ##sso ##uve ##rani ##tat lege ##n , zwei ent ##scheiden ##de aspekte , um den heute existieren ##den hunger zu mild ##ern . langer ##fr ##isti ##g muss das nach ##halt ##ige wachst ##um fur die weniger entwickelten lander gefordert werden . [SEP]

Legend: ■ Negative □ Neutral ■ Positive

True Label	Predicted Label	Attribution Label	Attribution Score
1	1 (0.70)	1	2.84

BERT-r2c-full-ft: Word Importance, checkpoint 500

[CLS] das problem an der wur ##zel zu pack ##en und die gegenwart ##ige krise zu uber ##wind ##en bedeutet , der menschlichen entwicklung vor ##rang ein ##zur ##au ##men . wir mussen in zwei richtung ##en vor ##gehen . kurz - und mittel ##fr ##isti ##g mussen wir den schwerpunkt auf die er ##nah ##rung ##ssi ##cher ##heit und die er ##nah ##rung ##sso ##uve ##rani ##tat lege ##n , zwei ent ##scheiden ##de aspekte , um den heute existieren ##den hunger zu mild ##ern . langer ##fr ##isti ##g muss das nach ##halt ##ige wachst ##um fur die weniger entwickelten lander gefordert werden . [SEP]

Legend: ■ Negative □ Neutral ■ Positive

True Label	Predicted Label	Attribution Label	Attribution Score
1	1 (0.75)	1	3.27

BERT-r2c-full-ft: Word Importance, checkpoint 600

[CLS] das problem an der wur ##zel zu pack ##en und die gegenwart ##ige krise zu uber ##wind ##en bedeutet , der menschlichen entwicklung vor ##rang ein ##zur ##au ##men . wir mussen in zwei richtung ##en vor ##gehen . kurz - und mittel ##fr ##isti ##g mussen wir den schwerpunkt auf die er ##nah ##rung ##ssi ##cher ##heit und die er ##nah ##rung ##sso ##uve ##rani ##tat lege ##n , zwei ent ##scheiden ##de aspekte , um den heute existieren ##den hunger zu mild ##ern . langer ##fr ##isti ##g muss das nach ##halt ##ige wachst ##um fur die weniger entwickelten lander gefordert werden . [SEP]

Legend: ■ Negative □ Neutral ■ Positive

True Label	Predicted Label	Attribution Label	Attribution Score
1	1 (0.71)	1	3.61

BERT-r2c-full-ft: Word Importance, checkpoint 700

[CLS] das problem an der wur ##zel zu pack ##en und die gegenwart ##ige krise zu uber ##wind ##en bedeutet , der menschlichen entwicklung vor ##rang ein ##zur ##au ##men . wir mussen in zwei richtung ##en vor ##gehen . kurz - und mittel ##fr ##isti ##g mussen wir den schwerpunkt auf die er ##nah ##rung ##ssi ##cher ##heit und die er ##nah ##rung ##sso ##uve ##rani ##tat lege ##n , zwei ent ##scheiden ##de aspekte , um den heute existieren ##den hunger zu mild ##ern . langer ##fr ##isti ##g muss das nach ##halt ##ige wachst ##um fur die weniger entwickelten lander gefordert werden . [SEP]

Legend: ■ Negative □ Neutral ■ Positive

True Label	Predicted Label	Attribution Label	Attribution Score
1	1 (0.71)	1	3.52

BERT-r2c-full-ft: Word Importance, checkpoint 800

[CLS] das problem an der wur ##zel zu pack ##en und die gegenwart ##ige krise zu uber ##wind ##en bedeutet , der menschlichen entwicklung vor ##rang ein ##zur ##au ##men . wir mussen in zwei richtung ##en vor ##gehen . kurz - und mittel ##fr ##isti ##g mussen wir den schwerpunkt auf die er ##nah ##rung ##ssi ##cher ##heit und die er ##nah ##rung ##sso ##uve ##rani ##tat lege ##n , zwei ent ##scheiden ##de aspekte , um den heute existieren ##den hunger zu mild ##ern . langer ##fr ##isti ##g muss das nach ##halt ##ige wachst ##um fur die weniger entwickelten lander gefordert werden . [SEP]

Legend: ■ Negative □ Neutral ■ Positive

True Label	Predicted Label	Attribution Label	Attribution Score
1	1 (0.81)	1	3.59

BERT-r2c-full-ft: Word Importance, checkpoint 900

[CLS] das problem an der wur ##zel zu pack ##en und die gegenwart ##ige krise zu uber ##wind ##en bedeutet , der menschlichen entwicklung vor ##rang ein ##zur ##au ##men . wir mussen in zwei richtung ##en vor ##gehen . kurz - und mittel ##fr ##isti ##g mussen wir den schwerpunkt auf die er ##nah ##rung ##ssi ##cher ##heit und die er ##nah ##rung ##sso ##uve ##rani ##tat lege ##n , zwei ent ##scheiden ##de aspekte , um den heute existieren ##den hunger zu mild ##ern . langer ##fr ##isti ##g muss das nach ##halt ##ige wachst ##um fur die weniger entwickelten lander gefordert werden . [SEP]

Figure 7: Layer Integrated Gradient saliency maps of input tokens contributing to the ground truth translationese label (here: translation). BERT pretrained for handcrafted feature prediction, and fine-tuned for translationese classification. Changes in attribution over the training checkpoints.

Probing GPT-3's Linguistic Knowledge on Semantic Tasks

Lining Zhang New York University lz2332@nyu.edu

Mengchen Wang New York University mw3723@nyu.edu

Liben Chen New York University lc4438@nyu.edu

Wenxin Zhang New York University wz2164@nyu.edu

Abstract

GPT-3 has attracted much attention from both academia and industry. However, it is still unclear what GPT-3 has understood or learned especially in linguistic knowledge. Some studies have shown linguistic phenomena including negation and tense are hard to be recognized by language models such as BERT. In this study, we conduct probing tasks focusing on semantic information. Specifically, we investigate GPT-3's linguistic knowledge on semantic tasks to identify tense, the number of subjects, and the number of objects for a given sentence. We also experiment with different prompt designs and temperatures of the decoding method. Our experiment results suggest that GPT-3 has acquired linguistic knowledge to identify certain semantic information in most cases, but still fails when there are some types of disturbance happening in the sentence. We also perform error analysis to summarize some common types of mistakes that GPT-3 has made when dealing with certain semantic information.

1 Introduction

GPT-3 (Brown et al., 2020) is a large neural language model (NLM) released in 2020, and it has realized state-of-the-art performance on various language tasks. Disregarding its achievement in recent years, however, few pieces of literature interpret well what would happen inside GPT-3, as well as the knowledge it has acquired or represented. This is also true for understanding linguistic phenomena, which represent all features and grammar that a linguist should study (Bhatt et al., 2011). Based on recent studies, like the task-agnostic methodology named CheckList (Ribeiro et al., 2020), it is revealed that NLP models have a high failure rate in testing linguistic phenomena, though they may perform well in many other language tasks. This paper contributes to the existing literature by making an effort on understanding GPT-3's knowledge of the linguistic phenomenon, especially with a focus on semantic information including tense and singularity or plurality of the number of subject and object of a given sentence.

The SentEval probing tasks (Conneau et al., 2018) introduce 10 probing tasks covering the aspects of surface information, syntactic information, and semantic information. In our study, we want to evaluate GPT-3's knowledge and understanding of linguistic phenomena, thus we focus on the aspect of semantic information. Specifically, we apply the semantic tasks (Tense, SubjNum, and ObjNum) to test GPT-3's linguistic knowledge to understand tense and singularity or plurality of the number of subject and object, which do not involve any replacement or inversion of source corpus. (See section 3.1 for details of these semantic tasks.)

For our experiment, we design zero-shot and few-shot prompts separately, which means different numbers of examples from the dataset appear in the prompt. We also set the binary choice question like "Is the number of the subject of the sentence singular or plural?" as the default prompt style, while designing another general prompt that allows GPT-3 to give its own answer to the general question. More details about prompt design can be found in Table 1. For the decoding method, we set temperature as 0, 0.5, 0.7, and 0.9 accordingly, where lower temperature means GPT-3 will take fewer risks when making the prediction. We test the semantic tasks from SentEval on GPT-3 with combinations of the above prompt and temperature, and calculate accuracy for each type of linguistic phenomena in the probing task.

Based on our experiment result, we find that GPT-3 has acquired some linguistic knowledge to understand semantic information like tense and singularity or plurality of subject and object, though it may be disturbed in some cases. Besides, we notice that designing the prompt with the general question might lead to model performance degradation. The model tends to provide irrelevant answers, since

Proceedings of the Fifth BlackboxNLP Workshop on Analyzing and Interpreting Neural Networks for NLP, pages 297 - 304
December 8, 2022 ©2022 Association for Computational Linguistics

Table 1: Examples of Different Prompt Design.

Prompt Design	Example
zero-shot prompt with **default** style	Is the sentence "It senses your movement." present or past?
zero-shot prompt with **general** style	What is the tense of the sentence "It senses your movement."?
few-shot prompt with **default** style	Is the sentence "He messed with you." present or past? ⇒ past Is the sentence "It senses your movement." present or past? ⇒?

no expected choice is provided as in the default prompt style. We also find that variation in temperature has a minor impact on GPT-3's performance. Further, it is unexpected that more examples in the few-short prompts confuse and hurt the model in some tasks, rather than providing more hints.

Our work contributes to the stream of the work on probing the large language models, which helps us better understand what linguistic properties the model has acquired or represented. Specifically, we provide better insights on GPT-3's linguistic knowledge of certain semantic information.

2 Related Work

In recent years, although pre-trained language models like BERT (Devlin et al., 2019) have achieved state-of-the-art performance in many NLP tasks, it is still difficult to figure out what linguistic information is learned by the language representations.

Probing tasks are designed to test whether language models have encoded linguistic phenomena in learned representations by training a probing classifier on these representations. In an early study of machine translation, Shi et al. (2016) convert source sentences into encoded representations by the neural machine translation model, and train a logistic regression model on these representations to predict syntactic labels. In another study, Adi et al. (2017) design tasks to measure what extent the sentence representation from CBOW (Mikolov et al., 2013) and LSTM auto-encoder encodes its length, the identities of words within it, and word order. Their results indicate that the probing task is an effective way to evaluate the language model's ability to learn linguistic information.

Thus, many recent works have made some efforts to profile neural language models (NLMs) (Marvin and Linzen, 2018; Warstadt et al., 2019; Miaschi et al., 2020). For example, Marvin and Linzen (2018) test whether the language model assigns a higher probability to the grammatical sentence than the ungrammatical ones, showing that the performance of the language model lags behind the human performance in recognizing the grammaticality of the sentence. Warstadt et al. (2019) also assess the NLM's ability on learning grammatical knowledge and show that the BERT has significant knowledge of some grammatical features in sentences. Miaschi et al. (2020) test the model's ability to understand linguistic features, such as sentence length and part-of-speech tagging (POS tagging). It reveals that "the more NLM stores readable linguistic information of a sentence, the stronger its predictive power". Many other works also focus on understanding the attention mechanism of NLMs (Tang et al., 2018; Jain and Wallace, 2019; Clark et al., 2019). For example, Clark et al. (2019) conduct an analysis on BERT's attention and show that "certain attention heads correspond well to linguistic notions of syntax and coreference".

Previous work has provided evidence of NLM's ability to learn linguistic knowledge from the data. Some work tries to understand whether the learned linguistic knowledge has a particular structure (e.g. hierarchical structure) (Belinkov et al., 2018; Lin et al., 2019). These works have developed important probing tasks that profile the different aspects of the linguistic knowledge of NLMs. We follow the approach to conduct our own experiments of probing tasks on exploring GPT-3's ability to understand linguistic phenomena.

3 Experiment

We test the semantic tasks (Tense, SubjNum, and ObjNum) from SentEval (Conneau et al., 2018) on GPT-3 with combinations of different prompt designs and temperatures, and calculate accuracy for each type of linguistic phenomena in the probing task.

3.1 Dataset

We use the SentEval dataset with a focus on probing tasks of semantic information. Specifically, we apply the semantic tasks of Tense, SubjNum, and ObjNum to test GPT-3's linguistic knowledge.

The Tense task is a binary classification task that predicts whether the tense of the main verb of a sentence is present (PRES) or past (PAST). The SubjNum task is also a binary classification task that predicts whether the number of the subject of a sentence is singular (NN) or plural (NNS). The ObjNum task is almost the same as the SubjNum task, but it predicts the number of the object of a sentence instead.

The original SentEval dataset has over 100 thousand of records for each probing task. Given the computational efficiency, we randomly sample a subset of 500 records for each semantic task of Tense, SubjNum, and ObjNum to run our experiments. The datasets and codes are available at `https://github.com/lining-zhang/GPT-3_Linguistic`.

3.2 Experimental Design

Baseline Experiment For our baseline experiment, we use the prompt from the OpenAI API ("QA prompt")[1], with some modifications on the instruction part of the prompt. This makes our default prompt zero-shot, which means no examples from the SentEval probing dataset appear in the prompt. We also design the question in the default prompt to directly specify the labels that GPT-3 should choose from. For the decoding method, we set the temperature to 0, which means GPT-3 will take fewer risks when making the prediction. For the engine, we use "text-davinci-002"[2] for all experiments, which is the most capable GPT-3 model for all kinds of tasks.

Default Prompt vs General Prompt For the default prompt style, we set the binary choice question like "Is the number of the subject of the sentence singular or plural?" to appear in the prompt. This default style specifies the exact answers that GPT-3 is expected to choose from. To investigate the effect of the prompt design, we also design another general prompt that allows GPT-3 to directly give its own answer to the general question like "What is the number of the subject of the sentence?". This general prompt style gives GPT-3 more freedom to generate its own answer without restriction to certain choices, but still with the risk that it may not be able to find the expected answer. The experiments of the default prompt and general prompt are all zero-shot. Examples of different prompt designs can be found in Table 1.

Temperature Variations To test the influence of temperature on model performance, we measure GPT-3's linguistic knowledge on the semantic tasks with the temperature variation of 0, 0.5, 0.7, and 0.9 accordingly. Both default and general prompts are tested.

Few-shot Experiment To test whether the model benefits from more examples, we provide randomly selected examples of the linguistic phenomena to create the few-shot prompt. Based on the assumption that the number of examples in the few-shot prompt might also have an effect on the model's performance, we vary the number of examples provided, while keeping all few-shot prompts in the default style and setting the temperature to 0. We experiment with two examples and five examples in the few-shot prompt separately. See appendix A for more few-shot learning examples.

Evaluation To evaluate GPT-3's performance on each semantic task, we compare the response returned by GPT-3 with the true label. If GPT-3 predicts the true label correctly, we will assign a new label of response type with a value of 1. If GPT-3 predicts the true label adversely, we will assign the label of response type with a value of 2. If the response GPT-3 returned doesn't hit any of the true labels, or even doesn't make sense given the context, we will assign the label of response type with a value of 3. Then we calculate the ratio corresponding to each label of response type to show GPT-3's performance on each type of linguistic phenomena in the semantic probing task.

3.3 Results

Based on the answers returned from GPT-3, we categorize the responses into three response types which indicate their prediction as correct, adverse, or irrelevant. Detailed proportions for each case can be found in Table 2 and the corresponding visualization can be found in Figure 1. Considering the case that GPT-3 cannot detect linguistics phenomena at all and tends to give responses simply by random guess, then the ratio of each label of response type would all be approximately 0.33.

In terms of the default prompt style, which provides options like "Is the tense of the sentence past or present?", we find that GPT-3 has acquired some linguistic knowledge to understand semantic information like tense and singularity or plurality of sub-

[1] `https://openai.com/api/`

[2] `https://beta.openai.com/docs/models/gpt-3`

Table 2: Experiment Results for Combinations of Different Prompt Design and Temperature.

Experimental Setting	Task Name	Correct Answer (Label 1)	Adverse Answer (Label 2)	Irrelevant Answer (Label 3)
Default Prompt Temperature=0	Tense	0.712	0.288	0
	SubjNum	0.74	0.254	0.006
	ObjNum	0.608	0.392	0
Default Prompt Temperature=0.5	Tense	0.718	0.28	0.002
	SubjNum	0.698	0.276	0.026
	ObjNum	0.596	0.404	0
Default Prompt Temperature=0.7	Tense	0.698	0.3	0.002
	SubjNum	0.684	0.3	0.016
	ObjNum	0.6	0.398	0.002
Default Prompt Temperature=0.9	Tense	0.698	0.294	0.008
	SubjNum	0.662	0.3	0.038
	ObjNum	0.584	0.408	0.008
General Prompt Temperature=0	Tense	0.668	0.308	0.024
	SubjNum	0.044	0.03	0.926
	ObjNum	0.26	0.19	0.55
General Prompt Temperature=0.5	Tense	0.67	0.306	0.024
	SubjNum	0.062	0.04	0.898
	ObjNum	0.212	0.174	0.614
General Prompt Temperature=0.7	Tense	0.678	0.29	0.032
	SubjNum	0.048	0.042	0.91
	ObjNum	0.208	0.144	0.648
General Prompt Temperature=0.9	Tense	0.662	0.288	0.05
	SubjNum	0.06	0.058	0.882
	ObjNum	0.208	0.134	0.658
Five-shot examples Temperature=0	Tense	0.67	0.33	0
	SubjNum	0.718	0.282	0
	ObjNum	0.674	0.326	0
Two-shot examples Temperature=0	Tense	0.7	0.3	0
	SubjNum	0.72	0.28	0
	ObjNum	0.702	0.298	0

ject and object. However, when general prompts are provided, we notice that it degrades GPT-3's performance slightly regarding the tense query, and heavily regarding the singularity or plurality query. This issue results from the fact that GPT-3 sometimes cannot distinguish "What is the number of subject/object of the sentences" from "What is the subject/object of the sentences". Thus, GPT-3 tends to choose irrelevant answers in this situation.

For the variation of temperature, we find that it has a minor impact on GPT-3's performance regardless of which type of prompt is given. For the Tense task, the highest ratio reached by the correct answer (Label 1) happens when the temperature is 0.5 with the default prompt style and 0.7 with the general prompt style. For SubjNum and ObjNum tasks in whatever prompt style, the ratio of Label 1 tends to decrease slightly or fluctuate as the temperature increases.

Besides, GPT-3 performs better in identifying the singularity or plurality of the subject than that of the object given the default prompt style. This circumstance may result from the fact that GPT-3 can infer the subject's singularity or plurality not only based on the subject itself, but also on the predicate of the sentence. On the other hand, the structure of the object of sentences can be more confusing than the subject's most of the time, introducing more challenges to GPT-3 in syntactic parsing.

We first conduct the experiment with five examples in a few-shot prompt for each semantic task. The experiment is also in default prompt style with the temperature = 0. We notice that GPT-3's performance degrades for the Tense and SubjNum tasks but increases for the ObjNum task. This phenomenon matches the observation that identifying the singularity or plurality of the object is more difficult compared to the subject given a zero-shot prompt in the default style. Thus, in the few-shot

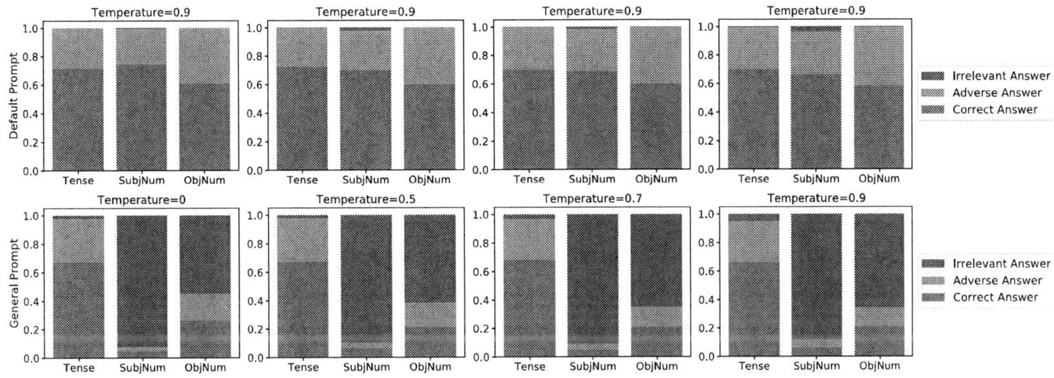

Figure 1: The Proportion of Different Answers Returned by GPT-3 for Each Combination of Prompt and Temperature

prompt, more examples are provided to support the ObjNum task which results in the increase. Besides, GPT-3 tends to be more confident in getting relevant answers, as the only percentage of the irrelevant answer which is not zero from the SubjNum task also goes to zero after several examples are provided in the few-shot prompt. After observing the degradation of model performance for the Tense and SubjNum tasks, we suspect that more examples obfuscate the model and reduce the number of examples to two in the few-shot prompt. We then observe an increase in model performance for all tasks, compared to results in the experiment with five examples. However, GPT-3's performance in the few-shot prompt still cannot rival the one from the baseline experiment for the Tense and SubjNum tasks, but improves for the ObjNum task.

4 Error Analysis

We perform the error analysis on records that GPT-3 does not answer correctly, which indicates the response is either adverse or irrelevant with Label 2 and Label 3 separately. We manually go through some records that get incorrect responses from GPT-3 to mark them with potential reasons and categorize them into several types of mistakes. However, this process requires a large amount of human annotations for each scenario to identify mistake types precisely, which may not be feasible in our case. Thus, this analysis may not exhaust all possibilities that GPT-3 might make mistakes when identifying certain linguistic phenomena and is not able to quantify the corresponding proportions, but it still provides some insights into how GPT-3 understands linguistic knowledge to some extent. Below is a brief summary of some common types of mistakes that GPT-3 has made when returning the response. Examples of each mistake type can be found in Table 3.

Disturbance of Quotation Mark For sentences that have partial content inside quotation marks as part of the dialogue, if the tense of the main verb is in past but the tense of the content inside quotation marks is in present, then GPT-3 will predict the tense as "present" incorrectly.

Disturbance of Concomitant Adverbial If the sentence has the present participle as the concomitant adverbial, but the tense of the main verb is in past, then GPT-3 will be disturbed by the adverbial and predict the tense as "present" incorrectly.

Identification of Negation If the sentence contains negation and the main verb followed by negation like "didn't" is in the present form, GPT-3 will ignore the context and return an incorrect "present" label for the whole sentence, focusing only on the form of the verb partially.

Disturbance of Clause If the sentence has a clause with a singular object, then GPT-3 will have difficulty identifying the object of the main sentence and its number.

Subject or Object Found, Not Its Number In some cases, GPT-3 finds the subject/object of the sentence, instead the number of the subject/object (singular or plural) as asked in the prompt.

5 Conclusion and Future Work

Based on our experiments and analysis, we find GPT-3 has acquired some linguistic knowledge to understand semantic information like tense and singularity or plurality of subject and object. Moreover, the variation in temperature does not have a big impact on GPT-3's performance, but design-

Table 3: Examples of Certain Error Types

Error Type	Task	Example	True Label	Predicted Label
Disturbance of Quotation Mark	Tense	"Beauty fades, but dumb is forever" Scarlet countered.	PAST	PRES
Disturbance of Concomitant Adverbial	Tense	Fake Mira commanded, pointing at Jace.	PAST	PRES
Identification of Negation	Tense	As if she truly didn't care whether or not someone loved her, as long as he at least pretended to.	PAST	PRES
Disturbance of Clause	ObjNum	Since the kiss that morning, Neal hadn't renewed his attentions.	NNS	NN
Subject or Object Found, Not Its Number	SubjNum	The rope around your waist will protect you if you fall.	NN	- (subject returned)

ing the prompt with the general question might lead the model to provide irrelevant answers. We also notice that the performance of identifying the number of the subject is commonly better than the performance in identifying objects, which explains why the ObjNum task benefits from the few-shot prompt. However, the few-shot learning experiment has a relatively degraded result for the Tense and SubjNum tasks, since more examples may obfuscate the model but the answer tends to be more relevant.

There are still some further works we could do based on the previous analysis. First, besides the baseline prompt and general prompt, there are still more combinations of different prompt designs and temperatures that we could test, suggesting that there might be more explorations when we analyze GPT-3's linguistic knowledge. Besides, our study mainly focuses on the semantic information of linguistic phenomena, which is restricted to a limited amount of probing tasks to test the model. A more exhaustive list of probing tasks or a carefully designed benchmark based on the error analysis could be created to better test the language model's linguistic knowledge in the future. Moreover, further human annotations could be applied in identifying mistake types for each scenario, which provides the quantitative measurement for each phenomenon where GPT-3 makes a mistake.

6 Acknowledgments

This work is finished as the course project for DS_GA 1012 Natural Language Understanding and Computational Semantics in Spring 2022 semester at New York University. We would like to thank our professor Samuel R. Bowman and our teaching assistant Richard Yuanzhe Pang for the suggestions for our paper, as well as Ruiqi Zhong for his initial proposal of this idea for this course.

References

Yossi Adi, Einat Kermany, Yonatan Belinkov, Ofer Lavi, and Yoav Goldberg. 2017. Fine-grained analysis of sentence embeddings using auxiliary prediction tasks. *ICLR 2017*.

Yonatan Belinkov, Lluís Màrquez, Hassan Sajjad, Nadir Durrani, Fahim Dalvi, and James Glass. 2018. Evaluating layers of representation in neural machine translation on part-of-speech and semantic tagging tasks. *arXiv preprint arXiv:1801.07772*.

Rajesh Bhatt, Owen Rambow, and Fei Xia. 2011. Linguistic phenomena, analyses, and representations: Understanding conversion between treebanks. In *Proceedings of 5th International Joint Conference on Natural Language Processing*, pages 1234–1242.

Tom Brown, Benjamin Mann, Nick Ryder, Melanie Subbiah, Jared D Kaplan, Prafulla Dhariwal, Arvind Neelakantan, Pranav Shyam, Girish Sastry, Amanda Askell, et al. 2020. Language models are few-shot learners. *Advances in neural information processing systems*, 33:1877–1901.

Kevin Clark, Urvashi Khandelwal, Omer Levy, and Christopher D Manning. 2019. What does bert look at? an analysis of bert's attention. *arXiv preprint arXiv:1906.04341*.

Alexis Conneau, German Kruszewski, Guillaume Lample, Loïc Barrault, and Marco Baroni. 2018. What you can cram into a single vector: Probing sentence embeddings for linguistic properties. In *Proceedings of the 56th Annual Meeting of the Association for Computational Linguistics (Long Papers)*, pages 2126–2136, Melbourne, Australia. Association for Computational Linguistics.

Jacob Devlin, Ming-Wei Chang, Kenton Lee, and Kristina Toutanova. 2019. Bert: Pre-training of deep bidirectional transformers for language understanding. In *Proceedings of NAACL-HLT 2019*, pages 4171–4186, Minneapolis, Minnesota. Association for Computational Linguistics.

Sarthak Jain and Byron C Wallace. 2019. Attention is not explanation. *arXiv preprint arXiv:1902.10186*.

Yongjie Lin, Yi Chern Tan, and Robert Frank. 2019. Open sesame: getting inside bert's linguistic knowledge. *arXiv preprint arXiv:1906.01698*.

Rebecca Marvin and Tal Linzen. 2018. Targeted syntactic evaluation of language models. *arXiv preprint arXiv:1808.09031*.

Alessio Miaschi, Dominique Brunato, Felice Dell'Orletta, and Giulia Venturi. 2020. Linguistic profiling of a neural language model. *arXiv preprint arXiv:2010.01869*.

Tomas Mikolov, Kai Chen, Greg Corrado, and Jeffrey Dean. 2013. Efficient estimation of word representations in vector space. *arXiv preprint arXiv:1301.3781*.

Marco Tulio Ribeiro, Tongshuang Wu, Carlos Guestrin, and Sameer Singh. 2020. Beyond accuracy: Behavioral testing of nlp models with checklist.

Xing Shi, Inkit Padhi, and Kevin Knight. 2016. Does string-based neural mt learn source syntax? In *Proceedings of the 2016 Conference on Empirical Methods in Natural Language Processing*, pages 1526–1534, Austin, Texas. Association for Computational Linguistics.

Gongbo Tang, Rico Sennrich, and Joakim Nivre. 2018. An analysis of attention mechanisms: The case of word sense disambiguation in neural machine translation. *arXiv preprint arXiv:1810.07595*.

Alex Warstadt, Yu Cao, Ioana Grosu, Wei Peng, Hagen Blix, Yining Nie, Anna Alsop, Shikha Bordia, Haokun Liu, Alicia Parrish, et al. 2019. Investigating bert's knowledge of language: Five analysis methods with npis. *arXiv preprint arXiv:1909.02597*.

A Appendix

We use the below examples to create the few-shot prompt. The binary value for the column of "Include in two-shot" indicates whether this example will be included in the few-shot prompt with two examples. By default, all the examples are included in the few-shot prompt with five examples.

Task Name	Include in two-shot	Example
Tense	1	Q: Is the tense of the sentence "He grunted And climbed to his feet, still holding me" present or past? A: Past
	1	Q: Is the tense of the sentence "It senses your movement" present or past? A: Present
	0	Q: Is the tense of the sentence "With a beer in his door hand and the window open to yell endlessly at everyone, he steered and shifted with the other hand" present or past? A:Past
	0	Q: Is the tense of the sentence, "His nostrils flare in reaction" present or past? A: Present
	0	Q: Is the tense of the sentence "Jack rolled and took me with him, capturing me on top of him, my head fitting perfectly into the hollow of his shoulder" present or past? A: Past
SubjNum	1	Q: Is the number of the subject of the sentence "Romulus was unreadable As ever" singular or plural? A: Singular
	1	Q: Is the number of the subject of the sentence "The wolves circled restlessly, their glowing yellow eyes fixed on the driver's door" singular or plural? A: Plural
	0	Q: Is the number of the subject of the sentence "There were several drips of whatever it was" singular or plural? A: Plural
	0	Q: Is the number of the subject of the sentence "An ape like Amy was not a cheap and stupid version of a human worker" singular or plural? A: Singular
	0	Q: Is the number of the subject of the sentence "Things were going even better than he had planned and it was all because of Misty" singular or plural? A: Plural
ObjNum	1	Q: Is the number of the object of the sentence "Practically purring with contentment, she rubbed her slightly bulging belly" singular or plural? A: Singular
	1	Q: Is the number of the object of the sentence "He flexed his biceps, and I groaned" singular or plural? A: Plural
	0	Q: Is the number of the object of the sentence "I served beers on autopilot" singular or plural? A: Plural
	0	Q: Is the number of the object of the sentence "The big man made a vague gesture" singular or plural? A: Singular
	0	Q: Is the number of the object of the sentence "The old woman could see my indecision" singular or plural? A: Singular

Table 4: Examples for Few-shot Prompt.

Garden Path Traversal in GPT-2

William Jurayj
Brown University
william@jurayj.com

William Rudman
Brown University
william_rudman@brown.edu

Carsten Eickhoff
Brown University
c.eickhoff@acm.org

Abstract

In recent years, large-scale transformer decoders such as the GPT-x family of models have become increasingly popular. Studies examining the behavior of these models tend to focus only on the output of the language modeling head and avoid analysis of the internal states of the transformer decoder. In this study, we present a collection of methods to analyze the hidden states of GPT-2 and use the model's navigation of garden path sentences as a case study. To enable this, we compile the largest currently available dataset of garden path sentences. We show that Manhattan distances and cosine similarities provide more reliable insights compared to established surprisal methods that analyze next-token probabilities computed by a language modeling head. Using these methods, we find that negating tokens have minimal impacts on the model's representations for unambiguous forms of sentences with ambiguity solely over what the object of a verb is, but have a more substantial impact of representations for unambiguous sentences whose ambiguity would stem from the voice of a verb. Further, we find that analyzing the decoder model's hidden states reveals periods of ambiguity that might conclude in a garden path effect but happen not to, whereas surprisal analyses routinely miss this detail.

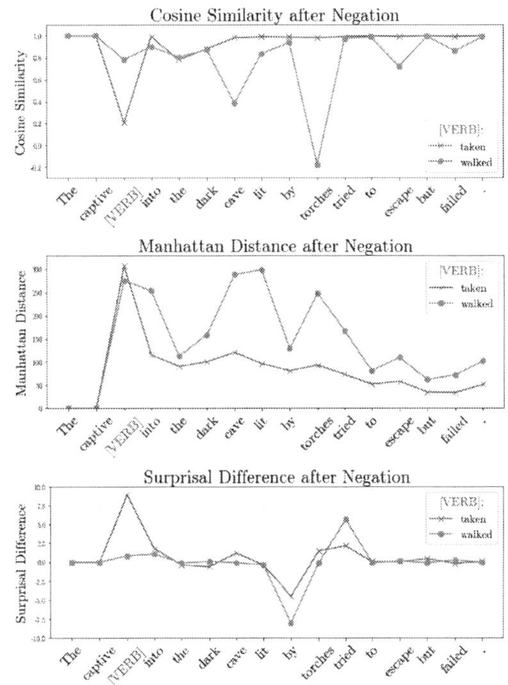

Figure 1: Hidden state relations (Top: cosine similarity, Middle: Manhattan distance, Bottom: surprisal difference) between negated and non-negated forms of garden path and unambiguous sentences. The ambiguous verb "walked" primes the effect later in the sentence, while the unambiguous "taken" avoids it. The verb "lit" introduces a similar ambiguity, which hidden state metrics show but surprisal misses because the next word "by" does not trigger a garden path effect.

1 Introduction

OpenAI's release of GPT-3 marked a major step in the field of massive language models, whose ability to generate news articles indistinguishable from those written by humans provides a salient example of the many social and political implications of these models (Brown et al., 2020; Wallace et al., 2019; Heidenreich and Williams, 2021). Within 2 years of BERT's release, over 150 studies have investigated BERT's structure, exploring how its internal representations enable powerful and flexible language comprehension (Coenen et al., 2019; Kovaleva et al., 2019; Tenney et al., 2019a; Rogers et al., 2020). A few such studies include a decoder model in the set of models examined, but do not specifically design their analyses around this type of architecture (Tenney et al., 2019b; Liu et al., 2019). Meanwhile, studies exploring GPT models alone tend to focus on properties of text generated from its language modeling head, and do not analyze the internal representations of the model in depth (Heidenreich and Williams, 2021; Brown et al., 2020).

Proceedings of the Fifth BlackboxNLP Workshop on Analyzing and Interpreting Neural Networks for NLP, pages 305 - 313
December 8, 2022 ©2022 Association for Computational Linguistics

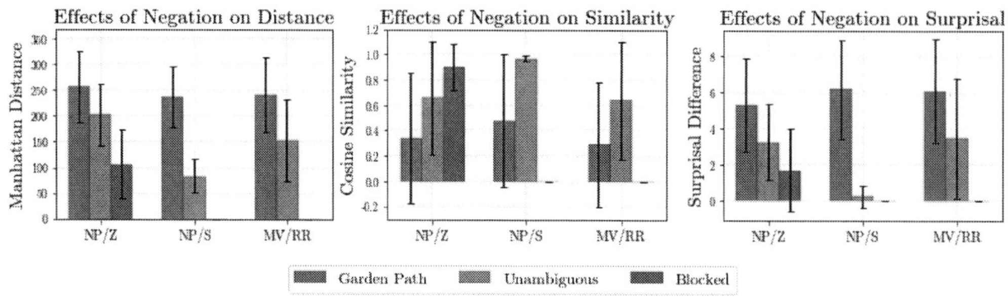

Figure 2: Left: Average Manhattan distances between sentence types and their negated forms. Center: Average Cosine similarities between sentence types and their negated forms. Right: Average surprisal differences between sentence types and their negated forms. Manhattan distances exhibit less variability than either cosine similarities or surprisal differences

The few studies that explore the hidden states of GPT-2 suggest an under-utilization of its massive latent space as representations are dominated by the presence of rogue dimensions (Ethayarajh, 2019; Cai et al., 2021; Rudman et al., 2021; Timkey and van Schijndel, 2021). As massive decoder models become more ubiquitous and powerful, it will become ever more important to understand the internal processes by which they generate content so they can be streamlined and improved upon.

In this paper, we use garden path traversal as a case study to demonstrate the value of directly analyzing properties of the embedding space in transformer decoder models. A garden path sentence is one where the parse that a reader expects at some point within the sentence is proven incorrect by the end of the sentence. We choose to explore this syntactic effect specifically because we believe the intuitive reaction a human has when reading such sentences provides a helpful frame for analyzing the behavior of a neural language model experiencing the same effect.

We expect that by looking at the hidden states from which next word likelihoods are computed, we can observe the same patterns that surprisal analysis reveals, while uncovering more nuanced trends that surprisal misses because it depends on the joint distribution of the hidden state and the next word. Moreover, we expect that Manhattan distances will exhibit less variance in the effect of negating a given sentence type than either surprisals or cosine similarities after a zero-mean transformation, because Manhattan distances are resilient to extreme values in a single dimension (Aggarwal et al., 2001). On the other hand, the next word likelihoods used to compute surprisal tend to depend heavily on these dimensions, while the zero-mean translation required to create meaningful angular differences around the origin mean that a few extreme dimensions expose cosine similarities to similarly high variances (Timkey and van Schijndel, 2021).

By analyzing how GPT-2 sequentially embeds tokens in space, we are able to identify how GPT-2 internally handles different garden path effects. Specifically, we show that GPT-2 recognizes potential but unrealized garden path effects using metrics that examine the model's hidden states, whereas surprisal analysis fails to reveal this finding. We argue that analysis of a decoder model's hidden states enables more robust analysis than can be done using the next word likelihoods alone, which themselves are distilled from these hidden states. The contributions of this study are as follows:

- to introduce the largest and most diverse dataset of garden path sentences currently available, along with construction functions to negate or extend the effect within each sentence,
- to demonstrate the advantage of analyzing syntactic properties such as garden path effects by examining geometric relationships between vectors in GPT-2's hidden states using Manhattan distance and cosine similarity,
- to motivate further study of the hidden states of transformer decoders as a more thorough alternative to the surprisal-based methods that are typically used to analyze language models.[1]

1.1 Related Work

Many studies into GPT or BERT involve fine-grained analyses of how the model handles specific syntactic phenomena, such as the garden path

[1]Code available at https://github.com/wjurayj/garden-path-gpt2

Sentence Type	Sentence Form	Sentence
NP/Z	Garden Path	When the dog scratched the vet took off the muzzle.
	Negated	When the dog scratched, the vet took off the muzzle.
	Blocked	When the dog scratched his owner the vet took off the muzzle.
	Unambiguous	When the dog struggled the vet took off the muzzle.
NP/S	Garden Path	The coach discovered the player tried to show off all the time.
	Negated	The coach discovered that the player tried to show off all the time.
	Unambiguous	The coach thought the player tried to show off all the time.
MV/RR	Garden Path	The horses raced past the barn fell into a ditch.
	Negated	The horses that were raced past the barn fell into a ditch.
	Unambiguous	The horses ridden past the barn fell into a ditch.

Table 1: Forms of NP/Z, NP/S, and MV/RR sentences included in our dataset, with the verb that triggers or would trigger the garden path effect underlined in red. Note that all of the perturbations can be combined to avoid the garden path effect, except for the blocked and unambiguous forms of the NP/Z sentence.

effect. Consider the sentence:

"Even though the girl phoned[,] the instructor was very upset with her for missing a lesson."

Without the comma, most readers will assume "the instructor" is the direct object of the verb "phoned", rather than the subject of the main clause's verb phrase, "was very upset" (van Schijndel and Linzen, 2019). Adding the comma immediately disqualifies the incorrect parse, nullifying the garden path effect. This method of preventing the effect is referred to as "negation" throughout this paper.

Analysis of garden path traversal is typically done by comparing the surprisal, or negative log likelihood, of the token that would trigger the garden path effect between garden path and negated sentences. The surprisal that a token induces from a language model can intuitively be understood to measure the amount of information that token adds to that model's representation of the sentence, as measured by the inverse of the degree to which the model anticipated that token. This is calculated using a language modeling head on top of GPT-2, and does not directly analyze the internal representations of the model from which these likelihoods are computed.

Previous studies into the navigation of these sentences find that sufficiently large models' relative surprisals at the disambiguating token between garden path and negated sentences show recognition of the garden path effect. However, these models systematically underestimate the magnitude of the effect observed in humans, suggesting that human recovery from an incorrect parse involves more than just the triggering token's lack of predictability (van Schijndel and Linzen, 2021, 2018). Further, using surprisal comparisons, Hu et al. (2020) show that GPT-2 recognizes garden path effects less successfully or consistently than smaller recurrent language models.

OpenAI has not released GPT-3's source code and parameters, so we instead analyze its predecessor GPT-2, which uses an almost identical architecture at a much smaller scale (1.5b parameters). Nonetheless, the methods we use to explore GPT-2's traversal of garden path effects can be easily generalized to study any decoder-based model.

2 Methods

2.1 Garden path sentence generation

The dataset used for these experiments builds on the combination of the NP/Z and NP/S sentences from Grodner et al. (2003) and the NP/Z and MV/RR sentences from Futrell et al. (2019), originally taken from Staub (2007) and Tabor and Hutchins (2004), and consists of 43 NP/Z sentences, 20 NP/S sentence, and 20 MV/RR sentences. Instead of building out side-by-side datasets of each type of sentence, however, we store the components of these sentences in tabular files, and include scripts to construct these sentences in various forms similar to those used by Futrell et al. (2019). Each sentence has a *garden path* and an *unambiguous* form, depending on whether the first verb allows for an ambiguous parse. Each of these forms can be *negated* with the addition of one or two tokens, which nullifies the garden path effect in an ambiguous sentence but makes no semantic difference in an unambiguous sentence. We provide this as a template to be extended indefinitely to meet the needs of future research. Examples of each sentence type's possible forms can be found along with a detailed description of these effects in Table 1.

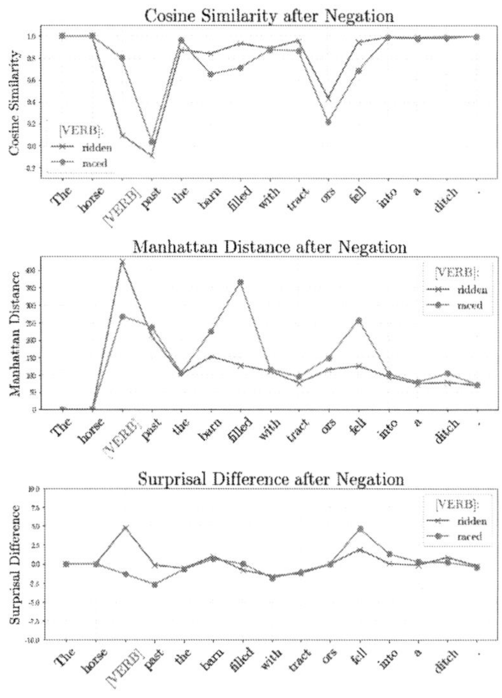

Figure 3: Hidden state relations (Top: cosine similarity, Middle: Manhattan distance, Bottom: surprisal difference) between negated and non-negated forms of garden path and unambiguous sentences. The ambiguous verb "raced" primes the effect later in the sentence, while the unambiguous "ridden" avoids it. Like in Figure 1, all metrics catch the garden path effect at the verb "fell", but only cosine similarity and Manhattan distance anticipate the possible effect at "filled"

2.1.1 NP/Z sentences

NP/Z is short for Noun Phrase/Zero complement. These are sentences where the first verb appears to take on a Noun Phrase as its direct object, but subsequently is revealed to have no (Zero) direct object at all (Futrell et al., 2019). The garden path effect in these sentences is caused by ambiguity about whether the verb of the leading subordinate clause has a direct object. These sentences have an additional *blocked* form, which nullifies its garden path effect by adding an explicit direct object to the leading verb. This is considered one of the stronger types of garden path effects, with an average increase in human reading time of 152 ms (Sturt et al., 1999).

The first NP/Z sentence in Table 1 evokes a garden path effect because the reader initially expects that "the vet" is the direct object of "scratched"; The negated form avoids the effect by using a comma to indicate the separation between the two clauses. The blocked form avoids the effect by adding the direct object "his owner" to block the ambiguity that triggers the effect, while the unambiguous form avoids the effect by replacing the transitive verb "scratched" with the intransitive verb "struggled" to avoid ambiguity around the verb's direct object.

Our dataset includes 43 distinct NP/Z sentences, and includes scripts allowing a user to easily transform these into unambiguous or blocked sentences. Moreover, each sentence has the option to include a negation, and an extension so as to increase the duration of the ambiguity.

2.1.2 NP/S sentences

NP/S is short for Noun Phrase/Sentential complement. These are sentences where the first verb appears to take the Noun Phrase as its direct object, but subsequently is revealed to have a sentence-like object as its complement (van Schijndel and Linzen, 2018). The garden path effect in these sentences is caused by ambiguity about whether the noun following the main clause's verb is that verb's direct object. This is considered one of the weaker types of garden path effects, with an average increase in human reading times of 50 ms (Sturt et al., 1999).

The first NP/S sentence in Table 1 evokes a garden path effect because the reader expects that "the player" is the direct object of the verb 'discovered' until the word "tried" reveals that it is her propensity to show off that the coach is discovering. The negated form avoids the effect by adding "that" before "the player" to eliminate the possibility that 'the player' is the verb's direct object. The unambiguous form avoids the effect altogether by using the verb "thought", which could not allow a person to be its direct object. Our dataset includes 20 distinct NP/S sentences, each of which can be negated, unambiguous, extended, or any combination thereof.

2.1.3 MV/RR sentences

MV/RR is short for Main Verb/Reduced Relative. These are sentences where prior to a disambiguator, the ambiguous verb could either be the main verb of the sentence or a verb that introduces a reduced relative clause (Futrell et al., 2019). The garden path effect in these sentences is caused by ambiguity about whether the past-tense verb of the leading subordinate clause is a past participle or the main verb of the sentence. This effect is considered

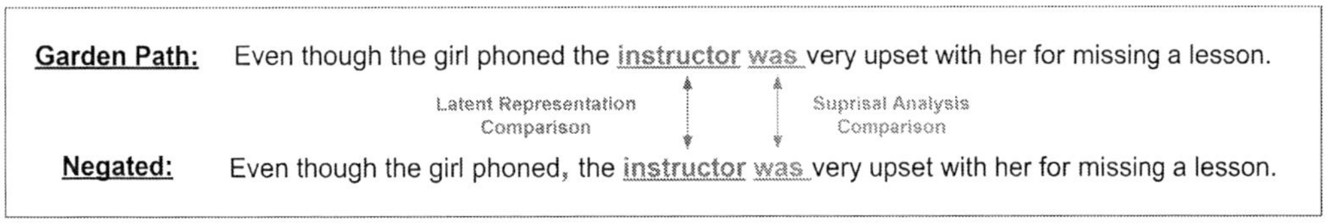

Figure 4: Method for comparing latent space metrics (cosine similarity, Manhattan distance) against surprisal difference.

stronger than that of an NP/S sentence, but reading time data to compare it with the other sentence types is not available.

The first MV/RR sentence in Table 1 evokes the garden path effect because the reader assumes "raced" is the main verb of the sentence, while the negated form negates this ambiguity by clarifying that "raced past the barn" is a descriptor for the horses rather than the main clause itself. Note that in some examples, the negating tokens are "who were" instead of "that were", but in both cases these tokens serve to un-reduce the relative participle. The unambiguous form avoids ambiguity altogether by replacing the ambiguous "raced" with the unambiguously passive "ridden". Our dataset includes 20 distinct MV/RR sentences, each of which can be negated, rendered unambiguous, extended, or any combination thereof.

2.2 Experimental design

The general structure of the tests we run is inspired by Futrell et al. (2019) and Hu et al. (2020). The key difference is that, where previous studies compare the model's surprisal at the disambiguating word, we examine the model's hidden state prior to this word. Figure 4 shows a visualization of this approach.

We compare each sentence to its negated form, computing the vector differences and cosine similarities between each token and its counterpart in the negated form (omitting the token[s] that were added to negate the garden path effect in that sentence type from the pairing process) after re-centering embeddings around the origin. We use Manhattan distance over Euclidean distance to compute scalars from the vector differences between sentences as is generally preferred in high dimensional spaces, where Euclidean distances are sensitive to the dimensions with the largest values (Aggarwal et al., 2001). Cosine similarities are computed after re-centering all vectors so that the distribution has a mean of zero, which prevents the metric from defaulting to near-maximum values and allows it to measure the true directional changes between vectors (Rudman et al., 2021). These side-by-side metrics are generated for all sentences' garden path and unambiguous forms, as well as for the blocked form of the NP/Z sentences.

We expect to see larger distances and lower similarities upon negation in garden path sentences than in unambiguous or blocked sentences. In the garden path sentences the negating tokens help to resolve some ambiguity, whereas in an already unambiguous sentence they will contribute minimally to the sentence's meaning prior to the triggering token.

3 Results & Discussion

Our analysis reveals several properties of GPT-2's experience of the garden path effect. Across all sentence types, Manhattan distances and cosine similarities show that the model reacts more heavily to negation of garden path sentences than it does to these sentences' unambiguous counterparts, as is reflected by surprisal analyses done here and in previous studies (Sarti, 2020).

Although our surprisal baselines mirror the trends seen in Manhattan distance, using Manhattan distances provides more consistent results compared to surprisal analysis. Our results demonstrating exceedingly high variance in the surprisal analysis is in line with the findings of Hu et al. (2020), who use surprisal to show that GPT-2 performs especially poorly and inconsistently on garden path effects. On the other hand, the high-level trends we expected to see are present across all metrics, with negation causing a less pronounced difference in unambiguous and blocked sentences than it does in garden path sentences. Whereas Figure 2 shows Manhattan distances to have relatively low variance compared to the other metrics we examine, cosine similarity and surprisal suffer from very high variances within each sentence form. We believe that this is due to Manhattan distance's resistance to GPT-2's rogue dimensions, which dominate cosine similarities after the zero-mean transformation because even relatively minor differences in a few of these dimensions will have a much more substantial effect on the angular difference than more major differences in many smaller dimensions would (Timkey and van Schijndel, 2021; Aggarwal et al., 2001).

Figure 1 illustrates how these high level trends appear within a given sentence. Here, the verb "tried" triggers the garden path effect, which is directly preceded by a spike in Manhattan distance and a dip in cosine similarity between the garden path and negated sentence forms as the model anticipates different continuations: in the garden path sentence the model is likely to predict some sort of punctuation or conjunction to end the clause, while in the negated form the model expects a verb to complete the clause that the ambiguous verb is subordinate to.

An interesting property of the specific example in Figure 1, "The captive walked into the dark cave lit by torches tried to escape but failed." is that the verb "lit" also triggers a momentary garden path effect; the sentence could, for instance, simply continue, "The captive walked into the dark cave lit the torches." In the first case, the verb "lit" is a reduced relative of "that was lit", which refers to the cave, whereas in the second case the captive is the subject of "lit", which is the main verb of the sentence and thus would trigger a garden path effect. Of course, the immediate next word "by" eliminates this possibility, which a human reader notices quickly enough that they do not experience the effect, but the decoder's causal attention mask allows it no such foresight.

This possibility is thus worth considering because it helps explain why there is a spike in Manhattan distance and a dip in cosine similarity at the preceding word, "cave". We believe the relative shallowness of the dip in cosine similarity before "lit" is due to the possible MV/RR ambiguity of the word, since even in the garden path case where punctuation can be expected, a verb such as "lit" can preempt an adjectival clause as it does here ("lit by torches"). This puts it in a curious superposition between introducing and triggering a garden path effect, at least until the next word "by" resolves this ambiguity. Notably, in the garden path form neither hidden state metric returns to its baseline value until after the verb "lit", because the model expects this verb leads a subordinate clause whereas in the negated form it considers both possibilities.

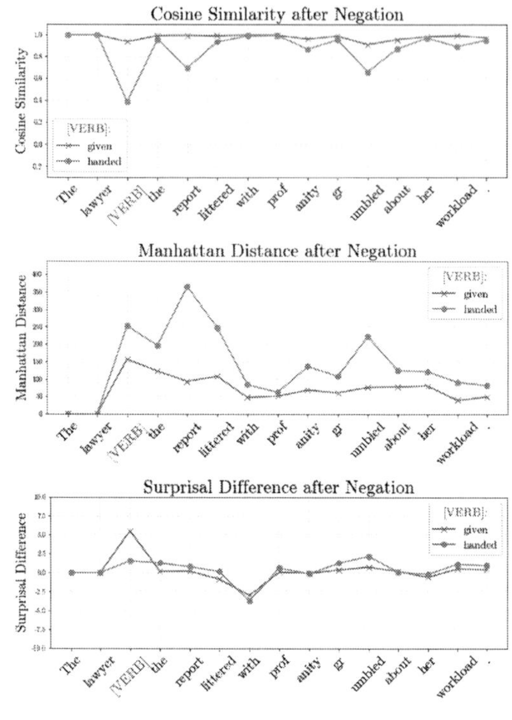

Figure 5: Hidden state relations (Top: cosine similarity, Middle: Manhattan distance, Bottom: surprisal difference) between negated and non-negated forms of garden path and unambiguous sentences. The ambiguous verb "handed" primes the effect later in the sentence, while the unambiguous "given" avoids it. Like in Figure 1, all metrics catch the garden path effect at the verb "grumbled", but only cosine similarity and Manhattan distance anticipate the possible effect at "littered"

On the other hand, the verb "tried" is not ambiguous in this way. The clause it might preempt, such as "tried for murder", would be improperly placed and awkward. Thus, the model's hidden states prior to the verb "tried" in the garden path and negated sentences are nearly orthogonal to each other, whereas they bear more similarity right before the verb "lit". Although surprisal spikes at the verb "tried" as well, the surprisal trajectory does not reflect the possible effect at "lit", illustrating the inadequacy of using this metric alone. This ambiguity, however, is only reflected in Manhattan distance and cosine similarity, and demonstrates how internal metrics can help us understand relationships between the model's syntactic states that surprisal analysis alone would miss. We argue that surprisal misses this effect because it depends entirely on the word that triggers a garden path effect rather than the state of the decoder prior to the trigger, which more holistically encodes the ambiguity that creates the environment where a garden path effect can occur. In this case, it seems that the prior likelihood of various constructions after 'lit' leads GPT-2 to suspect it leads a reduced relative clause (i.e. 'that was lit') and is not the sentence's main verb, but our distance metrics between the model's hidden states prior to this potential trigger show that GTP-2 nonetheless registers the possibility of a garden path effect. However, more work is needed to explore how exactly each of these metrics measures this abstract concept, and how sensitive they are to other syntactic and semantic effects.

We highlight two other examples of this phenomenon. In Figure 3, the preceding clause "The horse raced past the barn filled [...]" could be completed either with the actual continuation "with tractors [...]", or with a direct object for "filled", for instance: "The horse raced past the barn filled her trainer with admiration". In Figure 5, the clause "The lawyer handed the report littered [...]" could likewise either continue as shown, "with profanity [...]", or could instead be the main verb of a shorter sentence: "The lawyer handed the report littered as he walked across the street". Whereas surprisal overlooks the temporary ambiguities in these examples because it relies on the next word to trigger the garden path effect, hidden state metrics reveal them because they can directly measure the ambiguity itself.

Our analysis revealed a few unexpected results. Most prominent among these is the extent to which the addition of the negating token ("that") to unambiguous NP/S sentences leaves the hidden representation of the sentence unchanged. Across all metrics, the negated and garden path forms of NP/S sentences are closest together, showing that except in cases where it resolves a clear ambiguity, the negating token in these sentences contributes very little to the model's internal representation. The blocked form of NP/Z sentences shows a similar indifference to the negating token (in this case, the addition of a comma), which curiously does not extend to the unambiguous form.

4 Conclusion

This paper presents a suite of methods to analyze the internal representations of transformer decoder language models such as GPT-2, taking advantage of a richer reflection of the model's internal process than can be ascertained from the output of the language modeling head alone. We use Manhattan distance and cosine similarity between the hidden states of GPT-2 to show that the model is affected by garden path effects in ways that are predictable based on human readers' difficulty with these sentences. Although conventional surprisal analysis mirrors these effects in many cases, it exhibits higher variance than Manhattan distances, and misses certain nuances. On this basis, we argue that linguists should look to a decoder model's hidden state for a more complete picture of syntactic state than surprisal alone can report.

Our belief is that Manhattan distance should be the preferred metric for this type of analysis, but we invite researchers to introduce and explore new metrics to challenge this hypothesis. We hope that these early insights will help inspire deeper exploration of the hidden states of decoder-only language models. Possible directions for future work could more closely examine how information is transformed across different decoder layers within GPT-2, and might explore causes for differences between Manhattan distance and cosine similarity trajectories. The methods introduced in this study can also be used to explore decoder models' handling of arbitrary syntactic phenomena beyond garden path effects, such as verb subordination or negative polarity item licensing.

5 Limitations

One weakness of this type of analysis is the necessity of having side-by-side examples, with a single perturbation between them, to compare between. The beam search approach used by Aina and Linzen (2021) avoids this requirement, but still relies on the language modeling head, so more work is needed to integrate these benefits. Another difficulty is the size of the dataset; although larger than all previous datasets of garden path sentences, it only includes 83 distinct sentences, and while many more variations can be generated with the scripts we include, there is substantial overlap between these that makes training a model on these challenging. Finally, since weights for GPT-3 were not available at the time we conducted this research, our analysis is constrained to the smaller GPT-2.

References

Charu C. Aggarwal, Alexander Hinneburg, and Daniel A. Keim. 2001. On the surprising behavior of distance metrics in high dimensional space. In *Database Theory — ICDT 2001*, pages 420–434, Berlin, Heidelberg. Springer Berlin Heidelberg.

Laura Aina and Tal Linzen. 2021. The language model understood the prompt was ambiguous: Probing syntactic uncertainty through generation. *CoRR*, abs/2109.07848.

Tom B. Brown, Benjamin Mann, Nick Ryder, Melanie Subbiah, Jared Kaplan, Prafulla Dhariwal, Arvind Neelakantan, Pranav Shyam, Girish Sastry, Amanda Askell, Sandhini Agarwal, Ariel Herbert-Voss, Gretchen Krueger, Tom Henighan, Rewon Child, Aditya Ramesh, Daniel M. Ziegler, Jeffrey Wu, Clemens Winxter, Christopher Hesse, Mark Chen, Eric Sigler, Mateusz Litwin, Scott Gray, Benjamin Chess, Jack Clark, Christopher Berner, Sam McCandlish, Alec Radford, Ilya Sutskever, and Dario Amodei. 2020. Language models are few-shot learners.

Xingyu Cai, Jiaji Huang, Yuchen Bian, and Kenneth Church. 2021. Isotropy in the contextual embedding space: Clusters and manifolds. In *International Conference on Learning Representations*.

Andy Coenen, Emily Reif, Ann Yuan, Been Kim, Adam Pearce, Fernanda B. Viégas, and Martin Wattenberg. 2019. Visualizing and measuring the geometry of BERT. *CoRR*, abs/1906.02715.

Kawin Ethayarajh. 2019. How contextual are contextualized word representations? comparing the geometry of bert, elmo, and GPT-2 embeddings. *CoRR*, abs/1909.00512.

Richard Futrell, Ethan Wilcox, Takashi Morita, Peng Qian, Miguel Ballesteros, and Roger Levy. 2019. Neural language models as psycholinguistic subjects: Representations of syntactic state.

Daniel Grodner, Edward Gibson, Vered Argaman, and Maria Babyonyshev. 2003. Against repair-based reanalysis in sentence comprehension. *Journal of Psycholinguistic Research*, 32(2):141–166.

Hunter Heidenreich and Jake Williams. 2021. The earth is flat and the sun is not a star: The susceptibility of gpt-2 to universal adversarial triggers. pages 566–573.

Jennifer Hu, Jon Gauthier, Peng Qian, Ethan Wilcox, and Roger Levy. 2020. A systematic assessment of syntactic generalization in neural language models. In *Proceedings of the 58th Annual Meeting of the Association for Computational Linguistics*, pages 1725–1744, Online. Association for Computational Linguistics.

Olga Kovaleva, Alexey Romanov, Anna Rogers, and Anna Rumshisky. 2019. Revealing the dark secrets of BERT. *CoRR*, abs/1908.08593.

Nelson F. Liu, Matt Gardner, Yonatan Belinkov, Matthew E. Peters, and Noah A. Smith. 2019. Linguistic knowledge and transferability of contextual representations. In *Proceedings of the 2019 Conference of the North American Chapter of the Association for Computational Linguistics: Human Language Technologies, Volume 1 (Long and Short Papers)*, pages 1073–1094, Minneapolis, Minnesota. Association for Computational Linguistics.

Anna Rogers, Olga Kovaleva, and Anna Rumshisky. 2020. A primer in bertology: What we know about how BERT works. *CoRR*, abs/2002.12327.

William Rudman, Nate Gillman, Taylor Rayne, and Carsten Eickhoff. 2021. Isoscore: Measuring the uniformity of vector space utilization. *CoRR*, abs/2108.07344.

Gabriele Sarti. 2020. *Interpreting Neural Language Models for Linguistic Complexity Assessment*. Ph.D. thesis, University of Trieste.

Adrian Staub. 2007. The parser doesn't ignore intransitivity, after all. *J. Exp. Psychol. Learn. Mem. Cogn.*, 33(3):550–569.

Patrick Sturt, Martin Pickering, and Matther Crocker. 1999. Structural change and reanalysis difficulty in language comprehension. *Journal of Memory and Language*.

Whitney Tabor and Sean Hutchins. 2004. Evidence for self-organized sentence processing: digging-in effects. *J. Exp. Psychol. Learn. Mem. Cogn.*, 30(2):431–450.

Ian Tenney, Dipanjan Das, and Ellie Pavlick. 2019a. BERT rediscovers the classical NLP pipeline. *CoRR*, abs/1905.05950.

Ian Tenney, Patrick Xia, Berlin Chen, Alex Wang, Adam Poliak, R Thomas McCoy, Najoung Kim, Benjamin Van Durme, Sam Bowman, Dipanjan Das, and Ellie Pavlick. 2019b. What do you learn from context? probing for sentence structure in contextualized word representations. In *International Conference on Learning Representations*.

William Timkey and Marten van Schijndel. 2021. All bark and no bite: Rogue dimensions in transformer language models obscure representational quality. *CoRR*, abs/2109.04404.

Marten van Schijndel and Tal Linzen. 2018. Modeling garden path effects without explicit hierarchical syntax. *Cognitive Science*.

Marten van Schijndel and Tal Linzen. 2019. Neural network surprisal predicts the existence but not the magnitude of human syntactic disambiguation difficulty.

Marten van Schijndel and Tal Linzen. 2021. Single-stage prediction models do not explain the magnitude of syntactic disambiguation difficulty. *Cognitive science*, 45 6:e12988.

Eric Wallace, Shi Feng, Nikhil Kandpal, Matt Gardner, and Sameer Singh. 2019. Universal adversarial triggers for attacking and analyzing nlp.

Testing Pre-trained Language Models' Understanding of Distributivity via Causal Mediation Analysis

Pangbo Ban[†] **Yifan Jiang**[†] **Tianran Liu**[†] **Shane Steinert-Threlkeld**
Department of Linguistics, University of Washington
{pbban, yfjiang, tianranl, shanest}@uw.edu

Abstract

To what extent do pre-trained language models grasp semantic knowledge regarding the phenomenon of distributivity? In this paper, we introduce DistNLI, a new diagnostic dataset for natural language inference that targets the semantic difference arising from distributivity, and employ the causal mediation analysis framework to quantify the model behavior and explore the underlying mechanism in this semantically-related task. We find that the extent of models' understanding is associated with model size and vocabulary size. We also provide insights into how models encode such high-level semantic knowledge. Our dataset and code are available on GitHub.

1 Introduction

The ability to understand and utilize semantic knowledge (consciously or unconsciously) is essential to human reasoning process. Although significant progress has been made by large-scale pre-trained language models on many reasoning-required tasks, it is still unclear whether these models have reached a considerable level of competence in discerning and processing semantic knowledge. To break into the black box, recent studies employ various analysis methods and bring evidence that semantic knowledge (Bowman et al., 2015b; Ettinger, 2020; Jumelet et al., 2021) is encoded by pre-trained models. However, some issues still remain. First, due to the difficulty in being analyzed and probed for, many semantic phenomena are not touched on by NLP researchers, even though they have been studied by linguists for decades. Second, current analysis methods are not flawless. For example, Belinkov (2021) reviews some limitations of the probing classifier paradigm such as the spurious correlation between the probing classifier and the original model.

To address these issues, in this paper, we leverage causal mediation analysis (CMA), a new analysis framework introduced by Vig et al. (2020a,b), to test pre-trained language models' understanding of semantic knowledge, with a specific focus on predicative distributivity. As a complex linguistic phenomenon, predicative distributivity involves semantics, pragmatics, and psycholinguistics. With minimal pairs differing in distributivity, we look into whether pre-trained language models grasp the semantic difference, and how much a model component plays a role in such extent of understanding. Our contributions are as follows:

- We introduce DistNLI, a diagnostic NLI dataset which targets testing pre-trained language models' ability of discerning the property of predicative distributivity via minimal pairs of coordinated sentences (Section 3).
- We refine metrics used in the CMA framework, namely total effect (TE), natural indirect effect (NIE) and natural direct effect (NDE) to guarantee the effect decomposition. We apply the framework to the ternary NLI task (Sections 5.1 and 6.1).
- We find that pre-trained models with either more parameters or richer vocabulary show some understanding of distributivity. We also find that knowledge of distributivity is concentrated in middle layers and the level of concentration is patterned with the degree of understanding (Sections 4, 5.2 and 6.2).

2 Related Work

Distributivity A sentence with the verb predication applying to a group, e.g. *Sumon and Frank built a boat.*, can be interpreted into at least two readings: the distributive and the collective ones (Scha, 1981). In the distributive reading, the predication applies to each individual in the group (e.g.

[†]Equal contribution.

Proceedings of the Fifth BlackboxNLP Workshop on Analyzing and Interpreting Neural Networks for NLP, pages 314 - 324
December 8, 2022 ©2022 Association for Computational Linguistics

both Sumon and Frank individually/separately built a boat), whereas in the collective reading, the predication only applies to the group as a whole (e.g. Sumon and Frank built a boat *jointly*).

To theorize this linguistic phenomenon, Scha (1981) introduces the property of distributivity as a tool to formalize the collective and distributive senses of a predication. While Scha analyzes distributivity as a pure lexical property of different predicates, Link et al. (2002) propose that distributivity is a semantic operator comparable to *each*, which he defines as the 'D-operator'. Some later semanticists settle their analyses on the middle ground where the D-operator and the direct predication (based solely on the lexical property) theory are useful under different circumstances (Dowty et al., 1987; Roberts, 1987; Hoeksema, 1988; Verkuyl, 1993; Winter, 1997; De Vries, 2017; Champollion, 2017). Arguing that the predication of a simple sentence can be directly interpreted based on its lexical meaning while the analysis of a complex one will need a D-operator, Winter (1997) further defines P-distributivity and Q-distributivity, which correspond to the distributive sense under the direct predication and the D-operator respectively. For instance, *Azul and Marsha hold three balloons* falls in the category of Q-distributivity, since it is necessary to introduce the D-operator to analyze the distributivity given the group *Azul and Marsha*. The example *Yu and Vivian laughed*, on the other hand, is a case of P-distributivity, since it is apparent that the predicate *laughed* entails the distributivity originated from its lexical meaning.

Adopting the terminology proposed by De Vries (2017), we investigate the predicative distributivity in this paper by following the approach advocated by Winter (1997) and Champollion (2017) that collectivity and P-distributivity are categorized under the direct predication, which is paralleled to the D-operator that gives the Q-distributivity. We will call predicates which can be perceived in both distributive and collective senses ambiguous predicates in this paper, which corresponds to the mixed predicates in the previous literature. (De Vries, 2017; Champollion, 2017).

Natural Language Inference Natural Language Inference (NLI) is the task of determining whether one sentence (premise) entails, contradicts, or is neutral to another sentence (hypothesis). Early attempts include Chen et al. (2017) and Ghaeini et al. (2018) which are LSTM-based. Recent progress in pre-trained language models such as BERT (Devlin et al., 2019), RoBERTa (Liu et al., 2019), and DeBERTa (He et al., 2021) and NLI datasets like SNLI (Bowman et al., 2015a), XNLI (Conneau et al., 2018), and MNLI (Williams et al., 2018) provides more opportunities to tackle this task. Pre-trained models fine-tuned on NLI datasets often achieve satisfying performance.

However, diagnostic studies show that high scores achieved by neural models do not mean they truly understand the relationship between sentences. For example, McCoy et al. (2019) find BERT trained on MNLI instead leverages shallow heuristics to make predictions.

Causal Mediation Analysis Recently, several analysis methods have been proposed to reveal information that are learned and utilized by language models. One of them is causal mediation analysis (Robins and Greenland, 1992; Pearl, 2001), a statistical framework to identify direct and indirect effects of an intervention on an outcome of interest. It is first introduced as an analysis method to the NLP field by Vig et al. (2020a,b) to scrutinize gender bias in language models. More recent studies use it to explore linguistic phenomena such as syntactic agreement (Finlayson et al., 2021) and negation (Dobreva and Keller, 2021). The framework consists of three metrics: TE, NIE and NDE. TE is used to quantify how an *input intervention* (e.g., text edits) would affect a *response variable* (e.g., predicted probabilities). NIE and NDE are used to measure the mediated influence realized through an intermediate variable, or *mediator*, which can be a neuron, a whole layer, or an attention head. TE is usually decomposed into the sum of NIE and NDE. As Vig et al. (2020a,b) suggest, the CMA framework has great potential for extensions. Motivated by their work, in this paper, we apply the framework, which was limited to binary classification, to the NLI task and propose alternative definitions of the metrics for a more robust effect decomposition.

3 The DistNLI Dataset

3.1 Capturing distributivity with NLI

Although semanticists differ in the treatment of lexical distributivity (i.e., P-distributivity) in their theories, the evaluation of predicative distributivity generally relies on the validity of the inference from a predication of a group and the part with the *each* operator in the case of conjunction (e.g.

Premise	Hypothesis	NLI Label	Distributivity
Mia and Lin *laughed.*	Mia *laughed.*/Lin *laughed.*	Entailment	Distributive
Mia and Lin *pushed a rock.*	Mia *pushed a rock.*/Lin *pushed a rock.*	Entailment non-Entailment	Distributive Collective
Mia and Lin *gathered.*	*Mia *gathered.*/*Lin *gathered.*	N/A	Collective

Table 1: The relationship between distributivity and NLI labels illustrated by examples from DistNLI. The NLI label is determined by the type of the predicate in the premise, and *non-entailment* means that both *neutral* and *contradiction* are acceptable as true labels. Here, *pushed a rock* is an ambiguous predicate, so it can be assigned with both NLI labels.

Sumon and Frank each built a boat) (Dowty et al., 1987; Lasersohn, 1995; Winter, 1997; Champollion, 2017; De Vries, 2017).

Rooted in this definition, distributive predicates sanction the entailment relation between the plurality and its part, whereas collective or ambiguous predicates do not. Consequently, we use the NLI task to evaluate models' understanding of predicative distributivity. In our approach, the model's ability to discern distributivity is evaluated by the divergent prediction of models between predicates with differing distributivity. Table 1 demonstrates the relationship between distributivity and NLI labels. For instance, given the premise *Mia and Lin laughed* and the hypothesis *Lin laughed*, the model should predict the label as entailment based on the distributive predicate *laughed*. On the other hand, given the premise *Mia and Lin pushed a rock* and the hypothesis *Mia pushed a rock*, since *pushed a rock* is an ambiguous predicate, the model will exhibit a completely different performance if it grasps the disparity in semantics the distributivity exerts.

3.2 Data Generation

We generate a synthetic NLI dataset consisting of premise-hypothesis pairs with `[DP1] and [DP2] [Pred]` as premise and `[DP1]/[DP2] [Pred]` as hypothesis. `[DP1]` and `[DP2]` denote determiner phrases and `[Pred]` denotes a predicate. For example:

> **Premise**: Mia and Lin wore a mask.
> **Hypothesis**: Mia (Lin) wore a mask.

None of determiner phrase contains quantifiers in its structure, and both lexical and phrasal predicates are included (Champollion, 2017). Three kinds of noun phrases have been formulated, namely person, animal, and object, and it is guaranteed that no group nouns like *the committee* and conventionalized conjunctions like *Simon and Garfunkel* are included. The template is further instantiated with distributive and ambiguous predicates. We scrape existing categorized predicates from past publications on distributivity, and augment the list with predicates of similar pattern and characteristics regarding the semantic ambiguity in the information structure (Kroch, 1974; Taub, 1989; De Vries, 2017; Champollion, 2017; Coppock and Champollion, 2019). The augmented list aligns with the report of Safir and Stowell (1987) that most predications with indefinite cardinal as the determiner manifest the distributive feature.

3.3 Annotation

The annotation on predicative distributivity in this dataset consists of two stages. During the first stage, we recruit three graduate students, who are native speakers of American English with both linguistics and NLP background, to annotate grammatical sentences with predicates for whether they are distributive, collective or ambiguous. An example with pictures and explanation is given prior to the task. Considering the subtle nature of distributivity, we synthesize their judgements and discard highly controversial data points (i.e. predicates which received three distinct labels). During the second stage, the dataset is further confirmed by an expert in both Semantics and NLP to validate the result and guarantee a trustworthy dataset. The post-annotated data is split into the control group and the intervention group, with the former containing 164 pairs with distributive predicates and the latter containing 164 pairs with ambiguous predicates. The construction of the groups is explained in Section 5.1. They together form the final DistNLI dataset of 328 premise-hypothesis pairs.

Model	ConjNLI Total Acc	ConjNLI AND Acc	HANS Ent. Acc	HANS Non-Ent. Acc	DistNLI Dis. Acc	DistNLI Amb. Acc
DeBERTa-base	65.81	64.84	99.3	53.25	100.00	0.00
DeBERTa-large	66.61	65.99	99.89	54.81	100.00	0.00
DeBERTa-xlarge	65.01	64.84	100	42.33	100.00	0.00
DeBERTa-v2-xlarge	66.29	65.99	99.96	49.87	100.00	0.00
DeBERTa-v2-xxlarge	66.45	65.42	99.92	43.35	100.00	0.00
RoBERTa-large	64.53	64.55	99.65	46.61	100.00	0.61

Table 2: Pre-examination results on ConjNLI, HANS and DistNLI. For ConjNLI, **Total Acc** is the accuracy on the full ConjNLI data, and **AND Acc** is the accuracy on cases with *and* in the premise, hypothesis, or both. For HANS, **Ent. Acc** and **Non-Ent. Acc** stand for **Entailed Acc** and **Non-Entailed Acc**, which are the accuracy on entailed cases and non-entailed cases respectively. For DistNLI, **Dis. Acc** and **Amb. Acc** stand for **Distributive Acc** and **Ambiguous Acc**, which are the accuracy on the control group and intervention group respectively.

4 Models

4.1 Model Selection

We choose recent pre-trained models that are fine-tuned on MNLI as our target models. We try to control conditions as much as possible, such as model size and training setup. We use six models: DeBERTa (base, large, xlarge), DeBERTa-v2 (xlarge, xxlarge), and RoBERTa-large. RoBERTa-large shares the same vocabulary of size 50K as DeBERTa variants while DeBERTa-v2 variants increase their vocabulary size to 128K.

4.2 Pre-examination

Pre-trained language models can leverage various types of information learned from the training corpus to tackle the downstream tasks. The one we want to test in this paper is distributivity, but there is other related information models may use to make predictions, such as coordination, which is used to generate our dataset, or lexical overlap between the hypothesis and premise. To minimize the effect of these confounders, we run selected models over existing diagnostic NLI datasets, namely ConjNLI (Saha et al., 2020) and HANS (McCoy et al., 2019). In addition, we also report each model's accuracy on DistNLI as a preliminary evaluation of models' ability to recognize distributivity. Results on these datasets are shown in Table 2.

ConjNLI ConjNLI is an NLI dataset testing both Boolean and non-Boolean usage of conjuncts including *and*, *or*, *but*, and their combination with quantifiers and negation (Saha et al., 2020). We report each model's accuracy on the whole development set of ConjNLI as well as the subset where *and* exists in the premise, the hypothesis, or both. We find that all selected models perform reasonably well on ConjNLI, suggesting that they can handle diverse Boolean and non-Boolean coordinated sentences to a certain extent.

HANS HANS is an NLI dataset testing whether models have adopted syntactic heuristics, e.g., the lexical overlap heuristic, the subsequence heuristic, the constituent heuristic during pre-training (McCoy et al., 2019). HANS is annotated with *entailment* on which the heuristics make correct predictions, and *non-entailment* (*neutral* or *contradiction*) on which the heuristics make incorrect predictions. Therefore, if a model can perform perfectly on the entailed cases but fails on the non-entailed cases, it may exploit the heuristics. For selected models, we report their accuracy on both entailed and non-entailed cases. As expected, we find that all models achieve nearly perfect performance on entailed cases. Nevertheless, they reach much higher scores on the non-entailed cases compared to the experiment with BERT by McCoy et al. (2019). This indicates that these models rely less on syntactic heuristics to solve the NLI task.

DistNLI We report each model's accuracy on the control (distributive) group and the intervention (ambiguous) group. Because the control group is labeled with *entailment* and the intervention group is labeled with *non-entailment*, unsurprisingly results on DistNLI match the same pattern as that on HANS. However, the accuracy gap between the two groups is much bigger. Although this seems to suggest selected models heavily rely on syntactic heuristics and hence fail to recognize distributivity, results on ConjNLI and HANS show that selected models can handle at lease some of the non-Boolean coordinated sentences on which the heuristics provide no help. It is also worth noting that even for our recruited annotators, distributivity is a challenging phenomenon. Their responses demonstrate more variance in ambiguous predicates labeling. This implies accuracy may not be a good metric to evaluate models' understanding of distributivity since it does not account for the change of predicted probability when the decision is not flipped. Thus, we leverage the CMA framework for further investigation.

5 Total Effect

5.1 Experiment Design

Response Variable To quantify the model behavior, we follow the general idea proposed by Finlayson et al. (2021). We define the response variable y as the odds that a model (parameterized by θ) predicts *non-entailment* for a premise-hypothesis pair S_I, where I is the set of possible readings of S which may contain a distributive reading, a collective reading or both:

$$y(S_I) = \text{Odds}(\textit{non-entailment}|S_I) = \frac{P_\theta(\textit{non-entailment}|S_I)}{P_\theta(\textit{entailment}|S_I)} \quad (1)$$

The larger the $y(S_I)$, the more likely the model predicts *non-entailment* on the input pair S_I. With this definition, we can transform the original question into a binary task: whether models have a stronger preference over *non-entailment* given a premise-hypothesis pair with a particular predicate.

We hypothesize that if a model has some understanding of distributivity, *ceteris paribus*, an ambiguous pair should result in a larger predicted probability of *non-entailment* than a distributive pair, even if the model predicts *entailment* for both. In other words, $y(S_I)$ should be small when I only contains a distributive reading but relatively large when I contains both readings, provided that all other aspects of S are equal.

Input Intervention To isolate distributivity, we need a class of interventions to change possible readings of a given premise-hypothesis pair S while keeping everything else the same. Since it is intractable to directly modify the possible readings I, we choose to modify the surface form. For our data templates, I is determined by the predicate. Therefore, we define a do-operator `swap-pred`, which replaces the predicate in the given pair with a

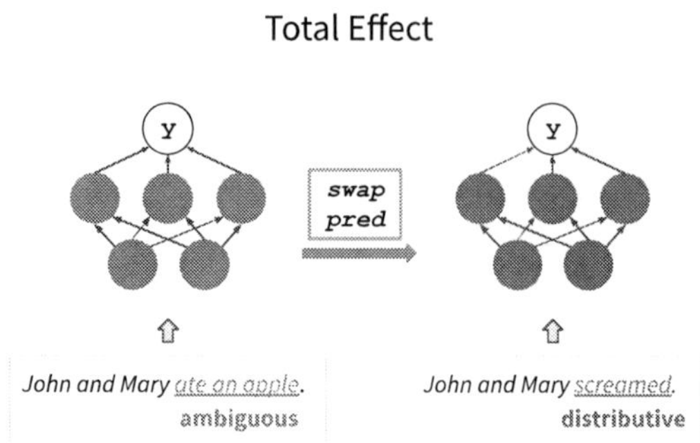

Figure 1: Total effect measures the relative change in y from the input intervention which alters the distributivity of the predicate in the sentence.

random sampled predicate of a different type, as illustrated in Figure 1.[1] We also define the `null` operator which preserves the original predicate. The response variable $y(S_I)$ can be redefined as $y_i(S_p)$ where i is a do-operator, S is a premise-hypothesis pair, and p indicates the type of the predicate in S:

$$y_{\texttt{null}}(S_p) = \text{Odds}(\textit{non-entailment}|S_p) \quad (2)$$

$$y_{\texttt{swap-pred}}(S_p) = \text{Odds}(\textit{non-entailment}|S_{p'}) \quad (3)$$

Leveraging these interventions, we can split the input dataset into two groups: the control group and the intervention group. Pairs in the control group have distributive predicates with the `null` operator applied. Pairs in the intervention group are the same sentences but with the `swap-pred` operator applied. Each pair in the control group can have one or more matches in the intervention group. For example, if *John and Mark smiled.* (premise) and *John smiled.* (hypothesis) is in the control group, *John and Mark built a house.* (premise) and *John built a house.* (hypothesis) could be its potential match in the intervention group.

Metric TE is used to measure how much a response variable y would change if we apply the `swap-pred` operator rather than the `null` operator. Instead of the odds difference definition used by previous studies (Vig et al., 2020b; Finlayson et al., 2021; Dobreva and Keller, 2021; Jeoung and Diesner, 2022), we adopt the odds ratio definition proposed by VanderWeele and Vansteelandt (2010). To make the scale more symmetric, we take the

[1]The illustration of TE and the following NIE figure are inspired by Vig et al. (2020a); Finlayson et al. (2021).

equivalent logarithmic version:

$$
\begin{aligned}
&\text{TE}(\texttt{swap-pred}, \texttt{null}; y, S_p) \\
&= \log\left(\frac{y_{\texttt{swap-pred}}(S_p)}{y_{\texttt{null}}(S_p)}\right) \\
&= \log\left(\frac{\text{Odds}(\textit{non-entailment}|S_{p'})}{\text{Odds}(\textit{non-entailment}|S_p)}\right)
\end{aligned}
\tag{4}
$$

We calculate the sample average total effect over DistNLI to estimate the average total effect over the population of all possible matched pairs:

$$
\overline{\text{TE}}(\texttt{swap-pred}, \texttt{null}; y) \mathrel{\widehat{=}} \mu_{\text{TE}} \tag{5}
$$

One benefit of this definition is that the total effect now inherits the interpretation of odds ratio, in addition to its own causal interpretation. Odds ratio is used to measure the strength of association between a response variable and an intervention. It compares the relative odds of the occurrence of an outcome of interest, given whether a particular intervention is performed (Szumilas, 2010). Therefore, by analogy with the odds ratio, we can interpret $\overline{\text{TE}}$ in three cases: (i) If $\overline{\text{TE}} > 0$, then the presence of ambiguous predicate in S causes higher odds of *non-entailment*; (ii) If $\overline{\text{TE}} = 0$, then there is no causal relationship between the type of the predicate in S and the model prediction; (iii) If $\overline{\text{TE}} < 0$, then the presence of ambiguous predicate in S causes lower odds of *non-entailment*.

Another benefit is that the lexical overlap heuristic is not a problem to our experiment, because $\overline{\text{TE}}$ measures the difference between sentences with swapped and unswapped predicates. If a model completely depends on the heuristic, $\overline{\text{TE}}$ will be close to 0 since the overlap between the premise and hypothesis remains the same when the input is intervened. In this case, no causal relationship is concluded between distributivity and the model prediction. If, however, we obtain a non-zero $\overline{\text{TE}}$, this should be due to factors other than the heuristic.

Since the size of DistNLI is relatively small, we perform the one-sample t-test with a significance level of 0.05 to infer about the average total effect over the full population. If $\overline{\text{TE}}$ is statistically significantly positive, we can conclude that the model has some understanding of distributivity.

5.2 Result and Discussion

Table 3 presents a one-sample t-test of the average total effect for each model. Except for DeBERTa-base, all models have a significantly positive $\overline{\text{TE}}$ with a significant level of 0.05. Based on the interpretation of $\overline{\text{TE}}$, these models are able to discern distributivity to some extent.

Model	Mean	SD	T	P-value
D-b	0.040	1.091	0.468	0.320
D-l	0.314	0.900	4.452	<7e-06
D-xl	0.351	0.507	8.844	<7e-16
D-v2-xl	0.856	0.796	13.724	<2e-29
D-v2-xxl	0.828	1.088	9.724	<3e-18
R-l	0.779	1.279	7.774	<4e-13

Table 3: One Sample t-test of $\overline{\text{TE}}$ for each model. Here, R stands for RoBERTa, D stands for DeBERTa, b stands for base, and l stands for large.

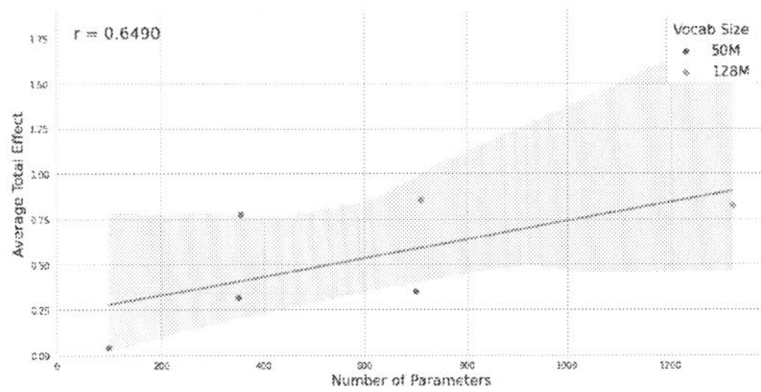

Figure 2: Relationship between $\overline{\text{TE}}$, the number of parameters and vocabulary size. Each point is a model.

Models with more parameters tend to show understanding of distributivity. We find that $\overline{\text{TE}}$ is positively correlated with the number of parameters, as shown by Figure 2 (r = 0.649). While there are confounders such as vocabulary size, number of layers, pre-training task, etc., the trend holds when we control for model architecture and only consider DeBERTa variants. This finding may suggest that larger models have a stronger ability to capture linguistic phenomena presented in the training corpus. Vig et al. (2020a) report an analogous result on gender bias. We also observe that the effect on $\overline{\text{TE}}$ vanishes when the number of parameters increases: as shown by Table 3, DeBERTa-large has a $\overline{\text{TE}}$ eight times greater than DeBERTa-base, but merely 0.04 lesser than DeBERTa-xlarge. This observation is in line with the finding of K et al. (2020) that the number of parameters has little effect on model performance after a certain threshold.

Models with richer vocabulary tend to show understanding of distributivity. We find that $\overline{\text{TE}}$ is associated with the size of vocabulary. As illustrated in Figure 2, DeBERTa-v2 variants have

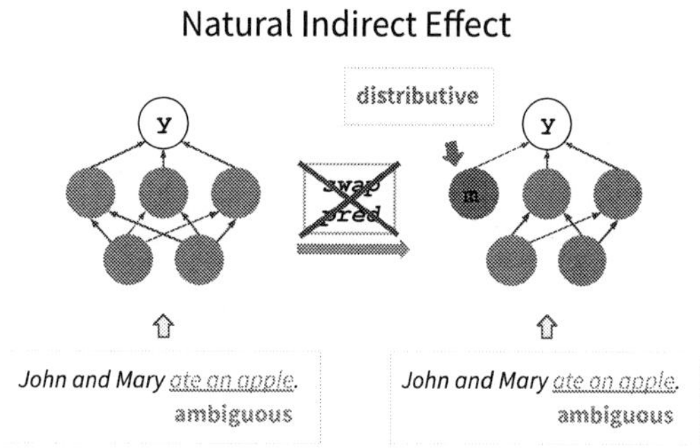

Figure 3: Natural indirect effect measures the relative change in y, given the presence of the input intervention, if every path into the mediator m is blocked by setting m to the value it would have been without the input intervention.

a $\overline{\text{TE}}$ of around 0.8, which is considerably larger than other models. We suspect this significant increase is due to their larger vocabulary size. Since distributivity is determined by the type of predicates, a richer vocabulary is expected to lead to a better semantic representation of predicates which in turn boosts $\overline{\text{TE}}$, although the effects of other confounders might not be ruled out.

6 Natural Indirect Effect

6.1 Experiment Design

Neuron Intervention To study the causal contribution of neurons, the hypothesized mediator in our experiment will be a single neuron or a group of neurons. Rather than investigating neurons for each input token independently (Vig et al., 2020a,b; Finlayson et al., 2021), we intervene on neurons for all input tokens simultaneously. This approach is computationally cheaper but still comprehensive enough to give a full picture of the underlying causal mechanism.[2]

Metric Natural Indirect Effect is used to measure how much the response variable y would change with the `swap-pred` operator applied, if we set the hypothesized mediator m to the value it would have been without rather than with the input intervention (demonstrated in Figure 3). Similar to TE, we use the log odds ratio and estimate the population average natural indirect effect:

$$\text{NIE}(\texttt{swap-pred}, \texttt{null}; y, m, S_p) = \log\left(\frac{y_{\texttt{swap-pred}}(S_p)}{y_{\texttt{swap-pred},m_{\texttt{null}}}(S_p)}\right) \tag{6}$$

where m is a hypothesized mediator and $m_{\texttt{null}}$ means that m is set to the value it would have been in the absence of the input intervention. We can also define NDE in a similar way:

$$\text{NDE}(\texttt{swap-pred}, \texttt{null}; y, m, S_p) = \log\left(\frac{y_{\texttt{swap-pred},m_{\texttt{null}}}(S_p)}{y_{\texttt{null}}(S_p)}\right) \tag{7}$$

VanderWeele and Vansteelandt (2010) prove that the log odds ratio definition of causal effects holds a decomposition property: TE $=$ NIE $+$ NDE even when there are interactions and nonlinearities.

The NIE and NDE defined above are in principle an implementation of what Robins and Greenland (1992) refer to as "total indirect effect" and "pure direct effect". The NDE given by Vig et al. (2020a,b) follows the same idea, but their NIE instead formulates the "pure indirect effect". A consequence is that the decomposition property is only guaranteed for linear models (Pearl, 2001; Vig et al., 2020a), which is a potential shortcoming as an analysis method for neural networks.

Given the decomposition property, $\overline{\text{NIE}}$ allows us to measure the magnitude of causal contribution a model component makes to the model behavior, which is quantified by $\overline{\text{TE}}$. In this respect, it potentially solves the problem of spurious correlation between the probing classifier and the original model (Belinkov, 2021). In our experiment, we use it to verify the causal relationship between the semantic information encoded in the original model and the prediction given by the NLI classifier. We can interpret the values of $\overline{\text{NIE}}$ similarly to $\overline{\text{TE}}$.

6.2 Result and Discussion

We experiment on models which pass the significance threshold.[3] Figure 4 illustrates the neuron-wise $\overline{\text{NIE}}$: for all models, most neurons have $\overline{\text{NIE}}$s around zero, but a few outliers can also be identified. In order to determine which neurons are responsible the most for the model behaviour, we also select the top 1% of neurons with highest individual $\overline{\text{NIE}}$s from each layer and evaluate the layer-wise $\overline{\text{NIE}}$. Figure 5 illustrates the layer-wise $\overline{\text{NIE}}$ obtained from selected neurons.

[2]Pilot experiments focusing on the `[CLS]` token, an approach used by Dobreva and Keller (2021), yielded mixed results, which is consistent with the findings of Reimers and Gurevych (2019) that the `[CLS]` token is not an ideal representation of sentence level meaning.

[3]Due to limited computational resources, DeBERTa-v2-xxlarge is excluded.

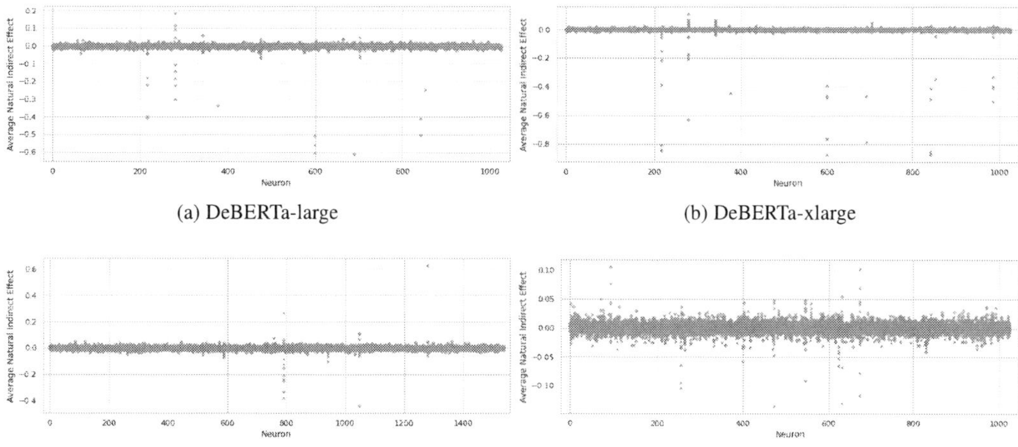

(a) DeBERTa-large (b) DeBERTa-xlarge

(c) DeBERTa-v2-xlarge (d) RoBERTa-large

Figure 4: Neuron-wise $\overline{\text{NIE}}$ of the models that pass the $\overline{\text{TE}}$ threshold. The x-axis represents the indices of neurons, which range from 0 to hidden size. The indices are not unique: neurons from different layers have the same index.

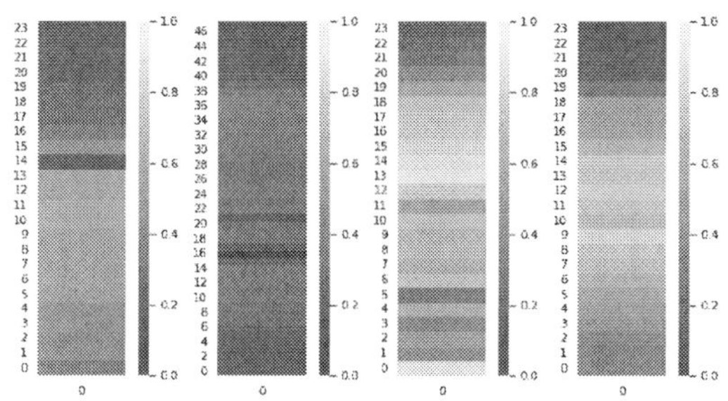

(a) (b) (c) (d)

Figure 5: Layer-wise $\overline{\text{NIE}}$ (top 1% neurons) of the models that pass the $\overline{\text{TE}}$ threshold. From left to right are DeBERTa-large, DeBERTa-xlarge, DeBERTa-v2-xlarge and RoBERTa-large. The y-axis represents layers and the color represents values of the $\overline{\text{NIE}}$.

Knowledge of distributivity is mostly concentrated in middle layers. We define the depth of a layer as its number divided by the total number of layers. Based on this metric, we can divide layers into three groups: early (0 - 0.33), middle (0.33 - 0.67), and final (0.67 - 1). In Figure 5, a concentration pattern of $\overline{\text{NIE}}$ is clearly shown by the color opacity of layers for all models. Specifically, middle layers have higher $\overline{\text{NIE}}$s than other layers. The exact layer where $\overline{\text{NIE}}$ peaks occur is more idiosyncratic, but still inside or near middle layers: 0.5 (layer #11) for DeBERTa-large, 0.73 (layer #35) for DeBERTa-xlarge, 0.54 (layer #13) for DeBERTa-v2-xlarge, and 0.42 (layer #9) for RoBERTa-large. This finding differs from the conclusion of Tenney et al. (2019) that semantic information is hardly localized in BERT-like models, although Jawahar et al. (2019) also report that most semantic tasks archive the best performance around middle layers.

Knowledge of distributivity is more concentrated in the models with higher degree of understanding. We find that the level of concentration of $\overline{\text{NIE}}$ patterns with the magnitude of $\overline{\text{TE}}$: $\overline{\text{NIE}}$s are concentrated in fewer neurons in DeBERTa-v2-xlarge and RoBERTa-large (both have a $\overline{\text{TE}}$ of about 0.8) than in DeBERTa-large and DeBERTa-xlarge (both have a $\overline{\text{TE}}$ of about 0.3). This finding is supported by the following observations: First, as shown by Figure 5, top 1% of neurons is sufficient to achieve the full total effect for the former two models, but not for the latter two models. Second, we notice that a few neurons have extremely higher $\overline{\text{NIE}}$ for the former two models. For example, neuron #1279 at layer #0 (located at the top right of Figure 4c) in DeBERTa-v2-xlarge has a $\overline{\text{NIE}}$ of 0.6735, much higher than most other neurons. According to the interpretation of $\overline{\text{NIE}}$, these neurons are causally and positively responsible for the model behaviour. The pattern is not observed in DeBERTa-large and DeBERTa-xlarge.

7 Conclusion

In this paper, we propose DistNLI, a diagnostic NLI dataset to examine to what extent pre-trained language models can discern the phenomenon of distributivity. By extending the CMA framework, we show that models including DeBERTa and RoBERTa have some understanding of distributivity, which provides further evidence that models have ability to encode high-level semantic knowledge, and reveal some interesting patterns related to the underlying mechanism of these models.

One direction for future improvement would be increasing the diversity of predicates and subjects in DistNLI. At present, we only look at subjects that are two coordinated DPs, but the phenomenon of distributivity applies to all noun phrases which denote groups and even without the utilization of conjuncts. It is possible that pre-trained language models can also differentiate more complicated combinations, as they are trained on large-scale text data. Another direction would be investigating how robust the CMA framework is to the definition of metrics, such as an empirical comparison between alternative definitions.

8 Limitation

Due to the specificity of the linguistic phenomenon involved and its size, this DistNLI dataset should only be used as a diagnostic dataset in the investigation of distributivity of verb predication. Also, occasionally some minimal pairs in the dataset could contradict with the world knowledge considering the nature of artificiality. On the one hand, the creators of this dataset have filtered out pairs that are tremendously deviant from the world knowledge by majority voting. On the other hand, even if there is still any deviating pair against the commonsense (i.e. *The lion and the seal found a habitat*), the distributivity manifested in such examples will not be confounded as long as the grammaticality is guaranteed, since the extent of deviance is constant between the premise and the hypothesis.

References

Yonatan Belinkov. 2021. Probing classifiers: Promises, shortcomings, and advances. *Computational Linguistics*, 48:207–219.

Samuel R. Bowman, Gabor Angeli, Christopher Potts, and Christopher D. Manning. 2015a. A large annotated corpus for learning natural language inference. In *Proceedings of the 2015 Conference on Empirical Methods in Natural Language Processing*, pages 632–642, Lisbon, Portugal. Association for Computational Linguistics.

Samuel R. Bowman, Christopher Potts, and Christopher D. Manning. 2015b. Recursive neural networks can learn logical semantics. In *Proceedings of the 3rd Workshop on Continuous Vector Space Models and their Compositionality*, pages 12–21, Beijing, China. Association for Computational Linguistics.

Lucas Champollion. 2017. *Parts of a whole: Distributivity as a bridge between aspect and measurement*, volume 66. Oxford University Press.

Qian Chen, Xiaodan Zhu, Zhen-Hua Ling, Si Wei, Hui Jiang, and Diana Inkpen. 2017. Enhanced LSTM for natural language inference. In *Proceedings of the 55th Annual Meeting of the Association for Computational Linguistics (Volume 1: Long Papers)*, pages 1657–1668, Vancouver, Canada. Association for Computational Linguistics.

Alexis Conneau, Ruty Rinott, Guillaume Lample, Adina Williams, Samuel Bowman, Holger Schwenk, and Veselin Stoyanov. 2018. XNLI: Evaluating cross-lingual sentence representations. In *Proceedings of the 2018 Conference on Empirical Methods in Natural Language Processing*, pages 2475–2485, Brussels, Belgium. Association for Computational Linguistics.

Elizabeth Coppock and Lucas Champollion. 2019. Invitation to formal semantics. *Manuscript, Boston University and New York University. eecoppock. info/semantics-boot-camp. pdf.*

Hanna De Vries. 2017. Two kinds of distributivity. *Natural Language Semantics*, 25(2):173–197.

Jacob Devlin, Ming-Wei Chang, Kenton Lee, and Kristina Toutanova. 2019. BERT: Pre-training of deep bidirectional transformers for language understanding. In *Proceedings of the 2019 Conference of the North American Chapter of the Association for Computational Linguistics: Human Language Technologies, Volume 1 (Long and Short Papers)*, pages 4171–4186, Minneapolis, Minnesota. Association for Computational Linguistics.

Radina Dobreva and Frank Keller. 2021. Investigating negation in pre-trained vision-and-language models. In *Proceedings of the Fourth BlackboxNLP Workshop on Analyzing and Interpreting Neural Networks for NLP*, pages 350–362, Punta Cana, Dominican Republic. Association for Computational Linguistics.

David Dowty et al. 1987. Collective predicates, distributive predicates, and all. In *Proceedings of the 3rd ESCOL*, pages 97–115. (Eastern States Conference on Linguistics), Ohio State University Ohio.

Allyson Ettinger. 2020. What BERT is not: Lessons from a new suite of psycholinguistic diagnostics for language models. *Transactions of the Association for Computational Linguistics*, 8:34–48.

Matthew Finlayson, Aaron Mueller, Sebastian Gehrmann, Stuart Shieber, Tal Linzen, and Yonatan Belinkov. 2021. Causal analysis of syntactic agreement mechanisms in neural language models.

In *Proceedings of the 59th Annual Meeting of the Association for Computational Linguistics and the 11th International Joint Conference on Natural Language Processing (Volume 1: Long Papers)*, pages 1828–1843, Online. Association for Computational Linguistics.

Reza Ghaeini, Sadid A. Hasan, Vivek Datla, Joey Liu, Kathy Lee, Ashequl Qadir, Yuan Ling, Aaditya Prakash, Xiaoli Fern, and Oladimeji Farri. 2018. DR-BiLSTM: Dependent reading bidirectional LSTM for natural language inference. In *Proceedings of the 2018 Conference of the North American Chapter of the Association for Computational Linguistics: Human Language Technologies, Volume 1 (Long Papers)*, pages 1460–1469, New Orleans, Louisiana. Association for Computational Linguistics.

Pengcheng He, Xiaodong Liu, Jianfeng Gao, and Weizhu Chen. 2021. Deberta: Decoding-enhanced bert with disentangled attention. In *International Conference on Learning Representations*.

Jack Hoeksema. 1988. The semantics of non-boolean "and". *Journal of Semantics*, 6(1):19–40.

Ganesh Jawahar, Benoît Sagot, and Djamé Seddah. 2019. What does BERT learn about the structure of language? In *Proceedings of the 57th Annual Meeting of the Association for Computational Linguistics*, pages 3651–3657, Florence, Italy. Association for Computational Linguistics.

Sullam Jeoung and Jana Diesner. 2022. What changed? investigating debiasing methods using causal mediation analysis. In *Proceedings of the 4th Workshop on Gender Bias in Natural Language Processing (GeBNLP)*, pages 255–265, Seattle, Washington. Association for Computational Linguistics.

Jaap Jumelet, Milica Denic, Jakub Szymanik, Dieuwke Hupkes, and Shane Steinert-Threlkeld. 2021. Language models use monotonicity to assess NPI licensing. In *Findings of the Association for Computational Linguistics: ACL-IJCNLP 2021*, pages 4958–4969, Online. Association for Computational Linguistics.

Karthikeyan K, Zihan Wang, Stephen Mayhew, and Dan Roth. 2020. Cross-lingual ability of multilingual bert: An empirical study. In *International Conference on Learning Representations*.

Anthony S Kroch. 1974. *The semantics of scope in English*. Ph.D. thesis, Massachusetts Institute of Technology.

Peter Lasersohn. 1995. Plurality, conjunction, and events, vol. 55 of. *Studies in Linguistics and Philosophy*.

Godehard Link et al. 2002. The logical analysis of plurals and mass terms: A lattice-theoretical approach. *Formal semantics: The essential readings*, pages 127–146.

Yinhan Liu, Myle Ott, Naman Goyal, Jingfei Du, Mandar Joshi, Danqi Chen, Omer Levy, Mike Lewis, Luke Zettlemoyer, and Veselin Stoyanov. 2019. Roberta: A robustly optimized bert pretraining approach. *arXiv preprint arXiv:1907.11692*.

Tom McCoy, Ellie Pavlick, and Tal Linzen. 2019. Right for the wrong reasons: Diagnosing syntactic heuristics in natural language inference. In *Proceedings of the 57th Annual Meeting of the Association for Computational Linguistics*, pages 3428–3448, Florence, Italy. Association for Computational Linguistics.

Judea Pearl. 2001. Direct and indirect effects. *Probabilistic and Causal Inference*.

Nils Reimers and Iryna Gurevych. 2019. Sentence-BERT: Sentence embeddings using Siamese BERT-networks. In *Proceedings of the 2019 Conference on Empirical Methods in Natural Language Processing and the 9th International Joint Conference on Natural Language Processing (EMNLP-IJCNLP)*, pages 3982–3992, Hong Kong, China. Association for Computational Linguistics.

Craige Roberts. 1987. *Modal subordination, anaphora, and distributivity*. Ph.D. thesis, University of Massachusetts Amherst.

James M Robins and Sander Greenland. 1992. Identifiability and exchangeability for direct and indirect effects. *Epidemiology*, pages 143–155.

Ken Safir and Tim Stowell. 1987. Binominal each. *North East Linguistics Society*, 18(3).

Swarnadeep Saha, Yixin Nie, and Mohit Bansal. 2020. ConjNLI: Natural language inference over conjunctive sentences. In *Proceedings of the 2020 Conference on Empirical Methods in Natural Language Processing (EMNLP)*, pages 8240–8252, Online. Association for Computational Linguistics.

Remko Scha. 1981. Collective, distributive and cumulative quantification. *Groenendijk, JAG; Janssen, TMV; and Stokhof, MBJ, editors*, pages 483–512.

Magdalena Szumilas. 2010. Explaining odds ratios. *Journal of the Canadian Academy of Child and Adolescent Psychiatry = Journal de l'Academie canadienne de psychiatrie de l'enfant et de l'adolescent*, 19 3:227–9.

Alison Taub. 1989. Collective predicates, aktionsarten and all. *University of Massachusetts Occasional Papers in Linguistics*, 15(2):16.

Ian Tenney, Patrick Xia, Berlin Chen, Alex Wang, Adam Poliak, R Thomas McCoy, Najoung Kim, Benjamin Van Durme, Sam Bowman, Dipanjan Das, and Ellie Pavlick. 2019. What do you learn from context? probing for sentence structure in contextualized word representations. In *International Conference on Learning Representations*.

Tyler J. VanderWeele and Stijn Vansteelandt. 2010. Odds ratios for mediation analysis for a dichotomous outcome. *American journal of epidemiology*, 172 12:1339–48.

Henk Verkuyl. 1993. *Distributivity and collectivity: a couple at odds*. Research Institute for Language and Speech. Utrech University.

Jesse Vig, Sebastian Gehrmann, Yonatan Belinkov, Sharon Qian, Daniel Nevo, Yaron Singer, and Stuart M. Shieber. 2020a. Causal mediation analysis for interpreting neural nlp: The case of gender bias. *ArXiv*, abs/2004.12265.

Jesse Vig, Sebastian Gehrmann, Yonatan Belinkov, Sharon Qian, Daniel Nevo, Yaron Singer, and Stuart M. Shieber. 2020b. Investigating gender bias in language models using causal mediation analysis. In *NeurIPS*.

Adina Williams, Nikita Nangia, and Samuel Bowman. 2018. A broad-coverage challenge corpus for sentence understanding through inference. In *Proceedings of the 2018 Conference of the North American Chapter of the Association for Computational Linguistics: Human Language Technologies, Volume 1 (Long Papers)*, pages 1112–1122, New Orleans, Louisiana. Association for Computational Linguistics.

Yoad Winter. 1997. Choice functions and the scopal semantics of indefinites. *Linguistics and philosophy*, pages 399–467.

Using Roark-Hollingshead Distance to Probe BERT's Syntactic Competence

Jingcheng Niu[RH] **Wenjie Lu**[R] **Eric Corlett**[R] **Gerald Penn**[RH]
University of Toronto[R] Vector Institute[H]
{niu,luwenjie,ecorlett,gpenn}@cs.toronto.edu

Abstract

Probing BERT's general ability to reason about syntax is no simple endeavour, primarily because of the uncertainty surrounding how large language models represent syntactic structure. Many prior accounts of BERT's agility as a syntactic tool (Clark et al., 2013; Lau et al., 2014; Marvin and Linzen, 2018; Chowdhury and Zamparelli, 2018; Warstadt et al., 2019, 2020; Hu et al., 2020) have therefore confined themselves to studying very specific linguistic phenomena, and there has still been no definitive answer as to whether BERT "knows" syntax.

The advent of *perturbed masking* (Wu et al., 2020) would then seem to be significant, because this is a parameter-free probing method that directly samples syntactic trees from BERT's embeddings. These sampled trees outperform a right-branching baseline, thus providing preliminary evidence that BERT's syntactic competence bests a simple baseline. This baseline is underwhelming, however, and our reappraisal below suggests that this result, too, is inconclusive.

We propose *RH Probe*, an encoder-decoder probing architecture that operates on two probing tasks. We find strong empirical evidence confirming the existence of important syntactic information in BERT, but this information alone appears not to be enough to reproduce syntax in its entirety. Our probe makes crucial use of a conjecture made by Roark and Hollingshead (2008) that a particular lexical annotation that we shall call RH distance is a sufficient encoding of unlabelled binary syntactic trees, and we prove this conjecture.

1 Introduction

BERT (Devlin et al., 2019) is a structurally rich system both because of its neural architecture and because of the knowledge it captures through pre-training. Many have studied the similarities between these architectures and linguistically motivated structures or processing pipelines through probing (Conneau et al., 2018; Jawahar et al., 2019; Tenney et al., 2019a; Zhu et al., 2022; Niu et al., 2022) to argue for an enigmatic "BERT revolution," into which large parts of previous research in computational linguistics are now subsumed.

In this paper, we present *RH Probe*[1], a novel encoder-decoder-based probing architecture that utilises Roark-Hollingshead (2008) syntactic distance (RH distance) to examine the overall capacity of BERT's comprehension of syntax.

We introduce this probing architecture because there still has been no definitive answer as to whether the knowledge that BERT acquires during its pre-training process can in fact serve as a replacement for a phrase-structure-based notion of syntax. Limited by their probing methodology, prior performance-based probing attempts only investigated individual, fine-grained linguistic phenomena, until Wu et al. (2020).

Wu et al. (2020) proposed *perturbed masking*, a parameter-free probing method that directly looks for traces of well-established linguistic structures such as constituency trees latent in BERT representations. The baseline used in Wu et al.'s (2020), a right-branching tree, is overly simplistic. Upon conducting a thorough reappraisal of their results, we found that their parameter-free constituency-tree parser only marginally outperforms a naïve, right-branching baseline, and their *impact matrix* which formed the basis of their analysis only has weak to no correlation with constituency tree information.

We believe Wu et al. (2020) has overly fixated on parameter-free probing. They want to address the criticism that, because traditional supervised probes introduce supervised data, we cannot directly attribute evidence of "knowledge" to the pre-trained base language model itself — perhaps

[1]The implementation and results of RH Probe are available online: https://github.com/frankniujc/rh_probe.

Proceedings of the Fifth BlackboxNLP Workshop on Analyzing and Interpreting Neural Networks for NLP, pages 325 - 334
December 8, 2022

everything is learned *post hoc* by the classifier through the probe dataset (Hewitt and Liang, 2019). But this risk can be mitigated. In particular, the ablation study is still a valid experimental design for probing (Zhu et al., 2022).

In our view, the only satisfactory evidence of "knowledge" that there has ever been in artificial intelligence has been the ability to use the model in question to perform inference. The present case should be no different. What we need then is parsing, or some other derivative task, which is easy to perform given a sufficient grasp of syntactic structure and much more difficult to perform without it, but in an experimental setting in which several sources of information are provided as input. BERT's output is one such potential source of information. Ablation studies then take the form of removing one or more of those sources during training. We also need alternative encodings of that knowledge for the purposes of comparison.

Roark-Hollingshead distance (2008) annotates word tokens in sequence but has been conjectured to encode unlabelled syntactic constituency trees. It is used by PRPN (Shen et al., 2018) as an important component of its internal model of tree structure that the network develops in the course of learning to parse unsupervised. RH distances are an important bridge between token sequences (language model) and arboreal structure (traditional syntax).

Therefore, we propose RH Probe, an encoder-decoder-based probing architecture. With RH Probe, we conduct two experiments: (1) an *ablation probe* that observes whether the removal of a feature source during training (language model output, RH distance, or part-of-speech (POS) information for reference) can decrease the probe's performance; and (2) an *"attack" probe* that observes whether randomization of certain features during testing can cause the performance to drop. The results of these experiments suggest that word embeddings contain important syntactic information, but that this information alone is not enough to reproduce traditional syntactic representations such as phrase structure in their entirety. In our experiments, we have also not been able to find any correlation between the quality of the language model and the amount of syntactic information.

After surveying previous probing methods, including probability probes, performance-based probes, and Wu et al.'s (2020) parameter-free probe, we introduce our RH Probe architecture and probing task design, including the definition of RH distance. We prove Roark and Hollingshead's (2008) conjecture that RH distance encodes unlabelled binary syntactic trees, and then present two experimental trials that use RH Probe to study the syntactic information carried by various sources. Our analysis of these results broadly confirms the existence of important syntactic information within BERT, but militates against the conclusion that this information alone can reproduce syntax in its entirety.

2 Probing for Syntax in BERT

2.1 Probability Probing

Since language models estimate the probability distribution over sequences of tokens, it is natural to compare the probability of a syntactically well-formed sentence with a syntactically ill-formed sentence; and reason about a language model's knowledge of syntax based on how often it can correctly assign a higher probability to the well-formed sentence. This practice of "probing" can trace its roots to Pereira (2000) on pre-neural language models. The same method is used in various work (Clark et al., 2013; Lau et al., 2014; Marvin and Linzen, 2018; Chowdhury and Zamparelli, 2018; Warstadt et al., 2019, 2020; Hu et al., 2020) to study neural language models from Mikolov et al. (2013) to contemporary large-scale models on different syntactic features, ranging from long-distance dependencies to anaphora.

Although simple and intuitive, this method of probing suffers two primary difficulties. First, probability is not a particularly good reflection of syntactic well-formedness. Other features of the input sequence, such as sequence length, token frequency, semantics, social bias, and even punctuation, can affect a language model's score. Second, this method of probing does not reflect the modern usage of language models after BERT introduced the pretrain/finetune paradigm. Although the probability distribution is still useful for text generation, language models are often used to encode a sequence of tokens into a vector space. But analysing probability alone does not provide insight into whether linguistic structures are latent in the language model's representations.

2.2 Performance-based Probing

To better reflect this new pretrain/finetune paradigm, *performance-based* probes (Adi et al.,

2017; Conneau and Kiela, 2018; Hupkes and Zuidema, 2018; Jawahar et al., 2019; Hewitt and Liang, 2019; Tenney et al., 2019a,b; Pimentel et al., 2020; Zhu et al., 2022) were introduced. These probes introduce the linguistic feature of interest as an auxiliary task and train a supervised classifier (often referred to as a *probe classifier* or *diagnostic classifier*) that takes BERT's embeddings as input. If this bolt-on classifier acquires good performance, people have concluded that the language model contains the relevant linguistic knowledge.

Overall, these probes use small classifiers with simple architectures to avoid introducing extra variables into the probing process — there is no good in explaining a black box with another black box. As a consequence, the auxiliary linguistic task design is also restricted to be simplistic and fine-grained (see Niu et al. (2022) for a more detailed discussion).

But as Hewitt and Liang (2019) presciently ask: "When a probe achieves high accuracy on a linguistic task using a representation, can we conclude that the representation encodes linguistic structure, or has the probe just learned the task?"

2.3 Perturbed Masking

This question is particularly salient for Wu et al. (2020), who resort to parameter-free probing based on the pairwise impact between tokens in a sentence. This impact is computed as the distance (either Euclidean or an information-theoretic difference in distributions) between the BERT representations of the sentence with the first token masked (with `[MASK]`) and the sentence with both tokens masked. Wu et al. (2020) theorized that tokens in the same constituent have higher impact scores among each other than with tokens outside the constituent. Using this pairwise impact score, they devised a matrix-based top-down parsing algorithm (MART) to induce constituency tree structures from BERT. Given an input sentence and its token impact information, the algorithm recursively chooses a splitting position that separates the sentence into two parts with the highest average impact between intraconstituent tokens, until a binary tree emerges. By evaluating those binary trees as constituency trees, they observed a better performance than simple right-branching and left-branching baselines.

Reappraising Wu et al. (2020) The performance increases are unfortunately slight. As shown in Table 1, MART only outperforms the right-branching baseline by a 1.3/2.3% F1 increase, whereas using RH distances in place of BERT vectors leads to considerably better F1 scores. Furthermore, a comparison of MART-generated trees to right-branching trees (with right-branching trees set as the reference) shows that MART-generated trees more closely resemble right-branching trees than constituency trees (Table 2).

To further investigate Wu et al.'s (2020) hypothesized connection between pairwise token impact and constituency, we can use it as a proxy for RH distance (as we will show in further detail in Section 3). When a token has a high RH distance from its predecessor, it means the two tokens' common ancestor is higher up in the syntactic tree, and therefore they are not both in a same, lower constituent

	MART	RB Tree	LB Tree	RH	Random
WSJ10	58.0	56.7	19.6	67.04	51.6
WSJ23	42.1	39.8	9.0	50.08	29.69

Table 1: Wu et al.'s (2020) MART F1 performance compared to two naïve baselines: right-branching (RB) trees and left-branching (LB) trees, and the substitution of RH distances (RH) or random vectors (Random) for BERT vectors within MART. MART barely outperforms the right-branching baseline with a 1.3/2.3% F1 increase on the two evaluation datasets.

	MART vs. Const. Tree	MART vs. RB Tree
WSJ10	58.0	78.6
WSJ23	42.1	56.1

Table 2: Parsing F1 comparison. The "Const. Tree" column shows the parsing F1 of MART evaluated with the original PTB annotations as gold standard. The "RB Tree" column shows the same evaluation, but with the right-branching trees as a baseline. MART generates trees more closely resembling right-branching trees than constituency trees.

Test Split	Direction	mean r	median r	macro r
WSJ10	t_{i-1}, t_i	0.3	0.365	0.159
	t_i, t_{i-1}	0.153	0.223	0.261
	sum	0.258	0.323	0.25
WSJ23	t_{i-1}, t_i	0.246	0.255	0.195
	t_i, t_{i-1}	0.195	0.218	0.213
	sum	0.259	0.273	0.242

Table 3: Correlation between pairwise token impact and constituent level (RH distance). Following Wu et al. (2020), we calculated the result on the WSJ10 and WSJ23 splits. The mean correlation (r) and median correlation between impact score and RH distance are reported. We can see weak to no correlation for both test splits.

So there should be a high anti-correlation between impact score and RH distance.

We report the Pearson correlation of these in Table 3. Wu et al.'s (2020) token impact matrix is asymmetrical. The impact of token t_i on t_{i-1} is different from the impact of t_{i-1} on t_i. Therefore we showed correlation results in three different ways: the impact of a token's predecessor on itself (t_{i-1}, t_i), the impact of a token on its predecessor (t_i, t_{i-1}), and the sum of the impacts in both directions (sum). We also used two methods of calculating Pearson's correlation. First, we compute the correlation between the impact scores and RH distances of every sentence and report the mean and median. Second, we compute the "macro" correlation between the impact score and RH distance of every pair of adjacent tokens. We can see there are weak to no positive correlations on both the WSJ10 and WSJ23 splits in either direction. We did not observe the expected, high negative correlation.

2.4 Discussion: Parameter-free Probing and Ablation Study

Parameter-free probing is not the only solution to Hewitt and Liang's (2019) criticism of performance-based probing. Ablation is widely recognised as a means of mitigating this issue. When we subtract a source of information or signal from the input to the probe classifier, decreased performance of the probe can be interpreted as good evidence that those removed features or signals contained task-relevant information to the neural network. While there is still an ongoing debate on how well the magnitude of this difference correlates to the relevance of the information (Hewitt and Liang, 2019; Pimentel et al., 2020; Zhu and Rudzicz, 2020), that does not change the validity of using performance decreases as evidence for the mere presence of knowledge.

Although parameter-free probing does not use supervised data, the clustering algorithm itself encodes rigid prior information about trees and what they should look like structurally (the Random scores of Table 1 can be construed as indications of syntactic information latent in the algorithm itself). Right-branching trees satisfy these constraints, and MART-generated trees are similar to right-branching trees. We propose to reinstate a supervised finetuning regimen, in which BERT's presence in the input can be compared to other lexicalized encodings of syntactic structure. Sequences of RH distances are one such encoding. POS tag sequences can arguably serve as an imperfect, indirect encoding of the same.

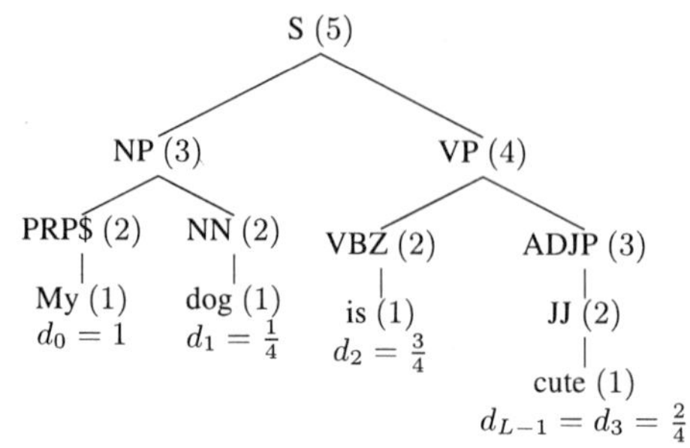

Figure 1: An RH distance calculation example. The height of nodes (h) are annotated in brackets.

3 RH Probe

3.1 Background: RH Distance

Before introducing our probing architecture, we need to introduce RH distance. Given a sentence $[t_0, t_1, \ldots, t_{L-1}]$, RH distance d_i is a measure of the syntactic distance between a token t_i and its predecessor t_{i-1}. It is calculated based on the height of the lowest common ancestor[2] of t_i and t_{i-1}. The precise calculations of both height and RH distances used in PRPN are somewhat parochial, but we adhere to them in equation 1 and figure 1 (r is the root of the tree) because this application of RH distance is perhaps the one best known to this audience.

$$\begin{aligned} d_i &= \frac{h(t_{i-1}, t_i) - 2}{h(r) - 1} \\ h(t_{-1}, t_0) &= h(t_{L-1}, t_L) = h(r) + 1 \\ h(u, v) &= h(u \cup v), \text{everywhere else} \end{aligned} \tag{1}$$

With RH distance information $[d_0, d_1, \ldots, d_L]$, it is sufficient to reconstruct the structure of an entire binary constituency tree. This was conjectured by Roark and Hollingshead (2008), but remained unproven until now. We will prove it in Section 3.5. Sequences of RH distance can be regarded as the encoding of an entire unlabelled constituency tree, and we can use this linear encoding of arboreal information to form the basis of our RH Probe architecture.

[2]The lowest common ancestor of two tree nodes u and v is denoted as $u \cup v$.

3.2 Probe Architecture

RH distance is a lexicalized measure, a sequence of which encodes the structure of certain constituency trees. We can use that information to create a series of probes into BERT's "understanding" of syntax. RH Probe has two modes of operation: an *ablative probe* observes the classifier's performance decrease when an input source is removed from training; and an *"attack" probe* observes its performance decrease after input features are obscured through randomization during testing (after a noise-free training).

3.3 Ablative Probe

The successful generation of a constituency tree is simple given the necessary structural information (RH distance), POS tags and internal node labels. Our ablation probe aims to determine whether language models provide crucial syntactic information in the presence of either RH distance or POS tags, neither of which directly encodes the labels of internal nodes.

To avoid providing structural hints to the probe in the decoder itself, we implemented an encoder-decoder probing architecture as shown in Figure 2. The output of the probe is a flattened version of the PTB parse trees. The terminal tokens are dropped to simplify the output space. The input is a concatenation of all the chosen input feature sources (word embedding, RH distance, POS tag embedding), as shown in Figure 3. For the choice of word embeddings, we use two different sizes of BERT, and also word2vec (Mikolov et al., 2013) as well as no embedding. word2vec vectors (300 dimensions) are significantly smaller than bert-base-cased vectors (784 dimensions), and so the 256-dimensional BERTtiny (Bhargava et al., 2021) was included for reference. When POS tags are provided, they are vectorised by the same embedding as the decoder, as POS tags are a subset of constituent tags.

Evaluation Metrics We want to evaluate whether the probe classifier can correctly predict the structure of the tree, as well as the pre-terminal and phrasal labels. Two of these three aspects correspond to possible input sources. Nevertheless, it is impossible to evaluate the quality of the labels completely independently of the structure. Therefore, we instead measure quality in two ways:

- **Tree Integrity** the average of a binary variable that is 1 iff the decoder's output can be successfully evaluated as a tree. This includes bracket balancing and constituent label location, but not the labels themselves.
- **Unlabelled Exact Match Accuracy** the average of a binary variable that is 1 iff the produced sequence is exactly correct, ignoring labels.

The overall quality of the trees is measured through:

- **Levenshtein (1965) distance** (the average of) the minimum number of insertions, deletions, or replacements of output tokens (including left or right brackets and constituent labels) to edit the decoder output to the the gold standard, normalised by the gold standard's sequence length.
- **Labelled Tree Exact Match Accuracy** the average of a binary variable that is 1 iff the produced sequence is exactly correct, including labels.

3.4 Attack Probe

The ablation task is not a probe into the disjointness of knowledge between two sources of information nor a probe into the relative weights of each information source. Therefore, we also introduce an *Attack Probe*. Figure 4 depicts this process. With a fully trained probe classifier, we evaluate the classifier's performance on perturbed input. By replacing one of the information sources (RH distance, word embeddings, or POS embeddings) with random noise, we can observe by how much the classifier's performance drops. A bigger performance drop can be interpreted as higher feature importance. The evaluation method is exactly the same as in the ablative task.

3.5 Proof of RH Conjecture

It can be proved that RH sequences uniquely encode unlabelled binary trees with no unary branches above the pre-terminal connections that they implicitly assume to be present at every word token. Roark and Hollingshead (2008) were the first to speculate about the expressive capacity of these sequences to encode syntactic trees. The definition of RH sequences itself provides a unique, constructive recipe for translating any such tree into an RH sequence. As for the reverse direction, the proof proceeds by induction on $h(r)$, the height of the root node. The base case is a single word, with a single pre-terminal, which is also the root, at height 2. This is encoded by a single RH distance of 1, which is the only length-1 RH sequence that can exist, and its tree is the only tree that can exist

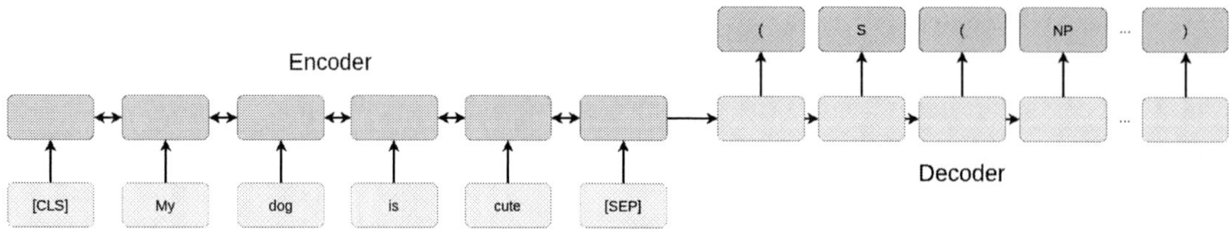

Figure 2: RH Probe Encoder-Decoder Architecture. The input features are fed into a bidirectional encoder, and the encoded representation of the sentence is decoded by a unidirectional decoder. The decoder outputs the flattened tree with all of the pre-terminal POS tags but no terminal tokens. The constituency tree of the example sentence *my dog is cute*, displayed in figure 1, will be flattened into `(S (NP (PRP$) (NN)) (VP (VBZ) (ADJP (JJ)))).`

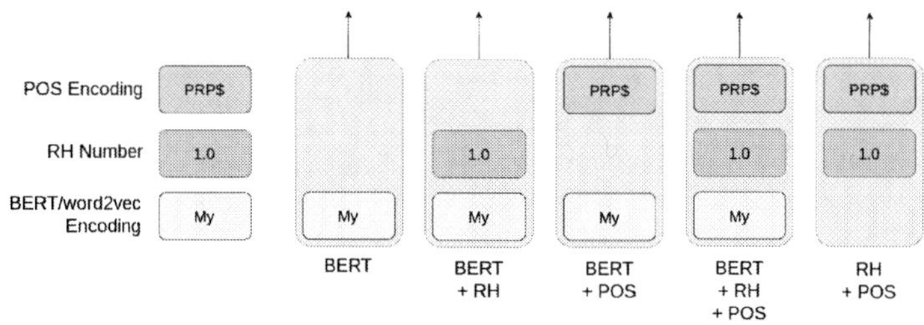

Figure 3: Ablation probe input selection. The input features are concatenated into one vector.

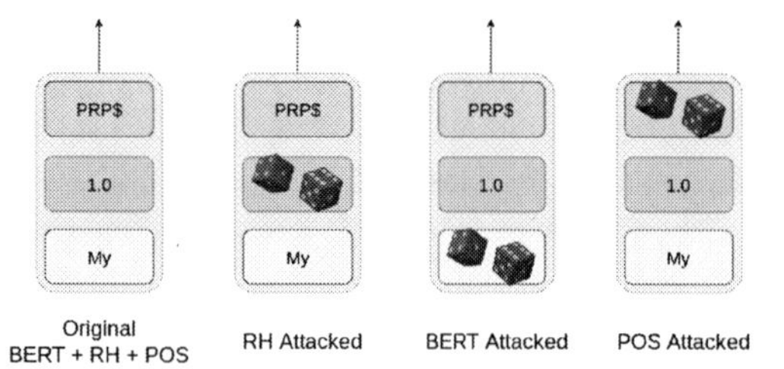

Figure 4: Attack Probe. Attack on different input means replace that input with random noise. Performance drop after this attack is then observed.

with a yield of 1, given the constraints on trees that we have assumed.

Assuming that all constrained trees of height $h(r) = n$ are uniquely encoded by RH sequences, we seek to show that any tree of height $h(r) = n+1$ is also uniquely encoded by reconstructing it from its RH sequence. Given the smallest number in a well-formed RH sequence, it is possible to infer the height of its corresponding tree. This number will be $\frac{1}{h(r)-1}$, since the witness to the height of the root $h(r)$ must contain a node of height 3, which, being of height greater than 2, must be the join of some adjacent pair of word tokens in our constrained trees. We posit joins of adjacent pairs in the tree that we are reconstructing wherever we see the number $\frac{1}{h(r)-1}$ on the second (right-hand) number of a pair. Note that no two adjacent word tokens can both have RH numbers of $\frac{1}{h(r)-1}$ in a well-formed RH sequence for our trees.

Let us now contemplate what the RH sequence of the remainder of the tree would look like. This remainder is itself a tree that satisfies our constraints, if we were to remove these adjacent, joined words, replacing them with a single, made-up token, and their join with a new, made-up POS tag, which would have height 2 rather than 3. Although it is not possible in general to predict what the new RH sequence would be if we were to remove one such pair from a tree, it is actually possible to predict what the new RH sequence would be if we removed all such pairs at once from the tree. This would remove all nodes of height 3. Every longest path to every node of height higher than 3 passes through exactly one height-3 node, which means that the root and the remaining joins in the new tree all decrement by exactly 1. So, without knowing the structure of the remainder of the tree yet, we can recalibrate the RH sequence to it: because we could infer $h(r)$ in the old tree, we can recover the unnormalized join heights by multiplying by $h(r)-1$, then decrement the unnormalized heights, and then renormalize using $h(r) - 2$ rather than $h(r) - 1$. This recalibrated sequence now corresponds to a tree of height one less, and so by the inductive hypothesis, its tree can be recovered.

Model	Tree Integrity	Unlabelled EM	Levenshtein	Labelled EM
BERT	0.124	0.0244	0.352	0.012
BERT + RH	0.177	0.0824	0.284	0.0269
BERT + POS	0.16	0.043	0.283	0.0344
BERT + RH + POS	0.181	0.055	0.268	0.0472
BERTtiny	0.11	0.0356	0.341	0.0161
BERTtiny + RH	0.168	0.065	0.301	0.0157
BERTtiny + POS	0.161	0.0464	0.293	0.0368
BERTtiny + RH + POS	0.168	0.0555	0.274	0.0435
word2vec	0.119	0.048	0.333	0.0178
word2vec + RH	0.179	0.0679	0.302	0.0236
word2vec + POS	0.18	0.0588	0.277	0.048
word2vec + RH + POS	0.209	0.0795	0.258	0.0642
RH	0.147	0.0774	0.322	0.0132
POS	0.162	0.0629	0.295	0.0509
RH + POS	0.165	0.0803	0.27	0.053

Table 4: Ablation probe result. For Levenshtein distance, the lower, the better. For the others, higher is better.

4 Experimental Setup

Constituency trees were obtained from the Penn Treebank (PTB) (Marcus et al., 1994). The corpus was processed and split into training/validation/test sets using Kim et al.'s (2019) scripts, available online[3]. Trees were binarized, as usual, but unary branches except for the pre-terminal connections were removed, in accordance with the limitations on the expressive capacity of sequences of RH distances.

A hyperparameter search was conducted using Optuna (Akiba et al., 2019) for 150 trials with `bert-base-cased` embeddings and no RH distances nor POS tags were provided as hints. The search result concluded with a 50 PTB-tag embedding size, a 0.0005 Adam (Kingma and Ba, 2015) learning rate, and a 5-layer GRU encoder-decoder with a 350 hidden-unit size. Finally, a beam search algorithm was implemented in the decoder with a width of 5. This set of hyperparameters was used for every probe conducted here. This hyperparameter selection process can be generalised to other large-scale pretrained language models.

5 Experimental Results

5.1 Ablation Probe Results

Table 4 shows our ablation probe results. Each probe was trained for 200 epochs and for each evaluation metric, we reported the test set performance on the epoch that has the best validation set performance. We note the following key findings:

Language models provide useful information for parsing. Performance is lower when no word embedding is provided (RH, POS, RH+POS). The removal of word embeddings derived from any type of language model decreases the probe's performance. This shows that language models can learn through pre-training information useful and recognizable to downstream syntactic tasks.

POS and RH distance provide performance increases across the board. With the labelled tree exact match ratio of BERTtiny *vs.* BERTtiny + RH being the only exception (0.04% performance increase), all settings when POS and RH distance information are removed result in a performance drop. Furthermore, we can observe a lower structural performance when RH distance is removed, and a lower overall performance when POS tags are removed. This is expected as RH distance only contains structural information. While language models contain useful syntactic information, the information they contain is still notably disjoint from syntax, as the removal of RH sequences and/or POS tags in the presence of BERT is also deleterious to performance.

Better language model $\neq$ more syntactic knowledge. Finally, the quality of the language model is not directly correlated to the probe's performance. If the central presupposition of performance-based probing is in fact true, that the magnitude of performance increases with the quantity of knowledge, then a better language model does not mean better understanding of syntax. BERTtiny and word2vec outperformed BERT(-base-cased) in several respects, and the hyperparameters were searched with the BERT model. While it may be controversial to compare the quality of BERT and word2vec, as it is not uncommon

[3]https://github.com/harvardnlp/compound-pcfg

Model	Attack	Tree Integrity		Unlabelled Acc		Levenshtein		Tree EM Acc	
		score	Δ	score	Δ	score	Δ	score	Δ
BERT + RH + POS	original	0.181	-	0.0675	-	0.263	-	0.0571	-
	attack RH	0.148	-0.0328	0.0261	-0.0414	0.334	0.0712	0.0219	-0.0352
	attack BERT	0.0803	-0.101	0.00455	-0.0629	0.467	0.205	0.0029	-0.0542
	attack POS	0.0629	-0.118	0.000828	-0.0666	0.516	0.253	0.0	-0.0571
BERTtiny + RH + POS	original	0.168	-	0.0642	-	0.273	-	0.0517	-
	attack RH	0.154	-0.0136	0.0435	-0.0207	0.319	0.0461	0.0373	-0.0145
	attack BERT	0.101	-0.0674	0.00745	-0.0567	0.407	0.134	0.00497	-0.0468
	attack POS	0.055	-0.113	0.000828	-0.0633	0.633	0.36	0.0	-0.0517
word2vec + RH + POS	original	0.209	-	0.0795	-	0.261	-	0.06	-
	attack RH	0.118	-0.0915	0.0207	-0.0588	0.369	0.108	0.0199	-0.0401
	attack w2v	0.115	-0.0935	0.00455	-0.0749	0.423	0.162	0.00207	-0.0579
	attack POS	0.0741	-0.135	0.000828	-0.0786	0.502	0.241	0.0	-0.06

Table 5: Attack probe results. The probe's test set performance after the attack is displayed in the score columns, and the magnitude of the performance drop is displayed in the Δ columns. All attacks are conducted on the epoch with the highest validation set tree integrity.

Metric	BERT	BERTtiny	word2vec
Tree Integrity	79.61%	54.17%	4.76%
Unlabelled EM	85.25%	84.47%	81.25%
Levenshtein	73.38%	28.05%	40.16%
Labelled EM	86.79%	86.67%	89.58%

Table 6: Relative "importance" of word embedding input, calculated as $\frac{S_{\text{embed}}-S_{\text{rh}}}{S_{\text{pos}}-S_{\text{rh}}}$, where S_{embed}, S_{pos}, S_{rh} represent the underlying measure after attacks on the respective information source.

to have simpler language modelling architectures outperforming more powerful ones (Edwards et al., 2020), BERT and BERTtiny share the same architecture.

5.2 Attack Probe Results

Table 5 presents our attack probe results. We trained each model for 200 epochs, found the epoch that gives the best tree-integrity performance on the validation set and then performed attack probing on that epoch. Some of the results are paradoxical. As with Section 5.1, language models apparently do not embody a complete account of syntactic information, but an attack on BERT brings a noticeably more adverse impact on performance than an attack, for example, on RH distance. This may be connected to the greater dispersion of BERT inputs over a larger dimensionality of input.

In other words, although RH + POS and BERT + RH + POS exhibit very close performance (Table 4) and RH is important for parsing, the model still weighs BERT more than RH distance. We can see in the second row of Table 5 that, over all measures, attacks on BERT always bring a more significant performance drop. This indicates that BERT's higher dimensionality makes information easier to extract better, increasing the model's generalizability to different downstream tasks. This advantage outweighs RH distance's provable adequacy as a representation of unlabelled binary syntactic trees.

We also note that the performance drop of attacking the word embeddings always stays between the performance drop of attacking the RH distance and that of attacking POS embeddings. However, this relative performance drop differs from language model to language model. Therefore, we calculate the relative importance of word embedding information as $\frac{S_{\text{embed}}-S_{\text{rh}}}{S_{\text{pos}}-S_{\text{rh}}}$, where S_{embed}, S_{pos}, and S_{rh} represent the measure S after attacks on the respective information source. As shown in Table 6, except for labelled EM, where every model gives similar scores that are very close to 0 (so the percentage is almost the same for every model), BERT has higher relative importance than the other two simpler language models. This indicates that although better language models do not necessarily contain more syntactic information, better language models will make information easier to pick out or extract for downstream classifiers, and therefore give better performance.

6 Conclusion

Does BERT know syntax? Our RH Probe results demonstrate that BERT contains important syntactic information, although this information alone cannot reproduce syntax in its entirety. Our empirical evidence is not subject to the criticism that the observed syntactic knowledge is not obtained by the language model through pretraining, but rather emerges from the probe classifier itself. The evidence is drawn from two carefully designed tasks, in which the substantial performance changes can be observed.

Nevertheless, we strongly agree with the insight (Wu et al., 2020) that the internal structure of BERT, although it may not embody a complete syntactic characterization of its input, can provide useful information for downstream applications. Recent probing attempts (Hewitt and Liang, 2019; Jawahar et al., 2019; Tenney et al., 2019a) have proved that the utility of knowledge acquired through pre-training is not limited to lexical semantics — word embedding also encodes syntax-adjacent information. Our probing results reinforce this argument through a more general examination of the relation between BERT and syntax.

References

Y. Adi, E. Kermany, Y. Belinkov, O. Lavi, and Y. Goldberg. 2017. Fine-grained analysis of sentence embeddings using auxiliary prediction tasks. In *Proceedings of ICLR*. OpenReview.net.

T. Akiba, S. Sano, T. Yanase, T. Ohta, and M. Koyama. 2019. Optuna: A Next-generation Hyperparameter Optimization Framework. In *Proceedings of ACM KDD*, pages 2623–2631.

P. Bhargava, A. Drozd, and A. Rogers. 2021. Generalization in NLI: Ways (Not) To Go Beyond Simple Heuristics. In *Proceedings of the Second Workshop on Insights from Negative Results in NLP*, pages 125–135. ACL.

S.A. Chowdhury and R. Zamparelli. 2018. RNN Simulations of Grammaticality Judgments on Long-distance Dependencies. In *Proceedings of COLING*, pages 133–144.

A. Clark, G. Giorgolo, and S. Lappin. 2013. Statistical Representation of Grammaticality Judgements: The Limits of N-Gram Models. In *Proceedings of the Fourth Annual Workshop on Cognitive Modeling and Computational Linguistics (CMCL)*, pages 28–36. ACL.

A. Conneau and D. Kiela. 2018. SentEval: An Evaluation Toolkit for Universal Sentence Representations. In *Proceedings of LREC*, pages 1699–1704.

A. Conneau, G. Kruszewski, G. Lample, L. Barrault, and M. Baroni. 2018. What you can cram into a single $&!#* vector: Probing sentence embeddings for linguistic properties. In *Proceedings of ACL*, pages 2126–2136.

J. Devlin, M.-W. Chang, K. Lee, and K. Toutanova. 2019. BERT: Pre-training of Deep Bidirectional Transformers for Language Understanding. In *Proceedings of NAACL*, pages 4171–4186.

A. Edwards, J. Camacho-Collados, H. De Ribaupierre, and A. Preece. 2020. Go Simple and Pre-Train on Domain-Specific Corpora: On the Role of Training Data for Text Classification. In *Proceedings of COLING*, pages 5522–5529.

J. Hewitt and P. Liang. 2019. Designing and Interpreting Probes with Control Tasks. In *Proceedings of EMNLP*, pages 2733–2743.

J. Hu, S. Chen, and R. Levy. 2020. A Closer Look at the Performance of Neural Language Models on Reflexive Anaphor Licensing. *Proceedings of SCiL*, 3(1):382–392.

D. Hupkes and W. Zuidema. 2018. Visualisation and 'Diagnostic Classifiers' Reveal how Recurrent and Recursive Neural Networks Process Hierarchical Structure (Extended Abstract). In *Proceedings of IJCAI*, pages 5617–5621.

G. Jawahar, B. Sagot, and D. Seddah. 2019. What Does BERT Learn about the Structure of Language? In *Proceedings of ACL*, pages 3651–3657.

Y. Kim, C. Dyer, and A. Rush. 2019. Compound Probabilistic Context-Free Grammars for Grammar Induction. In *Proceedings of ACL*, pages 2369–2385.

D.P. Kingma and J. Ba. 2015. Adam: A method for stochastic optimization. In *Proceedings of ICLR*.

J.H. Lau, A. Clark, and S. Lappin. 2014. Measuring Gradience in Speakers' Grammaticality Judgements. *Proceedings of the Annual Meeting of the Cognitive Science Society*, 36:821–826.

V.I. Levenshtein. 1965. Binary codes capable of correcting deletions, insertions, and reversals. *Soviet physics. Doklady*, 10:707–710.

M. Marcus, G. Kim, M.A. Marcinkiewicz, R. MacIntyre, A. Bies, M. Ferguson, K. Katz, and B. Schasberger. 1994. The Penn Treebank: Annotating Predicate Argument Structure. In *Human Language Technology: Proceedings of a Workshop Held at Plainsboro, New Jersey, March 8-11, 1994*, pages 114–119.

R. Marvin and T. Linzen. 2018. Targeted Syntactic Evaluation of Language Models. In *Proceedings of EMNLP*, pages 1192–1202.

T. Mikolov, K. Chen, G. Corrado, and J. Dean. 2013. Efficient Estimation of Word Representations in Vector Space. In *Proceedings of ICLR*.

J. Niu, W. Lu, and G. Penn. 2022. Does BERT rediscover a classical NLP pipeline? In *Proceedings of COLING*, pages 3143–3153.

F. Pereira. 2000. Formal grammar and information theory: Together again? *Philosophical Transactions of the Royal Society of London. Series A: Mathematical, Physical and Engineering Sciences*, 358(1769):1239–1253.

T. Pimentel, J. Valvoda, R. Hall Maudslay, R. Zmigrod, A. Williams, and R. Cotterell. 2020. Information-Theoretic Probing for Linguistic Structure. In *Proceedings of ACL*, pages 4609–4622.

B. Roark and K. Hollingshead. 2008. Classifying Chart Cells for Quadratic Complexity Context-Free Inference. In *Proceedings of COLING*, pages 745–752.

Y. Shen, Z. Lin, C. Huang, and A. Courville. 2018. Neural Language Modeling by Jointly Learning Syntax and Lexicon. In *Proceedings of ICLR*.

I. Tenney, D. Das, and E. Pavlick. 2019a. BERT Rediscovers the Classical NLP Pipeline. In *Proceedings of ACL*, pages 4593–4601.

I. Tenney, P. Xia, B. Chen, A. Wang, A. Poliak, R.T. McCoy, N. Kim, B. Van Durme, S.R. Bowman, D. Das, and E. Pavlick. 2019b. What do you learn from context? Probing for sentence structure in contextualized word representations. In *Proceedings of ICLR*.

A. Warstadt, A. Parrish, H. Liu, A. Mohananey, W. Peng, S.-F. Wang, and S.R. Bowman. 2020. BLiMP: The Benchmark of Linguistic Minimal Pairs for English. *Transactions of the Association for Computational Linguistics*, 8:377–392.

A. Warstadt, A. Singh, and S.R. Bowman. 2019. Neural Network Acceptability Judgments. *Transactions of the Association for Computational Linguistics*, 7:625–641.

Z. Wu, Y. Chen, B. Kao, and Q. Liu. 2020. Perturbed Masking: Parameter-free Probing for Analyzing and Interpreting BERT. In *Proceedings of ACL*, pages 4166–4176.

Z. Zhu and F. Rudzicz. 2020. An information theoretic view on selecting linguistic probes. In *Proceedings of EMNLP*, pages 9251–9262.

Z. Zhu, S. Shahtalebi, and F. Rudzicz. 2022. Predicting fine-tuning performance with probing. In *ACL BigScience Workshop*.

DALLE-2 is Seeing Double: Flaws in Word-to-Concept Mapping in Text2Image Models

Royi Rassin[*1], **Shauli Ravfogel**[*1,2] **Yoav Goldberg**[1,2]
[1]Bar-Ilan University [2]Allen Institute for Artificial Intelligence
{rassinroyi, shauli.ravfogel, yoav.goldberg}@gmail.com

Abstract

We study the way DALLE-2 maps symbols (words) in the prompt to their references (entities or properties of entities in the generated image). We show that in stark contrast to the way human process language, DALLE-2 does not follow the constraint that each word has a single role in the interpretation, and sometimes re-uses the same symbol for different purposes. We collect a set of stimuli that reflect the phenomenon: we show that DALLE-2 depicts both senses of nouns with multiple senses at once; and that a given word can modify the properties of two distinct entities in the image, or can be depicted as one object and also modify the properties of another object, creating a semantic leakage of properties between entities. Taken together, our study highlights the differences between DALLE-2 and human language processing and opens an avenue for future study on the inductive biases of text-to-image models.

Figure 1: The word *bat* is realized as two entities given the prompt *a bat is flying over a baseball stadium.*

1 Introduction

Large diffusion-based text-to-image models, such as DALLE-2 (Ramesh et al., 2022), generate visually compelling images that condition on input texts. Yet, the extent to which such models capture properties of human language, such as its compositional structure, has been doubted (Conwell and Ullman, 2022).

A very basic property in the interpretation of natural language utterances is that each word has a specific role in the interpretation, and there is a one-to-one mapping between symbols and roles. While symbols—as well as sentence structures—may be ambiguous, after an interpretation is constructed this ambiguity is already resolved. For example, while the symbol *bat* in *a flying bat* can be interpreted as either a wooden stick or an animal, our possible interpretations of the sentence are either of a *flying wooden stick* or *a flying animal*, but never both at the same time. Once the word *bat* has been used in the interpretation to denote an object (for example a wooden stick), it cannot be re-used to denote another object (an animal) in the same interpretation. Similarly, in *a fish and a gold ingot*, the word *gold* is used as a modifier of *ingot*.[1] Once it is used, it cannot be re-used to modify another object in the same interpretation, and also cannot be used as a standalone object.[2] Some linguists refer to this property as *resource sensitivity* (Salvucci et al., 2009).

We show evidence that—in stark contrast

*Equal contribution.

[1]We use the word "modifier" to refer to any word that influences the way another word is depicted in the output.

[2]Note that in some cases a single word can be used to modify several objects, for example, *a gold fish and ingot* can be interpreted as *a gold fish and a gold ingot.* These cases manifest in very specific syntactic configurations, and are well documented in linguistics. Indeed, the linguistic analysis of such cases are either based on mechanisms such as "duplication" of the word, or allude to a deeper version of the sentence in which the word appeared twice, and was dropped before production. While the reality behind these linguistic theories cannot be proven, the appeal to use such mechanisms as "duplication" or "deletion" (before realization) as explanations to the phenomena, highlights the naturalness of the "single use per symbol" principle.

Proceedings of the Fifth BlackboxNLP Workshop on Analyzing and Interpreting Neural Networks for NLP, pages 335 - 345
December 8, 2022

to humans—the text-to-image model DALLE-2 (Ramesh et al., 2022) does not respect this constraint. Indeed, we show that DALLE-2 exhibits the following behaviors that are inconsistent with the single-role principle:

- **A word or phrase is interpreted as two distinct (concurrently-incompatible) entities** and is consequently realized as multiple objects in the same scene. For instance, the prompt *a bat is flying over a stadium* is mapped to an image showing a baseball bat alongside the flying mammal (fig. 1).
- **A word is interpreted as a modifier of two different entities,**[3] and is consequently realized as a property of multiple objects in the scene. For instance, the prompt *a fish and a gold ingot* is mapped to an image showing a gold ingot as well as a goldfish (section 4.2).
- **A word is interpreted simultaneously as an entity and as a modifier of a different entity** and is consequently realized as an object in the scene as well as as a property of another object in the same scene. For instance, the prompt *a seal is opening a letter* is mapped to an image showing a seal holding a *sealed* letter (fig. 2).

Visually, the cases we highlight map to one of two failure modes from the perspective of the image designer / user: (a) sense-ambiguous words are hard to isolate, and the resulting images often exhibit the unintended sense together with the intended one (*homonym duplication*). (b) visual properties of one object in the image "leak" into other objects in the image (*concept leakage*).[4]

We also observe some *second order effects*, where a hypernym of the modifier word, or an implicit description of it, also triggers the duplication effect.

Taken together, the phenomena we examine provides evidence for limitations in the linguistic ability of DALLE-2 and opens avenues for future research that would uncover whether those stem from issues with the text encoding, the generative model, or both. More generally, the proposed approach can be extended to other scenarios where the decoding process is used to uncover the inductive bias and the shortcomings of text-to-image models.

Figure 2: The word *seal* is realized both as an object and as a modifier of another word (*letter*) in the prompt *a seal is opening a letter*, resulting in *concept leakage*. The prompt tends to generate *sealed* letters, while minimally-different prompts that do not contain the noun *seal* do not.

2 Previous Work

Promptly after the introduction of DALLE-2 (Ramesh et al., 2022), analyses of the system began to surface (Marcus et al., 2022; Conwell and Ullman, 2022). Conwell and Ullman (2022) showed that DALLE-2 does not understand spatial relations. Marcus et al. (2022) reported that if an object in the prompt is said to have some property, then the image will likely show that property somewhere, however, not necessarily on the correct object. We take this analysis a step further, showing that the same property sometimes simultaneously modifies several unrelated objects. Ramesh et al. (2022) allude to the phenomena we analyze: they mention the issues with binding separate attributes to separate objects, and hypothesize that it is because CLIP (Radford et al., 2021) embeddings do not explicitly bind attributes to objects. Accordingly, they observe that that reconstructions from the decoder often mix up attributes and objects. Concurrent to this work, Hutchinson et al. (2022) discuss under-specification in text-to-image generation, a condition which we find to be associated with some of the behaviors we identify; and Anonymous (2023) discuss several cases of "leakage", and propose an intervention in the decoding process that is aimed to mitigate them.

[3]While not under a syntactic configuration that allows such duplication.

[4]Importantly, we note that both phenomena rarely occur when explicit specification is provided, e.g, the prompt *a fruit bat is flying over a stadium* generates only the flying mammal. See Hutchinson et al. (2022) for a discussion on under-specification in text-to-image generation.

3 Methdos

Stimuli We construct linguistic stimuli (prompts) which evoke a behavior that is inconsistent with the single-use-per-symbol axiom. For the first case (words interpreted as two entities), we use *homonyms*, words that have two distinct senses. `DALLE-2` often generates two objects, one corresponding to each of the senses. For the modification cases, we construct the following prompts. For the case of a word that is interpreted as a modifier of two entities, we include prompts with two entities e_1 and e_2 and a modifier word m that is semantically compatible with both of them, but is only syntactically modifying the second one (For instance, "A *fish*$_{e_1}$ and a *gold*$_m$ *ingot*$_{e_2}$"). For the case of a word that is simultaneously interpreted as an entity as well as a modifier, we construct stimuli that contain two entities e_1 and e_2, such as that one of them is semantically associated with the other noun—for instance, "classic *butter*$_{e_1}$ and *peanuts*$_{e_2/m}$".

The complete list of stimuli is presented in tables 1, 2 and 3 in appendix A.1, together with samples of the generated images.

Control Stimuli In order to argue for the existence of a leakage of property P between two entities e_1 and e_2, we need to assess whether `DALLE-2` does not tend to depict e_2 with that property, regardless of e_1. For instance, if the default *groceries* for `DALLE-2` in different contexts is a groceries basket, it is hard to argue that it is the presence of the word *basket* in "a *basketball* near *groceries*" that elicited `DALLE-2` to generate a basket. With this in mind, we generate a set of control prompts, which are minimally-different variations over the challenge prompts, that were built so as to prevent the possibility of a leakage by changing either n_1 or n_2 alone, depending on which change can prevent the leakage in a given prompt. The full set of controls are also detailed in tables 2 and 3.

4 Results

We generate 12 images per stimulus, and report the average over all stimuli and images.

4.1 A single word realized as multiple entities

We have 17 stimuli that elicit `DALLE-2` to assign a single word two roles. Homonym duplication occurred in 80.3% of the 216 images. We found that, out of context, the vast majority of words are biased

left: *A bass lounging in a tropical resort in space, vaporwave.*
right: *a fan at a hot sport event.*

towards a particular sense, specifically, out of our 17 homonyms, only *bass* and *date* reveal homonym duplication without added context. Using *bass* as a prompt will[5] return an image of a *seabass* and a *guitar bass* or a *speaker bass*, and for *date*, `DALLE-2` will return a romantic couple, holding together a date (the fruit). Most of the homonym duplication prompts were created by including context related to the non-default role of the homonym. For instance, for the homonym *fan*, `DALLE-2` is biased towards the cooling device, but if we are to add context that is related to the other possible role a *fan* can have (a sports fan), and that still applies towards the cooling device, we will get both: *A fan at a hot sports event* (top of section 4.1).

4.2 A single word realized as a modifier of multiple entities

Main (left): *a **fish** and a **gold** ingot.*
Control (right): *a fish and an ingot.*

Given a pair of entities (e_1, e_2), we observe that the underspecified entity, e_2 is depicted by `DALLE-2` with properties from e_1: in the prompt *A fish and a gold ingot*, *gold* modifies *fish*, and the image consistently contains a golden fish.[6] This is

[5] Using just a homonym as a prompt does not consistently elicit the phenomenon as a prompt that includes context with the homonym.

[6] Interestingly, The golden fish also resemble goldfish, suggesting that priming effect also extends to compounds, even though the word *gold* in *gold ingot* is a part of a phrase with a compositional structure, while "goldfish" is not compositional.

likely because *fish* is an underspecified noun and *gold* is an amicable property to fish. In the control, *a fish and an ingot*, golden fish do not appear at all in the output.

For the two-properties case, we have 6 stimuli-control pairs. The output of the stimuli prompts display the shared property in 97.2% of the cases, while the control prompts show that property in only 15.2% of the cases.

4.3 A single word is realized as an entity and as a modifier of another entity

Main (left): *A* ***zebra*** *and a* ***street.***
Control (right): *A zebra and a gravel street.*

For the entity-to-property case, we have 10 stimuli-control pairs. On average, the stimuli prompts exhibit the shared property in 92.5% of the cases while the control prompt shows it in only 6.6% of the cases.

In similar fashion to the two-properties case, n_2 is depicted by DALLE-2 with properties from n_1, however, this time, n_1 is not a property, but an entity. To demonstrate, consider *a zebra and a street*, here, *zebra* is an entity, but it modifies *street*, and DALLE-2 constantly generates crosswalks, possibly because of the zebra-stripes' likeness to a crosswalk. And in line with our conjecture, the control *a zebra and a gravel street* specifies a type of street that typically does not have crosswalks, and indeed, all of our control samples for this prompt do not contain a crosswalk. When n_1 is a homonym, the entity-to-property case is more nuanced, for example, in *food and a cone hat, zoomed out photo*, the word *cone* modifies *food* by generating ice-cream cones, while its control: *food and a birthday hat, zoomed out photo*, a semantically and physically equivalent replacement of *cone*, does not lead to the generation of ice-cream cone.

4.4 Second-order stimuli

Main (left): *a tall, long-legged, long-necked bird and a construction site.*
Control (right): *a bird and a construction site.*

Concept Leakage can be taken a step further, by masking the affecting noun and receiving similar results: *a tall, long-legged, long-necked bird and a construction site* is describing *a crane and a construction site*, but nowhere in the prompt a *crane* is mentioned. Yet, it will cause DALLE-2 to generate two types of cranes: a bird crane, and a construction crane. We also observe that the bird-crane's head and legs share physical properties with the crane. From the same challenge prompt, the border between a bird-crane and a construction-crane is especially blurred. This behavior is not repeated when the description of a bird-crane is removed from the prompt: *a bird and a construction site.* This suggests that the model first maps entities into a concept space, and only then renders.

4.5 Other text-to-image-models

The empirical focus of this work is DALLE-2. In preliminary experiments, we found that DALLE-mini (Dayma et al., 2021)—a much smaller model—did not replicate the observed phenomena. Particularly, only the "common" word sense is depicted for homonyms. As for Stable-diffusion (Rombach et al., 2021), the phenomena seem to occur less frequently, particularly because in many times the model does not follow the prompt at all. Other models, such as (Saharia et al., 2022; Yu et al., 2022), are not publicly available. We hypothesize that—paradoxically—it is the lower capacity of DALLE-mini and Stable-diffusion and the fact they do not robustly follow the prompts, that make them appear "better" with respect to the flaws we examine. A thorough evaluation of the relation between scale, model architecture, and concept leakage is left to future work.

5 Conclusions

We demonstrate that across a set of stimuli, `DALLE-2` does not follow basic principles of symbol-to-entity mapping in language. This flaw is especially pressing given that `DALLE-2` is directed to the general population, where the majority of the users are probably not aware of the phenomenon.[7] Future work should trace back the issues we diagnose to specific components in the model, such as the text encoding or the generative decoder; and study its dependence on scale and architecture. Additionally, the development of post-hoc mitigation techniques is especially important, given that most users lack the resources needed to train the models from scratch.

6 Acknowledgements

We thank Carlo Meloni for his valuable feedback. This project received funding from the European Research Council (ERC) under the European Union's Horizon 2020 research and innovation programme, grant agreement No. 802774 (iEXTRACT).

7 Limitations

One limitation of this work is the focus on `DALLE-2` a commercial product, whose source code is not publicly available. As discussed, capacity issues prevented a thorough examination of the phenomena we focus on in other available models. We hope that additional models of similar scale will be released to the public in the future, enabling a more thorough examination. Additionally, our analysis is focused on a manually constructed set of stimuli, that were designed so as to surface the issues we focus on in the clearest way. Scaling the analysis would rely on automatic or semi-automatic generation of stimuli of the kind we use, which is a challenging task. Yet, we believe that such large-scale analysis is important in order to robustly quantify the issues we observe.

References

Anonymous. 2023. Training-free structured diffusion guidance for compositional text-to-image synthesis. In *Submitted to The Eleventh International Conference on Learning Representations*. Under review.

Colin Conwell and Tomer Ullman. 2022. Testing relational understanding in text-guided image generation.

Boris Dayma, Suraj Patil, Pedro Cuenca, Khalid Saifullah, Tanishq Abraham, Phúc Lê Khac, Luke Melas, and Ritobrata Ghosh. 2021. Dall·e mini.

Ben Hutchinson, Jason Baldridge, and Vinodkumar Prabhakaran. 2022. Underspecification in scene description-to-depiction tasks. *arXiv preprint arXiv:2210.05815*.

Gary Marcus, Ernest Davis, and Scott Aaronson. 2022. A very preliminary analysis of dall-e 2.

Alec Radford, Jong Wook Kim, Chris Hallacy, Aditya Ramesh, Gabriel Goh, Sandhini Agarwal, Girish Sastry, Amanda Askell, Pamela Mishkin, Jack Clark, Gretchen Krueger, and Ilya Sutskever. 2021. Learning transferable visual models from natural language supervision.

Aditya Ramesh, Prafulla Dhariwal, Alex Nichol, Casey Chu, and Mark Chen. 2022. Hierarchical text-conditional image generation with clip latents.

Robin Rombach, Andreas Blattmann, Dominik Lorenz, Patrick Esser, and Björn Ommer. 2021. High-resolution image synthesis with latent diffusion models.

Chitwan Saharia, William Chan, Saurabh Saxena, Lala Li, Jay Whang, Emily Denton, Seyed Kamyar Seyed Ghasemipour, Burcu Karagol Ayan, S. Sara Mahdavi, Rapha Gontijo Lopes, Tim Salimans, Jonathan Ho, David J Fleet, and Mohammad Norouzi. 2022. Photorealistic text-to-image diffusion models with deep language understanding.

Dario D Salvucci, Niels A Taatgen, and Jelmer P Borst. 2009. Toward a unified theory of the multitasking continuum: From concurrent performance to task switching, interruption, and resumption. In *Proceedings of the SIGCHI conference on human factors in computing systems*, pages 25, item 90.

Jiahui Yu, Yuanzhong Xu, Jing Yu Koh, Thang Luong, Gunjan Baid, Zirui Wang, Vijay Vasudevan, Alexander Ku, Yinfei Yang, Burcu Karagol Ayan, Ben Hutchinson, Wei Han, Zarana Parekh, Xin Li, Han Zhang, Jason Baldridge, and Yonghui Wu. 2022. Scaling autoregressive models for content-rich text-to-image generation.

[7]While the issues we focus on can easily go unnoticed when examining a randomly-selected set of outputs–which mostly look very good—our examination of carefully-selected stimuli clearly reveals them. We believe that such analysis is important, as human language is characterized by many long-tail phenomena.

A Appendix

A.1 Data

The full image-dataset can be accessed at `https://github.com/RoyiRa/DALLE2-Flaws-in-word-to-concept-mapping`.

The following tables contain the stimuli we use to test the reference system of `DALLE-2` .

Prompt	Duplication Ratio
A person wearing a **cone** hat is eating, a full body photo	7/12
A **bat** is flying over a baseball stadium	11/12
A **bass** lounging in a tropical resort in space, vaporwave	10/12
A **fan** at a hot sports event	12/12
A **crane** carrying a heavy material, fish in the background	12/12
A banker collecting **dough**	9/12
Two men having a loud **beef**, restaurant in the background	10/12
A model with an **hourglass** figure	12/12
A gentleman with a **bow** in the forest	11/12
A woman is pouring water into her **glasses**	9/12
A man stuck in a **jam**, eating	7/12
A great **ruler**	8/12
Apple commercial	12/12
A person with **metal nails**	6/12
date	7/12
a person with **chicken legs**, full body image	12/12
a **board** meeting	9/12

Table 1: List of stimuli for the **multiple entities** case (Section 4.1). The noun that is mapped to two entities is denoted with **bold**

Challenge and Control	Challenge Ratio	Control Ratio
a person **jay**walking and a *bird* A person crossing the street unlawfully and a bird	11/12	0/12
food and a **cone** hat, zoomed out photo food and a birthday hat, zoomed out photo	12/12	0/12
A *fish* and a **gold** ingot A fish and an ingot	12/12	0/12
A **basket**ball near *groceries* A football near groceries	12/12	5/12
A **lady**bug and a *person*, full body image A bug and a person, full body image	11/12	6/12
An *animal* alongside a **piggy bank** An animal alongside a table	12/12	0/12

Table 2: Challenge and Control Prompts in **word-to-multiple-modifiers** case (section 4.2). The modifier nouns in the Challenge prompts are denoted with **bold**, and modified nouns with *italic*

Challenge and Control	Challenge Ratio	Control Ratio
A **zebra** and a *street* A zebra and a gravel street	10/12	0/12
A **seal** is opening a *letter* A large water mammal is opening a letter	10/12	1/12
Two people play **squash** with *food* Two people play squash	12/12	0/12
a **pool** and a *table* a pool and a bar	10/12	0/12
A person is washing hair with **Dove** *shampoo* A person is washing hair with shampoo	12/12	0/12
an **armadillo** and an *elephant* a rhino and an elephant	12/12	0/12
a fish and an **elephant** a rhino and an elephant	12/12	0/12
A **cross** and a *sidewalk* A crucifix and a sidewalk	10/12	2/12
classic butter and **peanuts** classic butter and cucumbers	12/12	0/12
A **leopard** and a *piece of cloth* a leopard and a black towel	11/12	5/12

Table 3: Challenge and Control Prompts in the **word-to-entity-and-modifier** case (Section 4.3). The modifier nouns in the Challenge prompts are denoted with **bold**, and modified nouns with *italic*

Challenge and Control	Challenge Ratio	Control Ratio
An **armadillo** on a *sea* shore A dog on a sea shore	12/12	0/12
A **pinniped** is opening a *letter* A large water mammal is opening a letter	7/12	1/12
a **tall, long-legged, long-necked bird** and a *construction site* a bird and a construction site	12/12	0/12
A *person* and a **bug with red spots**, full body image A bug and a person, full body image	11/12	6/12

Table 4: Challenge and Control Prompts in **Second-Order Concept Leakage** (Section 4.4). The modifier nouns in the Challenge prompts are denoted with **bold**, and modified nouns with *italic*

Single word realised as multiple entities

*A person wearing a **cone** hat is eating, full body photo*

*A **crane** carrying a heavy material, fish in the background*

*A **fan** at a hot sports event*

*A **bat** is flying over a baseball stadium*

*A banker collecting **dough***

*A model with an **hourglass** figure*

*A **bass** lounging in a tropical resort in space, vaporwave*

*Two men having a loud **beef**, restaurant in the background*

*A gentleman with a **bow** in the forest*

*A woman is pouring water into her **glasses***

*A man stuck in a **jam**, eating*

*A great **ruler***

***Apple** commercial*

*A person with **metal nails***

date

*A **board** meeting*

*A person with **chicken legs**, full body image*

A word acting as a modifier of two different entities

Bold items are **entities**, and bold+underline is the **modifier**.

Main (left): *A **person jay**walking and a **bird***
Control (right): *A person crossing the street unlawfully and a bird*

Main (left): ***food** and a **cone hat**, zoomed out photo*
Control (right): *food and a birthday hat, zoomed out photo*

Main (left): *A **fish** and a **gold ingot***
Control (right): *A fish and an ingot*

Main (left): *A **basketball** near **groceries***
Control (right): *A football near groceries*

Main (left): *A **ladybug** and a **person**, full body image*
Control (right): *A bug and a person, full body image*

Main (left): *An **animal** alongside a **piggy bank***
Control (right): *An animal alongside a table*

Same word realised as an entity as well as a modifier of another entity

Bold item is the **entity**, bold+underline is acting as both **modifier and entity**.

Main (left): *A **zebra** and a **street***
Control (right): *A zebra and a gravel street*

Main (left): *Two people play **squash** with **food***
Control (right): *Two people play squash*

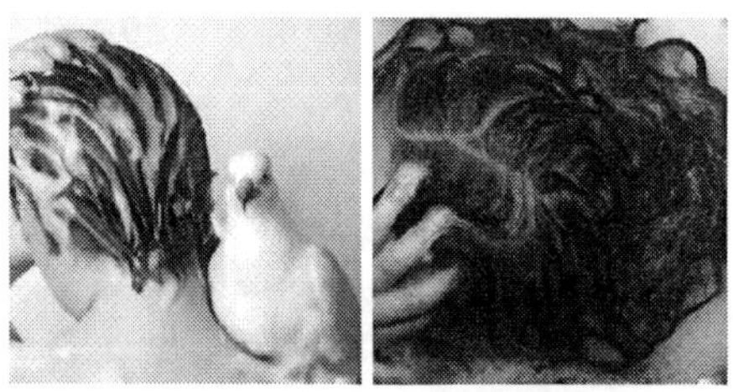

Main (left): *A person is washing hair with **Dove shampoo***
Control (right): *A person is washing hair with shampoo*

Main (left): *a **fish** and an **elephant***
Control (right): *a rhino and an elephant*

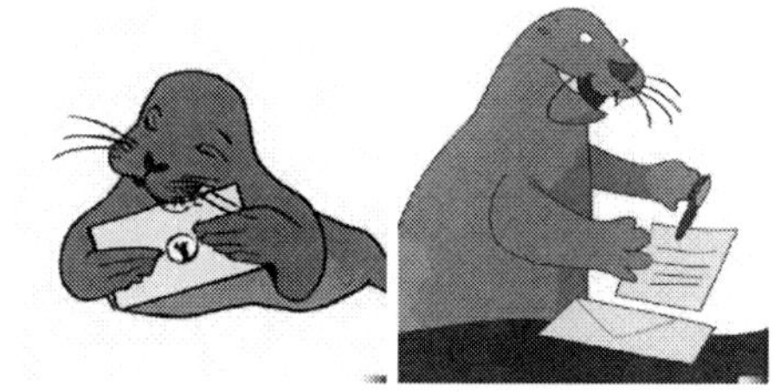

Main (left): *A **seal** is opening a **letter***
Control (right): *A large water mammal is opening a letter*

Main (left): *a **pool** and a **table***
Control (right): *a pool and a bar*

Main (left): *an **armadillo** and an **elephant***
Control (right): *a rhino and an elephant*

Main (left): *A **cross** and a **sidewalk***
Control (right): a crucifix and a sidewalk

Main (left): *classic **butter** and **peanuts***
Control (right): *classic butter and cucumbers*

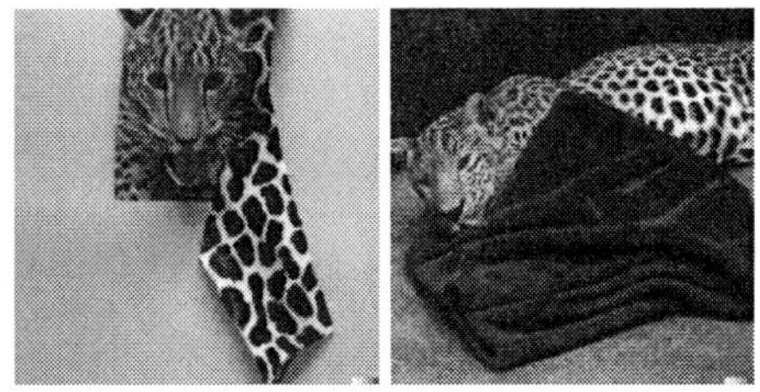

Main (left): *A **leopard** and a piece of **cloth***
Control (right): *a leopard and a black towel*

Second order concept leakage

Main (left): *A tall, long-legged, long-necked bird and a construction site*
Control (right): *a bird and a construction site*
Explanation: the *tall, long-legged, long-necked bird* is identified as a **crane** and realised as two kinds of cranes.

Main (left): *A pinniped is opening a letter*
Control (right): *A large water mammal is opening a letter*
Explanation: the *pinniped* interpreted as a **seal,** which is realised both as the actor and as a seal on the letter.

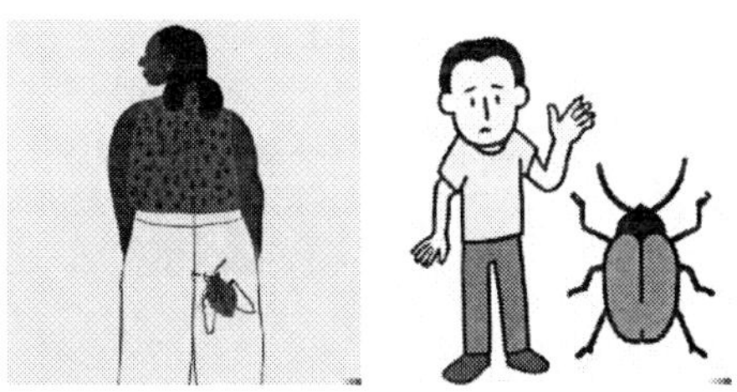

Main (left): *A person and a bug with red spots, full body image*
Control (right): *A bug and a person, full body image*
Explanation: The *bug with red spots* is identified as a **ladybug**, and the person is female (*lady*).

Main (left): *An Armadillo on a sea shore*
Control (right): *A dog on a sea shore*
Explanation: the *armadillo* has a **shell**, and there are shells on the beach.

Practical Benefits of Feature Feedback Under Distribution Shift

Anurag Katakkar*, Clay H. Yoo*, Weiqin Wang,
Zachary C. Lipton, Divyansh Kaushik
Carnegie Mellon University
akatakka,hyungony,weiqinw,zlipton,dkaushik@cmu.edu

Abstract

In attempts to develop sample-efficient and interpretable algorithms, researcher have explored myriad mechanisms for collecting and exploiting *feature feedback* (or *rationales*) auxiliary annotations provided for training (but not test) instances that highlight salient evidence. Examples include bounding boxes around objects and salient spans in text. Despite its intuitive appeal, feature feedback has not delivered significant gains in practical problems as assessed on iid holdout sets. However, recent works on counterfactually augmented data suggest an alternative benefit of supplemental annotations, beyond interpretability: lessening sensitivity to spurious patterns and consequently delivering gains in out-of-domain evaluations. We speculate that while existing methods for incorporating feature feedback have delivered negligible in-sample performance gains, they may nevertheless provide out-of-domain benefits. Our experiments addressing sentiment analysis, show that feature feedback methods perform significantly better on various natural out-of-domain datasets despite comparable in-domain evaluations. By contrast, performance on natural language inference remains comparable. Finally, we compare those tasks where feature feedback does (and does not) help.

1 Introduction

Addressing various classification tasks in natural language processing (NLP), including sentiment analysis (Zaidan et al., 2007), natural language inference (NLI) (DeYoung et al., 2020), and propaganda detection (Pruthi et al., 2020), researchers have introduced resources containing additional side information by tasking humans with marking spans in the input text (called *rationales* or *feature feedback)* that provide supporting evidence for the label. For example, spans like "underwhelming", "horrible", or "worst film since Johnny English" might indicate negative sentiment in a movie review. Conversely, spans like "exciting", "amazing", or "I never thought Vin Diesel would make me cry" might indicate positive sentiment.

These works have proposed a variety of strategies for incorporating feature feedback as additional supervision (Lei et al., 2016; Zhang et al., 2016; Lehman et al., 2019; Chen et al., 2019; Jain et al., 2020; DeYoung et al., 2020; Pruthi et al., 2020). Other researchers have studied the learning-theoretic properties of feature feedback (Poulis and Dasgupta, 2017; Dasgupta et al., 2018; Dasgupta and Sabato, 2020). We focus our study on the resources and practical methods developed for NLP.

Some have used this feedback to perturb instances for data augmentation (Zaidan et al., 2007), while others have explored multitask objectives for simultaneously classifying documents and extracting rationales (Pruthi et al., 2020). A number of papers exploit feature feedback as intermediate supervision for building extract-then-classify pipelines (Chen et al., 2019; Lehman et al., 2019; Jain et al., 2020). One common assumption is that resulting models would learn to identify and rely more on spans relevant to the target labels, which would in turn lead to more accurate predictions.

However, despite their intuitive appeal, feature feedback methods have thus far yielded underwhelming results on independent drawn and identically distributed (iid) test sets in applications involving deep nets. While Zaidan et al. (2007) found significant gains when incorporating rationales into their SVM learning scheme, benefits have been negligible in the BERT era. For example, although Pruthi et al. (2020) and Jain et al. (2020) address a different aim towards boosting interpretability—to improve extraction accuracy—their experiments show no improvement in classification accuracy by incorporating rationales.

On the other hand, Kaushik et al. (2020), introduced counterfactually augmented data (CAD) with the primary aim of showing how supplementary annotations can be incorporated to make mod-

Proceedings of the Fifth BlackboxNLP Workshop on Analyzing and Interpreting Neural Networks for NLP, pages 346 - 355
December 8, 2022 ©2022 Association for Computational Linguistics

els less sensitive to spurious patterns, and additionally demonstrated that models trained on CAD degraded less in a collection of out-of-domain tests than their vanilla counterparts. In followup work, they showed that for both CAD and feature feedback, although corruptions to evidence spans via random word flips result in performance degradation both in- and out-of-domain, when non-evidence spans are corrupted, out-of-domain performance often improves (Kaushik et al., 2021). These findings echo earlier results in computer vision (Ross et al., 2017a; Ross and Doshi-Velez, 2018) where regularizing input gradients (so-called *local explanations*) to accord with expert attributions led to an improved out-of-domain performance.

In this paper, we conduct an empirical study of the out-of-domain benefits of incorporating feature feedback in selected domains in NLP (sentiment analysis and NLI). We seek to address two primary research questions: (i) do models that rely on feature feedback generalize better out of domain compared to *classify-only* models (i.e., models trained without feature feedback)? and (ii) do we need to solicit feature feedback for an entire dataset or can significant benefits be realized with a modest fraction of examples annotated? Our experiments on sentiment analysis (Zaidan et al., 2007) and NLI (DeYoung et al., 2020) use both linear, BERT (Devlin et al., 2019), and ELECTRA (Clark et al., 2020) models, using two feature feedback techniques (Pruthi et al., 2020; Jain et al., 2020).

We limit our experiments to sentiment analysis and NLI only, although other tasks such as hate speech and propaganda detection might appear to be natural candidates to include in our study as well. Hate Speech detection is an inherently subjective task. For example, (Waseem, 2016) documented the disagreement between labels collected from the crowd and those annotated by experts. Similarly, (Ross et al., 2017b) documented that annotating hate speech itself is a hard task leading to low inter-rater agreement within the crowd as well. Thus, even though several hate speech classification datasets exist, in our view, they are not suitable for the research questions we ask in the paper—what might be labeled as hate by one annotator may not be labeled hate in another dataset by another annotator, making it difficult to attribute the impact on performance to generalization ability or some other factors (such as noisy labeling, or choice of labeling instructions, etc.). As for propaganda detection, while a dataset with high-quality labels and feature feedback annotations exists, the lack of additional datasets restricts our ability to train and evaluate the resulting models on a battery of out-of-domain datasets.

We find that sentiment analysis models fine-tuned with feature feedback on IMDb data see no improvement in in-domain accuracy. However, out-of-domain, sentiment analysis models benefit significantly from feature feedback. For example, ELECTRA and BERT models both see gains of $\approx$ 6% on both Amazon (Ni et al., 2019) and Yelp reviews (Kaushik et al., 2021) even when feature feedback is available for just 25% of instances. However, on NLI, we find that both iid and out-of-domain performance are comparable with or without feature feedback. We further find that while for sentiment analysis, rationales constitute only $\approx$ 21% of all unique tokens in the training set, for NLI they constitute $\approx$ 80%, potentially helping to explain why feature feedback is less useful there.

2 Methods and Datasets

We focus on two techniques (classify-and-extract (Pruthi et al., 2020) and extract-then-classify (Jain et al., 2020)), two pretrained models, and one (in-domain) dataset each for sentiment analysis and NLI that contain feature feedback. For both techniques, *feature feedback* annotations provide supervision to the extractive component. The classify-and-extract model jointly predicts the (categorical) label and performs sequence tagging predict rationales. The classification head and a linear chain CRF (Lafferty et al., 2001) share an encoder, initialized with pretrained weights.

The extract-then-classify method (Jain et al., 2020) first trains a classifier (*support*) on complete examples to predict the label, using its outputs to extract continuous feature importance scores. These scores are then binarized using a second classifier (*extractor*) which is trained on the feature importance scores from *support* and makes token-level binary predictions to identify rationale tokens in the input. A binary cross-entropy term in the objective of the extractor is used to maximise agreement of the extracted tokens with human rationales. Finally, a third classifier (*predictor*) is trained to predict the target (sentiment or entailment) label based only on these extracted tokens.

For both approaches, we experiment with two pretrained models (BERT and ELECTRA). We

Test set	Classify-only	Pruthi et al.	Jain et al.
BERT			
In-domain	$85.9_{0.7}$	$\mathbf{89.9_{2.3}}$	$\mathbf{90.4_{0.3}}$
CRD	$89.3_{0.7}$	$\mathbf{91.6_{0.7}}$	$87.5_{0.8}$
SST2	$77.6_{4.1}$	$79.3_{3.6}$	$75.6_{1.2}$
Amazon	$78.1_{4.9}$	$83.5_{3.1}$	$\mathbf{92.3_{1.2}}$
Semeval	$70.6_{5.7}$	$73.2_{2.6}$	$68.6_{2.2}$
Yelp	$86.8_{1.7}$	$85.7_{1.6}$	$\mathbf{91.6_{0.1}}$
ELECTRA			
In-domain	$93.2_{0.3}$	$91.8_{1.4}$	$93.1_{0.3}$
CRD	$91.6_{0.4}$	$\mathbf{93.7_{0.9}}$	$91.5_{0.7}$
SST2	$73.2_{1.3}$	$74.0_{1.2}$	$\mathbf{77.2_{1.4}}$
Amazon	$72.8_{2.0}$	$75.5_{2.1}$	$\mathbf{84.2_{1.6}}$
Semeval	$67.5_{4.5}$	$72.5_{1.8}$	$66.7_{3.0}$
Yelp	$79.0_{3.6}$	$\mathbf{84.6_{1.8}}$	$\mathbf{94.7_{0.2}}$

Table 1: Mean and standard deviation (in subscript) of accuracy scores of classify-only models, and models proposed by Pruthi et al. (2020) and Jain et al. (2020), fined-tuned for sentiment analysis. Significant results ($p < 0.05$) compared to the classify-only models are highlighted in bold.

Test set	Classify-only	Pruthi et al.	Jain et al.
BERT			
In-domain	$88.7_{2.0}$	$89.8_{0.8}$	$77.7_{0.1}$
RP	$62.9_{3.9}$	$66.6_{0.6}$	$57.9_{0.1}$
RH	$76.9_{3.5}$	$80.5_{1.9}$	$70.7_{0.2}$
MNLI-M	$69.7_{2.6}$	$68.1_{1.9}$	$69.8_{0.1}$
MNLI-MM	$71.5_{2.7}$	$69.2_{2.3}$	$66.2_{0.1}$
ELECTRA			
In-domain	$\mathbf{96.0_{0.2}}$	$95.0_{0.3}$	$85.4_{0.04}$
RP	$80.8_{1.0}$	$78.0_{0.6}$	$72.2_{0.1}$
RH	$88.9_{1.0}$	$88.7_{0.9}$	$79.7_{0.1}$
MNLI-M	$86.5_{0.9}$	$81.9_{2.1}$	$77.1_{0.1}$
MNLI-MM	$86.6_{0.8}$	$82.1_{2.0}$	$75.7_{0.1}$

Table 2: Mean and standard deviation (in subscript) of F1 scores of models fine-tuned for NLI with an increasing number of examples with feature feedback. Significant results ($p < 0.05$) compared to the classify-only models are highlighted in bold.

limit the maximum sequence length to 512 tokens and train all models for 10 epochs using AdamW optimizer (Loshchilov and Hutter, 2019) with a learning rate of $2e-5$ and a batch size of 8 and early stopping based on mean of classification and extraction F1 scores on the validation set. We replicate all experiments on 5 seeds and report mean performance along with standard deviation.

To see whether results are consistent across architectures, we also use a linear SVM (Zaidan et al., 2007) with a modified objective function on top of the ordinary soft-margin SVM, i.e.,

$$\frac{1}{2}||w||^2 + C(\sum_i \delta_i) + C_{\text{contrast}}(\sum_{i,j} \xi_{ij})$$

subject to the constraints $\vec{w} \cdot \vec{x}_{ij} \cdot y_i \geq 1 - \xi_{ij}\ \forall i, j$ where $\vec{x}_{ij} := \frac{\vec{x}_i - \vec{v}_{ij}}{\mu}$ are *psuedoexamples*, created by subtracting *contrast-examples* ($\vec{v}_{ij}$), input sentence void of randomly chosen rationales, from the original input ($\vec{x}_i$). We use term-frequency embeddings with unigrams appearing in at least 10 reviews and set $C = C_{contrast} = \mu = 1$. For each training example, we generate 5 psuedoexamples.

Datasets For sentiment analysis, we use an IMDb movie reviews dataset (Zaidan et al., 2007). Reviews in this dataset are labeled as having either *positive* or *negative* sentiment. Zaidan et al. (2007) also tasked annotators to mark spans in each review that were indicative of the overall sentiment. We use these spans as feature feedback. Overall, the dataset has 1800 reviews in the training set (with feature feedback) and 200 in test (without feature feedback). Since the test set does not include ground truth labels for evidence extraction, we construct a test set out of the 1800 examples in the original training set. This leaves 1200 reviews for a new training set, 300 for validation, and 300 for test. For NLI, we use a subsample of the E-SNLI dataset (DeYoung et al., 2020) used in Kaushik et al. (2021). In this dataset, there are 6318 premise-hypothesis pairs, equally divided across *entailment* and *contradiction* categories.

We evaluate on CRD (Kaushik et al., 2020), SST-2 (Socher et al., 2013), Amazon reviews (Ni et al., 2019), Tweets (Rosenthal et al., 2017) and Yelp reviews (Kaushik et al., 2021) for sentiment analysis, and Revised Premise (RP), Revised Hypothesis (RH) (Kaushik et al., 2020), MNLI matched (MNLI-M) and mismatched (MNLI-MM) (Williams et al., 2018) for NLI.

3 Experiments

We first fine-tune BERT and ELECTRA on the annotated IMDb dataset (Zaidan et al., 2007) following both classify-and-extract and extract-then-classify approaches. We evaluate resulting models on both iid test set as well as various naturally occurring out-of-domain datasets for sentiment analysis and compare resulting performance with classify-only models (Table 1). We find that both approaches lead to significant gains (when tested with t-test with $p < 0.05$) in out-of-domain performance compared to the classify-only method. For

Evaluation set	Fraction of Training Data with Rationales				
	No rationales	25%	50%	75%	100%
BERT					
In-domain	$85.9_{0.7}$	$\mathbf{87.7_{1.1}}$	$88.1_{2.4}$	$\mathbf{90.2_{1.5}}$	$\mathbf{89.9_{2.3}}$
CRD	$89.3_{0.7}$	$\mathbf{91.7_{0.6}}$	$\mathbf{92.3_{0.9}}$	$\mathbf{92.3_{0.3}}$	$\mathbf{91.6_{0.7}}$
SST2	$77.6_{4.1}$	$81.2_{0.6}$	$81.3_{0.7}$	$81.8_{0.6}$	$79.3_{3.6}$
Amazon	$78.1_{4.9}$	$\mathbf{85.3_{1.2}}$	$\mathbf{84.6_{1.7}}$	$\mathbf{84.0_{0.5}}$	$83.5_{3.1}$
Semeval	$70.6_{5.7}$	$\mathbf{77.8_{1.0}}$	$75.5_{0.8}$	$74.9_{0.8}$	$73.2_{2.6}$
Yelp	$86.8_{1.7}$	$86.9_{1.1}$	$85.8_{1.5}$	$85.4_{0.7}$	$85.7_{1.6}$
ELECTRA					
In-domain	$93.2_{0.3}$	$92.4_{0.9}$	$92.8_{1.2}$	$93.7_{1.9}$	$91.8_{1.4}$
CRD	$91.6_{0.4}$	$92.1_{0.8}$	$\mathbf{93.0_{0.6}}$	$\mathbf{93.1_{0.3}}$	$\mathbf{93.7_{0.9}}$
SST2	$73.2_{1.3}$	$73.1_{1.8}$	$72.3_{1.6}$	$72.3_{1.1}$	$74.0_{1.2}$
Amazon	$72.8_{2.0}$	$\mathbf{79.0_{1.8}}$	$\mathbf{75.7_{1.2}}$	$\mathbf{76.6_{1.8}}$	$75.5_{2.1}$
Semeval	$67.5_{4.5}$	$70.5_{1.5}$	$66.2_{1.5}$	$67.1_{2.2}$	$72.5_{1.8}$
Yelp	$79.0_{3.6}$	$\mathbf{84.5_{1.1}}$	$\mathbf{84.2_{1.7}}$	$\mathbf{84.3_{1.2}}$	$\mathbf{84.6_{1.8}}$

Table 3: Mean and standard deviation (in subscript) of accuracy scores of models fine-tuned for sentiment analysis using the method proposed by Pruthi et al. (2020) with different base models (BERT and ELECTRA) and increasing proportion of examples with feature feedback. Results highlighted in bold are significant difference with $p < 0.05$.

Evaluation set	Fraction of Training Data with Rationales				
	No rationales	25%	50%	75%	100%
BERT					
In-domain	$88.7_{2.0}$	$89.6_{0.4}$	$89.9_{0.4}$	$89.7_{0.4}$	$89.8_{0.8}$
RP	$62.9_{3.9}$	$67.6_{2.0}$	$67.4_{1.2}$	$68.6_{0.6}$	$66.6_{0.6}$
RH	$76.9_{3.5}$	$80.4_{1.1}$	$81.7_{1.6}$	$81.4_{0.7}$	$80.5_{1.9}$
MNLI-M	$69.7_{2.6}$	$67.6_{3.4}$	$68.1_{4.6}$	$68.8_{2.0}$	$68.1_{1.9}$
MNLI-MM	$71.5_{2.7}$	$68.8_{4.5}$	$69.2_{5.9}$	$69.8_{2.7}$	$69.2_{2.3}$
ELECTRA					
In-domain	$\mathbf{96.0_{0.2}}$	$95.1_{0.3}$	$95.0_{0.3}$	$95.0_{0.3}$	$95.0_{0.3}$
RP	$80.8_{1.0}$	$78.2_{1.3}$	$79.2_{1.1}$	$77.2_{1.3}$	$78.0_{0.6}$
RH	$88.9_{1.0}$	$88.0_{1.2}$	$88.4_{0.3}$	$87.9_{0.4}$	$88.7_{0.9}$
MNLI-M	$86.5_{0.9}$	$82.0_{2.8}$	$82.4_{1.6}$	$82.3_{0.9}$	$81.9_{2.1}$
MNLI-MM	$86.6_{0.8}$	$82.6_{2.8}$	$83.5_{1.4}$	$82.6_{0.8}$	$82.1_{2.0}$

Table 4: Mean and standard deviation (in subscript) of F-1 scores of models fine-tuned for NLI using the method proposed by Pruthi et al. (2020) with different base models (BERT and ELECTRA) and increasing proportion of examples with feature feedback. Results highlighted in bold are significant difference with $p < 0.05$.

instance, ELECTRA fine-tuned using the extract-then-classify framework leads to $\approx 15.7\%$ gain in accuracy when evaluated on Yelp. For NLI, however, training with rationales doesn't lead to any visible performance gain (Table 2).

As Pruthi et al. (2020) demonstrate better performance on evidence extraction for sentiment analysis compared to Jain et al. (2020), we use their method for additional analysis. For both sentiment analysis and NLI, we fine-tune models with varying proportion of samples with rationales and report iid and out-of-domain performance (Tables 3 and 4). Training with no feature feedback recovers the classify-only baseline.

On sentiment analysis, we find feature feedback to improve BERT's iid performance but find ELEC-

Test set	Classify-only	Zaidan et al.
In-domain	$75.2_{3.5}$	$79.1_{3.4}$
CRD	$48.3_{2.0}$	$\mathbf{58.2_{2.4}}$
SST-2	$49.7_{0.3}$	$\mathbf{65.6_{1.5}}$
Amazon	$50.9_{0.3}$	$\mathbf{68.7_{3.1}}$
Semeval	$49.8_{0.1}$	$\mathbf{58.0_{1.5}}$
Yelp	$55.7_{2.8}$	$\mathbf{74.8_{2.7}}$

Table 5: Mean and standard deviation (in subscript) of accuracy scores of classify-only SVM model versus SVM trained with feature feedback for sentiment analysis using Zaidan et al. (2007)'s method. Significant results ($p < 0.05$) compared to the classify-only models are highlighted in bold.

Task	Unigram	Bigram
Sentiment Analysis	21.37	11.20
NLI	79.54	35.49

Table 6: Percentage of unigram and bigram vocabularies that are marked as feature feedback at least once.

	Entailment	Contradiction
D_{all}	0.25	0.16
$D_{\text{rationale}}$	0.30	0.09

Table 7: Mean Jaccard index of premise-hypothesis word overlap (D_{all}) and rationale overlap ($D_{\text{rationale}}$) in the training set.

TRA's performance comparable with and without feature feedback. Feature feedback leads to an increase in performance out-of-domain on both BERT and ELECTRA. For instance, with feature feedback, ELECTRA's classification accuracy increases from 91.6% to 93.7% on CRD and 79% to 84.6% on Yelp. Similar trends are also observed when we fine-tune BERT with feature feedback. Interestingly, when evaluated on the SemEval dataset (Tweets), we observe that BERT fine-tuned with feature feedback on all training examples achieves comparable performance to fine-tuning without feature feedback. However, fine-tuning with feature feedback on just 25% of training examples leads to a significant improvement in classification accuracy. We speculate that this might be a result of implicit hyperparameter tuning when combining prediction and extraction losses, and a more extensive hyperparameter search could provide comparable (if not better) gains with 100%

Dataset	% Overlap	Label Agreement
Unigram		
CRD	60.3	51.3
SST2	64.6	66.5
Amazon	45.6	47.6
Semeval	30.9	60.3
Yelp	78.3	65.1
Bigram		
CRD	28.2	51.9
SST2	28.5	64.5
Amazon	19.6	49.9
Semeval	10.2	58.5
Yelp	46.8	65.3

Table 8: Rationale vocabulary overlap and label agreement between in-sample and OOD datasets.

data. Similarly, SVM trained with feature feedback (Zaidan et al., 2007) consistently outperformed SVM trained without feature feedback, when evaluated out-of-domain despite obtaining similar accuracy in-domain (Table 5 and Appendix Table 11). For instance, SVM trained on just label information achieved $75.2\% \pm 3.5\%$ accuracy on the in-domain test set, which was comparable to the accuracy of $79.1\% \pm 3.4\%$ achieved by SVM trained with feature feedback. But the classifier trained with feature feedback led to $\approx 19\%$ and $\approx 18\%$ improvement in classification accuracy on Yelp reviews and Amazon reviews, respectively, compared to the classifier trained without feature feedback.

For NLI, it appears that feature feedback provides no added benefit compared to a classify-only BERT model, whereas, ELECTRA's iid performance decreases with feature feedback. Furthermore, models fine-tuned with feature feedback generally perform no better than classify-only models when trained with varying proportions of rationales (Table 4) while classify-only models perform significantly better than the models trained with rationales when trained with varying dataset size. (Appendix Table 2). These results are in line with observations in prior work on counterfactually augmented data (Huang et al., 2020).

4 Discussion and Analysis

To further study the different trends on sentiment analysis versus NLI, we analyze feature feedback in both datasets. We find that 21.37% of tokens in the vocabulary of Zaidan et al. (2007) are marked as rationales in at least one movie review. Interestingly, this fraction is 79.54% for NLI (Table 6). While for movie reviews, certain words or phrases might generally denote positive or negative sentiment (e.g., "amazing movie"), for NLI tasks, it is not clear that any individual phrase should suggest entailment or contradiction generally. A word or a phrase might be marked as indicating entailment in one NLI example but as a contradiction in another. This may explain why training with rationales lead to no improvement in the NLI task.

We further construct vocabulary of unigrams and bigrams from phrases marked as feature feedback in examples from the sentiment analysis training set ($V_{\text{rationale}}$). We compute the fraction of unigrams (and bigrams) that occur in this vocabulary and also occur in each out-of-domain dataset. We find that a large fraction of unigrams from $V_{\text{rationale}}$ also exist in CRD ($\approx$ 60%), SST2 ($\approx$ 64%), and Yelp ($\approx$ 78%) data. (movie and restaurant reviews). However, this overlap is much smaller for SemEval ($\approx$ 30%) and Amazon ($\approx$ 45%) , which consist of tweets and product reviews, respectively. For these overlapping unigrams, we observe a relatively large percentage (50–65%) preserve their associated majority training set label in the out-of-domain datasets. Similar trends hold for bigrams, though fewer $V_{\text{rationale}}$ bigrams are present out-of-domain (Table 8). A model that pays more attention to these spans might perform better out of domain.

For each pair in the NLI training set, we compute Jaccard similarity between the premise and hypothesis sentence (Table 7). We compute the mean of these example-level similarities over the entire dataset, finding that it is common for examples in our training set to have overlap between premise and hypothesis sentences, regardless of the label. However, when we compute mean Jaccard similarity between premise and hypothesis rationales, we find higher overlap for entailment examples versus contradiction. Thus, models trained with feature feedback might learn to identify word overlap as predictive of entailment even when the true label is contradiction. While this may not improve an NLI model's performance, it could be useful in tasks like Question Answering, where answers often lie in sentences that have high word overlap with the question (Lamm et al., 2020; Majumder et al., 2021). Interestingly, our results on NLI are in conflict with recent findings where models trained with rationales showed significant improvement over classify-only models in both iid and out-of-domain (MNLI-M and MNLI-MM) settings (Stacey et al., 2021). This could be due to the different modeling strategy employed in their work, as they use rationales to guide the training of the classifier's attention module. Investigating this difference is left for future work.

5 Conclusion

In this paper, we investigate the practical benefits of using feature feedback in two well-known tasks in NLP: sentiment analysis and natural language inference. Using two techniques that were primarily introduced for boosting interpretability as the basis of our experiments, we find they also have an unexpected advantage in boosting model robustness. Our experiments and analyses offer insight into how these interpretability methods may encourage generalization in out of domain settings.

To answer our first research question, we show that models trained with feature feedback can lead to performance improvement in the sentiment analysis task but not in NLI. To answer our second question, we find that as little as 25% of the dataset can achieve the best performance in the out-of-domain setting in sentiment analysis, whereas no clear trends are visible in NLI. Our analysis reveals that a smaller percentage of vocabulary is selected as rationales in sentiment analysis compared to NLI, indicating rationale tokens in the sentiment analysis task contain more distinctive information than NLI. Rationale tokens are more likely to exist among entailment samples than contradiction, which may lead the model to correlate the existence of rationales with entailment.

References

Sihao Chen, Daniel Khashabi, Wenpeng Yin, Chris Callison-Burch, and Dan Roth. 2019. Seeing things from a different angle: Discovering diverse perspectives about claims. In *North American Chapter of the Association for Computational Linguistics: Human Language Technologies, (NAACL-HLT)*.

Kevin Clark, Minh-Thang Luong, Quoc V Le, and Christopher D Manning. 2020. Electra: Pre-training text encoders as discriminators rather than generators. In *International Conference on Learning Representations (ICLR)*.

Sanjoy Dasgupta, Akansha Dey, Nicholas Roberts, and Sivan Sabato. 2018. Learning from discriminative feature feedback. In *International Conference on Neural Information Processing Systems (NeurIPS).*

Sanjoy Dasgupta and Sivan Sabato. 2020. Robust learning from discriminative feature feedback. In *International Conference on Artificial Intelligence and Statistics (AISTATS).*

Jacob Devlin, Ming-Wei Chang, Kenton Lee, and Kristina Toutanova. 2019. BERT: Pre-training of Deep Bidirectional Transformers for Language Understanding. In *North American Chapter of the Association for Computational Linguistics: Human Language Technologies (NAACL-HLT).*

Jay DeYoung, Sarthak Jain, Nazneen Fatema Rajani, Eric Lehman, Caiming Xiong, Richard Socher, and Byron C Wallace. 2020. ERASER: A Benchmark to Evaluate Rationalized NLP Models. In *Association for Computational Linguistics (ACL).*

William Huang, Haokun Liu, and Samuel Bowman. 2020. Counterfactually-augmented snli training data does not yield better generalization than unaugmented data. In *First Workshop on Insights from Negative Results in NLP.*

Sarthak Jain, Sarah Wiegreffe, Yuval Pinter, and Byron C Wallace. 2020. Learning to faithfully rationalize by construction. In *Association for Computational Linguistics (ACL).*

Divyansh Kaushik, Eduard Hovy, and Zachary Lipton. 2020. Learning the difference that makes a difference with counterfactually-augmented data. In *International Conference on Learning Representations (ICLR).*

Divyansh Kaushik, Amrith Setlur, Eduard Hovy, and Zachary C Lipton. 2021. Explaining the efficacy of counterfactually-augmented data. *International Conference on Learning Representations (ICLR).*

John D Lafferty, Andrew McCallum, and Fernando CN Pereira. 2001. Conditional random fields: Probabilistic models for segmenting and labeling sequence data. In *International Conference on Machine Learning (ICML).*

Matthew Lamm, Jennimaria Palomaki, Chris Alberti, Daniel Andor, Eunsol Choi, Livio Baldini Soares, and Michael Collins. 2020. Qed: A framework and dataset for explanations in question answering. *arXiv preprint arXiv:2009.06354.*

Eric Lehman, Jay DeYoung, Regina Barzilay, and Byron C Wallace. 2019. Inferring which medical treatments work from reports of clinical trials. In *North American Chapter of the Association for Computational Linguistics: Human Language Technologies (NAACL-HLT).*

Tao Lei, Regina Barzilay, and Tommi Jaakkola. 2016. Rationalizing neural predictions. In *Empirical Methods in Natural Language Processing (EMNLP).*

Ilya Loshchilov and Frank Hutter. 2019. Decoupled weight decay regularization. In *International Conference on Learning Representations (ICLR).*

Sagnik Majumder, Chinmoy Samant, and Greg Durrett. 2021. Model agnostic answer reranking system for adversarial question answering. In *European Chapter of the Association for Computational Linguistics: Student Research Workshop (EACL SRW).*

Jianmo Ni, Jiacheng Li, and Julian McAuley. 2019. Justifying recommendations using distantly-labeled reviews and fine-grained aspects. In *Empirical Methods in Natural Language Processing and the International Joint Conference on Natural Language Processing (EMNLP-IJCNLP).*

Stefanos Poulis and Sanjoy Dasgupta. 2017. Learning with feature feedback: from theory to practice. In *International Conference on Artificial Intelligence and Statistics (AISTATS).*

Danish Pruthi, Bhuwan Dhingra, Graham Neubig, and Zachary C Lipton. 2020. Weakly-and semi-supervised evidence extraction. In *Empirical Methods in Natural Language Processing (EMNLP).*

Sara Rosenthal, Noura Farra, and Preslav Nakov. 2017. Semeval-2017 task 4: Sentiment analysis in twitter. In *International Workshop on Semantic Evaluation (SemEval).*

Andrew Ross and Finale Doshi-Velez. 2018. Improving the adversarial robustness and interpretability of deep neural networks by regularizing their input gradients. In *AAAI Conference on Artificial Intelligence.*

Andrew Slavin Ross, Michael C Hughes, and Finale Doshi-Velez. 2017a. Right for the right reasons: training differentiable models by constraining their explanations. In *International Joint Conference on Artificial Intelligence (IJCAI).*

Björn Ross, Michael Rist, Guillermo Carbonell, Benjamin Cabrera, Nils Kurowsky, and Michael Wojatzki. 2017b. Measuring the reliability of hate speech annotations: The case of the european refugee crisis. *ArXiv*, abs/1701.08118.

Richard Socher, Alex Perelygin, Jean Wu, Jason Chuang, Christopher D Manning, Andrew Y Ng, and Christopher Potts. 2013. Recursive deep models for semantic compositionality over a sentiment treebank. In *Empirical Methods in Natural Language Processing (EMNLP).*

Joe Stacey, Yonatan Belinkov, and Marek Rei. 2021. Natural language inference with a human touch: Using human explanations to guide model attention. *arXiv preprint arXiv:2104.08142.*

Zeerak Waseem. 2016. Are you a racist or am i seeing things? annotator influence on hate speech detection on twitter. In *NLP+CSS@EMNLP.*

Adina Williams, Nikita Nangia, and Samuel Bowman. 2018. A broad-coverage challenge corpus for sentence understanding through inference. In *North American Chapter of the Association for Computational Linguistics: Human Language Technologies (NAACL-HLT)*.

Omar Zaidan, Jason Eisner, and Christine Piatko. 2007. Using "annotator rationales" to improve machine learning for text categorization. In *Human language technologies: North American chapter of the association for computational linguistics (NAACL-HLT)*.

Ye Zhang, Iain Marshall, and Byron C Wallace. 2016. Rationale-augmented convolutional neural networks for text classification. In *Empirical Methods in Natural Language Processing (EMNLP)*.

A Appendix

Task	Examples
Sentiment Analysis (Positive)	. . . characters are portrayed with such saddening realism that you can't help but love them , as pathetic as they really are . although levy stands out , guest , willard , o'hara , and posey are all wonderful and definitely should be commended for their performances ! if there was an oscar for an ensemble performance , this is the group that should sweep it . . .
Sentiment Analysis (Negative)	. . . then , as it's been threatening all along , the film explodes into violence . and just when you think it's finally over , schumacher tags on a ridiculous self-righteous finale that drags the whole unpleasant experience down even further . trust me . there are better ways to waste two hours of your life . . .
NLI (Entailment)	**P:** a white dog drinks water on a mountainside. **H:** there is a dog drinking water right now.
NLI (Contradiction)	**P:** a dog leaping off a boat **H:** dogs drinking water from pond

Table 9: Examples of documents (and true label) with feature feedback (highlighted in yellow).

Task	Examples
Sentiment Analysis (Positive, Correct)	everyone should adapt a tom robbins book for screen . while the movie is fine and the performances are good , the dialogue , which works well reading it , is beautiful when spoken .
Sentiment Analysis (Positive, Wrong)	... very uncaptivating yet one gets the feeling that their is some serious exploitation going on here ...
Sentiment Analysis (Negative, Correct)	... using quicken is a frustrating experience each time i fire it up ...
Sentiment Analysis (Negative, Wrong)	... with many cringe-worthy 'surprises', which happen around 10 minutes after you see exactly what's going to happen ...
NLI (Entailment, Correct)	**P:** a woman cook in an apron is smiling at the camera with two other cooks in the background . **H:** a woman looking at the camera .
NLI (Entailment, Wrong)	**P:** a woman in a brown dress looking at papers in front of a class . **H:** a woman looking at papers in front of a class is not wearing a blue dress .
NLI (Contradiction, Correct)	**P:** the woman in the white dress looks very uncomfortable in the busy surroundings **H:** the dress is black .
NLI (Contradiction, Wrong)	**P:** a man , wearing a cap , is pushing a cart , on which large display boards are kept , on a road . **H:** the person is pulling large display boards on a cart .

Table 10: Examples (from out-of-domain evaluation sets; with true label and model prediction) of explanations highlighted by feature feedback models (highlighted in yellow).

Evaluation Set	Dataset size 300	600	900	1200
In-domain	$77.0_{3.9}$/$77.6_{2.2}$	$78.5_{3.2}$/$82.3_{2.0}$	$80.5_{1.7}$/$\mathbf{84.9_{1.6}}$	$75.2_{3.5}$/$79.1_{3.4}$
CRD	$48.0_{2.9}$/$\mathbf{56.4_{1.3}}$	$48.3_{2.5}$/$\mathbf{58.0_{2.7}}$	$48.4_{2.3}$/$\mathbf{58.7_{1.8}}$	$48.3_{2.0}$/$\mathbf{58.2_{2.4}}$
SST-2	$52.2_{1.6}$/$\mathbf{62.9_{1.0}}$	$50.9_{3.0}$/$\mathbf{64.0_{0.9}}$	$51.3_{3.1}$/$\mathbf{64.9_{0.9}}$	$49.7_{0.3}$/$\mathbf{65.6_{1.5}}$
Amazon	$51.8_{1.5}$/$\mathbf{65.9_{1.9}}$	$52.4_{2.0}$/$\mathbf{66.5_{1.2}}$	$52.0_{2.9}$/$\mathbf{69.9_{0.4}}$	$50.9_{0.3}$/$\mathbf{68.7_{3.1}}$
Semeval	$50.3_{1.4}$/$\mathbf{56.7_{1.1}}$	$50.3_{1.2}$/$\mathbf{56.4_{0.8}}$	$50.1_{0.5}$/$\mathbf{58.8_{1.3}}$	$49.8_{0.1}$/$\mathbf{58.0_{1.5}}$
Yelp	$60.2_{4.0}$/$\mathbf{72.0_{2.4}}$	$57.3_{7.1}$/$\mathbf{74.5_{1.5}}$	$61.2_{4.6}$/$\mathbf{74.8_{2.5}}$	$55.7_{2.8}$/$\mathbf{74.8_{2.7}}$

Table 11: Mean and standard deviation (in subscript) of accuracy scores of classify-only SVM models (left) presented alongside accuracy scores of models trained with feature feedback (right), with increasing number of training-samples for sentiment analysis using the method proposed by Zaidan et al. (2007). Results highlighted in bold show statistically significant difference with $p < 0.05$.

Evaluation Set	Dataset size 1500	3000	4500	6318
		BERT		
In-domain	$85.9_{6.0}$/$84.5_{2.0}$	$87.9_{0.4}$/$87.7_{1.0}$	$89.1_{0.4}$/$89.2_{0.2}$	$88.7_{2.0}$/$89.8_{0.8}$
RP	$61.8_{0.9}$/$62.8_{1.8}$	$63.3_{1.6}$/$64.2_{1.8}$	$63.7_{1.8}$/$\mathbf{66.8_{1.4}}$	$62.9_{3.9}$/$66.4_{1.7}$
RH	$74.5_{1.6}$/$71.8_{3.4}$	$77.0_{1.4}$/$77.3_{2.1}$	$78.3_{1.1}$/$80.4_{1.8}$	$76.9_{3.5}$/$80.5_{1.9}$
MNLI-M	$63.7_{3.1}$/$60.8_{3.2}$	$69.2_{1.8}$/$66.3_{2.2}$	$70.2_{0.9}$/$67.5_{3.1}$	$69.7_{2.6}$/$68.1_{1.9}$
MNLI-MM	$64.8_{4.3}$/$61.8_{4.3}$	$71.3_{2.3}$/$67.5_{2.8}$	$72.1_{1.2}$/$68.9_{4.2}$	$73.1_{1.9}$/$71.4_{1.1}$
		ELECTRA		
In-domain	$\mathbf{94.6_{0.2}}$/$92.7_{0.5}$	$\mathbf{95.1_{0.4}}$/$94.2_{0.3}$	$\mathbf{95.7_{0.2}}$/$94.4_{0.2}$	$\mathbf{96.0_{0.2}}$/$95.1_{0.3}$
RP	$78.4_{1.2}$/$75.2_{2.5}$	$78.5_{1.8}$/$77.2_{0.9}$	$\mathbf{81.2_{0.6}}$/$76.2_{1.2}$	$\mathbf{80.8_{1.0}}$/$78.0_{0.6}$
RH	$\mathbf{87.7_{0.7}}$/$85.2_{1.4}$	$88.1_{1.3}$/$87.3_{0.6}$	$\mathbf{89.4_{0.6}}$/$87.1_{1.0}$	$88.9_{1.0}$/$88.7_{0.9}$
MNLI-M	$\mathbf{82.8_{2.2}}$/$77.0_{1.8}$	$\mathbf{85.4_{1.8}}$/$78.9_{1.7}$	$\mathbf{86.0_{1.6}}$/$80.4_{2.1}$	$\mathbf{86.5_{0.9}}$/$81.9_{2.1}$
MNLI-MM	$\mathbf{83.6_{2.5}}$/$77.9_{2.1}$	$\mathbf{86.2_{2.1}}$/$79.9_{1.9}$	$\mathbf{86.1_{1.8}}$/$80.8_{2.2}$	$\mathbf{86.6_{0.8}}$/$82.1_{2.0}$

Table 12: Mean and standard deviation (in subscript) of F-1 scores of classify-only models/models trained with feature feedback, with increasing number of training-samples for NLI using the method proposed by Pruthi et al. (2020). Results highlighted in bold are statistically significant difference with $p < 0.05$.

Identifying the Source of Vulnerability in Explanation Discrepancy: A Case Study in Neural Text Classification

Ruixuan Tang
University of Virginia
rt5tb@virginia.edu

Hanjie Chen
University of Virginia
hc9mx@virginia.edu

Yangfeng Ji
University of Virginia
yangfeng@virginia.edu

Abstract

Some recent works observed the instability of post-hoc explanations when input side perturbations are applied to the model. This raises the interest and concern in the stability of post-hoc explanations. However, the remaining question is: is the instability caused by the neural network model or the post-hoc explanation method? This work explores the potential source that leads to unstable post-hoc explanations. To separate the influence from the model, we propose a simple *output probability perturbation* method. Compared to prior input side perturbation methods, the *output probability perturbation* method can circumvent the neural model's potential effect on the explanations and allow the analysis on the explanation method. We evaluate the proposed method with three widely-used post-hoc explanation methods (LIME (Ribeiro et al., 2016), Kernel Shapley (Lundberg and Lee, 2017a), and Sample Shapley (Strumbelj and Kononenko, 2010)). The results demonstrate that the post-hoc methods are stable, barely producing discrepant explanations under output probability perturbations. The observation suggests that neural network models may be the primary source of fragile explanations.

1 Introduction

Despite the remarkable performance of neural network models in natural language processing (NLP), the lack of interpretability has raised much concern in terms of their reliability and trustworthiness (Zhang et al., 2021; Doshi-Velez and Kim, 2017; Hooker et al., 2019; Jiang et al., 2018). A common way to improve a model's interpretability is to generate explanations for its predictions from the post-hoc manner. We call these explanations post-hoc explanations (Doshi-Velez and Kim, 2017; Molnar, 2018). Post-hoc explanations demonstrate the relationship between the input text and the model prediction by identifying feature importance scores (Du et al., 2019). In general, a feature with a higher importance score is more important in contributing to the prediction result. Based on feature importance scores, we can select top important features as the model explanation.

However, some recent works (Ghorbani et al., 2019; Subramanya et al., 2019; Zhang et al., 2020; Ivankay et al., 2022; Sinha et al., 2021) have observed explanation discrepancy when input-side perturbation is applied to the model. One question to this observation is what makes the explanation discrepant? Explanations generated by a post-hoc method (Ribeiro et al., 2016; Lundberg and Lee, 2017a; Friedman, 2001) depend on a model's prediction probabilities. If perturbations at the input side cause model prediction probabilities to change, post-hoc explanations may change accordingly.

In Figure 1 (a), we demonstrate a simple example of the process that generates explanations using a post-hoc method. The explanation is generated depending on the probability P. In Figure 1 (b), we demonstrate an example of the same process with perturbation at the input side. The explanation is generated depending on the probability $\bar{P}$. The output probabilities in the two examples are not the same, i.e. $P \neq \bar{P}$. In Figure 1 (a) and (b), it is noticeable that the feature importance score of the same feature has changed. For instance, the feature "love" has different importance scores in the two examples. Since feature importance scores are inconsistent, the explanations in the two examples are different. We call this *explanation discrepancy*, which will be introduced more in subsection 2.2.

However, the prediction label in Figure 1 (a), $\hat{y}$, and the prediction label in Figure 1 (b), $\bar{y}$, are equal, which is $\hat{y} = \bar{y} =$ POSITIVE. This indicates that input side perturbations may not flip the model prediction label, while can make output probabilities change, hence further leading to explanation discrepancy. We argue that, under input side perturbations, it is difficult to identify the source causing the explanation discrepancy. One intuitive justifica-

Proceedings of the Fifth BlackboxNLP Workshop on Analyzing and Interpreting Neural Networks for NLP, pages 356 - 370
December 8, 2022 ©2022 Association for Computational Linguistics

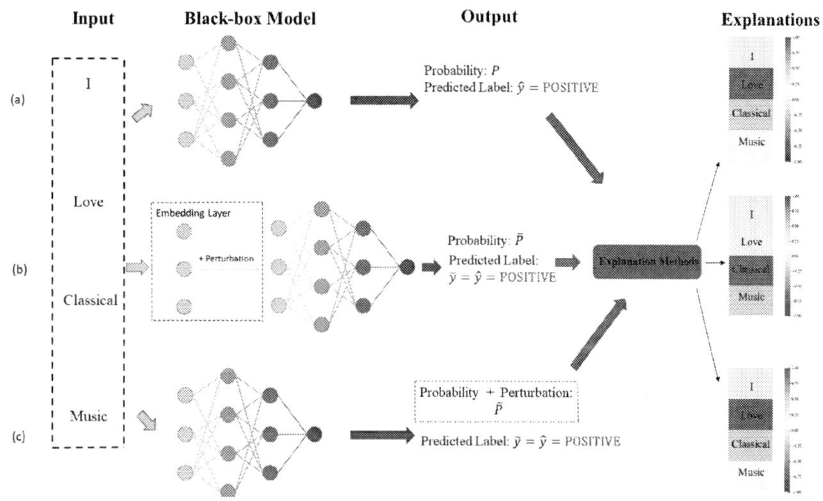

Figure 1: The pipeline of a simple example that post-hoc explanation methods generate explanations with (a) no perturbation applied. (b) perturbation applied at the input side. (c) perturbation applied at the output probabilities.

tion is that the perturbation at the input side has to pass through both the model and the post-hoc explanation method. Both the model and the post-hoc explanation method are possible factors that result in unstable explanations. For example, the model's prediction behavior may change under input side perturbations, that is focusing on different features to make predictions, hence resulting in the explanation discrepancy (Chen and Ji, 2020, 2022). Or the explanation method itself may be vulnerable to input perturbations, producing discrepant explanations. The instability may not be told from the prediction results, but reflected in the explanations, i.e., explanation discrepancy

In this paper, we propose a simple strategy to demonstrate the potential source that causes explanation discrepancy. To circumvent the potential influence of the model on the explanations, we design an *output probability perturbation* method by slightly modifying the prediction probabilities, as shown in Figure 1 (c). In this work, we focus on the model-agnostic post-hoc methods, LIME (Ribeiro et al., 2016), Kernel Shapley (Lundberg and Lee, 2017a), and Sample Shapley (Strumbelj and Kononenko, 2010), that explain the black-box models. If a similar explanation discrepancy can be observed when only output probability perturbation is applied, it would suggest that post-hoc explanation methods may be unstable because the potential influence from the black-box model has been blocked. Otherwise, we should not blame post-hoc explanation methods as the source of vulnerability in fragile explanations (Sinha et al., 2021; Subramanya et al., 2019).

2 Method

2.1 Background

For a text classification task, $\boldsymbol{x}$ denotes the input text consisting of N words, $\boldsymbol{x} = [\boldsymbol{x}^{(1)}, \cdots, \boldsymbol{x}^{(N)}]$, with each component $\boldsymbol{x}^{(n)} \in R^d$ representing the n-th word embedding. We define a black-box classifier as $f(\cdot)$ and its output probability of a given $\boldsymbol{x}$ on the corresponding label k is $P(y = k \mid \boldsymbol{x}) = f_k(\boldsymbol{x})$, where $k \in \{1, \ldots, C\}$ and C is the total number of label classes.

To explain a black-box model's prediction $\hat{y} = f(\boldsymbol{x})$, a class of post-hoc explanation methods approximate the model locally via additive feature attributions (Lundberg and Lee, 2017b; Ribeiro et al., 2016; Shrikumar et al., 2017). Specifically, these algorithms demonstrate the relationship between the input text and the prediction result by evaluating the contribution of each input feature to the model prediction result. These methods would assign a feature importance score to each input feature to represent its contribution to the prediction. We use LIME (Ribeiro et al., 2016) as an example.

Example: Post-hoc Explanation Method, LIME. It first sub-samples words from the input, $\boldsymbol{x}$, to form a list of pseudo examples $\{\boldsymbol{z}_{j=1}^{L}\}$, and then the contributions of input features are estimated by a linear approximation $f_{\hat{y}}(\boldsymbol{r}) \approx g_{\hat{y}}(\boldsymbol{r}')$, where $\boldsymbol{r} \in \{\boldsymbol{x}, \boldsymbol{z}_{j=1}^{L}\}$, $g_{\hat{y}}(\boldsymbol{r}) = \boldsymbol{w}_{\hat{y}}^{T}\boldsymbol{r}'$, and $\boldsymbol{r}'$ is a simple representation of $\boldsymbol{r}$, e.g. bag-of-words representation. The weights $\{w_{\hat{y}}^{(n)}\}$ represent importance scores of input features $\{\boldsymbol{x}^{(n)}\}$. Let $I(\boldsymbol{x}, \hat{y}, P)$ denote the explanation for the model prediction on $\boldsymbol{x}$, where $\hat{y}$ is the predicted label and P represents output probabilities.

2.2 Explanation Discrepancy

As mentioned in the previous section, the explanation discrepancy may happen when input perturbations are applied to the model. Let $I(\boldsymbol{x}, \hat{y}, P)$ and $I(\bar{\boldsymbol{x}}, \bar{y}, \bar{P})$ denote the explanation to the model prediction based on the original input $\boldsymbol{x}$ and the perturbed input $\bar{\boldsymbol{x}}$ respectively, where $\bar{\boldsymbol{x}} = \boldsymbol{x} + \varepsilon$, and ε is the perturbation at input. Similarly, we define $I(\boldsymbol{x}, \widetilde{y}, \widetilde{P})$ as the explanation to the prediction based on the perturbed output probability $\widetilde{P} = P + \varepsilon'$, where ε' is the perturbation on the output probability. Note that when ε and ε' are small, the model prediction stay the same, which is $\hat{y} = \bar{y} = \widetilde{y}$. The explanation discrepancy between $I(\bar{\boldsymbol{x}}, \bar{y}, \bar{P})$ and $I(\boldsymbol{x}, \hat{y}, P)$ is denoted as δ_{input}, and the discrepancy between $I(\boldsymbol{x}, \widetilde{y}, \widetilde{P})$ and $I(\boldsymbol{x}, \hat{y}, P)$ is denoted as δ_{output}.

We use Figure 1 in section 1 as an example to illustrate explanation discrepancy in details. The explanation, $I(\boldsymbol{x}, \hat{y}, P)$, in Figure 1 (a) is “Love", “Classical", “I" and “Music", in the descending order of importance scores. The explanation, $I(\bar{\boldsymbol{x}}, \bar{y}, \bar{P})$, in Figure 1 (b) is “Classical", “Music", “Love", and “I", in the descending order. The explanation, $I(\boldsymbol{x}, \hat{y}, \widetilde{P})$, in Figure 1 (c) is “Love", “Classical", “I" and “Music", in the descending order. Generally, after perturbation, explanation inconsistency reflects in two aspects. The first aspect is whether the overall ranking of the features based on their importance scores in the explanation remains the same. For example, “Love" ranks the first in the explanation in Figure 1 (a), while drops to the third in the explanation in Figure 1 (b). The discrepancy is denoted as δ_{input}. The second aspect is whether the top K important features in the explanation are consistent. For example, if $K = 2$, the first two important words in Figure 1 (a) are “Love" and “Classical", while those in Figure 1 (b) are “Classical" and “Music". The difference can also be denoted as δ_{input} mentioned above. Similarly, the same aspect of explanation discrepancy in Figure 1 (a) and Figure 1 (c) can be denoted as δ_{output}.

2.3 Output Probability Perturbation Method

As mentioned in section 1, the limitation of input perturbation methods is the difficulty in identifying the primary source that causes explanation discrepancy. Motivated by this, we propose the output probability perturbation method to circumvent the influence of black-box models.

Specifically, given an example $\boldsymbol{x}$, we add a small perturbation to the model output probabilities $\{P(y = k \mid \boldsymbol{x}) + \varepsilon'_{y=k}\}_{k=1}^{C}$. To guarantee the modified $\{P(y = k \mid \boldsymbol{x}) + \varepsilon'_{y=k}\}_{k=1}^{C}$ are still legitimate probabilities, we further normalize them as

$$\widetilde{P}(y = k \mid \boldsymbol{x}) = \frac{P(y = k \mid \boldsymbol{x}) + \varepsilon'_{y=k}}{\sum_{i=1}^{C}\{P(y = i \mid \boldsymbol{x}) + \varepsilon'_{y=i}\}} \quad (1)$$

The explanation in the case with output probability perturbation is computed based on the output probability $\widetilde{P}(y = \hat{y} \mid \boldsymbol{x})$. The proposed method well suits the motivation of investigating the source that causes explanation discrepancy. The main reason is that, unlike perturbation applied at the input side, the proposed method avoids the potential effects of the model's vulnerability on post-hoc explanations. We use LIME (Ribeiro et al., 2016) as an example to demonstrate the proposed method.

Example: Output probability perturbation in LIME algorithm. As denoted in subsection 2.1, $\boldsymbol{r'}$ is the bag-of-words representation of the original input text, $\boldsymbol{x}$. A simplified version [1] of LIME algorithm is equivalent to finding a solution of the following linear equation:

$$\boldsymbol{w}_{\hat{y}}^{T}\boldsymbol{r'} = \widetilde{\boldsymbol{p}}_{\hat{y}} \quad (2)$$

where $\widetilde{\boldsymbol{p}}_{\hat{y}} = [\widetilde{P}(y = \hat{y} \mid \boldsymbol{x}), \widetilde{P}(y = \hat{y} \mid \boldsymbol{z}_1), \ldots, \widetilde{P}(y = \hat{y} \mid \boldsymbol{z}_L)]^T$ are the perturbed probabilities on the label $\hat{y}$, and $\boldsymbol{w}_{\hat{y}}^{T}$ is the weight vector, where each element measures the contribution of an input word to the prediction $\hat{y}$. A typical explanation from LIME consists of top important words according to $\boldsymbol{w}_{\hat{y}}$. Essentially, the proposed output perturbation is similar to the perturbation analysis in linear systems (Golub and Van Loan, 2013), which aims to identify the stability of these systems. Despite the simple formulation in Equation 2, a similar linear system can also be used to explain the Shapley-based explanation methods

[1]Without the example weight computed from a kernel function and the regularization term of explanation complexity.

(e.g., Sample Shapley (Strumbelj and Kononenko, 2010)).

3 Experiment

3.1 Experiment Setup

Datasets. We adopt four text classification datasets: IMDB movie reviews dataset (Maas et al., 2011, IMDB), AG's news dataset (Zhang et al., 2015, AG's News), Stanford Sentiment Treebank dataset with binary labels (Socher et al., 2013, SST-2), and 6-class questions classification dataset TREC (Li and Roth, 2002, TREC). The summary statistics of datasets are shown in Table 1.

Models. We apply three neural network models, Convolutional Neural Network (Kim, 2014, CNN), Long Short Term Memory Network (Hochreiter and Schmidhuber, 1997, LSTM), and Bidirectional Encoder Representations from Transformers (Devlin et al., 2018, BERT).

The principle of CNN model is based on information processing in the visual system of humans. The core characteristics are that it can efficiently decrease the dimension of input, and it can efficiently retain important features of the input (Kim, 2014).

LSTM model is one advanced RNN model. Unlike the architecture of a standard feedforward deep learning neural network, it has feedback connections in the architecture, which helps to process sequential data (e.g., language and speech) (Hochreiter and Schmidhuber, 1997, LSTM).

BERT model is a Language Model (LM). In the NLP research, the main tasks of the BERT model are (1) Sentence pairs classification tasks and (2) Single sentence classification tasks (Devlin et al., 2018). In this work, we focus on the second task while we apply the BERT model in the experiment.

The prediction performance of the three models on the four datasets are recorded in Table 2.

Post-hoc Explanation Methods. We adopt three post-hoc explanation methods, Local Interpretable Model-Agnostic Explanations (Ribeiro et al., 2016, LIME), Kernel Shapley (Lundberg and Lee, 2017a), and Sample Shapley (Strumbelj and Kononenko, 2010). LIME, Kernel Shapley, and Sample Shapley are additive feature attribution methods. The additive feature method provides a feature importance score on every feature for each text input based on the model prediction.

LIME and Kernel Shapley are two post-hoc methods adopting a similar strategy. The first step is to generate a set of pseudo examples and their corresponding labels based on the black-box model's predictions on them (Ribeiro et al., 2016; Lundberg and Lee, 2017a). The second step is to train an explainable machine learning model (eg: linear regression, LASSO) with the pseudo examples (Ribeiro et al., 2016; Lundberg and Lee, 2017a). The difference between the LIME algorithm and the Kernel Shapley algorithm is in the way to calculate the weight of pseudo examples in the explainable model (Molnar, 2018). LIME algorithm relies on the distance between the original example and the pseudo example (Ribeiro et al., 2016). Kernel Shapley algorithm relies on the Shapley value estimation (Lundberg and Lee, 2017a).

Sample Shapley is a post-hoc method based on Shapley value (Shapley, 1953a), which stems from coalitional game theory. Shapley value provides an axiomatic solution to attribute the contribution of each word in a fair way. However, the exponential complexity of computing Shapley value is intractable. Sampling Shapley (Strumbelj and Kononenko, 2010) provides a solvable approximation to Shapley value via sampling.

Evaluation Metrics. In the experiment, we apply two evaluation metrics, Kendall's Tau order rank correlation score, and the Top-K important words overlap score (Chen et al., 2019; Kendall, 1938; Ghorbani et al., 2019) to evaluate the discrepancy between explanations (i.e., δ_{input} and δ_{output}).

As illustrated in subsection 2.2, explanation discrepancy can be evaluated in in two aspects. We use Kendall's Tau order rank correlation score to quantify the change of the overall ranking of feature importance scores in explanations. For example, in Figure 1 (a) and (b), we can apply Kendall's Tau order rank correlation score to identify how close the overall ranking of features in the two examples. If the score is close to 1, then the two explanations are similar. If the score is close to -1, then the two explanations differ significantly. We use Top-K important words overlap score to evaluate the discrepancy on the top K features in the explanations. This metric computes the overlap ratio among the top K features. In this work, we set $K = 5$.

Dataset	C	L	$\#train$	$\#dev$	$\#test$	vocab	threshold	length
IMDB	2	268	20K	5K	25K	29571	5	250
SST-2	2	19	6920	872	1821	16190	0	50
AG's News	4	32	114K	6K	7.6K	21838	5	50
TREC	6	10	5000	452	500	8026	0	15

Table 1: Summary statistics for the datasets where C is the number of classes, L is the average sentence length, # counts the number of examples in train/dev/test sets, vocab is the vocab size, and the threshold is the low-frequency threshold, and length is mini-batch sentence length.

Dataset	**CNN**	**LSTM**	**BERT**
IMDB	86.30	86.60	90.80
SST-2	82.48	80.83	91.82
AG's News	89.90	88.90	95.10
TREC	92.41	90.80	97.00

Table 2: Prediction accuracy(%) of the three neural network models (CNN, LSTM and BERT) on the four datasets (IMDB, SST-2, AG's News and TREC).

3.2 Explanation Discrepancy Comparison Experiment

To explore the primary source causing fragile explanations, we conduct a comparison experiment to evaluate and compare between explanation discrepancy δ_{input}, and explanation discrepancy δ_{output}. The definition of δ_{input}, and δ_{output} are introduced in subsection 2.2. δ_{input} denotes the discrepancy between the explanation generated by the black-box model with no perturbation, $I(x, \hat{y}, P)$, and the explanation generated by the black-box model with perturbation at the input, $I(\bar{x}, \hat{y}, \bar{P})$. While δ_{output} denotes the discrepancy of $I(x, \hat{y}, P)$ and the explanation generated by the black-box model with perturbation at the output probability, $I(\bar{x}, \hat{y}, \widetilde{P})$.

In this experiment, for output probability perturbation, we directly add random noise to the model output probabilities. For comparison, we add the noise to word embeddings for input perturbations (Liu et al., 2020). Both input side perturbation and output probability perturbation are applied with noise sampled from a Gaussian distribution, $\mathcal{N}(0, \sigma^2)$. We apply Gaussian noise because it is easy to control the perturbation level by modifying the variance of the Gaussian distribution σ^2. In experiments, we applied five different perturbation levels from "0" to "4". "0" means the slightest perturbation level, zero perturbation, while "4" represents the strongest perturbation level. The specific value of each perturbation level is shown in Table 3.

Note that for each level, the input side perturbations and the output probability perturbations are different because we select different perturbations for the input side and the output probability to reach a similar accuracy at each level. If the model's accuracy is not close at each level, it is difficult to evaluate the results.

Perturbation Source	**Level**	σ^2
Input Side (σ^2_{input})	0	0
	1	0.05
	2	0.1
	3	0.15
	4	0.2
Output Probability (σ^2_{output})	0	0
	1	0.25
	2	0.5
	3	0.75
	4	1

Table 3: Perturbation levels applied to the input and output respectively.

3.3 Results and Discussion

Figure 2 shows the results of the IMDB dataset. Due to the page limit, full results of other datasets are shown in Figure 4, Figure 5 and Figure 6 in Appendix A, which have similar tendencies. Kendall's Tau order rank correlation score plots are shown in Figure 2 (a), (b) and (c). Top-K important words overlap score plots are shown in Figure 2 (d), (e) and (f). Figure 2 (a) and (d) show the results of the LIME method. Figure 2 (b) and (e) show the results of the Kernel Shapley method. Figure 2 (c) and (f) show the results of the Sample Shapley method.

Kendall's Tau order rank correlation score evaluation results. Kendall's Tau order rank correlation score results indirectly illustrate the stability of post-hoc explanation methods. Furthermore, previous observation on the explanation difference can

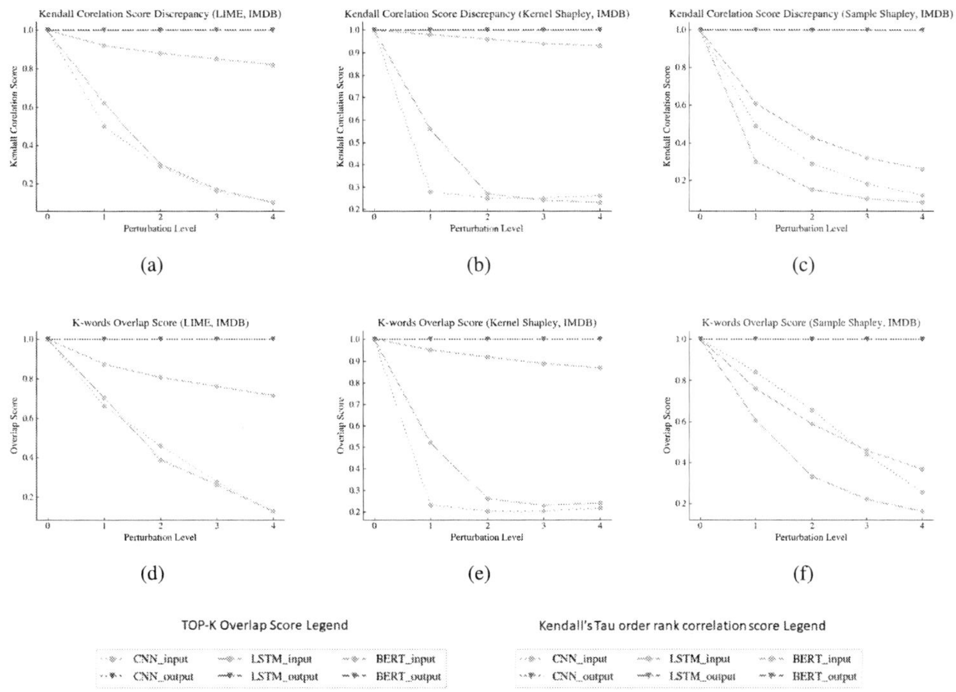

Figure 2: Comparison experiment results on the IMDB dataset; (a) and (d) demonstrate results using LIME method; (b) and (e) demonstrate results using Kernel Sharply method; (c) and (f) demonstrate results using Sample Sharply method.

be attributed to the potential influence caused by the black-box model. In Figure 2 (a), (b) and (c), the large gap between δ_{input} and δ_{output} is consistent across all three post-hoc explanation methods, LIME, Kernel Shapley and Sample Shapley. For output probability perturbations, it is noticeable that the values of Kendall's Tau order rank correlation scores remain the same with the perturbation level increasing from "0" to "4". This indicates that the overall ranking of feature importance scores are stable under output perturbations. Furthermore, the results suggest that for a given input, if x and prediction results stay unchanged, $\hat{y} = \widetilde{y}$, the only perturbation ε' at output probability is unlikely to influence explanations generated by the post-hoc methods. In other words, the explanation discrepancy observed in the previous study (Ivankay et al., 2022; Sinha et al., 2021) is unlikely caused by the post-hoc methods. Meanwhile, for the baseline results (perturbation applied at the input), it is notifiable that the values of Kendall's Tau order rank correlation scores decrease obviously with the increase of input perturbation intensity levels. This indicates that the black-box model is vulnerable to input perturbations, which causes fragile explanations. Based on the observations, we claim that the black-box model is more likely to be the primary source that results in fragile explanations.

Top-K word importance score evaluation results. Top-K word importance score evaluation shows the same result: the black-box model is the primary source causing explanation discrepancy. In Figure 2 (d), (e) and (f), δ_{input} against δ_{output} display an obvious discrepancy across the three post-hoc explanation methods. For output probability perturbations, δ_{output} shows no change in the overlap among the top K important words. This indicates that, for the top five important features in the explanation of each corresponding prediction result, output probability perturbations will not cause any difference. The results under this metric also illustrate that the black-box model is more likely to cause fragile explanations than explanation methods themselves.

3.4 Further Analysis on LIME Algorithm

According to the previous results, we have a conclusion that post-hoc explanation methods are stable.

We further analyze the stability of the explanation algorithms. We use the LIME algorithm (Ribeiro et al., 2016) as an example.

$$L(f_{\hat{y}}(\boldsymbol{r}), g_{\hat{y}}(\boldsymbol{r'}), \pi) = \sum_{\boldsymbol{r},\boldsymbol{r'} \in \boldsymbol{R}} \pi(f_{\hat{y}}(\boldsymbol{r}) - g_{\hat{y}}(\boldsymbol{r'})) \tag{3}$$

Equation 3 is definition of the loss function in LIME algorithm (Ribeiro et al., 2016). In the loss function, $\pi g_{\hat{y}}(\boldsymbol{r'})$ is denoted the kernel calculation function of the algorithm. $\boldsymbol{r'}$ represents the pseudo example based on the original example, $\boldsymbol{r}$. $g_{\hat{y}}(\boldsymbol{r'})$ represents the linear local explainable model on the pseudo example, $\boldsymbol{r'}$. Here, we use a general linear model representation to represent the explainable model, $g_{\hat{y}}(\boldsymbol{r}) = \boldsymbol{w}_{\hat{y}}^T \boldsymbol{r'}$. $\boldsymbol{w}_{\hat{y}}^T$ is the weight function of the linear model and it is the importance feature score calculation function as well. Equation 4 is the kernel calculation function of the LIME algorithm after expanding.

$$G = \pi g_{\hat{y}}(\boldsymbol{r}) = \pi \boldsymbol{w}_{\hat{y}}^T \boldsymbol{r'} \tag{4}$$

The form of the kernel calculation function can be interpreted as a general linear function, $Ax = b$. In the linear function, the condition number, (κ), is applied to evaluate how sensitive the linear function is due to a small change at the input and reflects in its output (Belsley et al., 2005). If the condition number, (κ), which is the largest eigenvalue in the matrix A divided by the smallest eigenvalue in the matrix A, is large, the solution x would change rapidly by a slight difference in b, which would cause sensitivity of the solution to the slight error in the input (Goodfellow et al., 2016). In Equation 4, $\pi \boldsymbol{r'}$ can be considered as the matrix A, and the feature importance score function $\boldsymbol{w}_{\hat{y}}^T$ can be considered as the solution x. If $\pi \boldsymbol{r'}$ is a stable linear system, the feature importance score function $\boldsymbol{w}_{\hat{y}}^T$ would be unlikely sensitive to a minor change at the linear system input side, and the corresponding post-hoc explanation method is stable. The form of the kernel calculation function can be interpreted as a general linear function, $Ax = b$. In the linear function, the condition number, (κ), is applied to evaluate how sensitive the linear function is due to a small change at the input and reflects in its output (Belsley et al., 2005). If the condition number, (κ), which is the largest eigenvalue in the matrix A divided by the smallest eigenvalue in the matrix A, is large, the solution x would change rapidly by a slight difference in b, which would cause sensitivity of the solution to the slight error in the input (Goodfellow et al., 2016). In Equation 4, $\pi \boldsymbol{r'}$ can be considered as the matrix A, and the feature importance score function $vecw_{\hat{y}}^T$ can be considered as the solution $\boldsymbol{r}$. If $\pi \boldsymbol{r'}$ is a stable linear system, the feature importance score function $\boldsymbol{w}_{\hat{y}}^T$ would be unlikely sensitive to a minor change at the linear system input side, and the corresponding post-hoc explanation method is stable. Since the kernel function is a pure numerical step without semantics involved. We conduct a simulation experiment to explore the stability of the LIME algorithm (Ribeiro et al., 2016).

Simulation Experiment and Results In the simulation experiment, the pseudo example, $\boldsymbol{r'}$, is a matrix with the size of sub-sampling size, m, multiple with the length of a sentence, l. We select $m = 200$, which is the actual sample size value we applied in the comparison experiment. For the sentence length, first, we simulate the case when sentence length is fixed, that is $l = 20$. Then, to compare condition number distribution when sentence length is different, we apply two more cases, that are $l = 30$, and $l = 40$. For each length, we simulate it for 500 iterations. For π, it is the distance between the original input to the sub-sampling based on the original input in the LIME algorithm (Ribeiro et al., 2016). In the simulation experiment, we apply cosine distance to represent the value of π.

Total iteration number	$\kappa \in [5, 6)$	$\kappa \in [6, 7)$
500	392	108

Table 4: Condition number (κ) distribution when $l = 20$

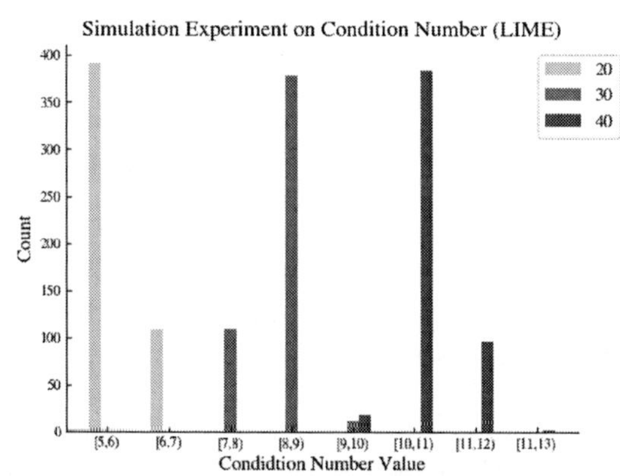

Figure 3: Simulation Experiment Result.

In Table 4, the result of the simulation experiment when the sentence length is fixed, $l = 20$, demonstrates that the majority of the condition number κ of the matrix $\pi \boldsymbol{r}'$ is lower than 7. In Goldstein's work, it suggests that the condition number of a stable or a well-conditioning matrix should be lower than 30 (Goldstein, 1993). It means that the feature importance score function, W, is less likely influenced by a small perturbation involved, which is also reflected in the real dataset results in the comparison experiment in subsection 3.3. In Figure 3, the result of the simulation experiment when sentence lengths are different shows that when the length of the sentence increases, the condition number κ of the matrix $\pi \boldsymbol{r}'$ increases with a tiny amplitude. The majority of the condition number κ of the matrix is lower than 13 when the length is from 20 to 40. Although the result demonstrates that the condition number κ would increase with sentence length increasing, the increasing amplitude is small and the majority of the condition number is lower than the threshold number. The result suggests that the matrix $\pi \boldsymbol{r}'$ in the LIME algorithm can remain a small condition number, which makes the linear system relatively stable. In other words, the LIME algorithm (Ribeiro et al., 2016) is a relatively stable post-hoc explanation method.

4 Previous Works

Post-hoc Explanation Methods Most works focus on explaining neural network models in a post-hoc manner, especially generating a local explanation for each model prediction. The white-box explanation methods, such as gradient-based explanations (Hechtlinger, 2016), and attention-based explanations (Ghaeini et al., 2018), either require additional information (e.g. gradients) from the model or incur much debates regarding their faithfulness to model predictions (Jain and Wallace, 2019).

Another line of work focuses on explaining black-box models in the model-agnostic way. Li et al. (2016) proposed a perturbation-based explanation method, Leave-one-out, that attributes feature importance to model predictions by erasing input features one by one. Ribeiro et al. (2016) proposed to estimate feature contributions locally via linear approximation based on pseudo examples. Some other works proposed the variants of the Shapley value (Shapley, 1953b) to measure feature importance, such as the Sample Shapley method (Strumbelj and Kononenko, 2010), the Kernel Shapley method (Lundberg and Lee, 2017a), and the L/C-Shapley method(Chen et al., 2018).

Model robustness Recent works have shown the vulnerability of model due to adversarial attacks (Szegedy et al., 2013; Goodfellow et al., 2014; Zhao et al., 2017). Some adversarial examples are similar to original examples but can quickly flip model predictions, which causes concern on model robustness (Jia et al., 2019). In the text domain, a common way to generate adversarial examples is by heuristically manipulating the input text, such as replacing words with their synonyms (Alzantot et al., 2018; Ren et al., 2019; Jin et al., 2020), misspelling words (Li et al., 2018; Gao et al., 2018), inserting/removing words (Liang et al., 2017), or concatenating triggers (Wallace et al., 2019).

Explanation Robustness Previous work explored explanation robustness by either perturbing the inputs (Ghorbani et al., 2019; Subramanya et al., 2019; Zhang et al., 2020; Heo et al., 2019) or manipulating the model (Wang et al., 2020; Slack et al., 2020; Zafar et al., 2021). For example, Slack's group fooled post-hoc explanation methods by hiding the bias for black-box models based on the proposed novel scaffolding technique (Slack et al., 2020). However, all of these works cannot disentangle the sources that cause fragile explanation. Differently, the proposed method mitigates the influence of model to the explanation by perturbing model outputs.

5 Conclusion

In this work, our main contribution is to identify the primary source of fragile explanation, where we propose an output probability perturbation method. With the help of this proposed method, observation results can illustrate a conclusion that the primary potential source that caused fragile explanations in the previous studies is the black-box model itself, which also illustrate that some limitations of prior methods. Furthermore, in subsection 3.4, we analyze the kernel calculation inside the LIME algorithm (Ribeiro et al., 2016). We apply the condition number of the matrix and simulation experiments to demonstrate that the kernel calculation matrix inside LIME has a low condition number. This result further suggests the stability of the LIME algorithm.

References

Moustafa Alzantot, Yash Sharma, Ahmed Elgohary, Bo-Jhang Ho, Mani Srivastava, and Kai-Wei Chang. 2018. Generating natural language adversarial examples. *arXiv preprint arXiv:1804.07998*.

David A Belsley, Edwin Kuh, and Roy E Welsch. 2005. *Regression diagnostics: Identifying influential data and sources of collinearity*. John Wiley & Sons.

Hanjie Chen and Yangfeng Ji. 2020. Learning variational word masks to improve the interpretability of neural text classifiers. In *Proceedings of the 2020 Conference on Empirical Methods in Natural Language Processing (EMNLP)*, pages 4236–4251, Online. Association for Computational Linguistics.

Hanjie Chen and Yangfeng Ji. 2022. Adversarial training for improving model robustness? look at both prediction and interpretation. In *Proceedings of the AAAI Conference on Artificial Intelligence*.

Jianbo Chen, Le Song, Martin J Wainwright, and Michael I Jordan. 2018. L-shapley and c-shapley: Efficient model interpretation for structured data. *arXiv preprint arXiv:1808.02610*.

Jiefeng Chen, Xi Wu, Vaibhav Rastogi, Yingyu Liang, and Somesh Jha. 2019. Robust attribution regularization. *arXiv preprint arXiv:1905.09957*.

Jacob Devlin, Ming-Wei Chang, Kenton Lee, and Kristina Toutanova. 2018. Bert: Pre-training of deep bidirectional transformers for language understanding. *arXiv preprint arXiv:1810.04805*.

Finale Doshi-Velez and Been Kim. 2017. Towards a rigorous science of interpretable machine learning. *arXiv preprint arXiv:1702.08608*.

Mengnan Du, Ninghao Liu, and Xia Hu. 2019. Techniques for interpretable machine learning. *Communications of the ACM*, 63(1):68–77.

Jerome H Friedman. 2001. Greedy function approximation: a gradient boosting machine. *Annals of statistics*, pages 1189–1232.

Ji Gao, Jack Lanchantin, Mary Lou Soffa, and Yanjun Qi. 2018. Black-box generation of adversarial text sequences to evade deep learning classifiers. In *2018 IEEE Security and Privacy Workshops (SPW)*, pages 50–56. IEEE.

Reza Ghaeini, Xiaoli Z Fern, and Prasad Tadepalli. 2018. Interpreting recurrent and attention-based neural models: a case study on natural language inference. *arXiv preprint arXiv:1808.03894*.

Amirata Ghorbani, Abubakar Abid, and James Zou. 2019. Interpretation of neural networks is fragile. In *Proceedings of the AAAI Conference on Artificial Intelligence*, volume 33, pages 3681–3688.

Richard Goldstein. 1993. Conditioning diagnostics: Collinearity and weak data in regression.

Gene H Golub and Charles F Van Loan. 2013. *Matrix computations*, volume 3. JHU press.

Ian Goodfellow, Yoshua Bengio, and Aaron Courville. 2016. *Deep Learning*. MIT Press. `http://www.deeplearningbook.org`.

Ian J Goodfellow, Jonathon Shlens, and Christian Szegedy. 2014. Explaining and harnessing adversarial examples. *arXiv preprint arXiv:1412.6572*.

Yotam Hechtlinger. 2016. Interpretation of prediction models using the input gradient. *arXiv preprint arXiv:1611.07634*.

Juyeon Heo, Sunghwan Joo, and Taesup Moon. 2019. Fooling neural network interpretations via adversarial model manipulation. *arXiv preprint arXiv:1902.02041*.

Sepp Hochreiter and Jürgen Schmidhuber. 1997. Long short-term memory. *Neural computation*, 9(8):1735–1780.

Sara Hooker, Dumitru Erhan, Pieter-Jan Kindermans, and Been Kim. 2019. A benchmark for interpretability methods in deep neural networks. *Advances in neural information processing systems*, 32.

Adam Ivankay, Ivan Girardi, Chiara Marchiori, and Pascal Frossard. 2022. Fooling explanations in text classifiers. *arXiv preprint arXiv:2206.03178*.

Sarthak Jain and Byron C Wallace. 2019. Attention is not explanation. *arXiv preprint arXiv:1902.10186*.

Robin Jia, Aditi Raghunathan, Kerem Göksel, and Percy Liang. 2019. Certified robustness to adversarial word substitutions. *arXiv preprint arXiv:1909.00986*.

Heinrich Jiang, Been Kim, Melody Guan, and Maya Gupta. 2018. To trust or not to trust a classifier. *Advances in neural information processing systems*, 31.

Di Jin, Zhijing Jin, Joey Tianyi Zhou, and Peter Szolovits. 2020. Is bert really robust? a strong baseline for natural language attack on text classification and entailment. In *Proceedings of the AAAI conference on artificial intelligence*, volume 34, pages 8018–8025.

Maurice G Kendall. 1938. A new measure of rank correlation. *Biometrika*, 30(1/2):81–93.

Yoon Kim. 2014. Convolutional neural networks for sentence classification. In *Proceedings of the 2014 Conference on Empirical Methods in Natural Language Processing (EMNLP)*, pages 1746–1751, Doha, Qatar. Association for Computational Linguistics.

Jinfeng Li, Shouling Ji, Tianyu Du, Bo Li, and Ting Wang. 2018. Textbugger: Generating adversarial text against real-world applications. *arXiv preprint arXiv:1812.05271*.

Jiwei Li, Will Monroe, and Dan Jurafsky. 2016. Understanding neural networks through representation erasure. *arXiv preprint arXiv:1612.08220*.

Xin Li and Dan Roth. 2002. Learning question classifiers. In *COLING 2002: The 19th International Conference on Computational Linguistics*.

Bin Liang, Hongcheng Li, Miaoqiang Su, Pan Bian, Xirong Li, and Wenchang Shi. 2017. Deep text classification can be fooled. *arXiv preprint arXiv:1704.08006*.

Xiaodong Liu, Hao Cheng, Pengcheng He, Weizhu Chen, Yu Wang, Hoifung Poon, and Jianfeng Gao. 2020. Adversarial training for large neural language models. *arXiv preprint arXiv:2004.08994*.

Scott M Lundberg and Su-In Lee. 2017a. A unified approach to interpreting model predictions. In *Proceedings of the 31st international conference on neural information processing systems*, pages 4768–4777.

Scott M Lundberg and Su-In Lee. 2017b. A unified approach to interpreting model predictions. In I. Guyon, U. V. Luxburg, S. Bengio, H. Wallach, R. Fergus, S. Vishwanathan, and R. Garnett, editors, *Advances in Neural Information Processing Systems 30*, pages 4765–4774. Curran Associates, Inc.

Andrew Maas, Raymond E Daly, Peter T Pham, Dan Huang, Andrew Y Ng, and Christopher Potts. 2011. Learning word vectors for sentiment analysis. In *Proceedings of the 49th annual meeting of the association for computational linguistics: Human language technologies*, pages 142–150.

Christoph Molnar. 2018. A guide for making black box models explainable. *URL: https://christophm. github. io/interpretable-ml-book*.

Shuhuai Ren, Yihe Deng, Kun He, and Wanxiang Che. 2019. Generating natural language adversarial examples through probability weighted word saliency. In *Proceedings of the 57th annual meeting of the association for computational linguistics*, pages 1085–1097.

Marco Tulio Ribeiro, Sameer Singh, and Carlos Guestrin. 2016. "why should I trust you?": Explaining the predictions of any classifier. In *Proceedings of the 22nd ACM SIGKDD International Conference on Knowledge Discovery and Data Mining, San Francisco, CA, USA, August 13-17, 2016*, pages 1135–1144.

Lloyd S Shapley. 1953a. A value for n-person games. *Contributions to the Theory of Games*, 2(28).

LS Shapley. 1953b. Quota solutions op n-person games1. *Edited by Emil Artin and Marston Morse*, page 343.

Avanti Shrikumar, Peyton Greenside, and Anshul Kundaje. 2017. Learning important features through propagating activation differences. In *International Conference on Machine Learning*, pages 3145–3153. PMLR.

Sanchit Sinha, Hanjie Chen, Arshdeep Sekhon, Yangfeng Ji, and Yanjun Qi. 2021. Perturbing inputs for fragile interpretations in deep natural language processing. *arXiv preprint arXiv:2108.04990*.

Dylan Slack, Sophie Hilgard, Emily Jia, Sameer Singh, and Himabindu Lakkaraju. 2020. Fooling lime and shap: Adversarial attacks on post hoc explanation methods. In *Proceedings of the AAAI/ACM Conference on AI, Ethics, and Society*, pages 180–186.

Richard Socher, Alex Perelygin, Jean Wu, Jason Chuang, Christopher D Manning, Andrew Y Ng, and Christopher Potts. 2013. Recursive deep models for semantic compositionality over a sentiment treebank. In *Proceedings of the 2013 conference on empirical methods in natural language processing*, pages 1631–1642.

Erik Strumbelj and Igor Kononenko. 2010. An efficient explanation of individual classifications using game theory. *The Journal of Machine Learning Research*, 11:1–18.

Akshayvarun Subramanya, Vipin Pillai, and Hamed Pirsiavash. 2019. Fooling network interpretation in image classification. In *Proceedings of the IEEE/CVF International Conference on Computer Vision*, pages 2020–2029.

Christian Szegedy, Wojciech Zaremba, Ilya Sutskever, Joan Bruna, Dumitru Erhan, Ian Goodfellow, and Rob Fergus. 2013. Intriguing properties of neural networks. *arXiv preprint arXiv:1312.6199*.

Eric Wallace, Shi Feng, Nikhil Kandpal, Matt Gardner, and Sameer Singh. 2019. Universal adversarial triggers for attacking and analyzing nlp. *arXiv preprint arXiv:1908.07125*.

Junlin Wang, Jens Tuyls, Eric Wallace, and Sameer Singh. 2020. Gradient-based analysis of nlp models is manipulable. *arXiv preprint arXiv:2010.05419*.

Muhammad Bilal Zafar, Michele Donini, Dylan Slack, Cédric Archambeau, Sanjiv Das, and Krishnaram Kenthapadi. 2021. On the lack of robust interpretability of neural text classifiers. *arXiv preprint arXiv:2106.04631*.

Xiang Zhang, Junbo Zhao, and Yann LeCun. 2015. Character-level convolutional networks for text classification. *arXiv preprint arXiv:1509.01626*.

Xinyang Zhang, Ningfei Wang, Hua Shen, Shouling Ji, Xiapu Luo, and Ting Wang. 2020. Interpretable deep learning under fire. In *29th {USENIX} Security Symposium ({USENIX} Security 20)*.

Yu Zhang, Peter Tiňo, Aleš Leonardis, and Ke Tang. 2021. A survey on neural network interpretability. *IEEE Transactions on Emerging Topics in Computational Intelligence*.

Zhengli Zhao, Dheeru Dua, and Sameer Singh. 2017. Generating natural adversarial examples. *arXiv preprint arXiv:1710.11342*.

A Figures of Comparison Experiments Result on SST-2, AG's News and TREC Dataset

In the section, we include comparison experiments results of the SST-2 dataset in Figure 4, the AG's News dataset in Figure 5, and the TREC dataset in Figure 6.

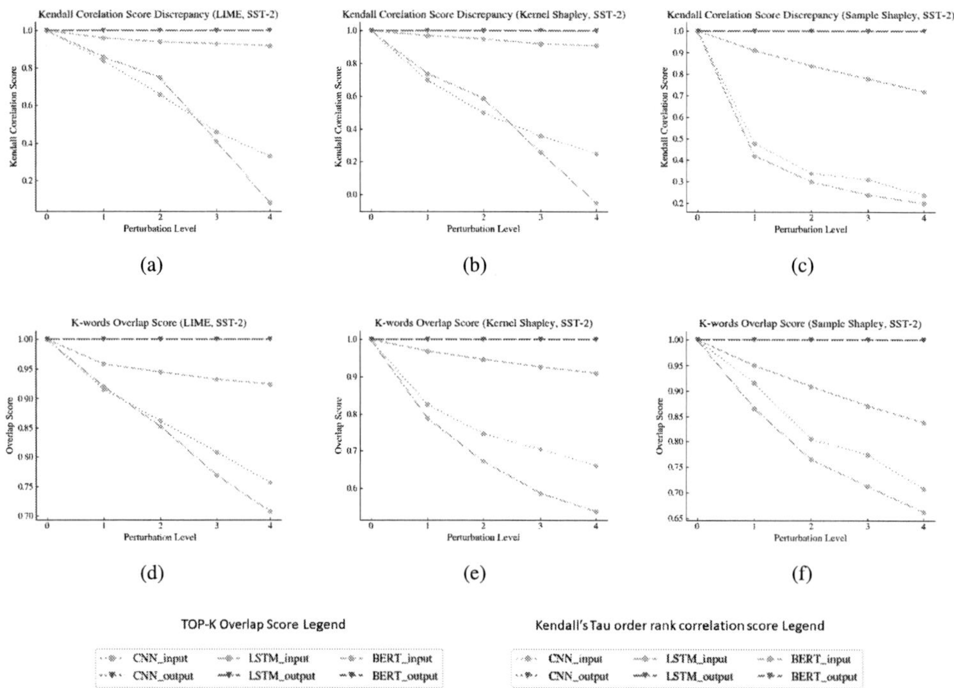

Figure 4: Comparison experiment results on the SST-2 dataset; (a) and (d) demonstrate results using LIME method; (b) and (e) demonstrate results using Kernel Sharply method; (c) and (f) demonstrate results using Sample Sharply method.

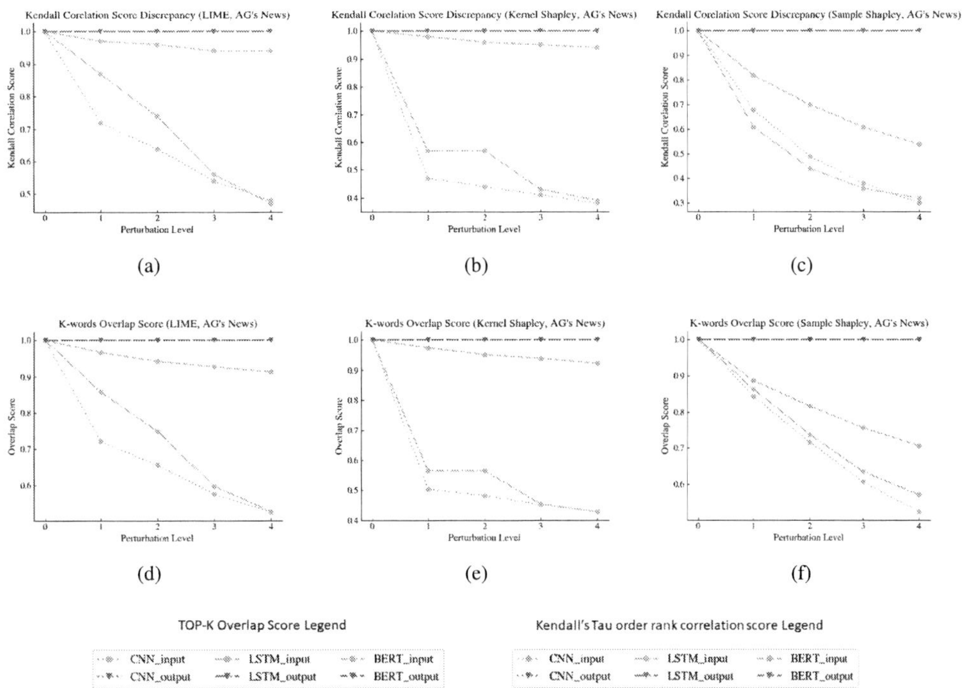

Figure 5: Comparison experiment results on the AG's News dataset; (a) and (d) demonstrate results using LIME method; (b) and (e) demonstrate results using Kernel Sharply method; (c) and (f) demonstrate results using Sample Sharply method.

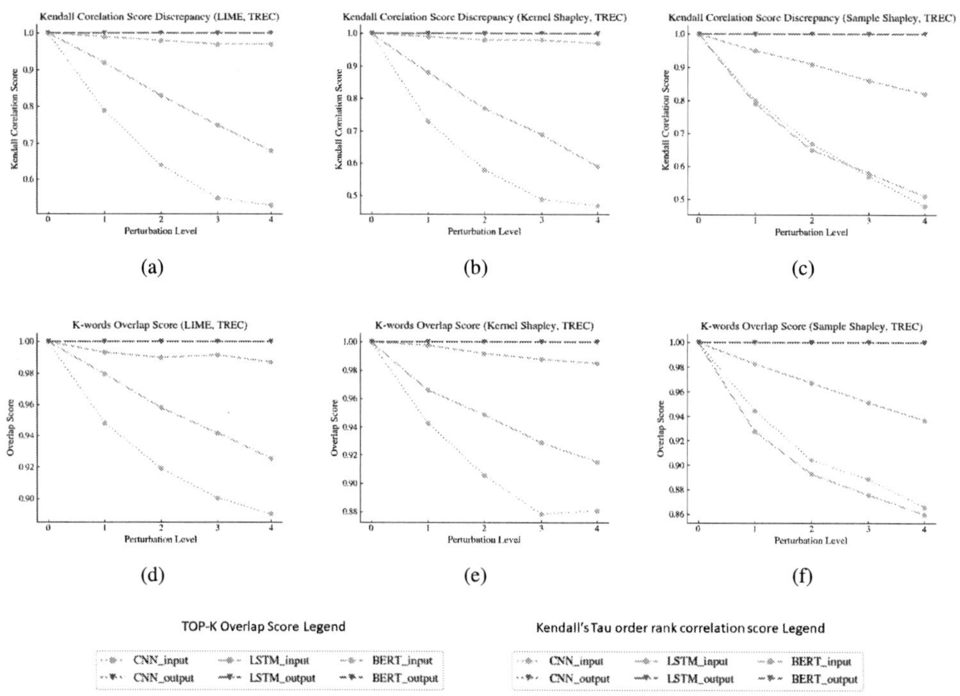

Figure 6: Comparison experiment results on the TREC dataset; (a) and (d) demonstrate results using LIME method; (b) and (e) demonstrate results using Kernel Sharply method; (c) and (f) demonstrate results using Sample Sharply method.

Probing Pretrained Models of Source Codes

Sergey Troshin, Nadezhda Chirkova*
HSE University
{stroshin, nchirkova}@hse.ru

Abstract

Deep learning models are widely used for solving challenging code processing tasks, such as code generation or code summarization. Traditionally, a specific model architecture was carefully built to solve a particular code processing task. However, recently general pretrained models such as CodeBERT or CodeT5 have been shown to outperform task-specific models in many applications. While pretrained models are known to learn complex patterns from data, they may fail to understand some properties of source code. To test diverse aspects of code understanding, we introduce a set of diagnostic probing tasks. We show that pretrained models of code indeed contain information about code syntactic structure, the notions of identifiers, and namespaces, but they may fail to recognize more complex code properties such as semantic equivalence. We also investigate how probing results are affected by using code-specific pretraining objectives, varying the model size, or finetuning.

1 Introduction

Deep learning and especially Natural Language Processing (NLP) methods have been widely and successfully adopted to process source code. Example tasks include code generation (Allamanis et al., 2015; Chen et al., 2021) where the task is usually formulated as to produce a code of a function given the natural description; code translation (Nguyen et al., 2013; Roziere et al., 2020a) where the model needs to translate from one programming language to another; and code summarization (Haiduc et al., 2010; Alex et al., 2020) where the task is to produce natural language (NL) description for a given code snippet. Deep learning is also widely used in discriminative tasks, such as automated bug search and repair (Hellendoorn et al., 2020).

In recent years, the focus has shifted from developing task-specific models incorporating prior knowledge about the task, to relying on general pretrained models of code such as CodeBERT (Feng et al., 2020) or CodeT5 (Wang et al., 2021). These models, once pretrained, can be finetuned on the downstream tasks with a little additional cost, surpassing task-specific models. While the performance of the models is high on a wide range of downstream tasks (Lu et al., 2021), the boundary between what the models know and where they fail remains hidden behind the complexity of the downstream tasks. The lack of interpretability of pretrained models limits their practical use. At the same time, a deeper examination of model's understanding of source code may increase developers' trust and broaden the applicability of pretrained models.

In NLP, there is an established probing approach for a more fine-grained examination of the knowledge of various aspects of the language, e.g. morphology, syntax, or discourse understanding (Belinkov et al., 2020; Tenney et al., 2019; Koto et al., 2021). Probing usually means training a linear model on top of hidden representations of a model for various simple tasks, e.g. to predict a part-of-speech tag, to detect whether a sentence was corrupted, or to estimate the number of objects in the main clause (Conneau et al., 2018a). Probing experiments may suggest ways to improve the quality of the pretrained model or provide recommendations on how to tune the model better in applied tasks (Belinkov, 2022).

Inspired by the insights probing provided in NLP, we develop probing tasks to understand the extent to which the current state-of-the-art pretrained models capture structural and semantic properties of source code. Our contributions are as follows:

- we introduce a set of syntactic and semantic probing tasks, suitable for testing diverse aspects of code understanding;
- we study an effect of the model choice, pre-

*Now at Naver Labs Europe

Proceedings of the Fifth BlackboxNLP Workshop on Analyzing and Interpreting Neural Networks for NLP, pages 371 - 383
December 8, 2022 ©2022 Association for Computational Linguistics

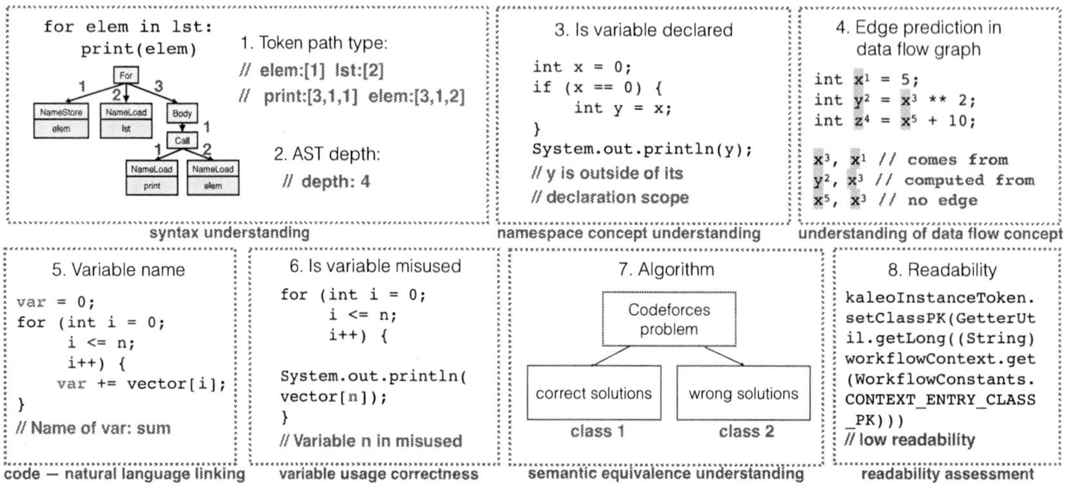

Figure 1: Illustration of the proposed probing tasks testing various aspects of code understanding.

training objective choice, and model size on probing results;

- we use probings to highlight which information about code is preserved by finetuned models in different downstream tasks.

We release our code[1].

2 Probing tasks

We probe pretrained models of code using linear regression or classification trained on top of code representations extracted from each layer of each model (layers weights are not finetuned) (Alain and Bengio, 2016).

We develop auxiliary tasks (with synthetic data or data borrowed from other works) that test models' understanding of various properties of source code: strict syntactic structure, the notions of data flow and namespaces, naming, semantic equivalence, and readability. We consider both *global* tasks (predicting a property of the whole code snippet) and *local* tasks (predicting a property of a particular token or a group of tokens). For each task, we introduce a simple but as strong as possible baseline. Figure 1 illustrates all tasks. For all classification tasks, we measure test error ($1 - accuracy$), and for "AST depth" regression task, we calculate the mean absolute error $MAE(y_{true}, y_{pred}) = \frac{1}{N}\sum_{i=1}^{N} |y^i_{true} - y^i_{pred}|$.

Notation. Pretrained models of code usually follow the standard NLP methodology: representing a code snippet as a sequence of subtokens, e. g. byte-pair encoding subtokens, and pretraining the model on a large corpora of source code using masked language modeling. We denote the sequence of subtokens as $s_1, \ldots, s_m$. Let us denote $t(s_i)$ a mapping from a subtoken s_i into a corresponding code token $t(s_i)$, e.g. for a subtoken sequence [`_(`, `_for`, `_public`, `_get`, `Status`], $t($`_get`$) =$ `getStatus`. For each subtoken s_i, we extract the model's embedding $\mathrm{w}^\ell_\mathrm{i} \in R^d$ for a particular layer ℓ, where d is the size of hidden representations.

2.1 Token Path Type

The first two probing tasks test whether pretrained models contain information about the syntactic structure of code. The first task consists of predicting the position of a token in the Abstract Syntax Tree (AST). Given a subtoken s_i and the corresponding embedding $\mathrm{w}^\ell_\mathrm{i}$, the task is to predict the path type from the root to the $t(s_i)$ token, e.g. $[1, 2, 1]$, meaning go to the first child, then to the second one, then to the first one. This task, which is a local task, is formulated as a classification problem by selecting target subtokens corresponding to 15 most frequent path types. As a baseline, we consider constant prediction w. r. t. a subtoken, i. e. we select the most frequent class (path type) for each subtoken in the vocabulary.

2.2 AST depth

The second syntactic task is defined on a code snippet level (global task) and consists of predicting the depth of the AST built from the snippet (regression problem). The baseline for this task is defined as a

[1]https://github.com/serjtroshin/probings4code

linear regression trained on a single feature – the number of tokens in the code snippet, this baseline outperforms the median depth baseline computed over the whole dataset.

2.3 Is Variable Declared

This task tests the model's understanding of the notion of namespaces. The model is asked, whether there is an "undeclared variable name" error for a particular expression with an identifier. For example, in the first code snippet the identifier y is correctly used after a declaration:

```
int x = 0;
if (x == 0) {
    int y = x; // declare
    System.out.println(y); // use
}
```

However, in the second snippet there is an error, since y is outside of the scope of it's declaration:

```
int x = 0;
if (x == 0) { int y = x; }
System.out.println(y); // y is undeclared
```

We generate positive and negative examples using the following procedure. For a code snippet, we find a variable name declaration, e.g. `float x = 0`. Next, we find a random place in code after the variable declaration where we can insert a printing expression e.g. `System.out.println(x);`, and define a label for binary classification analyzing variable scopes: is variable declared before used? The task is formulated for the mean subtoken embedding of the inserted variable name (local task). The baseline in this task is a constant prediction that the variable is declared.

2.4 Edge Prediction in Data Flow Graph

The next task measures to what extent a model encodes the information about the data flow. Given two tokens, the task is to predict a data flow edge between them. There can be no edge (negative example), a "comes from" edge, or a "computed from" edge. The task is formulated as classification of a pair of tokens (their mean embeddings over subtokens are concatenated), this is the local task.

In addition to existent data flow edges we select a roughly equal number of "no edge" examples by selecting random pairs of nodes from AST with suitable node types (e.g. pairs of identifiers, constants, etc.). As a baseline, we predict the most frequent edge type for the corresponding pair of tokens, which outperforms the most frequent class baseline.

2.5 Variable Name

The next task targets the ability to link code elements and their natural language descriptions. A model should predict a variable name, given a code snippet with all occurrences of the original name replaced with a placeholder `var`. This task requires semantic understanding of the variable's role in the program (local task).

We formulate this task as classification, targeting only 15 most popular identifier names. The feature vector is a mean hidden representation for all occurrences of the identifier in code. In such way, the model should be able to predict the identifier name based on the context in which the variable was used. The baseline in this task is defined by the bag-of-words model: we count occurrences of all subtokens in the code snippet, convert them to tf-idf values and train a linear classifier on these features. This baseline substantially outperforms the constant baseline which always predicts the most frequent variable name.

2.6 Is Variable Misused

The next local task tests the ability of the model to detect the variable misuse bug (Hellendoorn et al., 2020). We introduce variable misuse by randomly assigning "wrong" identifier name copying from another identifier from the same code snippet. We add "correct" code snippet for each "wrong" snippet, formulating the task as a binary classification problem, where the input is identifier's subtokens (mean embedding). The baseline is the bag of words predictor, which, for this task, is better than most frequent class predictor.

2.7 Algorithm

The next (global) semantic task also tests the ability of models to distinguish computationally equivalent codes from other codes. To obtain a dataset for this task, we select a simple problem from the CodeForces competition[2], which can be reformulated as to check if each character in a string has a neighbor equal to it. We download "wrong answer" and "accepted" Python submissions from the contest and filter out too long codes ($>$ 1000 characters) obtaining 550 "accepted" and 384 "wrong answer" submissions.

[2]https://codeforces.com/problemset/problem/1671/A

The task is to distinguish "correct" code from "wrong" and formulated as a binary classification problem. The task requires deeper understanding of the data and control flow since the "accepted" and "wrong answer" solutions are usually very similar visually. It should be hard for a model to make predictions based only on spurious surface or syntactic features to succeed in this task. As a baseline, we again use the bag-of-words model described above.

2.8 Readability

Finally, we consider a readability property of code. Readability defines how easy code is for the programmers to understand and maintain. Generally, readability depends on visual appearance of code (spaces, new lines etc), the meaningfulness of variable and function names, the quality of comments, and the particular algorithmic implementation (the same algorithm could be written in different ways, some of them more and some of them less readable). We use the 200 examples dataset provided by Scalabrino et al. (2018) and obtained by collecting a set of functions and asking developers to rate readability on the scale from 1 to 5 (several ratings per example). The task is then converted by the authors to binary classification by treating all snippets with rating $\leqslant 3.6$ as not readable and the rest ones as readable, as in Scalabrino et al. (2018). This is a global task and as the baseline we use the bag-of-words model which outperforms the constant most frequent class prediction.

3 Models

In this section, we briefly describe the models to be compared. We have selected several widely used pretrained models, which vary in the model architecture, pretraining objective, model size, and training datasets.

3.1 CodeBERT

CodeBERT (Feng et al., 2020) is one of the first attempts to pretrain a Transformer-based encoder model for source code representation learning and comprehension. It is a 12 layer encoder model based on RoBERTa-base (125M) (Liu et al., 2019) and trained with masked language modeling and replaced token detection objectives. The model is trained on 6M CodeSeachNet dataset (Husain et al., 2020), composed of functions from 6 programming languages (Java, Python, JavaScript, PHP, Ruby, Go) and NL comments.

3.2 GraphCodeBERT

GraphCodeBERT (Guo et al., 2021) extends the work of (Feng et al., 2020), by introducing data flow-related objectives. They encourage the models to learn structure-aware representations by predicting randomly selected "comes from" data-flow edges.

3.3 PLBART

Ahmad et al. (2021a) introduced a 140M parameter PLBART model with 6 encoder and 6 decoder layers. The model is based on the BART (Lewis et al., 2020) architecture. The authors released a PLBART[3] checkpoint pretrained on the data collected by Roziere et al. (2020b), which is 470M Java, 210M Python functions/methods, and pretrained the 47M NL descriptions. They release a PLBART_large checkpoint as well (400M, 12 layer encoder, 12 layer decoder).

3.4 CodeT5

CodeT5 (Wang et al., 2021) is an encoder-decoder model based on the T5 (Raffel et al., 2020) architecture and pretrained on 8.35M functions in 8 programming languages (Python, Java, JavaScript, PHP, Ruby, Go, C, and C#). The model combines the masked language modeling objective with code-specific objectives, including identifier tagging and predicting variable names. We experiment with two released model checkpoints[4]: CodeT5-base (220M) and CodeT5-small (60M).

3.5 CodeGPT2

CodeGPT2 (Lu et al., 2021) is a decoder only model based on GPT-2 architecture (Radford et al., 2019). The 117M model consists of 12 layers and is pretrained on the CodeSearchNet (Husain et al., 2020) dataset. We used *CodeGPT-small-java-adaptedGPT2* checkpoint[5], that is initialized from GPT-2 model and then trained on code corpus.

3.6 BERT

We also consider the text-based model, BERT, to understand the effect of code-specific pretraining. We use a 110M 12-layer BERT model (Devlin et al.,

[3] `https://github.com/wasiahmad/PLBART`

[4] `https://github.com/salesforce/CodeT5`

[5] `https://huggingface.co/microsoft/ /CodeGPT-small-java-adaptedGPT2`

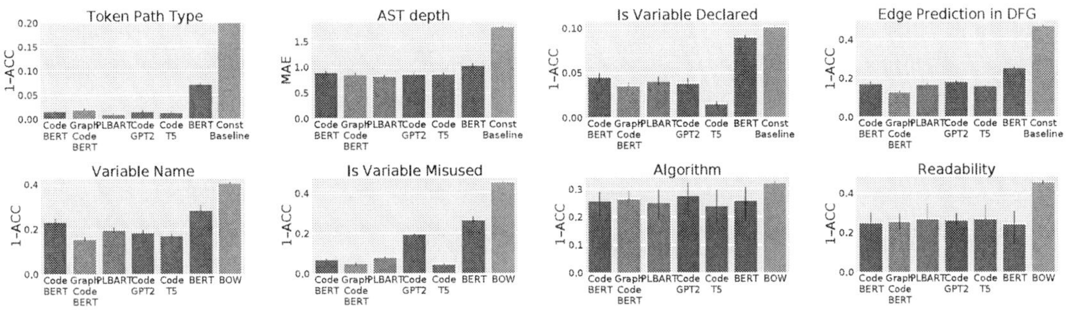

Figure 2: Results for the best performing layer representations, for all probing tasks. Metrics are the lower the better.

2019), *"bert-base-cased"* checkpoint from Hugging Face[6], trained on the Book Corpus (Zhu et al., 2015).

4 Experimental setup

4.1 Data and preprocessing

For our experiments which involve synthetic data (first 6 tasks), we use the test dataset provided by Ahmad et al. (2021a) consisting of 10k examples of Java functions and methods with removed comments and new line symbols, and standardized code snippets. For the two remaining tasks the datasets were mentioned in the task descriptions. For each pretrained model, we apply it's subtokenization procedure. All models have a limit of 512 input subtokens. We crop subtoken sequences that are longer than 512 subtokens. We use commonly used open access datasets intended for research purposes.

4.2 Probing details

For each probing task, we average results over four runs using 4-fold cross-validation. For each model, we use a single checkpoint as usually only one checkpoint is released.

Each pretrained model returns representations for a sequence of subtokens $s_1, \ldots, s_m$, e. g. from byte-pair encoding. When the task is formulated on a code snippet level, the layer-wise embeddings of the snippet are obtained by averaging subtoken embeddings, following (Koto et al., 2021).

For the probing models, we use linear models from scikit-learn (0.24.2) (Pedregosa et al., 2011), including *SGDClassifier* with logistic regression loss for classification tasks (we select optimal alpha parameter via grid search over $[0.0001, 0.001, 0.01, 0.1, 1, 10, 100]$ range, and set tolerance to 0.0001); and *RidgeCV* for regression tasks (grid search for alpha over $[0.0001, 0.001, 0.01, 0.1, 1, 10, 100]$ range). In addition to linear probings, we also probe pretrained models with a 3-layer MLP (see Appendix B), however, the results for MLP are similar.

[6] https://huggingface.co/bert-base-cased

5 Experiments

Our research questions are as follows:

- To what extent do the models pretrained on code capture information about source code properties?
- Does multitask pretraining with code-specific objectives provide richer representations?
- How does the model size affect probing results? Which representations are better: provided by the encoder or by the decoder? Which layers provide better representations?
- Does finetuning preserve syntactic and semantic information in different downstream tasks?

We used a single Tesla V100 GPU for the forward pass to collect embeddings, and 4 CPU for training linear models. Our total computational budget is 864 CPU hours and 20 GPU hours.

5.1 Comparison of different models

In this subsection, we study the performance of different pretrained models in all probing tasks. In this experiment, we report the results for the best performing layer representation for each model: the layer is chosen using the first fold and the results are averaged over three remaining folds. Figure 2 presents the results.

Overall, we observe that the probing performance of pretrained models exceeds the performance of the simple baseline in all tasks. However, in the semantic-related "Readability" and "Algorithm" tasks, the pretrained models are very close to the simple baseline and thus do not capture much more information relevant to these tasks. The BERT model pretrained on textual data performs worse than the models pretrained on code in all tasks except the semantic-related "Readability" and "Algorithm" tasks, where all pretrained models perform similarily. We conclude that *models pretrained on code contain knowledge about basic source code properties but lack a deeper semantic understanding of code.*

Comparing different models, we find that the models pretrained with code-specific objectives, GraphCodeBert and CodeT5, are better or on par with other models for all tasks. In "Edge Prediction in DFG", GraphCodeBERT performs best because it uses the edge prediction objective during pretraining. Similarly in "Variable is Undeclared", "Is Variable Misused" CodeT5 and GraphCodeBERT perform best potentially because they use the variable-related pretraining objectives. CodeGPT2 performs worse for "Is Variable Misused" task, because it only sees the left context which may be not enough to predict the misused variable. To sum up, *models pretrained with code-specific objectives, CodeT5 and GraphCodeBERT, show consistent gain for the tasks related to their pretraining objectives, over other models, pretrained with single objectives, or perform on par with them.*

To better understand how pretrained models perform on each task, we perform an ablation study masking different code components: identifiers, keywords, and punctuation. This ablation study is described in Appendix A. The main finding is that masking punctuation hurts the probing performance of the model pretrained on source code in almost all tasks, while masking language keywords and renaming identifiers do not have much effect (except the variable naming task where renaming identifiers has a significant effect).

5.2 Encoder vs Decoder

This subsection compares the representations of the encoder and the decoder. We consider representations of two encoder-decoder models, PLBART-base and CodeT5-base. Table 1 compares best performing encoder representations and best performing decoder representations for all probing tasks. We observe that *in almost all probing tasks, the decoder representations perform worse or on par with the encoder representations.* In some tasks, e. g. "Is Variable Misused", the decoder shows much worse results than the encoder. A possible explanation is that the aim of the encoder is to provide rich representations for the decoder, hence the encoder is more suitable for information extraction.

5.3 The effect of the model size

In this subsection, we are interested whether larger models capture more information about the source code properties than smaller models. Table 1 reports the performance of CodeT5-base and CodeT5-small models, and of PLBART-large and PLBART-base models (other models are not available in variable sizes). We find that *in three variable related tasks the larger models expectantly perform better than smaller models but in the majority of the tasks the performance is similar.*

5.4 Per-layer probing performance

We now analyse probing results for different Transformer layers. Figure 3 shows the per-layer performance of all considered pretrained models. In syntax-related, namespace-related, data flow-related, algorithm-related and readability-related tasks, *middle layers (4–10) usually provide the most informative representations.* In the "Variable Name" (and partly in "Is Variable Misused"), the last layers consistently perform better because the task is closely related to the masked language modeling objective which is usually solved on top of last layers.

5.5 The effect of finetuning

In this section, we study the effect of finetuning on probing results. Specifically, we are interested 1) whether finetuned models preserve information contained in pretrained models; 2) does pretraining enrich the representations of finetuned models, compared with the representations of models trained from scratch.

In this section, we focus on the PLBART model and finetune it for 5 downstream tasks: 3 generative tasks (Code Translation from Python to Java, Java Code Generation based on natural language descriptions, Java Code Summarization into textual description) and 2 discriminative tasks (Clone Detection, Defect Prediction). We use the AVATAR

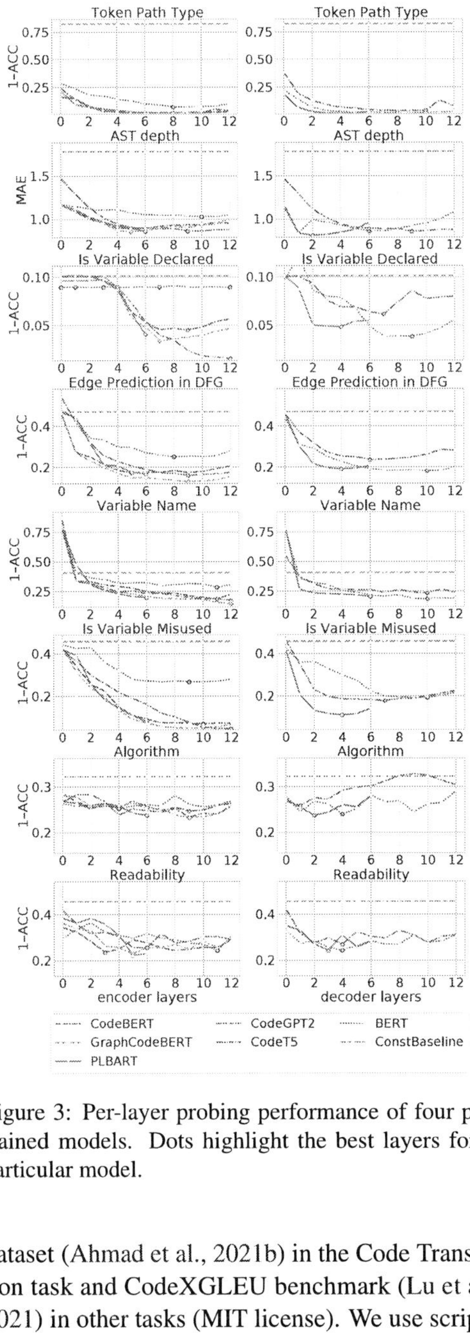

Figure 3: Per-layer probing performance of four pretrained models. Dots highlight the best layers for a particular model.

dataset (Ahmad et al., 2021b) in the Code Translation task and CodeXGLEU benchmark (Lu et al., 2021) in other tasks (MIT license). We use scripts for PLBART finetuning on these tasks provided in PLBART[7] and AVATAR[8] repositories.

Figure 4 compares 3 scenarios: the PLBART checkpoint after pretraining (leftmost bar), checkpoints after PLBART finetuning on each of 5 downstream tasks (dark bars), and checkpoints after training from scratch on each of 5 downstream tasks (semi-transparent bars). We also include baselines for reference.

[7]https://github.com/wasiahmad/PLBART

[8]https://github.com/wasiahmad/AVATAR

Models finetuned for discriminative tasks exhibit the highest information loss between the initial pretrained stage and the finetuned stage, which may indicate that models trained on these tasks rely on some spurious features, rather than on code syntax or semantics.

Among generative tasks, the Code Translation model exhibits almost no gap between pretrained and finetuned stages. This could be attributed to having code as both input and output of the task. Code Generation and Code Summarization models have code only as either the input or the output of the task, and usually exhibit a slightly larger gap.

As for models, trained from scratch for downstream tasks (semi-transparent bars), the overall trend is similar across the downstream tasks, but the absolute results are usually much worse, compared to finetuned models, and sometimes are close to simple baselines. *The downstream tasks alone do not provide high-quality code representations.*

6 Related Work

Probing became a universal tool in NLP for testing pretrained models' understanding or knowledge of various language aspects. A simple linear probing was used in (Gupta et al., 2015) to test whether referential knowledge is already encoded in word embeddings, while Köhn (2015) got insights into the behaviour of word embedding in terms of morphological and syntactical properties. Probing tasks were developed to evaluate sentence embeddings (Ettinger et al., 2016; Conneau et al., 2018b) whether they incorporate compositional, or surface (length of the sentence), syntax (tree depth, top constituent), and text semantics (e.g. tense of a sentence) knowledge. Hewitt and Manning (2019) proposed more complex probing tasks, questioning the possibility to parse the whole dependency trees from the sentence embeddings using a metric learning approach. More recent studies for language models include the study of emerging capabilities of large language models (Wei et al., 2022). We refer to Belinkov (2022) for a broad review of existing probing works in NLP.

In the context of source code, Karmakar and Robbes (2021) made the first steps towards probing pretrained models. However, they only consider four simple tasks and tree code models, CodeBERT, CodeBERTa and GraphCodeBERT. In contrast to their work, we propose a wider set of tasks, including several token-wise tasks, consider a wider

Task	PLBART encoder	PLBART decoder	CodeT5 encoder	CodeT5 decoder	PLBART base	PLBART large	CodeT5 small	CodeT5 base
Token Path Type	**0.011**	0.012	**0.013**	0.036	**0.011**	0.014	**0.012**	0.013
AST depth	0.866	**0.820**	**0.867**	**0.864**	**0.820**	**0.850**	**0.863**	**0.864**
Is Variable Declared	**0.042**	**0.049**	**0.014**	0.061	0.042	**0.019**	0.025	**0.014**
Edge Prediction in DFG	**0.167**	0.191	**0.161**	0.230	**0.167**	**0.167**	**0.162**	**0.161**
Variable Name	**0.186**	**0.194**	**0.162**	0.211	**0.186**	**0.165**	0.208	**0.162**
Is Variable Misused	**0.080**	0.112	**0.046**	0.176	0.080	**0.053**	0.064	**0.046**
Algorithm	**0.239**	**0.251**	**0.228**	**0.268**	**0.246**	**0.225**	**0.235**	**0.228**
Readability	**0.226**	**0.237**	**0.247**	**0.246**	**0.216**	**0.238**	**0.242**	**0.221**

Table 1: Encoder vs decoder performance for PLBART-base and CodeT5-base; and comparison of small vs large models: PLBART-base vs PLBART-large, and CodeT5-small vs CodeT5-base. Metrics: MAE for "AST depth", otherwise test error (1-accuracy).

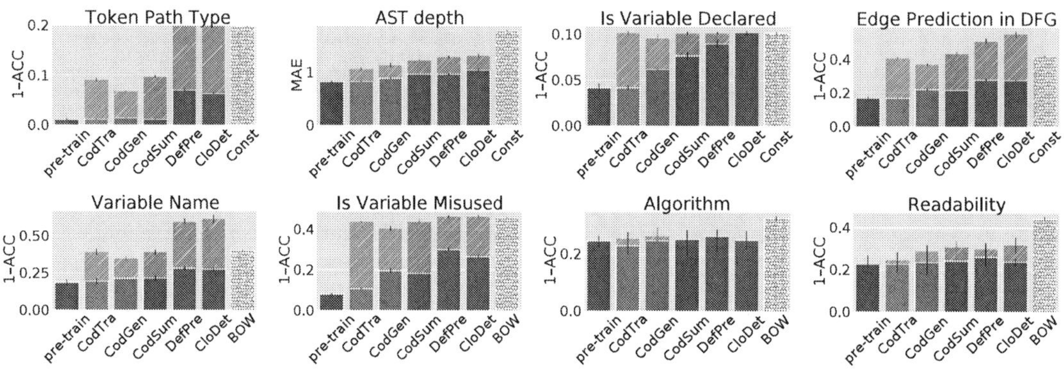

Figure 4: Results on the effect of finetuning. Pre-train (leftmost bar): pretrained-only checkpoint. The following bars: dark – finetuned models, semi-transparent – models trained from scratch. Results for 5 downstream tasks: Code Translation, Code Generation, Code Summarization, Defect Prediction, Clone Detection.

range of pretrained models, and investigate various dimensions, including different pretraining objectives, model sizes, and the effect of finetuning.

A line of work investigate pretrained models for code in different directions. anonymous authors (2022) show that CodeBERT relies on the high token overlap between query and code solving code search task rather than deeper syntax or semantic features, and Sharma et al. (2022) shows that BERT trained on code pays more attention to identifiers and separators. Our work provides another view on the analysis of pretrained models of code, from the probing perspective, and complements these results.

Recently created BIG-bench benchmark (Srivastava et al., 2022) contains a number of challenging code-related probing tasks for testing large language models capabilites, including programming synthesis and code summarization tasks, which are close to complex downstream tasks. In contrast, we aim at developing simple probing tasks targeting specific code understanding aspects.

7 Conclusion and discussion

We presented a diagnosis tool, based on probing tasks, that can be used to estimate to which extent deep learning models capture the information about various properties of source code in their hidden representations. Our results show that pretrained models of code do contain information about code syntactic structure, the notion of namespaces, data flow, code readability and natural language-based naming. However, pretrained models show limited understanding of code semantics, which means that their usefullness in applied tasks requiring semantic understanding of code may be limited.

Using code-specific pretraining objectives (CodeT5, GraphCodeBert) enriches the understanding of the code aspects addressed in the corresponding objective. This result may suggest practitioners to choose pretrained models which pretraining objectives are better aligned with the considered applied task.

We also found that finetuning may deteriorate the model's understanding of code properties, especially in classification downstream tasks. This may suggest including code-specific objectives in finetuning, especially if multi-stage finetuning (Pruksachatkun et al., 2020) is used.

Limitations

In this section, we discuss the limitations of our probing toolkit.

Our probing setup does not cover all possible aspects of source code. However, we were aiming at covering diverse properties of code.

Our experiments are limited to the two most popular high-level languages, which are usually used to evaluate pretrained model for code: Java (7 tasks) and Python (1 task). It would be interesting to compare the models on low-level languages like C/C++.

The linear models used for probings may appear limited in their capacity, however, they were successfully used in a lot of NLP probing approaches (Belinkov, 2022) and are well suitable for particular research questions considered in the paper. Moreover, we also experiment with a 3-layer MLP and find that our main results hold for MLP.

Finally, in this work, we only considered open-sourced pretrained checkpoints. It would be interesting to compare the performance of pretrained models across a wide range of model sizes.

Ethics Statement

The main goal of this paper is to provide an empirical study of the existent models. Since we do not propose new models, there are no potential social risks to the best of our knowledge. Our work may benefit the research community providing more introspection to the current state-of-the-art models.

Acknowledgments

The results were supported by the Russian Science Foundation grant №19-71-30020. The research was supported in part through the computational resources of HPC facilities at NRU HSE.

References

Wasi Ahmad, Saikat Chakraborty, Baishakhi Ray, and Kai-Wei Chang. 2021a. Unified pre-training for program understanding and generation. In *Proceedings of the 2021 Conference of the North American Chapter of the Association for Computational Linguistics: Human Language Technologies*, pages 2655–2668, Online. Association for Computational Linguistics.

Wasi Uddin Ahmad, Md Golam Rahman Tushar, Saikat Chakraborty, and Kai-Wei Chang. 2021b. Avatar: A parallel corpus for java-python program translation. *arXiv preprint arXiv:2108.11590*.

Takuya Akiba, Shotaro Sano, Toshihiko Yanase, Takeru Ohta, and Masanori Koyama. 2019. Optuna: A next-generation hyperparameter optimization framework. In *Proceedings of the 25rd ACM SIGKDD International Conference on Knowledge Discovery and Data Mining*.

Guillaume Alain and Yoshua Bengio. 2016. Understanding intermediate layers using linear classifier probes. *CoRR*, abs/1610.01644.

LeClair Alex, Haque Sakib, Wu Lingfei, and McMillan Collin. 2020. Improved code summarization via a graph neural network. In *2020 IEEE/ACM International Conference on Program Comprehension*.

Miltos Allamanis, Daniel Tarlow, Andrew Gordon, and Yi Wei. 2015. Bimodal modelling of source code and natural language. In *Proceedings of the 32nd International Conference on Machine Learning*, volume 37 of *Proceedings of Machine Learning Research*, pages 2123–2132, Lille, France. PMLR.

anonymous authors. 2022. Analyzing codebert's performance on natural language code search.

Yonatan Belinkov. 2022. Probing classifiers: Promises, shortcomings, and advances. *Computational Linguistics*, 48(1):207–219.

Yonatan Belinkov, Nadir Durrani, Fahim Dalvi, Hassan Sajjad, and James Glass. 2020. On the linguistic representational power of neural machine translation models.

Mark Chen, Jerry Tworek, Heewoo Jun, Qiming Yuan, Henrique Ponde de Oliveira Pinto, Jared Kaplan, Harri Edwards, Yuri Burda, and Nicholas Joseph et al. 2021. Evaluating large language models trained on code.

Nadezhda Chirkova and Sergey Troshin. 2021. Empirical study of transformers for source code. In *Proceedings of the 29th ACM Joint Meeting on European Software Engineering Conference and Symposium on the Foundations of Software Engineering*, ESEC/FSE 2021, page 703–715, New York, NY, USA. Association for Computing Machinery.

Alexis Conneau, German Kruszewski, Guillaume Lample, Loïc Barrault, and Marco Baroni. 2018a. What you can cram into a single $&!#* vector: Probing sentence embeddings for linguistic properties. In *Proceedings of the 56th Annual Meeting of the Association for Computational Linguistics (Volume 1: Long Papers)*, pages 2126–2136, Melbourne, Australia. Association for Computational Linguistics.

Alexis Conneau, German Kruszewski, Guillaume Lample, Loïc Barrault, and Marco Baroni. 2018b. What you can cram into a single $&!#* vector: Probing sentence embeddings for linguistic properties. In *Proceedings of the 56th Annual Meeting of the Association for Computational Linguistics (Volume 1: Long Papers)*, pages 2126–2136, Melbourne, Australia. Association for Computational Linguistics.

Jacob Devlin, Ming-Wei Chang, Kenton Lee, and Kristina Toutanova. 2019. BERT: Pre-training of deep bidirectional transformers for language understanding. In *Proceedings of the 2019 Conference of the North American Chapter of the Association for Computational Linguistics: Human Language Technologies, Volume 1 (Long and Short Papers)*, pages 4171–4186, Minneapolis, Minnesota. Association for Computational Linguistics.

Allyson Ettinger, Ahmed Elgohary, and Philip Resnik. 2016. Probing for semantic evidence of composition by means of simple classification tasks. In *Proceedings of the 1st Workshop on Evaluating Vector-Space Representations for NLP*, pages 134–139, Berlin, Germany. Association for Computational Linguistics.

Zhangyin Feng, Daya Guo, Duyu Tang, Nan Duan, Xiaocheng Feng, Ming Gong, Linjun Shou, Bing Qin, Ting Liu, Daxin Jiang, and Ming Zhou. 2020. CodeBERT: A pre-trained model for programming and natural languages. In *Findings of the Association for Computational Linguistics: EMNLP 2020*, pages 1536–1547, Online. Association for Computational Linguistics.

Daya Guo, Shuo Ren, Shuai Lu, Zhangyin Feng, Duyu Tang, Shujie LIU, Long Zhou, Nan Duan, Alexey Svyatkovskiy, Shengyu Fu, Michele Tufano, Shao Kun Deng, Colin Clement, Dawn Drain, Neel Sundaresan, Jian Yin, Daxin Jiang, and Ming Zhou. 2021. Graphcode{bert}: Pre-training code representations with data flow. In *International Conference on Learning Representations*.

Abhijeet Gupta, Gemma Boleda, Marco Baroni, and Sebastian Padó. 2015. Distributional vectors encode referential attributes. In *Proceedings of the 2015 Conference on Empirical Methods in Natural Language Processing*, pages 12–21, Lisbon, Portugal. Association for Computational Linguistics.

Sonia Haiduc, Jairo Aponte, Laura Moreno, and Andrian Marcus. 2010. On the use of automated text summarization techniques for summarizing source code. In *2010 17th Working Conference on Reverse Engineering*, pages 35–44.

Vincent J. Hellendoorn, Charles Sutton, Rishabh Singh, Petros Maniatis, and David Bieber. 2020. Global relational models of source code. In *International Conference on Learning Representations*.

John Hewitt and Christopher D. Manning. 2019. A structural probe for finding syntax in word representations. In *Proceedings of the 2019 Conference of the North American Chapter of the Association for Computational Linguistics: Human Language Technologies, Volume 1 (Long and Short Papers)*, pages 4129–4138, Minneapolis, Minnesota. Association for Computational Linguistics.

Hamel Husain, Ho-Hsiang Wu, Tiferet Gazit, Miltiadis Allamanis, and Marc Brockschmidt. 2020. Codesearchnet challenge: Evaluating the state of semantic code search.

Anjan Karmakar and Romain Robbes. 2021. What do pre-trained code models know about code? In *2021 36th IEEE/ACM International Conference on Automated Software Engineering (ASE)*, pages 1332–1336.

Arne Köhn. 2015. What's in an embedding? analyzing word embeddings through multilingual evaluation. In *Proceedings of the 2015 Conference on Empirical Methods in Natural Language Processing*, pages 2067–2073, Lisbon, Portugal. Association for Computational Linguistics.

Fajri Koto, Jey Han Lau, and Timothy Baldwin. 2021. Discourse probing of pretrained language models. In *Proceedings of the 2021 Conference of the North American Chapter of the Association for Computational Linguistics: Human Language Technologies*, pages 3849–3864, Online. Association for Computational Linguistics.

Mike Lewis, Yinhan Liu, Naman Goyal, Marjan Ghazvininejad, Abdelrahman Mohamed, Omer Levy, Veselin Stoyanov, and Luke Zettlemoyer. 2020. BART: Denoising sequence-to-sequence pre-training for natural language generation, translation, and comprehension. In *Proceedings of the 58th Annual Meeting of the Association for Computational Linguistics*, pages 7871–7880, Online. Association for Computational Linguistics.

Yinhan Liu, Myle Ott, Naman Goyal, Jingfei Du, Mandar Joshi, Danqi Chen, Omer Levy, Mike Lewis, Luke Zettlemoyer, and Veselin Stoyanov. 2019. Roberta: A robustly optimized bert pretraining approach. *ArXiv*, abs/1907.11692.

Ilya Loshchilov and Frank Hutter. 2019. Decoupled weight decay regularization. In *International Conference on Learning Representations*.

Shuai Lu, Daya Guo, Shuo Ren, Junjie Huang, Alexey Svyatkovskiy, Ambrosio Blanco, Colin B. Clement, Dawn Drain, Daxin Jiang, Duyu Tang, Ge Li, Lidong Zhou, Linjun Shou, Long Zhou, Michele Tufano, Ming Gong, Ming Zhou, Nan Duan, Neel Sundaresan, Shao Kun Deng, Shengyu Fu, and Shujie Liu. 2021. Codexglue: A machine learning benchmark dataset for code understanding and generation. *CoRR*, abs/2102.04664.

Anh Tuan Nguyen, Tung Thanh Nguyen, and Tien N. Nguyen. 2013. Lexical statistical machine translation for language migration. In *Proceedings of the 2013 9th Joint Meeting on Foundations of Software Engineering*, ESEC/FSE 2013, page 651–654, New York, NY, USA. Association for Computing Machinery.

Adam Paszke, Sam Gross, Francisco Massa, Adam Lerer, James Bradbury, Gregory Chanan, Trevor Killeen, Zeming Lin, Natalia Gimelshein, Luca Antiga, and Desmaison et al. 2019. Pytorch: An imperative style, high-performance deep learning library. In H. Wallach, H. Larochelle, A. Beygelzimer, F. d'Alché-Buc, E. Fox, and R. Garnett, editors, *Advances in Neural Information Processing Systems 32*, pages 8024–8035. Curran Associates, Inc.

F. Pedregosa, G. Varoquaux, A. Gramfort, V. Michel, B. Thirion, O. Grisel, M. Blondel, P. Prettenhofer, R. Weiss, V. Dubourg, J. Vanderplas, A. Passos, D. Cournapeau, M. Brucher, M. Perrot, and E. Duchesnay. 2011. Scikit-learn: Machine learning in Python. *Journal of Machine Learning Research*, 12:2825–2830.

Yada Pruksachatkun, Jason Phang, Haokun Liu, Phu Mon Htut, Xiaoyi Zhang, Richard Yuanzhe Pang, Clara Vania, Katharina Kann, and Samuel R. Bowman. 2020. Intermediate-task transfer learning with pretrained language models: When and why does it work? In *Proceedings of the 58th Annual Meeting of the Association for Computational Linguistics*, pages 5231–5247, Online. Association for Computational Linguistics.

Alec Radford, Jeff Wu, Rewon Child, David Luan, Dario Amodei, and Ilya Sutskever. 2019. Language models are unsupervised multitask learners.

Colin Raffel, Noam Shazeer, Adam Roberts, Katherine Lee, Sharan Narang, Michael Matena, Yanqi Zhou, Wei Li, and Peter J. Liu. 2020. Exploring the limits of transfer learning with a unified text-to-text transformer. *Journal of Machine Learning Research*, 21(140):1–67.

Baptiste Roziere, Marie-Anne Lachaux, Lowik Chanussot, and Guillaume Lample. 2020a. Unsupervised translation of programming languages. *Advances in Neural Information Processing Systems*, 33.

Baptiste Roziere, Marie-Anne Lachaux, Lowik Chanussot, and Guillaume Lample. 2020b. Unsupervised translation of programming languages. In *Advances in Neural Information Processing Systems*, volume 33, pages 20601–20611. Curran Associates, Inc.

Simone Scalabrino, Mario Linares-Vásquez, Rocco Oliveto, and Denys Poshyvanyk. 2018. A comprehensive model for code readability. *Journal of Software: Evolution and Process*, 30.

Rishab Sharma, Fuxiang Chen, Fatemeh Fard, and David Lo. 2022. An exploratory study on code attention in bert.

Aarohi Srivastava, Abhinav Rastogi, Abhishek Rao, Abu Awal Md Shoeb, Abubakar Abid, Adam Fisch, Adam R. Brown, Adam Santoro, Aditya Gupta, Adrià Garriga-Alonso, Agnieszka Kluska, Aitor Lewkowycz, Akshat Agarwal, Alethea Power, Alex Ray, Alex Warstadt, Alexander W. Kocurek, and Safaya et al. 2022. Beyond the imitation game: Quantifying and extrapolating the capabilities of language models.

Ian Tenney, Patrick Xia, Berlin Chen, Alex Wang, Adam Poliak, R. Thomas McCoy, Najoung Kim, Benjamin Van Durme, Samuel R. Bowman, Dipanjan Das, and Ellie Pavlick. 2019. What do you learn from context? probing for sentence structure in contextualized word representations. In *International Conference on Learning Representations*.

Yue Wang, Weishi Wang, Shafiq Joty, and Steven C.H. Hoi. 2021. CodeT5: Identifier-aware unified pretrained encoder-decoder models for code understanding and generation. In *Proceedings of the 2021 Conference on Empirical Methods in Natural Language Processing*, pages 8696–8708, Online and Punta Cana, Dominican Republic. Association for Computational Linguistics.

Jason Wei, Yi Tay, Rishi Bommasani, Colin Raffel, Barret Zoph, Sebastian Borgeaud, Dani Yogatama, Maarten Bosma, Denny Zhou, Donald Metzler, Ed H. Chi, Tatsunori Hashimoto, Oriol Vinyals, Percy Liang, Jeff Dean, and William Fedus. 2022. Emergent abilities of large language models.

Yukun Zhu, Ryan Kiros, Richard Zemel, Ruslan Salakhutdinov, Raquel Urtasun, Antonio Torralba, and Sanja Fidler. 2015. Aligning books and movies: Towards story-like visual explanations by watching movies and reading books. In *arXiv preprint arXiv:1506.06724*.

A Ablation study

In this section we perform an ablation study of different code components to understand which component of code is important for each of the probing tasks, i. e. identifier names, language specific keywords (e.g. “for", “if"), or punctuation (e.g. “(", “:", “<") . We experiments with two pretrained models: pretrained on code (PLBART) and text model (BERT). For ablation of identifiers, we rely on the methodology of (Chirkova and Troshin, 2021) and apply syntax-preserving anonymization, replacing identifiers inside a code snippet with placeholders (“var1", “var2", “var3"). To ablate language-specific keywords or punctuation, we simply replace them with “MASK".

The ablation results are presented in Figure 5. Overall, for all tasks the most influential component is punctuation: masking it hurts the quality the most, except for the “Variable Name" task, where anonymizing identifier leads to the worst quality. With punctuation being masked, PLBART model is close to the quality of the text BERT model or performs even worse.

In contrast, masking language-specific keywords does not hurt the performance significantly.

To conclude, the models pretrained on code rely heavily on punctuation, for almost all tasks, and also rely on identifier names for variable related tasks.

B MLP

Linear probings may appear limited, thus we also include the results for 3-layer MLP model for comparison. We implement an MLP in PyTorch (Paszke et al., 2019) with ReLU nonlinearity and hidden size 128. We train it with AdamW (Loshchilov and Hutter, 2019) optimizer with batch size 512 and we use Optuna (Akiba et al., 2019) with 10 trials to search over learning rate (high=0.1, low=0.0001, *log* domain) and weight decay (high=0.1, low=0.00001, *log* domain) minimizing error on validation set (0.1% of train set) for regression/classification tasks. We reduce learning rate by factor 0.1 with patience 5, use early stopping with patience 10, and maximum number of update 5000.

The results for MLP (Figures 6,7) are very similar to the results with linear models, both quantitatively and qualitatively. For edge prediction in data flow graph, MLP outperformes linear model significantly, but for other tasks the results are roughly the same.

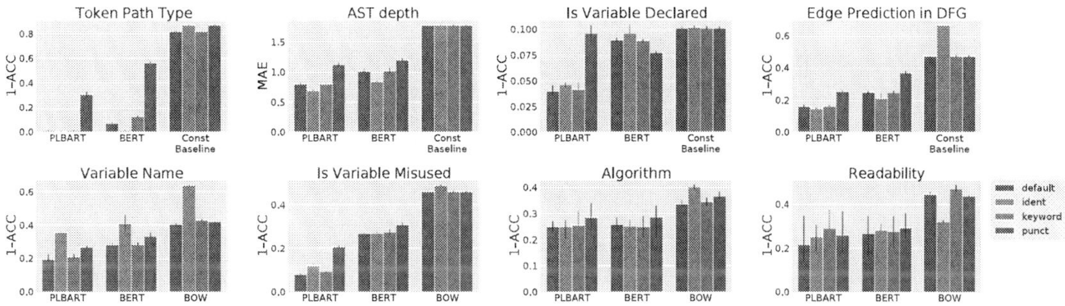

Figure 5: The results for ablation study: no ablation (default), anonymization of identifiers (ident), masking keywords (keyword), and masking punctuation (punct). Metrics are the lower the better.

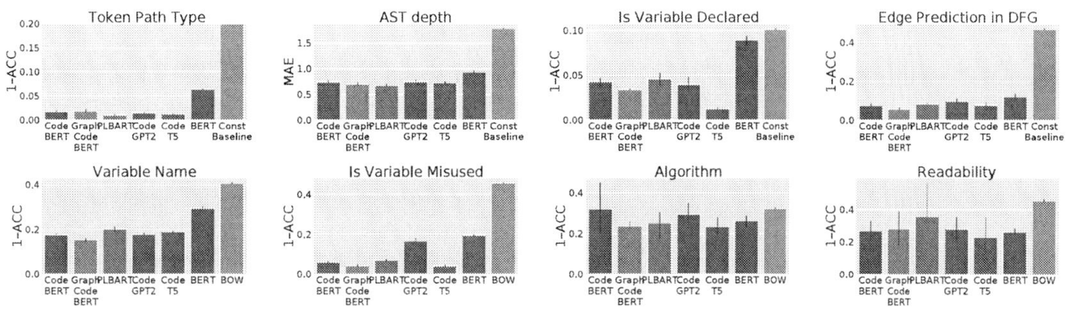

Figure 6: Results for the best performing layer representations, for all probing tasks, *3-layer MLP*. Metrics are the lower the better.

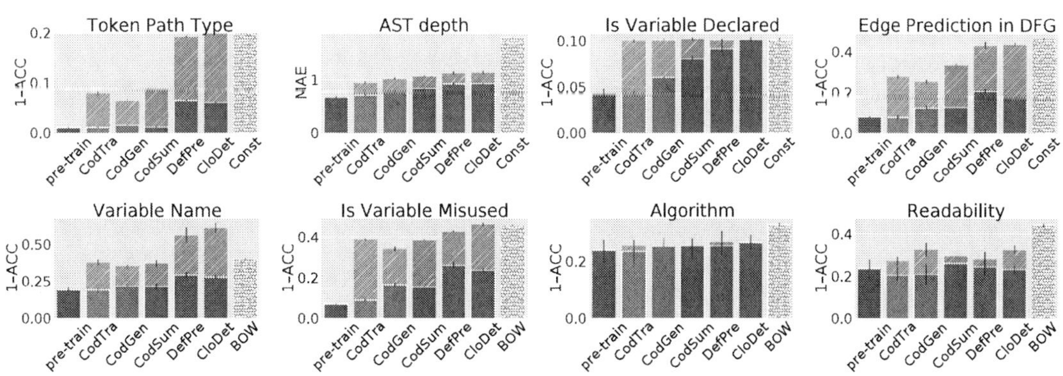

Figure 7: Results on the effect of finetuning, *3-layer MLP*. Pre-train (leftmost bar): pretrained-only checkpoint. The following bars: dark – finetuned models, semi-transparent – models trained from scratch. Results for 5 downstream tasks: Code Translation, Code Generation, Code Summarization, Defect Prediction, Clone Detection.

Probing the representations of named entities in Transformer-based Language Models

Stefan F. Schouten and **Peter Bloem** and **Piek Vossen**
Vrije Universiteit Amsterdam
Amsterdam, The Netherlands
{s.f.schouten,p.bloem,p.t.j.m.vossen}@vu.nl

Abstract

In this work we analyze the named entity representations learned by Transformer-based language models. We investigate the role entities play in two tasks: a language modeling task, and a sequence classification task. For this purpose we collect a novel news topic classification dataset with 12 topics called RefNews-12. We perform two complementary methods of analysis. First, we use diagnostic models allowing us to quantify to what degree entity information is present in the hidden representations. Second, we perform entity mention substitution to measure how substitute-entities with different properties impact model performance. By controlling for model uncertainty we are able to show that entities are identified, and depending on the task, play a measurable role in the model's predictions. Additionally, we show that the entities' types alone are not enough to account for this. Finally, we find that the the frequency with which entities occur are important for the masked language modeling task, and that the entities' distributions over topics are important for topic classification.

1 Introduction

The probability a language model should assign to a sequence depends not only on what is being said, but also on the context, i.e. who is saying it, where, when, and why? Some types of context such as (cultural) background knowledge may already be represented to some degree within pre-trained language models. However, recent work shows that when it comes to world knowledge language models and knowledge bases are complementary, and that various forms of integration are beneficial (Safavi and Koutra, 2021). Being able to condition on the context explicitly would be particularly useful when we consider, for example, more specific cultural knowledge or interpersonal knowledge, which are unlikely to be contained in pre-training corpora.

In order to integrate language models and knowledge bases effectively it is important to know precisely how these two sources of information complement each other. Entities are specifically interesting as they occur within characteristic contexts learnable by language models and at the same time provide access to knowledge graphs.

In this work we investigate what information is present in the entity representations of Transformer-based (Vaswani et al., 2017) language models. We also study whether some entities' representations contain more information than others and why. Finally, we show how much these aspects change after a pre-trained language model is fine-tuned.

For our investigation we choose News articles as our primary source of data. News articles often describe events that involve numerous entities. Which is the primary reason they have been used in the past for entity-related tasks such as NERC (Tjong Kim Sang and De Meulder, 2003), NEL (Hoffart et al., 2011), and coreference resolution (Pradhan et al., 2012). We fine-tune and evaluate our models for news topic classification and masked language modeling. For this purpose, we collect a new dataset of English news articles by following links cited on Wikipedia pages covering many newsworthy incidents (Vossen et al., 2018). Our data collection method allows for this dataset to easily be expanded with additional topics and languages in the future. Furthermore, the set of entities linked to from Wikipedia pages covering such incidents can also provide us with a 'short-list' of entities likely to be referenced in the news articles themselves. These entity links will allow integration with Wikidata, an avenue we wish to explore in future work.

Our analysis includes two complementary methods: diagnostic models (Veldhoen et al., 2016; Adi et al., 2016; Conneau et al., 2018) and a novel method of analysis we call entity mention substitution. *Diagnostic models* are trained on a relevant task (in our case entity recognition) with hidden representations of another model as input. The di-

Proceedings of the Fifth BlackboxNLP Workshop on Analyzing and Interpreting Neural Networks for NLP, pages 384 - 393
December 8, 2022

agnostic model is kept as simple as possible such that its performance can be attributed to the information being available in the hidden representation. *Entity mention substitution* measures the impact of various kinds of substitutions on the prediction of the model. If the impact is high we interpret this as evidence that the entity was important for the prediction. By manipulating which entities we choose as substitutes and by comparing the results to those of the diagnostic models, we answer the following research questions:

RQ1: When entities are mentioned in the input text, are they identified and used by Transformer-based language models?

RQ2: Does a Transformer-based language model either partially, or fully represent entities by their type?

RQ3: Do the answers to RQ1 & RQ2 depend on: **(a)** the frequency with which an entity-mention occurs in the data; and **(b)** the distribution of that entity across the news topics?

We make two important contributions. First, we collect a novel news classification dataset we call RefNews-12, which consists of 106,167 articles which cover 9,878 incidents grouped by 12 topics. Second, we analyze what information is present in entity representations in two ways. One concerns training and evaluating diagnostic models on entity recognition using only the model's hidden representations for entities as input. The other involves corrupting entity mentions in the data in various ways, showing how the model relies on the entities to make predictions.

We find that entities are identified in pre-trained models both before and after fine-tuning. Entities are also used to perform the task for which the model is trained or fine-tuned, even if they cannot be identified clearly by their representation. We also find that entities are represented by more than their type. Finally, our experiments suggest that the importance of the frequency with which entities occur and entities' distribution over topics is task-specific.

2 Related Work

The use of news articles to study the interaction of entities and topics is not new. Newman et al. (2006) mention that "news articles are ideal because they have the primary purpose of conveying information about who, what, when and where." We use them for the same reason, but focus on studying the entity representations in recent Language Models.

Previous investigations into the representation of entities in Language Models have come from various directions.

Broscheit (2019) investigates entity knowledge in pre-trained BERT through entity linking. They frame entity linking as a token classification problem over the entire vocabulary of 700K entities, thereby solving mention detection, candidate generation, and entity disambiguation simultaneously. When trained with BERT's weights frozen this method still obtains decent F1 scores (67.8 versus SotA of 85.8 by (Zhang et al., 2021)) on the AIDA benchmark (Hoffart et al., 2011). This indicates that BERT already assigns representations that are sufficiently distinct for entity linking to a lot of the entity tokens. We expect that this distinctness does not necessarily imply that entities are really treated by the model as individuals. Thus, we directly investigate the degree to which these entity representations are interchangeable.

Sorodoc et al. (2020) study whether pre-trained language models capture information helpful with the resolution of pronominal anaphora. They hypothesize that the model will learn helpful grammatical properties, but not semantic-referential information. To test this hypothesis they train diagnostic models and analyze how their performance varies as the variables of interest change. Their evidence suggests that language models do in fact learn some referential aspects, but that they are still much better at grammar. We also investigate the presence of semantic properties in representations of entities, but do so with different methods and include models that have been fine-tuned.

Biswas et al. (2021) use entity embeddings obtained from various language models to classify entities as one of 14 types. Interestingly, BERT embeddings obtain the lowest accuracy of the models tested. Where Biswas et al. (2021) embeds only the name of the entity, our work studies representations of entities that appear in context.

A number of other works do not investigate the representations of entities specifically, but test to what extent Language Models are able to reproduce relational world knowledge, which involves numerous facts about entities as well (Petroni et al., 2019; Roberts et al., 2020). For a recent survey of this type of research see Safavi and Koutra (2021).

3 Methodology

The following section describes the method by which we collect our data (3.1), and the two methods we used to perform our analysis (3.2, 3.3).

3.1 Dataset Collection

We collect a novel news topic classification dataset based on articles that are linked to from Wikipedia. For our investigation we prefer data that is categorized across a large number of (hierarchical) topics, which can be used to construct datasets of varying difficulties.

For this purpose we use the Multilingual Wiki Extraction Pipeline (Vossen et al., 2020). This tool takes as input a set of Wikidata Event Types and queries Wikidata for each type's set of incidents. For example, for the Wikidata Item 'homicide' (Q149086) the pipeline finds items that are instances of homicides, i.e. all items that link to it with the 'instanceOf' property. The incidents that we select are those Wikidata Items for which a time and place are known. These incidents' Wikipedia pages are then scraped for links to news articles. Besides the articles linked on the Wikipedia pages, we also include the page itself. The links to other Wikipedia pages can be used to supervise Named Entity Recognition and Entity Linking.

To obtain the initial set of Wikidata Event Types, we make use of IPTC's Media Topics standard. This standard consists of a hierarchical taxonomy of terms intended for use by media to categorize their productions. Along with the hierarchy of topics, IPTC also distributes a mapping of these topics to Wikidata. We query the Wikidata Event Types referenced in the mapping to obtain the number of incidents available for each topic.

The dataset we collect for the experiments in this paper are based on a selection of 12 diverse topics, each with a number of incidents that is manageable but sufficient. We call this dataset RefNews-12. See Table 1 for an overview of the selected topics, their Wikidata ID, the number of incidents, and the total number of articles we scraped.

RefNews-12 is based on news articles from a wide variety of publications, none of which we obtained (or attempted to obtain) permission from to redistribute their work. To circumvent this legal obstacle, we do not directly distribute the articles themselves, but rather a set of URLs. To further increase the reproducibility, each URL is also accompanied by the timestamp of a 'capture' in the Internet Archive's Wayback Machine from which we obtained our copy. This set can be used by any interested party to obtain a dataset near-identical to that used for the experimentation in this work. This set of URLs for the articles which constitute RefNews-12 can be found at `https://github.com/sfschouten/refnews`, along with instructions and code to collect the dataset.

3.2 Diagnostic Models

Diagnostic models[1] (Veldhoen et al., 2016; Adi et al., 2016; Conneau et al., 2018) are used to investigate if the representations learned by a system include information about some feature of interest. The diagnostic model is trained to predict this feature from the representations. Its architecture is chosen to be as simple as possible, which allows for the diagnostic model's performance to be attributed to the information in the representation.

3.3 Entity Mention Substitution

Substituting the entities mentioned in the data allows us to establish whether entities are important for news topic classification and masked language modeling. It also tells us whether entity representations capture the the entity's type. Finally, we use it to investigate if either of these things depend on the frequency of the entity in the data, or the entity's distribution over the classes.

The core of this method involves measuring the effect of the substitutions on the final prediction. If a model's prediction consistently does not change after substitution then clearly the original entities' representations are not meaningfully different from the substitute representations. By identifying a few key ways in which entities can be (dis)similar, and substituting such that one particular property is either changed or kept the same, we can test if that property is present in the model's representations.

Specifically, we hypothesize that the effect of a mention's replacement depends on at least the following variables.

Type Equality Whether or not the original and substitute entities are of the same type. If type is present in the representations, then substituting by entities of the same type should give better performance than if we substitute for random entities.

[1] Also known by various other names, including 'diagnostic classifiers', 'auxiliary prediction tasks' and 'probing tasks'.

IPTC Name	Wikidata ID	#Incidents	#Articles
homicide	Q149086	938	25,123
natural disaster	Q8065	1,103	10,900
referenda	Q43109	722	5,627
transportation accident and incident	Q11822042	1,822	16,551
sport event	Q167170	518	7,188
coup d'etat	Q45382	339	3,416
educational testing and examinations	Q27318	1,352	8,168
record and achievement	Q1241356	2,352	15,034
armed conflict	Q350604	137	4,155
sports transaction	Q18515440	196	4,018
primary election	Q669262	193	2.612
transport	Q7590	206	3,375
Total		9,878	106,167

Table 1: RefNews-12: topics, number of incidents and articles.

Frequency How frequently the original and substitute entities occur in the training data. We expect that the embeddings associated with more frequently occurring entity mentions will have acquired more distinctive representations during training, and thus have a greater impact on the model's predictions.

Topic Shift How much difference there is between the distribution over topics of the original and substitute entity mentions. For example, if 'entity1' is only mentioned in articles of topics A and B and we replace it with 'entity2' which is only mentioned in articles of topics C and D; then we would expect that to have a greater impact than if we had replaced 'entity1' with an entity that is mentioned in a collection of articles with similar topics.

4 Experiments

This section details our experimental setup.

4.1 The (fine-tuned) language models

We use DistilBERT as our model of choice for all experiments. This decision was made because of resource constraints, specifically because we train multiple instances for each setting in order to calculate model uncertainty. DistilBERT is a 40% smaller distilled version of BERT (Devlin et al., 2019). While much smaller, it retains much of BERT's original performance. Choosing this model allows for a smaller computational budget.

We fine-tune DistilBERT seven times on RefNews-12 for both news topic classification and masked language modeling. Each time the classification head's parameters are initialized using a different seed. For topic classification we also train a model with the same architecture but from initialization (rather than using pre-trained weights).

All models are trained with a batch size of 72. The base learning rate is set to 0.0005, and subject to 2000 steps of warmup followed by a linear decay. They are evaluated on the validation split every 500 batches and training is stopped early if the performance does not improve 5 times in a row.

4.2 NER diagnostic models

We train diagnostic models on the CoNLL-2003 dataset (Tjong Kim Sang and De Meulder, 2003). We choose this dataset, because like RefNews-12, it consists of news articles. This procedure reveals to what degree the hidden representations can be used to predict which tokens are part of named entities. We train them for a pre-trained DistilBERT and the seven instances of DistilBERT fine-tuned on RefNews-12 for both tasks. A different classifier is trained for each layer of each model instance, revealing at what layer entities are most clearly represented. To put the results of the diagnostic classifiers in perspective, we also train them on an untrained randomly initialized model. The diagnostic classifiers are trained with the same hyperparameters as above, but without a learning rate warmup.

4.3 Replacing entity mentions

We perform a series of experiments where we replace entity mentions that occur in RefNews-12's news articles. We do not have gold-standard entity mention labels for all of RefNews-12 (only the Wikipedia pages have mention annotations through hyperlinks), so we use an additional DistilBERT model[2] that has been fine-tuned for Named Entity Recognition and Classification to obtain silver-standard labels instead.

Replacing the entity mentions may result in two kinds of changes in the model's predictions. First, our intervention may cause the model to confidently predict something else, this might mean that a different entity consistently causes a different topic to be predicted. However, if the manipulated inputs are sufficiently different from the training distribution, they may also cause greater model uncertainty, making predictions more arbitrary. We can use our independently seeded instances to differentiate between these two scenarios. The seven independently seeded model instances can be thought of as samples from an approximate posterior over the model's weights (Gustafsson et al., 2020). Thus, we use the variation in the predictions of these seven instances to approximately measure model uncertainty. Specifically, we evaluate the uncertainty using the method suggested in (Lakshminarayanan et al., 2017), which is to sum the KL Divergence between each model instance's prediction and the average of those predictions.

4.3.1 [MASK] Token Baseline

In this first baseline we replace entity mentions by the [MASK] token. This prevents the model from being able to use the information captured by the entity representations directly. However, both BERT and DistilBERT's training objective included predicting masked-out tokens in English text. Therefore the model may be able to reconstruct some of the missing information. Thus, we expect this to have relatively little effect on the performance and uncertainty of the pre-trained and fine-tuned models.

4.3.2 Random Token Baseline

The second baseline involves the mentions being replaced by random tokens. In this case the model has to identify the tokens that are out of place first, before it has the option of ignoring them. Thus we expect a somewhat larger effect on model performance. Contrary to the first baseline we expect this second baseline to come with significant model uncertainty, because this intervention should produce inputs the model did not see during training.

[2]https://huggingface.co/elastic/distilbert-base-cased-finetuned-conll03-english

4.3.3 Random Mention

In this variant we substitute entity-mentions by a different randomly selected mentioned entity. With this substitution, the model may have a harder time identifying and ignoring the substitution, because other entities will not seem particularly out of place compared to random tokens. Therefore, if the named entities are important to complete the task at hand, and their representations are meaningfully different, we would expect the model to confidently predict something else. This would look like a large shift in the prediction where the shift is similar for each model instance (low uncertainty). If the model's performance is comparable to the baselines, we interpret this as evidence that either all entities are represented more or less the same way, or their differences are ignored in practice.

4.3.4 Type Invariant

The next step is to replace mentions only by others of the same type. If even entities of the same type are still represented in meaningfully different ways, we expect the performance to stay below the baselines. This would be evidence that entities are represented distinctly even within their type. However, if performance is comparable to the baselines, we interpret this as evidence that entities must be represented no more distinctly than their type.

4.3.5 Most Frequent

The final substitution we make is based on the frequency with which entity mentions occur in the data. We select the substitute mentions from the 100 most frequently occurring entities. If substituting for more frequently occurring entities affects the performance more than substituting for random entities, then the most frequent entities' representations must have encoded more information relevant to the task.

4.3.6 Correlation with shift in frequency and topic distribution

Finally, we calculate the correlation between two metrics and the loss of each model. For the first metric we calculate the difference in log-frequency between the original and substitute entities, averaged over each substitution per sequence. For the second metric we calculate how each entity is distributed across the topics. We then calculate the KL divergence of the original distribution from the substitute distribution, also averaged over each substitutions per sequence.

5 Results

Using the experimental results we can now answer our research questions. Figure 1 shows the results of the entity mention substitution experiments. Figure Figure 2 shows the accuracies obtained by the diagnostic classifiers. Table 2 shows the correlation coefficients obtained described in 4.3.6.

In Figure 1a we can see a significant drop in mean accuracy between both *original* and random-tokens (from 84.1% / 85.9% to 74.7% / 78.4% for From init. / Fine-tuned respectively, both with p<0.001), and between *random-tokens* and *random-mention* (from 74.7% / 78.37% to 70.4% / 75.99% with p<0.001 / p=0.008). Replacing a mention with another mention leaves a sentence that is more coherent than when it is replaced with random tokens. Despite this, we observe lower accuracy for *random-mention*. It seems that for topic classification the model is capable of ignoring random tokens, but cannot do the same for the random mentions. Instead, the model's predictions are considerably different with the substitute entity mentions, decreasing the accuracy as a result. From the model uncertainty in Figure 1b we can see that the drop in accuracy is not caused by increased uncertainty (uncertainty decreases from 0.150 for *random-tokens* to 0.107 for *random-mention*). We interpret this as evidence that the model uses entity mentions in its prediction.

Unfortunately, we cannot conclude the same from the masked language modeling results in Figure 1c. For this task the performance does not worsen going from *random-tokens* to *random-mention* (from 5.80 / 4.37 to 4.95 / 2.82). We also cannot make the same argument when comparing between *mask* and *random-mention*, because although the performance does deteriorate (from 3.73 / 1.83 to 4.95 / 2.82), this may also be explained by the uncertainty going up (from 0.098 to 0.147, no uncertainty for pre-trained). However, results from the diagnostic classifiers (Figure 2) do indicate that the identification of entities is beneficial for masked language modeling, since their performance increases compared to the Random and Pre-trained baselines.

Furthermore, the diagnostic classifiers indicate that entities are identified in pre-trained and fine-tuned language models to a much greater degree than in models trained from initialization for topic classification.

In conclusion, entities are identified and used by the fine-tuned models for the topic classification task. However, for models trained from initialization entities are not easily identifiable from their representations. Despite that, their presence is still used by the model to perform the topic classification task. For masked language modeling we only have evidence of them being identified, but not of them being used. Thus, the answer to **RQ1** (*"When entities are mentioned in the input text, are they identified and used by Transformer-based language models?"*) is that entities are identified by language models, but whether they are used in practice depends on the task that the model is fine-tuned for.

Looking at the *type-invariant* substitution in Figure 1a we can see that there is no significant difference in accuracy compared to the *random-mention* substitution. By comparing to *random-tokens* however, we can see the same pattern as we saw for *random-mention*: accuracy and uncertainty are both down (accuracy from 74.7% / 78.4% to 70.5% / 75.4%, uncertainty from 0.275 / 0.150 to 0.197 / 0.098). So even when substituting for mentions of the same type the model is still confidently changing its prediction, indicating that type is at least not the only aspect being looked at when predicting topics.

In setting out to answer **RQ2** (*"Does a Transformer-based language model either partially, or fully represent entities by their type?"*) we have not been able to present new evidence indicating that type is used by Transformer-based language models, but we have demonstrated that entities are not generally represented only by their type.

The substitution by the most frequently mentioned entities for the topic classification task as seen in Figure 1, shows a drop in performance compared to *random-mention*, but this is paired with a (modest) increase in uncertainty. Thus, the results of this particular experimental setting are inconclusive. However, in Table 2 we can see that there are dependencies between the performances

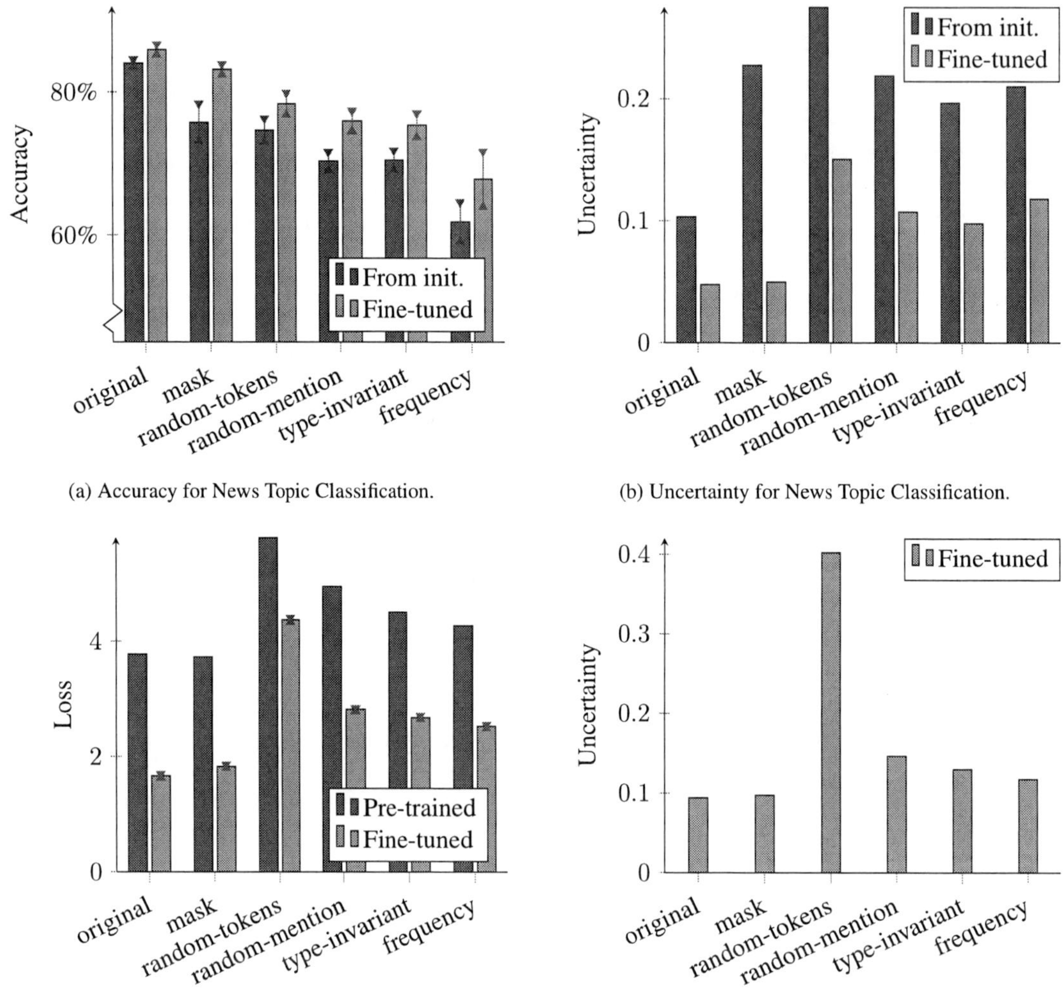

(a) Accuracy for News Topic Classification.

(b) Uncertainty for News Topic Classification.

(c) Loss for Masked Language Modeling.

(d) Uncertainty for Masked Language Modeling.

Figure 1: Performance metrics and uncertainty estimates obtained while performing Topic Classification and Masked Language Modeling for our entity-mention substitution experiments using our RefNews dataset. Error Bars display 95% confidence intervals indicating sensitivity to random initialization.

Task	Training	Variable	random-mention	type-invariant
TopicCLF	From init.	Frequency	0.00 ± 0.01	-0.01 ± 0.02
		Topic	0.10 ± 0.01	0.17 ± 0.01
	Fine-tuned	Frequency	0.00 ± 0.01	-0.02 ± 0.01
		Topic	0.10 ± 0.01	0.19 ± 0.01
MaskedLM	Pre-trained	Frequency	0.15	0.19
		Topic	-0.03	0.00
	Fine-tuned	Frequency	0.07 ± 0.00	0.13 ± 0.00
		Topic	-0.03 ± 0.01	-0.02 ± 0.01

Table 2: Pearson correlation between difference in frequency/topic and the model's loss while performing masked language modeling or topic classification for our entity-mention substitution experiments.

obtained on either task and the average difference in frequency and topic distribution. For the models trained on MaskedLM when the difference between the frequency of the original and substitute entities increases so does the loss of the model. The same is true for the difference in topic distribution on the model fine-tuned for topic classification. Therefore our answer for **RQ3** (*"Do the answers to RQ1 & RQ2 depend on: **(a)** the frequency with which an entity-mention occurs in the data; and **(b)** the distribution of that entity across the news topics?"*) is that both the identification and use of entities, and the extent to which they are represented by their type each depend on frequency and topic distribution. Specifically, the frequency is depended on for the masked language modeling, and the topic distribution for the topic classification task.

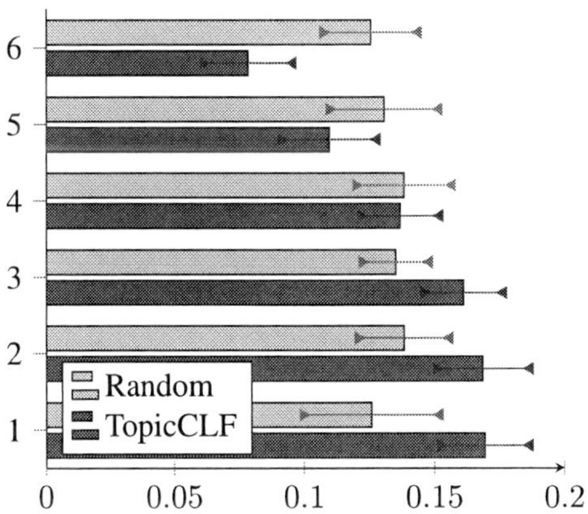

(a) Randomly initialized (untrained) model compared to topic classifier trained from initialization.

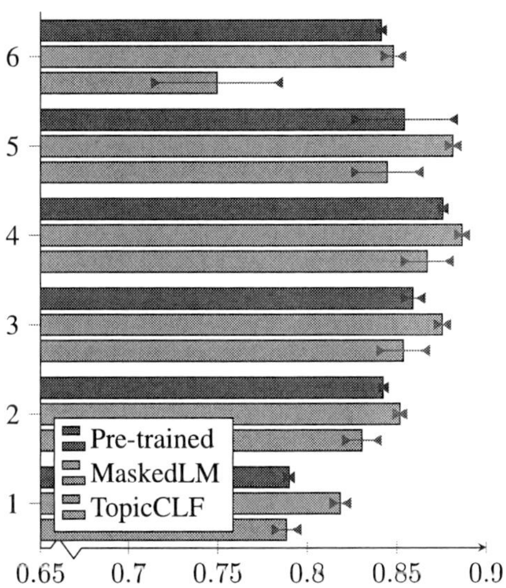

(b) Pre-trained and fine-tuned models.

Figure 2: Diagnostic classifier F1 score (x-axis) on NER for each layer (y-axis) of various models. Error bars display 95% confidence intervals indicating sensitivity to random initialization (of the diagnostic model, and in the case of the fine-tuned models also the model being probed).

6 Conclusion

We have presented RefNews-12, a novel news topic classification dataset. This dataset was collected by scraping Wikipedia articles for links. This collection method allows it to be expanded with additional topics and languages in the future. Because the Wikipedia pages also link to the pages of entities relevant to the incident, the dataset can be bridged easily to knowledge from Wikidata.

We have investigated entity representations in Transformer-based language models. We find that after having been fine-tuned for news topic classification these models do identify and use the entities to accomplish the task at hand. Although, whether they are used also depends on the task for which the model is trained. Our results also show that on average these language models do not represent entities only by their type. Entities are used by the model as distinctly different even within the same type. Finally, we have shown that the frequency with which an entity occurs in the data does not play a significant role in models performing topic classification. Nor does the topic distribution play a significant role in masked language modeling.

We obtained our results by altering the inputs of a model and measuring the change in performance. Crucially, to allow us to draw conclusions from these results we also control for model uncertainty. We believe this general methodology can be used to probe for many kinds of properties. As such it provides an additional probing technique which can be used to strengthen existing experimental evidence in the future.

7 Limitations & Future work

Our results are based on DistilBERT, which is a relatively small model. Because of this, the results are not necessarily representative of all Transformer-based language models. A further limitation is that our experiments are only performed with our RefNews-12 dataset, and the only downstream task we evaluate on is topic classification. Finally, the entity types we use are limited to the highest level of types (locations, organizations, persons and miscellaneous). It is possible that at more fine-grained levels entity representations do become less and less distinct.

In future work, we mean to address these limitations by including larger models and other datasets to show if the same patterns hold on all Transformer-based models including on other data and tasks. Also, by including entity linking in future experimentation, we will be able to extract entity-types from knowledge bases such as Wikidata, and perform substitutions exclusively within those much more fine-grained types.

Acknowledgments

This research was supported by Huawei Finland through the DreamsLab project. All content represented the opinions of the authors, which were not necessarily shared or endorsed by their respective employers and/or sponsors.

References

Yossi Adi, Einat Kermany, Yonatan Belinkov, Ofer Lavi, and Yoav Goldberg. 2016. Fine-grained Analysis of Sentence Embeddings Using Auxiliary Prediction Tasks.

Russa Biswas, Radina Sofronova, Mehwish Alam, Nicolas Heist, Heiko Paulheim, and Harald Sack. 2021. Do Judge an Entity by Its Name! Entity Typing Using Language Models. In *The Semantic Web: ESWC 2021 Satellite Events*, Lecture Notes in Computer Science, pages 65–70, Cham. Springer International Publishing.

Samuel Broscheit. 2019. Investigating Entity Knowledge in BERT with Simple Neural End-To-End Entity Linking. In *Proceedings of the 23rd Conference on Computational Natural Language Learning (CoNLL)*, pages 677–685, Hong Kong, China. Association for Computational Linguistics.

Alexis Conneau, German Kruszewski, Guillaume Lample, Loïc Barrault, and Marco Baroni. 2018. What you can cram into a single $&!#* vector: Probing sentence embeddings for linguistic properties. In *Proceedings of the 56th Annual Meeting of the Association for Computational Linguistics (Volume 1: Long Papers)*, pages 2126–2136, Melbourne, Australia. Association for Computational Linguistics.

Jacob Devlin, Ming-Wei Chang, Kenton Lee, and Kristina Toutanova. 2019. BERT: Pre-training of Deep Bidirectional Transformers for Language Understanding. In *Proceedings of the 2019 Conference of the North American Chapter of the Association for Computational Linguistics: Human Language Technologies, Volume 1 (Long and Short Papers)*, pages 4171–4186, Minneapolis, Minnesota. Association for Computational Linguistics.

Fredrik K. Gustafsson, Martin Danelljan, and Thomas B. Schon. 2020. Evaluating Scalable Bayesian Deep Learning Methods for Robust Computer Vision. pages 318–319.

Johannes Hoffart, Mohamed Amir Yosef, Ilaria Bordino, Hagen Fürstenau, Manfred Pinkal, Marc Spaniol, Bilyana Taneva, Stefan Thater, and Gerhard Weikum. 2011. Robust Disambiguation of Named Entities in Text. In *Proceedings of the 2011 Conference on Empirical Methods in Natural Language Processing*, pages 782–792, Edinburgh, Scotland, UK. Association for Computational Linguistics.

Balaji Lakshminarayanan, Alexander Pritzel, and Charles Blundell. 2017. Simple and Scalable Predictive Uncertainty Estimation using Deep Ensembles. In *Advances in Neural Information Processing Systems*, volume 30. Curran Associates, Inc.

David Newman, Chaitanya Chemudugunta, Padhraic Smyth, and Mark Steyvers. 2006. Analyzing Entities and Topics in News Articles Using Statistical Topic Models. In *Intelligence and Security Informatics*, Lecture Notes in Computer Science, pages 93–104, Berlin, Heidelberg. Springer.

Fabio Petroni, Tim Rocktäschel, Sebastian Riedel, Patrick Lewis, Anton Bakhtin, Yuxiang Wu, and Alexander Miller. 2019. Language Models as Knowledge Bases? In *Proceedings of the 2019 Conference on Empirical Methods in Natural Language Processing and the 9th International Joint Conference on Natural Language Processing (EMNLP-IJCNLP)*, pages 2463–2473, Hong Kong, China. Association for Computational Linguistics.

Sameer Pradhan, Alessandro Moschitti, Nianwen Xue, Olga Uryupina, and Yuchen Zhang. 2012. CoNLL-2012 Shared Task: Modeling Multilingual Unrestricted Coreference in OntoNotes. In *Joint Conference on EMNLP and CoNLL - Shared Task*, pages 1–40, Jeju Island, Korea. Association for Computational Linguistics.

Adam Roberts, Colin Raffel, and Noam Shazeer. 2020. How Much Knowledge Can You Pack Into the Parameters of a Language Model? In *Proceedings of the 2020 Conference on Empirical Methods in Natural Language Processing (EMNLP)*, pages 5418–5426, Online. Association for Computational Linguistics.

Tara Safavi and Danai Koutra. 2021. Relational World Knowledge Representation in Contextual Language Models: A Review. In *Proceedings of the 2021 Conference on Empirical Methods in Natural Language Processing*, pages 1053–1067, Online and Punta Cana, Dominican Republic. Association for Computational Linguistics.

Ionut-Teodor Sorodoc, Kristina Gulordava, and Gemma Boleda. 2020. Probing for Referential Information in Language Models. In *Proceedings of the 58th Annual Meeting of the Association for Computational Linguistics*, pages 4177–4189, Online. Association for Computational Linguistics.

Erik F. Tjong Kim Sang and Fien De Meulder. 2003. Introduction to the CoNLL-2003 Shared Task: Language-Independent Named Entity Recognition. In *Proceedings of the Seventh Conference on Natural Language Learning at HLT-NAACL 2003*, pages 142–147.

Ashish Vaswani, Noam Shazeer, Niki Parmar, Jakob Uszkoreit, Llion Jones, Aidan N Gomez, Łukasz Kaiser, and Illia Polosukhin. 2017. Attention is All you Need. In *Advances in Neural Information Processing Systems*, volume 30. Curran Associates, Inc.

Sara Veldhoen, Dieuwke Hupkes, and Willem H. Zuidema. 2016. Diagnostic Classifiers Revealing how Neural Networks Process Hierarchical Structure.

Piek Vossen, Filip Ilievski, Marten Postma, Antske Fokkens, Gosse Minnema, and Levi Remijnse. 2020. Large-scale Cross-lingual Language Resources for Referencing and Framing. In *Proceedings of the 12th Language Resources and Evaluation Conference*, pages 3162–3171, Marseille, France. European Language Resources Association.

Piek Vossen, Filip Ilievski, Marten Postma, and Roxane Segers. 2018. Don't Annotate, but Validate: a Data-to-Text Method for Capturing Event Data. In *Proceedings of the Eleventh International Conference on Language Resources and Evaluation (LREC 2018)*, Miyazaki, Japan. European Language Resources Association (ELRA).

Wenzheng Zhang, Wenyue Hua, and Karl Stratos. 2021. EntQA: Entity Linking as Question Answering.

Decomposing Natural Logic Inferences for Neural NLI

Julia Rozanova[1], **Deborah Ferreira**[1], **Mokanarangan Thayaparan**[1],
Marco Valentino[1] and **André Freitas**[1,2]
Department of Computer Science, University of Manchester, United Kingdom[1]
Idiap Research Institute, Switzerland[2]
{firstname.lastname}@manchester.ac.uk

Abstract

In the interest of interpreting neural NLI models and their reasoning strategies, we carry out a systematic probing study which investigates whether these models capture the crucial semantic features central to natural logic: *monotonicity* and *concept inclusion*. Correctly identifying valid inferences in *downward-monotone contexts* is a known stumbling block for NLI performance, subsuming linguistic phenomena such as negation scope and generalized quantifiers. To understand this difficulty, we emphasize monotonicity as a property of a *context* and examine the extent to which models capture relevant monotonicity information in the vector representations which are intermediate to their decision making process. Drawing on the recent advancement of the probing paradigm, we compare the presence of monotonicity features across various models. We find that monotonicity information is notably weak in the representations of popular NLI models which achieve high scores on benchmarks, and observe that previous improvements to these models based on fine-tuning strategies have introduced stronger monotonicity features together with their improved performance on challenge sets.

1 Introduction

Large, black box neural models which achieve high scores on benchmark datasets designed for testing *natural language understanding* are the subject of much scrutiny and investigation.

It is often investigated whether models are able to capture specific semantic phenomena which mimic human reasoning and/or logical formalism, as there is evidence that they sometimes exploit simple heuristics and dataset artifacts instead (McCoy et al., 2019; Herlihy and Rudinger, 2021).

In this work, we consider the rigorous setting of *natural logic* (MacCartney and Manning, 2007). This is a highly systematic reasoning principle relying on only two abstract features, each of which is in itself linguistically complex: *monotonicity* and *concept inclusion word-pair relations*. It underlies the majority of symbolic/rule-based and hybrid approaches to NLI and is an important baseline reasoning phenomenon to look for in a robust and principled NLI model.

Downward monotone operators such as negation markers and generalized quantifiers result in the kinds of natural logic inferences which are often known to stump neural NLI models that demonstrate high performance on large benchmark sets such as MNLI (Williams et al., 2018): this has been identified in behavioural studies based on targeted challenge test sets, such as in Yanaka et al. (2019a) and Geiger et al. (2020).

In this work, however, we present a **structural** study: we investigate the extent to which the features relevant for identifying natural logic inferences, especially context monotonicty itself, are captured in the model's internal representations. To this end, we carry out a systematic *probing* study.

Our contributions are may be summarized as follows:

1. We perform a structural investigation as to whether the behaviour of *natural logic* formalisms are mimicked within popular transformer-based NLI models.

2. For this purpose, we present a joint NLI and semantic probing dataset format (and dataset) which we call NLI-XY: it is a unique probing dataset in that the probed features relate to the NLI task output in a very systematic way.

3. We employ thorough probing techniques to determine whether the abstract semantic features of *context monotonicity* and *concept inclusion relations* are captured in the models' internal representations.

4. We observe that some well-known NLI models demonstrate a systematic failure to model

Proceedings of the Fifth BlackboxNLP Workshop on Analyzing and Interpreting Neural Networks for NLP, pages 394 - 403
December 8, 2022

context monotonicity, a behaviour we observe to correspond to poor performance on natural logic reasoning in downward-monotone contexts. However, we show that the existing HELP dataset improves this behaviour.

5. We support the observations in the probing study with several *qualitative analyses*, including decomposed error-breakdowns on the **NLI-XY** dataset, representation visualizations, and evaluations on existing challenge sets.

2 Related Work

Natural logic dates back to the formalisms of Sanchez (1991), but has been received more recent treatments and reformulations in MacCartney and Manning (2007) and Hu and Moss (2018). Symbolic and hybrid neuro-symbolic implementations of the natural logic paradigm have been explored in Chen et al. (2021); Kalouli et al. (2020); Abzianidze (2017) and Hu et al. (2020).

The shortcomings of natural logic handling in various neural NLI models have been shown with several *behavioural* studies, where NLI challenge sets exhibiting examples of downward monotone reasoning are used to evaluate performance of models with respect to these reasoning patterns (Richardson et al., 2019; Yanaka et al., 2019b,a; Goodwin et al., 2020; Geiger et al., 2020).

In an attempt to better identify linguistic features that neural models manage or fail to capture, researchers have employed *probing* strategies: namely, the *diagnostic classification* (Alain and Bengio, 2018) of auxiliary feature labels from internal model representations. Most probing studies in natural language processing focus on the *syntactic* features captured in transformer-based language models (Hewitt and Manning, 2019), but calls have been made for more sophisticated probing tasks which rely more on contextual information (Pimentel et al., 2020).

In the realm of semantics, probing studies have focused more on *lexical* semantics (Vulić et al., 2020): word pair relations are central to monotonicity reasoning, and thus form part of our probing study as well, but the novelty of our work is the task of classifying context monotonicity from intermediate contextual embeddings.

3 Problem Formulation: Decomposing Natural Logic

Natural logic inferences (as formalized in Sanchez 1991; MacCartney and Manning 2007) are usually described with respect to *substitution* operations. Certain word substitutions result in either forward or reverse entailment, while others result in neither. This is the basis for a calculus of determining entailment from substitution sequences (MacCartney and Manning, 2007; Hu et al., 2020; Hu and Moss, 2018).

Broadly speaking, we wish to determine whether well-known transformer-based NLI models mimic the reasoning strategies of natural logic. However, as neural NLI models are black box classifiers that only see a premise/hypothesis sentence pair as its input, it is not immediate how to compare its process to a rule-based system.

To this end, we consider a formulation of natural logic which describes its rules in terms of concept pair relations and *context monotonicity* (similar to Rozanova et al. 2021).

3.1 Inferences From Concepts and Contexts

Consider the following example of a single step natural logic inference, which we will decompose into semantic components relevant to its entailment label:

		NLI Label
Premise	I did not eat any **fruit** for breakfast.	Entailment
Hypothesis	I did not eat any **raspberries** for breakfast.	

The hyponym/hypernym pair (raspberries, fruit) exemplifies a more general relation which we will refer to as the *concept inclusion* relation $\sqsubset$, (and dually, *reverse concept inclusion* $\sqsupset$). This mimics the subset relation of the set-based interpretations of the predicates *raspberry* and *fruit*.

In the above example, they occur in a shared **context**, namely the sentence template

"I did not eat any ____ for breakfast".

Such a context may be treated as a term substitution function f

$$f : (\mathcal{X}, \sqsubseteq) \rightarrow (\mathcal{S}, \Rightarrow)$$

between a set of concepts $\mathcal{X}$ (ordered by the concept inclusion relation) and the set $\mathcal{S}$ of full sentences ordered by entailment - we demonstrate this substitution in table 1.

X	$f(X)$
raspberries	I did not eat any **raspberries** for breakfast
fruit	I did not eat any **fruit** for breakfast

Table 1: In the example, the substitution function f behaves on the concept inputs as shown.

3.2 Context Monotonicity

We say that f is *upward monotone* ($\uparrow$) if it is order *preserving*, i.e.

$$\forall_{X,Y}(X \sqsubseteq Y \text{ implies } f(X) \Rightarrow f(Y))$$

and that f is *downward monotone* ($\downarrow$) if it is order *reversing*, i.e.

$$\forall_{X,Y}(X \sqsupseteq Y \text{ implies } f(X) \Rightarrow f(Y)).$$

Given a natural language context f, any pair of grammatically valid insertions (X, Y) (e.g. ("raspberries", "fruit")) yields a sentence pair $(f(X), f(Y))$. Treating $f(X)$ as a *premise* sentence and $f(Y)$ as a *hypothesis* sentence, a trained neural NLI model can provide a classification of whether $f(X)$ entails $f(Y)$.

In summary, these two abstract linguistic features, *context montonicity* and *concept inclusion relation*, jointly determine the final gold entailment label of this type of NLI example.

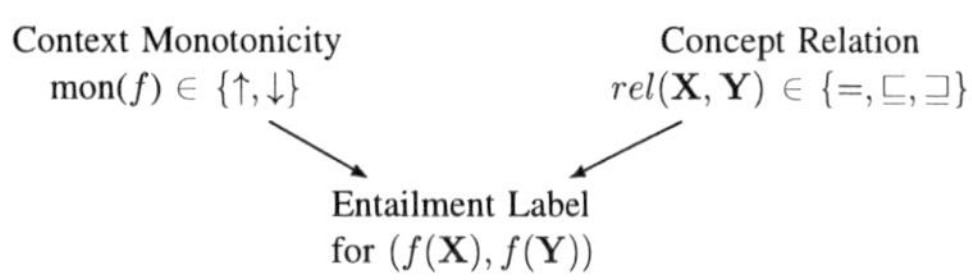

4 NLI-XY Dataset

We follow this formalism as the basis for the **NLI-XY** dataset. This is the first probing dataset in NLP where the auxiliary labels for intermediate semantic features influence the final task label in a rigid and deterministic (yet simple) way, with these features being themselves linguistically complex. As such, it is a "decomposed" natural logic dataset, where the positive entailment labels are further enriched with labels for the monotonicity and relational properties which gave rise to them. This allows for informative qualitative and structural analyses into natural logic handling strategies in neural NLI models.

The NLI-XY dataset is comprised of the following:

			Auxilliary Label
Context	f	I did not eat any ___ for breakfast.	$\downarrow$ (downward monotone)
Insertion Pair	(X,Y)	(fruit, raspberries)	$\sqsupseteq$ (reverse concept inclusion)
			NLI Label
Premise	$f(X)$	I did not eat any fruit for breakfast.	Entailment
Hypothesis	$f(Y)$	I did not eat any raspberries for breakfast.	

Table 2: A typical NLI-XY example with labels for context monotonicity, lexical relation and the final entailment label.

1. A set of *contexts* f with a blank position (indicated with a lower case 'x' or an underscore), annotated with the context monotonicity label.
2. A set of *insertion pairs* (X, Y), which are either nouns or noun phrases, annotated with the concept inclusion word-pair relation.
3. A derived set of premise and hypothesis pairs $(f(X), f(Y)$ made up of permutations of (X, Y) insertion pairs through contexts f, controlled for grammaticality as far as possible.

We present examples of the component parts and their composition in table 2.The premise/hypothesis pairs may thus be used as input to any NLI model, while the context monotonicity and insertion relation information can be used as the targets of an auxiliary probing task on top of the model's representations.

We make the NLI-XY dataset and all the experimental code used in this work is publically available [1]. We constructed the NLI-XY dataset used here as follows:

Context Extraction We extract context examples from two NLI datasets which were designed for the behavioural analysis of NLI model performance on monotonicity reasoning. In particular, we use the manually curated evaluation set MED (Yanaka et al., 2019a) and the automatically generated HELP training set (Yanaka et al., 2019b). By design, as they are collections of NLI examples exhibiting monotonicity reasoning, these datasets mostly follow our required $(f(X), f(Y))$ structure, and are labeled as instances of upward or downward monotonicity reasoning (although the contexts are not explicitly identified).

[1] Anonymized github link.

We extract the common context f from these examples after manually removing a few which do not follow this structure (differing, for example, in pronoun number agreement or prepositional phrases). We choose to treat determiners and quantifiers as part of the context, as these are the kinds of closed-class linguistic operators whose monotonicity profiles we are interested in. To ensure grammatically valid insertions, we manually identify whether each context as suitable either for a singular noun, mass noun or plural noun in the blank/"x" position.

Insertion Pairs Our (X, Y) insertion phrase pairs come from two sources: Firstly, the labeled word pairs from the MoNLI dataset (Geiger et al., 2020), which features only single-word noun phrases. Secondly, we include an additional hand-curated dataset which has a small number of *phrase-pair* examples, which includes intersective modifiers (e.g. ("brown sugar", "sugar")) and prepositional phrases (e.g. ("sentence", "sentence about oranges")). Several of these examples were drawn from the MED dataset. Each word in the pair is labelled as a singular, plural or mass noun, so that they may be permuted through the contexts in a reasonably grammatical way.

Premise/Hypothesis Pairs Premise/Hypothesis pairs are constructed by permuting insertion pairs through the set of contexts within the grammatical constraints. Such a permutation strategy may generate examples which are not consistently *meaningful*, but we see the monotonicity reasoning pattern as sufficiently rigid and syntactic that it is of interest to observe how models treat less "meaningful" entailment examples that still hold with respect to the natural logic formalism: for example, "I did not swim in a person" entails "I did not swim in an Irishman" at a systematic level. This does raise a question of whether we do (or even should) observe certain systematic behaviours on out-of-distribution examples: we leave the further investigation of this matter for future work.

Lastly, we note that the data is split into train, dev and test partitions *before* this permutation occurs, so that there are **no shared contexts or insertion pairs** between the different data partitions, in an attempt to avoid overlap issues such as those discussed in (Lewis et al., 2021). The full dataset statistics are reported in table 3.

Partition	(X,Y) Relation	Context Monotonicity Up ↑	Down ↓	Total
train	$\sqsubseteq$	671	543	1214
	$\sqsupseteq$	671	543	1214
	None	244	222	466
	Total	1586	1308	**2894**
dev	$\sqsubseteq$	598	389	987
	$\sqsupseteq$	598	389	987
	None	220	242	462
	Total	1416	1020	**2436**
test	$\sqsubseteq$	1103	1066	2169
	$\sqsupseteq$	1103	1066	2169
	None	502	516	1018
	Total	2708	2648	**5356**

Table 3: Dataset statistics for the NLI-XY dataset. We employ an **aggressive** $30, 20, 50$ train-dev-test split for a more impactful probing result, as probing is meant to demonstrate the *ease of extraction* of features. In particular, higher test accuracy with a smaller training set is a more convincing probing result than one with a large training set and small test set.

5 Experimental Setup

Our experiments are designed to investigate the following questions: Firstly, how do NLI models compare in their learned encoding of context monotonicity and lexical relational features? Secondly, if a model successfully captures these features, to what extent do they correspond with the model's predicted entailment label? We investigate these questions with a detailed probing study and a supporting qualitative analysis, using decomposed error break-downs and representation visualization.

5.1 Model Choices

We consider a selection of neural NLI models based on BERT like transformer language models (such as BERT (Devlin et al., 2019), RoBERTa (Liu et al., 2019) and BART (Lewis et al., 2020)) which are fine-tuned on one of two benchmark training sets: either SNLI (Bowman et al., 2015) or MNLI (Williams et al., 2018). Of particular interest, however, is the case where these models are trained on an additional dataset (the HELP dataset from (Yanaka et al., 2019b)) which was designed for improving the overall balance of upward and downward monotone contexts in NLI training data. We use our own random $50-30-20$ train-dev-test split of the HELP dataset (ensuring unique contexts in every split), so that there is no overlap of contexts between the fine-tuning data and the few HELP-test examples we used as part of our NLI-XY dataset[2].

5.2 Probing Tasks

The NLI-XY dataset is equipped with two auxiliary feature labels which are the targets of the probing task: context monotonicity and the relation of the (X, Y) word pair (referred to as concept inclusion relation or lexical relation). We now describe the details of the intermediate representations we choose as inputs to the probing tasks:

Target Representation The standard practice for word-pair relation classification tasks is to concatenate the contextual representation vectors for the (X, Y) word pair (taking the mean vector for multi-token words). We argue that this is a good representation choice for probing context monotonicity as well: as we are considering transformer-based bidirectional encoder architectures, the context (including the order) of each token in the input sequence informs the representation of each token in the final layer. As such, we propose that since contextual information is implicitly encoded, it is feasible to expect that a token's vector representation may encode contextual features such as context monotonicity. As both the X and the Y word occur in the same respective context, we are comfortable probing the concatenated (X, Y) representation for contextual features, and note that it allows for easy comparison with the word pair relation probing results.

Probing Methodology For each auxiliary classification task, we use simple linear models as probes. We train 20 probes of varying complexities using the *probe-ably* framework (Ferreira et al., 2021).

The complexities are represented and controlled as follows: For linear models, we follow Pimentel et al. (2020) in using the nuclear norm of the linear transformation matrix as the approximate measure of complexity, as it is a continuous approximation of the transformation matrix rank. Naively, a strong accuracy on the probing test set may be understood to indicate strong presence of the target features within the learned representations, but there has been much discussion about whether this evidence is compelling on its own. In fact, certain probing experiments have found the same accuracy scores for random representations (Zhang and Bowman, 2018), indicating that high accuracy scores are meaningless in isolation. Hewitt and Liang (2019) describe this as a dichotomy between the representation's encoding of the target features and the probe's capacity for *memorization*, and propose the use of the *selectivity* measure to always place the probe accuracy in the context of a controlled probing task with shuffled labels on the same vector representations. For each fully trained probe, we report both the test accuracy and the *selectivity* measure: tracking the selectivity ensures that we are not using a probe that is complex enough to be *overly expressive* to the point of having the capacity to overfit the randomised control training set. The *selectivity* score is calculated with respect to a *control task*. At its core, this is just a balanced random relabelling of the auxiliary data, but Hewitt and Liang (2019) advocate for more targeted control tasks with respect to the features in question and a hypothesis about the model's possible capacity for *memorization*. For the lexical relation classification control task, we assign a shared random label for all identical insertion pairs, regardless of context. Thus, a probe which is expressive enough to "memorize" individual labels of word pairs would attain high accuracy on this control task. Analogously, the context monotonicity classification control tasks assigns shared random labels to identical contexts.

5.3 NLI Challenge Set Evaluations

As well as the NLI-XY dataset (which can function as an ordinary NLI evaluation set), for completeness we report NLI task evaluation scores on the full MED dataset (Yanaka et al., 2019a), which was designed as a thorough stress-test of monotonicity reasoning performance. Furthermore, we report scores on the HELP-test set (from the dataset split in Rozanova et al. 2021): this data partition was not used in the fine-tuning of models on HELP, but we include the test scores here for insight.

5.4 Decomposed Error Analysis

The compositional structure and auxiliary labels in the NLI-XY dataset allow for qualitative analysis which may enrich the observations. To this end, we construct decomposed error analysis heatmaps which indicate whether a given premise-hypothesis data point $(f(X), f(Y))$ is correctly classified by an entailment model. These are structured with individual (X, Y) insertion pairs on the vertical axis and contexts on the horizontal axis. For brevity (and because this is representative of our observa-

[2] We use the *transformers* library (Wolf et al., 2020) and their available pretrained models for this work.

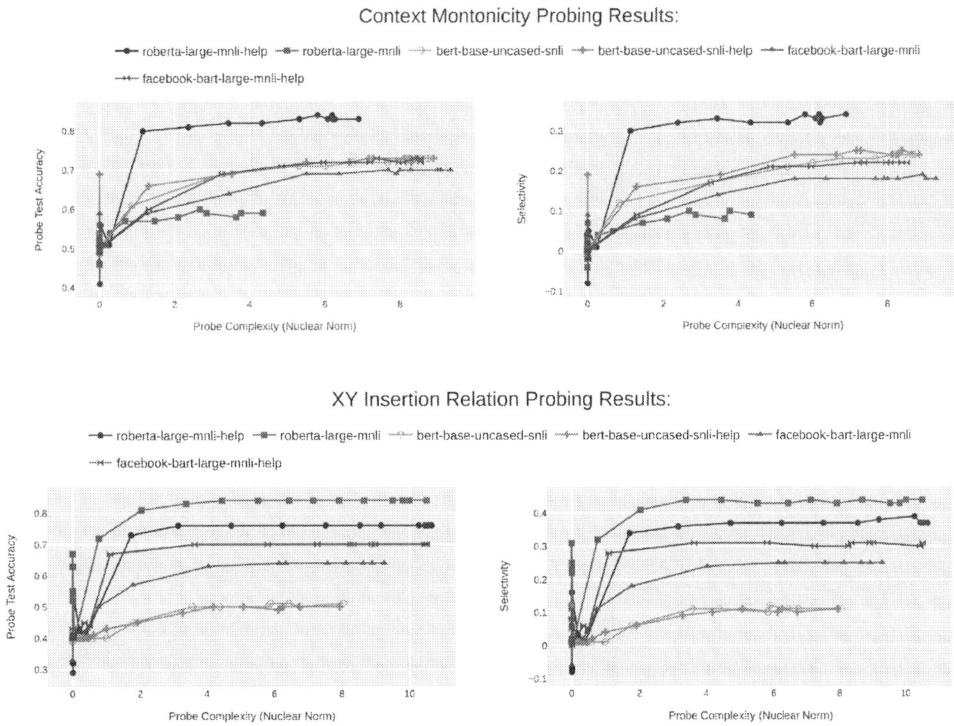

Figure 1: Linear probing results for all examined models.

tions), we include only the error breakdowns for the two sublasses of the positive entailment label: where the context monotonicity is upward and lexical relation is forward incusion, and where the context monotonicity is downward and the lexical relation is reverse inclusion.

6 Results and Discussion

6.1 Probing Results

The results for the linear probing experiments for both the *context monotonicity classification* task and the *lexical relation* classification task may be found in figure 1, with a summary score of accuracy at maximum selectivity visible in table 4. The results of the control tasks are taken into account as part of the selectivity measure, which is represented on the right hand plot for each experiment.

It is particularly notable that large models trained only on the MNLI dataset have inferior performance on context monotonicity classification. This corresponds with the further qualitative observations, suggesting that even in some of the most successful transformer-based NLI models, *there is a poor "understanding" of the logical regularities of contexts and how these are altered with downward monotone operators.*

6.2 Comparison to Challenge Set Performance

A summary of the probing results (presented as accuracy at maximum selectivity) can be compared with challenge set performance in table 4. Evaluation on the challenge test sets is relatively consistent with monotonicity probing performance, in the sense that there is a correspondence between poor/successful modeling of monotonicity features and poor/successful performance on a targeted natural logic test set. As these challenge sets are focused on testing monotonicity reasoning, this is a result which strongly bolsters the suggestion that explicit representation of the context monotonicity feature is crucial, especially for examples involving negation and other downward monotone operators. Furthermore, we generally confirm previous results that additional fine-tuning on the HELP data set has been helpful for these specialized test sets, and add to this that it similarly improves the explicit extractability of relevant context montonicity features from the latent vector representations.

NLI Models	Fine-Tuning Data	Feature Probing		NLI Monotonicity Challenge Sets		
		Context Monotonicity (%*)	XY Insertion Relation (%*)	HELP-Test (%)	MED (%)	NLI-XY (%)
roberta-large-mnli	-	59.00	84.00	36.69	46.10	59.01
roberta-large-mnli	HELP	84.00	76.00	**97.63**	**78.22**	**80.68**
facebook/bart-large-mnli		70.00	64.00	43.61	46.54	60.59
facebook/bart-large-mnli	HELP	73.00	70.00	88.99	77.16	79.34
bert-base-uncased-snli		73.00	51.00	63.55	49.38	49.09
bert-base-uncased-snli	HELP	73.00	51.00	66.80	46.13	44.79

Table 4: Summary NLI challenge test set and probing results for all considered models. *Probing results are summarized with the *accuracy at max selectivity*.

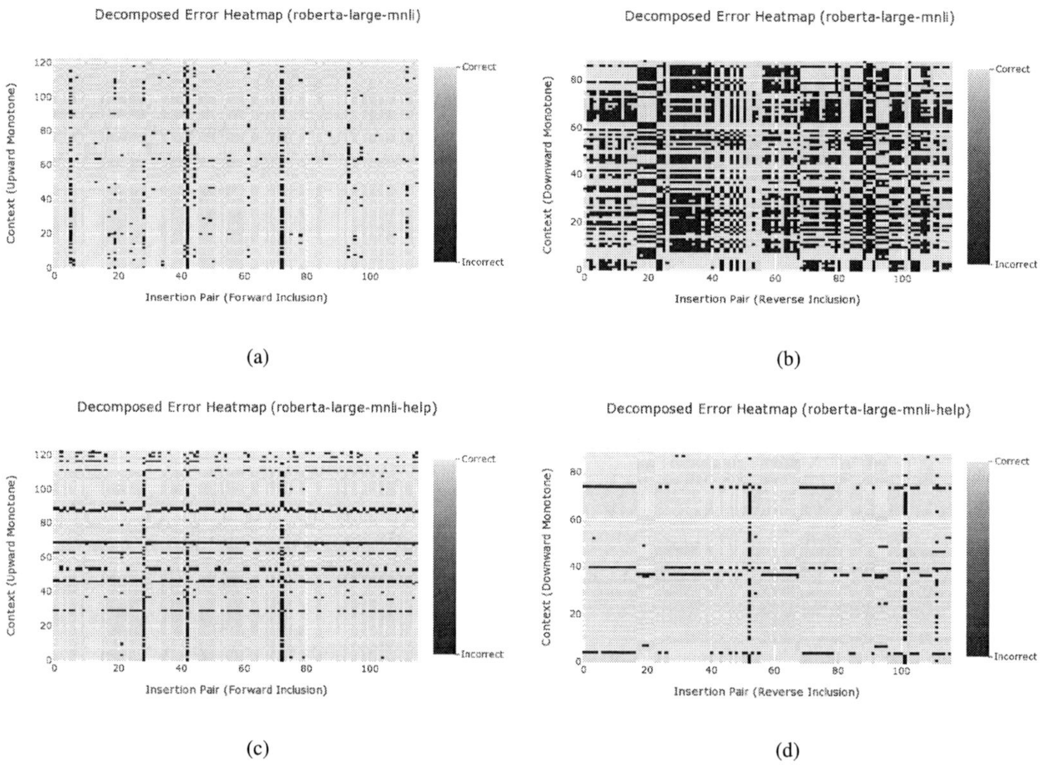

Figure 2: Decomposed error heat maps for portions of the NLI-XY dataset corresponding to the indicated context monotonicity and insertion relations (blank positions are present as only grammatical insertions were included in the dataset.)

6.3 Qualitative Analyses

Error Break-Downs An error heat map according to decomposed context monotonicity and word-pair insertion relation can be seen in figure 2. We are less concerned with the accuracy score (on NLI challenge sets) of a given model as with the behavioural *systematicity* visible in the errors, as we are not interested in noisy errors which may be due to words or phrases from outside the training domain. Consistent mis-classification for all examples derived from a fixed context or insertion pair are actually *also* strongly suggestive of a regularity in reasoning. The decomposed error analyses paint a striking picture: we generally see that models trained on MNLI routinely fail to distinguish between the expected behaviour of upward and downward monotone contexts, despite generally achieving high accuracies on large benchmark sets. This is in accordance with observations in Yanaka

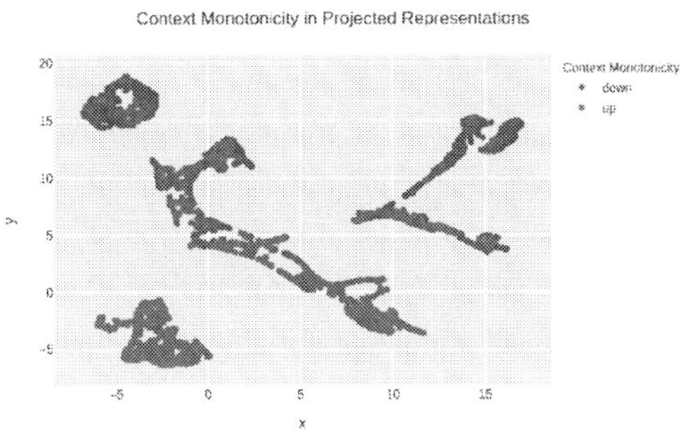

(a) roberta-large-mnli-help

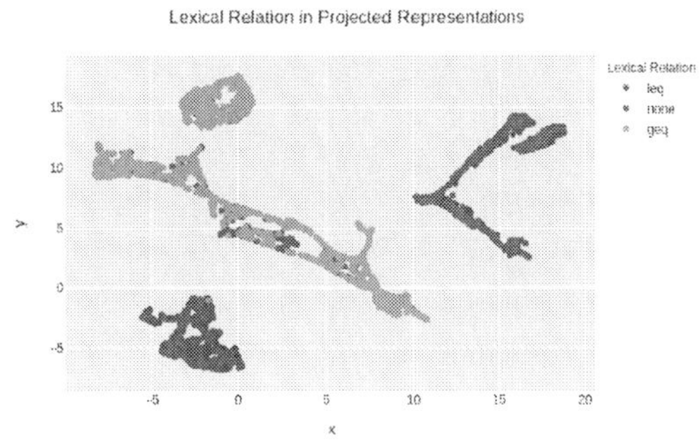

(b) roberta-large-mnli-help

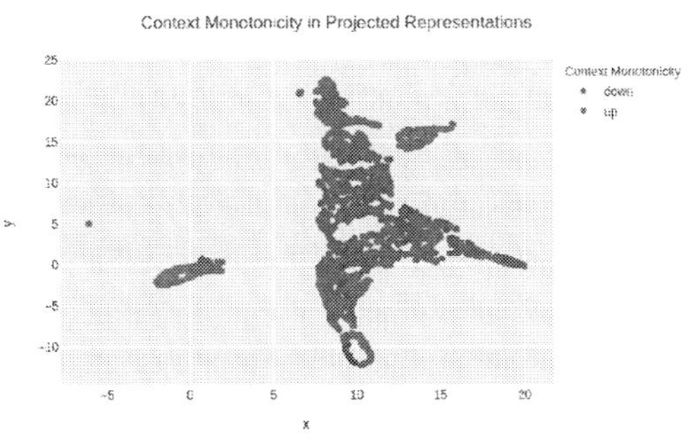

(c) roberta-large-mnli

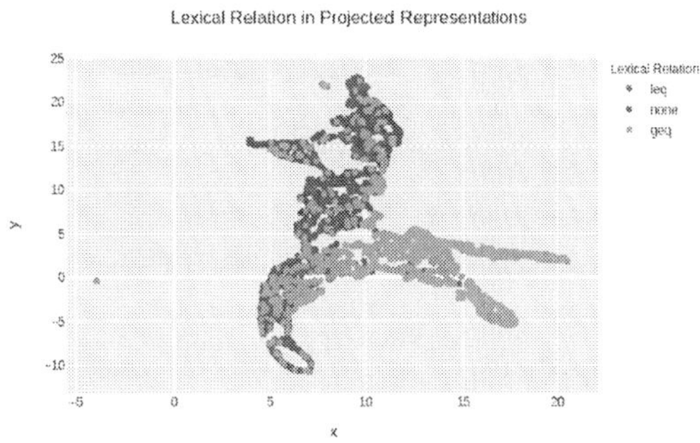

(d) roberta-large-mnli

Figure 3: UMAP projections of selected classification token representations comparing roberta-large-mnli and the improved roberta-large-mnli-help, which shows greater distinction between context monotonicity features.

et al. (2019b) and Yanaka et al. (2019a), where low accuracy on the downward-monotone reasoning sections of challenge sets points to this possibility. Howver, they show consistently show strong behavioural regularity with respect to concept inclusion. Even when the contexts are downward monotone, they still treat them systematically as if they were *upward* monotone, echoing the concept insertion pair relation *only*: they completely fail to discriminate between upward/downward monotone contexts and their opposite behaviours.

Visualization In figure 3, each data point corresponds to an embedded example (contextual XY word pair representation) in the NLI-XY dataset, with the left and right columns colored with the *gold* auxiliary labels for context monotonicity and concept inclusion relations respectively. These illustrate the probing observations: in the well-known roberta-large-mnli model, concept inclusion relation features are distinguishable, whereas context monotonicity is very randomly scattered, with no emergent clustering. However, the roberta-large-mnli-help model shows an improvement in this behaviour, demonstrating a stronger context monotonicity distinction.

7 Conclusion

In summary, the NLI-XY has enabled us to present evidence that explicit context monotonicity feature clustering in neural model representations seems to correspond to better performance on natural logic challenge sets which test downward-monotone reasoning. In particular, many popular models trained on MNLI seem to lack this behaviour, accounting for previous observations that they systematically fail in downward-monotone contexts.

Furthermore, the probes' labels also have some explanatory value: both entailment and non-entailment labels can each further be broken down into sub-regions. This qualifies the classification with the observations that the data point occurs in a cluster of examples with a) upward (resp. downward) contexts and b) a forward (resp. backward) containment relation between the substituted noun phrases. In this sense, the analyses in this work can thus be interpreted as an explainable "decomposition" of the treatment natural logic examples in neural models.

References

Lasha Abzianidze. 2017. LangPro: Natural language theorem prover. In *Proceedings of the 2017 Conference on Empirical Methods in Natural Language Processing: System Demonstrations*, pages 115–120, Copenhagen, Denmark. Association for Computational Linguistics.

Guillaume Alain and Yoshua Bengio. 2018. Understanding intermediate layers using linear classifier probes.

Samuel R Bowman, Gabor Angeli, Christopher Potts, and Christopher D Manning. 2015. A large annotated corpus for learning natural language inference. In *EMNLP*.

Zeming Chen, Qiyue Gao, and Lawrence S. Moss. 2021. Neurallog: Natural language inference with joint neural and logical reasoning.

Jacob Devlin, Ming-Wei Chang, Kenton Lee, and Kristina Toutanova. 2019. BERT: Pre-training of deep bidirectional transformers for language understanding. In *Proceedings of the 2019 Conference of the North American Chapter of the Association for Computational Linguistics: Human Language Technologies, Volume 1 (Long and Short Papers)*, pages 4171–4186, Minneapolis, Minnesota. Association for Computational Linguistics.

Deborah Ferreira, Julia Rozanova, Mokanarangan Thayaparan, Marco Valentino, and André Freitas. 2021. Does my representation capture X? probe-ably. In *Proceedings of the 59th Annual Meeting of the Association for Computational Linguistics and the 11th International Joint Conference on Natural Language Processing: System Demonstrations*, pages 194–201, Online. Association for Computational Linguistics.

Atticus Geiger, Kyle Richardson, and Christopher Potts. 2020. Neural natural language inference models partially embed theories of lexical entailment and negation. In *Proceedings of the Third BlackboxNLP Workshop on Analyzing and Interpreting Neural Networks for NLP*, pages 163–173, Online. Association for Computational Linguistics.

Emily Goodwin, Koustuv Sinha, and Timothy J. O'Donnell. 2020. Probing linguistic systematicity. In *Proceedings of the 58th Annual Meeting of the Association for Computational Linguistics*, pages 1958–1969, Online. Association for Computational Linguistics.

Christine Herlihy and Rachel Rudinger. 2021. MedNLI is not immune: Natural language inference artifacts in the clinical domain. In *Proceedings of the 59th Annual Meeting of the Association for Computational Linguistics and the 11th International Joint Conference on Natural Language Processing (Volume 2: Short Papers)*, pages 1020–1027, Online. Association for Computational Linguistics.

John Hewitt and Percy Liang. 2019. Designing and interpreting probes with control tasks. In *Proceedings of the 2019 Conference on Empirical Methods in Natural Language Processing and the 9th International Joint Conference on Natural Language Processing (EMNLP-IJCNLP)*, pages 2733–2743, Hong Kong, China. Association for Computational Linguistics.

John Hewitt and Christopher D. Manning. 2019. A structural probe for finding syntax in word representations. In *Proceedings of the 2019 Conference of the North American Chapter of the Association for Computational Linguistics: Human Language Technologies, Volume 1 (Long and Short Papers)*, pages 4129–4138, Minneapolis, Minnesota. Association for Computational Linguistics.

Hai Hu, Qi Chen, Kyle Richardson, Atreyee Mukherjee, Lawrence S. Moss, and Sandra Kuebler. 2020. MonaLog: a lightweight system for natural language inference based on monotonicity. In *Proceedings of the Society for Computation in Linguistics 2020*, pages 334–344, New York, New York. Association for Computational Linguistics.

Hai Hu and Larry Moss. 2018. Polarity computations in flexible categorial grammar. In *Proceedings of the Seventh Joint Conference on Lexical and Computational Semantics*, pages 124–129, New Orleans, Louisiana. Association for Computational Linguistics.

Aikaterini-Lida Kalouli, Richard Crouch, and Valeria de Paiva. 2020. Hy-NLI: a hybrid system for natural language inference. In *Proceedings of the 28th International Conference on Computational Linguistics*, pages 5235–5249, Barcelona, Spain (Online). International Committee on Computational Linguistics.

Mike Lewis, Yinhan Liu, Naman Goyal, Marjan Ghazvininejad, Abdelrahman Mohamed, Omer Levy, Veselin Stoyanov, and Luke Zettlemoyer. 2020. BART: Denoising sequence-to-sequence pre-training for natural language generation, translation, and comprehension. In *Proceedings of the 58th Annual Meeting of the Association for Computational Linguistics*, pages 7871–7880, Online. Association for Computational Linguistics.

Patrick Lewis, Pontus Stenetorp, and Sebastian Riedel. 2021. Question and answer test-train overlap in open-domain question answering datasets. In *Proceedings of the 16th Conference of the European Chapter of the Association for Computational Linguistics: Main Volume*, pages 1000–1008, Online. Association for Computational Linguistics.

Y. Liu, Myle Ott, Naman Goyal, Jingfei Du, Mandar Joshi, Danqi Chen, Omer Levy, M. Lewis, Luke Zettlemoyer, and Veselin Stoyanov. 2019. Roberta: A robustly optimized bert pretraining approach. *ArXiv*, abs/1907.11692.

Bill MacCartney and Christopher D. Manning. 2007. Natural logic for textul inference. In *Proceedings of the ACL-PASCAL Workshop on Textual Entailment and Paraphrasing*, pages 193–200, Prague. Association for Computational Linguistics.

Tom McCoy, Ellie Pavlick, and Tal Linzen. 2019. Right for the wrong reasons: Diagnosing syntactic heuristics in natural language inference. In *Proceedings of the 57th Annual Meeting of the Association for Computational Linguistics*, pages 3428–3448, Florence, Italy. Association for Computational Linguistics.

Tiago Pimentel, Naomi Saphra, Adina Williams, and Ryan Cotterell. 2020. Pareto probing: Trading off accuracy for complexity. In *Proceedings of the 2020 Conference on Empirical Methods in Natural Language Processing (EMNLP)*, pages 3138–3153, Online. Association for Computational Linguistics.

Kyle Richardson, Hai Hu, Lawrence S. Moss, and Ashish Sabharwal. 2019. Probing natural language inference models through semantic fragments. *CoRR*, abs/1909.07521.

Julia Rozanova, Deborah Ferreira, Mokanarangan Thayaparan, Marco Valentino, and André Freitas. 2021. Supporting context monotonicity abstractions in neural nli models.

V. Sanchez. 1991. Studies on natural logic and categorial grammar.

Ivan Vulić, Edoardo Maria Ponti, Robert Litschko, Goran Glavaš, and Anna Korhonen. 2020. Probing pretrained language models for lexical semantics. In *Proceedings of the 2020 Conference on Empirical Methods in Natural Language Processing (EMNLP)*, pages 7222–7240, Online. Association for Computational Linguistics.

Adina Williams, Nikita Nangia, and Samuel Bowman. 2018. A broad-coverage challenge corpus for sentence understanding through inference. In *Proceedings of the 2018 Conference of the North American Chapter of the Association for Computational Linguistics: Human Language Technologies, Volume 1 (Long Papers)*, pages 1112–1122. Association for Computational Linguistics.

Thomas Wolf, Lysandre Debut, Victor Sanh, Julien Chaumond, Clement Delangue, Anthony Moi, Pierric Cistac, Tim Rault, Rémi Louf, Morgan Funtowicz, Joe Davison, Sam Shleifer, Patrick von Platen, Clara Ma, Yacine Jernite, Julien Plu, Canwen Xu, Teven Le Scao, Sylvain Gugger, Mariama Drame, Quentin Lhoest, and Alexander M. Rush. 2020. Transformers: State-of-the-art natural language processing. In *Proceedings of the 2020 Conference on Empirical Methods in Natural Language Processing: System Demonstrations*, pages 38–45, Online. Association for Computational Linguistics.

Hitomi Yanaka, Koji Mineshima, Daisuke Bekki, Kentaro Inui, Satoshi Sekine, Lasha Abzianidze, and Johan Bos. 2019a. Can neural networks understand monotonicity reasoning? In *Proceedings of the 2019 ACL Workshop BlackboxNLP: Analyzing and Interpreting Neural Networks for NLP*, pages 31–40, Florence, Italy. Association for Computational Linguistics.

Hitomi Yanaka, Koji Mineshima, Daisuke Bekki, Kentaro Inui, Satoshi Sekine, Lasha Abzianidze, and Johan Bos. 2019b. HELP: A dataset for identifying shortcomings of neural models in monotonicity reasoning. In *Proceedings of the Eighth Joint Conference on Lexical and Computational Semantics (*SEM 2019)*, pages 250–255, Minneapolis, Minnesota. Association for Computational Linguistics.

Kelly Zhang and Samuel Bowman. 2018. Language modeling teaches you more than translation does: Lessons learned through auxiliary syntactic task analysis. In *Proceedings of the 2018 EMNLP Workshop BlackboxNLP: Analyzing and Interpreting Neural Networks for NLP*, pages 359–361, Brussels, Belgium. Association for Computational Linguistics.

Probing with Noise: Unpicking the Warp and Weft of Embeddings

Filip Klubička and **John D. Kelleher**
ADAPT Centre, Technological University Dublin, Ireland
{filip.klubicka,john.kelleher}@adaptcentre.ie

Abstract

Improving our understanding of how information is encoded in vector space can yield valuable interpretability insights. Alongside vector dimensions, we argue that it is possible for the vector norm to also carry linguistic information. We develop a method to test this: an extension of the probing framework which allows for relative intrinsic interpretations of probing results. It relies on introducing noise that ablates information encoded in embeddings, grounded in random baselines and confidence intervals. We apply the method to well-established probing tasks and find evidence that confirms the existence of separate information containers in English GloVe and BERT embeddings. Our correlation analysis aligns with the experimental findings that different encoders use the norm to encode different kinds of information: GloVe stores syntactic and sentence length information in the vector norm, while BERT uses it to encode contextual incongruity.

1 Introduction

Probing in NLP, as defined by Conneau et al. (2018), is a classification problem that predicts linguistic properties using dense embeddings as training data. The framework rests on the assumption that the probe's success at a given task indicates that the encoder is storing information on the pertinent linguistic properties. Probing has quickly become an essential tool for encoder interpretability, by providing interesting insights into embeddings.

In essence, embeddings are vectors positioned in a shared multidimensional vector space, and vectors are geometrically defined by two aspects: having both a **direction** and **magnitude** (Hefferon, 2018, page 36). Direction is the position in the space that the vector points towards (expressed by its dimension values), while magnitude is a vector's length, defined as its distance from the origin (expressed by the vector norm) (Anton and Rorres, 2013, page 131). It is understood that information contained in a vector is encoded in the dimension values, which are most often studied in NLP research (see §6). However, information can be encoded in a representational vector space in more implicit ways, and relations can be inferred from more than just vector dimension values.

We hypothesise that it is possible for the vector magnitude—the norm—to carry information as well. Though it is a distributed property of a vector's dimensions, the norm not only relates the distance of a vector from the origin, but indirectly also its distance from other vectors. Two vectors could be pointing in the exact same direction, but their distance from the origin might differ dramatically.[1] A similar effect has been observed in the literature: for many word embedding algorithms, the norm of the word vector correlates with the word's frequency (Schakel and Wilson, 2015). E.g. in fastText embeddings the vectors of stop words (the most frequent words in English) are positioned closer to the origin than content words (Balodis and Deksne, 2018); and Goldberg (2017) notes that for many embeddings normalising the vectors removes word frequency information. Additionally, the norm plays an integral part in BERT's attention layer, controlling the levels of contribution from frequent, less informative words by controlling the norms of their vectors (Kobayashi et al., 2020). It stands to reason that the norm could be leveraged by embedding models to encode other linguistic information as well. Hence, we argue that a vector representation has two **information containers**: vector *dimensions* and the vector *norm* (the titular *warp* and *weft*). In this paper, we test the assumption that these two components can be used to encode different types of information.

To this end, we need a probing method that provides an intrinsic evaluation of any given embed-

[1] Mathematically, two vectors can only be considered equal if both their direction and magnitude are equal (Anton and Rorres, 2013, page 137).

Proceedings of the Fifth BlackboxNLP Workshop on Analyzing and Interpreting Neural Networks for NLP, pages 404 - 417
December 8, 2022

ding representation, for which the typical probing pipeline is not suited. We thus extend the existing probing framework by introducing random noise into the embeddings. This enables us to do an intrinsic evaluation of a single encoder by testing whether the noise disrupted the information in the embedding being tested. The right application of noise enables us to determine which embedding component the relevant information is encoded in, by ablating that component's information. In turn, this can inform our understanding of how certain linguistic properties are encoded in vector space. We call the method *probing with noise* and demonstrate its generalisability to both contextual and static encoders by using it to intrinsically evaluate English GloVe and BERT embeddings on a number of established probing tasks.

This paper's main contributions are: (a) a methodological extension of the probing framework: *probing with noise*; (b) an array of experiments demonstrating the method on a range of probing tasks; and (c) an exploration of the importance of the vector norm in encoding linguistic phenomena in different embedding models.

2 Method: Probing With Noise

Our method is an extension of the typical probing pipeline (steps 1-6), incorporated as steps 7 and 8:

1. Choose a probing task
2. Choose or design an appropriate dataset
3. Choose a word/sentence representation
4. Choose a probing classifier (the probe)
5. Train the probe on the embeddings as input
6. Evaluate the probe's performance on the task
7. **Introduce systematic noise in the embedding**
8. **Repeat training, evaluate and compare**

Usually, the evaluation score from step 6 is used as a basis to make inferences regarding the presence of the probed information in embeddings. Different encoders are compared based on their evaluation score and the probe's relative performance can inform which model stores the information more saliently. Though ours may seem like a minor addition, it changes the approach conceptually. Now, rather than providing the final score, the output of step 6 establishes an intrinsic, *vanilla baseline*. Embeddings with noise injections can then be compared against it in steps 7 and 8, offering a relative intrinsic interpretation of the evaluation. In other words, using relative information between a vector representation and targeted ablations of itself allows for inferences to be made on where information is encoded in embeddings.

The method relies on three supporting pillars: (a) random baselines, which in tandem with the vanilla baseline provide the basis for a relative evaluation; (b) statistical significance derived from confidence intervals, which informs the inferences we make based on the relative evaluation; and (c) targeted noise, which enables us to examine where the information is encoded. We describe them in the following subsections, starting with the noise.

2.1 Choosing the Noise

The nature of the noise is crucial for our method, as the goal is to systematically disrupt the content of the information containers in order to identify whether a container encodes the information. We use an ablation method to do this: by introducing noise into either container we "sabotage" the representation, in turn identifying whether the information we are probing for has been removed. Though we introduce random noise, our choice of how to apply it is systematic, as it is important that the noising function applied to one container leaves the information in the remaining container intact, otherwise the results will not offer relevant insight.

Ablating the Dimension Container: The noise function for ablating the dimensions needs to remove its information completely, while leaving the norm intact. It should also not change the dimensionality of the vector, given that a change in the dimensionality of a feature also changes the chance of the probe finding a random or spurious hyper-plane that performs well on the data sample. Maintaining the dimensionality thus ensures that the probability of the model finding such a lucky split in the feature space remains unchanged.

Our noise function satisfies these constraints: for each embedding in a dataset, we generate a new, random vector of the same dimensionality, then scale the new dimension values to match the norm of the original vector. This invalidates any semantics assigned to a particular dimension as the values are replaced with meaningless noise, while retaining the original vector's norm values.

Ablating the Norm Container: To remove information potentially carried by a vector's norm while retaining dimension information, we apply a noising function analogous to the previous one: for each embedding we generate a random norm value, and then scale the vector's original dimension values to match the new norm. This randomises vector magnitudes, while the relative sizes of the dimensions remain unchanged. In other words, all vectors will keep pointing in the same directions, but any information encoded by differences in magnitude is removed.[2]

Ablating Both Containers: The two approaches are not mutually exclusive: applying both noising functions should have a compounding effect and ablate both information containers simultaneously, essentially generating a completely random vector with none of the original information.

2.2 Random Baselines

Even when no information is encoded in an embedding, the train set may contain class imbalance, and the probe can learn the distribution of classes. To account for this, as well as the possibility of a powerful probe detecting an empty signal (Zhang and Bowman, 2018), we need to establish informative random baselines against which we can compare the probe's performance.

We employ two such baselines: (a) we assert a random prediction onto the test set, negating any information that a classifier could have learned, class distributions included; and (b) we train the probe on randomly generated vectors, establishing a baseline with access only to class distributions.

2.3 Confidence Intervals

Finally, we must account for the degrees of randomness, which stem from two sources: (1) the probe may contain a stochastic component, e.g. a random weight initialisation; (2) the noise functions are highly stochastic (i.e. sampling random norm/dimension values). Hence, evaluation scores will differ each time the probe is trained, making relative comparisons of scores problematic. To mitigate this, we retrain and evaluate each model 50 times reporting the average score of all runs, essentially bootstrapping over the random seeds.

To obtain statistical significance for the averages, we calculate a 99% confidence interval (CI) to confirm that observed differences in the averages of different model scores are significant. We use the CI range when comparing evaluation scores of probes on any two noise models to determine whether they come from the same distribution: if there is overlap in the range of two possible averages they might belong to the same distribution and there is no statistically significant difference between them. Using CIs in this way gives us a clearly defined decision criterion on whether any model performances are different.

3 Data

In our experiments we use 10 established probing task datasets for the English language introduced by Conneau et al. (2018). The goal of the multi-class *Sentence Length* (SL) probing task is to predict the length of the sentence as binned in 6 possible categories, while *Word Content* (WC) is a task with 1000 words as targets, predicting which of the target words appears in a given sentence. The *Subject* and *Object Number* tasks (SN and ON) are binary classification tasks that predict the grammatical number of the subject/object of the main clause as being singular or plural, while the *Tense* (TE) task predicts whether the main verb of the sentence is in the present or past tense. The *Coordination Inversion* (CIN) task distinguishes between a sentence where the order of two coordinated clausal conjoints has been inverted or not. *Parse Tree Depth* (TD) is a multi-class prediction task where the goal is to predict the maximum depth of the sentence's syntactic tree, while *Top Constituents* (TC) predicts one of 20-classes of the most common syntactic top-constituent sequences. In the *Bigram Shift* (BS) task, the goal is to predict whether two consecutive tokens in the sentence have been inverted, and *Semantic Odd Man Out* (SOMO) is a task predicting whether a noun or verb was replaced with a different noun or verb. We use these datasets as published in their totality, with no modifications.[3] We also consider these tasks to represent examples of different language domains: surface information (SL,WC), morphology (SN,ON,TE), syntax (TD,TC,CIN) and contextual incongruity (BS,SOMO). This level of abstraction can lend itself to interpreting the experimental results, as there may be similarities across tasks in the same domain (note that Durrani et al. (2020) follow a similar line of reasoning).

[2]We are conscious that vectors have more than one kind of norm, so choosing which norm to scale to might not be trivial. We have explored this in supplementary experiments and found that in our framework there is no significant difference between scaling to the L1 norm vs. L2 norm.

[3]`https://github.com/facebookresearch/SentEval/tree/master/data/probing`

4 Experiments

4.1 Models and Implementation

Given the current prominence of contextual encoders, such as BERT (Devlin et al., 2019), ELMo (Peters et al., 2018b) and their derivatives, they are an obvious choice for the application of our method. However, rather than compare different contextual encoders, we prefer to draw a contrastive comparison with a static encoder, such as GloVe (Pennington et al., 2014), which is a distributed representation based on a word to word co-occurrence matrix. This provides insight into both models and demonstrates the method's generalisability to more than one type of encoder. In our experiments we examine BERT and GloVe embeddings.

Note that all the probing datasets we use are framed as classification tasks at the sentence level (see §3), so our experiments require sentence representations. We use pretrained versions of BERT and GloVe to generate embeddings for each sentence. The BERT model generates 12 layers of embedding vectors with each layer containing a separate 768-dimensional embedding for each word, so we average the word embeddings in BERT's final layer, resulting in a 768-dimensional sentence embedding. We take the same mean pooling approach with GloVe, which yields a 300-dimensional sentence embedding for each sentence. While BERT uses sub-word tokens to get around out of vocabulary tokens, in the rare instance of encountering an OOV with GloVe, we generate a random word embedding in its stead.

In each set of experiments, the sentence embeddings are used as input to a Multi-Layered Perceptron (MLP) classifier, which labels them according to the probing task. We evaluate the performance of all probes using the AUC-ROC score.[4] Regarding implementation and parameter details, we used the bert-base-uncased BERT model from the *pytorch_pretrained_bert* library[5] (Paszke et al., 2019), a pre-trained GloVe model[6] and for the MLP probe we used the scikit-learn MLP implementation (Pedregosa et al., 2011) using the default parameters.[7,8]

4.2 Chosen Noise Models

As described in §2, we remove information from the norm by sampling random norm values and scaling the vector dimensions to the new norm. However, considering that vectors have more than one calculable norm, the scaling can be done to match more than one norm value. We have examined the effects of scaling to both the L1 and L2 norms, as they are most widely used in NLP, and found that applying our norm ablation noise function to scale to either norm removes information from both norms (see Table 3).[9] In order to streamline the results presentation, henceforth when discussing norm ablations we only report results pertaining to scaling to the L2 norm.

To ablate information encoded in the dimension container, we randomly sample dimension values and then scale them to match the original norm of the vector (see §2).[10] We expect this to fully remove all interpretable information encoded in the dimension values, making the norm the only information container available to the probe. Applying both noise functions together on the same vector should remove any information encoded in it.

Finally, we use the vanilla BERT and GloVe sentence embeddings in their respective evaluations as vanilla baselines against which the models with noise are compared. Here the probe has access to both information containers: dimensions and norm. However, it is also important to establish the vanilla baseline's performance against the random baselines: we need to confirm whether the information is in fact encoded somewhere in the embeddings.

[4] `https://scikit-learn.org/stable/modules/generated/sklearn.metrics.roc_auc_score.html`

[5] `https://pypi.org/project/pytorch-pretrained-bert/`

[6] The larger common crawl vectors: `https://nlp.stanford.edu/projects/glove/`

[7] activation='relu', solver='adam', max_iter=200, hidden_layer_sizes=100, learning_rate_init=0.001, batch_size=min(200,n_samples), early_stopping=False, weight init. $W \sim \mathcal{N}\left(0, \sqrt{6/(fan_{in} + fan_{out})}\right)$ (scikit relu default). See: `https://scikit-learn.org/stable/modules/generated/sklearn.neural_network.MLPClassifier.html`

[8] Code available here: `https://github.com/GreenParachute/probing-with-noise`

[9] This contrasts with applying a normalisation function to the vector, where normalising to one of the norms removes information encoded in that norm, but retains, or even emphasises the information in the remaining norm, making normalisation an unsuitable ablation function (see §A for details).

[10] The random norm and dimension values are sampled uniformly from a range between the minimum and maximum norm/dimension values of the respective embeddings on all 10 datasets. BERT norm range: [7.1896,13.2854], BERT dimension range: [-5.427,1.9658]; GloVe norm range: [2.0041,8.0359], GloVe dimension range: [-2.5446,3.1976]

GloVe											Key
Model	SL		WC		SN		ON		TE		*Surface Info.*
	auc	±CI	auc	±CI	auc	±CI	auc	±CI	auc	±CI	SL: Sentence Length
rand. pred.	.5006	.0013	.4995	.001	.4996	.002	.4999	.0023	.4981	.0022	WC: Word Content
rand. vec.	.4999	.0011	.5006	.0009	.499	.0022	.4998	.0024	.4997	.0024	*Morphology*
vanilla	.9475	.0005	.9974	.0001	.8114	.0014	.7805	.0013	.8632	.0014	SN: Subject Number
abl. N	.9384	.0005	.994	.0001	.8058	.0016	.7743	.0018	.8594	.0013	ON: Object Number
abl. D	**.5481**	.0013	**.504**	.0011	.5003	.0022	.4994	.0024	.5013	.0025	TE: Tense
abl. D+N	.5001	.0011	.4999	.0008	.4987	.0024	.4994	.002	.4998	.0021	*Syntax*
Model	CIN		TD		TC		BS		SOMO		CIN: Coordination
	auc	±CI	auc	±CI	auc	±CI	auc	±CI	auc	±CI	Inversion
rand. pred.	.5004	.0022	.5005	.0012	.5005	.0009	.4998	.0022	.4999	.0026	TD: Parse Tree Depth
rand. vec.	.4993	.0022	.5002	.0014	.5004	.0009	.4989	.0023	.4991	.0023	TC: Top Constituents
vanilla	.5493	.0019	.7799	.0012	.9512	.0004	.5017	.0021	.5291	.0021	*Incongruity*
abl. N	.5437	.002	.7689	.001	.9438	.0004	.5034	.0024	.5235	.002	BS: Bigram Shift
abl. D	.5003	.0023	**.5137**	.0012	**.5331**	.0013	.499	.0026	.5005	.0021	SOMO: Semantic
abl. D+N	.5004	.0021	.501	.0013	.4996	.0011	.4996	.0024	.5007	.0019	Odd Man Out

Table 1: Experimental results on GloVe models and baselines. Reporting average AUC-ROC scores and confidence intervals (CI) of the average of all training runs. Cells shaded light grey belong to the same distribution as random baselines, dark grey cells share the vanilla baseline distribution, while scores significantly different from both the random and vanilla baselines are unshaded, while the most pertinent scores are marked in bold.

4.3 Results

Detailed experimental evaluation results for GloVe and BERT on each of the 10 probing tasks are presented in Tables 1 and 2 respectively. Note that all cells shaded light grey belong to the same distribution as random baselines on a given task, as there is no statistically significant difference between the different scores[11]; cells shaded dark grey belong to the same distribution as the vanilla baseline on a given task; and all cells that are not shaded contain a significantly different score than both the random and vanilla baselines, indicating that they belong to different distributions. The scores most pertinent to the result discussion are marked in bold.

GloVe results: The vanilla GloVe vectors outperform the random baselines on all tasks except BS. This is not surprising, as BS is essentially a local-context task, and GloVe does not encode context in such a localised manner. In all other tasks, at least some task-relevant information is encoded in the embeddings. Having established the vanilla results as a baseline for the ablations, we examine which information container encodes the relevant information: dimension or norm.

Generally, the results show that the answers are task-dependent. In the SN, ON, TE, CIN and SOMO tasks, there is a substantial drop in the probe's performance after ablating the dimension container and it is immediately comparable to random baselines. Furthermore, performance does not significantly change after also ablating the norm, indicating that for these tasks no pertinent information is stored in the norm, and that all the information the probe uses is stored in the dimensions.

However, the results for the SL, WC, TD and TC probes tell a different story. Once the dimension container is ablated from these vectors, although the performance drops markedly compared to vanilla, it does not quite reach the random baseline performance as observed in the above tasks.[12] These results indicate that for these tasks the relevant information is not contained *only* in the dimension container. Furthermore, when the dimension and norm ablation functions are applied together, this induces a further performance drop, and the resulting performance scores become comparable to the random baselines. This indicates that the vectors with ablated dimension information still contain residual information relevant to the task, which is removed when also ablating the norm, pointing to the fact that the norm contains some of the relevant information *regardless of what is encoded in the vector dimensions*.

We should note here that, while it is true that in

[11]We highlight that the *rand. vec.* baseline is equivalent to the scenario where both dimensions and norm are ablated (*abl. D+N*). While the two scenarios are arguably the exact same condition, we include both of them in the results presentation to demonstrate a consistent application of our methodology, where we consider *rand. vec.* to be a baseline, and the *abl. D+N* a sense-check of our ablation functions.

[12]This is true even in the case of WC, where the difference is really quite small, yet still statistically significant. Note that the WC task is a particularly unusual classification task, as there are 1000 possible classes to predict, which could explain the statistical significance of such a small difference.

	BERT										Key
Model	SL		WC		SN		ON		TE		*Surface Info.*
	auc	±CI	auc	±CI	auc	±CI	auc	±CI	auc	±CI	SL: Sentence Length
rand. pred.	.5002	.0006	.4996	.0012	.4995	.0021	.4988	.0022	.5007	.0021	WC: Word Content
rand. vec.	.5003	.0004	.4997	.0009	.5006	.002	.4996	.0024	.4993	.0021	*Morphology*
vanilla	.9733	.0011	.982	.0003	.9074	.0008	.8674	.0019	.9135	.0008	SN: Subject Number
abl. N	.973	.0008	.9783	.0003	.9078	.0008	.8658	.0017	.9118	.0012	ON: Object Number
abl. D	.5047	.0008	.5013	.0011	.4992	.0021	.5004	.0023	.5007	.0019	TE: Tense
abl. D+N	.4997	.0008	.5	.0013	.5006	.0024	.4994	.0024	.4983	.0021	*Syntax*
Model	CIN		TD		TC		BS		SOMO		CIN: Coordination
	auc	±CI	auc	±CI	auc	±CI	auc	±CI	auc	±CI	Inversion
rand. pred.	.5007	.0022	.4999	.0012	.5001	.0013	.5011	.0020	.499	.0018	TD: Parse Tree Depth
rand. vec.	.5014	.0019	.4999	.0012	.5001	.0013	.5005	.0024	.5001	.0021	TC: Top Constituents
vanilla	.7472	.0016	.7751	.0016	.9562	.0002	.9382	.0006	.6401	.0013	*Incongruity*
abl. N	.7492	.0018	.7709	.0016	.9547	.0004	.9371	.001	.6396	.0017	BS: Bigram Shift
abl. D	.5049	.0021	.5004	.0013	**.5093**	.0019	**.556**	.0025	**.5272**	.002	SOMO: Semantic
abl. D+N	.5015	.0035	.5	.0012	.5001	.001	.4972	.0035	.4997	.002	Odd Man Out

Table 2: Experimental results on BERT models and baselines. Reporting average AUC-ROC scores and confidence intervals (CI) of the average of all training runs. Cells shaded light grey belong to the same distribution as random baselines, dark grey cells share the vanilla baseline distribution, while scores significantly different from both the random and vanilla baselines are unshaded, while the most pertinent scores are marked in bold.

all tasks ablating the norm alone causes a statistically significant drop in performance, this finding on its own should not be taken as an indicator that the norm encodes task-relevant information. Given how consistently small the drop is across all tasks (<0.1), this is more likely an artefact of an interaction between the noising function and the GloVe vectors. The more reliable indicator of where the information is encoded is the experiment on dimension ablations compared to ablating both dimension and norm: if for a particular task performance remains above random after ablating dimensions, but drops to random when ablating both dimensions and norms, this shows that the norm is encoding at least part of the relevant information.

BERT results: The vanilla BERT vectors outperform random baselines across all tasks, including the BS task. When ablating the dimensions on most tasks, the probe's performance drops dramatically and is comparable to random baselines. It does not change after also ablating the norm, indicating that no pertinent information is stored in BERT's norm container for these tasks. However, the BS and SOMO tasks show that some of the task information is stored in BERT's norm, as the performance drop when ablating dimensions is not comparable to random baselines, and only reaches that once the norm is also ablated. The same is true for the syntactic TC task, which is also the only BERT result that shows a similar trend as GloVe, though it seems that BERT stores far less TC information in the norm than GloVe does.

Ultimately, our experimental results allow us to make a number of general inferences: (a) the norm is indeed a separate information container, (b) on most tasks the vast majority of the relevant information is encoded in the dimension values, but can be supplemented with information from the norm, (c) though the information contained in the norm is not always very impactful, it is not negligible, (d) different encoders use the norm to carry different types of information, (e) specifically BERT stores information pertinent to the BS, SOMO and TC tasks in the norm, (f) while GloVe uses it to store SL, WC, TC and TD information.

4.4 Norm Correlation Analysis

While we have demonstrated that information can be encoded in the norm, we wish to also understand the relationship between the norms and the probed information. We explore this with a Pearson correlation analysis: we test the correlation between each vector norm and the sentence labels on each probing task dataset.[13] The correlation results are presented in Table 3, and largely support our result interpretations from §4.3,[14] including that applying

[13]The Pearson test only works on continuous variables, but it is still possible to calculate with categorical variables if they are binary, by simply converting the categories to 0 and 1.

[14]In cases such as WC and TC where there are more than two categorical variables we can perform a Kruskal-Wallis test to determine a statistically significant difference between the categories. This does not quantify the difference in the same way as a Pearson test, and does not allow us to determine whether the correlation is positive or not, nor how strong it is. Instead we can only say that we performed the test and found

Task	Vectors	GloVe		BERT	
		L1	L2	L1	L2
SL	Vanilla	-0.7278	-0.3758	-0.1564	-0.1039
	Abl. norm	-0.1893	-0.0025	-0.0417	-0.0013
SN	Vanilla	0.0360	0.0268	0.0071	0.0146
	Abl. norm	0.0036	-0.0033	-0.0035	-0.0021
ON	Vanilla	0.0013	0.0008	-0.0736	-0.0583
	Abl. norm	0.0009	0.0013	-0.0181	-0.0010
TE	Vanilla	0.1152	0.0571	0.0542	0.0413
	Abl. norm	0.0277	-0.0031	0.0097	-0.0030
TD	Vanilla	-0.0817	0.1908	-0.0415	-0.0251
	Abl. norm	-0.0665	0.0016	-0.0163	-0.0045
CIN	Vanilla	-0.0019	-0.0094	-0.0755	-0.0638
	Abl. norm	0.0029	0.0018	-0.0152	-0.0015
BS	Vanilla	0.0040	0.0002	-0.3866	-0.3238
	Abl. norm	0.0022	0.0006	-0.0978	-0.0005
SOMO	Vanilla	-0.0464	-0.0222	-0.2414	-0.2305
	Abl. norm	-0.0105	0.0000	-0.0420	0.0021

Table 3: Pearson correlation coefficients between the class labels and vector norms for vanilla vectors and vectors with ablated norms.

our noise function to ablate the norm fully removes the information from the norms: the correlation between either norm and the class labels drops to ≈ 0,[15] indicating that information encoded by the norm and any distinguishing properties it may have had have been removed.

The data shows that most task labels do not exhibit a correlation with the vanilla GloVe norm. There is a moderate positive correlation between TD and the L2 norm, but not the L1 norm, and a weak positive correlation between TE and the L1 norm, but not the L2 norm. There is a high correlation between the SL labels and both norms, showing that GloVe uses the norm to encode sentence length, as reflected in our experiments in §4.

When it comes to vanilla BERT, most task labels do not exhibit a correlation with the norms. However, both norms have a weak negative correlation with SL, and a moderate negative correlation with BS and SOMO. The latter two are most highly correlated with BERT's norm, which also aligns with our experimental findings in §4.

5 Discussion

The correlation coefficients in Table 3 can be interpreted in terms of how these linguistic phenomena are encoded in vector space. A negative correlation coefficient means that larger norms indicate a negative class, while a positive coefficient means that larger norms indicate a positive class. For example, the negative correlation in SL-GloVe and SL-BERT indicates that longer sentences are positioned closer to the origin. The same interpretation holds for BERT embeddings on the BS and SOMO tasks; e.g. in SOMO a sentence containing an out of context word is positioned closer to the origin.

It is interesting that BERT's norm stores information on the BS and SOMO tasks specifically. Their common thread is a violation of the local context of the affected words: though the overall context and structure of the sentence is unaffected, there is a small, localised disruption in co-occurrences. Hence, these tasks capture contextual incongruity. Given that we know that BERT is a contextual encoder, and that its self-attention uses the vector norm to control the levels of contribution from less informative words (Kobayashi et al., 2020), we suspect that this gives it the capabilities to accurately model these short-distance dependencies and word co-occurence probabilities, concepts which strongly correspond to local contextual incongruity. BERT is evidently capable of encoding this signal well, and seems to be using its norm to supplement the encoding of the phenomenon in such a way that it positions sentences exhibiting local contextual incongruity closer to the origin, relative to sentences that do not contain it. Furthermore, BERT's ability to model incongruity via the norm could essentially be frequency-based, similar to how some word embeddings encode word frequency in the norm. In contrast, GloVe is a static encoder and exhibits no indication that it stores this information in the norm, or indeed any ability to accurately model this phenomenon at all, but uses the norm to store surface-level and syntactic information.

We emphasise the importance of the norm as it expands our understanding of the way information is encoded in vector space, but it could also have important implications for downstream tasks involving operations on vectors: e.g. the calculation of a cosine similarity measure normalises the vectors being compared. This nullifies the information in the norm, reducing the comparison to one of directions (i.e. dimensions), and any linguistic information encoded in the norm will be lost and unaccounted for when making the comparison.

the results to be significant, indicating some correlation.

[15]Except in GloVe-SL-L1 where the coefficient 'only' drops from strongly correlated to weakly correlated.

6 Related Work

Probing has been proposed seemingly independently by different groups of NLP researchers (Ettinger et al., 2016; Shi et al., 2016; Veldhoen et al., 2016; Adi et al., 2017) and has gained significant momentum in the community, helping to explore different aspects of text encodings (e.g. Hupkes et al. (2018); Giulianelli et al. (2018); Krasnowska-Kieraś and Wróblewska (2019); Tenney et al. (2019a); Lin et al. (2019); Şahin et al. (2020); Liu et al. (2021); Arps et al. (2022)). Probes trained on various representations successfully predict surface properties of sentences (Adi et al., 2017; Conneau et al., 2018), POS and morphological information (Belinkov et al., 2017a; Liu et al., 2019), as well as syntactic (Zhang and Bowman, 2018; Peters et al., 2018a; Tenney et al., 2019b), semantic (Belinkov et al., 2017b; Ahmad et al., 2018; Conia and Navigli, 2022), and even number (Wallace et al., 2019), emotions (Qian et al., 2016), idiomaticity (Salton et al., 2016; Nedumpozhimana and Kelleher, 2021; Garcia et al., 2021; Nedumpozhimana et al., 2022) and world knowledge information (Ettinger, 2020), among others (Belinkov and Glass, 2019; Rogers et al., 2020; Koto et al., 2021; Ousidhoum et al., 2021; Aghazadeh et al., 2022).

Furthermore, some dichotomies have emerged in the literature, due to nuanced differences in the presuppositions behind probing approaches. Ravichander et al. (2020) distinguish varying points of view on embeddings, highlighting a difference between *instrumentative* and *agentive* probing. Vig et al. (2020) view probing as a method of analysis and distinguish two types of methods: *structural* and *behavioural*. Additionally, Pimentel et al. (2020) and Voita and Titov (2020) take an information-theoretic perspective on embeddings, highlighting the tension between probing identifying the mere *presence* of information, versus its *extractability*. We position our work as being **instrumentative**, i.e. we view embeddings as tools that extract and store knowledge from text; we consider our probing method to be **structural**, i.e. it provides insight into how information is encoded within the representation and the vector space; and the goal of our work is to identify the **presence** of information in embedding components. It is important to clearly signpost this position in order to avoid confusion and emphasise that our chosen approach is sufficient to address our research questions.

Meanwhile, recent work calls for greater rigor in evaluation approaches in NLP (McCoy et al., 2020; Sadeqi Azer et al., 2020; Card et al., 2020), advocating for more widespread use of statistical tests on common benchmarks. Probing has attracted similar criticism: Hewitt and Liang (2019) have shown that under certain conditions, above-random probing accuracy can be achieved even when probing for linguistically-meaningless noise. Recent work addresses some of these problems by constructing counterfactual representations in order to compare the performance of the probe with and without the pertinent information (Feder et al., 2020). Similarly, Elazar et al. (2020) remove the relevant information from the representation, allowing a comparison of probe performance with and without the removed information; not unlike the intrinsic probe of Torroba Hennigen et al. (2020) who focus on isolating the dimensions that encode relevant information. In essence, these recent efforts address the issue of relativising probe interpretations by removing information from the encoding; in that sense, our work finds its place alongside them. However, our method is not meant to remove specific information, but is more exploratory in nature, with a focus on understanding where within an embedding certain information is encoded. Our use of confidence intervals gives us a way to claim statistically significant differences in our evaluations, offering a more principled basis for result interpretation.

Our work also contributes to the relatively scarce study of the role of the norm: Adi et al. (2017) explain its correlation with SL information due to the central limit theorem (which we see does not apply to BERT as its vector values are not centred around zero). Hewitt and Manning (2019) show that the squared L2 norm of BERT and ELMo corresponds to the depth of the word in a parse tree (a finding we could not confirm as they probe embeddings at the word level, unlike our work). In contrast, work on the role of dimensions as carriers of specific types of information is plentiful (e.g. Karpathy et al. (2015); Qian et al. (2016); Bau et al. (2019); Dalvi et al. (2019); Lakretz et al. (2019)). Work complementary to ours (Torroba Hennigen et al., 2020) which focuses on the dimension container also highlights the need for an intrinsic probe of embedding models, and shows that most linguistic properties are reliably encoded by only a handful of dimensions, a finding consistent with Durrani et al. (2020) and Durrani et al. (2022).

7 Conclusion

We have developed a method of enquiry that provides geometric insights into embeddings and show experimental evidence that both BERT and GloVe embeddings use two separate information containers to store different types of linguistic information. Our findings show that BERT primarily uses the norm to store contextual incongruity information and positions incongruous sentences closer to the origin. Meanwhile, GloVe stores much more syntactic information in its norm than BERT, but does not store contextual information at all, and mainly stores surface-level information in the norm.

Probing with noise can shift perspectives and broaden our understanding of embeddings, demonstrated by our experiments which provide novel insights into contextual and static encoders. However, they are by no means exhaustive: deeper and further applications of the method, such as exploring a host of other representations, different pooling strategies or tracking behavior across embedding layers, exploring word-level tasks or folding in additional datasets, are all fruitful avenues for future work. Fortunately, the method is robust enough to be applied to any encoder and any dataset, whether it is at the word or sentence level, which allows for systematic further study.

Limitations

While our insights into how linguistic information can be encoded in embeddings are valuable on their own merit, our experiments mainly serve the purpose of validating the *probing with noise* method, in demonstrating that it can produce relevant insights on different types of embeddings. Hence we did not have scope to more thoroughly pursue many of the topics touched upon in the paper.

One example is our choice in generating sentence embeddings needed to probe for sentence-level information. The encoders we have used generate word-level embeddings, so we average the word embeddings in each sentence, as this is one of the most popular ways to generate sentence representations. However, there are other known approaches available to choose from, such as max pooling and min pooling, or, when it comes to BERT, using the CLS token.[16] Indeed, rather than a pooling strategy, using direct sentence-level representations such as doc2vec (Le and Mikolov, 2014) or SentenceBERT (Reimers and Gurevych, 2019) might also be prudent, as well as applying the method to word-level representations, for which this paper did not allow scope.

Similarly, we have consistently used only one probing classifier, an MLP with default parameters, and we cannot say whether parameter tuning or different probes would yield different results. These choices were made consciously, in order to avoid adding more variables to our line of enquiry and increasing the complexity of our experiments, yet it is still a limitation in the sense that we do not know whether the findings generalise to other probes.

It is also worth noting that the correlation study in §4 comes with the limitation of only describing linear relationships, whereas it is possible that connections between variables can be non-linear. We argue that this demonstrates the value of our method, which allows for a non-linear probe to test for non-linear relationships. While even this limited correlation test can provide interesting insights, much more can be done to study both the norm and the dimension container—we have just barely scratched the surface. Indeed, we have considered only the most fundamental geometric properties of vectors, yet vectors have other (distributed) properties that could potentially be considered distinct information containers in their own right, such as the vector's minimum and maximum value, their ratio, the entropy in the vector etc. Thankfully the principles underpinning our method can be expanded to include other types of noise that help discriminate other possible geometric properties of embeddings as information containers.

These points speak to the more general limitations of our research: like any empirical work, we measure behaviours on a number of data points and draw conclusions from these measurements. Thus there is a risk that our findings hold only for the datasets on which we measured or the models which were used to measure, be it encoders, probes or probing tasks, and it is possible that our findings might not generalise to other settings. While this issue is more epistemological than it is specific to our work, we must keep it in mind. Now, having demonstrated that a signal is detectable in our particular setting, a more comprehensive host of studies is needed to draw more general conclusions.

Another source of uncertainty stems from our use of off-the-shelf GloVe and BERT embeddings:

[16]Presumably, we may have observed a crisper effect in BERT encoding incongruity using min or max pooling, given that the BS task mainly affects only a few vectors in a sentence.

they have been trained on completely different datasets of dramatically varying sizes and content. To truly test the interaction of their architectures with our method, the training data used to train their word embeddings should be identical between both encoders, however implementing this was not feasible in practice. Granted, using off-the-shelf varieties does provide insight into the functioning of well-known and commonly used embeddings, but it consequently limits the comparability of their results as we cannot confidently distinguish whether differences in probe performance are due to differences in encoder architecture or training data.

While we acknowledge a number of the work's limitations, we stress that all our choices have been made in a sound, informed and methodologically consistent manner. Here we simply highlight just how many choices have been made along the way, and how quickly the number of alternative paths grows the further back up the decision tree we look. While we believe that the work is fundamentally sound, each choice could have made for a drastically different suite of experiments and could potentially have yielded different results. In fact, we find this to be a very exciting motivator for future work, as this long list of "missed opportunities" only goes to show how young and rich this research area still is and how many more avenues there are to explore.

Acknowledgements

This research was conducted with the financial support of Science Foundation Ireland under Grant Agreements No. 13/RC/2106 and 13/RC/2106_P2 at the ADAPT SFI Research Centre at Technological University Dublin. ADAPT, the SFI Research Centre for AI-Driven Digital Content Technology, is funded by Science Foundation Ireland through the SFI Research Centres Programme, and is co-funded under the European Regional Development Fund.

References

Yossi Adi, Einat Kermany, Yonatan Belinkov, Ofer Lavi, and Yoav Goldberg. 2017. Fine-grained analysis of sentence embeddings using auxiliary prediction tasks. In *Proceedings of ICLR, 2017.*

Ehsan Aghazadeh, Mohsen Fayyaz, and Yadollah Yaghoobzadeh. 2022. Metaphors in pre-trained language models: Probing and generalization across datasets and languages. In *Proceedings of the 60th Annual Meeting of the Association for Computational Linguistics (Volume 1: Long Papers)*, pages 2037–2050, Dublin, Ireland. Association for Computational Linguistics.

Wasi Uddin Ahmad, Xueying Bai, Zhechao Huang, Chao Jiang, Nanyun Peng, and Kai-Wei Chang. 2018. Multi-task learning for universal sentence embeddings: A thorough evaluation using transfer and auxiliary tasks.

Howard Anton and Chris Rorres. 2013. *Elementary linear algebra: applications version.* John Wiley & Sons.

David Arps, Younes Samih, Laura Kallmeyer, and Hassan Sajjad. 2022. Probing for constituency structure in neural language models.

Kaspars Balodis and Daiga Deksne. 2018. Intent detection system based on word embeddings. In *Artificial Intelligence: Methodology, Systems, and Applications*, pages 25–35, Cham. Springer International Publishing.

Anthony Bau, Yonatan Belinkov, Hassan Sajjad, Nadir Durrani, Fahim Dalvi, and James Glass. 2019. Identifying and controlling important neurons in neural machine translation. In *International Conference on Learning Representations.*

Yonatan Belinkov, Nadir Durrani, Fahim Dalvi, Hassan Sajjad, and James Glass. 2017a. What do neural machine translation models learn about morphology? In *Proceedings of the 55th Annual Meeting of the Association for Computational Linguistics (Volume 1: Long Papers)*, pages 861–872, Vancouver, Canada. Association for Computational Linguistics.

Yonatan Belinkov and James Glass. 2019. Analysis methods in neural language processing: A survey. *Transactions of the Association for Computational Linguistics*, 7:49–72.

Yonatan Belinkov, Lluís Màrquez, Hassan Sajjad, Nadir Durrani, Fahim Dalvi, and James Glass. 2017b. Evaluating layers of representation in neural machine translation on part-of-speech and semantic tagging tasks. In *Proceedings of the Eighth International Joint Conference on Natural Language Processing (Volume 1: Long Papers)*, pages 1–10, Taipei, Taiwan. Asian Federation of Natural Language Processing.

Dallas Card, Peter Henderson, Urvashi Khandelwal, Robin Jia, Kyle Mahowald, and Dan Jurafsky. 2020. With little power comes great responsibility. In *Proceedings of the 2020 Conference on Empirical Methods in Natural Language Processing (EMNLP)*, pages 9263–9274, Online. Association for Computational Linguistics.

Simone Conia and Roberto Navigli. 2022. Probing for predicate argument structures in pretrained language models. In *Proceedings of the 60th Annual Meeting of the Association for Computational Linguistics (Volume 1: Long Papers)*, pages 4622–4632, Dublin, Ireland. Association for Computational Linguistics.

Alexis Conneau, German Kruszewski, Guillaume Lample, Loïc Barrault, and Marco Baroni. 2018. What you can cram into a single $&!#* vector: Probing sentence embeddings for linguistic properties. In *Proceedings of the 56th Annual Meeting of the Association for Computational Linguistics (Volume 1: Long Papers)*, pages 2126–2136, Melbourne, Australia. Association for Computational Linguistics.

Bhavana Dalvi, Niket Tandon, Antoine Bosselut, Wen-tau Yih, and Peter Clark. 2019. Everything happens for a reason: Discovering the purpose of actions in procedural text. In *Proceedings of the 2019 Conference on Empirical Methods in Natural Language Processing and the 9th International Joint Conference on Natural Language Processing (EMNLP-IJCNLP)*, pages 4496–4505, Hong Kong, China. Association for Computational Linguistics.

Jacob Devlin, Ming-Wei Chang, Kenton Lee, and Kristina Toutanova. 2019. BERT: Pre-training of deep bidirectional transformers for language understanding. In *Proceedings of the 2019 Conference of the North American Chapter of the Association for Computational Linguistics: Human Language Technologies, Volume 1 (Long and Short Papers)*, pages 4171–4186, Minneapolis, Minnesota. Association for Computational Linguistics.

Nadir Durrani, Fahim Dalvi, and Hassan Sajjad. 2022. Linguistic correlation analysis: Discovering salient neurons in deepnlp models. *arXiv preprint arXiv:2206.13288*.

Nadir Durrani, Hassan Sajjad, Fahim Dalvi, and Yonatan Belinkov. 2020. Analyzing individual neurons in pre-trained language models. In *Proceedings of the 2020 Conference on Empirical Methods in Natural Language Processing (EMNLP)*, pages 4865–4880, Online. Association for Computational Linguistics.

Yanai Elazar, Shauli Ravfogel, Alon Jacovi, and Yoav Goldberg. 2020. When bert forgets how to POS: Amnesic probing of linguistic properties and MLM predictions. *arXiv preprint arXiv:2006.00995*.

Allyson Ettinger. 2020. What bert is not: Lessons from a new suite of psycholinguistic diagnostics for language models. *Transactions of the Association for Computational Linguistics*, 8:34–48.

Allyson Ettinger, Ahmed Elgohary, and Philip Resnik. 2016. Probing for semantic evidence of composition by means of simple classification tasks. In *Proceedings of the 1st Workshop on Evaluating Vector-Space Representations for NLP*, pages 134–139, Berlin, Germany. Association for Computational Linguistics.

Amir Feder, Nadav Oved, Uri Shalit, and Roi Reichart. 2020. CausaLM: Causal model explanation through counterfactual language models. *arXiv preprint arXiv:2005.13407*.

Marcos Garcia, Tiago Kramer Vieira, Carolina Scarton, Marco Idiart, and Aline Villavicencio. 2021. Probing for idiomaticity in vector space models. In *Proceedings of the 16th Conference of the European Chapter of the Association for Computational Linguistics: Main Volume*, pages 3551–3564, Online. Association for Computational Linguistics.

Mario Giulianelli, Jack Harding, Florian Mohnert, Dieuwke Hupkes, and Willem Zuidema. 2018. Under the hood: Using diagnostic classifiers to investigate and improve how language models track agreement information. In *Proceedings of the 2018 EMNLP Workshop BlackboxNLP: Analyzing and Interpreting Neural Networks for NLP*, pages 240–248.

Yoav Goldberg. 2017. Neural network methods for natural language processing. *Synthesis Lectures on Human Language Technologies*, 10(1):117.

Jim Hefferon. 2018. *Linear Algebra*. openintro.org.

John Hewitt and Percy Liang. 2019. Designing and interpreting probes with control tasks. In *Proceedings of the 2019 Conference on Empirical Methods in Natural Language Processing and the 9th International Joint Conference on Natural Language Processing (EMNLP-IJCNLP)*, pages 2733–2743, Hong Kong, China. Association for Computational Linguistics.

John Hewitt and Christopher D. Manning. 2019. A structural probe for finding syntax in word representations. In *Proceedings of the 2019 Conference of the North American Chapter of the Association for Computational Linguistics: Human Language Technologies, Volume 1 (Long and Short Papers)*, pages 4129–4138, Minneapolis, Minnesota. Association for Computational Linguistics.

Dieuwke Hupkes, Sara Veldhoen, and Willem Zuidema. 2018. Visualisation and 'diagnostic classifiers' reveal how recurrent and recursive neural networks process hierarchical structure. *Journal of Artificial Intelligence Research*, 61:907–926.

Andrej Karpathy, Justin Johnson, and Fei-Fei Li. 2015. Visualizing and understanding recurrent networks. *CoRR*, abs/1506.02078.

Goro Kobayashi, Tatsuki Kuribayashi, Sho Yokoi, and Kentaro Inui. 2020. Attention is not only a weight: Analyzing transformers with vector norms. In *Proceedings of the 2020 Conference on Empirical Methods in Natural Language Processing (EMNLP)*, pages 7057–7075, Online. Association for Computational Linguistics.

Fajri Koto, Jey Han Lau, and Timothy Baldwin. 2021. Discourse probing of pretrained language models. In *Proceedings of the 2021 Conference of the North American Chapter of the Association for Computational Linguistics: Human Language Technologies*, pages 3849–3864, Online. Association for Computational Linguistics.

Katarzyna Krasnowska-Kieraś and Alina Wróblewska. 2019. Empirical linguistic study of sentence embeddings. In *Proceedings of the 57th Annual Meeting of the Association for Computational Linguistics*, pages 5729–5739, Florence, Italy. Association for Computational Linguistics.

Yair Lakretz, German Kruszewski, Theo Desbordes, Dieuwke Hupkes, Stanislas Dehaene, and Marco Baroni. 2019. The emergence of number and syntax units in LSTM language models. In *Proceedings of the 2019 Conference of the North American Chapter of the Association for Computational Linguistics: Human Language Technologies, Volume 1 (Long and Short Papers)*, pages 11–20, Minneapolis, Minnesota. Association for Computational Linguistics.

Quoc Le and Tomas Mikolov. 2014. Distributed representations of sentences and documents. In *International conference on machine learning*, pages 1188–1196. PMLR.

Yongjie Lin, Yi Chern Tan, and Robert Frank. 2019. Open sesame: Getting inside bert's linguistic knowledge. In *Proceedings of the 2019 ACL Workshop BlackboxNLP: Analyzing and Interpreting Neural Networks for NLP*, pages 241–253.

Nelson F. Liu, Matt Gardner, Yonatan Belinkov, Matthew E. Peters, and Noah A. Smith. 2019. Linguistic knowledge and transferability of contextual representations. In *Proceedings of the 2019 Conference of the North American Chapter of the Association for Computational Linguistics: Human Language Technologies, Volume 1 (Long and Short Papers)*, pages 1073–1094, Minneapolis, Minnesota. Association for Computational Linguistics.

Zeyu Liu, Yizhong Wang, Jungo Kasai, Hannaneh Hajishirzi, and Noah A. Smith. 2021. Probing across time: What does RoBERTa know and when? In *Findings of the Association for Computational Linguistics: EMNLP 2021*, pages 820–842, Punta Cana, Dominican Republic. Association for Computational Linguistics.

R. Thomas McCoy, Junghyun Min, and Tal Linzen. 2020. BERTs of a feather do not generalize together: Large variability in generalization across models with similar test set performance. In *Proceedings of the Third BlackboxNLP Workshop on Analyzing and Interpreting Neural Networks for NLP*, pages 217–227, Online. Association for Computational Linguistics.

Vasudevan Nedumpozhimana and John Kelleher. 2021. Finding BERT's idiomatic key. In *Proceedings of the 17th Workshop on Multiword Expressions (MWE 2021)*, pages 57–62, Online. Association for Computational Linguistics.

Vasudevan Nedumpozhimana, Filip Klubička, and John D. Kelleher. 2022. Shapley idioms: Analysing bert sentence embeddings for general idiom token identification. *Frontiers in Artificial Intelligence*, 5.

Nedjma Ousidhoum, Xinran Zhao, Tianqing Fang, Yangqiu Song, and Dit-Yan Yeung. 2021. Probing toxic content in large pre-trained language models. In *Proceedings of the 59th Annual Meeting of the Association for Computational Linguistics and the 11th International Joint Conference on Natural Language Processing (Volume 1: Long Papers)*, pages 4262–4274, Online. Association for Computational Linguistics.

Adam Paszke, Sam Gross, Francisco Massa, Adam Lerer, James Bradbury, Gregory Chanan, Trevor Killeen, Zeming Lin, Natalia Gimelshein, Luca Antiga, Alban Desmaison, Andreas Kopf, Edward Yang, Zachary DeVito, Martin Raison, Alykhan Tejani, Sasank Chilamkurthy, Benoit Steiner, Lu Fang, Junjie Bai, and Soumith Chintala. 2019. Pytorch: An imperative style, high-performance deep learning library. In H. Wallach, H. Larochelle, A. Beygelzimer, F. d'Alché-Buc, E. Fox, and R. Garnett, editors, *Advances in Neural Information Processing Systems 32*, pages 8024–8035. Curran Associates, Inc.

F. Pedregosa, G. Varoquaux, A. Gramfort, V. Michel, B. Thirion, O. Grisel, M. Blondel, P. Prettenhofer, R. Weiss, V. Dubourg, J. Vanderplas, A. Passos, D. Cournapeau, M. Brucher, M. Perrot, and E. Duchesnay. 2011. Scikit-learn: Machine learning in Python. *Journal of Machine Learning Research*, 12:2825–2830.

Jeffrey Pennington, Richard Socher, and Christopher Manning. 2014. Glove: Global vectors for word representation. In *Proceedings of the 2014 conference on empirical methods in natural language processing (EMNLP)*, pages 1532–1543.

Matthew Peters, Mark Neumann, Luke Zettlemoyer, and Wen-tau Yih. 2018a. Dissecting contextual word embeddings: Architecture and representation. In *Proceedings of the 2018 Conference on Empirical Methods in Natural Language Processing*, pages 1499–1509.

Matthew E. Peters, Mark Neumann, Mohit Iyyer, Matt Gardner, Christopher Clark, Kenton Lee, and Luke Zettlemoyer. 2018b. Deep contextualized word representations. *CoRR*, abs/1802.05365.

Tiago Pimentel, Josef Valvoda, Rowan Hall Maudslay, Ran Zmigrod, Adina Williams, and Ryan Cotterell. 2020. Information-theoretic probing for linguistic structure. In *Proceedings of the 58th Annual Meeting of the Association for Computational Linguistics*, pages 4609–4622, Online. Association for Computational Linguistics.

Peng Qian, Xipeng Qiu, and Xuanjing Huang. 2016. Investigating language universal and specific properties in word embeddings. In *Proceedings of the 54th Annual Meeting of the Association for Computational Linguistics (Volume 1: Long Papers)*, pages 1478–1488, Berlin, Germany. Association for Computational Linguistics.

Abhilasha Ravichander, Eduard Hovy, Kaheer Suleman, Adam Trischler, and Jackie Chi Kit Cheung. 2020. On the systematicity of probing contextualized word representations: The case of hypernymy in bert. In *Proceedings of the Ninth Joint Conference on Lexical and Computational Semantics*, pages 88–102.

Nils Reimers and Iryna Gurevych. 2019. Sentence-BERT: Sentence embeddings using Siamese BERT-networks. In *Proceedings of the 2019 Conference on Empirical Methods in Natural Language Processing and the 9th International Joint Conference on Natural Language Processing (EMNLP-IJCNLP)*, pages 3982–3992, Hong Kong, China. Association for Computational Linguistics.

Anna Rogers, Olga Kovaleva, and Anna Rumshisky. 2020. A primer in BERTology: What we know about how BERT works. *Transactions of the Association for Computational Linguistics*, 8:842–866.

Erfan Sadeqi Azer, Daniel Khashabi, Ashish Sabharwal, and Dan Roth. 2020. Not all claims are created equal: Choosing the right statistical approach to assess hypotheses. In *Proceedings of the 58th Annual Meeting of the Association for Computational Linguistics*, pages 5715–5725, Online. Association for Computational Linguistics.

Gözde Gül Şahin, Clara Vania, Ilia Kuznetsov, and Iryna Gurevych. 2020. LINSPECTOR: Multilingual probing tasks for word representations. *Computational Linguistics*, 46(2):335–385.

Giancarlo Salton, Robert Ross, and John Kelleher. 2016. Idiom token classification using sentential distributed semantics. In *Proceedings of the 54th Annual Meeting of the Association for Computational Linguistics (Volume 1: Long Papers)*, pages 194–204, Berlin, Germany. Association for Computational Linguistics.

Adriaan MJ Schakel and Benjamin J Wilson. 2015. Measuring word significance using distributed representations of words. *arXiv preprint arXiv:1508.02297*.

Xing Shi, Inkit Padhi, and Kevin Knight. 2016. Does string-based neural MT learn source syntax? In *Proceedings of the 2016 Conference on Empirical Methods in Natural Language Processing*, pages 1526–1534, Austin, Texas. Association for Computational Linguistics.

Ian Tenney, Dipanjan Das, and Ellie Pavlick. 2019a. BERT rediscovers the classical NLP pipeline. In *Proceedings of the 57th Annual Meeting of the Association for Computational Linguistics*, pages 4593–4601, Florence, Italy. Association for Computational Linguistics.

Ian Tenney, Patrick Xia, Berlin Chen, Alex Wang, Adam Poliak, R Thomas McCoy, Najoung Kim, Benjamin Van Durme, Samuel Bowman, Dipanjan Das, et al. 2019b. What do you learn from context? probing for sentence structure in contextualized word representations. In *7th International Conference on Learning Representations, ICLR 2019*.

Lucas Torroba Hennigen, Adina Williams, and Ryan Cotterell. 2020. Intrinsic probing through dimension selection. In *Proceedings of the 2020 Conference on Empirical Methods in Natural Language Processing (EMNLP)*, pages 197–216, Online. Association for Computational Linguistics.

Sara Veldhoen, Dieuwke Hupkes, and Willem H Zuidema. 2016. Diagnostic classifiers revealing how neural networks process hierarchical structure. In *Workshop on Cognitive Computation: Integrating Neural and Symbolic Approaches (at NIPS)*.

Jesse Vig, Sebastian Gehrmann, Yonatan Belinkov, Sharon Qian, Daniel Nevo, Simas Sakenis, Jason Huang, Yaron Singer, and Stuart Shieber. 2020. Causal mediation analysis for interpreting neural nlp: The case of gender bias. *arXiv preprint arXiv:2004.12265*.

Elena Voita and Ivan Titov. 2020. Information-theoretic probing with minimum description length. In *Proceedings of the 2020 Conference on Empirical Methods in Natural Language Processing (EMNLP)*, pages 183–196, Online. Association for Computational Linguistics.

Eric Wallace, Yizhong Wang, Sujian Li, Sameer Singh, and Matt Gardner. 2019. Do NLP models know numbers? probing numeracy in embeddings. In *Proceedings of the 2019 Conference on Empirical Methods in Natural Language Processing and the 9th International Joint Conference on Natural Language Processing (EMNLP-IJCNLP)*, pages 5307–5315, Hong Kong, China. Association for Computational Linguistics.

Kelly Zhang and Samuel Bowman. 2018. Language modeling teaches you more than translation does: Lessons learned through auxiliary syntactic task analysis. In *Proceedings of the 2018 EMNLP Workshop BlackboxNLP: Analyzing and Interpreting Neural Networks for NLP*, pages 359–361, Brussels, Belgium. Association for Computational Linguistics.

A Appendix A

A.1 Analysis of L1 and L2 Normalised Embeddings

Table 4 presents an extended Pearson correlation analysis that includes correlations between class labels and the norms of L1- and L2-normalised vectors, in addition to vanilla vectors and vectors with ablated norm information using our noising function as described in §2.

As supported by Goldberg (2017, page 117), the results show that normalising the vectors removes information encoded in the norm. This also comes

Task	Vectors	GloVe		BERT	
		L1	L2	L1	L2
SL	Vanilla	-0.7278	-0.3758	-0.1564	-0.1039
	L1 normal.	-0.0013	0.7161	0.0032	0.2195
	L2 normal.	-0.7027	0.0001	-0.2223	0.0001
	Abl. norm	-0.1893	-0.0025	-0.0417	-0.0013
SN	Vanilla	0.0360	0.0268	0.0071	0.0146
	L1 normal.	0.0028	-0.0228	-0.0010	0.0087
	L2 normal.	0.0255	-0.0019	-0.0086	-0.0003
	Abl. norm	0.0036	-0.0033	-0.0035	-0.0021
ON	Vanilla	0.0013	0.0008	-0.0736	-0.0583
	L1 normal.	-0.0016	0.0048	-0.0015	0.0892
	L2 normal.	-0.0004	-0.0015	-0.0901	0.0037
	Abl. norm	0.0009	0.0013	-0.0181	-0.0010
TE	Vanilla	-0.1152	-0.0571	-0.0542	-0.0413
	L1 normal.	-0.0020	0.1040	-0.0023	0.0659
	L2 normal.	-0.1071	-0.0006	-0.0691	-0.0018
	Abl. norm	-0.0317	-0.0007	-0.0116	0.0010
TD	Vanilla	-0.0817	0.1908	-0.0415	-0.0251
	L1 normal.	0.0005	0.3133	0.0021	0.0645
	L2 normal.	-0.3159	-0.0026	-0.0652	0.0000
	Abl. norm	-0.0665	0.0016	-0.0163	-0.0045
CIN	Vanilla	-0.0019	-0.0094	-0.0755	-0.0638
	L1 normal.	0.0000	-0.0062	-0.0047	0.0846
	L2 normal.	0.0065	0.0064	-0.0850	0.0034
	Abl. norm	0.0029	0.0018	-0.0152	-0.0015
BS	Vanilla	0.0040	0.0002	-0.3866	-0.3238
	L1 normal.	-0.0015	-0.0048	0.0004	0.4333
	L2 normal.	0.0056	-0.0019	-0.4357	0.0024
	Abl. norm	0.0022	0.0006	-0.0978	-0.0005
SO MO	Vanilla	-0.0464	-0.0222	-0.2414	-0.2305
	L1 normal.	0.0031	0.0401	0.0035	0.2213
	L2 normal.	-0.0392	-0.0014	-0.2219	0.0023
	Abl. norm	-0.0105	0.0000	-0.0420	0.0021

Table 4: Pearson correlation coefficients between the class labels and vector norms for vanilla vectors, L1 and L2 normalised vectors, as well as vectors with ablated L2 norm containers.

with a caveat: normalisation only removes information from the same order norm as the normalisation algorithm. We can observe this in the table: applying an L1 normalisation algorithm to the vectors seems to completely remove any information encoded in the L1 norm, as the correlation drops to ≈ 0. The same happens to the correlation with the L2 norm when applying L2 normalisation. However, surprisingly, it seems that a given normalisation algorithm impacts the other norm as well. For example, in the BS task L2 normalisation nullifies the L2 norm's correlation with the class labels, but in turn strengthens that correlation for the L1 norm, which intensifies from -0.39 to -0.44. On the other hand, L1 normalisation causes the same strengthening of correlation in the L2 norm, but also changes the sign—the L2 norm's correlation with BS class labels increases from -0.32 to 0.43.

This shows that on certain tasks, not only is the other norm unaffected by a normalisation procedure, but its correlation with the task labels increases. We observe this to varying degrees in SL, ON, TE and BS. Furthermore, while the correlation weakens in SOMO, it still exhibits the latter behaviour—the sign changes when the vectors are L1 normalised, but not when they are L2 normalised. This is prevalent across all datasets, even in cases where the correlation between norm and class labels is ≈ 0.

This analysis supports our decision from §2 to use a different noising function to remove information from the norm container, as only the vectors with fully ablated norms have an ≈ 0 correlation with both the L1 and L2 norms.

Look to the Right: Mitigating Relative Position Bias in Extractive Question Answering

Kazutoshi Shinoda[1,2] **Saku Sugawara**[2] **Akiko Aizawa**[1,2]
[1]The University of Tokyo
[2]National Institute of Informatics
shinoda@is.s.u-tokyo.ac.jp
{saku,aizawa}@nii.ac.jp

Abstract

Extractive question answering (QA) models tend to exploit spurious correlations to make predictions when a training set has unintended biases. This tendency results in models not being generalizable to examples where the correlations do not hold. Determining the spurious correlations QA models can exploit is crucial in building generalizable QA models in real-world applications; moreover, a method needs to be developed that prevents these models from learning the spurious correlations even when a training set is biased. In this study, we discovered that the relative position of an answer, which is defined as the relative distance from an answer span to the closest question-context overlap word, can be exploited by QA models as superficial cues for making predictions. Specifically, we find that when the relative positions in a training set are biased, the performance on examples with relative positions unseen during training is significantly degraded. To mitigate the performance degradation for unseen relative positions, we propose an ensemble-based debiasing method that does not require prior knowledge about the distribution of relative positions. We demonstrate that the proposed method mitigates the models' reliance on relative positions using the biased and full SQuAD dataset. We hope that this study can help enhance the generalization ability of QA models in real-world applications.[1]

1 Introduction

Deep learning-based natural language understanding (NLU) models are prone to use spurious correlations in the training set. This tendency results in models' poor generalization ability to out-of-distribution test sets (McCoy et al., 2019; Geirhos et al., 2020), which is a significant challenge in the field. Question answering (QA) models trained on intentionally biased training sets are more likely

Context	... This changed in **1924** with formal requirements developed for graduate degrees, including offering Doctorate (PhD) degrees ...
Question	The granting of Doctorate degrees first occurred in what year at Notre Dame?
Relative Position	-1
Context	... The other magazine, The Juggler, is released **twice** a year and focuses on student literature and artwork ...
Question	How often is Notre Dame's the Juggler published?
Relative Position	-2

Table 1: Examples taken from SQuAD. Underlined words are contained in both the context and question. **Bold** spans are the answers to the questions. In both the examples, answers are found by *looking to the right* from the overlapping words. See §2.1 for the definition of the relative position.

to learn solutions based on spurious correlations rather than on causal relationships between inputs and labels. For example, QA models can learn question-answer type matching heuristics (Lewis and Fan, 2019), and absolute-positional correlations (Ko et al., 2020), particularly when a training set is biased toward examples with corresponding spurious correlations. Collecting a fully unbiased dataset is challenging. Therefore, it is vital to discover possible dataset biases that can degrade the generalization and develop debiasing methods to learn generalizable solutions even when training on unintentionally biased datasets.

In extractive QA (e.g., Rajpurkar et al., 2016), in which answers to questions are spans in textual contexts, we find that the relative position of an answer, which is defined as the relative distance from an answer span to the closest word that appears in both a context and a question, can be exploited as superficial cues by QA models. See Table 1 for the

[1]Our codes are available at https://github.com/KazutoshiShinoda/RelativePositionBias.

Proceedings of the Fifth BlackboxNLP Workshop on Analyzing and Interpreting Neural Networks for NLP, pages 418 - 425
December 8, 2022 ©2022 Association for Computational Linguistics

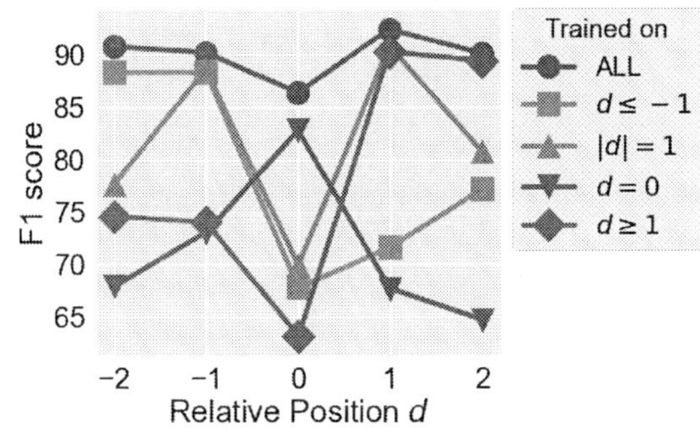

Figure 1: F1 score for each relative position d in the SQuAD development set. "ALL" in the legend refers to a QA model trained on all the examples in the SQuAD training set. The other terms refer to models trained only on examples for which the respective conditionals are satisfied. BERT-base was used for the QA models. The accuracy is comparable to ALL for examples with seen relative positions, but worse for others. Please refer to §2.1 for the definition of d.

examples. Specifically, we find that when the relative positions are intentionally biased in a training set, a QA model tends to degrade the performance on examples where answers are located in relative positions unseen during training, as shown in Figure 1. For example, when a QA model is trained on examples with negative relative positions, as shown in Table 1, the QA performance on examples with non-negative relative positions is degraded by 10 $\sim$ 20 points, as indicated by the square markers (■) in Figure 1. Similar phenomena were observed when the distribution of the relative positions in the training set was biased differently, as shown in Figure 1. This observation implies that the model may preferentially learn to find answers from seen relative positions.

We aim to develop a method for mitigating the performance degradation on subsets with unseen relative positions while maintaining the scores on subsets with seen relative positions, even when the training set is biased with respect to relative positions. To this end, we propose debiasing methods based on an ensemble (Hinton, 2002) of intentionally biased and main models. The biased model makes predictions relying on relative positions, which promotes the main model not depending solely on relative positions. Our experiments on SQuAD (Rajpurkar et al., 2016) using BERT-base (Devlin et al., 2019) as the main model show that the proposed methods improved the scores for unseen relative positions by 0$\sim$10 points. We demonstrate that the proposed method is effective in four settings where the training set is differently filtered to be biased with respect to relative positions. Furthermore, when applied to the full training set, our method improves the generalization to examples where questions and contexts have no lexical overlap.

2 Relative Position Bias

2.1 Definition

In this study, we call a word that is contained in both the question and the context as an overlapping word. Let d be the relative position of the nearest overlapping word from the answer span in extractive QA. If w is a word, $c = \{w_i^c\}_{i=0}^N$ for the sentence, $q = \{w_i^q\}_{i=0}^M$ for the question, and $a = \{w_i^c\}_{i=s}^e$ $(0 \leq s \leq e \leq N)$ for the answer, the relative position d is defined as follows:

$$f(j,s,e) = \begin{cases} j-s, & \text{for } j < s \\ 0, & \text{for } s \leq j \leq e \\ j-e, & \text{for } j > e \end{cases} \quad (1)$$

$$D = \{f(j,s,e) | w_j^c \in q\} \quad (2)$$

$$d = \text{argmin}_{d' \in D} |d'| \quad (3)$$

where $0 \leq j \leq N$ denotes the position of the word w_j^c in the sentence, $f(i,s,e)$ denotes the relative position of w_i^c from a, and D denotes the set of relative positions of all overlapping words.[2] Because QA models favor spans that are located close to the overlapping words (Jia and Liang, 2017) and accuracy deteriorates when the absolute distance between the answer span and the overlapping word is considerable (Sugawara et al., 2018), the one with the lowest absolute value in Equation 3 is used as the relative position.[3]

2.2 Distribution of Relative Position d

Figure 2 shows the distribution of relative position d in the SQuAD (Rajpurkar et al., 2016) training set. This demonstrates that the d values are biased around zero. Although the tendency to bias around zero is consistent for the other QA datasets, there are differences in the distribution between the datasets. See Appendix B for more details. This

[2]Because function words as well as content words are important clues for reading comprehension, D in Equation 2 can contain function and content words.

[3]There are a few cases where d in Equation 3 is not fixed to one value. However, such examples are excluded from the training and evaluation sets for brevity.

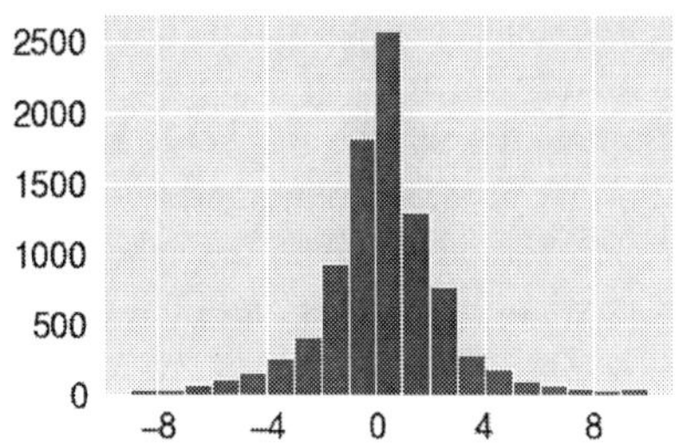

Figure 2: Histogram of relative position d in the SQuAD training set.

difference may be caused by how the datasets were collected or to the contexts' domains. Therefore, building a QA model that does not overfit a specific distribution of relative positions is necessary.

3 Method

3.1 Debiasing Algorithm

For debiasing algorithms, we employ BiasProduct and LearnedMixin (Clark et al., 2019; He et al., 2019), which are based on product-of-experts (Hinton, 2002), following Ko et al. (2020). In both methods, after an intentionally biased model is prepared, the cross-entropy loss is calculated using a product of the biased and main models. The biased model is fixed when minimizing the loss to train the main model. Only the main model is used to make predictions during testing. Following existing research (Seo et al., 2017; Devlin et al., 2019), the model $\hat{p}$ outputs the probabilities $\hat{p}(s)$ and $\hat{p}(e)$ of the start position s and the end position e of the answer span, and the loss function is the sum of the cross-entropy of the start and end positions. For simplicity, $\hat{p}(s)$ and $\hat{p}(e)$ will be denoted as $\hat{p}$.

3.1.1 BiasProduct

In BiasProduct, the sum of the logarithms of the output probability b of the biased model and the output probability p of the main model is given to the softmax function to obtain $\hat{p}$, as follows.

$$\hat{p} = \text{softmax}(\log p + \log b) \tag{4}$$

This encourages the the main model to learn examples where the biased model make incorrect predictions, rather than examples that contain biases allowing the biased model to make correct predictions.

3.1.2 LearnedMixin

BiasProduct strongly depends on the output probability of the biased model. The main model can be made more robust by using LearnedMixin, which predicts whether the main model can trust the prediction of the biased model for each example.

$$\hat{p} = \text{softmax}(\log p + g(c, q) \log b) \tag{5}$$

where $g(\geq 0)$ is a learnable function that takes q and c as inputs.

3.2 Biased Model

We describe how to construct the biased model described in §3.1. The first model, Answer Prior, is a fully rule-based model with a prior probability of answer span. The second, the Position-only model, is a QA model trained with only binarized contexts from which models can know only which token is an overlapping word.

3.2.1 Answer Prior (AnsPrior)

We first use a simple heuristic called AnsPrior as a biased model. AnsPrior empirically defines the prior probabilities of the start and end positions of the answer span a according to the distribution of the relative position d in a training set. The prior probability b_i that a word w_i^c in a sentence is a start or end of the answer is defined as follows for each of the subsets of the training set that satisfies one of the four conditions shown in the legend of Figure 1.

$$b_i = \begin{cases} \mathbb{1}\left[w_{i+1}^c \in q\right]/Z, & \text{for } d \leq -1 \\ \mathbb{1}\left[(w_{i+1}^c \in q) \vee (w_{i-1}^c \in q)\right]/Z, & \text{for } |d| = 1 \\ \mathbb{1}\left[w_i^c \in q\right]/Z, & \text{for } d = 0 \\ \mathbb{1}\left[w_{i-1}^c \in q\right]/Z, & \text{for } d \geq 1 \end{cases} \tag{6}$$

where $\mathbb{1}$ denotes an indicator function (e.g., $\mathbb{1}\left[w_{i+1}^c \in q\right]$ returns 1 if w_{i+1}^c is contained in q, otherwise it returns 0) and Z denotes a normalizing constant. These prior probabilities are based on a heuristic that assigns equal probabilities to the possible answers in the training set. Therefore, they are inflexible as they are prior probabilities specific to the distribution of relative positions of a training set.

3.2.2 Position-only model (PosOnly)

We propose PosOnly as a biased model that can be used without prior knowledge about the distributions of relative positions in training sets. PosOnly accepts as input the sequence of binary variables indicating if a word in a context is overlapped

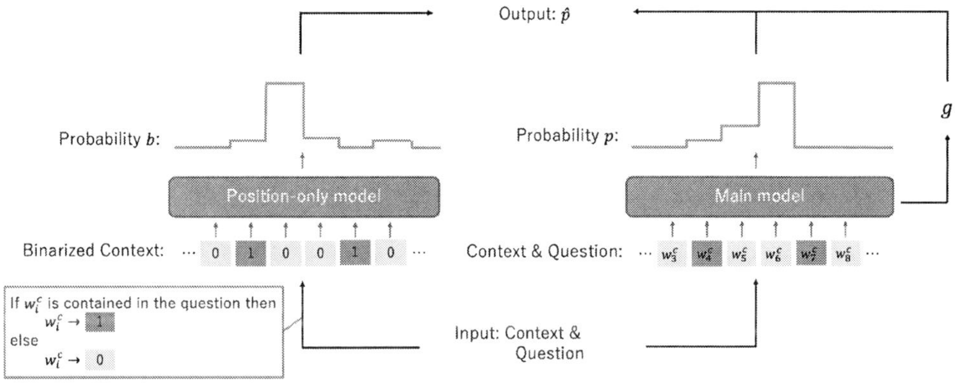

Figure 3: Illustration of LearnedMixin with Position-only model (PosOnly) as a biased model. The output $\hat{p}$ is used for computing the loss, and the probability p is used for inference.

with a question. The only information available to PosOnly to predict answer spans is the relative distances from the overlapping words. Hence, it is expected to learn solutions using the relative positions regardless of how biased the relative positions of the training set are. The illustration of LearnedMixin with PosOnly is shown in Figure 3.

4 Experiments

4.1 Generalization to Unseen Relative Positions

Dataset SQuAD 1.1 (Rajpurkar et al., 2016) was used as the dataset. The training set is filtered to be biased in four different ways to assess the applicability of our methods. The four subsets were constructed by extracting only examples whose relative positions d satisfied the conditions $d \leq -1$, $|d| = 1$, $d = 0$, and $d \geq 1$. The sizes of the subsets are 33,256, 30,003, 21,266, and 25,191, respectively. The scores of BERT-base trained on the full training set are also reported for comparison. For evaluation, we reported the F1 scores on subsets of the SQuAD development set stratified by the relative positions.

Method We compare four combinations of two learning methods for debiasing, BiasProduct and LearnedMixin, and two biased models, AnsPrior and PosOnly. BERT-base (Devlin et al., 2019) was used for both the main model and PosOnly. We also evaluate the BERT-base with standard training as the baseline. The training details are given in Appendix A.

Results Table 2 shows the results. First, when the full training set is used (ALL), the performance of the BERT-base baseline exceeds 90 points when $|d| = 1, 2$, whereas it drops by about eight points when $|d| \geq 3$. As shown in §2.2, there is a correlation between the accuracy for a specific range of relative positions and the frequency of examples whose relative positions are in the corresponding range in the training set.

The results of the BERT-base baseline trained on subsets where the distribution of relative position d was intentionally biased strengthened the credibility of this hypothesis. For example, when the standard training was performed only on examples with relative positions $|d| = 1$, the F1 score decreased by less than two points for $|d| = 1$ compared to ALL, whereas the F1 score decreased by 10$\sim$15 points for $|d| \neq 1$. A similar trend was observed in the BERT-base baseline trained on other subsets. This suggests that the model exploited spurious correlations regarding relative positions in the biased subsets to make predictions.

We compare the four proposed debiasing methods under the same conditions of relative positions in the training sets. For the debiasing algorithms, LearnedMixin produced higher F1 scores than BiasProduct in most cases. This result shows the effectiveness of learning the degree to which the predictions of a biased model should be utilized for training the main model. For the biased models, PosOnly was superior to AnsPrior for improving the generalization ability to examples with relative positions unseen during training, i.e., the scores in white cells in Table 2. LearnedMixin-PosOnly outperformed LearnedMixin-AnsPrior by about 5 points when trained on $d = 0$ and tested on $d \leq -3$, and when trained on $d \leq -1$ and tested on $d \geq 3$.

Trained on	Model	Evaluated on $d \leq -3$	$d = -2$	$d = -1$	$d = 0$	$d = 1$	$d = 2$	$d \geq 3$
ALL	BERT-base	82.19	90.82	90.25	86.47	92.49	90.14	81.43
$d \leq -1$	BERT-base	78.17	88.34	88.38	67.82	71.62	77.22	69.54
$d \leq -1$	BiasProduct-AnsPrior	73.00	84.34	85.61	46.32	25.23	64.91	59.06
$d \leq -1$	LearnedMixin-AnsPrior	79.07	89.27	89.01	68.52	72.35	80.43	70.31
$d \leq -1$	BiasProduct-PosOnly	75.04	83.90	83.22	73.80	81.35	81.79	73.27
$d \leq -1$	LearnedMixin-PosOnly	77.00	86.72	86.25	74.26	82.66	82.81	75.94
$\|d\| = 1$	BERT-base	65.62	77.69	88.70	69.96	90.88	80.84	66.42
$\|d\| = 1$	BiasProduct-AnsPrior	60.44	75.07	56.44	49.32	52.37	72.85	57.98
$\|d\| = 1$	LearnedMixin-AnsPrior	73.42	83.39	88.70	74.24	90.47	85.51	73.52
$\|d\| = 1$	BiasProduct-PosOnly	72.41	80.59	84.01	73.34	87.61	83.11	72.09
$\|d\| = 1$	LearnedMixin-PosOnly	73.76	80.63	86.10	74.50	89.64	82.98	72.04
$d = 0$	BERT-base	60.75	67.94	73.11	82.85	67.72	64.74	52.88
$d = 0$	BiasProduct-AnsPrior	56.25	65.15	69.05	81.07	65.10	62.95	49.43
$d = 0$	LearnedMixin-AnsPrior	59.66	69.62	72.53	83.06	68.04	66.03	53.29
$d = 0$	BiasProduct-PosOnly	62.97	67.88	70.22	78.66	66.69	69.12	59.88
$d = 0$	LearnedMixin-PosOnly	65.09	70.47	72.51	81.32	68.29	68.47	59.54
$d \geq 1$	BERT-base	68.03	74.63	74.08	63.21	90.28	89.44	75.42
$d \geq 1$	BiasProduct-AnsPrior	58.63	63.13	29.08	39.22	88.53	88.34	72.29
$d \geq 1$	LearnedMixin-AnsPrior	70.71	77.22	76.82	66.67	90.87	89.75	76.31
$d \geq 1$	BiasProduct-PosOnly	68.54	78.13	78.58	70.72	85.17	81.59	72.90
$d \geq 1$	LearnedMixin-PosOnly	71.17	80.41	79.97	71.33	87.53	84.33	74.24

Table 2: F1 scores for each subset of the SQuAD development set. The cells with relative position d seen during training are indicated by gray. For gray cells, the scores tend to remain close to those in the case where the full training set is used (ALL). Conversely, the scores for the other white cells tend to be lower than ALL.

In contrast, regarding the scores on examples with relative positions seen during training (i.e., the scores in the gray cells in Table 2), LearnedMixin-AnsPrior was superior to LearnedMixin-PosOnly. As pointed out in Utama et al. (2020), the trade-off between accuracies on in- and out-of-distribution test sets was observed in our cases. Mitigating the trade-off for relative positions is future work.

4.2 Effect of Mitigating Relative Position Bias in Normal Settings

Although we verified the effectiveness of our methods on intentionally biased datasets in §4.1, the proposed biased model, PosOnly, can also be applied to training on standard datasets because it does not require prior information about the distribution of relative positions, unlike AnsPrior. To investigate the effect of our method in a normal setting, we first trained PosOnly on the full training set. We then trained BERT-base as the main model on the full training set using BiasProduct or LearnedMixin with PosOnly as the biased model.

The results are shown in Table 3. LearnedMixin-PosOnly improved the generalization to a subset where questions and contexts have no common words (i.e., $c \cap q = \phi$), with little performance degradation on the other subset (i.e., $c \cap q \neq \phi$). This observation implies that our method might mitigate the reliance on overlapping words in a normal setting. However, the size of the subset $c \cap q = \phi$ is only 15, which makes the above conclusion unreliable. Future work should increase the size of this subset and verify its effectiveness.

5 Related Work

Recent studies have found that NLU models tend to learn shortcut solutions specific to the distribution of the training sets. In natural language inference,

Trained on	Model	Evaluated on $c \cap q \neq \phi$	$c \cap q = \phi$
ALL	BERT-base	87.94	67.11
ALL	BiasProduct-PosOnly	84.83	59.88
ALL	LearnedMixin-PosOnly	87.37	80.44

Table 3: F1 scores for two subsets of the SQuAD development set. Each model is trained on the full SQuAD training set. c indicates the context, and q indicates the question. ϕ indicates the empty set. The scores for each relative position are given in Appendix C.

models can use spurious correlations regarding lexical items (Gururangan et al., 2018) and lexical overlap (McCoy et al., 2019). In extractive QA, existing studies have shown that models can learn several kinds of shortcut solutions. Weissenborn et al. (2017) showed that a substantial number of questions could be answered only by matching the types of questions and answers. Sugawara et al. (2018) demonstrated that only using partial inputs is sufficient for finding correct answers in most cases. Ko et al. (2020) indicated that the absolute position bias of answers could severely degrade the generalization. Shinoda et al. (2021) showed that question generation models can amplify lexical overlap bias when used for data augmentation in QA.

Sampling training and test sets from different distributions (Jia and Liang, 2017; Fisch et al., 2019; Lewis and Fan, 2019; Ko et al., 2020) is one of the most effective frameworks to assess whether models can learn generalizable solutions. In this study, we also employed the framework to analyze the generalization capability from a new perspective of relative position bias, and developed effective debiasing methods for this bias. Specifically, we used the same loss functions as Ko et al. (2020), and proposed new biased models in this study.

6 Conclusion

We showed that an extractive QA model tends to exploit relative position bias in training sets, causing the performance degradation for relative positions unseen during training. To mitigate this problem, we proposed new biased models that perform well with existing debiasing algorithms on intentionally filtered training sets. Furthermore, when applied to the full training set, our method improved the generalization to examples where questions and contexts have no common words. Future work includes refining the definition of relative position bias that is more learnable for QA models, mitigating the trade-off between the accuracies for seen and unseen relative positions, and increasing the size of the test set with no lexical overlap between question and context.

Acknowledgements

We would like to thank the anonymous reviewers for their valuable comments. This work was supported by JST SPRING Grant Number JPMJSP2108 and JSPS KAKENHI Grant Numbers 22J13751 and 22K17954. This work was also supported by the SIP-2 "Big-data and AI-enabled Cyberspace Technologies" by the New Energy and Industrial Technology Development Organization (NEDO).

References

Christopher Clark, Mark Yatskar, and Luke Zettlemoyer. 2019. Don't take the easy way out: Ensemble based methods for avoiding known dataset biases. In *Proceedings of the 2019 Conference on Empirical Methods in Natural Language Processing and the 9th International Joint Conference on Natural Language Processing (EMNLP-IJCNLP)*, pages 4069–4082, Hong Kong, China. Association for Computational Linguistics.

Jacob Devlin, Ming-Wei Chang, Kenton Lee, and Kristina Toutanova. 2019. BERT: Pre-training of deep bidirectional transformers for language understanding. In *Proceedings of the 2019 Conference of the North American Chapter of the Association for Computational Linguistics: Human Language Technologies, Volume 1 (Long and Short Papers)*, pages 4171–4186, Minneapolis, Minnesota. Association for Computational Linguistics.

Adam Fisch, Alon Talmor, Robin Jia, Minjoon Seo, Eunsol Choi, and Danqi Chen. 2019. MRQA 2019 shared task: Evaluating generalization in reading comprehension. In *Proceedings of the 2nd Workshop on Machine Reading for Question Answering*, pages 1–13, Hong Kong, China. Association for Computational Linguistics.

Robert Geirhos, Jörn-Henrik Jacobsen, Claudio Michaelis, Richard Zemel, Wieland Brendel, Matthias Bethge, and Felix A. Wichmann. 2020. Shortcut learning in deep neural networks. *Nature Machine Intelligence*, 2(11):665–673.

Suchin Gururangan, Swabha Swayamdipta, Omer Levy, Roy Schwartz, Samuel Bowman, and Noah A. Smith. 2018. Annotation artifacts in natural language inference data. In *Proceedings of the 2018 Conference of the North American Chapter of the Association for Computational Linguistics: Human Language Technologies, Volume 2 (Short Papers)*, pages 107–112, New Orleans, Louisiana. Association for Computational Linguistics.

He He, Sheng Zha, and Haohan Wang. 2019. Unlearn dataset bias in natural language inference by fitting the residual. In *Proceedings of the 2nd Workshop on Deep Learning Approaches for Low-Resource NLP (DeepLo 2019)*, pages 132–142, Hong Kong, China. Association for Computational Linguistics.

Geoffrey E Hinton. 2002. Training products of experts by minimizing contrastive divergence. *Neural computation*, 14(8):1771–1800.

Robin Jia and Percy Liang. 2017. Adversarial examples for evaluating reading comprehension systems. In *Proceedings of the 2017 Conference on Empirical Methods in Natural Language Processing*, pages 2021–2031, Copenhagen, Denmark. Association for Computational Linguistics.

Diederik P Kingma and Jimmy Ba. 2014. Adam: A method for stochastic optimization. *arXiv preprint arXiv:1412.6980*.

Miyoung Ko, Jinhyuk Lee, Hyunjae Kim, Gangwoo Kim, and Jaewoo Kang. 2020. Look at the first sentence: Position bias in question answering. In *Proceedings of the 2020 Conference on Empirical Methods in Natural Language Processing (EMNLP)*, pages 1109–1121, Online. Association for Computational Linguistics.

Mike Lewis and Angela Fan. 2019. Generative question answering: Learning to answer the whole question. In *International Conference on Learning Representations*.

Tom McCoy, Ellie Pavlick, and Tal Linzen. 2019. Right for the wrong reasons: Diagnosing syntactic heuristics in natural language inference. In *Proceedings of the 57th Annual Meeting of the Association for Computational Linguistics*, pages 3428–3448, Florence, Italy. Association for Computational Linguistics.

Pranav Rajpurkar, Jian Zhang, Konstantin Lopyrev, and Percy Liang. 2016. SQuAD: 100,000+ questions for machine comprehension of text. In *Proceedings of the 2016 Conference on Empirical Methods in Natural Language Processing*, pages 2383–2392, Austin, Texas. Association for Computational Linguistics.

Minjoon Seo, Aniruddha Kembhavi, Ali Farhadi, and Hannaneh Hajishirzi. 2017. Bidirectional attention flow for machine comprehension. In *International Conference on Learning Representations*.

Kazutoshi Shinoda, Saku Sugawara, and Akiko Aizawa. 2021. Can question generation debias question answering models? a case study on question–context lexical overlap. In *Proceedings of the 3rd Workshop on Machine Reading for Question Answering*, pages 63–72, Punta Cana, Dominican Republic. Association for Computational Linguistics.

Saku Sugawara, Kentaro Inui, Satoshi Sekine, and Akiko Aizawa. 2018. What makes reading comprehension questions easier? In *Proceedings of the 2018 Conference on Empirical Methods in Natural Language Processing*, pages 4208–4219, Brussels, Belgium. Association for Computational Linguistics.

Prasetya Ajie Utama, Nafise Sadat Moosavi, and Iryna Gurevych. 2020. Mind the trade-off: Debiasing NLU models without degrading the in-distribution performance. In *Proceedings of the 58th Annual Meeting of the Association for Computational Linguistics*, pages 8717–8729, Online. Association for Computational Linguistics.

Dirk Weissenborn, Georg Wiese, and Laura Seiffe. 2017. Making neural QA as simple as possible but not simpler. In *Proceedings of the 21st Conference on Computational Natural Language Learning (CoNLL 2017)*, pages 271–280, Vancouver, Canada. Association for Computational Linguistics.

A Training Details

The number of training epochs for each model was 2, the batch size was 32, the learning rate decreased linearly from 3e-5 to 0, and Adam (Kingma and Ba, 2014) was used for optimization.

B Distribution of Relative Position d

The frequency distribution of relative positions in the SQuAD, NewsQA, TriviaQA, and NaturalQuestions development sets is shown in Figure 4. Although there are differences among the datasets, they all show that the relative positions are biased around 0.

C Results on the Full Training Set

The detailed scores of our methods when trained on the full training set are shown in Table 4. Compared to the BERT-base baseline, LearnedMixin-PosOnly can maintain the score in each column.

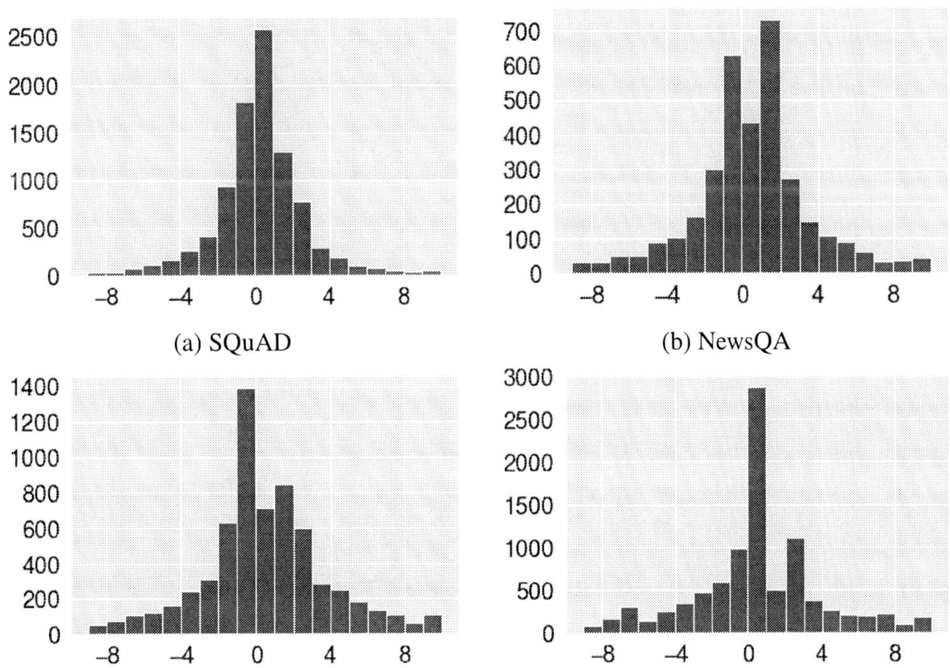

(a) SQuAD (b) NewsQA (c) TriviaQA (d) NaturalQuestions

Figure 4: Histograms of relative position d in the SQuAD, NewsQA, TriviaQA, and NaturalQuestions development sets.

Trained on	Model	Evaluated on						
		$d \leq -3$	$d = -2$	$d = -1$	$d = 0$	$d = 1$	$d = 2$	$d \geq 3$
ALL	BERT-base	82.19	90.82	90.25	86.47	92.49	90.14	81.43
ALL	BiasProduct-PosOnly	81.04	85.72	86.89	83.53	88.47	87.16	80.61
ALL	LearnedMixin-PosOnly	82.48	90.63	90.15	85.69	91.33	89.14	81.21

Table 4: F1 scores for each subset of the SQuAD development set.

A Continuum of Generation Tasks for Investigating Length Bias and Degenerate Repetition

Darcey Riley and **David Chiang**
University of Notre Dame
{darcey.riley,dchiang}@nd.edu

Abstract

Language models suffer from various degenerate behaviors. These differ between tasks: machine translation (MT) exhibits length bias, while tasks like story generation exhibit excessive repetition. Recent work has attributed the difference to *task constrainedness*, but evidence for this claim has always involved many confounding variables. To study this question directly, we introduce a new experimental framework that allows us to smoothly vary task constrainedness, from MT at one end to fully open-ended generation at the other, while keeping all other aspects fixed. We find that: (1) repetition decreases smoothly with constrainedness, explaining the difference in repetition across tasks; (2) length bias surprisingly also decreases with constrainedness, suggesting some other cause for the difference in length bias; (3) across the board, these problems affect the mode, not the whole distribution; (4) the differences cannot be attributed to a change in the entropy of the distribution, since another method of changing the entropy, label smoothing, does not produce the same effect.

1 Introduction

Neural language models serve as the core of modern NLP technologies, but they suffer from "inadequacy of the mode" (Eikema and Aziz, 2020; Zhang et al., 2021), in which the sentences with the very highest probability under the model exhibit various pathological behaviors. Specifically, machine translation suffers from *length bias*, where the generated translations are too long or (more often) too short (Murray and Chiang, 2018; Stahlberg and Byrne, 2019), while story generation suffers from *degenerate repetition*, where the generated text repeats words or phrases unnecessarily (Holtzman et al., 2020).

It has frequently been assumed that length bias and degenerate repetition are both aspects of a single phenomenon; for instance, it is very common for papers studying MT to reference issues observed in story generation. However, MT and story generation exhibit very different problems, and have been addressed using very different solutions. So it is worth pausing for a moment to ask how they relate. Are they truly two symptoms of the same problem? Why do different tasks exhibit different degenerate behaviors?

Stahlberg et al. (2022) and Wiher et al. (2022) attribute the differences to *task constrainedness*: given a particular input, how many different possible correct answers might there be? For example, grammatical error correction (GEC) and speech recognition are more constrained; image captioning and MT are in the middle; and story generation, dialogue, and pure unconditioned generation from the language model (UCG) are least constrained. However, constrainedness is only one of many differences among these tasks. They also differ in the length of the inputs and outputs, the size of the models, and so on. So although these papers provide compelling circumstantial evidence that the differences can be explained in terms of constrainedness, they do not rule out alternative hypotheses.

In this paper, we introduce a new experimental framework which lets us directly adjust constrainedness while keeping everything else (architecture, number of parameters, type of output data) fixed. We expect that, if task constrainedness really is responsible for the differences in degenerate behaviors seen across tasks, then these behaviors should vary smoothly as we adjust constrainedness. We find this to be true for degenerate repetition: we see basically none for pure MT, and an increasing amount as we lower the constrainedness down to UCG. This is consistent with the literature, which reports repetition as a problem in UCG, but not MT.

On the other hand, for length bias, we discover, to our knowledge for the first time, that length bias actually *increases* for less constrained tasks. This is inconsistent with the literature, where length bias is commonly reported for MT but very rarely re-

Proceedings of the Fifth BlackboxNLP Workshop on Analyzing and Interpreting Neural Networks for NLP, pages 426 - 440
December 8, 2022 ©2022 Association for Computational Linguistics

ported for UCG. We conclude that the difference, then, is either due to some other factor besides constrainedness influencing the model's probability distribution, or that it can be attributed to the different decoding strategies commonly used for the different tasks.

In addition, we present results showing that both length bias and degenerate repetition are problems exclusive to the mode; they do not in general affect random samples from the distribution. Lastly, we explore one possible explanation for why length bias and repetition differ across constrainedness levels: that it is because less constrained tasks have higher entropy. We find that this cannot be the explanation, as another method of increasing the entropy, label smoothing, has very little effect on these phenomena.

2 Related Work

Closely related to our work are two recent papers by Stahlberg et al. (2022) and Wiher et al. (2022), which also explore how degenerate phenomena differ across tasks. Stahlberg et al. (2022) study two more-constrained tasks, MT and GEC. Using exact search and beam search, they find that, for GEC, the distribution is peaked around a few very high-probability outputs, and that, unlike MT, it does not suffer from inadequacy of the mode.

Wiher et al. (2022) study tasks in the same constrainedness range as we do, from MT to UCG. Although their main focus is on evaluating different decoding strategies (where they confirm the trend seen in the literature, that more constrained tasks favor mode-seeking strategies, while less constrained tasks favor sampling-based methods), they look, as we do, at how degenerate repetition and length bias differ across tasks, finding that these phenomena vary across tasks and decoding methods.

Our contribution here is to provide a more rigorous empirical analysis of why these behaviors differ across tasks. Both Stahlberg et al. (2022) and Wiher et al. (2022) attribute the differences they observe to task constrainedness, and Stahlberg et al. (2022) quantify task constrainedness by looking at how much the references differ across a multi-reference test set, but neither is able to directly control task constrainedness while keeping all else fixed. Tor our knowledge, our method is the first to study the effect of task constrainedness on degeneration in a completely controlled way.

3 An Experimental Framework for Controlling Task Constrainedness

The tasks which have been compared before (GEC, MT, story generation, and others) all differ along multiple dimensions besides constrainedness: they use different architectures, different numbers of parameters and amounts of training data, and they produce different length outputs (one sentence for MT, many sentences for story generation), among other distinctions. This makes it difficult to study whether task constrainedness is actually responsible for the differences observed between these tasks. We therefore seek a way of controlling the constrainedness directly, via some sort of "knob" that we could adjust. In this section, we introduce an experimental framework that allows us to do so.

3.1 Truncation

We begin with an ordinary MT dataset and a desired constrainedness level s, which can be 0 (UCG, the least constrained task) or 100 (MT, the most constrained task in our setup) or anything in between. In our experiments, we choose $s = 0, 10, \ldots, 100$. For each value of s, we truncate each source sentence in the dataset to $s\%$ of its original length. To be precise, if $x = x_1 \cdots x_n \cdot \texttt{EOS}$ is the original sentence (after separating punctuation, but before BPE), we let $n' = \lceil n \cdot s\% \rceil$ and truncate the sentence to $x_1 \cdots x_{n'} \cdot \texttt{EOS}$. See Table 1 for an example German source sentence and all of its truncations.

We apply this truncation to all of the source sentences in the train, dev, and test data, leaving the target sentences intact. This way, as s decreases, the model has to predict the target side given less and less information about what it might contain. Or, to think of it another way, as s decreases, there become more and more possible "correct" answers, since the truncated source sentence could be the prefix of many possible full source sentences, and a translation of any one of them can be considered a valid solution to the task.

3.2 Experimental details

We use the German-to-English (de-en) and Chinese-to-English (zh-en) datasets from IWSLT 2017 (Cettolo et al., 2012), consisting of transcribed TED talks. We use the standard dataset for training, the 2010 development set for development, and the 2010–2015 test sets for testing, following the split by Kulikov et al. (2021). Table 2 shows the size of each of these sets, after removing copy noise (pairs

s (%)	length	tokens
0	0	EOS
10	3	Sch@@ on heute EOS
20	7	Sch@@ on heute spru@@ d@@ elt in EOS
30	8	Sch@@ on heute spru@@ d@@ elt in einigen EOS
40	13	Sch@@ on heute spru@@ d@@ elt in einigen f@@ la@@ chen Se@@ en EOS
50	14	Sch@@ on heute spru@@ d@@ elt in einigen f@@ la@@ chen Se@@ en in EOS
60	19	Sch@@ on heute spru@@ d@@ elt in einigen f@@ la@@ chen Se@@ en in Al@@ as@@ ka Me@@ than EOS
70	21	Sch@@ on heute spru@@ d@@ elt in einigen f@@ la@@ chen Se@@ en in Al@@ as@@ ka Me@@ than von selbst EOS
80	22	Sch@@ on heute spru@@ d@@ elt in einigen f@@ la@@ chen Se@@ en in Al@@ as@@ ka Me@@ than von selbst aus EOS
90	24	Sch@@ on heute spru@@ d@@ elt in einigen f@@ la@@ chen Se@@ en in Al@@ as@@ ka Me@@ than von selbst aus dem Wasser EOS
100	25	Sch@@ on heute spru@@ d@@ elt in einigen f@@ la@@ chen Se@@ en in Al@@ as@@ ka Me@@ than von selbst aus dem Wasser . EOS

Table 1: Prefixes of an example German source sentence, for all values of s. Lengths do not include EOS.

	de-en	zh-en
train	205,898	231,259
dev	888	879
test	8,079	8,549

Table 2: Sizes of our training, development, and test datasets.

where the source and target are identical) from the data (Ott et al., 2018).

We preprocess the data using BPE tokenization (Sennrich et al., 2016). To ensure that the experimental setup is as similar as possible for all values of s, we learn BPE on the full, untruncated dataset. Then, once BPE has been learned, we apply it to the truncated data. Initially, we experimented with both joint and separate BPE, but found very little difference between them, so we present results for joint BPE only.

For our MT system, we use the Transformer model (Vaswani et al., 2017); specifically, we use a fork of the Transformers without Tears library (Nguyen and Salazar, 2019).[1]. We use identical hyperparameter settings for both language pairs and all values of s; these are the same as the Transformers without Tears base configuration, except that we use 6 layers and 4 heads.

We trained our systems both with and without label smoothing (Szegedy et al., 2016), thinking that, because label smoothing changes the shape of the distribution, it might impact the results. We discuss the effect of label smoothing in §6; in all other sections we look only at systems trained without it. All of our results are averaged across three random restarts.

Fearing that BLEU scores might not provide a meaningful enough signal for $s < 100$, we tried using both dev BLEU and dev perplexity to lower the learning rate and control early stopping; these gave very similar results, so we only present results for the systems tuned using dev BLEU.

To better view the natural properties of the distribution, we do not use any length normalization during decoding. We decode up to a maximum length of 300 tokens.

We make our full experimental setup publicly available on GitHub.[2]

3.3 Sanity checks

We verify via BLEU score that we have trained our systems successfully. Although, for the purposes of our experiment, it is not necessary to use a state-of-the-art MT system, we nonetheless achieve reasonable BLEU scores of 34.7 and 17.5 for de-en and zh-en respectively for the $s = 100$ systems, using the standard beam size of 4 for decoding. Predictably, lowering s also decreases the BLEU score, as can be seen in Figure 2.

As an additional sanity check, we confirm that varying s does indeed change the spread of the distribution in the expected way. Using 1000 samples for each sentence in the test set, we estimate the entropy (Figure 1a), and find that it decreases as s increases. In addition, following Ott et al. (2018), we look at the portion of the total probability mass covered by all of the unique samples, and find that, although the number of unique samples decreases as s increases (Figure 1c), the total probability mass covered increases (Figure 1b).

4 Degeneracy in the Mode

In this section, we look at how length bias and repetition vary as we vary the constrainedness parameter s.

[1] https://github.com/darcey/transformers_without_tears/tree/mt-interpolation-paper

[2] https://github.com/darcey/mt-interpolation

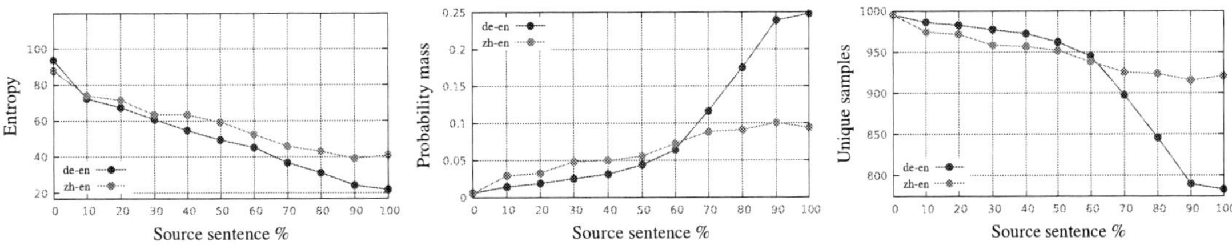

(a) Per-sentence entropy (nats) (b) Total probability mass (c) Number of unique samples

Figure 1: Increasing constrainedness increases the peakedness of the predictive distribution as expected. Every data point is based on 1000 random samples for each sentence in the test data.

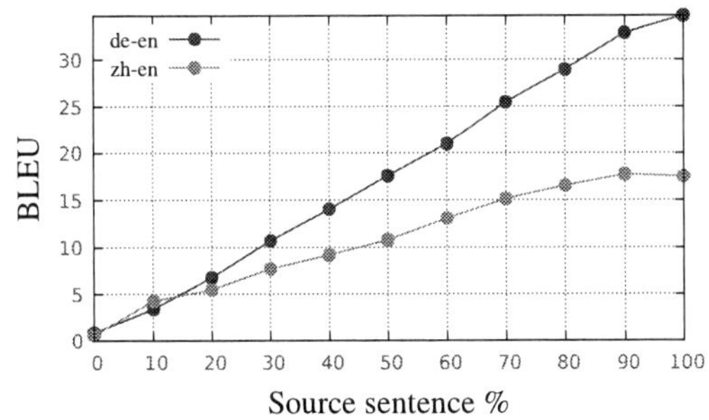

Figure 2: Predictably, BLEU score decreases smoothly as we decrease s.

4.1 Length bias

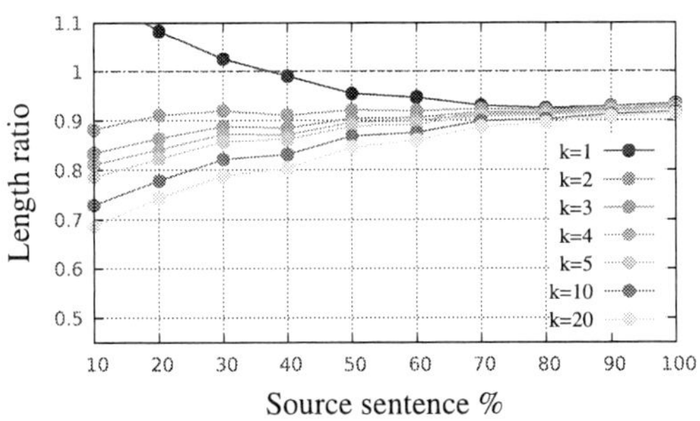

(a) German–English

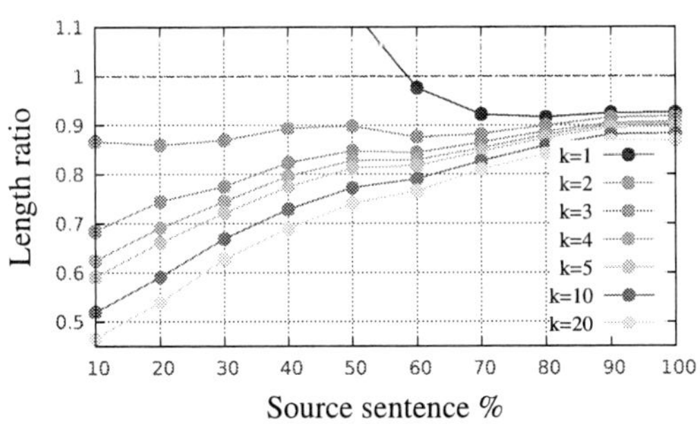

(b) Chinese–English

Figure 3: Length ratio versus source sentence percentage (s), for various beam sizes (k). For high s, there is a slight bias towards shorter outputs that increases mildly with k, whereas for low s, we see extreme bias, towards longer or shorter outputs depending on k.

Length bias is a problem where the length of the output consistently differs from the length of the reference; the term typically refers to sentences being too short. In NMT, length bias is such a major and well-known problem that nearly all systems correct for it using some kind of length normalization during decoding (Wu et al., 2016; Koehn and Knowles, 2017; Murray and Chiang, 2018).

In NMT, length bias gets worse the closer one approaches the mode of the distribution. It has been repeatedly shown that, as beam size increases, bringing the output translation closer to the mode, the length bias becomes more extreme. In fact, the mode of the distribution is often simply the empty string itself (Stahlberg and Byrne, 2019).

On the other hand, length bias has been understudied in less constrained tasks such as story generation or UCG. We know of just two reports of this problem: for story generation, Holtzman et al. (2020) report worsening length bias as beam size increases, with immediate stopping when using beam sizes ≥ 64, and Wiher et al. (2022) found length bias for beam sizes $k = 5, 10$; however, neither of these is the main result of their respective papers.

This difference in emphasis seen in the literature would seem to suggest that length bias only affects MT, and does not affect less constrained tasks like story generation. Thus, if constrainedness were fully responsible for the difference seen in the literature, then we would expect to see length bias decrease with constrainedness, becoming less of a problem for less constrained tasks.

To test this, we measure how length bias changes as we vary s. To quantify length bias, we compute the (micro-averaged) *length ratio*,

$$\ell(T) = \frac{\sum_{(h,r)\in T} |h|}{\sum_{(h,r)\in T} |r|}$$

where T is a test set consisting of pairs (h, r), where h is a hypothesis (output) sentence and r is a reference sentence.

Figure 3 shows how length ratio changes as we vary both s and the beam size k.[3] Consistent with previous findings, we find that standard NMT suffers from considerable length bias, with the problem worsening as beam size k increases. But to our surprise, as s decreases, we find that not only does length bias worsen, but that the dependence on beam size grows stronger and stronger. This is surprising given the lack of concern with length bias in the literature on less constrained tasks. To our knowledge, we are the first to report a result like this, where length bias actually worsens as task constrainedness decreases.

We can think of two explanations for this result. The first is that there are other factors besides constrainedness affecting the length bias seen across tasks. We suspect that the length of the reference outputs might be a major part of this; models like GPT-2 are trained to produce much larger chunks of text than our systems, which typically just output one sentence at a time. The second is that this is an artifact of the decoding processes used. Most of the literature on NMT uses mode-seeking decoding strategies such as beam search, while literature on less constrained generation favors sampling-based approaches. So it could in fact be that all unconstrained systems also suffer from length bias, but it simply doesn't show up because beam search is not used with those systems.We also note that it may be more difficult to study length bias in less constrained tasks, since there is not necessarily a roughly "correct" length the way there is in MT.

A last interesting result is that, for $k = 1$ (greedy search), the length ratio actually increases for decreasing s, ending up well above 1. This agrees with a recent result reported by Wiher et al. (2022), who found that, for the relatively unconstrained task of story generation, beam sizes $k = 5, 10$ returned texts that were too short, while greedy search returned texts which were far too long.

4.2 Repetition

Degenerate repetition is a well-known problem where the model gets stuck in a loop, repeating the same n-grams over and over again. It so strongly affects less constrained tasks like story generation (Holtzman et al., 2020) that these tasks avoid mode-seeking strategies altogether, preferring sampling-based approaches. Since pure random sampling also produces low-quality output, most work on this topic has focused on finding a balance between mode-seeking and pure sampling, either by truncating the distribution during sampling (Fan et al., 2018; Holtzman et al., 2020; Basu et al., 2021; Zhang et al., 2021; Nadeem et al., 2020; DeLucia et al., 2021), or by using some combination of sampling and search (Massarelli et al., 2020), though Welleck et al. (2020) address the issue via training rather than search, by modifying the objective function to discourage repetition.

In contrast, to our knowledge, degenerate repetition has not been reported in the literature on NMT. (Our anecdotal experience is that degenerate repetition is a familiar sight in MT, but not a serious problem in well-trained systems.) If the difference between story generation and MT can be explained by their constrainedness, as previous work has suggested, then we should expect to see repetition increase smoothly as we decrease s.

This is, in fact, exactly what we find. Figure 4 shows the amount of repetition for German-to-English, measured as the percentage of unique n-grams which appear in each search result (that is, for each search result, the number of n-gram types divided by tokens), as compared to the reference. (The Chinese-to-English results are similar, and can be found in Appendix B.) We find that, as s decreases, repetition increases considerably. Consistent with the literature, we see basically no evidence of repetition in pure MT, where the amount of repetition almost perfectly matches that seen in the references. But as s decreases, so does the percent of unique n-grams, until for $s = 10$ there is very clear evidence of repetition. We therefore feel confident in concluding that task constrainedness adequately explains the difference in the level of concern paid to repetition in the literature for different tasks.

One interesting thing to observe is that, as beam size increases, repetition actually decreases. We suspect that this might be due to the effect of length bias: as shown in the previous section, higher beam sizes tend to return shorter sentences, and these seem less likely to experience degenerate repetition (though it is certainly possible to have both problems at once).

[3] These graphs (and all of our beam search results) exclude the $s = 0$ case, which turn out to be nearly meaningless: since the source sentence is identical (namely, the empty string) for each sentence pair in the test set, the beam search results will also be identical, meaning that the decoder will simply generate $|T|$ copies of the same sentence. So any properties of that one sentence will be magnified. The results under beam search for $s = 0$ are therefore little better than noise.

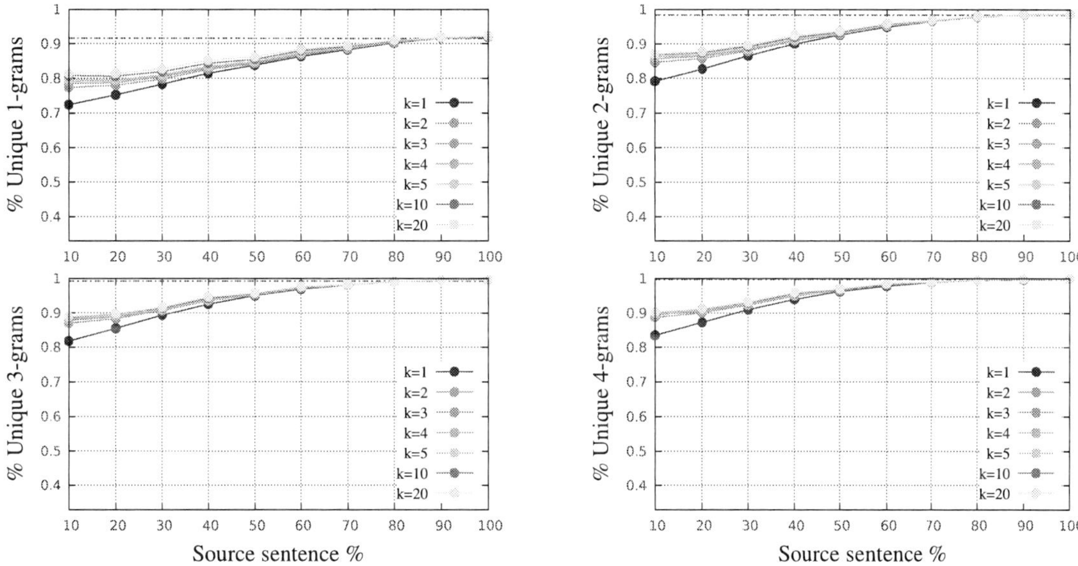

Figure 4: Amount of repetition versus source sentence percentage (s), for various beam sizes (k). Repetition is measured as the percentage of unique n-grams in a sentence; the graphs show this for different values of n. The repetition rate of the reference is plotted as a dashed grey line. Across all values of n, the percent of unique n-grams drops as s decreases. These graphs show German-to-English results only; see Appendix B for Chinese-to-English.

4.3 Discussion

It is illustrative to examine some strings generated by our systems. Table 3 shows the translations for one sentence from the test data; others can be found in Appendix B. Consistent with our results, we see length roughly decrease along with s. We also see some concrete examples of degenerate repetition for the lower s values. As is typical, the same phrase is repeated over and over, separated by commas or "and".

In addition to length bias and repetition, we can also observe that, as s decreases, the content of the generated strings diverges further and further from the reference. But we notice that, qualitatively, as it does this, the outputs get increasingly boring. This fits with what others have reported (Holtzman et al., 2020), that beam search simply produces tedious and boring output for less constrained tasks.

Another observation is that some of these sentences are simply ungrammatical. While grammatical errors are very common among random samples, it is interesting to see them even at these high probabilities.

5 No Degeneracy in Samples

In addition to looking at search results, we also look at samples from the distribution. For each system and for each sentence in the test set, we take 1000 samples, and discover that the samples do not suffer from either degenerate repetition or length bias (Figs. 5 and 6). This underscores that these problems are specific to the mode, and are not properties of the distribution as a whole.

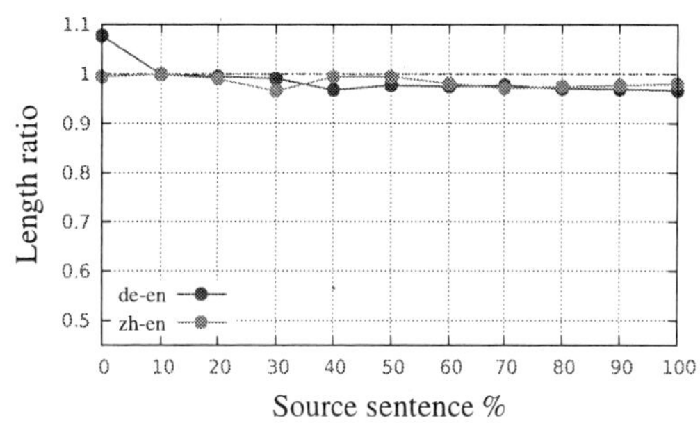

Figure 5: Length ratio of samples versus source sentence percentage (s), for both language pairs. The samples only suffer from very slight length bias, and only for higher values of s.

For low values of s, this should not be particularly surprising; sampling-based decoding approaches such as top-k (Fan et al., 2018) and top-p (Holtzman et al., 2020) are favored for these tasks specifically to avoid the degenerate mode.

Yet it may be surprising to see that the pure MT (s = 100) outputs do not suffer from degeneracy either. Since MT papers rarely explore properties of the full distribution beyond the mode, one might

s (%)	Output found using beam search, k = 4
0	And I said, "Well, I'm going to show you a little bit."
10	When Steve Lopez said, "You know, I'm not going to be here."
20	When Steve Lopez, Columni, who is the first person in the world, he's the first person in the world, and he's the first person in the world.
30	When Steve Lopez, Columni, the Los Angeles Times, he said, "You know, I'm going to go to school."
40	When Steve Lopez, Columnist, the Los Angeles Times, one day, he said, "You know, we're going to have to do this."
50	When Steve Lopez, Columnist, the Los Angeles Times, one day through the Pacific Ocean Ocean, I started to think about it.
60	When Steve Lopez, Columnist in Los Angeles Times, one day through the streets in the center of the city, the city of New York.
70	When Steve Lopez, Columnist, the Los Angeles Times, one day through the streets of Los Angeles, the city of London.
80	When Steve Lopez, Columnist, the Los Angeles Times, one day went through the streets at the center of Los Angeles, I heard this story.
90	When Steve Lopez, Columnist, the Los Angeles Times, one day went through the streets at the center of Los Angeles, he heard a wonderful story.
100	When Steve Lopez, Columnist at the Los Angeles Times, walked through the streets at the center of Los Angeles, he heard a wonderful music.
ref	One day, Los Angeles Times columnist Steve Lopez was walking along the streets of downtown Los Angeles when he heard beautiful music.

Table 3: Beam search (k = 4) outputs for a sentence in the test dataset, shown across all values of s. Illustrates both length bias and degenerate repetition.

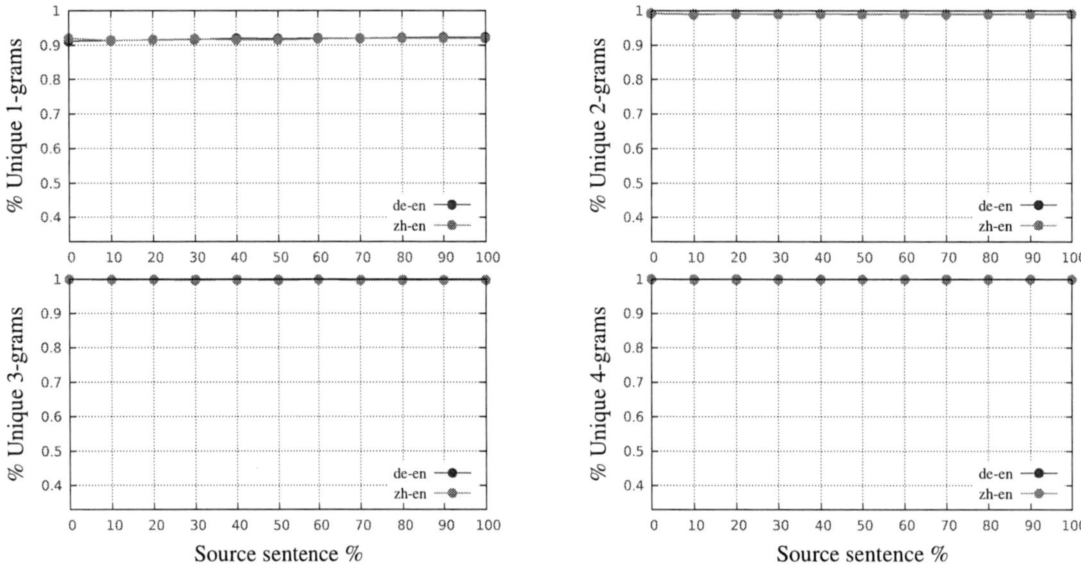

Figure 6: Amount of repetition versus source sentence percentage (s), for various values of n, computed over 1000 random samples for each sentence in the test data. The samples show no evidence of degenerate repetition whatsoever; the level of repetition matches extremely closely to the reference (shown as a dashed grey line which is completely hidden behind the sampling results).

get the false impression that length bias is a problem that affects most sentences in the distribution. Figure 5 shows that this is definitely not the case. This supports the argument by Eikema and Aziz (2020) that it is a mistake to focus too much on the mode during decoding.

6 Label Smoothing and Degeneration

We now begin to examine exactly what it is about task constrainedness which affects the amount of degeneration. One possible explanation is that, as we vary s, we vary the distribution's peakedness: the distribution becomes much less peaked as s decreases (as shown in §3.3). To examine whether differences in peakedness fully explain the level of degeneration, we contrast with a different method of adjusting peakedness: label smoothing. Label smoothing (Szegedy et al., 2016) is an alternative to the standard cross-entropy loss function. Instead of comparing the next-word distribution against a one-hot vector, it compares against a mixture of a one-hot vector and the uniform distribution. It is commonly used in modern NMT systems, and has generally been found to be helpful, though the reasons why are still being investigated (Müller et al., 2019; Lukasik et al., 2020; Gao et al., 2020).

Label smoothing has the effect of smoothing the distribution over more output tokens at each timestep. This has a big effect on the peakedness, as shown in Fig 7. But, as we will show, it has almost no impact on either length bias or repetition. (All the graphs in this section show German-to-

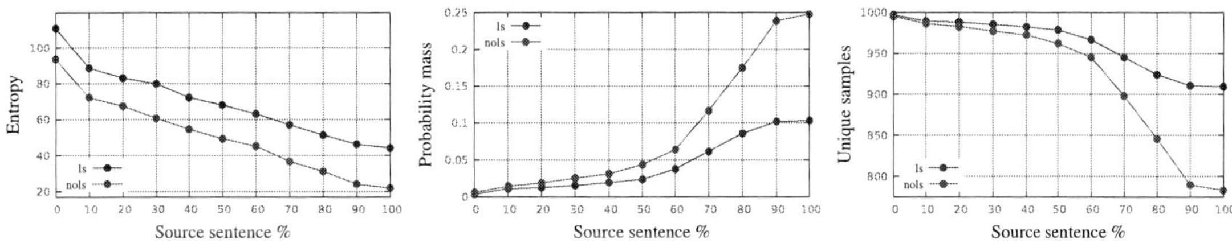

(a) Per-sentence entropy (nats), de-en (b) Total probability mass, de-en (c) Number of unique samples, de-en

Figure 7: Effect of label smoothing (ls) on the peakedness of the distribution, compared with no label smoothing (nols), for German-to-English (see Appendix C for Chinese-to-English). Label smoothing consistently increases entropy and decreases total probability mass across all values of s.

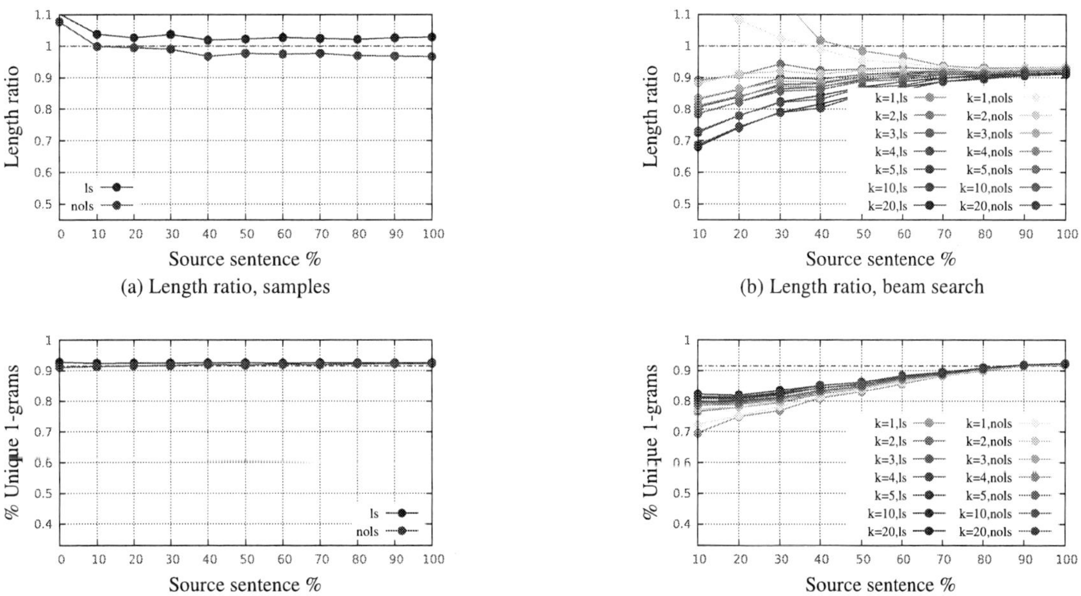

(a) Length ratio, samples (b) Length ratio, beam search

(c) Repetition, samples (d) Repetition, beam search

Figure 8: Length ratio of translations and percentage of unique 1-grams versus source sentence percentage (s), both with label smoothing (ls) and without (nols). Results for samples are computed based on 1000 samples for each test sentence; results for beam search vary across beam sizes (k). For samples, label smoothing increases the length ratio from slightly below the reference length to slightly above it; otherwise it has no discernible effect. (These results are for German-to-English; see Appendix C for Chinese-to-English.)

English only; the Chinese-to-English results are similar and can be found in Appendix C.)

The biggest effect we see is in Figure 8a, which shows how adding label smoothing impacts the length bias when sampling. Here, label smoothing changes the length bias from just below 1 to just above 1, giving sentences which are, on average, very slightly longer than the reference.

However, although label smoothing affects length bias for the overall distribution, we see essentially no effect on length bias when using beam search (Figure 8b).[4] Similarly, Figures 8c and 8d show the effect of label smoothing on 1-gram repetition, for both search and sampling; there is essentially no effect. (We found this to be true for other values of n as well.)

From this, we can conclude that it is not merely the spread of the distribution which causes these degenerate behaviors to occur. There must be some other property of task constrainedness which is influencing them. We leave further investigation of what that property might be to future work.

7 Conclusion

We introduced a new experimental framework for directly controlling the level of task constrainedness, by truncating sentences on the source side of an MT system. Using this experimental framework, we analyzed how task constrainedness affected degenerate behaviors.

For less constrained tasks, we observe three failure modes: beam search decoding that is too short, greedy decoding that is too long and repetitive, and random samples that are disfluent. We note that the same three failure modes are also displayed by a simple unigram language model: since every sentence contains EOS, the highest-probability output must be empty (just EOS with no real words); since $P(\text{EOS}) < P(\text{the})$, a greedy search will choose *the* over and over; and random samples from a unigram distribution are of course disfluent. So the simplest explanation may be that the neural models used here are still insufficiently sensitive to context.

For more constrained tasks, these effects are much milder. The presence of the source sentence seems to be sufficient to all but eliminate repetition and noticeably improve fluency. Although some work on RNN models for NMT focused on adding coverage models to reduce skipping and repeating of source words (Tu et al., 2016; Mi et al., 2016; Li et al., 2018), Transformers seem to suffer from these problems far less. As Transformers were originally designed for the $s = 100$ case, one direction for future research may be to investigate modifications of the Transformer that are better-suited to less constrained tasks.

[4] We do note, however, that Peters and Martins (2021) did find that label smoothing affected length bias in the mode of the distribution.

Acknowledgements

We thank Toan Nguyen for his help with the `transformers-without-tears` library, and Ari Holtzman for useful discussion.

This material is based upon work supported by the National Science Foundation under Grant No. CCF-2019291. Any opinions, findings, and conclusions or recommendations expressed in this material are those of the authors and do not necessarily reflect the views of the National Science Foundation.

References

Sourya Basu, Govardana Sachitanandam Ramachandran, Nitish Shirish Keskar, and Lav R. Varshney. 2021. Mirostat: A neural text decoding algorithm that directly controls perplexity. In *International Conference on Learning Representations*.

Mauro Cettolo, Christian Girardi, and Marcello Federico. 2012. WIT3: Web inventory of transcribed and translated talks. In *Proceedings of the 16th Annual conference of the European Association for Machine Translation*, pages 261–268, Trento, Italy. European Association for Machine Translation.

Alexandra DeLucia, Aaron Mueller, Xiang Lisa Li, and João Sedoc. 2021. Decoding methods for neural narrative generation. In *Proceedings of the 1st Workshop on Natural Language Generation, Evaluation, and Metrics (GEM 2021)*, pages 166–185, Online. Association for Computational Linguistics.

Bryan Eikema and Wilker Aziz. 2020. Is MAP decoding all you need? the inadequacy of the mode in neural machine translation. In *Proceedings of the 28th International Conference on Computational Linguistics*, pages 4506–4520, Barcelona, Spain (Online). International Committee on Computational Linguistics.

Angela Fan, Mike Lewis, and Yann Dauphin. 2018. Hierarchical neural story generation. In *Proceedings of the 56th Annual Meeting of the Association for Computational Linguistics (Volume 1: Long Papers)*, pages 889–898, Melbourne, Australia. Association for Computational Linguistics.

Yingbo Gao, Weiyue Wang, Christian Herold, Zijian Yang, and Hermann Ney. 2020. Towards a better understanding of label smoothing in neural machine translation. In *Proceedings of the 1st Conference of the Asia-Pacific Chapter of the Association for Computational Linguistics and the 10th International Joint Conference on Natural Language Processing*, pages 212–223, Suzhou, China. Association for Computational Linguistics.

Ari Holtzman, Jan Buys, Li Du, Maxwell Forbes, and Yejin Choi. 2020. The curious case of neural text degeneration. In *International Conference on Learning Representations*.

Philipp Koehn and Rebecca Knowles. 2017. Six challenges for neural machine translation. In *Proceedings of the First Workshop on Neural Machine Translation*, pages 28–39, Vancouver. Association for Computational Linguistics.

Ilia Kulikov, Maksim Eremeev, and Kyunghyun Cho. 2021. Characterizing and addressing the issue of oversmoothing in neural autoregressive sequence modeling. arXiv:2112.08914.

Yanyang Li, Tong Xiao, Yinqiao Li, Qiang Wang, Changming Xu, and Jingbo Zhu. 2018. A simple and effective approach to coverage-aware neural machine translation. In *Proceedings of the 56th Annual Meeting of the Association for Computational Linguistics (Volume 2: Short Papers)*, pages 292–297, Melbourne, Australia. Association for Computational Linguistics.

Michal Lukasik, Srinadh Bhojanapalli, Aditya Menon, and Sanjiv Kumar. 2020. Does label smoothing mitigate label noise? In *Proceedings of the 37th International Conference on Machine Learning*, volume 119 of *Proceedings of Machine Learning Research*, pages 6448–6458. PMLR.

Luca Massarelli, Fabio Petroni, Aleksandra Piktus, Myle Ott, Tim Rocktäschel, Vassilis Plachouras, Fabrizio Silvestri, and Sebastian Riedel. 2020. How decoding strategies affect the verifiability of generated text. In *Findings of the Association for Computational Linguistics: EMNLP 2020*, pages 223–235, Online. Association for Computational Linguistics.

Haitao Mi, Baskaran Sankaran, Zhiguo Wang, and Abe Ittycheriah. 2016. Coverage embedding models for neural machine translation. In *Proceedings of the 2016 Conference on Empirical Methods in Natural Language Processing*, pages 955–960, Austin, Texas. Association for Computational Linguistics.

Rafael Müller, Simon Kornblith, and Geoffrey E. Hinton. 2019. When does label smoothing help? In *Advances in Neural Information Processing Systems*, volume 32. Curran Associates, Inc.

Kenton Murray and David Chiang. 2018. Correcting length bias in neural machine translation. In *Proceedings of the Third Conference on Machine Translation: Research Papers*, pages 212–223, Brussels, Belgium. Association for Computational Linguistics.

Moin Nadeem, Tianxing He, Kyunghyun Cho, and James Glass. 2020. A systematic characterization of sampling algorithms for open-ended language generation. In *Proceedings of the 1st Conference of the Asia-Pacific Chapter of the Association for Computational Linguistics and the 10th International Joint Conference on Natural Language Processing*, pages 334–346, Suzhou, China. Association for Computational Linguistics.

Toan Q. Nguyen and Julian Salazar. 2019. Transformers without tears: Improving the normalization of self-attention. In *Proceedings of the 16th International Conference on Spoken Language Translation*, Hong Kong. Association for Computational Linguistics.

Myle Ott, Michael Auli, David Grangier, and Marc'Aurelio Ranzato. 2018. Analyzing uncertainty in neural machine translation. In *Proceedings of the 35th International Conference on Machine Learning*.

Ben Peters and André F. T. Martins. 2021. Smoothing and shrinking the sparse Seq2Seq search space. In *Proceedings of the 2021 Conference of the North American Chapter of the Association for Computational Linguistics: Human Language Technologies*, pages 2642–2654, Online. Association for Computational Linguistics.

Rico Sennrich, Barry Haddow, and Alexandra Birch. 2016. Neural machine translation of rare words with subword units. In *Proceedings of the 54th Annual Meeting of the Association for Computational Linguistics (Volume 1: Long Papers)*, pages 1715–1725, Berlin, Germany. Association for Computational Linguistics.

Felix Stahlberg and Bill Byrne. 2019. On NMT search errors and model errors: Cat got your tongue? In *Proceedings of the 2019 Conference on Empirical Methods in Natural Language Processing and the 9th International Joint Conference on Natural Language Processing (EMNLP-IJCNLP)*, pages 3356–3362, Hong Kong, China. Association for Computational Linguistics.

Felix Stahlberg, Ilia Kulikov, and Shankar Kumar. 2022. Uncertainty determines the adequacy of the mode and the tractability of decoding in sequence-to-sequence models. In *Proceedings of the 60th Annual Meeting of the Association for Computational Linguistics (Volume 1: Long Papers)*, pages 8634–8645, Dublin, Ireland. Association for Computational Linguistics.

Christian Szegedy, Vincent Vanhoucke, Sergey Ioffe, Jon Shlens, and Zbigniew Wojna. 2016. Rethinking the Inception architecture for computer vision. In *2016 IEEE Conference on Computer Vision and Pattern Recognition (CVPR)*, pages 2818–2826.

Zhaopeng Tu, Zhengdong Lu, Yang Liu, Xiaohua Liu, and Hang Li. 2016. Modeling coverage for neural machine translation. In *Proceedings of the 54th Annual Meeting of the Association for Computational Linguistics (Volume 1: Long Papers)*, pages 76–85,

Berlin, Germany. Association for Computational Linguistics.

Ashish Vaswani, Noam Shazeer, Niki Parmar, Jakob Uszkoreit, Llion Jones, Aidan N. Gomez, Łukasz Kaiser, and Illia Polosukhin. 2017. Attention is all you need. In *Advances in Neural Information Processing Systems*, volume 30. Curran Associates, Inc.

Sean Welleck, Ilia Kulikov, Stephen Roller, Emily Dinan, Kyunghyun Cho, and Jason Weston. 2020. Neural text generation with unlikelihood training. In *International Conference on Learning Representations*.

Gian Wiher, Clara Meister, and Ryan Cotterell. 2022. On Decoding Strategies for Neural Text Generators. *Transactions of the Association for Computational Linguistics*, 10:997–1012.

Yonghui Wu, Mike Schuster, Zhifeng Chen, Quoc V. Le, Mohammad Norouzi, Wolfgang Macherey, Maxim Krikun, Yuan Cao, Qin Gao, Klaus Macherey, et al. 2016. Google's neural machine translation system: Bridging the gap between human and machine translation. arXiv:1609.08144.

Hugh Zhang, Daniel Duckworth, Daphne Ippolito, and Arvind Neelakantan. 2021. Trading off diversity and quality in natural language generation. In *Proceedings of the Workshop on Human Evaluation of NLP Systems (HumEval)*, pages 25–33, Online. Association for Computational Linguistics.

A Additional results on repetition

Here we show some additional outputs from our systems. Figure 10 graphs the amount of repetition for the Chinese-to-English systems; we see similar results to the German-to-English systems, but with an even more pronounced decrease in repetition for higher beam sizes k.

Figure 9 displays the same results, but graphed in terms of n. (We look at beam size $k = 1$ since repetition is most pronounced in that case.) This graph shows a surprising consistency across n; although the effect is most pronounced for 1-gram repetition, we still see quite a bit of degenerate repetition even up to 6-grams, suggesting that the phrases which are being repeated are quite long.

B Additional outputs from our model

As a supplement to Table 3, we present some additional outputs from our system, which show similar trends.

C Additional results on label smoothing

Here we present additional results on label smoothing, for the Chinese-to-English language pair. These results are quite similar to the ones observed for German-to-English. Again, we see a substantial difference in the peakedness of the distribution. And again, we notice a slight change in length ratio for the samples, but otherwise, we observe essentially no effect of label smoothing on degenerate behavior.

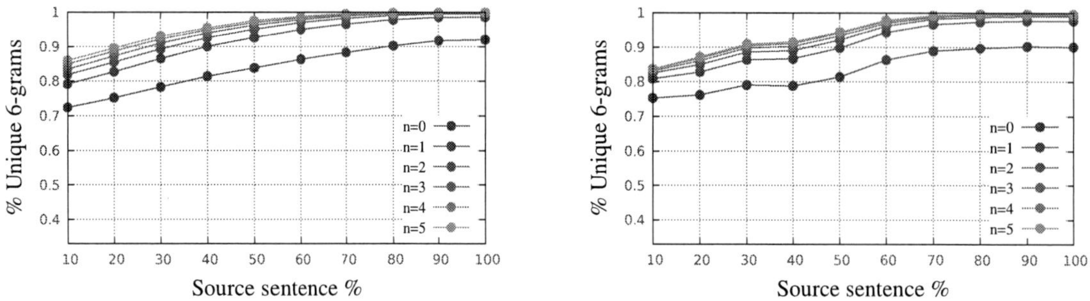

(a) German–English

(b) Chinese–English

Figure 9: Amount of repetition, measured as the percentage of n-grams in the sentence which are unique, versus source sentence percentage (s). This is mostly the same information shown in Figures 4 and 10, but viewed in a different way: here, we look at just one beam size ($k = 1$, for which the repetition was most pronounced), and compare multiple n. All values of n show a similar pattern, with considerable repetition observed even for 6-grams for low s.

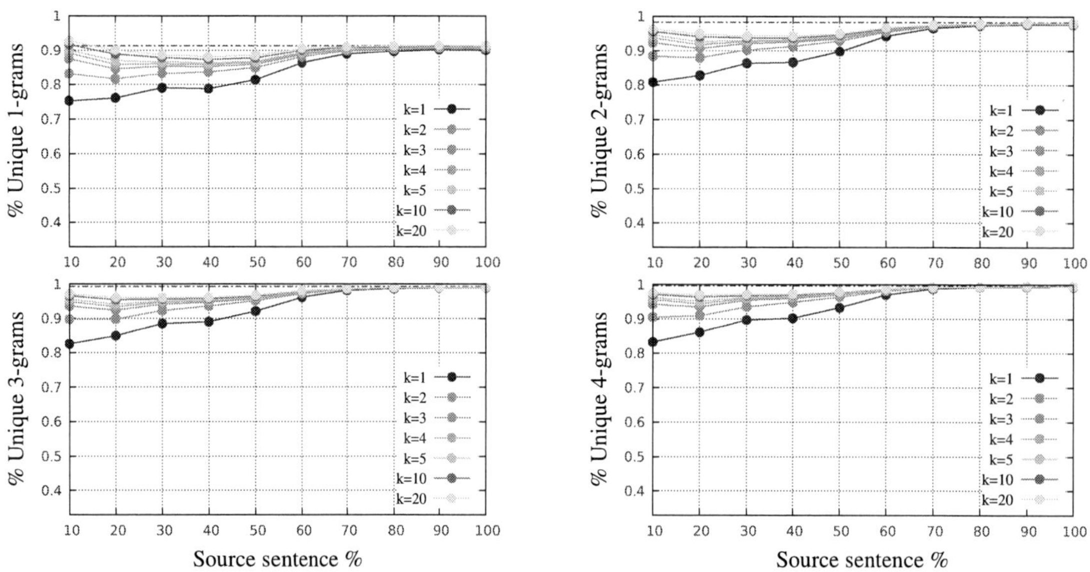

Figure 10: Amount of repetition versus source sentence percentage (s), for various beam sizes (k). (Graphs show Chinese-to-English results only.) Repetition is measured as the percentage of unique n-grams in a sentence; the graphs show this for different values of n. The repetition rate of the reference is plotted as a dashed grey line. As in German-to-English, the percent of unique n-grams drops as s decreases across all values of n, while repetition actually becomes less of a problem for higher values of k.

s (%)	Output found using beam search, $k = 4$
0	And I said, "Well, I'm going to show you a little bit."
10	A few years ago, I was in the hospital, and I was in the hospital.
20	A few years ago, when I was a kid, I was a kid.
30	A few years ago, here at TED, I'm going to tell you a little bit about this.
40	A couple of years ago, at TED, I'm going to tell you a little bit about this.
50	A couple of years ago, at TED, Peter Peter asked me, "What are you doing?"
60	A couple of years ago, here at TED, Peter Skillman introduced a book called "The Sun."
70	A couple of years ago, here at TED, Peter Skillman introduced a design competition called "The House."
80	A few years ago, here at TED, Peter Skillman introduced a design competition called "The Government."
90	A few years ago, here at TED, Peter Skillman made a design competition called "The Marshmallow Child."
100	A few years ago, here at TED, Peter Skillman introduced a design competition called "The Marshmallow Child."
ref	Several years ago here at TED, Peter Skillman introduced a design challenge called the marshmallow challenge.

Table 4: Beam search ($k = 4$) outputs for a sentence in the test dataset, shown across all values of s.

s (%)	Output found using beam search, k = 4
0	And I said, "Well, I'm going to show you a little bit."
10	A child, a child, a child, a child, a child, a child, a child, a child.
20	A child who is living in the world today is a child, a child, a child, a child, a child, a child, a child.
30	A child who's born in New Delhi today will be born in a new world, a new world, a new world, a new world.
40	A child born today in New Delhi can expect to be a child who has been born in the United States.
50	A child who's born in New Delhi today can expect to be as long as they're born, and that's where they are.
60	A kid who can be born in New Delhi today would expect to live as long as they were, and that's what they were doing.
70	A child born in New Delhi today will expect to live as long as the richest child in the world.
80	A child born in New Delhi today will expect to live as long as the richest man on the planet.
90	A child born today in New Delhi can expect to live as long as the richest man in the world, 100 years ago.
100	A child born today in New Delhi can expect to live as long as the richest man in the world 100 years ago.
ref	A kid born in New Delhi today can expect to live as long as the richest man in the world did 100 years ago.

Table 5: Beam search (k = 4) outputs for a sentence in the test dataset, shown across all values of s.

s (%)	Output found using beam search, k = 4
0	And I said, "Well, I'm going to show you a little bit."
10	Today, I'm going to show you a couple of examples of how this works.
20	Today, I don't know how many of you have heard of this, but I think it's a very important thing.
30	Today, I don't know, maybe it's going to go up today, but I'm going to tell you a little bit about what I'm going to talk about today.
40	Now, I don't know, maybe someone in this room came to me and said, "You know, I'm going to go to school."
50	Today, I don't know, maybe someone in Lagos came to a place where I was born, and I didn't know what to do.
60	Today, I don't know, maybe somebody in Lagos came into an airplane this morning, and it's going to be like, "Oh, I'm going to die."
70	Now, I don't know, maybe someone in Lagos this morning went into an airplane, and it's going to go to Los Angeles, and it's going to be a big deal.
80	Today, I don't know, maybe someone in Lagos came to an airplane this morning, and it's just going to Los Angeles, in the middle of the Central Sea.
90	Today, I don't know, maybe someone in Lagos is going to go to an airplane this morning, and he's going to go to Los Angeles, right now he's gone.
100	Today, I don't know, maybe someone in Lagos climbed into an airplane this morning, and it's just going to Los Angeles right now, it's over Ohio.
ref	Today, I don't know, maybe a guy got on a plane in Lagos this morning, and he's flying to LAX, right now he's over Ohio.

Table 6: Beam search (k = 4) outputs for a sentence in the test dataset, shown across all values of s.

s (%)	Output found using beam search, k = 4
0	And I said, "Well, I'm going to show you a little bit."
10	If you look at it, you can see that it's a little bit different.
20	If you're 10 teams, you're going to have to be able to do that.
30	If you have 10 teams, you have 10 teams, and you have 10 teams, and you have them.
40	If you have 10 teams, typically, you have 10 teams, and you have 10 teams.
50	If you have 10 teams that are typically predicting, you're not going to be able to do that.
60	If you have 10 teams that are typically predicted, you get 10 teams, and you get 10 teams.
70	If you have 10 teams that typically go, you get about six teams per second.
80	If you have 10 teams that typically go ahead, you get about six, the two teams.
90	If you have 10 teams that are typical, you get about six, the stable structures.
100	If you have 10 teams that go typically, you get about six that have stable structures.
ref	If you have 10 teams that typically perform, you'll get maybe six or so that have standing structures.

Table 7: Beam search (k = 4) outputs for a sentence in the test dataset, shown across all values of s.

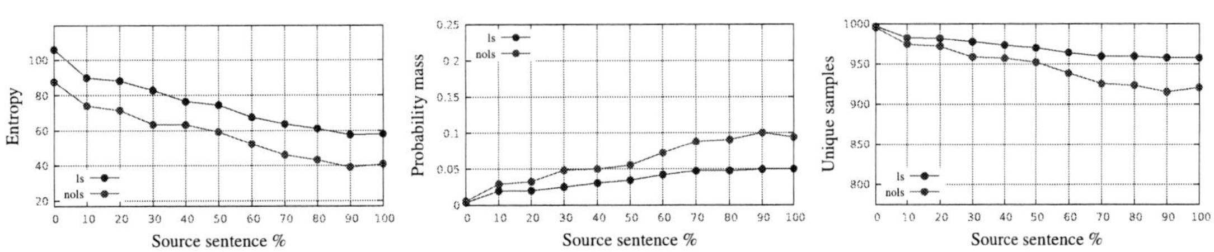

(a) Per-sentence entropy (nats), zh-en (b) Total probability mass, zh-en (c) Number of unique samples, zh-en

Figure 11: Effect of label smoothing (ls) on the peakedness of the distribution, compared with no label smoothing (nols), for Chinese-to-English. As with German-to-English, label smoothing consistently increases entropy and decreases total probability mass across all values of s.

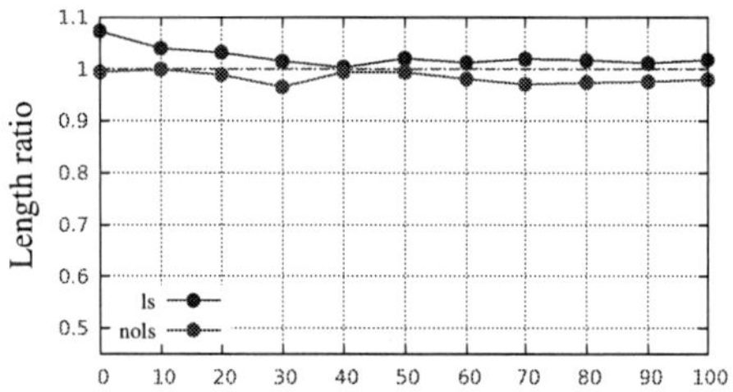

(a) Length ratio, samples

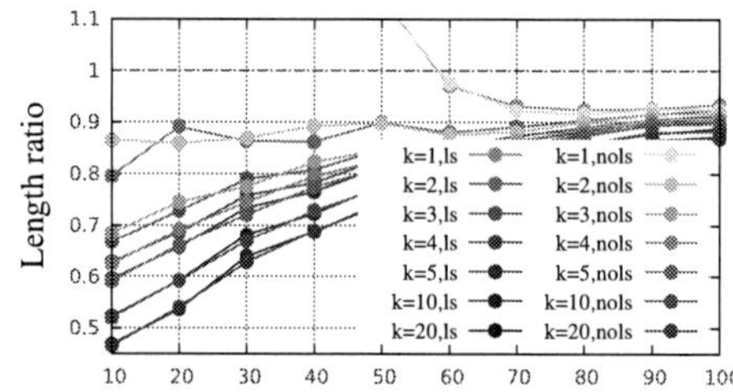

(b) Length ratio, beam search

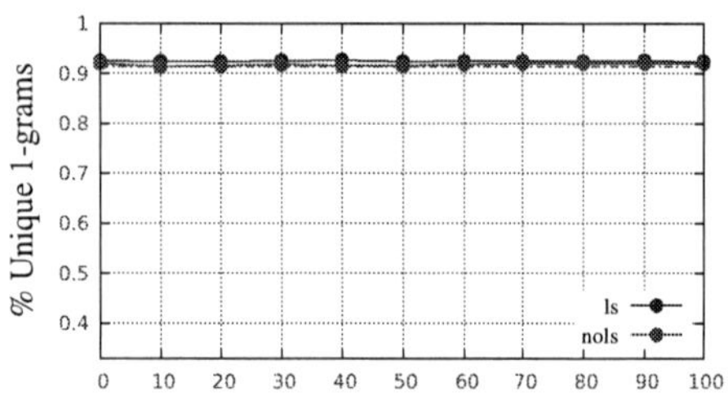

(c) Repetition, samples

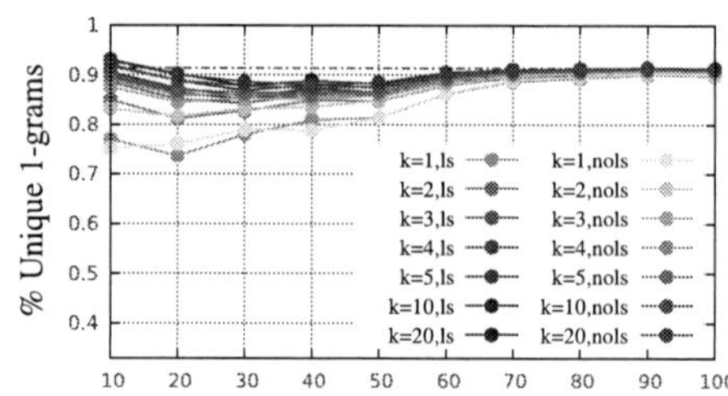

(d) Repetition, beam search

Figure 12: Length ratio of translations and percentage of unique 1-grams versus source sentence percentage (s), both with label smoothing (ls) and without label smoothing (nols). Results for samples are computed based on 1000 samples for each test sentence; results for beam search vary across beam sizes (k). As with the German-to-English results, we find that, for samples, label smoothing increases the length ratio from slightly below the reference length to slightly above it; otherwise it has no discernable effect.

Universal and Independent: Multilingual Probing Framework for Exhaustive Model Interpretation and Evaluation

Oleg Serikov[‡♠♡], **Vitaly Protasov**[‡], **Ekaterina Voloshina**[$], **Viktoria Knyazkova**[♡], **Tatiana Shavrina**[‡$]

[‡] Artificial Intelligence Research Institute, [$] SberDevices,
[♡] HSE University, [♠] DeepPavlov lab, MIPT

Abstract

Linguistic analysis of language models is one of the ways to explain and describe their reasoning, weaknesses, and limitations. In the probing part of the model interpretability research, studies concern individual languages as well as individual linguistic structures. The question arises: are the detected regularities linguistically coherent, or on the contrary, do they dissonate at the typological scale? Moreover, the majority of studies address the inherent set of languages and linguistic structures, leaving the actual typological diversity knowledge out of scope. In this paper, we present and apply the GUI-assisted framework allowing us to easily probe a massive number of languages for all the morphosyntactic features present in the Universal Dependencies data. We show that reflecting the anglo-centric trend in NLP over the past years, most of the regularities revealed in the mBERT model are typical for the western-European languages. Our framework can be integrated with the existing probing toolboxes, model cards, and leaderboards, allowing practitioners to use and share their standard probing methods to interpret multilingual models. Thus we propose a toolkit to systematize the multilingual flaws in multilingual models, providing a reproducible experimental setup for 104 languages and 80 morphosyntactic features. GitHub

1 Introduction

Probing methods shed light on the black box of the neural models in unearthing the linguistic features encoded in them. Probing sets a standard setup with various internal representations from the model and uses an auxiliary classifier to predict linguistic information captured in the representation.

As probing research results have come up with contradictory results on different languages and language models, there appears to be a methodological need for a meta-study of the accumulated knowledge and a need to standardize the experimental setup. At the same time, the fixation of the setup and hyperparameters should allow the reproduction of a wide range of experiments, such as multilingual probing, like X-Probe (Ravishankar et al., 2019a) and Linspector (Sahin et al., 2020), layer-wise probing (Fayyaz et al., 2021), chronological probing (Voloshina et al., 2022).

Often, data for probing experiments is based on already known competition data, benchmarks, and gold standards. To obtain consistent results, such data must be high-quality, manually validated, and carefully include multiple languages. For this reason, in this work, we use the Universal Dependencies data (de Marneffe et al., 2021) as a source of multilingual data with a validated and standardized complete morphological and syntactic annotation, which will allow us to accumulate the assimilation of specific linguistic phenomena in many languages at once. Probing these languages on the respective annotated linguistic categories would reveal how models seize the typological proximity of languages.

Therefore, the general probing methodology should include (according to Conneau and Kiela (2018)) 1) a fixed set of evaluations based on what appears to be community consensus; 2) a fixed evaluation pipeline with standard hyperparameters; 3) a straightforward Python interface.

This paper aims to extrapolate the multilingual linguistic diversity on the proven and tested SentEval-like methodology.

We state our contribution as follows:

- We develop a framework for exhaustive multilingual probing of the language models, with a complete enumeration of all grammatical characteristics and all languages available in Universal Dependencies while maintaining the standard SentEval format.
- We provide a setup for better and explanatory aggregation and exploration of the massive

Proceedings of the Fifth BlackboxNLP Workshop on Analyzing and Interpreting Neural Networks for NLP, pages 441 - 456
December 8, 2022 ©2022 Association for Computational Linguistics

probing results with thousands of experiments for each model.

- We illustrate the possibilities of the framework on the example of the mBERT model, demonstrating new insights and reassuring the results of previous studies on narrower data.

Performing probing studies on such a large scale addresses the vision outlined in Nichols (2007) and contribute to a new dimension to linguistic typology research, as the revealed structures are encapsulated in tools and data inseparably tied to nowadays linguistic nature. Our framework provides users from different fields, including linguists, with a new point of view on the typological proximity of languages and categories.

2 Related Work

Different attempts were made to interpret behavior and hidden learned representation of language models. For example, Hoover et al. (2020) investigated the attention-heads of the BERT model on word tokens connectivity level. Wallace et al. (2019) presented an interpretation framework where they improved a visual component of the model prediction process on several NLP tasks for the end-user.

Flourishing after the ACL debates on semantic parsing[1], the probing methodology has developed its own model interpretation tools. Thus, **SentEval framework** (Conneau and Kiela, 2018) includes various types of linguistically-motivated tasks: surface tasks probe for sentence length (SentLen) and for the presence of words in the sentence (WC); syntactic tasks test for sensitivity to word order (BShift), the depth of the syntactic tree (TreeDepth) and the sequence of top-level constituents in the syntax tree (TopConst); semantic tasks check for the tense (Tense), the subject (resp. direct object) number in the main clause (SubjNum, resp. ObjNum), the sensitivity to random replacement of a noun/verb (SOMO) and the random swapping of coordinated clausal conjuncts (CoordInv).

Linspector (Şahin et al., 2019) includes 15 probing tasks for 24 languages by taking morphosyntactic language properties into account, including case, verb mood, and tense, syntactic correctness, and the semantic impossibility of an example. While lacking the simplicity of the SentEval approach, the framework provides both a linguistically-grounded and multilingual setup. We are significantly expanding both the list of languages and properties being examined.

Probe-X (Ravishankar et al., 2019b) has expanded SentEval setup with 5 additional languages, while **NeuroX framework** (Dalvi et al., 2019) also introduced novelty, but proposed to enrich the methodology to allow for cross-model analysis of the results, supporting neuron-level inspection.

2.1 Probing Critique

We would state a few problems why some of the probing practices are methodologically problematic.

First, the probing interpretation result can differ from paper to paper, creating various conclusions from different authors. While Jawahar et al. (2019) achieves from 69.5-96.2% accuracy on the SentLen SentEval probing task (BERT model), they state that this info is somehow represented at the bottom layers. The work (Ravishankar et al., 2019b) achieves 38-51% accuracy on SentLen (RNN encoder) and states that "recurrent encoders show solid performance on certain tasks, such as sentence length." This drastic difference in result interpretation (“somehow” vs. “extremely strong”) leads to misrepresenting the factual results. Conflicting evidence within the field of BERTology can be found in Rogers et al. (2020), see Sec 3.1 and 4.3.

Secondly, the results on similar tasks can be obtained with unstable success if the hyperparameters are not fixed or exhaustively described: for example, study (Jawahar et al., 2019) finds that "BERT’s intermediate layers encode a rich hierarchy of linguistic information, with surface features at the bottom, syntactic features in the middle and semantic features at the top," while the work by Tikhonova et al. (2022) on mBERT shows, that the model does not learn the linguistic information. More meta-research is needed to explore the contradictory results obtained by the community.

2.2 Task Representation

In the survey of post-hoc language model interpretation (Madsen et al., 2021), the linguistic information-based tasks fall into the groups of the highest abstraction and the top-informativeness of properties used. This group of projects includes tasks based on the various theoretical language levels: from part-of-speech tagging to discourse.

[1]https://aclanthology.org/volumes/W14-24/

Languages While the most tasks are English-based, there appear the non-English monolingual frameworks: French-based probing (Merlo, 2019), Russian-based SentEval (Mikhailov et al., 2021), Chinese word masking probing (Cui et al., 2021). The multilingual benchmarks have paved the way for multilingual probing studies by collecting the necessary data.

Linguistic features Most language-based tasks tend to be based on morphology or syntax, deriving from SentEval methodology. Thus, higher-level tasks can concentrate both on monolingual discourse evaluation (Koto et al., 2021) (mostly English-based by now), as well as the multilingual discursive probing based on the conversion of the existing multilingual benchmarks (Kurfalı and Östling, 2021) (XNLI, XQUAD).

3 Framework Design

This section describes the probing framework and the experimental setup part.

The main goal is to probe how well a model assimilates language constructions during training. For the framework, we want to form an end-to-end solution that can be applied to different models, work on diverse data, and simplify the process of getting insights from the results.

Based on that, the challenges we have are the following:

1. The data we use in the training and evaluation parts must be in the standard format no matter what language we deal with.
2. The probing process should be universal for different models. Based on it, we also need to collect detailed results for further analysis.
3. Since we aim to work with diverse data, we should contain instruments to simplify the process of getting insights from the results. If we do not handle this problem, we can have bunches of results that would be difficult to interpret and provide findings for.

Thus, we can represent our framework as a tool with different instruments. The first one is aimed at pre-processing data for probing, which is commonly a classification task. The second one is a probing engine supporting popular probing techniques such as diagnostic classification. And the last one is a visualization instrument which should ease the process of interpreting the findings.

3.1 SentEval Format Converter

We found the SentEval format to be generally good and universal in the data composition for classification tasks. Since we have such a vast resource as Universal Dependencies for different languages, we can transform the data into the SentEval format and compose different classification tasks based on the language categories we can get.

UD annotation consists of several parts: lemmas, parts of speech, morphological features, and universal dependencies relations. The converter to SentEval format is focused on morphological features. As Table 1 illustrates, morphological categories are written in the sixth column with their category values separated by the equals sign, for example, in *Number=Sing*, *Number* is a category and *Sing* is a category value. It took us 8 hours to process by the SentEval converter on 96 CPUs for absolutely all archives.

For each morphological category found in a given file, the converter generates a new file in SentEval format according to the following steps:

```
Data: CONLLU files or a directory to such
      files for one language
Result: a file in SentEval format
read files;
find all morphological categories;
foreach categories do
    foreach sentences do
        if category is in sentence then
            get a category value
    end
    stratified split on three samples;
    write to a file
end
```

Algorithm 1: The conversion process

If split UD data into train, validation, and test sets, we do not change this split. In other cases, we split data into three sets, so the distribution of category values in the original text will be kept in each set.

If a sentence contains several words with the same morphological categories, the closest to the sentence node word is taken, preventing the one sentence from being repeated several times. Table 1 depicts the example of *Tense* category, the value of word *stopped* will be taken, as it is the root of the sentence.

```
# sent_id = weblog-typepad.com_ripples_20040407125600_ENG_20040407_125600-0055
# text = That too was stopped.
1	That	that	PRON	DT	Number=Sing|PronType=Dem	4	nsubj:pass	4:nsubj:pass	_
2	too	too	ADV	RB	_	4	advmod	4:advmod	_
3	was	be	AUX	VBD	Mood=Ind|Number=Sing|Person=3|Tense=Past|VerbForm=Fin	4	aux:pass	4:aux:pass	_
4	stopped	stop	VERB	VBN	Tense=Past|VerbForm=Part|Voice=Pass	0	root	0:root	SpaceAfter=No
5	.	.	PUNCT	.	_	4	punct	4:punct	_
```

Figure 1: The example of UD annotation

Format	Data entry
Conll-U	# sent_id = weblog-typepad.com_ripples_20040407125600_ENG_20040407_125 # text = That too was stopped. 1. **That** that PRON DT Number=Sing I PronType=Dem 4 nsubj:pass 4:nsubj:pass _ 2. **too** too ADV RB _ 4 advmod 4:advmod _ 3. **was** be AUX VBD Mood=Ind I Number=Sing I Person =3I Tense=Past I VerbForm=Fin 4 aux:pass 4:aux:pass _ 4. **stopped** stop VERB VBN Tense=Past I VerbForm=Part I Voice=Pass 0 root 0:root SpaceAfter=No 5. . . PUNCT . _ 4 punct 4:punct _
SentEval	tr Past That too was stopped .

Table 1: Example of CONLL-U format and its conversion to SentEval: Tense classification, train set.

3.2 Multilingual Data

We take 289 repositories, including the data of 172 languages available at the GitHub of Universal Dependencies , updated in May 2022.[2]

While parsing files, we face several problems inherited from UD. 71 of the repositories do not contain any CONLLU files. Three Japanese repositories and Korean and Frisian Dutch repositories contain different annotations from standard UD annotations. The data from 16 repositories (Akkadian, Cantonese, Chinese (2), German, Japanese, Hindi, Irish, Kangri, Maltese, Neapolitan, South Levantine Arabic, Swedish Sign language, Swiss German, Old Turkish, Tagalog) do not contain morphological annotation. Also, some repositories include correctly annotated data but are not suitable for classification problems because all the examples contain only one value of all the categories, for example, only examples with class *Plural* are left for the category Number (Cantonese, Chukchi, Frisian Dutch, Hindi English, Japanese, Kangri, Khunsari, Makurap, Maltese, Nayini, Neapolitan, Old Turkish, Soi, South Levantine Arabic, Swedish Sign Language, Swiss German, Telugu, Vietnamese).

After filtering, we have data from 104 languages from 194 repositories (see Appendix A.1). From the typological point of view, these languages belong to 20 language families, and the Basque language is an isolate. Although almost half of the languages are from the Indo-European family, the data include several under-studied language families. Many of the languages in our data are endangered or even extinct. The UD data is distributed based on Creative Commons and GNU-based licenses, varying from language to language[3]. Extracting the tasks for every grammatical category results in 1927 probing datasets.

3.3 Probing Engine

3.3.1 Encoders

In the experiments, we consider the layers of encoder-based models and their ability to acquire language data and perform well on probing tasks. Using the output of the model's layers, we can get contextualized token embeddings for elements of the input text. For that reason, we can consider several options for embedding aggregation: **CLS** where the text is presented as the embedding from "[CLS] "token, **SUM** and **AVG** where the sentence vector is a sum or average of embeddings of all text tokens.

3.3.2 Classifiers and metrics

After the embeddings are obtained, we train a simple classification model based on the encoder layers' representation and task data labels. We consider linear (Logistic Regression) and non-linear (MLP) classifiers. As the metrics for performance evaluation, we use *accuracy* score and weighted F_1 score in case of unbalanced classes.

[2]https://github.com/UniversalDependencies

[3]https://lindat.mff.cuni.cz/repository/xmlui/page/licence-UD-2.1

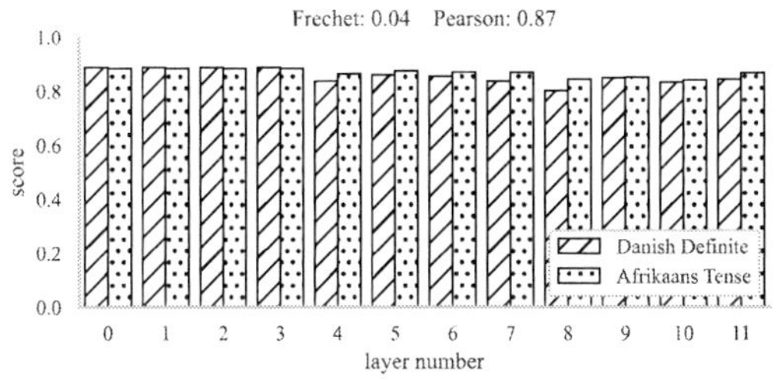

Figure 2: An example of δ_F and r scores calculation between the two probing experiments

3.4 Aggregation

The engine is meant to produce probes of a particular category in a particular language. We provide additional grouping and visualization tools to allow for meaningful interpretation of such large result sets. They are meant to highlight similar experiments and visualize them on the world map.

The default configuration follows the classical probing experiments and uses layers' numbers as X axes. Yet the more novel setup can be chosen, e.g. treating the $< \text{language}, \text{category} >$ features pairs as X-axis instead.

The defined atomic experimental axis allows to characterize larger groups of experiments via their pooled value (such as mean-pooled by categories value in Figure 6), or even cluster them (e.g., using pairwise experiments similarity as in Figure 3).

3.4.1 Similarity Metrics

We support two metrics of scoring the experiments' pair-wise similarity. Both of them are calculated for the experiment results curves. [4] *Frechet distance* (δ_F) provides a natural way to compare curves taking into account both the similarity of curves' shapes and their absolute positioning on the chart. Unlike that, for *Pearson correlation* (r) absolute positioning is irrelevant.

While r formalizes the notion of "coherent" or "similar" behavior of models' layers, δ_F complements it with exact values similarity constraint (see Figure 2).

Frechet distance Given the simultaneous iterative step-by-step walkthrough from the start to the end points of both curves, one could freely vary the step size for every curve at every iteration. By the proper choice of step sizes during the walkthrough, one could guarantee that the optimal distance between curves' respective points will never be exceeded during the iteration process. That optimal distance is called Frechet distance and is formally calculated as follows: $\delta_F = \inf_{a,b} \{\max_t \{d(A_a(t), B_b(t))\}\}$, where t denotes iteration steps, a, b combinations correspond to various step size strategies, and A, B are the functions respective to the curves.

Pearson correlation coefficient Pearson correlation measures the strength of linear dependence of two samples: $r_{xy} = \frac{\sum x_i y_i - n\bar{x}\bar{y}}{(n-1)s_x s_y}$, where s_α is the standard deviation of sample α and $\overline{\alpha}$ is this sample mean.

3.4.2 Visualization

We provide the GUI (see Figure 3) to allow us to configure the similarity thresholds and explore the particular categories' results on a geospatial chart.

GUI allows setting off the δ_F and r absolute values thresholds and specifying particular languages and categories to be shown.

4 Evaluation Setup

To present the whole procedure of our probing framework working process, we decided to run the experiments only for two multilingual transformer encoder-based models: the 12-layer mBERT model (Devlin et al., 2018)[5] and the 24-layer XLM-RoBERTa model (Conneau et al., 2019)[6]. We used embeddings from "[CLS]" token for each text sample as it is widely accepted. As the classifier, while supporting LogReg and MLP, we choose Logistic Regression due to its higher *Selectivity* (Hewitt and Liang, 2019). The classifier was trained on 10 epochs using cross-entropy loss and *AdamW* (Loshchilov and Hutter, 2017) optimizer. A separate classifier was trained for each feature of all languages and each layer.

To eliminate the problem of different sizes of the datasets, we run the classifier five times and then take an average result to avoid the classifier bias. The results were evaluated by F_1 weighted score because of the unbalanced data for most probing tasks. From Universal Dependencies, using our SentEval converter, we obtained 1927 probing tasks for 104 languages. During the training, we noticed

[4]By probing curve we refer to the typical probing chart. Layers, or other probed parts of a model, and the respective results are visualized as a curve on a linear chart.

[5]https://huggingface.co/bert-base-multilingual-cased

[6]https://huggingface.co/xlm-roberta-large

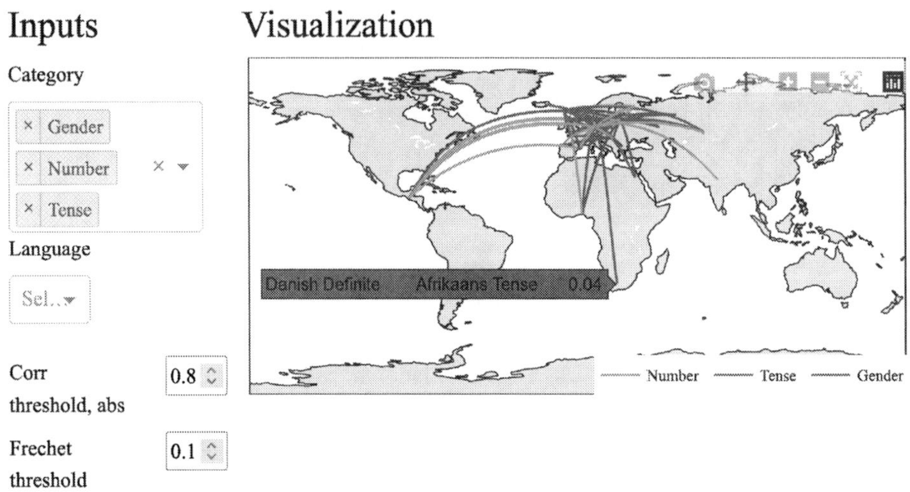

Figure 3: GUI screenshot: Similarity between languages learned by mBERT based on different probing tasks.

that some samples contain long sentences with token numbers of more than 512. We propose two options for handling it correctly: truncate sentences to 512 tokens or dispose of all of these sentences.

5 Results and Insights

5.1 General Results

We received a massive multilingual probing task bundle of 1927 tasks using all the converted data for 104 languages. It took us 10 hours to probe through all the files on one NVidia Tesla GPU V100.

We thus conducted the probing of the mBERT and XLM-R models to figure out the capabilities of the models, as follows:

1. to generalize linguistic information language-wise: grouping the average results a) by layers (Figure 5), b) by each feature in each language (Figure 4).
2. to generalize linguistic information feature-wise, grouping the average results by each layer and by each language (Appendix A.2).
3. to explore the results feature-wise: a) by searching for similarities in layer-wise feature representations) by exploring individual feature results grouped by language and layer (Appendices A.4, A.5), c) by creating the geospatial visualizations of the similar features.

The model evaluation results are presented in Figure 4: the figure clearly shows the sparseness with which all features are presented in each language. Basic features such as Number, PronType, and Tense are among the most frequent ones. The example of the geospatial visualizations of the similarly learned features is presented in Figure 3

5.2 mBERT and XLM-R Multilingual Abilities and Insights

Given the mBERT model as an example, as for the categories *Number* and *PronType*, which are the most common across languages, the best scores were achieved at the 3rd and 6th layers, respectively. In the case of all categories, mBERT showed the best result at the 5th layer. In Appendix A.4 and A.5 the heatmaps for all languages with these categories can be found. As for the average results by all categories, see Appendices A.2 and A.3. Figure 5 depicts average language scores for Number and PronType and among all categories.

As mentioned above, we evaluated two models, mBERT and XLM-R, on our data. On average, their performance is similar. However, the scores of XLM-R are slightly worse than the ones of mBERT. By the categories, mBERT shows the best performance in Hungarian, Chinese, Urdu, Welsh, and Slovak. The worst results were shown in Tupinambá and Akuntsu. XLM-R's top languages include the same language in a different order (Chinese has the best quality).

On Javanese and Akuntsu, XLM-R shows the worst quality. The models show the best quality on high-resource languages and have worse representations of under-resourced non-Indo-European languages.

Among the factors that can impact the models'

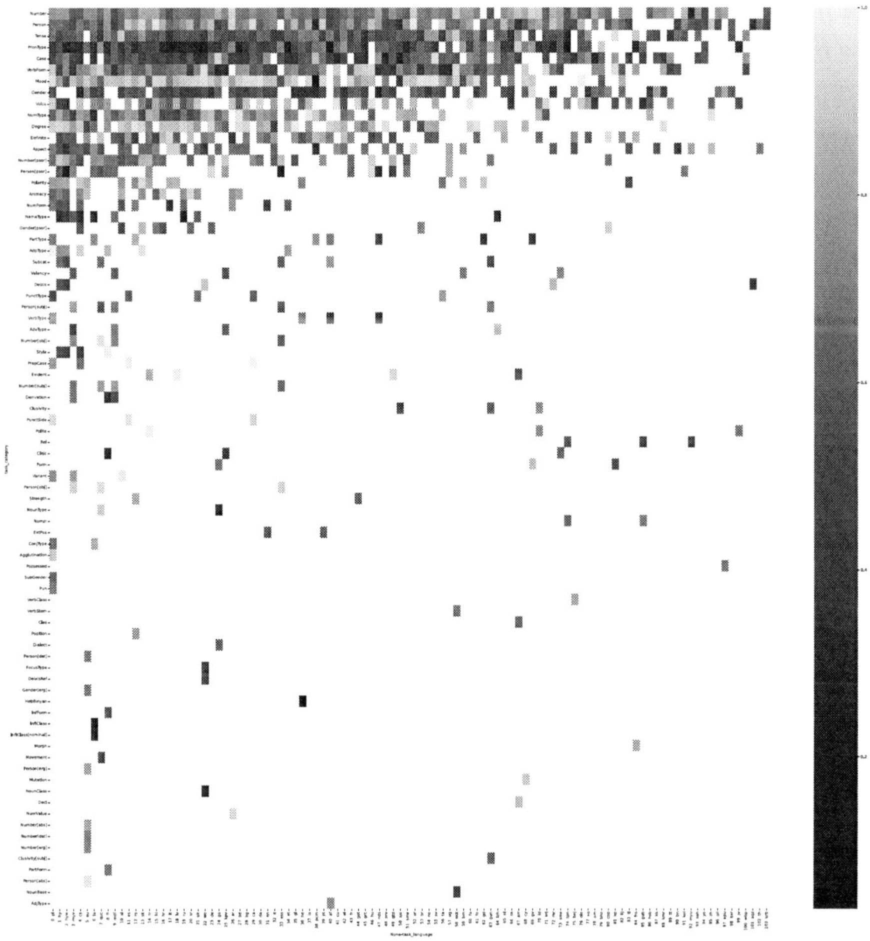

Figure 4: mBERT results grouped by languages and average feature probing score on all layers

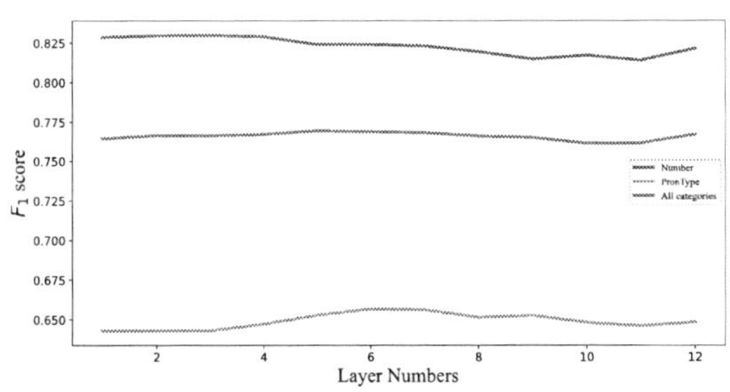

Figure 5: Distribution of scores by model's layers depending on the categories which are used across languages.

performance on different languages, the following might be the most essential: script, language genealogy, and typological features of languages.

To research the effect of script and language genealogy on the results, we run an ANOVA test since we have more than two families or scripts. The test reveals a strong correlation between a language family and the models' performance ($p = .0005$ for both XLM-R and mBERT).

We also run an ANOVA test to see if another significant difference in performance on languages with different scripts exists. The test shows that script did not impact the final performance ($p = .52$ for mBERT and $p = .39$ for XLM-R). The reported difference in the performance may be caused by the set of categories or the dataset size. Independently, other works (Pires et al., 2019; Wu and Dredze, 2019) claim that mBERT shows language neutrality regarding both a language and its script. Our results support that level of performance does not depend on a script, as models show high results on languages with Arabic-based (Persian, Urdu) or Ge'ez scripts (Amharic).

Yet, the models might be biased towards Standard Average European languages (SAE) (Haspelmath, 2001), as it solves tasks on the categories found in SAE languages better than on the other language-specific categories. For example, the top-10 of the best recognised categories include *Person[abs], PunctSide, Person[obj], Agglutination* [7], *Mutation, Degree, Decl, Mood* [8], *Evident*[9], and *Polarity*[10]. Agglutination and Mutation are highly imbalanced towards one class, and other categories, except for Evident, are widespread in European languages.

On the other hand, top-10 worst categories are following: *NumValue, InflClass, NounClass, HebBinyan, Clitic, ExtPos, Derivation, NameType, InflClass[nominal], FocusType*. These categories are language-specific and are not found in SAE languages. Apart from that, if a category typical for SAE gets a different set of values, the model performs much worse. The model generally shows good results on *Case* and significantly worse results for Hungarian and Amharic with a different set of values for *Case*.

Chi et al. (2020) prove that mBERT has a joint subspace of universal syntactic relations. Since we cannot fully prove if mBERT has a joint subspace of morphological features because, as mentioned before, some morphological features are not universal. However, we can see if there is any correlation between categories across all languages based on how different layers learn these features, according to Frechet distance. Most categories do not have a correlating category. However, there are several compelling cases to mention. mBERT generally learns Evident and Mood similarly, and in some languages, such as Bulgarian, Evident is regarded as a value of *Mood*. Other than that, Definite and Number have a little distance, which might be expressed with one morpheme, as in Scandinavian languages. The same is valid for Number and Person categories that are learned similarly by mBERT.

[7]Only used for Polish past participles

[8]Mood express modality, such as indicative, imperative, conditional

[9]Evidence is the morphological marking of a speaker's source of information (Aikhenvald, 2006)

[10]Polarity shows if words can be used only in negative or positive contexts

There is not enough evidence to claim that mBERT has a joint subspace for morphological features because categories have different sets of values, and mBERT performs better on SAE categories. Yet, it shows some generalization abilities on the similarity of morphology across languages.

6 Future Work

As part of future work, we plan to include syntactic markup in research and an interface with a CQL-like[11] query language for authors. The ability to set conditions on a subcorpus of examples will give the researchers the freedom to create custom and linguistically motivated probing tasks while the rest of the experiment parameters will be fixed. One can imagine, e.g., the probing of the model on the `[tag="NP"]` query, exploring the results specifically on the noun phrases. We believe that, in this respect, the tasks of probing and interpreting the results of the model become close to the tasks of corpus linguistics and searching through corpora for statistical testing of hypotheses.

7 Conclusion

The typological variety of linguistic features composes the general nature of language. To address the lower-abstract parts of this nature, we introduced the Universal Probing framework, which allows the researchers to run and aggregate massive amounts of probing experiments in a fixed and reproducible setup.

The current framework version includes an experimental setup from 104 languages and 80 grammatical features. The framework can be used for language model interpretation with various architectures, and the results can also be easily incorporated into the model cards checklist. It can be used in more language-wise transfer learning and typological studies with multilingual models.

We hope that the community will use our work in order to interpret, evaluate and compare the language models, leading to better and more explainable NLP. The framework and all the data are open-source under Apache 2.0 license `https://github.com/AIRI-Institute/Probing_framework`.

[11]`https://www.sketchengine.eu/documentation/corpus-querying/`

8 Limitations

By now, it is also worth mentioning the UD data dependencies of the framework. The problems in the UD data, such as annotation errors, formatting errors, and version instability, could potentially affect the resulting probing framework. As described in Section 3.2, we have eliminated obviously problematic fragments; however, more deeply incorporated inaccuracies may drag on, surviving conversion to the SentEval format. Some inconsistencies in the accepted annotation format affected the quality of model embeddings: such categories as PunctSide (Catalan, Finnish, Icelandic, Polish, Spanish), NameType (Armenian, Classical Chinese, Czech, Erzya, etc.) are rare and have a very different distribution from language to language and are expected to be at the bottom of the list. The categories accepted in the UD for one specific language are also poorly solved: Agglutination (Polish), Mutation (Welsh), HebBinyan (Hebrew), NounClass (Wolof), NumValue (Arabic, Czech).

We use the latest available UD release (version 2.10)[12]. As stated on the project's website, the next release (v2.11) is scheduled for November 15, 2022, so data curation and updates will be necessary to incorporate the newer and better UD annotation into the framework.

The proposed framework allows for different probing methods to be used similarly, including the widely criticized ones (Belinkov, 2022). Researchers relying on the presented framework should carefully pick the proper methods in their probing studies. For example, we've introduced the control task (Hewitt and Liang, 2019) consisting of averaging the probing performance across several probing experiments. This reduced the possibility of a probing task erroneously receiving a high score due to the small size of the testing data.

9 Ethical Considerations

9.1 Possible Misuse

The framework's usage implies working concerning standard practices during model pre-training, such as controlling that the test data (e.g., UD corpora) are excluded from the training corpus. Using UD data during pre-training or fine-tuning the model can lead to indicative and biased results of model interpretation.

[12]Version 2.10 treebanks are available at http://hdl.handle.net/11234/1-4758. 228 treebanks, 130 languages, released May 15, 2022.

9.2 Data-specific Problems

9.2.1 Dataset Characteristics

The dataset covers the languages described in Section A.1. The probing dataset statistics are also presented in Section A.1.

9.2.2 Generalization

The UD data can be considered mostly validated, as it involves multiple institutions to develop and test the annotation standards, as well as the corpus data itself. However, besides data quality, usage of the data should address such characteristics as quantity: that is why we have automatically excluded the UD categories having only one value within a category in all available languages. For all other categories, the data for the classification task were not limited in any way; the train/val/test data division was preserved.

Potentially, other data-dependent problems (see also the resulting data dependencies in Section 8) could be:

- genre bias in specific languages;
- personal style/resource bias in specific languages;
- collocation of the specific features: some features can possibly occur within the same contexts (sentences), which makes the solution of the classification problem within the probing setup noisy for the tested language model.

Nevertheless, we consider the UD corpora to be sufficiently reliable and the most complete of the available data for a detailed low-level multilingual probing study of the models.

9.2.3 Data Quality

In addition to the above, we draw attention to the question of the language representation problems in the UD. According to the Ethnologue database [13], there are more than 4000 languages with developed writing systems, while only 172 of them are presented in the UD in general, and even less (104) were qualified to be included in the framework format.

As we understand that the presented language set is not typologically sampled, we proceeded from the criterion of completeness, not balance. If necessary, we encourage willing researchers to sample their subsamples from our data to follow typological sampling.

[13]https://www.ethnologue.com/enterprise-faq/how-many-languages-world-are-unwritten-0

References

Alexandra Y Aikhenvald. 2006. Evidentiality. oxford: Oxford university press, 2004.

Yonatan Belinkov. 2022. Probing classifiers: Promises, shortcomings, and advances. *Computational Linguistics*, 48(1):207–219.

Ethan A Chi, John Hewitt, and Christopher D Manning. 2020. Finding universal grammatical relations in multilingual bert. *arXiv preprint arXiv:2005.04511*.

Alexis Conneau, Kartikay Khandelwal, Naman Goyal, Vishrav Chaudhary, Guillaume Wenzek, Francisco Guzmán, Edouard Grave, Myle Ott, Luke Zettlemoyer, and Veselin Stoyanov. 2019. Unsupervised cross-lingual representation learning at scale. *CoRR*, abs/1911.02116.

Alexis Conneau and Douwe Kiela. 2018. Senteval: An evaluation toolkit for universal sentence representations. *ArXiv*, abs/1803.05449.

Yiming Cui, Wanxiang Che, Ting Liu, Bing Qin, and Ziqing Yang. 2021. Pre-training with whole word masking for chinese BERT. *IEEE/ACM Transactions on Audio, Speech, and Language Processing*, 29:3504–3514.

Fahim Dalvi, Avery Nortonsmith, D. Anthony Bau, Yonatan Belinkov, Hassan Sajjad, Nadir Durrani, and James Glass. 2019. Neurox: A toolkit for analyzing individual neurons in neural networks. In *AAAI Conference on Artificial Intelligence (AAAI)*.

Marie-Catherine de Marneffe, Christopher D. Manning, Joakim Nivre, and Daniel Zeman. 2021. Universal Dependencies. *Computational Linguistics*, 47(2):255–308.

Jacob Devlin, Ming-Wei Chang, Kenton Lee, and Kristina Toutanova. 2018. Bert: Pre-training of deep bidirectional transformers for language understanding.

Mohsen Fayyaz, Ehsan Aghazadeh, Ali Modarressi, Hosein Mohebbi, and Mohammad Taher Pilehvar. 2021. Not all models localize linguistic knowledge in the same place: A layer-wise probing on BERToids' representations. In *Proceedings of the Fourth BlackboxNLP Workshop on Analyzing and Interpreting Neural Networks for NLP*, pages 375–388, Punta Cana, Dominican Republic. Association for Computational Linguistics.

Martin Haspelmath. 2001. The european linguistic area: Standard average european. In Wulf Oesterreicher Martin Haspelmath and Wolfgang Raible, editors, *Language Typology and Language Universals, Handbücher zur Sprach- und Kommunikationswissenschaft*, pages 1492–1510. Mouton de Gruyter, Berlin.

John Hewitt and Percy Liang. 2019. Designing and interpreting probes with control tasks. *ArXiv*, abs/1909.03368.

Benjamin Hoover, Hendrik Strobelt, and Sebastian Gehrmann. 2020. exbert: A visual analysis tool to explore learned representations in transformer models. In *ACL*.

Ganesh Jawahar, Benoît Sagot, and Djamé Seddah. 2019. What does BERT learn about the structure of language? In *Proceedings of the 57th Annual Meeting of the Association for Computational Linguistics*, pages 3651–3657, Florence, Italy. Association for Computational Linguistics.

Fajri Koto, Jey Han Lau, and Tim Baldwin. 2021. Discourse probing of pretrained language models. In *NAACL*.

Murathan Kurfalı and Robert Östling. 2021. Probing multilingual language models for discourse. In *Proceedings of the 6th Workshop on Representation Learning for NLP (RepL4NLP-2021)*, pages 8–19, Online. Association for Computational Linguistics.

Ilya Loshchilov and Frank Hutter. 2017. Fixing weight decay regularization in adam. *CoRR*, abs/1711.05101.

Andreas Madsen, Siva Reddy, and A. P. Sarath Chandar. 2021. Post-hoc interpretability for neural nlp: A survey. *ArXiv*, abs/2108.04840.

Paola Merlo. 2019. Probing word and sentence embeddings for long-distance dependencies effects in French and English. In *Proceedings of the 2019 ACL Workshop BlackboxNLP: Analyzing and Interpreting Neural Networks for NLP*, pages 158–172, Florence, Italy. Association for Computational Linguistics.

Vladislav Mikhailov, Ekaterina Taktasheva, Elina Sigdel, and Ekaterina Artemova. 2021. RuSentEval: Linguistic source, encoder force! In *Proceedings of the 8th Workshop on Balto-Slavic Natural Language Processing*, pages 43–65, Kiyv, Ukraine. Association for Computational Linguistics.

Johanna Nichols. 2007. What, if anything, is typology?

Telmo Pires, Eva Schlinger, and Dan Garrette. 2019. How multilingual is multilingual bert? *arXiv preprint arXiv:1906.01502*.

Vinit Ravishankar, Lilja Øvrelid, and Erik Velldal. 2019a. Probing multilingual sentence representations with x-probe. In *RepL4NLP@ACL*.

Vinit Ravishankar, Lilja Øvrelid, and Erik Velldal. 2019b. Probing multilingual sentence representations with X-probe. In *Proceedings of the 4th Workshop on Representation Learning for NLP (RepL4NLP-2019)*, pages 156–168, Florence, Italy. Association for Computational Linguistics.

Anna Rogers, Olga Kovaleva, and Anna Rumshisky. 2020. A primer in BERTology: What we know about how BERT works. *Transactions of the Association for Computational Linguistics*, 8:842–866.

Gözde Gül Sahin, Clara Vania, Ilia Kuznetsov, and Iryna Gurevych. 2020. Linspector: Multilingual probing tasks for word representations. *Computational Linguistics*, 46:335–385.

Maria Tikhonova, Vladislav Mikhailov, Dina Pisarevskaya, Valentin Malykh, and Tatiana Shavrina. 2022. Ad astra or astray: Exploring linguistic knowledge of multilingual bert through nli task. *Natural Language Engineering*, page 1–30.

Ekaterina Voloshina, Oleg Serikov, and Tatiana Shavrina. 2022. Is neural language acquisition similar to natural?a chronological probing study.

Eric Wallace, Jens Tuyls, Junlin Wang, Sanjay Subramanian, Matt Gardner, and Sameer Singh. 2019. Allennlp interpret: A framework for explaining predictions of nlp models. *ArXiv*, abs/1909.09251.

Shijie Wu and Mark Dredze. 2019. Beto, bentz, becas: The surprising cross-lingual effectiveness of bert. *arXiv preprint arXiv:1904.09077*.

Gözde Gül Şahin, Clara Vania, Ilia Kuznetsov, and Iryna Gurevych. 2019. Linspector: Multilingual probing tasks for word representations.

A Appendix

A.1 Languages information and statistic

After the processing of Universal Dependencies, 104 languages left. Here is a table with the languages, their families, and the number of examples that we used in the experiments.

Language	Family	Examples	Language	Family	Examples
Afrikaans	Indo-European	19646	Komi Zyrian	Uralic	5682
Akkadian	Afro-Asiatic	15037	Korean	Koreanic	3314
Akuntsu	Tupian	79	Kurmanji	Indo-European	9134
Albanian	Indo-European	380	Latin	Indo-European	1048162
Amharic	Afro-Asiatic	7166	Latvian	Indo-European	393694
Ancient Greek	Indo-European	566076	Ligurian	Indo-European	2304
Apurina	Arawakan	176	Lithuanian	Indo-European	81462
Arabic	Afro-Asiatic	484604	Livvi	Uralic	835
Armenian	Indo-European	37117	Low Saxon	Indo-European	623
Assyrian	Afro-Asiatic	152	Manx	Indo-European	13536
Bambara	Mande	4829	Marathi	Indo-European	6340
Basque	-	191646	Mbya Guarani	Tupian	5503
Beja	Afro-Asiatic	347	Moksha	Uralic	3133
Belarusian	Indo-European	445666	Munduruku	Tupian	164
Bengali	Indo-European	156	Naija	Atlantic-Congo	42928
Bhojpuri	Indo-European	1525	North Sami	Uralic	21639
Breton	Indo-European	5206	Norwegian	Indo-European	631651
Bulgarian	Indo-European	238822	Old Church Slavonic	Indo-European	118508
Buryat	Mongolic-Khitan	6832	Old East Slavic	Indo-European	153393
Catalan	Indo-European	305522	Old French	Indo-European	45115
Chinese	Sino-Tibetan	18865	Persian	Indo-European	183678
Classical Chinese	Sino-Tibetan	93864	Polish	Indo-European	860418
Coptic	Afro-Asiatic	22150	Portuguese	Indo-European	197481
Croatian	Indo-European	193156	Romanian	Indo-European	543203
Czech	Indo-European	831540	Russian	Indo-European	270189
Danish	Indo-European	104906	Sanskrit	Indo-European	25885
Dutch	Indo-European	241808	Scottish Gaelic	Indo-European	27907
English	Indo-European	414215	Serbian	Indo-European	94856
Erzya	Uralic	17458	Skolt Sami	Uralic	989
Estonian	Uralic	557773	Slovak	Indo-European	218032
Faroese	Indo-European	21133	Slovenian	Indo-European	286196
Finnish	Uralic	624845	Spanish	Indo-European	660046
French	Indo-European	686410	Swedish	Indo-European	213496
Galician	Indo-European	15878	Tagalog	Austronesian	380
German	Indo-European	311259	Tamil	Dravidian	12602
Gothic	Indo-European	99064	Tatar	Turkic	250
Greek	Indo-European	49364	Thai	Tai-Kadai	612
Guajajara	Tupian	409	Tupinamba	Tupian	593
Hebrew	Afro-Asiatic	112866	Turkish	Turkic	746291
Hindi	Indo-European	321197	Turkish German	Indo-European	21160
Hungarian	Uralic	41102	Ukrainian	Indo-European	139882
Icelandic	Indo-European	503790	Upper Sorbian	Indo-European	5241
Indonesian	Austronesian	47426	Urdu	Indo-European	96902
Irish	Indo-European	93264	Uyghur	Turkic	40174
Italian	Indo-European	395470	Warlpiri	Pama-Nyungan	128
Javanese	Austronesian	290	Welsh	Indo-European	17026
Kaapor	Tupian	99	Western Armenian	Indo-European	71303
Karelian	Uralic	1475	Wolof	Atlantic-Congo	21518
Karo	Tupian	1845	Xibe	Tungusic	4226
Kazakh	Turkic	15082	Yakut	Turkic	213
Kiche	Indo-European	11534	Yoruba	Atlantic-Congo	1151
Komi Permyak	Uralic	325	Yupik	Eskimo-Aleut	2281

A.2 mBERT's layers F_1 scores for all languages and categories.

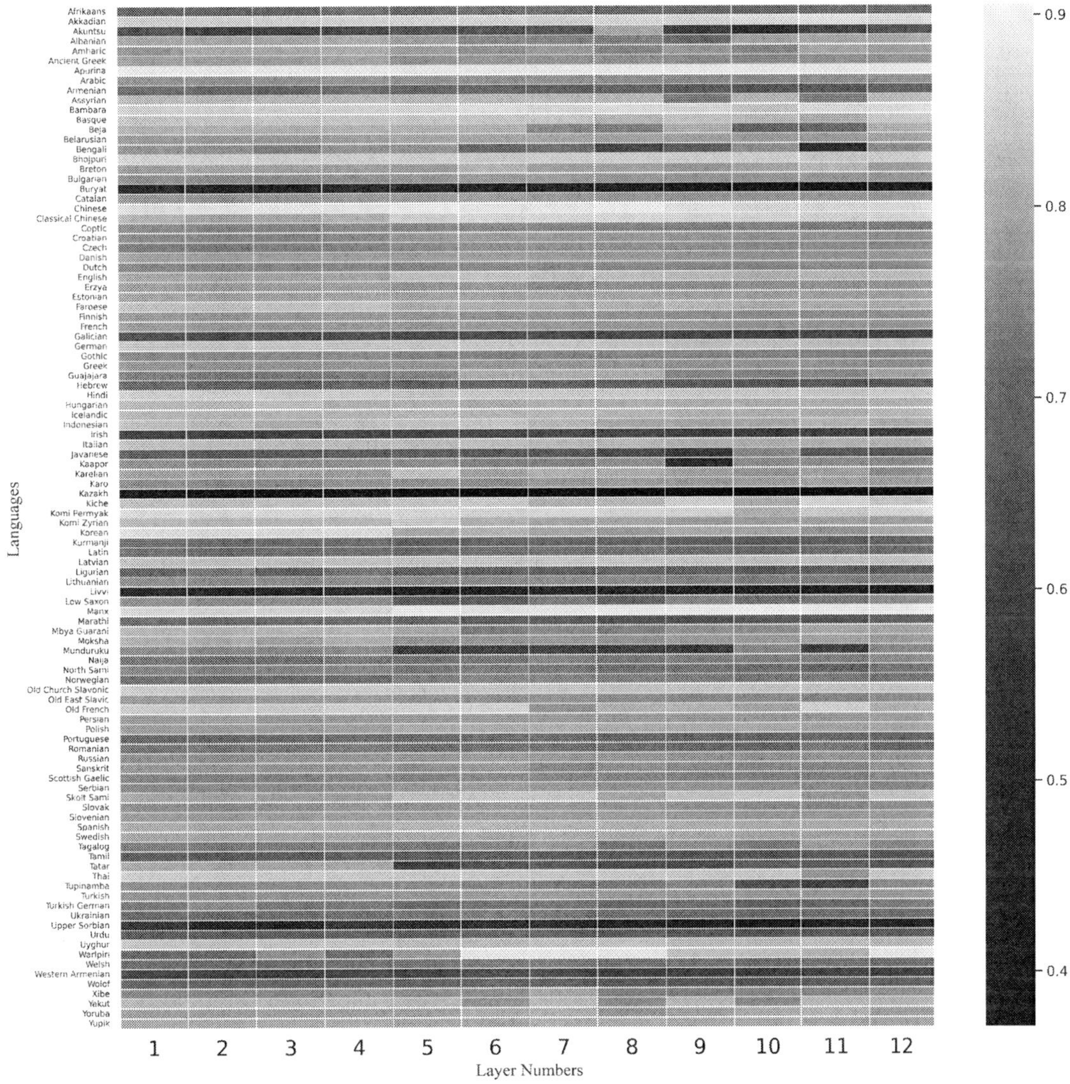

Figure 6: Distribution of average model scores by layers for languages measured on all categories.

A.3 XLM-R results grouped by languages and average feature probing score on all layers

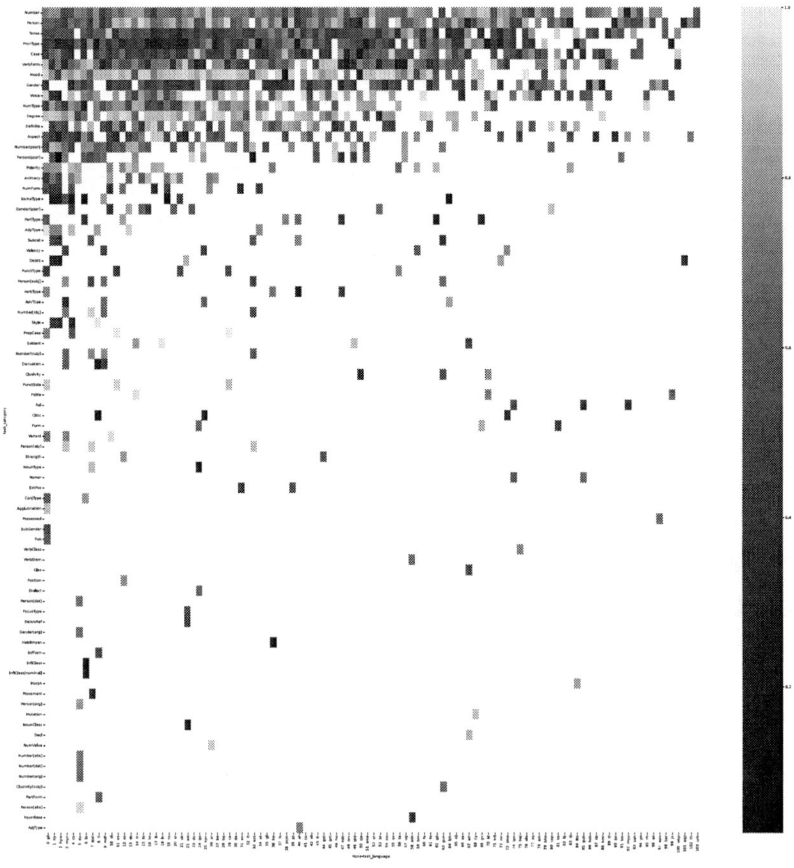

Figure 7: XLM-R results grouped by languages and average feature probing score on all layers

A.4 Model's layers F_1 scores for all languages on category "Number".

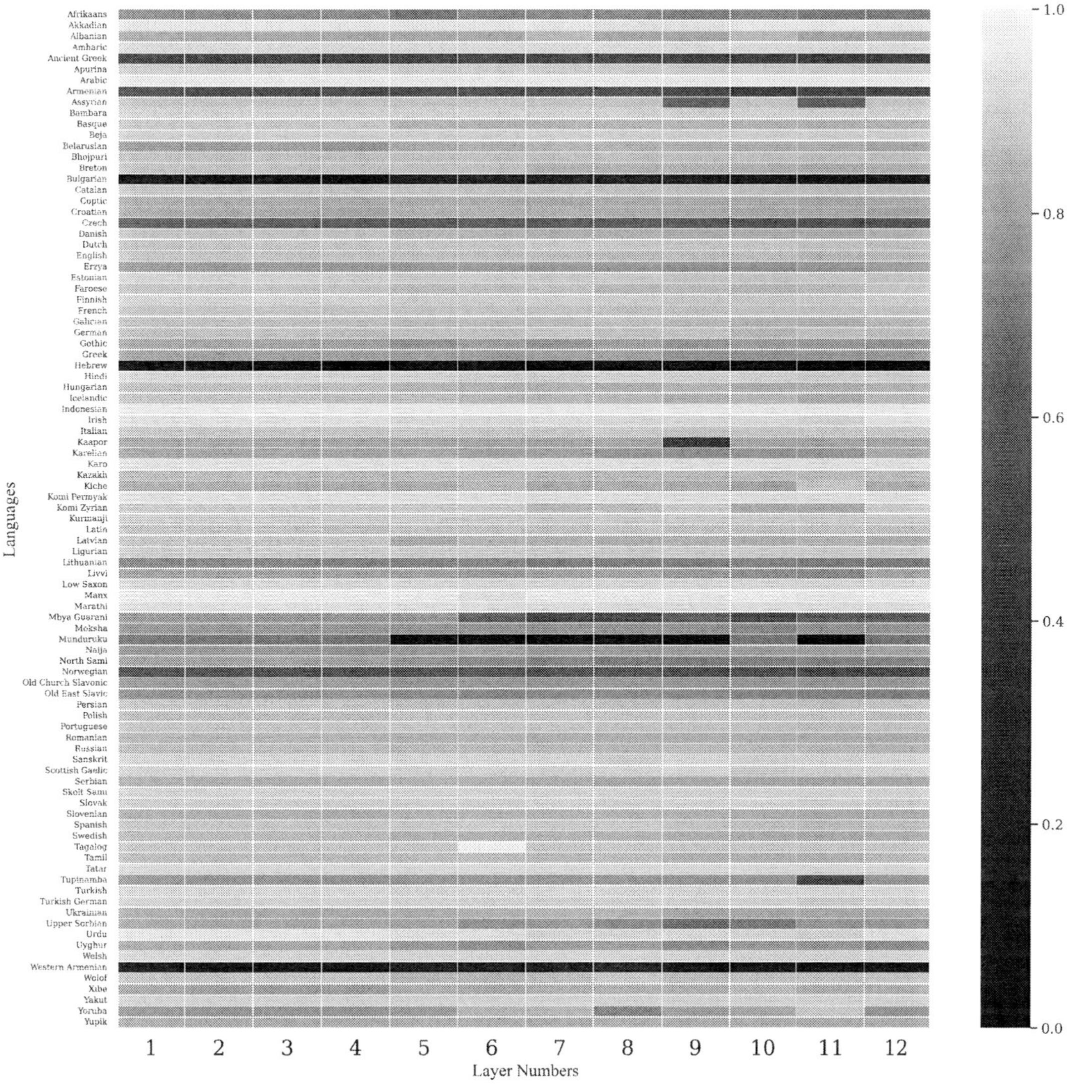

Figure 8: Distribution of model scores by layers for languages measured on category *Number*.

A.5 Model's layers F_1 scores for all languages on category "PronType".

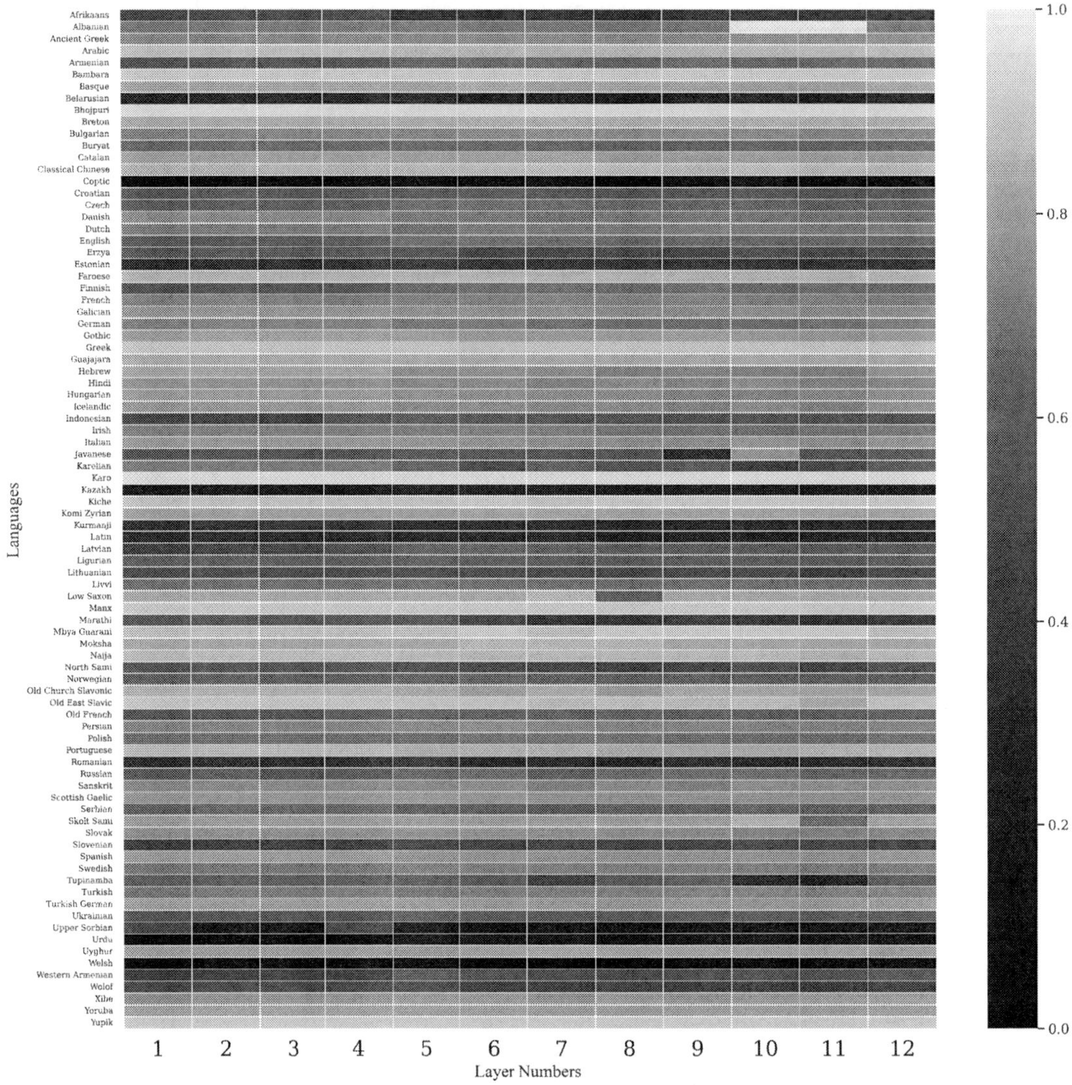

Figure 9: Distribution of model scores by layers for languages measured on category *PronType*.

Author Index

Association for Computational Linguistics
209 N. Eighth Street
Stroudsburg, Pennsylvania 18360

CURRAN ASSOCIATES INC.
proceedings.com

ISBN 978-1-7138-9104-8